PRESTONPANS

A Social & Economic History across 1000 years

Edited by
Annemarie Allan, Jane Bonnar
and Gordon Prestoungrange

Prestoungrange
University Press

Burke's Peerage
and Gentry

ISBN 978-0-85011-047-0

Prestoungrange University Press with Burke's Peerage & Gentry for
The Barons Courts of Prestoungrange and Dolphinstoun
227/229 High Street, Prestonpans
East Lothian, Scotland EH32 9BE

Design & Typesetting by utimestwo, Collingtree, Northamptonshire
Printed & bound in Great Britain by William Clowes Ltd, Beccles, Suffolk

SPONSORS

We would like to thank the following people who have sponsored this book

Sheila Baird
Nigel & Jan Barker
Douglas Boyd
George Brown
J Deacon
Heather Macdonald
Anne McEwen
Ronald Myles
Philip D Petrie
Andrew Ralton
Rennie Weatherhead
Duncan, Mathew and Julian Wills

CONTENTS

FOREWORD
by Dr Gordon Prestoungrange
Baron of Prestoungrange

This is the most extensive anthology of historical research ever to be published on Prestonpans. McNeill [1902] had of course a century ago created his most excellent book *Prestonpans & Vicinity* on which we have built but he was a raconteur and we have not attempted that approach here. Jane Bonnar, as the Prestoungrange Arts Festival's founding Director, set out the guidelines fresh from her own adult studies of Scottish History at Edinburgh University. Scholarly they were to be and both under Jane's leadership and latterly with Annemarie Allan in the editorial chair, that is how they have remained. So my very first responsibility here is to thank all the authors for what they have achieved. I sincerely trust that readers will find them as fascinating as I have and value them as greatly.

The history recounted in these pages shows beyond any doubt at all that Prestonpans was a major centre of the industrial revolution in Scotland. And the reason for this significant role was the presence of excellent coal close by the Firth of Forth making transportation relatively straightforward. Coal of course provided the energy that boiled that very water to 'pan' salt and gave the town founded by 'priests' from Newbattle Abbey its name. And the heir to the Abbey's lands at The Reformation was none other than my predecessor as Baron of Prestoungrange, the smart Clerk at the Abbey who claimed and gained 'sitting tenant rights' from the monarch.

Coal mining also yielded suitable clays for pottery and brick making and for earlier glass making by Italian migrants. It facilitated chemical production and soap making. It provided jobs for waves of immigrants from Ireland. The entire workforce were consumers for agricultural output generally, market gardens in particular and for breweries like Fowler's and distilleries like Glenkinchie to quench everyone's thirst. Morrison's Haven on the Firth of Forth was a major port for over 400 years carrying trade around the nation and abroad including Sweden from whence came the Gothenburg Principles enshrined in Scotland's temperance history at the beginning of the 20th century not least at The Trust Tavern [now known as The Prestoungrange Gothenburg].

Since coal mining was the engine of it all, when the mines finally closed in the 1960s the town's livelihood closed too. All the dependent industries failed to survive and there were no jobs to be had. Unemployment with dependency on grant programmes including European Union support became the order of the decades that followed. Whilst the housing stock and social facilities were certainly reconstructed the young necessarily commuted to Edinburgh using the excellent rail, road and bus links or migrated away from home to make their living and live their lives afar. This continues to be the case as I write although there is lately an added dimension. There is currently a boom in new housing not for indwellers of The Pans per se but for a new wave of immigrants who have found employment in Edinburgh but find living in The Pans more cost effective. This raises the spectre of Prestonpans' destiny as an Edinburgh suburb unless it can once again stand up and out in its own right as a town.

As one who grew up in suburbia and was closely aware of the social challenges such urban patterns engender, I for one do not relish such an outcome. The history so well described and analysed in these pages shows that much can be achieved when the mind is determined and the resultant action is focused. And as is extensively illustrated in the sister volume to this book, *The Murals and Art Treasures of Prestonpans,* a valiant effort is in hand to leverage our history through the arts to create a distinctive identity once again. The Gothenburg lives again, and real ales including the famed Wee Heavie are being brewed. That regeneration has won acclaim from East Lothian, from English Heritage and from CAMRA taking their top awards. Thousands of visitors are already coming to Prestonpans to see our story told in murals and to enjoy our environment. Bold plans are afoot both to pan salt again and to interpret and present the 1745 Battle Victory of Bonnie Prince Charlie to myriad visitors on a year round basis. This determination in Prestonpans is increasingly acknowledged in the Scottish media and around the world in the global murals community with the holding of its biennial Global Conference on Murals Art and Cultural Tourism in The Pans in August 2006. And as Chapter 23 recounts that is why our totem pole has been carved summarising the town's history using the traditional art form of the NW Pacific Coast peoples. Surprising it may be to some, indeed to many, but then so was Bonnie Prince Charlie's dawn attack on General Sir John Cope's Hanoverian forces on September 21st 1745!

As Baron of Prestoungrange since 1997 I have been privileged to convene Scotland's last Baronial Courts, to Pardon the town's 81 Witches, to Condemn the last Miscreants to the Stocks, to strive to uphold feudal values and offer all such aspects of traditional feudal leadership that I can. It is the least I can and ought to do if I am to earn let alone retain with popular esteem my right to carry my historic title. I resolved to come to The Pans in my retirement years not knowing what to expect because my grandfather had worked in Prestongrange Pit whilst my mother was born and brought up in Newbiggin in Musselburgh. And it was an added bonus that my great-great uncles were Willie Park Senior and Mungo Park, the fabled golfers. I have never had the chance to regret that decision for a moment and I sincerely thank all those who have made me so welcome here and who have expressed appreciation for what feudalism can still aspire to achieve in the 21st Century!

East Lodge
Prestonpans
06.06.06

CONTRIBUTERS

Julie Aitken

Julie Aitken was born in Port Seton and lives in Prestonpans. She was educated at Preston Lodge High School and graduated University of Edinburgh Access Course in 1998. She is an active member of Prestonpans Heritage Association and works as Co-ordinator of the Day Care Centre for Elderly in Prestonpans. She is a keen local historian.

Annemarie Allan

Annemarie Allan was born in Edinburgh and lives in Prestonpans. Her mother's family were part of the mining community at Morrison's Haven and she has always had a strong interest in the history of the local area. After taking a degree in Literature at Stirling University she worked as a teacher, librarian and information officer with the Scottish Arts Council. She now works as a freelance researcher/writer in particular as Editor of *The Prestoungrange Historical Series*. She was a major contributor to the Prestonpans Chapter of the *Millennium Statistical Account of East Lothian* published in 2004.

Chris Allan

Chris Allan has strong family connections with Prestonpans and the surrounding area. He graduated from Napier University in 1996 with a degree in Journalism and his interests are politics and social issues. He lives in Gullane and works in Edinburgh.

David Anderson

David Anderson was educated at Dunbar Grammar School and Edinburgh University, graduating with a PhD in Inorganic Chemistry. Post-doctoral work at University of Alberta and University of Sussex was followed by teaching at Moray House College of Education. He has been with East Lothian Museum Service since 1994 and has worked on a variety of collections based projects and as a Museum Assistant at Prestongrange. He has most recently worked as SCRAN Project Officer, compiling images and records relating to East Lothian's cultural heritage.

Sonia Baker

Sonia Baker holds a First Class Honours degree in Scottish Historical Studies from the University of Edinburgh (1999), and was awarded two prizes for her research work. From 2000–2004 she was the editor of the seven-volume *East Lothian Fourth Statistical Account* 1945–2000. Sonia is currently Scottish history consultant for the Reader's Digest *The Story of Where You Live*.

Kirsty Black

Kirsty Black was educated in Lochgilphead, Argyll. She obtained a BA(Hons) in Social Sciences, History and Sociology from Glasgow Caledonian University in 1999. She currently works in the 'News and Information Research' Section of BBC Scotland's Information and Archives Department in Glasgow.

Jane Bonnar

Jane Bonnar was educated at West Calder High School and the University of Edinburgh, graduating with MA(Hons) in Scottish Historical Studies. She organised The Power, the Port and the People and Gone to Pot Exhibitions for East Lothian Council. She worked as Museum Assistant at Prestongrange Industrial Heritage Museum before joining the Prestoungrange Arts Festival as Founder Director in 1998. Since 2004 she has taught at Musselburgh Grammar School where she is now Head of History.

Colin Boyd

Colin Boyd was born in Peebles and has had trains in his blood and on his mind ever since he watched them from his bedroom window there. He joined the Scottish Railway Preservation Society in 1963 as a virtual founder member aged 14 and when he left school two years later he became an apprentice with Ferranti in Leith with the Citadel line running beneath the school.

He became actively involved with the Lochty Railway in Fife every other Sunday and soon met Ann who was destined to be a railway wife before long. By 1976 they had both found Prestongrange.

Allan Burnett

Allan Burnett was educated at University of Edinburgh, graduating with MA (Hons) in Scottish Historical Studies. He has worked with the National Libraries of Scotland, the National Archives of Scotland and is currently Sub-Editor of Scotland's Story partwork.

Craig Ward

Craig Ward was born in Glasgow in 1969. He graduated from Strathclyde University in 1993, with a degree in English and Philosophy. After graduating he based himself in Antwerp, Belgium, in order to pursue a career in music. He has been guitarist in the band dEUS (sic) since 1995. Their albums include In A Bar Under The Sea and The Ideal Crash. He currently lives in Edinburgh

Matthew Carter

Matthew Carter was born in Huddersfield and holds his BSc in Environmental Science and Geography from Bradford University.

Bob Hopkins

Bob Hopkins BA (Law) lives in Dunbar in East Lothian, and has a very long-standing interest in those whose lives helped to shape the history of the county. He is a frequent magazine contributor on famous East Lothian figures most particularly in *East Lothian Life* and gives talks to local history groups on famous residents from their own areas.

Annie Lyall

Annie Lyall was born and educated in Edinburgh. In 1999, she graduated in Scottish Historical Studies at Edinburgh University and won Fraser MacKinstosh prize for her writing on Highland History. She specialised in early mediaeval history and carried out research on Dupplin Cross for the Royal Museum of Scotland. She is a Fellow of the Society of Antiquities of Scotland.

Michael of Albany

Michael of Albany was born in Belgium and came to Scotland in 1976 aged 18. His book *The Forgotten Monarchy of Scotland – The True Story of the Royal House of Stewart and the Hidden Lineage of the Kings and Queens of Scots* was on the Scottish and US Best Seller Lists for months when published in 2002.

Gordon Prestoungrange

Dr Gordon Prestoungrange, Baron of Prestoungrange, was educated at Reed's School, Cobham, and at Reading, The Open and Cranfield Universities where he gained respectively BA in Political Economy, MPhil in Educational Administration and PhD in Marketing & Logistics. He also holds MSc in Management Action Learning from Colorado USA. After an initial five years in marketing research and advertising, he became a lifelong University faculty member holding professorships in Canada, the USA, Australia, Finland and England. He devoted much time to publishing, establishing a major house, and authoring more than 30 books. He is currently Publisher of *Burke's Peerage & Gentry*. He became Baron in succession to Sir James Grant-Suttie in 1997 and is a Trustee of the Barons Courts of Prestoungrange & Dolphinstoun and Battle of Prestonpans Heritage Trust.

Andrew Ralton

Andrew Ralton was born and lives in Prestonpans. He was educated at Preston Lodge High School. His work at the Scottish Rights of Way and Access Society (ScotWays) as Assistant Secretary led to his current role as East Lothian's EU Nortrail Project Officer. Previous jobs included working with Thomas Nelson in Edinburgh and also as a Museum Assistant at Prestongrange Industrial Heritage Museum. He pursued Heritage Studies at Jewel and Esk Valley College; Rural Recreation at the Scottish Agricultural College in Auchincruive and Tourism Management at Queen Margaret University College, Edinburgh where he graduated with a First Class Honours in 1999.

Ewan Wilson

Ewan Wilson graduated from University of Edinburgh with a Fine Art Degree and has written articles on art history. He currently works as Museum Assistant at Prestongrange Industrial Heritage Museum, a post he has held since 1998. A keen local historian, with a sound knowledge of Prestongrange

Industrial History, he has researched for Museum exhibitions and produced contemporary images of the site.

Julian Wills

Dr Julian Wills, Baron of Dolphinstoun, is Managing Director of LJ Lifestyle Limited and a Partner in Sharp Hine and Burgess LLP. He holds his BSc from London University, his MSc in Geology and PhD in Geotechnical Engineering from the University of Newcastle upon Tyne. He worked initially in that professional area before becoming involved in online management education with IMCA and residential property development.

1
Prestongrange House

Sonia Baker

INTRODUCTION

Prestongrange House is an impressive mansion located in its own policies between Prestonpans and Musselburgh at the far western extremity of the county of East Lothian, Scotland. The house is situated about half a mile from the sea, and has extensive views north over the Firth of Forth, towards Fife.

In 1958, the property was purchased by the Coal Industry Social & Welfare Organisation (CISWO), and is held in trust by the Musselburgh Miners' Charitable Society. As a golfing sub-section of the latter, Prestongrange is the home course of the Royal Musselburgh Golf Club.

The history of Prestongrange House is easier to trace for some periods than for others; from the nineteenth century, much can be pieced together from documentation and from the standing evidence of the house as it is today. However, earlier evidence intrinsic to the building itself is hard to find, and even harder to trace in written sources. Fortunately, the history of such a house is more than the building itself: the people who owned (or rented) the house, and the accompanying Grange, provide the key to Prestongrange House's past, and there is quite a lot of information on them. Thus it is their history that this work addresses.

Rear view of Prestongrange House (now Royal Musselburgh Golf Clubhouse). Courtesy of Ms Sonia Baker

Prestongrange House and its policies have had some very influential owners over the last nine centuries. For example, the sixteenth century Ker family, and the eighteenth century Grants were both closely involved with the Scottish ruling elite. Prestongrange was to prove to be a profitable property, with its agricultural base enhanced over time by income from other sources. Its wealth was initially built on wool, and as early as the twelfth century, coal was mined from shallow outcrops. As technology developed to allow deeper and more extensive mining, so coal production increased. The proximity of the harbour at Morrison's Haven aided the development of additional industries such as salt, soap, glass, brick and tile, and pottery production. All of these developments provided an income for Prestongrange's owners, apparently peaking in the mid nineteenth century, when their surplus income was used by the Grant-Suttie family to employ WH Playfair – one of Scotland's leading architects – to add to and to embellish Prestongrange House.

Such an extended history presents much of Scottish history in microcosm; it also is a lot to take in. Because of this, brief summaries of the relevant periods

Staircase to South Entrance
Courtesy of Ms Sonia Baker

are provided, to enable the reader to place events that occur to and around the various owners, in a broader Scottish context. Until the eighteenth century, details are given of the monarchy, as several of Prestongrange's owners were closely aligned to the court. For the later periods, this type of information is of less import, as the aegis of power influence of the House's owners, like their contemporaries in both Scotland and Europe, was more closely tied to their immediate locality.

1 THE EARLIEST RECORDS – THE LATE 12TH AND EARLY 13TH CENTURIES[1]

Kings of Scots

David I (1124–53)
Malcolm IV (1153–65)
William I [the Lion] (1165–1214)

From the time of David I, there was an influx of Anglo-Norman, and later, an increasing number of Anglo-Scottish, supporters of the crown. Monasticism grew and, with it, a concomitant increase in royal and noble patronage of monastic foundations (David I founded the Abbey of St Mary, Newbattle, in 1140). From 1192 Scotland was seen as a 'special daughter of Rome', and church matters were resolved with Rome direct, not via English Archbishops. Problems persisted over the Anglo-Scottish border, which impacted on Lothian and Northumbria. Loyalties of landowners – many had land in both Scotland and England – were divided, and this was especially tricky in time of war, often pushing King/aristocrat relationships apart. Under David I, there were good Anglo-Scottish relationships, which wobbled under Malcolm, and declined rapidly with William.

The de Quincy family

Like so many Anglo-Scottish families of the period, the de Quincy family roots lay in the Norman knights who came to Scotland with David I,[2] when he returned to Scotland from a lengthy stay in England at the court of Henry I (firstly as a prisoner, later by choice). Robert de Quincy was a younger son of Saer de Quincy I and Maud de Senlis,[3] but it was his marriage to Orable (also known as Oribilis, and also as the Countess of Mar) which appears to have brought him land[4] in both Fife and the Lothians. While Prestongrange may well have been included in these lands, one source suggests that it was given to de Quincy by King William I in 1165.[5]

From 1171–1178, Robert held the post of Justiciar of Lothian,[6] and he was evidently active in politics in the southern heartland of Scotland as he appears to have witnessed several royal acts there.[7] The owner of Prestongrange was an important member of William the Lion's court circle although in 1170 Robert de Quincy found it necessary to make arrangements to pay off some of his creditors. However, his fortunes evidently improved as, by 1190, he had inherited extensive lands in Huntingdon; it is thought he died in 1200.[8] He had close links to David, Earl of Huntingdon, the brother and heir of King William I: not only was the Earl a distant relation[9] to de Quincy, but had also acted as surety for Robert on the 1170 Prestongrange Charter. The grandson and namesake of David I would have been a powerful ally.

The 12th Century Charter[10]

This Charter of 1170, detailing the terms of a 20 year lease between Pain de Hedleia for Newbattle Abbey,[11] and Robert de Quincy provides the earliest evidence of the traceable history of the site of Prestongrange. The document provides a brief description of the site, what the Cistercian monks were to get as their part of the bargain, and introduces the de Quincy family as its twelfth century owners – albeit in a feudal system where the King retained ultimate ownership.

Robert de Quincy offered the Newbattle Cistercian monks a 20 year lease on Prestongrange in return for the settlement of a debt of 80 pounds of silver, which he appears to have borrowed from Aaron of Lincoln. A later Charter of 1179 x 1189, in the names of both Robert de Quincy and his son Saer IV, confirms the grant of land to Newbattle,[12] and in the early 13th century, the Newbattle Cartulary recorded further Charters, confirmed by both William the Lion and the Pope, in which the land at Prestongrange was given 'in free alms' to Newbattle. The monks were thus expected to say prayers for the original benefactor – Robert de Quincy – but they were, in terms of secular services, under no further obligation to the family. This is the arrangement that continued unhindered until the mid-sixteenth century, when the Reformation shifted land ownership out of the churches and into the secular sphere.

The name Prestongrange initially appears to suggest some sort of monastic settlement, but in fact the name was already in use at nearby Preston – the Priests' Town – before Prestongrange was leased to the Church. This is confirmed by the wording of the 1170 Charter of

> ... lands at Preston, later Prestongrange...[13]

Evidently, priests were already working the land, and extracting coal and salt from the area now known as Prestonpans, which lies on the coast a few miles from Prestongrange. The second part of the name 'grange' referred to a 'farming establishment', particularly in relation to a farm

> belonging to a religious house or a feudal lord, with granaries for the storage of crops, and titles in land[14]

The Charter granted the Cistercians pasture for 700 sheep, and for oxen to work the land; meanwhile Robert and his men were still able to cultivate their own land there. The monks were also to have

> ... all other easements, water, grass and fuel for the grange, except for [Robert's] demesne peatery...

and it stipulated that

> ... such buildings as the monks have received with the land they are to return at the end of the lease, or else 30/- having removed whatever is theirs whether buildings or other things...[15]

The Charter then, suggests that any buildings extant in 1170 on the grange were fairly utilitarian agricultural buildings; there is no mention of any sort of dwelling house. It is not known what accommodation the monks enjoyed during almost four centuries of occupation of Prestongrange.

What became of the de Quincys?

Saer de Quincy IV, Robert's son, married Margaret of Beaufort, daughter of Robert 3rd Earl of Leicester, thereby becoming (in 1207) 1st Earl of Winchester. In addition, Saer IV benefitted from a further inheritance when he unexpectedly succeeded a nephew, re-uniting two branches of the family, and consolidating their wealth. Saer's son Robert became the 2nd Earl of Winchester, and he in turn made a propitious marriage to Hawisia, sister to the Earl of Chester;[16] this Robert became Constable of Scotland.

Similar patterns of Anglo-Scottish interplay through marriage were common in late 12th and early 13th century aristocratic circles; servants and loyal retainers too, followed their lords north[17] and, over time, many moved up the social scale. Land ownership in both Scotland and England might be acceptable in peace time, yet could pose immense problems of identity and loyalty in time of war. Indeed, Robert the Bruce made his supporters choose between their lands, and their Kings.[18]

Unfortunately, throughout the 12th to 16th centuries, war between Scotland and England was a recurring theme. Outright invasion, by both sides, and more minor skirmishes over border disputes occurred time and time again, and Northumbria and the rich lands of the Lothians bore the brunt of it. While the unsettled nature of their Lothian lands may have been part of the reason why the de Quincy family gave the monks Prestongrange, it would have been genuine religious piety that promoted their gift. Grants in free alms were gifts in perpetuity, in return for which they expected only the monks' prayers and God's grace.

So, in the longer term, Lothian remained in the front line: it was usually the first part of Scotland to be invaded – understandably, given its position relative to England, the usual aggressor. Nevertheless, the Cistercian monks at Prestongrange appear to have weathered this turbulent time; no records have yet appeared to clarify this period, but Prestongrange was still in the possession of Newbattle Abbey in the sixteenth century, when a more detailed, yet still fragmented picture of its known history, begins to emerge. Even then, some large gaps and questions remain.

2 PRESTONGRANGE'S OWNERS FROM THE REFORMATION, AND WHAT ABOUT THAT MOST INTERESTING CEILING?

Kings & Queens of Scots

James IV (1488–1513)
James V (1513–1542)

1513–24:	minority intermittently under Albany Regency
1524–28:	minority under Douglas, Earl of Angus
1528–42:	rule as adult

Mary, Queen of Scots (1542–1567 – abdicated)

1542–61:	minority under	i) 1543–54 Earl of Arran
		ii) 1554–60 Marie de Guise
1561–67:	rule as adult	

James VI (1567–1625)

1567–70:	minority rule under Moray Regency
1570–72:	minority rule under Lennox, and then Mar, Regencies
1572–78:	minority rule under Morton Regency (he was executed 1581)
1579–82:	influence of Esme Stuart, Earl, later Duke, of Lennox
1582–83:	Ruthven Raid: they captured James, who then escaped
1583–85:	influence of James Stewart, Earl of Arran
1585–1625:	rule of Scotland as adult
1603:	Union of the Crowns - absentee Kingship. As James I of England: Court moved to London
1603–25:	rule of England as adult

A complex period, full of intrigue, encompassing several very lengthy periods of minority rule, which in turn led to ever-changing power-play between different factions of the nobility. In addition, English ambitions to inveigle a marriage between the very young Catholic Queen Mary, and their (Protestant) King Edward VI came to a head in what Walter Scott later called 'The Rough Wooing' (1540s). The resultant disputes, skirmishes and occasional battles left their scars on the borderlands, including the Lothians.

As was happening elsewhere in northern Europe, the Reformation – when Catholicism was superseded by Protestantism (in Scotland, it was later refined to Presbyterianism) – eventually ushered in profound changes at every level of society; however, initial progress was both very piecemeal and gradual. The process of changing lifelong Catholic beliefs was slow, led by a dedicated Protestant minority; there was, for a long time, the possibility that the country would revert to Catholicism. In Scotland, the rise of Protestantism was further complicated by the fact that Mary, Queen of Scots was, and remained, a Catholic. On her abdication in 1567, her one-year-old son James became King and, even after years of minority under an ever-changing array of Regents, proved to be a well-regarded monarch. In spite of the economic problems that beset Scotland at the end of the sixteenth century, his Government provided the country with a considerable degree of stability.

Moving with the times: the rise of the Ker family

From the twelfth century, Prestongrange's fortunes were tied to those of Newbattle Abbey. Come the sixteenth century, the Commendator (later, he became Abbot), of Newbattle was an ambitious and acquisitive man called Mark Ker. These were not perhaps qualities which today would be associated with a man of the cloth, but by being in the right place at the right time, and perhaps by acting when others might hesitate, Mark Ker[19] soon made some impressive career moves. This second son of the powerful Sir Andrew Ker of Cessford, Warden of the Middle March (a border family that was no stranger to fighting for its rights), was born in Edinburgh Castle in 1517; he was educated at college in St Andrews. Like many other younger sons who had little hope of an inheritance, Mark Ker pursued a career in the Church; in a society where land and property bequeathed power and status, the Church itself was a rich and powerful player, although increasingly uncertain of its future in the face of change already sweeping Europe.

Mark Ker was firstly (1536) granted the income from Maison Dieu, Jedburgh, and eleven years later, on 5 May 1547,[20] was appointed by the Pope to the Abbey of Newbattle, and thus to receive, on behalf of the Abbey, the concomitant income from agriculture, coal and salt. The longevity of the existing Abbot, James Haswell, meant that Mark Ker had to wait a further ten years until he could succeed to the Abbacy. Meanwhile, from 1549 he operated as commendator, an administrative post to which individuals were generally nominated by the Crown, and appointed by the Pope. This placed him in control of Newbattle's income, without the inconvenience of playing any part in the religious life of the Abbey, nor of taking any restricting vows. His role was fairly typical for the period when, across Europe, secular clergy were taking an increasing part in running Church property.

After Abbot Haswell's demise in 1557, Mark Ker speedily exercised his new powers, using the feuing system to grant land in exchange for cash. Part of Prestongrange[21] appears to have been feued to his nephew, Alexander Home: another 'arrangement' made by Mark Ker in 1558, was the feuing of other Newbattle lands to his son, Mark. The child's mother was Helen Leslie, a widow with two children, to whom his father was not, at the time, married:[22] unmarried clerical paternity was not unusual, but it does perhaps indicate that Mark Ker's ambitions did indeed lay more in the secular, than in the religious, realm.[23] His liaison with Helen Leslie gives a further hint of where his own allegiances lay: her family were in favour of religious reform, tended to be pro-English and anti-French, and to that end had been associated with the murder of Cardinal Beaton (who had supported Marie de Guise) twelve years earlier.

Unsurprisingly, Mark Ker emerged from the upheaval of those Reformation years as a Protestant, with his hold of the Newbattle lands intact. That he was able to weather the uncertainties of the time is remarkable; if Catholicism had won through, he might have lost everything. As it was, the new Protestant Kirk was slow to seek to acquire the old church's wealth, giving the likes of Ker plenty of time to secure it for themselves.

What is more, thereafter Mark Ker's name appeared regularly in various documents relating to State events: in 1558, he sat in Parliament, and on 26th April 1560 put his signature to the Covenant to 'defend the evangell of Christ'.[24] He sat in the Reformation Parliament in August the same year, and again in 1563. Mark Ker was appointed an Extraordinary Lord of Session in 1569, and made it to the Privy Council by September that year. On Regent Morton's resignation in 1578, Ker appears to have been one of the twelve appointees to the replacement Government,[25] and, two years on, he was an auditor of the Exchequer. Ker's astuteness ensured he remained a step ahead of trouble; he opposed the Ruthven Raids of the extreme Protestant faction, and thereafter became less involved with day-to-day political events, passing his office of Commendator to his son, Mark, in October 1581. He remained a member of the Privy Council up to the year of his death, 1584. His widow, Helen Leslie, died on 26 October 1594, having lived her last ten years at Prestongrange. They left four sons, and one daughter: the latter, Katherine, and the third son, George, favoured the Catholic faith. Such religious dissonance within families was common.

The Prestongrange ceiling[26]

In 1560, Mark Ker re-acquired the Abbey lands he had feued away a few years earlier, naming his wife and son as beneficiaries. At some point in this period, Ker was transforming Newbattle Abbey into an impressive private residence; Sanderson considers it unlikely that he actually lived there, and points to the existence of a

> house at Prestongrange, comfortably furnished, to which Helen Leslie retired towards the end of her life.[27]

Evidence relating directly to Prestongrange House continues to prove elusive; nevertheless, a chance discovery during renovation work at the House in 1962, provided a further insight – and raised more questions – about Prestongrange's sixteenth century owners, Helen Leslie and her husband, Mark Ker. When the removal of a later plaster ceiling revealed an earlier painted finish, it became clear that, by at least 1581 – the date on the ceiling – there had been a substantial house on the site. Comments made by art historians in the early 1960's suggested that the ceiling was designed for a much larger room than the one in which it was discovered. Other than that, there is very little substantiated evidence available to indicate what the sixteenth century Prestongrange was like.

It is possible that Mark Ker and Helen Leslie had invested their wealth in building a 'new' tower house, on the old site. Sanderson gives Mark Ker's net estate on death at £16,046, 5 shillings (Scots, although this is unstated), when the average laird left an estate of around £2,000.[28] Given that, from 1547, East Lothian had been devastated by the English occupation during the latter phases of the 'Rough Wooing', and that the Battle of Pinkie, September 1547, took place just outside Musselburgh, it is hard to see how Prestongrange, at that time a Catholic, monastic property, would have escaped undamaged.

It is thus entirely valid to suggest that any buildings at Prestongrange may have been destroyed, and that, as did many of his contemporaries,[29] Mark Ker indulged himself in building a new house or considerably adding to an existing building. That either are possible is supported by the standing evidence: the most easterly section has smaller windows than the central part of the bulding, and the floors are at different levels.[30] From Ker's last testament it is clear that he had a gardener, George Tait, at Prestongrange, as well as a grieve – Robert Watson; while the latter may be quite common, the presence of a gardener appears to imply that there were parts of the property's policies that needed a particular type of maintainence, and it is likely that there was a substantial house set in those policies.

In addition, Mark Ker chose to embellish his house with an unusual painted ceiling. While many of these late sixteenth/ early seventeenth century houses had painted ceilings; Mark Ker's taste was somewhat earthier than most. At Culross Palace (c1608), Sir George Bruce chose moralising stories: the owner of Pinkie House (c1603), Sir Alexander Seton, favoured heraldry and Latin and Greek inscriptions: Mark Ker's selection of images reflect a bawdier side of life. The Prestongrange ceiling – now at Merchiston Tower, Edinburgh[31] – portrays a series of lively if rather grotesque and, at times perhaps, almost obscene, figures. Various interpretations on this were made at the time of discovery, with suggestions of a link to witch-craft seemingly having credence.[32] Academic views today on the prevalence, or otherwise, of witch-craft in sixteenth century Scotland,[33] reveal a pressing need for the interpretation of this ceiling to be re-visited; it is currently thought that the figures represented comic actors in German folk-plays.[34] It seems more likely that the Kers delighted in the sexually suggestive imagery, rather than the decoration being tied to devil-worship and witch-craft. Quite what Mark Ker's and Helen Leslie's successors thought of the ceiling is not recorded; it probably came as no surprise to their son, and grandson, but perhaps the later residents of Prestongrange found it a little difficult to live with.

3 THE MIXED FORTUNES OF THE SEVENTEENTH AND EARLY EIGHTEENTH CENTURY OWNERS

Kings & Queens of Scots

James VI (1567–1625)
- 1585–1625: rule as adult – Scotland
- 1603: Union of the Crowns – absentee Kingship. As James I of England: Court moved to London
- 1603–1625: rule as adult – England

Charles I (1625–1649) – executed 1649, in England
- Commonwealth under Oliver Cromwell (1651–1659)
- Scotland incorporated in England

Charles II (1649–1684)
- 1649–1659 nominal King
- Restoration 1660

James VII/II (1685–1688)
- 1688 leaves country – Roman Catholic convert

William & Mary (1689–1702)

Anne (1702–1713)
- 1707 Acts of Union: Scotland and England as equal partners – Great Britain

George I (1714–27)

George II (1727–60)

A turbulent period, with Scotland and England united under one monarch in 1603, yet remaining separate, and each with its own Parliament. During the early years of the seventeenth century there was a shuffling of power amongst the wealthy in Scotland, once James VI had decamped to the London court. The problems created by having one monarch for two countries were many; absentee kingship stimulated a 'tightening-up' of the systems by which government ran. For example, in 1619 an Act[35] was passed which introduced an examination and a thesis as criteria for the office of Advocate, whereas previously no qualifications were required.

Mid century saw civil war in England, Scotland and Ireland – for a range of reasons. There was a period of enforced union as Commonwealth under Oliver Cromwell as Lord Protector, and once again the Lothian area was used as a battlefield. The upheaval of war led to economic disruption, and the seventeenth century marks a distinct change in trading patterns, with the rise of numerous burghs of barony which competed in the domestic market. The coal and salt industries existed side by side, the latter using the low grade coal in the distillation process.

With a change of owners in around 1609, the emphasis on Prestongrange moved towards a more localised viewpoint, although some of those who owned the property were to play an important role in Scotland's government. The Union of the Parliaments in 1707 led to more upheaval as the hub of politics became concentrated on London. Not everyone approved of the Acts of Union, and of the removal of the Stuart dynasty from the Scottish throne. Jacobite claims continued with varying degrees of vigour, to 1745, to be eventually quelled at the Battle of Culloden, when the supporters of Bonnie Prince Charlie were routed by the King's armies. This was not a clear English/Scottish confrontation, as each side had supporters from both nationalities; the reprisals that followed Culloden reflected that, after almost forty years of conflict, the Hanoverian regime wished to annihilate any possibility of further warfare in a part of Britain widely regarded as barbaric.

The Earls of Lothian – Mark Ker's son and grandson

Mark Ker was succeeded by his eldest son, also Mark who, before his father's death, had already shown an inclination to serve his monarch. In 1567, Queen Mary confirmed that he had a right to the commendator role at Newbattle after his father,[36] and on his father's retiral, he took over his commendator duties in 1581. The year before, Mark Ker (younger) had been made a gentleman of the bedchamber to the young James VI, and was appointed Master of Requests in 1581[37] not only was Ker's right to the Newbattle lands confirmed by the King in 1584, but in 1587 he was one of the few people to retain his hold on what had previously been church property, when all else was being gathered back into crown ownership. Dated 28 July 1587, the Charter granted by James VI gave Mark Ker and his heirs male

> ... the whole lands of the suppressed monastery of Newbattle, including the baronies of Newbattle and Prestongrange...[38]

The official acquisition of the barony of Prestongrange, and its associated courts, would have confirmed Ker's social status in the area: barony courts enforced a range of national legislation, but it was their influence over the locality that was of greater importance. The barony court (essentially under the aegis of the landowner) disciplined tenants, and settled disputes. The tenants were thus placed in a vulnerable position, while the holder of the barony profited from fines and forfeitures.[39]

From 1581, Ker also took over his father's political duties on the Privy Council and as an extraordinary lord of session; he was present at many important committee meetings until his death in 1609. By 1591, Mark Ker had been given the title of Lord Newbattle, and in 1606 that of Earl of Lothian. On his death on 8 August 1609, it is evident that he had nurtured his inheritance, as his net estate was worth nearly £37,000.[40] Mark Ker's wife, Margaret Maxwell, died at Prestongrange on 8 January 1617, and it seems likely that she and her husband had made Prestongrange their main home after his mother's death in 1594. They had a large family of five sons and seven daughters. Their eldest son, Robert, became 2nd Earl of Lothian, and it is thought that he disposed of Prestongrange fairly soon after his father's death in 1609, although primary evidence of this has proved elusive.[41] The question then raised is why? Why did he need to sell off part of his inheritance, when that inheritance was so immense? And even though it is likely that the Kers were, by this time, no longer owners of Prestongrange, the story of their problems is enlightening and aids understanding of the problems of the period. It also helps to put the demise of a later owner, William Morison, in 1737, into context.

The 2nd Earl of Lothian is known to posterity as the one who committed suicide. On 6 March 1624, at Newbattle, he gave instructions that he was not to be disturbed and, barring the door, wounded himself with a dagger, and then cut his throat.[42] Fanciful explanations have abounded over the years for the reasons behind his action, with one of the most popular being that he killed himself as a result of dabbling in witchcraft. Other stories have linked the Ker family to witchcraft (see the section on the Prestongrange ceiling above), but may all be dismissed. Robert Ker, like many of his contemporaries, was beset by debt.

Brown points to the combination of warfare, poor harvests and high inflation as being the driving forces behind 'noble indebtedness' which was a common problem amongst the nobility: in the seventeenth century, it was the only way to maintain a noble lifestyle, and credit was easily available.[43] Another contributing factor that Brown[44] highlights is that if a widow survived, as did Margaret Maxwell, she had a right to the liferent of the property – about a third of the estate; thus Robert Ker would have been unable to realise that income until 1617. Having eleven siblings may also have tied up his inheritance.

When set against Robert Ker's likely share of his father's enormous estate, it seems hardly believable that someone could get into such a fix.[45] That the family was still well regarded by the Crown is apparent: James VI even intervened to rescue the Newbattle estate from the creditors. As Ker had probably sold Prestongrange to John Morison fourteen years earlier, and as the sale of property was generally the last resort of landowners, it is likely that Ker was in serious trouble long before he killed himself.

The Morisons: almost 150 years at Prestongrange – c1609–1745

Information on Prestongrange's new owners, John Morison – bailie of Edinburgh – and his wife Katherine Preston – daughter of the Lord

President,[46] is minimal; it appears that there were family links to other East Lothian families – the Hepburns of Smeaton, and the Sutties.[47] It is not known exactly when they bought Prestongrange, nor when their second son, Alexander, inherited it.

However, as a member of Scotland's legal elite, Alexander Morison's history is better known and recorded.[48] Born in 1579, he died at Prestongrange on 20 September 1631;[49] his wife was Helenora, daughter of William Mauld, merchant and burgess of Edinburgh, whom he married 6 September 1610. Admitted to the Faculty of Advocates on 25 January 1604, he became a lord of session – Lord Prestongrange – on 14 February 1626. The following year, Alexander Morison appears with the title of Senator of the Court of Justice,[50] and was elected rector of Edinburgh University. High office did not preclude Alexander from either borrowing or lending money (£40,000 Scots on one bond), although in doing this, he was not unusual amongst his contemporaries.[51]

His wife survived him by 34 years,[52] but it is not known whether she, or the next Alexander Morison, later Lord Prestongrange, made Prestongrange their home. For this period, the evidence is once again patchy: Alexander had only one son, William,[53] and at least two daughters, the second of which, Christian, married William Bennet of Grubet on 6 April 1665.[54] Like his father, Alexander too lent and borrowed money,[55] and some of these debts were to return to haunt his son, William. William's date of inheritance is unclear, although one source suggests he 'succeeded his father in the lands of Prestongrange in 1684':[56] his father seems to have been around until at least 1691, but was definately dead by 1711. William's wife, Janet Rochheid, died in 1716,[57] at around the time that his hold on reality began to fade.

William himself had a parliamentary career that spanned some 40 years, and he sat both in the pre-Union Scottish, and the post-Union British, parliaments: in 1707, he had won the Haddingtonshire seat against Andrew Fletcher of Saltoun. It thus appeared that he was a successful, and wealthy, landowner. However, by 1734, the lords of session had appointed Alexander Tytler (writer in Edinburgh) as factor to Morison's lands and estates,[58] and were aware of the possibility that

> the lands and baronie of Prestongrange shall be rouped and sold by the lords of session...

In effect then, Morison's property was sequestrated by the lords of session in order to pay his debts: he died abroad, in 1739.[59]

There is little doubt that William was a man who would exploit any opportunity to his advantage: he is recorded as being perhaps hesitant to pay his dues relating to the coal road access across the neighbouring Pinkie lands.[60] And with about 63% of his non-agricultural income being derived from salt, Morison was certainly guilty of by-passing the laws on salt duty, being twice found guilty between 1719 and 1721. Evidently the penalties charged – £430 Scots – were minimal compared with the profits gained.[61] However, while Green puts his demise down to the fact that

> in London, William Morison unfortunately took to gambling and lost his money, with the result that he became moody and strange[62]

and he indeed owed an enormous amount of money to Colonel Charteris – a noted gambler – there was more to William Morison's downfall than just gambling. One of Alexander Morison's debts, relating to money borrowed by him from Nisbet of Dirleton, in 1691, was only resolved in William Morison's favour in 1703.[63] A very complex case developed alongside this one, this time between William Morison and Nisbet of Dirleton, which appears to have lasted from the 1690s through to 1733;[64] it concerned monies gifted to William Morison's sister, Joan, who had married into the Nisbet of Dirleton family and, in the process acquired a step-daughter. This lady, Lady Scott, because of the law of entail, could not inherit her father's estate, and felt that the heir of entail – who had agreed to give the bond to Joan Morison – had no right to do so. In spite of numerous discharges of the bond, and deaths of Lady Scott, the original pursuer, the case continued being heard in court, appealed against, and returning to court, until 1733, when the records, though not the case, end.

By the second decade of the eighteenth century, a further agenda appears to this case, when letters are being sent, by the Nisbet faction,[65] to various members of the aristocracy appealing for their support. They were successful in getting the Duke of Roxburghe, Lord Belhaven and, through the last, the Duke of Argyl and Lord Islay on their side against Morison. William Scot's comment is also revealing about the way that the Anglophile, post-Union parliament operated

> ... all the entreat in my power is useless against the English... the lawiers in the house determines it seldom or never coming to a vote. PS as [to] my own opinion, I must indeed say that Prestongrange will reverse the decree, it having to my judgement little foundation in law...[66]

The same document also records a letter from Robert Dundas, solicitor, who agreed to act for Nisbet, even though he had already been approached by Morison to act on his behalf. It looks rather as if the Scottish establishment were acting as a unit to condemn someone who perhaps was not actually, in this instance at least, guilty.

Nevertheless, other surviving documents do suggest that William Morison was living beyond his means. Perhaps he was a man who lived on the edge of what was legal, as his affairs on death proved to be a nightmare to sort out. Important documents that would have clarified whether his (sizeable) debts to the family of Colonel Charteris had been discharged, were noticeably absent. Because of the state of his affairs on his death, various official papers were drawn up relating to the estate, providing later readers with almost as many questions as answers.

The *Minutes for the Creditors of Prestongrange*[67] show that, by 1716, Morison had two bonds from Colonel Charteris, totalling £14,305 sterling, with no evidence of them being discharged.

> ... it is well known that Prestongrange had no funds to pay such a sum, but out of the rents of his estate here in Scotland so that if either Prestongrange or his factors had applied so considerable part of the rents towards payments of these 2 debts it is incredible but that proper documents of such payments would have been taken. It cannot be alleged that Prestongrange's writings have been abstracted or embezzled, and as no

documents are produced, or any the least evidence offered to instruct payment of so considerable sum other than this null-doquet subjoined to the Act which, if genuine, appears to have been instituted in the view of a sale of lands which never took effect...

... it is indeed possible that Prestongrange would have another duplicate, what became of that the creditors cannot tell. There would have been repeated diligences for recovery [in] Prestongrange's writings, but considering in what great confusion his affairs were, how negligent he was, and yet his residence was very uncertain, sometimes at Edinburgh, sometimes in the country, very frequently in London,[68] there can scarce be any doubt that many of his writings have been mislaid or lost which probablie will never be recovered...

Acting as a curator for Francis Charteris of Ampsfield (Colonel Charteris' grandson) was the Lord Justice Clerk, Andrew Fletcher of Miltown, who managed to locate copies of the bonds in the Charteris papers. He also located a further bond for £1746 19 shillings 5 pence sterling dated 26.5.1726, and another for £820 dated 22.6.1722.

Other documents indicate that the rot did not stop there: Morison appeared to request assistance over a loan for £15,125,[69] and an appraisal of the debts due to the creditors was, by the 1740s, given at £24,472 5 shillings 8 pence, while the estate was valued at around £26,000.[70]

Another document generated as a result of Morison's situation was a *Memorial Concerning Prestongrange* in 1736.[71] This provides the following information:

Money	
Barony of Prestongrange	£1151 1 shillings 2 pence
Barony of Dolphinstone	£ 779 15 shillings
Barony of Muirfoot	£2313 6 shillings 8 pence
Barony of Lethinhopes	£5626 6 shillings 2 pence
plus wheat and bere	

The above is the just rental of the estate of Prestongrange... besides 84 hens, 82 carriages,[72] 16 darques of peats, 12 darques of selling trees, 20 grazing sheep and 3 turfes of hay, all payable out of the barony of Muirfoot

The factors account will show what the casual rent of coal and salt has amounted to for these several years bygone.

There is no proof of the value of the lands

It also gives a list of debts, and the factor appointed by the lords of sequestration. In contrast to earlier figures, the sum of the whole debt is given as £382,011 12 shillings, which, if accurate, is a huge sum of money.

The executor of the 'defunct William Morison' was his son-in-law, Viscount Arbuthnot, who registered Morison's will on 30 July 1741;[73] the estate evidently took a lot of sorting out. Perhaps the most interesting document of all is given as Folio 269, which is a three and a half page list of William Morison's goods: for the first time, there is real evidence of what was in his home, and it does seem likely that the list related to the contents of

Prestongrange House. The detail given of the rooms in which the furniture was placed is also enlightening, and goes a long way to illustrate the layout of the House at this time. There were listed, a kitchen, a dining room with a room off, a [?aigly] gray room and a high gray room, a gallery with a room off, a first and second room off the staircase, and a nursery. It is almost a century until later records provide further evidence of Prestongrange's interior, and the two descriptions are hard to correlate. Nevertheless, the list is revealing.

List of William Morison's goods: 1741

2 silver candle snuffers [and assorted other silver]
a 1lb piece of gold

a blew moyhair bed with yellow lynning
a feather bed
4 pair English blankets in very bad state
4 pieces arras hangings
one pair yellow window hangings
a fine Japanese cabinet and table
a fine glass
2 bigg chairs
4 small chairs
4 bigg pictures and gilded frames
3 other pictures
10 framed prints
4 unframed
a grate
old shutters
2 small bells
pair of pistols

In the kitchen
a large grate and gallows
3 spits
one old brass pan, drainer and saucepan
brass poll with cover
copper oven pan and saucepan
old white iron sconce
marble mortar
linen

2 tables in the room next the dining room
4 chairs and 2 sconces

In the dining room
2 tables, 4 chairs
5 pieces worsted arras and a small piece
a grate

In the [?aigly] gray room
bed with yellow moyhair and a feather bed and bolster
3 pair of single blankets
2 armed chairs and 10 other
a grate
a table
hanging of the room
piece of glass
chest of drawers, and another
a table

In the high gray room
bed with silk hangings
feather bed mattress
bolster and pillow
3 pair blankets
hangings of the room
chest of drawers
a glass
a table
3 armchairs
6 other chairs
and a table
2 pictures
a chimney

In the room of the gallery
a bed hung with Irish shot
feather bed, a bolster, 2 pillows
hangings
a grate
3 small and a bigg chair

In the gallery
one small cabinet
a dutch ambrey
chest of drawers

Wardrops 5 old trunks
2 old chests

In the first room of the staircase
one bed lined with green stuff

one feather bed, small and bolster
one blanket and room hanging

In the 2nd room of the staircase
a bed hung with blew stuff
a feather bed and bolster
grate, 3 chairs and a table

Nursery
one old feather bed and 2 [?]
a table and timber box

Kitchen
assorted linen and napery (a long list)
plates and trenchers

This list indicates a well furnished home, with plenty of goods of value, and would have been fairly typical of a home of the wealthy class. From the early years of the eighteenth century, consumerism had grown in importance, and so it is possible that Morison's acquisition of home comforts pre-dated his slide into disrepute which effectively brought the Morison family's ownership of Prestongrange to an end. Its next resident was the very respectable William Grant, who purchased the Baronies of Prestongrange and Dolphinstone on 19 May, 1745.[74]

4 LORD ADVOCATE WILLIAM GRANT AND HIS DAUGHTERS

George II (1727–60)
George III (1760–1820)
1811–1820: Regency under Prince George, later George IV

From 1745, the Whig establishment were deeply concerned to bring the Highlands of Scotland into what they regarded as the civilised world. They were unable, or unwilling, to see that Gaelic culture had its own civilisation, in much the same way that they could see no validity in the claims of the Jacobite supporters. From mid-century, heavyweight legislation was introduced to limit the rights of the Gaelic people, and hand-in-hand with this went the desire to educate them, in English, a process which had begun after the 1715 rebellion. These efforts eventually had the desired result, in that Gaelic declined, and the erstwhile clan chiefs of the Highlands and Islands transformed themselves into landowners, a process that began in the south and west, and moved slowly north and east. In turn, the changes the landowners introduced in land tenure triggered the emigration of the better-off, and was also instrumental in the emergence of Highland regiments in the British army, as the young Highlanders sought regular employment off the land. Parallel to these changes in the Highlands was the growing industrialisation of the Lowlands; the proto-industry of the early years of the eighteenth century provided the base on which many industries grew, and, from around the 1770s, expansion was rapid, although patchy. Changing agricultural practices, like enclosure, had been in place in the rich lands of the Lothians since early in the eighteenth century, and the population had already begun to be pushed off the land: they were thus available to provide the workforce for the expanding industrial sector.

This period sees an increase in the importance of the role of the families that dominated the Lothians. Most were inter-related. From 1742, the Dalrymples of North Berwick and the Fletchers of Saltoun combined to agree that they would share the representation of the county and the burgh parliamentary seats, on alternate years; by the 1760s the arrangement was beginning to go awry, as the 'sharing' disintegrated. Incidentally, the number of voters they were pursuing was c55 in 1768, and c75 in 1789. Their disagreement was brought into focus by the appearance of a third candidate – a cousin to Dalrymple – Sir George Suttie of Balgone, North Berwick, who was backed by Robert Dundas of Arniston, the Lord President of the Court of Session. Suttie and Dundas were related by marriage – each being married to a daughter – Agnes and Jean – of William Grant of Prestongrange.

William Grant[75]

William Grant (1701–1764), was the second son of the learned Francis, Lord Cullen, and was an archetypal Scottish Whig: he was a lawyer and a supporter of the established Church,[76] the Union, and the Hanoverian crown. One of his associates was Archibald Duke of Argyll, to whom William owed his political advancement. At the time of his purchase of Prestongrange in 1745, William Grant was a member of the Faculty of Advocates; since 1731, he had held the posts of both principal clerk and of procurator for the Church of Scotland, as well as being a Member of Parliament for the Elgin burghs (1747–1754). From 1737 to 1742, Grant had been solicitor general, and was appointed lord advocate on 26 February 1746: having his portrait painted by the leading Scottish painter Allan Ramsay places Grant at the heart of the cultural and intellectual world that Edinburgh's early Enlightenment elite inhabited. He was clearly a well-regarded member of the Scottish professional elite.

Lord William Grant by Allan Ramsay
Courtesy of The Scottish National Portrait Gallery and the National Gallery of Scotland

Post-Culloden, Grant is said to be the author of a pamphlet responding to the Jacobite claim to the throne, which unreservedly takes the Hanoverian stance. This comes through in his politics: as a commissioner for fisheries and manufactures (1738) and as one of those responsible for the legislation introduced after the '45, he had several opportunities to put his beliefs into practice. He was one of the commissioners for the annexed estates (1755), and saw the Highlands as ripe for '... civilising and improvement...'.[77]

By 1754, Grant had lost his post of lord advocate (probably due to illness) and also resigned from Parliament. Later the same year, he was appointed as an ordinary lord of session and took the legal title of Lord Prestongrange; by some accounts, he was a better judge than lawyer. However, although he was not above using his position to press-gang local troublemakers to be 'recruits',[78] when faced with problems on his own estates, he took pains to avoid '... strife or confrontation...'.[79] Because of his political duties, William Grant probably had little time to spare for his new estate, which may explain his reputation locally for being rather mean; he certainly had to leave for London '... before he had settled in...', and so continued to employ Alexander Tytler as factor, and his manager, Mr John Rainin, who oversaw the estate as well as the salt and coal works. When Rainin died '...suddenly of an apoplexy...', Grant was relieved that Rainin's son was able to take over.[80]

Grant made very few references to Prestongrange in his surviving letters; however, soon after buying the estate he wrote

> ... I came here this night to visit a nursery which Mrs Grant has fitted up in this old house, in my absence[81]

Prestongrange was clearly rather old-fashioned, and the nursery must have been for their one-year-old daughter, Christian. Dogged by ill health in his later years, it has been suggested that the death of Christian, in 1761, aged 16, contributed greatly to his decline in health. A later reference to workmen being '... employed about this house...' frustratingly omits to state what work they were doing.[82] Since it is thought that a new plaster ceiling was installed sometime in the eighteenth century, masking the sixteenth century painted one, here perhaps is a hint of when it was done; there again perhaps it is not.

William Grant does seem to have supported the development of the industrial aspects of the area. He wanted to repair the harbour, and even asked the Duke of Argyll to visit it:[83] he was also instrumental in getting the pottery industry started. Grant died at Bath, taking the waters, on 23 May 1764;[84] he was survived by his wife, Grizel Millar (whom he married in 1729, and who died in 1792 in Canongate, Edinburgh) and their remaining three daughters.

Four daughters and an entail

William Grant is thought to have been the writer of the 'Memoirs of the History of the Family of Grant': his view on the role of history is revealing:

> the pleasure and the utility of History is universally acknowledged – and the same motives that make it reasonable to research in general histories the memorable transactions of kingdoms, the descents of kings, and the resolution and fate of governments render it no less reasonable to preserve in private in particular, histories or memoirs, the genealogy, the actions and the changes in private families of distinction and eminency[85]

He also commented on the way that the inheritance of a baronetcy must go through the male line, as it was a military honour.[86] By 1756, it was clear that he and his wife were unlikely to have a male heir; William Grant then drew up a deed of entail[87] leaving Prestongrange to Archibald Grant of Moneymusk. This document refers to Prestongrange as '... the manor place...' and lists the associated lands: the lands of Prestongrange, the lands of Salt Preston, the miln and miln lands of Prestongrange, the harbour called Aicheson's Haven and harbour milns, and sea milns.

William evidently had a re-think as, in 1760, he drew up a new deed of entail,[88] wherein he detailed the line of inheritance that he wished his family to follow. Perhaps it was the production of a male heir in 1759, by his second daughter, Agnes, to her husband Sir George Suttie,[89] that swayed him: his eldest daughter Janet was still childless after eleven years of marriage. The new entail instructed that each daughter, in age order, should inherit, followed by '... the heirs male of her body...'.

Consequently, on William Grant's death, his eldest daughter, Janet (c1729-1818), inherited Prestongrange, which she held as Countess of Hyndford for over half a century. Apart from intermittent entries in the Haddington Sheriff Court Records – because the estate was subject to a deed of entail – little documented evidence survives from Janet Grant's period as owner. She evidently initiated some agricultural works, as the Sheriff Court Records show between 1775 and 1784, where the building of several March dykes are noted.[90] She died childless, and so the estate passed in 1818 to Agnes' son (Agnes having died in 1809), who took the additional name of Grant to become Sir James Grant-Suttie of Prestongrange and Balgone.

William Grant's third daughter, Jean, made an equally auspicious marriage, to Robert Dundas of Arniston, the elder half-brother of Henry Dundas, one of the most powerful British politicians of the time. This assured that the next generation retained the family's close links to the governing circle.

5 THE GRANT-SUTTIES: OWNERS IN THE INDUSTRIAL AGE

Summary

By the nineteenth century, the hold of the upper classes on government had begun to loosen. From 1832, a Member of Parliament had a larger electorate to satisfy and, as a consequence, the increasing demands of politics saw a lessening of participation by the minor nobility. Population growth, especially in the urban areas, was one of the main contributing factors to change. The 1832 Reform Act (Scotland), gave the franchise to the middle classes; by 1868 it had been extended to the skilled workers, and more working men had the vote by 1884. Women were amongst those considered not eligible for the vote; nineteenth century society remained, in many respects, patriarchal.

This period saw an increase in the amount of documentation as more land changed hands, and as industry grew apace. Estate plans were produced, often to keep track of land sold for industry: changing land use can also be traced from mid-century, from the Ordnance Survey maps of the country. Industrial growth continued, further stimulated by the introduction of new technologies, and by the expanding railway network, which facilitated the movement of goods further afield, as well as by increasing demand. By the third quarter of the century, this growth was matched by an increasing concern about the plight of the workforce; some proprietors were actively involved in the improvement of conditions, whilst others were rather more dilatory. As the coal workers were not only employed by the colliery owner, but also accommodated, their lives were entirely reliant upon the whims of the owners who, in many instances, exploited their positions.

The fourth to the sixth Baronets

Sir George Suttie [d1783], 3rd Bt.
  m. Agnes Grant (on 7 June 1757) [d1809]
  three sons; five daughters

Sir James Suttie [1759–1836], 4th Bt. from 1783
from 1818 (aged 59) took name of Grant-Suttie, when he inherited Prestongrange from his aunt, Janet, Countess of Hyndford
m. Catherine Isabella Hamilton (on 16 April 1792)
one son, George; two daughters, Grace & Janet

Sir George Grant-Suttie [1797–June 1878], 5th Bt. from 1836 (aged 39)
m. Lady Harriet Charteris (in 1829), a daughter of the Earl of Wemyss & March
four sons, James, Francis, George & Robert;
two daughters, Margaret and Catherine

Sir James Grant-Suttie [1830–Oct 1878], 6th Bt. from June 1878 (aged 48)
m. Lady Susan Harriet Innes-Ker (on 5.8.1857), daughter of the Duke of Roxburghe
one son, George; three daughters, Susan Harriet,
Harriet and Victoria Alberta

The tenure of the Grant-Suttie family at Prestongrange House coincides with the expansion of the estate and surrounding area as an industrial complex. Paradoxically, while the increase in income from its industrial base had enabled the Grant-Sutties to engage in conspicuous consumption, ultimately, it was the proximity of the coal workings that contributed to the decline in the property's amenity value. The history of this family in the Victorian age is fairly typical, with its rise and subsequent fall in fortune. What later came to be a major problem in wealthy families post First World War, hit the Grant-Sutties much earlier. The unexpected death of the 6th Baronet barely four months after the death of his father not only placed severe financial demands on the estate, but also left it in the hands of a minor, the 7th Baronet being barely eight years of age. While his mother, Lady Susan, was a very capable woman, because of the attitudes of Victorian society towards women, there was no question that she could cope alone; hence while she was named as her husband's executrix, the running of the estate was governed by an assortment of legal advisors. Almost inevitably, once the day-to-day business of such a property moves outwith the hands of an interested owner, all sorts of problems arise. So the death of the 6th Baronet in 1878 probably marked the turning point for the fortunes of the Grant-Sutties, and for Prestongrange House. Nevertheless, prior to that, the family had thrived, particularly under the care of the 5th Baronet; their industrial interests are dealt with elsewhere, so it is the family detail that is addressed below.

At the time he inherited Prestongrange from Janet, Countess of Hyndford, in 1818, the 4th Baronet, Sir James Suttie was a Member of Parliament for Haddingtonshire; he served in three parliaments, retiring from politics in 1826. There is extant a plan which shows the improvements made to Prestongrange Estate to 1825 (with an overlay of the 1877/1878 cropping plan).[91] Little else is known of him. Neither of Sir James' daughters married, and were not elderly when they died – Grace on 15 October 1821 and Janet on 7 January 1836, a few months before her father. The Grant-Suttie archive not only indicates that Janet Grant-Suttie's home was at 63 George Street, Edinburgh, but it also provides an inventory of her moveable property after her death in January 1836.[92] The house was probably owned by the family,

Coat of Arms above North Entrance
Courtesy of Ms Sonia Baker

but this does show that it was possible for unmarried daughters to live away from home. Amongst the references to linen and china, there is a reference to

'...my curiosities, specimens of lava, marbles etc...'[93]

indicating that Janet, like many other men and women of the time, loved collecting the many extraordinary things that their expanding world had to offer. This private passion for collecting the unusual was paralleled by the collections of the wealthy and great that later came to make up the contents of the museums of the later nineteenth century.

The family archive (NAS GD357) also contains a list[94] of those who attended the fourth baronet's funeral on 16 May 1836; this gives a good indication of the 'good and the great' of the locality, at the time. There are no women listed.

Robert Suttie esq
George Suttie Esq
Robert Dundas of Arniston
William Pitt Dundas Esq
Captain Henry Dundas
Lord Melville
Lord Ramsay
James Hamilton Esq
Major Hew Dalrymple
David Anderson Esq of St Germains
Sir David Baird Bt.
Sir David Kinloch Bt.
Sir Thomas Buchan-Hepburn Bt.
Sir Alexander Hope Bt.
The Rev Mr Balfour Graham
Captain Brown
James Balfour esq of Whittinghame
Sir John Hall Bt.
James Hunter, Earl of Thurstone
Robert Hay Esq of Lawfield
The Earl of Lauderdale
Sir George Warrender Bt.
Archibald Todrick Esq
The Reverend Mr Cunningham, Prestonpans
John Borthwick Esq of Crookston

It seems unlikely that Sir James and his family ever lived at Prestongrange House; he was residing at the Suttie house at Balgone, North Berwick at the time of his death in 1836,[95] and the only mention of Prestongrange in the inventory of his personal estate was that the grass parks there were to be let by roup (auction).[96] The letters between William Playfair and George Grant-Suttie, relating to Playfair's work on the alterations to Prestongrange House, date from 1830, so it would appear that Sir James had handed over the House to his heir, 32 year-old George and his wife Lady Harriet, soon after their marriage in 1829, and before his death in 1836. According to their marriage contract, George was given an annuity of £3,000 on which to live.

Over his 42 years' ownership, Sir George Grant-Suttie, the fifth Baronet, was perhaps the most influential and successful member of the Grant-Suttie family to own Prestongrange House. His time at Prestongrange coincided with the boom time in the coal industry, and he had managed to implement two distinct phases of improvement on the House itself (see the section on Playfair at Prestongrange below). In spite of this conspicuous consumption, on his death in 1878, his estate was valued at £48,609 11 shillings 8 pence; Sir George died a wealthy man.

The relationship between Sir George and his wife lasted 31 years. It started auspiciously

> '... having conceived a mutual love and affection for one another...'[97]

and produced six children; like their aunts, the two daughters, Margaret and Katherine did not marry, but lived away from home, with their youngest brother Robert, at Tilney Street, Park Lane, London. At some stage, Margaret (at least) moved back to Prestongrange House, to assist her ailing mother, who died in May 1858. A letter, thought to date from 1852, Margaret Suttie wrote to a family friend, Mrs Harrington, telling of her mother's frailty:

> ... she has not been able to sit up and write for many months, or else she would have written to you before... my dearest mother under went an operation in August and another a few weeks ago, and I am very sorry to say that we do not see the improvements we hoped for. She is very seldom able to be off the sofa and suffers a great deal...

Lady Harriet was evidently very ill. Margaret Suttie then went on to comment on her brothers

> ... we expect Georgey and Bob down on Friday from their school and we had such a delightful account of Francis from Lord George saying he was such an excellent officer which has given us all much pleasure...

and on the House

> ... we are delighted with Prestongrange. The house is so nice, I do not think you would know it again, it is so very much changed...[98]

The garden too was evidently being improved: the shrubberies were thinned out

> ... admitting light and air into this fine old, but now modernised mansion...'

and the hothouses were extended

> ... so as to give more room for exotics and other choice conservatory flowers...'.[99]

Perhaps some twenty years as a widower explains Sir George's later neglect of the House; it was not lack of money. In November 1876, the local minister was berating him for the lack of investment in the local community, and pointing to the

> ... need of some additional provisions for the pastoral oversight and religious instruction of the very largely increased population which the colliery and other public works on your estate are now bringing to this parish...

and asks for

> ... an indication of what you would recommend, and are prepared to contribute out of your large increase in revenue from the new population...[100]

There is no record extant of Sir George's response, although the next month, he was writing of his intention to build a school.[101] Two years later, his death at Grantham House, Putney Heath, Surrey,[102] which he had rented for six months, handed Prestongrange House and estate to his son, James, the 6th Baronet and his wife Lady Susan. An interesting document[103] lists the rental of the Prestongrange and Balgone Estates for the final year of Sir George's life, perhaps produced when inventories of his possessions were being compiled.

The death of the 6th Baronet – leaving an estate of £15,059 15 shillings 2 pence – so soon after that of his father, set in train a sequence of events which must have been extremely hard on his widow and four children. On Sir James' death, his family was living at Maines House, Chirnside, and they were only able to move to Prestongrange House after some considerable repairs and renovations were carried out. It

> ... had been allowed by the late Sir George Grant-Suttie to fall into a neglected state as regards both the Mansion House and offices and the grounds which involved very considerable expense on draining, gas fitting, painting etc. before the place could be made habitable as a residence...[104]

A new water and gas supply were also provided. It

> ... has been arranged that Lady Susan shall occupy Prestongrange House rent free in view that the heir is to reside with her... that the garden and grounds shall be upheld at the expense of the heir and that Lady Susan shall pay at market rates for all produce supplied to her from the garden. The gardener has also been instructed to make arrangements for having such of the garden produce as shall not be required by Lady Susan disposed of to the best advantage at sight of Mr Yule...[105]

However, the condition of Prestongrange House was the least of Lady Susan's problems. On Sir George's death, his heir, James, inherited the entailed estates; his other surviving children – Francis, Robert, Margaret and Catherine

– also had a claim on the estate. Because their brother, James, was to die so soon, it meant that the claim of the older generation took precedence over that of Lady Susan's family. The details of the inheritances had been set down in marriage contracts of 1829 and 1857, as well as being tied to an entail.[106]

In 1865, Sir George had, with his sons' knowledge, disentailed the property, and then set up a new deed of entail, which settled £20,000 on his younger children, and settled the same amount on James' younger children. Ten years later, Sir George added a further £20,000 on his younger children (as long as this did not exceed 3 years rental from the entailed estate); at the time it would have appeared to be a positive bequest, and the estate could probably have carried out Sir George's request, and recovered.

With the untimely death of the 6th Baronet, and the decline in the returns from coal, by 1878 the estate was struggling to pay its way. Nonetheless, the sons and daughters of Sir George pursued their claim on the estate; eventually the court of session was called upon to make a decision. On 12.5.1881 it was decided that they would get only £7044 19 shillings over and above the first £20,000, secured on a loan.[107] At the time, the two ladies were living at St Agnes, Cannes, France, while Francis lived in London, and Robert at The Lodge, North Berwick. Only £11,600 was left towards the inheritances of Sir James' three daughters.

As a comparison, there is a list of the servants at Prestongrange and at Balgone, together with their wages[108] which indicates how much of a dissonance there was between rich and poor at this time.

Mary MacDonald Housemaid £20 yearly + 10 shillings/ week board wages
Margaret Dobson ditto £7 yearly + 8 shillings/week board wages
the above are half yearly servants; their wages are paid
up to Whitsunday 1876 and board wages to July

Prestongrange policies
John Edington 14 shillings per week + 4 bolls potatoes yearly
Peter Dudgeon 14 shillings per week
the above are supposed monthly servants and are paid
up to 8 June

Details are given for farms at Dolphinston, St Clements Wells and Rockville garden, Balgone House, Gamekeeper (Ninian B Erskine), Home Farm Balgone and Foresters, Balgone.

Conspicuous consumption: Playfair at Prestongrange[109]

When George Grant-Suttie employed William Playfair[110] (1790–1857) in 1830 and again in 1850, to design and implement additions to Prestongrange House, he was employing one of the most important architects of the period, in Scotland; the others were William Burn and James Gillespie Graham. Known chiefly for his public buildings, Playfair was a largely self-taught designer, never having been 'trained'; this gave his approach to design a particularly personal touch. He was also very conscious of accommodating the physicalities of a site in his designs, and his preference for following the 'nature of the ground'. This can be seen in his treatment of Calton Hill and the area to the North, the layout of which he was, from 1818, closely involved with, although, for a number of reasons, his plan was not fully executed.[111]

William Playfair by J.T. Smyth after Sir John Watson Gordon
Courtesy of The Scottish National Portrait Gallery and the National Gallery of Scotland

Playfair's public works in and around Edinburgh were mostly in a Classical style. They included the City Observatory and, with Cockerell, the (famously unfinished) National Monument on Calton Hill; the Royal Institution (now the Scottish Academy) and, later in his life, the National Gallery of Scotland, both on the Mound; The Advocates' (now Signet) Library staircase and the Surgeons' Hall, Nicolson Street. His work on the gateway and terraces of Heriot's Hospital and on the Free Church College leaned towards the Gothic, with a variable degree of success. However, Playfair's Edinburgh *piece de resistance* was Donaldson's Hospital, which was erected between 1842 and 1851: this was not a Classically inspired building, but one clearly influenced by Romanticism and the Picturesque. Its many towers, mullioned windows, and buttresses were gleaned from the Medieval and post-Reformation periods, and the style later manifested itself under the guise of Scottish Baronial, a sort of Gothic Romantic plus Scottish vernacular. Youngson's descriptions of Donaldson's as '... frivolously ornamented...' and of a '... light-hearted and fanciful touch...' sum up Playfair's design[112] most appropriately.

In the absence of Playfair's working drawings and correspondence (just two letter books[113] and a few separate letters remain, and only his finished designs were retained), it is only possible to guess at his processes of inspiration. He only worked on private buildings (and Prestongrange House was a private commission) for a close circle of people, all of whom he would have known well.[114] The houses he worked on were luxurious and, partly because of his inability to devolve any of his work, partly because of his attention to detail, he was not a cheap architect to employ. He even turned down work if he felt it undeserving of his abilities.[115]

Very early on in his career, in the 1830s, he was working on existing properties – like Craigcrook Castle, Cramond, Grange House and Prestongrange House – enlarging and modernising them, all the while ensuring that his efforts were, externally at least, virtually indistinguishable from the original. Gow has said that Playfair '... adjusted the tower house vocabulary...':[116] Playfair's designs for Prestongrange bear this out. Externally, the House echoed its earlier tower house roots, sitting safe and secure on its site; internally, the layout was modernised, yet every detail (and Playfair was very conscientious about detail) spoke of quality – both of design and materials – and of comfort. Sixty-two drawings[117] survive out of seventy listed for the 1830 period, when Prestongrange House was first being altered for George Grant-Suttie (later 5th Bt.) and his wife Lady Harriet, shortly after their marriage: the main addition was a solid North tower, complete with the owner's coat of arms and motto – Nothing Hazard, Nothing Have – over the entrance. In 1837, Playfair was back, designing an Eastern Lodge and gateway – twenty-seven drawings for these – and in 1845, he designed a range of offices and stables: forty drawings survive. From c1845, Sir George and Lady Harriet had commissioned some more additions for the House: the final plans were submitted, and work on the House was begun by 1850. Eighty-three drawings survive. This time, Playfair added a massive tower to the West.

Playfair's drawings are very beautiful; they bear the mark of an artist whose commitment to quality almost leaps off the page. Every decoration – inside and out – was drawn in detail; even the ornamentation to the roof-line, the star, the thistle, the crescent and the fleur-de-lis, were drawn out to scale. These last were symbols of power in the late medieval to early modern period,[118] and Playfair may have either been adding to what was extant, or creating anew in the older style; he certainly used them in great abundance all over the estate buildings. So it seems that the Romantic was his preferred style, allied both to any history a house might have had already, and to the site; his work at Floors (1837–45) for the Duke of Roxburghe is perhaps the most ebullient of all his private designs. Nevertheless, in his public works, it was rather later in his life before he felt able to suggest Romantic flights of fancy to his commissioning clients.

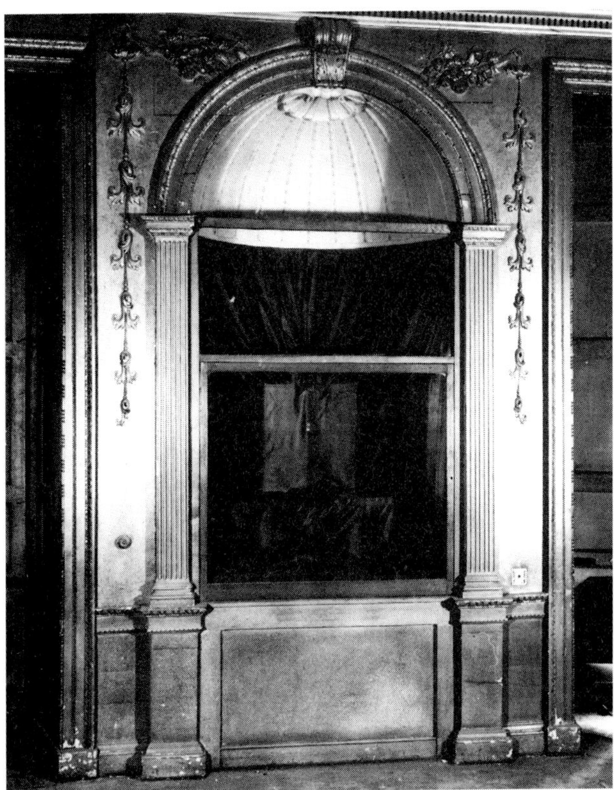

View of Alcove
Crown Copyright: RCAHMS

To have Playfair to work on your House was a real cachet; it also was costly. In 1853, Playfair submitted his bill to Sir George: he appears to have usually charged 5% of the amount of expenditure. In this instance, this was estimated at £231 10 shillings 6 pence; but for Sir George, Playfair had arranged to charge 2.5%, plus his travelling expenses – in total £138 10 shillings.[119] This was consumption at its most conspicuous. As Prestongrange estate was entailed, any investment in the property could be recorded in the Sheriff Court records, and a proportion of the sums spent set against the property when the heir of entail inherited. In the private papers there is reference to an 'Account of money expended by Sir George Grant-Suttie ... on Additions to Prestongrange Mansion House',[120] but the works listed seem to be totally out of proportion to the work indicated by Playfair's drawings. The amount of money mentioned are far below those referred to by Playfair.[121] Work at Balgone, North Berwick (the other family home) is also recorded.

View of Fireplace
Crown Copyright: RCAHMS

It is hard to know why so little of the work was recorded, either in the family papers (although the relevant documents could be missing) or in the Sheriff Court records. It might be that the bulk of the work was not eligible – although the Sheriff Court records contain pages of information relating to similar works on other owners' properties. It perhaps implies that either the heir of entail would not agree to the work being set against the estate (assuming some degree of consensus was necessary), or that the financial situation of Sir George and the estate were such that it was deemed as unnecessary. It seems more likely that it was the latter.

6 INTO THE TWENTIETH CENTURY: A NEW ROLE FOR AN OLD HOUSE

Sir George Grant-Suttie [1870–1947], 7th Bt. from October 1878 (aged 8) unmarried

succeeded by his relative [who inherited via his grandfather, Francis, 2nd. son of the 5th Bt.]

Sir George Philip Grant-Suttie [1938–1997], 8th Bt. from 1947 (aged 9) m. Elspeth Mary

Dr Gordon Prestoungrange [1937–], Baron from 1998

The family's history in this period is particularly difficult to piece together, as the contents of the NAS GD357 collection peter out. From local newspaper reports it is clear that Lady Susan played a role as 'lady of the manor' in the area, and lived, with her family, at Prestongrange House. Her three daughters each married – Susan Harriet in 1878 to the Earl of Stair, Harriet in 1886 to the 2nd baronet of Woollahra and the third, Victoria Alberta, in 1896 to the Reverend George Smith, Minister of Prestonpans. Their brother George, the seventh Baronet, was educated at Eton and Oxford, and then seems to have lived most of his life in Hampshire, leaving the estate to be administered by his mother, and then by the family lawyers, who acted as his *curator bonis*.[122] In essence, Prestongrange House was thus run by lawyers from 1876 onwards. This, combined with a more general decline in the fortunes of the gentry led almost inevitably to change. Such a large House needed a lot of maintenance, which cost money, and problems of staffing increased as industry offered increased wages, and more attractive working conditions. Once Lady Susan died in October 1909, the House lay empty.[123] The Inland Revenue Survey of 1912–14 is revealing about the state of the property:

> A well built but not very conveniently arranged house of considerable age. Owing to proximity of Collieries, it is not a readily lettable subject, and the only bathroom in the house being on the third floor is also a distinct disability. There is a rather attractive flower garden and a walled orchard which latter has recently been separately let.

and the Survey also gives a description of the layout:

> *Ground Floor* contains kitchen scullery, housekeepers room, 2 butlers pantries, wine cellar, 4 servants bedrooms – 2 of which are in court wing.

First Floor Hall, Library and Drawing Room (both large) dining room, business room and schoolroom, 2 bedrooms and WC, besides 4 smaller bedrooms.

Second Floor Large bedroom with maids room and lavatory off, and 5 other bedrooms, 1 with dressing room.

Third Floor and attics, 7 rooms and a bathroom.

The stable offices are substantial structures comprising 2 stables of 7 stalls and 2 loose boxes each, harness room, boiler house and coachhouse, besides a house or houses of 6 rooms over same. At back of stable there is also a washhouse byre for 6 cows and old coachhouse in poor condition.

At the garden there is a rather poor gardener's house, brick built and containing 2 apartments. There is also a quantity of glass which however is in very middling order.[124]

So, Prestongrange House, despite its earlier owners' expenditure, was suffering from neglect once again. The war years delayed still further the letting of the property; nonetheless, with hindsight, it proved fortuitous that the eventual tenant, in 1924, was The Royal Musselburgh Golf Club.

The Royal Musselburgh Golf Club (RMGC) at Prestongrange[125]

The RMGC is the fifth oldest golf club in the world: founded in 1774, its early history was played out on the 9 holes of the Musselburgh links, which was located on the site of the present race course. It took 100 years before the epithet of 'Royal' was added, when the 24 year old Duke of Connaught (one of Queen Victoria's sons) became the Club's Honorary President. By the middle of the 1920s, the RMGC had outgrown its Musselburgh site, and was looking for alternative accommodation; Newhailes was one possibility, but Prestongrange was chosen and, from 1924, the RMGC rented both House and policies.

The course was designed by James Braid (1870–1950), one of the leading golfers of his day; he won four Open Championship in the early 1900s, and was, in 1902, one of the founder members of the Professional Golfers' Association. He also designed the course at Gleneagles. James Braid and three other leading players – JH Taylor, Harry Vardon and Sandy Herd – played an exhibition round at Prestongrange to celebrate the new course. The Club seems to have attracted members from many different walks of life, including members of the mining community.

So Prestongrange House remained in the Grant-Suttie family, but was home to the RMGC for the next 33 years. Quite how much work, if any, was done to the property is difficult to ascertain; the surveyor's reports (see below) for 1960 suggest that the House continued to be neglected during this period. In 1947, George, the seventh Baronet, died and the estate passed to his nine year-old relative, George Philip; probably because of his youth, and because the family then lived in Canada, the estate remained in the hands of lawyers, until, in 1956, it was decided that Prestongrange House and policies were to be sold. The RMGC were given first option on the property, but could not raise the money. This last caused some embarrassment, and there appears to have been mention of a law suit as the RMGC had made an offer, and were then unable to honour their offer. Another player, CISWO (together with the Musselburgh Miners' Charitable Society), now entered Prestongrange's story.

Prestongrange as a Miners' Welfare Trust: 1958 to date[126]

In the 1950s, the coal industry was booming; production was high, and the communities that the industry depended upon were both large and vibrant. The miners and their families came, as they still do today, under the pastoral eyes of the Coal Industry & Social Welfare Organisation, and one of the activities that CISWO encouraged was golf. The National Coal Board Golf Championships had been a feature of the social schedule of the mining industry for some time and, while the membership of the RMGC was not dominated by members of the mining community (115 of 270 members were miners[127]), it was thought that the loss of this amenity to the community would have quite an impact. So when CISWO was approached by coal industry employees who were also RMGC members, to consider purchasing Prestongrange House and policies, the suggestion was considered and accepted, and the property eventually purchased on behalf of the Musselburgh Miners' Charitable Society. The RMGC was to continue using the course, and the club house, as a golfing sub-section of the Musselburgh Miners' Charitable Society. Evidently there were some members of the RMGC who could not cope with this change of ownership, and who left; yet the only way that the RMGC was going to continue was through such a partnership.

CISWO introduced a fairly unusual management programme, in that the administrative committee was to comprise of CISWO members who were also RMGC members together with officials of the No 2 District Welfare Committee of CISWO. The ethos behind this was written into CISWO's constitution, the aims of which, while CISWO has had to adapt to the changes that have occurred over the past 40 years, largely remain the same today.[128] From taking up Charitable status in 1993, the constitutional objectives of CISWO and the Musselburgh Miners' Charitable Society are to

> ... provide facilities for such forms of recreation and other leisure-time occupations as are conducive to the improvement of the conditions of living of the inhabitants of Musselburgh, Port Seton, Prestonpans, Cockenzie and the neighbourhood thereof within the Society's sphere of operations as defined from time to time and in particular (but not exclusively) such of the inhabitants as are members of the Mining Community provided that nothing herein contained shall authorise the application of the Property to purposes which are not in law charitable.[129]

So in effect, Prestongrange was bought by a miners' social organisation, to be run by miners, for the mining community, with the long term aim of providing for a wider range of social welfare activities, alongside golf. This ethos came to fruition in 1962 when James Bush, a miner, was appointed Captain of the RMGC.

In the late 1950s, the facade of Prestongrange House hid a horror story: as one of the architectural surveys revealed

> The house is built of stone, and is commodious, although rather rambling for the purpose of a club house. It appears to have been neglected, with the result that in certain parts rain has been getting in and damage has been done to plasterwork and woodwork. There has been dry rot in parts of the building and some timber repairs have been carried out. Much of the outside stonework is decaying and ornamental roof finials have been removed for safety. To make the house attractive and comfortable much repair work would be required to roofs, stonework, woodwork and plasterwork. The cost would be considerable.[130]

and while CISWO knew of that the building was in poor condition, and that that was reflected in the purchase price, a further report revealed that the

> existing clubhouse would require either very extensive repairs and improvements, or that a new clubhouse would have to be built[131]

Fears of dry rot in the roof were to be realised and further investigations into the condition of the building revealed more problems. The consensus of opinion was that a new clubhouse was an urgent requirement; it seems that the golf course was far more important to the new owners than the House. As early as 1951, before the sale of the property was under consideration, there had been talk of demolishing the House.[132] In 1960, the area office of CISWO proposed the building of a new club house; this was rejected by the CISWO Council, which suggested that any proposal should cater also for for the non-golf playing membership. As a result, part of House was to be rehabilitated, and an extension built to accommodate such as bowling, and other activities. Finance remained a problem, even though a grant was given.

The discovery of the painted ceiling[133] during renovation work created an enormous challenge for the new owners. With no additional funds on which to draw, and a half-completed renovation programme, they called in as many experts as possible to proffer advice. Eventually, the ceiling was relocated to Merchiston Tower, leaving the Prestongrange programme behind schedule, and the owners rather bemused; as TWS Morgan had commented

> it was appreciated that some of the paintings were, to say the least, not in good taste, and it might be necessary to conceal them[134]

The eventual solution saved much embarrassment – and money. Such historical artifacts are costly to renovate, and even costlier to maintain; interestingly though, one wonders what the reaction may have been in the climate of the 1990s, in comparison to that of the 1960s. Also, the much vaunted 1960s extension, providing bowling facilities and a large hall area, perhaps would have had a little more difficulty in meeting the planning regulations today; like its contemporary, the University Library in George Square, it is a building very much of its time.

Today, Prestongrange House and policies remain in the ownership of CISWO's Musselburgh Miners' Charitable Society, and its golfing sub-section the Royal Musselburgh Golf Club has the use of the course and the Club House and facilities. Over and above the RMGC's own competitions, two golf competitions are held for workers from the much diminished mining communities – the Annual Retired Mineworkers' Golf Competition (previously the Annual Golf Championship for Retired Personnel) in June (begun in 1961), and the Annual Scottish Coalfield Golf Championships on the first Monday in May. This last competition is the successor to the Scottish Divisional Golf Championship Final (begun 1952), the final of which seems to have been held at Prestongrange from 1964–68. Re-organisation in the industry in 1968 resulted in a re-naming of the competition to the Scottish Mineworkers' Golf Championship, which, after a break in 1984, was re-started in 1985 under its present name. From 1970, the winners of the previous year's final at the RMGC have gone on to represent Scotland in the National Competition for Mineworkers; they won the first three years of this, and the 1974 final was held at Prestongrange.

Today, a range of 'social' golf days are held, in aid of charities and for local causes such as the East Lothian Children's Playgroup (for less able children). Indoor bowls remain a popular activity, as does snooker. The weight lifters, so much a feature of Prestongrange in the 1960s, have now moved to Edinburgh.

With the decline in employment in the mining sector, CISWO's brief to deal with the whole community through Miners' Welfare has changed to encompass a development strategy for the whole community – whether associated with mining or not. Nevertheless, as many of today's communities comprise the children and grandchildren of past miners, CISWO's remit almost inevitably retains, at its heart, the mining community: and the whole community which lives around Prestongrange is no exception.

* * *

On the death of the 8th Baronet in 1997 the remaining baronial lands of Prestoungrange were acquired by Dr Gordon Prestoungrange from the Manor of Milton Malsor in Northamptonshire. His interest in the barony arose from Lilian Audrey Park, his mother who was born in Musselburgh in 1902, and his grandfather's career as a miner at Prestongrange Colliery at the dawn of the 20th Century. He also numbered among his ancestors Willie Park Senior and Mungo Park, both winners of the Open and well known to the RMCC. Since his accession and recognition by The Lord Lyon, he has re-established the Baron Court as a non-profit organisation to facilitate the socio-economic regeneration of Prestonpans, and to revive some of the traditions of the feudal age which can bring benefit and enjoyment in the 21st Century. In 2006 he and Lady Prestoungrange took up residence in the Eastern Lodge which William Playfair had designed in 1837.

CONCLUSION

The story of Prestongrange House is one of a long occupied site, of a number of illustrious owners, and of other less well known residents whose mark, nonetheless, the old House retains. It is a story of lives that impinged on great events in Scotland's history, and of lives that made no impact at all on the national scene. Most noticeable of all, it is a story of variable fortunes, often won by one generation, and lost by another.

In the second half of the twentieth century, CISWO's commitment to Prestongrange has witnessed enormous social and economic change, including change in the coal industry. Having taken on the property at a time when it seemed that the industry would continue to thrive, CISWO has weathered the storms of the 1970s and 1980s, and finally reached the changed cultural environment of the 1990s. The decline in the coal sector has been matched by an increase in the leisure and heritage industries. The adverse influences – the proximity of the colliery – that made Prestongrange House so 'unlettable' in 1912–14 have now gone. Its position on the edge of the Firth of Forth is an admirable one, and its proximity to Edinburgh desirable. There is a nice irony here. The descendants of many of those who laboured to provide earlier owners with luxuries, now themselves enjoy the amenities that the House has to offer. It seems that the future for Prestongrange looks better today than it has done for almost a century.

BIBLIOGRAPHY

Primary Sources

As per footnotes in text:
CISWO Records (CISWO); contact CISWO, 2nd Floor, 50 Hopetoun Street, Bathgate, West Lothian, EH48 4EU
Edinburgh University Library (EUL), George Square, Edinburgh
National Archives of Scotland (NAS), Princes Street, Edinburgh – was SRO
National Library of Scotland (NLS), George IV Bridge, Edinburgh
Royal Commission for Ancient and Historical Monuments (RCAHMS), 16 Bernard Terrace, Edinburgh
Haddingtonshire Courier
Regesta Regum Scottorum p280, no 241

Secondary Sources

Anderson, AO, *Early Sources of Scottish History: AD500–1286* (1922)
Balfour Paul, J (Ed), *The Scots Peerage* (1907)
Barrow, GWS, *Kingship and Unity: Scotland 1000–1306* (1981)
Barrow, GWS, *The Kingdom of the Scots: Government, Church and Society from the 11th–14th Centuries* (1973)
Barrow, GWS, 'A 12th Century Newbattle Document' in *Scottish Historical Review* XXX (1951)
Black, DJ, 'A Step up for Playfair' in *The Scottish Field* (August 1977)
Brown, KM, 'Noble Indebtedness in Scotland between the Reformation and the Revolution' in *Historical Research: the Bulletin of the Institute of Historical Research* Vol LXII (1989)
Brunton, G & Haig, D, *An Historical Account of the Senators of the College of Justice from its Institution in MDXXXII* (1832)
Checkland, O & S, *Industry and Ethos: Scotland 1832–1914* (2nd ed 1989)
Cohn, N, *Europe's Inner Demons: the Demonization of Christians in Mediaeval Christendom* [Ch 8] (1975, 1993)
Colvin, H, *A Biographical Dictionary of British Architects: 1600–1840* (1978)
Craigie, WMA, *A Dictionary of the Older Scottish Tongue from the 12th Century to the End of the 17th Century* (1938, 1951)
Daiches, D (Ed), *The New Companion to Scottish Culture* (1993)
Dickinson, WC, *Scotland from the Earliest Times to 1603* (1961)
Dilworth, M, 'The commendator system' in *The Innes Review*, XXXVII (1986)
Donaldson, G, Scotland: *James V to James VII* (1965)
Elliott, A & May JA, *A History of Golf*
Glendinning, M MacInnes, R & MacKechnie, A, *A History of Scottish Architecture from the Renaissance to the Present Day* (1996)

Gouldsborough, P, *Formulary of Old Scottish Documents* (1985)
Gow, I, 'Playfair: a Northern Athenian' in *RIBA Journal* (May 1990)
Gow, I, 'WH Playfair, Architect to the Modern Athens' in *RIAS Diary* (1988)
Grant, A, *Independence and Nationhood: Scotland 1306–1469* (1984)
Grant, FJ (Ed), *The Faculty of Advocates in Scotland 1532–1943* (1944)
Green, CE, *East Lothian* (1906)
Harvie, C, *No Gods and Precious Few Heroes: Twentieth Century Scotland* (3rd Ed 1998)
Howard, D, *The Architectural History of Scotland: Scottish Architecture from the Reformation to the Restoration 1560–1660* (1995)
Lenman, BP, *Integration and Enlightenment: Scotland 1746–1832* (1981)
Lynch, M, *Scotland: a New History* (1991)
McNeill, P, *Tranent and its Surroundings* (1883)
McNeill, P, *Prestonpans and Vicinity* (1902)
McNeill, PGB & MacQueen, HI (Eds), *Atlas of Scottish History to 1707* (1996)
McWilliam, C, *The Buildings of Scotland: Lothian except Edinburgh* (2nd ed 1980)
McWilliam, C, 'Modern Athenian' in *Scotland's Magazine* (August 1957 pp 20–21)
Mitchison, R, *Lordship to Patronage: Scotland 1603–1745* (1983)
Moody, D, 'Notes on William Grant of Prestongrange' to be published in *The New Oxford Dictionary of National Biography* (c 2002)
Mosley, C (Ed), *Burke's Peerage & Baronetage* (106th ed 1999)
Murdoch, A, *The People Above* (1980)
Murray, G, Apted, MR & Hodkinson, I, 'Prestongrange and its Painted Ceiling' in *Transactions of the East Lothian Antiquarian and Field Naturalists Society* Vol X (1966) pp 92–132
Namier, L & Brooke, J, *History of Parliament: the Commons 1754–1790* vol III (1964)
Napier University, *Merchiston Tower* (undated pamphlet)
Ritchie, RLG, *The Normans in Scotland* (1954)
Sanderson, MHB, *Mary Stewart's People* [pp166–178] (1987)
Scott, H, *Fasti Ecclesiae Scoticanae: The Succession of Ministers in the Church of Scotland from the Reformation* Vol I: Synod of Lothian & Tweedale (1915)
Stair Memorial Encyclopaedia *The Laws of Scotland*, Vol II (1990)
Stringer, KJ, *Earl David of Huntingdon, 1152–1219: a Study in Anglo-Scottish History* (1985)
Tranter, N, *The Fortalices and Early Mansions of Southern Scotland: 1400–1650* (1935)
Whatley, CA, *The Scottish Salt Industry 1570–1850* (1987)
Whyte, I & K, *The Changing Scottish Landscape 1500–1800* (1991)
Wormald J, Court, *Kirk and Community: Scotland 1470–1625* (1981)
Youngson, AJ, *The Making of Classical Edinburgh: 1750–1840* (1988 ed)

NOTES

1 I am grateful for Dr S Boardman's comments on this section
2 Stringer, KJ, *Earl David of Huntingdon, 1152–1219: a Study in Anglo-Scottish History* (1985) p. 179
3 Ibid. p. 130
4 Ibid. p. 130, Anderson, AO, *Early Sources of Scottish History: AD500–1286* (1922), p. 487 Ritchie, RLG, *The Normans in Scotland* (1954), p. 285
5 McNeill, P, *Tranent and its Surroundings* (1883) p. 2
6 Barrow, GWS, 'A 12th Century Newbattle Document' in *Scottish Historical Review* XXX (1951) p. 42. A Justiciar was a Royal official who supervised the Sheriffs; there were only 2 Justiciaries – one to the South and one to the North of the Forth.
7 Barrow, GWS, *The Kingdom of the Scots: Government, Church and Society from the 11th–14th Centuries* (1973), p. 102

8 Barrow (1951) op. cit., p. 42
9 Stringer, op. cit., p. 27
10 Barrow (1951) op. cit., pp. 41–49
11 Stringer, op. cit., p. 277 note 19
12 *Regesta Regum Scottorum*, p. 280, no 241
13 Barrow (1951) op. cit., p. 41
14 Craigie, WMA, *A Dictionary of the Older Scottish Tongue from the 12th Century to the End of the 17th Century* (1938, 1951) Vol II, p. 693
15 Barrow (1951) op. cit., p. 49
16 Anderson, op. cit., p. 487
17 The de Brus (later Bruce) and Steward (later Stewart) families, both of Norman origin, came to Scotland in this period; the former probably with David I c1124, the latter in 1136. Lynch, M, *Scotland: a New History* (1991), pp. 56, 57
18 The fortunes of the de Quincy family prospered for several years on the back of a series of fortuitous marriages; it seems that the male line eventually died out, and the three remaining co-heiresses managed to marry a trio of husbands, who in c1318, gave their support to the English Edward II against Robert the Bruce. McNeill, op. cit., p. 3
19 Sanderson, MHB, *Mary Stewart's People* (1987) pp. 166–178 provides extensive detail on Mark Ker
20 Balfour Paul, J (Ed), *The Scots Peerage* (1907), Vol V, p. 453
21 Sanderson, MHB, op. cit., p. 167
22 Ibid., p. 171, suggests that Mark Ker and Helen Leslie were married by 1567
23 Ibid., p. 175 states that Mark Ker also had a natural daughter, Margaret, who gave birth to his grandson sometime before 1557
24 Balfour Paul, J, op. cit., p. 453
25 Sanderson, MHB, op. cit., p. 173
26 See also the section on the Twentieth Century
27 Ibid., p. 173
28 Ibid., p. 175
29 Wormald J, *Court, Kirk and Community: Scotland 1470–1625* (1981), Chapter 10, pp. 160–176 lists Crathes, Midmar and Castle Fraser as examples of developments on 'the native style, the tower house' p. 171 Howard, D, *The Architectural History of Scotland: Scottish Architecture from the Reformation to the Restoration 1560–1660* (1995) illustrates the style of this period; Chapter 3, pp. 48–96
30 Apted, M in Murray, G, Apted, MR & Hodkinson, I, 'Prestongrange and its Painted Ceiling' in *Transactions of the East Lothian Antiquarian and Field Naturalists Society* Vol X (1966) p. 102
31 The Prestongrange Ceiling at Merchiston Tower, Napier University, Edinburgh is normally open to the public **by appointment only**. Telephone: PR & Marketing Unit on 0131 455 6311. As of December 1999, the site is closed for essential maintenance
32 Murray, G, Apted, MR & Hodkinson, I, 'Prestongrange and its Painted Ceiling' in *Transactions of the East Lothian Antiquarian and Field Naturalists Society* Vol X (1966) pp. 92–132
33 Cohn, N, *Europe's Inner Demons: the Demonization of Christians in Medieval Christendom* [Ch 8] (1975, 1993)
34 Napier University, *Merchiston Tower* (undated pamphlet) p. 5
35 Grant, FJ (Ed), *The Faculty of Advocates in Scotland 1532–1943* (1944), p. iii
36 Sanderson, MHB, op. cit., p. 175
37 Balfour Paul, J, op. cit., p. 455
38 Ibid., p. 456
39 McNeill, PGB & MacQueen, HI (Eds), *Atlas of Scottish History to 1707* (1996), p. 201
40 Sanderson, MHB, op. cit., p. 177
41 Murray, G, Apted, MR & Hodkinson, I, op. cit. p. 98
42 Brown, KM 'Noble Indebtedness in Scotland between the Reformation and the Revolution' in *Historical Research: the Bulletin of the Institute of Historical Research* Vol LXII (1989), p. 260
43 Ibid., p. 275
44 Ibid., p. 266
45 Ibid., p. 273 note 49 indicates that, in c1622, Ker had forfeited a £40,000 caution on behalf of Sir John Kerr of Jedburgh, thus pushing his finances out of control. Why he did this is not explored

46 Grant, FJ, op. cit., p. 155
47 NAS GD357/43/1 1627
48 Brunton, G & Haig, D, *An Historical Account of the Senators of the College of Justice from its Institution in MDXXXII* (1832) p. 27
49 NAS CC8/8/55 fo 224
50 NAS GD124/2/22 1627
51 NAS GD124/2/22 1627 Assignations; GD124/2/47 discharge of 1627 bond GD357/43/1 1627 Procuratory by Mr Alexander Morison: demand for bond £40000 Scots. For notes on 'discharge' see Gouldsborough, P, *Formulary of Old Scottish Documents* (1985)
52 NAS CC8/8/55 fo 224 1665
53 NAS CC8/8/86 fo 181 GD20/1/813 reference to William Morison of Prestongrange, only son of said Alexander, now deceased 1711
54 NAS GD6/1367 1665
55 NAS GD6/2156 1634 Debt Discharge GD20/1/813 1668 Assignation by Master Robert Gordon to Sir Alexander Morison who, on a bond dated 16, 17, 18 March 1668, borrowed 14,000 merks Scots – this bond reappears on 6 April 1717 in GD20/1/813
56 Murray, G, Apted, MR & Hodkinson, I, op. cit., p. 99
57 NAS CC8/8/86 fo 181
58 NLS Charter 1019 5.4.1734 NLS MSS 10851 re Alexander Tytler acting for the creditors of Prestongrange 10.2.1736 although NLS MSS 16809 fo 116–123 indicates Tytler was Prestongrange factor 1729–34
59 NAS CC8/8/104 fo 267 will registered 30.7.1741
60 NLS MSS 14757 fo 92–143 1695–1697 NLS Charter 11832 and Charter 11833 1696
61 Whatley, CA, *The Scottish Salt Industry 1570–1850* (1987) pp 71 & 117
62 Green, CE, *East Lothian* (1906) p. 63
63 NAS GD6/2094 12 November 1703
64 NAS GD6/2094 1688–1733 GD6/2156
65 NAS GD6/2156 1715, 1718, 1719
66 NAS GD6/2156 12.3.1719
67 NLS MSS 17706 fo101, 102, 106, 220
68 NLS MSS 16352 fo 87 1725 – Morison's house was in 'Chelsay'
69 NLS MSS 16352 fo 87, August 1725
70 NLS MSS 17712 fo 68, undated, probably 1742
71 NLS MSS 17713 fo 48
72 Mitchison, R, *Lordship to Patronage: Scotland 1603–1745* (1983) p. 96 explains that 'carriages' referred to '... fetching goods, particularly cutting and bringing in peats.' and that this was a service often carried out as a means of paying the rent in a society where the economy was based less on money and more in goods.
73 NAS CC8/8/104 fo 267 30 July 1741
74 NLS MSS 3720 1745
75 Moody, D, 'Notes on William Grant of Prestongrange' to be published in *The New Oxford Dictionary of National Biography* (c 2002) I am grateful to David Moody for making his notes available to me. William Grant appears in Robert Louis Stevenson's *Catriona*, the sequel to *Kidnapped.*
76 NLS MSS 17528, fo 46 1747
77 NLS MSS 16679, fo 48–50 1752
78 NLS MSS 16700, fo 129 1757 letter to Lord Milton on getting constables '... searching, seizing and bringing to the next meeting persons fit to be recruits...'
79 NLS MSS 16675, fo 77 1751
80 NLS MSS 3720, p. 1 1745
81 NLS MSS 16623, fo 238 11 August 1746
82 NLS MSS 16671, fo 32 19.11.1750
83 NLS MSS 16687, fo 234 1754
84 NAS CC8/8/119.2 1764
85 NLS MSS 10970, p. 2 1752
86 NLS MSS 10970, p. 102 1752
87 NAS GD357/46/2 1756
88 NAS GD357/43/18 GD357/44/7
89 NAS GD357/44/3 The third baronet was the eldest son of Sir James Suttie of Balgone, second baronet, and of Elizabeth Dalrymple, third daughter of Sir Hugh Dalrymple of North Berwick

90 NAS SC/40/67/1 SC40/67/13
91 NAS RHP 41333/2
92 NAS GD357/51/2 7.1.1836 GD357/51/3 & GD357/51/7 Inventory: 1839
93 NAS GD357/51/6
94 NAS GD357/50/3 16.5.1836
95 NAS GD357/50/1 1836
96 NAS GD357/50/6
97 NAS GD357/44/7 Contract of marriage between George Grant-Suttie and Lady Harriet
98 NLS MSS 8191, fo 169
99 Haddingtonshire Courier: 6.6.1862
100 NAS GD357/34/10 Letter to Sir George Grant-Suttie 17.11.1876 from Dr Struthers Prestonpans Manse
101 NAS GD 357/34/11 14.12.1876
102 NAS GD357/40/21 21.1.1878
103 NAS GD357/39/1 1877–78
104 NAS GD357/87 pp. 243, 244 8.8.1879
105 NAS GD357/87 p. 268
106 NAS GD357/87 pp. 167–213 and GD357/24/7
107 NAS GD357/87 p. 393
108 NAS GD357/40/17 4.7.1878
109 An excellent summary of Playfair's work on the House is given by Apted in Murray, G, Apted, MR & Hodkinson, I, 'Prestongrange and its Painted Ceiling' in *Transactions of the East Lothian Antiquarian and Field Naturalists Society* Vol X (1966) pp. 92–132
110 for a full interpretation of Playfair's career see: Gow, I 'Playfair: a Northern Athenian' in *RIBA Journal* (May 1990) and Gow, I 'WH Playfair, Architect to the Modern Athens' in *RIAS Diary* (1988)
111 Youngson, AJ, *The Making of Classical Edinburgh: 1750–1840* (1988 ed) pp. 155, 156
112 Ibid, pp. 281, 282
113 Letterbooks for 1830–33 and 1840–45 are held by the Special Collections in the University of Edinburgh library: they also hold his collection of drawings, which are available on microfilm. Others of Playfair's letters are held in various collections in the National Library of Scotland, Edinburgh.
114 NAS GD18/5847 1.11.1849 Indicates that Sir George Grant-Suttie was on the Board of Management for the designs for the Mound, Edinburgh. Playfair's work on Prestongrange House began c1830, so it is clear that they knew each other before 1849.
115 Gow, I (1988) op. cit., under 'Playfair's Life of Work' [no page numbers]
116 Ian Gow, informal conversation December 1999
117 Playfair's collection of drawings is held by the University of Edinburgh, reference P19. A copy of the list of the drawings is appended as Annex A
118 Howard, op. cit., p. 55
119 NAS GD357/28/3 18.1.1853
120 NAS GD357/15/1 to 4 1852–1872
121 Edinburgh University Library: Playfair Letterbooks: No 4 – 1830 pp. 1, 5, 8, 9, 20, 121, 146, 181. No 7 – 1840 pp. 288, 503
122 Stair Memorial Encyclopedia, *The Laws of Scotland*, Vol II (1990), paragraphs 1232–1237 on the role of a *curator bonis*; 'a curatory of those under mental disability'.
123 NAS VR99/21-29 1909–1927
124 NAS IRS 64/92 p. 102
125 CISWO files: extracted from an unpublished article by J Bush, 15.5.1962. A new publication on the History of the RMGC is to be published shortly
126 Thanks are due to Ian McAlpine, CISWO's Operations Manager (Scotland) for his assistance in making the CISWO files available, and also to Tom Hardie and his team at Prestongrange House.
127 CISWO files: 14.3.1957 lette from TWS Morgan, CISWO Divisional Social Welfare Officer, Edinburgh to RS Sutherland, CISWO, London
128 The Trustees are now the President, the Vice-President, the Secretary and the Treasurer of the Management Committee
129 CISWO files: from the Constitution and Regulations of the Musselburgh Miners' Charitable Society (1993)
130 CISWO files: letter from Cassells, Architect's Section, Welfare Branch 9.11.1956
131 CISWO Preliminary Investigation Report, c 1960

132 CISWO files: 18.1.1951 letter from Architect to the RMGC Secretary
133 As discussed earlier, relative to Mark Ker and Helen Leslie
134 CISWO files: report of meeting 20.11.1962 with Michael Apted

2
Acheson/ Morrison's Haven

What Came and Went and How?

Julie Aitken

INTRODUCTION

The site of the harbour at Morrison's Haven lies between the towns of Musselburgh and Prestonpans at the western end of the county of East Lothian, Scotland. The harbour site and environs form part of an area of land reclamation by the South of Scotland Electricity Board (now ScottishPower). As part of the coastal walkway, the site is maintained by the county's Ranger Service and also links into the nearby Prestongrange Mining Museum which provides an interesting and informative diversion for walkers of the route. If you are unaware of its existence, the harbour is easy to overlook particularly in summer when the remains of its stone piers are clothed in a mantle of brambles and wild flowers. The wooden pillars, which supported the timber wharf, now protrude from the grass in what was the harbour basin. They are easy to mistake for an addition to the wooden barrier erected along the roadside by East Lothian Council in a bid to deter travelling folk from inhabiting the grassy expanse between the road and the seashore. Clearly visible down on the beach is the roundel which was at one time the base for the light at the harbour mouth, and what looks at first sight to be nothing more than a strip of rocks, proves on closer inspection to be the ruinous remnants of the pier. The beach around the harbour is also a testimony to the past industries of the immediate area – the sand abounds with pottery shards, oyster shells, fireclay bricks and shale (a by-product of coal mining), all of which were exported via Morrison's Haven. The harbour's life began and ended with coal and fishing. From the outset coal was loaded and shipped from its piers and fishermen sheltered their boats in its safe embrace. It is therefore fitting that its life should have ended with the demise of mining in the locality and with the ruined skeleton of a fishing vessel buried amidst the rubble that fills the basin.

Landward view of Morrison's Haven Harbour featuring trading ships or 'bushes'

Courtesy of Mrs A. Allan

Morrison's Haven was home to a harbour for almost five hundred years. Originally known as Newhaven, this name was used intermittently until the 18th century, along with the name Acheson's Haven after Alexander Atkinson of Salt-Prestoun (now Prestonpans). In 1700, William Morison,[1] then the owner of Prestongrange Estates, applied to The Scottish Parliament for permission to build a Harbour at Morrison's[2] Haven and so we arrive at the name by which the area is still known today.

Prestonpans was an important industrial area in the 18th century and, as such, its port was equally significant. Its varying fortunes reflect events in Scotland, and the characters linked to the harbour were of importance in Scottish history. The significance of Morrison's Haven is difficult to appreciate when looking at the overgrown, grassy site that is all that remains of the harbour today.

FOREIGN TRADE IN MEDIEVAL SCOTLAND

The sea routes used by the Scottish merchant ships from the 12th century onwards were first navigated by the Vikings, a race of warrior seamen from Scandinavia. During the 8th to 10th centuries, the Vikings raided the coasts of Europe, conquering and settling all over the British Isles and colonising the shoreline of France. The seafaring skills of the Vikings were legendary. Viking folklore tells of the "Saga of Eric the Red" who made an epic voyage from Iceland to Greenland and of his son Leif's journey to the country today known as North America – 500 years before Columbus. The Vikings, through marriage and time, became integrated into the communities they had once invaded.[3] The Viking influence in Scotland is far reaching, but their most important legacy, from the point of this discussion of foreign trade, are the sea routes they established for the purpose of invasion, which were later used by traders and craftsmen looking for overseas trade.

By the 12th century the Burghs of Berwick and Perth were Scotland's most important centres of foreign trade, exporting wool and woollen cloth produced by the Burgh's Scots, Fleming, Anglo-Norman and French inhabitants.[4] Scotland's economy was firmly rural based and this was reflected in the export trade which largely consisted of products from the rural 'hinterlands', particularly wool and hides. This was a time when town and country were very much dependent upon one another for survival. The countryside produced goods and labour and the towns purchased both. Central to the whole system were the monasteries with their sheep farms in the country and their grain stores in the towns.[5]

This system continued largely intact for several centuries until the 16th century, and even then Scotland's economy remained predominantly pastoral, relying upon the export of its produce for revenue to import manufactured goods not available at home. However, by the 1580's the product range had expanded to include coal and salt, both of which were being exported to the Netherlands in increasing quantities. The 1590's saw Scots trade well established and the merchant vessels, in order to search out new markets for their trading purposes, ventured as far south as Spain and north into Sweden. The main export trade remained in wool, skins, hides and other animal products such as tallow, which was used in the production of candles, while manufactured goods and luxury foodstuffs continued to be imported. Scotland also exported 'hawkers', rogue traders better known in the Baltic ports they favoured as "Kramerwaren". They traded in cheap, coarse, woollen cloth made in Dundee for export from the majority of east coast ports.

Thus the state of late sixteenth Scottish international trade was becoming increasingly more sophisticated than when the Port of Newhaven, to the west of Prestonpans, began its life in 1526.[6]

FROM NEWHAVEN TO ACHESON'S HAVEN

The first official recording of a harbour at Prestongrange was made in April, 1526, when James V, whilst visiting Newbattle Abbey, granted the monks 'licentium spedialem unum portum in loco nuncupate Gilbertis-draucht infra dictas terras (i.e. de Prestoungrange) edificandi', or, permission to build a harbour at Prestongrange. This charter was ratified by Parliament in October of that year. Although it is now recognised that the monks wanted a harbour to facilitate the shipping of their coal and salt, the stated purpose for building the harbour was to provide a 'safe haven' for local fishermen who, in the absence of one, had experienced loss of boats and lives. The harbour at this time was known as Newhaven and the presence of a fishing fleet may indicate that some sort of shelter already existed which the monks simply wanted to upgrade. The adversity faced by the fishermen and the need for a 'safe haven' was further confirmed in 1552, by a charter proclaiming a new burgh at nearby Preston which stated that "...the fishermen beyond the sea shore below the lands of Preston and Prestonpans have in past times sustained considerable losses".[7]

From 1540 onwards, Newbattle Abbey, in a bid to raise funds to meet its growing tax obligations to the crown, was forced to feu a large proportion of its lands.[8] Therefore, in 1541 when James V confirmed the charter of 1526, a second charter was included, granted by the Abbey, in favour of one Alexander Atkinson (Acheson) giving him feu-ferme of the harbour.[9] The charter stated that Acheson was permitted to build the harbour (approximate size being one Scots acre, or one and a quarter of today's acres), repair boats there and operate a tide mill. Acheson was also given a 'lie grene' [field], adjoining the harbour on which to erect buildings as required. Indeed, a map of 1850 includes a building named as 'Aitchieson's Lodge' lying just to the east of the harbour.[10] Acheson is described in the second charter as a "servitor" of the Abbey, implying that aside from being the sitting tenant and feuar of the harbour, he was also in service to the Abbey. Assuming building work began around 1541, it was evidently completed quickly to allow its proprietor to begin trading – in 1542 Alexander Acheson, as 'custumar', was in a position to present accounts.[11] His accounts for 1544 show that the goods that passed through the port that year, were fish, hides, salt, tar and lead.[12] The fish, hides and salt would be exported, the tar (used to repair boats) and lead imported. Success did not continue for Acheson, as foreign trade at the harbour was put on hold for a while in 1563 when the Scottish Parliament, concerned at "the derth and scantiness of fewell" prohibited the export of coal.[13]

During the Acheson's tenancy, ownership of the harbour passed by Royal Charter from the Monks of Newbattle into the hands of Mark Ker, Earl of Lothian, in 1587.[14] What happened to the Acheson family does not seem to have been recorded but their link with the harbour that shared their name and appears to have been in their hands for at least 50 years seems to have ended around 1602 when they simply disappeared from the area. One local theory is that the two Acheson brothers who jointly ran the concern at the beginning of the 17th century, for some unknown reason sold their very profitable shipping business and emigrated with their respective families to America. It is even suggested that Dean Acheson, the USA's Secretary for Foreign Affairs in the 1950's, is a direct descendant of these very men![15] At any rate, while customs accounts for Acheson's Haven were produced regularly throughout the sixteenth century, by 1602 the harbour features in a report listing ports with no custumar,[16] indicating that the Acheson's had indeed moved on to pastures new. Parish records show that in 1602, two Acheson brothers were elders in the church and session records show that between them they had a number of children baptised there.[17] Their memory lives on in the modern town of Prestonpans by virtue of a street bearing their name – Acheson Drive.

FROM ACHESON'S HAVEN TO MORRISON'S HAVEN

In 1609, John Morison of Edinburgh, a Bailie, purchased the Estates of Prestongrange from the executors of the 2nd Earl of Lothian, Robert, the son and heir of the aforementioned Mark Ker.[18] It was under the stewardship of John Morison's grandson, William that the harbour was to enjoy one of its busiest periods with vessels trading from as far afield as Maryland, North America. John Morison's son and heir, Alexander, purchased the lands and barony of Prestongrange in 1617,[19] presumably when he inherited the estate from his father. Alexander Morison was an Edinburgh Advocate, academic and one time Rector of Edinburgh University. His friend Jupiter Carlyle of Inveresk wrote of Morison that he was,

> "...so imaginary and credulous as to believe that close by his creek of Morison's Haven was the place where St John wrote the Apocalypse, because some old vaults had been discovered in digging a mill-race for a mill that went by sea-water."[20, 21]

Morison's belief was grounded in the fact that the Masons belonging to the "Ludg of Aitchison's heavine" met annually at the harbour on St John's Day. Minutes of a meeting of master tradesmen held at Falkland on the 31st October 1636 record a discussion on the Lodge at "Atcheson-Haven". Their concern was to put an end to "certain abuses in the 'airtis and craftis' of masons, wrights, shipwrights, coopers, glaziers, painters, plumbers, slaters, plasterers, etc." which gives an insight to the type of employment to be found around the harbour in the mid 17th century.[22] There is still a Lodge of Aitchison's Haven, based in nearby Musselburgh, but it only shares the name of the original Lodge which ceased to exist in 1853.[23]

Trade

In the 17th century, the majority of Scottish vessels trading on the continent were Dutch built, varying in size between 30 and 80 tons each. Commonly known as "bushes", they made up two thirds of the shipping based in East Lothian's harbours.[24] The size of the boats, their relative frailty, and the unpredictable weather of the North Sea meant foreign trade was a summer affair. In the winter months, merchants were restricted to trade with England, hugging the coast as they sailed from port to port.

Dunbar Trade

In the 1680s, Customs Records show Morrison's Haven as home to the Customs House for all trade between Fisherrow Harbour and Aberlady (Dunbar covered Gullane down to the Berwickshire border). Records also indicate that an average of 58 boats per annum used Morrison's Haven while Dunbar's yearly average was 16 boats. Dunbar's main trade was in fish, which was not subject to duty, and boats carrying cargoes of fish would not therefore be entered in the records. Taking this into account, the shipping usage of Dunbar would most likely have been much heavier. A distinct shift in trade was occurring at this time. The traditional exports of the pre-industrial age were abandoned for the manufactured goods and raw materials of the industrial age; salt, coal, and so on were becoming more important and therefore attracted custom's duty. Dunbar's foreign exports consisted of uncured herring to Newcastle-upon-Tyne, cured red and white herring for the continent (particularly catholic Poland, France and on a smaller scale to Spain) and, in times of good harvests, grain.

Foreign exports for Morrison's Haven were primarily salt and coal, with a secondary trade going on in eggs for London (with little hope of a profit if rough seas were encountered!) a few pairs of stockings and a few ells of cloth.[25] Fifty per cent of the boats recorded by customs men at Morrison's Haven carried coal; between November 1684 and November 1685, 28 colliers berthed at Morrison's Haven to load up with coal. Seventeen of these boats were from the Netherlands: nine bound for Zierikzee in Zealand, five for Rotterdam, one to Veere (which was the main Scot's trading port in the Netherlands) and one to an unspecified Dutch destination. Of the remainder, six were headed for France, three to London, one to Hamburg and a further ship to an unknown port of call. Although this would appear to imply that a substantial amount of coal was being exported, each collier could carry on average a mere thirty tons which makes the total recorded coal export for the year in question less than one thousand tons. Presumably, most of the coal mined in the Prestonpans area went towards fuelling the domestic fires that earned Edinburgh its nickname of "Auld Reekie" or to feed the coal hungry salt industry. Another recorded market for the salt industry was the English fishing fleets heading for the Icelandic fishing grounds and calling into Morrison's Haven to take on salt, presumably to use as a preservative for their catches until they were able to get it to market. Prior to the civil wars in England and Holland, both countries had provided important outlets for Prestonpans salt. However, the disruption caused by the wars resulted in the salt merchants having to look for markets further afield, and the focus of their trade shifted to the Baltics and Germany.[26]

Exports

As mentioned earlier, the harbour was home to a fishing fleet so naturally Prestonpans traded in harvests from the sea, but of a more exotic nature than that of Dunbar. Indeed, an entry in the Report Book of Prestonpans for 1691 shows one William Ritchison, master of the *King's Fisherman* of London entering Morrison's Haven with an empty hold, and leaving with a cargo of Lobsters. The report book also shows an English ship picking up a cargo of some 12,000 oysters bound for Riga, Latvia. Shellfish were also sent to Norway, but the main trade was with London, Newcastle, Yorkshire and Yarmouth. Kelp, a useful fertiliser, was also harvested and exported for the English market. As mentioned, in times of glut grain was exported. When, in 1679 and 1685 the continental harvests failed and East Lothian produced more than local markets required, record amounts were sent overseas. Tallow was exported to Holland, and all sorts of animal skins (including dog), together with linen, woollen cloth and a small amount of gloves and stockings were sent abroad via Morrison's Haven.[27, 28]

Imports

As well as indicating the growing industrialisation of the area, the export and import markets also point to the increasing sophistication of Scots society. The crews of the Dutch colliers coming in "empty", in anticipation of their coal loads, would earn themselves some extra money by bringing luxury foodstuffs such as "currants, raisins, figs and prunes; oranges and lemons; sugar loaf and sugar candy". These goods would have originally been exported from France and Spain, and then re-imported into Scotland by the collier crewmen. An import of absolute necessity for the industry of the area was timber. In the spring, boats carrying coal for Holland would set sail from Prestonpans and having off-loaded their coal would then head for Norway and a return cargo of timber. Norway is recorded as providing 40% of East Lothian's imports at this time.[29] East Lothian had exhausted its natural supply of wood but still required quantities of timber for the mining industry (shoring up the coal face), agricultural use (manufacture of carts and other implements), building of houses etc., and for barrel making as most fishing exports were salted and packed into barrels. Once the cargo was loaded, any remaining space was stuffed with "burnwood" for the domestic hearth – belief at this time was that coal burning was not conducive to good health and there was always an eager market for household firewood.

Morrison's Haven dealt with many other industrial imports including iron plate, which was used in the manufacture of the salt pans and which was imported from the Swedish ports of Gothenburg, Stockholm and Norkopping, with three boat loads required yearly to satisfy the local market. Flax, the raw material of the linen industry was imported from Danzig, together with hemp for the rope manufactories, with two or three Prestonpans ships making the trip annually to secure supplies. Dyestuffs were imported from Zierikzee in Holland. Pitch and tar (both required to repair ships and make them watertight) were vital imports from Holland for an area that relied so heavily on its merchant vessels. English hops were imported and used by the numerous breweries in Prestonpans and the surrounding area.

In order to raise money for the royal coffers, double customs duty was levied against foreign registered ships bringing cargoes into Scotland from the end of the 17th century. Competition from foreign ships was an ongoing concern for local merchant seaman and this extra tax on their rivals must have been very welcome.[30] However, the double duty could be avoided. Custom records for 1702 report that two Dutch ships bound for Berwick and driven into Morrison's Haven to shelter from a storm were willing;

> "...to sell cargo, being onions, to Scotsmen, provideing the same be entered for a single duty"

The Leith Customs office were apparently aware of this loophole, when they replied;

> "...Wee doe suspect that there may be some Trick in the matter, and therefore desires you to expixet the same to the bottom. But rather than part with [the onions], If you find their Designs to be honest, we allow you to enter them at Single Duty."[31]

The importance of the harbour at this time should not be underestimated. From the 1680's onwards, English and continental trade at the port flourished, with customs records for 1680 and 1686 suggesting that as much as 10% of Scotland's trade with foreign ships passed through Morrison's Haven.[32] While this growth can be attributed to the fact that the industries in the vicinity of the harbour were producing goods that were much in demand in foreign markets, the industries themselves prospered because of their very proximity to a thriving port. Even the local fishermen were astute enough to alter their traditional catches from herring, etc., and diversify into the luxury food market by providing lobsters and oysters for Europe's finest dinner tables. The system for levying customs duty became more sophisticated with the introduction of increased taxes and double duties for foreign cargoes, but then so too did the trader become more sophisticated in his methods of avoiding having to pay them.

WILLIAM MORISON'S GLASS MANUFACTORY

While accounts show that his father was more at home in Edinburgh's intellectual circles, William Morison appears to have been very much involved with the harbour he inherited in 1684. With the blessing of the Scottish Parliament he had established a glass manufactory "...within his own Bounds at Atchesons Haven, Alias Morisons Haven" by April 1697 which was ratified, by Act of Parliament, in Edinburgh on the 5th August 1698

> "....whereby the Countrey about is not only furnished with bottles, which are sold at very modest and easie rates: But likewayes there are made several other Sorts and Species of Glasses, which were never heretofore Manufactured within this Kingdom, such as Mirror or Looking Glass Plates, Coach-Glasses, Spectacle Glasses, Watch Glasses, Moulded Glasses, and Window Glasses".[33]

The 1698 Act also indicates that Morison had gone to great lengths to ensure the quality of the glass he was producing as he went to the trouble of "...bringing home from abroad expert Workmen for the said Work".[34] Morison was granted a monopoly within Scotland for the manufacture of such products so long as he kept up the quality and affordable prices. Suitable punishments were threatened for anyone who attempted to manufacture, or even import, goods similar to those produced at the glasswork. Despite these measures protecting Morison's enterprise, the glassworks was only in operation for a few short years, before it failed. Perhaps he could not maintain a suitably high quality for the "easie" prices he was obliged to charge.

LATE 17TH CENTURY TO THE MID 18TH CENTURY

Edinburgh's port of Leith held an almost complete monopoly on the import of wine and commanded 80% of the wool and hides market. Even the coal trade did not escape the clutches of the capital city, with 65% of outward trade passing through Leith. Morrison's Haven, like other small ports, had to diversify in order to survive. Therefore, a huge miscellany of goods passed through its entrance accompanied by an equally diverse range of traders, from the fishermen and their fish, to colliers and coal, to members of the upper classes importing necessities for their own households. The following account from the Bye-book of Prestonpans for 1692, offers a small window on the world of a 17th century Scottish Lord

> "...In the Ship called the Ann of Prestonpans, William Melville, Master from London...for the use of the Earle of Levin: an collace with furniture value 300 po:Scotts, a box with a hat wch my Lord wore at London, a box with nyn pounds Jaculat value 27 po: Scotts, two lanthorns, six pound cannary seed for birds, two barrells apples, a box with twentie pound wax candles, a bundle of trees".[35, 36]

The Earl of Levin's imports show just how varied and personal a ship's cargo could be.

Such was the importance of the harbour in the 17th century, that in 1698 an Act of Parliament was passed which permitted the resident's of Acheson's Haven to hold a weekly market and an Annual Fair. At this time, the Mercat Cross in the nearby Burgh of Preston provided the annual meeting place of the Chapmen of the Three Lothians, the largest group of Chapmen in Scotland.[37, 38] The Chapmen of the Three Lothians were an extremely wealthy guild and boasted business interests all over the globe, from gold and diamond mines in India to yearly shipments of huge quantities of fur from Hudson Bay, some of which must surely be included amongst the "skins" recorded as trade at the Haven.[39] It can be easily assumed that the weekly market at Acheson's Haven, with its assortment of goods from all over Europe, would have proved an irresistible draw for the Chapman wishing to add variety to the wares he had to offer his customers.

Although the majority of wines and spirits came through Leith, Edinburgh did not command every such cargo. In 1705, two Norwegian ships from the port of Bergen sailed into Morrison's Haven with a cargo of "...brandie, claret and cherrie sack among their deals and timber baulks".[40] Occasionally, a Dutch boat would enter the harbour carrying German wines and beers. English ships brought tobacco, along with soap, bricks, paper and ropes, all industries which were to become established in the area in the future, but which for the present had to be imported. At the absolute luxury end of the market were imported English hats and gloves, along with Dutch silk and whalebone, de rigeur items for the fashionable ladies and gentlemen of the day. Delft china from Holland and *Russia Leather* from Danzig also made welcome cargoes and each autumn saw the arrival of cargoes of apples and onions, surplus to the Dutch harvests and imported in ships from Zierikzee making a last trading run before the winter weather set in.

In 1700, William Morison petitioned for an 'imposition' 'for building an harbour at Morrison's Haven';[41] the first recorded improvements at the harbour since Acheson's work around 1541. The fact that Morison's petition uses the word "build" implies that at this time major rebuilding works took place as opposed to improvements or repairs.

Smuggling

By 1707 there was considerable activity at Morrison's Haven, particularly with Dutch and French ships. In fact, together with the port at Queensferry, Morrison's Haven was the focus for the Dutch trade.[42] Imported goods were for the Scots market and were also smuggled – at great profit for those prepared to take the risk – into Berwick in the North of England along with tobacco and salt. The boats smuggling goods into England would return laden with cargoes of wool which were then re-exported via Morrison's Haven into France, along with legitimate exports of malt, salt and coal. Anglo-French relations at this time were not good, and as a result the two countries did not officially trade.[43]

Prestonpans was notorious for smuggling. In 1656 Thomas Tucker, Cromwell's agent in Scotland, lamented the fact Morrison's Haven provided the population of Prestonpans with "...a very opportune place for the carreying out and bringing in of goods unto or from any shippe that shal be lying in the roade, if not looked after".[44] Indeed, the Prestonpans' smugglers in 1686 had a friend in the customs officer of that time, Mr James Nimmo, a man who had the ability to run with the hares and hunt with the hounds. He was famed amongst merchants for leaving his records blank for them to complete at their own discretion. This almost backfired on him when he received a visit from his superior, the itinerant surveyor from the port of Leith. However, having been forewarned of the call, Nimmo was able to climb into his office via the window, amend his record book and nip back out, just in time to usher his boss in through the office door. God was on his side that day – as he states in his journal, ".....the Lord wonderfully and mercifully guided me in this hurrie of surprise, praise, praise to Him!"[45]

Nimmo also comments on the local attitude to men in his position, stating that he believed "....we were taken as enemies to the most part of the paroch, and they for the most pairt traders and many of them endevouring to run their Goods privatlie ashoar without entering and payeing the King's Customs".[46] Indeed, local hatred and mistrust of the King's men was highlighted in a case presented to the Privy Council in 1699. Robert Mitchell, a ship's master, was believed to be using his house as a store for illicit goods and two customs waiters who were despatched from Leith to investigate the matter duly discovered "...several anchors of Sack and Brandy and Matts of Tobacco".[47] Upon the removal of these items from their hiding place in the Mitchell home, the two men were confronted by a crowd of two hundred men and women. The angry throng proceeded to attack them "... and fell desperately upon these waiters and did Beat, Bruise and Bleed them to an admirable hight and robbed them of ffourteen pound Scots money and Took their papers and wold actually have murdered them, hade not the Collector and some others come up to divert them".[48]

There is still a widely held belief in Prestonpans that several of the older houses of the town, most notably Walford on the High Street, and Hamilton House in Preston Village, have secret doorways hidden within their walls which open into smugglers tunnels leading down to the beach. A lookout point, built into the sea wall opposite Prestongrange Kirk stands testimony to the problem smuggling in Prestonpans once posed for the state. This vantage point would have afforded the customs man a bird's eye view of any ship approaching the harbour, while giving him plenty time to reach quayside before she berthed. Harry Galloway, a miner at Prestongrange, had some interesting information on the smuggler's tunnels;[49]

> "Old houses had to be knocked down to build the block of flats you see next to the Dragon's Lair, across the High Street from the [Safeway] supermarket. Well, when they got down to the founds, the men got a shock, because they went right through the roof of an old smuggler's tunnel leading down to the beach. They couldn't trace it back because it was blocked with all the rubble, but those flats are built with a pillar holding up the one corner that stands in the tunnel."[50]

It stands to reason that a town inhabited by men who tunnelled underground to earn a living, would also be able to turn those skills to underhand activities if they were so inclined.

The Effect of the Union and the end of the Morison Era

The Union of Parliaments between England and Scotland in 1707 proved to be the beginning of the end of foreign trade at Morrison's Haven at this time. The Westminster Parliament imposed duties and taxes which meant that the illicit trade which had been going on with the North of England was no longer profitable although it still occurred to a lesser extent. The pre-Union smuggler, in fact, became the post-Union merchant. He had already established contacts in various previously illicit markets and had experience of the established routes for bringing cargoes in. In reality all he had to do was carry on as normal, except now he was an honest citizen where once he had been a black marketeer. A prime example of this is the Glasgow Tobacco Lords of the 1750's – pre-Union enemy of the state turned post-Union success story.

In what is recorded as one of the last great trading years of this period, 1719 saw 41 cargoes delivered at Morrison's Haven, amongst which;

> "...19 were imported in ships belonging to the town. Of these cargoes 21 were wholly from Norway, 6 from Sweden, 1 from Dantzic, 2 from Dantzic & Norway, 2 from Bremen, 5 from Rotterdam, 2 from Havre de Grace and St Martin, 1 from Oporto, and 1 from Maryland in North America".[51]

The vessel from North America came into port carrying "102 hogsheads" of tobacco, and then sailed onto the Port of Leith with the remainder of her cargo after having off-loaded 59 hogsheads at Prestonpans. The duties imposed after the Union of 1707 caused a slow but sure decline in the foreign trade of the Port, and then when several of the town's ships were lost at sea, the harbour suffered a setback from which it never truly recovered.[52]

In 1734, the Prestongrange Estates were sequestrated and William Morison died abroad in 1739. Towards the end of his life, he apparently lost interest in his affairs, most notably from the time of his wife's death in 1716 and during this period the lease of the colliery at Prestongrange was offered for sale in the Caledonian Mercury in 1729. The advert read, "...The coal of Prestongrange is fit for the sea as well as land sale, there being a good harbour at Morison's Haven not far distant from the said coal."[53] Whether the lease was taken up is a matter of doubt as by 1746 the mines had stopped producing due to ongoing problems with flooding. The year 1745 saw Prestongrange come into the ownership of the Grant (later Grant-Suttie) family, who were to be its last private owners, and who saw the resuscitation of the mining industry at Prestongrange – to greater heights than ever before – and oversaw the final days of the harbour.

Production problems at the mine and the resulting lack of coal for sale, led to the foreign colliers moving to pastures new in search of their cargoes. This, added to the post-Union duties and loss of vessels, would have further contributed to the fact that trade had ground to a complete halt by 1743, and the port's clientele were forced to go elsewhere in pursuit of foreign goods. According to the records 'No person of enterprise, or capacity, or possessed of sufficient stock, made any persevering efforts to re-establish it [foreign trade at Morrison's Haven]."[54]

LATE 18TH CENTURY

By 1796, foreign trade at Morrison's Haven had apparently picked up again.[55] It was noted that trade in "brownware" pottery from Prestonpans was in demand in such far off market places as North America, the West Indies and most of the European sea-ports. The various local potteries also depended upon the accessibility of the harbour for importing clay from Devonshire, flint from Gravesend and lead from London, Hull and Newcastle. The Prestonpans Vitriol Company (formerly the chemical works of Messrs Roebuck and Garbet), were producing and exporting their products at an incredible rate.[56] In excess of fifty men were employed, working round the clock, to produce Oil of Vitriol, White Ashes, Aquafortis, Spirit of Salt, Sulphuric Acid, Glauber Salts, and also Powdered Manganese for use in the bleaching process. These products were much in demand by Scottish bleachers for bleaching linen cloth and by the printing industry, and were also exported around Europe. As well as exporting via Morrison's Haven, the chemical works also imported their raw materials; these being brimstone from Leghorn and saltpetre from the East India Company of London, required in the production of Oil of Vitriol, and also sulphur shipped from Italy.[57]

One unexpected import of which evidence is still found today at Morrison's Haven is the several species of flora not native to Scotland. Soil was at one time used to weight vessels sailing "empty" to collect a cargo and was jettisoned on arrival in port to make room for cargo. Today's plants are the descendants of those seeds collected along with the soil to be used as ballast.

MILLS AT MORRISON'S HAVEN

Tide Mills

The 1526 Charter granted permission to operate a tide-mill at Prestongrange, and by 1587, the Register of the Great Seal mentions two tide mills working at Acheson's Haven, both of which were employed in milling grain.[58] Tide mills were peculiar to the East Coast of Scotland, but still remained rare mainly due to the ready accessibility of conventional waterpower. At least four sites existed in the Firth of Forth at Crail, Burntisland, Blackness and Acheson's Haven.[59]

By the mid-17th century, Prestonpans and its port were at the heart of an area of rapid industrialisation; its two tide mills, together with several other water-mills driven by the mine adits[60] and at least one windmill were required to satisfy the area's need for power. By the late 1700's, the tide mills were grinding flint for the Prestonpans pottery industry. The entrepreneurs, Garbett and Cadell jointly founded a pottery in 1751, one of several in the area, which combined the ground flint with lead to produce lead silicate for glazing their white stoneware and china pottery.[61] According to the Statistical Account, only one of the harbour mills was involved in the flint industry, complimented by a second flint mill to the east of the harbour area which was powered by a mine adit.[62]

That the harbour was known by the names Port au Moulin, in 1553, and Milhaven, as an alias in 1607, would indicate that tide mills did in fact exist and were an important feature of the harbour.[63] However, money making venture apart, a tide mill at the Haven was a necessity for another reason – the harbour was notorious for silting up. The position of the mill and reservoir was such that the pond filled up with each incoming tide, and then the stored water, as well as driving the mill machinery, was used to flush out the silt from the harbour mouth.[64] The entrance to the harbour was extremely narrow and without the existence of the mill, would have quickly become impassable.

Sawmills and Bleachingfields

A map dated 1854 showing the Prestongrange coastline features a sawmill operating at Morrison's Haven.[65] Despite no other evidence for the existence of a sawmill, a case can readily be made for one. Of the two tide mills to be found at Burntisland, one was apparently used as a saw mill as early as the late 16th century, although the first documentary evidence is a map dated 1843.[66] It is reasonable to assume that a sawmill would have operated at Prestongrange, based on the amount of timber being imported. Timber imported from Morrison's Haven, perhaps cut at the sawmill, was purchased for Lord Milton's new project, a Bleachingfield at Saltoun.[67] The advances made in the chemistry of bleaching, and especially John Roebuck's experiments with oil of vitriol and powder of manganese at the Prestonpans works, resulted in the bleaching of linen becoming one of the earliest "factory" type operations.[68] During August and September of 1747, 123 cart loads of timber from Prestonpans were sent to Saltoun, along with iron and tiles purchased from the Cockenzie merchant, Cadell, which would have been, in all probability, imported at Morrison's Haven. The creation of the Bleachingfield took four years to complete, required in excess of 400 cartloads of materials and cost £2,123 13s 6d.

Fisherfolk and Oysters

Oysters

The first industry mentioned in connection with the harbour at Morrison's Haven was that of fishing, and although various kinds of fish, including herring and skate were caught in the waters off Prestonpans, the main harvest of the fishermen was Oysters. A 1896 report on the profitability of the Prestongrange estate contains a map showing the extent of "Sir George Grant Suttie's Oyster Fishing Grounds circa 1870". They stretched from the Eskmouth at Musselburgh at the Western edge to Prestongrange Kirk at the Eastern edge, and reached six miles out into the Firth of Forth.[69]

The golden age for the oyster fisher was between 1773– 1786 when the "scalps" (the Scots name for an oyster bed) were providing in excess of 6,000 oysters per boat per day, and ten boats operated out of Morrison's Haven.[70] Each of the ten local boats required a crew of five men, at a time when the Statistical Accounts show that Prestonpans had only 23 regular fishermen.[71] The remaining twenty-seven men would have been made up of "onca's"; men on call to some other trade, but who turned their hand to fishing in season to supplement their income.[72] During the 1770's the oysters went by land to Glasgow and Edinburgh as well as by sea to London and Hull. The oysters sent for the London market at Billingsgate were packed in barrels, each containing 1200 of the shellfish. Arriving in London around mid-May, the oysters were deposited in the Thames estuary to be fattened up, before being dredged once more the following September, for sale and consumption. The best Prestonpans oysters were known as Pandores, so called because they were to be found bordering the salt pans, or at the "pan doors".[73] If Pandores were considered a delicacy by those outwith Prestonpans, some locals considered them a special treat too. Mary Morgan born 1905 off the High Street, Prestonpans, remembers the fishing community in Prestonpans, especially the oysters;

> "...My uncle went to the fishing........ he had his own wee boat. He used to get maybe half a dozen oysters in his [bait] nets, and he would keep them for grandfather Thomson. He loved oysters. He would just open up the shells, scoop them out and swallow them down"[74]

The oyster season traditionally ran during those months with an "R" in their names – September to April – and at least three times during this period a boat would set sail for Newcastle carrying a cargo of between thirty and forty thousand oysters. Boats used for exporting fish were traditionally open decked and as such came home empty as, without a deck, there was nothing to protect a valuable cargo from sea spray. The type of boat used for the Newcastle run would have been 38′ from stem to stern with no deck, a 33′ keel, a depth of 4′8″ and a beam of 12′9″. The oyster fishing boats themselves were much the same design although smaller, being only 26ft stem to stern. One story, much retold, is of the night the trade boat left Morrison's Haven at 3am, loaded with her cargo of oysters, and reached Newcastle at 4pm that same day – a record time of thirteen hours. Fishing is, and always has been, a dangerous occupation. There are two accounts of violent storms causing loss of life and vessel, one on the 6th December 1847,[75] and another on the 13th January 1908 at which time emergency loans were offered to the fishermen to replace their lost boats.[76] There can be no reference to the oyster fishermen of Morrison's Haven without mentioning their dredging song, described both as "curious", and "not unpleasant". The men sang the plaintive, haunting air from the commencement of dredging until the catch was hauled onto the boat. In the early morning, with a mist lying over a calm, still sea, they must have provided an eerie sound indeed.

In 1786, trade in Prestonpans oysters ceased because their scarcity, due to overfishing, meant high prices. The Prestongrange grounds were also fished by Dutch and English boats whose catch was in demand all over Europe. Local fishermen used a method of dragging the oysters which was very labour intensive and oysters unsuitable for sale were returned to the sea till the next time. The foreign boats used an entirely different method whereby everything on the sea bed was dredged and taken, large or small, edible or not. This was considered the main cause for the scalps decline. Indeed, by 1796, catches were down to around 500 oysters per boat per day, and oysters earned the fishermen 15d (old pennies) for 100 but by the time the catch reached the markets of Newcastle, the price per 100 had jumped to two shillings.

Oyster spat, (eggs), were also exported to replenish the English oyster beds in Kent and Essex, and this coupled with over-fishing and increasing pollution from the mines, led to the industry dying out. The English and Dutch boats stopped coming around 1871, and while local fishermen continued to dredge, the main purpose of the exercise was now to obtain bait for their lines.

COAL MINING AND EXPORTS – EARLY 19TH CENTURY TO THE END OF THE HARBOUR'S TRADING LIFE

When Prestongrange came into the ownership of William Grant in 1745, the coal mine was flooded and, as a result, foreign trade at the harbour was almost non-existent. Yet another Advocate, Grant was also one time Lord Advocate and Member of Parliament, and with such a busy life, employed a Factor and Manager to oversee his estates and interests at Prestongrange.[77] The harbour would appear once more to be a free port by 1753, with no one person required to take responsibility for necessary repair works as was demonstrated when the heritors and some of the feuars "...applied to Parliament and obtained an act for imposing a duty of two pennies Scotch on each Scotch pint of ale brewed, brought into, and vended in the parish; the money arising from which was to be applied for repayment of a sum to be advanced ......and for repairing Morison's Haven."[78] The harbour is shown on a contemporary map as being open mouthed to the east and west ends with a barrier of natural rock embellished with dressed stone providing a pier which could only be reached

Landward view of Morison's Haven Pier
East Lothian Council, David Spence Collection

during high tide by boat, or on foot when the tide was out.[79] Fishing would appear, once again, to be the main industry of the harbour. The mining community of Prestonpans, with the mine out of production, no money coming in and hungry families to feed, must all have looked seawards. It was not until Sir James Grant Suttie inherited the estate in 1818 that the fortunes of the miners, and therefore those of Morrison's Haven, revived.

Landward view of Morison's Haven Harbour with Prestongrange Colliery in the distance

East Lothian Council, David Spence Collection

That Sir James Grant Suttie was able to consider reopening the mine at Prestongrange, was due to the development of new machinery allowing easier removal of water from the coal face. That it was worthwhile investing thus in the mines at Prestongrange was indicated in a report commissioned from a Civil Engineer named John Buchanan whose recommendations were also taken into account when the harbour was rebuilt in 1876. Sir James' heir, Sir George Grant Suttie inherited Prestongrange in 1828 and by 1830, had leased the mining operations to the English Company owned by one Mathias Dunn. However, Dunn's expenditure on the necessary machinery to get the mines working again, was not recompensed by the profit raised by the price of the coal he produced and by 1840 the pit was once more flooded with no tenant. Things finally began to look up in 1850 when the Prestongrange Coal and Iron Company took up the lease. Based in Cornwall, the Prestongrange Company was responsible for shipping via Morrison's Haven, the giant beam engine that now forms the focal point of the present day mining museum.[80] They were also responsible for the construction of; "...a large no. of commodious cottages, two storeys in height for their [workforce] accommodation at a short distance eastwards from the Harbour".[81] Increased output at the modernised and extended colliery meant that Morrison's Haven was unable to cope with the higher level of exports and re-building works were undertaken in 1875 when the Haven is recorded as receiving a major facelift for the third time in its existence. These works were completed in 1877 and were described as "..improvements and increase in harbour size, to coincide with the opening of Prestonfield coalfield, at a cost of £10,000".[82] The works included the installation of a railway line to allow an engine hauling hutches [barrows] to transport coal from the pit-head to the colliers waiting in the harbour. Also included on the wharf was a piece of lifting equipment to allow ease of transfer of the coal from hutch to hold, known universally by the men who used it as the "side cowper" [side tipper]. A further rail line connected the Firebrick Works to the harbour and sewage pipes, chimney pots, firebricks and bricks were also shipped overseas. As previously mentioned, the works carried out were planned by John Buchanan a Civil Engineer. He had recommended that as well as deepening the harbour basin, "...a concrete pier 80 ft in diameter and 4 ft above the high water mark.....be erected at the extreme west point."[83] Once the works were completed, the harbour could still not be considered large, and was able to accommodate colliers no larger than 600 tons, with no more than one boat at a time in the harbour basin. The boats arriving to take out the coal also brought in timber props for use in mines.

Sir James Grant Suttie's accounts for the year 1877–78 show that the Prestongrange Coal and Iron Company Limited were obliged to find the following sums for the rental of their premises. The yearly fixed rent for Prestongrange Colliery and Minerals was £2,000.00. For the miner's houses at various sites around Prestonpans, including Morrison's Haven, £148.00. The rental for the harbour itself was the princely sum of £20.00 with a further £180.00 for the five acres of land at Morrisons Haven "on a long lease". Morrison's Haven Park and Pipe Park rental came to £110 2s 6d with the land for the railway and housing at Cuthill costing a further £22 18s 8d.[84]

The Summerlee Coal and Firebrick Company, from Coatbridge in the West of Scotland, acquired the mine in 1895 and remained the proprietors until nationalisation in 1947. The Summerlee Company brought in many Irish immigrant workers, the majority of whom inhabited the houses at Morrison's Haven.[85] The Brickworks remained in operation until the mid 1970's, when even political intervention could not save them from closure. Tommy Thomson, who began his working life as an apprentice brickmaker from age 14 can remember; "...a local petition to the MP to keep the brickworks going, but they were doomed for closure and nothing could save them."[86] Of course, by this time, Morrison's Haven was long gone and trade was conducted by road and by rail. The export market, pre 1939, is shown to be "Holland, Denmark, Germany and other European countries".[87] The salt industry also made use of the harbour until the end. Although no longer producing salt on site, rock salt was imported from Cheshire, which was then processed at the Prestonpans works.[88] This produced a source of great delight for local children, as John Wilson recalls;

"....I used to go along to Morrison's Haven when I was wee and I can mind of the boats bringing in salt rock. They used to put it in sea-water to get the salt out. It was amber coloured and we used to pinch it and sook it like a sweetie."[89]

View of Morison's Haven Harbour towards the end of its life, featuring the trapped 'Topaz'
East Lothian Council, David Spence Collection

By the mid 1930's the harbour was used solely by "pleasure craft" and the odd fishing boat and even these were forced to move on once the silt began to reclaim the basin. The 'Topaz', the last vessel ever to enter the harbour mouth, was unable to get back out and was abandoned to her fate as a diving board for local children. Johnny Berg recollects;

We used to swim in the harbour. If you could not swim that was alright because you could just jump in off the old wreck, and hold onto a trunk – there were always trunks (10ft pit props!) floating in the water and you just grabbed one. The water was aye warm because the water pumped out of the pit went into the harbour. It was great.

The Haven's end was as inglorious as its history had been glorious. Concern for the safety of the children who used the decaying harbour as a swimming pool prompted the decision, in the mid 1950's, to fill it in. Rubbish from the mine was used as infill and the engine and hutches that were once used to carry coal to the waiting ships, now brought rubble to be "side cowped" into the harbour basin itself. A County Council Scheme involving Prestonpans, Tranent and Port Seton was set up whereby domestic refuse was collected and "used in a reclamation project at Morrison's Haven."[90]

Eastward view of Morison's Haven, Prestonpans showing land reclamation process
East Lothian Council, David Spence Collection

On Wednesday May 22nd 1957, the Edinburgh Evening News carried the headline:

–MORISON'S HAVEN–
One-Time Customs Port with Flourishing Export-Import Trade
–IS NOW NO MORE–

The article goes on to tell that the "...The ubiquitous bulldozer and tipping truck, snarling symbols of an age of rapidly changing values, have completed yet another victory over the laboriously wrought achievements of the past." The ancient port that had withstood the test of five centuries, times of war and peace, and a constant battering from the elements, had outlived its use for twentieth century man. The once prosperous industries of Prestonpans, the saltworks, the potteries, the breweries, the collieries, were either no longer in existence, or coming to the same end as the harbour which had served them so well and so long. Modern day Prestonpans has, on the surface, little to distinguish it from similar towns which like itself now serve simply as an extension to Edinburgh's commuter belt. However, a look at the history of the town might just leave you nostalgic for the days when our ancestors mingled and traded daily with people of all nationalities and were adventurous enough to sail the seven seas in a tiny wooden boat, in search of their cargoes. Which begs the question; of the periods covered, which was the more cosmopolitan and worldly wise? Certainly not 21st century man, although he would believe himself to be so.

WHO OR WHAT WAS JOHNNIE MOAT?

When the section of the coastal walkway, which covers Prestonpans was being formed, the contractors undertook to retrieve Johnnie Moat from his watery grave and reinstall him on his perch on the Girdle Rocks from which he was toppled during a violent storm in the 1950's. He can be found just below the tide line, directly behind the new East Lothian Council Offices on the High Street at Aldhammer. So who, what, is Johnnie Moat? As he exists now, Johnnie Moat is a huge whinstone boulder over six feet tall, nine feet long and six feet wide. Local legend has it that he was brought to Prestonpans during the ice age by a glacier, or even blown out of Arthur's Seat, Edinburgh when that volcano was active and erupting. Another piece of local lore claims that so long as Johnnie sits on the Girdle Rocks, Prestonpans will enjoy prosperity. If he falls, dark days are to come. The original Johnnie Moat, was either harbour master or customs man at Acheson's haven during the 16th century.[91] The girth of the man and that of the great boulder were considered to be so similar, that the stone was given his name.

THE FORT

The rebuilding works of 1875 uncovered the remains of a 16th century fort, described as a "three cornered building with gun-holes in it."[92] The Rev. Dr. John Struthers, Minister of Prestonpans, had in 1853 furnished the Ordnance Survey officers with information about the fort. He claimed it was constructed circa 1547 by one John Acheson of the Scot's Guard in Paris who came to Scotland on the business of the French King with a recommendation for Mary of Guise.[93] Although this claim cannot be supported by written evidence, a case can be made for it being grounded in fact, over and above the obvious connection of the Officer's name [Acheson] with that of the Haven. The date, 1547, is the time of the so-called "Rough Wooing" of Mary, Queen of Scots. Both the English and French royal houses wanted links through marriage to Scotland; the French with an eventual eye on the English throne, and the English to secure themselves from the French threat, and also to put an end to the financially draining wars with Scotland. To this end, the English built a chain of at least twenty fortresses along the east coast from Berwickshire to Dundee, and the French counterattacked by building an opposing chain at sites including "Eyemouth, Dunbar and Inchkeith".[94] It is more than possible that the remains uncovered at the harbour belonged to this era.

THE LAST WORD

The last word on the harbour at Morrison's Haven should go to the people who knew it best – those who lived, worked and played there. The majority of written histories about the ancient port give the end of its commercial life as the year 1914 (with the exception of Angus Graham who opts for the end of the First World War). However, Harry Galloway, who was employed at Prestongrange and vividly remembers the colliers in the harbour, did not come to work in the area as a miner until 1925. Likewise, Tommy Thomson, a brickmaker with the Summerlee Company, did not begin work until 1923 but he, too, recalls the boats calling in for loads of bricks and pipes.[95] Surely the collective memory of the people whose lives and workplaces revolved around Morrison's Haven cannot be wrong and, therefore we can confidently state that the harbour was in commercial operation until the late 1920's at the very least.

In concluding this discussion of the Harbour of Acheson/ Morrison's Haven it is important to consider several points. Firstly, the exports and imports of the harbour and the places they were shipped to and from, serve as an indication of the changing times. We can see how the harbour at the beginning of its life dealt in the trade of the day, mainly rural produce, but was able to adapt to the advent of industrialisation. How its very proximity and accessibility allowed the industries, which grew up around it and the coal mining at Prestongrange, to prosper and how they in turn supported the harbour. Throughout the life of the harbour, fishing and the fishermen are a recurrent theme. That the harbour was the base for a customs house indicates official recognition that the business transacted there was of high significance. Further, the manner in which the activities conducted at the harbour were restricted (or went underground as demonstrated by the operations of the smugglers) by the legislation they attracted; for example, customs duties levied, Acts of Parliament prohibiting coal exports and so on. Waterpower was an important feature at the Haven and thought should be given to the ingenious manner in which the tide mills at the harbour were put to good use by the industries in its vicinity. Finally, the ironic manner in which things have apparently come full circle. Gone are the coal, salt, chemicals and pottery for export and we once more import manufactured goods not available at home. And what of Scotland's exports? Once again we hark back to the 16th century and export fish [salmon and shellfish], woollen cloth [tartan and cashmere] and foreign visitors still visit us as traders, but now in the guise of the tourist. Smuggling is also making a comeback and Customs and Excise reports seem to feature increasingly in the news, lamenting the black-market in alcohol and tobacco. So the imports and exports and clandestine activities of 21st century Scotland mirror those of the 16th century and it is as if the industries that evolved from the 16th century onwards, like the harbour itself, never existed.

How many 'R's As a footnote, the editor adds that there is no agreement on whether one or two 'r's is correct. As such, here and throughout this whole volume, we have indulged all authors to spell it as they wish!

APPENDIX I
ORAL HISTORY TRANSCRIPTIONS

THE FISHER FAMILY

Mary Morgan, born 1905 off the High Street, Prestonpans

"There used to be a right fishing community in Prestonpans. The men all wore the Guernseys, and their own style of hat, and they held a walk once a year through the town when they did all their business. My Grandfather Thomson was a fisherman, and he and my grannie, Peepie Mag, she was born in Cockenny, [Cockenzie] *lived off the High Street on the seaside. You went doon a wee brae and up a stair to get to their house but they're [the houses] all away now. My granny mended the nets in the summer. She hung them up on the window snib and I can mind her needle flying out and in at a fair speed. On a Saturday night it was aye salt herring for supper. My grandfather Thomson brought it back in a barrel from the winter fishing and I used to like to see into the barrel when the lid came off. The fishes were laid out right bonny, round and round in layers of salt. My granny would lift a fish out of the barrel and lie it on top of a pan of tatties and that*

was Saturday night's supper. She didn't salt the water, the fish did it for her.

My uncle went to the fishing as well and he had his own wee boat. He used to get maybe half a dozen oysters in his nets and he would keep them for grandfather Thomson. He loved oysters. He would just open up the shells, scoop them oot and swallow them doon.

The other thing I can mind of Morrison's Haven is the boats coming in with the rock salt. It used to get loaded off the boats onto a horse drawn cart and taken along to the 'Pans to get refined.

THE MINER

Harry Galloway, b1900 Hamilton and moved to Prestonpans to work in the pits in 1925

"...I worked in the Links and Grange pits as a miner. Morrison's Haven as I mind was not that big, and I only ever saw the one boat in it at a time. Mind you, these were the big coal boats that came in for the coal out the pit. The coal wagons came right across the road from the pit in single file and went alongside the boat and side cowped the coal into it. The coal was shipped foreign with the bricks and that from the brickworks, but I'm not sure where it all went to. I remember the last coal boat that ever came into the harbour. It came from Copenhagen and the reason it has stayed in my mind is the harbour was getting right bad for silting up and the boat could not get out by itself. A tug was called down from Leith but could not come till the next day and we all went down to the harbour to see the wee tug pull the coal boat out into the deep water. Looking back now, it was fitting that the last boat should have got such a send off. If I mind right it would have been about 1929 or maybe even 1930.

I'll tell you another thing about Morrison's Haven. There was more coal came up that siding in the hutches and got shipped than came up the pit. Do you know how that was? The weightman checked the weight of the hutches coming up the pit and one of the miners noticed that every hutch was going down as weighing eight and a half. So this miner, he went into the second weight box and shoved the second weightman out the road and jumped on top of the hutch, and still it only showed eight and a half. So now all the men knew something was not right. One of the men got two facemen to go and check with him and they saw that the weights were tied with a length of rope, and even if you had ten hundredweight in your hutch it would only go out at eight and a half. It was the mine owners that did it so the men never knew how much coal they were digging and the wages could get kept down."

The 'Pans is built on old mine workings and smuggler's tunnels. When they were building the new Preston Lodge High School [circa 1967] *the ground collapse underneath the workers and they found they had caved in an old tunnel. Folk said it was the old mine shaft of the monks. Another thing, some old houses had to be knocked down to build the block of flats next to the Dragon's Lair [an old house], across the High Street from the [Safeway] supermarket. Well, when they got down to the founds, the men got a shock, because they went right through the roof of an old smuggler's tunnel leading down to the beach. They couldn't trace it back because it was blocked with all the rubble, but those flats are built with a pillar holding up the one corner that stands on the tunnel. It used to be called the tramp's tunnel, for a tramp sometimes slept in it".*

THE BRICKWORKER

Tommy Thomson b1909 East Seaside, Prestonpans (next to site of Fowler's Brewery, now both demolished)

"...I got a job in the kilns when I was fourteen years old, making the bricks. The kilns were hot all day for firing the clay, and at night tramps would sleep inside them because it was aye warm, they never really cooled down. I mind of Morrison's Haven. Boats used to come in with trees for the pit and they took away coal and the clay pipes from the brick works. We put the pipes into bogeys at the brick works, and run them over the road to the harbour to get loaded onto the boats for shipping abroad.

The clay for the bricks came out a pit next to the Grange pit. It was right good for the brickmaking."

THE RESIDENT

(Unknown lady) b1912. Came to live with aunt at Morrison's Haven 1920–1943. Memories related by her daughter Ann-Marie.

"...My mother and her sister were left orphaned after her mother died in the flu epidemic and her father was killed in the war. Her aunt, Mrs Clark, took both girls to live with her family at Morrison's Haven.

My mother told us about the ships that came into the harbour. The children would all race down to the pier whenever they saw a ship approaching, all desperate to get there first and be "the winner". My mother told us about the time she put all her effort and concentration into racing the other children, so that she forgot to stop running and went right off the end of the pier and into the harbour itself. She had on a blue dress and when she was fished out, all the dye had come off her frock, and her skin was dyed blue! She also told us about the occasion when one of the sailors taught her to shoot a rifle. She was only about twelve years old at the time and could not really talk with the man, as he was Scandinavian and his English was poor. Anyhow, she went home and astonished everyone with the information that she had learned to fire a rifle that day!

My mother's two uncles were drowned in the harbour. She remembered it happening but I can't recall the date – around the mid-1920's I would think. They had both been drinking, it was a Saturday night, and they decided to take a rowing boat out. They just got outside the harbour entrance when the boat capsized. No-one was able to save them and they both drowned. It is ironic because they both survived working in dangerous conditions down a mine but died in their leisure time in the harbour they had known all their lives.

Many of the families at Morrison's Haven were Irish and came with the Summerlee Company from Coatbridge. The family names my mother remembered from Morrison's Haven are:

TRACY CLARK GUNN McAULEY

These names can all still be found in the area today. When the Passionist Fathers took over Drumohr [a large mansion house in grounds about a mile to the south west of Morrison's Haven], all the Morrison's Haven girls took to religion in a big way. The fathers wore long black cloaks and looked very dashing and romantic and all of a sudden everyone was desperate to say Novenas and go to confession!

My mother also used to tell us that during the Second World War, the aeroplane carrying Rudolf Hess on his escape bid, flew over the Haven!!

MORRISON'S HAVEN REMEMBERED

John Wilson b1926 Crown Square, Prestonpans

"...I worked in Prestonlinks Colliery which was owned by the Edinburgh Coal Company. Prestongrange miners lived at the other end of the 'Pans in the Cuttle (Cuthill) and their pit was owned by the Summerlee Coal Company. There was some rivalry went on with the miners, I can tell you. I used to go along to Morrison's Haven when I was wee and I can mind of the boats bringing in salt rock. They used to put it in sea-water to get the salt out. It was amber coloured and we used to pinch it and sook it like a sweetie.

During the war even the buses were blacked out, and when I used to get the bus home from Edinburgh, there was a stop at Morrison's Haven. There was a level crossing to let the pug cross the road to the harbour from the pit, and that's where the bus stopped. The conductor was called "Lugs" (Andrew "Lugs" Hamilton of Prestonpans) and he had to shout every stop because it was so dark and you could not see where you were. I can mind him shouting "Morrison's Haven!"

John Berg b 1924 in Summerlee Street, Prestonpans

"...I worked in the Grange pit as a miner and so did my dad. My mother used to tell me that before I was born she worked down the mine as well. She did not cut the coal, but she used to push the hutches filled with coal from the pit across the road to the harbour, and then load it onto the boats. Boats came in from Germany and Holland. They brought in trees – timber to use as props in the pit. They took away with them the coal that was dug out of the pit. When the women stopped pushing the hutches, they used wee ponies to pull them, and then it was the pug that did the job. When the boats came in, all the fast women from round about used to hang around the harbour with their handbags – I'll not tell you what for, you can use your imagination!

We used to swim in the harbour. If you could not swim that was alright because you could just jump in off the old wreck and hold onto a trunk – there were always trunks (10ft pit props!) floating in the water and you just grabbed one. The water was aye warm because the water pumped out of the pit went into the harbour. It was great.

Anne Tough (née Potter, 1931–2000) Came to Prestonpans in 1940 from Lanarkshire.

"...My family moved to Prestonpans in 1940 as my father got a job at Prestongrange pit as an Underground Oversman. We first lived at Summerlee Street, then No 1 Front Street. The harbour was still there at the time but I don't think it was used for boats. Apart from the old wreck, I don't remember seeing any other boats. We used to dive off the wreck and swim in the harbour. I'm surprised no-one was ever killed.

There were houses at Morrison's Haven then. Tam Paton lived in the bottom one and used to sell fruit and vegetables from his house. During the war when everything was rationed and scarce, you would hear that he had got bananas or oranges delivered and everyone would rush up to Morrison's Haven and there would be a huge queue.

THE END OF AN ERA

John McNeill b1914 Musselburgh. Moved to Prestonpans in 1929

"...I never worked down a mine, but I spent thirty-six years of my working life as a surface worker, first at the Links Pit and then at the Grange from about 1943 till 1960. I worked mainly as a labourer and worked as part of the gang that filled in the harbour at Morrison's Haven when it was reckoned to be getting too dangerous. The wooden pier and supports were all rotting away and it was an accident just waiting to happen. We used stones and rubbish that dam up from the pit, it was brought over by the pug and normally dumped on the foreshore for the tide to wash away. We barrowed it from the bogeys and tipped it in the harbour. We used cement to seal it all, mixing it on site and as quick as we got it made, we tipped it in. I do not know how many barrows we used but we were weeks at it. It was a sad end. We buried the old boat that lay in the harbour and if folk dug about they would probably still find it and bottles and all sorts of other rubbish we put in there.

The labouring squad kept their tools, the picks and spades and pinchers, in a building the colliery put up, just beside the harbour. They kept good stones that came up the pit and built this sort of igloo shaped building. Two brothers, the McGinns, used to live in it for a house. It had a fireplace and everything in it. The colliery did not mind them being there because they were like unofficial nightwatchmen for the place and kept the bairns away from the harbour. The McGinns used to gather sea coal and sell it to make some money. The pug used to come over to the foreshore every day from the Grange, the same pug that used to bring the coal over to the coal boats for shipping, but by this time the coal was going up to Edinburgh for selling. Anyway, the bogey's would be full of rubbish from the pit and the pug would bring them over, and would side cowp the rubbish from the pit onto the foreshore and the tide would come in and out and wash it all away. There was not supposed to be any rubbish but, of course there was and that's what folk used to call sea coal. It really came up from the pit and the tide brought it in after it was dumped.

George Berrick b1933. Moved to Prestonpans in 1966

"...Although I did not come to live here until 1966, I have known Prestonpans most of my working life, first as a lorry driver with the council and then as a meter reader for the South of Scotland Electricity Board. The first time I saw Morrison's Haven was in 1956/7 and it was in a ruinous state then, sort of filled in but you could still make out that it had been a harbour. The pier supports were still there and the wreck of an old wooden boat. The houses there were ruinous also, two blocks of them, and at that time, Tommy Gunn, a councillor owned them. One had been used as a grain drier and had split practically in two with the weight of the grain. In the 1960's, the council contracted me out as a driver to the SSEB when Cockenzie Power Station was being built on the site of the old Links pit and

we filled in what was left of the harbour with waste ash. I don't know what happened, but somehow or another, the old harbour was recognised as being a historical feature. I think it was about 1965, when the SSEB were made to take all the ash out of the harbour basin and reinstate it to the condition it was in when they put the ash into it.

APPENDIX II
IMPORTS AND EXPORTS

Morrison's Haven – Exports by date

1543	• Coal. • Salt. • Hides.	
Pre 1660	• Salt.	• England, Holland & Sweden.
Post 1660	• Salt.	• The Baltics, England, Germany & Holland.
1684–1685	• Coal.	• France, Hamburg, London & Netherlands.
1686	• Oysters.	• Riga, Latvia.
Late 1600's	• Eggs, Stockings & Cloth. • Kelp. • Tallow • Skins (Wool, Lamb, Hair even Dog Skins), Malt, Salt & Coals. • Salt, Tobacco, French and Dutch goods.	• London. • Newcastle. • Holland. • France. • England.
Post 1698	• Glass. • Stoneware & Brownware. • Oil of Vitriol, Aquafortis, Spirit of Salt, Glauber Salts & White Ashes, Sulphuric Acid	 • Europe, North America & West Indies. • Europe.
1777–1786	• Oysters	• Hull, London & Newcastle.
1788–1796	• Salt	• Stockholm.
1790–1800	• Grain, Coal & Salt.	•
1845	• Oysters	• Hartlepool, Newcastle & Shields.
1887-1930's	• Coal, Bricks & Claypipes.	• The Baltics, Germany.

Morrison's Haven – Imports by date

Date	Goods	Origin
1544	• Pitch, Lead	• Netherlands
1620–1645	• Iron Plate.	• Sweden
Pre 1707	• Wool.	• England
1705	• Brandy, Claret & Cherrie Sack • Beer. • Tobacco. • Soap, Bricks, Glass, Paper & Rope. • Wrought Copper & Brass, Wrought Iron & Steel, Swedish Copper Kettles, Iron Cooking Pots. • Hats and Gloves. • Russia Leather • Dutch Silk, Whalebone & Delft.	• Norway • Germany • America via England • England & Holland • Rotterdam • England • Danzig • Holland
1719	• Variety of Goods. • Tobacco • Timber. • Bar-iron. • Flax & Hemp. • Currants, Raisins, Figs, Prunes, Oranges, Lemons, Sugar Loaf & Sugar Candy. • Hops. • Apples and Onions. • Wine.	• Norway, Sweden, Dantzig. Bremen, Rotterdam, Harve de Grace, St. Martin & Oporto • Maryland • Norway • Sweden • The Baltics • England & Holland (countries of origin, Spain and France) • England (Newcastle) • Holland • Europe
Late 1700's	• Clay • Flint. • White & Red Lead. • Saltpetre. • Brimstone. • Timber. • Grain, Raw Materials for acid works	• Devonshire, England • Gravesend, England • Hull, London & Newcastle • East India Company, London • Leghorn • Norway
Pre 1812	• Sulphur	• Italy
Pre 1843	• Tallow	• Australia
1887–1930's	• Timber for Pit Props • Rock Salt.	• The Baltics • Cheshire, England

APPENDIX III
MORRISON'S HAVEN MISCELLANIA FROM *THE HADDINGTONSHIRE COURIER*

8th June 1860
The fishing reports for this date showed that the majority of Prestonpans' boats had left for the summer fishing grounds, found along the north coast of Scotland, or down in Yarmouth, England. Prior to setting sail, the fishermen indulged themselves in a nip of The Glenlivet, following "...a time-honoured custom." All told, a combined fleet of approximately one hundred boats from Morrison's Haven and Cockenzie harbours departed.

8th August 1862
Four new cases of infectious diseases in the Western District of East Lothian are confirmed – all occurring at Morrison's Haven. The illnesses in question were; 3 cases of crysipelas and one case of scarlatina.

24th December 1875
The extensive alterations to the haven, undertaken by the Prestongrange Coal and Iron Company Limited are reported at this time as being finally completed after the said Company had become lessees of the site a mere two years prior. The paper reports that during this two year period, "...a great enterprise has been exhibited", with the building of a large brick and tile works and branch railway lines laid down. It also comments on the elaborate arrangements made for the pumping out of a "drowned-out pit known as the Low Pit". It is noted that present coal production at the site is almost 1000 tons per week and once the Low Pit is again workable, a futher 500 tons can be expected to be added to this output. A large trade in the manufacture of firebricks and pipes is also noted.

23rd March 1893
A report on the annual Fisherman's Walk informs that upon conclusion of official business, Office Bearers elected and so on, a collection was made which raised £3.00, described as a "handsome sum" in aid of the Royal Infirmary. The assembly then marched through the town accompanied by the Newtongrange Brass Band, and ended up at Prestongrange House where a dance had been laid on by Lady Susan Grant-Suttie for the Fisherfolk and her own servants and estate workers. The report concludes that the streets of Prestonpans were full of dancing fisher families until a very late hour.

30th June 1893
A successful fishing expedition to the Irish grounds with crews averaging a very profitable £120 each is reported on this date. Apparently, the Irish fishermen and their families were falling over one another to offer hospitality to their Scottish peers and a great deal of friendly socialising occurred. The Prestonpans men left, vowing to return.

14th July 1893
A rendevous of an unpleasant nature, with a foreign fishing boat, is reported. At the Lowestoft fishing grounds, a Belgian vessel armed with a "razor-sharp

prow", drove through the nets of a Prestonpans boat with the result that six new nets were lost. That the crime was a deliberate one can be deduced from the fact that the Skipper of the offending, Ostend registered, boat had taken the care to cover the registration number of his ship with a rag. Reports indicate that the Scottish fisherman's experience in the English grounds were not nearly so positive as that in Ireland, described above. It was even claimed to be almost impossible to get an English fisherman standing quayside to catch a rope thrown from another [Scots] ship coming in to berth. The Scottish fisherman's motto in English waters was always "Safety in Numbers".

24th November 1893
Violent storms out in the Firth of Forth resulted in a 600 ton German steamer called the Alsen of Hamburg, to come aground on the reefs west of Morrison's Haven. The ship had been heading for Methil in Fife when the storm forced her to put down her anchor in a bid to ride out the gales. Despite the best efforts of her crew, the winds proved too forceful and, firing off distress flares and sending out "Mayday" signals, she was washed aground. A tug came out from Leith in an attempt to get her off the rocks but it was not until almost 24 hours after their ordeal began, that the 16 strong crew were able to get off their stricken ship. The rescue took four trips to complete and once ashore the Harbourmaster at Morrison's Haven took charge of finding beds and a warm meal for the grateful men. When the storm had blown itself out, the next high tide floated their ship with surprising ease from the rocks that had appeared to hold her so fast, and astonishingly she was relatively undamaged and able to continue with her voyage. These same storms also washed a life boat bearing the name "Lark, Sunderland" ashore at the Haven, but as no boat of that name was in the vicinity of the Forth at the time, no lives were considered lost or in danger.

APPENDIX IV
IMPORTANT DATES

1526 Existence of harbour established which is known as Newhaven. At this time it measured 1.5 Scots acres, including "lie greene" (area for paddock/garden/ buildings) with permission to build a tide mill.

1541 Harbour improved by "feuar" Alexander Acheson, and takes new name, Acheson's Haven.

1700 Harbour extensively remodelled by William Morison, owner of Prestongrange Estates (from this date increasingly known as Morrison's Haven).

1753 Repairs to Harbour undertaken after monies raised by tax levied on ale consumed, manufactured or vended in Parish of Prestonpans. Plan shows depth of harbour at 13 ft with the pier having natural rock to the seaward side, and dressed stone to the interior. At this time the harbour appears to be open mouthed to the East and West. Presumably the pier could only be reached by boat when the tides were in or on foot when they were out. (1753 map, Peck & Co. See Appendix V – List of Maps)

1796 Tide mill in operation grinding flint for potteries.

1799 Map shows the harbour in its familiar form, with the east end enclosed. (1799 map, Forrest. See Appendix V – List of Maps.

1853 A survey at this time produced a map showing Morrison's Haven with a school and the tide mill operating as a saw mill. (1853 map, 6″ County Series. See Appendix V – List of Maps)

1875–7 Major improvements carried out by Prestongrange Coal and Iron Company Limited. Increase in depth of harbour basin and new pier built to accommodate increased mining and fireclay operations in area. Rail lines from pit head and brick works leading to harbour wharf, installed. 1930's Harbour area shown as being almost 2 acres in size, internal area = 720 ft by 160 ft with entrance width of 70 ft. (1907 map, 25″ County Series. See Appendix V – List of Maps)

1930's Harbour used by pleasure boats and fishing craft, until silt prohibits boats entering or leaving. One ship named the "Topaz" left to rot in harbour basin. She was later blown up and buried when the harbour was in-filled.

1957 Harbour filled in using refuse and debris from the mine.

APPENDIX V
MAPS

1753 *A plan of Morison's Haven as it now stands, 6th August 1753* Peck & Co., George Street, Edinburgh

1799 Forrest's map of 1799 one of earliest OS maps of area.

1825 Prestongrange Estate Upon a Reduced Scale from the Plans or Surveys of J Ainslie and William Forrest, 1812, with improvements since to 1825. Scottish Records Office Ref: RHP 41333/2

1849 Plan of Prestongrange Policy, the property of Sir George Grant Suttie, Bart., 1849. Scottish Records Office Ref: RHP 10006

1850 Plan of Morrison's Haven ascribed to J Fergusson and dated 1850

1853 6″ County Series Surveyed 1853. Sheet 8, Haddingtonshire.

1870 Report by Dr Fulton 1896 showing Sir George Grant Suttie's Oyster Fishing Grounds. East Lothian District Council Local History Centre.

1907 25″ County Series Surveyed 1893, Revision of 1906, Published 1907. Sheet IV.8 Edinburghshire. Sheet VIII.8 Haddingtonshire.

BIBLIOGRAPHY

Primary Sources

Graham, A., *Morrison's Haven* Proceedings of the Society of Antiquities of Scotland (1962) (1969)

Shaw, J., *Water Power in Scotland 1550–1870* (1984)

Smout, T. C., *The Trade of East Lothian at the End of the 17th Century*. Transactions of the East Lothian Antiquarian and Field Naturalists Society: Vol IX (1963)

Sinclair, W., Trotter, J., Chapter on Prestonpans pp. s 61–88 *Statistical Account of Scotland*; Vol 17 (1793–99)

Secondary Sources

Balfour, P. J., (ed) *The Scots Peerage* (1907)
Cunningham, W. B., Chapter on Prestonpans pp. s 304–316 *New Statistical Account of Scotland*; Vol II (1845)
Gibson, W., *Fishing in Old East Lothian* (1994)
Gould, R., *Early British Freemasonry* (1926)
Gray and Jamison (eds) *East Lothian Biographies*
Groome, F., *Ordnance Gazeteer of Scotland* (1903)
Hume Brown, P.. *Early Travellers*
Lindgren, D., *The Firth of Forth in Old Picture Postcards* (1989)
Lynch, M., *Scotland: A New History* (1992)
McAuley, J. D., *A Short History of Prestonpans* (1981)
McNeill, P., *Prestonpans & Vicinity: Historical, Ecclesiastical and Traditional* (1884)
Martine, J., *Reminiscences and Notices of Ten Parishes of the County of Haddington* (1984)
Scott-Moncrieff, G., (ed) *The Narrative of Mr James Nimmo 1654–1709* (1889)
Snodgrass, C. P., *Third Statistical Account of Scotland: The County of East Lothian* (1953)

Manuscripts

Acts of Parliament of Scotland, Vol X, p. 231a
Act of Parliament and Ratification, Edinburgh 5th August 1698
Exchequer Roll Vol XVII (1537–42) p. 458
Exchequer Roll Vol XVIII (1543–56) p. 68
Laing Manuscripts, Vol II, 490/2, Prestonpans, University of Edinburgh Library
Laing Manuscripts, Vol II, 1705, p. 491, Prestonpans Bullion Book
National Archives of Scotland, Ref GD357/39/1, 1877–78.
Records of the Privy Council, July 1699–May 1703 p. 7
Register of the Privy Council of Scotland, Vol VI (1599–1604) p. 373
Register of Great Seals 720: 10th November 1552

Newspaper Articles

Edinburgh Evening News, 22nd May 1957
Haddingtonshire Courier, 8th June 1860
Haddingtonshire Courier, 8th August 1862
Haddingtonshire Courier, 24th December 1875
Haddingtonshire Courier, 23rd March 1893
Haddingtonshire Courier, 30th June 1893
Haddingtonshire Courier, 14th July 1893
Haddingtonshire Courier, 24th November 1893

NOTES

1 When used in reference to the harbour, the name "Morrison" is spelt with two "r's". In reference to the family of that name it is spelt with one 'r' – "Morison"
2 Ibid
3 Kenneth mac Alpin, King of the Scots, married one of his daughters to the Norwegian King Olaf III of Dublin
4 The first Scottish towns to develop were based on the English burgh system, introduced by David I. The term "Burgh" granted legal entitlements to the town including the right to trade and to not have to pay tolls throughout kingdom
5 Lynch M. *Scotland: A New History* (1984), p. 63
6 The trade of Morrison's Haven, both exports and imports are dealt with throughout this essay, complimented by a comprehensive list of imports and exports attached as Appendix II

7 720 Register of Great Seals of Scotland: 10th November 1552
8 Lynch, op cit., p. 182
9 That is to say owner's rights over the harbour and its business for the term of his lease
10 See Appendix V – Fergusson's Map
11 Exchequer Roll, Vol. XVII (1537–42),p. 458
12 Exchequer Roll, Vol. XVIII (1543–56), p. 68
13 Edinburgh Evening News 22nd May 1957
14 Balfour, P. J. (ed) *The Scots Peerage* 1907 p. 456
15 For this information I am grateful to Mr John Hogg, local historian and resident of Prestonpans
16 Register of the Privy Council of Scotland, Vol. VI (1599–1604), p. 373
17 McNeill, P. *Prestonpans & Vicinity* (1902) p. 253
18 Gray & Jamieson (Eds) *East Lothian Biographies* p. 99
19 For reference see Graham, A. *Morison's Haven* (1961–62), p. 300
20 Alexander "Jupiter" Carlyle's father was minister for the parish of Prestonpans
21 Gray & Jamieson., op cit., p. 99
22 R Gould, *Early British Freemasonry* (1926) p. 446
23 This information comes from Brother Robert Guiney, a Mason from the fishing village of Port Seton who has seen sight of the Minute Book of the Lodge of Aitchison's Haven. This Minute Book, entitled "The Buik of the Actis and Ordinans of the Nobile Maisteris and fellows of Craft of the Ludg of Aitchison's heavine", is now in the Hands of the Grand Lodge and is one of its most prized possesions. The dates of meetings contained therein, the earliest being the 9th January 1598, pre-date those of the Lodge of Edinburgh (Mary's Chapel) No 1
24 Trade of East Lothian at End of 17th Century by T C Smout (1963) The Transactions of the East Lothian Antiquarians & Naturalists Society. Vol IX (1963), p. 70
25 Smout, op.cit., p. 73
26 Smout, op.cit., p. 72
27 Smout, op. cit., p. 73
28 These last two items were most likely imported from England and then re-exported for the foreign markets
29 Smout, op.cit., p. 73
30 In 1620, Parliament dealt with a complaint the foreign ships were given preferential treatment over local boats at various harbours along the east coast. The Parliament found the complaint to be justified and ruled local trade be served first. (Edinburgh Evening News, 22nd May1957)
31 University of Edinburgh Library, Laing Manuscripts Vol. II, 490/2 Prestonpans
32 Smout, op.cit., p. 69
33 Act of Scottish Parliament (and Ratification), Edinburgh August 5, 1698
34 Ibid
35 Smout, op.cit., p. 75
36 The Dictionary of the Older Scots Tongue was able to give the translation for "Jaculat" as being "chocolate". However, they could not come up with a translation for "collace"
37 Traders who travelled the length and breadth of the countryside with their laden pack horses – the prototype of today's door to door salesmen! They held an account with the Bank of England, and at one time, were in credit to the tune of over ¨ 1,000,000 pounds sterling!! (Martine *Reminiscences of Ten Parishes* (1894) p. 166)
38 Statistical Account of Scotland, Vol 17, p. 79
39 Martine, op.cit., p. 167
40 University of Edinburgh Library, Laing Manuscripts II, p491 Prestonpans Bullion Book 1705
41 Acts of the Parliament of Scotland, Vol. X, p. 231a
42 SAOS, op cit., p. 73
43 This was at the time when the French monarchy/government supported the Stuart cause and were regarded as enemies of the British throne
44 Hume Brown, P. *Early Travellers* p. 166
45 Scott-Moncrieff, G. (Ed), *The Narrative of Mr James Nimmo, 1654–1709*, Scottish History Society 1889 pp. 96–97
46 Ibid
47 Records of the Privy Council, July 1699–May 1703 P7
48 Ibid
49 See appendix I for full transcipt of oral histories
50 The Dragon's Lair is an old house which borders the green commemorating the poet and song writer, Rabbie Burns, on the High Street. The amusing thing about this tale is that the

aforementioned look out point is situated on the sea wall of the Burn's memorial, meaning that the smuggler's would have been passing right under the noses of the customs men!

51 SAOS, op cit., p. 73
52 Ibid., p. 73
53 Ann-Marie's ref 38
54 SAOS, op.cit., p. 73
55 SAOS, op cit., p. 67
56 Roebuck and Garbet worked in partnership in Birmingham as consultant chemists. They founded a sulphuric acid work in Birmingham in 1746 and came to Prestonpans in 1749 to establish another. Here they met up with William Cadell, a merchant of Cockenzie. The trio were responsible for various enterprises including several potteries (some at Prestonpans) and mills as well as their chemical works, but most famously for establishing the Carron Ironworks in 1759
57 McAuley, J D., *A Short History of Prestonpans* (1981) p. 12
58 Shaw, J.P. *Water power in Scotland* , (1984) p. 14–16
59 Ibid., p. 15
60 The mine adits were used as outlets for water being pumped from the mine workings. In a mine such as Prestongrange where flooding was a constant problem, the level of water being pumped would, and did, provide for a mill
61 Shaw op.cit., p. 471
62 SAOS, op.cit., p. 74
63 Graham, Angus, *Morison's Haven* (1961–62) p. 300
64 See Appendix V – List of Maps. Forrest's Map of 1799 shows how, when the tide was out, the stored water, upon release, would flood through the harbour mouth, removing any debris
65 See Appendix V – List of Maps, 1853 6" County Series
66 Shaw, op.cit., p. 14
67 Shaw, op cit., p. 242
68 Where it had previously taken place outdoors, over a period of months and involved all-natural products, linen bleaching now became an industrialised process taking place indoors in a relatively short space of time, using chemicals
69 Report by Dr Fulton 1896, East Lothian District Council Local History Centre
70 SAOS, op.cit., p. 69
71 Ibid., p. 85
72 Gibson, W., *Fishing in Old East Lothian* (1994), p. 15
73 A street situated approximately halfway between the site of the Saltworks and that of the Harbour is still known as Pandores Walk
74 See Appendix I – Oral History Transciptions, Mary Morgan
75 Hislop, J.F. *Notes on Relief paid to Fishermen at Prestonpans* (1847)
76 Gibson., op cit., p. 53
77 National Library of Scotland, Manuscript 3720 p. 1 1745
78 SAOS op.cit., p. 76
79 See Appendix V – List of Maps, Peck & Co., 1753
80 The Engine was dismantled from its original place in the Cornish tin mines and shipped in pieces to be reassembled at Prestongrange
81 Haddingtonshire Courier, 24th December 1875
82 Ibid
83 Ibid
84 The National Archives of Scotland, Ref GD357/39/1, 1877–78
85 See appendix I. Oral History Transcriptions, Ann-Marie Allan
86 See appendix I. Oral History Transcriptions, Tommy Thomson
87 Third Statistical Account of Scotland, (1953), p. 213
88 Snodgrass, C. P., *The Third Statistical Account of Scotland, The County of East Lothian* p. 216
89 See Appendix I. Oral History Transcriptions, John Wilson
90 Snodgrass, op.cit., p. 205
91 McNeill., op cit., p. 157
92 Ibid, p. 254
93 Graham, op.cit., p. 303
94 Lynch, op.cit., p. 206–7
95 See Appendix I, Oral Histories Transcriptions, Harry Galloway and Tommy Thomson

3

Sourcing Brickmaking Salting and Chemicals at Prestongrange

David Anderson

1 INTRODUCTION

The **refractory** (bricks, tiles, pottery and glass) and **chemical** industries (salt, acids, soaps and bulk chemicals) of Prestongrange and Prestonpans Parish are of great antiquity. They are inextricably linked, both amongst themselves and to the production of coal in the immediate vicinity and the availability of good water, both salt and fresh: in effect, an early integrated industrial complex. However, additional speciality materials had to sourced from outwith the UK. There are thus geographical and geological components to be considered in any assessment of their history and development. I understand pottery will be treated in a full paper by itself and so will only mention the subject where it impinges upon brick and tile making.

Beehive Brick Kilns, Prestongrange Colliery Brickworks
Scottish Mining Museum Trust

The industries under discussion can be considered to have a known history of at least eight centuries, although it would be natural to extrapolate certain aspects further back in time: thus salt, coal, and clayworking are likely to have been of importance at an even earlier period. Over the course of these eight centuries, the industries have employed substantial proportions of the local inhabitants in conditions which range (to the contemporary eye) from the barbaric to simply appalling. In general, primary producers (the actual workers) seldom enjoyed any rights over their produce, their lives being dictated by landowners and entrepreneurs. However, it is becoming clear that certain groups of workers, with special skills or expertise, might have been able to 'dictate' their terms, at least at some times. Some of the landowners and entrepreneurs were national figures, with significance beyond the confines of the immediate locality. Others were in advance of their time and initiated remarkable projects at the forefront of industrial development. All the industries under consideration are extinct in the Prestonpans and Prestongrange locality. Some survived into the twentieth century, but insurmountable economic, technological and cultural trends combined to lead to progressive closures. There is much that is beyond the scope of this brief; however, in attempting to draw together the story of these industries, pointers may be suggested for other researchers, who may desire to 'fill in the gaps'.

Treatment

Each theme will be developed on a chronological basis, tracking development across the years and highlighting key (or known) individuals or 'types' and characteristic products, methods or consequences of the industries. Key sites have been identified wherever possible and again, individuals are linked to places. The several themes are cross-linked wherever appropriate. Each theme is introduced to set its context and a conclusion attempts to summarise the impact of the industry locally, regionally, nationally, and further afield (if important).

2 SALT

Most accounts of Prestongrange rightly begin with salt. However, they place the start of this industry with the proprietorship of Newbattle Abbey; this probably ignores a significantly longer association with the neighbourhood.

Chemistry and Technology

Brine is a complex solution of positive and negative solvated ions, generally about 3.5% of the whole by weight. By increasing the concentration of these ions, simply achieved by evaporation of the water, they will precipitate at different rates. First come relatively insoluble sulphates, mostly calcium sulphate in the dihydrate form: Gypsum. This often caused problems for unskilled salters – encrusted gypsum in the pan caused hot spots and hence both corrosion and uneven boiling, both increasing inefficiency. Then after further boiling comes sodium chloride, common salt, which comprises over 70% of the ionic content of brine. Precipitation by boiling yields 'sea salt' in 95–98% purity. 'Sunday salt', which crystallised in large plates when the pans were allowed to cool on the Sabbath, is of higher purity and was therefore prized, but needed to be ground before use. The impurities in sea salt, or Scotch salt, meant that imported 'Bay salt', first from Bourgneuf Bay in France and later from the Iberian Peninsula, was often preferred for the table. More will be said on the quality of salt. The remaining liquor in the pan contained hydroscopic calcium and magnesium chlorides and sodium and magnesium sulphates. These 'bitters' (alternatively 'bittern') hardly ever crystallised under normal conditions, although sodium sulphate sometimes precipitated on cold nights (when the pan fires were out). To early panners the bitters were a useless by-product, often thrown away, sometimes used as animal feed, sometimes used as a washing solution for window glass. During the seventeenth century chemists began to isolate the constituents of the bitters: the identification of Glauber's Salt, sodium sulphate heptahydrate, in 1624 has been taken to be the beginning of the chemical revolution of common salting: bottled in solution as Oil of Salt Liniment it was one of the last products of the Scottish Salt Company in the twentieth century.

The amount of sodium sulphate could be increased by the action of sulphuric acid (see on) on common salt, when it is formed with the evolution of hydrochloric acid gas (it was also formed when low quality sulphurous coal was used to fuel the pans: the sulphur oxides formed by burning the coal react with brine and white encrustations of sodium sulphate grew round the pan rim). The action of sulphuric acid on the bitters increased the proportion of magnesium sulphate (Epsom salts), which then precipitated (also with the evolution of HCl gas). By the eighteenth century the range of salts refined at salt works with simple chemical processes had grown to include magnesium carbonate, magnesium chloride, magnesium oxide and others. By the nineteenth century salt was increasingly being used in the artificial formation of soda, which had supplanted natural alkalis in the soap and glass industries. In general, it can be said that diversification into the productive use of a once waste product helped to sustain the profitability of salting.

To win the salt, seawater had first to be collected and fed to the boiling pan. Often it rested in an intermediate 'bucket pot' above the tideline, where solids could settle (and a small amount of natural evaporation would take place). The pans were shallow and wide to maximise evaporation and heated from below by a dispersed bank of embers to evenly spread the heat. Once made of lead, iron plates were used for pans as soon as a practicable size of plate could be fabricated. In the sixteenth century there was a dearth of iron, which held back the industry – at this time there were as many as 38 pans in the immediate Prestonpans area. Limekilns Iron Works in Fife bore most of the demand for iron plates in the succeeding century. Empirical improvements appeared over the years, practical solutions to the mechanics of producing clean, dry sodium chloride. Alexander Hamilton's Salt Pans (Outlet designs, Edinburgh, c1980) describes some of these – creech cogs to collect the least soluble calcium sulphate, wells to drain the bitterns or concentrate of very soluble salts remaining when the sodium chloride precipitated, and the use of blood products to sequester organic matter, inadvertently drawn into the pans, so it could be drawn off. Further improvements included the introduction of 'Brander pans' by innovative saltmasters in the eighteenth century. Brander pans were fired from a furnace (rather a raised firebed, an iron grille to support the fire, ashes falling through to be raked) instead of the simple ground level bed of embers under the traditional sole pans; they were also larger: both furnace and size meant they were more economical (at Grange Pans further up the Forth, Dr John Roebuck continued to experiment in the 1760s, producing a pan so large – it was 55 by 32 feet – that it required 10 men to tend it; it never really worked effectively and was only in operation for five years).

Imports of Cheshire rock-salt (via Liverpool) improved the purity of the final product and tripled the nominal output, allowing a draw every charge of the pan, but at the concomitant cost of buying what had been a 'free' raw material. The last real innovation was to mechanise the intake of brine, by means of force pumps driven by steam engines, saving on the labour of manually charging the pans (the economy won by installing pumps justified their capital expense). By the nineteenth century the fuel ratio of previous centuries, which had been somewhere between 6:1 and 8:1, was reduced to about 3:1; this was still much higher than that achieved by the Cheshire producers. The material produced even after all these changes was still of inferior quality, with a tendency to be deliquescent (absorbing atmospheric moisture), sometimes gray in colour, and sometimes bitter to the taste: all a consequence of impurities and the rate at which salting was forced. Experiments which slowed the process showed that fine quality could be achieved, but not at a competitive cost (although the last surviving panworks in Prestonpans, Mr Alexander's, produced salt of 'fine quality' by the mid-nineteenth century according to the New Statistical Account).

Outline History of Salt and Saltprestone

Salt extraction is one of humanities oldest technologies, with a rich northern European archaeological record. Hundreds of salt extraction sites have been recognised along coastlines and by brine springs, characterised by distinctive shallow ceramic pans. While many sites are reckoned to have been seasonal, familial operations, industrial scale sites have also been found. There is little doubt that this technology was adopted by the ancient peoples of the British Isles, both the Celtic peoples who occupied the Lothian area at the time of the Romans and their Anglian successors in the second half of the first millennium. Indeed, the Roman presence would provide a stimulus for any salt extraction which then existed and the economy and organisational dictates of the Anglian kingdom would demand an input of salt.

It must be admitted that there is no direct evidence for any longer history, but it can be inferred from:

1. the presence of the Roman Inveresk Fort and the Celtic centres of Traprain and Edinburgh, all of which would demand commodities, and both cultures knew salt could be extracted from seawater;
2. Althammer House in Prestonpans, which recalls the name of one of the burgh's constituent villages and is an Anglian name, as is the first part of the oldest recorded name for Morison's Haven: 'Gilbert's Draucht' (where Gilbert is from the Old English Gislbe(o)rht; Black, Surnames of Scotland). Both suggest a considerable Anglian presence. Salt working might be expected to be a seasonal activity within the Anglians predominantly agricultural economy and
3. the charters to Newbattle Abbey can be read as the monastery succeeding to an already established estate; it was after all intended as a donation whereby the revenue accrued to the Abbey (and the goodwill of the Abbey accrued to the spiritual well-being of the De Quincys, the donors). For a translation see David Spence, Early Charters Relating to Coalmining, Transactions of East Lothian Antiquarian and Field Naturalists, 1984; and
4. the simple fact of the density of settlement and agriculture in the area creating a steady demand for salt.

Having mentioned the Abbey charters it must be noted that the Cistercians were no strangers to industrial developments, the improvement of their estates being a central imperative of their economy and culture. Newbattle was working saltpans on an industrial scale further up the Forth before Prestongrange was donated. Although there is no mention of coal mining in the first of the De Quincy charters, the specific mention of 'carbonneris' in the second suggests the inheritance of facilities which were already established. This is a key point: coal was being worked when the Abbey acquired the land and, although they were certainly involved in development of mining, there must have been a reason for the pits earlier existence. The De Quinceys, father and son, as the previous landowners may have had a hand in earlier developments.

The presence of the Abbey would certainly stimulate the large scale production of salt using comparatively cheap fuel (arable East Lothian was long cleared and had limited supplies of wood and peat, which were in demand for domestic use) and the brinier water of the Prestonpans shore.

Better returns could be expected compared to their earlier operations. However, the basic operation of a pan was to remain unchanged for several centuries – even if the details of development remain obscure. Salting references are scarce in contemporary records but the religious houses and the crown secured possession of much of the industry and statutes were promulgated to protect the workers. At one time a Master of the Royal Saltworks existed; interestingly, the King's Pan Craig lies near Prestongrange, perhaps marking an early Royal saltworks. Occasional inferences might be drawn about the industry from other sources such as Treasury statements and Accounts, placenames and folk stories. The 'Salter's Way', the route from Newbattle Abbey to their lands and holdings around Prestongrange is an example of the latter. After the easy coal of the Great Seam outcrop near (the now) Bankton House had been exhausted the route reputedly saw a two-way trade of Eskside coal down and Pretonpans salt up. Salt appears in a list of regularly taxed goods at the burgh of Berwick in the period before 1303 and salt was reckoned to be one of the foremost exports of Scotland during the reign of James VI. There are more documentary sources surviving in the sixteenth century, when lay proprietors were a significant feature of the industry.

In the Prestonpans area the transition to lay ownership was almost universal. In the late fifteenth century Sir Nicholas Flemyn, chaplain at Seton Collegiate Church, was the occupier of a single pan at 'Saltprestone', and perhaps represents an intermediate stage as benefices were secularised and ownership transferred from Church to lay proprietors. Other saltworks were in the hands of burgesses (citizens of nearby burghs) and local 'indwellers' (a lower social ranking), c.f., the Achesons of Prestonpans. Most of the owners of the sixteenth century had single or double pan operations, essentially family operations or superintended by a Grieve: one such family can be traced in the Grant-Suttie Papers at the SRO. Thus, George Mott had charter of a saltpan from Mark Ker of Prestongrange in 1559. Many of these small-scale owners were to disappear as works were consolidated under the ownership of landed proprietors. Next, a daughter of George Mott consolidated her sisters' shares, which they inherited in 1595, and sold on to Mark Achesone of Mylnehevin (Morison's Haven) in 1597 (GD1/402/28, et seq.). The Achesones were only one rung below the landed gentry and controlled the Abbey's old harbour. Some years later the pans passed from the Achesones (Sir Patrick of Clancairney) to Alexander Morisone of Prestongrange.

However, small scale undertakings remained the norm in the Prestonpans area (in later centuries an untypical position in the Scottish salt industry). Even most of the pans on Prestongrange Estate were in the hands of people of modest rank. For example in the early eighteenth century John Greig, indweller, and Richard Henderson, sailor. Others were merchants, both local and from Edinburgh. A total of eleven works around Prestonpans remained outside the hands of the landed proprietors in the early eighteenth century. However, their output has been estimated as only 2,000 bushels each per pan p.a. when the Scottish average was 4,500. The remaining works were on a considerably larger scale, c.f. the 40 pans owned and operated by the Winton Estates at Cockenzie and their individual outputs were higher.

The golden age of the Scottish salt industry lasted from the latter sixteenth century to the middle of the nineteenth. It has been the subject of a scholarly investigation by Christopher Whatley, who has assiduously assembled statistical and social information relating to the Salt Industry 1570–1850 (published by the Aberdeen University Press, 1987). Some of his key points include noting the low operational efficiency of everyday panning throughout most of the period (above), with occasional bursts of better performance when demand was up (e.g., the Napoleonic Wars) and towards the end of the period when efficiency was essential in the fight for survival against Cheshire rocksalt competition. Additionally, he makes it clear that the industry survived only because of the skill (and obstinacy) of the saltmasters in securing a virtual monopoly in the home market and manipulating and interpreting legislation to suit themselves. That this was done in the face of competition which destroyed a comparable industry on Tyneside, in the face of anti-competitive English legislation, and with a product which was notoriously poor, is remarkable. Scots salters could make high quality salt (see Sunday salt and slow evaporation, above) but the amount of time a Scottish pan was down (for repair – beiting – or natural interruptions: storms damaging the pans and bucket pots or even weed clearing from the latter) meant that when pans worked they had to be driven hard, taking a draw every 24–28 hours. The scale of production is illustrated by figures compiled by Whatly. Thus, Forth Estuary saltworks produced 95% of Scotland's salt in 1716–17, of which Prestonpans parish (including Prestongrange) accounted for 29% (of that total; 67,400 bushels). At the end of the century the Forth's share had marginally declined to 88%, but the Prestonpans proportion within this had risen to 37.3% (107,500 bushels).

Whatly accounts for the landed interest, including the proprietors of Prestongrange, by considering both the gathering industrial revolution and the need of the estates for ready cash. Early industrial developments in Scotland were small scale, with the exception of the investments of the Board of Trustees in establishments such as bleachfields (inspired by Fletcher of Saltoun). Comparatively, saltworks once called for large investments – not just pans, but girnels, salters' housing, and reserves for unpredictable repairs. An estate could absorb these costs amongst their other operations. As the eighteenth century progressed and the industrial revolution took off, the capital stock tied in saltworks paled into insignificance. There was also a century long (slow) decline in demand and valuations decreased in real terms; quite markedly towards the last productive years of the industry. In the mid nineteenth century a working pan could be had for the annual rent of £50–60; only fifty years before pans could be let for several hundred pounds. In view of this decline, although it explains why estates absorbed pans as small scale operators succumbed to liquidity problems, another reason must be sought for the estates' interest in panning.

Most of the landowners in Prestonpans and its vicinity were coal proprietors: and the two industries were interlocked. Salt sales might make marginal mining operations profitable. Further, in the seventeenth and early eighteenth centuries income from salt could form a considerable part of an estate's cash income (Scotland was notoriously short of moveable capital and cash). At Prestongrange in 1716–17 (SRO CS 96/4520: Factor's Account Book of Prestongrange 1716–23), income from salt amounted to 63% of the non agricultural income, the rest being spread over coal, cloth, and bottles (the remnant product from Morison's glass-making enterprise). As the agricultural income was predominantly in kind, cash from salt sales could go a long way towards plugging an estate's liquidity gap. So the Morisons of Prestongrange were at an advantage over their immediate inland neighbours. Their accumulated cash reserves were noted by Rev. Alexander 'Jupiter' Carlyle – William Morison was very rich, sufficiently so to fund a political career (although it all went in the bright lights of London and gambling dens). Other proprietors invested their salt revenues in improving and sinking coal pits, and subsidising their tied colliers when pits were inoperable (a frequent occurrence). The colliers, when unpaid and despite their unfree status, could be 'mutinous' and it was expensive to return absconders through law.

The saltmasters operated their industry to a background of distinctive legislation. By 1707, at the Union of Parliaments, a file of 361 pages of 'all statutes relating to salt' was drawn up. As well as quality, differential taxes, customs dues and other imposts meant that Scottish salt often competed against other supplies with 'one hand tied behind its back' in the eighteenth century export market. Lobbying, exercise of interest and political influence could turn the situation around in the home market and the landed proprietors were intimately connected with the Government of Scotland. Bay salt had been heavily taxed: in the 1650s a Colonel Aytkins and his colleagues, the tacksmen of the excise of Bay salt, were investigated for importation such that '*no other merchant finds a market*' (Records of the Conventions of Royal Burghs of Scotland, ed. JD Marwick, Edinburgh, 1866–90). An investigating committee was appointed and proposed an inhibiting tax of £12 Scots per boll. Thus, the saltmasters managed a virtual domestic monopoly throughout the eighteenth century, aided by times of dearth in other supplies for one reason or another. In 1687 it was observed that '*salt masters intend to make a monopoly*' prejudicial to Royal Burghs (Conv. of Burghs) and although the monopolists did not succeed then, the Convention was well aware it needed to be on guard against further attempts. One of the few uses to which imported salt could be legitimately put was to preserve fish, an exemption secured by another powerful lobby group. Despite public complaint, virtually all domestic salt had to come from Scottish pans. The saltmasters in the neighbourhood of Edinburgh also gained from the growth of the city; the salt wife walking to Edinburgh and hawking her wares through the streets is a remembered figure. Steady sales there and to the immediate area were Prestonpans saltmasters' main market. By the Old Statistical Account (1796) there were 14 saltmasters and agents employing a similar number of assistants (persons employed in saltpans with their families totalled 47, giving between 10 and 15 able bodied adult male labourers). The statistical analysis of the account estimated a grand total of 205 workers in Scotland, the majority clustered on both sides of the Forth.

The salt proprietors grouped themselves into a Salt Association ('*the Proprietors of Salt Works on the Firth of Forth*' also known as '*the Society*') to co-ordinate action. As well as acting to restrict imports, they operated as a cartel regulating the output of domestic pans and 'fixing' domestic prices. Most small operators were ignored by the Society and even some of the landed proprietors felt no need to join (such as those with a nearby city market), but all benefited as the Society seldom had less than 55% of the industry in its own hands. Their strategy was simply to set an agreed output per pan to force up prices in their relatively secure domestic market. Quota breaking was enforced by fines, the confiscated salt sometimes being distributed amongst other producers but at other times dumped on export markets or the Icelandic fisheries. The Society remained strong until the last decade of the eighteenth century, having accomplished their objectives for about twenty years They managed a decline in output from over 300,000 bushels p.a. to around a quarter million while increasing prices from around 1/1d per bushel to 1/6d; as costs at a well managed pan were 9–10d this implies a profit of around 100% before the Society's tax of 2d a bushel. However, growing public disquiet at unfair pricing and a change in Government attitudes to taxes signalled changes. In Ayrshire, the Forth Society faced another threat: imported rocksalt. Their biggest challenge to the end of the eighteenth century had been keeping Cheshire competition out of Scotland. Now there were promoters who actively sought to supplant brine by refining rocksalt (and break the existing monopoly in their own interest). Despite plaintive appeals to Parliament and to patriotism, with a solemn undertaking to reduce domestic prices, the differential tax between English and Scottish salt was eroded in 1798, when the ratio was changed from 30% to 55%. Only the Napoleonic Wars now protected the industry, and other industrial users (e.g., chemists, bleachers and calico printers) had gained as much economic clout as the Society; they all needed plentiful, cheap salt. Further, fisheries were being supported and developed by Government subsidies and their supporters argued against cumbersome official procedures involved in getting the salt they needed. With the arrival of peace in 1815, the writing was on the wall. In 1823 all duties were repealed; within two years, large legal shipments of rocksalt had arrived in Scotland and the industry was devastated. In the next generation, railway transport was just one more problem to overcome for the survivors.

The surviving nineteenth century salters, by now concentrated in Prestonpans, Joppa and Cockenzie, attempted to meet the competition by importing rock salt themselves. Added to brine it meant salt could be drawn on every boiling instead of the traditional 1 in 3. Pigot's Directory, 1825–6 tellingly records the survivors in that year:

Cockenzie:	Francis Cadell
Prestonpans:	Andrew Alexander
Cuthill:	William McLean
Cuthill:	Robert Laidlaw
West Pans:	Robert and George Gordon (Potters: a supply of glaze for their works?)
West Pans:	Nicol Watson
Joppa:	John Baxter & Company
Portobello:	Joseph Astley (Physical salts, a medicinal manufacturer)

By 1860 (Slater's Directory of Scotland) only the Cadells (now Hew Francis), Alexanders (now William), Joppa (now under Alexander Nisbet) and the pharmaceutical salter (now Robert and Thomas Smellie of the Wellington Chemical Works) were in business, but there was a slight resurgence a few years later (Slaters, 1867) with old works at Magdalen (Robert Irving) and Musselburgh Links (Alexander McKinley & Co), Pinkie Works (John Grieve; a coalmaster) reopened and joining the three other survivors. Perhaps the growth of brick and tile works was stimulating local production – vast amount of salt ware required as glazes, and quality wasn't a problem. However, any respite was short lived. By 1878 (Slater's) four works survived:

Cockenzie:	P&C Forman
Prestonpans:	William Alexander, John Sharpe, manager
Pinkie:	John Grieve
Joppa:	Alexander Nisbet & Son

Shortly afterwards, the Scottish Salt Company was formed, most surviving saltmasters becoming founding shareholders. When Peter McNeil came to write his History of Prestonpans (John Menzies, 1902), only William Alexander Meek was operating working pans, a twin unit. Under the Scottish Salt Company the surviving pans were able to carve out a niche. The quality of the salt was much improved, and in demand as coarse cooking salt. Oil of Salt and Saladine Ointments had their adherents and the Joppa pans diversified into pipeclay whiting (for doorsteps). The company survived for fifty years, coming through the Second World War only marginally reduced. However, although the demand for salt remained fairly steady, the company's other products were no longer selling. When the last Scottish salt pan closed in Prestonpans during 1959 (Cockenzie closed in 1939), no one could be found to repair it. At the same time, the supply of Cheshire rock-salt dried up (it was diverted to road spreading); an attempt was made to import salt, but it coincided with the pan failure and only one boiling was made.

After a few years spent packing English salt in Scottish Salt Company packets, the Company was wound up and the story of Scottish Salt came to an end. [Editor: Plans have been mooted since 2004 to attempt to recreate a 'boutique' sea salt enterprise in Prestonpans.]

3 CHEMICALS AND SOAP

Sulphuric Acid

In the middle of the eighteenth century a new industry began in Prestonpans. Two English scientists and entrepreneurs selected the area to develop a new process for making sulphuric acid (oil of vitriol). John Roebuck and Samuel Garbett are profiled in Appendix I. The partners were already experienced in both commerce and technology: they raised the seed-money for their new plant from a gold recovery process in Garbett's home city of Birmingham, where they had also carried out the preliminary development work for the new plant. Their process revolutionised the production of the acid, slashing the price by a third and laying the foundations for an explosion in the heavy chemical industry. Their instinct for secrecy, commercial protection and patent avoidance led them to Prestonpans in 1749, where they set up the world's first successful large scale sulphuric acid manufactory. The presence in Edinburgh of one of Roebuck's old tutors, Professor Francis Home, who had experimented with sulphuric acid for linen bleaching and Lord Milton's (Andrew Fletcher of Saltoun) push for bleaching and linen making in Scotland through the Board of Manufactures were probably other considerations. Indeed, Roebuck and Garbett engineered an introduction to Milton through Rev. Alexander Carlyle of Inveresk; Carlyle quite took to Garbett, but he held a lesser opinion of Roebuck (see: the Autobiography of Dr. Alexander Carlyle of Inveresk, Foulis, London and Edinburgh, 1910). The market for bleaching agents on East Lothian's many commercial fields was considerable. Bleaching required first a mild alkali (extracted from wood or kelp ashes, acting to strip out oils and dirt), followed by acid treatment, the best of which was soured milk, although the treatment took 5 days. The old bleach, soured milk, could not be secured in sufficient quantity: in the 1730s Cockburn of Ormiston's bleachfields at Ormiston and Glenkinchey employed over 90 hands under John Christie and John Drummond; Fletcher's in 1746 was on a similar scale. In the eighteenth century owners of public bleachfields were granted an immunity of duties on 'whitening materials' (bleaches; Conv. of Burghs). The intention was to boost the linen trade and the effect was to increase demand for bleaches, as well as soap and ashes (alkalis) needed by the trade. Once adopted, oil of vitriol was not only more plentiful and cheaper, but also took only five hours to do the same task as soured milk.

To some extent the Prestonpans chemical industry was also a natural spin-off from salting. Increasingly in the eighteenth century by-products had been found commercial uses and salt itself was becoming an important feedstock for other processes (covered in more detail with salt, above). By the eighteenth century, basic chemicals were needed in bulk at economical rates. Prestonpans provided a skilled workforce (experienced in the toxic and corrosive environment of the plant), ready supplies of fuel, easy transportation links and, perhaps above all, privacy and security and a nearby market. Security was enhanced by a high wall round their plant (the '*Secret Works*') – a fact which has passed into local legend (MacNeil, Prestonpans).

The secrecy was essential because the basis of Roebuck and Garbett's new process was simply to exchange fragile glass retorts for robust lead equivalents, although they may have refined the preparation and balance of their ingredients (a mixture of sulphur and saltpetre). Roebuck's first vessels had a 200 cubic foot capacity and held 4 inches of water with the reagent on lead pedestals, where it could burn; the combustion took a month (with replenishment of combustibles in the vessel), the process being that the sulphur, burning in air, yields sulphur dioxide; this combines with the nitre to yield sulphur trioxide and sodium nitrite. Solvated sulphur trioxide is sulphuric acid. The process is inefficient and yields amounts of highly toxic gases – a great problem not only for the workers in the plant, but also the local environment. By 1785 there were 100 chambers, some of them larger than the original designs.

Further evidence of the operation of the plant comes from a variety of sources. Between 1784 and 1786 a nearby competitor was Dr Francis Swediaur who petitioned for the erection of a salt-works at Port Seton (where he was already established; OSP 181:23) where he intended to make soda (sodium carbonate) by the application of sulphuric acid to salt. Fanjus St Fond, a visitor, left a record (Fanjus Sant Fond, 1799, Volume 1) of the corrosive nature of the atmosphere around Prestonpans, its effect on brass (which turned green in hours), and the hellish conditions under which the workers laboured. He attributed it to the vapours from salting, but to our eye the acid works would be the natural culprit. He also provides testimony on '*the suffocating smell at a distance*' and '*the high wall concealed even chimneys*'. In a comment in a Local History (History of the Regality of Musselburgh, James Paterson) another plant, at Fisherrow, was seen to cause concern to local fishermen. They complained the effluent was wasting their musselbeds; mussels were essential for baiting their lines. Finally, Thomas Pennant (A Tour of Scotland, 1769) graphically captures the salters' (and by extension the acid workers') lot with his comment '*nothing ever exhibited such an idea of the infernal regions as the horrid furnace and the poor miserable naked wretches attending it*'.

Although the Works could produce sulphuric acid at a third of the historic cost, the secret was one which could be applied by anyone else, once out. Despite inducements and binding indentures their workforce was potentially the main source of leaks and it is believed that the secret was stolen by decamping workers who sold it to the highest several bidders they could find: soon all sulphuric acid was made in lead retorts. However, such was the demand for cheap acid that for a number of years the leaks were irrelevant and the profits enabled both partners to go on to greater enterprises with a third, the local man William Cadell: together they founded the Carron Iron Works, in 1759. The Prestongrange Works was left in the hands of Garbett's former apprentice (Carlyle, Autobiography) Peter Downey as manager in 1766. About then, Garbett bought out his partner Roebuck (who squandered large sums on adventures in coal mining and salt panning as well as the Works at Carron). The partners still had mind of their joint responsibilities as in 1772 they sought the protection of a patent (Old Session Papers 116:18) for their process.

After Roebuck had sold on, the enterprise traded as Samuel Garbett and Company. Like many such concerns, when the proprietor ran into trouble, in this case in-fighting between the directors and a 'boardroom coup' at Carron, sequestration was the result. Garbett and Company folded in 1772. Its future was secured, because in 1774, the Company traded as Glassford, Downey & Company: the new controlling partner was Henry Glassford of Dougalston, a Glasgow industrialist. Patrick Downey died around 1790, and a James Mackenzie, also of Glasgow appears as the Company's agent in that city up to 1807 and also between 1810–20; he was also associated with the Caledonian Pottery there. Then, in 1795, the pollution caused by the works was the subject of a legal action between a resident, Elizabeth Howieson, on one part and the new manager, John Gilmour, on the other part for Henry Glassford. These trying conditions were not helped by six competitors in Glasgow, a large plant at Burntisland and others in the immediate neighbourhood. All of them were experiencing difficult times because of further technological advances, mainly the developments under Tennant at St Rollox (below).

However, St Rollox was in the future and the Company was still trading at the time of the Old Statistical Account, 1796; the name was then the Prestonpans Vitriol Company and it supported 188 people, suggesting a staff of around 40–45 hands, a considerable number: in 1784 the Company's operation had been the largest acid works in Great Britain and had secured a great export market. Prestonpans Customs accounts from Downey's time, March 1768 to March 1769, record the export of 750 bottles of green glass and 84554 pounds of oil of vitriol. Applying figures given in the OSA, oil of vitriol fetched 3d per pound and was sold in 140lb bottles (supported in wicker baskets, which each cost three shillings). Therefore the exports above were valued just under £2200 – a great sum. The scale of the Works was probably still comparable in the 1790s, but the next decade was difficult and the Company disappears from the record until in the light of the evidence from sasines in the Haddingtonshire Register, Laird Fowler, the proprietor of the Prestonpans brewery and the successor to the Cadells in many of their enterprises (he also backed their pottery company) had secured the premises.

There has been a curious tendency for researchers to place 'the Secret Works' at a site on the west of Prestonpans, to the north of the High Street (See, for example, Patrick MacVeigh, Scottish East Coast Potteries). A sasine registered on 15 May 1879 (Index, Haddingtonshire) notes '*several connected tenements of land lying in a triangle in the Harlawhill of Prestonpans with the buildings thereon, on the south side of the High Street ... on which lands the works of the Vitriol Company of Prestonpans and part of the accommodation of the late Brewery Company ... were erected and situated*'. This site is contiguous with the present Preston Links shopping complex and supermarket (and in the east and south of the High Street – well away from MacVeigh's location; the problem appears to be confusion with the site of Belfield's Pottery, which had been a saltworks and, for a period, a chemical works). In 1879 the site was in the hands of John Fowler and Company, as it had been for some years.

It is not clear when Fowler or his successor Hislop gained the Works, either as an operating concern or for its assets, although the evidence from Glasgow would suggest after 1820 (Scottish Pottery Historical Review 4, p73). At some point in the very early nineteenth century it was operating next to their Prestonpans Distillery Company on an adjacent part of the site and the land was mortgaged to provide funds for Brewery development. It would have faced increasingly difficult trading conditions. As early as 1785 Roebuck's protege James Watt was introduced to the properties of chlorine as a bleach; by 1788 his father-in-law James McGrigor was using it to bleach linen. Then in 1799 Charles Tennant of St Rollux patented a process for the bulk synthesis of chloride of lime. Within a few years, it was the bleach of choice, available at a fraction of sulphuric acid's price. In 1800 Tennant made 25 tons of bleach; by 1825 he was producing 1000 tons p.a. and the acid plants were disappearing. There is no mention of the Vitriol Company in Pigot's Directory of 1825–6 and any chemical making at Prestonpans continued solely as an adjunct to the surviving saltworks or the soapworks.

The Chemistry of Soapmaking

Soap is the alkali metal (sodium, potassium) salt of stearic acid. Stearic moities are found in nature combined in tallow, an ester of stearic acid and glycerol (alternatively, propantriol – a molecule with three alcohol moieties). Under conditions of alkaline hydrolysis the stearate is formed and the triol regenerated. This means, by boiling tallow with an alkali it can be split into its component parts. When the ionic content of the solution is changed – by loading it with salt – soap separates and floats to the top where it can be collected. Subsequent cleaning, drying and perfuming gives a solid which can be melted and moulded, or simply cut into blocks, or flaked. Different feedstocks, such as vegetable, nut or tree oils yield variants on the theme. Soap cleans by 'solubilising' dirt particles: it coats them in such a way that they are mobilised and can be rinsed out.

Soap was discovered long before the chemical explanation above. A scenario where animal fat drips onto hot embers on an open cooking fire, followed by quenching of the fire, would leave a naturally formed soap deposit amongst the ashes. This means that soap would be discovered countless times in prehistory (if the ashes were used for scouring) before the connection with fat was noticed. For a long time it was a domestic industry: it did not become industrialised until the eighteenth century. The well known process was scaled up in the first manufactory, set up in 1703, and soap had joined the Industrial Revolution. It quickly attracted a prohibitive excise duty or tax which held back advances in production, but its main markets, the cloth finishing industries were growing equally as fast and demand continued to grow. As noted above, in the 1730s, bleachfields were common in Scotland. Many of them had, initially at least, their own soapmaking facility. Soap was essential for finishing the cloth and, like the case of bleaching agents, specialists soon took over the manufacture and supply of the commodity. By the end of the eighteenth century the larger soapmaking plants were capable of producing several million pounds per annum.

Soap Making at Prestonpans

In the middle of the eighteenth century, Thomas Paterson was established as a soap boiler in Prestonpans on a site to the West of the Brewery, on the North (seaward) side of the High Street. He had the advantage of an agricultural hinterland (supplies of tallow), nearby fuel (coal), alkali (potash could be made from kelp, which the previous century had been burnt for the glass industry (John Ray, 1662) and, of course, plentiful supplies of salt and a local market of both domestic and industrial users. Although the Prestonpans OSA is silent, the plant was there because it appears in Pigot's Directory of 1825–6 in the hands of Thomas and William Patterson. The latter features in a complimentary report in the New Statistical account where '*Mr Paterson's Soapworks*' were '*thriving*' and importing supplies of tallow from as far afield as Australia. By 1852 (Slater's) the soapworks was in the hands of a relative of the Patersons, James Mellis: after the 1860s the company name became James Mellis and Company, and remained so until closure.

It was always a small affair employing only a few hands, but some of these spent their whole working lives there. There was little necessity for technological improvement and it appears that some of the Victorian equipment may have been used for many years in the twentieth century. Robert Scott in writing the Industrial History of Prestonpans for Mining Technology, 1980, covers the soapworks. There were three old iron boiling vats, about 10 feet high and 6 feet across, which had originally been heated by open fires; three more modern vats were cylindrical steel retorts of a similar size. In later years both sets were heated by steam pipes. The range of fats and oils imported by the company increased during the twentieth century and was not restricted to animal fats, but palm oil and other vegetable oils were used as appropriate feedstocks for different soaps and some detergents were also manufactured. The by-product glycerol, some of which was retained for moisturising soaps was occasionally otherwise in demand: during the First World War it was collected for processing into explosives.

The product range was at some times quite extensive. Fine perfumed soaps and toilets soaps, large blocks for flaking and clothes washing, soft soaps and leather soaps, detergents and others were all produced. An advertisement (Haddingtonshire Register and Almanac, John Hutchinson, Haddington) in 1918 lists soft soaps sold from the firkin (41/2 gallons) to 1lb tin, Speedwell Soap Powder sold from 7lb to penny packets, as well as toilet and bar soaps. Despite this, the factory was closed in the late nineteen fifties, a victim of the advertising power and the economies of scale of the giant chemical companies which still dominate production today.

4 GLASS

Glass is processed silica in combination with a variety of other materials, all of them commonly available now and in the past. Purification has always been a problem, but colouring glass to disguise unattractive hues was an early known skill (it was accomplished by deliberately allowing a contaminant of known effect into the melt). Hardness, melting point and optical characteristics are all aspects of glass which can be controlled to some degree, and most of these attributes had been arrived at empirically by medieval glassmakers long before scientific reasons were formulated. Glassworks require a skilled workforce, both for the making and the fabrication of glass objects and both sides of the trade have always been amongst the elite of the working classes. However, as late as the sixteenth century, there were few glassmakers in Britain, their products being regarded as a rich man's luxury. With the development of the country's first flint glassworks at London's Crutched Friars Lane in 1557 (David Bremner, Industries of Scotland, Adam and Chas. Black, Edinburgh, 1869), its use began to spread. In 1615, the application of coal as a fuel brought down costs and throughout the seventeenth century, further immigration of skilled hands raised the standards of the native industry: the Duke of Buckingham's Venetians at Lambeth were Britain's first mirror makers in 1675. An excise was briefly applied in 1695, and then again in 1745 (for a century). Although the first period caused problems for Scottish glassmakers, the production grew until, for a time, it was Scotland's third greatest export, by value.

Glassmaking in Britain is first mentioned (after the Roman period) in 674AD, when the Church at Wearmouth, near Durham, was employing workmen from abroad. This was a pattern which continued over the centuries, as mentioned above, and it was repeated in Scotland, where the origins of glassmaking were probably the initiative of Hay of Wemyss, who had a patent from James VI (Scottish Industrial History 7.1 1984 p34). Glass-wrights were working in Scotland in the early seventeenth century, their output of window glass being regulated by defining Act between 1624–26 (CRB). As early as 1662, there was production in the Prestonpans area. In August of that year, John Ray described (Hume Brown, Early Travellers in Scotland, James Thin, 1973) his journey from North Berwick to Leith. He wrote '*By the way also we saw glasses made of kelp and sand mixed together, and calcined in an oven. The crucibles which contained the melted glass, they told us, were made of tobacco-pipe clay*' (kelp was still being collected in the early 1800s: Musselburgh Council Records). This suggests that the Morisons of Prestongrange had a glass making facility at least as early as that year, and probably earlier; certainly the local area afforded all the raw materials.

The next significant figure is William Morison of Prestongrange. 'Jupiter' Carlyle of Inveresk was intimately connected with the Morison family and has left several impressions of William. He writes (Alexander Carlyle: Anecdotes and Characters of Times, Oxford University Press, 1973) that Morison was MP for East Lothian in the first UK Parliament, standing against Fletcher of Saltoun; he had previously sat for Haddingtonshire in the Scots Parliament. He had had a considerable fortune, based on his family estate and the industries and farms developed on it but by 1732 the estate was sequestered by his creditors. Carlyle believed that this had been caused by Morison's involvement with a notorious gambler, Colonel Charteris. In another anecdote, in the course of development work at Morison's Haven Mill Morison had encountered a series of vaults underground, perhaps part of the 'fort' noted on early maps just to the west of the harbour, which were believed by the credulous Laird to be part of the 'infernal regions'.

Morison's beliefs notwithstanding, he pursued a vigorous policy on his estates. On the fifth of August 1697 he obtained an Act and ratification in favour of the Glass Manufactory at Morisons Haven from the Scots Parliament. This Act followed an earlier one in favour of the Leith Glassworks of George Mackenzie, Viscount Tarbat, who had had a similar Act on 8th October 1689 (Monica Clough, The Leith Glassworks, Scottish Industrial History, 5.1, 1982).

However, the acts differ in some detail. That to Tarbat extends a prohibition to competitors making green glass bottles, chemists and apothecaries glass ware; that to Morison suggests his works would enjoy '*the whole privileges, liberties and immunities granted by the former acts ... at any time bygone*', therefore perhaps superseding Tarbat's. Morison's stated product list included special glasses such as Mirrors, coach glasses, spectacles, watch glasses and window glasses '*never heretofore manufactured within this Kingdom*', as well as common bottles and his application was supported by samples. The application further mentions the expenses in getting skilled workmen to make these new products, suggested the normal glassowners augmentation of local skills by paying for new from abroad. Morison and his partners would also have a fair idea that Tarbat had difficulties with marketing, transport and, not least, English competition so the terms of the act were written to expressly forbid anyone else making the new glasses for nine years and also prohibited importing these articles on pain of confiscation. It was perhaps these very imports, probably a consequence of the glass excise, that prompted this clause in Morison's Act.

Viscount Tarbat was the nearest direct competitor to Prestongrange and Morison. Tarbat had found trading conditions difficult, as mentioned above, and failed in the early eighteenth century (despite petitioning in 1701 for further protection from English exports). As the reverse export was impossible because of the legal position favouring English exporters he was in an invidious position. Morison seems to have weathered this period, and gained a niche for bottles (the finer products seeming having disappeared), or so at least the estate accounts of 1716–23 would indicate (above). Shortly afterwards, we find the glassworks site in the hands of one of the Prestonpans potters, and the site remained in that industry until most of the works were demolished to make way for the industrial railway lines of the colliery and brickworks of the later nineteenth century.

5 BRICKMAKING

Bricks, tiles and heavy ceramics

Bricks are generally defined as prismatic rectangular units of burnt clay, however both standards and definitions have varied over time, changing as the industry evolved. Bricks have historically been made in a variety of ways. The earliest were hand moulded, brickmakers extracting and preparing their clay with little mechanical assistance. There was no appreciable technological advance until the nineteenth century when mechanisation permitted the use of a wider range of raw materials (such as fireclay, shales, and coaly shales (locally *blaes*)) and gave greater output (at lower cost) of more consistent quality. Often in Scotland, clays and shales have been worked as a by-product of the coal industry; this is particularly true of the industrial development of the Prestongrange Works. Thus, several of the coal seams comprising the East and Mid-Lothian coal basin are underlain by significant depths of fireclay and contain bands of, or are roofed with, blaes. The attractions of the latter arise from a proportion of combustible material integral to the blaes which can supplement fuel during firing. 'Self-firing' is a useful economy exploited from the late nineteenth century, when sophisticated kilns were developed to utilise this feature. Such was the demand for the resulting 'composition' or common bricks that Prestongrange Pit was by the years after Nationalisation (1947–1961) increasingly devoted to the supply of the adjacent brickworks.

Tiles are closely associated with brickmaking but in particular to improvements in farming after about 1800. When it is understood that the bulk of the many nineteenth century tile-works produced field drainage tiles (and not roofing pantiles) the latter connection is clear. East Lothian was at the forefront of land improvement, led by luminaries such Lord Belhaven of Biel, Cockburn of Ormiston and the Fletchers of Saltoun. Many other landowners, such as the Grant-Sutties of Prestongrange and Balgone were quick to follow their example. In the later nineteenth century drain-tile manufacture became an adjunct to heavy ceramics production, essentially comprising everything from roofing and floor tiles; speciality bricks and furnace fittings; chimney cans and firebacks; a diverse range of garden wares such as edging, rustic furniture, bird baths and planters; water and gas pipes; drainage and sewerage traps; to sanitary wares such as sinks, cisterns, toilets, and the like. This market was developed at the Prestongrange Brick and Tile Works under a variety of owners until it closed.

Brickmaking

The Romans used clay to make bricks and tiles (both roof and drainage) and were probably responsible for the technology's introduction to the British Isles (see also Salt, above). The presence of a major Roman fort and viccus or civil settlement at nearby Inveresk suggest that native British inhabitants would be exposed to both the technology of brickmaking and salting, although no evidence exists to suggest that either process survived during the Dark Ages.

The spread of continental Monasticism in the medieval period saw a revolution in both technologies. Decorative tiles were produced to floor ecclesiastical structures, some being imported from the continent, but others certainly manufactured locally. The Franciscan Priory at Dunbar had a tiled floor, St Mary's Church in Haddington likewise. A good example of a tile kiln was excavated at North Berwick and examples of its tiles are to be found in the National and East Lothian Council Museum Service Collections. This kiln was almost certainly worked by an emigree European tiler, from stylistic similarities to European examples. From the extent of the tilework now discovered, other undiscovered kiln sites must have existed in the locality.

Brick became popular in Britain in the mid 1400s, in areas where there was abundant clay but little useful building stone. However, in Scotland there was an abundance of good building stone (and subsequently a powerful and organised (operative) masonic guildery (or lobby) hindered the development of brickmaking for construction). Here, roofs of significant buildings continued to be finished in stone slabs and slates and common dwellings used sod, heather and other natural materials, right throughout the late medieval period and into the industrial age. Gradually, there was a change. One Tobaccos Knowes (Tobias Knox?) received a patent for '*the making of bricks under several conditions*' prior to 1643 (Conv. of Burghs). Bricks were convenient and could be quite cheap to produce. By 1784, brickmaking was of sufficient importance to attract an Excise duty of 2/6 per thousand bricks. Later duties were applied on the basis of size: in 1835 the common brick tax had increased to the rate of 5/10 per thousand. The same rate was applied universally in 1839, because the differential rate had 'obstructed the development of dwellings for the poorer class' (David Bremner, Industries of Scotland); the effect of the tax had certainly been to inhibit brick manufacture: in 1802, 714 million bricks were made annually; after abolition (1840), 1725 million.

Colliery and Beehive Brick Kilns, Prestongrange Colliery
Scottish Mining Museum Trust

After the Union of Parliament, Scotland's landowners and the main agricultural producers had to compete in a wider market. Several looked south to see the farming revolution underway there and imported new ideas. New villages were created as '*policies*' and parks grew around country seats. Lord Belhaven at Biel expounded upon the ideal stackyard and steading layout, specifying the housing conditions which the farm servants might enjoy. Cockburn of Ormiston experimented with long leases on his estate and encouraged his farmers to explore new methods in cultivation, rotation and the application of fertilisers. New technology meant that new land could be ploughed and with liming and draining could be made fertile. Old style field drains involved trenching and packing stones. Porous earthenware tiles and pipes did the same job much more simply and their production boomed. They could be made by hand from any suitable clay deposit and fired using available resources in a clamp or temporary kiln. There were excellent deposits of suitable clay at the surface all along the coast from Portobello right through to Prestonpans and there have been countless tileworks exploiting these resources.

Once, fireclay and blaes were worked simply to give room around the coals with which they were associated. Refractory materials such as fireclay have high resistance to high temperature and can be used to retain heat and line furnaces. It was not until the early 1830s that reserves of high quality fireclays were proved in Scotland: by 1900 they were being exploited by over sixty separate companies. Natural fireclays have 26–43% alumina; soda, potash and iron content all reduce the effective refractoriness; basic raw materials can be treated to increase their refractoriness (KW Sanderson, the Scottish Refractory Industry 1830–1980, 1990). The reserves around the Mid and East Lothian Coalfield were such that even in the 1970s, the Lothian Region

Structural Plan considered (but discounted) fireclay reserves and noted 1.5 million, workable tons of blaes in the Dolphinton-Wallyford area.

Brickmaking at Prestongrange and Prestonpans

At the time of the Old Statistical Account, there were two works in Prestonpans itself. One was near the Old Kirk (Edinburgh Advertiser, 1789: the Old Kirk tile works had its clay onsite, supplying nearby potteries as well) and employed six men at a shilling (5 pence) a day. In 1795 they fired 13 kilns of tiles at 10,000 tiles per load paying 3 shillings and 6 pence per 12 hundredweight of coal; they also made 107,000 bricks, probably in clamps because no kilns are mentioned. The other works lay further to the west (a site called Ravenscroft) on the seaside, digging its clay from a three acre site immediately adjacent. It was slightly smaller, because it fired 9 kilns of 9000 tiles; the work was carried on by 3 men at 7s each per week. At this period bricks fetched 17 shillings and 6 pence (with half a crown duty included) per thousand and a thousand tiles was £2 13 shillings (including 8 shillings duty); the tax had been introduced in 1784. An article in the Scottish Pottery Review, The Old Kirk Pottery (at) Prestonpans by Gerald Quail, assembles valuable information and detailed references to both brick and tile works. An expert tiler and his assistant could turn out 4–5 thousand daily (for a long time hand labour had the advantage of greater economy than machines). Drain pipes, however, were more economically made by machine (although Belfields of Prestonpans developed a line in glazed, hand thrown gas pipes in the 1840s). Bricks and tiles also may have been made at the pottery beside Morisons Haven at Prestongrange: there was certainly an appropriate source of clay, and later events suggest that it may have been applied to this purpose for some time. Customs Accounts for the port of Morisons Haven have been analysed and show that between 1742–1770, 29 entries towards the end of the period relate to the export of bricks. A total of 443,400 and 218,000 brickstones went out in this period (Scottish Pottery Historical Review, 4, p. 18).

In the last decade of the eighteenth century, Caddell, Anderson & Co. of the Old Kirk Pottery and Brickworks leased the smaller, Ravenscroft Works from the owner Alexander Banks, through his nieces the Misses Clapperton, as well as continuing their own Works. Both are located on Forest's Map of Haddingtonshire, 1799. From the sasines relating to the Ravenscroft, it lay adjacent to Northfield Estate on the north side of the road (therefore by the seashore) with three acres of claypits, and so was within the bounds of the ancient Barony of Prestongrange. The works had been founded around 1770 and passed from an Edinburgh builder, Thomas Russell to the lessees above and subsequently their successors, the pottery company Anderson & Co. However, relations between the company and the landowner's agent Miss Clapperton were bad to begin with and deteriorated, leading to a series of actions at the Court of Session. The reasons for the dispute centre on a decline in tile demand which set in around 1805, after Anderson and Company had enjoyed several years of profitable operation. The tileworks came up for a renewed lease in 1813, which was secured by the holders now trading as David Thomson & Company. However, David Thomson had backed a salt manufacturer (and sulphur manufacturer) Mr Walker, in 1814. Walker's works lay even further west and it would appear that he had diversified from salt to other related chemicals, perhaps also including sulphuric acid. In 1817 Walker failed, Thomson's bond was called in, and the pottery's sleeping partner, Fowler of Prestonpans Brewery, intervened to prevent his interest (capital) disappearing. Both pottery and brick and tile works were advertised for sale, the latter clearly not in an operating condition as the claypits were under a crop of barley and grass. The advertisement suggests that the product range was pretty limited – only undifferentiated bricks and tiles are mentioned. It was sold for £240 to Hew Francis Cadell of Cockenzie.

Attention can now be shifted to Prestongrange where the pottery had come into the hands of the Gordons of Bankfoot. Once again, the Court of Session Papers are a valuable source: a prolonged dispute arose between the lessees, George and Robert Gordon, and the proprietor of Prestongrange, Sir George Grant-Suttie. The core of the dispute appears to have been clay dug from the nearby deposits on Grant-Suttie's estate (the site is still obvious today, on the edge of the Golf Course). The Gordons were also making industrial ceramics in contravention of their lease. The Gordons tenure at Morison's Haven is covered more fully in the Chapter on Potteries.

Having disposed of the Gordons, the Grant-Sutties began to make bricks and tiles on their own account. The Works came under the estate factors, or managers, and appears to have been of a small scale. In 1837, it was under the control of George Leach, described as Clerk (he also served under Grant-Suttie's colliery manager Robert Moore, at Birsley; Pigot's Directory). The Grant-Suttie Papers in the SRO include a sequence of documents relating to the family's industrial undertakings after Mattias Dunn's Prestongrange Pit was sunk (the Beam Engine shaft); the documents relate to annual balances and the colliery and brickmaking operations in the period up to the formation of '*the English Company*' in the 1870s. The management of the Works changed hands several times; for example Slater's Directory notes James Myles, Brickworks Colliery manager, 1852. From 1841, the decennial censuses begin to flesh in the operation of the Works on a personal level, as employees can be identified living in premises leased from the estate at Morison's Haven and at Cuthill to the east.

To pick just one of the censuses, that of 1871 identifies several of the workers at Grant-Suttie's Brickworks, most residing at Morison's Haven. The brickmakers were William and James Anderson, from Stirling. The record of their families suggests that their association came via one of the neighbouring sites in Inveresk Parish (Levenhall or West Pans, perhaps) although they had been employed in the Prestonpans area for at least six years. The works were in the charge of Edward Yule, the estate's factor, land agent and colliery manager, who resided at Ravensheugh Cottage. Yule retained this position for a number of years. In 1873–4 he is recorded as Factor, residing at Ravensheugh (Valuation Roll); James Anderson was by then Tilework Manager. The Grant-Suttie operation was into its last years. Physical evidence from the site (the remains of the 1874 ventilation duct on Shaft No 2, sunk in that year) suggests that the output in this period did not include fireclay products: the duct is composed of hand moulded, red terracotta bricks.

The full industrial development of the Prestongrange site commenced in the early 1870s with the arrival in the Prestonpans area of Richard Kitto, a Cornishman (see Appendix II). His main interest was mining – but not necessarily coal. He and his partners secured a lease of Prestongrange minerals and the existing infrastructure owned by the Grant-Sutties. This development is first marked in the 1874–5 Valuation Roll when the Prestongrange Colliery Company is in possession of the colliery and workmen's houses at Cuthill. The most important feature of this year, however, is that Grant-Suttie retained the Brick and Tile Works in his own hands (via Yule and James Anderson). In the same year the Colliery Company was reformed as the Prestongrange Coal and Iron Company, with Kitto as Managing Director and several Middlesborough magnates on the Board, and took over the Brickworks. By 1878, the company could boast to be '*manufacturers of every description of Fireclay goods*'. After several years of successful trading the Company lost way and was wound up in 1880. Throughout this period it is clear that the Brick and Tile Works had formed part of the new company infrastructure and had been comprehensively developed (Slater's Directory, 1878): no longer simply a rural tileworks supplying material for the estate, but a major heavy ceramics plant utilising the underground reserves of fireclay to fabricate a wide range of products. A major increase in the labour force, both for the Colliery and the Brickworks, was accommodated in a new housing estate at Cuthill. However, the older part of the workforce seem to disappear: the Andersons disappear from the record when the Prestongrange Coal and Iron Company took over – possibly as early as the later part of 1874.

After the company failure, operations continued under a liquidator. There are a number of workmen identified in the 1881 census who must have continued in employment. Trades mentioned include fireclay and sewage piper makers and finishers, brickmakers, brickwork labourers and a foreman, Robert Fishlock (most of these lived in the company's housing estate at Cuthill and some had worked for the Grant-Sutties). The brickworks manager was James Campbell, residing at Morisons Haven Harbour House.

Out of the ashes rose the Prestongrange Coal and Firebrick Company, with more directed objectives. Coal was still exported to the Middlesborough ironmasters, but investment in fireclay was made more prominent, probably reflecting prevailing market conditions. The evidence of the site (mainly surviving bricks) and museum artefacts (East Lothian Museum Service Collections, National Museums of Scotland Collections) shows a large output of machine-made composite bricks, fireclay special bricks (hand-moulded) and a large variety of salt-glazed wares. The last consists of pipes, traps, chimney cans, sanitary wares, and decorative urns and garden pieces. All of these materials were in great demand in Edinburgh and the local district. Indeed, advertisements suggest that fireclay products became the company's main product (Slater's Directory, 1893); depots were opened at Leith and Granton, as well as Morisons Haven. The Prestongrange site was managed for the company by Francis Rawling Luke (of Redburn House, to the immediate west of the site), in succession to his father GB Luke. Larger artefacts from this period might be distinguished by a glassy, green-blue interior slip-glaze, probably compounded from flint; many shards survive on the site and a few single objects (East Lothian Museums Service Collections and National Museums of Scotland Collections). A full page advertisement from this period (ELMS Collections) includes a woodcut showing that the brickworks had spread to occupy much of the area of the existing site. The large moulding halls are evident as are a variety of bottle and downdraught kilns and the railway is in place with spurs into the Brickworks. In the background of the view is the tall chimney of the Company's powerplant, a boilerhouse supplying steam to pumps and stationary engines.

Shortly after the entry in Slater's 1893 Directory, the Prestongrange Coal and Firebrick Company was also wound up, succumbing to outstanding liabilities in May 1893. Once again the site was operated in receivership by an Edinburgh CA, AAW Carter. The new owners were the Summerlee Coal and Iron Company who entered in 1895 and operated until Nationalisation in 1947. Summerlee invested heavily in infrastructure: the power station to generate electricity, a new workers housing estate, coal washers, new underground pumps, an extended railway network, and new kilns were erected. Summerlee is believed to have replaced 15 beehive style kilns with 9 round kilns for glazed pipes and they were responsible for large scale clearance of older properties on their land, mainly unoccupied and very old cottages and tenements lying on the seaward side of the road from Cuthill to Morison's Haven. Thus were probably lost the last remains of many of the Prestongrange saltpans (Haddingtonshire Courier,15/2/1914).

Slater's Directory of 1907 records John Haliday as manager of the site. He appears in several surviving photographs, standing confidently with his staff. He, like the other managers, resided close to the Works in the cottage at Ravensheugh; their occupancy of this house gave rise to the local name for the road behind, which is still current: Manager's Brae. The earlier bottle kilns were replaced by the suite of domed downdraft kilns which survived (with continual repair and replacement) until site closure. In 1910 brickmaking was facilitated by the erection of a Hoffmann continuous kiln (Appendix III), another feature which was operated until closure and stands today. About the time the kiln was built, Sumerlee published a catalogue under the 'Prestongrange Company' imprint, which illustrates and lists the entire product range (some 500 different articles). A large export trade was worked up with the Low Countries and Germany, although Morison's Haven was soon abandoned due to silting. The overseas trade came to an end at the outbreak of the Second World War, but the domestic market remained strong.

The workforce was high throughout the whole of Summerlee's tenure, often over a thousand hands, more than 200 of whom were associated with the Brickworks. The site employed 786 underground and 202 hands above in 1924, a high proportion of the latter working at the Brick and Tile Works; a

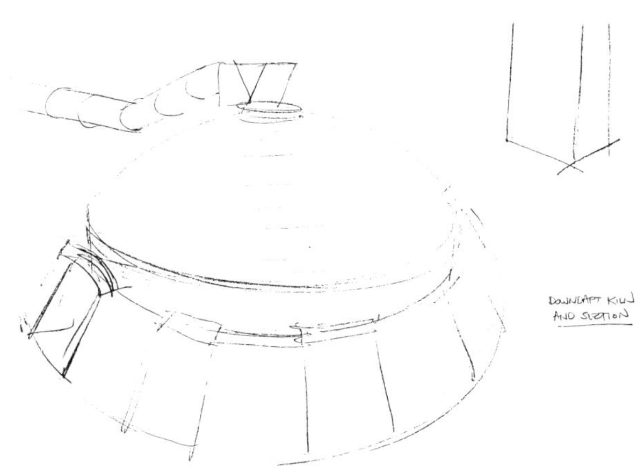

Drawing of Downdraft Kiln
East Lothian Council, David Spence Collection

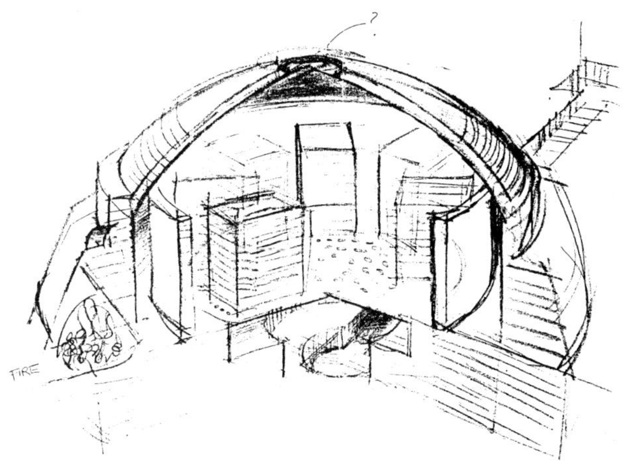

Section of Downdraft Kiln
East Lothian Council, David Spence Collection

significant proportion of the former supplying their raw materials (fireclay, blaes, coal) from the pit (Andrew S Cunningham, Mining in Mid and East Lothian, Thin and Orr, 1925). Even in the 1950s, the Third Statistical Account (1953) records that the Brick and Tile Works employed over 100 hands. By this period both it and the colliery had been nationalised (1947). The raw material still came from the adjacent colliery and was used for building bricks, pipes and chimney cans and special orders on demand. Most articles were machine made, but many continued to be hand moulded – a skilled task calling for experience. Several of the senior tradesmen spent their whole working life at the Brickworks: a number who started in 1914 were still there in the 1960s and one at least saw the plant through right to closure.

The last minerals were brought from the pit in 1961 as the Coal Board concentrated on the super pits of Bilston Glen and Monktonhall. The Brick and Tile Works passed to the newly formed Scottish Brick Corporation in 1969, with a declining workforce and infrastructure. It was operated for six more years, finally closing in 1975, a victim of transport costs because all raw materials and fuel had now to be brought onto the site. All the owners of the twentieth century have left their (literal) mark, in the frogging (recess) on the bricks which are found around the local area: bold PRESTONGRANGE (Summerlee), NCB–PG (Coal Board), and SBC (the Corporation).

6 CONCLUSION

The industries discussed above have all ended in the Prestongrange and Prestonpans area. They have left few substantial physical traces, although there is probably a wealth of archaeology at a number of local sites. All that remains are a few placenames, some walls, the surviving industrial buildings of the Prestongrange Industrial Heritage Museum and souvenirs, artefacts and products held in the community and at museums and archives.

But the industries were not transient affairs: even the shortest lived, the glassworks, lasted for around sixty years, nearly two full working lives, and salting has a documented history of eight centuries. In their time thousands of hands were employed. The local population was enriched by the immigration of skilled workers and later exported its own skilled hands (sometimes legitimately, sometimes not – the Secret Works). Some of the businesses were family affairs, some part of landed estates, some part of industrial conglomerates. Their products were used locally, nationally and internationally (counting England here, because for most of the period it was a foreign country) and were exported against frequent tax and excise barriers. Some of the industries enjoyed periods of monopoly in their home markets and at other periods went through phases of cut-throat competition. The owners might be local people, either landed or not, or from outside. Some were of national importance, such as Roebuck, who brings the best of the eighteenth century Scottish Enlightenment to Prestonpans, and others have passed as unremarked by surviving sources as the vast majority of the workers. Some made their home locally, such as Kitto of the 'English Company who died in Prestonpans, others were absentee landlords, like Henry Glassford, whose manager went to court for him.

For the most part people laboured in (to the modern eye) appalling conditions which would have significant effects on their health, but they had jobs which required a degree of skill (some more so than others), had a freedom of movement within the local economy (despite what the law might say) and a steady income at most times.

Only two of the industries – salt and glass – have been the subject of comprehensive academic study, and then only as part of the Scottish whole. There is scope, and the resources in many collections, to further investigate Prestongrange's many industries.

BIBLIOGRAPHY

Sources consulted

The three *Statistical Accounts (Old, 1796; New, 1845; and Third, 1953)* and *Martine's Reminiscences (of the Parishes of East Lothian)*, republished by East Lothian Library Service, 1999) provide background studies of Prestonpans and Prestongrange of varying detail at approximately 50 year intervals. For the nineteenth century, *Pigot's Directory of Scotland (1825–6, 1837)* and *Slater's Commercial Directory of Scotland* (consulted various years 1852– 1907) provided detail on industrial concerns at Prestonpans and Prestongrange and their nearby competitors. The series of volumes compiling the *Proceedings of the Convention of Royal Burghs* also provided useful information. Local publications such as Alexander Hamilton's *Salt Pans* (*Outlet Design,* c1980) and *The Pans Remembered* (East Lothian District Library, 1986) provide local anecdotes and folklore. Peter McNeill's three volumes, all of which have been republished by East Lothian Library service are of similar value; they are *Prestonpans and District,* its companion volume, *Tranent*, and a novelisation, *Blawearie*, which gets under the skin of the local inhabitants of two centuries past.

Also of use were articles in *Scottish Pottery Historical Review*, the Journal of the Scottish Pottery Society, where interest in the Prestonpans area extends beyond their core brief. CA Whatley has investigated the *Scottish Salt Industry, 1570–1850* (Aberdeen University Press, 1987) in depth and his book contains detailed references to source material; the same author's paper published in the *Transactions of the East Lothian Antiquarian and Field Naturalists Society (A Saltwork and the Community: The Case of Winton, 1716–1719, Transactions of the ELAFNS, 18, 1984)* provides a detailed exposition of the operation of eighteenth century saltpans nearby to Prestongrange. See also, *Scottish Salt-making in the Eighteenth Century: A Regional Survey,* Scottish Industrial History, 5, 1982. General industrial texts, such as the *Companion to the Industrial Revolution* by Clifford Lines (*Facts on File*, 1990) were also useful. East Lothian Museums Service Collections, in particular the *David Spence Bequest*, provided additional information as did the resources of the East Lothian Library Service Local History Centre: in addition to *newspaper cuttings, study packs, parish information*, and scarce publications relating to East Lothian, the Centre holds complete runs of *Valuation Rolls of the Parish (and Burgh) of Prestonpans* (from 1855), the *Haddingtonshire/East Lothian Courier* (on microfilm) and the indexes to the *Register of Sasines for the Sherrifdom of Haddingtonshire*. Background on Roebuck, Garbett, Cadell and Morison came from a variety of sources, including Carlyle (referenced in the text) and RH Campbell's, *The Carron Company*, (Oliver and Boyd, 1961).

Early charters relating to Prestongrange are published in *Transactions of the ELAFNS*, (David Spence, volume 14, 1984), which series also contains material of local interest. The complete *Chartulary of Newbattle Abbey* was published by the Bannatyne Club in 1849 (*Registrum Sancta Maria de Neubotle*).

Other relevant sources

A work in progress, Gillian Harding's survey of early Scottish Glassmaking (Ph.D. Edinburgh University, to be published) will undoubtedly increase knowledge on the early history of the glassmaking industry at Prestongrange and vicinity.

The Scottish Record Office contains a wealth of material on the industries of Prestonpans and Prestongrange. To highlight just a few, there are records of the Scottish Salt Company (*SRO GD454/* and bundles therein) including daybooks, cashbooks, letter books and accounts. There are eighteenth century tacks (rentals) of Prestongrange saltpans (*SRO GD24/17/642*) and details relating to the Colliers and Salters Bill of 1775 (*SRO GD18/1123; GD172/503*). There are even sketches by John Fowler Hislop, the brewer, who had antiquarian interests and deposited his papers therein (*SRO GD172/862*). There is also relevant material in the National Library of Scotland, Edinburgh University Library, the City of Edinburgh Central Library, and even the collections of Glasgow Libraries.

APPENDIX I
ROEBUCK, GARBETT AND CADELL

Sheffield born **John Roebuck** (1718–94) was the son of a cutler and one of a large family. He attended Grammar School and Northampton Academy, before becoming a student at Edinburgh University during the period when Cullen, Home and Black revolutionised the science of chemistry and its application to industrial processes. He graduated in medicine in 1737 and undertook advanced studies at Leyden, graduating MD in 1743. He afterwards practised medicine in Birmingham and developed a side-line as a consulting chemist to industry, which brought him into contact with the entrepreneurial Samuel Garbett. Roebuck has been described as the 'ideas' man of the partnership. He seems to have taken enthusiastically to each new project that came along, sometimes with success but ultimately ending his productive career with a series of failures in the early 1770s.

With Garbett, he became expert in refining precious metals, setting up a plant in Steelhouse Lane which generated sufficient profits to float other ventures. The business faced a bottleneck in the supply of sulphuric acid (then known as oil of vitriol), essential in the refining process and also in demand as a metal cleaning agent. At Steelhouse Lane they developed a process which revolutionised production, as described in the main text. He was the partner who selected the site for their next venture, having identified a gap in Scotland's iron production facilities, he prospected diligently until he found the most suitable site, passing up on Musselburgh Links in so doing. At Carron he became interested in the work of James Watt, taking him under his wing (and into partnership), effecting introductions and commissioning one of Watt's engines for his mines. However, always interested in the next new thing, he raised capital from his various interests and ventured into ceramics, coal-mining and saltpanning, adventures which failed.

Samuel Garbett's (1717–1805) background is obscure. He was of a similar age to Roebuck, but his earlier circumstances would appear to have been modest and his education poor. He was working successfully in the Birmingham brass industry when he met Roebuck, and was already his own master and comparatively wealthy. A man of modest tastes at home, contemporaries generally liked him and admired his steady business head, describing him as '*acute with great understanding*'. In partnership with Roebuck he seems to have maintained his erratic partner's discipline and focus: it was only when acting independently that Roebuck failed. However, Garbett suffered bankruptcy himself, with a fight for control of the Carron Works ending in failure and the further failure of partners back in Birmingham. He too ceased to figure from the early 1770s.

William Cadell of Cockenzie was a scion of a local merchant family which had originated in Haddington and was based at Cockenzie House, just along the coast from Prestonpans. He exercised considerable entrepreneurial skills in developing an extensive trade in general merchandise, based on his family's control of pits lying on the north east of Tranent, the gravity tramway to Cockenzie Harbour and his interests in what was the East of Scotland's most productive pottery in Prestonpans. He invested in many local concerns and was prepared to come in with Roebuck and Garbett in their ambitious plans for the Iron Works at Carron. He also controlled iron mills at nearby Cramond.

APPENDIX II
THE ENGLISH COMPANIES

The Memorandum of Association of the *Prestongrange Coal and Iron Company* (locally remembered as *The English Company*, a name also applied to its successor) was filed on 30/9/1874 (BT2/584, Files of Dissolved Companies) and lists the principal shareholders at outset as:

Name / Occupation	Place	Shares
Richard Luke Middleton Kitto Coalmaster	Prestongrange	1000 shares
Isaac Wilson Ironmaster	Middlesburgh (sic)	300 shares
Alexander Hogg Naysmyth Mining Engineer	Musselburgh	100 shares
Thomas Brentnall Merchant	Middlesburgh	1000 shares
Henry Brentnall Ironmaster	Middlesburgh	50 shares
Fred. Sam. Brentnall Ironmaster	Middlesburgh	50 shares
George Bainbridge Solicitor	Middlesburgh	100 shares

This group is dominated (2500 shares) by the proposed buyers of Prestongrange's raw materials, which were prospected to include ironstone (of which there are a number of seams at Prestongrange all of which were probably not economically viable then, let alone now). However, the high quality coals had a history of being suitable for iron founding and this was probably the principal interest of the Middlesborough ironmasters and their financiers. The company was consolidated from earlier agreements between RLM Kitto, T Brentnall, and the Cornish mining engineer, Matthew Loam on one part and the landowner Sir George Grant-Suttie on the other. The details of the earlier agreements specifically mention fireclay, along with coal, ironstone and limestone. Kitto, Brentnall and Loam's embryonic company was probably floated to raise the capital required to rehabilitate the pit and the engine works proposed by Loam. The opportunity was taken to secure the brick and pipe works at the same time – a good move considering the subsequent story of the site.

The company entered voluntary liquidation on 3 June 1880, when FW Carter, Edinburgh, was appointed liquidator. He seems to have ensured some continuity until the company was finally wound up on 14 February 1884. The principal problems appear to have been mineralogical – the iron and limestone was never worked and there were problems with coal output – and personal – Kitto, the Managing Director had cash flow difficulties (see GS) and later died, removing the company's guiding hand.

However, on 25 February 1882 a Certificate of Incorporation (BT2/1092) was filed for the *Prestongrange Coal and Firebrick Company*. The shareholders included members of the previous company (John Gjers, Middlesborough who had bought in, perhaps after Kitto's death) as well as new blood (for example, Robert Stephenson, Middlesborough, and CE Mills, a locally based mining engineer). The consortium had acted in advance of their incorporation by securing leases, property, equipment and stock for £45,000 at the public auction of the previous company's goods on 9 November 1881. The new company installed GB Luke as company secretary and site manager, a position inherited by his son, Francis R Luke. Advertisements from the latter's administration emphasise the ceramics production above coal. The Company survived until 1893, before it too went into receivership and the site was ultimately sold to the Summerlee Iron Company.

APPENDIX III
THE HOFFMAN KILN

Circular pattern Hoffman kilns were introduced into Britain in 1858 by Friedrich Hoffman, a German engineer. The first were used for firing pottery and burning lime; their advantage was that they could be worked continuously, the burning zone rotating through a kiln's chambers in succession. The principle was adapted and improved within a very few years and the style proliferated across Britain, finding new applications in brickmaking, for which industry it became one of the most significant types. Oblong kilns became the standard pattern after 1870 and the chimneys were soon off-set to one side on a floor heated by ducts carrying flue gases. Hoffman kilns were particularly well suited to the firing of composition bricks made from blaes. The only criticism levelled at them was a lack of fine control, problems with staining and scorching from fuel contacting the bricks and lack of high temperatures (for more specialised products: solved at Prestongrange by the suite of eleven round downdraught kilns). Prestongrange got its first Hoffman in 1910, and the chimney still stands. It was replaced by another in 1937, built by Cleghorn of Newmains, which operated until the Works closed in the mid 1970s and is still standing.

Hoffman Kilns were worked by teams on piece-work: setters, working in advance of the fire, and the burnt team, clearing the fired bricks and redding the chambers. An expert, waged employee worked the kiln roof and controlled the operation. The setters built green brick stacks, positioning voids below the roof vents (through which coal would later be added) and constructing flues and channels amongst the bricks to ensure even burning. A temporary wall was constructed to terminate the filled chamber and the exterior gate was 'stuffed' or closed with bricks. Another chamber was then set, and so on. Behind the burning zone the burnt team, working in singlets and with leather hand protectors, unloaded hot bricks from the kiln. To get them, they first unblocked the gate; an inrush of air helped to keep them cool. In passing over the bricks the air was increasingly warmed as it was drawn to the burning zone. Some of the air was diverted along the spinal conduits to heat the green bricks in advance of the burning zone. The remainder fed the fire and was discharged to the chimney, carrying away the volatiles released in the burning process. meanwhile the green bricks were heated until the chamber temperature was above the flashpoint of coal: when added, it spontaneously combusted. At this point, the combustion gases were diverted (underground) into the chimney flues, raising the temperature of the drying floor outside and predrying the green bricks stacked there. After a burning period which was judged empirically (cold iron in a vent was moistened when the bricks were still curing), no more coal was added and the bricks began to cool down. By this time the head of the fire would be several chambers further on.

Hoffman kilns required 12–14 chambers for regular operation on a continuous process. The Prestongrange kiln has 24, suggesting a higher load bearing capacity – or periods when the output could be doubled. Each chamber stacked 11,000 bricks, suggesting a potential annual output of between 3 and 6 million bricks.

4
Industrial Ownership and Relations at Prestongrange

Allan Burnett

INTRODUCTION

Prestongrange colliery is situated near Prestonpans, on the edge of the old County of Haddingtonshire, in East Lothian. The 21st Century sees it entering its 900th year as a known mining concern. Its story has been a long and dramatic one.

Known events begin with the monks of Newbattle Abbey, who were granted the right to excavate coal around the turn of the 13th Century. Thanks to the dearth of surviving material the earliest years of coal production at Prestongrange have an almost mythical quality. Colourful images of coal-fired boiling salt-pans tended by an army of eager monks taking a break from illuminating the scriptures are set against secular developments in landholding and social hierarchy.

In later years, serious issues come to the fore such as slavery, the dangers of working in the mines, and the role of coal in the gradual development of the Scottish economy. With the material extant from the 18th Century comes a greater appreciation of some of the personalities involved, even though these are exclusively those of the mine-owners rather than the colliers.

The history of the colliery at Prestongrange really comes alive, though, in the 19th Century. This, after all, was when coal became the keystone of the modern Industrial Revolution. Throughout this period there was a belief that there was money to be made in coal. The estate owners of the period, the Grant-Sutties, made it their business to ensure that the mine was constantly worked and developed.

The running of Prestongrange presented its managers with challenges that often proved difficult to overcome. Repeated market crises, lack of managerial skill, and the colliery's Achilles' Heel – flooding – constantly undermined efforts to make the mine a commercial success. This forced the abandonment of three successive commercial ventures in only twenty years during the last quarter of the Century.

The early decades of the 20th Century were the golden-years of the industry, and under the management of the Summerlee Company the colliery reached its peak. Throughout this period, however, the miners and their families never shared in the great financial rewards reaped by the coalowners, and this generated much resentment.

The 19th and 20th Centuries also saw the miners break the shackles of slavery and force an improvement in their circumstances. But it was a slow process. The social and economic advances of the age increased the expectations of greater rights and freedoms, and later better pay and working conditions, leading to a struggle between the miners and the Prestongrange lairds which was sometimes bitter and violent. The successful struggle of the colliers and salters to break the shackles of serfdom in the 1790s had later echoes in the industrial disputes of c.1870–c.1930, though the gains made by the miners in the latter period were far less in the context of the times.

Management and Unions declaring Prestongrange as 'Managed by the NCB on behalf of the people' in 1947
East Lothian Council, David Spence Collection

The tide of progress expansion turned after the First World War. The collapse of the British economy in the 1920s and 30s was followed by coal losing its pre-eminence as an industrial resource and fuel. After WWII, the pace of decline at Prestongrange accelerated rapidly, despite the initial flicker of hope offered by the National Coal Board. With low morale among the workforce clearly in evidence in the early 1960s, the pit ceased working in 1962.

Since that time, Prestongrange has in some senses been reborn – as a visitor attraction. It is now a fine example of East Lothian's industrial heritage and is in the care of the Prestongrange Industrial Heritage Centre.

PIONEERS AND SLAVES 1200–1811

The first known coal-owners of Prestongrange appeared well over 800 years ago in the form of cistercian monks from the abbeys of Holyrood and Newbattle. In 1184 they were granted the use of a healthy portion of the lands of Tranent by local magnate, Robert de Quincy. Around this time the monks made a settlement near the shore of the Firth of Forth which became known as Preston, meaning Priest's town. The name 'Prestongrange' refers to the farmhouse and granary, or 'grange', which the monks erected nearby. The monks were industrious herders of oxen and sheep, and they shepherded their livestock on the meadows near the grange, where they also conducted another activity, peat cutting. They cut their peats in a part of the meadows known as the Tranent peaterie, where there are numerous surface-deposits of coal, or 'heughs', which the monks began excavating at some point in their early history.

It's difficult to say with complete confidence how the monks first discovered coal at Prestongrange. A well known local antiquarian writing at the turn of the 20th Century gives two alternate accounts from local tradition of how the monks may have stumbled upon this hidden treasure. One is that the monks may have uncovered the coal cutting peat, while the other places the find in much more dramatic circumstances. As they watched their flocks in the meadows by night the monks kindled fires around them, possibly for warmth, more probably in order to hold at bay the wild animals that wandered the country in those days. One night, they inadvertantly lit a fire directly on top of a barely concealed coal outcrop, causing the ground to catch fire, and in this most spectacular fashion the coal was discovered. Whether or not either of these traditions is accurate, we know that by around 1210, a charter had been issued by Seyer de Quincy, a descendent of Roger, granting the monks the right to quarry coal.

It should be remembered that the dating of these early charters is not in itself a completely reliable indicator as to when the lands of Prestongrange were first used for coal extraction, or for other purposes. The wording of the charter of 1184, for instance, indicates that the monks had already been using the land for several decades. Similarly, the 1210 charter does not preclude the possibility that they had been taking coal from the ground several years prior to that date (how else would the signatories of the charter have known that the coal was there in the first place?). What we can reliably assume is that it was decided some time around 1210 that the monks needed permission to cut coal, which is quite a different matter. If these charters in fact confirm what were already well established activities, it could be suggested that the abbeys had been cutting coal since the time of Newbattle's establishment in 1140, perhaps earlier.

Their use of coal demonstrates that apart from being centres of religion and learning in medieval Scotland, Newbattle and Holyrood were also early centres of industry. Coal burned more slowly than wood, and had a much greater heat output than peat, making it ideal for heating large buildings like castles and monasteries. It was also used to distil sea-water to make salt, a vital food preservative in the days before refrigeration. The monks set-up a manufactury in which huge open iron pans were filled with sea water and boiled until the water evaporated to leave salt crystals. The name Prestonpans or Salt-Preston evolved as the area became synonymous with the monks' activities there, and salt-panning was to continue at Prestonpans for hundreds of years. Other sites where this early activity took place can be identified by the suffix 'pans' to place-names such as Kennetpans and Grangepans. The coal excavated at Prestongrange was also used to some extent by blacksmiths instead of charcoal, and masons used it to burn limestone in the making of mortar for buildings.

To transport coal and salt, a road was constructed from Newbattle Abbey to Prestongrange some time during the 12th or 13th Centuries. It became known as the Salters road. Recent research suggests this example of a medieval road may be typical, contradicting the conventional wisdom that roads in this period were poor or non-existent. Part of the Salters road still exists today in places. Perhaps the most easily found is where it crosses the Maidens Bridge over the South Esk near Newbattle golf course. The Maidens Bridge may date from around 1165, underlining the probability that the cistercians were transporting coal by that date.

Although they made many advances, these early industrialists found that the Prestongrange coal contained flaws and impurities which undermined its usefulness. They quarried what was referred to in the Newbattle charter as both *carbonarium*, coal, and *carbones marinos fodiendi*, or ‘stinking sea-coal’. The coal did indeed ‘stink’, and as a result was unpopular in two important respects. In an age before the introduction of the domestic fireplace and ‘lum’ or chimney, such an unpleasant substance could not be used to heat the ordinary home, or for such purposes as smoke-curing foodstuffs. As a result, the main fuels used by ordinary people continued to be charcoal, timber and peat. Meanwhile, the sulphur in the coal which caused the foul smell was an even more serious drawback. Sulphur and other impurities restricted the use of the coal in metal refining, preventing it from realising its full industrial potential.

As the monks expanded their operations in close proximity to the Forth, they would have also encountered a more serious problem. Flooding. The seam which they worked was the one which outcrops nearest the surface, known as the Great Seam. Initially flooding would not have posed a serious problem as, probably until at least the 14th Century, the monks’ excavations were of the most primitive type, being simple surface excavations. As time wore-on however, they began to tunnel for considerable distances into the coal crop. Burrowing through the Great Seam, they extended their tunnels beneath the Forth at a distance of 10 feet below sea level. Some of the old workings made by the monks are still in existence but the methods they used to prevent water pouring in remain a mystery. The answer may lie in the way the monks built their tunnels. They would leave the upper part of the coal unexcavated, instead fashioning it into the form of an archway, which may have had some bearing on the flow of water. Alternatively the monks probably had to make sporadic forays into the tunnels to excavate when they could, and then abandon them whenever flooding became a problem. They almost certainly relied on nothing but the grace of God to prevent the roof caving in. As later visitors have observed, some of the old workings are just like the vaults of a cathedral.

Despite such difficulties, Prestongrange seems to have prospered during the 15th Century. According to the accounts of the Lord High Treasurer of Scotland, coal from the Prestongrange area helped fuel the fireplaces of the Royal Household of James III (1460–88). We don’t know precisely how much was used, only that it was ordered in “loads”. Uses to which coal was being put by this time continued to include the burning of lime in kilns, as well as boiling pitch for caulking ships, melting lead for windows and bullets and blacksmith’s work associated with making cannon.

Although its expansion was mainly due to local factors, the success of the mining operation had a great deal to do with its exportation further afield. Evidence that coal was a widely sold commodity is found in government records from 1425, when the Scottish Parliament seems to have been sufficiently concerned about illicit trade costing the government money, it passed an Act requiring local authorities to appoint invigilators. Geographically, Prestongrange was well placed to participate in a wider marketplace. It and the other earliest known mines of importance in Scotland were all driven into the hillsides of the Lothians, south-east Fife and Clackmannan – all on the edge of the Forth estuary. Before the arrival of canals, turnpike roads and waggonways, coal seams which outcropped near tidal waters were the only ones from which coal could be easily transported over great distances, by ship. The beauty of having such an operation located on the east coast in particular was that Prestongrange managers could export their coal not only to other parts of Scotland, but even further afield, to mainland Europe.

The export trade seems to have been small but regular. Andrew Halyburton, an early Scottish Ambassador in the Netherlands, records a number of coal shipments in his ledger between 1492 and 1503. The Newbattle inmates used pack-horses and carts to transport coal and wood down the Salters Road in some quantity. These commodities were then exported along with salt to Scandinavia and the Netherlands. In return came luxury goods such as oysters and French claret.

By the 1520s, the import and export of goods through the area was so extensive that a new harbour was built nearby to facilitate trade. The natural sea haven in which the harbour was built seems to have already been a longtime place of shelter for seafarers, and a busy east-coast port. Permission to build a harbour on the lands of Prestongrange was granted at Newbattle on 22 April 1526 by Royal Charter. It seems that the grant was made not to the Abbot of Newbattle, but for an enterprising local magnate called Alexander Acheson, who re-named the port Acheson's Haven. For over a hundred years the Achesons were highly successful traders through the port and it rivalled Leith in its importance for a time with the erection of a custom-house whose jurisdiction covered an area stretching from Portobello to the mouth of the Tyne. The haven, which later became known as Morisons Haven, can still be found on the map, but is now landlocked.

The coming of the Achesons represented wider national changes which were afoot as the position of the old religious houses was weakened towards the mid-16th Century. Nevertheless, it seems the monastic industrialists still wielded control of coal production in 1548. The monks of Newbattle were among those called on to provide extra coal for an army of between six and eight thousand men as they battled to eject an English occupying force in nearby Haddington. During the previous year the Scots were defeated at the Battle of Pinkie, at Haddington, and local inhabitants were forced to hide underground in the mines to escape the invading English army.

In the 1550s, with the onset of the Reformation in Scotland, four centuries of development ended in catastrophe for the monks at Prestongrange. It might be added glibly that this was the least of their worries as their monasteries and property were destroyed. While the Reformation didn't penetrate the whole of Scotland for at least another hundred years, in the area in and around Edinburgh the Reformers quickly took-over the old political, social and industrial hierarchies, and monastic orders like Holyrood and Newbattle were put to flight.

There is a well known saying respecting the Reformation, however, which is that many religious and secular officials "didn't lose their jobs" as a result. In the case of Newbattle, although the monastery was smashed, the Abbot himself was brought under the influence of the Reformed Church. Coal operations did suffer during this period, however, as in 1563, the export of coal was banned for a time. The process of restructuring at Newbattle was complete when the son of the last Abbot, Mark Ker, was made a loyal follower of the new hierarchy and created Baron of Newbattle in 1592 – a title which included the lands of Prestongrange.

Also in 1592 an Act was passed which exempted miners from taxes, charges and proclamations, whether in time of peace or war, and all their "families, guids, and gear," taken under regal protection. Further, it was declared that "any wrong or oppression done to them directly or indirectly would be severely punished, as done contrary to his majesty's special safeguard."

That same year another Act of Parliament declared "That for the better punishment of the wicked crime of wilfully setting fire to coal heuchs by ungodly persons, from motives of private revenge and spite, this crime should for the future be treason, and that whoever was found guilty of the same should suffer the punishment of treason in their bodies, lands and goods." A known case arising from this Act was that of a Lothian coalminer who had set fire to a coal-heuch. He was hanged at the Mercat Cross of Edinburgh and beheaded. His head was then sent out to the mine where he had worked and impaled on a pole by the pit head as a warning to others.

The next Act of Parliament connected with mining has rightly been described by a historian of the parish as "a horrible one". This was the infamous act of 1606 which recinded all former acts and reduced colliers and salters to a social status which was little short of common slavery. By this Act their service was to be perpetual. In other words, if the owner sold the work the labourer had no option but to go with it. Karl Marx traced the origins of the 19th (and 20th) Century class-conflict between workers and industrialists to the effects of this Act, which created the slavery of 'serfdom'.

Centuries before this, the monks of Newbattle had used slave labour in the mines, but that regime had long since been done away with. In those days, in order to provide labour for their mining and salt-panning works, the monks utilised a regime of slave owning known as neyfship. We know that under that system colliers were 'owned' by their masters, but little detail has survived as to the character of that relationship. The last successful claim for ownership of a collier through neyfship was in 1364.

The 1606 Act was motivated by simple economic imperatives. As mining operations progressed, the landowners needed larger amounts of labour to work the coal faces. By 1620, a Forth-valley landowner, Sir George Bruce, was said to have a pit shaft on his lands at Culross which extended for a mile underground, and this would have required extensive human resources. But mining remained desperately difficult and dangerous work in those days, and as a result was an extremely unpopular occupation. The only assured way of establishing a secure labour force, therefore, was to place people in bondage.

Women and children suffered terribly as they too were driven down into the mines to undertake some of the most arduous tasks. Because of their small size, boys were made to cut coal in tight, confined spaces, whilst women and girls were mostly given the task of bearing coal up to the surface. This was a terribly arduous task, known as 'hewing', which required large baskets full of coal to be hauled up steep wooden ladders and treacherous gangways. This situation only began to be relieved latterly, when the mechanised system of the "gin" was introduced. This device, which comprised a bucket on the end of a large pulley wheel driven round by a horse was cumbersome and slow, but it relieved the toil of the hewers to some extent and remained in operation well into the 19th Century.

One of the chief culprits responsible for the 1606 Act was the Earl of Winton, whose reason given to explain its introduction was one which ironically hinted at the future, when miners would one day fight back: "...it was feared that in the course of time people would not be found willing to engage in such arduous and unrenumerative labour".

Around the same time an extensive programme of restructuring of landholding was being undertaken by the crown. This process resulted in the creation of the Barony of Prestongrange in 1609 which seems to have been accomplished by severing the lands of Preston from its ancient bond to Tranent, and then dividing it in two. The new lands may have initially been named East and West Preston, but became known as Preston and Prestongrange respectively. In 1617, the barony of Preston was granted by charter to Sir John Hamilton, and it included the village of Preston and town of Prestonpans, while the new baronetcy of Prestongrange had already been acquired by one Sir George Morison.

This first Baronet of Prestongrange came from the north-eastern corner of Scotland. His father held the lands of Troup in Banffshire and Pitfour in Aberdeenshire. Comparatively little is known about George Morison himself, as indeed is the case with the subsequent Morisons of Prestongrange. It seems that they continued, however sporadically, to work the coal at Prestongrange. They also took over Achesons Haven, renaming it Morisons Haven, and continued trading through that port.

George Morison was succeeded by his son, Alexander. The Prestongrange lairds were the patrons of the parish of Prestonpans and records show ministers being presented with office by Sir Alexander in 1638 and 1647. In 1682 the next Sir Alexander Morison of Prestongrange was fined 900 merks for failing to prevent a riot from occurring when the local schoolmaster took the pulpit under the direction of the diocesan Bishop. The minister, James Buchan, had been deprived of his office for his involvement in the religious controversies of the time. Alexander could count himself lucky – his neighbour Sir William Hamilton of Preston had been fined 1800 merks "for looking on and laughing".

Around 1710 the parish minister, the Rev. Robert Horsburgh, complained that his church was unsafe because of the extent of the coal "wastes" beneath. For some months his congregation was obliged to meet in a barn at Preston. Repairs were eventually executed after long litigation. Meanwhile, in 1711, Sir James Morison of Prestongrange, who had recently been involved in a dispute over the rights to the Prestongrange Coal Road access, married his daughter to John 5th Viscount Arbuthnott, later a Jacobite who supported Prince Charles in the '45 Rising.

The estate passed out of the hands of the Morison dynasty and, in 1746, was purchased by William Grant, the Lord Advocate of Scotland, at a judicial sale. William was one of three sons and five daughters of Sir Francis Grant of Cullen, a judge and political writer. Francis Grant was a remarkable character. At the Convention of Estates of 1689, whilst only 28 years old, he had given a famous speech supporting William of Orange in which he argued that King James VII had "forfeited" his right to the throne. Although a committed supporter of the Union of 1707, Grant nevertheless defended the right of the Church of Scotland to maintain its independence, and the right of Scots to choose their own monarch.

William's career was equally distinguished. He followed his father into the legal profession and quickly became a high-flyer at the Scottish bar. He also attained a senior role in the Church of Scotland. In 1737 he was appointed Solicitor General and rose to become Lord Advocate in 1738. William also inherited much of his father's politics, and was instrumental in defending the government from the Jacobite Rising of 1745–6. After the Rising was defeated he advocated leniency in the subsequent prosecutions of the Jacobites, arguing that severity would only serve to undermine efforts to encourage Scots to accept the Union with England. Despite being largely ignored in this, he was left the credit of having performed his duties "regulated by a principle of equity, tempering the strictness of the law." William took a seat on the bench as Lord of Session in 1754 as Lord Prestongrange, later becaming Lord Justice Clerk. He was one of the Commissioners for improving the fisheries and manufactures of Scotland, and afterwards one of the Commissioners for the Annexed Estates which dealt with lands confiscated from the Jacobites. He died at Bath in 1764.

The spectacular career of William Grant contrasts with the period of relative inactivity which seems to have set in at Prestongrange under the Grant succession. Most of the second half of the 18th Century witnessed the colliery being left in a state of disuse. According to the Rev. John Trotter, a Prestonpans parish minister writing in 1791, it had not been worked since at least 1760. This is backed up in evidence taken by a Royal Commission of 1841–2. The evidence also tells us about the conditions endured by the collier-serfs of Prestongrange during the 18th Century.

The 1842 Commission reveals that collier-serfs experienced breathtaking cruelty at the hands of the Lords of Prestongrange. If they wanted to work the colliers often had to seek coal-hewing employment at other nearby collieries. However, their bondage to the Barons of Prestongrange prevented them from attempting to find work elsewhere without permission which rarely, if ever, seems to have been given. The Commission itself was set up to head-off of a wave of public sympathy which had built up as a result of a growing middle-class awareness of the awful conditions perpetuating in the mines. It is a valuable document in the history of 19th Century social reform.

The grim treatment of colliers by the Lairds of Prestongrange is attested to by the evidence of two independent witnesses. The examples of treatment of colliers which they refer to seem to relate primarily to what they witnessed in their own lifetimes, although there is little doubt that this was a continuation of an established pattern. The laird being principally referred to, therefore, would be William Grant's heir, John Carmichael of Castlecraig and 4th Earl Hyndford. John succeeded to the baronetcy of Grant of Prestongrange in 1764 as a result of his earlier marriage to William's eldest daughter Janet in 1749. The Grants' attitude towards their colliers was harsh even by the standards of the day, as is revealed by the eloquent testimony of those who had suffered under them.

Interviewed by the commissioners in 1841, the 81-year-old Walter Pryde recounted how he was first yoked to the coal work at Prestongrange when he was nine years old. At that time he and his family were all "slaves to the Prestongrange Laird". Walter remembered that even if they had no work at the colliery he and his family couldn't look for employment elsewhere without a written license and agreement to return, and even then the laird or the tacksman selected their place of work. If they did not do as they were commanded, they were placed by the necks in collars known as 'juggs' and fastened to the wall. An even more brutal punishment was being "made to go the rown", in which the victim was tied facing the horse at the gin, and was then made to run round backwards all day.

At this time the Prestongrange hewers were paid four pence for a tub weighing four cwt., and could send up to six to eight tubs, but had to pay their own bearers out of the money, so that they never took more than 8s to 10s a week. Walter added that the money "went much further than double would now", suggesting that in respect of pay at least, things were not much better in 1841 than they had been in the days of serfdom.

An insight into the terrible living conditions colliers' families had to endure is given when Walter stated grimly that of their 11 children, five were still alive. He continued by remarking that there were few men who lived to his age who had worked in the pits. He added that his wife was 82, and incredibly she had worked at coal bearing until she was 66 years of age. Walter said that he and his wife were very poor and would die were it not for their neighbours and son, "who has a large family and can ill afford to give".

Another ex-collier at Prestongrange, Robert Inglis, aged 82, recollected that his Father and Grandfather had been "slaves to the laird of Preston Grange". After the works had stopped, presumably some time in the 1760s, he and his family received license from the then tacksman, Mr Peter Hunter, to work a nearby colliery. But, Robert added, "we could not get work, as the neighbours kenned that the Laird of Prestongrange would send the sheriff after us and bring us back".

The totality of the bondage was so great that the lairds had the power of taking colliers who had left to join the Royal Navy, or to bring back any who had enlisted in the army. Robert's evidence highlighted the "ill feelings [which] existed towards colliers and salters years past", when he testified that they were commonly buried in unconsecrated ground. His evidence ends with the statement, "If colliers had been better treated they would have been better men". Such simple logic strikes at the heart of the issue of social reform, and why it was so necessary.

The lifetimes of Walter Pryde and Robert Inglis were turbulent years in the history of Scotland as ordinary people across the country expressed great dissatisfaction with those who owned the nation's wealth and power. In 1797, people from the Parish of Prestonpans, which included Prestongrange, were involved in protests which culminated on the 29th of August in an event known as the 'Tranent militia riot'. This led to the subsequent massacre by government forces of a dozen people, and injury to twenty others. Most of the protestors were colliers.

While Prestongrange's neighbour, the Laird of Preston, led local civil forces against the protestors, the wanton brutality shown by British soldiers demonstrates the unbridled hatred of collier-serfs that existed within their ranks. One soldier mocked a wounded man by pretending to shoot him in the head, while another shot a woman in the face at close range, firing the bullet in front of her so that the gunpowder burned her features.

The Scottish civil authorities turned a blind eye to the atrocities in Tranent, but by this time the state and the coalowners were being forced to react to a workforce which was increasingly unprepared to enter into work in mines under such conditions. The astute political partership of Prime Minister William Pitt and his Scottish Home Secretary Henry Dundas brought the complete abolition of serfdom in 1799. But this seemingly great act of statesmanship was not borne out of concern for those in bondage – quite the opposite, in fact. It was considered on one hand to be a necessary evil if they were to curb the peoples' desire for more radical reform, and on the other it was a response to the economic realities of the day. The demand for coal was increasing and the industry needed labour. The politicians hoped that giving colliers freedom would both satisfy the needs of the coalowners and at the same time foster loyalty and obedience among the people to the existing hierarchy.

John Carmichael Grant of Prestongrange did not live to see the abolition of serfdom. He was survived by Janet, until she too passed away in 1818. The baronetcy of Grant of Prestongrange was then succeeded by her nephew, Sir James Suttie of Balgone, whose accession marks the beginning of the modern industrial age at Prestongrange.

INTO THE INDUSTRIAL AGE 1818–1894

During the tenure of the Grant-Sutties, industrial coal production at Prestongrange began in earnest. The connection between the houses of Grant of Prestongrange and Suttie of Balgone from which Sir James Grant-Suttie traced his inheritance had been established in 1757 with the marriage of Janet's younger sister Agnes to James' father, Sir George Suttie of Balgone. Sir George had been a keen advocate of 'Improvement', an ideology focused particularly on the development of commercial agriculture, and a forerunner of 19th Century industrialism. He would no doubt have been impressed by the Century-long advance of the Industrial Revolution and its enormous impact on coal mining operations at Prestongrange. A symbol of the dawn of this new era, and a major local factor behind the development of Prestongrange during this period, was the extraordinary transformation of the city of Edinburgh.

In just a few decades, Scotland's capital overturned its noxious image as 'Auld Reekie' to reveal the gleaming 'Athens of the North'. Spurred-on by the wealth flowing from Britian's colonial trade, many of Edinburgh's elite gentry, bankers, merchants and lawyers simply abandoned their dwellings around the impoverished 'Auld Toun', migrated across the Nor Loch, and took up residence in the gleaming neo-classical New Town. Although the vast bulk of Edinburgh society continued to dwell in somewhat less utopian circumstances, the whole city nonetheless witnessed a profound change. As the 19th Century rolled on, industrial advance caused a further heightening of commerce, wealth and social expectations. The changes which took place in Edinburgh during this time were to have a direct impact on the coal fields in the Lothians as the achievements of the city, as well as burgeoning industrial enterprises around and about it, were matched by a growing demand for fuel. By 1825, only 60 years after the first plans for the New Town had been drawn-up, Edinburgh's transformation was virtually complete.

The year 1825 also heralded great changes at Prestongrange. On one hand it saw the demise of the mine's oldest customer, Prestonpans, as a result of the removal of duty on cheaper salt from overseas, while on the other it witnessed the colliery's own development as a serious mining concern. A Newcastle mining engineer, Matthias Dunn, took out a lease at Prestongrange from Sir James to mine coal on a much larger scale than anything which had gone before.

Another sign of industrial 'take-off' occured in June when a second mining agreement was made, this time with a Portobello developer named William Lindsay. The agreement allowed Lindsay to quarry stones at the Land Eye quarry at Prestongrange for one year. Lindsay was to pay £25 rent and an eighth of all sales above £150. Meanwhile, a great deal of fencing, draining and enclosing was going on on the estate, and threshing machines were now being used in the fields.

Matthias Dunn, meanwhile, continued his operation for thirteen years. In 1829 he sunk two shafts, 28 yards apart, to work deeper coals. One 10 foot square shaft was for winding and the other, 10 feet by five, was used for pumping. He would soon introduce a revolutionary new development which markedly improved water management within the mine, and would later be adopted elsewhere. Twenty-three fathoms of cast iron rings known as 'tubbing' were placed in the shaft. It was estimated that this prevented feeders of water equal to 1150 gallons per minute from flooding the pits.

But Dunn's operation also experienced great difficulties which eventually combined to force him to quit. His capacity to trade outwith the Lothian area was limited as he and his contemporaries faced stiff competition from south of the border. During this period much of the coal sold beyond the Tay was English. The coal fields of the Forth valley were high-cost producers and, it seems, were unable to compete extensively with the well-organised mines and coal shipping of Newcastle-upon-Tyne. Meanwhile, despite his technical advances, Dunn found that flooding continued to be a major problem at Prestongrange. In unfavourable circumstances, he gave-up the running of the colliery around 1838. His lasting achievement was to provide a good platform for further exploitation of the Prestongrange coals as and when the market made it viable. This next occurred during the tenure of the second Grant-Suttie of Prestongrange, Sir George, who succeeded his father in 1836.

Sir George Grant-Suttie (1797–1878), an officer of the Scots Fusileer Guards from 1817–18, had the colliery up and running again by 1848. He seems to have made some good returns, such as in 1855 when he sold almost £2000 worth of coal. But Sir George found, as Dunn had before him, that flooding continued to be a major problem. His neighbours, too, experienced similar difficulties. In January 1860 Sir George received a letter from C & A Christie, owners of nearby Walliford colliery, requesting permission to dig a ditch to drain water out of their coal workings and onto his lands at Walliford.

By this time, the employment-structure was significantly altered as a result of the increased emancipation and improved lot of working people. In 1843, the Mines Act had prohibited the employment of women underground and boys under the age of ten. This was a move supported by Sir George (although he had not yet had experience of running the mine at Prestongrange). To the Royal Commission of 1841–2 he remarked, "...I beg leave to state to you my conviction, that the employment of women in the mines of Scotland is one of the reasons which tends to depreciate the character and habits of the collier population; and that to remedy this evil a legislative enactment is required..." But he also added that government should act to keep miners wages low as they were "already too high".

Sir George's true position on labour relations, a deeply conservative one which was hinted at in 1841–2, was revealed when he began running the mine at Prestongrange. His 1848 Notice of Contract between himself and the miners and other colliery workers which was more strict than many for the period, and although it did have some clauses which entertained philanthropic gestures, the tone was generally oppressive and seems to betray a yearning for the days when mine-owners could treat their colliers as they pleased. Sir George was not alone in his attitude to his workforce. His neighbour, Lord Lothian, was also noted for his hard-line stance on working conditions.

In an amusing aside, Sir George's sometimes reactionary and conservative approach to life in the changing world of the mid-19th Century is highlighted in a letter of his from 13 March 1850. He describes being thwarted in an attempt to meet his neighbour, Lord Aberdour to discuss the boundary between their two estates, by that most vexing by-product of the modern age – the railway timetable: "Ma[de] an attempt to meet you at Dalmahoy to-day, which failed from my having got out at Gogar in place of Ratho, and after walking to within sight of your gate finding that I had not more than time to get back for the quarter to four train. – So much for the *Railways*."

It is questionable whether Sir George would have had the capacity to engage successfully with the advancing modern world without the efforts of his 'right-hand', a man named Edward Yule. Yule performed the roles of estate factor, colliery manager and agent and while he seems to have been competent at certain of his duties, the running of the coal mine presented him with a tough challenge with which he didn't have a great deal of success. Several of the colliery's business relationships on record from Yule's time in charge ended in disaster. In fairness, the mid-19th Century was an evolutionary period full of uncertainty and unprecedented challenges, and between them, Sir George and Edward Yule were able to keep Prestongrange colliery a going concern for nearly a quarter of a Century.

The evidence surviving from the 1860s portrays Prestongrange as lurching, rather than striding, through the industrial age. In April 1865 Prestongrange began trading with a coal agent in Edinburgh by the name of James Orr. Orr's premises in Edinburgh was in Mary Kings Close, an old hidden street under the Royal Exchange, infamous for having witnessed terrible scenes of plague, persecution and fire in the 17th Century and now widely believed to be haunted. Officially the company's address was 14 Royal Exchange, but it was an unpropitious location nonetheless.

Orr was paid a commission of seven and a half per cent on the value of the coal he sold. His agreement included taking responsibility for all bad debts and paying for his coal monthly at a price proportional to its value on the Edinburgh market. He was also allowed a temporary arrangement to help him get started of 16 shillings per week to assist in paying the wages of the men employed in his depot. Some time in 1867, however, Orr became seriously ill and for many months was unable to attend to business. As his condition worsened, his wife's brother Gilbert P Simpson was brought in to manage the business. James Orr died around the beginning of August 1868.

After Orr's death, Yule seems to have rather mismanaged affairs by allowing things to amble along on a string of verbal agreements and assumptions. A verbal agreement was made that Simpson should carry on the agency on his own account, and enter the company in the Colliery Ledger in the name of G P Simpson. After that date the coals were also invoiced in Simpson's name. In October 1868, Simpson brought down his younger brother, John, from England to join him in the business and it was then carried on in the name of G P Simpson and Co. Yule drew out a memorandum of agreement as to the agency which he left with the Simpsons for signature but it was never returned to him.

Despite this, Yule continued to act on good faith. Simpson arranged with Mrs Orr that he would carry on at the Prestongrange Agency for her benefit till the end of December 1868. Yule later stated that he believed that this was probably why the agreement had not been signed and returned by the Simpsons, as in effect the company was still legally in the possession of James Orr's widow. At the same time, several of the monthly accounts between

August & December 1868 were paid by Mrs Orr's cheques and Yule later said that he believed they must all have been paid in this way.

Things became increasingly messy in the new year. In January 1869 Gilbert Simpson backed out of the Agency and became manager of Dykehead Colliery near Motherwell, leaving his brother John to carry on the business. Around that time Simpson agreed with Mrs Orr that she should take care of the agency's outstanding business for the months of October 1868 to January 1869 and that she would send Yule a cheque for January's sales when they became due. Yule seems to have been apprehensive at this point that he didn't have the opportunity of seeing Mrs Orr personally and that his applications for payment of the January sales had to be made through her two brothers.

The payment for January's sales was not received, and it was so often deferred that Yule later claimed that he then began to doubt whether Mrs Orr had made *any* arrangement with her brother that she would pay for the January sales. Yule seems to have written a stern letter to her on the subject on 7 July. She then acknowledged her liability and handed over £20. Mrs Orr then refused to accept any further responsibility for the debt and Yule seems to have been left with at least £40 unrecovered. This relatively minor affair was a harbinger of worse to come, however.

In June 1871 the colliery ran into trouble with a coal merchant in Leith, James Dykes (later Dykes and Hawks). Throughout the course of the year, Yule was consistently unable to keep-up the agreed level of coal supply. He cited in his defence mining difficulties, but Dykes seems to have gained the impression as time went on that he was being treated like a mug. He observed that on several occasions when others were receiving wagons from Prestongrange, he was also due yet received none. At almost every turn he had to write to Yule asking where his next payload of coal was. After a time, as Yule continued to claim mining difficulties were the source of the problem, he suggested that if he could supply Dykes with dross, then the demands of the contract would be met. Dykes accepted, but remarked acidly; "It is a strange thing that you can send the dross and not the coal. Do try and treat me a little more in accordance with our contract and avoid this extra expense..." He later added that "of course you are aware at what fearful loss other collieries have carried out their contracts ... this would be but a "flea-bite" [to Sir George] in comparison to them". The affair further degenerated, as the colliery continued to fail to supply the requisite amounts of coal on time, and ended in litigation in September 1872.

That same year, views were exchanged in respect of a proposed Mine-owners Association showed that Sir George had a draconian attitude towards his workforce, reminiscent of the days of bondage, that was out-of-step with the prevailing mood of other coalowners. He wrote from his holiday villa on the French south-coast that he wanted a confederacy of mine owners which stipulated that men could not be employed unless they presented a certificate from their former employers. The proponents of the Association remarked that such a condition was "of doubtful legality". Further, the Association was to lay down rules for the regulation of miners' wages, which Sir George also opposed. Sir George's individual obstinacy reflected the mindset of many of the landowner-industrialists of the day – they were just not used to the concept of modern regulatory bodies and associations. The Lothian mine owners tried several times without success to organise themselves into a long-term federation to protect their interests from the increasing threat posed by organised labour, but until 1907 they were usually only able to convene at moments of crisis. That year, however, they formed a long-standing Association which would also liaise with a body ostensibly designed to ease tension in the industry, created in 1899, the Scottish Coal Conciliation Board. But such developments were part of a later era of modern industrial relations which was only beginning to emerge during Sir George's tenure.

In May 1872 Sir George entered into a one-year contract to supply the Edinburgh Gas Light Company with 3,000 tons of Parrot Coal, even though the colliery was still failing to meet his obligations to Dykes and Co. in Leith. This new contract again proved disasterous for both parties, and also ended in litigation in November of that year. Severe flooding of the seams meant that Prestongrange had been unable to supply Edinburgh Gas Light with anything like what had been agreed. The Edinburgh Company doubted whether this had been the real reason behind the poor supply, and the colliery was forced to procure an independent report on the state of the Parrot Coal seam. Sir George was vindicated by the report's findings in 1873, which mentioned that the mine was so badly flooded the engineer was unable even to get near the Parrot Coal seams.

As early as the winter of 1871–2 Sir George decided that he had had enough of trying to run the colliery and was exploring how he would permit an independent party to set-up a company to work there. The fatigue Sir George felt at this time seems to be attested to later by his refusal to become a director of the new company despite repeated pleas that his experience would be of great benefit. He stated that; "I must decline to becoming company director... as I reside so short a period of the year in Scotland." This is unlikely to have been the main reason, as he had already happily run the colliery himself for many years as a mostly absentee landlord. He was now, though, in his mid-seventies. A combination of old age and weariness at having struggled for so long to successfully work the mine seem to have contributed to his decision to relinquish the running of the operation.

On 25 September 1873 a 99-year lease was entered into between Sir George and the three partners of a new company, Englishman R L M Kitto, Mathew Loam from Liskeard, and Thomas Brental, also an Englishman, from Middlesbrough. The company was to be called the Prestongrange Coal and Iron Co.

It was agreed that the sale would encompass all property connected with the running of the mine. Legally, there were two basic types of property, 'moveable' and 'immoveable'. The 'moveable' property, which alone was valued at £18,000, was basically anything which was used by the mine but was not physically 'nailed to the ground' in some way. This vast array of items included wagons, buckets, blasting tools, fire lamps, pithead cages, the sawmill with its four saws, and the horses with their carts and harnessess (except for one pony which Sir George wanted to keep). 'Immoveable' items were things which were stuck to the ground, like winding apparatus, rails, certain ropes and rods, and the pit engines and their engine-houses. The distinction between the two types of property was important, as 'immoveable' property was also heritable, and therefore automatically became the property of Sir George's heir when he died. The engine at No.1 pit was described as "One Beam Engine 60" Cylinder with walking beam and balance beam complete". The engine at No.2 was recorded as being "One Horizontal Engine 12" Cylinder 4 flat-stroke in good working order". The process of definining what property was 'moveable' as opposed to 'immoveable' was a complex one which seems to have taken up much of Sir George's time as he prepared the colliery for sale. It is an interesting example of changes to landed estates wrought by the Industrial Revolution, demonstrating that new ways of thinking were required to make sure that pieces of mechanical property especially were given appropriate legal definitions.

In 1874, Prestongrange Coal and Iron began trading as a limited company. It used two shafts in its operations, one at Morrisons Haven and the other at Birslie. The No. 2 shaft was redeveloped to work the Jewel Seam and No. 1 shaft used to pump the massive amounts of water from the mine. A beam pumping-engine made by Harvey and Company of Hayle in Cornwall was installed. It was shipped to Morrisons Haven and erected in a massive stone pump-house at the head of No. 1 shaft. The front wall of the house was six feet thick to support the weight and motion of the thirty-three foot cast iron beam. The machine was so vast that the pump rod alone weighed 100 tons. This huge engine would remain a Prestongrange stalwart until its final decommissioning in 1954.

It's not clear whether the decision to purchase this engine was inspired by Sir George, but he certainly seems to have been a fan of Cornish engineering. In 1860 Sir George got himself into trouble for appearing to slander a Scottish engine maker, James Landale. Landale threatened legal action after Sir George remarked that Cornish-made pumping engines were superior to those manufactured in Scotland.

If the Grant-Suttie management team was fairly lacklustre in terms of its business skill, the new partnership was a seriously weak regime – though it did face a serious and unexpected downturn in the coal market which hit just as it was trying to establish itself.

Just as Prestongrange Coal and Iron was making a massive outlay on equipment and machinery, it found itself faced with a serious economic crisis. When the directors entered into dialogue with Sir George in 1872 the value of coal was as high as it had ever been, but by the time the company started trading in 1874 the markets had slumped. The company tried to offset its financial problems by cutting miners' wages to one shilling per day and extending working hours. This was in contravention of the 8-hour day maximum which the government had introduced in 1873.

The miners responded to these measures by going on strike. The *Scotsman* newspaper reported that out of 2,000 men on strike in the Lothian area, 800 were from East Lothian, 140 of whom were from Prestongrange. With the direction and financial support provided by the fledgling Mid and East Lothian Miners' Association, the miners held out for seven weeks. On 20 May 1874, Mathew Loam wrote to Sir George stating; "I am now returned from Preston where we have had a meeting to make our financial arrangements for the current year. As these will involve many heavy payments for the new machinery etc, and we are deprived – through strikes and other circumstances – of a large portion of our returns, upon which we had relied, I write for myself and co-lessees to ask if you will kindly defer the payment of the last instalment of your purchase money and commute it into a permanent loan, when due in September next, at interest from that date".

Suttie gave his consent to the debt being turned into a loan, but both he and Yule seem to have been unhappy that the company had run into such severe difficulty so early on. When the company wrote to Sir George on 4

September requesting that Suttie's lawyers prepare the necessary documents for the agreed loan, they did their best to make encouraging noises about the company's progress with its development of the site; "You will be glad to learn that in a few days, extra exertions will be made to complete the new works."

Despite advances procured from the general growth of the coal industry, poor management and flooding in the pits seem to have formed a plague which refused to leave the colliery. While there is little surviving detail of the years 1875–6, it seems that it had sufficient trade to keep its head above water, but little else. The lack of managerial foresight is highlighted by the fact that the directors didn't get the accounts audited until 1877 – over three years after they began trading as a limited company.

That same year, operations at the Birslie pit had to be suspended for several months due to a rash of water flooding into the workings. Because much of the water drained into other areas, the company were unable to extend new excavations as planned. They wrote to Yule requesting that he make arrangements "for the carrying of this water, and cutting [of] any connections [from the new areas] which lead into old workings".

In January 1878, the future was looking very doubtful for the company. Its Annual Report to its shareholders made clear that the output from the new Morrisons Haven pit in particular had not lived-up to expectations: "although steady progress has been made during the past year, it has not been so rapid as your directors could wish, or were led to expect at the end of the previous year. Twelve months ago our Mining Engineer was most sanguine that our Morrisonshaven pit would now be giving us 500 tons of coals per day. As a fact, however, only during the past few months has a maximum of 400 tons a day been reached from the whole of the pits [with] Morrisonshaven seldom exceeding 250 tons, or just half of what we had hoped to get by this time."

While 1878 was a very sad year personally for the Grant-Suttie family, the financial condition of the colliery company, too, was deeply depressing. Sir George died in August 1878 at Grantham House, Putney Heath, Surrey, aged 80. He was succeeded in 1878 by a third generation Sir James (1830–78) whose tenure would be sadly brief, lasting for only four months. Meanwhile, the Company blamed its worsening financial state on the continuing depression in the coal trade and the "unavoidable" delay in the development of its property. On the face of it, these claims seemed to hold water. However, Sir George and his agents seem to have become suspicious that the company's directors were not in such a dire financial state of affairs as they claimed.

In its anxiety for the future of the operation, the estate seems to have engaged in some 'snooping' into the condition of the company. They contacted an English bank who dealt with the Prestongrange Coal Co. to try and find out some information on the health of the company. On September 2 1878, the bank wrote back to Sir James Grant-Suttie's lawyers stating that they understood the company to be doing reasonably well. It was, as far as they understood it, "a going concern". Further, they had information that the company was negotiating the purchase of some houses near the works for some of the colliery management staff which suggested that "things were not so very bad."

On 8 August the company's lawyers tried to shift the blame for the colliery's poor state of affairs onto the estate. They argued that the company had gone to great expense in erecting very powerful machinery to work coal on the foreshore and under the sea-bed of the Forth with the assurance from the late Sir George that his baronetcy included mineral rights to these areas. As it turned out the crown had retained the right of ownership of the coal under the sea, and it prevented the company from working there. Had the company been able to work this coal they would have had access to a field with vast potential extending for some 2,500 acres. Further, they stated that Sir George had also assured them that there was 80,000 tons of Great Seam coal available at the Morrisons Haven pit, provided the water was pumped out. What they discovered was that there was nowhere near 80,000 tons available, and instead had to fix expensive underground machinery to work coal from a neighbouring estate. Sir George made them pay wayleave so that they could work the Jewel Seam at Birslie, only for them to find that after a large outlay on equipment the water levels there were twice as heavy as at Morrisons Haven.

To add insult to injury, Sir George had still insisted that the company pay their fixed rent in full, despite these problems having come about as a result of his overblown claims about the mine's potential. They asked that they only be charged royalties on the coal which they actually wrought, and that they be freed from paying what they considered to be an "excessive" amount of fixed rent, arguing that the field was incapable of supporting a fixed rent of £2,000.

An omen of further misfortune was the early death of Sir James Grant-Suttie in October of that year. He was only 48 years old. This left the estate to the fourth Grant-Suttie, George, who was only eight when he succeeded his father. On 23 November 1878 the company wrote to the young Sir George's trustees reporting a considerable loss for the previous year. They stated that the directors and their shareholders were aware of the fact that they had not only failed to make any profit, they had also been unfortunate enough to have suffered very heavy losses in several "unprecedented" business transactions. The immediate upshot of this was that the company was unable to pay a dividend to its shareholders. The situation was so bad that four of the Directors had had to tide the company over "the recent depression" by each paying £1,000 to the Company's bankers. But in mitigation they added that, notwithstanding the lack of success that the company's operations had met with so far, in the face of high rents, mining difficulties, and continued commercial depreciation, they were thankful that the company's position was not worse.

The company wrote to the young Sir George's trustees in December 1878 stating that "without very considerable concessions the works cannot be carried on, with them however, the present time of depression can be tided over, and steps taken so that, immediately on the revival of trade, the estate may be developed to its fullest capabilities." Two days later, the Company issued its Annual Report which detailed the depressing situation for the benefit of the company's shareholders: "Your Directors are doing their best in these difficult and anxious times to keep the works going on a limited scale, and without further loss, but the time is not distant when the constitution of the company will require revision and modification commensurate with the altered condition of things". In other words, a minor miracle was now required if the company was to be saved from collapse.

Acting upon a recommendation by one of their own agents, the estate relented on the issue of fixed rent and agreed to reduce it to £1,000. It was recognised that if the company folded, a fixed rent of £2,000 would stand little chance of attracting new interest given the amount of coal which could be extracted at that time. They also realised that it was imperative that the mine be kept open, even if it had to be run somehow by the estate. If the Morrisons Haven pit were abandoned and the wastes allowed to fill with water the expense of pumping it out again and repairing the mines would be prohibitive.

The company directors were then permitted to surrender their lease.

In February 1879, the Prestongrange Coal and Iron Company ceased trading having run up large debts. It owed £35,000 to "a Scotch bank", had incurred losses of between £6,000 and £10,000, and was unable to pay the second half of the rent for 1878. It was recommended that the trustees of the young Sir George sequestrate the property of the colliery immediately. The company then went into voluntary liquidation and was run by the liquidator, Frederick Walter Carter until 1881. The company was forced to hand over the steam engines and other machinery which were sequestrated. The demise of the Company at a time when the coal trade had still not recovered had dire consequences for the estate.

F W Carter attempted to sell the lease throughout the winter of 1880–1. The lease, which including the expensive plant and fittings which had belonged to the lessees, failed to find a purchaser even with the considerable modifications of its conditions, such as the halved rent. In the spring of 1881 Carter intimated his intention to cease working the Colliery.

A saviour was eventually found in 1882 when business partners John Greis, Robert Stephenson and Charles Ellison moved in and set up a new company. The new men received considerable concessions from the estate to help them make the running of the colliery a success. These concessions were doubly essential since the value of coal was still in serious decline at this time. The sale price had been reduced from £60,000 to £45,000. As well as the reduced rent, the new men also got wayleaves reduced from two pence to one penny per ton, breathing space to make up losses and the right to expand the coal works by boring at Morrison's Haven and sink a pit there within five years.

The new company was to be called the Prestongrange Coal and Fire-Brick Company, and in September of that year it became the official owner of the colliery. However, while it was certainly better organised than the previous company, Prestongrange Coal and Fire-Brick met with limited success. Indicative of this was the company's plan to sink a 3rd shaft at Morrisons Haven, which never came to fruition.

Prestongrange Coal and Fire-Brick continued working the pits until a slump in the market and strike action by the miners forced it to relinquish the mine in 1894. It was around this time, however, that the coal trade entered a new phase of prosperity far in excess of anything witnessed before, and Prestongrange itself was soon to expand greatly under new and dynamic ownership.

MAJOR PHASE AND EVENTUAL ECLIPSE 1894–1962

The Prestongrange Colliery and estate was sold by the 24-year-old Sir George Grant-Suttie to the Summerlee and Mossend Iron and Steel Company in 1894. The coming of this new owner heralded a dramatic and long-term upturn in the fortunes of the colliery. At this time only two seams were being worked, the eight-foot thick great seam and the four-foot Jewel seam. The Summerlee

Company, which was much larger than any of the previous companies, was able to re-equip the pit, sink a third ventilation shaft and open out the deeper Beggar seam. This helped increase output to 500 tons a day, increasing the colliery's competitiveness. The quality fireclay produced at Prestongrange which went to make firebricks, tiles and pipes also increased in volume. Morrisons Haven began exporting a large amount of fireclay products as well as coal. There were two berths for the fireclay works and four coaling berths, all connected by railways or tramways to the colliery and kilns. Vessels of up to 280 tons could enter the harbour and by 1900, almost one a day was leaving with exports. The company went on to manufacture 5,500 tons of clay products a year.

The commercial success which the Summerlee company brought to Prestongrange owed a great deal to the pedigree of its founding family, the Neilsons. Over the course of the 19th Century, three succeeding generations made their mark in the engineering, coal, iron and steel industries. By the time they acquired Prestongrange they had established themselves as major players in the West of Scotland business world.

For over fifty years until the Prestongrange colliery was nationalised, the Neilsons lorded over the affairs of Prestongrange, its miners and their families. The new company moved many mining families from Lanarkshire to Prestonpans to work their newly acquired pit, building a street of brick upstairs-downstairs housing and brashly naming it Summerlee Street. This was indicative of a level of overbearance on the miners' lives which would come to be deeply resented in future years.

The leading partner in the Summerlee Company was John Neilson, a third-generation member of the family. In order to appreciate what John Neilson and the Summerlee Co. brought to Prestongrange, some understanding is perhaps required of the role which his father and grandfather's generations played in establishing the foundations on which his success was based.

The first generation of the Neilson dynasty were two brothers, John Neilson and James Beaumont Neilson. James became a star of the industrial age after he invented the hot-blast process, patented in 1828, which enabled blackband ironstone to be successfully smelted using local splint coal in small furnaces – drastically reducing costs of production. James was therefore very much a catalyst whose iron-smelting process enabled a whole host of ironmasters to spring up in the west around Airdrie and Coatbridge. James Beaumont's brother, John, on the other hand, earned his reputation at his Oakbank Engine works and foundry where all branches of mechanical engineering from boilermaking to blast furnace and colliery engines were made.

For the second generation of the Neilson family, the 1830s saw the launching of their notable careers as engineers and iron founders. The elder John Neilson's sons, Walter, William and Hugh, formed an energetic trio which ran the iron works at Summerlee and Mossend. Walter in particular demonstrated from an early age his abilities as a first-class engineer. In 1843 William formally founded a partnership of the Mossend Iron Company which ran a malleable iron works for the manufacture of wrought iron at Mossend, near Holytown. By 1868, Summerlee, which was by now a co-partnership of Walter and Hugh, had eight blast-furnaces. Like many of their contemporaries, the Neilsons owned or leased their own coal and ironstone mines not only in Lanarkshire but in several counties in Scotland.

By 1886 the three brothers had passed away, and the third generation of Neilsons united the two works into one company, the Summerlee and Mossend Iron and Steel Company. The chairman of the company was John Neilson, the son of Walter. He was accompanied by a proliferation of the dynasty which resulted in nine members of the family being registered as partners. Mossend later closed due to the effects of poor labour relations and diminishing returns. Meanwhile Summerlee, with John Neilson at the helm, grew in strength by concentrating more on coal and pig-iron. In fact, a most important part of the company's business by this time was coal mining.

The acquisition of Prestongrange in 1894 marked the beginning of a period in which the Neilsons began to really push themselves into the coal trade. Within fifteen years, the number of miners employed by the company rose from 1,700 to over 4,100. By 1910, the company had eight mines, had ditched the unprofitable Mossend works, and was focusing itself solely on iron and coal.

For all their great achievements, however, the Neilsons, like so many coal owners of this period, valued their own profits far and above the livelihoods of the miners and their families. When problems arose with the system of coal production at the pit, or there was a slackening of the coal market, the coal owners sought to ensure that the miners absorbed as much of the impact as possible by cutting wages and extending working hours.

In March 1912 miners at Prestongrange, along with twenty-three other pits in Mid and East Lothian, joined colleagues across Britain in strike action, demanding a minimum wage of six shillings per day. The existing set-up was grossly unfair, since, although a man and a boy would usually make a joint earning of ten or eleven shillings per day – the man making seven and the boy three – some men never made more than about four shillings a day. Poor earnings were due to circumstances beyond the miners' control such as old age, lack of strength or skill, or having to work difficult seams. During the strike the miners were financially supported by the local Miners Association. It lasted for five weeks and won the concession from the government of a Minimum Wage Bill, which proposed impartial boards whose job would be to work out the rate of minimum wage in the various districts across the country, according to the prevailing conditions in each. But it was not the victory that the miners had hoped for – there was still no fixed national minimum wage.

The post-war spirit of rewarding the workers for their efforts during WWI was partly responsible for the miners winning some statutary improvements in pay and conditions in 1919. But when the coal market collapsed the following year, faced with falling profits, the coal owners opted for their traditional tactic of squeezing the workforce. In response, Prestongrange miners were involved in a three-month long national strike in 1921. This forced further concessions from the government. But in July 1925 a further squeeze from coal owners caused Prestongrange miners to join colleagues in strike action again. This dispute was but a precursor for *the* industrial conflict of the Century in Britain, which took place the following year.

Through the spring and early summer of 1926 there was a gradual build-up of tension between the Prestongrange miners and the Summerlee Company. On 2 February several complaints were laid before the board of the Mid and East Lothian Miners Association that the 7-hour day ruling was being violated. In February, 500 men were left idle at Prestongrange's No. 2 pit for eight days as a result of an industrial dispute in the haulage industry. The conservative-

Rescue Team, Prestongrange Colliery
Scottish Mining Museum Trust

leaning local newspaper, the *Haddingtonshire Courier*, sought to soften the situation by reporting a "general slackness" in the East Lothian pits at this time. At first this was attributed to bad weather and a resultant lack of shipping, but by the end of March even the *Courier*'s conservative reporting could not hide the crisis which was looming. The paper seized on evidence of a slight improvement at the beginning of April, but by the second quarter of that month things had begun to get even worse. 50 pit ponies were withdrawn from Prestongrange on 28 April – an indication that Summerlee was expecting a long fight.

On 30 April, there was a packed emergency meeting at Prestonpans town hall to discuss what action the miners should take in response to the wage cuts and redundancies being imposed by the government and the coal owners. They opted to fight back with strike action, and on 7 May it was reported that the East Lothian pits had closed down completely. The mining families of Prestongrange had joined workers across Scotland and the rest of Britain in one of the most significant events to have occured in these islands in the 20th Century, the General Strike of 1926. During the strike, the deadlock between trade unions and the government was so great that it brought the whole country almost to the brink of a political revolution.

Within weeks the government's anti-strike general, Winston Churchill, skilfully orchestrated every resource at his disposal – radio, print, civil and military forces. Interestingly, in East Lothian as with elsewhere, the police as a highly visible arm of civil authority were the focus of particularly intense hatred from the miners. In Tranent the police station was stoned and policemen were attacked. Meanwhile, Churchill successfully called the TUC's bluff. Was it really prepared to attempt a workers revolution? The answer was no. The TUC called off the strike and demoralised workers went back to work having won nothing. But while other industries returned to work, hundreds of thousands of miners remained resolute, and continued the strike.

Miners at Prestongrange were no exception to this. On August 13, a crowd of 6,000 turned out at Prestongrange park to greet A J Cook, the General Secretary of the British Miners Federation. He received a rapturous response when he told the audience that the Federation would surrender nothing to the coal owners and the government. On 8 October, Prestongrange miners voted by a large majority to reject government proposals aimed at ending the deadlock. They agreed that the proposals fell far short of what was required. Miners across the country carried on their strike into the winter, but after many hard months they were eventually forced to concede defeat. It was a decisive victory for the status-quo, and a workers' revolution was never a serious prospect after that.

It is not hard to understand why the miners were particularly strong in resisting the punitive measures imposed by the coalowners and the government during times of economic depression. Coal was at the base of heavy industry, and as a result felt the hardest impact when the economy contracted. From their point of view, miners worked in an essential occupation which was still one of the most difficult and dangerous, and yet they were also being robbed of their livelihoods.

A sense of the unfairness of the miners' circumstances is perhaps captured by a deeply tragic occurrence that took place at Prestongrange on the 9th of April 1926. A miner named John Reid was crushed to death in the Three-foot seam when the roof of the tunnel he was in collapsed. The inquest into his death took place in June while the miners were locked in confrontation with the coal owners and the government. Shortly before 10 o'clock on the morning of 9 April, Robert Martin, one of the men working in the Three-foot seam, heard the distant sound of a hutch coming down the passageway towards him. As the hutch seemed to be drawing nearer, he heard a rumbling sound. Robert alerted a nearby colleague, George Archibald, and the two men went to investigate. About fifty or sixty feet (15–18 metres) down the passageway they found the hutch standing by a pile of stone and rubbish which had fallen from the ceiling. All that could be seen of John Reid was the light of his lamp which shone out from beneath the rubble.

The men had to go round by another road to the other side of the rubble before they could reach the stricken man. They cleared away the stones to find John in a sitting position with his head bent right down to the floor of the tunnel. He was dead when they found him. A boulder weighing four to five cwts. had smashed against his neck with another large stone resting on top of it. It was reckoned that a freak movement of the roof had caused one of the supporting timbers to split, allowing eight or nine tons to fall on him.

This event is perhaps coldly symbolic of the manifest unfairness of the miners' situation. The evidence given by the witnesses demonstrates that, after hundreds of years of development at Prestongrange, the possibility of a horrific death in darkness and isolation was something which the miners still faced every day of their working lives. Just as it was the miners and not the Neilsons who bore the personal costs of accidents in the mine, so it was the miners and their families who shouldered the collapse in the coal market.

While the effects of the industrial disputes following the post-war depression left many miners and their families with nothing, by the time John Neilson died in 1935 at the age of ninety-five, he had amassed a massive personal fortune. Thanks to the favourable circumstances he was born into, he had been able throughout his life to use his talents to their full potential, leaving his children a portfolio of shareholdings in J & P Coats, Distillers, ICI, various railway interests and an estate worth almost £155,000. Had the Neilsons and their fellow coal owners a greater appreciation that their money would never have been made without the efforts of their miners, a great deal of misery could have perhaps been avoided

After the heady days of the early 20th Century, the coal trade went into a long decline from which it never recovered. The vast British Empire began contracting rapidly. As the colonial peoples were regaining their freedom, trade opportunities in every sector of British industry diminished. The ship building and heavy industries were in a state of collapse, and as they had been major consumers of coal, this spelled disaster for the industry. There were other new threats as well. Alternative forms of energy, oil especially, were starting to impinge on coal's traditional market territories.

Between the mid 1920s and the outbreak of the Second World War, the Prestongrange workforce was decimated and its trade greatly reduced. While it had, in its small part, helped the state-run war machine achieve victory in 1945, after the war the mine was a shadow of what it had been thirty years before. Prior to 1939 a large export trade in its clay products had been carried on with Denmark, Holland, Germany and other European countries, but after 1945, sales were only in the home market.

The harbour at Morrisons Haven was now a derelict. Since 1914, coal and bricks had been sent away by rail and road. Despite its obsolescence, however, the harbour did, by the 1950s, find a new and novel use for itself as a 'swimming pool' used by local youngsters – thus continuing to at least provide some sort of benefit to the local community.

Subtle evidence of the decline of the colliery's size and standing is also found with the combining of Prestongrange and nearby Prestonlinks Miners' Galas into one event in 1946, and the changing of the name to the Town Children's Gala.

As part of its post-war national reconstruction, the Labour government attempted the rehabilitation of the coal industry by bringing the collieries under national control, and as part of this process the National Coal Board bought Prestongrange in 1947. The full complement of coal seams at Prestongrange were now being worked. From shallowest to deepest there was the Great Seam, Diver Seam, Clay Seam, Five-foot Seam, Jewel Seam, Beggar Seam, No.1 Diamond Seam and No. 2 Diamond Seam. The NCB carried out extensive redevelopment work at the pit which included new pit-head baths which were opened in September 1952 by sixty-six year old William Cunningham, a miner who had spent nearly all of his fifty-two working years at the colliery. Such events were supposed to encourage optimism, but again it was a hope that soon subsided.

In 1953 Prestongrange had a workforce of only 660, and it was remarked that the colliery was now becoming "highly mechanised". The plethora of varied occupations which used to exist at the mine had gone, making it increasingly difficult to distinguish the different roles of colliery workers. The majority of its employes still lived in East Lothian, taken to and from the colliery by bus. The NCB provided canteen services which were used by at

Prestongrange Bowling Club, First Bowl by W. Ford, J.P., B.E.M., on 25th April 1953
East Lothian Council, David Spence Collection

least half of the employees. Another benefit was the Welfare Institute, and recreational facilities which were under development. The residue of earlier political struggles was evidenced by the continued survival of a small Communist Party organisation. Alongside the colliery, the Brick and Fireclay works continued their operations in which around 120 people were employed. Although the principle products were made by machines, many things were also hand-moulded. These works were described at the time as "modern and equipped with the latest machinery."

As with the rest of the country in the post-war era of hope in the future, expectations of the NCB at Prestongrange were initially high. They soon subsided, however, as demand for coal bottomed-out. Coal increasingly gave way to oil, gas and nuclear power. Domestic consumers in the Edinburgh area increasingly used oil, gas and electricity to heat their homes. In 1960, meetings of the Colliery Consultative Committee were dominated by the problem of absenteeism and low morale. During most of that year, almost a fifth of the entire workforce was absent and there were repeated problems with theft and vandalism. The local trade union representatives gave poor attendance at the meetings, and didn't seem to contribute much when they did turn up. This sorry state of affairs is perhaps most poignantly illustrated by the poor showing and support for the colliery football team.

The NCB itself does not seem to have been a particularly conscientious landowner. It attempted in 1951 to build an aerial ropeway from Prestongrange that would tip waste directly into the sea. This raised the prospect of total despoilation of the coastline, as had happened elsewhere. Their "dastardly proposal" was only thwarted when the Town Clerk of Edinburgh served them with an interdict.

With even the newly built super-colliery at nearby Monktonhall already facing an uncertain future, Prestongrange was deemed surplus to National requirements and shut down in 1962. Some miners were lucky enough to be relocated to other nearby collieries, but even for most of these, the writing was on the wall as dozens of collieries throughout Scotland closed over the course of the 1970s and 80s. One thing that the miners all shared was the certainty that their occupation was fighting a losing battle against an array of aggressive outside factors. Like other workers, many erstwhile Prestongrange miners and their children have since witnessed years of uncertainty and unemployment amidst the ever-changing character of the late-20th Century Scottish workplace.

EPILOGUE 1963–2000

Although its life as a working mine was at an end, the curtain by no means went down for good on the mine at Prestongrange in 1962. More than a glimmer of light has been brought to its latter-day history by the creation of the Industrial Heritage Centre, which is flourishing today. It was set up by former colliery manager and local MP, David Spence, who arranged the purchase of the site after it was closed by the NCB. Prestongrange's pump-house had become a listed building in 1940, and on this basis Spence managed to prevent the NCB from moving in the demolition gangs in 1963.

The Heritage Centre announced its maturity in the late 1980s with a flurry of advertising which highlighted the role it played in providing a valuable educational resource as well as being a pleasant visitor attraction. At present, highlights of the site include the survival of the Grant-Sutties' massive Cornish pumping engine as well as the working pugs, tough little workhorse locomotives, formerly used by the Summerlee Company. The Heritage Centre ensures that, while the Prestongrange miners and mineowners are now long gone, their fascinating 1000 year history will continue to illuminate the 21st Century.

CONCLUSION

The relationship between the industrial owners of Prestongrange and their miners has been a consistently fascinating one. The distinction of the earliest mine-ownership on record in the British Isles leads on to a history which clearly reflects the general patterns in the development of the coal industry and labour relations in Scotland, whilst also having its own unique features.

The Prestongrange Lairds and coal owners like Sir William Grant, Sir George Grant-Suttie and John Neilson provides the story with an array of interesting characters whose careers help explain prevailing attitudes and developing patterns among the old landed and later capitalist elite.

Colourful events such as the Battle of Pinkie, the Tranent Massacre, and the General Strike of 1926 punctuate the importance of the colliers as a human resource, their own worth as a hard-working people, and their long and often tragic struggle for emancipation and justice.

While the industrial history of Prestongrange is worthy of a much more significant study than this one, it is hoped that this small contribution nonetheless succeeds in highlighting the major developments and personalities involved.

Some Further Reading

Prestonpans and Vicinity: Historical, Ecclesiastical and Traditional by Peter MacNeill (Leicester, 1902)
Mining in Mid and East Lothian by A.S Cunningham (Edinburgh, 1925)
Mining The Lothians by Guthrie Hutton (Edinburgh, 1998)
The Story of Prestonpans from Contemporary Records 1790s– 1950s Edited by Sir John Sinclair (East Lothian District Council, 1995)
Essays in Scottish Labour History Edited by Ian MacDougall (Edinburgh, 1978).

ACKNOWLEDGEMENTS

I would like to gratefully acknowledge the help of the staff at the National Library of Scotland, the National Archives of Scotland, East Lothian Local History Centre, and the Edinburgh Central Library for their help and assistance.

My particular thanks are due to Mr Colin Johnson of the NAS and Mr Ian MacDougall of the Scottish Workers History Society. Any errors and omissions included in this work are of course entirely my own fault.

5

Horses, Steam and Electric Engines at Prestongrange

Annemarie Allan

THE NEED FOR COAL

Like most of Scotland's coal, the Lothian coalfield is a basin-shaped series of layers, or seams, interspersed with other material. Over millions of years, movements in the earth caused folds or faults in the seams, while the invasion of molten material from deeper within the earth's crust created solid rock barriers within the coal and burnt areas, where coal was destroyed or reduced to cinders. The basin shape means that in some places coal originally lay on or near the surface, especially near the edge of the coalfield, or where the land surface is worn away by rivers or the sea.[1]

This is, of course, a very simple description of a complex geological process, but it is important to understand a little of the nature of the coalfield and the earliest methods of working the coal in order to understand the how and why of later developments in the use of power at Prestongrange.

It is clear from the charter granted to the Cistercian monks of Newbattle Abbey in the early 12th Century by Seyer de Quincey, Earl of Winchester, that coal was already well established as an alternative source of fuel to replace the rapidly diminishing supplies of timber in the Lowlands. This charter allowed the monks to establish a coal-works and quarry (carbonarium et quarrarium) to work coal seams between the Whytrig Burn and the boundaries of Pinkie and Inveresk. This charter is evidence that coal works on the Prestongrange lands are among the earliest recorded in Scotland.[2] However, it is not known exactly which outcrops of coal were being worked by the monks and it is important to remember that, since the lands known as Prestongrange were extensive, it is not possible to assume that these early records refer to the locality of the later mine.

The earliest types of mine were Bell Pits and Drift Mines. The Bell Pit, as its name suggests, was a pit dug into the earth and hollowed out at the level where the coal was found. The circular chamber created beneath the surface was not a stable structure and mining only continued until the sides threatened to collapse inwards. At this point the hole was abandoned and another started elsewhere. Drift mines, also known as 'ingaun e'es' (ingoing eyes), were opened where natural dips in the surface, such as a river bed, shoreline or glen, meant it was possible to dig into the side and extract the coal until the threat of collapse in the tunnel prevented further mining.

At this time, coal was not a popular fuel for domestic use, as the smoke and fumes were considered dangerous to health. Although it was used to heat large monastic and noble houses in Scotland, an Act passed in 1306 forbade the use of coal in London.[3] Nonetheless, coal mining has been associated with trade and industry from earliest times. James V gave permission for a harbour, known originally as Acheson's Haven, later Morrison's Haven,[4] and the Abbey was also granted the right to transport coal from workings beside the river Esk for shipment in small boats, along the road still known today as Salter's Road.[5] The packhorses made the return journey with salt from the salt pans and goods taken in trade for the salt and coal they shipped at the harbour.

The monks of Newbattle took up their right to mine coal against a background of political and social instability. In 1261, Haddington was one of the Lothian towns burned in a raid by the English. The later 13th Century was a period of relative calm, but, by the beginning of the 14th, Scotland was embroiled in a series of wars with England which lasted for 150 years.[6] Throughout this period, the Abbey of Newbattle worked the coal until, by the middle of the 15th Century the most accessible supplies were exhausted and it became necessary to dig deeper.

As supplies of timber became even scarcer, the demand for coal increased. But supply was limited by difficulties in transportation and the exhaustion of accessible seams. Roads at this time were not easy to travel: they were muddy, potholed and poorly maintained.[7] By the 16th Century, the supplies of coal available by traditional mining methods were becoming inadequate to meet demand, yet at the same time, there was a growing interest in the use of coal for industry. Hector Boece's 'History', published in 1527 states:

> "In Fyffe ar won black stanis quilk ha sa intollerable heit quhair they are kendillit that they resolve and meltis irne, and are therefore richt proffitable for operation of smithis"
>
> *['In Fife are quarried black stones which have such intolerable heat when they are kindled that they resolve and melt iron and are therefore right profitable for operation of smithies']*[8]

At the beginning of the 16th Century, the annual output of Scottish coal was less than 40 thousand tons, still mined from small-scale workings for local supply. Yet up to six tons of coal were needed to produce one ton of salt – and the manufacture of salt was enormously profitable.

A further pressure on the demand for coal was lack of colliers: during the Reformation, church lands passed into the hands of individuals such as Mark Ker, who was granted the estates of Newbattle Abbey in 1587.[9] The labour force represented by the monks and others who lived and worked on the Abbey lands was lost. Attempts were made both to protect coal supplies and to ensure an adequate supply of labour: in 1609, the export of coal was forbidden and in 1606, colliers were reduced by law to a form of slavery which lasted till 1775.[10]

The need to increase supply led to deeper workings and an increasing problem with flooding, a constantly recurring theme at Prestongrange throughout the centuries. The quantity of water which these early mineworkings were faced with is demonstrated by the fact that water flowing from mineworkings provided water supplies for Prestonpans and other villages.[11] Drift mines were free of water only as long as the tunnel cut into the coal seam was angled to allow water to drain naturally. Later workings used a method known as 'Pit and Adit' whereby a drainage tunnel, known as an 'adit' or 'day-level' was dug with an outlet below the mine workings, so that gravity caused the water to flow down and away from the workings.

THE HORSE GIN

Diggings at this time were to a depth of 70–90 feet, with coal being carried to the foot of the mine shaft by bearers, then carried up a spiral stair or a series of ladders to the surface. Such mines were known as "stair pits". Alternatively, a rope was lowered to the pit bottom and attached to baskets or tubs filled with coal, then hauled to the surface.[12] This early haulage was the origin of the first true mining machine, the 'horse gin'.

The 'Whin' or 'Scotch Gin' did not replace the stair pit, probably because there was little, if any, public concern for the use of human labour in mines and because maintaining a horse-gin was expensive compared to the use of a drainage tunnel. The gin was operated by means of a windlass (a horizontal axle) on the surface. The windlass was attached to a drum. As the drum turned, it raised or lowered buckets attached to a rope, bringing coal or water to the surface.[13] The motive power for the windlass was supplied either by a horse harnessed to the axle or by water, often the water flowing from old day levels: a nearby flint mill at Cuthill was powered by this method in the 1700s.[14]

Sir John Clerk, a prominent mining figure in the 17th Century, states:

> "One horse will serve for a sink [depth] from 10 to 20 fathoms...and two are necessary for a sink from 20 to 60 fathoms."[15]

There is evidence of the use of gin pits on the Prestongrange estate in a document dating from 1748. This document also refers to a "drowned pit" and, although we cannot be sure of exact locations, (a pit at Dolphingston, for example, was also referred to as Prestongrange) we know that mining ceased at Prestongrange due to flooding in 1746.[16] An estate plan dated 1825, based on an earlier plan of 1741, refers to a "water gin sink"[17] and a report on the Prestongrange coalfield in 1825 also mentions a gin pit.[18] Horse gins remained in operation in East Lothian until the 1840s: a list of machinery and equipment on the Prestongrange estate in 1872, made for inheritance purposes, mentions

> "Gin engines for raising coal; and Gins worked by horse power."[19]

From the personal reminiscences of Walter Pryde, we learn that horse gins were in operation in 1760, although his description is not concerned with raising coal:

> "I was yoked to work coal at Preston Grange when I was nine years old. We were then all slaves to the Preston Grange laird...if we did not do his bidding...the men's hands were tied in face of the horse at the gin, and made run backwards all day."[20]

As pits deepened, another major problem was air. With poorer ventilation, there was the additional danger of 'Blackdamp' or 'Chokedamp', a mixture of nitrogen and carbon dioxide which used up oxygen, leaving little or no breathable air. 'Firedamp' or methane – an inflammable gas which accumulated at the work face – brought the danger of explosion, but this was rarely present at depths of less than 200 feet. The most lethal of the gases present in mine workings is what is known as 'Whitedamp'. This is carbon monoxide, a colourless, odourless gas so poisonous that it can kill very swiftly indeed.[21]

The earliest solutions to such 'bad air' was to build a fire in the workings to create a draught and improve air circulation. As mines deepened, this method was adapted and refined into a two-shaft system, one to draw the air down, another to allow air to pass back to the surface, with doors between to prevent the returning air bringing explosive fire damp in contact with the furnace. A carelessly-tended furnace in a pit at Lower Birsley in the early 1800s resulted in a fire which burned for many years. As for the unfortunate furnace-keeper,

> "Whether [he] escaped or perished in the flames is uncertain, but he was never more heard of in that locality"[22]

By 1700, output of coal was probably around 4 million tons a year.[23] Demand was rising against a background of increasing difficulty in bringing it to the surface. Horses could be used underground only where the size of the workings permitted and the labour of raising coal and transporting it above ground was still largely dependent on human labour.

There were many efforts to improve mining methods, perhaps the most notable being Sir George Bruce's Moat Pit in Fife, with its two shafts, one on land and one below the high water mark in the Forth, protected by means of an artificial island.[24] The Moat Pit demonstrated the improvements in ventilation that could be achieved by the sinking of two shafts instead of one. In general, however, by the beginning of the 18th Century, these efforts had reached their limit.

The Union of the Parliaments of Scotland and England in 1707 brought further difficulties in the form of competition from English goods: the salt industry, for example, though it survived in Prestonpans well into the 20th Century, began a decline from which it never recovered. In 1719, 41 cargoes arrived at Morrison's Haven harbour, 19 of these in ships belonging to Prestonpans. By 1743, due to shipping losses and taxation imposed after union, the harbour trade had ceased.[25] English merchants were determined to protect their own markets and Scotland's efforts to develop trade with the colonies was marked by costly failures.

NEWCOMEN & WATT

It is against this background that Thomas Newcomen's patent for a steam engine in 1705 heralded the dawn of the industrial age. Newcomen's engine worked by a combination of steam and condensation. Fire heated water to form steam inside a cylinder, then the steam was cooled until it returned to the form of water. This created a vacuum inside an enclosed space. A piston inside the cylinder would rise in response to the generation of steam and fall as a result of atmospheric pressure on the vacuum when the steam was cooled and the power generated by this principle could be applied to the raising of coal or water.[26]

But Thomas Newcomen's "fire engine" did not offer an instant solution. These early engines were massive and stationary. Once erected, they could not be readily dismantled and transported elsewhere, although in many cases this did happen. Moreover, the cost of buying an engine included the cost of years of research and experimentation. Newcomen's engine was enormously expensive to install and maintain. For the first such engine erected in Scotland, in Stirlingshire, the costs were as follows: a royalty payment of £80 per annum for eight years, installation cost of £1007 (excluding engine house) and £200 a year to the engineers for maintenance as well as half the colliery profits.[27]

The history of coal working in Scotland has always been tied to economics. Sir John Clerk, writing in 1672, considered the use of equipment to drain coal workings as viable only where a seam was more than 4′ thick, of a depth of less than 500 fathoms and close to a regular market for the coal.[28] The problem with Newcomen's engine was that it was only economically worthwhile for large mining ventures and in the case of the small pits of East Lothian there was not enough guarantee of profit to make such costs worthwhile. It is the need to balance the cost of extracting coal against its saleable value that explains the closure of Prestongrange Pit in 1746.[29]

East Lothian pits therefore made little headway in the use of steam power until about 1780, when James Watt's modifications to Newcomen's original design promised a future for mines such as Prestongrange. Watt's engine separated the action of steam and condensation, resulting in a more practical machine, more mobile and easier to maintain.[30]

Throughout the 18th and 19th Centuries, coal consumption had continued to rise as coal became an increasingly acceptable fuel for household use and steam power encouraged machine development in industry and agriculture. In 1812, William Murdoch, a contemporary of James Watt, created a method by which gas extracted from coal could be used for lighting. The process of extracting gas also produced other elements, including coal-coke and tar, thus marking the start of a developing industry based on the by-products obtainable from coal.[31] As industrial usage began to diversify, differences in the nature of coal seams became more important. Murdoch's gas lighting, for example, initially required the brightly burning coal known as 'cannel coal' and the East Lothian seam known as the "Parrot" was mined for such coal.[32]

The scene would appear to be set for a resurgence in mining in Scotland and this was, indeed, the case. But East Lothian was not at the forefront of this revival, for a number of reasons. Firstly, the coal seams of East Lothian, with their problems of flooding and the depths of the seams, could not compete with other parts of Scotland where coal seams were more easily accessible. It was in West and Central Scotland, where coal seams were both relatively shallow and technically challenging that major industrial development took place. Developments in the iron industry, allowing coal-coke to be used to smelt iron, led to the erection of the first furnace at Carron, in Stirlingshire, close to ore deposits at Bo'ness and coal at Kinnaird and the early 18th Century also saw the beginnings of the shipbuilding industry on the lower Clyde.[33]

Furthermore, the 18th Century was not a stable political period for Scotland. The Jacobite risings of 1715 and 1745 resulted in changes in land ownership in East Lothian[34] and the county itself was a battleground for opposing armies. It was not possible to work the coals under these circumstances, as the old song demonstrates:

> "Hey! Johnnie Cope are ye waukin' [wakened] yet? Or are your drums a beatin' yet? If ye were waukin' I wad wait, To gang to the coals I' the mornin'."[35]

The commonest method of extracting coal at this time was known as "stoop and room": an "oversman" would calculate and mark out pillars of coal to support the roof and the collier would work on the remaining coal. The areas where coal was cut away were the rooms, the pillars were the stoops. Obviously, leaving such large sections of unworked coal behind was a source of great temptation: it was not unknown for colliers to ignore the danger and remove coal from these stoops:

> "Care must be taken not to suffer Coaliers to impair these pillars, as they commonly do for their own advantage."[36]

In spite of difficulties, East Lothian mine owners made continual efforts to share in industrial expansion and take advantage of new equipment. In 1741, almost 100 years before the sinking of the first modern shaft at Prestongrange, the area was identified as a possible site for the sinking of an engine pit and accompanying working pits to a depth of 50 fathoms.[37] An advertisement in the Caledonian Mercury in 1729 shows that owners were aware of the potential of the new engines for Prestongrange:

> "...the...Coal of Prestongrange...is fit for the Sea as well as Land Sale, there being a good harbour at Morison's Haven not far distant from said Coal which, when formerly wrought, produced a very considerable rent, both by Land and sea Sale...If any persons may have a mind to take a lease of said Coal and Salt Pans jointly or seperately, may set down under the old Level, 12 or 24 Fathoms where there is Coal which will last for many years. And the water may be thrown by a Fire Engine into the Level or otherwise..."[38]

Of course, this advertisement also demonstrates an unwillingness to bear the costs of setting up such a "fire engine". Nevertheless, mine owners were eager to make what headway they could and were closely involved with developments elsewhere in Scotland. The Cadell family, for example, were local mine owners, but also had a founding interest in the Carron Ironworks mentioned earlier.[39]

TURNPIKES & WAGGONWAYS

Where East Lothian could make improvements was in methods of coal transportation. Money was made available for road improvements by the introduction of the Turnpike System to Scotland in the middle of the 18th Century, when barriers were set up to make sure that road users paid a contribution towards the cost of upkeep. The roads linking Prestonpans, Wallyford and Tranent were such roads.[40] Coal for local trade was carried by human bearers, with horse or donkey used for longer journeys.[41] However, the turnpike system does not seem to have generated much improvement in the transportation of Lothian coal to the city of Edinburgh. In the early 18th Century:

> "...the state of the roads did not admit of vehicles of any kind being employed in connection with coals or any heavy traffic"[42]

and conditions did not seem to have greatly improved 100 years later:

"carts are badly constructed, and frequently not five inches deep at the sides...the condition of the horses accords somewhat with the construction of the cart...the general weight brought to the city is 12 cwts. to 15 cwts."[43]

Given these circumstances, it is hardly surprising that Lothian mine owners were at the forefront in the development of an alternative system, the waggonway, where wagons were hauled by horses along wooden or metal rails. The Tranent and Cockenzie waggonway, laid in 1722, was the earliest in Scotland. It was initiated by the London-based York Buildings Company, who acquired land in the aftermath of the rebellion of 1715. It was eventually taken over by the Cadells, who replaced the wooden rails with cast iron in 1815.[44]

Other waggonways included the Edinburgh and Dalkeith Railway, also known as the 'Innocent Railway', initially constructed in 1831, with a branch line laid to Fisherrow in Musselburgh in 1834. Up until its takeover by the North British Railway in 1845, this line, which is now a pedestrian and cycle path, transported up to 300 tons of coal each day. The Innocent Railway is also notable for its use of a stationary steam engine to draw waggons upward where the slope was too steep for horses.[45] Another waggonway was Sir John Hope's Pinkie railway, running between Pinkiehill and Fisherrow in 1814.[46] When we consider that a horse could pull about 48 cwt. up a slope on these waggonways, compared to a human bearer in a stairpit hauling about 3 cwt., it is evident why Cadell's Tranent and Cockenzie waggonway was well used for over 160 years, until the coming of the North British Railway line and its steam locomotives.

Since steam power was used largely for pumping water and raising coal, there was initially little change to methods of underground working. In about 1840, traditional "stoop and room" was challenged by a new method, known as "longwall", which used timber to support a wider coal face so that greater quantities of coal could be extracted more easily.[47] However, this change in mining methods still relied on human power to cut and carry coal. Not all seams could be worked by this method and this was particularly true of some East Lothian mines, including Prestongrange. Longwall had replaced stoop and room in many mines by the end of the 19th Century, but at Prestongrange, stoop and room continued in certain seams well into the 20th.[48]

As seam workings extended further underground, bearers were used to transport coal from the face to the tunnels and then to the pit bottom. These were usually women or girls. But this was not simply because women were regarded as a convenient source of unskilled labour: men had the strength to work the coal, but women had the stamina to haul it.

"...the miner always preferred the girl to the boy, for, strange as it may appear, a woman or girl could always carry about double the weight of coal that a man or boy could."[49]

As long as a ready supply of human labour was available, the only incentive to improve underground haulage was that faster haulage meant more coal was shifted and therefore profits were increased. Baskets carried on the back were eventually replaced by the use of wooden boxes which were harnessed to the 'putter' as the women were called, then dragged to the pit bottom. Later, wheeled wagons known as 'slypes', or 'hutches' were pulled along roadways and eventually, many of these roadways were laid with rails to speed up the movement of coal.[50]

The passing of laws to prevent women working underground meant that by 1844 there were no more female bearers in East Lothian mines. There were two direct results of the change in the labour force brought about by the 1842 Act: an increase in both the number of railed tunnels and the use of ponies for underground haulage.[51] However, horses could only be used in passages wide enough to allow them to move freely. Smaller ponies were particularly valued: in 1858, a total of 400 shetland ponies were bought from the Shetland Islanders by one single dealer alone. By 1860, the cost of a shetland pony had increased fourfold.[52]

Steam-powered machinery did not, therefore, replace the horse and at least one reason for this is demonstrated in the following story from a local pit. When the miners finished their shift, they discovered that the horse which operated the gin was busy elsewhere:

> "...the men...shouted for hours for the "bucket", but did not get up until the horse came back from delivering an order."[53]

It would not have been possible to dismantle a winding engine, use it to power a wagon for deliveries, then reassemble it to lift the miners out of the pit at the end of their shift – the horse was a great deal more flexible than an engine.

Horse shoeing at Prestongrange
East Lothian Council, David Spence Collection

View of Prestongrange colliery with horse and gig in the forefront
East Lothian Council, David Spence Collection

RAILWAYS

Although the application of steam to pumping and winding engines was recognised from the earliest days of steam power, its application to transportation was an equally important one, resulting in the development of a country-wide railway network between the years 1800 and 1870.

Watt's 'improved' steam engine design was not, initially, appropriate for use with a moving vehicle. The mechanism was too heavy and unwieldy and further modifications were required before it could be used to power transportation.[54] Nevertheless, by 1815, at the close of the Napoleonic Wars, early mobile engines were making an appearance and by 1825, the Stockton and Darlington Railway was hauling goods wagons by steam power. Experiments in steam powered engines for transportation were under way in the West of Scotland by 1817.[55] Both East and West Scotland were equally enthusiastic about this innovative transport method and its potential to revolutionise coal transportation. A large steam engine used about one ton of coal and the labour of two men – driver and fireman – to pull about 550 tons of coal for 60 miles.

The Innocent Railway, with its stationary engine, was authorised by the crown in 1826. In 1836, the Edinburgh, Leith and Granton Railway received royal assent and by 1842, the Edinburgh and Glasgow line had joined the major cities of the East and West coasts with stations at Haymarket in Edinburgh and Queen Street in Glasgow. From 1840 onwards, railway lines proliferated at a great rate. In the 1840s, most of the Lothian lines, had been absorbed by the North British Railway and rails were converted to a standard gauge (ie the distance between the rails), so that locomotives could travel from one line to another.[56]

By 1846, the Edinburgh to Berwick railway line was taking coal from Cadell's waggonway at Meadowmill for transportation elsewhere.[57] The coastal mines of East Lothian and others inland were linked via a series of marshalling yards and junctions, not only to the shipping ports of Leith and Granton and the city of Edinburgh, but to anywhere else they could compete economically with other pits. It was because of the new rail network, the advances in pumping and lifting equipment and the enormous appetite of the developing iron and gas industries for Scotland's coal, that the owner of Prestongrange, Sir James Grant Suttie, became interested in expanding the mining operations on his estate.

THE GEDDES REPORT

In 1824, John Geddes prepared a report on the Preston Grange Coalfield.[58] This report is a fascinating look at the industrial landscape around Prestonpans in the early 19th Century, including the area round the Wallyford mine, at that time owned and operated by the Marquess of Lothian.

There were four main elements to Geddes' report: the amount of coal remaining in various parts of the estate, the water courses underground, the cost of establishing a new mine and the accessibility of transport and markets for the coal, given the proposed "Rail-way to Edinburgh and Haddington."[59] Any recommendation, therefore, was closely linked to the twin elements of machinery and transportation.

Geddes was supplied with some estate plans, although these did not cover the whole extent of mineworkings on the estate. Such earlier plans as existed, of both the surface and the workings beneath, showed that old seam workings often linked one pit with another below the surface.[60] The problem of identifying the relationships between this network of old workings made it extremely difficult to identify the most economic location for a new mining operation.

Some of his calculations of available coal were based on the result of borings near Dolphinstone, which involved drilling small holes down from the surface to determine what lay beneath. Elsewhere, Geddes was forced to rely on observations of the land surface, comments from the owner, the memories of tenants currently living on the estate and what few documents were available.

> "These calculations can not however be depended on as absolutely exhibiting the remaining coal. They are assumed from data which are rather uncertain nothing being known of the extent of the old Wastes, or of the true line [ie the slant] of the old Dip-head levels."[61]

Geddes was extremely careful to avoid any categorical statements. With many 'ifs' and 'buts', he concluded that significant amounts of coal exist on the estate, particularly to the north, ie towards the Firth of Forth. His observation of the presence of ironstone, confirmed in a plan of 1825,[62] offers an insight into the dominance of the west of Scotland in terms of its ironworks:

> "The working of Ironstone in the lands of Preston Grange could not at present be attended with profit, there being no ironwork to consume the same nearer than Carron and these works can be supplied with this material at a cheaper rate in their immediate neighbourhood."[63]

Geddes also observed that the Prestongrange coals were a continuation of seams worked by the Wallyford mine, therefore a new coal working deeper than the existing Wallyford mine would be likely to cause flooding in the new workings. His calculation of the depth required for a new pit was 50 fathoms, while the Wallyford pit as this time extended only to a depth of 39 fathoms. This was important in terms of the pumping equipment which would have to be installed at Prestongrange. Another option, to track the course of the old day levels, or drainage channels, to the sea and renew and extend them, would, he concluded, be "difficult and expensive".[64]

Geddes was extremely wary of offering categorical advice on the best way for Grant Suttie to ensure maximum profit from his mining operations. He presents two options: either to lease the property to Wallyford mine, in which case the expense of the erection of

> "an engine of sufficient power on the Preston Grange Lands"[65]

would be unnecessary. Alternatively, the property could be leased to another tenant, who might be expected to bear the costs of such an engine themselves. By the beginning of the 19th Century, the cost of equipment to work the coal at deep levels was promoting the move from individual to company ownership.

An appendix to this report in April 1825, by Robert Bald, a civil engineer and surveyor, was inclined to be more positive.[66] From old colliery plans, John Geddes' report and a survey of his own, Bald concluded that a combination of clearing out part of the old day level and the erection of an engine would result in enough drainage to allow further mining to take place, though southward rather than under the Forth. However, he does inject a note of caution:

> "...as there is every reason to apprehend that the quantity of water will be very considerable, the power of the Engine would, consequently, require to be great."[67]

Bald also proposed

> "The whole machinery and Fitting of the Colliery to be done at the Tenants expence: the landlord to have it in his power at the end of the Lease to take the whole, or any part of the Machinery he may choose according to the valuation of men mutually chosen."[68]

MATTHIAS DUNN

The leasing of land by George Grant Suttie to Matthias Dunn in 1830 and the sinking of the No. 1 shaft to reopen the mine after more than 65 years, marks the birth of the modern Prestongrange mine.[69] Dunn, from Newcastle, was a prominent mining engineer at the forefront of developments in mining technology. His shaft introduced the first iron 'tubbing' or shaft lining (previously, a combination of stone, timber and clay had been used) to Scotland, and the drainage of water was by a steam pumping engine.[70]

A plan of the mine workings drawn up in 1838 by George Buchanan (which also includes later, undated additions)[71] identifies a waggon road from the pit bottom to the workings and there is evidence that Dunn and his manager, Moore, replaced the use of bearers with wheeled rails.[72] The coal was lifted onto these rails by means of a crane, then transported by waggon along the rails. However, in 1838, Dunn gave up the lease and by 1840 the workings were flooded yet again. It would seem that both owner and leesee learnt a bitter lesson: the market for coal, with its rise and fall in prices together with the enormous expense of the machinery involved required restraint on both sides in the pursuit of profit.

> "..the casualties of coal-mining are such as to entitle a tenant of capital and enterprise to good consideration from his landlord and that landlords often get punished for failing to do this."[73]

However we can be grateful for this disagreement between owner and leesee – it was probably responsible for the existence of Buchanan's plan.

CORNISH BEAM ENGINE ARRIVES

In 1850, the Prestongrange Company took over the lease. They re-sunk Dunn's shaft to the Beggar seam as a pumping pit and sunk No. 2, the Jewel shaft. This company, based in Cornwall, were responsible for the erection of the beam engine, shipped to Prestongrange in parts and assembled on site. Cornish tin mines had long been used to deep workings and this type of engine was commonly known as a Cornish Beam Engine.[74] We gain some insight into the effect of such massive machines on pre-industrial society from a description of a similar engine seen by the poets Wordsworth and Coleridge on a trip to Scotland in 1803:

> "...it was impossible not to invest the machine with some faculty of intellect; it seemed to have made the first step from brute matter to life and purpose, showing its progress by great power."[75]

The original pump installed by Matthias Dunn was presumably on the surface, as was common in the early days, for safety reasons. The Cornish engine had two main pumps below ground, one at the depth of the Great Seam, 420 feet below the surface and another halfway between the Great Seam and the surface, plus another, lower pump at the level of the Beggar Seam, at a depth of 766 feet. Pumps were driven by steam from the surface and could pump water out of the pit at a rate of 650 gallons per minute.[76] Given the quantities of water, it is clear that without steam power, there would have been no possibility of extracting coal at Prestongrange at these depths.

In 1850 the junction for the mineral railway, linking Prestongrange Colliery with the main East coast line was opened.[77] The inventory of George Grant Suttie's estate in 1872 includes:

> "Rails, sleepers and other articles...used in the formation and working of Railways for conveying Coals from the pit head to any Railway or other place where they are sold or disposed of."[78]

The inventory also mentions sleepers and other equipment for use on underground railed roadways.

After 1876, when Morrison's Haven harbour was rebuilt, railway lines ran from the mine and there were facilities for loading coal onto ships for the overseas trade, as well as a tram line running to the harbour from the Summerlee brickworks.[79] The landscape of the mine was radically different from the grass covered slopes of today. The area was covered in a network of buildings which housed workshops, engine houses, locomotive sheds and stables for horses, a network of railway lines and sidings, and a link to a stone quarry close to where Sam Burns' yard is today. The mineral railway connecting the mine to the main line included further junctions and storage sidings for wagons beside the main line.[80]

The estate inventory lists a wide range of equipment in use shortly before the installation of the beam engine in 1874, although again, it is important to bear in mind that this was equipment in use throughout the Prestongrange estate.[81] Two "water" engines are referred to, one with one and the other with two boilers, the latter described as old. This, perhaps, was the engine installed at the time of the original sinking of the No. 1 shaft by Matthias Dunn.

Mention is also made of "air pumping machines", though these are not fully described and are unlikely to be of recent development since there was little, if any, interest in the use of fans to circulate air until the end of the 19th Century. Ventilation at this time was still by means of a furnace near the pit bottom. Suspicion amongst mine owners regarding innovations in ventilation were to some extent justified: some early mechanical ventilators were up to 40 feet in diameter and their installation was no easy task.[82]

Also included in this inventory is reference to a gig engine with winding apparatus and ropes, so it is likely that horse gins were still in use, although another entry referring to

> "old materials of Gig and water engine with pipes and pump rods and Boiler"[83]

makes it clear that much of what was in operation at this time was a combination of old and new.

In spite – or perhaps because – of the massive investment represented by the beam engine, the Prestongrange Company failed in 1893,[84] but after a gap of only two years, the mine was taken over, by The Summerlee Coal and Iron Company, who leased Prestongrange from 1895 until nationalisation over fifty years later.

SUMMERLEE COAL & IRON

This company, based in Coatbridge, had strong links with the West of Scotland, which was at the forefront of industrial innovation. The parent company produced iron as well as pumping and winding engines for mines throughout the country. Summerlee was responsible for the first iron steamboat built in the early years of the Clydeside shipping industry. The company owned eight blast furnaces in Coatbridge and were owners or leesees of over 10 collieries, mostly around Glasgow and the West, as well as the Prestongrange Colliery in East Lothian and its associated brick and fireclay works.[85]

Summerlee had the breadth of experience and the financial wherewithal to develop Prestongrange and the early 20th Century were years of unparalleled growth and expansion, when Prestongrange coal played its part in fuelling Scotland's industrial development.

The pace of change in these years brought about a proliferation of legislation. In earlier centuries, laws were primarily concerned to make sure that the profits to be made from coal mining were liable to taxation, that the coal seams were protected from damage and that an adequate workforce was available to work the coal.[86]

Although legislation in the later 19th and early 20th Centuries still concerned itself with these issues, many of the new laws dealt with the need to regulate the use of equipment, which was constantly evolving. Regulations were exhaustive, covering use and storage of explosives, boilers, engines, furnaces, haulage, winding, coal sorting, horses, locomotives and associated equipment above and below ground.[87] With the advent of electricity, an even greater weight of legislation was added to what was already in force and coverage was, if anything, even more detailed.

By 1870, the national rail network was largely complete. Scottish lines extended both up and down the country, meeting up with English lines to complete the network of rail transportation. Coal mines were linked to industry by a network of mineral railways, junctions and canals and Scotland's industries were competing ably in national and international markets. Small railway companies had been absorbed, to form such giants as the North British Railway, standardisation of main railway lines was complete and economic conflict with England had shrunk to the level of mere rivalry.[88]

Many of the iron companies of the west expanded their operations to include the building of steam engines for the rail network. Manufacturers such as the firm of Andrew Barclay of Kilmarnock not only built steam locomotives for use at Prestongrange,[89] they also provided materials for other types of steam engine. They were, for example, responsible for manufacturing new pump barrels, rams and valves for improvements to the pumping capacity of the Cornish beam engine in 1905: the Summerlee Iron Company carried out the installation.[90]

The style and capacity of engines and wagons developed for industrial haulage in the early days remained largely unchanged. Wagons were wood, of 10–12 ton capacity; traffic on mineral railways was slow, averaging about 11 kilometers an hour, partly because braking systems for wagons had to be operated manually and engines had to be stopped while this was in progress. Industrial haulage was concerned with heavy loads travelling relatively short distances, but by the early years of the 20th Century, main line train services were increasingly interested in speed and economy in the fuel they used and the design of main line and industrial locomotives began to diverge.[91] A report on the testing of Prestongrange coal on the 9.30 am Edinburgh to Carlisle passenger train in 1909 found it to be:

> "...a very swift coal, not at all durable...the several different wagons contained various qualities...re wagon no. 16968 – all dirt. The coal is ... fairly good steam coal but burns away quickly when the engine is working very heavily... not a suitable coal for heavy express work."[92]

At Prestongrange, as with other mineral railways, specific sidings were earmarked for particular destinations. A map dated 1911[93] lists the location of wagons for land sale in the south, others for Leith north and south, for Granton and closed wagons for "shipment", presumably abroad. The sorting of coal into different types and different destinations was an important one. As mentioned earlier, different coals were suitable for different purposes, some for household use, others for industry.

However, industrial development at this time was not problem free: the 19th Century saw the birth of the labour force as a political power, marked by disputes between owners and workers in the form of strikes and lock-outs.[94] But famine in Ireland brought a steady stream of immigrants to the West coast, eager for employment[95] and the extensive mining operations resulting from the application of steam power to the mining industry required a much increased labour force. In 1900, there were 439 employed at Prestongrange Pit, 61 above ground and 378 below – by 1910, this total had risen to 873, 153 above and 720 below.[96] Many of these were immigrants from Ireland who gradually moved eastward into the Lothians, bringing radical change to the traditional mining communities of East Lothian.

As mineworkings at Prestongrange reached deeper below the surface, pressure increased on existing methods of operation. A second edition of Buchanan's map in 1882,[97] indicates that much of the coal below the land had either been exhausted, in the case of the Great Seam, or were arrested by areas of burnt coal or areas where folds in the seams created rock barriers. At the same time, improvements in boring techniques allowed engineers to test for the presence of coal in previously inaccessible areas, while improvements in shaft construction and haulage machinery meant that coal could be lifted from deep workings.[98]

By the turn of the century, only the Clay and Five-foot Seams were being worked under the land. Other workings extended seawards, from between 300–900 feet below sea level, working the Great (still by stoop and room), the Jewel and the Beggar Seams.[99] The extent of these workings brought rapid change to the machinery in use.

The traditional furnace method of ventilation was inadequate to meet the demands of depths where the temperature itself became an issue: a depth of 900 feet would mean a temperature increase of approximately 18 degrees Fahrenheit, excluding the additional heat generated by human labour and the operation of machinery. Furthermore, the air entering and leaving the shafts caused significant draughts, resulting in wind velocities at times of over 1 kilometre per minute. These elements, together with the need to circulate breathable air and avoid the gathering of poisonous or explosive gases, created a need for improved methods of ventilation.[100]

Early equipment was large, steam-powered and relied on a revolving fan. Later "axial flow" fans used a series of blades which did not change the direction of air flow and therefore required less energy to run.[101] In 1900, the fan in operation at Prestongrange was a 22 inch Guibal fan, 7 feet wide.[102] In 1906, a new shaft, No. 3, was sunk to provide additional ventilation.[103]

The quantities of water associated with Prestongrange had always been problematic. By the 1890s, the Cornish engine, even with additional support from steam and hydraulic engines below ground, was certainly finding it difficult to cope. On several occasions, the strain proved too great and significant repairs had to be made. By 1900, an hydraulic engine, using water pressure to run the pumps, was in the process of construction as an additional means of pumping water away from the workings.

"Conditions at Prestongrange...were such that a much higher pressure [than that supplied by a normal hydraulic pump] of drive water was required, consequently a ram pump, driven by a steam engine, was installed on the surface...The steam engine and ram pump were designed and manufactured by the Summerlee Iron Company."[104]

ELECTRIC POWER

By 1910, an electric turbine pump had been installed at the pit bottom, which pumped water at 3 times the previous rate.[105]

Steam power for underground haulage was initially used only on tracks which were too steep to allow ready haulage by horse or human. Full wagons were attached by rope and pulled up the incline by steam power: empty wagons ran backwards simply by the effect of gravity. By 1841, high-pressure steam winding engines were introduced to Scottish pits and a number of systems came into use.[106]

At Prestongrange, by 1900, the system was Endless Rope Haulage, where a continuous rope travelled along the tunnels which connected the pit bottom to the workings. This system was driven by two engines located on the surface, using steel ropes. There was also an elevator for raising the dross left after the coal was removed "capable of raising fifty tons per hour". The Endless Rope system was also used to lift coal to the surface.[107] Hemp (vegetable fibre) ropes were used as winding ropes at some East Lothian collieries as late as the 1880s,[108] but presumably, given the weight being lifted, at Prestongrange, these, too, were steel.

Generally speaking, throughout the 19th Century, little effort was put into the sorting and cleaning of coal: in the middle of the century:

"What is now called 'coal preparation' was virtually unknown. The object was round coal, and to that end the drawer had to fill his hutch with a harp shovel, i.e., one with slots through which the dross passed and was flung back in the waste."[109]

By 1900, at Prestongrange, this situation had changed radically. Although human labour was still used to sort coal from stone, much of the process was mechanised: tumblers were used to shake coal and fireclay free of surrounding matter as well as screens and riddles (metal grilles) which sorted the coal into different sizes. Loading the coal onto wagons was also a mechanised process.[110]

A washer for cleaning coal was installed at Prestongrange as early as 1895, claiming the distinction of being the first in the county. There was also great interest in the use of conveyor mechanisms to move the coal. Although the "jigger" conveyor, which carried coal along in pans, was not marketed until just before World War I, the General Manager at Prestongrange, David Marr Mowat had developed and installed his own version of this machine by about 1907.[111]

The narrowness and steep angle of many coal seams in Scotland encouraged development in coal cutting equipment. Unfortunately, early experimentation was hampered by the lack of a metal strong enough to withstand the abrasion from the coal seam. By the late 1880s, further refinements to these machines and the emergence of suitably strong metals resulted in the production of a number of mechanical coal cutters.[112]

All of these developments in mining equipment and methods must be viewed against the background of motive power: in 1850, steam engines were the only source of mechanical power and by 1900, developments had largely been in the form of refining steam engines to increase power by the addition of compressed air or hydraulic power to steam engines. In the 1850s, almost all machinery in use in East Lothian collieries was steam-driven.[113] As steam power evolved, machinery became less massive and more suitable for use in underground workings. Adaptations which combined steam power with the use of compressed air increased the efficiency of smaller machines, allowing them to use the force exerted by the compression of air to generate greater power and reduce energy loss.[114]

Throughout this time, horses, working alongside men and machines, continued to be valued as an essential part of mining operations. Although these animals rarely saw the light of day, the legislation surrounding the use of horses at pits is clear evidence of care: regulations directed that properly experienced people should care for horses and that properly regulated tests were conducted to be sure animals were healthy. Horses were to be housed in decent-sized stalls in a clean, well-ventilated stable away from haulage or travelling roads. They were not to work unless fit, properly shod, with proper harness and eye-guards and were not to be worked in places too small for them to pass through comfortably. At the end of their shift, they were to be supplied with wholesome food and pure water and should be examined, cleaned and groomed. A record book had to be kept and an annual report made, and any pain, injury, ill-treatment or overworking to be reported.[115]

However, it was not horses, steam, hydraulics or compressed air, but the growth of electrical power which had the potential to generate changes almost as far reaching as those resulting from the harnessing of steam power in the 19th Century. Electricity was in a process of constant development, but its application to mining methods was limited by the danger of explosion from sparks generated by the operation of electrical engines.[116] Nevertheless, although steam power continued as a major source of energy, electrical engines were seriously challenging its use in many areas.

Before 1910, when the electric turbine pump was installed to pump water from the workings at Prestongrange,

> "...all the electrical power for the pit was supplied by a 140 kw DC generator driven by a horizontal steam engine...[and] a little old dynamo for the lights driven by a 'grasshopper' which was accounted the sweetest running engine in the place"[117]

It is interesting to note in passing that the respect people had displayed towards the early engines was by now replaced in many cases by affection. Perhaps this was due to their smaller size, but clearly people had developed a very personal relationship with mechanical equipment, a situation which remains true even today.

Electrical power was seen to be as far reaching as steam had been a hundred years before, part of an evolutionary process which would continue into the future. Steam, compressed air and hydraulic pumps would be replaced by electrically powered equipment because it was:

> "...more easily transported, with less loss in transmission [ie the amount of power generated relative to the amount of power put to use]. It

revolutionised underground transport because it was far easier to install a haulage motor than to make and maintain a road for a horse."[118]

The applications of electric power seemed endless: safer lamps for miners; smaller machinery which could cut coal from seams too narrow or awkward to reach; deeper mineworkings supported by electrical ventilation, pumping and haulage and lifting equipment; faster movement of coal from the face, with automated loading and sorting to speed up the process from coal cutting to railway siding or dock.[119] The technology to transform the railway network existed as early as 1897, when Rudolph Diesel developed a working model of an engine which combined oil as fuel and electrical power.[120]

UNDER INVESTMENT BLIGHTS DEVELOPMENT

However, the optimism of these early years did not last. By 1915, industrial growth in Scotland had begun to die away and developments in the use of mechanical power became piecemeal and erratic. Statistics for coal production between 1800 and 1935 reveal the increases in output resulting from the application of machine mining. But equally, regional and national variations in coal production show how growth in the late 19th and early 20th Centuries had became years of stagnation and decline.[121]

In 1800, the total coal output for the whole of Britain was 10 million tons. By 1870, Scotland alone produced 15 million tons and by 1913, the Scottish coalfields were producing 42 and a half million tons. Two years later, output in Scotland had dropped to 35 and a quarter million tons a year and this decline in output continued almost uninterrupted until, by the end of World War II, the Scottish output had shrunk to a little over 20 million tons a year.

The second important element in these figures is the comparison they offer between different coal-producing areas: in 1880, Lanarkshire produced 54.81% of Scotland's coal, by 1910, the figure was 43.29% and by 1935, only 28.62%. For East and Mid Lothian, the reverse was true: 5.67% in 1880, 9.87% in 1910 and 15.37% in 1935.[122]

From 1915 onwards, coal production in Scotland was diminishing. At the same time, the coalfields of Lanarkshire, where industrial development was at its height, were shrinking and the smaller coalfields of the Lothians were proportionally increasing their contribution to the shrinking total of Scotland's coal production.

The extraction of coal in the west of Scotland had been the impetus which fuelled industrial development of equipment and machinery – but accessible coal seams were becoming exhausted by intensive mining and new seams were often too technically difficult to exploit.[123] Greater reliance was placed on supplies of East Lothian coal, but the slowing pace of coal mining in the west affected industrial development throughout Scotland.

Furthermore, the fact that electrical power was increasingly put to use in the 1920s and 1930s gives a misleading impression of progress during these years. The technical innovation that promoted the use of electrical machinery was essentially a 19th Century development.[124] A clearer indication of the pace of industry after World War I is seen in the fact that the application of electric power did not advance at the rate typified by the early years of steam.

In 1905, coal cutting machines in Scotland were producing two and a quarter million tons of coal, but only about 50% of these were electric.[125] Even though electrically powered machines were produced as far back as 1887, compressed-air machines were in use well into the 20th Century.[126]

Similarly, although coal conveyors were patented as early as 1902, these were far from universal: even in the 1940s, Prestongrange did not have a continuous belt conveyor for shifting coal.[127] There was little investment in equipment such as power loaders which could take full advantage of the speed of the belt conveyor and the pace of production remained tied to the manual loading of the belt at the face. Although some collieries did invest in electrical equipment – Elphinstone Colliery near Tranent purchased an electrically-driven coal cutter in 1890,[128] the use of electricity in East Lothian was not widespread in the early years of the 20th Century. At the start of the century, most mining machinery, including that in use at Prestongrange, still relied largely on steam power and even as late as 1910 only one East Lothian pit (Woodall) was using electric power for coalcutting.[129]

The reason for such a slow pace of development was both economic and technical. Mine owners were increasingly unwilling to invest in new equipment, claiming that increases in government taxation did not allow them a fair return on their investment.[130] By and large, electrical power replaced steam as a major motive force only where the changeover was a fairly straightforward process without significant alterations to tunnels and seam-workings, or where it was essential to maintain the workings – for example in the case of electrical pumping equipment at Prestongrange. The establishment of the Mining Institute of Scotland in 1878[131] had been intended to support and expand knowledge and experience, but without investment, new techniques could not be developed.

Not until nationalisation, when the government took over the coal mines in 1946–7 was there any large-scale redevelopment capable of taking full advantage of the potential of electric power. And, by that time, the concept of "rationalisation" meant that this was only undertaken at existing collieries if the expense was justified in terms of profit.[132] Mines which required too much investment were earmarked for closure. This was certainly not the future envisaged by mineworkers, engineers and managers in the early years of the 20th Century. To them, no doubt, it seemed that electrical power promised a future where technical development and increased coal production would continue long into the future.

The period between the first and second World Wars was typified by an increasing sense of decay in the mining industry. The building of welfare institutes, pithead bathhouses etc gives an impression of progress and certainly conditions for workers improved.[133] But as far as equipment was concerned, East Lothian mines, including Prestongrange were increasingly operating on outmoded or elderly machinery. A sense of the atmosphere in these years can be found in local press reports:

> "The annual holidays began on Friday, when the pits closed down for ten days. The duration of the holiday is exceptionally long, considering the quiet time...at some of the pits lately..."[134]

> "In a military sense the war is over and won, but in an economic sense it is raging as keenly and bitterly as the military war ever did."[135]

The struggle between owners and workers over conditions of employment was another contributing factor to mechanical deterioration: when pits stopped production due to industrial action or lock outs by owners, maintenance procedures could not be carried out and the extent of flooding in some East Lothian pits meant they were permanently closed and machinery lost.[136]

A list of equipment in use 1939, reveals some significant facts about coal mining at Prestongrange at the outbreak of World War II[137]: No. 2 pit, the Jewel, still used a steam hoist, although the air shaft at the harbour had an electric winder. A Norton engine with a 60 horsepower motor had replaced the original steam power for the washer installed in 1895, but electrical power was still supported by machinery installed in 1910 and 1916. A number of pumps and some drilling equipment listed is manufactured by Siemens, a German firm (which is still in existence) whereas most earlier machinery had been manufactured in Scotland.

What this demonstrates is that Scotland had lost its industrial lead. Whereas 19th Century growth allowed engineers to make full use of the applications of steam power, the period of stagnation following World War I meant that electrical power never developed its full potential at Prestongrange. Furthermore, the growing interest in alternative sources of power meant that coal was losing its attraction as a major fuel source. In the 1950s, hydro-electric power was in the process of development,[138] then later oil and gas from the North Sea, nuclear energy and, more recently, wind and wave power have all made a contribution to Scotland's energy resources.

Miners' reminiscences of their days at Prestongrange during World War II give a good idea of how little development had taken place since the early years of the century:

> "...during the war, there were no many what you call belt runs...it was what you called a road...a man had a hutch and a pony..the ponies pulled the hutches...they were pretty strong but they could only pull one because there were nae room...where the coal was lyin'..."[139]

Some innovations in equipment took place at this time, thanks to the lend-lease arrangement with the United States, when equipment was supplied to industry in Britain. Prestongrange benefited with the introduction of a machine known as a "joyloader", which speeded up the process of coal cutting.[140] But loss of manpower during the war, the cost of mechanisation and the fact that owners were not prepared to invest in case of subsequent nationalisation meant that by the end of the war, Prestongrange pit was in the final stages of the decline which led to its closure in 1962. In 1948, East Lothian produced 870,000 tons of coal – 230,000 tons less than in 1939.[141]

A map, loosely dated 1947,[142] shows the deterioration since the early years of the century. The pre-war trade with Europe was never adequately re-established, especially at small harbours such as Morrison's Haven. By this time, the railway line to the harbour and the harbour crane were gone. A large number of railway lines around the mine had been lifted and there was little in the way of industrial addition – most new building was related to the welfare of the workforce, pithead baths, and an ambulance house, for example. The only piece of equipment added was one extra washer.

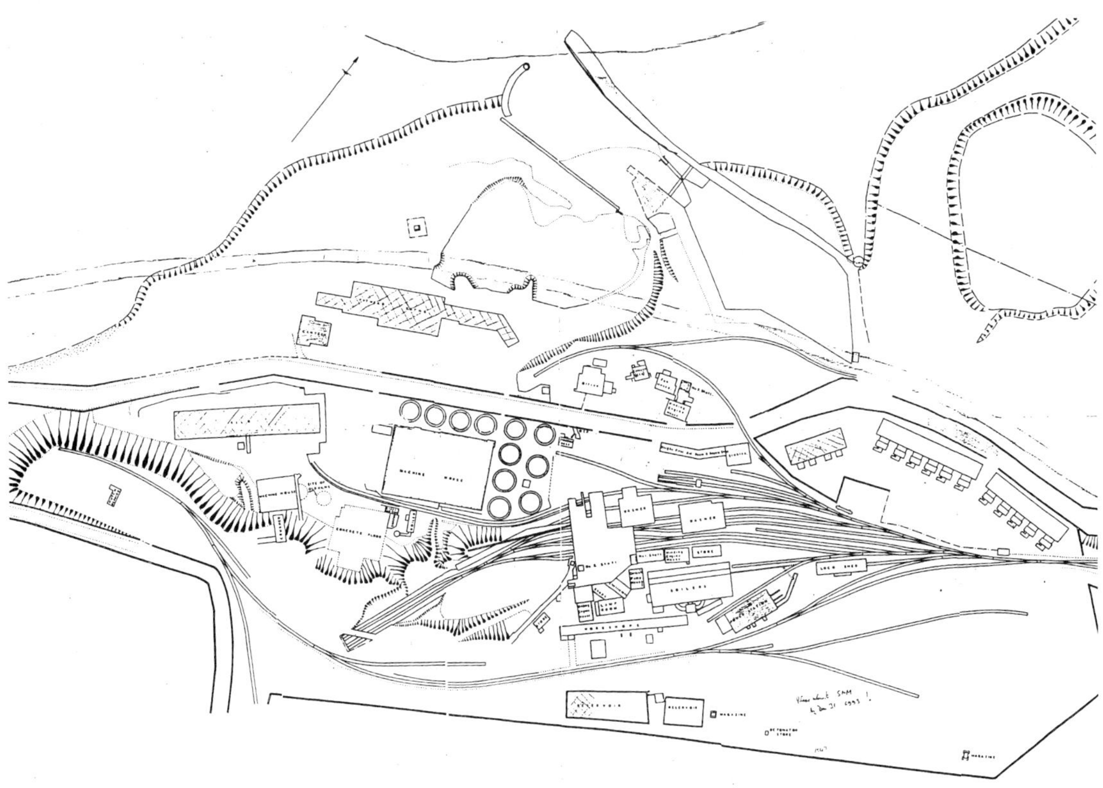

Map showing Sidings at Prestongrange colliery c.1943
Courtesy of the National Archives of Scotland

NATIONALISATION'S INVESTMENT PROGRAMME

Nationalisation in 1947 brought large scale redevelopment for Scotland's coalfields, including the sinking of new pits, with wide tunnels of reinforced concrete, haulage engines and mechanised cutting, conveying sorting and washing.[143] For a short time, there was a mood of optimism, reinforced by improvements in working conditions. In 1953, the estimated coal reserves in the East Lothian coalfield were 1230 million tons, extending up to three miles under the Forth.[144] and although some coal seams at Prestongrange were worked out, a great deal of coal remained. East Lothian employment estimates in 1950[145] show 694 people employed at the mine and suggest a projected employment figure of 755 between 1961 and 1965. But although productivity figures at Prestongrange were not low,

> "Prestongrange, with its narrow roadways was not suitable for mechanisation."[146]

Despite innovation on a larger scale in other East Lothian mines, Prestongrange was only one of many pits identified as uneconomic. Between 1959 and 1965, 13 East Lothian mines closed, bringing mining in East Lothian to an end,[147] except for open cast mining such as that conducted at

Coal trucks entertain the local miners' children
East Lothian Council, David Spence Collection

Blindwells, which, strangely enough, represents a large-scale return to the drift mine of the early centuries. At the closure of Prestongrange mine in 1962, the number of workers employed was 696, almost exactly what it had been 12 years earlier.[148]

A visitor to the quiet, grass-covered site of Prestongrange colliery today will find it difficult to imagine the bustle and vigour of the mine in the early years of the 20th Century, just as the mine workers at the time would have found it hard to believe that their way of life, so well established and solidly based, would have disappeared only 70 years later. In the days of full production, the air was filled with the hum of electric generators, the deeper beat of the pumping machines, the constant clamour of men and machinery as haulage engines transported the coal to harbour and railway line. At the brickwork, lorries waited to be loaded with bricks and pipes still warm from the firing, while the women of Morrison's Haven were engaged in their constant battle against the ever-present dust and children were everywhere busy about their lives.

Through the buildings and equipment remaining today, it is possible to chart the whole progress of Prestongrange, from the sinking of Matthias Dunn's original shaft. The beam engine house, surrounded by relics of pumping engines, electrical ventilation and winding machines, remains as a tribute to the art of those early engineers in that so much of it remains intact, nearly 130 years after it was erected. There are wagons which were used for transporting coal both underground and on the surface, and the steam engines which pulled them offer another demonstration of the strength and durability of Scottish engineering. The steam crane is not the original one used at Prestongrange and is an interesting anomaly: although it is of English manufacture, the building of steam cranes was in fact a Scottish specialisation.[149] The pithead baths and the canteen, clearly later additions, show how the working conditions of miners changed over the years. No trace of the horses remains, though they, like the people, were there at the start of mining at Prestongrange and survived well into the 20th Century, through their usefulness in terms of mobility, flexibility and strength.

Above: Lothians Southern Engine No. 17 at work at Prestongrange

Below: Prestongrange Steam Engine No. 7 entertains visitors at Prestongrange Museum
East Lothian Council, David Spence Collection

BIBLIOGRAPHY

Primary Sources

McKechnie, J and Macgregor, M, *A Short History of the Scottish Coal-Mining Industry*, National Coal Board, Scottish Division (publications), 1958
McMarland, P, Interview Transcript (Duncan Graham Russell), Open University Project "Wartime Trouble at the Pits – the East Lothian Case", 1998
McMarland, P, Interview Transcript (William Bush), Open University Project "Wartime Trouble at the Pits – the East Lothian Case", 1998
National Coal Board, Scottish Division, Lothians Area, *Prestongrange Colliery Manpower Deployment Summary*, 1962, Spence Collection
Statistics on employment at various mines, ref: 7.35, 1900, 1910

East Lothian Libraries and Museums

East Lothian Libraries: Collection on Mining:
Dott, G, letter accompanying notes for *A Century of East Lothian Mining*,
Dott, G, Notes for *A Century of East Lothian Mining*, August 1958
Dott, G, *A Century of East Lothian Mining*, from *Haddingtonshire Courier*, 20 Nov, 1959
East Lothian County Council Survey Report, 1953
East Lothian Libraries: the Last Pits in East Lothian, Dates of Abandonment
East Lothian Libraries, Mining at Prestongrange: some source extracts with a commentary, no date
Snodgrass, C, Third Statistical Account, 1953

Local History Centre

Harvie, C, *Scotland's Earliest Railway, Scotsman*, Sat 7 April, 1962
Shaw, JP, *Water Power and Rural Industry*, 1989

National Library of Scotland

Narrative of the Management of Coal Work at Prestongrange from 2 April 1748, National Library of Scotland

Scottish Records Office

Memorandum to enable Engine Maker to prepare Inventory of Valuation of Moveable and personal Property at Sir George Grant Suttie's Collieries, from 'List of Engines and Machinery', 1872
Report regarding the Preston Grange Coalfield the Property of Sir James Suttie Baronet, 1824, plus appendix 1825

West Register House

Dott, G, *Early Scottish Colliery Waggonways*, 1947
Report on Tests of Locomotive Coals, 1909–10
Plan of Prestongrange Colliery Sidings and maps 1898 – 1912

Loose papers

Dott, G, Notes on Three Early Plans of Prestongrange, Nov 1943
Dott, G, Notes on Three Early Plans of Prestongrange – additional sheet no. 2
Dott, G (?) Notes on Prestongrange Estate Plans 1796–1812 (no date)
Edinburgh Society of Model Engineers, Notes on Cornish Beam Engine at Prestongrange Colliery, 1950
Engineering Branch, Notes on Hydraulic Pumps at Prestongrange Colliery, 1968
Engineering Branch, Notes on the Origin of the Summerlee Iron Co. Ltd., 1968

List of Equipment at Prestongrange 1939
Prestongrange Winning: Account of Sinking of Shaft by Matthias Dunn

Secondary Sources

Cunningham, A S, *Mining in Mid and East Lothian: History of the Industry from Earliest Times to Present Day*, 1925
Edgington, D, *Old Stationary Engines*, 1996
Greig, J, (ed), *Scots Minstrelsie*, Vol II, 1892, p. 200
Hayes, G, *Industrial Steam Locomotives*, 1998
Keay, J and Keay, J, (eds), *Collins Encyclopaedia of Scotland*, 1994
Lynch, M, *Scotland: a New History*, 1992
McNeil, Tranent and its Surroundings, 1883
The Story of Prestonpans from Contemporary Records 1790s– 1950s, East Lothian District Library, 1995
Wordsworth, D, *Recollections of a Tour Made in Scotland*, 1803

Maps

Ordnance Survey sheets IV.8 (Edinburghshire), VIII (Haddingtonshire), 1907: Prestonpans Parish 1908
Map of Prestongrange Colliery (hand-dated 1947 on original)

Newspapers, Journals and Periodicals

Duckham, Baron F, *Some Eighteenth-Century Scottish Coal Mining Methods: the "Dissertation" of Sir John Clerk, Industrial Archaeology*, Vol 5, No 3, August 1968
Caledonian Mercury, 13 June, 1727
Colliery Guardian, 17 August 1900
Haddington Courier, 25 July 1924, 7 November 1924
National Coal Board Diary, 1937: legislation
Transactions of the Institute of Mining Engineers, Vol CI, Part 12, September 1942

Other

The Innocent Railway, Lothian Regional Council Leaflet, 1990
L'il Beginnings Miniature Horses Website: http://www.xcelco.on.ca/~mchorses

NOTES

1 McKechnie, J and Macgregor, M, *A Short History of the Scottish Coal-Mining Industry*, 1958, pp. 19–33
2 Ibid, p. 35
3 Ibid, p. 36
4 Cunningham, A S, *Mining in Mid and East Lothian: History of the Industry from Earliest Times to Present Day*, 1925, p. 4
5 Ibid, p. 5
6 Lynch, M, *Scotland: A New History*, 1992, ch. 8
7 Op cit., McKechnie, J and Macgregor, M, p. 14
8 Ibid, p. 39
9 Keay, J and Keay, J, (eds), *Collins Encyclopaedia of Scotland*, 1994, p. 737
10 McNeil, *Tranent and its Surroundings*, 1883, pp. 17–18
11 Ibid, p. 39
12 Ibid, facing p. 25
13 Duckham, Baron F, *Some Eighteenth-Century Scottish Coal Mining Methods: the "Dissertation" of Sir John Clerk, Industrial Archaeology*, Vol 5, No 3, August 1968, pp. 223–224
14 Shaw, JP, *Water Power and Rural Industry in East Lothian*, 1989

15 Op cit., Duckham, Baron F, p. 224
16 Narrative of the Management of Coal Work at Prestongrange from 2 April 1748, National Library of Scotland
17 Dott, G, *Notes on Three Early Plans of Prestongrange*, Nov 1943
18 Geddes, J, *Report Regarding the Preston Grange Coalfield the Property of Sir James Suttie Baronet*, 1825, p. 1
19 Memorandum to enable Engine Maker to prepare Inventory of Valuation of Moveable and personal Property at Sir George Grant Suttie's Collieries, 1872
20 Op cit., McNeil, p. 22
21 Op cit., McKechnie, J and Macgregor, M, pp. 93–95
22 Op cit., McNeil, p. 15
23 Op cit., Keay, J and Keay, J, p. 174
24 Op cit., McKechnie, J and Macgregor, M, p. 42
25 *The Story of Prestonpans from Contemporary Records 1790s–1950s: Part One – the Statistical Account of Scotland 1791–1799*, pp. 15–16
26 Op cit., McKechnie, J and Macgregor, M, p. 76
27 Op cit., Cunningham, A S, p. 13
28 Op cit., Duckham, Baron F, p. 219
29 Op cit., Dott, G, *Notes on Three Early Plans of Prestongrange*, p. 3
30 Op cit., McKechnie, J and Macgregor, M, p. 48
31 Ibid, p. 52
32 Dott, G, *A Century of East Lothian Mining, Haddingtonshire Courier*, 20 Nov, 1959
33 Op cit., Keay, J and Keay, J, p. 545
34 Dott, G, *Early Scottish Colliery Waggonways*, 1947, p. 15
35 Greig, J, (ed), *Scots Minstrelsie*, Vol II, 1892, p. 200
36 Op cit., Duckham, Baron F, p. 228
37 Op cit., Dott, G, *Notes on Three Early Plans of Prestongrange*, p. 3
38 *Caledonian Mercury*, 13 June, 1727
39 Harvie, C, *Scotland's Earliest Railway, Scotsman*, Sat 7 April, 1962
40 Op cit., Geddes, J, p. 1
41 Op cit., McNeil, p. 17
42 Op cit., Cunningham, A S, p. 33
43 Ibid, p. 52
44 Op cit., Dott, G, *Early Scottish Colliery Waggonways*, pp. 15–16
45 *The Innocent Railway*, Lothian regional Council Leaflet, 1990
46 Op cit., Dott, G, *Early Scottish Colliery Waggonways*, p. 21
47 East Lothian Libraries, Mining at Prestongrange: some source extracts with a commentary, no date, p. 2
48 *Colliery Guardian*, 17 August 1900, p. 340
49 Op cit., McNeil, p. 28
50 Op cit., Cunningham, A S, p. 40
51 Ibid, p. 54
52 L'il Beginnings Miniature Horses Website: http://ww.xcelco.on.ca/~mchorses/
53 Op cit., Dott, G, *A Century of East Lothian Mining*
54 Hayes, G, *Industrial Steam Locomotives*, 1998, p. 10
55 Op cit., Keay, J and Keay, J, p. 800
56 Op cit., Hayes, G, p. 5
57 Op cit., Dott, G, *A Century of East Lothian Mining*
58 Op cit., Geddes, J
59 Ibid, p. 6
60 Op cit., Dott, G, *Notes on Three Early Plans of Prestongrange*, p. 2
61 Op cit., Geddes, J, p. 6
62 Prestongrange Estate Plans 1796–1812 (no date)
63 Op cit., Geddes, J, p. 2
64 Ibid, p. 3
65 Ibid, p. 7
66 Bald, R, Appendix to Report Regarding the Preston Grange Coalfield, 1825
67 Ibid, p. 9
68 Ibid, p. 11
69 Op cit., Dott, G, *A Century of East Lothian Mining*
70 Account of sinking of shaft by Matthias Dunn, titled "Prestongrange Winning"

71 Op cit., Dott, G, *Notes on Three Early Plans of Prestongrange*, p. 4
72 Ibid, p. 5
73 Op cit., Dott, G, *A Century of East Lothian Mining*
74 Edinburgh Society of Model Engineers, *Notes on Cornish Beam Engine at Prestongrange Colliery*, 1950
75 Wordsworth, D, *Recollections of a Tour Made in Scotland*, 1803
76 Op cit., *Edinburgh Society of Model Engineers*, p. 2
77 Dott, G, Notes for *A Century of East Lothian Mining*, August 1958
78 Op cit., Memorandum to enable Engine Maker to prepare Inventory
79 Op cit., Dott, G, Notes for *A Century of East Lothian Mining*
80 Map: Prestonpans Parish 1908
81 Op cit., Memorandum to enable Engine Maker to prepare Inventory
82 Op cit., McKechnie, J and Macgregor, M, p. 67
83 Op cit., Memorandum to enable Engine Maker to prepare Inventory
84 Op cit., Dott, G, Notes for *A Century of East Lothian Mining*
85 Engineering Branch, *Notes on the origin of the Summerlee Iron Co. Ltd.*, 1968
86 Op cit., McNeil, pp. 13–19
87 National Coal Board Diary, 1937
88 Op cit., Keay, J and Keay, J, pp. 800–801
89 Op cit., Hayes, G, pp. 13–14
90 Op cit., Edinburgh Society of Model Engineers
91 Op cit., Hayes, G, p. 3
92 Tests of Locomotive Coals, 1909–10
93 Diagrams and plan of colliery sidings at Prestongrange, 1898, 1912
94 Op cit., Lynch, M, p. 410
95 Op cit., Lynch, M, p. 395
96 Index of collieries – employment figures, 1900, 1910
97 Op cit., Dott, G, Notes on Three Early Plans of Prestongrange – additional sheet no. 2
98 Op cit., McKechnie, J and Macgregor, M, pp. 62–74
99 Op cit *Colliery Guardian*
100 Op cit., McKechnie, J and Macgregor, M, pp. 93–94
101 Ibid, p. 66
102 Op cit., *Colliery Guardian*
103 List of equipment at Prestongrange, 1939
104 Engineering Branch, *Notes on Hydraulic Pumps at Prestongrange Colliery*, 1968
105 Op cit., Dott, G, *A Century of East Lothian Mining*
106 Op cit., McKechnie, J and Macgregor, M, pp. 70–71
107 Op cit., Dott, G, *A Century of East Lothian Mining*
108 Ibid
109 Ibid
110 Op cit., *Colliery Guardian*
111 Op cit., Dott, G, *A Century of East Lothian Mining*
112 Op cit., McKechnie, J and Macgregor, M, pp. 75–76
113 Op cit., Dott, G, *A Century of East Lothian Mining*
114 Op cit., McKechnie, J and Macgregor, M, p. 81
115 Op cit., National Coal Board Diary
116 Op cit., McKechnie, J and Macgregor, M, p. 82
117 Op cit., Dott, G, *A Century of East Lothian Mining*
118 Ibid
119 Op cit., McKechnie, J and Macgregor, M, pp. 83–84
120 Edgington, D, *Old Stationary Engines*, 1996, p. 6
121 *Transactions of the Institute of Mining Engineers*, Vol CI, Part 12, September 1942
122 Ibid, pp. 431–432
123 Ibid, p. 433
124 Op cit., McKechnie, J and Macgregor, M, p. 82
125 Op cit., *Transactions of the Institute of Mining Engineers*, p. 434
126 Op cit., McKechnie, J and Macgregor, M, p. 82
127 McMarland, P, Interview Transcript (William Bush), Open University Project "Wartime Trouble at the Pits – the East Lothian Case", 1998
128 Op cit., McKechnie, J and Macgregor, M, p. 82
129 Op cit., Dott, G, *A Century of East Lothian Mining*

130 Op cit., *Transactions of the Institute of Mining Engineers*, p. 439
131 Op cit., McKechnie, J and Macgregor, M, p. 61
132 Ibid, pp. 85–87
133 Ibid, p. 88
134 *Haddington Courier*, 25 July 1924
135 Ibid, 7 November 1924
136 Dott, G, letter accompanying notes for *A Century of East Lothian Mining*
137 Op cit List of equipment at Prestongrange, 1939
138 Op cit., McKechnie, J and Macgregor, M, p. 107
139 Op cit., McMarland, P, Interview Transcript (William Bush)
140 Ibid
141 Snodgrass, C, Third Statistical Account 1953, p. 107
142 Map of Prestongrange Colliery, (1947?)
143 Op cit., McKechnie, J and Macgregor, M, p. 88
144 Op cit., Snodgrass, C, p. 109
145 *East Lothian County Council Survey Report*, 1953, p. 40
146 McMarland, P, Interview Transcript (Duncan Graham Russell), Open University Project "Wartime Trouble at the Pits – the East Lothian Case", 1998
147 East Lothian Libraries: the Last Pits in East Lothian, Dates of Abandonment
148 National Coal Board, Scottish Division, Lothians Area, Prestongrange Colliery, *Manpower Deployment Summary* 1962
149 Op cit., Hayes, G, p. 29

6

Health Hazards over the Centuries at Prestongrange

Kirsty Black

SERVITUDE TO FREEDOM

> 'Mother took me down four years ago, as father had died of typhus. I work with three brothers and one sister, usually 10 and 12 hours, many times longer, as we wait our turns for the gig to draw up the cart; I am not very strong, as my thigh bone was broken two years since by the cart. All the family have had typhus within the last three years, and I have had it twice. Putting is very sore work; the coal weighs four cwt., and the cart is nearly as heavy. Mother has ceased to work for two years; she is fashed with pains in the stomach, owing to hard labour.'[1]

This is the testimony of a twelve year old boy who worked down an East Lothian colliery in the mid nineteenth century. It gives some idea of the conditions and the health hazards which existed for those who worked underground at this time.

There had been mining in the area of East Lothian around Prestonpans since the thirteenth century when, in 1210, a charter was granted to monks living in this area which allowed them to mine for coal.[2] By the latter part of the eighteenth century, Scotland and Britain experienced a period of rapid industrial expansion; an escalating rate of population growth and urbanisation.[3] Next to textile and agricultural workers coal miners rapidly became one of Scotland's largest working-class groups. In Scotland, however there were two main difficulties within the coal industry at this time: the labour supply and drainage. The latter will be discussed later, the former related to the serfdom in which miners lived and worked. This did not encourage people into the industry.[4]

In 1606 an Act of Parliament prevented the employment of salters and colliers unless they could prove that they had been released from their last place of employment.[5] In 1701 an Act of Parliament made colliers and salters serfs bound for life to a colliery owner and outside the powers of Scotland's Habeas Corpus Act of the same year. The latter Act stated that 'the imprisonment of persons without expressing the reasons thereof, and delaying to put them to trial is contrary to law'.[6] Further legislation in 1762 meant that the colliery owner had the power to move colliers to whereever they had work for them, and the collier had no powers to resist. This is demonstrated in the letter on the following page, recorded in the Prestongrange Collier Books, which was written to Lord Grange by six of his colliers in 1746, requesting that they be allowed to continue working at a neighbouring mine whilst Prestongrange mine was closed.

It has been argued that while serfdom limited a collier's freedom it did not equate directly with low wages. In fact by the 1770s the push to remove serfdom came not from the colliers and salters themselves, for whom this life contract offered an element of employment security, but from industrialists and mine owners, primarily in the west of Scotland, who were concerned with

'UNTO YE Honourable ye Lord Grange, at Prestongrange, ye petition of Robert Pride, James Pride his son, James Pride, Robert Thomson, and William Ines, all collers belonging to his Lordship:

> Humble shewerh, that we are all your Lordship's servants, and is willing to serve your Lordship qn yt you have work for us; but since yt your Lordship's work is not going at Prestongrange, we are at ye tyme is at Pinky, under Mr Robertson, and not far from your Lordship, if yt qn yt you are pleased to fit your work in Prestongrange we are near to be gatton qn yt your Lordship pleases. And at ye tyme John Binel, oversman to ye Duke of Hamilton, is hard upon us in stopping us of bread, where we now are by lifting out of ys work to place us in yt sd Duke's work at Bawerestness. And now ye workman yt is there sweres yt of yt we go to yt work yt they shall be our dead. And now we humbly beg yt you out of your clemency and goodness will keep us from guing to yt place, where our lives will be in so much danger, and we your Lordship's humble petitioners shall ever pray.'[7]

Figure 1: Copy of Pride's Petition to Lord Prestongrange (1746)

labour shortages and high rates of pay.[8] The result of this turn away from serfdom was two pieces of legislation. The Act of 1775 acknowledged firstly the state of servitude in which colliers and salters lived and secondly that there were insufficient colliers and salters in Scotland to meet the countries needs. It stated:

> '... the emancipating or setting free of the Colliers, Coal bearers and Salters in Scotland, who are now in a State of Servitude, gradually and upon reasonable Conditions ... would be the Means of increasing the Number of Colliers, Coal bearers and Salters, to the great Benefit of the Publick, with out doing any injury to the present Masters ...'.[9]

This legislation did not decree that every collier, coal bearer and salter was to be immediately freed but rather that those under 21 years of age would be freed after 7 years service; those ages 21 to 35 after 10 years service; those aged 35 to 45 after 7 years service and those over 45 years of age after 3 years. This was to be replaced with the 'long contract' which would bind colliers, coal bearers and salters to their employment for a minimum of 1 year whilst those under 18 years of age would be tied into apprenticeships for between 3 and 7 years.[10] In fact it was not until 1799 that miners finally got their freedom. This was as a result of a second Act which amended the first and freed any colliers still living in servitude.[11] What all of this meant was that by the time Prestongrange sunk its first shaft in 1829 its colliers were free, although still bound by long contracts.

THE HEALTH HAZARDS

Critical hazards to health and general safety which confronted underground workers during the nineteenth century were drainage, ventilation, haulage and lighting. Each of these presented specific difficulties within this environment which shaped the roles and experiences of men, women and children.

Prestongrange colliery sank its first main shaft in 1829; the second in 1840 and the third in 1873. Discussion of the period from 1829 'until the closure of Prestongrange Colliery in 1962–3 will enable identification of the experiences within East Lothian and Prestongrange colliery. It will also highlight attempts to improve the situations through technological and legislative developments; improvements in safety precautions, which had to be combined with a need for efficiency and productivity in coal production; and as a result of increased knowledge and awareness of medical and health problems.

Drainage

The problem of drainage has always been present in mining. When a hole is dug it will fill with water, a problem which increases depending on the depth of the hole. The drive to improve drainage came from increasing demands for coal to meet the domestic and industrial needs of a rapidly developing nation.[12] This need for more coal led to the sinking of shaft pits and as they became deeper so the problems associated with drainage increased. Church[13] pointed out strongly that a great threat to sinking pits in the nineteenth century was the presence of water and hence drainage was vital. He identified several early methods which were used to remove water from a pit: these included water tubs or kibbles which would have been carried up by hand, then by a horse gin and later by a steam pump. An example of a typical one-horse gin from East Lothian in the mid nineteenth century can be seen in Figure 2 opposite. From the 1780s Watt's steam engine was used in mills and factories and to propel trains and ships.[14] The development of the steam engine necessitated the increased use of coal as a power source.

The limitations of horse gins were clear, in wet pits, such as some of those in the East of

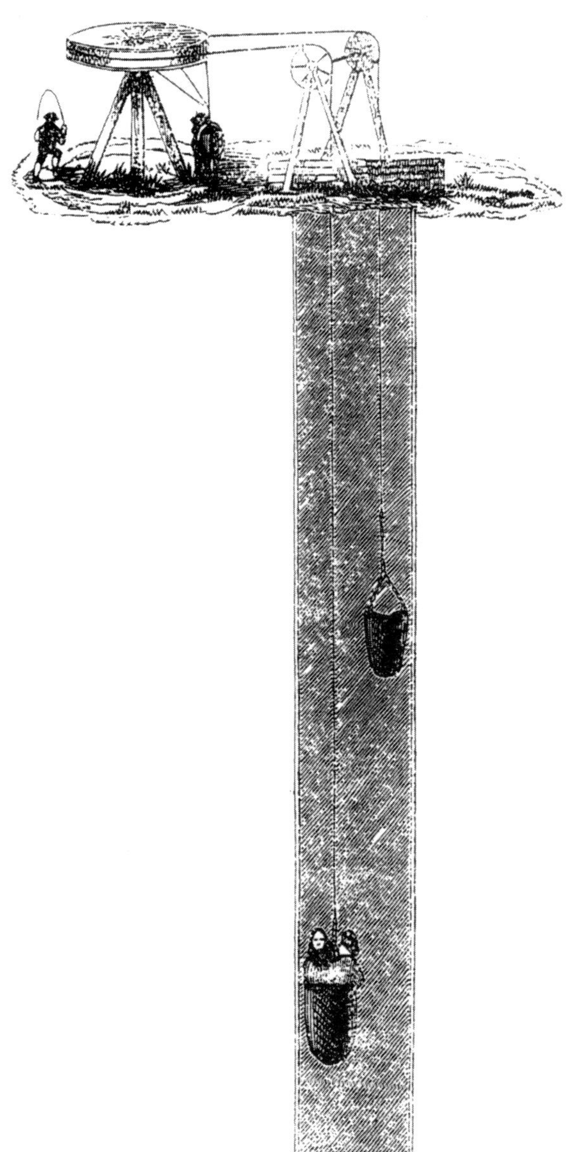

Shaft, drawing up by one-horse gin

Figure 2: One horse gin
Source: First Report of the Commissioners of Mines (1842): Appendix, p.382

Scotland. It was difficult to remove a large quantity of water in buckets raised on chains, pulled by a horse and this prevented pits from being dug to any great depth. Accordingly as steam power was introduced into British industry coal was no exception in the attempts to harness this power. Therefore while the growth of steam power necessitated increased production of coal it also helped to facilitate its own production. Early attempts included the development of the 'Newcomen engine' in the early eighteenth century.

The ineffective drainage of collieries was a potential health hazard for all those working within the mine. Prestongrange colliery was situated on the coast, on the shores of the Firth of Forth, and the proximity to water made mines even more likely to be wet: 'those near to a coast or a river were often excessively wet... In Scotland it was not unusual for miners to come up the pit at night drenched to the skin with water'.[15] This was reiterated by the findings of the Commissioners appointed to report to the Children's Employment Commission in 1842. They said of the East of Scotland that underground 'the roads are most commonly wet, but in some places so much so as to come up to the ankles; and where the roofs are soft the drippy and slushy state of the entire chamber is such that none can be said to work in a dry condition.'[16] The water colliers and coal bearers worked in often contained chemicals, and salt, which would soak into their clothing and harnesses, rubbing the skin raw.[17]

In the case of Prestongrange colliery, the problem of flooding was such that in 1840 when the Royal Commission's enquiries were being conducted the mine was actually closed due to flooding so none of its employees were interviewed.[18] Despite this the Commission did cover a wide range of mines in East Lothian so it is reasonable to assume that the experiences described in other mines were similar to those of Prestongrange when it was operational. In 1872 a Cornish Beam Engine was finally installed at Prestongrange colliery which enabled the colliery to be drained much more efficiently.

Ventilation and Explosion

A second health hazard in coal mining was ventilation.The main hazards here were a lack of oxygen, the presence of gases and the risk of explosion. As drainage methods improved so pits became deeper. Deeper shafts and hence larger mines meant a greater need for efficient ventilation due to the risk of pockets of gas developing. Two of the earliest gases identified were: 'choke damp' which caused suffocation, and 'fire damp' which created the risk of explosion. Early methods of detecting the presence of gas included carrying a candle on a pole to alert colliers to any pockets of gas before they reached them and carrying a bird in a cage, because the bird would be more sensitive to the effects of gas. Neither was particularly scientific or effective. However, irrespective of the presence of gas, for colliers to be able to work hewing coal, or for any of the other tasks which were performed below ground it was necessary to ventilate mines.

By the 1830s the use of wooden partition doors along the length of roads underground was common. These trap doors enabled the air to be channelled throughout the mine. Trap doors were relatively effective in ventilating coal mines in the first half of the nineteenth century but there were serious flaws and risks involved in this method. When the trap doors were correctly operated they would ventilate the mine, but the primary problem here was that if they were left open this would reduce the flow of air and increase the risk of

Figure 3: A Trapper Boy
Source: First Report of of the Commissioners of Mines for the Children's Employment Commission (1842) Vol 189. Appendix: Reports & Evidence from Sub Commissioners. HMSO: London, P444

explosion. This job of opening and closing the doors was therefore given to the trapper. A trapper was usually a young child, generally a boy, who had the task of sitting at one of these trap door and opening it to allow colliers or coal bearers through and then closing it again. An example of a trapper at work can be seen in Figure 3 over in an illustration taken from the Report of the Royal Commission into the Employment of Children in Mines.[19]

In that Report it was stated that 'in regards to ventilation, the coal mines in the East of Scotland are in general in a deplorable state ... the main principles of ventilation in many parts of Scotland are ill understood, and as illpracticed as understood, to the great danger of the workmen, they can exist in this state, but accidents are constantly happening'.[20] Several of the testimonies which the Commissioners collected were from trappers who spoke of the long hours, of sitting alone in the dark and often in wet conditions, waiting to open their door.[21] It was not only however that young primary school aged children, were employed below ground but that they were given a job as important as the efficient working of a ventilation system which is significant here. The safety and ultimately the lives of the mine and all of those working within it were put into the hands of children.[22]

The Mines and Colliers Act of 1842 made illegal the employment of women and children under 10 years of age underground. It also prevented the operation of winding gear from being given to children under 15 years of age. This was another example of the way that the lives and health of all those who worked in a colliery had been put at risk by allowing children to operate important pieces of equipment.[23]

By the 1840s the incorporation of two shafts and the use of furnace ventilation had become popular. This involved lighting a fire at the bottom of the 'up shaft' which operated like a chimney, hot air rose up this shaft and as a result sucked fresh air down the second shaft to ventilate the mine.[24] It is reasonable to assume that this was a method used by the middle of the nineteenth century at Prestongrange Colliery since a second shaft was dug in 1840. Even as late in the century as 1882, by which time Prestongrange had three shafts, shafts number 1 and 2 were still operated on the furnace method.[25] In fact the number 2 shaft actually had three furnaces in operation in 1882, which highlights the point made by Church that the furnace method of ventilation could be enhanced by the use of several furnaces.[26]

As mines got larger it became increasingly difficult to maintain a sufficient flow of air using furnace ventilation. Were a furnace to be extinguished it was not easy to relight. It was difficult to carry out repairs in the up shaft, since there was a furnace burning at the bottom of it. As a result the risk of injury in this up shaft was great.[27] A further problem was the risk of explosion. For the flow of air created by a furnace to effectively ventilate a mine the underground roads had to be well maintained. If they were not of a high standard then pockets of flammable and explosive gases could gather in poorly ventilated areas which increased the risk of explosion with the naked flames of a furnace. Not only did the roads which were in use have to be maintained, but any old or discarded workings also had to be continually ventilated to prevent a build up of gases within them. The health hazards as a result of explosion meant not just the risk of burns for those working underground but also there was the risk of the fall or collapse of the roof or sides of an underground road, creating the threat of being trapped or crushed. Any of these were sufficient to cause death.[28]

Unfortunately this was the case at Prestongrange. There are no comprehensive reports of all minor accidents at Prestongrange Colliery but some of those reported to the Inspectors of Mines in the years 1880 to 1900 can be seen in Figure 4. Explosions did occur, and although it is not possible to say exactly what the causes of those explosions were, in some cases it is a reasonable assumption to make that had there been a completely effective ventilation system the explosion in 1882, and those caused by fire damp in 1884, and again in 1894 would not have occurred.

What is also worthy of attention is the fact that the miners at Prestongrange were well aware of the inadequacies of their ventilation system. In 1861 a group of miners from across East Lothian met to discuss the problem of ventilation systems. With the exception of three mines, of which Prestongrange was not one, all were found to be defective. The meeting decided to apply to the Inspectors of Mines to improve the situation and decided to gather a petition together to send to the Home Secretary highlighting the problem.[29]

None of the accidents above produced fatalities, but there were fatal accidents as a result of explosions at Prestongrange. One such accident occurred in 1877 and was the result of bad ventilation and inappropriate lighting, according to the Haddingtonshire Courier of the day. Not only did they claim the accident was preventable, but it left a fireman dead. The article was titled 'Explosion of Fire Damp at Prestongrange:

> 'On Monday morning, George Sneddon, fireman, while examining the workings ... before the miners commenced their shift proceeded to the end of the pit workings, when an explosion of fire damp occurred which injured him so badly that he has since died in the infirmary. Another miner ... was also slightly burned about the arms. We believe the unfortunate deceased was provided with a Davy Lamp in addition to the one commonly used by miners where the workings are considered free from fire damp. It is not known how the accident occurred but it is safe to affirm that had the Davy lamp been used the unfortunate casualty would not in all probability have occurred.'[30]

DATE	OCCUPATION	AGE	ACCIDENT	INJURIES	TIME ABSENT
2.5.1882	Collier		Fall of roof or sides	Arm fracture	94 days
8.7.1882	Collier	25	Fall of roof or sides	Spine injury	
19.9.1882	Oncostman	40	in an explosion	Burned	41
19.9.1882	Oncostman	50	in an explosion	Bruised	1
16.12.1882	Drawer	35	Miscellaneous underground	Bruised	left
15.6.1883	Sinker	30	Miscellaneous underground	Bruised	
25.9.1883	Drawer	13	In shaft	bruised	left
5.11.1883	Collier	25	Miscellaneous underground	Spinal injuries	left
14.3.1884	Hewer	40	Fall of roof or sides	Fractured collarbone	10
16.7.1884	Hewer	32	Fall of roof or sides	Cut on head	90
13.10.1884	Inspector	50	Explosion of Fire Damp	Burned	
18.10.1884	Drawer	48	Fall of roof or sides	Internal injuries	
22.10.1884	Hewer	15	Fall of roof or sides	Collarbone fracture	28
5.12.1884	Drawer	17	Miscellaneous underground	Arm fracture	6
20.12.1884	Drawer	15	Miscellaneous underground	Hand fracture	
14.3.1888	Collier		Fall of roof or sides	Scalp wound	left
29.3.1888	Fitter		On surface	Shoulder dislocation	left
25.5.1888	Drawer		Miscellaneous underground	Hand injury	21
2.8.1888	Collier		Fall of roof or sides	Shoulder injury	21
2.8.1888	Collier		Fall of roof or sides	Foot injury	28
2.8.1888	Collier		Fall of roof or sides	Hand injury	left
26.10.1888	Bottomer		On surface	Hand injury	
27.12.1888	Oversman		Miscellancous underground	Eye injury	10
18.2.1892	Collier	38	Miscellaneous gunpowder	Burned	42
18.2.1892	Collier	32	Fall of roof or sides	Bruising & injuries	
4.3.1892	Collier	43	Fall of roof or sides	Bruising & injuries	
2.5.1892	Oversman	35	In shaft: crushed by cage	Internal & external	
11.11.1892	Collier	50	Fall of roof or sides	Bruising & injuries	
27.12.1892	Collier	42	Fall of roof or sides	Bruising & injuries	
24.7.1893	Miner	57	Fall of roof or sides	Bruising & injuries	
8.2.1894	Drawer	19	Drawing before tubs when hit		
13.2.1894	Drawer		fall of clay		
18.5.1894	Drawer		Fall of roof or sides		
8.6.1894	Miner		Explosion of fire damp		

Figure 4: Table of Non Fatal Accidents at Prestongrange

Source: Report on the Eastern Districts of Scotland in HMSO: Report of the Inspectors of Coal Mines. *Each incident taken from the report of the year of its occurrence 1882–1900*

During the second half of the nineteenth century the use of fans to ventilate mines increased. In 1882 Prestongrange was using one mechanical ventilator, a Guibal fan.[31] The striking difference between the use of furnaces and the use of fans, aside from the obvious prevention of the health hazards described above, is the difference in the current of air provided. In 1882 at

Prestongrange the furnace ventilation in operation in shafts number 1 and 2 were averaging air currents of between 100 and 250 yards in length. However, the fan in use in shaft number 3 was producing an air current of between 1900 and 2100 yards in length.[32] This was a striking improvement in ventilation, but there was still not room for complacency.

Lighting

In early mines light was provided by the use of a candle's naked flame. This provided a third health hazard since the presence of explosive gases in the atmosphere made such a practice dangerous. Because of this, improvements in lighting and ventilation were closely related. An early attempt to combat the problem of suitable lighting was the development, in 1815, of the Davy Safety Lamp, pioneered by scientist Sir Humphry Davy.[33]

The Davy Safety Lamp used a wire gauze to protect the flame, preventing it from coming into contact with volatile gases. In fact the flame would change colour if there were any gases present. In principle, therefore, safety lamps such as the Davy lamp and those which followed it should have made working in coal mines safer.

There were three main disadvantages to the safety lamp however. The first was that safety lamps were considered a defensive rather than a standard practice, and were only used where it was deemed necessary. In fact naked lights remained the standard form of lighting in Scotland as late as 1913 when there were only 0.3 safety lamps in use for every underground worker, against the national average of 0.85.[34] The second disadvantage of the early safety lamp was that it was possible for them to be extinguished or for a breeze to extend their flame outside of the protective gauze, once again creating a risk of explosion. The third disadvantage was probably the most pressing concern for miners themselves. It was generally acknowledged that Davy lamps were safer, but their level of illumination was eight times weaker than a paraffin lamp. Hewers, or coal face workers depended on the amount of coal they cut for their wages. Yet if they worked with Davy lamps they could not see the coal face as well, nor could they identify any possible dangers as easily. They depended on good light for job efficiency and also for safety, so they would remove the gauze from safety lamps and also take candles with them to enable them to see better.[35]

In 1835 a House of Commons Committee who reviewed Safety Lamps described them as dangerous, stating that they improved safety only in suitable conditions and if properly used. In 1843 a South Shields Committee further stated the dangers of safety lamps in general, claiming ironically that 'no lamp is safe unless in a well ventilated area'. It also stated that while the Mueseler lamp was safer than a Davy lamp it was still only half as bright as a candle.[36] What this demonstrated was that while science was making progress with regards to safety and lighting, the primary task still remained to convince miners themselves to use them. The historian Anthony Burton pondered why, with clear examples of explosions and deaths in every colliery would miners continue using naked flames, and further why would their employers allow it, and continue to send them into inadequately ventilated mines.[37] The solution to this dilemma was the search to find a common ground between efficiency and safety. Brighter light provided better vision, better vision provided greater efficiency at work and also the perception of greater safety for those working underground.

Despite this clear acknowledgement of the potential hazards to health inherent in lighting, the Coal Mines Acts of 1872 and 1887 failed to make the use of safety lamps compulsory. Consequently miners continued to be injured and killed because of inappropriate lighting and the use of naked flames. At Prestongrange Colliery in 1887 a serious accident resulted in the loss of three lives. The deceased were James McEwan, a fireman, Fredrick Curtis, a miner and his fourteen year old son Francis. The cause of the accident was an explosion of fire damp, and is reported to have been so severe as to have been heard at the pit head. Fortunately there was a workers' strike in progress at the time otherwise the accident may have been a great deal worse.[38]

The Coal Mines Act of 1911 eventually required that only locked safety lamps were to be used underground and that where safety lamps had been introduced the use of naked flames was to be made illegal. This Act further stipulated that after 1913 only colliery owners could provide safety lamps and that they could only be opened or checked at appointed lamp stations and by competent and appointed persons. However this Act of 1911 stated that safety lamps should only be made absolutely compulsory if there was a dangerous level of fire damp present.[39] What this Act did do however was to ban all those working underground from carrying anything which could produce a spark or light, such as matches, cigarettes or a pipe and it appointed officials who had the authority to search anyone going underground for such banned substances. An example of a search sheet from the 1950s is in Figure 5 over. Anyone caught in possession of matches or cigarettes could be prosecuted for this contravention of safety policy. At Prestongrange an incident was reported to the Inspector of Mines in 1914 where a twenty year old miner, John Adams, had been badly burned as a result of an explosion of fire damp underground which had been caused by the use of a naked flame.[40] Clearly such an example demonstrates that the 1911 Act was not totally effective. Indeed this example clarifies the way miners' own behaviour contributed to the problems in lighting and ventilation which had been voiced for over a century and which were responsible for many deaths and accidents at Prestongrange.

By 1917 the number of accidents due to the presence of gases was growing. It was again suggested that the cause of these accidents was a combination of problems in ventilation and lighting and had the use of safety lamps been universal then some could have been prevented.[41] The Inspector's Report on the condition of mines in the Eastern District of Scotland in 1883 stated the the two reasons for the slow uptake of electric lighting were the cost and the perception it was only experimental.[42] By the early twentieth century electric lighting was becoming common on the main underground roads, but had not reached the smaller passages or the coal face. In 1911 there were over 1 million miners in Great Britain, but only 4298 portable electric lights in use.[43] In Scotland the numbers of lamps used were recorded by the Inspectors of Mines. In 1910 they recorded 549 non shielded and 232 shielded Davy Safety Lamps, 211 Clanny Safety Lamps, 415 Mueseler Safety Lamps, many hundreds of other safety lamps but only 14 Electric Lamps. By 1911 they reported 135 electric lamps in their district.[44]

By this time, however, a shortage of lamps was not the only problem with electricity. The suppliers of other safety lamps capitalised on a suspiciousness about them which is evidenced by advertisements printed at the time. Colliers were concerned that if electric lamps broke underground there would be a risk of further explosions and accidents. Despite this by 1923 the Lothians

SERIES 570.

FORM P.40.

SEARCH OF UNDERGROUND WORKERS FOR SMOKING MATERIALS

Mines and Quarries Act, 1956, Section 66(2)

Date	Shift	No. In Shift	Number Searched	Result (Enter 'NIL" or specify articles found, and on whom)	Signature(s) of Authorised Person(s) making the Search, and of Witnesses (if articles were found)	Signatures of Workmen Searching the Authorised Searcher

Countersigned: ____________ Under-manager. ____________ Date

____________ Manager. ____________ Date

Figure 5: 1956 Form for search of underground Workers for smoking material
Source: National Coal Board *(1954) Diary for Search of Underground Workers for Smoking Materials* (Mines & Quarries Act 1954, Section 66). HMSO: London

were highly regarded for their level of electrification, and mechanisation. Prestongrange was one of the largest pits in the area, employing 899 workers and one of the few pits to use electric lighting.[45]

Haulage

By the turn of the twentieth century haulage was one of the two main causes of fatal accidents in coal mines, the other main cause was falls from the roof or sides of underground roads and passages.[46] Haulage as a source of hazard was not a new phenomenon. In 1842 the Royal Commission report clearly illustrated the health hazards which existed as a result of the system of haulage used in coal mines. The basic problem was that once coal had been cut it then had to be transported from the coal face to the shaft and thence from the base of the shaft to the surface. There were two main methods of transporting coal from the coal face to the main shaft in the first half of the nineteenth century. The first was to carry it. This was a job carried out by 'coal bearers'. The second was to push or pull it in a cart, carried out by 'coal putters' or 'drawers'. The other distinguishing feature of these jobs was that they were commonly carried out by women or children.

Burton stated that the employment of women as coal bearers was exclusive to Scotland by the middle of the nineteenth century, and in fact was localised in the east. The Report of the Commissioners in 1842 corroborates this statement and described the job of coal bearers as being to 'carry coal on their backs in unrailed roads with burdens varying from three quarters of a cwt. to three cwt.' It further describes the occupation as being predominantly carried out by female or child labour, and peculiar to the Lothians. The report stated that these women and children would work for 12 to 14 hours daily in the 'damp, heated and unwholesome atmosphere of the coal mine.'[47] The illustrations in Figure 6 below are from that report. The report had many examples of testimonies from coal bearers. Consider the following from Isabella Reid a twelve year old coal bearer:

> 'I am wrought with sister and brother, it is very sore work; cannot say how many rakes or journeys I make from pit's bottom to wall face and back; thinks about 30 or 25 on average; the distance varies from 100 to 250 fathoms. I carry about 1cwt and a quarter on my back; have to stoop much and creep through water which is frequently up to the calves of my legs. When first down fell asleep while waiting for coal from heat and fatigue. I do not like the work, nor do the lassies, but they are made to like it. When the weather is warm there is difficulty in breathing, and frequently the lights go out.'[48]

Figure 6: Coal bearers
Source: First Report of the Commissioners of Mines (1842): Appendix, pp. 386–7

Margaret Jaques, a seventeen year old coal bearer also offered testimony:

> 'I have been seven years at coal bearing; it is horrible sore work ... I make 30 rakes a day with two cwt of coal on my creel. It is a guid distance I journey, and very dangerous on parts of the road. The distance fast increases as the coals are cut down.'[49]

Further testimonies highlight more coal bearing hazards, for example, a loss of footing or a fall or if a strap which secured the coal to the bearer broke, carrying such a weight of coal could cause serious injury to the bearer. The report stated that the oppression of coal bearing injured women for life, leaving them with damaged or crushed legs,ankles and backs. It also stated that they often continued to work whilst pregnant and that the women believed that their miscarriages were a result of their work.[50]

The second method of transporting coal to the main shaft was the use of 'putters', or 'drawers'. In this case a cart was filled with between three and ten cwts of coal and either pushed by the 'putters' or dragged by the 'drawers' to the main shaft. The putter would be harnessed over the shoulders and back to their cart (see Figure 7). The 1842 Commissioners' report described putting as next in level of severity and physical oppression to coal bearing. It pointed out

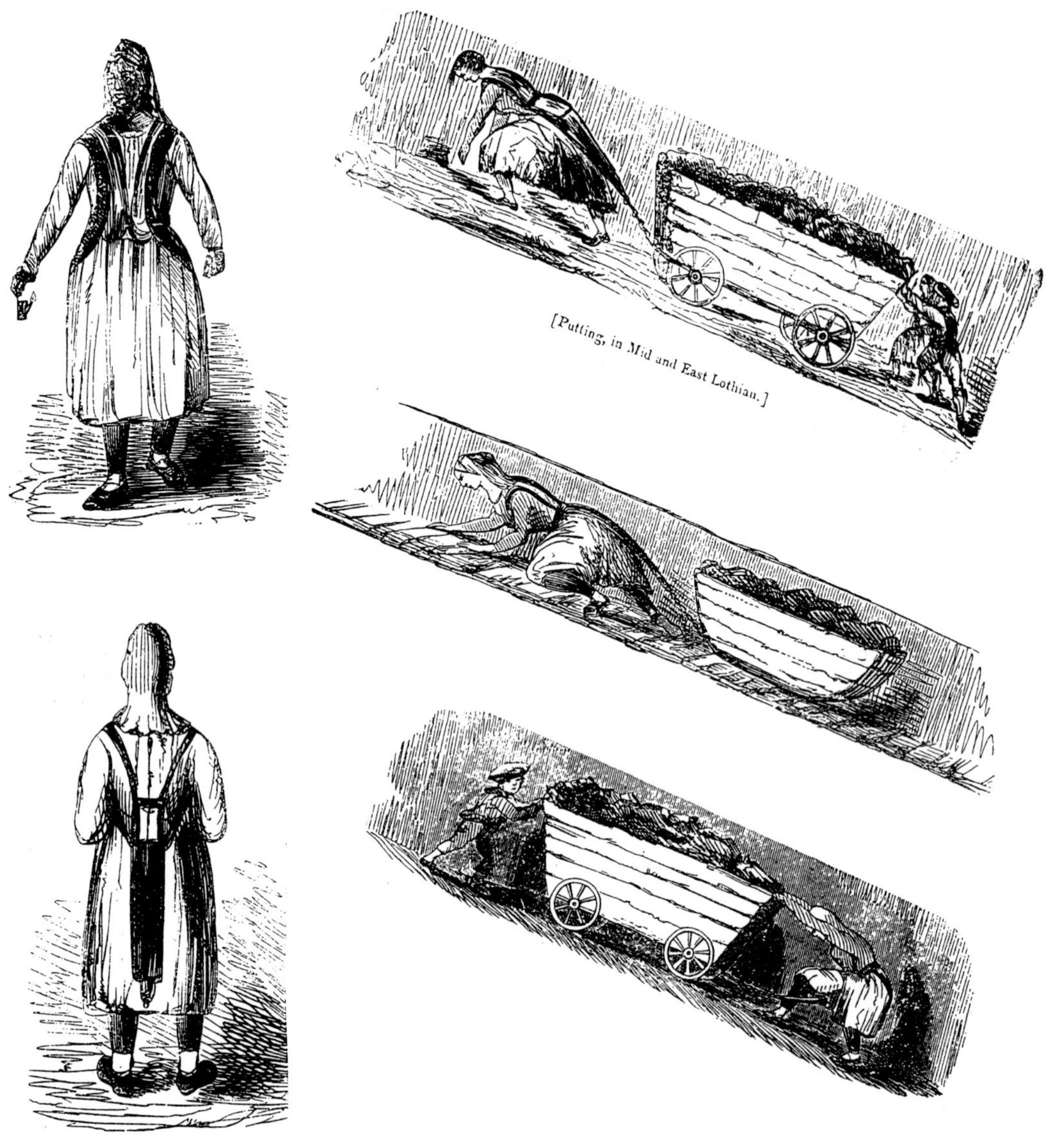

Figure 7: Putters and drawers
Source: First Report of the Commissioners of Mines (1842): Appendix, pp. 388–9 and First Report of the Commissioners of Mines (1842), pp. 94–5

that as with coal bearing often the roads along which workers transported the coal were steeply sloped and wet with ceilings of less than three foot high. In such conditions the putters had to crawl on their hands and knees.[51]

The list of non fatal accidents at Prestongrange between 1880 and 1900 demonstrates that although the 1842 Coal Mines Act removed women and children under ten years old from the mines, the hardships for drawers continued. Nine of the thirty five recorded accidents happened to drawers and of the nine injured drawers the youngest was 13 and the oldest 48, with four of these aged under twenty. These statistics must not be assumed to be definitive of all accidents at Prestongrange Colliery during this period. There were almost certainly many more haulage accidents, but accidents were so frequent that many were not recorded. A further confusion with these statistics is what they omit to say. They do not always explain whether the injured person recovered or if they returned to work. It is possible that of those with no details in the column 'time absent' may have returned underground, however in the case of a drawer injured in 1884, a report in the Haddingtonshire Courier from the following year stated that he had died as a result of his injuries.[52] Haulage accidents did not only injure drawer, putters or coal bearers. A report in the Haddingtonshire Courier in 1861 highlights the danger and injuries suffered by one particular collier as a result of run away coal wagons.

> 'On the 8th, David Innes, collier, residing at Cuthill met with an accident, while working in the Prestongrange coal pit. He was walking before a wagon down an incline and had to turn in order to ascertain the cause of a sudden stoppage of the wagon, when it came away again, and running down upon him before he could move out of the road, crushed his legs and body pretty severely.[53]

Coal was therefore transported, through narrow, wet roads which could be over 200 yards long and which sloped to assist drainage, to the bottom of the main shaft. The second aspect of haulage was to raise the coal to the surface.[54] For bearers this could involve carrying the coal up steps or ladders, as can be seen in Figure 8 over.

Later methods of raising coal included horse gins (see Figure 2), followed by steam driven pumps and mechanical and electric pumps in the twentieth century. By the 1830s and 40s steam pumps operated iron ropes and cages, and the women and young children were replaced by ponies and later railways. A statement given to the Royal Commission of 1842 by Sir George Grant Suttie Bart., the owner of Prestongrange colliery at the time, proves that he did employ women and children before 1842, and further identifies the need for the legislative change to remove women and children from coal mines:

> 'I have no control whatever over the colliers in my employment; the engagement on their part is nominal; as, although a fortnight's notice is stipulated for previous to leaving their employment, it is in point of fact of no avail; the colliers, men women and children go to their work at whatever hour of the night or day they think proper, and work just as long as they choose. There is in all the mines in this district, a greater or less number of women and children employed; and I beg leave to tell to you my conviction that the employment of women in the mines of Scotland is one of the reasons which tends to depreciate the character and habits of the collier population; and that to remedy this evil a legislative enactment is required

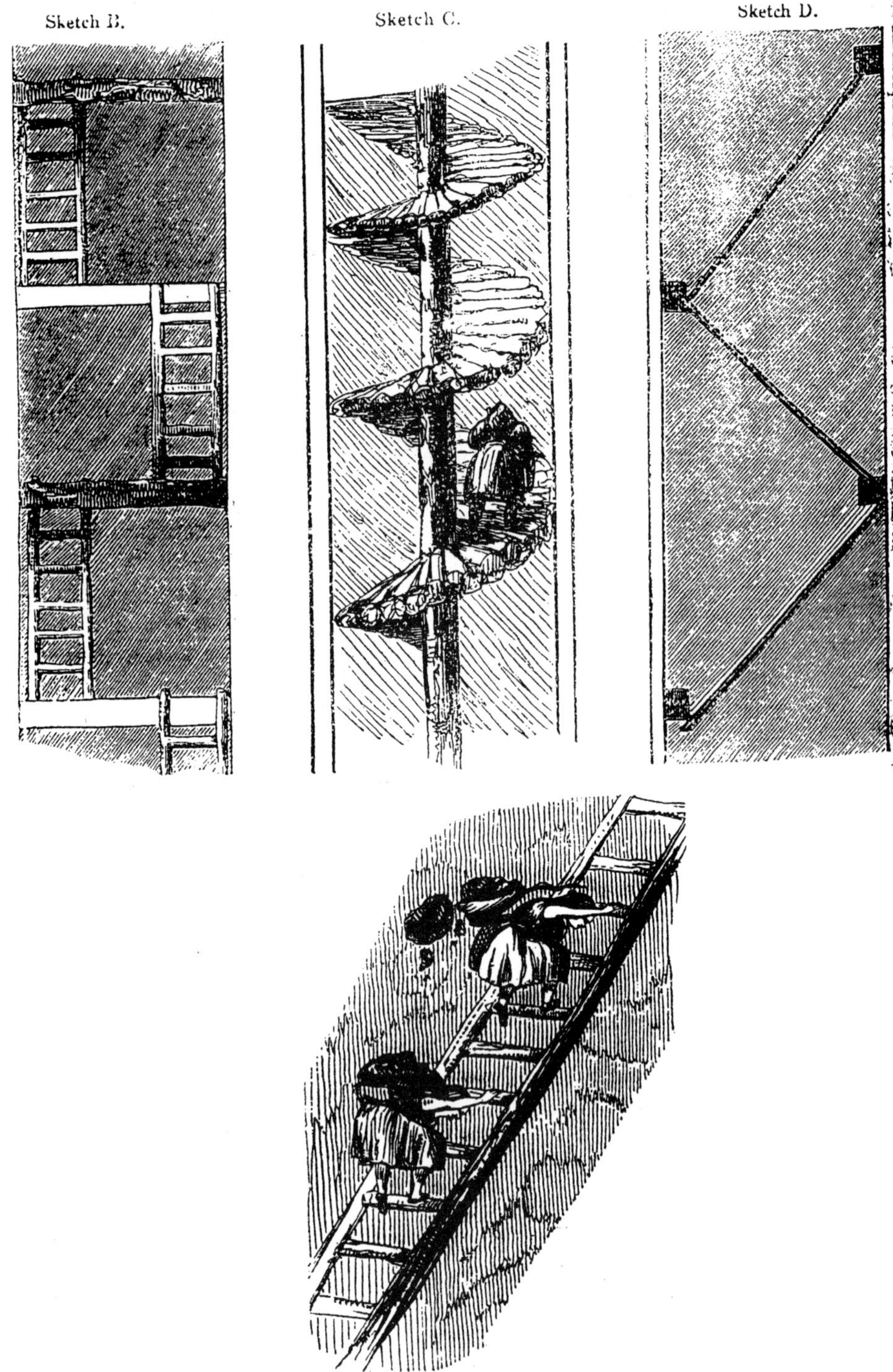

Figure 8: Coal Bearers steps & Ladders
Source: First Report of the Commissioners of Mines (1842): Appendix, p. 382

as any resolution on the part of one or two mine proprietors, not to employ women or children would be injurious to them, without tending at all to remedy the evil ...'[55]

The examples given from the nineteenth century prove that men and teenaged boys continued to be employed as drawers at Prestongrange Colliery after the underground employment of women and young children ceased. A piece of evidence to suggest that Prestongrange colliery employed women and children underground, pre 1842, as coal bearers is the diagram of Prestongrange colliery taken from the Prestongrange Colliery Book which details the depth and thickness of seams in use and in which coal bearers are present. See Figure 9.

Colliers worked long hours in dark and cramped conditions.

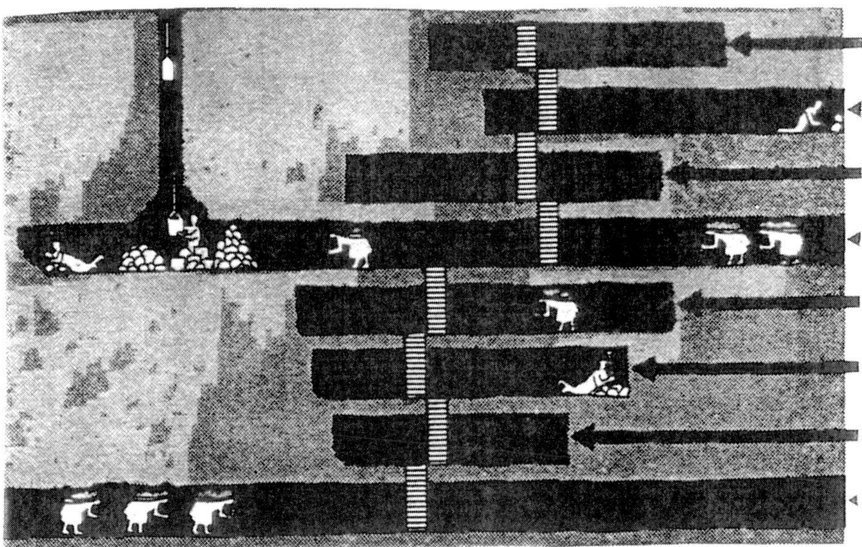

1 Seam from the Grass or Superfice of the Earth called the Great Seam is nine feet thick and lies twenty fathom below the grass.

2 Seam is called Diver Coall is three and a half feet thick and lyes nine fathom below the Great Seam.

3 Seam is called the Splenty Coall is three feet thick and lyes Eight fathom below the Diver Coall.

4 Seam is called the five foot Coall is about five foot thick and lyes four fathom below the Splenty Coall.

5 Seam is called the Rough Coall and is about three quarters of an Ell thick and lyes four fathom below the five foot Coall.

6 Seam called Souterclout Coall is four foot thick and lies twenty six fathoms below the Rough Coall.

7 Seam is called Beggar's Coall is three foot and a half thick and lyes six fathoms below the Souterclout Coall.

8 Seam is called Splenty Coall is three and a half foot thick and lyes eight fathom below the Beggar Coall.

Figure 9: Diagram of the seams of coal at Prestongrange
Source: Poster of Collier Serfs at Prestongrange Colliery, at Scottish National Mining Museum at Newton Grange

'... underground work was different from all others. The pit was a world apart – dark, dusty, insanitary and unpredictable and very often hot, stuffy, wet and cramped as well.'[56]

It is hard to calculate the number of working hours since travelling time to and from the coal face in long and narrow passages must be added. At Prestongrange, workings on the Great Seam actually extended for two miles under the Firth of Forth so colliers would have to travel this distance each day to get to and from the coal face.[57] Scottish coal was hard with narrow seams, and the work required 'constant exertion and twisting of the body, that unless a person had been habituated to it from his earliest years, he cannot submit to the operation. The work could involve 'lying full length in a thirty inch seam, or sitting with the body bent to one side.'[58]

Falls of Roof and Sides

The second main cause of fatal accidents in coal mines was falls from the roof or sides of coal seams.[59]

The pictures in Figure 10 demonstrate the cramped working conditions of colliers. They show examples of men working in spaces so cramped that they were required to lie on their sides to excavate the coal. They also show how easily an accident could occur and how serious that could be in such cramped conditions. One in particular highlights the danger inherent in the use of

Figure 10: Photographs of Colliers at work
Source: Part of the collection at Newton Grange: Scottish National Mining Museum, references 1997: 568, 1997: 568a & 1997: 261.

Figure 10 continued

wooden supports to hold up the roof of the coal seam, as it shows a support which had split and was being repaired. The Haddingtonshire Courier repeatedly reported accidents at Prestongrange Colliery as a result of falls from the roof or sides of coal seams. In 1865 a collier had two ribs broken and was badly bruised when a large quantity of coal fell on him. A more serious roof fall in 1870 left one collier with head injuries and one leg broken at both the ankle and knee, while another collier involved in the same accident walked away with only some bruising. In 1877 another miner was involved in a fall of two tons of coal from the roof of a seam. He suffered serious internal injuries however it was believed that he escaped death only because of the soft nature of the ground on which he stood.[60]

Accidents at Prestongrange were sometimes fatal. The 1842 Commissioners Report detailed three deaths.[61] The table in Figure 11 over details only the deaths reported to the Inspectors of Mines between 1858 and 1914. Ten of the seventeen deaths listed were a result of a fall from the roof or side of a seam.

This list is not inclusive of all the fatal accidents which occurred at Prestongrange. The Haddingtonshire Courier during the nineteenth century reported on many others for example the case of a 23 year old collier who died in 1883 and another in 1886, both as a result of a fall of coal and stone from the roof of a seam.[62] Unfortunately work related deaths continued into the twentieth century. During both wars many colliers joined the armed forces and there were concerns about the dilution of labour and the possible increased risk to health and safety which this could cause.[63] At Prestongrange

DATE	NAME & AGE	OCCUPATION	ACCIDENT
1858	Alexander Watson	Collier	Fall of coal
12.2.1883		Stone Miner	Roof fall
14.5.1898	Robert Harline, 17	Brusher	Deceased had turned out a loaded tub onto a haulage road … the roof came in over a length of 25 foot, completely burying him.
31.12.1901		Labourer	Killed when run over by a train of wagons powered by a locomotive on the surface.
23.4.1902	James Walker, 34	Reddsman	Deceased was laying rails on underground roadways when a mass of stone fell on him.
18.11.1902	William Walters, 14	Haulage attendant	Deceased fell in front of a moving loaded tub on a steep underground roadway.
24.9.1904	Joseph Stafford, 24	Brusher	Deceased was engaged in cutting needle holes in side walls for crowns, when the roof fell in on him.
24.2.1905	William Craig, 20	Sinker	Shaft enlarged for pumping and winding coal from 35 fathoms, so scaffolding removed to allow sinkers to work. When sinker later descended the shaft, forgetting the absence of scaffolding, stepped out cage and plunged a further 15 fathoms.
10.3.1910	James Curren, 37	Brusher	The chain attached to a tub slipped and ran back, fatally injuring deceased.
28.4.1910	Henry Somers, 15	Haulage boy	Failed to separate chains attached to tubs, one caught under a rail and jammed the deceased between the wall and a hutch.
6.10.1910	Thomas Gorman, 24 & Thomas Campbell, 48	Stone mine drivers	A roof fall swung out over 10 sets of timbers, three men were buried, all were extricated alive, but two later died.
1.12.1910	Hugh McConnell, aged 63	Fireman	Killed on entering a new seam to check its safety, carrying a safety lamp and a naked light which ignited the gas present.
1913	aged 39	Road repairer	Killed in fall of stones from the side.
23.10.1914	James Johnston, 36 & James Couper, 32	Miners	Straightening the line of the upper portion of a conveyor face when the roof above them, over an area of 9ft 8inches by 5ft 10 inches collapsed and buried them.
15.11.1914	William Boyd, 19	Pony driver	Knocked down by a 15 wagon locomotive.
14.10.1922	Edward Gunn, 26	Drawer	Killed by the falling of a large stone.

Figure 11: Table of fatal accidents at Prestongrange
Source: Report on the Eastern Districts of Scotland in HMSO: Report f the Inspectors of Coal Mines. *Each incident taken from the report of the year of its occurrence 1883–1922*

there were three deaths reported to the Inspector of Coal Mines in 1914 alone,[64] but it would be foolhardy to attribute those incidents simply to the outbreak of war several months earlier.

The outbreak of the Second World War again resulted in high levels of recruitment among colliers. Production and employment levels fell and once again Britain found it difficult to match coal supplies with demand levels. By 1942 the government was acutely aware of the need to maintain coal production within Britain and so in 1942 the Ministry of Fuel and Power was created by Anthony Bevin to control the industry. Continued labour shortages led to the creation of the 'Bevin Boys'. These were boys who, on reaching conscription age, were selected using a ballot system to go and work in the coal mines. It was said of the Bevin Boys however that they did little to increase production levels but that since they came from a broad spectrum of society, through the ballot system they may have helped to publicise both the nature of colliers work and the conditions in which they worked.[65]

LONG TERM HEALTH EFFECTS

There are two types of health hazard which coal mining presented. The first includes accidents, for example, the risk and level of occurrence of explosion. This group of hazards are to some extent quantifiable in relation to specific experiences at Prestongrange. However colliers worked day to day in a dangerous and hazardous environment, small accidents or injuries were often accepted as being a result of the nature of the job, so there are not comprehensive records of accidents or injuries, as was stated by Charles Brister:

> 'It has always been the tragedy of the miner that no one sees him at work. Even in this world of mass communication his life remains very much a closed book except to those who are near and know him well... Certainly the miner is a brave man for he faces daily that which he fears most.'[66]

The second significant group of hazards include long-term health problems such as arthritis, lung disease or eye problems such as nystagmus which colliers experienced. This group is more difficult to quantify since Prestongrange employees medical records are private. A further problem is that some of the health problems experienced by colliers are not immediately evident and indeed may only become a problem after a collier has retired, or stopped working e.g. rheumatism. Therefore, inevitably, any discussion of such problems in relation to Prestongrange Colliery will ultimately be of a more general nature than any discussion of the occurrence of deaths or serious injuries arising from accidents within the mine.

Benson identified four sources of health hazards within the coal industry. The first was the physical nature of the work; the second was the impurity of the air in coal mines; the third was the poor illumination underground and the fourth health hazard was insanitary and dirty conditions.[67] The 1842 Commissioners Report into the employment of children in mines stated that:

> 'About the age of twenty few colliers are in perfect health, almost all being more or less affected with difficulty of breathing, cough and expectoration, either occurring occasionally or in a permanent form. ... After the thirtieth year it is rare to find a healthy collier ... perhaps not one in ten could pass the necessary examination to enter as a soldier'[68]

It claimed that after thirty breathing would become worse, coughing would seldom cease and muscular strength would decline. The report claimed to find relatively few miners surviving beyond 50 years old. It further stated that chronic bronchitis was one of the most common diseases found.[69]

The conditions which led to illness and disease are the same conditions which gave rise to the danger of health hazards from accidents. The photographs in Figure 10 and the illustrations in Figures 3, 6 and 7 clearly depict the uncomfortable and difficult physical nature of the work in collieries such as Prestongrange. Health problems which have been attributed to these include rheumatism, arthritis and bent hand, knee and elbow. The poor quality of the air underground and the presence of impurities, gases and coal dust in the air led to further health hazards which included headaches; pneumoconiosis (miners' asthma); chronic bronchitis and in the East of Scotland specifically silicosis (black spit) as a result of inhaling stone dust. A lack of good, clear and safe lighting has been linked to headaches, giddiness, night blindness and nystagmus, which caused a vibration or a flickering of the eye balls. Nystagmus became more common with the introduction of early safety lamps, but would improve if the sufferer stopped going underground to work. Finally insanitary and unhealthy conditions could lead to diseases of the blood. These problems were not unknown in East Lothian in the nineteenth century as the Haddingtonshire *Courier* article dated 21 November 1879 demonstrated.

> 'IS COAL MINING A HEALTH OCCUPATION?
> The impartial inquiry into the varying merits of different occupations would it appears to me have some difficulty in finding any advantages accruing to the operative in coal mining, or indeed mining in any form. To be obliged to leave the light and the fresh, open air, and descend into comparative and sometimes absolute darkness in the bowels of the earth, where the best efforts fail to induce fresh air to enter sufficiently and to lie on his side or back on damp or wet ground and drive his pick against the coal bank either horizontally or from below upwards, the nearest approach he can attain to the upright posture being sitting or stooping; to breath continually during working hours a close and gas charged atmosphere; to begin life by crawling on hands and knees while pushing with his head 'corves' laden with coal, and to end it prematurely old, shaken with cough and exhausted by expectoration – if indeed some explosion of fire damp has not sooner ended suddenly an existence doomed at best to painful termination – these are plain every day incidents in the life of miners.'[70]

This article does however go on to discuss how accustomed the human frame can become to such conditions, and in fact implied that coal miners suffered less in reality than was often suggested. It stated that 'coal mining is not necessarily a particularly unhealthy or particularly dangerous occupation'.[71]

Despite this suggestion, developments were made to improve the health, situation and safety of collieries and to minimise the risk of health hazards as a result of various Acts of Parliament throughout the nineteenth and twentieth centuries. This reflected a greater understanding and awareness of health and illness and saw a great many developments in health and safety regulations within mines. An 1850 Act called for the appointment of Inspectors for Coal Mines, and by 1855 they had been given the power to establish safety regulations. In 1851 the Royal School of Mining was established and by 1872 mine managers had to pass government competence exams.[72]

Another safety measure was the use of firemen. They were required to descend into a mine before the first shift of workmen to check the pit to ensure it was safe and a fireman had to be below ground at all times if colliers were below.[73] At least three fireman lost their lives at Prestongrange colliery, one as late as 1910. He entered a new seam carrying both a safety lamp and a naked flame.[74] The firemen were given inspection sheets on which to record

Report of Inspection by Fireman. Coal Mines Act, 1911.

I hereby certify that I have inspected every part of the mine situated beyond the

Strike out words in italics for report of Inspection during shift. ________________________Station, and in which workmen are to work or pass during the shift, *and all working places in which work is temporarily stopped within any ventilating district in which the men have to work* and that the following is a full and accurate report of my Inspection.

19	Between the Hours of	A.M. or P.M.		SIGNATURE
	&			
	&			
	&			
	&			
	&			
	&			
	&			
	&			
	&			
	&			
	&			
	&			
	&			
	&			
	&			
	&			

Figure 12: Report of inspection by fireman
Source: HMSO (1912) Fireman's Pocket Diary or Daily Report Book. William Craig & Sons, Colliery Printers & Publishers: Coatbridge

their examination of the mines. Such a sheet, based on the regulations of the 1911 Coal Mines Act is given below (Figure 12).

Sanitation and Welfare

As this awareness of health and safety grew during the nineteenth century so the problem of poor sanitation became more pressing both above and below ground. There were no toilets below ground in the nineteenth century so old workings would be used instead which meant that for colliers 'eating, drinking, urinating and defecating all went on side by side'.[75] A further problem was that there were no set meal times when colliers would stop work and take a break to eat. This meant they would eat where they worked and when they wanted without taking a proper break. Not only did these activities continue side by side, there were no means of washing their hands and since colliers would often have to move around on their hands and knees the need for sanitary provisions became all the more pressing. In fact it was reported that some colliers would even drink the stagnant water that lay underground.[76] The problem of

The RAT MENACE

The Rat Catcher is here.
Help him to clear your Section.
Don't throw away bread etc.,
Keep your crusts in your piece box
and
KEEP YOUR HEALTH.

Issued by The National Coal Board.
Fife Area.

Figure 13: Hygiene poster
Source: Widdas W., Ministry of Fuel and Power (1954) Report for the Scotland Division of H.M. Inspector of Mines for 1953. *Under the Coal Mines Act 1911. HMSO: London, p. 17*

eating underground and leaving rubbish, crumbs or uneaten food behind is highlighted in the poster in Figure 13.

During the twentieth century the development of health and safety measures and general improvements to colliery areas began to accelerate. In 1920 the Miners Welfare Act acknowledged the lack of amenities and also the lack of recreational provision in collieries and the surrounding areas and set about developing miners institutes, parks and sports grounds etc.[77] By 1921 Inspectors of Mines detailed four key areas for the Health and Safety provisions in mines. The first was regulation and inspection, which involved the development of codes of practice and regulations concerning safety lamps, ventilation, haulage and roof supports etc. The second was focussed on the Safety in Mines Research Board, which looked into the causes and effects of diseases such as beat hand, beat knee and nystagmus, and questioned the effects of inhalation of stone dust. The third area of health and safety involved the statutory testing and analysis of safety lamps, explosives, mine air and dust samples to ensure high standards of safety and air. The final area considered was the use of mine exams to ensure that those who went underground had some knowledge of the environment they were entering.[78]

Between 1900 and 1947 the national level of fatalities within collieries was approximately one fatality for every 800 employees, decreasing to 1 in 1500 by the end of the period. Edmond claims that collieries in the Lothians were generally representative of this pattern.[79] By 1923 Prestongrange employed 988 workers, but fortunately although deaths did continue to occur the death rate does not seem to have been as high as the national average given above which would have equated to approximately one death every second year. However, even well into the twentieth century accidents did occur. For example in 1945 a collier was killed when a large piece of ice fell onto the cage in which he was descending causing a fatal head injury. There was another death in 1956, as a result of an explosion this time.[80]

Rescue Teams and Safety First

In the 1920s the Safety First campaign was instituted to try to raise awareness and to change behaviour to ensure greater health and safety. In 1922 the Safety in Mines Research Board set up a competition among rescue teams. The rescue teams had two tasks underground: to rescue lives and to penetrate and recover sections of underground workings.[81] The rescue competition was based on these basic needs. The competitions were set up in four regional areas. The competition in the Lothians was held at the mining department attached to Heriot Watt College. For many it was the highlight of the year.[82] The test had three parts, firstly a gallery test with mine research apparatus e.g. an underwater test could be set; secondly there was an oral examination for everyone in a team with questions on regulations, apparatus, plan reading, signalling and testing for gas; finally there was a test of the use of artificial respirators and oxygen reviving equipment.[83] Once a winner and a runner up had been found in each of the four regions, Coatbridge, Cowdenbeath, Edinburgh and Kilmarnock, the successful eight would go forward to the overall final.

Prestongrange Colliery won this competition on several occasions, as can be seen in Figure 14 which shows two of Prestongrange's winning teams, one probably from the 1920s and others in 1958–9. They won in 1956, 1957, 1959 and in 1962 which was National Safety Year.[84]

Figure 14: Photographs of Rescue Teams
Source: Part of the collection at Newton Grange: Scottish National Mining Museum, references 1998: 1338, 1997: 314 and 1997: 301

In 1923 the Inspectors of Mines reported little activity with the 'Safety First' movement despite twelve months activity. The idea of this campaign was to promote health and safety and to make miners aware of the need to take appropriate precautions.[85] By 1924 the Safety First campaign was issuing monthly posters and was encouraging managers of mines to display them to raise awareness.[86]

Despite the increased publicity involved in the campaigns for health and safety, even when the National Coal Board (NCB) took over the running of all Britain's coal mines in 1947, the protective equipment used by colliers was still generally only a safety hat, knee pads and boots, even goggles were a rarity.[87]

NATIONAL COAL BOARD IMPROVEMENTS

Once in control the NCB set about improving health and safety provisions in mines. It was thought that perhaps mines being owned by so many small operators meant that there was not sufficient funds for large scale modernisation and improvements so the Labour governments nationalisation of the industry was to pool these resources and set about improvements.[88] In 1952 the construction of the pit head baths at Prestongrange was completed. It was formally opened on 12 September 1952.[89] The Prestongrange baths were the one hundredth installed by the NCB in Scotland and were built at a cost of £63,578. The facilities included washing and storage for 969 men; a canteen; a bicycle store for 50 bicycles and room for 6 cars. The total cost of NCB improvements thus far was over £354,000 and provided facilities for 7,500 men. The funds came from the NCB and the Miners Welfare Fund.[90] The pit head baths and canteen can be seen in the photograph in Figure 15. These improvements at Prestongrange continued in 1953 with the completion of the Prestongrange Medical Centre.[91]

Figure 15: Pit Head Baths and Canteen
Source: Scottish Mining Museum. NGSMM.1996.2464

In 1952 the Inspectors' report stated that only 18% of the total accidents in Scotland were not preventable. It stated that 15.9% would have been prevented if rules had not been breached and a further 50% prevented by using ordinary caution.[92] This was a pattern which was to continue.

Despite all of the improvements which were made one issue continued to stand out. Was it the duty of management to ensure safe working conditions or were accidents and ill health the result of the workers lack of regard for safety and their own health? This is a dilemma for which there can be no definitive answer. What is clear is that the health and the lives of the people who work in any colliery is the responsibility not only of themselves but also of all those with whom they work and all those for whom they work.

Duckham suggested that mining accidents on a large scale and the death and devastation which that could bring to a community could be compared only with war and the 'decimation of a local regiment'. Prestongrange was fortunate in this respect. Although there were health hazards, safety risks and accidents there was never a large scale disaster. What Duckham implied was that the frequency of small scale accidents, injury and disease which has been shown to exist at many collieries, including Prestongrange, in fact 'dulled perceptiveness and blunted sympathy'. What is meant by this is that accidents, injuries and health hazards were an every day part of the job, something which no one liked but which was still generally accepted. He further suggests that this led to complacency both from the workers themselves and from the management, who would each blame the other for inadequacies in the standards of health and safety within coal mines.[93]

CONCLUSION

Over the course of the active life of Prestongrange Colliery from 1829 until 1963 there were many different health hazards to which the workers were exposed. They ranged from difficulties with drainage, ventilation, haulage, lighting and falls each of which brought with it a risk of injury, accident, ill health and death. Throughout this period, however, mining had not stood still. It had progressed from human to mechanical and electrical labour. Nor had the problem of health hazards remained static. Throughout the period there were developments based on technology, a greater understanding of medical and health problems and legislative developments all of which made Prestongrange Colliery, and all others, safer and better regulated places to work. That is not to say that all the risk and the hazards were removed from the occupation, nor even that the progression was rapid and wide ranging in the early days. However the risks were reduced, and continued to be reduced after the closure of Prestongrange, provided that miners and managers alike avoided complacency and adhered to the necessary regulations.

BIBLIOGRAPHY

Primary Sources

Manuscripts and documents

Campbell R.H. & Dow J.B.A. (1968) *Source Book of Scottish and Economic History.* Basil Blackwell: Oxford.

Cunningham Rev. W.B. (1845) *The New Statistical Account of Scotland: Volume II, Linlithgow–Haddington–Berwick.* William Blackwood and Sons: Edinburgh and London.

Poster of Collier Serfs at Prestongrange Colliery, held in Prestongrange folder at Scottish National Mining Museum in Newton Grange.

Sinclair J. (ed.) (1975) *The Statistical Account of Scotland*: Volume II, The Lothians (1791–99). E.P. Publishing Ltd.

Snodgrass C.P. (1953) *The Third Statistical Account of Scotland*: *The County of East Lothian.* Oliver and Boyd: Edinburgh and London.

Transactions of the East of Scotland Mining Students Association Volume 1 (1923).
Transactions of the East of Scotland Mining Students Association Volume 2 (1924).

Parliamentary Papers and Government Publications

First Report of the Commissioners of Mines for the Childrens Employment Commission (1842) Parliamentary Papers Volume 188. HMSO: London.

First Report of the Commissioners of Mines for the Childrens Employment Commission (1842) Volume 189. Appendix: Reports and Evidence from Sub Commissioners. HMSO: London.

Ashley T., *Report for the Scotland Division: HMSO (1938) Mines & Quarries: Annual Reports of (a) Secretary of Mines, (b) H.M. Chief Inspector of Mines, (c) H.M. Inspector of Mines for 1937*. Harrison & Sons: London.

Atkinson J. B. Esq., Report on the Eastern Districts of Scotland in: HMSO (1893) *Report of the Inspectors of Coal Mines for 1892*. George Edward Eyre & William Spottiswood: London.

Atkinson J. B. Esq., Report on the Eastern Districts of Scotland in: HMSO (1894) *Report of the Inspectors of Coal Mines for 1893*. George Edward Eyre & William Spottiswood: London.

Atkinson J. B. Esq., Report on the Eastern Districts of Scotland in: HMSO (1895) *Report of the Inspectors of Coal Mines for 1894*. George Edward Eyre & William Spottiswood: London.

Atkinson J. B. Esq., Report on the Eastern Districts of Scotland in: HMSO (1897) *Report of the Inspectors of Coal Mines for 1896*. George Edward Eyre & William Spottiswood: London.

Atkinson J. B. Esq., Report on the Eastern Districts of Scotland in: HMSO (1901) *Report of the Inspectors of Coal Mines for 1900*. Darling & Son Ltd: London.

Atkinson J. B. Esq., Report on the Eastern Districts of Scotland in: HMSO (1902) *Report of the Inspectors of Coal Mines for 1901*. Darling & Son Ltd: London.

HMSO (1912) *Fireman's Pocket Diary or Daily Report Book*. William Craig & Sons, Colliery Printers & Publishers: Coatbridge.

Houston H. R., Ministry of Fuel and Power (1953) *Report for the Scotland Division of H.M. Inspector of Mines for 1952*. Under the Coal Mines Act 1911. HMSO: London.

Hyde H., Ministry of Fuel and Power (1959) *Report for the Scotland Division of H.M. Inspector of Mines for 1958*. Under the Coal Mines Act 1911. HMSO: London.

Hyde H., Ministry of Fuel and Power (1960) *Report for the Scotland Division of H.M. Inspector of Mines for 1959*. Under the Coal Mines Act 1911. HMSO: London.

Hyde H., Ministry of Fuel and Power (1961) *Report for the Scotland Division of H.M. Inspector of Mines for 1960*. Under the Coal Mines Act 1911. HMSO: London.

Hyde H., Ministry of Fuel and Power (1962) *Report for the Scotland Division of H.M. Inspector of Mines for 1952* for 1961. Under the Coal – Mines Act 1911. HMSO: London.

Hyde H., Ministry of Fuel and Power (1963) *Report for the Scotland Division of H.M. Inspector of Mines for 1962*. Under the Coal Mines Act 1911. HMSO: London.

Masterton J., *Report for the Scotland Division: HMSO (1922) Mines & Quarries: Annual Reports of (a) Secretary of Mines, (b) H.M. Chief Inspector of Mines, (c) H.M. Chief Inspector of Mines for 1921*. Harrison & Sons: London.

Masterton J., *Report for the Scotland Division: HMSO (1923) Mines & Quarries: Annual Reports of (a) Secretary of Mines, (b) H.M. Chief Inspector of Mines, (c) H.M. Chief Inspector of Mines for 1922*. Harrison & Sons: London.

Masterton J., *Report for the Scotland Division: HMSO (1924) Mines & Quarries: Annual Reports of (a) Secretary of Mines, (b) H.M. Chief Inspector of Mines, (c) H.M. Chief Inspector of Mines for 1923*. Harrison & Sons: London.

Masterton J., Report for the Scotland Division: HMSO (1925) *Report for the Scotland Division: HMSO (1922) Mines & Quarries: Annual Reports of (a) Secretary of Mines, (b) H.M. Chief Inspector of Mines, (c) H.M. Chief Inspector of Mines for 1924*. Harrison & Sons: London.

McLaren R., Report on the Eastern Districts of Scotland in: HMSO (1903) *Report of the Inspectors of Coal Mines for 1902*. Darling & Son Ltd: London.

McLaren R., Report on the Eastern Districts of Scotland in: HMSO (1905) *Report of the Inspectors of Coal Mines for 1904*. Darling & Son Ltd: London.

McLaren R., Report on the Eastern Districts of Scotland in: HMSO (1906) *Report of the Inspectors of Coal Mines for 1905*. Darling & Son Ltd: London.

McLaren R., Report on the Eastern Districts of Scotland in: HMSO (1910) *Report of the Inspectors of Coal Mines for 1909*. Darling & Son Ltd: London.

Ministry of Fuel & Power (1955) *Coal Mines Act 1911: Regulations and Orders Relating to Safety and Health* (Supplement to the 1953 edition). HMSO: London.

Moore R. Esq., Report on the Eastern Districts of Scotland in: HMSO (1874) *Report of the Inspectors of Coal Mines for 1873*. George Edward Eyre & William Spottiswood: London.

Moore R. Esq., Report on the Eastern Districts of Scotland in: HMSO (1882) *Report of the Inspectors of Coal Mines for 1881*. George Edward Eyre & William Spottiswood: London.

Moore R. Esq., Report on the Eastern Districts of Scotland in: HMSO (1883) *Report of the Inspectors of Coal Mines for 1882*. George Edward Eyre & William Spottiswood: London.

Moore R. Esq., Report on the Eastern Districts of Scotland in: HMSO (1884) *Report of the Inspectors of Coal Mines for 1883*. George Edward Eyre & William Spottiswood: London.

Moore R. Esq.,Report on the Eastern Districts of Scotland in: HMSO (1885) *Report of the Inspectors of Coal Mines for 1884*. George Edward Eyre & William Spottiswood: London.

Moore R. Esq., Report on the Eastern Districts of Scotland in: HMSO (1889) *Report of the Inspectors of Coal Mines for 1888*. George Edward Eyre & William Spottiswood: London.

National Coal Board (1954) *Diary for Search of Underground Workers for Smoking Materials* (Mines & Quarries Act 1954, Section 66). HMSO: London.

Steele A. H., *Report for the Scotland Division: HMSO (1922) Mines & Quarries: Annual Reports of (a) Secretary of Mines, (b) H.M. Chief Inspector of Mines, (c) H.M. Chief Inspector of Mines for 1948*. Harrison & Sons: London.

Walker W., Report on the Eastern Districts & of Scotland in: HMSO (1911) *Report of the Inspectors of Coal Mines for 1910*. Darling & Son Ltd: London.

Walker W., Report on the Eastern Districts of Scotland in: HMSO (1912) *Report of the Inspectors of Coal Mines for 1911*. Darling & Son Ltd: London.

Walker W., Report on the Eastern Districts of Scotland in: HMSO (1914) *Report of the Inspectors of Coal Mines for 1913*. Darling & Son Ltd: London.

Walker W., Report for the Scotland Division: HMSO (1915) *Report of the Inspectors of Coal Mines for 1914*. Harrison & Sons: London.

Walker W., Report for the Scotland Division: HMSO (1919) *Report of the Inspectors of Coal Mines for 1915–18*. Harrison & Sons: London.

Walker W., Report for the Scotland Division: HMSO (1920) *Report of the Inspectors of Coal Mines for 1919*. Harrison & Sons: London.

Widdas W., Ministry of Fuel and Power (1954) *Report for the Scotland Division of H.M. Inspector of Mines for 1953*. Under the Coal Mines Act 1911. HMSO: London.

Widdas W., Ministry of Fuel and Power (1955) *Report for the Scotland Division of H.M. Inspector of Mines for 1954*. Under the Coal Mines Act 1911. HMSO: London.

Widdas W., Ministry of Fuel and Power (1956) *Report for the Scotland Division of H.M. Inspector of Mines for 1955*. Under the Coal Mines Act 1911. HMSO: London.

Widdas W., Ministry of Fuel and Power (1957) *Report for the Scotland Division of H.M. Inspector of Mines for 1956*. Under the Coal Mines Act 1911. HMSO: London.

Widdas W., Ministry of Fuel and Power (1958) *Report for the Scotland Division of H.M. Inspector of Mines for 1957*. Under the Coal Mines Act 1911. HMSO: London.

Williams R., Report on the Eastern Districts of Scotland in: HMSO (1858) *Report for the Scotland Division of H.M. Inspector of Mines for 1857*. George Edward Eyre & William Spottiswood: London.

Newspapers and Periodicals

Glasgow Herald September 12 1952.

Haddingtonshire Courier 1861–1962.

Musselburgh & Portobello News 1942–1951.

Secondary Sources

Ashton T. S. (1964) *The Coal Industry of the Eighteenth Century*. Manchester University Press.

Benson J. (1989) *British Coal Miners in the Nineteenth Century: A Social History*. Longman: London and New York.

Burton A. (1976) *The Miners*. Futura Publications Ltd.: Norwich.

Calder A. (1997) *The Peoples War: Britain 1939–45*. Jonathan Cape: London.

Campbell R.H (1971) *Scotland since 1707: The Rise of an Industrial Society*. Basil Blackwell: Oxford.

Church R. (1986) *The History of the British Coal Industry*: volume III 1830–1913. Clarendon Press: Oxford.

Devine T.M. (ed.) (1990) *Conflict and Stability in Scottish Society*. John Donald Publishers LTD. : Edinburgh.

Devine T.M. & Finlay R. J. (1996) *Scotland in the Twentieth Century*. Edinburgh University Press: Edinburgh.

Devine T.M. & Mitchison R. (Ed.) (1998) *People and Society in Scotland*: Volume I. 1760–1830. John Donald Publishers Ltd.: Edinburgh.

Dickson A. & Treble J.H. (ed.) (1998) *People and Society in Scotland*: Volume III, 1914–1990. John Donald Publishers LTD: Edinburgh.

Duckham H. & B. (1973) *Great Pit Disasters in Britain 1700 To The Present Day*. David & Charles Newton Abbot.

East Lothian District Library (1986) The Pans Remembered.

Edmond T. W. (1981) *Reflections on the Life and Times of the Edinburgh Collieries Company Ltd*.

Fraser W.H. & Morris R.J. (Ed.) (1995) *People and Society in Scotland*: Volume II. 1830–1914. John Donald Publishers LTD. : Edinburgh.

Hobsbawm E. J. (1968) *Industry and Empire*. Pelican Books: Great Britain.

John A. V. (1980) *By the Sweat of Their Brows: Women Workers at Victorian Coal Mines*. Croom Helm: London.

Johnson P. (1994) *20th Century Britain: Economic, Social and Cultural Change*. Longman: London & New York.

Lynch M. (1998) *Scotland a New History*. Pimlico: London.

MacNeill P. (1902) *Prestonpans and its Vicinity: Historical, Ecclesiastical Traditional*. Remploy Ltd.: Leicester.

MacNeill P. (1883) *Tranent and its Vicinity: Historical, Ecclesiastical and Traditional*. Remploy Ltd.: Leicester.

McAdam R. & Davidson D. (1955) *Mine Rescue Work*. Oliver & Boyd: Edinburgh & London.

McCaffrey J. (1998) *Scotland in the Nineteenth Century*. MacMillan Press LTD.: London.

More C. (1989) *The Industrial Age: Economy and Society in Britain 1750–1985*. Longman: London and New York.

Orwell G. (1989) *The Road to Wigan Pier*. Penguin Books: London.

Scottish Records Office (1983) *The Coal Miners*.

www.scran.ac.uk (Internet Site).
Smout T.C. (1997) *A Century of the Scottish People 1830–1950*. Fontana Press.
Smout T.C. (1998) *A History of the Scottish People 1560–1830*. Fontana Press.
Tulloch A. P. (1989) *Prestonpans in Old Picture Postcards*. European Library: Zaltbommel, Netherlands.

NOTES

1 First Report of the Commissioners of Mines for the Childrens Employment Commission Volume 189. Appendix: Reports and Evidence from Sub Commissioners (1842) HMSO: London, p. 65
2 P. MacNeill (1902) *Prestonpans and its Vicinity: Historial, Ecclesiastical and Traditional*. Remploy Ltd.: Leicester, pp. 9–10
3 T. C. Smout (1998) *A History of the Scottish People 1560–1830*. Fontana Press, p. 230
4 Ibid, p. 403. R.H Campbell (1971) *Scotland Since 1707: The Rise of an Industrial Society*. Basil Blackwell: Oxford, p. 128
5 T. C. Smout (1998) p. 168. And T.M. Devine & R. Mitchison (Ed.) (1998) *People and Society in Scotland*: Volume I. 1760–1830. John Donald Publishers LTD: Edinburgh, p. 237
6 First Report of the Commissioners of Mines (1842): Appendix, p. 385
7 First Report of the Commissioners of Mines(1842): Appendix, p. 385. T. C. Smout (1998) pp. 403–404. P. MacNeill (1902), p. 13
8 T.M. Devine & R. Mitchison (Ed.) (1998), p. 197
9 R.H. Campbell & J.B.A. Dow (1968) *Source Book of Scottish Economic and Social History*. Basil Blackwell: Oxford. p. 143
10 Ibid, p. 144
11 R.H. Campbell & J.B.A. Dow (1968), p. 145. T.C. Smout (1998) pp. 403–4
12 R.H. Campbell (1971), p. 128
13 R. Church (1986) *The History of the British Coal Industry*: volume III 1830–1913. Clarendon Press: Oxford, p. 317
14 C. More (1989) *The Industrial Age: Economy and Society in Britain 1750–1985*. Longman: London and New York, p. 114
15 J. Benson (1989) *British Coal Miners in the Nineteenth Century: A Social History*. Longman: London and New York, p. 34
16 First Report of the Commissioners of Mines for the Childrens Employment Commission (1842) *Parliamentary Papers* Volume 188. HMSO: London, p. 61
17 J. Benson (1989), p. 34
18 First Report of the Commissioners of Mines (1842), Appendix, p. 380. P. MacNeill (1902), p. 16
19 R. Church (1986), p. 362: illustrations
20 First Report of the Commissioners of Mines (1842), p. 60
21 First Report of the Commissioners of Mines (1842): Appendix, p. 444
22 A. Burton (1976) *The Miners*. Futura Publications Ltd.: Norwich, p. 116
23 T.C. Smout (1997) *A Century of the Scottish People 1830–1950*. Fontana Press, p. 95
24 R. Church (1986), p. 315
25 R.Moore Esq., Report on the Eastern Districts of Scotland in: HMSO (1883) *Report of the Inspectors of Coal Mines for 1882*. George Edward Eyre & William Spottiswood: London, p. 295
26 R. Church (1986) , p. 321
27 Ibid, p. 321
28 A. Burton (1976), p. 31 and R. Church (1986), p. 321
29 *Haddingtonshire Courier* 5 April 1861
30 *Haddingstone Courier*, 1 June 1877. The firemen were the men who would go down the pit each day before a shift began to ensure that it was safe for colliers to work in
31 R. Moore Esq., (1883), p. 295 & P. MacNeill (1902), p. 19
32 R. Moore Esq., (1883), p. 295
33 A. Burton (1976), p. 115
34 R. Church (1986) , p. 327
35 R. Church (1986) , p. 325–7 & J. Benson (1989), p. 33
36 R. Church (1986) , p. 325–9
37 A. Burton (1976), p. 115–6

38 *Haddingtonshire Courier* 2 September 1887
39 Ministry of Fuel & Power (1955) *Coal Mines Act 1911: Regulations and orders relating to safety and health* (Supplement to the 1953 edition), HMSO: London, pp. 44–50
40 W. Walker, Report for the Scotland Division: HMSO (1915) *Report of the Inspectors of Coal Mines for 1914*. Harrison & Sons: London, p. 67
41 W. Walker, Report for the Scotland Division: HMSO (1919) *Report of the Inspectors of Coal Mines for 1915–18*. Harrison & Sons: London, p. 25
42 R. Moore, Esq., Report on the Eastern Districts of Scotland in HMSO (1884) *Report of the Inpectors of Coal Mines for 1883*. George Edward Eyre & William Spottiswood: London, p. 98
43 J. Benson (1989), p. 33
44 W. Walker, Report on the Eastern Districts of Scotland in HMSO (1911) *Report of the Inspectors of Coal Mines for 1910*. Darling & Son Ltd: London, p. 28. W. Walker, Report on the Eastern Districts of Scotland in HMSO (1912) *Report of the Inspectors of Coal Mines for 1911*. Darling & Son Ltd: London, p. 47
45 C.P. Snodgrass (1953) *The Third Statistical Account of Scotland: The Country of East Lothian*. Oliver and Boyd: Edinburgh and London, p. 48
46 T.W. Edmond (1981) *Reflections on the Life and Times of the Edinburgh Collieries Company Ltd*, p. 89
47 First Report of the Commissioners of Mines (1842), pp. 28–9
48 Ibid, p. 29
49 First Report of the Commissioners of Mines (1842), p. 29
50 First Report of the Commissioners of Mines (1842), pp. 29–30
51 Ibid, pp. 29–30
52 *Haddingtonshire Courier* 9 January 1885
53 Ibid, 12 July 1861
54 A. Burton (1976), p. 33
55 First Report of the Commissioners of Mines (1842): Appendix, p. 470
56 J. Benson (1989), p. 32
57 www.scran.ac.uk, SCRAN ID:000-000-014-910-C
58 A. Burton (1976), p. 32
59 Edmond T.W. (1981), p. 89
60 *Haddingtonshire Courier* 28 July 1865, 7 October 1870, 4 May 1877
61 First Report of the Commissioners of Mines (1842): Appendixn, p. 394
62 *Haddingtonshire Courier* 13 January 1883 and 30 April 1886
63 C. More (1989), p. 222
64 See table of fatal accidents in Figure 12
65 A. Calder (1997) *The Peoples War: Britain 1939–45*. Jonathan Cape: London, pp. 438–9
66 C. Brister *This Is My Kingdom*, as quoted in T.W. Edmond (1981)
67 J. Benson (1989), pp. 44–46
68 First Report of the Commissioners of Mines (1842): Appendix, pp. 411–12
69 Ibid, p. 412
70 *Haddingtonshire Courier*, 21 November 1879
71 Ibid, 21 November 1879
72 A. Burton (1976), p. 117
73 R. Church, (1986) d, p. 256
74 See table in figure 15. The others were mentioned earlier and occurred in 1877 and 1887; *Haddingtonshire Courier*, 1 June 1877 and 2 September 1887
75 J. Benson (1989), p. 33
76 First Report of the Commissioners of Mines(1842), pp. 121 and J. Benson (1989) , p. 34
77 C.P. Snodgras, (1953), p. 64
78 J. Masterton, Report for the Scotland Division: HMSO (1922) *Mines & Quarries: Annual Reports of (a) Secretary of Mines, (b) H.M. Chief Inspector of Mines, (c) H.M. Inspector of Mines for 1921*. Harrison & Sons: London, pp. 32–38
79 T.W. Edmond (1981), p. 86
80 *Haddingtonshire Courier* 24 January 1945 and 29 June 1956
81 R. McAdam & D. Davidson (1955) Mine Rescue Work. Oliver & Boyd: Edinburgh & London, p. 108
82 T. W. Edmond (1981), p. 90
83 J. Masterton, Report for the Scotland Division: HMSO (1924) *Mines & Quarries: Annual Reports of (a) Secretary of Mines, (b) H.M. Chief Inspector of Mines, (c) H.M. Inspector of Mines for 1923*. Harrison & Sons: London, pp. 35–36

84 W. Widdas, Ministry of Fuel and Power (1957) *Report for the Scotland Division of H.M. Inspector of Mines for 1956*. Under the Coal Mines Act 1911. HMSO: London, p. 19. W. Widdas , Ministry of Fuel and Power (1958) *Report for the Scotland Division of H.M. Inspector of Mines for 1957*. Under the Coal Mines Act 1911. HMSO: London, p. 20. H. Hyde, Ministry of Fuel and Power (1960) *Report for the Scotland Division of H.M. Inspector of Mines for 1959*. Under the Coal Mines Act 1911. HMSO: London, p. 26. H.Hyde, Ministry of Fuel and Power (1963) *Report for the Scotland Division of H.M. Inspector of Mines for 1962*. Under the Coal Mines Act 1911. HMSO: London, p. 274 H.Hyde, Ministry of Fuel and Power (1963) *Report for the Scotland Division of H.M. Inspector of Mines for 1962*. Under the Coal Mines Act 1911. HMSO: London, p. 274

85 J. Masterton (1924), p. 33

86 J. Masterton, Report for the Scotland Division: HMSO (1925) *Mines and Quarries: Annual Reports of (a) Secretary of Mines, (b) H.M. Chief Inspector of Mines, (c) H.M. Inspector of Mines for 1924*. Harrison & Sons: London, p. 45

87 T. Ashley, Report for the Scotland Division: HMSO (1948) *Mines & Quarries: Annual Reports of (a) Secretary of Mines (b) H.M. Chief Inspector of Mines, (c) H.M. Inspector of Mines for 1939–47*. Harrison & Sons: London, pp. 36–7

88 P. Johnson (1994) *20th Century Britian: Economic, Social and Cultural Change*. Longman: London & New York & C. More (1989)

89 *Glasgow Herald*, 12 September 1952

90 *Haddingtonshire Courier* 19 September 1952

91 W. Widdas (1954), p. 20

92 H.R. Houston, Ministry of Fuel and Power (1953) *Report for the Scotland Division of H.M. Inspector of Mines for 1952*. Under the Coal Mines Act 1911. HMSO: London, p. 4

93 H. & B. Duckham (1973) *Great Pit Disasters in Britian 1700 to the Present Day*. David & Charles: Newton Abbot, pp. 14–16

7
Model Housing for Prestongrange Miners

Annie Lyall

The pitman homeward treads his weary way,
Glad to behold the faintest light of day:
To change his garb, and sit beside the coal
He help'd from yon tremendous hole.[1]

INTRODUCTION

The housing of the working classes was an issue of growing dominance in Britain, as in other industrialised nations, during the second half of the 19th century and the first half of the 20th. The outcome of this housing debate has had significant consequences for British housing policy. This chapter will look at miners' housing during this period, stressing the Scottish experience and especially that at Prestongrange. The reason for highlighting miners' housing, as opposed to shipbuilders, railway or factory workers housing, does not simply lie in the fact that mining is a primary topic of this book. In an era when the housing debate was a core issue in the political life of the nation, miners' housing had a distinctive role to play.

To trace this story, this chapter has been divided into five sections. The first section delves into the background of coal industry housing, taking it up to last part of the 19th century and comparing it to other working class housing in Scotland. This demonstrates why miners' housing was a special case, raising problems and issues peculiar to it. The term 'model' applied to houses will be looked at, its origins and what that label meant in practise for miners' housing, especially at Prestongrange. Working class attitudes were changing and an acceptance of conditions that could be described as inherently dirty was giving way to a mood of rising expectations as the nation went towards the First World War.

Miners' houses were functional, built to shelter the workers and their families who lived in them. It is the story of these people, their feelings, and the attitudes of the rest of society towards their communities, that is embodied in the buildings, such as those at Prestongrange in Cuthill and Morrison's Haven. To appreciate what life in these homes might have been like, the second section looks behind the doors of miners' houses to see the families who lived there and the hardships they endured. Public opinion towards working class housing conditions was changing and the issue staked a claim on the political agenda that it was to hold for decades to come.

The third section picks up the story at the end of the First World War looking at various means of addressing the housing problem during the 'Homes Fit for Heroes' campaign of the 1920's and how it affected the miners living around Prestonpans. In the inter-war years, a mounting campaign to improve miners' housing met inevitable opposition but the seeds of its eventual success had been sown.

The Second World War brought a temporary halt to the saga but in the fourth section it begins again with the nationalisation of the coal industry in 1946. Putting nationalisation into effect lifted the lid on the problem of miners' housing yet again and renewed pressure for a permanent solution. At Prestongrange, the fate of the old miners' houses reached its inevitable conclusion in the 1950's and new 'model' houses appeared. Evidence of the progress that had been made towards better living conditions for miners will be seen in the proposals for a 'new' Scottish mining town in Fife.

In the last section, a somewhat different note will be struck with a selection of memories. These will give an idea of the spirit of mining communities, the way they spent their leisure time and how some people from the "kittle" saw their community at Prestongrange.

HOUSING BEFORE THE 20TH CENTURY

19th century coal mining was a labour intensive operation. In order to have a supply of labour convenient to the pit shaft, coal owners were often forced to provide housing because many pits were located in rural areas, far from centres of population. The numbers involved could mean that such housing schemes were villages in themselves where everyone was supported directly or indirectly by the local pit. In many cases, building houses for miners was an absolute necessity in order to mine coal from the pit.

There were advantages and disadvantages to this arrangement for both coal owners and miners. From the coal owner's point of view, building large numbers of workers houses in rural areas might be essential but was also an expensive and unproductive capital outlay. The houses would be needed only for the duration of the life of the pit. That life depended on the amount of coal available in the seam, the duration and buoyancy of the coal market, and technological developments in the industry. This is one of the reasons why coal owners often spent as little as possible on houses for their workers. Also there was little incentive for coal owners to renovate houses and bring the facilities up-to-date if they thought the pit might be abandoned within the next few years. If a pit closed, realising any financial return on the houses was unlikely. Often there was no other work to be had in the neighbourhood and a ghost town was created. As early as 1853 a writer commented that "Houses and pits are often simultaneously abandoned and the place presents a most desolate appearance".[2]

There were additional problems associated with providing housing in newly developing rural coalfields. Drainage, sanitation and water supply could pose particular difficulties which were often accentuated by the large numbers of miners involved.[3] Access could also be a problem. Rows of miners' houses might be built beside a good public road, maintained by the rates, but they might be constructed in a field with access by a private road, possibly poorly built and badly maintained, cutting the inhabitants off, even from the local tradesman's carts.[4] The most common plan for a group of miners' houses was a series of parallel rows of connected houses, like the Cuthill houses at Prestongrange. One row was often a mirror image of the next. These long rows might be unbroken and without back doors, condemning those living in the middle of the row to a long walk in order to make use of washhouse and sanitary facilities behind the houses. It is easy to see why Campbell suggests that the term 'flung down' describes the planning aspect of many miners' rows.[5]

There were advantages for coal owners in owning the housing stock in which their workers lived. They could put the houses very close to the pit making them convenient for work, particularly when walking was the working man's common mode of transport. This had the added advantages of encouraging good attendance and making it more difficult for the colliers to seek other employment.[6] As was demonstrated by the 1842 unrest in the coal fields, owning their employees houses gave coal owners a power over their workforce denied to other industrialists.[7] During one strike, for example, a mine owner was able to threaten to cut off the water supply to his collier's village, unless they paid for the water to be pumped from the mine.[8] This extension of the coal owner's control beyond the workplace and into the home was a significant aspect of mining culture which set it apart from other trades. In 1877 when colliers in the west of Scotland won a battle against their employers for higher wages, they were also able to negotiate lower rents, demonstrating that the system could occasionally work the other way.[9]

This relationship between employment and housing is significant. It is probable that the balance worked more commonly in favour of the coal masters. As landlords they were able to guarantee security of rental payments from their tenants. Regulations listed in an 1856 report on the "State of the Population in the Mining Districts" show that rent was deducted direct from the miner's salary.[10] Eviction was not a problem for the coal owner either, as employees could be forced out of colliery housing on the day they finished or were discharged from work.[11]

Colliery expansion during the 19th century was driven by the demands of the industrial revolution. In Scotland, many of the earliest coalfields to be efficiently exploited for commercial use were in the west, in counties such as Lanarkshire, Ayrshire, Stirlingshire and Dunbartonshire, where miners' housing on a larger scale started to be built. Colliers housing from an earlier era was still in use. Typical early colliers' houses were stone built with thatched or turf roofs. Any concept of rustic charm is banished by this description of such collier's housing written in 1842.[12] The inadequacy of the roofs was such that they let in "... wind and rain ...".[13] Both thatch and rafters were unlikely to be renewed when required which meant that they might become rotten and "infested with bugs, which occasionally dropped down". Add to this the "... paper, bundles of rags, and old hats ..." which were stuffed into windows in place of missing glass and, on occasion, the "... straw strewed in the corner of the apartment, serving as a bed for the family." and some picture of the depths to which colliers housing might sink in this period becomes apparent.[14] This particular description comes from the Tranent district, close to Prestongrange.

Without running water, sanitary arrangements in miners' houses consisted of dry-closets and refuse went on ash-pits or middens, both separate from the houses, which had to be cleaned out by a scavenger who would take the filth away by cart. The frequency and effectiveness of his visits depended on the colliery owners who hired him.

It was in a mid-19th century mining community at Legbrannock, near Holytown in Lanarkshire that James Keir Hardie (1856–1915), was born. He started work in the pits at Quarter at the age of ten, as a trapper. He was destined to work to improve miners' housing conditions, first as organising secretary of the Ayrshire Miners' Union and later as one of the first labour MP's elected to Parliament in 1892.

It is interesting to make comparisons between miners' housing and working

Example of the effects of neglect and lack of maintenance in early Miners' Housing
Courtesy of Central Regional Council Archives Department

class housing generally in Scotland during the 19th century. Government policy, or lack of it, had relied on market forces to meet the need for working class housing. In the cities, this had resulted in landlords "making down", or subdividing, older houses while new housing often consisted of filling in open spaces in inner city areas.[15] Many 19th century miners' houses were single rooms, known as single ends, or two rooms, known as but-and-bens. By the standards of the day this would not have seemed unusual. Glasgow had 226,723 one-apartment houses when the 1861 census was taken and 8,000 of these were windowless.[16] It is estimated that "almost one-third of Scotland's people were living in dwellings of one room" at this time.[17] Overcrowding was endemic in working class housing and housing expectations were low. What is important from the point of view of miners' housing, is to try to discover when it was much the same as other working class housing and when or why it started to get left behind. In this respect it is interesting to note that by the 1890's the number of Glasgow's one-apartment houses had dropped sharply to 36,000,[18] demonstrating an improvement in housing conditions which indicates changing attitudes towards them.

One initiative, indicative of such change, can be seen in Edinburgh. In the spring of 1861, a new company, called The Edinburgh Co-operative Building Company Limited, was established to build houses for artisans.[19] The houses were planned on a basic three room model, with internal water closet and coal cellar. Many of the shareholders of this company were artisans who intended to live in the houses they built and they aimed to combine quality of construction with low expenditure.[20] Among the pioneering spirits behind this movement was the Reverend Doctor James Begg (1808–1883), a minister with the Free Church of Scotland. Begg published a book in 1873, entitled *Happy Homes for Working Men and How to Get Them*,[21] demonstrating a concern, felt by many, that the quality of working class housing had a crucial role to play in the serious social problems of the day. The 1860's also witnessed the appointment of Scotland's first Medical Officers of Health, whose work provided evidence of the links between poor housing and bad health. These men were to play an important role in bringing the state of miners' housing to the attention of the nation.

The Edinburgh movement is a good example of the idea behind 'model' homes. They were ideal homes not only in design but also because they took into account the profit margins necessary for builders and landlords.[22] The term 'model' in connection with dwellings first arose in connection with lodging-houses, established in the 1840's by philanthropists, who instituted various "regulations intended to secure the comfort and the orderly conduct of the inmates."[23] The term was later abused by proprietors whose lodging-houses did not meet the necessary requirements.[24] In the case of miners' 'model' housing, the comfort of the tenants often appears to have taken a lower priority than the landlord's ability to impose orderly conduct on his tenants and secure the colliery company's profits.

This paints the general picture, but what of Prestongrange? Up to the early 1870's, mining was obviously carried out on a small enough scale that miners' houses were scattered over the estate. The row of five miners houses at Bankfoot,[25] beside Cuthill, probably similar in construction to other early colliers' houses, are examples. All this was to change. Sir George Grant Suttie leased out the mining operations on his estate to the Prestongrange Coal & Iron Company Limited of Middlesbrough in late summer 1874. Across the county boundary in Midlothian, so many landlords did the same in this period, that noble coalmasters control of mining enterprises was slashed from 60% in 1842 to 7% by 1880.[26]

It is arguable that miners' welfare and housing suffered as a result. Many noble coal owners had begun to treat their colliers with a benevolent paternalism that was an extension of the way they managed the rest of their estate.[27] In 1873 the Earl of Lothian, who owned substantial estates in Midlothian and built good houses for his miners,[28] agreed with Sir George that mine owners should agree a common policy covering the treatment of their mines and miners.[29] However he refused to become a part of such an association if it was based on colliery practices in the west of Scotland, because of the difference in their methods.[30] Here Lothian puts his finger on an important aspect in the development of Scottish mining in the period. With the introduction of ironmasters into the coal industry in the west, colliery organisation in that region was changing to meet the demands of increasing scale and higher production, often at the cost of miners' welfare. This situation was spreading eastwards and would encompass the whole Scottish coal industry in the 19th century,[31] destroying the relationship between noble coal owners and their colliers.

Prestongrange appears to have been fortunate that Sir George would seem to have continued as a more conscientious and sympathetic landowner than most. He suggested to Lothian, for instance, that the labouring population in the South of Scotland might need "...special interference in their favour". Lothian, on the other hand, felt their situation was better than ever before[32] –

but better than what? Until the complete Emancipation Act, passed as late as 1799, miners and their families, alone amongst British labourers, had been bonded to coal owners for life, their position not unlike that of serfdom. This not only separated them as a community from other labourers and affected the attitudes of society towards miners, but also meant that there was little to force the introduction of better conditions in their industry. The 19th century might have seen conditions for miners and their families improve significantly, but they had started from a very low base.

The Prestongrange Coal and Iron Company set about planning the exploitation of the coalfield and, in July 1874, Mr. Jones, the Secretary of the Iron and Steel Institute of Great Britain submitted a report on this to the Company.[33] He estimated that a financial investment of £30,000 would be necessary to cover the cost of harbour repairs, a branch railway and a new shaft, while half as much again would be needed, over a period of three years, to build two hundred workmen's houses.[34] This figure was based on single shift working, although the company's managing partner, Mr. Kitto, was contemplating two or even three shifts per day, increasing profits, but also the number of houses that would be required.[35] The original site for these houses was at Morrison's Haven, beside the pit shaft, an important consideration if Mr. Kitto's shift work, with its awkward hours, was to be instituted. Such proximity to the pit was common but meant that miners' housing was often subject to subsidence due to the mine workings below which caused cracking and broken plasterwork in the houses.[36]

In November, when plans for the building of the houses were already well advanced, Sir George suggested that an open field site to the south of Cuthill be considered instead, partly because of a proposed Fire Clay Manufactory on the Morrison's Haven site.[37] Situated between Prestongrange and the western end of Prestonpans, Cuthill already had a small community living in stone-built houses on the coast, whose inhabitants had worked mostly in the pottery and salt works.[38] The contrast between the 'modern' Cuthill and the dilapidated, old dwellings beside which it was springing up must have been quite striking.[39] The following autumn sixty miners' houses were being built at Cuthill, with a further one hundred and fifty planned, when the Company sought a loan of £6,000 from Sir George to cover increased costs in harbour repairs, proposing the sixty houses as collateral.[40] The Prestongrange company had not chosen the best time for their expansion, as the boom years of coal and iron, with their high profits, had came to an end in the mid-1870's, and the future of the coal market was less certain.[41]

It is unlikely that tighter financial constraints affected the design of the houses. During 1875–6, one hundred and seventeen houses were built at Cuthill in five blocks of two storeys each. Front Street and Middle Street had arrived. This choice of street names is typical of the unimaginative approach taken towards the construction of such mining communities. For the first time in this area the new houses were built of brick, which was cheaper than stone, and might also reflect the fact that the company organising the construction came from England, where brick was popular. The roofs were slated, which would last longer than thatch. These houses reflected a new scale and commercialism in the coal industry and their style was to become as typical of Scottish miners' rows as English.

Alternate doors in the rows led either straight into the ground floor or up a wooden staircase to the floor above and each house consisted of two rooms, which would have been considered reasonably spacious by Scottish working class standards of the day.[42] In some cases both floors were occupied as one house, presumably enabling a larger number of people to be accommodated. This might mean that more than one family lived there, as letting out rooms to lodgers was common practice, sometimes forced on tenants by the coal company. However, taking in lodgers was also one of the very few methods a miner's wife might add to the family income.[43]

These first Cuthill houses had no internal running water or sanitation but each house had a brick built and slated outbuilding containing an ash closet and a coal house. This would have been perfectly acceptable by the standards of the day but they were built much too close to the houses, risking the spread of disease and assuring the presence of unpleasant smells for the householders.[44] In 1894, John Martine wrote about several of the parishes in East Lothian and referred to Cuthill as a small village, on a low hill, with "a long row of excellent miners and workmen's houses" which demonstrates the favourable impression the houses made in the late 19th century.[45] Martine says that the place was then known as "the Cuttle" and oral tradition had it that the origins of this name lay in the fact that, the sinking of minerals below ground, had caused the local burn to change course cutting the hill in two.[46]

One person who watched these houses being built was the local minister in Prestonpans, Dr. Struthers. He wrote to Sir George in November 1876 casting some interesting light on the new mining community at Cuthill.[47] Visits to families within this large and rapidly increasing section of the parish, prompted Dr. Struthers to suggest that this shifting population, which had largely migrated from the west, should have the services of a missionary.[48] Dr. Struthers bluntly demanded what Sir George intended to do for this community, pointedly linking its mushrooming growth and the inadequacy of welfare provision available, to the greatly increased income from his estates that Sir George must now be enjoying.[49] Sir George's reply was courteous and equally to the point: "I am disposed to build at my sole expense and maintenance a handsome school..." and " ...a room in connection with it to be used as a place for public worship on Sundays and as a reading room on other days."[50]

Sir George was as good as his word and the miners' children were henceforth educated at Cuthill School. It was a fine red sandstone building with high windows, designed so that light could get in but children could not look out. It stood on the other side of the road from Front Street and was so close to the sea shore that, in bad weather, waves broke over the back wall of the playground.

Sir George died in 1878. His son, James, died later that same year, leaving a boy of eight as the new laird, a situation that was likely to weaken the family's connection with the community at Cuthill. Whilst it is tempting to bemoan the loss of such individual acts of paternalistic benevolence, such as the building of the school at Cuthill, such philanthropy was proving ineffective against the demands of Scotland's new industrialised society. Just as a new spirit of commercialism had moved into working practices, so a greater spirit of professionalism was beginning to grow in welfare, taking it out of the realms of philanthropy and into the world of politics.

In 1895, the Summerlee and Mossend Iron and Coal Company Limited took over the Prestongrange enterprise, following the demise of the Prestongrange Coal and Iron Company Limited. The origins of Summerlee were in Coatbridge in Lanarkshire and they had taken over Mossend, a company from Motherwell. Development at Prestongrange was again to be subject to pressures and

Eastward view of Cuthill School, Morison's Haven, Prestonpans
East Lothian Council, T.J. Knight Collection

influences from the west. Summerlee started building forty-four miners houses that same year at Morrison's Haven, comprising two double-storey blocks. The main differences in design between these houses and Front and Middle Streets were that the first floor houses were reached by outside stone staircases which had coal cellars underneath and, instead of individual ashpits, there was an additional building for every eight houses, which contained two washhouses, four water closets and ashpits.[51]

Summerlee's next housing development was at Cuthill with the construction of the first twenty-nine houses of Summerlee Street, completed in 1900.[52] By the time Summerlee Street was finally finished, there were five blocks of thirty-two houses each and the Cuthill community had increased by some one hundred and sixty households, most of whom used water wells by the staircases.[53] The last 32 houses to be built on Summerlee Street, during the First World War, were of a higher standard, containing baths, water closets and sinks.[54] Locally these houses appear to have become known as Bath Street,[55] for obvious reasons. Whilst the term 'model' to describe the Morrison's Haven and Cuthill miners' houses might seem somewhat exaggerated in present day terms, it fairly reflects their standard compared to other working class housing at the time and the fact that there were many miners much worse off than they were. This was particularly the case in the west of Scotland where many pits were reaching the end of their productive life, causing maintenance of the housing stock to be neglected. However, in common with the majority of miners' housing, the Cuthill houses had not been built to last and would start to lag behind as working class housing generally improved.

The greatly increased supply of miners housing can be assumed to have been connected to the expansion of the pit which included the sinking of a deep shaft at Prestongrange in 1906 to work the under-sea coal. There was a general increase in population in the area during this period. Between 1871 and 1911 the population of Prestonpans rose from 2,069 to 4,722, while nearby Cockenzie doubled in size.[56] Increased output was undoubtedly one factor in this population increase, but another may be assumed to be the higher than average family size common amongst miners. In 1901, miners, along with crofters, averaged just over seven children per family, compared with professional groups who averaged four.[57] Family size was another significant factor in the housing of miners. Large families were still a feature of mining communities ten years later when the 1911 census was taken.[58] It is arguable that the isolated position of many mining communities meant that these larger than average families might also be relied upon to replenish the labour force in the pit.

Having looked at how the Cuthill community was becoming established, it is time to return to the national picture in Scotland by the end of the 19th century. The number of colliery-owned houses stabilised in 1890 at approximately 140,000.[59] Scottish miners' housing offered the cheapest accommodation nation-wide,[60] but it was "...almost universally inferior..." and conditions were "...worse than in any other region".[61] In other areas, such as the north-east of England, signs of improvement were becoming evident by the last decades of the century.[62]

Scottish miners were not uncritical of the conditions under which so many of them lived. The Secretary for Scotland received deputation's of miners in 1909 and 1911 as part of a campaign mounted to highlight the plight of their communities. One aspect of a growing awareness of the effects of their living conditions on miners and their families was a set of reports commissioned by the Local Government Board. These reports were prepared by various Medical Officers of Health of mining communities in Scotland because the close relationship between diseases, such as typhoid and tuberculoses, with domestic habit and environment, and the infectious nature of such diseases, was becoming better understood.[63] By 1900, with improving sanitation, fear of typhus was receding, but tuberculosis, in all its forms, was still the major killer after heart disease.[64]

One of these reports, written by John McVail in 1911, was on miners' housing in Stirlingshire and Dunbartonshire.[65] It demonstrates changing attitudes towards the disgraceful condition of some miners' housing. McVail's report is analytical in style and undramatic in language, but still makes chilling reading. Parts of it must have made uncomfortable reading for coal owners, but his grasp of the underlying reasons for the situation, his ability to see all sides of the question and his sincere humanism, make his report useful evidence of the situation as it existed. The tone of his report is positive, concentrating not only on the various problems encountered but also on solutions.

McVail divides the different types of miners' rows in his area into two main categories, those built before and those after the Building Bye-laws brought in after the 1897 Public Health (Scotland) Act.[66] On this basis, Front and Middle Streets at Cuthill fall into the first category and Summerlee Street into the second. Plans for new buildings after 1897 had to be submitted for County Council scrutiny on health grounds, although their scope was so limited that even as basic a facility as the supply of water within houses was not included.[67]

Information on the houses built before 1897 demonstrates why miners' rows were becoming an emotive topic in the working class housing debate. Accurate statistical information was not available but McVail used 1,643 of the 1,881 houses built prior to 1897 for comparison.[68] Only 119 had the use of water closets, some were without any sanitation facilities whatever, none contained baths, only 45 had indoor water, 470 had no coal houses and the vast majority of drains were open channels.[69] These figures demonstrate that hundreds of families were condemned to a degrading standard of living, even by the standards of the day, where disease might almost be classed as an occupational hazard because of its close links with colliery employment.

Of the 873 miners houses built in Stirlingshire and Dunbartonshire between 1897 and 1911, 735 had two rooms[70] and a good proportion of more modern houses contained a scullery and even running water.[71] 589 out of McVail's 873 houses had an indoor water supply though the other 264 had only outside water.[72] This demonstrates that the majority of new houses in the area included many up-to-date facilities but, like other miners' housing, they were probably hastily erected and cheaply built, requiring a high level of maintenance which was unlikely to be provided.

What is particularly interesting about this report is the light it sheds on the administration of these housing estates. Refuse removal, including the manual removal of sewage, comes top of the list of problems. McVail could not understand why the necessity of employing scavengers on a frequent, and not just a regular, sometimes monthly, basis was not understood.[73] He proposed that Local Authorities should be given powers to take colliery villages into their own scavenging districts to ensure higher standards of public health.[74] With groups of houses too small in number to warrant Local Authority intervention, the problem simply became one of expense, an easy matter for mine owners to rectify.[75] It can be assumed that he understood only too well that reluctance to spend money was one of the root causes of the problem.

Responsibility was the key. McVail's solution was that larger mining communities should come under the umbrella of Local Authorities.[76] Between them the 1892 Burgh Police Act and the 1894 Local Government Scotland Act had combined to strengthen local government in terms of its responsibility for various municipal functions and the welfare of the poor. As a solution to the problem of conditions on miners' rows, putting them under the direct control of Local Authorities was to become a growing cry but Scotland, at the turn of the century, was going to take time to adjust to that concept.

FAMILY LIFE

One group regularly singled out for praise by McVail were miners' wives. Until the mid-19th century, whole families had worked down the pit. Public concern prompted the 1842 Royal Commission on the Mines. This revealed such startling facts about women being "chained, belted, harnessed, like dogs in a go-cart" whilst they pulled loads of coal, that the first protective labour legislation for women was enacted.[77] The 1842 Mines Act made it illegal for all women, and any children under the age of ten, to work down the mines. One aspect of this, was the expectation that it would be a major step towards improving the miner's standard of living.[78] Their wives were exchanging one full-time occupation, for which they received a salary, for another, for which they did not. Without employment, it may be assumed that earlier marriage became a feature of mining communities and that this was consequently a contributing factor to the larger than average size of miners' families.

Domestication of miners' wives was also a significant feature behind the term 'model' relating to miners' housing. Both men and women could now carry out socially approved roles[79] conducive to the "comfort and orderly conduct" of the household. Mining communities had changed from "virtually lawless and primitive communities, hastily erected, attracting a restless population, into something more representative of, and acceptable to, mid-Victorian standards."[80] This concept would seem to lie behind Dr. Struther's appeal to Sir George Grant Suttie in 1876 on behalf of the community at Cuthill.

A child's description of his mother's working day shows how hard miners' wives worked in the home:

> "She would be up at three in the morning to prepare a breakfast and a bait for my eldest brother, a hewer, who started at four o'clock. When he went to work she would try and snatch an hour's sleep before going through the same routine for one of my younger brothers, a datal worker, whose shift started at six. Meanwhile, father, who had started his night shift the previous evening at ten, would be coming out of the pit at six and going home for his breakfast and bath in front of the fire. By the time father had finished breakfast and bathed in the zinc tub in front of the fire it would be time for the three younger children to get ready for school. Even when they had been packed off to school mother had no time to rest. The hewers only worked a six-and-a-half to seven hour shift and she had to prepare a dinner for my eldest brother returning from the early shift. The children would be home from school for their mid-day meal before he had finished washing in front of the fire. In all probability father would get up and have something with the children at mid-day and then go to the local for a pint. When the children went back to school mother had to prepare for the afternoon shift at 2 p.m. when me and my two other brothers went down the pit. By the time his bath water was off the kitchen floor it was nearly time for the school children to be home for tea. Father would be back from the pub by tea-time and he would try to get a couple of hours sleep before night shift started at ten. Mother's work was not finished yet – in fact the biggest job of the day was to come. After 10 p.m. the three brothers who had gone to work at 2 p.m. would be home and mother not only had to prepare their dinner but she also had to boil water in the pan and kettle on the fire for their baths. Altogether, it would take anything up to two hours before they were finished. Consequently, it was always after midnight before mother got to bed at the end of a normal day – and the alarm clock would be ringing at three o'clock for the start of the next."[81]

It is a lengthy description but it was a long day which must have been physically very demanding. There is no mention made of the clothes washing that was also a feature of her day or the wet garments that must often have been draped around the one or two-room house when it was too wet for them to dry outside. Privacy was a luxury that could not be afforded within the home. Outside the home was no better if latrines had to be shared by several families, like the village of Drongan in Ayrshire, where fifteen families shared one earth closet.[82] Critics agree that this particular hardship was a greater affliction for women than men.

The role of children can also be seen to have changed. The 1872 Scottish Education Act made attendance at school compulsory between the ages of five and thirteen. The foundation of the Scottish National Society for the Prevention of Cruelty to Children, in 1884, demonstrated people's changing attitudes towards their offspring who came to be valued in a new light and to hold a central role within the family.[83]

As has been said, the only latrines in many miners' rows often consisted of foul-smelling ash-middens or privy-middens, good breeding grounds for flies which could then infect food. The design of the rows was such that children would play on the midden heaps, which made the outbreak of diseases, like typhoid, inevitable. McVail found that communities with no sanitation facilities, where people used the surrounding countryside, were sometimes better off than ones where rubbish and excrement were not regularly removed.[84] If there was an outbreak of typhoid, enough was known about the spread of disease to arrange for daily removal of waste, at least as long as the outbreak lasted. Open channels for drainage also facilitated the spread of disease, if not regularly cleaned, but the introduction of underground drains usually improved matters.

It was, therefore, "a matter of genuine surprise and admiration", surrounded as they were by such filthy conditions, not to mention the dirt and contamination brought back from the pit and the lack of facilities for coping with this, that miners' wives achieved such a high degree of cleanliness and order in their homes.[85] The Herculean nature of their task might make it interesting to dip into the psychology behind this, to learn a little more about mining communities like those at Prestongrange. Douglas and Wildausky assert that there is a strong connection between the society in which people live and those risks they choose to worry about or ignore.[86] Each society gives different priorities to different risks and, in order to belong to a particular society, people adopt common fears and values. Communities link certain risks and their adverse consequences to moral defects, so that knowing why people ignore some risks and lay emphasis on others, will demonstrate much about their community. Miners' wives faced the very real dangers encountered by their menfolk working down the pit for "between 1868 and 1919 a miner was killed every six hours, seriously injured every two hours and injured badly ... every two or three minutes"[87] They could do nothing about this nor about the squalid, insanitary, industrial conditions by which they were surrounded or the filthy midden heaps that served as their children's playground. However, they placed a high priority on the standard of cleanliness within the home. This leads to the assumption that a dirty home would have been the object of social criticism and even an indication of some moral deficiency. Keeping their houses clean must have been a major challenge, but it was one area where they could make a difference and their personal effectiveness would be judged on their success. Due to the identical nature of the houses on miners' rows, comparisons would have been easily made.

Although women in mining communities could do little to improve their circumstances, there was increasing public pressure for better housing. It is arguable that this made the miners' housing issue politically sensitive enough to be taken more seriously by politicians, who served an expanded electorate after the Reform Acts of 1868 and 1884. Men like Keir Hardie and William Adamson (1863–1963), who became West Fife's first miner M.P. in 1910, spoke from personal experience when they appealed in the House of Commons on behalf of those who lived in mining communities. Little could be achieved on the issue during the First World War but, by the time the armistice was signed in 1918, action was already being taken. The housing issue now occupied a central position in the political sphere.

HOMES FIT FOR HEROES

Originally set up in response to the 1912 Rent Strike, a year when unprecedented political action was taken by miners in a national strike, the Royal Commission on the Housing of the Industrial Population in Scotland finally reported in 1918. Of the twelve Commissioners, David Gilmour was Secretary of the Lanarkshire Miners' County Union and Charles Augustus Carlow was head of the Fife Coal Company, ensuring that the issue of miners' housing would be adequately covered.[88] The evidence submitted to the Commission by Thomas McKerrey and James Brown, of the Ayrshire Miners' Union, demonstrates that the miners' campaign for better housing was active and that the most disreputable housing was still in use.[89] Along with detailed descriptions of the dreadful state of repair into which many houses in Ayrshire mining communities had fallen, the submission proposed a plan for workmen's houses, prepared by a teacher of building construction, and a list of suggested remedies.[90] The first remedy consisted of putting a Closing Order on many of the houses, considered beyond repair.[91] The second was that miners' homes should not be provided by employers since "the tenants in many cases fear, rightly or wrongly, that it is not to their interests to complain to the employer to whom they are indebted for their employment about the condition of their houses".[92] Much of the blame for the state of the houses was attributed to this attitude which led to an acceptance of the worst conditions for fear of unemployment.[93] The Commission concluded that Scottish working class housing was "much, much worse" than its English counterpart.[94]

Following the end of the war and a General Election in 1918, Lloyd George became leader of a coalition government with a promise to build 'homes fit for heroes'. In January, 1919 the Miners Federation of Great Britain put a set of proposals covering wages and conditions of employment before the new Government. They also called for state ownership of the mines to be introduced under a scheme of joint administration by miners and the state. The government's refusal to

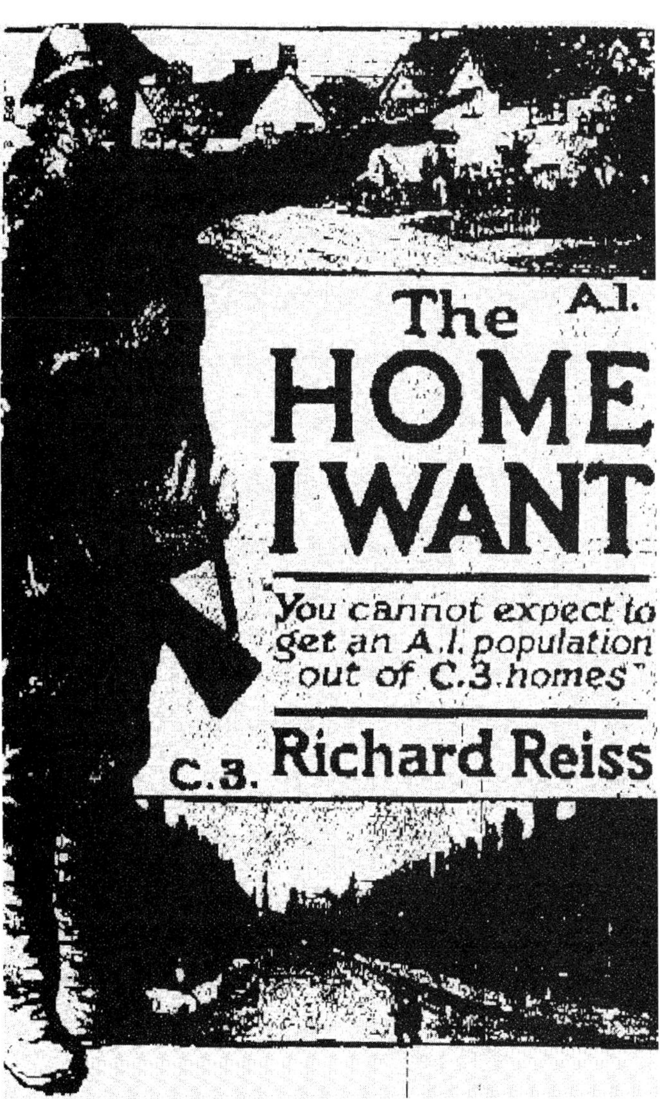

'Homes for Heroes' publicity where army health standards were applied to housing, dated 1918.
Courtesy of the Bodleian Library

meet these demands led to an overwhelming majority of miners backing strike action. To avert this, Lloyd George offered another Royal Commission, to include in its brief: wages, conditions, future organisation and the housing issue. Half the members of the commission were to be appointed by or approved by the Miners' Federation. The Prime Minister's strategy succeeded in averting a strike and the Coal Industry Commission, under the Chairmanship of Mr. Justice Sankey, began work at the beginning of March, 1919.

The Sankey Commission reported later that same month, condemning the system in the mining industry as it stood and recommending nationalisation.[95] One of the chief witnesses to the Commission was John Robertson, Scottish President of the Miners Federation and his evidence on housing conditions in the industry, which came from first hand experience, publicised the squalid, unhealthy and overcrowded nature of the housing conditions in which many Scottish miners lived.[96] Mr. Justice Sankey attacked such housing as "a reproach to our civilisation. No judicial language is sufficiently strong or sufficiently severe to apply to their condemnation."[97]

Government voiced support for the Sankey Commission's findings and the strike threat was lifted in April under the impression that the Government would implement the Commission's recommendations.[98] In August, Lloyd George rejected nationalisation and the most tangible asset that the mining industry gained from the Sankey commission was the setting up of the 'Miners' Welfare Fund', financed by the introduction of a levy of one penny on each ton of coal produced. The aim of the Fund was to finance 'the social well-being, recreation and conditions of living' of coalminers although housing itself was not included.[99]

The specific exclusion of housing from the Welfare Fund's activities may be misleading. Housing conditions were significantly affected because one of the Fund's priorities was the provision of pithead baths. These were obligatory on the continent and had been in use in Germany for the previous twenty-five years.[100] As far back as 1853, an author on conditions in mining communities had not only stressed the importance of such baths for miners' health but had gone into detail on how they might be cheaply run using some of the quantities of newly condensed steam run off into "hot ponds" at the pithead.[101]

The installation of pithead washing and changing facilities removed the need to wash men and their clothes at the end of each shift, easing the workload of miners' wives and improving the atmosphere and amenity of the house itself.[102] Moreover it meant that the public no longer saw the miner going home after his shift, black with filth, red-eyed and often stooped. Instead, he headed home looking like any other workman, improving the public's perception of miners.[103] The introduction of pithead baths was slow but by 1945 somewhere in the region of 63% of miners had the use of such facilities.[104]

Lloyd George's reaction to the miners' demands in March 1919 reflected, not only a desire to avert strike action, but also government fear of a growing mood of dissatisfaction in the country. It was felt this might lead to revolution, as had recently happened in Russia, if the returning soldiers could not be persuaded that "the bad old days" were a thing of the past.[105] The government promised to build half a million homes which would be completely new in concept.[106] This policy was influenced by the Garden City Movement, the roots of which lay in industrial housing for the working classes.

Other industries also appreciated the advantages to be gained from owning the houses in which their employees lived, but their approach was different from that of coal owners. As early as 1887 Lever Brothers had moved their soap factory to an open site on the Mersey and built a factory-village which they called Port Sunlight. In 1895 Cadbury followed suit at Bourneville near Birmingham. These communities enjoyed a standard of housing and an environment that was a vast improvement on previous working class housing.[107] This could genuinely claim to be 'model' housing. The concept pleased socialists and capitalists alike by transforming working people's living conditions on the one hand and leading to an increase in productivity which might be expected from a more contented workforce on the other.[108]

Density was the major difference in Garden City layouts which aimed to achieve eight houses to an acre and to give each house its own reasonably-sized garden.[109] It is interesting to note that the same year Bourneville was being laid out on garden city lines, Summerlee were building forty-four miners' houses on a one acre site at Morrison's Haven.[110] In the instance and spread of disease, especially tuberculosis, overcrowding and housing density were important factors.[111] Another aspect from which the garden city movement was determined to get away was the long straight rows of houses like those at Prestongrange.[112] One of the original architects behind the garden city movement was Raymond Unwin, who went on to play an important part in the design of state housing after the War.[113]

Another influence on Government housing policy after the war was the Tudor Walters Report, published in November, 1918. This Committee, comprising distinguished experts in the housing field, assumed that it was necessary to achieve "an improvement in the general standard of housing and more importantly that the standard of housing demanded by the working class had risen in the past and would continue to do so in the future."[114] As a measure of the importance government placed on the housing issue, the 1919 Housing Act was passed enabling Local Authorities to become major suppliers of housing.

As far as Scotland was concerned the 'Homes Fit for Heroes' campaign was a failure. Barely 2,000 houses were built by 1920 whilst 48,000 were constructed in England.[115] Government support for its housing policy was short-lived but the principle of Local Authority housing meeting much of the population's housing needs had been established and the standard expected had been laid down by the Tudor Walters Report.[116]

The effects of the Local Government Act (Scotland) 1889 were becoming more apparent in the rising power and influence of Local Government institutions. For example, between 1919 and 1939, East Lothian County Council undertook a building programme of some five and a half thousand houses and the reconditioning of many properties to meet the requirements of the County Sanitary Inspector.[117] The second highest number of houses built in one area were in Preston and Prestonpans where 437 Local Authority funded houses were built.[118] A building programme of this magnitude needed a great deal of investment in utility services. In 1938, East Lothian Water Board was set up and the following year was supplying over 90% of the water consumed in the County.[119] The Portobello Power Station provided the power supplied by the Lothians Electric Power Board which started the public supply of electricity in 1923.[120] The coastal situation of places like Prestonpans meant that sewage was mainly disposed of into the sea, in time honoured fashion, but efforts were now being made to restrict the number of outfall sewers on beaches, concentrating on fewer, larger outflows.[121] Education was

Sketch of a group of four miners' cottages at 'Preston Garden City', dated 1925
East Lothian Council, David Spence Collection

brought under the direct control of the Local Authority who built three secondary schools in the interwar period, one of which was at Prestonpans.[122]

The mining community around Prestonpans directly benefited from the garden city movement. In 1924–1925 Edinburgh Collieries Limited, owners of Preston Links Colliery, commissioned Mr. A.E. Horsfield, an Edinburgh architect, to lay out a housing scheme on garden city lines at Preston.[123] These miners homes were one-storey, three-roomed dwellings with bathrooms and sculleries which were in "striking contrast to the dingy long rows and squares which were features of the mining hamlets of fifty and a hundred years ago". They were also quite a contrast with Cuthill just down the road. In the 1920's debate centred on the positive aspects of improvement in miners' housing, whilst negative aspects, such as the small proportion of the problem that was actually being addressed, were ignored.

Conditions in mining communities in East Lothian, including Cuthill, played a prominent part in the miners' housing campaign early in 1924. Prestonpans district was one of nine mining areas specifically mentioned in talks between Lord Novar, the Secretary for Scotland, a deputation of Scottish Labour M.P.'s, and John Robertson.[124] These talks resulted in the preparation of a report on housing conditions in mining areas in East Lothian, drawn up by a Scottish Board of Health Housing Inspector.[125] Conditions were likely to be so similar, that Local Authorities in other mining areas were asked to take measures to deal with the defects highlighted by the East Lothian report.[126]

This report enables a check to be carried out on the progress of the Cuthill and Morrison's Haven houses. There were 1,012 miners' houses in East Lothian in 1924, the vast majority of which belonged to colliery companies, although 100 houses, let mostly to miners, had recently been put up by the Local Authority, using Government subsidy.[127]

Within the parish of Prestonpans there were 370 miners houses. The 44 houses at Morrison's Haven were considered to be "well constructed and all in good order", with "fairly good" access.[128] 128 of the Cuthill houses were described as broadly similar to those at Morrison's Haven. The Inspector was critical of the close proximity of each block of houses to the next which did not allow "a sufficiency of sunlight and ventilation".[129] Some of the facilities had been updated in Front and Middle Streets. Privies had recently been replaced by water closets although the Inspector felt the back yards were small.[130] Some of these yards had been cleared away and "a water Closet and sink with water laid on" was now provided in the scullery of each house.[131] The Inspector noted that there was daily refuse removal, a good water supply and that the amenities were of a good enough standard that he could make no practical suggestions to improve them further.[132]

Modernisation of the facilities of the Cuthill houses may stem from the "healthy rivalry" which the Inspector found had grown between the Edinburgh Colliery Company, which ran the Preston Links pit, and the Summerlee Coal and Iron Company, which ran the Prestongrange pit.[133] Prestonpans miners were often referred to as 'Grange' men, or 'Links' men. These companies may have been using housing as an incentive in competing for labour, especially skilled labour, as Scotland lost a disproportionate number of servicemen in the war and many of those who survived, emigrated rather than return to their former life.[134] If only such market forces could have been brought to bear on miners' housing earlier. The Inspector's other comment on the pleasant landscape and situation the miners' enjoyed in the Prestonpans area is interesting when compared to a problem experienced in the narrow South Wales' valleys where miners' houses were "deprived of sun and air."[135]

One of the key signs that the miners' housing campaign was beginning to have a serious impact was that the coal owners felt obliged to put their side of the case. A pamphlet published by a 'Scottish Architect' in the 1920's gives the arguments from the coal owner's side.[136] These include the fact that it was not their business to supply houses for their employees,[137] and that cost was a prohibitive factor against building more desirable housing for miners.[138] It is fair to say that schemes built on garden city lines were expensive. The pamphlet also suggests that miners' housing problems should be dealt with by the Local Authority,[139] a conclusion also reached by John McVail. Government had already rejected nationalisation which might have been one way to achieve this.

The General Strike in 1926 followed by depression and unemployment in the thirties aggravated the financial and social problems of mining communities. The miners stayed on strike for six months, and during this time a soup kitchen was opened at Cuthill School, serving those in need with a bowl of soup and a bread roll.[140] Many were prompted to leave the coalfields, or migrate from one to another in search of a better standard of living and many mining communities shrank as a result. Between July 1923 and July 1937, the numbers of insured workers in the coal industry nationally fell by 27%, whilst in Scotland this figure was 32%.[141] Demoralisation amongst miners was so acute that three years into the Second World War the ministry of information was concerned to find a general attitude that "we would be as well off under Hitler" in the Scottish coalfields.[142]

NATIONALISATION AND LOCAL GOVERNMENT

After the Second World War, the Coal Industry Nationalisation Act, 1946, finally delivered nationalisation but also a new twist in the tale of miners' housing. The 140,000 colliery houses due to be taken over by the National Coal Board were not considered to be assets with "coal industry value", only "subsidiary value" and the Board were keen not to pay excessive compensation for them.[143] Once more, miners' housing became the subject of dispute. The Board considered the houses as part of a going concern, whereas coal owners were looking for compensation which reflected replacement or open market value for the houses.[144] It was the old problem of the inter-relationship between pits and housing. In Scotland the dispute went to court but, after negotiation, the case was adjourned and a formula, known as the "Newbiggin Formula" worked out.[145] Owners could appeal against a housing valuation to a tribunal composed of representatives from both sides and any decision of this body would be final.[146]

The vesting date for the Board's take-over was lst January, 1947. At Prestongrange, Sir George Grant Suttie, as superior, was due compensation for the land on which the miners' houses at Morrison's Haven and Cuthill stood.[147] In May that year Sir George died, leaving his successor, a minor living in Canada, to receive compensation.[148] The young man's lawyers claimed £260 for the superiorities but settled for the Board's award of £240 in 1949, finally bringing the Grant Suttie's long connection with the mining community to a close.[149]

The Board's valuation of the forty-four houses at Morrison's Haven was signed in 1951.[150] The valuer was unimpressed by the houses which had no hot water or hand basins and roofs which required constant attention because of proximity to the colliery.[151] In his view they would be subject to a closing or demolition order within the next ten years.[152] He was even less impressed by Front Street, one block of which had already been demolished by 1951. The houses had outside water closets, roofs lacking any form of sarking or felt, and were bug-infested so that three of the houses were already empty and deemed to be uninhabitable.[153] Never built to last, they had certainly reached the end of their useful life by 1951.[154]

No valuation exists for Middle Street which, photographic evidence shows, had been demolished in the mid-1940's along with one block of Summerlee Street.[155] The four remaining blocks, containing 128 houses, had no hot water and the coal boilers in the sculleries were burnt out and obsolete. The Board valuer recommended immediate roof and plasterwork repairs but warned that these houses would also probably be subject to a closing order within the next ten years.[156] Elizabeth Neilson remembers this era when "flittings" from Cuthill took place daily as families were rehoused and more and more houses fell empty.[157]

It was June, 1954 before the Board began settling the last compensation claims for colliery housing but it was pleased that the final figure paid was lower than it might have been.[158] It was less pleased with the houses themselves and it's attitude towards them has a familiar ring to it. They did not want to take on the responsibility of managing the newly-acquired miners' houses and wanted to hand them over to Local Authorities, a proposal which had been made before.[159] East Lothian County Council were offered what remained of the miners' housing at Prestongrange.[160]

East Lothian County Council's annual budget on housing in 1950 stood at nearly £290,000, demonstrating their importance as a housing authority by this time.[161] Three years later, the County Council had 278 houses they considered substandard, of which 144 belonged to the Board and 103 of these were in the Prestonpans area.[162] The Council were drawing up a slum clearance plan which would close the old Coal Board houses at Prestonpans and rehouse the tenants in Local Authority houses.[163] It is not difficult to see the Local Authority's hand behind the demolition that had already taken place at Cuthill, some of which had been necessary in order to widen and straighten Prestonpans High Street.[164]

A new era in the housing of miners had dawned. East Lothian County Council had become involved in drawing up housing policies to meet mining employment prospects as early as 1944.[165] Their attempts to link housing policy to projected production targets in the industry had resulted in frustrations similar to those that coal owners had met in the past.[166] Now, solutions could be worked out on a regional basis. The location of miners' housing mattered less when men could be taken by bus to whichever pit had work for them.[167] Thus it was no longer necessary to live beside the pit, spelling the end of mining communities as they had existed until then. A 1958 aerial photograph shows that the Cuthill community had gone by that time but, in what had been fields to the south of Cuthill, the appearance of new houses and roads demonstrates that the County Council were fulfilling their commitment to provide housing of a good standard which was available for miners as for other applicants.[168] The influence of the garden city movement may be seen in the layouts of these new Local Authority schemes of houses and gardens set on the ground above Cuthill.

Miner returning home from work after using the 'new' NCB Bathhouse (c 1950)
East Lothian Council, David Spence Collection

It is interesting to look at how planning for a new mining town was handled in the 1950's. First its aims were set out: "The primary purpose of the New Town is to house the miners who will work in the new Rothes Pit now being sunk near Thornton, and other miners who work in adjoining areas. It is expected that these will be miners transferred from declining coal-fields in Lanarkshire and Central Fife and they will, of course, bring their families with them."[169] Significant progress had been made since colliers' families from declining Lanarkshire coalfields arrived at Prestongrange in the 1870's. No thought was given to achieving a balanced employment structure for them so that miners would only form one in eight of the community as they were to do at Glenrothes. Sir George Grant Suttie's choice of a site for housing, its hasty construction and the donation of a school at Cuthill, pales by comparison with the planning effort involved in the proposed facilities for housing, education, welfare, recreation, roads, and

View of Prestongrange featuring NCB 'improvements' such as (from right) Road Transport, Bathhouse, Cafeteria
East Lothian Council, David Spence Collection

drainage which the General Manager of Glenrothes New Town was co-ordinating long before construction began.

MEMORIES

Living in new urban settings was bound to be very different for miners and their families after the hard and demanding life of the old mining communities. Memories of the old days are full of enthusiasm and concentrate on the amusing aspects of the situation whilst elements of hardship are simply shrugged off.

People brought up in the "Kittle" remember the games of their childhood; skipping, marbles, or "joukin the waves" in the school playground, where the penalty for getting it wrong was to get soaked.[170] They remember all the visits to the cinema, Cadona's in Prestonpans, nicknamed "the scratcher", and scrambling over rocks at the sea shore on the way home.[171] The annual Grange Miners Gala Day was also remembered. It was a huge treat involving a great procession to Cuthill park, with tea, cakes, ice-creams and sweets on the grass, followed by sports and prizes for the winners.[172] In the inter-war years, dancing was popular with young people who reeled, waltzed and did square dances, and then went to Antonelli's chip shop for large bags of fish and chips.[173] Football was a popular sport. Even if there was no money to buy a real ball, tennis balls or rags bound with string were used instead.[174] Young boys graduated into the local league to play for teams like "Summerlee Thistle" and the "Bing Boys", fighting it out for the trophy that Mr. McGuire, a miner from Summerlee, had donated.[175]

Should the passing of those times be mourned? One woman remembers living in Front Street with her grandmother in the early 1900's. Before school each day the child had to fetch two pails of fresh water from the well beside the Front Street Post Office, collect rolls from the baker for her grandfather's breakfast when he returned from the pit, and still clean out the fire and dispose of the ashes before heading to school.[176] There was no rest for her on Sundays either, because twenty-two pails of water had to be collected to fill the barrels for Monday's wash.[177] There is pride in the way she writes of this contribution she made to the running of the household but the hard physical work it entailed should not be under-estimated. Memory is selective and good at blocking out or dulling that which it would rather forget. Reading such accounts of life in Cuthill, deprivation illnesses, like rickets, or those from poor sanitation, like dysentery, do not feature, yet feature they did.

There is one particularly wistful note in these memories. Planning for housing had come a long way by the 1950's but, the obvious advantages of better housing tended to disguise the radical nature of the move people were being asked to make. The houses were a vast improvement on what had gone before and often tenants had gardens they could enjoy, but the community was broken up. The wonderful spirit of the "Kittle" was lost and the new housing schemes seemed like "graveyards" by comparison.[178] This community spirit grew out of the physical effort each individual had to put into belonging to such communities. Much of the evidence that has been looked at demonstrates the lack of privacy in old mining communities but that was also one of their lifelines. Everyone in mining communities knew everyone else's business, down to the amount they earned, but they also knew when neighbours needed help or when someone was up to no good. There was no such thing as a closed door in the "Kittle" but once inside their new houses, tenants were able to shut the door so that the old ways of maintaining their community no longer worked, posing different problems and demanding new solutions.

BIBLIOGRAPHY

Primary Source Material

City Art Centre, Edinburgh, Exhibition *Housing the People*, November 1999.

East Lothian Local History Centre: East Lothian County Council Survey Report, 1953, Valuation Rolls, Valuation Rolls for the County of East Lothian

David Spence Collection – Naysmith, J. *As I Remember,* (1992) *Haddingtonshire Courier*

National Archives of Scotland: Valuation Field Book material from Lloyd George's Doomsday Valuation and relevant maps of Inland Revenue Service. Housing of Miners in Scotland, CB 7/10

Extracts from the Report on the Royal Commission on Housing, 1917

Scottish Board of Health: Housing Conditions in Mining Areas, 1924

National Coal Board, Scottish Division: NAS Compensation Unit material dated 27.6.1951

Correspondence 1954 and Recommended scales and valuation of of Houses and details of legal dispute

Paper on the New Town of Glenrothes, Fife, October, 1950

National Library of Scotland, Map Library: Maps of Prestongrange and Prestonpans from 1853–1960

RCAHMS Aerial Photographs of Prestpans Area: 1946, 1947, 1953, 1958, and 1960.

Registers of Scotland, Property Search Records, County of East Lothian.

Scottish Mining Museum, Lady Victoria Colliery, Newtongrange: McVail, J.C., Medical Officer of Health, *Housing of Scottish Miners: Report on the Housing of Miners in Stirlingshire and Dunbartonshire*, (1911)

Scottish Architect, *The Housing of Miners in Scotland: A Review of the Position*, (circa 1920)

Department of Planning & Building Control and Environmental Health of Midlothian District Council.

Secondary Source Material

Anderson, M. & Morse, D.J. 'The People', in Fraser, W.H., & Morris, R.J. (eds), *People and Society in Scotland, Vol 11*, (1995)

Butt, J. 'Working Class Housing in the Scottish Cities, 1900–1950', in Gordon, G. & Dicks, B., (eds), *Scottish Urban History*, (1983)

Campbell, R.H. *Scotland Since 1707: The Rise of an Industrial Society*, (1985)

Checkland, O. & S. *Industry and Ethos: Scotland 1832–1914*, (1989)

Church, R. *The History of the British Coal Industry, Vol 3, 1830–1913*, (1986)

Cunningham, A.S. *Mining in Mid and East Lothian: History of the Industry from Earliest Times to Present Day*, (1925)

Donaldson, R. 'From Six to Twelve' in East Lothian District Council, *The Pans Remembered*, (1986)

Douglas, M. & Wildausky, A. *Risk and Culture*, (1982)

Elliott, E.J., (Ed) *Historical Sources for Central Scotland: 2: The Coal Industry 17–20 Centuries*, (1978)

Hardy, A. *The Epidemic Streets: Infectious Disease and the Rise of Preventive Medicine, 1856–1900*, (1993)

Harvie, C., *No Gods and Previous Few Heroes: Scotland Since 1914*, (1993)

Hassan, J.A. 'The landed estate, paternalism and the coal industry in Midlothian, 1800–1880', in *Scottish Historical Review*

MacFarlane, A. 'Fond memories of my Childhood', in East Lothian District Library, *The Pans Remembered*, (1986)

McNeill, P. *Prestonpans and Vicinity*, (1902)

Martine, J. 'Reminscences and notices of Ten Parishes of the County of Haddington, Parish of Prestonpans', in East Lothian District Library, *The Story of Prestonpans from contemporary records, 1790's–1950's*. (1995)

Neilson, E. 'Cuthill', in East Lothian District Library, *The Pans Remembered*, (1986)

Nisbet, D. 'Not a Trace Left', in East Lothian District Library, *The Pans Remembered*, (1986)

Oakley, A. *Housewife*, (1976)

Oxford English Dictionary, Vol VI, The Philological Society, (1961.

Page Arnot, R. *A History of the Scottish Miners*, (1955)

Pipes, R.J. *The Colonies of Stockbridge*, (1998)

Rodger, R., *Housing the People – The Colonies of Edinburgh*, (1999) To accompany exhibition of same name, available RCAHMS

Scottish Record Office (NAS) *The Coalminers* (1983)

Snodgrass, Catherine P. 'The Parish of Prestonpans in the Third Statistical Account of Scotland, 1953', in East Lothian District Library, *The Story of Prestonpans from contemporary records, 1790's–1950's*, (1995)

Supple, B. *The History of the British Coal Industry, Vol 4, 1913–1946: The Political Economy of Decline*, (1987)

Strawhorn, J., *Notes on the Evidence Submitted to the Royal Commission on Housing (Scotland) by Thomas McKerrey and James Brown from the Ayrshire Miners' Union*, (1976)

Swenarton, M. *Homes Fit for Heroes: The Politics and Architecture of Early State Housing in Britain*, (1981)

Tindall, F., *Memoirs & Confessions of a County Planning Officer*, (1998)

Tulloch, A.P., *Prestonpans in Old Picture Postcards*, (1989)

Traveller Underground, A. *Our Coal and Our Coal-Pits: The People in Them, and the Scenes Around Them*, (1853)

Turner, L., *Chopwell's Story*, pub. Gateshead Metropolitan Borough Council Department of Education. No date.

NOTES

1 A Traveller Underground, *Our coal and Our Coal-Pits*, (1853) p. 190
2 Op cit., A Traveller Underground, p. 189
3 Church, Roy, *The History of the British Coal Industry, Vol 3 1830–1913*, (1986) p. 609
4 McVail, John C., MD., LL.D., County Medical Officer, *Housing of Scottish Miners: Report on the Housing of Miners in Stirlingshire and Dunbartonshire*, (1911) p. 55
5 Campbell, R.H., *Scotland Since 1707: The Rise of an Industrial Society*, (1985) p. 144
6 Op cit., Church, p. 601
7 Checkland, O & S., *Industry and Ethos: Scotland 1832–1914*, (1984), p. 87
8 Op cit., McVail, p. 47
9 Op cit., Checkland, p. 88
10 NAS publication, Document 22, p. 24, quoted from *Report for 1856 of the Commissioner on the State of the Population in the Mining Districts,* (1856), Appendix B, p. 58, Item IV.
11 Ibid. Item II
12 NAS publication, Document 21, p.23, *Report on the Sanitary conditions of the Labouring Population of Scotland* (1842) S. Scott Alison, M.D. on 'The Sanitary conditions in Tranent and colliery districts', p. 85.
13 Ibid
14 Ibid.
15 Op. cit., Checkland, p. 108
16 Ibid. p. 109
17 Ibid.
18 Ibid. p. 111

19 For a full description of this movement look at Pipes, Rosemary J., *The Colonies of Stockbridge*, (1984)
20 Ibid.
21 Begg, James, D.D., *Happy Homes for Working Men and How to Get Them*, (1873)
22 From Housing Exhibition at City Art Gallery, Edinburgh, November 1999
23 *Oxford English Dictionary*
24 Ibid.
25 NAS, Valuers Field Books, IRS/110/115
26 Hassan, John A., 'The landed estate, paternalism and the coal industry in Midlothian, 1800–1880', in *Scottish Historical Review*, pp. 73–74
27 Ibid. p. 88
28 Ibid.
29 NAS GD/357/69/13
30 Ibid.
31 Op cit., Campbell, p. 104
32 NAS GD/357/69/13
33 NAS GD/357/74/19
34 Ibid.
35 Ibid.
36 Page Arnot, R., *A History of the Scottish Miners*, (1955) p. 135
37 NAS GD/357/74/27
38 Snodgrass, Catherine P., *The Parish of Prestonpans in the third Statistical Account of Scotland, 1953*, p. 78
39 McNeil, P., *Prestonpans and Vicinity: Historical, Ecclesiastical & Traditional*, (1902) pp. 247–8
40 NAS GD/357/74/26
41 Op cit., Campbell, p. 105
42 NAS Valuers Field Books IRS/144
43 Op cit., Church, p. 633
44 NAS Valuers Field Books IRS/144
45 Martine, John, *Reminiscences and Notices of Ten Parishes of the County of Haddington: Parish of Prestonpans, 1894*, p. 61
46 Ibid. p. 63
47 NAS GD/357/34/10
48 NAS GD/357/34/10
49 Ibid.
50 NAS GD/357/34/11
51 NAS Valuers Field Books IRS/145/146
52 NAS Valuation Rolls for the County of Haddington/East Lothian Years 1900–1901
53 NAS Valuers Field Books IRS/145/146
54 NAS DD6/ll73 Report by Scottish Health Department Housing Inspector, 1924, p. 2
55 Tindall, Frank, *Memoirs and Confessions of a County Planning Officer*, (1998), p. 141
56 *East Lothian County Council Survey Report*, 1953
57 Anderson, M. & Morse D.J., in Fraser, W. Hamish and Morris, R.J. (Eds) *People and Society in Scotland, Vol II*, (1995), p. 40
58 Ibid.
59 Op cit., Church, p. 599
60 Ibid. p. 604
61 Ibid. p. 607
62 Ibid. p. 608
63 Hardy, A., *The Epidemic Streets: Infectious Disease and the Rise of Preventive Medicine, 1856–1900*, (1993), p. 211
64 Ibid.
65 Op cit., McVail
66 Ibid. p. 16
67 Ibid. p. 7
68 Ibid. p. 34
69 Ibid. p. 36
70 Ibid. p. 20
71 Ibid. p. 23
72 Ibid.
73 Ibid. p. 37
74 Ibid. p. 38

75 Ibid.
76 Ibid.
77 Oakley, Ann, *Housewife* (1976), pp. 43–4
78 Cunningham, A.S., *Mining in Mid and East Lothian: A History of the Industry from Earliest times to present Day,* (1925), p. 64 and 66
79 Ibid. p. 64
80 Op. cit., Church, p. 634
81 Turnbull, Les., *Chopwell's Story*, Copyright L. Turnbull, published by Gateshead Metropolitan Borough Council Department of Education. no date given p. 21
82 Strawhorn, John, MA, PhD, FEIS, Evidence submitted to the Royal Commission on Housing (Scotland) by Thomas McKerrey and James Brown from the Ayrshire Miners' Union, (1979), p. 6
83 Op. cit., Oakley, p. 31
84 Op. cit., McVail, p. 39
85 Op. cit., Page Arnot, p. 136
86 Douglas, Mary & Wildausky, Aaron, *Risk and Culture*, (1982), pp. 1–15
87 Op. cit., Church, p. 584
88 Op. cit., Page Arnot, p. 134
89 Strawhorn, John, *Evidence Submitted to the Royal Commission on Housing (Scotland)* by Thomas McKerrey and James Brown from the Ayrshire Miners' Union (1979)
90 Ibid. pp. 72–73
91 Ibid. p. 73
92 Ibid. p. 73
93 Ibid. p. 73
94 Harvie, Christopher, *No gods and Precious Few Heroes: Scotland since 1914*, (1981), p. 29
95 Op cit., Page Arnot, p. 147
96 Ibid. p. 146
97 Coal Industry Commission Act, 1919 by the Hon. Mr. Justice Sankey quoted in op.cit. Page Arnot, p.146
98 Op cit., Page Arnot, p. 148
99 Supple, Barry, T*he History of the British Coal Industry, Vol. 4, 1913–1946*, (1987) p. 474
100 Ibid.
101 Op cit., A Traveller Underground, p. 190
102 Op. cit., Supple, p. 475
103 Ibid.
104 Ibid. p. 477
105 Ibid. pp. 189–90
106 Swenarton, Mark, *Homes Fit for Heroes: The Politics and Architecture of Early State Housing in Britain*, (1981), p. 5
107 Ibid. p. 6
108 Ibid.
109 Ibid. p. 14
110 NAS IRS 64/92/111
111 Op.cit., Hardy, p. 240
112 Op.cit., Swenarton, p. 18
113 Ibid. p. 5
114 Ibid. p. 93
115 Op.cit. Harvie, p. 30
116 Op.cit., Swenarton, p. 93
117 East Lothian County Council Survey Report, 1953
118 Ibid. p. 10
119 Ibid.
120 Ibid. p. 11
121 Ibid. p. 10
122 Ibid.
123 Op.cit., Cunningham, pp. 75–76
124 NAS DD6/1173 *Minutes of Meeting with Secretary for Scotland*, (1924) p. 27
125 NAS DD6/1173 *Letter from Scottish Board of Health to Scottish Office in London*, 22nd February, 1924
126 Ibid.
127 NAS DD6/1173 Report by Scottish Health Department Housing Inspector, 1924. p. 2
128 Ibid. p. 9
129 Ibid.

130 Ibid.
131 Ibid.
132 Ibid.
133 Ibid. p. 12
134 Op. cit., Harvie, p. 24
135 Op. cit., Supple, p. 459
136 A Scottish Architect, *The Housing of Miners in Scotland: A Review of the Position*, (circa 1920)
137 Ibid. p. 3
138 Ibid.
139 Ibid. p. 15
140 Donaldson, Robert, 'From Six to Twelve' in *The Pans Remembered*, 1986, East Lothian District Library
141 Op. cit., Supple, p. 491
142 Op. cit., Harvie, p. 41
143 NAS CB 7/3
144 Ibid.
145 Ibid.
146 Ibid.
147 NAS CB 26/351/1
148 Ibid.
149 NAS CB 26/351/2
150 Ibid.
151 Ibid.
152 Ibid.
153 Ibid.
154 Ibid.
155 RCAHMS B17–106G/Scot/UK11, 7274
156 NAS CB 26/351/2
157 Nielson, Elizabeth, 'Cuthill' in *The Pans Remembered*, (1986) East Lothian District Library, p. 19
158 NAS CB 7/3/96
159 East Lothian County Council Survey Report, 1953
160 Ibid. p. 33
161 Ibid. p. 11
162 Ibid. p. 25
163 Ibid.
164 Op cit., Tindall, p. 141
165 Ibid.
166 Ibid. p. 39
167 Ibid.
168 RCAHMS F21/543/RAF/402., Aerial photograph September 1958
169 Preston, Frank, 'New town of Glenrothes, Fife, October, 1950, in *The Journal of the Institution of Municipal Engineers*, Vol. 77, No.8, 6th February, 1951
170 Op.cit., Neilson, p. 18
171 Ibid. p. 19
172 Op.cit., Donaldson, p. 8
173 Naysmith, Janet, *As I Remember, Janet Naysmith (Nee Cunningham) 1903–1995*, p. 4 http:// www.maths.strath.ac.uk/-caas66/homepage/preston/html
174 Op. cit., Donaldson, p. 7
175 Ibid. p. 8
176 Op. cit., Naysmith, p. 2
177 Ibid. p. 3
178 Op. cit., Donaldson, p. 7

8
Water at Prestongrange and Pumping it out

Ewan Wilson

INTRODUCTION

Coal has been worked on the site of Prestongrange for over seven hundred years. There is no question that the other industries that developed in and around the area owed their existence to its abundant presence. In order to tap the rich resource a solution had to be found to the major limiting factor – that of drainage.

This chapter briefly surveys the history of Prestongrange and its development. It then examines the development of the key machine that was to address the problems of drainage at Prestongrange, the Beam Engine. The history of its development and that of steam is addressed and then the history of Prestongranges Beam Engine is told.

This machine was extremely important to the site and today is now one of only four in the United Kingdom. It is a tribute to the importance of this huge machine that regardless of its immense size it was still considered as portable. Beam engines were transported all over the country and even exported to Europe and America.

Dorothy Wordsworth recorded in her 'A Tour of Scotland' the reaction she and the poets Coleridge and William Wordsworth on seeing a beam pumping engine in 1803 at Wanlockhead.

> "Our road turned to the right, and we saw, at the distance of less than a mile, a tall upright building of grey stone, with several men standing upon the roof, as if they were looking out over battlements. It stood beyond the village, upon higher ground, as if presiding over it – a kind of enchanter's castle, which it might have been, a place where Don Quixote would have gloried in. When we drew nearer, we saw coming out of the side of the building, a large machine lever, in appearance like a great forge-hammer, as we supposed for raising water out of the mines. It heaved upwards once in half a minute with a slow motion, and seamed to rest to take a breath at the bottom, its motion being accompanied with a sound between groan and 'jike'. There would have been something in this object very striking in any place, as it was impossible not to invest the machine with some faculty of intellect: it seemed to have made the first step from brute matter to life and purpose, showing its progress by great power. William made a remark to this effect, and Coleridge observed that it was like a giant with one idea. At all events, the object produced a stricking effect in that place, where everything was in unison with it".[1]

The beam engine at Prestongrange provided a solution to the problem of pumping the water out of the mines. Today it provides the site of Prestongrange with an inspiring building that houses an incredible piece of machinery. The relevence of the beam engine to Prestongrange remains as ever of great importance.

HISTORY OF THE SITE OF PRESTONGRANGE

Summary

1184	Cistercian Monks
1210–19	Coal working begins
1560	Reformation
1749	Coal production ceases
1829	Prestongrange Colliery sinks its first shaft
1874	Beam engine installed
1895	Site purchased by Summerlee & Co.
1947	Nationalisation
1954	Beam engine ceases
1962	Colliery closes

Early Developments

In 1184 the Cistercian Monks of Newbattle were granted land at Prestongrange to expand their salt-panning trade. This development gave the town of Aldhammer as it was known its new name of Salt Preston. The land they received was a stretch of marshland, a stone quarry and a coal heugh. They were given this land as alms from Sehr de Quincy, the head of a prominent Anglo-Saxon family who owned land in both Mid and East Lothian.

The Monks quickly exhausted the exposed coastal outcrops of coal, which they were using to accelerate the evaporation process of seawater to produce salt. In order to help transport needed coal from Newbattle to their salt pans the Monks built the Salter's Road.

In 1210 and 1219 the Monks were granted rights to actively work the coal in the Prestongrange quarry and therefore they significantly expanded the scale of their salt panning activities in the area.

The advent of the Reformation resulted in the Monks tenure over Prestongrange ending by 1560. At the end of the Sixteenth Century landowners took control of both the salt pans and the mines.

Growth of Industry

> "Prestonpans...named Salt Preston at the beginning of the last century is the burgh of Barony, and a part of the custom – house.....It is noted for its extensive manufactures, particularly of salt, stone, and earthenware, of brick and tile. The revenue arising from the manufacture of salt in Prestonpans, Cockenzie and Cuthill amounts to 17,000 or 18,000 pounds per annum. A manufacture of oil vitriol, acquafortis, and spirits of salt is also carried on to a greater extent: and the same company manufactures great quantities of Glaubers salts"[2]

All of these industries were thriving in the area in this time, the 1800's. This was due to the geographical merits of the site of Prestonpans. The locality of Edinburgh was by then an established commercial market place and there was abundant local fireclay which could be used to produce brick. Prestonpans had men and women with the kind of entrepreneurial vision that so characterised the progressive age of the Industrial Revolution and also skilled tradesmen and labourers to provide the workforce for the new industries.

Extensive communication links were already fully in place in 1819. Prestonpans had long established sea links that dated back to at least the Sixteenth Century. In the spring of 1526 King James V paid a visit to Newbattle and whilst on this journey he granted a local land-owning family called Acheson the rights to build a port. The port went on to flourish and at a later date it was purchased by Morrison and renamed Morrison's Haven.

Morrison was responsible for amongst other things the production of Sulphuric acid (or Vitriol), glass made from local seaweed and salt that was panned which gives Prestonpans its name.

Through the renamed Morrison's Haven clay would arrive from Devonshire, flint from Gravesend and white and red clay from London and Hull. Exports would be steamed most commonly to Edinburgh, but also back down the East Coast of England. Without this safe port trade growth in the area would have been severely restricted.

> "The harbour of Prestonpans, called Morrison's Haven, has about ten feet of water at spring tides, but might be deepened so as to draw twelve: it is esteemed a safe harbour."[3]

The site was developed by a series of owners who each expanded the site and sunk new pits. Matthias Dunn stated that in 1830 that 'he sank the Great Seam Pit'.[4] Ownership was then passed on to Sir George Suttie. An English company Brenton and Loam then managed the site from approximately 1868 to 1870.[5] The management of the site was soon taken over by Geares & Mills of Middlesborough who operated from around 1870/1874. Summerlee Coal and Iron Company then took over from Geares & Mills in 1895. Summerlee Iron Works was originally established in Coatbridge in 1837 under the name Messers Wilson & Co.[6]

A picture emerges at Prestongrange of one of Britain's earliest industrial estates being in rude health. In truth however things were less streamlined. Despite a long history of mining at Prestongrange coal from further afield was being imported into the area, this was costly in transport and tax but still more profitable.

The reason for the inaccessibility of the local raw coal was that the mineshafts had been flooded in 1749. In order to fulfil the potential of the area and enjoy the boom years and huge profit margins the resultant self-sufficiency would bring, a means had to be found to drain the water.

The solution to this problem was an example of one of the key features of the Industrial Revolution. This was an intensely fertile and competitive time, more than any other period in history, where necessity was the mother of invention. The problem of drainage was continually arising and being addressed at this time throughout the country. The developed solution would solve many similar problems of drainage as experienced at Prestongrange all over the country.

THE DEVELOPMENT OF THE BEAM ENGINE

The Cornish Beam Engine

It is easy today to underestimate the impact the steam engine. Until its advent there were no other locomotive forces other than wind, water and muscle. Steam engines eventually drove mills, fed canals, operated docks, supplied water and opened up the country with the advent of rail. In examining statistical accounts it has been estimated that in or before 1800 there were approximately sixty-one Newcomen type or other steam engines in Scotland with approximately four or five in East Lothian.[7]

The invention of the steam engine revolutionised mining freeing exponentially more mineral and fossil fuel wealth, allowing a scale of development that was unprecedented. However it was a long road from the initial breakthrough which occurred while Queen Anne sat on the throne (1704–14), to the monument of craft and science in maturity that is the Cornish Beam Engine of Prestongrange.

The 'Cornish Boiler' and the 'Cornish Beam Engine' were so named because in that time of massive development nowhere outside Cornwall was developing faster or more comprehensively in the area of mining. There was a huge escalation in the demand for coal, tin, copper, tungsten and other mineral wealth. This created a demand from other areas of the country that wished to emulate these thriving Cornish industries. A market opened up in the production of such equipment that could be sold and was portable.

The so-called Cornish cycle utilised the high-pressure steam available along with the doubled-up power strokes of the 'parallel motion' innovations of James Watt. This produced enormous fuel savings on all that had come before.

> "The typical Cornish engine had it's huge beam mounted on the strength end wall of the engine house so that the mechanism was indoors, and the end of the beam with the pumprods extending down the mineshaft was in the open air. The pumprods were composed usually of Oregon pine, in section usually 18 inches square and often weighing in the case of a deep mine, up to a hundred tons. The first pump was in a sump at the bottom of the mine and the water was raised in lifts with intermediate tanks and pumps, worked from offsets on the same pumprods, every few hundred feet. It was not necessarily pumped to the surface, but often to a tunnel or adit driven to come out on a low ground miles away… What the engine did was to raise the pumprods and, with them, the plungers in the pumps, thus filling them with water. When the steam valve shut, the rods descended again under their own great weight, an 'equilibrium valve' opening at the right moment to allow the expanded steam to fill the space below the piston as it rose. Closure of this valve as the piston approached the top of it's stroke cushioned the descent of the rods, bringing them gently to rest so that the pumps could take the water at their own natural speed. This valve was invariably known to the engine-men of old as the 'Uncle Abram' valve. The engine then passed at the top of it's stroke until the cataract allowed the steam valve to open and repeat the cycle."[8]

Influential Inventors

Thomas Newcomen (1663–1729)

The road starts with a Dartmouth ironmonger and brassfounder, Thomas Newcomen. Newcomen however died in obscurity in 1729. His pivotal role in changing the world has gone unrecognised despite the fact that his engines began to spring up throughout Britain and Europe in the years before his death.

Newcomen's discoveries began when he realised that if an upright cylinder with a sliding piston was filled with steam that was then condensed, a vacuum would be formed and the pressure of the atmosphere would drive the piston down with force. Although his theory was sound and he knew that the pressure of the atmosphere was around fifteen pounds per square inch he struggled to get the steam to condense rapidly enough. It was chance that intervened after years of failure to solve the problem.

A tiny flaw in the brass cylinder he had been using allowed a tiny spray of water to leak into the inside. This provoked the rapid condensing of steam that was sought and the piston then came down with an unprecedented speed and force. After this chance discovery he installed a tiny spray.

> "Newcomen arranged a great wooden beam, pivoted at the middle, on the specially strengthened wall of the engine-house, and to one end of the beam he attached the piston by length of a chain. The cylinder was mounted vertically mouth upward to the other end of the beam, again hanging by a chain. Newcomen attached the heavy rods fixed down the mineshaft to the pump at the lowest level. The weight of the rods pulled up the piston in the cylinder and sucked in the steam from the boiler mounted below; then the steam condensed by the water-jet, the piston descended to fill the vacuum and the pumprods were raised, pumping up the water. The valve admitting the steam to the cylinder and that controlling the water-jet were worked from a rod hung from the beam. Water covered the top of the piston to help seal the gap between the piston and cylinder since there was no machine tool available to produce a smooth cylinder bore that was sufficiently accurate".[9]

As early as 1762 there was an example of an engine with a seventy-four inch diameter cylinder in operation in England that was powered by four boilers. This is four inches larger than the far later Cornish Beam Engine of Prestongrange.[10] The cost however of installing one of Newcomens 'fire engines' was great and a deterrent to their use. The third engine of this type installed in Scotland at Edmonstone in 1726/27 was stated as costing £1008 without taking into account the cost of the engine house.[11] It became apparent therefore that Newcomen's 'fire engines' although great were in need of improvement and refining.

John Smeaton (1724–1794)

John Smeaton was the worthy successor in the long battle to pump water from one place to another. He took great steps in improving the steam engine which had previously been no more sophisticated than the greater the burden, the larger the machine.

Smeaton had a background in iron forging and founded the Carrock Iron-works. This experience greatly aided his ability in improving the efficiency of steam engines. In 1760 he markedly improved the effectiveness of the machine by increasing the size of the steampipes.[12]

He also improved the controls of the machine in developing the 'cataract'. This was a weighed lever with a tin cup at one end which was enclosed in a water tank. Water was poured into the cup, which would be heavy enough when full to tilt the lever. This in turn would open the steam valve, which was attached to the other end of the lever, while at the other end the cup would empty. By regulating the speed with which the cup was refilled with water one could control the speed of the engine.[13]

Smeaton's other great contribution to the age of steam was the standardising of the capacity of the engine. This became important as the trade in Beam Engines began to expand. The buyers could outline their needs and receive a machine of the scale to meet their expectations. Smeaton's "duty" was the amount of water in millions of pounds that could be raised one foot high by a bushel of coal (94 pounds).

This move was indicative of the state of the changing times in two important ways. Firstly that the trade in industrial machinery had increased and was expanding and secondly that there was a move away from the trail and error engineering advances of the past towards a much more practical scientific approach.

James Watt 1736–1819

James Watt at the Steam Engine by J.E. Lauder
Courtesy of The Scottish National Portrait Gallery and the National Gallery of Scotland

James Watt in 1765 invented the separate condenser, which was the next great breakthrough in the design of the Beam Engine. By this point in time the Beam Engine had been in manufacture and application for over sixty years.

Watt realised that the efficiency could be increased if the cylinder could be kept hot at all times rather than cooling every time water was admitted to condense the steam and provide a stroke. His solution was to design a separate condenser below the cylinder that was kept cool by emersion in water. The cylinder was equipped with an extra valve at its bottom through which the exhausted steam could enter the condenser. There a water jet reduced it to water effecting a vacuum that enabled the engine to continue operation. Water was removed from the condenser by merit of a pump, which also removed the dead air resultant in the condensing of steam. This water often subsidised the boiler in itself which was rendered more economical as it was not required to heat it from cold.[14]

The cylinder was provided with an insulated case and a steam jacket to prevent it from cooling. Watt realised by closing the top of the cylinder that he could admit steam to the piston alternately at either side. This resulted in the doubling of the power strokes that the machine could produce. This change was impossible to put into place however while the beam remained attached to the piston within the cylinder by a chain. This was due to the fact that the piston would have to exert a positive push on the beam as well as the pull previously exerted. A rod would be required to work through the closed cylinder cover, however the problem with that was that the piston would move vertically up and down. At the same time the end of the beam to which it was attached must by necessity describe circles in the air as it rises and falls. The result of these actions would be the bending of the piston rod. Watts solution to the problem of guiding the rod inflexibly on the path that was required of it was known as 'parallel motion'

> "The top of the rod was attached to the beam by a swinging link and two pairs of hinged rods were provided, one pair attached to either side of the top of the piston rod and the other pair attached to a part of the framing or the building itself. The movement of the guide rods is susceptible of a rather beautiful geometric solution, and it was the invention of which James Watt was said to have been most proud."[15]

Watt went on to design the rotative engine where the beam was attached to a circular crank replacing at a chop the unpredictable water wheel as a source of power. This also removed the need for man power to bear the coal from the steam to the surface. With a series of rail trucks wound by the wheel on an endless rope the job could be done at a fraction of the time and expense. These rotative engines were soon as widespread as pump engines. Watt and his partner Boulton patented all their designs and monopolised the industry until their patent expired in 1800.

After this cessation there came a renewed vigour in the search for greater efficiency and the upshot of this new found freedom came to be known as the Cornish Engine. Post 1800 timber disappeared from the engine framing. The beam and other moving parts were replaced almost over night by cast iron.

Richard Trevithick 1771–1883
Richard Trevithick with the advent of high-pressure steam made a major breakthrough in power and economy. This was made possible by what became known as 'the cornish boiler'. This was a cylindrical ensemble of riveted wrought iron with a fire grate cum flue down the middle. It could be mounted on wheels and afforded designers steam at fifty pounds per square inch. Previously the maximum available had only been four pounds per square inch.

All the inventors played a major part in the design and improvement of developing steam. The development of steam driven machinery was key to the invention of the beam engine that was to solve the problem of drainage at Prestongrange.

THE PRESTONGRANGE BEAM ENGINE

Why Prestongrange Needed a Beam Engine

Sporadic working of the coal seams continued on the site of Prestongrange for centuries in much the same fashion. The coal was simply dug out along the line of an outcrop at the base of a rise in the ground or along the coast where it was also to be found. If the seam was flat but shallow a vertical hole would enable access. When the coal supply became exhausted the particular hole would be abandoned and a new one begun elsewhere.

In the sixteenth century a new method of counteracting the drainage problem inherent in mining was introduced known as 'pit-and-adit'. It was described in 1878 as a method where hewers

> "have driven thair awin coill to this time and with such like lavell (level) and shall cause the water to have passage fra the back of the coill callit the coill dammys (dams) In sic manner as they have draven the lave of thair coill and mak twa fute (foot) dry at the back of said coill dammys. And also they shall open the conductis (conduit) thereof and in such a manner as the level seruis to be driven of their awine (own) coill to the boundaries of Pinkie and Inveresk that the water may hae anis (one) passage to the sey (sea)"[16]

Put simply the 'adit system' allowed rudimentary shafts to be sunk and worked for longer. It disposed of the water by channels cut in the coalface that would lead to the 'day-level' (surface). From there the water would run to the sea or to another watercourse.[17]

Through this system hundreds of gallons of water were drained every minute into the Forth. Some of these 'adits' were for their time truly formidable feats of engineering and provided a temporary answer to the problem of drainage. As described in 1621

> "...the greatest of these Gaes (faults), that I know (runs) from Archison's Haven, which hath been cut by Preston Grange, for a level (adit) to his coal, and goes from that to Seton ... and hath been cut at Seton, for serving the level of coal now wrought at Tranent"[18]

However still it was not unusual for the mines to be closed due to flooding because of faults in the seam.

By 1749 all easily accessible coal on the site had been used and there followed a gap in coal production as once again the volume of water became unmanageable for the technology of the day. Until the opening of the Prestongrange Colliery in 1829 coal was imported for use by the Prestongrange Industries from collieries such as Tranent and Inveresk at great expense. One of the brick and tile works needed 21 cart loads of coal and culm (dross) to fire 3000 bricks in their kiln.

Prestongrange was rich in coal but the shallowest untapped seam was four hundred feet underground. To cope with the enormous amount of water between them and it miners had to wait for the advent of steam and the beam engine.

The current Cornish Beam Engine was bought to replace the inadequate twenty-six inch cylinder pump and its auxiliaries that had been in place since the colliery had reopened in 1829. The colliery had been reopened by Matthias Dunn who had soon introduced the innovation of 'cast iron tubbing' that enabled the mine to access the 'Great Seam' which was to be found 420 feet below the surface. This seam was seven to nine feet in thickness and extremely rich.

'Cast iron tubbing' was a system of iron plates the circumference of the shaft. These were established at opportune points in areas where water pools invariably accompany a seam of impermeable stone. The 'tubs' are designed to hold the water back from the areas of the shaft being worked while the water is pumped away from the other side. If the iron plates begin below the water level and are fitted directly to the impermeable stone the water pressure seals them in place.

Dunn established three such tubs in the shaft. He estimated that as the water pressure naturally rises as the quantity of water held back increases, the bottom tub at three hundred and ten feet (52 fathoms) was sustaining a pressure the equivalent of six thousand three hundred and thirteen tons. The engine that was in place could barely cope with such a huge volume of water. As so often had happened on the colliery site the capacity for the mines to be open and worked became increasingly more erratic due to the problems of drainage.

History of Prestongrange's Beam Engine

The Cornish beam engine was purchased for use at Prestongrange Colliery in 1874. The engine is credited to the engineers Hocking and Loam and was purchased from Havey & Co's of Hayle. They were generally acknowledged to be the largest foundry in Cornwall. The seventy-inch cylinder machine was bought in 1874 then transported by sea and installed at Prestongrange.

By 1874 the boom time in Cornwall was past and competition from other areas, particularly the North of England, had ensured that they no longer had it their own way. Prestongrange was not the beam engine's first berth but there it remained operational for eighty years keeping the mines of that colliery pumped dry.

The Cornish Beam Engine of Prestongrange was built in 1853 by J.E Mare at the Plymouth foundry. It was originally sited on Porters shaft, Wheal Exmouth and Adams silver-lead mine at Christow in South Devon. It was then moved first to Wheal Neptune in Perranuthnoe in 1862 and again to another Great Western in 1869.

In 1873 it was purchased by Harvey & Co. who provided a new beam that shortened the shaft stroke from twelve foot to ten foot and lengthened the pistonrod. A year later in 1874 they sold the beam engine to Prestongrange Colliery. The beam engine was erected at Prestongrange by Matthew Loam of Liskard.

The beam engine made this long journey in part due to the long standing connections that existed between Cornwall and the Lothians. Thirty years before the beam engine was transferred Matthew Loam's father had purchased a Perran Foundry 60-inch engine from the Dolphiston pit, which is close to Prestongrange. Loam was also married to Patience Kitto who belonged to an influential Cornish family.

Newly cast beam arrives
East Lothian Council, David Spence Collection

The beam engine was 'according to local residents, shipped in parts to Prestongrange'[19] into the adjacent Morrison's Haven and installed in

Beam Engine exterior
East Lothian Council

the location where it still remains. This was a considerable feet as the weight of the machine was in excess of thirty tons. It was raised into position by stages with a series of jacks whilst at the same time the engine house was constructed around it. The completed structure has a reinforced front wall seven feet thick in order to support the weight of the beam.

The beam engine with its newly shortened stroke improved things on the site. The average working speed was three and a half strokes per minute with a pumping capacity of 650 gallons per minute, or six million gallons per twenty-four hours.

In 1895 Summerlee Iron Company took over the management of the Prestongrange Colliery. In 1905 they decided to increase the capasity of the mine shaft pumps. In order to do this they installed twenty-eight inch diameter rams on the two top lifts 'at the Great seam level, and one about midway between that and the surface, raising the water in two stages'.[20] The other 'at the beggar level, below the great seam, was a pump 17 inches in diameter, which pumped to the Great seam lodgement'.[21]

This work was carried out by Messers Andrew Barclay Sons & Co. Ltd. from Caledonia Works in Kilmarnock. New pump rods were also installed 'The pumprods, of Oregon pine, are 23 inches square from the surface to the top lift pump and the total weight of the pumprods, rams, crosshead and side rod, is about 105 tons'.[22]

In order to install the pumps and pumprods a 'steam driven worm geared winch'[23] was erected adjacent to the shaft 'the rope passing over a pulley mounted on a massive wood and steel frame erected over the pumping space in the shaft'.[24] This then became a permanent fixture allowing any further repairs to be made to the pumps and pumprods.

Due to the installation of these larger pumps a strengthening truss had to be added. This was required as calculations showed that the beam strength was no longer capable of bearing the increased load. The strengthening truss was designed and manufactured by the Summerlee Iron Company. The Chief Engineer of the company at the time was Mr Wm. Bryson.[25]

In order to fit the strengthening truss a boring bar had to be designed that was driven by a small steam engine. This boring bar was used to drill the larger holes on the side of the beam. These holes then 'received the pins in the eyes of the tiebars'.[26] In order to ensure that the beam was not over stressed when tightening the 'tiebars' a series of levers were attached to the beam that measured the 'deflection'. All the work of installing the new additions was the responsibility of the mechanical engineer who was a Mr David Smellie.[27]

Beam Engine interior
Scottish Mining Museum Trust

CONCLUSION

Once the beam engine was in place at Prestongrange the colliery enjoyed a fruitful period of activity where the mine was kept drained and the technology and the techniques for the removal of coal moved on apace. This however was at the mercy of the efficiency and reliability of the beam engine and the drainage related apparatus. A defining feature of the question of drainage, mundane as it may seem, is that it is a problem that must be constantly addressed. The water will always come flooding in again as fast as it ever did if not always addressed and dealt with.

This was clearly illustrated in 1916 when a pistonrod fractured at the top of a stroke. In falling it broke the cylinder bottom and also cracked the cylinder wall. As a result of this incident the mining in the colliery had to be stopped until repairs could be made. A new bottom had to be cast and the wall sealed by caulking the cracks with red lead and linseed oil before then clamping them together. The mine was then reopened but only after the repairs had been made and the time it took to once again drain the rapidly filling mine. Stoppages for any reason were increasingly more costly due to the efficiency at which the coal could be harvested.

Steam Cylinder
Scottish Mining Museum Trust

Apart from another similar event in 1938 the engine ran smoothly and admirably for The Summerlee Coal and Iron Company. It also maintained it record after nationalisation in 1947

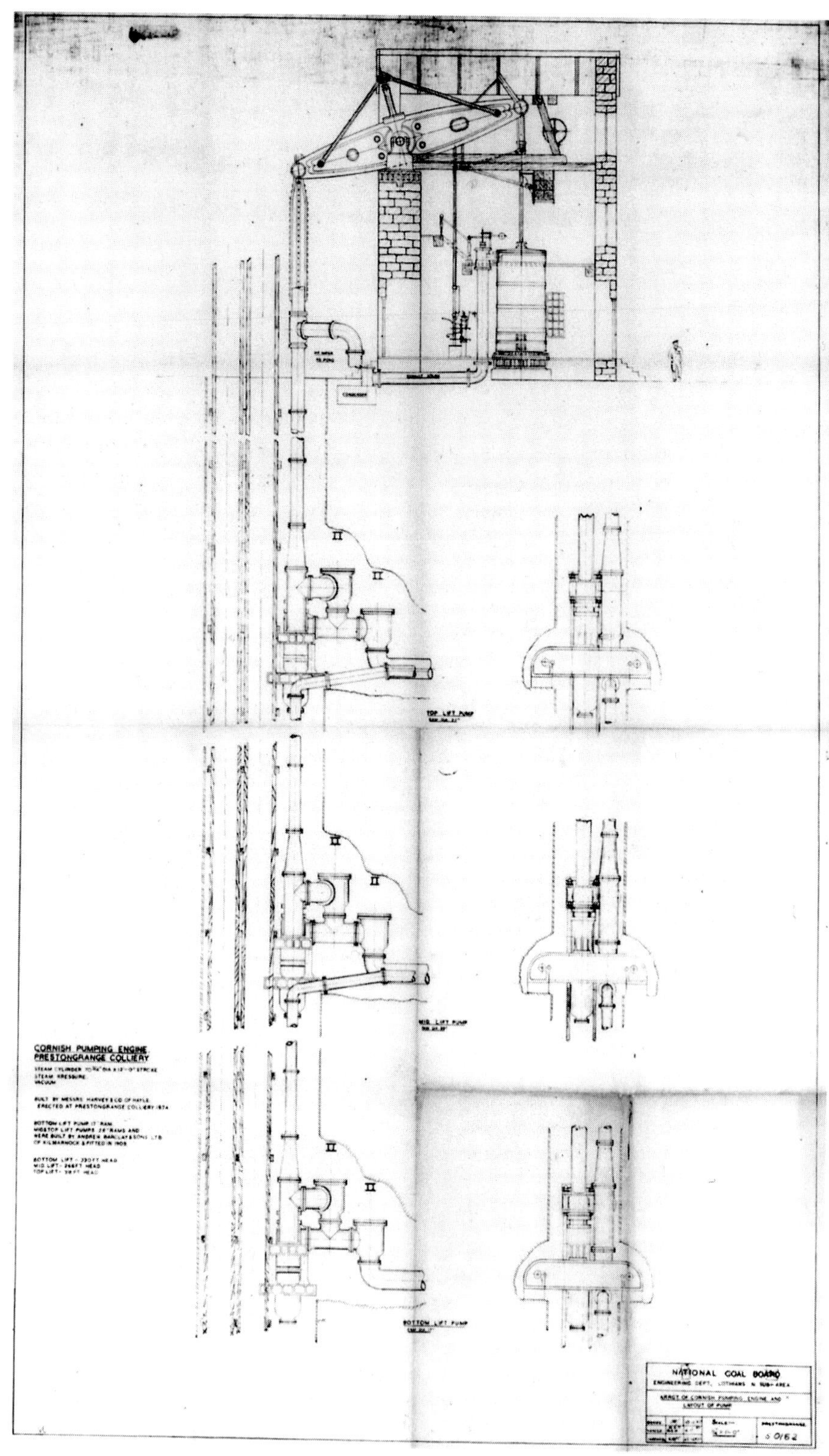

Diagram of Beam Engine workings
East Lothian Council, David Spence Collection

for the National Coal Board. Problems with breakdowns from 1952 heralded the end of the pump's use. In 1952 the pump became fractured 'about 30 fathoms from the surface' this was due to the stress after continuous years of working.[28] In 1953 the discharge valve burst, this valve was approximately six foot in diameter. The repairs were carried out by Mr Armstrong.[29]

In 1954 a fracture appeared in the 'stool-pipe which supported the whole vertical column to the surface'.[30] Attempts were made to repair the machine and cast a replacement. The cost of producing a 'pattern for one pipe only' was viewed as too expensive and the 'Cornish Pump retired from active service'.[31]

In 1954 the beam engine was replaced by the vastly smaller but more efficient electrical pumps. The solution to drainage on the site became little more than a stopgap measure. Coal after this period was increasingly being supplanted with other fossil fuels. Open cast mines were being established that were able to undercut the price of coal from the deep mines. Most importantly the cost in manpower and the expense of bringing up the coal was become increasingly expensive. In the 1950's the mines ran for no less than two miles under the Firth of Forth causing increased problems of drainage and flooding. This added cost of draining the mine finally tipped the balance.

In 1962 the colliery closed its doors for the final time. Many of the other associated industries that had originally been attracted to the area as a result of the coal closed shortly after. These changes in the local industries changed the area forever. Drainage, the problem that had plagued every owner for seven hundred years remained.

BIBLIOGRAPHY

Brown, K, *Prestongrange 70–inch Cornish Engine – A Myth Exploded,* 1982

Conrad-Patrick, *Early Documents Relating to Mining in Scotland,* 1878

Crowley, T E, *Beam Engines,* 1976

Clerk, Sir John, 11 1740

Dott, G, *History of Prestongrange Colliery,* The Spence Collection 1950

Duckham, Baron F, *Early Application of Steam Power at Scottish Collieries,* Spence Collection

Duckham, Baron F, *Some Eighteenth Century Scottish Coal Mining Methods: The Dissertation of Sir John Clerk,* Industrial Archaeology Vol. 5 No. 3 August 1968

Dunn, M, *Narrative of the Sinking Prestongrange Engine,* 1837

McNeil, P, *Prestonpans & Vicinity: Historical, Ecclesiastical & Traditional,* 1884

Shaw, J, *Water Power in Scotland 1550 1870,* 1984

Sinclair, *Hydrostatics,* 1672

Snodgrass, C P, *Third Statistical Account of Scotland: The County of East Lothian,* 1953

Spence Collection (Housed at East Lothian Museums Service, Dunbar Road, Haddington)

Webster, D, *Topographical Dictionary of Scotland,* 1819

Zweig, F, *Men in the Pits,* 1948

Websites

National Museums of Scotland	www.nms.ac.uk
Scottish Cultural Access Network	www.scran.ac.uk
National Library of Scotland	www.n/s.ac.uk

NOTES

1 Spence Collection (Letter from Tindall, F P)
2 Webster, D.
3 Webster, D. p. 565
4 Dott, G.
5 Ibid.
6 Dott, G.
7 Duckham
8 Crowley, T.E.
9 Crowley, T.E.
10 Crowley, T.E.
11 Duckham p. 222
12 Crowley, T.E.
13 Crowley, T.E.
14 Crowley, T.E.
15 Crowley, T.E.
16 Conrad-Patrick
17 Conrad-Patrick
18 Sinclair
19 Spence Collection
20 Spence Collection
21 Spence Collection
22 Spence Collection
23 Spence Collection
24 Spence Collection
25 Spence Collection
26 Spence Collection
27 Spence Collection
28 Spence Collection (Letter from Mr J. Close 1968)
29 Spence Collection (Letter from Mr J. Close 1968)
30 Spence Collection (Letter from Mr J. Close 1968)
31 Spence Collection (Letter from Mr J. Close 1968)

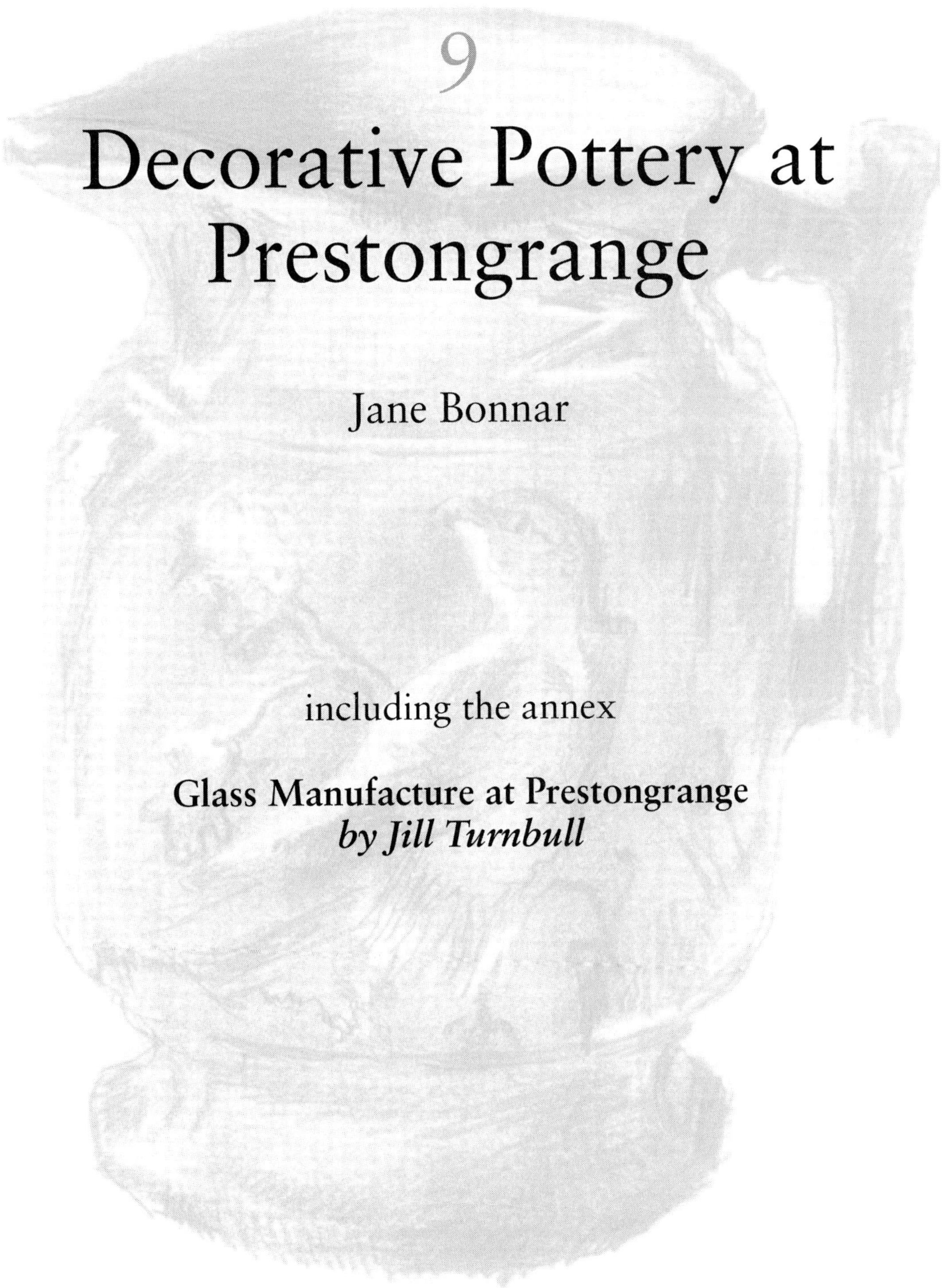

9

Decorative Pottery at Prestongrange

Jane Bonnar

including the annex

Glass Manufacture at Prestongrange
by Jill Turnbull

This analysis is complemented by the Prestongrange Virtual Pottery Exhibition to be found on the Internet at http://www.prestoungrange.org

ACKNOWLEDGEMENTS

Thanks are due to the following people: The Manor of Milton & The Scottish Baronies of Prestoungrange & Dolphinstoun, East Lothian Council Library & Museums Service, Huntly House Museum, Prestongrange Industrial Heritage Museum, Scottish Mining Museum, The David Spence Collection, Royal Commission on the Ancient and Historical Monuments of Scotland, Coal Industry Social Welfare Organisation, Napier University Edinburgh, National Galleries of Scotland, National Archives of Scotland, The Scotsman Publications Ltd, City of Edinburgh Museums and Galleries, National Museums of Scotland and all others who helped with information and photographs.

The version published here in 2006 has had the benefit of emedations from Graeme Cruickshank, Curator to the Prestonpans Pottery Exhibition: 2007 and Chairman of the Scottish Pottery Society in Edinburgh.

The Annex by Jill Turnbull was added to this version in 2006.

Whereas every effort has been made to trace the copyright of quoted material, any omissions are inadvertent and the author will happily rectify these, on request.

1 SITES

This work is neither about the manufacturing process of Prestonpans pottery, nor a guide to attributing and valuing Prestonpans pottery. It rather focuses on the 'potworks' of the principal potteries in Prestonpans and vicinity and the families who owned them. The intention is to bring to life the story of a craft community whose wares have given much enjoyment and whose story has been all but disregarded thus far.

Prestonpans forms part of East Lothian and is found on the east of Scotland. Situated on the south coast of the Forth estuary, around eight miles east of Edinburgh, Prestonpans had all the elements required for a successful pottery industry; local clay, water and coal mined nearby. The working harbour of Morrison's Haven enabled the necessary additional materials of china clay and flint to be brought to the site from the South of England. In the nineteenth century, the main potteries were those of William Cadell & Company, West Pans, Gordon's and Belfield & Company. All were in close proximity to each other, stretching from the west of Prestonpans eastwards to where the town bounds Musselburgh.

Pottery manufacture was not concentrated in Prestonpans, however, as the resources that made pottery production possible were found in other parts of Scotland. The largest and best-known Glasgow firm was that of J. & M.P. Bell & Co., which was producing white earthenware from c1842–c1910 in an attractive array of transfer-printed milk-jugs and dinnerware. Kirkcaldy also had a thriving pottery industry, with a number of potteries in production at the end of the 19th century, dominated by David Methven & Sons who

Close proximity of Potteries

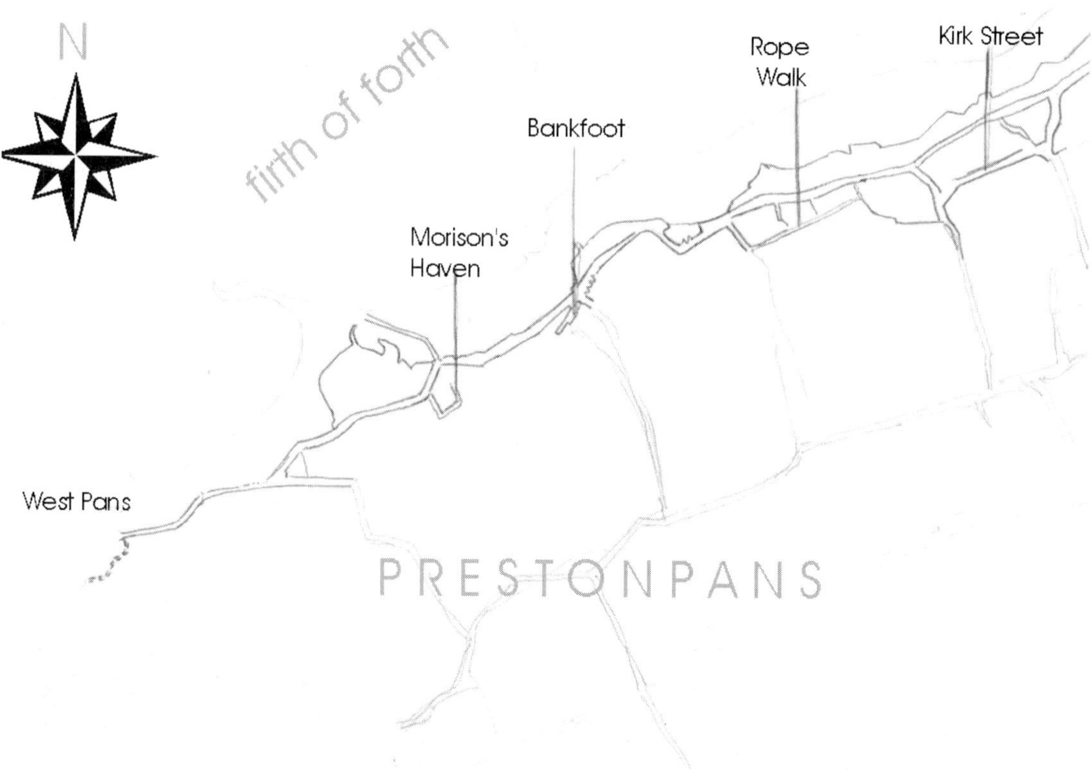

produced white dinnerware, bowls and mugs and brown teapots and other domestic items. However, at the advent of pottery making in Prestonpans, the Glasgow potteries were producing a vast amount of rather unimaginative transfer-printed ware [although Bell's export patterns were to go on at the end of the century to be rated some of the most exciting of any period in Scottish Pottery]. Prestonpans' potters, especially at West Pans, chose to concentrate on high quality, sophisticated wares and offered a welcome to the itinerant craft potters needed to produce them although it had competitors, some close, by in Musselburgh, Portobello, Bo'ness, Alloa, Greenock and Aberdeen.

Today, there are few living remains of the kilns and workshops and it is only with the help of old maps that we can pinpoint the extent of the potteries. Remnants of the products can be found on the beach at Morrison's Haven, where damaged and imperfect pieces were dumped. Different kinds of domestic pottery shards can be found of, mainly, tableware such as bowls, cups, plates and small jars. Pieces of round earthenware saggars, which held the pottery when it was put into the kiln, are found, together numerous three-legged clay stilts or 'craws' taes' used to separate each piece of ware to stop them from sticking together in the saggars.

The potteries have however left some mark on the landscape. At Prestongrange Industrial Heritage Museum, eleven circular kiln foundations indicate the scale of Prestongrange brick and tile works which catered for the building trade, manufacturing bricks, chimney pots, drainage pipes, outdoor garden urns and fountains. [But only in Portobello are thre just one and a half kilns remaining – the only such in Scotland – as a reminder of the great industry.] The pedestrian walkway from Tranent to Prestonpans (known

Beach finds

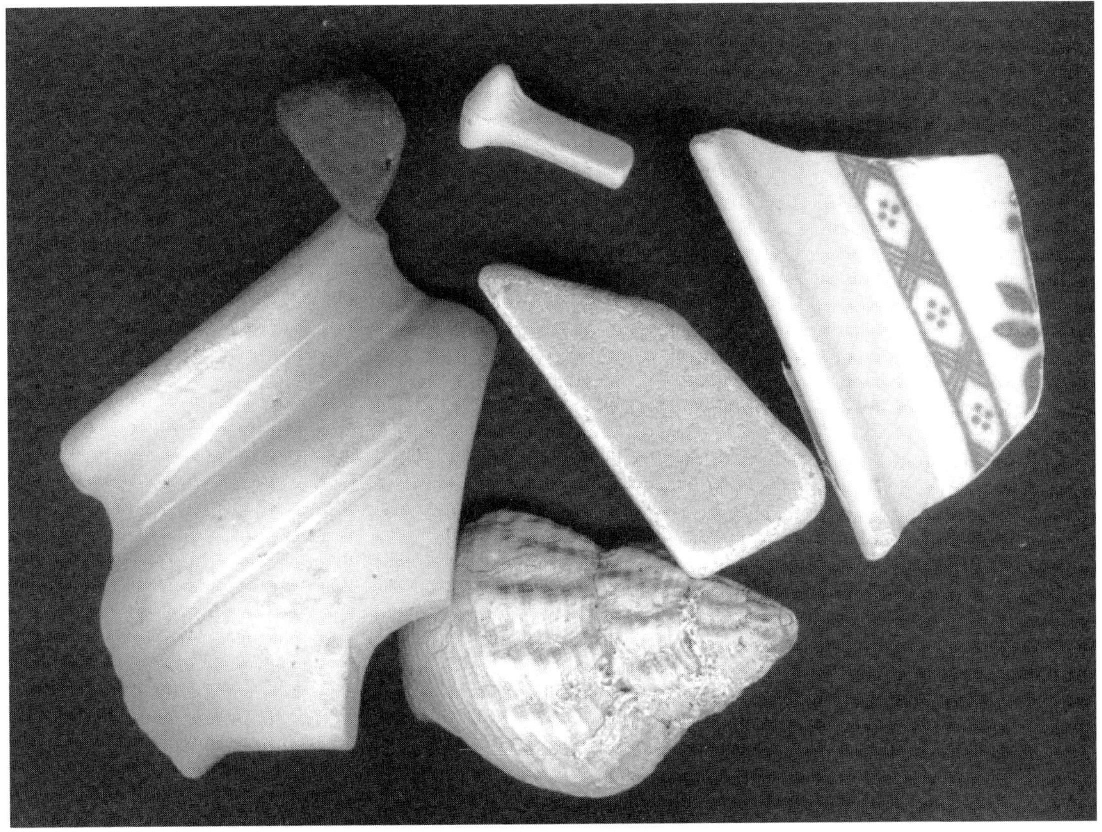

locally as 'The Heugh') reminds us that clay for the potteries was brought by (Scotland's first) narrow gauge waggonway from a clay pit in Birsley, Elphinstone. Many examples of Prestonpans ware are now family heirlooms or collectibles, treasured almost as much as the memories of the 'potworkers'.

2 POTTERY

Why was the pottery industry concentrated in the coastal region of East Lothian? Early eighteenth century conditions provided all resources required allowing the industry to take-off. A good quality local clay from Upper Birslie Plantation (or 'Clay Holes'), coal mined at Prestongrange and nearby Elphinstone, water power at Morrison's Haven Harbour and Pinky Burn, a working harbour at Morrison's Haven bringing in china clay and flint and a central position giving access to markets – all contributed to success in the nineteenth century. Such favourable conditions were not sustained. As clay deposits ran out and clay became more expensive, twentieth century production declined. Also, due to silt build-up, the harbour at Morrison's Haven had to be filled in, undermining transport facilities. The final blow was the increase in foreign competition which meant reduction in demand for Scottish pottery.

Pottery production began in Scotland fully 6000 years ago with finds including a beaker at Birsley near Prestonpans dated at around 2000BC. But a new phase began in Scotland in the early eighteenth century, with domestic-use pottery being manufactured according to consumer demand and expenditure. The turning point came mid-century when plaster moulds (which produced clumsy, irregular shapes) were abandoned around for white enamelled earthenware or delftware, which in turn were made possibly by the introduction of new lead glazes and double firing.[1] The introduction of transfer printing, painting including gilding and colour meant that the Prestonpans potteries could ably cater for the local demand for inexpensive decorated ware of good quality.[2] Their success was built on innovative design and the ability to keep production costs down.

Changes in design were led by William Litter's introduction in the early 1760s of the use of Scottish Cobalt to produce a deep blue product. The later introduction of mineral oxides meant creamware could be stained to produce a 'tortoise-shell' effect, a speciality of Cadell's pottery.[3] Gordon's utilised local clays to make terracotta, jet, basalt wares and black lustre ware, while using imported china clay to make more ornamental pottery. Rising demand for such products was stimulated from the social revolution of the early nineteenth century when each social strata sought to emulate their social superiors.[4] The average Scots family was increasingly paid in cash, rather than in kind, and had achieved a greater degree of comfort, security and prosperity. Houses were better equipped and meals became more elaborate.[5] So, the demand for quality pottery increased and was furnished at this time by Charles Belfield & Co. from their Kirk Street site.

Domestic salt glazed ware did remain popular, not only for its domestic usefulness but its industrial use too. Amongst other products, Cadell's made stoneware bottles for holding Prestonpans Ale.[6] Gordon's potteries eventually diversified into brick and tile manufacture, around 1812, to meet the demands of the growing industrial sector. Belfield's was first to make 'white' pottery –

WC's basins and sinks that were constantly in demand from Edinburgh and Leith Plumbers.

Over time, a pattern emerged in the demand for pottery. The mid-eighteenth century saw high demand for ornamental, novelty, one-off products, later to be superseded by demand for all kinds of tableware, toiletware and stoneware, it featured quality craftsmanship and lively colour. The mid-nineteenth century growth of Edinburgh and the associated industrial structures increased the need for building materials. By the late nineteenth century, demand had shifted to ornamental pottery ranging from plaques and garden tiles to figurines. It could be said of Scottish pottery then that it took its impetus from the fashion of the day. However, this statement undermines the fact that there are characteristics common to all domestic products; low relief ornamentation in shades of green, yellow, blue and brown, combining good design and workmanship with a strong sense of proportion and form.

Fashion was one reason for the apparent growth surges in the pottery industries, but what about mechanisation? Certainly, the early eighteenth century saw the introduction of steam power in flint/glaze milling, and indeed, Morrison's Haven had a steam operated flint mill by the 1850s. However, expansion in Prestonpans pottery production relied more on innovative body/glaze composition, improved factory organisation and adoption of new technology. Considering the twenty-percent failure rate in production due to breakage's and faulty firing, it follows that fragile materials were discarded; off-white salt glaze was considered more fragile than brown, so substitution took place, not just in Prestonpans but nationally. The quality of clay available in Scotland determined what new glazes; moulds and designs were introduced. Cash for any design innovation was very limited, so any new use for available materials was eagerly adopted.[7]

Changes of materials and designs were made successful by partial mechanisation; such as the introduction of the potters' wheel (for throwing) and the lathe (to extract excess clay). The pottery process still required human manipulation however, as exemplified in Belfield's invention of a system of hand pressing pipes.[8] Similarly, although mechanised jolley, jigger and batting machines produced flatwares, manual techniques were still required for standardised items, slipcasting and pressmoulding.

The issue of mechanisation highlights three points. Firstly, the quality of available clay determined glaze, composition and the amount of mechanisation required. Secondly, mechanisation was only adopted where it facilitated the use of new materials and designs. Finally, uneven and partial mechanisation meant that craft skills remained very important.

Such a complex mix of manual and mechanised production had to be well planned and well organised; hence the reason for the distinctively entrepreneurial element to Prestonpans pottery production. For most owners, pottery was only one of many business interests. Even Cadell's, one of the largest of the Prestonpans pottery firms, highly capitalised and commanding world markets, was almost a sweetener to William Cadell's business empire. As potteries were only part of larger enterprises, they tended to collapse when entrepreneurs lost interest or other interests demanded more time. Cadell, for instance, used his business connections as a local merchant, landowner and shipowner to distribute the pottery's produce via Morrison's Haven harbour through Cadell's existing trade links in Scandinavia, Russia, North America,

Spain and Italy.[9] However, when Cadell decided it was time for a new venture, to establish an ironworks, he left the pottery business in the hands of his son. Similarly, in 1811, the Gordons looked to pottery because they had capital, facilities and access to clay. That domestic pottery production was reduced in scale however, in response to increased demand for brick, tile and pipes.

Aside from the fact that Prestonpans pottery firms were all run by entrepreneurs, two of the four had another common feature – family orientation. The Cadell family had three simutaneous operations in Prestonpans, run by William Senior, his son and his nephew. Similarly, George Gordon and his three sons ran Gordon's Pottery. Arguably, such family orientation allowed these two Prestonpans potteries to expand rapidly because it was in the best interests of the family to make the project work. In addition, descent from a line of potters meant family members had a wealth of practical experience.

As the pottery industry proved increasingly profitable even previously inexperienced local businessmen were tempted to participate. One example is John Fowler, a local brewer, who helped fund the Kirk Street pottery in 1796, when it was run by David Thomson & Co.

All four of the main Prestonpans pottery production businesses ran along the same lines; workers were employed on a casual basis when demand was particularly high and production closed down when the business became unprofitable. As a consequence of this almost 'disposable' nature of the Prestonpans potteries and workforce, no one family forged strong associations with the industry, unlike the successful Wedgewoods in England. This may be symptomatic of Scottish business practice of not putting all one's eggs in the same basket, or perhaps a reflection of the changeable nature of the then Scottish economy.

In summary, the history of the potteries at Kirk Street, Bankfoot and West Pans followed the same path. In terms of location, all pottery owners chose East Lothian because of the readily available natural resources. In terms of range of wares, the demand for fashionable pottery was met by innovative use of existing materials and new technology. In terms of factory organisation, the Prestonpans potteries were most notable for their good designs and excellent workmanship, which meant that the manual part of the manufacturing process was maintained well beyond mechanisation. Finally, despite the diversity of ownership, the reason for the decline of pottery production is arguably similar in each case; potteries were only part of larger enterprises, and tended to be abandoned when a more profitable venture came along.

3 OWNERS

William Cadell & Company – 1750–1840

In 1750, William Cadell (1708–1777), a merchant from Haddington undertook the construction of a pottery in Prestonpans, situated in Kirk Street, to the west of the old Parish church. His family had been associated with industrial and commercial development in the area as, from 1732, Cadell leased Cockenzie House, the Boat Shore Harbour, some Salt Pans and coal pits at Tranent. The property was owned by the York Buildings Company, a London based property developer. So, by 1750, William Cadell was an accomplished merchant shipowner, land owner and entrepreneur, who traded from the harbour at Port Seton, exporting coal amongst other things to Edinburgh, and salt to Hanseatic ports, Norway and the Baltic.[10]

Cadell's Prestonpans Pottery was specifically designed to make creamware,[11] leading to McVeigh's assertion that Prestonpans is the home of creamware in Scotland.[12] A variety of mineral oxides were used to stain the creamware producing a mottled 'tortoise-shell' effect.[13] This technique remained a speciality of Cadell's until 1755, when the range expanded to include white saltglazed stoneware.[14] Further expansion came in 1789, when the company contemplated manufacturing glazed brownware '...Pigs, at five pence per dozen ...'; if this venture was successful, Cadell's intended to build workers' housing.[15]

In 1759, William Cadell left Cockenzie to join with John Roebuck and Samuel Garbett in founding the Carron Iron Works near Falkirk, the first large ironworks in Scotland; later, the partnership purchased the Cramond Iron Mills, near Edinburgh.[16] William Cadell passed the Kirk Street Pottery to the management of his son, John Cadell (1740-1814), leaving the former managers, William Cadell's nephew (also William) and his wife Margaret Cadell (nee Inglis), free to establish a pottery of their own at Bankfoot.[17]

Prestonpans Tu'penny Ale bottle

Situated half a mile west along the town boundary William Cadell (nephew) built a pottery on the Bankfoot site, which consisted of a 'Tenement of land with houses, biggings, yards, corn barn, malt barn and kiln steep-stove'.[18] Bankfoot originally specialised in basic brown earthenware, using local clay which was plentiful in the area. To produce a glazed brownware range, flints were ground at a nearby mill let to Margaret Cadell by the then owner of Prestongrange, Janet, Countess of Hyndford and Baron of Prestoungrange.[19] White clay, which gave a finer product, was later imported from the South of England to recreate the Creamware of the original Kirk Street pottery. Bankfoot also produced salt-glazed stoneware bottles, particularly used for holding the famous Prestonpans (tu'penny) Ale.[20]

William Cadell & Co. was a relatively large pottery, employing 40 men and 30 boys in 1791 and selling articles of earthenware to a value of upwards of £5,000 per annum.[21] John Cadell's pottery in Kirk Street, Prestonpans employed 40. Margaret Cadell (now widow) employed 12 at Bankfoot, including Adam Cubie, master potter.[22] All the Cadell potteries benefited from the business connections of William Cadell Snr, who built up a thriving export business in Prestonpans pottery.[23] Building on his existing trading links from the port of Morrison's Haven, about a mile west of Prestonpans, Cadell exported pottery along his existing merchant shipping lines to Scandinavia, Russia, North America, Spain and particularly Italy.[24] Pattern books featuring pottery were distributed by Cadell's various agents, which showed Cadell's awareness of the power of advertising and faith in his product.[25]

In 1777, John Cadell purchased Cockenzie House and the lands formerly leased from the now sequestrated York Buildings Company and the Cadells began their 140-year reign as Lairds of Cockenzie.[26] The pottery business failed to keep pace with this success however, as the late eighteenth century saw a general decline in pottery business. In light of this, Caddell decided to reorganise the pottery and, in 1786, considered engaging Richard Adams from Cobridge, Staffordshire. Adams may have been experienced and enthusiastic, but he failed to impress John Cadell and was not appointed.[27] Decline in business ultimately led to Margaret Caddell (nee Inglis) giving up Bankfoot to the Gordons in 1795; John Cadell gave up Kirk Street a year later, to David Thomson & Co.[28] David Thomson was a Potters' Society and Committee member, which status attracted large amounts of finance from John Fowler, brewer, and his partner Robert Hislop. David Thomson & Co. operated successfully from Kirk Street until around 1813–1814.[29]

When David Thomson died in 1819, the pottery passed to Hamilton Watson, Thomson's manager, competent potter and one time President of the Potters' Box Society.[30] Watson recruited a manager in J.J. Foster, master potter, originally from Newcastle.[31] The Kirk Street Pottery was now 'Watsons' and was responsible for the change in technique from the basic hand painting of clear or self-coloured glaze to transfer printing. The original design was first painted then engraved onto a copper plate, transferred to tissue paper and then rolled to the ware. Hamilton Watson remained owner of the Kirk Street pottery until 1838, when his business affairs were sequestrated and Foster left for Reid's Pottery in Musselburgh.[32]

In its 90 year lifespan to 1840, under the leadership of family members for the first 46 years, the Cadell pottery tradition in Prestonpans can be credited on three counts. Firstly, for introducing Creamware pottery to Scotland. Secondly, for establishing an international market for Prestonpans Pottery. Finally, for constructing purpose-built potteries in which to perpetuate the Prestonpans pottery tradition.

West Pans Pottery – 1764/5–1817

West Pans is situated three miles westwards of Prestonpans, on the seaward side of the road to Edinburgh. Opposite there is a knoll or hill which takes its name 'Drumore' (the 'big ridge') from Gaelic. West Pans had all the basic pottery making elements; clay, coal, salt and waterpower (provided by Pinky Burn). While the monks of the Cistercian order at Newbattle settled in the area in the twelfth century, and in all probability produced pottery, the first specific record appears in 1754, when the Burgh Council of Musselburgh ordered a Samuel Lambas to pay for the right to dig clay.[33] Pottery production, on a significant scale, began, in the 1760s, when William Littler arrived at West Pans, after the failure of his factory at Longton Hall in Staffordshire. Littler is respected today as the founder of Scotland's porcelain industry, but he was as highly regarded by his contemporaries who elected him honorary burgess of Musselburgh in 1764.[34]

The Littler pottery range included basic wares in white and brown, stoneware, creamware and earthenware.[35] Mapped in 1766 as a 'china work', Littler specialised in soft paste porcelain using clay from the Pan Brae, a pit on the side of the Drummer Ridge. Littler's work is characterised by a deep blue colour, achieved by utilising Scottish cobalt from Alva at the head of the Firth of Forth, refined by Roebuck at his chemical works in Prestonpans.[36] Littler had a tendency towards producing raised floral and leaf patterns on jugs, dishes and tureens as well as lustre decorated crests and coats of arms. Such decorations reflected not only the importance of aristocratic patronage, but also the West Pans tradition of 'novelty' and 'one-off' items.[37] Despite the admiration of his contemporaries and the patronage of the gentry, the pottery closed in 1777 principally because Littler was unable to produce porcelain at an affordable price.[38]

The West Pans pottery was reopened in 1784 with the arrival of Robert Bagnall, a Glasgow potter who had been forced to abandon his own, successful, pottery business after riots in the city. In 1779, the Bill before parliament to repeal the Penal Code against Roman Catholics in Scotland met with violent opposition by the Committee of Correspondence. Fired by Lord George Gordon's speech making, mobs destroyed Catholic meeting houses and shops in Edinburgh and Glasgow; Robert Bagnall had a pottery at Turine Street which was set on fire in Februrary 1779. Similarly, rioters destroyed the contents of his pottery warehouse in King Street. Although Bagnall received a small amount of compensation from Glasgow Town Council, he eventually went bankrupt and moved to West Pans to take over Littler's pottery, which he operated as a creamware pottery until 1792.[39]

Suffering a decline in sales, Bagnall attempted re-organisation. However, the pottery went bankrupt and was re-opened by Bagnall's creditors, trading as the West Pans Stoneware Company. A William Smith was succeeded, in 1813, by David Wilson and James Gibson who produced brownwares, until 1817.[40]

West Pans Pottery

Gordon's Pottery – 1772–1842

About 1750, a Newcastle potter, Anthony Hilcote, leased the pottery at Morrison's Haven Harbour, situated at the western extremity of Prestonpans. In 1772, Janet Grant, Countess of Hyndford (c1729–1818) granted a nineteen-year lease to Rowland Bagnall, potter and alchemist, and a George Gordon, then a clerk at the Glass House Company, Leith. The Partnership was given rights to ground at Morrison's Haven, including a Sea Mill and a number of houses from which Anthony Hilcote had carried out 'pottery work'.[41] The partnership planned to make cream coloured ware, black tortoise-shell and white ware.[42] However, Bagnall died on 22 February 1773 leaving his wife Elizabeth who, under the Partnership Agreement, had no hereditary entitlements and was removed. In 1774, Gordon personally moved into the pottery at Morrison's Haven along with his two sons, George (2nd) and Robert, both potters.[43] Initially, fuel for the Morrison's Haven pottery came from Elphinstone colliery, but the increasing success of the Gordon's pottery concern allowed them to take over the lease of the colliery at Wallyford.

By the end of the eighteenth century, Gordon's was exporting, and in 1795 took over Bankfoot pottery from William Cadell and Margaret Inglis. Bankfoot was situated to the west of Prestonpans on the landward side of the main road, which ran along the coast to Edinburgh. To the east lay the small promontory known as the Cuttle, or 'Cuthill'. To the south was the estate of Prestongrange and to the west, Morrison's Haven Harbour. Bankfoot was described, in 1766, as 'a Tenement of land with houses, biggings, yards, corn barn, malt barn and kiln steep stove'.[44] Bankfoot proved a suitable location for industrial pottery production because of the readily available, good quality clay from Upper Birslie Plantation or 'Clay Holes' in the Barony of Falside.[45] The existence of Prestongrange and Elphinstone coalfields conveniently provided coal suited to firing and the harbour and main Edinburgh Road provided transportation for produce.

Bankfoot, under the Cadells, had to 1790, produced glazed brown ware. This range was carried on by the Gordons, and by the first quarter of the nineteenth century this pottery was producing a wide variety of good quality earthenware.

By George Gordon (the elder)'s death in 1809, pottery production was a success. Robert was the proprietor of two feus, described as;

> lying over against the harbour of Milhaven, now called Morrison's Haven, betwixt the ... harbour on the north and west ... and the other called the Salt Girnee ... bounded by the Sea Craig on the north [46]

Conditions were attached to the nineteen year lease (1772– 1791) for Morrison's Haven granted by Janet, Countess of Hyndford, exemplifying how she advocated the movement towards agricultural 'improvement', an ideology which focused on the development of agriculture and which was a forerunner to later nineteenth-century industrialisation. Gordons had to provide a carriage of six carts and two horses on Janet Grant's demand, from Prestongrange to within a radius of ten miles, as well as infilling any clay excavation to make way for crops the following year.[47]

By 1812, Gordons operations at Morrison's Haven had expanded to include brick and tile making while pottery production continued and increased. Gordons' now leased the Bankfoot pottery to a Charles Belfield, whose three kilns at the Cuttle complemented Gordons' existing two.[48] Gordons' further expanded their pottery operations by taking over the bankrupt Prestonpans Vitriol Company's premises in Prestonpans.[49]

Gordons' success lay in the ability to continually manufacture products suited to the demands of the consumer. Plaster moulds used up to the 1740s were superceded by more sophisticated methods and wares were enhanced by transfer printing, painting, guilding and colouring. The change allowed Gordons' to cater for local demand for inexpensive decorated ware.[50] Initially producing coarse slipware pottery, Gordons' later produced white enamelled earthenware, whiteware or delftware. However, this proved unsuitable for domestic use because it was too brittle and was liable to crack. So, from 1770 when it was discovered in Devonshire, china clay was utilised.[51] Gordons' thereafter produced white and decorated ware in an extensive variety of shapes and patterns. Indeed, from inventories of Gordons' goods sent to buyers, about fifty per cent of the goods were whiteware.[52]

Gordons' looked to available resources to expand their range; local clays were utilised to make terracotta and jet, or basalt wares, including black *lustre* teapots, toy figures, banded bowls, enamelled pressed jugs, lustre bowls, lustre cream ewers and lustre sugar boxes.[53] Gordons' most popular printed pattern plates included 'Bird and Fly', the monarchy, nautical scenes and fruit designs. The range also featured hugely popular blue and white transfer printed ware, known patterns of which included Willow, Asiatic Pheasant, and Lady of the Lake. In addition, Robert Gordon probably produced hand painted pieces; his father had been a 'master potter', Robert was apprenticed to James Ramsay (an Edinburgh painter) for six years and he acted as Clerk at the 1799 Annual General Meeting of the Prestonpans Potters' Society, of which he was a member.[54] Whatever their style, Gordons' pieces can be identified by the impressions R. & G. Gordon with a *crown*, *Geo. Gordon*, or simply *Gordon*.

Despite adequate local resources and innovative designs, the success of Gordons' did not endure. Robert was prosperous enough to become a founding member of the East Lothian Bank in 1810,[55] but his fortunes suffered when one of the cashiers disappeared with the funds in 1822, and the partners were left liable for the substantial loss.[56] Other events conspired against him.

In 1818, Sir James Grant-Suttie, 4th Baron of Balgone and Prestongrange (1759–1836) had inherited the land at Prestongrange. The Grant-Suttie/Gordon relationship got off to a bad start with Grant-Suttie taking the Gordons to court over the disrepair of the housing and the Sea Mill at Morrison's Haven.[57] Gordons' had originally leased the 'flint mill at the foot of Prestongrange Avenue for a period of 14 years' from the Countess Hyndford in 1812.[58] The lease included an agreement that Countess Hyndford's 'heirs and successors ... warrant [the Gordons'] ... peaceable possession of said mill'. This was not entirely adhered to when, in 1826, a grievance was raised by Grant-Suttie that the power of the mill had been diminished as '... caused and continued by the negligence, or by the permission of the Gordons".[59] Such disrepair was presumably due to the Gordons indebtedness over the East Lothian Bank crisis. Whatever the case, Grant-Suttie refused to renew the Gordons soon to expire lease and began litigation banning Gordons' from winning the clay at Morrison's Haven.

It would seem that the action against Gordons' was part of Grant-Suttie's plans to consolidate his lands. Although, Grant-Suttie's treatment of the Gordons seems heavy handed, it is worth bearing in mind that Grant-Suttie moved to Prestongrange after retiring as Member of Parliament for Haddingtonshire; he was used to applying legal power to his will. In 1832, Grant-Suttie complained that a 'small stripe of ground' to which Grant-Suttie had legal right on the north side of the Edinburgh Road had been 'taken of them when the old road was changed from ... the south side of the houses and yards at the harbour at Morrison's Haven to ... the north side of the Houses and yards'.[60] It emerged that reallocation of the road was 'in consequence of an Act of Parliament' which had moved Morrison's Haven Harbour westwards. The move was only feasible because of land reclamation efforts instigated by the Gordons, where 'the ground in dispute may have been gradually formed by the accumulation of rubbish from ... [Gordons] manufactures'.[61] In effect, Grant-Suttie wrongly blamed Gordons' for his loss of a small strip of ground to facilitate improvements to the road system.

Further, Grant-Suttie still insisted that Gordons' pay him compensation for any clay they took for making brick. His pedantic view was that this was contrary to the terms of their lease, which stated that clay could only be used to make bricks for the pottery. His perception was that Gordons' were allegedly making excessive amounts of bricks and transporting them elsewhere.[62]

Later in 1832, a petition was served on 'Geo. Gordon, Potter at Morrison's Haven' claiming that he had 'thought fit to take off the turf of a part of the ... links grounds next [to] the Harbour with the intention apparently of carrying it off and applying it to some other purpose'.[63] In February 1833, an agent was assigned to survey and measure the grounds in question, and Gordons' were not only requested to 'replace any Turf that may have been taken from the ground ... and [banned] ... from removing any more', but a claim was made that Gordons' were liable in all expenses.[64] Again, it was noted that the piece of ground in question was now much bigger because of Gordons' reclamation efforts, indeed it was deemed that the ground belonged to Gordons'. It thereafter came to light that Grant-Suttie had ordered East Lothian Road Trustees to 'remove the turf and the soil ... with the view to blasting the Craig below'. This apparently '... had been done maliciously, and in order to annoy' the Gordons.[65] Unhappy with this allegation, Grant-Suttie ordered the case to be put before the Lord President. The case was ultimately dismissed in 1837, when it was deemed that no expenses were due by either party.; the death of Sir James Grant-Suttie the previous year was noted in the dismissal, and perhaps his successor saw more clearly the futility of the action.[66] However, if Grant-Suttie's actions had failed to exact any financial gain from the Gordons, he did succeed in removing them from the premises at Morrison's Haven.

The most notable feature of Gordons' pottery production history was their determination to remain in the pottery trade. The mid-nineteenth century saw pottery operations in decline, throughout the area, as one contemporary observed;

> 'Of late [1831], all operations of potting, with the exception of two small works for brownware ... [have] been suspended, to the serious disadvantage of numerous and manifold interests'.[67]

Robert moved to a small brownware pottery at Rope Walk, Prestonpans to be succeeded, in 1839, by his brother George Gordon (3rd). George Gordon (2nd) took over management of the pottery at Bankfoot but was soon struggling financially and was ultimately sequestrated, in 1828, for not paying his coal account to Grant-Suttie.[68] George Gordon (2nd) probably moved to the old vitriol works at Prestonpans; he already owned the site and the existence of two beehive kilns, suggests he used the premises as a pottery.[69] In 1840, he took on a five-year lease of the main Cadell Pottery in Kirk Street, Prestonpans. By this time, the pottery included 'three kilns and adjacent building along with the two dwellinghouses on the main street and small garden behind'.[70] By the end of his first year, Gordon had to relinquish the lease because he could not afford the rent arrears of £17 10s.[71] Subsequently, any existing Gordons' pottery stock was sold and, in 1841, George Gordon (2nd) was ordered out of the pottery, a year before his death in 1842 when all debts of Gordons' were discharged.[72]

The Gordons dominance of Prestonpans pottery production ended in 1842, after seventy years of producing pottery from premises in Kirk Street and Rope Walk in Prestonpans, Bankfoot and Morrison's Haven.

Belfield & Company – c1835–c1935

With the demise of Gordons' domination of the Prestonpans pottery industry, two potters – Andrew Mitchell and Charles Belfield – were only too happy to set up another pottery, intitially trading as Mitchell & Belfield and, by 1847, as Charles Belfield & Co.[73] Charles Belfield was familiar with both pottery and Prestonpans; he had previously managed Gordons' at Bankfoot and his father, James Belfield had probably originated from one of the Staffordshire potteries. James had established a pottery on the site of the old Salt manufactory of Robert Laidlaw – the property known as 'Seacliff' – on the north side of the west end of the High Street in Prestonpans.

Water Jug c1880 attributed to Bellfield's

At this time, the older potteries of Prestonpans were in difficulty and Belfields' is known to have bought a large amount of bankrupt stock from Watson's Pottery. The Victorian Era had begun and the average Scots family had better equipped kitchens and meals became more elaborate. The result was that demand for large quantities of quality pottery increased and Belfields' expanded to include premises on the south side of the High Street facing Rope Walk.[74]

Belfields' was best known for its fine quality sanitary ware and brown (or Rockingham) glazed tea and coffee pots. Their range included Majolica ware, everyday kitchen ware and high quality relief moulded plates featuring leaf decoration and/or leaf shape and coloured with a variety of deep oxide and lead glazes in green, yellow and brown.

Belfields' product range expanded in a different direction from previous Prestonpans pottery producers in that Belfields' ultimately specialized in drainpipes. Indeed, Charles Belfield invented (but did not patent) a system of hand pressing pipes of about thirty-seven centimetres long, wider at one end than the other. Some were utilised at Prestonpans for water drainage and gas while the remainder was transported to Forfarshire for use as water pipes.[75]

In 1850, Charles Belfield died, leaving the business to run as a family concern until shortly before the death of John Clark Belfield, in 1941, the last remaining potter in the family. This was not the end of industrial pottery production in the area however, as bricks and other fireclay goods continued to be produced at Morrison's Haven by a variety of companies until the early 1970s. However, Belfields' remains the most technically accomplished of the Prestonpans potteries, with a continuous record of family ownership lasting over one hundred years.

4 THE POTTERY COMMUNITY

In 1792, the *Statistical Account of Scotland* reported that Prestonpans Parish had a working population of 1435, of which 252 'Persons ... [and their families were] employed in the potteries'.[76] This was by no means the high point in the history of Prestonpans Pottery production; Bankfoot had just ceased production and was about to resume, and Gordons' had yet to start. In the meantime, Cadells' was the biggest employer with a workforce of upwards of 70, with about 35 employed at Morrison's Haven. This workforce comprised of men, women and children – the pottery community of Prestonpans – who established rules and work practices designed to protect their identity and themselves.

Pottery production has many elements that distinguish it from other manufactories. Firstly, production took several different processes, therefore requiring a workforce trained in their own particular skill. Secondly, an extensive product range was coupled with a low level of mechanisation. Thirdly, because technological change only occurred strategic points of the process, manual manipulation remained an essential part of the process. Put together, these elements ensured a complex sub-division of labour, which in turn resulted in a definite hierarchy within the potteries. This was best shown in the contract hiring system.

Pottery owners contracted individual craft potters to head the pottery hierarchy. Craft potters were chosen because of their manual dexterity and deep knowledge of technology, clay, its composition and its behaviour. Craft potters frequently brought their own work groups to produce a 'count' of ware, and managed the staff by determining wages and delegating supervision.[77] George Gordon was an eighteenth century example of a successful Prestonpans pottery owner with no experience of pottery production. To compensate for his inexperience, Gordon, in 1772, entered into partnership with Rowland Bagnall, potter and alchemist. Gordon advanced the money necessary for carrying on the pottery work, while Bagnall was to receive '16s per week of wages'. Bagnall only received half of this wage, however, the other half was to be left to accumulate to 'help the Company's stock till the trade should be able to afford the whole'.[78] It is interesting that while Gordon was confident that Bagnall had the ability to generate 'trade', a financial incentive was put in place to ensure that he did.

Prestonpans had many craft potters, all were itinerant and were temporarily employed by different potteries. Adam Cubie, master potter for William Caddell at Bankfoot, helped Cadell's widow to carry on the pottery, until his own death in 1791. Jonathan Foster, pottery engraver, worked at all of the Prestonpans potteries, until c1800, when he became manager of Watsons'. John Jenkins, journeyman and copperplate engraver, came to Scotland in 1820 and was employed for a time at Gordons'. The master potter at Belfields' was Andrew Mitchell, who managed an increasing number of staff: the workforce rose from twenty-one in 1851 to thirty-nine by 1861.

By today's standards, life at the Prestonpans 'Potworks' was bad and poorly paid. Potwork was not a glamorous job, but messy, repetitive and hard work. Before the 48-hour week was introduced, in the early 1920's, most 'potworkers' endured a 60-hour, 6-day week. Potwork did, however, constitute a valuable source of employment, with many members of the same family working in the potteries at different skills.

Men were mostly employed in creating pottery in the workshop area. 'Throwers' made the different pots, cups, saucers and plates, while 'turners', finished-off and made smooth the pieces before hardening them off in a warm kiln. Thereafter male 'carriers' transported pieces to the biscuit kiln, to be dipped in glaze, then back to the glaze kiln for around three days firing. Men were paid on piece-work, and only kilnmen or master potters, were paid a weekly wage. Aside from creating pottery, men were responsible for counting the ware, cleaning water pots, firing stoves and carrying coal.[79]

Women were often employed in the handlers' shop, making handles for cups and teapots, while others made spouts. Clay had to be cut up, manually manipulated and put in a box, from which equal quantities of clay emerged which would be set in a handle shape mould. Potworks used a high proportion of female labour, particularly in the decorating process. After baking, the pieces went to a painting shop, where the workers were regarded as superior to other sections of the workforce.[80] Up to the nineteenth century, child labour was a way of life in the Prestonpans manufactories, with ten-year-olds spending one day at work, one day at school, before entering full-time employment at around thirteen years of age.

Whatever the gender of the Potworker, in the mid-1800s all risked two industrial diseases. As lead was one of the main ingredients in the glazes, anyone in the glazing process was particularly vulnerable to lead poisoning. Additionally, pneumoconiosis (lung damage) could be contracted by inhaling the flint dust particles used in the clay mixture.[81] Consequently, potteries were sited away from residential areas because of the atmospheric pollution caused when the kilns were fired; in 1792, an average of 24 tons of coal were consumed per week at Kirk Street.

The abundance of natural resources attracted many manufactories to Prestonpans, which meant that although potters were numerous they did not dominate entirely the areas working population; colliers were more numerous than potters. However, colliers lived and worked in even more depressing surroundings than the potworkers and were treated as 'serfs' (or slaves) of the pits who, up to 1799, were contracted for life to personally provide labour, and that of their families. In contrast, while skilled potters also had to provide assistants, who were normally family members, they never had to commit themselves or their families to lifetime allegiance to one employer. Potters and coalworkers may have shared the same locality and had similarily strong links between home and work, but they had different experiences in terms of skill. Coalworkers comprised of largely non-skilled labourers, convicts and unemployed agricultural workers, while potters were acknowledged as highly skilled craftsmen, noted for their independence, pride, thriftiness and prudence.

Potters then, were well respected in the local community and also well represented. Such a large proportion of the local workforce had to have a large impact on the community. To ensure that impact was a positive one, in 1766, a 'Potters' Friendly Society' was established. Various benefits were attached to membership of the Society, including an annual 'Potters Day' parade (on the First Friday of June) and access to the 'Prestonpans Potters Box'. Managerial potters introduced the 'Box' to administer support for the remaining members of the pottery community during retirement, sickness and bereavement. Monthly dues were collected by members for the 'benefit of all' and were fairly high at one pence ha'penny per month, if living within 10 miles and every quarter if outwith. Benefits included sickness payments, retirement pension, widow's pension, maintenance for orphans and compensation on death of a child. Costly subscriptions and the scope of the aid on offer indicate not only how realistic benefits were but also the wealth of the potters.[82]

Fishwife Figurine

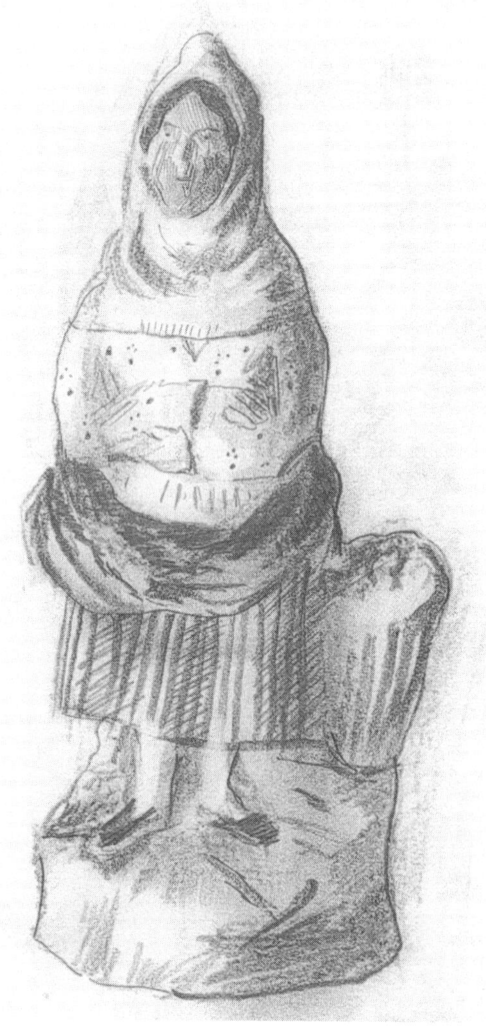

Members of the Society had to strictly adhere to its written Rules, which included penalties for inappropriate behaviour. For instance, any 'backbite or threat' incurred a fine, as did non-attendance at Annual General Meetings. Swearing on the Sabbath and any sort of theft meant exclusion from the Society. Burials had to be attended by all members within a two-mile radius or they were fined. *Mortality Cloths* were provided by the Society for use at members' funerals, including those of members' unmarried children, who had heritable benefit of the cloth.83 Possibly due to demand or the inconvenience of transporting the cloths, a 1785 ruling forbade the use of mortality cloths ten miles outwith Prestonpans (members received 5s instead).[84]

Establishing a workers' society may, to the twenty first century mind, suggest some sort of trade unionism, however, there are no political references in the *Prestonpans Potters' Society Rule Book*. Indeed, pottery owners, John and William Cadell, encouraged the benevolent measures, made subscriptions and chaired committee meetings which were made up of Boxmaster, two Key Keepers, a society member and clerk, all of whom were elected annually.[85] Any identifiable undertones are those of Protestantism. For example, at a meeting in 1779, for opposing the Repeal in favour of Popery, the Society agreed that the measure would threaten the interest of the 'Protestant Religion and the Civil Liberties of this Country'. And, along with 'Other Society's of Scotland', namely Hammermen, Weavers, Shoemakers, the Potters resolved to use every Constitutional measure to oppose the repeal.[86]

It was not only in times of personal tragedy that members could rely on Box benefits, as members could count on the Society to act to alleviate potential problems. For example, in July 1800 a shortage of corn moved the Society to purchase and distribute grain amongst its members thus acting to prevent hunger.[87] So, aside from monetary benefits, the Society offered the Prestonpans pottery community protection, identity and a collective voice.

In summary, Prestonpans potters had a distinctive experience of work compared to their industrial and agricultural contemporaries. Firstly, the complex production process meant sub-division of labour, resulting in a definite hierarchy. Secondly, itinerant specialists who imported designs and techniques managed an indigenous workforce. Lastly, in an area dominated by manufactories, the pottery workforce emerged as respected and highly skilled craftsmen armed with a published code of conduct.

5 CONCLUSION

The history of the potteries of Prestonpans, Morrison's Haven and West Pans follow the same path. In terms of location, all the pottery owners chose East Lothian because of readily available natural resources. In terms of range of wares, the demand for fashionable pottery was met, determined by technology and innovative use of existing materials. In terms of workforce organisation, the Prestonpans potteries are most notable for their good design and excellent workmanship, made possible by maintaining the highly skilled, manual part of the process beyond mechanisation. Finally, despite the diversity of ownership, the reason for the decline of pottery manufacture is arguably similar in each case; potteries were only part of larger enterprises, which tended to collapse when more profitable ventures came along. In all instances, the success of the Prestonpans pottery community was based on hard toil, adaptability and self-preservation, evident in the two hundred-year association with Prestonpans.

BIBLIOGRAPHY

Primary Sources

Manuscripts & Documents

Sinclair, W. *Statistical Account* (1793/99)

Snodgrass, C.P. *Third Statistical Account of Scotland : The County of East Lothian* (1953)

The Story of Prestonpans from Contemporary Records, 1790s–1950s (1995)

National Archives of Scotland (NAS)

CC 8/17/39 – Partnership Agreement between R. Bagnall and G. Gordon. Dated 12

May 1773.
GD357/49/1 – New Issue, Gordon's vs. Suttie, 1826.
GD357/49/2 – Turfcase interlocutor Suttie. Bart vs. Gordons. 21/11/1832.
GD357/49/25 – Edinburgh, 16 December 1834.
GD357/49/26 – Plan of Two Feus of Messrs. Gordon, Morison's Haven. Surveyed 9 February 1883.
GD357/49/27 – 1st Division, 20 January 1835. Additional Appendix to the Reclaiming note for Sir James Grant-Suttie, Bart against Lord Corehouse's Interlocutor
GD357/49/3 – Petition and Complaint of Sir James Grant Suttie of Prestongrange and Balgone, Baronet, 10/11/1832
GD357/49/31 – Note for Sir George Grant Suttie to order process of Advocation to the Roll along with Declarator. 22 February 1837.
RS27/175/173 – Register of Sasine entry, recording Mr. W. Cadell and Elizabeth Inglis' ownership of Bankfoot.
SC40/20/5
SC 40/20/12 – Summons. Elizabeth Bagnall vs. Geo.Gordon, 1774.
SC40/20/70
SC 40/20/126 – Decreet Absolvi for and for Expences Charles Ramsay one of the Partners of the Potterie Co. at Prestonpans against James Anderson, Potter at Prestonpans (1790).
SC40/20/196. Execution of Sequestration. Trustees of Wm. Cadell, deceased and George Gordon. Dated 03 July 1841.

Maps

Armstrong – Map of the Lothians, 1773
Forrest – Map of Haddingtonshire, 1799
Mather – Plan of Sea-Coast from Kerr's Toll House by Prestonpans to Seton Sands, 1766
Ordnance Survey – Tranent Village and Surroundings, 1854
Ordnance Survey – Prestonpans, 1854, 1907, 1914, 1957, 1960

Newspapers and Periodicals

East Lothian Courier
East Lothian News
Haddingtonshire Courier
Scottish pottery Studies
Scottish Pottery Historical Review
Transactions of the East Lothian Antiquarian & Field Naturalists' Society

Secondary Sources

Cameron, A. Bank of Scotland, 1695–1995: A Very Singular Institution (1995).
Campbell, R.D. *Captain Cadell and the Waikato Flotilla* (1995).
Cruickshank, G. 'Scottish Spongeware' in *Scottish Pottery Studies No. 1* (1982)
Cruickshank, G. 'Scottish Saltglaze' in *Scottish Pottery Studies No. 2* (1982)
Dalgleish, G., Haggarty, G. & McVeigh, P. (eds) *Pots at the 'Pans – The Potteries of Prestonpans, Musselburgh and Portobello* (1990)
Fleming, J.A. *Scottish Pottery* (1973).
Green, C.E. *East Lothian* (1907)
Louden, D. & Whitfield, Rev. W. *East Lothian Studies* (1891)
Macaulay, J.D. *A Short History of Prestonpans* (1981)
McNeill, C. *Kirkcaldy Potteries* (1998)
McNeill, P. *Tranent and its Surroundings* (1884)
McNeill, P. *Prestonpans & Vicinity: Historical, Ecclesiastical and Traditional* (1902, reprinted 1984)
McVeigh, P. *Scottish East Coast Potteries 1750–1840* (1979)
McVeigh, P. *The Creamware Potter: East Coast of Scotland – 1750–1840* (1980)
Paul, I. *The Scottish Tradition in Pottery* (1948)
Shaw, J. *Water Power in Scotland 1550-1870* (1984)

Shirlaw, J. 'Potters at Morrison's Haven c1750–1833 and the Gordon's at Bankfoot (1795–1840) in *Scottish Pottery Historical Review* (1998)

Trotter, J. Rev.Mr. 'Parish of Prestonpans' in Sinclair, J. *The Statistical Account of Scotland* (1975)

Whipp, R. *Patterns of Labour; Work and Social Change in the Pottery Industry* (1990)

NOTES

1 Paul, I. *The Scottish Tradition in Pottery* (1948), p2

2 Whipp, R. *Patterns of Labour; Work and Social Change in the Pottery Industry* (1990), p17.

3 Dalgleish, G., Haggarty, G. & McVeigh, P. (eds) *Pots at the 'Pans – The Potteries of Prestonpans, Musselburgh and Portobello* (1990)

4 Whipp, *Patterns.*, op cit., p18.

5 Paul, *Scottish Tradition*, op cit., p3.

6 Fleming, J.A. *Scottish Pottery* (1973), p158

7 The introduction of Spongeware is a clear example of a technique discovered by accident. Women transfer printers began applying glaze with discarded sponges, to great effect

8 McNeill, P. *Prestonpans & Vicinity: Historical, Ecclesiastical and Traditional* (1902), p104

9 Dalgleish, G., Haggarty, G. & McVeigh, P. (Eds.) *Pots at the 'Pans – the Potteries of Prestonpans, Musselburgh and Portobello* (1990)

10 Campbell, R.D. *Captain Cadell and the Waikato Flotilla* (1995), p1

11 Creamware is cream coloured earthenware with superior style and finish

12 McVeigh, P. *Scottish East Coast Potteries 1750–1840* (1979), p7

13 McVeigh, P. *The Creamware Potter: East Coast of Scotland – 1750–1840* (1980)

14 Dalgleish, G., Haggarty, G. & McVeigh, P. (Eds.) *Pots at the 'Pans – the Potteries of Prestonpans, Musselburgh and Portobello* (1990), McVeigh, *Creamware*, op cit

15 NAS SC 40/20/12. Decreet Absolvi for and for Expences Charles Ramsay one of the Partners of the Potterie Co. at Prestonpans against James Anderson, Potter at Prestonpans (1790)

16 Campbell, R.D. *Captain Cadell and the Waikato Flotilla* (1995), p1

17 NAS RS 27/175/173

18 Ibid

19 NAS SC40/20/5 & NAS 40/20/70. For nineteen years to 1790

20 Fleming, J.A., *Scottish Pottery* (1973), p158

21 Trotter, J. Rev. Mr. 'Parish of Prestonpans' in Sinclair, J. *The Statistical Account of Scotland* (1791), p570–1

22 Shirlaw, J. 'Potters at Morrison's Haven c1750–1833 and the Gordon's at Bankfoot 1795–1840' in *Scottish Pottery Society Historical Review* (1997), p1; The total population of Prestonpans town, in 1791, was 1492, with the number employed in the potteries and their families, totalling 252; Trotter, *Statistical Account.* op cit., p570–1.

23 McVeigh, *Creamware*

24 Dalgleish, op cit.

25 McVeigh, *Scottish East*, op cit., p13

26 Campbell, *Captain Cadell*, op cit., p1

27 Trotter, *Statistical Account*, op cit., p570

28 *Potters Box Society Rule Book*

29 Ibid

30 Ibid

31 McVeigh, *Scottish East*, op cit., pp34–41

32 Shirlaw, *Potters*, op cit., p3

33 McVeigh *Scottish East*, op cit., pp47–9

34 Ibid., p51. 'Honorary' indicating that Littler did not own the land, he leased it from a superior

35 McVeigh *Creamware*, op cit., (1979)

36 Trotter, *Statistical Account*, op cit., p142

37 McVeigh, *Scottish East*, op cit., pp51–64

38 Dalgleish, G, *Pots*, op cit
39 *The Prestonpans Potters Rule Book (1766–1807)*
40 Dalgleish, *Pots*, op cit
41 Shirlaw, *Potters*, op cit., p1
42 NAS CC 8/17/39 – Partnership Agreement between R. Bagnall and G. Gordon. Dated 12 May 1773
43 NAS SC 40/20/12 – Summons. Elizabeth Bagnall v Geo. Gordon, 1774
44 NAS RS27/175/173 – Register of Sasine entry, recording Mr. W. Cadell and Elizabeth Inglis' ownership of Bankfoot
45 McNeill, *Prestonpans*
46 NAS GD 357/49/25 – Legal Papers Grant Suttie v Gordon, Edinburgh, 16 December 1834
47 NAS RD5/263/p719 – Renewal of Hyndford/Gordon lease for Morrison's Haven, flint mill and land adjacent to Bankfoot
48 *East Lothian News* 06 April 1979; Charles Belfield and his son James, who started Belfield's pottery, both were originally employed in Gordon's (e1800–1830)
49 NAS SC40/20/196. Execution of Sequestration. Trustees of Wm. Cadell, deceased and George Gordon. Dated 03 July 1841
50 Whipp, *Patterns*, op cit.,
51 Paul, *Scottish Tradition*, op cit., p2
52 Shirlaw, *Potters*, op cit., p2
53 Fleming, *Scottish Pottery*, op cit., p252; Shirlaw, *Potters* op cit., p2
54 Ibid., p2; Scottish Record Society *Register of Edinburgh Apprentices, 1756–1800; The Rulebook of the Prestonpans Potters' Society, 1793–1801*
55 The East Lothian Bank had been formed on the premise of agricultural prosperity and speculated in wheat and barley prices
56 Cameron, A. *Bank of Scotland, 1695-1995: A Very Singular Institution* (1995), p107.
57 Ibid., p3
58 NAS GD357/49/1 – New Issue, Gordon's v Suttie, 1826
59 Ibid
60 NAS GD357/49/3 – Petition and Complaint of Sir James Grant Suttie of Prestongrange and Balgone, Baronet, 10/11/1832
61 Ibid
62 McVeigh, *Scottish East*. op cit., pp90-91
63 NAS GD357/49/2- Turfcase interlocutor Suttie. Bart v Gordons. 21/11/1832
64 Ibid; GD357/49/25 – Edinburgh, 16 December 1834
65 NAS GD357/49/26 – Plan of Two Feus of Messrs. Gordon, Morison's Haven. Surveyed 9 February 1883
66 NAS GD357/49/27 – 1st Division, 20 January 1835. Additional Appendix to the Reclaiming note for Sir James Grant Suttie, Bart against Lord Corehouse's Interlocutor; GD357/49/31 – Note for Sir George Grant Suttie to order process of Advocation to the Roll along with Declarator. 22 February 1837.
67 *The Story of Prestonpans from Contemporary Records: 1790s-1950s* (1995), p52
68 Shirlaw, J. op cit., p3
69 Ibid., p2
70 NAS SC 40/20/196. Execution of Sequestration. Trustees of William Caddell, deceased and George Gordon. Dated 03 July 1841
71 Ibid
72 NAS GD357/49/30 – Discharge dated 14 July 1842 of 'all Bonds or Debts due by George Gordon, Senior or Robert Gordon, or George Gordon, Junior; Shirlaw, J. op cit., p3
73 Shirlaw, *Potters*, p2
74 McVeigh, *Scottish East*, op cit., p107
75 McNeill, *Prestonpans*, p115
76 Trotter, *Statistical Account*, op cit., p589–91
77 Whipp, *Patterns*, op cit., pp53–55
78 NAS SC 40/20/12 Summons. Elizabeth Bagnall and George Gordon. 1774

79 McNeill, C. *Kirkcaldy Potteries* (1998), p46
80 Ibid., p42
81 Whipp, *Patterns*, pp53–55
82 *The Prestonpans Potters' Rule Book (1766–1807)*
83 Trade and craft guilds owned at least one mortality cloth; a heavy cloth embroidered with the guilds' emblem which was draped over the coffin at funerals. Funds from the hire of the mortality cloth were used towards poor relief and/or funeral expenses.
84 Ibid
85 Ibid
86 Ibid
87 Prestonpans Potters'

ANNEX

GLASS MANUFACTURE AT PRESTONGRANGE
by Jill Turnbull

Glass on an industrial scale has been made in Scotland for very nearly 400 years and one of the very earliest production sites was Morrison's Haven, now known as Prestongrange. It was particularly suitable because the Forth coal was regarded as the only type which could be used in the newly developed coal-burning glass furnaces, since it burned cleanly and produced less sulphur than coal from elsewhere. The safe harbour, availability of other local raw materials such as sand and fireclay, and proximity of Edinburgh were additional advantages, as they were to the pottery and other industries which later flourished there.

The first patent of monopoly to make glass in Scotland was obtained by Sir George Hay of Netherliff, later the first Earl of Kinnoull (1572–1634), in 1610.[1] He licensed other people actually to produce the glass for payment of a fee, and it was under such an agreement that the first glassworks was built at Morrison's Haven in 1622. Hay's licensee was probably a Scot called James Ord, but the expert glassmaker who built the furnace was a Venetian, Leonardo Michinelli, one of the skilled foreign workmen on whom the early industry depended.

Michinelli was funded to the amount of £400 sterling by Edinburgh merchant William Dick, acting on behalf of an English glassworks owner.[2] It is not necessary here to discuss the politics behind such patronage, but the basic aim was to undermine the English monopoly holder, Sir Robert Mansell, by supporting his Scottish rival Sir George Hay.

The Italian glassmakers brought their Catholic families with them to Scotland, and they took Mass at Seton House, home of the Earl of Winton. From time to time Sir Robert Mansell managed to force them to return to England and the Morrison's Haven glassworks were closed. In the 1630s, however, a Dutchman, Sir Philibert Vernatti, built a new furnace there,[3] and brought in another team of Venetians, eleven of whom are known by name. Vernatti's glassworks was managed by his brother Maximilian and appears to have been a successful enterprise.

Glass was a very expensive luxury in the 17th century, owned only by the wealthy. The most prestigious drinking glasses were those imported directly from Venice, but the facon-de-venise glasses made by ex-patriot Venetians

Stems of façon-de-venise glass from an inn assemblage at Bagshott made at Sir Robert Mansell's glassworks 1620–40 (Photograph: Dr Hugh Wilmott)

were also in demand. It is an indication of the success of the Scottish glassworks that in 1626 no fewer than 890 dozen crystal glasses, valued at £267 (sterling), and 142,500 other glasses, worth £593 15s were exported from Scotland to London for sale.[4]

The more expensive drinking glasses would have been hand blown and would probably have resembled those discovered recently in London. They were made at the Broad Street glasshouse owned by Sir Robert Mansell and manned by a workforce similar to the Scottish one (see illustrations). The majority of cheaper glasses would probably have been blown into a mould, involving less hand work, and may well have consisted largely of tumblers and similar vessels.

Sir Philibert Vernatti died circa 1646, his glassworks closed down and all but two of the Venetians left Morrison's Haven. The remaining family – the Visitellas – continued to make glass at Westpans, but glassmaking at Morrison's Haven ceased for some fifty years.

In 1698, the then owner of the estate, William Morrison, Baron of Prestongrange (1663–1739), decided to restart the glassmaking business, this time producing bottles and plate glass for mirrors.[5] He built a glassworks containing two furnaces and then formed a co-partnership with thirteen local people, ranging in status from a wright to Sir William Binning, each of whom bought a share for £50 sterling. The fifteenth shareholder was a French glassmaker Daniel Tittory who had been working at Newcastle.[6] He signed a nine year contract that he and his two sons, Daniel and Nathaniel would make:

'as good and sufficient broad window glass and glass bottles as any that were made in Newcastle.'

Over the next few months William Morrison bought out the other shareholders and by the end of 1699, he was the sole owner. Mirrors and window glass were probably made for a short time, but bottles were the main product of the glassworks throughout its history. There were many ups and downs in the fortunes of the glassworks and William Morrison himself over the ensuing years. The Tittorys left at the end of their contract and a new workforce was engaged, there were disputes, legal wrangles and problems with management, none of it helped by the fact that Morrison served as an MP in the London Parliament after 1707 and was absent for much of the time .[7]

Glassmaking continued however, until about 1727, by which time William Morrison was virtually bankrupt and the business was owned by the York Buildings Company, which invested heavily in a new glasshouse and raw material, in the hope of producing plate glass for mirrors and window glass. That venture came to nothing, however, glassmaking ceased, and the site eventually became the home of the Gordon's pottery.

Unlike a pottery, a glassworks leaves behind little in the way of datable or useful archaeological material but occasionally glass bottle seals survive. Glass has always been recycled as 'cullet', which is put into the furnace with the other ingredients. At Morrison's Haven, the sheer fragility of the facon-de-venise soda glass mitigates against the chance of finding any pieces of the glass made by the Venetians in the early 17th century, and it remains to be seen whether any bottle glass survives. More durable is the very distinctive slag and waste created by the failure of the pots in which the glass was melted, allowing the molten glass to escape and solidify on the fire below. Archaeological excavations carried out at Morrison's Haven in 2005 have recovered both these types of waste.

In a bid to create a high enough temperature to melt the glass ingredients, coal burning furnaces were built with large underground flues, designed to funnel air from outside the glasshouse under the fire. These tunnels were lined with stone or brick and were large enough for men to remove the ash from beneath the hearth. It will be interesting to see whether the arched tunnels discovered at Morrison's Haven are the flues built for the later period of glassmaking there, during the 1720s. Whatever evidence is recovered, there is no doubt that this was one of Scotland's earliest and most important small industrial sites, and should be valued as such now and for the future.

Wine glass from same assemblage with mould-blown bowl and stem (Photograph: Dr Hugh Wilmott)

Jill Turnbull has spent the last ten years researching the history of Scottish glass making. In 2001 the Society of Antiquaries of Scotland published her book *The Scottish Glass Industry, 1610–1750*, which was based on her doctoral thesis for the University of Edinburgh, and she has since written a number of journal articles on the subject. She is currently researching the period 1750–1900.

NOTES

1 Acts of The Parliaments of Scotland [APS] APS4 515
2 National Archives of Scotland [NAS] RD11/150
3 Register of the Privy Council of Scotland [RPS], 2nd Ser 5, 513

4 Godfrey, ES *The Development of English Glassmaking 1560-1640*, Oxford University Press, 1975, 211
5 APS10, 180
6 NAS CS18/188
7 Turnbull, J *The Scottish Glass Industry, 1610–1750* (Society of Antiquaries of Scotland 2001) pp 187–227

10

Geology and the Environment at Prestoungrange

Matthew Carter and Julian Wills

1. INTRODUCTION

The Barony of Prestoungrange has been worked for its geologically derived resources, including brickearth, clay, peat and of course coal, for nearly 1000 years. The extraction of these resources combined with the production of salt, glass and pottery on the site around the beam engine and Morrison's Haven inevitably had a significant impact on the environment.

This study comprises a brief history of the site to give an indication of the diverse industrial activities that have taken place there. The key industry, which attracted other industries to the area, was coal, which made possible the production of salt, pottery and bricks.

The geology of the barony was critical to the facilitation of these industries. The East Lothian basin runs north to south, from the Firth of Forth at

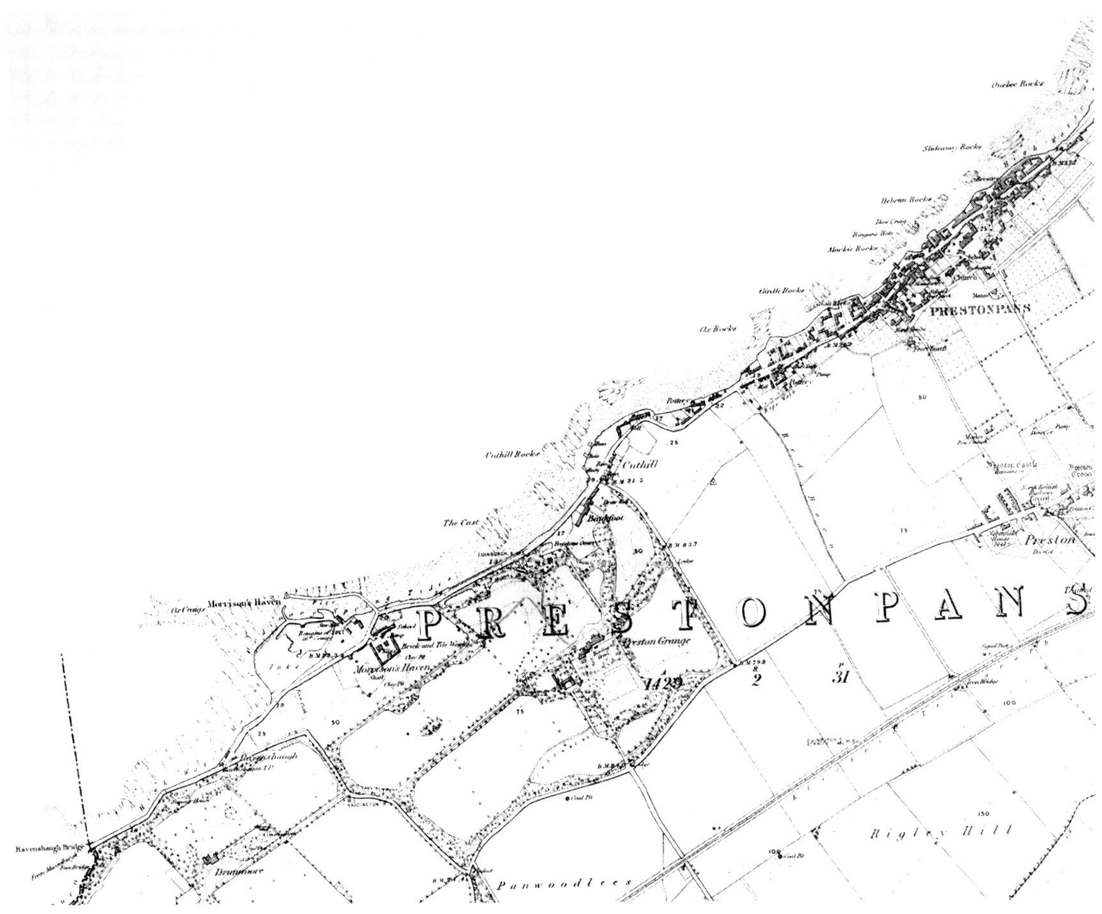

Prestonpans and Morison's Haven in 1853 (OS 1:10 560 Haddington Sheet 8)

Musselburgh southwards along the Esk valley. The area is underlain by limestone and coal measures of the Carboniferous Period and Old Red Sandstone of the Devonian Period.

Coal production at Prestongrange Colliery, however, has been plagued with the problem of flooding discussed at length by Ewan Wilson in No. 8 in this series, *Water at Preston-grange and Pumping it Out*. The other industries that located at Prestoungrange may have had a greater short term success, but none of them endured as long as coal mining.

The environmental impacts of the industries concerned and the substantial efforts to clean up the site are also discussed in conclusion of this study.

2. INDUSTRIAL HISTORY OF PRESTOUNGRANGE

In order to understand the environmental impacts of the industries that have been located at Prestoungrange through the last millennium it is important to provide a brief history of the barony and surrounding area.

The Monks of Newbattle and Holyrood Abbeys were granted permission to use the lands at Prestoungrange late in the twelfth century. By the end of the first decade of the thirteenth century they had also been granted the right to quarry for coal which passed along the 'Salters Road' between Prestoungrange and Newbattle. The monks found that coal was a more efficient source of energy for heating and salt production and it was the early production of salt as a preservative by panning that gave Prestonpans its name. The monks became skilled miners and worked the Great Seam going as low as 4m below the level of the Firth of Forth.

Coal became a very tradable item during the following centuries and the location of Prestoungrange made it an ideal shipping location. Salt was also being shipped from the Prestonpans coastline and in 1526 specific permission was sought to build a harbour. By this time, however, it was no longer the monks that were the major miners and shippers. The application for the harbour was made by Alexander Acheson, a name familiar to all those who know the history or live in Prestonpans.

Trading suffered during the religious Reformation and the lands themselves were transferred to the Kerrs and then the Morisons. Acheson's Harbour in due course became known as Morrison's Haven after extensive rebuilding and then ultimately the Grants and Grant-Sutties held the barony after the two Kingdoms were united until the end of the 20th century.

In 1697 formal permission to build a glass factory at Morrison's Haven was given. Glass had actually been produced on a large scale in Prestonpans for many decades previously. Coal production at the mine was sporadic at this time with the endemic problem of flooding returning again and again to halt production.

The major significant industrial era at Prestoungrange started during the early ownership of the Grant-Sutties under Sir James. Coal mining began in earnest. In 1825 Matthias Dunn took out a personal lease to mine on a larger scale than had been seen previously and four years later sunk two shafts, lined with iron rings to help prevent flooding. However, even with pumps in place Dunn could not stop the mines from flooding and production again ceased in 1838. Sir James' son, Sir George, re-opened the mine himself in 1848 but was soon to encounter the same fate as Dunn.

In 1872 the Cornish Beam Engine was shipped in and installed which heralded the onset of much new industrial activity. Kitto, Loam and Brental took out a 99-year lease and formed the Prestongrange Coal and Iron Company. The No.2 Shaft was used for extracting coal from the 'Jewel Seam' and the beam engine was situated on No.1 Shaft to pump out the water. However, due to the drop in price of coal, miners' strikes and the heavy debts incurred from company formation the Prestongrange Coal and Iron Company survived only until 1879.

In 1881 three more industrialists, Gneiss, Stephenson and Ellison established a successor company, the Prestongrange Coal and Firebrick Company. This enterprise operated for thirteen years until the same forces as previously forced closure. It was at this time that brickworks were created on the scale we can still see today, and bricks were produced on a substantial scale at Prestoungrange.

In 1894, Sir George Grant-Suttie sold the industrial estate including the colliery to the Summerlee and Mossend Iron and Steel Company. This new company sank a third shaft for ventilation purposes and bore down to the 'Beggar Seam'. They extracted coal and fireclay for use at the brickworks and for export. Around 1900, Morrison's Haven was exporting in excess of 5000 tons of clay products. But the next twenty years were to prove very difficult for the whole of the country as it passed through World War I, miners started demanding much improved conditions and more money, and then the price of coal collapsed. It all culminated in the General Strike of 1926.

The Summerlee and Mossend Iron and Steel Company remained afloat longer than all other enterprises until in 1947 when it was acquired by the new statutory corporation, the National Coal Board. At the end Morrison's Haven had long fallen into disuse through silting up and the coal and other outputs were despatched by rail and road.

During the next fifteen years six seams were worked and the colliery and brickworks employed nearly 800 staff. Morrison's Haven was infilled in 1957 and in 1962 the NCB closed the mine.[4]

These industries and many more have left their mark on the environment around Prestonpans. Some are clearly still visible; some are not so obvious such as the chemical bi-products arising through the production of coal.

3. GEOLOGY OF THE PRESTONPANS AREA

Broadly speaking, the geology of Scotland can be divided into regions, each area exhibiting similar geological characteristics. Prestongrange, indeed East Lothian, falls into the fault valley region of Scotland known as the Midland Valley. The Midland Valley is defined to the north by the Highland Boundary Fault and to the south by the Southern Upland Fault.

Rocks from the Devonian period are overlain by Carboniferous rocks, which dominate the region. It is the Carboniferous rocks that are of most interest and will be looked at most closely in this section, as these were the rocks from which coal, limestone, fireclay, ironstone and shales were extracted and used for industry. Rock from the Devonian period had a lesser effect on Prestongrange. Upper Old Red Sandstone was used primarily as building material, and can still be seen at Morrison's Haven today.

The presence of these Carboniferous rocks was the fundamental determinant of central Scotland's industrial development from East Lothian across to Glasgow and Ayr.

Formation of Sedimentary Deposits

Although there are many igneous rock formations in Scotland, these tend to be towards the northern and upland areas such as the Grampians. The Midland Valley is, relatively speaking, lower and flatter than most of Scotland, indeed Prestonpans is virtually at sea level. Sedimentary deposits dominate the rock structure although there are areas, such as the Pentland Hills and the Ochil Hills, where igneous deposits can be found at the surface due to the weathering and erosion of weaker overlying rocks.

Prestongrange is dominated entirely by rocks from the Carboniferous Period and beach deposits of the Pleistocene Period and exhibits no igneous rocks.

As mentioned previously, the materials that enabled industry to locate along the southern shore of the Firth of Forth were extracted from sedimentary deposits. Weathering (breaking of rocks by in-situ processes) and erosion (breaking of rocks by moving processes) disintegrates rocks into small enough fragments so that they can be transported. Once broken down, water, ice and wind transport rock fragments to where they will eventually be lithified, often via intermediate environments such as river flood plains.

Sedimentary rocks are usually formed in wet conditions and are deposited in one of four water environments – a riverbed (fluvial), a lakebed (lacustrine), the sea (marine) or a river delta. As sediments settle on the bed of the water body they compact sediment previously deposited and in turn are compacted by subsequent sediment deposition. Sediments consisting of relatively large fragments, such as sand, also need to be cemented together by naturally occurring elements such as iron oxide (FeO_2) and calcium carbonate ($CaCO_3$) to lithify them. Some cementation elements colour the rock giving it a reddish or yellowish look. Combining compaction, cementation and internal heat from the earth causes lithification of the sediment.

When considering the time periods involved, it is possible to visualise how the East Lothian sediments were lithified. The Carboniferous period alone lasted approximately 72 million years, which not only makes it possible to see how the rocks were formed, but also how the cyclic deposition of the rocks occurred.

Cyclic deposition is the process by which strata are laid down in a series of facies or a sequence of strata. In the Midland Valley there are many different localised facies, but a typical one would consist of coal measures and seat earth overlying non-marine limestones and sandstones. At the base of the sequence, marine limestones and sandstones would be present. This cyclic deposition partly explains the reason behind the varying depths of different coal seams, as one facies overlies another creating 'beds' of coal deposits.

The cycles of facies were formed as a result of ground subsidence and eustatic (sea level) change. The weight of the strata formed caused, and is still causing, the ground to subside, which allows more beds to be formed above previously formed strata. If the ground did not subside, then facies would be created laterally, building up usually towards the source of the sediment.

The Midlothian basin is a good example of localised subsidence, and evidence from boreholes drilled in the area shows cyclic deposition occurred across the whole region. The major eastern coalfields of the Midland Valley are located around the Midlothian basin, making it one of the best areas for the location of coal reliant industries, such as those located at Prestoungrange.

Coal Formation

The creation of coal is predominantly dependent on climate and as it is formed from the remains of plants the climate needs to be humid and wet to stimulate plant growth. Such a climate is not found today in Britain.

However, during the Carboniferous period it may seem surprising to learn Britain was located between 5° North and 5° South of the equator. That gave a very wet, humid climate just as the equatorial regions experience today. It was during this time that there was very high level of plant growth which led to the formation of the very extensive British Isles coal measures.

Coal is formed under the same conditions as other sedimentary rocks. Laid down in swampy, boggy conditions, the plant matter is compressed and altered in almost fully anaerobic conditions, such that coal ranges in carbon purity of 70–98%. The coal extracted at Prestoungrange will, in the most part, be lignite (approx. 70% carbon purity) and bituminous coal (approx. 80% carbon purity), both good sources of heat. Where the purity is less, there will be more contaminants in the coal, such as sulphur and iron, both of which create environmental problems when it is burned.

The cyclic deposition described above enabled many beds of coal and peat to be laid down over one another some, if thick enough, creating the seams that were worked at Prestongrange Colliery.

There were many other Carboniferous deposits that have been important industrial materials such as peat (used by the monks of Newbattle Abbey at the dawn of the last millennium), and fireclay (used in the potteries and brickworks of the area). These were laid down under the same conditions as the coal and exhibit similar characteristics, the only difference being the level of carbon content and plant remains.

Sandstones

Any sand deposited during the Carboniferous period would have been compressed to form the Millstone Grit that dominates the area around the periphery of the Midlothian basin. Millstone Grit is an excellent building material evident in the housing of the Cornish beam engine and some of the local housing as well.

The Red Sandstone that is present, most notably in part of Morrison's Haven's wall, is not present at Prestoungrange but has been transported approximately 10km from near Niddrie, south of Edinburgh's centre. The reason for the stone's colour is that the sediments which formed the stone were laid down during the Devonian period, which preceded the Carboniferous period. During this time the climatic conditions were very different from those in the Carboniferous. They were dry, arid conditions due to Britain being located between 5 and 10 degrees south of the equator where, as today, conditions were very dry and scattered with deserts.

The sediments that made up the Upper Old Red Sandstone were laid down in a fluvial or lacustrine environment. Examining the fossils of species that were trapped in the sediments reveals the depositional environment, as marine and non-marine species are almost exclusive to one environment. This technique is used widely to identify horizons in stratigraphical sequences throughout the world.

The Rocks that Influenced Industry

The Lower Carboniferous (Dinantian)

The Carboniferous Limestone Series was the first series of the Carboniferous period to be deposited in the Midland Valley and is split into two groups, the Calciferous Sandstone Measures and the Lower Limestone Group (see Fig. 3.1).

The series contains many strata including limestones, oil shales and throughout the Lower Limestone Group sandstones and coals are also present. However, in East Lothian, coals are relatively thinly bedded and therefore not workable and the oil shales seams are absent.

The Upper Carboniferous (part of the Silesian subsystem)

The Upper Carboniferous is the sub-period during which the majority of the workable coal seams and the fireclays were deposited and is split into the Namurian (Millstone Grit Series) and the Westphalian (Coal Measures) described below.

The Namurian

This series is split into three groups, making up the Millstone Grit Series; the Limestone Coal Group at the base, the Upper Limestone Group and the Passage Group (formerly Scottish Millstone Grit).

The Limestone Coal Group consists of some very productive coal seams, present only in the Central Coalfield (to the west of Edinburgh) and not so much in East Lothian. Much of the central and western Scottish coal industry was based on the Limestone Coal Group.

The Upper Limestone Group provides no workable coal seams throughout the entire Midland Valley region, but instead having thick beds of limestone and sandstone. No workable coal is a result of either the physical or climatic conditions (or both) changing, and plant growth reducing.

The Passage Group has many of the sought after raw materials, but the coal and ironstone beds, although numerous, are thinly bedded and therefore unworkable. The Upper and Lower Fireclays included in this group are of economic value mined for use in the production of bricks and ceramics. This is the last group of the Millstone Grit Series and underlies the Westphalian Coal Measures.

The Westphalian

These comprise the Lower (Westphalian A), Middle (Westphalian B) and Upper (Westphalian C and D). The coal measures of the Westphalian provided the raw materials that enabled the rise of industry throughout Britain.

The Lower and Middle measures exhibit similar characteristics, both laid down under similar conditions to those found in the Namurian. The Upper Measures were mostly laid down under drier and sandier conditions, due to the British Isles moving northwards away from the equatorial/ tropical climate and into a more arid one.

The facies comprise strata, including coal, sandstone, siltstone and mudstone, laid down in a fluvio-deltaic environment.

Collectively the Lower and Middle Coal Measures were known as the 'productive coal measures' and as mentioned above, had up to 20 workable seams. At the Prestongrange Colliery accessing the coal was the most difficult factor, which is well documented, but once the physical problems were overcome, extraction took place from eight seams. These seams were not particularly deep by modern standards and were from the Lower and Middle Coal Measures, drilled to a depth of 766 feet below ground level i.e. the Beggar Seam. (This is disputed from other sources, which state the Beggar Seam to be just 462 feet.)

Many seams in the Upper Coal Measures were either poorly developed or later oxidised by exposure to air and/or water and were given the name 'Barren Red' due to the colouration caused by this oxidation. The partial destruction of these coal seams meant that it was only economical to mine from the Lower and Middle Measures.

The Geology of Prestongrange Colliery

Over the course of 250 years, Prestongrange Colliery has had many owners and been closed due to flooding on numerous occasions. Coal has been extracted from eight different seams, ranging from 35 metres (120 feet) below ground level to in excess of 150 metres below ground level (500 feet). The seams are part of the Lower and Upper Coal Measures and not very thickly bedded, between 1 and 2.5 metres thick, making working conditions very difficult.

There were two shafts drilled at Prestongrange sunk by Matthias Dunn in 1829. One shaft (No.2) was used for lifting coal to the surface and the other shaft (No.1) was used to pump water latterly using the giant Cornish beam engine until its retirement in 1954. Plans to sink a third shaft by the Prestongrange Coal and Fire-Brick Company were stopped by a drop in coal prices and miners strikes, which forced the company out of business in 1894.

Figure 2

When the coal industry was nationalised in 1947, all eight Prestongrange seams were being worked. These seams were (top down): Great Seam, Diver Seam, Clay Seam, Five-foot Seam, Jewel Seam, Beggar Seam and No.1 and No.2 Diamond Seams. These seams vary in name from previous records, which pre-date nationalisation.

Fireclay extraction

The Passage Group, and to a lesser extent the Lower Coal Measures, contain valuable deposits of fireclay, which were especially useful for the refractory industries including glass, pottery and brick. Coaly shales that were a by-product of mining were used in the production of bricks and were abundant at Prestongrange due to a high clay content in the soils (clay weathers into shale).

There are also beds of fireclay scattered across the Midlothian basin. It has been shown in historical records that Morrison's Haven received a large amount of clay imports from London and Cornwall.

	LITHOSTRATIGRAPHY		SERIES	SUBSYSTEM
Upper	Upper Coal Measures	Coal	Westphalian C–D	
	Middle Coal Measures		Westphalian B	
Carboniferous	Lower Coal Measures	Measures	Westphalian A	Silesian
	Passage Group	Millstone		
(Pennsylvanian)	Upper Limestone Group	Grit	Namurian	
	Limestone Coal Group	Series		
Lower	Lower Limestone Group	Carboniferous		
Carboniferous	Calciferous Sandstone Measures	Limestone	Viséan	Dinantian
(Mississippian)		Series	Tournasian	
Devonian	Upper Old Red Sandstone			

Figure 3 Stratigraphy of the Carboniferous

4. ENVIRONMENTAL IMPACTS OF INDUSTRY AT PRESTOUNGRANGE

The numerous industries that located at Prestoungrange over the centuries have each caused their own particular environmental problems although clearly the colliery and the brickworks create the most visible effects. Less noticeable are the effects of salt, oil of vitriol (sulphuric acid) and glass production processes. These industries often left contaminants in the ground itself.

All the major environmental issues likely to arise will accordingly be addressed here in sequence.

Coal

There are many environmental impacts associated with coal mining. The most visible impact at Prestongrange is the large area of land, to the south of the beam engine, covered with colliery spoil that is now vegetated with trees. Other environmental issues that arise from coal mining include subsidence, water pollution, slope stability and visual disamenity.

Colliery Spoil

Colliery spoil is often described as 'overburden', comprises waste rock such as sandstones and siltstones, poor grade coal, iron pyrite and other minerals including quartz, silica, aluminium, sulphur (included in the coal), heavy metals (e.g. copper, nickel, zinc), magnesium, potassium, sodium and iron (see Goodman & Chadwick[9]).

Spoil 'heaps', as they are commonly known, are often formed in conical piles, or as mini plateaux on hillsides. Aesthetics is not a problem at Prestoungrange but there is a real impact on the ecology and water quality of the area due to the low level construction and grading of the spoil.

Spoil from collieries falls into one of two categories – fresh spoil and weathered spoil. The two have very different characteristics both physical and chemical. Firstly, fresh spoil tends to have a pH value of between seven and eight. Weathered spoil can be very acidic, values as low as pH 2.5. Secondly, as spoil weathers, the size of particles within it decreases which may lead to problems of stability.

To reclaim an area of colliery spoil it is necessary to put pollutants at a depth greater than 1metre to stop the oxidation of iron pyrite and then to cover the area with clean topsoil (In the case of many new open cast sites, the original soil is stripped at the commencement of mining.)

The oxidation of iron pyrite contained within colliery spoil is the main cause of ecological problems associated with coal mining. Iron pyrite (FeS_2) is a naturally occurring compound in Carboniferous rock and when in contact with oxygen and water oxidises as follows:

$$FeS_2 + 3.5\ O_2 + H_2O \Rightarrow Fe^{2+} + 2SO_4^{2-} + 2H^+$$

The resulting compounds are iron, sulphates (which combine with other elements) and hydrogen, which are combined with a lower pH value, toxic soils, water contamination and an increase in temperature. The deterioration of soils in and around spoil heaps means that only species tolerant to these ecological extremes can survive, yet vegetation is needed for the reclamation of colliery sites. The area indicated in the map below (Figure 4) is the area in which colliery spoil has been deposited, regraded and revegetated. This area is now vegetated with alder (*Alnus*), hawthorn (*Crataegus monogyna*) and birch (*Betula*), all very good for reclaiming coal environments, and also other deciduous species of trees. On the surface it is possible to see pieces of equipment left behind, brick fragments, coal and metal all being very evident. Looking beneath the surface it is possible to see how the coal has affected the soil. Over much of the area the soil is distinctively darker in colour than the soil found in neighbouring areas.

Another effect of pyrite oxidation is the pollution of ground and surface water, popularly known as 'acid mine drainage'. Due to Prestongrange's long and difficult history with flooding, large volumes of water have passed through

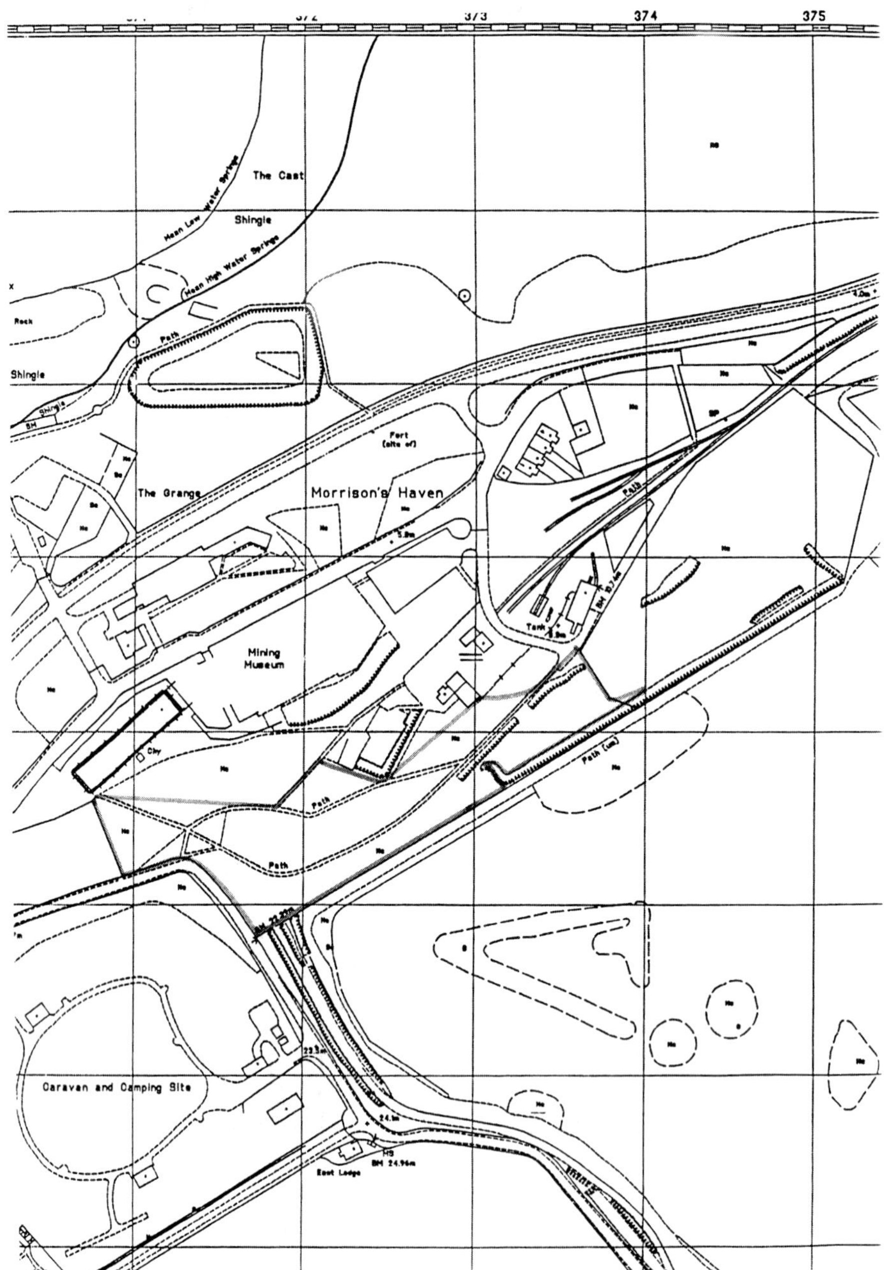

Figure 4 Map of areas known to be covered by colliery spoil

the mine's workings and shafts. The effects of oxidisation will have influenced this water, which is the cause of acid mine drainage.

Acid mine drainage is a by-product of the mining industry that is very distinctive, due to its yellow-orange colouring of watercourses and sulphurous odour. (Runoff water at the Industrial Museum frequently demonstrates this effect.) The chemical equation for the reaction is similar to the above, only that due to large water volumes the reaction products are Iron Hydroxide ($Fe(OH_3)$) and Sulphuric Acid (H_2SO_4).

$$FeS_2 + 3.75\ O_2 + 3.5\ H_2O \Rightarrow Fe(OH)_3 + 2\ SO_4 + 4H$$

The effects to watercourses of acid mine drainage can, in severe circumstances, destroy ecosystems by having two direct effects: (i) lowering the pH value of the watercourse thereby directly killing organisms, and (ii) coating river beds and shorelines thereby stopping plant and algae growth. Organisms are killed because the acid water reduces the sodium ions in the blood, which in turn reduces the amount of oxygen in blood (Reinhardt[10]). The iron hydroxide in the water will coat itself onto the river bed or shoreline turning the bed a yellow-orange colour and making it difficult for plants to survive and produce oxygen for the animals and fish, thereby reducing population numbers. Such pollution long ago made impossible the continuation of the oyster farming at Prestoungrange.

Water contamination caused by mining can be reduced through a number of techniques including limestone channels and artificial wetlands. These are as close to natural treatment as is possible and are effective for lower levels of contamination and are relatively cheap. Other techniques involve using alkaline chemicals to neutralise the acidic chemicals in the water. Such chemicals include calcium carbonate, calcium oxide, calcium hydroxide and sodium carbonate, all of which have the aim of raising pH and removing metal concentrations from the watercourse.

Chemical treatments, however, are considerably more costly. Compared to limestone, which can be bought for around £10/ton, even hydrated lime costs around 6 times as much (from Skousen et al. 1999, via Reinhardt).

The surface evidence indicates little acid mine drainage at the Prestongrange Colliery. Discoloured water is present around the winding gear adjacent to the beam engine but this is likely to be the effects of rainwater being discoloured by rusting equipment and structures. However, it is impossible to see what is the current extent of any underground contamination that has taken place as the colliery was closed and all shafts sealed in 1962.

Particulate matter in water (held in suspension) may also have a detrimental effect on fish health in that their feeding habits may be forced to change. This may be as a direct result of food being destroyed, or it may be that increased particulate matter leads to a decrease in algae and therefore dissolved oxygen levels. As there are no watercourses around the Prestongrange site, the direct effect on fresh water organisms is likely to be close to zero but the shoreline will be differently affected.

Due to the large volumes of water that Prestongrange Colliery has had to contend with, any contaminated water created has a greater chance of being transported away from the colliery than an inland colliery due to its proximity to the Firth of Forth. This means that any contamination may well have been carried out towards the North Sea or diluted by the large volumes of water passing through the mine.

Subsidence

Subsidence is another extensive problem associated with areas of mineral extraction. There appear to be no such problems affecting the area around Prestongrange but there have been extensive works carried out to level and reclaim the site so any subsidence may have been hidden from view.

Subsidence affects many regions of Britain and is particularly prevalent in the Midlands and the salt fields of Cheshire. The diagram below illustrates a typical case of mining subsidence in similar geological structures.

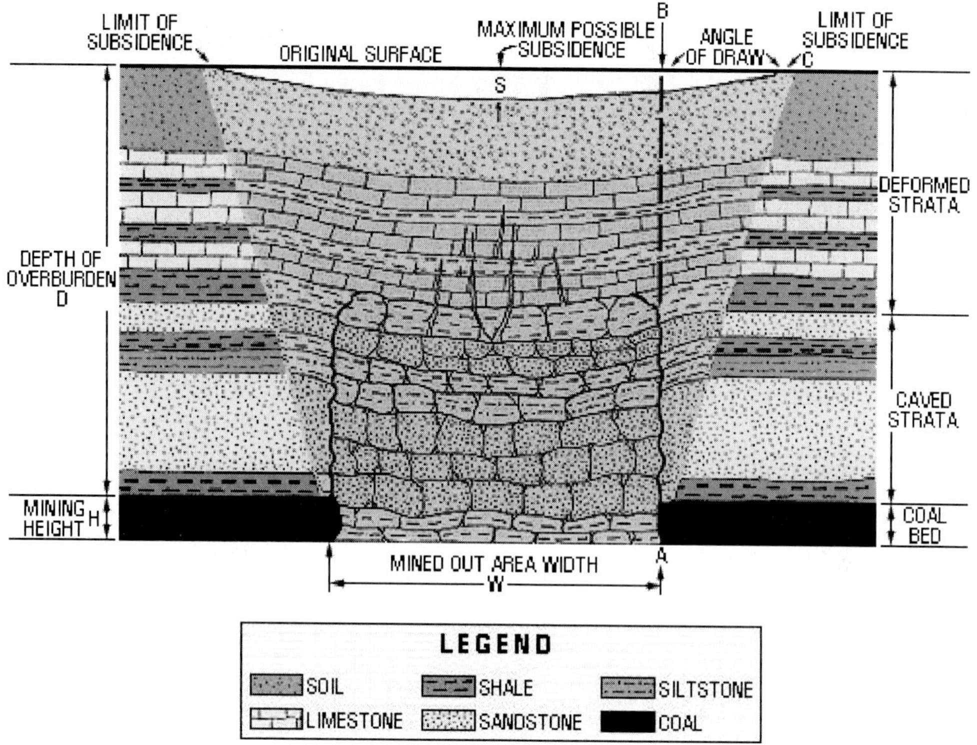

Figure 5 Subsidence
West Virginia Geological and Economic Survey

There is good reason to suspect subsidence at Prestongrange, and even more in the area of Prestonpans at large. Coal mining, both on the surface and underground has been undertaken since the twelfth century and across the millennium mining methods have changed considerably. If mining was undertaken below the surface then it is likely that 'bell pits' were used, illustrated in Figure 6. From this it can be seen how easily subsidence may occur if the walls of the pit collapsed inwards.

Later methods included 'stoop and room' and 'longwall'. The stoop and room method involved mining coal in 'rooms' leaving 'stoops', pillars of coal, to support the roof. The longwall method, as the name suggests, involved cutting a wall of a seam of coal, using artificial props to support the roof. After pit closure, the temporary supports are either removed or left to rot away, which will readily create the situation illustrated in Figure 5.

The owners of any development that suffers subsidence can make a claim for the damages from the government, the costs of which can be recovered to a certain amount through the Coal Mining Subsidence Act 1991 (The Coal Authority[11]). Measures can be taken to avoid subsidence in new developments by undertaking surveys of historical land use. If however the subsidence is happening to an existing development then structural measures can be taken such as flexible services (gas, water etc), strengthening and deepening of foundations and more flexible building materials, timber replacing concrete.

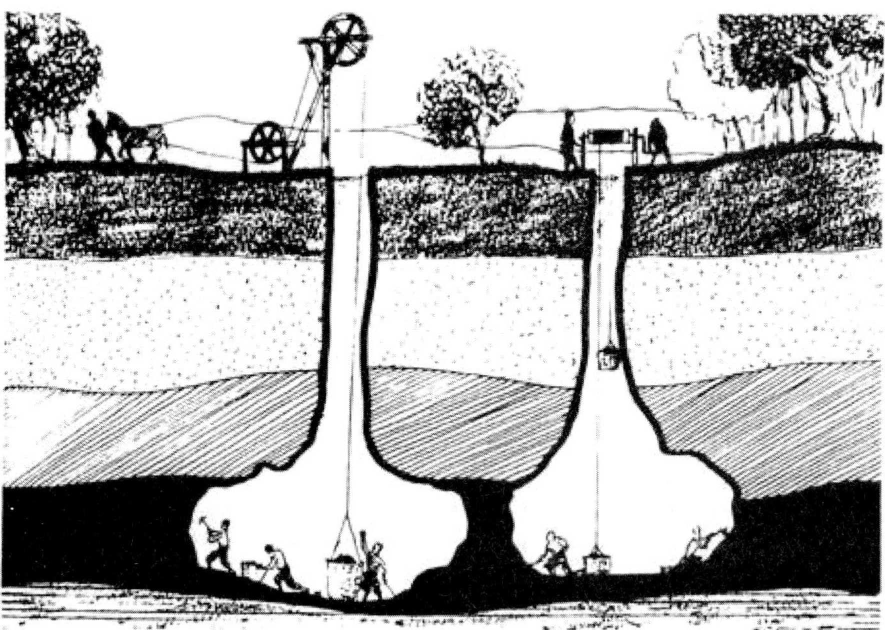

Figure 6 Bell Pit
Courtesy of Keele University via Coal Mining in Staffordshire (Staffordshire Multimedia Archive[12])

Coal Dust

Coal dust is also a problem of coal mining, however, it tends to occur only when the mine is operational or if there are bare spoil heaps, so the problem is no longer an environmental issue at Prestongrange. At the time of mining, dust was the cause of many bronchial illnesses, but the majority of cases will have been caused by dust from underground mining, as there are no records of large scale surface mining in the area around Prestonpans.

General Reclamation

Apart from the problems described above, the site must also undergo regrading. The land must be levelled out, stopping any potential stability problems and new topsoil laid over areas that are to be revegetated. Revegetation is usually carried out with agricultural crops or through forestry and the most widely used crops are oilseed rape, cereals and wheat. Trees best suited to these conditions are alder and birch. A grass cover is also essential for securing the topsoil and stopping it being wind blown (see Hester and Harrison[13]).

Salt

Of all the industries that located themselves around Prestonpans, salt is the most significant historically and has the most direct ecological problems for the environment after the colliery.

Salt was the first product to come out of Prestongrange and the town of Prestonpans owes its name to the industry. Previously known as 'Saltprestone', the name Prestonpans is derived from 'Priests' town' and 'pans' relating to the salt pans.

The production of salt dated back to the Monks of Newbattle Abbey who were producing it as a food preservative but later it was used in the production of other materials such as glass and soap (see Anderson[14]).

Salt production hit a peak in the early eighteenth century, when cheap imports from the Cheshire salt fields made production far more efficient, as the salt was purer than the Firth of Forth marine salt. This was at a time when Morrison's Haven was a thriving harbour, a fact which was undoubtedly central to Prestongrange's success.

Sulphuric Acid (Oil of Vitriol) was also produced around Prestonpans and is also a by-product of salt production. It is as harmful to the environment as sodium and chlorine compounds and is dealt with below.

Salt	Percentage
Sodium Chloride	2.68%
Magnesium Chloride	0.32%
Magnesium Sulphate	0.22%
Potassium Chloride	0.07%
Calcium Sulphate	0.12%
Other salts	0.01%
Water	96.58%

[N.B. From every kilogram of seawater, approximately 35g of salt will be obtained]

Figure 7 Approximate Composition of Sea Water (Cheetham Salt[15])

The production of salt is not only potentially hazardous to the environment at the time of panning but later because salts left in the ground can lead to health problems for plants, animals, fish, soil and humans.

The process itself, until the onset of the industrial revolution, involved using iron or lead pans to evaporate seawater to leave salt crystals in the pan. This process was not very detrimental to the environment, but the waste being poor grade salt, will normally have been deposited around the area and have been leached into ground water.

During the process of salt production chemicals such as Sulphuric Acid (H_2SO_4) are produced, which have a detrimental effect on the environment, but once sodium (Na) and chlorine (Cl) pass into the ground they can kill whole communities of plants and micro organisms. The presence of excess sodium or chlorine in the environment increases pH from around pH5.5 to as high as pH10, as sodium replaces calcium in an anion exchange, making soil less hospitable for vegetation. Sodium also makes soils less permeable and may even cause a 'hard pan'; a layer of salt encrusted soil, to form, which prevents plants from getting at groundwater.

The salt also has the effect of reducing the moisture content of the soil, making it more difficult for vegetation to grow.[16] Root growth hindrance means the plant is less able to access water unless it is a halophyte or salt loving plant (see US Salinity Laboratory[17]).

It is very difficult to regain an ecosystem after salt processes, whether human or natural, have affected it. The location of Prestongrange may help to ameliorate these effects, due to its proximity to the sea. The natural state of the ground and groundwater may be expected to have higher benchmark salinity than further inland and the local vegetation and micro-organisms to reflect this.

Heavy Metals

Heavy metals are elements also known as transition metals and are found in the middle section of the Periodic Table. In relation to mineral waste, they are often compounded with a salt or are oxidised and can be released into watercourses if leaching occurs. Some of the commonest heavy metals associated with the coal and brick industry tend to be iron, copper, lead and zinc.

The salts that these are often compounded with create sulphates, hydroxides, and carbonates and, with respect to the brickworks, silicates. Oxides are readily formed when the spoil material is weathered and iron, copper and zinc form oxides which may later be transported into watercourses, or left in the soil to hinder revegetation.

Iron pyrite is once again a major contributor to contamination as can be seen from the reactions below and purely through exposure to water and oxygen can produce a wide range of other chemicals.

$$FeS_2 + H_2O + 3.5\ O_2 \Rightarrow FeSO_4 + H_2SO_4$$

This reaction produces iron sulphate and sulphuric acid. These then combine with water in the following equation to produce ferric sulphate and water:

$$2FeSO_4 + 2H_2SO_4 + 0.5\ H_2O \Rightarrow Fe_2(SO_4)_3 + H_2O$$

The following reaction combines ferric sulphate, sulphuric acid and water to produce an iron hydroxide and further sulphuric acid:

$$Fe_2SO_4 + H_2SO_4 + 0.5\ O_2 \Rightarrow 2Fe(OH)_3 + 3H_2SO_4$$

Copper in the spoil may bond with sulphur to produce copper sulphide, and reacts with ferric sulphate and water to produce copper sulphate, iron sulphate and sulphur. The sulphur then may bond with oxygen and water to produce sulphuric acid as can be seen in the final equation.

$$Cu2S + 2\ Fe_2(SO_4)_3 + 2H_2O \Rightarrow 2CuSO_4 + 4FeSO_4 + S$$

$$2S + 3O_2 + 2H_2O \Rightarrow 2H_2SO_4$$

From these equations it can be seen that many of the compounds are reproduced, which means that some of these reactions are cyclic. This can make it difficult to stop the reactions, which needs to be achieved fully, to completely reclaim the site.

The effects to humans are very small, apart from the mine workers, who may have inhaled metals through the colliery dust and would have been at far greater a risk underground. The effects of the metals on vegetation can be more damaging. Only species tolerant to the metals and their compounds will be able to locate on the spoil and the species present can identify which contaminants are present. The level of plant mortality depends on the composition of the soil, nitrate levels, organic content, for example. For animals, problems arise when levels in cells or blood rise to toxic levels, having a direct effect on their health. Very little can be done to remove metal particulate matter from a stream.

The area around Prestongrange consists of coarse grass, consistent with that of a coastline, and there is therefore no reason to suspect any high concentration levels are present in the subsoil. If problems were to occur with high metal concentrations, then 'specialist' vegetation may be used to reclaim the area. Examples of such plants include the sweet clover (*Festuca arundinacea*) and tamarisk (*Tamarix pentandra*).

Brick, Tile and Glass

The historical production of bricks at Prestongrange is the best preserved industrial monument with the exception of the Cornish beam engine. The remaining Hoffman Kiln and the foundations of the 'beehive' kilns show the extent to which this industry grew at Prestongrange. The brick, tile and porcelain industry is not as widely known as coal mining for its contaminative effects, but the chemicals used in finishing products and the heat generated through firing can have a detrimental effect on the environment.

Figure 8 Beehive Kiln

Clay was not dug at Prestongrange, it lies too close to the coast and the underlying rock is Carboniferous in age; it was imported from the Upper Birslie Plantation.[18] The site of Prestongrange was used due to its coal resources and Morrison's Haven, at that time a gateway for exporting numerous products from all over the Lothians. Later, the harbour became useful for importing china clay from the south of England, a cheaper and higher quality of clay.[19]

The extracted natural clay from the area around Upper Birslie is known as 'Fireclay' and the formula is [in most cases] $Al_2O_3.Si_2O_2.2H_2O$ being a form of Kaolinite clay. It comprises approximately 40% aluminium oxide, 45% silicon oxide and 15% water. Also included in the clay varying but small concentrations of iron, magnesium, titanium sodium, potassium and free silica.[20]

The metals contained in the clay may be released into the environment and cause their own problems but the main by-product is hydrogen fluoride (HF). This substance which can attack concrete, glass, cast iron and other products containing silica. It is used to increase the porosity of ceramics, polish glass and enamelling which are all processes used in industries that have been located at Prestongrange. Hydrogen fluoride in plants can cause mutations of the roots[21] which may lead to death of the plant. At the Prestongrange brickworks there appears to be no indication of any detrimental effect on the vegetation around the kilns. Where the concrete around the Hoffman Kiln and beehive kilns is cracked, vegetation is attempting to break through from beneath the surface indicating the subsurface is in a reasonably healthy condition.

Aluminium and silica (originally in the form of an oxide) may be leached out of any waste deposited in spoil heaps, and is therefore a potential hazard to the surrounding environment. Heavy metals have been dealt with, but aluminium is also a concern as it may combine with water and oxygen to form hydroxides and acids which in high enough concentrations kill plants.

Glass is also a product of silica and silicates. The production of glass is reported to have taken place at Morrison's Haven from 1697 but lasted only a few years.[22] The process of making glass involves mixing silica (in sand), potash, zinc, and metals for colouring, for example, iron (green) and cobalt (blue). Once mixed, the mixture is heated to extremely high temperatures up to 1600 degrees Centigrade.[23]

Using chemical elements such as iron, cobalt and selenium in the production of glass leads to problems of heavy metal contamination and thermal pollution in the soil beneath the surface. If there is heavy contamination, as has been seen in St Helens, Lancashire, then it may be necessary to remove some or all of the contaminated material from the site, or treat it with bioremediation techniques on the site in question.

The long history of the Prestongrange colliery site and Morrison's Haven means that there has been much activity on the site and the movement of the ground material means that any contaminants are more than likely untraceable back to one particular industry.

Sulphuric Acid

There are records of sulphuric acid (oil of vitriol) being produced in Prestonpans from 1749 when John Roebuck and Samuel Garbett opened a plant. The primary use of the acid was for the bleaching of linen as experiments had found it to be faster than any other product of its time.[14]

The production of sulphuric acid was hazardous and the health effects on the workforce and the surrounding area could be very damaging. Advancements in methods since the days of Garbett and Roebuck means that production is now safe and environmental concerns are addressed, but the environmental impact of production in the eighteenth and nineteenth century received little or no attention.

Sulphuric acid is produced via one the following equation sequences.

- *Sulphur burns in oxygen (air) to form sulphur dioxide*

$$S + O_2 \Rightarrow SO_2$$

The gaseous acid is then put into solution, where it reacts with water to form sulphurous acid:

$$SO_2 + H_2O \Rightarrow H_2SO_3$$

Using further oxygen, the sulphurous acid is then oxidised to form sulphuric acid:

$$H_2SO_3 + O \Rightarrow H_2SO_4$$

- *Dissolving sodium trioxide in water*

$$2S + 3O_2 \Rightarrow 2\ SO_3$$

$$SO_3 + H_2O \Rightarrow H_2SO_4$$

Neither of these procedures are one hundred per cent efficient and therefore gases escape into the environment having health effects on both humans and vegetation. The effects of sulphuric acid on humans are extreme. Small drops internally are usually fatal and inhaling the vapour may cause serious lung damage.[24]

Further to this, combined with the production of salt, other harmful chemicals are produced. Sodium chloride (found naturally in seawater), when mixed with sulphuric acid forms sodium bisulphate and hydrochloric acid.[25]

$$NaCl + H_2SO_4 \Rightarrow NaHSO_4 + HCl$$

If sulphuric acid enters a watercourse it will most likely kill all species even at low concentrations and remains in water afterwards as a sulphate.[26] This is also true of hydrochloric acid.

The effect of acid rain is well documented and sulphuric acid is one of its components. Much research has been undertaken into methods of remediating areas affected by acid rain and is available through numerous sources. However, it is not likely to have been relevant at Prestongrange as the local sulphuric acid industry has not been recorded as being present at the Prestongrange site and the production of salt is unlikely to have produced quantities of acid sufficient to cause environmental harm.

Thermal Pollution

Thermal pollution is not a widely known type of pollution but it can cause change in ecosystems and effect ecology. Heat generated from the brick kilns, and to a lesser extent salt pans, created temperatures up to 1600 degrees Centigrade.

There are no natural watercourses adjacent to where the brick kilns stood, only groundwater. This however will still have an impact on the ecology. Warmer water, and therefore soil, leads to a decrease in dissolved oxygen levels, a decrease in photosynthesis rates and the death of some organisms leads to a higher biochemical oxygen demand.[27] The heat generated would evaporate all water out of the ground within the top few centimetres making life very difficult for shallow rooted plants, mosses and lichens close to the kilns.

Ash from Cockenzie Power Station

When coal is burned to produce electricity, the residual ash left is known as pulverised fuel ash. This substance is grey in colour and has been dumped (legally) along the shoreline from the power station west to the lagoons located to the west of Prestongrange Industrial Museum. (Way-leave along the baronial lands on the foreshore has been given for an ash slurry pipe that is covered over and provides an excellent scenic walkway.) The ash can be found around Morrison's Haven, on the open coastline and also around the area where previously there were railway lines between the beehive kilns and the

Figure 9 Eastward view of Morrison's Haven, Prestonpans showing land reclamation process

beam engine – it has indeed been used to level the area now pleasingly covered with grass.

Pulverised fuel ash has much the same properties as coal spoil as it is just the residue after coal has been burned and therefore contains similar contaminants including chlorine, sodium and heavy metals. The ash, however, is relatively inert and in its stable state, as at Prestongrange, is unlikely to cause any environmental problems.

The Local Industrial Railways

Prestoungrange at the time when the colliery, brickworks and Morrison's Haven were fully operational, had railway lines running across the works and to the Haven. Railway land can be highly contaminative, but risks to humans and plants are less than contaminants from other industries. Oil leaked by engines may have contributed hydrocarbon contamination to the ground but the volumes of any oil dropped around the works are likely to be relatively small and in their liquid phase. The oils will most likely have been saturated by soil or ballast.

If oil were to penetrate the soil there would be a detrimental effect on organisms within the soil and for the soil itself. The effects of oils on the environment have been well documented and information is available from the Scottish and English Environment Agencies.[28, 29] Oil coats the surface of water bodies, thereby reducing the light penetrating the water. This means that algae and plants cannot photosynthesise as effectively and reducing the oxygen level of the water. This combined with the direct action of coating animals and fish may kill whole communities. If the oil releases vapours and large volumes are allowed to build up then there may be risk of explosions, but only if concentrations reach 1% by volume.

Due to the large scale of development at the Prestongrange site, many areas would have been covered with made surfaces preventing oil reaching the natural sub-soil. The lack of freshwater lakes or streams also means that there will have been little or no adverse effect to wildlife. Also, the nature of industry located there contributed contaminants far worse than oil dropped by railway vehicles.

Conclusion

The long past of the Prestongrange Colliery and brickworks and other associated industries had the potential to leave ecological problems for the following decades, even centuries. However, the lack of intensity, arising from a ceasing of activity before the onset of the late twentieth century, has meant that the site remains in a relatively clean state. Work has been carried out to level the site and remove the railway lines and there is the obvious demolition of the beehive kilns, which is an archaeological tragedy. The infilling of Morrison's Haven in 1957[18] was also a tragedy, the Haven being a potent symbol of the site's rich industrial past. Covering of the area with ash from Cockenzie power station has meant that many traces of local industry have disappeared.

The revegetation of the area to the south of the beam engine has undoubtedly helped the site recover from the industrial processes and the site is now undergoing natural processes of reclamation to bring the areas of contamination by coal back to life.

5. CONCLUSIONS

The Prestongrange works have been fully industrialised for the past 500 years and has the potential to be a highly contaminated site. The environmental impact of industrial activity, however, appears to very small in comparison to what might have been. The areas around the brick kilns and the colliery equipment and the area to the south of works have been layered with colliery spoil and pulverised fuel ash. To reclaim that it was necessary to cover the area with clean topsoil and revegetate it, achieved with alder, birch and grass. Other species have appeared which is a benefit to the area showing the reclamation work carried has clearly been successful and the shallow sub-soil is reasonably healthy.

Overall, the Prestongrange site and the area around Morrison's Haven is in good condition. There is little known about what exactly has been used to fill the Haven. Bricks from the demolition of the beehive kilns and ash from the power station are obvious sources. Whatever has occurred in the past will not be remembered for the pollution caused but for the monuments that remain such as the Cornish beam engine and Morrison's Haven as well as for the history told out in the studies of which this is the tenth.

These historical and analytical studies are already providing the basis for Schools' educational visits to the Museum and for artists to create murals and to reproduce Prestonpans pottery and brickworks artefacts in the years ahead. As the hoped for increase in tourism materialises visitors will find a clean environment in which to enjoy themselves and to appreciate the industrial history of Prestoungrange.

REFERENCES

1 Wilson, Ewan: *Water at Prestongrange and Pumping it Out*, No. 8 Prestoungrange University Press, 2000
2 Burnett, Allan: *Industrial Ownership and Relations at Prestongrange,* No.4 Prestoungrange University Press, 2000
3 Black, Kirsty: *Health Hazards over the Centuries at Prestongrange*, No. 6 Prestoungrange University Press, 2000
4 Aitken, Julie: *Morrison's Haven, What Came and Went and How?,* No.2 Prestoungrange University Press, 2000
5 British Geological Survey: *Geological Memoirs: No.5* (1985), HMSO
6 British Geological Survey *Research Report RR/99/07*
7 Black, Kirsty: *Health Hazards over the Centuries at Prestongrange*, No. 6, Prestoungrange University Press, 2000
8 Burnett, Allan: *Industrial Ownership and Relations at Prestongrange,* No. 4, Prestoungrange University Press, 2000
9 Goodman, G. T. & Chadwick, M. J. (1978): *Environmental Management of Mineral Waste.* Sijthhoff & Noordhoff, Holland
10 *Acid Mine Drainage In Pennsylvania Streams: "Ironing Out" The Problem* (Carrie H. Reinhardt)
11 The Coal Authority – www.coal.gov.uk
12 Staffordshire Multimedia Archive – http://archive.sln.org.uk
13 Hester, R. E. and Harrison, R. M.: *Contaminated Land and its Reclamation* (1997), Thomas Telford
14 Anderson, David: *Sourcing Brickmaking Salting and Chemicals at Prestongrange,* Prestoungrange University Press, 2000
15 Cheetham Salt – www.cheethamsalt.com.au
16 www.papercamp.com/sci29.htm
17 United States Salinity Laboratory
18 Bonnar, Jane: *Decorative Pottery at Prestongrange*, Prestoungrange University Press, 2000
19 *Gone to Pot*, East Lothian Council, 2000
20 Lee, P. William.: *Ceramics* (1961), Reinhold Publishing Corporation
21 United States Environmental Protection Agency: *Chemical Profile 7664-39-3*
22 Aitken, Julie: *Morrison's Haven: What came and went and how?* Prestoungrange University Press, 2000
23 Iron and Glass – www.ironandglass.com
24 United States Environmental Protection Agency: *Chemical Profile 7664-39-9*
25 Sulphuric Acid, University College, Cork, 2000, Donal O'Leary
26 European Fertilizer Manufacturers Association
27 Earthforce – www.earthforce.org
28 Scottish Environment Agency – www.sepa.org.uk
29 The Environment Agency – www.environment-agency.gov.uk

Other Sources

Fluoride Action Network: *Cytogenetic Effects of Gaseous Fluorides on Grain Crops, Fluoride*, Vol. 26 No.1 23-32 1993 www. fluoridealert.org/grain.htm

Gibson, J.: *Coal and the Environment*, Northwood Science Reviews, 1984.

11

Agricultural Improvement at Dolphinstoun

Chris Allan

INTRODUCTION

The Dolphinstoun Barony lies inland of Prestongrange House and south of Prestonpans, between Birslie and Wallyford. Its farm lands and buildings straddle the old toll road between Musselburgh and Tranent. The barony itself has formed part of the lands or 'policies' attached to Prestoungrange from the seventeenth century.

For many centuries, until the intellectual flowering which came to be known as the 'Age of Enlightenment', farming at Dolphinstoun followed the traditional pattern of agriculture in Scotland. From the second half of the eighteenth century until the later years of the nineteenth, the application of scientific method to both industrial and agricultural practices brought significant innovations to farm management in Scotland. These innovations were destined to change the Scottish landscape beyond recognition. This examination of changes in farming methods in the baronial lands of Dolphinstoun offers an insight into the practical, social and technological innovations which were instrumental in bringing about this change, and considers the evidence for their impact at Dolphinstoun in particular.

In order to appreciate the magnitude of these changes, it is first necessary to provide an overview of the landscape of East Lothian prior to the beginning of the eighteenth century.

1. BEFORE 1700

In the opening years of the eighteenth century, nine out of ten people lived by working on the land and farming in Scotland followed a pattern which had been established for generations.[1] In exchange for goods or labour, feudal landowners leased their land to tenant farmers who, in turn, relied on landless labourers for their workforce. Farming was not for profit, but subsistence, ie, the tenants and labourers relied on the produce of the land to support themselves and to provide a share of the produce to the landlord. Each person farmed a number of sections or 'rigs'. These rigs were exchanged from time to time to make sure that everyone had a share of the best and worst rigs.[2] This 'runrig' system, common throughout Scotland at this time, was not, however, a system designed to maximise productivity. Samuel Smiles of Haddington, writing about the lowlands of Scotland in the early eighteenth Century, states:

The powerhouse of the farm until the introduction of tractors in the 1920s. Shown here are five pairs of plough horses and two carthorses with their dedicated handlers in Dolphinstoun farmyard (about 1910)

> "In the interior there was little to be seen but bleak moor and quaking bogs…each farm consisted of 'out-field,' or unenclosed land, no better than moorland, from which the hardy black cattle could scarcely gather herbage enough in winter to keep them from starving. The 'in-field' was an enclosed patch of ill-cultivated ground, on which oats and 'bear', or barley, were grown; but the principal crop was weeds."[3]

There was little interest in improving crop yields or farm buildings. The feudal system of sharing the land between a group of tenants with limited tenancy rights and consequently little security, did not encourage farmers to work towards increasing the future fertility of their land.

Farmhouses at this time were not the substantial dwellings of later years. Farm labourers generally inhabited 'cot-houses', single-roomed, thatched cottages built of local materials with walls of turf, mud, or stone covered with clay. The homes of the tenant farmers were not much better indeed "the greater part of the farmhouses were very mean and, except in having more apartments, differed very little in point of comfort, from the cottages of their servants"[4]. Typically, these buildings were single storey, with the housing for livestock a continuation of the living space.[5]

The pre-improvement farm comprised an infield, an outfield and common land or moorland. The infield was closest to the farm dwellings and received what little manure the farm produced. It was, therefore, the land which received the benefit of enrichment. Generally three crops – peas or beans, barley and oats – were grown in annual rotation on each section. However, since the land was not allowed to lie uncultivated in any season, crop yields were poor, rarely more than three times the amount sown.[6] The three-crop rotation was sometimes extended to include wheat as a fourth crop. There is evidence that wheat was grown in East Lothian during prehistoric times and even later[7, 8]: "I speak from the authority of record, when I states (sic) that wheat was certainly a regular crop in this county and used as bread in the 12th century."[9] By the 17th century, though, wheat was no longer a cultivated crop in the Highlands and in the Lowlands was rare enough to be something of a marvel: "When the first crop of that grain was tried on a field near Edinburgh, about the middle of the last century [ie 1750], people flocked to it as a wonder."[10]

The outfield was usually sown with oats. However, only around half of the area was used to grow crops at any one time, the remainder being left unsown for two years, then used as pasture. Since two years was not long enough to produce good pasture for grazing animals, their manure was of poor quality. This in turn affected the quality of the harvest when the land was later sown with oats. On the whole, farm animals were in poor condition as there was a lack of winter fodder and poor grazing meant that very few animals were kept alive from one year to the next. The outlying moor, or common land, provided further pasturage for stock, as well as supplying turves for building work and compost. Most of this land was open land, with no walls or fences and little effort was made to improve the quality of the land by drainage or otherwise.[11]

Traditionally, ploughing was done using a heavy single-sided 'swing plough'[12] pulled by a team of oxen, not horses. These ploughs required substantial effort; at least four oxen and often more to pull it and a team of workers to assist. Furthermore, the plough was made of both wood and iron and required considerable upkeep due to frequent damage.[13] After ploughing, grain was sown by hand or 'broadcast'. This was a slow, labour-intensive process as the sower was required to carry the seed and could therefore use only one hand. Furthermore, it required an expert worker to make sure it was distributed evenly. At harvest, crops were cut using a sickle. A team of harvesters worked their way across the rigs, cutting, binding and stacking the sheaves before they were transported to grain sheds, where the sheaves were 'threshed', to separate the seed from the chaff by beating the heads with a flail.[14] Storage facilities for crops were minimal and often poorly designed and threshing by hand often meant that the grain lay too long on the damp barn floor so that much of the seed was spoiled before threshing was complete.[15]

Before 1700, some attempts were made to increase the fertility of the land by the use of seaweed and lime to enrich acid soil.[16] However, activities such as this were limited by two factors: the difficulty of transporting materials on ill kept roads and a poor understanding of how various substances, particularly animal products, could be a valuable resource in increasing crop yields: "...the uses of manure were as yet so little understood that, if a stream were near, it was usually thrown in and floated away, and in summer it was burnt."[17] Use of seaweed was limited to land near the shore. Lime, although highly valued as a source of soil enrichment, was only used where the land lay within five miles of the outcrops of carboniferous stone which were quarried for lime.[18]

There is very little evidence remaining of the type of agriculture followed in the barony of Dolphinstoun before the nineteenth century. However, a strong indication that land management at Dolphinstoun was typical of 17th century East Lothian, and of Scotland as a whole, is indicated in maps of the total Prestoungrange Lands in the late nineteenth century which give details of the crops grown there.[19] These maps specify names only for the fields nearest the farmhouse, ie Kinnegar, Angle, Foreshot and the Barnyard. The outlying fields are numbered 1-6 Backfield and the remainder numbered 1–4 Brae. This strongly suggests that in the past, farming had followed the typical Scottish pattern, with an infield (the named fields), and outfield (the Backfields) and the moor or common land (the Braes).

2. THE ENLIGHTENMENT

After the Act of Union in 1707, Scotland's Parliament was disbanded and political control of the country was transferred to Westminster until 2000. With this loss of self determination, it could have been expected that Scotland would lose any impetus for development. Surprisingly, instead of a decline, the country at this time experienced a vigorous period of intellectual growth. Perhaps Scotland felt it had to prove that, despite its loss of sovereignty, it had not lost its capacity for innovation.

From the universities of Glasgow and Edinburgh, the philosophical concept of an 'Age of Reason', developed by philosophers such as David Hume, spread the notion of a universe bound by laws which could be described and acted upon. This concept of order is exemplified in the building of Edinburgh's 'New Town', with its classical style and ordered streets and gardens. The new thought formed the core of a scientific method which applied mathematics and physics to the natural world, developing an understanding of the physical implications of these laws. Through the activities of a range of innovators, this was translated into practical developments in both agriculture and industry.

Developing markets in the English colonies offered Scottish merchants great opportunity for profit. There was therefore great interest in mechanical innovations which could speed up processes of production. The development of steam powered engines (first by Thomas Newcomen and then James Watt) offered a new source of power with a wide range of applications. Inventions designed to improve methods of extracting the raw materials of industry such as coal and iron, increased the rate of production of goods.

The cost of producing such machinery was high. This, together with the fact that these early machines were of massive construction, requiring a great deal of space and constant maintenance, meant that manufacturing was transformed from a home to a factory-based industry. The increasing population in the growing industrial towns demanded a change in agricultural practices. The old style subsistence farming was no longer adequate to meet the needs of this population and gave way to profit-based agriculture supplying the town dwellers.

Another major incentive was a parallel progress in transportation. In the early eighteenth century, such roads as existed were all but impassable at certain times of the year and were filled with potholes which filled with mud in wet weather and were almost impossible to travel across when it was dry.[20]

By the middle of the eighteenth century, a turnpike system was introduced in Scotland. This system required road users to pay a charge for travelling on the roads which was used to fund road maintenance. Barriers were set up on all major routes and travellers were obliged to pay a toll before they were allowed past this barrier. Many place names in the Lothians originate from this eighteenth century innovation: Crewe Toll, Tollcross, Cameron Toll etc. Dolphinstoun was itself the location of such a toll and nineteenth century census returns provide details of both the residents of Dolphinstoun and those at Dolphinstoun Toll.[21] The tollkeeper was generally rigorous in exercising his duties. Peter McNeill, writing in 1905, recounts the story of a group of young men who arrived at Ravensheugh Toll close to Prestongrange Mine but were refused the right to pass through without paying for the pony they had with them: "They made a dash to get through behind a machine, but were caught. 'Not so fast my lads!' said the tollkeeper, 'not so fast!". The young men were obliged to carry the pony along the road to avoid paying the toll.

The turnpike system brought about a dramatic improvement in road conditions. This, together with the expanding railway network in the latter half of the nineteenth century, opened the way for new markets not only for industrial goods, but also for agricultural produce. Furthermore, improved roads offered Scottish farmers the opportunity to widen the market for their cattle and Dolphinstoun barony was well placed to supply Edinburgh and new markets in England.

Though many individuals focused their attention on industrial innovations in the growing cities, status and income was still very much tied to the ownership of land. As the nobility turned their attention more to England, a new middle class, including lawyers, academics and merchants, bought or married into land ownership and many of them were keen to apply scientific method to agricultural improvement.

3. THE AGRICULTURAL REVOLUTION

Awareness of the poor management of agricultural resources in Scotland already existed at the dawn of the eighteenth century: the first printed work on agriculture in Scotland was published in 1697: 'Husbandry Anatomized: or an Enquiry into the Present Manner of Teiling and Manuring the Ground in Scotland'. This publication, by an Edinburgh publisher, James Donaldson, based its discussion on the assumption of a 60 acre holding divided into one third infield and two thirds outfield. This was followed in 1699 by 'The Countrey-Man's Rudiments: or An Advice to the Farmers in East Lothian How to Labour and Improve their Ground', by John Hamilton, second Lord Belhaven. This publication is clear evidence that East Lothian landowners had an active interest in increasing the fertility of their land:

> "...lyme therefore your clay land in the Summer, fallow it at Lambas [Lammas], Harrow it well after the first frost, seedfur [prepare the seed bed] and sow it some time in February and you may expect a good Crop of Oats that same year."

The county's proximity to the city of Edinburgh gave it an ideal location to test both practical and theoretical developments and the natural fertility of the soil encouraged landowners to develop its potential. John Walker, from Beanston, near Haddington, exemplifies the fact that East Lothian landowners and tenants were at the forefront of agricultural development. A tenant of

Thomas, 6th Earl of Haddington, he conducted the first experiments with fallowing, ie leaving the land uncultivated for one or more seasons.[22]

Probably the most significant East Lothian contributors to agricultural developments in the seventeenth and eighteenth centuries were Adam and John Cockburn, of Ormiston. In 1702, as manager (and subsequently owner of the estate), John Cockburn introduced autumn ploughing, winter-sown wheat, field enclosure and long-term leases of 30 years and over for tenants. John Cockburn also established a brewery and a distillery in Ormiston, as well as encouraging the growing of flax and providing opportunities for estate workers to develop the skills necessary for spinning linen yarn.[23]

Market gardening was a major interest. Although as a Member of Parliament he was based in London, Cockburn maintained a close interest in his estates at Ormiston, developing several schemes including fruit growing and tree plantations. Although by 1805, barley had become a much less common crop in East Lothian, it was grown in the neighbourhood of Ormiston for the distillery established by Cockburn, which is now a museum. A distillery still operates near Ormiston today at Glenkindie:

> "The top-grade barley grown in the Lothians is the direct legacy of the Society of Improvers of Knowledge of Agriculture, a revolutionary eighteenth-century body that put Scotland in the forefront of the European farming scene at the time. The society was founded by John Cockburn of the village of Ormiston".[24]

The establishment of The Society of Improvers in the Knowledge of Agriculture was another of Cockburn's major achievements. It provided a forum in the early years of the eighteenth century for the exchange of ideas amongst landowners throughout Scotland.

Unfortunately, despite being innovative, these schemes were costly. John Cockburn bankrupted himself and was ultimately forced to sell the land he had invested so heavily in for over 40 years. It was probably Cockburn, among others, that the great Scottish economist Adam Smith had in mind when he wrote in 1776:

> "He embellishes perhaps four or five hundred acres in the neighbourhood of his house, at ten times the expense which the land is worth after all his improvements; and finds that if he was to improve his whole estate in the same manner, and he has little taste for any other, he would be a bankrupt before he had finished the tenth part of it."[25]

The Cockburns are particularly interesting in that they demonstrate the broad interests of these early improvers. The 'agricultural' and 'industrial' revolutions were not, in fact, separate events: the opportunities represented by a science-based approach to production applied to farming practice as well as industry and landowners were equally interested in both. Furthermore, increased crop production, changes in type of tenancies and the change from rig farming to enclosed fields were not, of themselves, sufficient to supply Scotland's growing city-based population. New equipment and machinery were required to speed up production and roads and railways were needed to transport food as well as raw materials and finished products.

Although landowners were heavily involved in innovative developments, the reorganisation of farming methods was in many cases applied in practice by the new breed of tenant farmer. These tenants, with more secure and longer leases, and a growing interest in farming for profit, were conscious of the benefits of enhancing the productivity of the farms they leased. A tenant farmer who shared the landowners interest in agricultural improvement was a valuable asset to the owner:

> "The proportion of land cultivated by proprietors is inconsiderable, a circumstance which may be accounted for, partly by the non-residence of some of them, and chiefly by there being no necessity for gentlemen to execute improvements at their own expense, in order to get them effected."[26]

Increased productivity meant new machinery, new crops and new methods of land management. All the traditional elements of farm activity – ploughing, sowing, harvesting and threshing – were subject to scrutiny and change. By 1780, the Carron Company ironworks was producing a new style plough developed by James Small from Berwickshire.[27] The old Scottish plough was replaced by a lighter plough, requiring less maintenance, which could be pulled by horses instead of oxen and which created a furrow on both sides, thereby reducing the time required and the uneveness of the soil. The Statistical Account of Scotland from the 1790s describes these changes on the farmland around Prestonpans: "Horses alone are employed in husbandry work. Horse-hoeing was introduced about 24 years ago...Small's plough with two horses is generally used." The Statistical Account further states that by this time almost all of the parish of Prestonpans was enclosed, mainly with walls rather than hedges, which were somewhat unpopular due to the fact that hedges gave shelter to birds which fed on the crops.[28]

Seed was sown in straight lines or 'drills' using a machine known as a 'fiddle' which regulated the amount of seed as it fell to the ground (later replaced by more sophisticated machinery developed in England by Jethro Tull, which buried the seed as it was sown). The scythe gradually replaced the sickle as a harvesting tool until it, in turn, was replaced by mechanical reapers, the first of which was invented in 1828. Threshing the grain to remove the chaff and leave the seed was mechanised by 1786,[29] with mills, initially using water or horse, then steam as the power source to drive the equipment. Steam driven mills were relatively common in East Lothian, due to the availability of coal.[30]

By the beginning of the nineteenth century, East Lothian farms were cultivating a much wider variety of crops than before: wheat, barley, oats, beans, pease, rye, vetch, potatoes, yams, various types of turnip and flax.[31] Cabbage was not a common crop, although it was widely grown in the area around Prestonpans:

> "About Prestonpans, a vast number of cabbage plants are annually raised, which serve the greater part of the county, and probably supply a good deal beyond the limits of it to the west. These plants have so high a character, that scarcely any other can find a market while they are to be got."[32]

Clearly, the eighteenth century thatched mud-walled cottages and peasant life of the farmworkers described by Samuel Smiles[33] was not appropriate to the new breed of tenant farmer. Nor did the lack of facilities for livestock suit the new methods of farming: cattle were driven from all over Scotland to markets in England and storage was required for fodder as well as housing to keep animals in good condition throughout the winter.

In addition to crops and livestock, close attention was given to what the new-style farmstead, suitable for the more prosperous tenant farmer, should comprise. By 1805, the average acreage of a mixed arable farm was 200 acres,[34] significantly larger than the 60 acre holding assumed by Donaldson in 1697. Lord Belhaven, in 1699, offered advice on the layout of farm buildings,[35] but "nearly 100 years were to pass before it could be called general".[36] Somerville, in 1805, advises that a proper farm steading should comprise separate housing for cows, hogs and poultry, barns, stables, feeding-houses, granaries and buildings to store equipment. Barns intended for grain storage should have raised floors to keep the crop away from the damp ground and the farmhouse itself should include:

> "...two good sitting rooms and from four to six sleeping apartments for the family, besides closets, garret rooms for servants etc.; the kitchen should be behind the house and the dairy, brew-house, store-house, laundry, etc. in the wings."[37]

4. PRESTOUNGRANGE LANDS AND BARONS

At the dawn of the age of agricultural improvement, the Prestoungrange Lands were in the hands of the Morison family, who were owners of Prestoungrange and Dolphinstoun from 1624 till 1734. However, the last Morison to own Prestoungrange, William Morison, was given to gambling and in 1734, the property was 'sequestrated' to pay his debts.[38]

In any case, there was little likelihood that East Lothian could have made significant progress in improvement in the first half of the eighteenth century. The Jacobite rebellions of 1715 and 1745 brought war and unrest to the county and were responsible for significant changes in land ownership, when supporters of the Stuart claim to the throne such as the Seton family, significant landowners in East Lothian, were stripped of their lands.[39]

Moreover, although the enclosure of land into large areas farmed by individual tenants had been promoted by legal statutes in the 16th and 17th centuries, these statutes did little, of themselves, to change the type of farming in East Lothian:

> "...it may be truly said, with very few exceptions, that the eighteenth Century was nearly half-run before much attention was bestowed making inclosures for the purpose of promoting agriculture."[40]

William Morison died in 1739 and by 1745, the property had come into the hands of William Grant, the second son of Francis, Lord Cullen. He purchased the Baronies of Prestoungrange and Dolphinstoun in 1745.[41]

William Grant had four daughters, a circumstance which caused him some concern in terms of the future of the Prestoungrange estate, since the estate would be shared among them on his death. Landowners at this time were interested in expanding their estates, not reducing them. They were also concerned to leave their property to male inheritors rather than female, since the property laws relating to married women at this time would result in the estate passing into the husband's family, not the wife's. An entailed property is one which is left to an individual family member. Sir William's first choice of entail was therefore to add his property to that of the other members of the Grant family, by leaving it to his elder brother. He drew up a deed of entail in 1756 in which he left Prestoungrange to Archibald Grant of Monymusk.[42]

William's elder brother, Grant of Monymusk, is known as the 'father of Scottish agriculture'. As the eldest son of Lord Cullen, he took over the Monymusk Estate in 1716. After setting up permanent residency on the estate in 1734 he began a programme of agricultural improvement designed to pay off his debts and set an example to other lairds. These improvements included land clearance, enclosure, the planting of fodder crops such as turnips, crop rotation and forestation programmes. Although these improvements were met with some degree of mistrust, particularly by his tenants, improved yields and better security eventually quelled such opposition. Archibald Grant died in 1778, fourteen years after his brother William.[43] Archibald Grant's example proved to other landowners that agricultural improvement was a potentially profitable enterprise. It is interesting to speculate what the impact might have been on Dolphinstoun baronial lands if this enthusiastic and highly successful agricultural improver had inherited the estate of Prestoungrange instead of his niece, Janet Grant.

However, when William's daughter Agnes, wife of Sir George Suttie, gave birth to a boy in 1759, William Grant changed the entail so that the estate was left to his eldest daughter Janet, Countess of Hyndford, and then to the first son that any of his daughters might have.[44] This meant that, by means of the entail, the estate would remain intact.

Entailed property had significant implications in terms of the relationship between landowners and their tenant farmers: Robert Somerville, writing in 1805, states:

> "The laws of entail...operate more directly against proprietors, and rather indirectly against farmers, but chiefly against the public...it is impossible that proprietors of estates, which are strictly entailed, can ever enter as heartily into the spirit of improving, as those who are differently circumstanced."[45]

Somerville's argument was that an owner with only a life interest in a property who would not necessarily be able to leave the estate to his own nearest relatives, would not be as willing to make improvements, such as tree plantations, to benefit future generations. Furthermore, any tenancy agreements would be of shorter term, ie only within the life expectancy of the current owner and therefore tenants too would be less interested in improvements which would not necessarily benefit themselves.

It may be largely due to the entail that there is little evidence of experiment and improvement on the Prestoungrange lands, including Dolphinstoun, when the estate was owned by William's eldest daughter Janet, Countess of Hyndford. Janet Grant inherited the estate from her father in 1764 and took over full control after the death of her husband in 1783. Lady Hyndford ran the estate until her own death in 1815. Apart from the building of a number of dykes, there is no evidence of agricultural improvement at Dolphinstoun during this time.[46]

This does not mean that Janet Grant neglected the estate. On the contrary, in 1789 she took the opportunity to extend it when she purchased the farmlands of Myles and Birslie,[47] formerly part of the estate of the Earl of Seton and forfeited after his involvement in the Jacobite uprising of 1715.[48] Excellent maps were drawn. By the time her nephew, Sir James Grant Suttie inherited in 1818, the estate included the farms of Dolphinstoun, Dolphinstoun Mains, St. Clements Wells, Myles and Birslie, as well as the land immediately surrounding Prestongrange House.

A further reason for limited interest in improvement at Prestoungrange might well have been a lack of incentive. While other landowners were working to improve the fertility of their land by means of fertilisers, fallowing and innovations in crops and rotation, the lands around Prestonpans were already noted for their fertility: "The soil...is a light, black, rich loam, of a quality considerable different from the greater part of the county."[49]

The richness of the soil, combined with the ready market in Edinburgh, was no doubt also the reason for so many market gardens in the neighbourhood of Prestonpans, including one at Dolphinstoun: 'The land appropriated either to sale, gardens or nurseries...is situated chiefly in the parishes of Dunbar, Haddington and Prestonpans.[50]

A market garden existed at Dolphinstoun Farm throughout the nineteenth Century and remained for the most part in the control of the same family. The earliest census records in 1841[51] includes the family of Thomas Gray, who ran the market garden. Thomas Gray at this time was 78 years old, therefore the family had presumably been in residence for a good many years at this date. By 1881, the Gray family were still involved with the market garden.[52] The area of the garden ground can still be easily seen surrounding the dovecot, which itself, is perhaps the only relic of pre-improvement farm life at Dolphinstoun.[53]

These were presumably the circumstances which limited the degree of interest in agricultural improvement at Dolphinstoun. However, when Agnes Grant, daughter of William Grant and niece of Archibald Grant, married Sir George Suttie, she married into a family with as strong an interest in agricultural improvement as her own.

Sir George Suttie was the son of Sir James Suttie of Balgone, near North Berwick. The Suttie family had a long established presence as landowners in East Lothian[54] and Sir George was a significant agricultural innovator, although his influence was at a more local level than that of Archibald Grant.

Sir George is credited with a number of agricultural improvements on his Balgone estate. In his youth, he travelled to Flanders as a soldier and also spent time in the county of Norfolk, in England. In both these places, he observed how farmers were introducing a new method of crop rotation. The English innovator 'Turnip' Townsend, demonstrated how the introduction of turnips into crop rotation not only aided the fertility of the land, but provided ample fodder for overwintering animals. This 'Norfolk' system was first introduced to Scotland by Cockburn of Ormiston,[55] but it was Sir George who made the first serious attempts at the system in Scotland:

> "soon after the year 1750, he [Sir George] introduced the regular Norfolk system of horse-hoed turnip, barley, clover, wheat, upon his own farm, which he successfully followed until the infirmities of age induced him, in a great measure, to give up agriculture."[56]

This was not Sir George's only innovation: methods of enclosure varied: in

Lady Susan Grant Suttie (back row 2nd from left) with some of the wives and children of staff at Dolphinstoun Farm, part of the family's estate. Lady Susan became well known in the Prestonpans area for her interest in the local community (about 1900)

some cases, hedges were planted, in others, stone walls. This latter method, however, was relatively costly. Sir George devised 'stone pailing', a method of making thorn hedges fenceable by building a wall, about 2 feet high, immediately behind the hedge to provide a solid foundation. He also pioneered a type of 'outfield culture' whereby the land was left fallow then sown with oats. This crop was followed by clover which was then ploughed into the soil before the next crop was sown, resulting in significant improvements in the quality of the subsequent harvest.[57]

Sir George was the father of Sir James Suttie, who changed his name to Grant-Suttie (becoming Sir James Grant-Suttie of Prestoungrange and Balgone) in 1818, when the Prestoungrange estate passed to him on the death of his aunt, Janet, Countess of Hyndford.

There is no evidence that he left his existing home on the Balgone Estate. However, although his son, Sir George Grant-Suttie, did not inherit the Prestoungrange estate until the death of his father in 1836, he is listed as resident at Prestoungrange House in the census report of 1841[58] and probably lived there before this date. Significant improvements were made to the property in 1830,[59] a circumstance which implies that Sir George Grant-Suttie had a personal interest in the quality of the accommodation. Moreover, the record of a tenancy agreement for Dolphinstoun Farm for the period 1833 to

Men, women and children who comprised most of the outdoor and some indoor staff at Dolphinstoun Farm. Because of the advent of machines and horse drawn cultivators the number of workers, although still substantial, was much reduced from just a few years before (about 1910).

1852 identifies Sir George as responsible for the Dolphinstoun Barony even before inheriting it in 1836.[60] Sir George Grant-Suttie was therefore responsible for the major changes which took place at Dolphinstoun Farm between the period 1855–1875.

By the nineteenth century, the Grant Sutties were major East Lothian landowners:

> "Sir Walter Hamilton-Dalrymple of Leuchie House, divides much of the property with Sir George Grant Suttie, sixth Bart...of Balgone and Prestoungrange, the Dalrymple estate within the shire comprising 3039 and the Suttie 8788 acres."[61]

and Sir George evidently had a strong interest in the relationship between landlord and farm tenant. In 1871, he published a pamphlet entitled 'On Land Tenure and the Cultivation of the Soil'.[62] Although this publication is essentially a political argument against the theories of John Stuart Mill, one of the nineteenth Century's most famous political theorists, it does offer an insight into the relationship between landlord and tenant on the Prestoungrange lands in the second half of the nineteenth Century.

Mill was a prolific writer, who advocated the concept of 'collective agriculture' and was a founder member of the Society for the Reform of Land Tenure. His 'Principles of Political Economy', published in 1848[63] was intended to provide a theory of economics which would replace that of eighteenth century economist Adam Smith, who maintained that: "Those who live by rent, those who live by wages and those who live by profit...are the three, great, original and constituent orders of every civilised society."[64]

Sir George's pamphlet (reprinted as Appendix 3) forcibly attacks Mill's arguments for reform on a number of issues, firstly, that Mill's ideas are valueless because a moral standpoint without belief in God and the established order is impossible: "It is the general opinion that no sane man can be an Atheist". Secondly, using France as an example of how increasingly divided plots of land impoverishes the community and leaves no opportunity for agricultural improvement, Sir George maintains that: "...peasant-proprietorship and division of the land are alike incompatible with improved cultivation or increased production." Thirdly, Sir George rejects Mill's arguments on the basis that his opinions are based on theory alone, not derived from any real experience of agriculture and that he had attempted to apply these theories to a country, ie Scotland, where the situation is quite different from that in the remainder of Britain and in Europe: in Scotland, argues Sir George, landowners encourage: "progressive agriculture..., expending their capital in permanent improvements and by encouraging and granting long leases to a superior class of tenant-farmers."[65]

Clearly, Sir George Grant Suttie felt strongly that a landlord who maintained an active interest in the land and property occupied by his tenant farmers was not only entitled to make a profit from those lands, but would also be contributing to the advancement of agricultural methods. Economic advantages for landlords were justified by their own investments on their estates, a point of view which evidence clearly indicates was put into practice on the Prestoungrange and Dolphinstoun lands.

5. DOLPHINSTOUN FARM

At Dolphinstoun Farm, little remains of any buildings from the eighteenth century or earlier, except for the 'beehive' dovecot typical of those built before the late 1800s.[66] The dovecote is close to a raised bank which is all that remains of a building already in ruins by the beginning of the nineteenth century, its origins long forgotten:

> "The estate of Prestongrange, including the lands of Dolphinston, Morisonshaven &c., long belonged to Lady Hyndford. It is now the property of Sir George Suttie, Bart, of Balgone...In the hamlet of Dolphinston a ruin of broken walls and gables is to be seen, which is supposed to have been a monastic establishment in its day."[67]

An alternative history is offered by P. McNeil[68] who suggests that Dolphinstoun may have originally been a fortified dwelling, or 'fortalice', and its position, midway between Fa'side and the lands of Preston, meant that the inhabitants frequently changed sides in local disagreements. However, there is no positive information for who originally settled at Dolphinstoun, nor how the farm got its name. Indeed records of baronial lands show that it was previously known as Colthrople.

A major source of information on agricultural practices at Dolphinstoun during the first half of the nineteenth century is the tenancy agreement for Dolphinstoun Farm between James Mitchell and Sir George Grant Suttie mentioned earlier.[69] This agreement demonstrates a radical change from the

Every farm in the 1920s still kept a number of heavy horses, mainly for ploughing but also to draw cultivators, or as here pulling a load of hay. Thomas Hope driving the cart was a long serving member of the workforce at Dolphinstoun Farm. Mainly employed as a ploughman he, like the horse, had to be versatile.

previous 'laissez faire' approach on the part of landowners during the early eighteenth century and before. By this time, feudal owners required legal guarantees that tenants would maintain the farmland efficiently and would return it to the owner in a fertile condition on completion of the lease. Instead of short-term joint tenancies, often with no written agreement, this formal document refers to a leasehold agreement between the landlord and a single tenant of 19 years duration, from 1833 to 1852. Even with the entail, it seems, landlords could offer far more security to their tenants than before.

The agreement details the 'Proposed mode of culture of the farm at Dolphinston' and is very specific in terms of the tenant's obligations, especially in the last three years of the lease. It specifies what proportion of the land should be returned on completion of the lease as fallow land and grass, the order of crop rotation and the exact quantities of fertiliser to be applied to the land between crops. Evidently, the innovative ideas of the previous century regarding crops, fallowing and pasture land are now accepted practice at Dolphinstoun Farm.

Of major significance is the contrast between the earlier ignorance of the use of fertilisers and the recognition of its importance and its value in this document. It is perhaps entertaining to imagine the scene when: "Dung shall be brought to the farm of equal value to what was removed...and the Dung so brought to the farm shall be put in heaps and shown to the Landlord or some person authorised by him."[70] But this is a clear indication of the value placed on manure as a fertiliser by this date and demonstrates the attention the landowner paid to the good management of his lands even when they were farmed by others.

Similarly, the condition that the grass seed to be sown in the last three years should be paid for by the tenant, but selected by the landlord and that it should be "grass seeds of the best description"[71] makes it clear that this agreement between landlord and tenant is intended to ensure that the land is returned to the landlord on completion of the lease in the best possible condition.

It has already been mentioned that landowners had a dual interest in the agricultural and industrial improvements of the eighteenth and nineteenth centuries. The notion of a rural economy based on a combination of agriculture and industry exemplified by the activities of John Cockburn was typical of many East Lothian landowners. Not only did their lands provide food for the increasing population which inhabited the growing cities, their lands were also the source of the coal, iron and clay which provided the raw materials of developing industries.

By 1850, modern mining was well established at Prestongrange Colliery[72] on lands leased to tenants who brought with them the expertise and finance to develop the mine. At the same time, investment in modernisation was taking place on the farm lands which comprised the Prestoungrange Policies. Unlike John Cockburn, Sir George did not bankrupt himself by his efforts: he concentrated instead on provision of suitable accommodation for a prosperous tenant farmer, housing for workers and buildings to house livestock, especially cattle.

In 1857, a programme of improvement began at Dolphins-toun Farm with the erection of two new cottages, alterations and repairs to the Farmhouse and drainage works on the farm itself.[73] Although the drainage works may well have been carried out in response to the poor summers of 1856 and 1857, when East Lothian harvests were badly affected by rain,[74] it cannot be assumed that the building of these drains was part of a process of agricultural improvement. Mining had been taking place in the area surrounding Prestonpans for over 500 years and beneath the surface there was a network of old mine workings. Water flowing through these workings created drainage problems for any new mineworkings at sea level. Prestoungrange Colliery was on the shore and was therefore particularly susceptible to flooding; these drainage works may have been undertaken to prevent flooding at the mine rather than for agricultural reasons. Certainly, Sir George Grant Suttie was no stranger to the pitfalls of draining boggy land. On his Balgone estate there was "a little loch...formed... after vain and expensive attempts had been made to drain a morass."[75] For whatever reason, drainage work was carried out between May and October 1857, using tiles supplied by Sir George's own brick and tileworks on the Prestoungrange estate.

More direct evidence for Sir George's commitment to the permanent improvements is available from estate records of the period 1857–1864. Between 1857 and 1861, the farmhouse at Dolphinstoun was extensively renovated and a number of new cottages built, in keeping with the new style of single tenant farmer living separately from other farm workers, who no longer had a share in the tenancy agreement.[76]

Between 1862 and 1864, building work at Dolphinstoun concentrated on provision for livestock and farm equipment.[77] Whereas earlier cattle cribs had been unroofed and open to the front, using the walls of existing buildings for

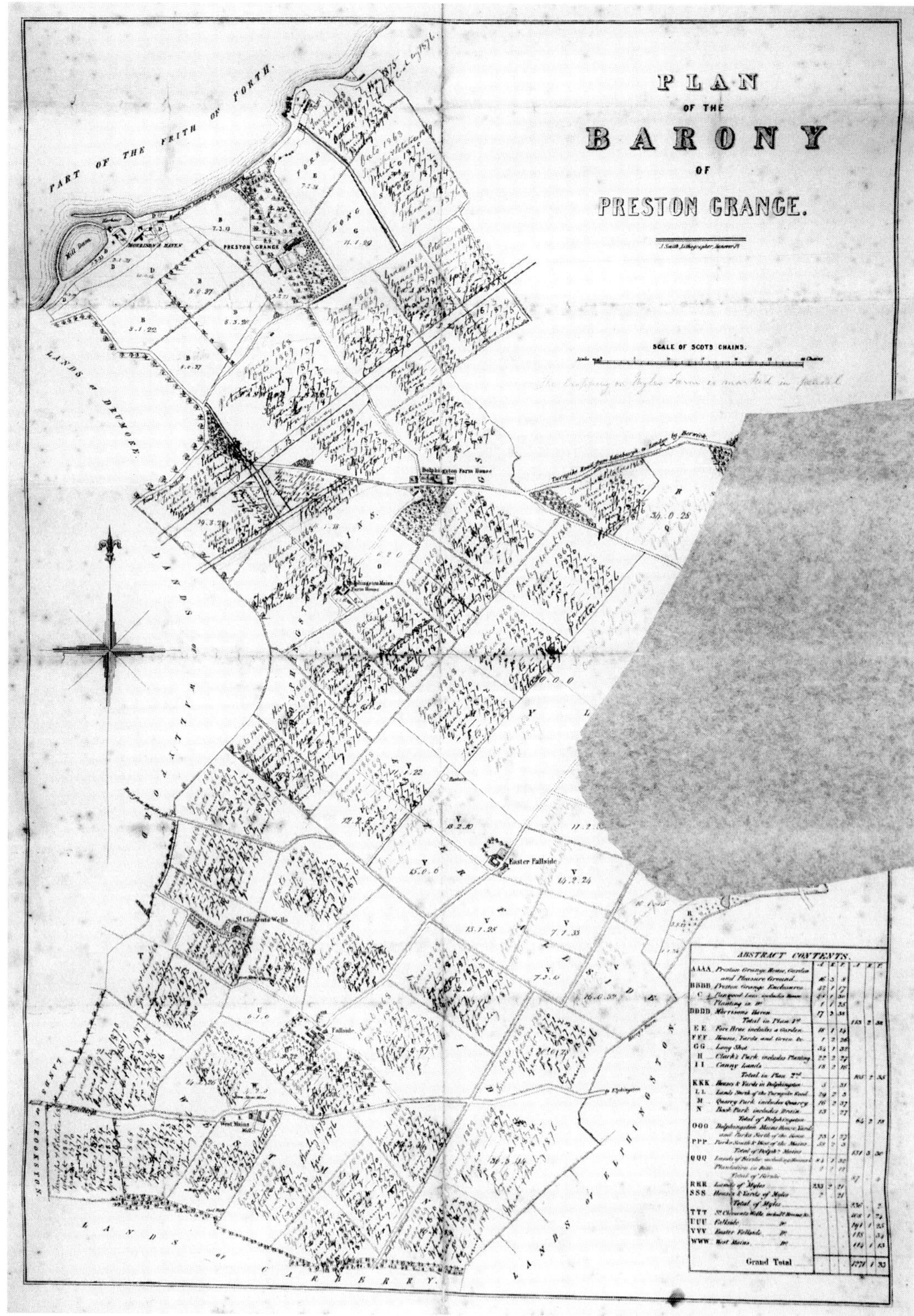

The agricultural output of all the baronial lands including Dolphinstoun in the late 19th Century (I)

support, the cattle courts erected at Dolphinstoun were more substantial structures, roofed to provide good shelter in the winter along with roofed feeding cribs for the animals.

> "The special features that distinguish East Lothian farms are: cart and granary sheds, horse mills, tall chimneys, doocots and cattle-courts...Cattle were traditionally kept in cattle-courts during the winter; hence the large size and often symmetrical design of steadings. Four to six courts could house as many as a hundred cattle fed on turnips and other crops stored in a central shed."[78]

With the exception of the chimney, this offers a good picture of the layout of Dolphinstoun Farm in the second half of the nineteenth century. Livestock farming no longer consisted of limited numbers of ill-fed cattle grazing on land arranged according to the old infield/outfield system and left to fend for themselves through the winter. These new arrangements, together with the new style of crop rotation which provided turnips and hay as winter fodder, meant that large numbers of animals could be housed and fed on the farm.

In terms of those living on the farm, the period between 1841, the date of the first census, and 1881 was one of great change. Dolphinstoun in 1841 was a small community, comprising mainly agricultural labourers. By 1861, the class of tenant and their style of living has changed: there is a housekeeper registered, a Land and a Farm steward, a forester and two young men whose occupation is given as clerks. Although the number of agricultural labourers had fallen, by 1881, there had been an increase in their number, presumably due to the erection of new cottages. However, the building of cattle courts meant that the type of work had changed somewhat, with more emphasis on livestock. By this time, due to increased mechanisation of farm processes, the number of workers required to work the crops had diminished dramatically: according to the Royal Commission on Labour in 1893 "in 1820...to cultivate, reap and deliver five different crops...would have taken 53 days, while in 1892 the same operations would be performed by those using modern methods in 35 days".[79]

Other changes to the lives lived by agricultural workers can be inferred from census information on place of birth. In 1861, Thomas Todd, born in Peebleshire, married an East Lothian woman and all their children, aged between sixteen and five, were born in the same place, ie Tranent.[80] However, in 1881, George Purves, agricultural labourer, has four children registered as born in three different locations in East Lothian.[81] Clearly, by this date, many farm workers were not long term residents of one area, but travelled around East Lothian depending on where work was available. Except for the Gray family, who ran the market garden and whose name appears on the census records throughout this period, no family names remain consistent between 1841 and 1881, and only three appear on more than one census form.

Those living in the farm cottages were also no longer necessarily employed on the farm itself. The re-opening of mine workings on Prestoungrange lands is presumably the reason for the presence of colliery employees – a gatekeeper, an 'oversman' and an engineman.[82] This reflects a national trend in the later decades of the nineteenth century. In 1851, 30% of the adult male population of Scotland was employed in agriculture. By 1901, many had left the land to find work in mines, factories and industry and only 14% were agricultural

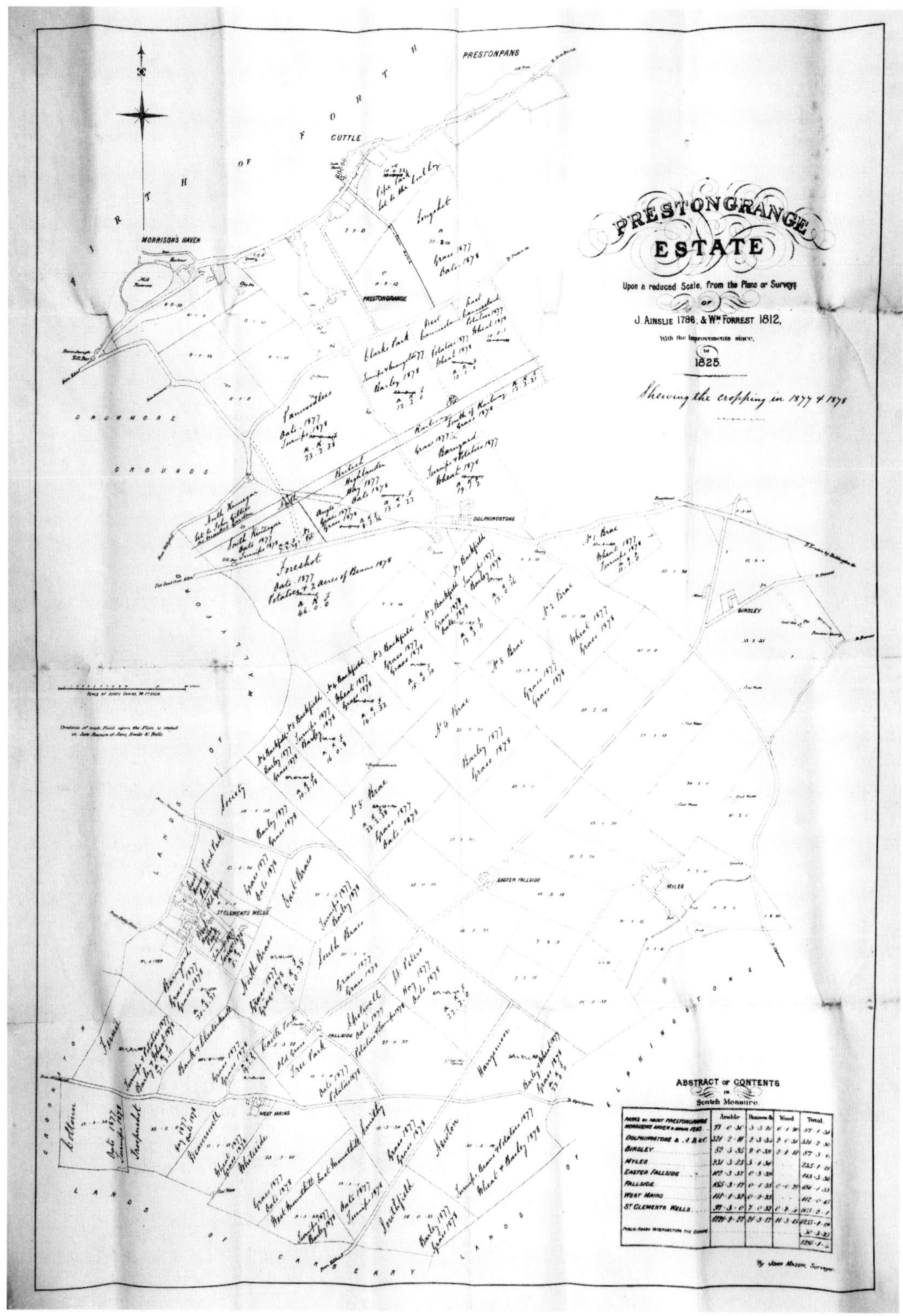

The cropping of all the baronial lands of Prestoungrange Estate at the end of the 19th Century (II)

workers.[83] The census also lists a grocer, a mason and a blacksmith, who like the colliery employees, had valued skills to offer and were therefore likely to expect more comfortable accommodation than that enjoyed by farm labourers in the past:

> "Instead of being four square walls covered with thatch, having a small hole twelve or fifteen inches square, with a fixed piece of glass, for a window...on many estates they had been rebuilt in a commodious and comfortable manner."[84]

Evidence also exists of a closer relationship between landowner and farm: in 1878, Dolphinstoun Farm had no tenant.[85] This, together with the listing of a land and a farm steward in the census return for 1861 and a farm grieve in 1881,[86] suggests that Sir George Grant Suttie, or his employees at this time had a more direct involvement with the running of the farm.

By 1868, maps of Dolphinstoun with details of fields and the crops to be grown there[87] reveal that nothing remains of the old runrig system except the names of the fields. The cropping for the period 1868–1878[88] show that the land is no longer divided according to the old 'infield/outfield' system and the traditional three-crop rotation of oats, pease and beans has been replaced with a wider range of crops in all fields: oats, turnip, barley, potatoes, wheat and grass.

Much of the land is given over to pasture which, together with the turnip crop, would support increased numbers of livestock in both summer and winter. The estate inventory of 1878,[89] lists cattle, sheep and horses. No oxen are part of the inventory, their greater strength no longer required to pull the new-style, lighter, double furrow plough, which also forms part of the inventory.

The inventory also lists the tools and equipment used on the farm. In addition to a variety of ploughs and harrows, there are reaping machines, weighing machines and a potato washer, these last two evidence of produce farmed for sale. These, and the presence of a threshing mill and engine, clearly demonstrate that farming at Dolphinston had, by this period, become highly mechanised.

Potatoes are no longer restricted to the farm gardens – they are now a major crop, grown in sufficient quantities not only for local consumption, but for the markets in Edinburgh and beyond.[90] Wheat is now widely grown and the small quantity of beans is further evidence that the old style of subsistence farming, with crops grown to feed the farmworkers and any surplus used as payment for tenancies to the landowner, is no longer a significant element. The inclusion of 'tares' – corn weed grown as fodder – shows that even the weeds described by Samuel Smiles in his description of early eighteenth century Scottish farm practices[91] now have a clear function in the good management of the farm. Animal fertiliser, listed as 'straw dung' in the 1878 inventory, is now considered valuable enough to be listed as part of the farm's resources.

6. THE ALTERED LANDSCAPE

By the final years of the nineteenth century and the beginning of the twentieth, East Lothian farmers had established a world wide reputation:

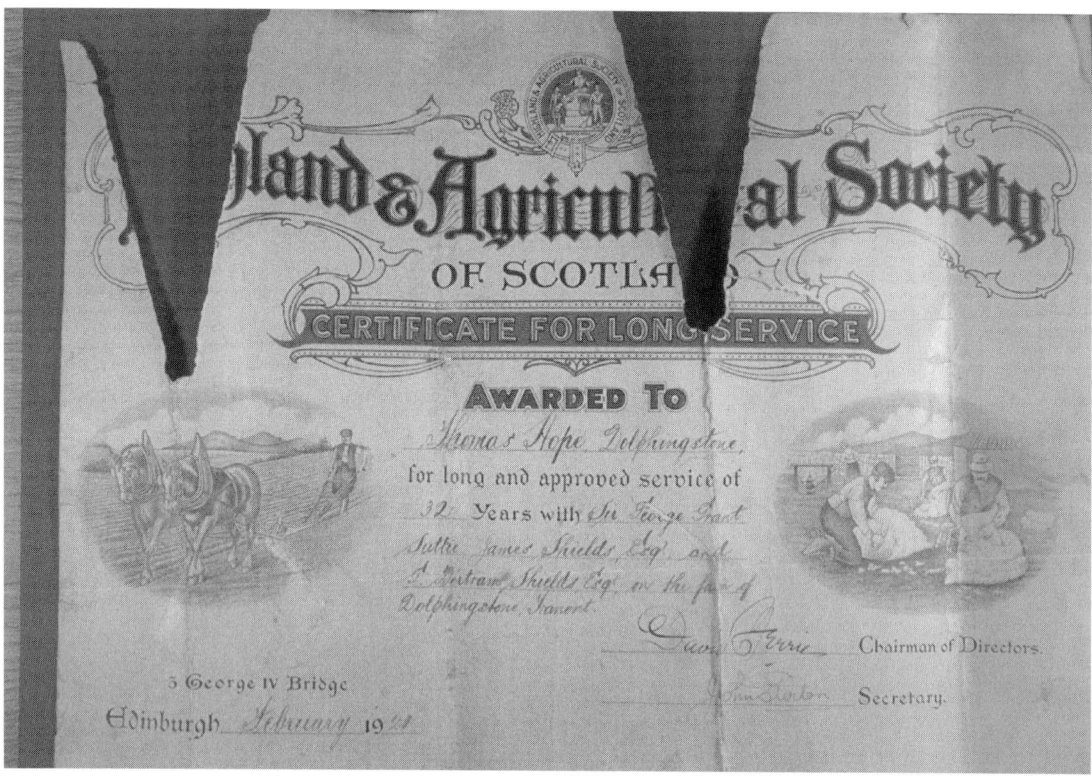

Thomas Hope was a senior ploughman at Dolphinstoun Farm and worked there for 32 years. This certificate was awarded to acknowledge his long service at a time when it was more common for farm staff to move regularly, sometimes annually.

> "The farmers of the Lothians have for long been celebrated for their skill and progressiveness...and they are recognised as the foremost in Scotland, which means the world, for a readiness to introduce new methods, and to utilise the discoveries of experimental science."[92]

The farming community by this date displays a vigorous interest in all aspects of agricultural life: the first Scottish Women's Rural Institute, intended to provide an female equivalent of the Farmer's Institute for men, was established at Longniddry in 1917.

The agricultural lands of Prestoungrange and Dolphinstoun were at the forefront of this dynamic farming community:

"June 16th 1880 was a real 'red-letter day' in a very wide surrounding district. The Agricultural Show on that day was being held for the first time within the Prestoungrange policies, and work in every shape and form, and all around, was brought to a stand for that day."[93]

Early experiments with enriching land with fertilisers had become standard and widespread; in 1903, guano was being imported to North Berwick as part of the programme of intensive crop feeding.[94] McNeil, writing in 1905, quotes 'The Scottish Farmer' on the quality of produce in the farmland near Prestonpans:

"...it is now an accepted fact that the quantities of leek and cabbage plants grown in the Musselburgh, Levenhall, Pinkie, and Prestonpans districts, are considerable greater than the combined outputs of all the farmers and gardeners in all the other parts of Scotland."[95]

Although much of this was the produce of the market gardens, it is evidence of the quality of the area which includes Dolphinstoun Farm where, according to McNeil, the tenant farmer at Dolphinstoun in 1902, Mr. Shields, is "one of the most enlightened and industrious agriculturalists in East Lothian".[96]

However, landowners and tenant farmers were not driven solely by the desire to maintain the county's reputation for innovation and good management. The new-style farms of the nineteenth and twentieth centuries were designed to generate as much profit from the soil as possible. From the 1870s onwards, East Lothian farms were in competition with foreign imports which reduced the sale price of crops and livestock.[97] The machinery they depended on to maximise their yields was expensive to maintain and there was a constant drain of agricultural workers leaving the country to find work in the industrialised cities.[98] The driving force of economic imperatives required that farmland should be developed to its full potential.

Nevertheless, the Third Statistical Account of the Parish of Prestonpans in 1953 makes it clear that in the second half of the twentieth century, a willingness to experiment and innovate was still a significant element in local agriculture and could still prove financially worthwhile

"...recent developments carried out by the Lowe Brothers at Burnside, East Loan, have produced a system of multiple cropping by forcing hitherto unknown in this country...vegetables of the finest quality are grown in regular succession and enormous annual crop production is realised from a comparatively small area."[99]

Dolphinstoun too, maintained its emphasis on maximising crop yields. The Third Statistical Account describes the farm at Dolphinstoun as an "intensively cultivated" farm, where "vegetables and early potatoes are grown in rotation with cereals and other farm crops."

In common with many other areas of East Lothian, farming still goes on today at Dolphinstoun. Little remains, though, of the: "funny-looking low-tiled houses... pleasant to behold always, with their whitewashed fronts, and flower pots each side the door, and so happy and clean-looking were the people, it was ever a pleasure to behold alike the village and the villagers". [100]

APPENDIX 1

References

1 Scottish Executive, *A Forward Strategy for Scottish Agriculture*, Edinburgh, 2000
2 Ibid
3 Samuel Smiles, *The Life of Thomas Telford*, chapter IV, text from http://www.bookrags.com
4 A. Fenton, *The Rural Economy of East Lothian in the 17th and 18th Century*, from *Transactions of the East Lothian Antiquarian and Field Naturalists' Society*, Vol 9, 1963
5 R. Somerville, *A General View of the Agriculture of East Lothian*, London, 1805, p.33
6 Op cit., Fenton

7 Ibid
8 T.S. Muir, *Cambridge County Geographies: East Lothian*, Cambridge University Press, 1915, p. 81
9 G. Buchan-Hepburn, *A General View of the Agriculture and Rural Economy of East Lothian*, Edinburgh, 1794, p. 48
10 Op cit., Smiles, chapter IV
11 Op cit., Fenton
12 Food and Farming Education Service, *Farmfacts Leaflet 2*, www.foodandfarming.org
13 Op cit., Fenton
14 Op cit., *Farmfacts Leaflet 4*
15 Op cit., Somerville, p. 36
16 I. White, *Grain Production in East Lothian in the 17th Century, from Transactions of the East Lothian Antiquarian and Field Naturalists' Society*, Volume XV, 1976
17 Op cit., Smiles, chapter IV
18 Op cit., White
19 NAS: RHP 41332/1, RHP 41333/2, RHP 41382/2
20 Op cit., Smiles, chapter IV
21 LHC: Census Enumeration Books, 1841, 1861, 1881
22 Op cit., Somerville, p. 92
23 *History and Topography of Ormiston Parish*, http://www.sportstune.com/elothian/towns/history/ormiston.html
24 Brown, Gordon, *The Whisky Trails*, 1995, from http://www. uisge.com/ud/glenkinchie.html
25 Adam Smith, *An Enquiry into the Nature and Causes of the Wealth of Nations*, 1776, text from http://www.socs.mcmaster-ca/ ~econ/ugcm/3113/smith/wealth/
26 Op cit., Somerville, p. 31
27 Op cit., Fenton
28 John Sinclair, *The Statistical Account of Scotland 1791–1799*, Vol.17, ps. 63–64
29 Op cit., *Farmfacts Leaflet 3*
30 R. Dunnett, *East Lothian Farm Buildings: an Architectural and Historic Survey*, East Lothian County Planning Committee, 1968
31 Op cit., Somerville, p. 103
32 Op cit., Somerville, p. 161
33 Op cit., Smiles, chapter IV
34 Op cit., Somerville, p. 36
35 John Hamilton, second Lord Belhaven, *The Countrey-Man's Rudiments: or, An Advice to the Farmers in East Lothian How to Labour and Improve their Ground*, 1699, from op cit. Fenton
36 Op cit., Fenton
37 Op cit., Somerville, pp. 35-36
38 *Memorial concerning Prestongrange*, NLS MSS 17713 fo. 48, 1736
39 Keay, J. and Keay, J. (eds), *Collins Encyclopaedia of Scotland*, 1994, p. 863
40 Op cit., Buchan-Hepburn, p. 20
41 NLS MSS 3720. *Purchase of Baronies of Prestongrange and Dolphinstone*, 1745
42 NAS GD 357/46/2
43 Op cit., Keay, J. and Keay, J, 485
44 NAS GD357/43/18, and GD357/44/7
45 Op cit., Somerville, p. 263
46 NAS SC40/67/1, NAS SC40/57/13
47 McNeill, P, *Prestonpans and Vicinity*, 1902 , p. 245
48 Op cit., Keay, J. and Keay, J, p. 863
49 Op cit., Somerville, p. 161
50 Op cit., Somerville, p. 160
51 Op cit., Census Enumeration Books, 1841
52 Op cit., Census Enumeration Books, 1881
53 *Rural Buildings of the Lothians, Conservtion and Conversion no.1: Guide for Practitioners*, Historic Scotland, 2000, p. 30
54 A Fenton, *The Begbie Farm Account Book 1729-70, from Transactions of the East Lothian Antiquarian and Field Naturalists' Society*, Vol 10, 1966
55 Op cit., Somerville, p. 103
56 Op cit., Buchan-Hepburn, p.56
57 Op cit., Buchan-Hepburn, p. 57

58 Op cit., Census Enumeration Books, 1841
59 S. Baker, Playfair at Prestongrange, from *Prestongrange House*, Prestoungrange University Press, 2000
60 NAS/GD357/37/1: *Proposed mode of culture of the farm at Dolphinston*
61 Frances Groome (ed), *Ordnance Gazetteer of Scotland*, London 1903
62 Sir G. Grant Suttie, *On Land Tenure & the Cultivation of the Soil*, Edinburgh, 1871, NAS GD 357/32 (reprinted as Appendix 3 here)
63 John Stuart Mill, *Principles of Political Economy*, summary from http://www.publicbookshelf.com:great books
64 Op cit., Adam Smith
65 Op cit., NAS GD 357/32
66 Op cit., *Rural Buildings of the Lothians*, p. 30
67 John Martine (EJ Wilson ed), *Reminiscences and Notices of Ten Parishes of the County of Haddington*, Haddington 1894, p.169
68 Op cit, McNeil, ps 259-260
69 Op cit., GD357/37/1
70 Ibid
71 Ibid
72 A. Allan, *Horses, Steam and Electric Engines at Prestongrange*, Prestoungrange University Press, 2000, p. 19
73 NAS GD 357/15/6
74 R. Skirving, *On the Agriculture of East Lothian*, 1871
75 Op cit., T. S. Muir, p. 19
76 NAS GD357/15/6, GD357/15/7, GD357/15/8, GD357/15/10
77 NAS GD357/15/10, GD357/15/12
78 Op cit., Dunnett
79 T. C. Smout, *A Century of the Scottish People: 1830-1950*, London 1986, p. 61
80 Op cit., Census Enumeration Books, 1861
81 Op cit., Census Enumeration Books, 1881
82 Op cit., Census Enumeration Books, 1881
83 Op cit., Smout, p. 61
84 Op cit., Fenton
85 NAS GD357/39/1
86 Op cit., Census Enumeration Books, 1861, 1881
87 NAS: RHP 41332/1, RHP 41333/2, RHP 41382/2
88 Ibid
89 NSA GD35/40/3
90 Op cit., Groome
91 Op cit., Smiles
92 Op cit., Muir, p. 57
93 Op cit., McNeill, p. 108
94 Op cit., Groome
95 Op cit., McNeill, p. 237
96 Op cit., McNeill, p. 260
97 Op cit., Smout, p. 61
98 Op cit., Smout, p. 61
99 *The Story of Prestonpans from Contemporary Records 1790s– 1950s: Statistical Account 1953*, East Lothian District Libraries, 1995
100 Op cit., McNeill, p. 259

APPENDIX 2

Bibliography

Primary Sources

R. Dunnett, East Lothian Farm Buildings: an Architectural and Historic Survey, East Lothian County Planning Committee, August 1968

Sir G. Grant Suttie, On Land Tenure & the Cultivation of the Soil, Edinburgh, 1871 (NAS GD 357/32) (Reprinted here as Appendix 3)

The Story of Prestonpans From Contemporary Records, 1790s–1950s, East Lothian District Library, 1995

National Archives of Scotland:

NAS RHP 41332/1 – Part of Plan of the Barony of Prestongrange with cropping 1868–1876
NAS RHP 41333/2 – Improvements to Barony of Prestongrange estate to 1825, with overlay of 1877/1878 cropping plan
NAS RHP 41382/2 – Plan of the Barony of Prestongrange with cropping 1875–77
NAS SC40/67/1 and SC40/67/13 – Sheriff Court records relating to the building of dykes on the Prestongrange Estate
NAS GD357/15/6 – Improvements to farm and dwellings
NAS GD357/15/7 – Improvements to Dolphinstone farmhouse
NAS GD357/15/8 – Improvements to Dolphinstone farmhouse
NAS GD357/15/10 – Costs for erection of cottages and cattle sheds at Dolphinstone
NAS GD357/15/12 – Erection of cattle sheds at Dolphinstone
NAS GD357/32 – On land tenure and the cultivation of the soil
NAS GD357/37/1 – Proposed mode of culture of the farm at Dolphinston
NAS GD357/40/3 – Estate inventory, Dolphinston
NAS GD357/43/18 and GD 357/44/7 – Deeds of entail 1759
NAS GD357/46/2 – Deed of entail, 1756

National Library of Scotland

NLS MSS 17713 fo. 48, 1736: Memorial concerning Prestongrange
NLS MSS 3720, 1745: Purchase of the Baronies of Prestongrange and Dolphinstone

Secondary Sources

A. Allan, Horses, Steam and Electric Engines at Prestongrange, Prestoungrange University Press, 2000
S. Baker, Playfair at Prestongrange, from Prestongrange House, Prestoungrange University Press, 2000
George Buchan-Hepburn, A General View of the Agriculture and Rural Economy of East Lothian, Edinburgh, 1794
A Fenton, The Rural Economy of East Lothian in the 17th and 18th Century, from: Transactions of the East Lothian Antiquarian and Field Naturalists' Society, Vol 9, 1963
A Fenton, The Begbie Farm Account Book 1729-70, from: Transactions of the East Lothian Antiquarian and Field Naturalists' Society, Vol 10, 1966
A Forward Strategy for Scottish Agriculture, Scottish Executive, Edinburgh, 2000
Frances Groome (ed), Ordnance Gazetteer of Scotland, London 1903
Keay, J. and Keay, J. (eds), Collins Encyclopaedia of Scotland, 1994
P. MacNeil, Prestonpans and Vicinity, 1903
John Martine (EJ Wilson ed), Reminiscences and Notices of Ten Parishes of the County of Haddington, Haddington 1894
T.S. Muir, Cambridge County Geographies: East Lothian, Cambridge University Press, 1915
Rural Buildings of the Lothians, Conservtion and Conversion no.1: Guide for Practitioners, Historic Scotland, 2000
Robert Skirving, On the Agriculture of East Lothian, 1871
T. C. Smout, A Century of the Scottish People: 1830–1950, London 1986
R. Somerville, A General View of the Agriculture of East Lothian, London, 1805
I. Whyte, Grain Production in East Lothian in the Seventeenth Century, from: Transactions of the East Lothian Antiquarian and Field Naturalists' Society, Vol XV, 1976

Additional Sources

G. Brown, The Whisky Trails, 1995, from http://www. uisge.com/ud/glenkinchie.html

Food and Farming Education Service, Farmfacts Leaflets 1-4: www.foodandfarming.org

James Halliday, Scotland – A Concise History, from http:// www.electricscotland.com/history/chap.9.htm

History and Topography of Ormiston Parish, http://www. sportstune.com/elothian/towns/history/ormiston.html

John Stuart Mill, Principles of Political Economy, summary from http://www.publicbookshelf.com:great books

Samuel Smiles, The Life of Thomas Telford, chapter IV, text from http://www.bookrags.com

Adam Smith, An Enquiry into the Nature and Causes of the Wealth of Nations, 1776, text from http://www. socs.mcmaster-ca/~econ/u/3113/smith/wealth

APPENDIX 3

ON

LAND TENURE

AND

THE CULTIVATION OF THE SOIL

BY

SIR GEORGE GRANT SUTTIE
BARONET

WILLIAM BLACKWOOD AND SONS
45 GEORGE STREET, EDINBURGH; AND
37 PATERNOSTER ROW, LONDON
MDCCCLXXI

LAND TENURE

AND THE

CULTIVATION OF THE SOIL

LAND TENURE and the Cultivation of the Soil are at this moment attracting the notice of the most civilised nations in Europe.

The Government of France has instituted inquiries of the most searching and minute description in regard to them.

The system of land tenure and the cultivation of the soil naturally act and react on each other; they have, and must continue to have, a direct and powerful influence on the political organisation of all civilised nations.

The tenure of land and the agricultural organisation of Britain are altogether different from that of France; and on that difference it seems evident that much of the difference in the political organisation of the two countries depends.

The advocates of monarchy and of republican institutions naturally take widely different views of this subject, and in the discussion of agricultural questions, political opinions often enter in a way to obscure the truth. In discussing these questions, it therefore seems important to separate, as far as possible, the material from the political question.

The material question is—How to raise the greatest amount of produce from the soil of a country for the use of its inhabitants with the least expenditure of their labour?

This seems a fair statement of the material question; and this or some definition of a similar nature ought never to be lost sight of in discussing these questions. It is therefore satisfactory to find, from his Edinburgh speech, that Mr Bright retains perfect freedom to judge and decide on the system of land tenure and cultivation of the soil best adapted to the position of Great Britain and Ireland; and that he is equally adverse to laws which compel the minute division of land, as to laws which tend to its too great accumulation. This is certainly a statesman-like view of these most important and difficult questions—difficult especially as regards Ireland – and contrasts most favourably with the extreme views industriously promulgated by certain political philosophers, who have acquired a name and influence by their metaphysical writings. In Mr S. Mill's estimation, the possession, tenure, and cultivation of land are all defective in this country when compared with others. The land system in this country differs from every other country in Europe, and differs for the worse. As regards landlords, Mr Mill says the community has too much at stake in the proper cultivation of land, and in the conditions annexed to the occupancy of it, to leave these things to the discretion of a class of persons called landlords, who have shown themselves unfit for the trust.

As regards the cultivation of the soil, Mr Mill informs the farmers of England, that from Denmark or the Sound to Calais on one side, and from the Firth of Forth to Dover on the other, there is no blinking the fact that better crops are grown on land of equal quality over the whole extent when compared with England. On the best-farmed parish in Scotland or England, more land is wasted in borders of fields and in roads unnecessarily wide because they are bad, and bad because they are unnecessarily wide, than would maintain the poor of the parish.

Speaking of the labouring population, he says: "If, therefore, the choice were to be made between Communism with all its chances , and the present state of society with all its sufferings, and if this or Communism were the alternative, all the difficulties, great or small, of Communism, would be but as dust in the balance." He then proceeds: "When I speak either in this place or elsewhere of the labouring classes, or of labourers as a class, I use these phrases in compliance with custom, and as descriptive of an existing, but by no means a permanent or necessary, state of social relations. So long, however, as the great social evil exists of a non-labouring class, labourers also constitute a class, and may be spoken of, though only provisionally, in that character." These opinions are taken from a work by Mr Mill, intended to replace or supersede 'The Wealth of Nations,' which work, 'The Wealth of Nations,' he states in his preface, is in all parts imperfect, and in many obsolete—that is, out of fashion, as Mr Mill now seems to be with the electors of Westminster.

These opinions appear to me so singular as to approach insanity. It is the general opinion that no sane man can be an Atheist. In 'Mill on Comte' the following passage occurs, page 133: "Though conscious of being in an extremely small minority, *we* venture to think that a religion may exist without belief in a God, and that religion without a God may be even to Christians an instructive and profitable subject of contemplation." To ordinary mortals, a religion without a God is about as intelligible a proposition as a metaphysician without a mind.

There is a prevailing idea amongst a class of metaphysical philosophers that peasant-proprietors and minute division of the soil afford a certain remedy for all the ills that afflict humanity. The perusal of the 'Enquête Agricole,' a work published by the authority of the French Government, must disabuse the mind of Mr Mill—that is, if he has a mind to be disabused of all such Utopian dreams. In France, things are exactly the reverse of what they are in England. Here, in general, a landlord has a number of tenants; there a tenant has, in general, a number of landlords. This will not surprise, when it is considered that in France there are above seven millions of landlords, and of that number only sixty thousand have more than £12 of rental.

This inquiry by the French Government is well worthy of attention, from the immense amount of information it affords as to the existing social condition of France. One hundred and sixty-one questions are put by the Government. These questions have been sent to every commune and parish in France; and answers, both written and verbal, have been returned to the different Prefects, who have drawn up long and able reports upon them. I will proceed to make a few remarks on some of the most important touched upon. The first in importance is the continued subdivision of the land. This is evidently giving the Government and the French nation great anxiety. From the evidence there appears to be a total absence of capital amongst the owners of land; and that, as a rule, no capital is applied by the landlord to what in this country would be termed permanent improvements. All classes, without exception, deplore the effects of the law which compels the equal division of property amongst the children. The strongest feeling exists amongst the great mass of the small landed proprietors to preserve their properties from destruction after their death, and prevent their estates being cut up into the numerous small portions which, by the present law, is imperative. This feeling is so strong as to give rise to the most singular and unlooked-for results. The mass of the small landowners, being unable to leave their land to one child, seem decided to have only one child to leave it to: from the evidence, this fact is beyond a doubt. A fact such as this, no less strange than true, deserves to be made the subject of philosophical inquiry; and as Mr Mill has taken the fair sex under his peculiar protection, it is a subject he may now devote his leisure to investigate with advantage; and he may be able to ascertain whether the phenomena arise from physical or metaphysical causes. From the evidence, it is clear that all the educated classes in France desire some change in this law, to mitigate the evils now attending it; but no one ventures to propose its abolition, or even any change in the principle of the law of equal division of the father's property amongst his children. One change is very generally pointed out as possible— that is, to allow the father to leave his land to one child, provided he can leave an equal amount of movable property to the others.

The families of from seven to eight millions of landowners—that is, nearly the whole population—have now a direct interest in maintaining the existing law. Any alteration in it would, therefore, seem impossible.

Fortunately, in this country, no such barrier as yet exists to the alteration of any law which the matured opinion of the country decides to be at variance with the welfare of the community.

To all who have the slightest knowledge either of British or Foreign agriculture, it would be a waste of time to show that peasant-proprietorship and division of the land are alike incompatible with improved cultivation or increased production.

The contrary opinion is, however, maintained by a class of writers, and of this class is Mr Mill, who has risen to distinction by his work on political economy. In it he asserts that the statesman and landlords of England show an insular ignorance of every system of agriculture except their own. Mr Mill's ideas of agriculture are certainly INNATE, since they are evidently *not derived from experience. He states that as land was not made by man, he who appropriates more of it than* enough, usurps the rights of others. The question of *enough* is one to be solved only by a deep thinker such as Mr Mill. Not being either a

Communist or a Positivist, I may fail in the attempt. But to begin with a dwelling-house—a cottage, with two good rooms and a kitchen, is by many considered enough for a labourer with a family of children: a lofty library, more than equal to the whole cottage, with dining and drawing room of at least equal dimensions, besides other apartments, may not be considered *enough* by Mr Mill. Mr Bright, who in his Edinburgh speech indulges in some good-humoured satire at the expense of Scotch lairds, intended apparently to amuse, certainly not to instruct his audience, proceeds, nevertheless, to give the said lairds credit for the good sense they have shown by encouraging progressive agriculture in Scotland. He evidently does not, like Mr Mill in his 'Political Economy', take for granted that there is only one system of agriculture in existence from the Firth of Forth to Dover; on the contrary, he seems aware that the Scotch agricultural system differs in many essential respects from that of the midland and southern districts of England; and he credits the Scotch lairds with expending their capital in permanent improvements, and by encouraging and granting long leases to a superior class of tenant-farmers. And there can be no doubt that to these two causes must in a great measure be attributed any superiority possessed by Scotch agriculture. There is, however, a third cause equally influential; that is, the capital advanced by landlords to tenants by deferred rents. In the best-cultivated districts of Scotland, a tenant entering on a farm under a nineteen or twenty-one year lease, sows, reaps, and disposes of the first crop before being called on to pay a sixpence of rent. The first half-year's rent is not due till he has been in possession of the houses and the greater proportion of the farm one year and nine months: in point of fact, he receives on loan from his landlord, for the whole term of his lease, one year and a half's rent without interest. If for such conduct the Scotch lairds deserve the pity of Mr Bright, what must be his feelings for English squires and Irish landlords?

The too great accumulation either of land or of money in the hands of individuals is unquestionably an evil, and laws which tend to prevent the natural division and dispersion of property, whether real or movable, ought to be abolished.

Since writing the above, the Land Tenure Association has been inaugurated under the patronage of Mr J. S. Mill. In a pamphlet explanatory of the objects of this Association, he begins by remarking that Mr Disraeli's Reform Bill of 1867 will shortly educate the landlords of the Kingdom into the belief that private property in land is a mistake, and that the land ought to be resumed and managed by the State, compensation being made to the proprietors. Judging from the past, Mr Disraeli's ability as a schoolmaster is such that, aided by Mr Mill, it is impossible to say what he may not accomplish; and he may thus finish the education of the landed proprietors by putting an end to their existence as such.

Mr Mill does not appear to have made up his mind as to the best method of cultivating the soil of the United Kingdom; he is in doubt whether it should be by co-operative farms on a large scale, or by peasant-proprietors on a small one. Co-operative farming, having as yet no existence except in the imagination of Mr Mill, need not at present be considered: but it is far otherwise with his favourite system of farming by peasant-proprietors. On this question a vast amount of authentic information exists, which, strange to say, Mr Mill seems determined to ignore. The 'Enquête Agricole' is a work never alluded to either by Mr Mill or any other writer, such as Mr Fawcett, who takes somewhat similar views of these subjects. This is explained by the facts established in the 'Enquête' being entirely at variance with their views. The position of the peasant-proprietors of France is shown to be miserable, and daily becoming more so in many districts. Cultivation will be all but impossible, and the position of the Metayer farmer is, if possible, worse.

The first article in Mr Mill's programme is to remove all fiscal and legal impediments to the transfer of land. The 'Enquête Agricole' proves that this is the great and universal grievance of the French peasant-proprietor; and the fact that in one commune of 2000 acres, divided into 5000 separate parcels, each parcel paying a tax to Government on every transfer, shows a state of affairs requiring no farther comment. The second article in the programme is the abolition of primogeniture. No such law has existed in France for generations; it is for Mr Mill to explain to his Association and to the public the *moral* consequences attributed by numerous witnesses to the absence of this law.

As to the boasted efficiency of peasant cultivation in adding to produce, the fact stated in the Agricultural Statistics just published is an ample and sufficient answer. The produce of wheat in France is 17 bushels per acre; in Britain it is 28.

PRINTED BY WILLIAM BLACKWOOD AND SONS, EDINBURGH.

12
Fowler's Brewery

– Famous since the '45

David Anderson

1. INTRODUCTION

Writing in the late eighteenth century, the Reverend John Trotter recorded in the *Statistical Account of the Parish of Prestonpans* that 'in the year 1754 there were 16 brewers whereas there are only 5 brewers now'. By the mid-twentieth century, there was only one. It traded from the Prestonpans Brewery under the name John Fowler and Company Limited and had established a national reputation as a brewer of strong bottled ales. In 1960 it was absorbed into a brewing conglomerate and did not long survive. Most of Scotland's provincial breweries suffered a similar fate. However, such was the reputation of the established Prestonpans brands a 'Fowler's Wee Heavy' strong ale is still available today, although it bears little relation to the original.

Metal advertising sign to be found outside public houses and off licences

Who the early brewers of Prestonpans were is obscure. Reliable sources are few. However, the Prestonpans parish records of births, marriages and deaths were exceptionally well kept and the professions of many individuals are recorded. The Register of Sasines of the County of Haddingtonshire is preserved in the National Archives of Scotland; it is a chronological list of property transactions. The entries often record considerable detail of individual premises but this source is probably incomplete – short lived changes of use and lessees rather than proprietors within a long tenure of a property are generally not recorded. But the occurrence of brew houses and maltings within the bounds of Prestonpans is noted with some regularity. Individual testaments also provide collaborative detail. Despite the limitations of the sources, it is possible to sketch in and assign some dates to a number of early brewing families and indicate the location of some of their works. Some of these concerns can be followed through the eighteenth century, observing on the way the appearance of Robert Fowler. Fowler, and his successors, survived in the trade while all local competitors ceased trading. The firm grew throughout the nineteenth century even if at some times the leaders of the family firm diversified their interests into other areas of business, including land, potteries and distilling.

After the middle of the nineteenth century, it was the 'other interests' of a descendant of the Fowlers that brought about the sale of the company – he was a firm believer in Temperance. The new owners refloated the brewery as a limited company, which continued to flourish for a further century. Indeed, it become one of the burgh's largest employers as other major industries in the area went into decline or were superseded. Given the robust reputation of the company's products, its sale and closure in the early 1960s came as a great surprise. The decision was irreversible however and brought to an end another of Prestonpans' fine old traditions.

2. BREWING IN THE EIGHTEENTH CENTURY

Brewing in Scotland

Many Scottish brewing operations counted as little more than cottage industries in the early part of the eighteenth century. They were generally of a small scale and catered to a purely local market. Frequently, breweries and maltings were run as one operation and, equally as often, the proprietor might have other sources of income. Many of them were innkeepers, farmers or merchants. In the grain growing districts of Scotland there was a multiplicity of breweries in every town, with a focus on Edinburgh where there was an organised Brewer's Guild and where the country's first large brewery had been established at Leith. This prompted the growth of a number of other large concerns, which began the process of centralising the industry in fewer, larger units. After the Union of Parliaments in 1707 legislative changes, including increased duties, appear to have provided impetus for centralisation and a progressive decline in the number of breweries is recorded – although the surviving units were increasingly of a greater scale with correspondingly larger outputs (Ian Donnachie, *The Brewing Industry in Scotland*, John Donald Publishers, 1979).

Much of their output would be unfamiliar to today's real ale enthusiasts. Hops are presently universally used as a flavouring and bittering agent but until the end of the eighteenth century their use was almost unknown in Scotland. Appendix 3 indicates the ingredients that might be used for porter around 1800. Breweries in rural areas generally remained small-scale and could even be seasonal producers. Around 1,000 barrels (each of around 36 gallons) would be an average output.

Brewing in Prestonpans

In the early eighteenth century Prestonpans was an unremarkable seaside settlement extending along a single street running east to west by the shore. There were associated but separated settlements at Preston, around the old market cross and tower, Cuthill, to the west and Morrison's Haven even further west. Much of the surrounding land was still owned by the barons at Preston (lands to the east) and Prestoungrange (lands to the west) who normally retained their feudal superiority to property within the town.

The principal trades of the town and district during the 1720s, as recorded in the Parish Records, included good numbers of mariners and fishermen, colliers and salters (the traditional industries) as well as weavers, gardeners, masons, smiths and wrights (of all sorts), tailors, shoemakers, a variety of customs-house men and excisemen and even Archibald Heriot, a wigmaker. A large number of individuals are simply recorded as 'workmen' having no specified trade. In addition to those noted there was an upper class of merchants, farmers and shipmasters and notice of a few 'glasshouse workmen' indicate that Morrison's glassworks was still in production. A tilemaker, forerunner of hundreds of potters, appears in the records during 1731. The liquid wants of the inhabitants were supplied by the subjects of the present investigation, who appear as brewers, maltsmen and coopers (although this last group also supplied their wares to the fish curing trade).

Brewers between 1720–32 were James Anderson, James Hetherwick and Thomas Robertson (who had progressed to the description 'merchant' by 1728). In the same period the malt trade was represented by a maltster, John Couper, and maltmen, James Peacock, George Mitchell, William Muat, Patrick Shepherd, James Jack (who is described further as maltster in 1728), Patrick Thomson, and James Shiel.

Between 1740 and 1765 an increased number of brewers appear some of whom, from the consistent witnesses associated with recorded events, can be grouped with maltsters and merchants, perhaps business partners. For example, Peter Thain (brewer), Alexander Nevoy (maltster) and James Johnston (maltman and periodically workman) all appear as primary entries and as witnesses for each other. William Warroch, a member of a prominent local merchant and property owning family, also appears sometimes as their witness and after 1752 James Johnston is associated with Robert Nicol, another brewer. A superficial reading of these entries in the Parish records suggests a three-handed brewery and maltings (brewer Thain succeeded later by Nicol with maltster Nevoy assisted by Johnston) with possible backing from the Warrochs. Similarly, the brewers John Melvil and William White appear to be associated with John Warroch, and each other.

By the 1780s a significant number of potters had appeared in the Prestonpans workforce and the proportion of gardeners (commercial market gardeners) had also increased. The new trade of vitriol worker had gained a significant place. Increasing industrialisation suggests the town would, of necessity, be growing also, providing a reliable local market for brewed products. Agricultural changes were well in hand and the county's grain crop was reckoned amongst the best in Scotland. Much of the crop was absorbed by Edinburgh but maltings, breweries and distilleries were a feature of all the county's towns and many villages. The Statistical Account numbers five brewers in Prestonpans around this period and the Parish Records record the same number of brewers in that decade: William Law, William Foggie, Robert Watt, John Fowler and Mr James Dow. The latter's designation suggests that he occupied a respected position – almost above trade; he is subsequently noted as a merchant. In the 1790s, Robert Hamilton, Thomas Bryson, William Low, Mr James Dow, George Broadfoot, John Fowler and James Cunningham are extant in the records with the designation brewer. However, excluding Dow and Laird Fowler the remaining five might represent the practising brewers – there is no doubt, for example, that fifty years later James Cunningham (at the age of 75) was Fowler's head brewer (*Census, 1841*, Prestonpans Parish). In the 1790s, George Broadfoot is the likeliest candidate for a similar position (John Fowler stood witness to the christening of one of his children), but any one of the five might have been employed in a similar capacity.

The location of these breweries is just as problematic. One lay in the Prestoungrange barony in 1794 but was probably non-working, being used as a bakery (No 976, *Register of Seisins*, Haddington First Series, 1781–1820). It was formerly worked by one Adam Robertson (related to Thomas Robertson of the 1720s) and comprised 'a piece of yard with tenement or mansion house consisting of halls, chambers, malt kiln, corn barn, malt barn, bake house and oven with dwelling house adjacent and houses gardens at the Saltworks of Prestongrange'. The notice of Robertson is therefore additional to those brewers noted above for the end of the eighteenth century but, as he is described as 'farmer and brewer', it may be that the works was leased or worked by an employee at that time. His relative Thomas was also doubly described, first as brewer and then as 'merchant'. In 1825 Robert Burnet purchased another defunct site close by Morrison's Haven: 'land with brew-houses, and salt girnel, and lofts over against the harbour' (404, *Register of Seisins*, Haddington First Series, 1821–30).

The Gordons, one of the Prestonpans pottery families also later owned a property by the harbour that once contained 'brewhouses' They had it from Mary Henderson, daughter of a shipmaster (Nos 1420 and 1438, *Register of Seisins*, Haddington First Series, 1781–1820). In 1798 and 1800 transactions also record another defunct brewery nearby, passing through the hands of the Allen family, candlemakers (Nos 931 and 1080, Register of Seisins, Haddington First Series, 1781–1820) to William Anderson, potter. In 1802 a tenement called the Bankhill was sold which also included a maltings. Another was at Preston, near Northfield House and the remainder probably lay along either side of the High Street. The four main Fowler sites, each with their ancient malt barns are good candidates. That lying on the North side of the High Street opposite Harlaw Hill certainly was once a brewery. The records show 'brewery, maltings, granaries, store' disposed by J Fowler and R Hislop to the Prestonpans Distillery Company in May 1825 (368, *Register of Seisins*, Haddington First Series, 1821–30).

In 1784 the brewer James Dow inherited a piece of ground through his wife's family. But this and several other property transactions of the Dow family shed little light on the location of their brewery. Similarly, Robert Fowler's purchase of the Old Brewery (entry 214 251, *Index to the Particular Register of Sasines*, Edinburgh, Haddington, Linlithgow and Bathgate, 1771–1780) on 2 August 1774 is also couched in extremely general terms. Without subsequent knowledge it would be very difficult to assign a location to the record, which reads 'All and haill the houses, small barn and brewery presently possessed by the said Robert Fowler himself by tack let by the said Mr David Dalrymple the 11th June 1771, with a piece of ground lying to the west of said house bordered on the south by the garden of the said David Dalrymple lately purchased from Alexander Dalziel, bordered on the west by the subjects belonging to John Warroch on the east by a piece of ground or yard presently let by the said tack possessed by the said Robert Fowler and on the north by the High Street of Prestonpans. With permission to make an opening on the yard in the east for opening or shutting the cock on his malt steep'.

Dalrymple, an advocate, owned several properties in Prestonpans and he had been Fowler's landlord for at least part of Fowler's tenure of the tack or lease of the brewery (Fowler being described as 'farmer' in the document, and his son John as 'gardiner'). Peter McNeill (*Prestonpans and Vicinity*, 1902) suggested that this site had been utilised as a brewery for a considerable period. 'What is known as the old brewery, situated to west of Dovecot Gardens, is known to have been built about 1720. Buildings were not erected long ago to last a century and a half only, but many centuries, and this, judging by appearances, may safely be set down as being built a couple of centuries previous to that date'. Quite when Fowler began brewing is only ever mentioned in passing – but 1745 is consistently given as the year.

The purchase of the brewery gave the Fowlers their first step on the property ladder. The brewery was of a scale that might be compared to the arrangement still in use at Traquair House today (http://www.traquair.co.uk/beer.html). There, only two men are required to produce 600 barrels annually although Fowler would have needed additional hands to make his own malt.

During Robert Fowler's time and that of his son, local competition diminished as other breweries nearby ceased production. Poor harvests giving rise to fluctuating grain prices and narrow margins (a danger if a succession of brews spoiled) were all perils to the small brewer (Donnachie, 1979) but, from the 1790s, records show a steadily increasing output on the national scale. Those that had weathered bad spells could look forward to expanding markets, and would prosper with good business sense which included perhaps a touch of sharp practice. Excise duties were also a variable burden and evidence has survived that John Fowler could be quite unscrupulous in 'cheating the gauger'.

3. THE EARLY NINETEENTH CENTURY

Laird Fowler's Progress

John Fowler must have given up his market garden at an early stage to take an active part in the brewery. He is always mentioned as a brewer in the Parish Records. After inheriting the brewery from his father, he seems to have increased the reputation of its ales and consequently was soon looking to extend the installed capacity. This was achieved around 1820 by enlarging the brewhouse through raising the height of the roof, repositioning vessels to maintain the advantage of gravity, and adding new ones. Barnard notes that a 'peculiarly shaped ten-barrel brewing copper, and a quaint-looking old pump' lingered in the Old Brewery seventy years later (Alfred Barnard, *Noted Breweries of Great Britain and Ireland,* 1889–91 – see Appendix 1). The profit from Laird Fowler's operations enabled him shortly thereafter (1828) to build a new brewery on the north side of the High Street, absorbing a site that had once been used as a distillery. In the 1880s the smallest brewing copper on the new site was of 35 barrel capacity, one of a sequence of increasing size, as noted by Barnard (see Appendix 1). It may have been installed originally in the Old Brewery and then been transferred to the new in 1828. The scale would be about right for the period and contrasts strongly with the 10 gallon copper, which was probably the installed plant John Fowler inherited.

At this period, apart from Brown's Brewery in Haddington and the growing Fowler's, all other East Lothian's breweries were small-scale affairs. They seldom had a fixed plant worth more than a few hundred pounds and a comparable amount of stock. Most could be operated by a few hands and many were still adjuncts to the proprietor's main business, usually farming

(Donnachie, 1979). Fowler also followed this pattern by purchasing Hallydown, an estate near Eyemouth – from which he gained his sobriquet 'Laird'. All the stories about this character mention that he took an active hand in the brewing process, so his interests appear to have reversed the usual trend. In his case his land was an adjunct to his brewery, and not the other way around.

Laird Fowler's business sense is revealed by his progressive purchases of parcels of land around Prestonpans. Sometimes he acquired these when a bond, or loan, he had issued was not redeemed. In this way property of the Drysdale Brothers, grocers in Tranent, passed to Fowler (362, *Register of Seisins*, Haddington First Series, 1821–30). At other times, often in partnership with his nephew and successor Robert Hislop, the purchases were made outright. In 1824 they purchased land at Nethershot which stayed in the Company's hands until 1960. In 1830 Fowler also purchased property in Tranent from a spirit dealer.

Fowler also snapped up property that could be rented to his workers. On 8 April 1801 he registered seisin of houses and gardens 'near the east end of Prestonpans' on the south side of the road, purchased from one Margaret Marshall. This property was still in Company's hands when the buildings were condemned and the Town Council built new houses on the site (1054, *Register of Seisins*, Haddington First Series, 1781–1820).

John Fowler and Robert Hislop also diversified into supporting other business ventures. Prestonpans' original pottery, that set up by the Cadell family at Kirk Wynd, was refloated in 1796 under the leadership of David Thomson. Fowler and Hislop provided much of the finance necessary for the new company. Thomson died in 1819 and his manager, Hamilton Watson, took over until the business failed in 1838 (Jane Bonnar, *Decorative Pottery at Prestongrange*, 2000). Reference has already been made to Prestonpans Distillery Company. This firm was formed around the middle 1820s. Its principal site was on the south side of the High Street, around where the Tesco store stands today. But distilling needs maltings as much as brewing and Fowler and Hislop transferred their site on the north side of the street to the Distillery. At a later stage (1841) the company's distiller lodged with Robert Hislop and his family.

The Fowler's Brewhouse on the north side of the main street in Prestonpans. The louvred windows allowed the air to cool the malt liquor before fermentation.

The main Fowler's Brewery from the south west with three storey maltings and the kiln beyond

The distillery was founded at a period when an Excise Act harmonising duty between Scotland and England had come into force (1814, see H. Charles Craig, *The Scottish Whisky Industry Record*, 1994). This presented great opportunities for enterprising Scots, as Scottish duty declined. An annual fee of £10 was required. After that duty of 2s per proof gallon was levied. Before 1823 there were 303 licensed stills, many small. After 1824 there were 337 and much of the new had a capacity of over 500 gallons.

The Prestonpans Distillery Company underwent a succession on name changes: HF Cadell & Company, HF and W Cadell, and just before it closed, Hislop & Company. The connections between the Cadells and the Fowler clan went deeper than potteries and distilleries. In August 1841 Martha Hislop, Robert's daughter, married Henry Cadell.

Finally, there is one piece of evidence that for much of his tenure, Laird Fowler had local competition. A document dated 15 February 1821 found in a time capsule unearthed in a local building under demolition apparently stated 'there is at present in town two breweries' ("Buried Treasure" in *Tales of the Pans*, Prestonpans Local History Society, 2000).

Growth and development

Robert Hislop inherited his uncle's business on his death. By 1839 Hislop had been the brewery manager for some considerable time, but it is unlikely given what is known of Laird Fowler's character, that his uncle in any way took a back seat in the day-to-day running and direction of the brewery when he was alive. Recorded dispositions indicate that the two men had entered into a formal partnership since at least 1820. Fowler registered his inheritance in terms of a disposition made on 15 March 1820 (168, *Register of Seisins*, Haddington First Series, 1841–50). In 1839, the Rev. W Bruce Cunningham, compiler of the New Statistical Account of Prestonpans Parish, was moved to remark that 'the brewery of Mr Fowler has long been signalized by the high character of its ales. There is perhaps no similar manufactory in Scotland that has for so long a period sustained its well-earned celebrity. Nor is it probable that in Mr Hislop's management it will be less famous in the future than it has been in the past'.

Fowler's embossed bottle

And it is clear than Hislop was successful in his management. The brewery now had no local competition and was able to reabsorb the property belonging to the Distillery Company. After an obscure period in the middle 1840s, that firm re-emerges as Hislop & Company. By 1851 the Distillery's property was counted as an integral part of the Brewery, the suite of maltings on the north side of the High Street remaining an integral part of the facility until the end, and the Harlaw Hill site provided room to develop new facilities as some of the older ones were condemned.

At the time when Robert Hislop's tenure of the Brewery drew to an end, it is possible to venture to estimate the scale of his facility. In the period October 1862 – December 1863, the 22 brewers then licensed in the county of Haddingtonshire produced 44,070 barrels (1.59 million gallons) of ales and paid an average duty of £648 (*Haddingtonshire Courier*, 24 April

1863). On average, then, each brewer still produced only around 1000 barrels. Even as a generation before, there was great variability in the size of the county's breweries. Statistics tabulated by Ian Donnachie (Appendix II, Donnachie, 1979) give an indication of the variability. Burnett's Dunbar Brewery was valued at £800; Brown's of Haddington at £3300. Unfortunately, Donnachie gives no analogous figure for Fowler's. In view of the valuation when the Hislops sold in 1865 for around £20,000, it was likely to be nearer Brown's than Burnett's in size.

Shortly after brewing statistics above were published, the Dunbar Brewery was advertised for roup (auction) (Haddingtonshire Courier, 17 March 1865). Its stock of barrels was 5 butts, 15 hogsheads, 600 half hogsheads, 150 quarter hogsheads, one copper and a mash tun. The plant had 4 fermenting tuns but there is no evidence of conditioning vessels. That process we must assume likely took place in cask. The site this brewery and its maltings occupied was about half the extent of Fowler's Old Brewery in Prestonpans. The Dunbar Brewery was one of the smaller in East Lothian and the Courier notice was in fact a signal of its permanent closure. Only the very largest – Brown's of Haddington and Fowler's of Prestonpans – or those with virtually no local competition – such as Dudgeon's of Belhaven – were able to survive a round of closures in the first half of the century. Those that did survive were well placed to cater to an increasing population in the county, and in Prestonpans.

The last Proprietor with Temperance Scruples

John Fowler Hislop inherited responsibility for Fowler's Brewery from his father in 1865, on the latter's retirement from active business. The new proprietor had started in the brewery trade at a young age, being already recorded as 'brewer' in the Census of 1841. But in later life he became a staunch follower of the temperance movement and found that his beliefs were not compatible with this part of the family's interests. These may also have been the reason behind the family's closure of the Prestonpans Distillery around 1850. Certainly, local opinion thought so. McNeill relates: 'It was a highly prosperous concern all the time it lasted, and did not go down through want of funds to keep the concern moving, but rather, it is understood, was allowed to die out through conscientious scruples on the part of new successors'. The distillery buildings were thrown down and the site afterwards secured for a flour mill. This was a short-lived venture. A shortage of water-power blighted the works and it was never a paying concern. It was eventually destroyed by fire.

Temperance scruples were probably the prime motivation for the family's sale of the brewery just as John Fowler Hislop came into his inheritance. Whatever the reason, the result was that the brewery was sold to a new limited company trading as John Fowler and Company Limited.

4. COMMERCE AND CAPITAL FROM 1865–1969

The Brewery's sale by the family proprietors to a new company under the freshly introduced legislation ushered in a new chapter in Prestonpans' brewing history. From 1865 the sequence of formal changes necessarily recorded under the Act afford a window upon the concerns of its leaders. As a Limited Liability Company, annual returns were perforce registered along with Special Resolutions presented for the approval of the shareholders. The increasing professionalism of the Board can be seen in its concerns to develop the company by regenerating the brewery fabric and plant. There was a distinct emphasis on producing high quality bottled ales brewed from malt made by the company from mostly local grain. As time passed the increasing distribution reach of the company was demonstrated by it branching out to support retailers through loans and by its purchase of an estate of tied houses. The Board was helped in its aims by stability. It was seldom more than four members strong and only ten individual directors served between 1902 and 1957. The focus of the company was helped by its choice of leaders. Three successive Managing Directors, namely RH White, JD Ross, and JB Laing were promoted from the position of Head Brewer.

The New Beginning

John Fowler and Company was incorporated under the Companies Act of 1862 as a limited company on 14 October 1865. From that time to the voluntary liquidation of the company in 1969 annual returns and other documents were registered and these have been preserved in the *National Archives of Scotland*. They are kept in West Register House in Edinburgh. Other papers have survived to be deposited in the *Scottish Brewing Archive* in Glasgow.

The documents reveal that the incoming directors who had purchased the brewery in 1865 as a going concern from the Hislop family were mostly Edinburgh based. They were Alexander Wood (25 shares), John MacKay (10), Walter Reid (20), Thomas Sprot WS (10), Alexander Murray WS (12), Andrew Paterson (5), and John Forman (10). Only Reid had an East Lothian address. Paterson acted as Company Secretary, recording 'the Brewery, High Street, Prestonpans' as the official company address. The company's *Memorandum of Association* states that its main purpose was to carry out brewing and other processes at the Brewery in Prestonpans and to progress the business of the company by purchase and construction as necessary.

The company was established with a nominal capital of £30,000, comprising 300 shares of £100 each. By the time of the first Annual General Meeting on 21 March 1866 a call of £60 on each share had been issued and all 300 had been sub-scribed: the company thus raised £18,000. The founders held 92 shares and most of the other shareholders (again with mainly Edinburgh addresses) had holdings of between 3 and 25, costing £180 – £1500. John Fowler Hislop held 25 shares and was still being noted as 'brewer'. His son, Robert Hislop, farmer, held 10.

At the first AGM the company's directors were listed as Alexander Wood (Chairman), Walter Reid, John MacKay, Thomas Sprot, John Nairn Forman, Andrew Wood and George Wood. The company's head brewer, William B Neilson, also held 5 shares. Shortly after that first AGM the company registered a Special Resolution with the intent of raising the firm's nominal capital from £30,000 to £100,000 by creating 700 new shares and offering them to the existing shareholders or to the public. Only 20 were seemingly issued. Over the next few years no more shares were issued and such transactions that took place simply traded on the 320 that had been issued. The sale and purchase of shares was recorded annually and a subsequent register of shareholders reveals that Robert Hislop sold his holding on 25 April 1867, followed by his father on 10 September 1867. Thus, the Fowler/ Hislop family interest in the company they had founded came to an end. The same register shows that the company's brewer was at that time Joseph Robertson, holding 1 share.

The company was by that time a major landholder in Prestonpans, the terms of the sale having included all the Brewery's five discrete sites along Prestonpans High Street, as well as land at Burnrigg and Nethershot. Shortly after it was formed, in December 1866, a set of plans was drawn up by R Thornton Shiells, an architectural practice in Edinburgh which are now in West Register House, *RHP* 23482/3. They were based on surveys made by James Hay in 1851 for Robert Hislop.

The main brewery complex was at the north side and east end of Prestonpans High Street, on a narrowing wedge of land. It was constructed around a series of three courtyards, perhaps a product of the sequential incorporation of adjacent properties by Laird Fowler and Hislop. The easternmost, or 'cattle yard' was dominated on the seaward side by a range of 'vaults' or conditioning cellars and on the landward by a large stable. One of the brewery's wells was located in this yard. Next came a heterogeneous mixture of buildings housing bottling and storage facilities with, on the seaward side Laird Fowler's old counting house, once the company office. Dominated by a tall chimney to the west of this complex was the engine house: it housed the brewery's power plant. The engine house was integrally linked to the main brewery which surrounded it, extended west along the High Street and terminated in a block running down to the sea. Within the courtyard thus formed were maintained a cistern and reservoir, fed from the well to the east and another (the original source) on the other side of the road at the 'Old Brewery'. This facility was set back from the High Street, on the south side. It was flanked to east and west by two wings. Further to the east was a dwelling (also once another office site) and behind it a series of workshops. The original brewery well lay behind the south-east corner of the Old Brewery building with a redundant cistern behind it. This part was, in John Fowler's time, actually outwith the family's property.

To the east of the Old Brewery, also on the south side of the High Street, the company owned a number of dwelling houses and gardens which were rented to workers. They were mainly coopers and draymen from the evidence of the decennial censuses.

At Harlaw Hill to the west of the Old Brewery, the Company possessed the site of the town's old Vitriol Works. This concern had continued to produce sulphuric acid and other chemicals into the early nineteenth century. The Works ceased to produce chemicals around 1820–1825, by which time Laird Fowler was certainly in control of part of the site. In Fowler's time this site was the home of Prestonpans Distillery. After that ceased trading in the middle 1840s it will be recalled that there was a short-lived attempt to mill flour. On the plan the largest building on this site is named 'Old Mill'. The remaining facilities in 1851 comprised dwelling houses, stables, the brewery's carpentry shop (at the extreme east end) and, adjacent to the Old Mill, Maltings No1. A well on this site provided water for the maltings and up the hill the Brewery owned a substantial dwelling house and garden which was often occupied by the Head Brewer and once the Hislops' own home. On the opposite, north side of the road lay the Brewery's main malting complex. At least three individual malthouses are noted on the plan, together with a bottling house and more company dwellings.

This, then, was the extent of the Brewery's working plant. Except for minor changes in the boundaries the actual Brewery property was unchanged when the Company was wound up in the mid-twentieth century. Over the course of time much of the old accommodation was altered to keep pace with new methods and standards. Similarly, many of the dwelling houses were condemned and subsequently replaced with Council housing.

The property of the company could of course be utilised as a tangible asset. On 16 May 1870, the Scottish Fire Insurance Company disburdened itself of a bond which had been taken out on 2 August 1866 by the new directors. By mortgaging the Brewery they had raised £5000 (62, *Index to the Register of Seisins*, Haddingtonshire, 1869–70) for investment. Their next act was to raise £8000 on the same day from the same property, this time from the Heritable Securities Investment Association Limited (63, as above), which probably paid off the £5000 and left £3000 to invest further.

A Change of Leadership

Apart from minor changes in the structure of the share capital and occasional changes amongst the shareholders, the next significant event for the company was the death in service of Alexander Wood, the Company's Chairman, in May 1884. In the official returns of this period there is no record of the composition of the Board of Directors, but William Cumming, with 40 shares was the largest shareholder. An Edinburgh based engraver, Robert White had, since 1870, been assiduously increasing his holding by small increments and was certainly by now prominent in the company's affairs. The compiler of the Prestonpans entry in '*Noted Breweries of Great Britain and Ireland*' considered that White had been the direct successor of Hislop, but this is clearly wrong as shown above although the White family were quick to build their shareholding. Robert White was the father of Robert Hunt White, who first appears as a shareholder in his own right in 1887. In 1890 the latter is recorded in the Register as brewer and by 1892 his address was being given as 'Preston House, Prestonpans'.

These share transactions mark the rise to dominance of the White family in the affairs of the company. When White senior died in 1887, his estate was administered for several years by James Pringle, an Edinburgh brewer, and Robert Hunt White himself, who may have replaced his father on the Board. A balance sheet for the year to 25 December 1890 survives in the *Scottish Brewing Archive* (JF 4/1/1). The company had gross sales worth £54,240 and a gross profit of £13,717 was recorded. £3840 was distributed to shareholders, a 15% dividend.

A sign of the changing strategy of the directors over this period was a Special Resolution registered on 8 July 1899. Its essence was an extension of the company's allowed business practice by new clauses inserted into the Memorandum of Association. One alteration was to allow the company to purchase property and advance money by loan. It may be significant that a number of small shareholdings appear at the same period. These were owned by a number of innkeepers and spirit merchants in Prestonpans, Edinburgh and further afield. The Resolution further indicated that the company intended 'to carry on its business more economically or more efficiently to attain its major purposes by new or improved means, to enlarge its area of operation, and to carry on other business'. Its principal objects were then considered to be malting and brewing with authority to acquire, enlarge and extend the brewery and other premises in Prestonpans occupied by the company. Barnard assessed the effects of these changes as a doubling of the brewery's output but unfortunately there is no detailed financial information to confirm this (see Appendix 1).

In 1902, a list of directors was appended to the company's returns for the first time since the Company's incorporation. They were Alfred Bryson (10 shares, solicitor, Edinburgh), James F Mackay (10, WS, Edinburgh), George Henry Carphin (10, chartered accountant, Edinburgh, who was also a director of Edinburgh's United Breweries Limited amongst others) and Robert Hunt White (10, brewer, Preston House, Prestonpans). However, White and Pringle continued to administer the 71 shares registered to White's deceased father. Robert White thus had control of twenty five percent of the company's issued shares, a situation that lasted to 1904 when the register shows that the estate had been settled. Three equal portions of the 71 went to other members of the White family and Robert inherited 20 in his own name.

At this period no indication was given of the directors' roles. Peter McNeill, writing in 1902, gave the following assessment of the company around that year: 'at the present time there are forty men and boys connected with the brewery. There are ten travellers employed daily pushing the trade throughout the country, and a staff of six clerks continually in the office. There are also two agencies connected with the business, one established at Glasgow, the other at Leith. In order to show what gives employment to all these hands, it may be added there are no less than 6,000 quarters of malt used annually, turning out from 24,000 to 25,000 barrels of thirty-six gallons each, representing a money value of from £60,000 to £65,000'.

From 1909 considerable financial detail was added to the annual returns although the form notes that the company was not required to supply such detail. In that year, the Company had book assets of £39,455. These comprised the brewery itself, valued at £9200, and a 'new maltings' valued at £1200. Land holdings at Burnrigg and Nethershot came to £3,840, around £1,500 was set aside for a new water supply, stock and moveable property was valued at around £9,500 and the company had debtors of over £16,000 – as a consequence of regular trading. Its liabilities included a special reserve fund of £5,000, a small bank loan of £734 and accounts due to creditors of around £2,000. The year's balance at the credit of the profit and loss account was the sum of £3467. 8s. 6d.

The company returned remarkably steady figures until 1919 during which period the Board was unchanged. In the year after the Great War ended, the Company's book assets jumped by around £20,000, accounted for by increases in the value of stock, moveable property, utensils and debts due. This was all reflecting post-war inflationary pressures. The company continued to trade profitably in what was an uncertain market, and the returns begin to show that George Carphin was Company Chairman and Robert H White Managing Director. White was at this period resident at Magdala Crescent, Edinburgh, although he had occupied Castlepark in Prestonpans before the Great War. In the return of 1924 the company's prosperity is noted by the appearance of two brewers, JD Ross of Prestonpans and James Davidson residing in the company's Harlaw Hill property, both of whom had a single share.

Feeder tank and filter – a result f major investment in the 1920s

Staff portrait at the Brewery in 1929

Succession and Investment

In 1924 the Company's reserve fund having been built up to £6400, a Special Resolution was registered to capitalise that fund and consequently the shareholders received £20 for each share they held on 29 March 1926 i.e. as JD Ross's shareholding was then 5 shares he received £100. Ross also benefited from the first change in the Board since at least 1902 when he replaced Alfred Bryson when he retired at the end of 1927. Under new Articles of Association adopted in 1930, the company began to distribute an annual dividend that was set initially at 15% (or the sum of £3,840 after tax. An additional director, James Philip Logie Robertson, an Edinburgh chartered accountant, joined the Board in preparation for the retirement of George Carphin and Robert White in March 1931. He died during August the same year. JD Ross succeeded as Managing Director and by 1933 was also Chairman of the Board. In June 1933 John Knox Morrison replaced James Mackay, who had died in March of that year after serving as a director for 39 years. Ross took an active part in the future direction of the brewery operation. He visited suppliers such as William Rankin and Sons of Glasgow to review their crown corking machines for which Fowler's was testing a new design. He established agencies for the Company's bottled ales. Devon was supplied with 12 guinea Crown Ale (wee Heavy) at 5/3d per boxed dozen splits and he also set up a Scottish network of travellers. WJ McAinsh was appointed on 29/6/1931 on a salary of £300 with commission of 5% on bulk sales, 1d per dozen splits and 1/2d per dozen pints of Pale Ale and Prestonpans Beer. (JF 8/1/1/1, *SBA*).

Fowler's Twelve Guinea Prestonpans Ale

From 1935, the reports provide an insight into developments within Prestonpans at the brewery. First, the directors issued a warning that some of the company's buildings had been scheduled for demolition and that consequently provision for extensive renewal was foreseen. Such eventualities did not prevent the annual dividend rising to 17.5% announced February 1936 and then to 20% in February 1937. The 1938 report indicated that the renewal of plant was well underway and that there was a probability of further compulsory demolition and reconstruction. The directors intimated that they were following a strategy of conserving liquid resources to cover these eventualities. Consequently, the dividend was maintained at 20% although the scale of profit on trading would have borne an increase. An idea of the scale of reconstruction was indicated. £5536 had been spent on the brewery buildings and the book asset value was increased proportionately.

During 1938 the directors invested heavily in plant and technology. A new process for naturally maturing and conditioning beer was adopted. The directors considered that this innovation would bring the preparation of beer for bottling 'as near perfection as it is ever likely to be' – no mean boast. This new plant was at that time the first of its type to be installed in Scotland. It

Bottling, labelling and capping bottles at Fowler's Brewery

Bottling hall workers standing behind a crate conveyor

was in operation by November 1938 and the directors were glad to report in February 1939 'a marked improvement in the appearance and quality of the company's bottled ales'. A complementary renewal of the bottling plant was reported to be well in hand and it was anticipated that that department 'will be the most efficient and thoroughly up to date' when completed.

The next year a new problem was reported. Another of the old maltings had been condemned as unsafe and the directors had found it necessary to provide for the extension of one of the more modern maltings to maintain capacity. Despite the outbreak of war, the arrangements to carry out the work had been underway before that event and consequently permits for building materials had been secured. It may be assumed that if the building's problems had been noticed a few months later, the permits would have been much harder to come by. The war further affected the operational side of the company because, despite increasing output, increased taxation ate into profit. The increased output was secured in difficult circumstances as materials were harder to come by. Provision also had to be made for an accumulated backlog of repairs, anticipating likely heavy expenditure when restrictions were relaxed. During the war, the death of John Morrison saw the Company Secretary, Alaister Henry Crerar WS, join the Board. He was the first of the company's Secretaries ever to attain Board status.

Despite the difficult war years and their aftermath, Fowler's programme of investment in the 1930s stood it in good stead. When emergency taxation was reduced, 1946–1947 brought in a phenomenal profit on trading of over one hundred thousand pounds. Contrast this with 1938–1939 when the equivalent sum was £13,455. However, account has to be taken for inflation over the same period. The company's assets increased in book value from around £80,000 to £252,000. Underlying the inflationary boost was very real growth and the Board increased the annual dividend to 60%. In February 1950 they were able to report that 'in view of the very satisfactory results which have been more than maintained over the past few years despite the general depression in the brewery trade and of the decreased value of the pound, the Directors feel themselves justified in proposing the larger dividend suggested' – a dividend of 100%. The shareholders divided a total of £17,600. One reason for the success of the company in this period may well have been the war itself. During that period there was a marked decline in distilling (*Scientific Survey of South-eastern Scotland*, BAAS, 1951), a situation that continued after the war. Fowler's concentration on bottled ales, and its excellent distribution network probably benefited from this decline by supplying an alternative product where other breweries were at a disadvantage.

The Final Decade

The 1950s opened with the Board embarked upon a plan to adjust the company's share structure. A Special Resolution registered on 26 April 1951 proposed that the existing 1000 shares of £100 be each divided into two shares of £50. This meant there were 640 existing shares. The Resolution further proposed that the General Reserve Fund of £48,000 be capitalised as 960 shares of £50 to be distributed amongst the shareholders on the basis of three new for every two held. This meant that 1,600 of the nominal 2,000 shares were in circulation. The Board recommended a dividend of 45% equivalent to 112.5% of the previous capital of £32,000.

In March the following year a second Special Resolution proposed a further change in the company's share structure. The share capital was to be increased to £300,000 (6,000 shares at £50) and £160,000 was to be capitalised as 3,200 ordinary shares of £50 that were distributed pro rata two for every existing one. Now 4,800 shares would circulate. Fowler's sought and received special permission required from the Treasury for this distribution and in March 1953 reported that the required £160,000 was found from the General Reserve Fund (around £122,000), an excess profits tax post-war refund of around £30,000 and £9,000 from a Future Taxation Reserve. As issued capital was now £240,000, the dividend became 15%, exactly equivalent to the previous year's figure of 45%. In 1954 the three directors capitalised the General Reserve once more, distributing one new share for every five held and bringing the total in circulation to 5,760.

JP Logie Robertson retired from the Board on 21 March 1957 prompting the promotion of James Barclay Laing, head brewer at Prestonpans, and Alexander Darroch, JD Ross's long standing secretary or personal assistant, to the Board. Laing and Darroch became Joint Managing Directors, Ross deciding that he was overextended by holding both that position and the Chair. He was then around 66 years old and had been with the company at least 33 years. Laing was resident in the company's Harlaw Hill House. Darroch lived in Gosford Road, Longniddry close to Ross, who resided at 'Sorgenfri', Kings Road there. The appointments of Laing and Darroch were only the ninth and tenth to the Board in the 56 years since the returns of 1902. However, on 21 July 1960 Captain James Paton Younger CBE was most significantly appointed as an additional director of the company. A senior member of a long-standing Scottish brewing family, Younger was a director of the Northern Breweries of Great Britain Limited as well as holding four other brewery company directorships.

Prestonpans Beer with trademark Preston Cross

Younger's appointment was a consequence of great changes in the company. Within months, JD Ross had also gone. He resigned on 1 October 1960. Before then, at the 95th Annual General Meeting on 9 March 1960, he was able to report that the company's net book assets had exceeded £1 million for the first time. The profit on trading came in that year at £123,640 and £29,400 was distributed to shareholders in the annual dividend. The company sold bulk ale worth around £150,000 and bottled ale worth £261,000, an indication of the company's traditional strengths (JF 4/1/2, SBA). At that time the bottled range included Strong Ale (wee Heavy) splits; Sweet Stout, Export Ale, India Pale Ale, Pale Ale, and Prestonpans Beer in small bottles and the last two were also offered in large bottles. The company paid out somewhere between £40–50,000 in salaries, wages and commissions.

It was this very strong position which made the company a target for takeover. The brewing industry at that time was going through further technological and marketing transformations making larger scale operations a commercial necessity. None of the shareholders truly identified with Prestonpans per se. So in May 1960 all the issued share capital of the company was acquired by Northern Breweries Limited with promises to keep the brewery going. The only public notification had been a single paragraph article in the *Haddington Courier* 15 April 1960:

> 'Messrs Fowler ... announced last week that Northern Breweries had made (an offer) to acquire the whole of the share capital. The Board regard the offer as fair and recommend acceptance'.

The actual share transfer was recorded on 19 August 1960, on which day the independent existence of John Fowler and Company Limited came formally to an end.

This was the reason why Captain Younger appeared on the Board. The new owners were placing their own men. It was the reason for Ross' retirement. Younger was immediately appointed Chairman. Ross' departure was followed by those of Laing on 30 September 1961 and Crerar on 24 January 1962. A manager and director of United Caledonian Breweries to which Northern belonged, William RC Elliot, joined the Board on 27 February 1962. Alexander Darroch, the last of the original directors, soon followed his colleagues to be replaced by The Honourable GHK Younger who joined the Board on 23 October 1962.

Closure and Liquidation

The reasons why the Board agreed to the takeover offer from Northern Breweries are not recorded in the official returns. They would clearly have been given a good price and have received the promises they wanted to hear about the brewery staying open. But the eventual outcome was not that.

From a commercial perspective their timing was probably right. With hindsight we can see that to have survived the following two decades as a small brewery on the national scene would have been very difficult. Some of course did and still flourish forty five years later. But most sold out in the brewery merger mania of that time.

It may be that, having most successfully weathered the difficult post-war years in a strong position, it was believed that the company's assets – strong, popular brands and a chain of tied houses – would benefit from being part of a larger concern. However, given the prevailing climate it is hard to believe that closure had not been considered a very likley consequence of the directors' recommendation to sell. And so it was. To Northern Breweries/United Caledonian, John Fowler was small beer. The Chief Accountant of Fowler's was able to report, two years after the share offer was accepted in October 1962, that 'production at the brewery in Prestonpans ceased in May this year and the machinery and plant has been and is at present being transferred' (JF 1/4/1, *SBA*).

The 98th AGM on 18 April 1963 showed the result of these momentous changes. The dividend, after providing for depreciation and taxation, came in at £8,690 despite this being accrued over 15 months as the reporting year was brought into line with other group companies. The company's assets were marked down by around £100,000. Licensed premises were sold and the company's assets were transferred as at 1 January 1963 to United Caledonian Brewers. The company's estate was valued at £493, 395 (JF 1/4/1, *SBA*). It comprised a suite of around forty public houses scattered across the central belt of Scotland and a two small '7 day' hotels. Only a few were near the brewery. These included the *Fa'side Inn*, Wallyford; *Robin's Neuk*, Macmerry;

the *Johnnie Cope*, *Queens Arms* and *Railway Tavern* in Prestonpans; and the *Dolphin* in Whitecraig. To keep these and the thousands of individual accounts supplied the company had at the end maintained a fleet of 25 varied lorries.

The in-house publication '*United News*' of Autumn 1961 stated the new owner's policy:

> 'to be successful the Group aims to develop its local business and its national brands side by side. Neither is complete without the other'. But 'there have already been changes in our regional product ranges, and doubtless there will be more in the future'. Any changes would be made 'with full consideration of all the relevant factors' in the 'general interests of the group as a whole'. Although 'regional drafts and bottled beers will remain the backbone for a long time and their rationalisation and improvement is a continuous activity' (UCB 12/4/1, *SBA*).

The figures for the financial year to the end of 1962 shows the profit on trading had declined to £46,000, a third of the level to which JD Ross had brought them and representing the last few months of trading. The 99th AGM baldly makes this clear. 'There was no trading by the company during the year'. The Company existed as a shell for a few more years its only purpose being to secure loans raised on its property. The fixed plant, including the bottling plant installed with such pride before the war, was stripped out of the brewery buildings to be utilised elsewhere. Most went to Alloa. The valuation recorded on 30/9/1961 showed the assets of the Brewery valued at £890,540 – counting everything down to the office typewriters and the gardener's tools. The inventory is preserved at the Scottish Brewing Archive (UCB 10/2/3) – a fully detailed snapshot. The estate of tied houses, brands, trademarks, goodwill and other intangible assets were rationalised or applied in a small way elsewhere.

The last acts of the Board were to enter voluntary winding up. A Declaration of Solvency was registered on 5 March 1969 and Robert Campbell Ward, CA, of Glasgow, was appointed Liquidator a week later. Finally, at a General Meeting of John Fowler and Company Limited at 110 Bath Street, Glasgow on 14 October 1969 an Extraordinary Resolution was passed: 'that the books and papers of the Company be handed over by the Liquidator to Tennant Caledonian Brewers Limited and that they be retained by them for a period of two years and thereafter be destroyed'. Fowler's was no more.

5. FAMOUS SINCE THE '45

The closure of the brewery came at a period when the town's pits were also marked down to be shut, the last saltworks had ceased to produce and survived on packing, and the pottery and soapworks had also gone. This latest blow was a great shock to the community. Since the days of Robert Fowler and his son 'the Laird' the brewery had been a fixture in the town. Many Prestonpans families could boast of several generations of brewery workers and were able to draw on a pride and a tradition built over nearly two centuries. The brewery had accreted a wealth of stories and tales, some of which had surely grown in the telling. The best are well worth repeating here.

Some of the following has been drawn from Peter McNeill's history, *Prestonpans and Vicinity*, a wonderful evocation of old Prestonpans and its characters, first published during 1902. The detail and feeling that McNeill realises is of times long gone. Consequently, it has been felt justified to let his words speak for themselves where appropriate and the material has been simply lightly edited with explanatory pieces inserted. Many of the additions were sourced at East Lothian Council Library Service's Local History Centre, particularly material that originally appeared in other publications and newspapers. McNeill quotes extensively from a descriptive volume 'Barnard's Noted Breweries of Great Britain and Ireland'. The description of the late Victorian brewery plant and its means of operation afforded by this work has been appended in its entirety as Appendix 1.

Robert Fowler

Very little is known of Robert Fowler. There were Fowlers in Prestonpans at the start of the eighteenth century. Robert was the son of a wright, John Fowler, and Margaret Miller. From his marriage to Martha Neil there were several children, at least four girls and one boy, John. In the Parish records, where any appellation is given to Robert, it is 'brewer', after a single mention as 'farmer'. It is not clear if he owned any farmland. As he does not appear in the 1770 *Directory of Land Ownership*, which measured plots down to 4 acres, such land as he had was probably leased see LR Timpeley (ed.), *Directory of Landownership* c1770, 1976. Both John and Robert were well respected in Prestonpans, appearing in the Parish records many times as witnesses to others' families christenings and marriages – including the potter, Antony Hilcote.

Laird Fowler

John Fowler was born on July 9th 1756 and died at the advanced age of eighty-three in 1839. In early documents he is recorded as a market gardener. There were many such in Prestonpans, and many small but economic gardens lying between Salt-Preston and Preston village around the cross. Most of them were operated on a lease-hold basis but John Fowler was able later to become a landowner in his own right.

Fifty years after Laird John Fowler had died there were still stories told about him. One is given in Bernard's account: 'Laird Fowler brewed entirely by rule of thumb. It was, therefore, his custom to test the gravity of the mash by tasting it. On one occasion he was going his rounds and, as usual, dipped his finger in the mash-tub. Calling out to his man, he said, "Jamie, put in anither bag o' maut". To which Jamie curtly replied, "There's owre muckle in't a'ready". The Laird frowned, and silenced him with the remark, "The maut's nane o' yours, Jamie, but mine"'. Bernard concluded from this tale that the Laird believed in giving good value, and this was probably the cause of his wonderful success.

Peter McNeill provides two more tales. 'Laird Fowler was a hearty old man. He seemed not only to know, and be known, by everybody but hailed every one in passing in his own familiar way. One day, it is told of him, when Lords Wemyss and Blantyre were passing the brewery he hailed their lordships very familiarly, got them to dismount, enter, and have a horn of his new brewed beer'.

'Old Laird Fowler was no prophet, but he always knew when the gauger was coming and as sure as he arrived a good dinner awaited him. While the dinner was being discussed all hands were called at once to the store rooms. These were speedily cleared out, the full barrels being all run up into the old back garden and hid beneath the wide-spreading currant bushes. So as a rule when the gauger entered the store-rooms he found nothing but empty barrels, but no sooner was his back turned than the empties were turned out and the full barrels returned to the store rooms'.

Barnard's tale was repeated in slightly different terms by John Martine of Haddington in his '*Reminiscences of the Parishes of Haddington*' writing in the 1880s. Martine had also been a brewer so the tale had probably entered the mythology of the local profession. He adds with an interesting observation on innovation: 'Laird Fowler was a well-known man in town and country in his day. The best kinds of ale he made were very strong, quite different from the weak, mild ales of the present day. There was no bitter ale in his time except his extra hopped table beer'. Martine also observes that 'Mr Fowler acquired a deal of land and property in Tranent and Prestonpans Parishes, and was Laird of Hallydown, a fine estate near Eyemouth'.

Robert Hislop

Hislop's public activities had no less effect on Prestonpans than his commercial concerns. He, together with James Mellis (soapmaker), Henry Wakelin (Inland Revenue), Charles Kerr (merchant), James Petticrew (merchant), and James Bellfield (potter), and twenty-three other householders in Prestonpans made an application to the Sheriff of Haddington in February 1862 (*Haddingtonshire Courier*, 07 February 1862). Their purpose was to secure agreement that, in terms of a Parliamentary Act for Regulating Police (and other matters), that Prestonpans was a 'Populous Place' as defined by the Act. The result was the formation of the Burgh of Prestonpans.

However, even after the formation of the Burgh, the clout of the Brewery and its ex-proprietors in public affairs was of some interest locally. The formation of the Police Board and Burgh meant that local rates were implemented by the elected Commissioners. This soon led to local dissent, an early rate-payers protest. At the election of 1868 (*Haddingtonshire Courier*, 06 May 1868, 24 July 1868, 7 August 1868) the cry was 'No Commissioners' and 'No Taxes'. The popular perception was that the old Board had been dominated by a claque of 'Brewery Party' candidates. At the stormy meeting arranged to elect a new board, James Bellfield commented "I would be willing to serve the community; but I am not disposed to be a servant of the Brewery Company". Mr Ferguson Joseph, manager of the company; John Edgar, a company clerk, and James Sheils, brewer, were also nominees; others were seen to be in the company's interest. The discontented party won the day eventually and a new leet of Commissioners was elected to serve the Burgh and proposed by 'limiting the expenditure ... they would secure the health and comfort of the lieges and ... save their pockets'.

A few months later the *Haddington Courier* reported on the outcome of the day when a group of local men appeared before the Bar charged as part of a 'riotous assembly' outside the Queens Arms (Grant's) Inn, which 'wickedly and feloniously' disrupted election proceedings. The jury decided that the men had suffered enough in paying for their defence and by appearing in court and, taking into account the excitement in Prestonpans, found them all not guilty.

Behind the affair would seem to be a general public discontent about the new Burgh administration. As the brewery had recently changed hands a certain high-handedness was attributed to the employees of the brewery who, being resident in Prestonpans, had ventured to place their skills at the disposal of the community.

Robert Hislop died in January 1872 during his 83rd year. The notice of his death in the Haddingtonshire Courier noted his passing 'would be lamented by those who once owned him as master' and the community lost 'one who was wont to be looked up to with respectful regard' (*Haddingtonshire Courier*, January 19 1872).

John Fowler Hislop

John Fowler Hislop was a man of many interests. A firm believer in the merits of temperance, his principles probably led to the sale of the brewery. Like his father and great-uncle, he took an active part in Prestonpans' community life, serving several terms on the Parochial Board (*Haddingtonshire Courier*, 17 June 1865; 22 June 1866), for many years as Chairman. The Board administered the district's poor-roll and schools amongst other statutory duties. Fowler and his daughter, Miss Annie Fowler, later served on the School Board representing the Free Church interest. In 1873 this led to an unprecedented competitive election against a leet of Established Church candidates when John Fowler lost his seat.

Fowler and his family philanthropically organised lectures, musical evenings and concerts for the community. Some of the themes presented were wide-ranging for example when the Rev. Gillespie of Edinburgh gave an account of China in January 1861. After the sale of the Brewery he moved to Castlepark and devoted much of his time to antiquarian pursuits, becoming expert on aspects of the history of Prestonpans and district. His newspaper clippings books are still a source of information and contain many items of scare ephemera produced in Prestonpans and recording the activities of the nineteenth century (*Local History Centre*, Haddington).

Reminiscences

- One of the last notices of the Company as a functioning concern was a Farewell Dance, organised by the firm's Caledonian Social Club, a short lived innovation of the new owners. It was held in the Johnnie Cope and the last of the old directors, Mr Alexander Darroch, took the opportunity to say a few words. He implied that things had certainly not gone according to plan but can he really have been so naive. He observed, "it was rather disturbing that after so many years together they now had to take leave of one another. Despite strenuous efforts to keep the brewery functioning on a 100 per cent basis they had failed". Rather disturbing? It was a body blow to the town. A large percentage of the employees knew already that they were losing their jobs or being transferred with only around 30 staying on at Prestonpans. Yet despite the nature of the occasion, the night seems to have been a successful one with presentations, prizes and dancing competitions (*Haddingtonshire Courier*, 9 March 1962).

- During the twenties, AM Smith began work in the brewery in the cooperage. His account of his first working days appears in *Prestonpans Remembered*, East Lothian District Council, 1986. This was his second job. He had spent 8 months at Bankton Colliery – and he was still only 14, starting work at 6.15 and continuing, with breaks until 5.00 pm. He remembered that JD Ross was a 'real go-ahead person, very strict, but very fair' who recognised that there was a good market in pushing bottled ales, particularly strong ale. Mr Smith reckoned it was through Ross's influence that the first girls (a dozen) were taken on in the bottling plant that had been installed. This pilot scheme was so successful that Ross convinced the Board to invest in the plant that has been noticed here earlier. A national campaign promoted the ale as '*Fit for a thorough-bred*' or '*Makes weak men stronger*', and of course '*Famous since the '45*'.

Back in the cooperage, Mr Smith was put through a rigorous apprenticeship, receiving training on the job and at night-school in Edinburgh. Success in the latter brought a bonus of £2. His training stood him in good stead as he spent 37 years in the cooperage, observing that 'not one modern machine was installed; every job was done by hand, brute strength and muscle'.

- Others also had memories of the brewery. Janet Naysmith in a memoir (As I Remember, http://www.maths.strath.ac.uk/~caas66/homepage/preston.html) recalled that the First World War was a time of change. 'Like most companies, the brewery relied heavily on women doing work which would never before have been attempted by them. These tasks were malting, handling kegs at the loading bay and scrubbing tuns with long handled brushes after the beer had been fermenting for several days. When the men returned the women left the heavier work. However as the brewery was a thriving complex many of the girls retained their employment. Modernisation of the bottling plant meant the streets would clatter with the sound of the girl's clogs as they went to and from work. Alas now all is quiet'.

- Then again, working in a pub like the Queens Arms, one of Fowler's, could give certain advantage. One of the barmen there organised an annual Sunday jaunt. A bus was hired from Wiles, a local company. It was loaded with 'crates of Wee Heavies, no restrictions, and off they went'. Wiles ensured that a teetotal driver was on duty (Annette Gilroy, Wiles Buses in *Tales of the Pans*, 2000).

- Another ex-worker, Margaret Black, has also published an account of her time at John Fowler & Co Brewers in *Tales of the Pans*, 2000. This gives an insight into many of the brewery operations. Margaret worked in the office, from where she was able to gain an insight into many aspects of the operation and, over the course of time, the traditions of the firm, such as the annual trip to the Lammermuirs to gather heather to make up into brooms. She concludes with a fitting assessment: "Fowler's has been described as being 'a lovely wee Brewery'. As far as cleanliness and hygiene are concerned it was second to none. There was always a good rapport between the Brewing Room and the Excise Officer, and merchants and travellers who called. I think it is true to say that it was a happy environment.

  At the time of the takeover we were informed on Mr Taylor's authority that 'there will be no changes'. But we only remained open for two years. Some employees were made redundant, others were given jobs in the new head office in Eglinton Crescent or in Murray's which was still open, but that is another story!"

ACKNOWLEDGEMENTS

This work would have been impossible without the resources of several institutions. Both the National Archives of Scotland and The Scottish Brewing Archive have deposits of material relating to Fowler's Brewery. Reference is made in the text to material obtained at these places. The Local History Department of East Lothian Council's Library Service has comprehensive and detailed resources on East Lothian, including Prestonpans, comprising microfilmed editions of the local press, parish and census records, indexes of sasines and much more, again cited in the text where appropriate. The Local History Centre also collects unpublished work and publishes contemporary material. Panners' interest in history has resulted in a number of publications over the years, such as '*The 'Pans Remembered*' and the recent '*Tales of the 'Pans*'. Those, and other similar sources, often provide a detailed insight into old Prestonpans unavailable elsewhere. Individual works are referenced throughout the text.

While all proper care has been taken to ensure these references are comprehensive, any omissions are the error of the author, for which apologies are tendered.

APPENDIX 1
FOWLER'S BREWERY, A VICTORIAN DESCRIPTION

The following extract came from Volume 4 of Alfred Barnard's '*Noted Breweries of Great Britain and Ireland* (1889–91)' and has been extracted from Peter McNeill's '*Prestonpans and Vicinity*'. It affords a comprehensive description of the Prestonpans Brewery operation in the late Victorian period at a time when Robert Hunt White was leading its development. Some notes have been appended to the end. See also the Introduction to Brewing, Appendix 3 here.

After a preamble describing the foundation and development of the brewery in the hands of the Fowlers and their successors the Hislops, Barnard compliments the White family, confirming the managing role of Robert Hunt White in passing, and then describes the brewery.

> 'The ales of Prestonpans have become a household word in Scotland, and their reputation dates back more than a century. J. Parker Lawson, in his work, speaks of Prestonpans ale as a celebrated beverage, and the brewery extensive. But we must now hasten to make our readers acquainted with this venerable brewery and its fine business.
>
> On the east side of the ancient town of Prestonpans stands Laird Fowler's brewery, and, in close proximity, its numerous subsidiary maltings. The walls, and one or two outlying buildings of the original brewery, are still standing, and contain, among other things, a peculiarly shaped ten-barrel brewing copper, and a quaint-looking old pump, which formed a portion of the ancient plant. Equally interesting is the laird's dwelling-house, a roomy low-pitched building, which has been altered into a counting-house and offices, joined on to which is a new structure, containing a board room, managing partner's office, a sample room, and lavatories.[1]
>
> The new brewery, built by Laird Fowler, is opposite the old one, covers

upwards of an acre of ground, and is situated close to the margin of the sea on the north side. The premises consist of a number of massive stone buildings, grouped around a courtyard, the most important of which comprise the brewhouse, fermenting rooms, and *above-ground* cellars. So close are these buildings to the sea, that in rough weather the waves dash up against their walls, in magnificent style, as they did during the time of our visit.

Some of the malthouses are even more ancient than the old brewery, having been erected in the seventeenth century. Beneath the ground floor of one of them, now used for storing ales, are subterraneous caverns called the 'Catacombs', which are curiously constructed and of great extent.[2] Another of the maltings formed part of an extensive distillery, which, in the days of James II, was famous for its whisky.[3]

On entering the offices of Mr R. H. White, the managing director, we were entertained by that gentleman with a brief history of the brewery. Afterwards we were introduced to the head brewer, Mr Armstrong, who directed us through the brewery, and finally took us to the maltings. We commenced our observations at the malthouse, a two-storied building to the left of the entrance, and adjoining the brewhouse. It is used for receiving and storing malt from the various malthouses and contains, on the ground floor, the mill chamber. The room is paved with stone, and contains one of Milne's malt mills, enclosing a pair of pressed rollers capable of crushing thirty-five quarters of malt per hour. Before reaching the rolls the malt is most effectually screened in the following manner. The malt hopper is situated about 18 feet from the rolls, and the malt is conveyed thither by a propeller 11 feet long inside a cylinder.[4] This propeller is fashioned to act as conveyor and polisher and delivers into the malt screen. We do not remember having seen anything like it before. It was designed by Messrs Milne & Son to meet the special requirements here and has been found to work admirably. When the malt has been crushed between the rolls it is carried by an elevator to the top of the building, and thence, by an Archimedean screw to the gristcase depending over the tuns. The remainder of this floor is used for storing cumins in sacks and for a fitter's shop.

Pursuing our way upstairs to the top floor we passed an enormous flywheel connected with the shafting of the main engine which is for driving the mill machinery and working the pumps.

The whole extent of the large room above is used for storing malt and, fixed in the floor, is a hopper into which the sacks are tipped, when the malt disappears as fast as it is put in.[5]

Before following the crushed malt to its destination we have something to say about the water used which plays such an important part in a brewery. The brewing liquor is drawn from a well 80 feet deep situated in the old brewhouse[6] which has supplied the brewery for two centuries, and is of the finest quality. It is particularly free from objectionable matter which, along with the first-class material always used, accounts for the excellent keeping qualities of even the lightest ale made. Through an opening in the wall we passed into the brew-house, a square structure with an open roof and a paved floor. On the north side reached by a staircase in the centre, is a broad gallery, on which the coppers are erected and over them, at a slight elevation, a special copper tank for heating brewing water which holds 100 barrels. On the floor of the house, which measures 50 feet square, are three cast-iron mash-tuns having a total capacity of forty quarters – viz., eight, twelve, and twenty quarters. The difference in the capacity of these vessels indicates the successive and proportionate increase of the trade during the last half century. These tuns, all of which are fitted with covers, telescopic spargers[7], and slotted iron draining plates, are commanded by an extra size portable Steel's mashing machine which possesses a 5 feet gun-metal cylinder and runs on wheels.

In the basement of the building is a very capacious under-back for receiving the contents of all the mash-tuns, and from whence the wort is pumped direct to the coppers.

Following our guide, we ascended to the copper-stage to take a peep at the insides of the three coppers which hold respectively thirty-five, seventy, and eighty barrels. They are all supplied with boiling fountains and are heated by fire. As we approached them the copper-man, as he is called, was emptying the hops from the bags into the boiling wort and their fragrance soon filled the air with appetising odour. The hop-store, afterwards visited, occupies the upper floor of the beer-bottling house and is capable of holding 300 pockets.

Leaving the coppers behind us, we descended to the mashing floor to inspect the hopback built into a recess on that level. It is a square vessel, holding ninety barrels and beneath it, sunk into the floor, is a receiver 10 feet deep into which the strained wort runs. From there it is pumped to the coolers by a powerful three-throw pump. We next bent our steps to the top of the adjoining building where the cooling department is situated. On our way thither a capacious tank was pointed out to us, holding 200 barrels which receives the waste water from the refrigerator. It commands a large oval heating tank heated by exhaust steam and its contents are used for flushing down the tun-rooms, for cask-washing, and other purposes.

The cooling room is a spacious and lofty chamber some 50 feet in length with louvred walls. How the wind from over the sea whistled through those louvres and how glad we were to turn our backs on this chilly place! Nearly the whole of the floor is covered by an open cooler in the centre of which is a fan driven round by steam-power. At the east end of the room is fixed a large refrigerator of the Morton type cooling wort at the rate of forty barrels per hour. From this level a few steps lead down into the fermenting house, 110 feet in length, which contains a range of fermenting rooms extending its whole distance. They are well lighted, most effectively ventilated, and kept beautifully sweet and clean. The fermenting process conducted in this brewery is that known to brewers as the cleansing system.

In the No. 1 room, first entered we were shown three copper-lined fermenting vessels fitted with modern attemperators and each holding seventy barrels. The tops of these vessels, as well as those afterwards visited, are reached by a latticed staging through which we could see the busy workmen in the racking and other rooms below.

The second chamber contains five fermenting squares constructed of massive blocks of slate each vessel holding about sixty barrels and weighing many tons. Passing through a lofty doorway we came to the No. 3 fermenting room, the last of the series, which contains five more of these ponderous slate vessels lined with copper, two of which hold forty-five and three sixty barrels.

Bearing round to the left we reached the yeast room where the barm is stored either for pitching purposes or for sale to the distillers, beyond which is the finings factory where we saw heaps of the finest quality of isinglass being manipulated for fining the beers. Ascending some steps we reached two settling-back rooms situated over a portion of the cellars, one of which contains six settling squares lined with copper and having attemperators, and the other the same number of settling-backs but constructed of slate. There is also a capacious vat for finishing stout and porter.

Our next visit was to the cellars which are situated on the ground level and have a frontage to the sea of 260 feet. They are four in number all laid with cement. Together, these cellars will store upwards of 5,000 barrels. At the time of our visit they contained more than half that number spread out on the floor. In order, however, to make room for the increasing trade it has been found necessary to add considerably to the cellarage accommodation. The space where the old stabling stood has been utilised for this purpose and a handsome addition made to the cellars with a loading-stage, etc., for wagons, the floor being arranged at a convenient height for this purpose.

From the No. 4 cellar we made our way into the beer-bottling store, situated in a fine building over which is the hop store. Here the famous Prestonpans specially brewed ale, as well as the twelve-guinea Crown Ale, is bottled. The operations are conducted in the same manner as at other large breweries. Adjoining is an empty-bottle store and beyond the sampling cellar, where a sample cask of every brew is staged for reference, etc.'

NOTES

1. The Old Brewery on the south side of the High Street
2. The 'Catacombs' are further elaborated on by Peter McNeill in *Prestonpans and Vicinity*. Much of the oldest parts of the seaside settlements of Prestonpans, Cuthill and Morrison's Haven had extensive, ancient cellarage
3. This is not the distillery floated by the Cadells, John Fowler and Robert Hislop in the 1820s–40s. That was at Harlaw Hill on the opposite side of the street and further west. Prior to that function the distillery building had formed part of the Vitriol Works (perhaps the main manufactory lying as it did in the centre of the site). However, the observation is an indication of the antiquity of some of the buildings lying within the 'new' brewery complex and of the variety of uses to which they were once applied. It might also mean that this site could be added to the list of Prestonpans Breweries explored in the first discussion – an eighteenth century brewery differed in little respect from a distillery once the equipment was stripped out
4. A variant on the Archimedean screw subsequently mentioned adapted so that tumbled malt would be efficiently stripped of husks and presumably with walls fretted to separate waste
5. The complexities and capacities of much of the Brewery equipment afforded many opportunities for accident to the unwary worker. This account appeared in the *Haddingtonshire Courier* on 14 August 1863: 'on Thursday last a sad accident occurred in the malting premises of Messrs Fowler & Co. Malt is usually stored in large separate compartments of wood, which reach to a height of several storeys, and have their outlet below in various funnel shaped openings by which malt is removed in bags as required. While drawing off bags, the content of one of these compartments, getting coved out beneath and ceasing to run freely, a young lad who was employed about the works went up into one of the upper divisions and either leaping down on the malt or falling through the open joisting was immediately engulphed. A person ran to the boy's assistance but life was quite extinct. He was about 15 years of age and the principal support of his widowed mother'
6. RHP 23482, surveyed in 1851 by James Hay, shows this well clearly. It lay behind the south-east corner of the old brewery itself set back on the south side of the High Street. It is one of two wells marked on the plan at this site but is the only one connected to the new brewery by water pipes. The brewery also drew water from a second well at the east end of the new brewery site between the stables and the 'vaults', the above-ground cellars alluded to above. The old wells were often the source of tales in their own right: see Appendix 2
7. Brewing terms are explained in Appendix 3

APPENDIX 2
A TALE OF THE OLD BREWERY WELL
(FROM PETER MCNEILL, PRESTONPANS AND VICINITY, 1902)

'About the beginning of last century (1827) the proprietor of those gardens towards the east end of the village in which the old draw-well, known as the brewery well, is situate, sent three of his workmen to have the well thoroughly cleaned out. No one knew when this well had been sunk, and no one knew that it had ever been thoroughly cleansed before. Down went two of the men, and the third, Bill Baxter, well known previously as an artful dodger, elected to stay above ground the first day and row the rubbish up. "About mid-day they struck oil" in the form of stone jars all apparently choke-full with mud, and seeing that they were not home made, the men at the bottom took great care in sending them up entire. All had been sent up but one, and when searching for more, one of the men at the bottom of the well accidentally struck the jar with his spade and broke it, when out tumbled quite a number of foreign silver coins.

'The men at the bottom, not wishing to raise any suspicion of what they had discovered, cried up to Bill Baxter to rest himself for an hour or so, "because they had broken a jar and wished to fish its contents out of the water". "All right", replied Bill, "and I will take care that nobody gets here to disturb you while engaged in fishing". An hour passed. Two hours passed, and only when about another half hour had gone the two men were 'rowed' to the top. But there was no Bill Baxter there to welcome them. Bill had learned what the jars contained long before his fellows at the bottom of the well, and engaged a man to make sure that they would not get up till he had time to be out of the way. He hired, and drove into Leith with the jars and contents, and disposed of all of them. He was never again heard of but once, from America, but he never returned.

'The proprietor and the two workmen divided the contents of the broken jar amongst them. They were Dutch silver coins, and all about the size of crown pieces. These coins are well remembered yet in the village, and some as curiosities may still be in keeping of the natives. They were of the 14th or 15th century. But how the jars and contents came to be deposited there is a mystery. The general opinion is that some piratical gang had to do with the business, and had forgotten all about them. This may be so, but perhaps the people in Prestonpans had to do with the piratical gang, otherwise they might not have known there was a brewery well in the garden. Subsequently there was another jar got in the well, filled with coins relating to the Stuart dynasty. Several of them are yet in possession of the proprietors of these grounds. It is quite possible that they were all deposited there for security during the '45 Rebellion'.

N.B. This tale, if accurate, may represent the finding of a local merchant's hidden reserves. It is unlikely in the extreme that the events of the '45 could cause such a deposit. However, the local disruption of the Cromwellian period around 1650 and the association of Morrison's Haven with that General may provide a more authentic cause.

APPENDIX 3
BREWING BEER – AN OUTLINE

The brewing trade has a language all of its own. To illustrate some of the terms this note will follow the process from grain to ale. Although the equipment might have altered over the years both Robert Fowler of the eighteenth century and JB Laing of the later twentieth would have been each at home in the other's facility.

East Lothian's breweries relied upon local barley, a prime resource much in demand as well by Edinburgh's trade. It was soaked in a tank (steep, steep-stone, malt steep, stoup) and allowed to germinate on a covered floor. This procedure activates (and maximises) enzymes in the grain. Germination was halted by transferring the malt into a kiln (distinctive square buildings with tapering, conical roofs topped with a vent) for drying. Care was taken to ensure complete drying by hand turning, the work of a 'maltman' under the direction of a 'maltster'. Even in the Victorian period, powered automated dryers were available but to produce the best malt many works continued to use open floors. The degree of roasting produced different (coloured) grades of malt. Pale malt, produced at low temperature and with all of its enzymes intact, was usually made. Crystal and Chocolate malts were made by longer roasting and tended to be used for 'colour' and texture in the finished product.

A quantity of malt, crushed, rolled or cracked before use, often measured as 'quarters'(1 quarter = 8 bushels; 1 bushel = 8 gallons), was placed in the mash-tun, a squat vessel usually made of copper. (It must be noted here that Fowler's retained their own, archaic scale of measurement and details are given by Margaret Black in her memoir in *Tales of the Pans*.) Frequently other grains and grain derivatives were used to augment the malt. The malt sat on a horizontal partition in the mash tun, which was fretted with drain-holes. Hot water from a tank was sprinkled over the malt via a 'sparger', any of numerous forms of sprinkler or agitation device. The water activates the enzymes present in the malt, which then convert starch to soluble sugars forming a solution termed 'wort'. Wort was collected in an 'under-back' or receiving tank before being pumped to the copper. The copper generally took the form of a deep, circular open-topped vessel made or sheathed in that metal. The capacity was measured in barrels (1 barrel = 36 gallons), and they were heated directly (an under furnace) by steam pipes or by boiling fountains. At this stage hops or other bittering agent were added and as required 'colour' or a caramel solution. The use of hops is of comparatively recent origin in British brewing. We have already seen that one observer believed Fowler's were the first to use them in East Lothian. Their preservative effect afforded a distinct advantage to both the keeping and transporting properties of the finished product. Prior to the use of hops a wide variety of agents was used to provide flavour. One recipe for porter which was popular in East Lothian and a staple of nineteenth century breweries recommends the use of treacle and 'colour' (caramel solution) with liquorice root, salt of tartar (sodium tartrate), and capsicum to taste!

The wort was strained via a hop-back and receiver and cooled before being made up to volume with water. At this stage its specific gravity was measured for the purposes of calculating duty. The duty was once expressed as a value per barrel and, having been at a stable rate for many years, the duty rate was extrapolated to the name of the ale itself – thus 60/-, 70/-, 80/-.

From the cooler the wort passed to fermenting vessels where 'barm' (fresh yeast solution skimmed from the top of an earlier fermentation) was 'pitched'. The vessels were either copper or stone lined and were open-topped. Attemperators regulated the temperature of the liquor, which after fermentation passed to settling tanks (settling-backs) from where it was filtered, fined and finished by a conditioning stage usually in cask (barrel) in the establishment's cellars. Some breweries might hold conditioned beer in a conditioning tun if it were to be bottled. Others would bottle from the cask for smaller amounts. 'Fining' was the final process of clarifying the beer. Finings were prepared from gelatin, originally derived from the air bladders of freshwater fish such as sturgeon but subsequently prepared from animal hide or hoof and some seaweeds. Fowler's had their own finings factory. The effect of fining was to sequester the last remaining particulate matter in the beer and deposit it as a sticky precipitate at the bottom of the cask or bottle.

As many of these stages were conducted in open vessels and as the process required the use of a whole sequence of vessels, scrupulous attention had to be paid to cleanliness. The fermenting houses in particular were often tiled throughout and copious amounts of water were used to wash down building interiors and vessels. At one stage, the Fowlers in particular would have had a distinct advantage in this regard as the Prestonpans' chemical (and soap) industry would have been well placed to provide bleaches and detergents that other brewers would have had more difficulty in securing.

Postscript

In 2004 Fowler's Ales (Prestongrange) under the brand name of Prestonpans Ales was brewed once again under the leadership of Craig Allan, a distant descendent of a Fowler's cooper and brewer. Working from a microbrewery at the Prestoungrange Gothenberg 80/=, IPA, Porter and in 2006 a '45 wee heavie have all been successfully launched.

13

The Prestoungrange Gothenburg

The Goth's first 90 years and the coming decade

Gordon Prestoungrange

Permissions

The photographs included in this text, the proceeds of which go to charity, are reproduced with permission of those who hold copyright, including East Lothian Library Services Local History Collections, the Royal Commission on the Ancient and Historical Monuments of Scotland, Alister Tulloch and Stenlake Publishing of Glasgow. We are most grateful to them for this assistance.

INTRODUCTION

The Goth, as it is affectionately known in Prestonpans, played a significant part in the town's social life throughout the 20th Century, closing its doors some 90 years after they first opened in 1908. In 1998 Scott Murray, the Lions and Scotland rugby star, and his father John, purchased it to transform into their private family residence upstairs and a bistro below. But they were not able to achieve that ambition and in 2001 they passed the baton to the Baron and Lady of Prestoungrange to see it through. This short history of The Gothenburg Public House in Prestonpans has been collated so that as the doors reopen in 2003 a better understanding can exist of:

- why *The Goth* was built and by whom;
- what the real connection was with Gothenburg (Goteborg) in Sweden;
- how, as best as fragmentary documentation and recollection allows, *The Goth* fared over its first 90 years;

Drinking selflessly for the good of Dalkeith (not Prestonpans) photographed as part of the annual parade to raise funds for the Edinburgh Royal Infirmary. The company built Dalkeith's Black Bull pub, but strangely there are no records of consequent improvements to the town. In the 1930s the Gothenburg constitution changed to the extent that it lost popularity with both members and the public, resulting in the movement dying out.
from Rhona Wilson, Old Dalkeith, Stenlake Publishing, Glasgow

The Gothenburg sign from 1986

- how other 'Gothenburg' initiatives fared across Britain;
- when the architecture and interior decor of *The Goth* were designated as an important element in the town's heritage; and
- where and how it is planned for *The Goth* to go forward over the next decade to 2013 when its doors will proudly claim to have stood open for Panners for a century.

As the story unfolds it will be clearly seen that it has not been 90 years of unremitting philanthropic delight. The Edinburgh founders survived for just a single a decade in Prestonpans before they sold out to the English in London! The Gothenburg ethos was never as strongly felt in Prestonpans as occurred elsewhere because of its absentee owners in Edinburgh and London. Other Gothenburg-inspired public houses in Scotland, most spectacularly Dean Tavern at Newtongrange, have been and still are far better exemplars of the principles and beliefs espoused by their very local founders.

None of which is intended to be churlish about the past. It quite simply is what it was. And as we approach the reopening the espoused principles and beliefs of the founders are very much back on parade for the first time since 1919. 21st Century 'ownership' is re-vested in the town itself in the person of each and every future patron who crosses the threshold of *The Goth* from 2003.

But before we get into the future, we must surely get back to the past. (And in telling the tale rough estimates of present day 2002 monetary values will be give in brackets alongside the nominal values at the time.)

1. 1908 AND ALL THAT

Prestonpans was certainly buzzing with speculative blether throughout 1908 as its new Gothenburg Public House was being constructed. Not for its promoters, the East of Scotland Public House Trust, the delays and consultations associated with planning consents, building and fire regulations, health, safety and the rest of today's palaver. From the day they purchased the lands and raised £2000 (£400 000 at today's prices) from Thomas Nelson's family Trust by way of a secured loan in 1908, to the day the doors opened, was less than 12 months.

The press gave brief objective reports on good construction progress and finally factual confirmation of its formal opening at the beginning of December. No records have yet been found of brass or pipe bands a-playing or 'happy hours' although surely there must have been some celebrations to mark the event. Maybe the weather in early December 1908 was none too encouraging and everyone was better off indoors by the grand fireplaces. This was how the local newspaper reported:

James Fewell with his family and staff circa 1909 outside the Trust Tavern

> *"The new Gothenburg ... premises which have now been opened ... are picturesque and quaint in character, being of that pleasing style associated with the old English hostelries of bygone centuries. The blending of colour with the red stone and brick in the lower portion of the walls in contrast to the white harling of the upper walls and chimneys, and gables is very effective, while the grouping of red tiled roofs, heavy projecting timbered gables, and the quaint lattice windows, all go to secure a most picturesque and appropriate new building to the environs of historic Prestonpans.*
>
> *Although the exterior is medieval in character, the internal planning and arrangements compare favourably with modern restaurants and tea rooms now recently erected in large cities. The street floor is occupied by tavern, dining room, kitchen, and the most modern lavatory equipment, while the upper floor is occupied by a spacious, quaintly designed temperance restaurant and tea rooms which commands extensive views of the Firth and its coastlines.*
>
> *To meet the wants of pedestrians and cyclists in good weather, there is in the rear of the building a well laid out tea garden."*

Maggie Fewell takes up the story as best we can recount. Her father, James Fewell, was the Gothenburg's second manager, taking over very soon after the opening from a Mr. Mercer. James had been Assistant Manager from the outset, and when Mr Mercer was transferred to The Red Lion in Culross Fife,

James Fewell with the bar staff circa 1909 with boards promoting snacks and sandwiches. He remained as Manager until 1927

another Gothenburg style public house acquired by the East of Scotland Public House Trust in 1907, he was the obvious choice to succeed.

By all accounts, including those of his daughter, he ran a truly excellent establishment right through the war years until 1927. He was always to be seen, and the 1909 photographs we have support the folklore, in a black tie with the premises immaculate. In fact his reign as manager saw both the coming and the going of the East of Scotland Public House Trust with its Swedish style, community based, vision for temperance. The East of Scotland Public Houses Trust sold out all its interests to Earl Grey's London based Trust House Limited in 1919.

Maggie Fewell, writing to the Prestonpans Historical Society in 1984 from her family home in Norfolk, remembered it vividly and remarkably well some 75 years later:

> *"There was a large circular bar with big fireplaces on each side of it, and mahogany bar tables on iron legs, and also comfortable seats. There was a large dining room where women could come in the evenings to have a drink and their children were allowed to accompany them, although this was not actively encouraged. Upstairs there was another big dining room where all types of functions were catered for including weddings, Burns' Dinners, Masonic meetings and many others.*
>
> *A daily supply of hot coffee and rolls was provided free for the men who came from the early shift and* The Scotsman, Sporting Life *and evening papers were also supplied for the men to weigh up form if they wished.*
>
> *My father was a stickler for cleanliness and the green-tiled bar was always kept highly polished. Should any child dare to draw on the outside walls a*

barman was immediately detailed to take Prestonpans soap and a scrubbing brush to clean it off, so always keeping the premises spotlessly clean both inside and out.

My father received a bonus on food and soft drinks but nothing on the sale of beer and spirits. Hot pies were available and sandwiches cut on request – they cost 2d (£1.60) and 1d (80p) doorstep style with roast beef.

Each autumn a dominoes competition started, ending at Christmas. Prizes were joints of beef in various weights as well as bottles and half bottles of whisky, rum and port. The meat would be cooked for anyone who did not have the facility at home, the wives bringing bowls for dripping and gravy. This food was paid for by the Trust as were the soup kitchens in use during the various Pit strikes. The soup kitchens would serve good Scotch broth plus a thick slice of bread for each of the men's families.

During the Great War a section of the upstairs dining room was blocked off for the military who were assigned to patrol the coast. There was a wooden staircase leading to a balcony which led into the dining room. This contained a messing room used by the men billeted there – some seven men of the RSF – and at the same time sixteen officers of the Argylls also fed there, despite the difficulty of finding staff with so many women doing munitions work. My mother, aided by one Army cook, three friends and myself did all the catering for these men as well as continuing to provide coffee and rolls for those men still working at the Pit.

The East of Scotland Public House Trust was eventually wound up because so many members had lost their lives in the Great War, and The Gothenburg became part of the London-based Trust Houses Limited which changed the whole format taking any profits for themselves. However, by that time the miners had pit head baths – a great blessing to the men and their wives. And plans to build the Miners' Institutes had begun. My father, who was a local Councillor and Bailie left Prestonpans for Bellingham, Nr Catford in London in 1927 for a Barclay Perkins house where there were no bars at all and men could bring their womenfolk and children, have food and drinks at tables and were waited upon by waiters and waitresses and able to watch a show. This was an extension of the Gothenburg idea."

2. WHY THE GOTH WAS BUILT AND BY WHOM

The Goth in Prestonpans was the creation of a group of investors who had registered their new Company in Edinburgh on April 22nd 1901, and their Prospectus offering 50 000 × £1 (£200) shares was issued on May 13th with a closing date on or before 20th May that same year. An initial payment of 1/- (£10) was required, and up to 3d or 25% of that 1/- could be accorded as commission to a broker.

From the very outset they may well have had a new Gothenburg in Prestonpans on their list of potential locations for their bold temperance initiatives, but they began in earnest elsewhere. In 1903 they acquired The White Hart Inn in Grassmarket, Edinburgh and built The Gothenburg at Glencraig, Ballingry in Fife. In 1905 they acquired The Anchor Bar in Kincardine, Fife, The Town Hall Bar in Dufftown, Banff and finally The Mansion House in Prestonpans. Their Company was known as the East of Scotland Public House Trust and was a copycat initiative for several others already occurring across the British Isles. But why were they and others doing it?

Today we are continually aware of the escalating problems arising from the use of drugs ranging from tobacco up and down the hazardous chain of consequences. *The Goth's* founders were most especially aware of the problems arising from excess of alcohol. These problems were scarcely new then and they have certainly not gone wholly away in contemporary times. But at the end of the 19th Century and the dawn of the 20th there was a very great determination amongst the caring classes, most especially religious leaders and early social welfare analysts and reformers such as the Rowntrees, to do something sensible beyond advising one and all to 'take the pledge' of abstinence.

There was at that time only a mild manifestation of that clamour that eventually led across the Atlantic to total but ineffectual prohibition by Amendment to the US Constitution and to patterns of prohibition across Canada with the exception of Quebec. Nationalisation or municipal socialism were, however, a fashionable and hotly debated proposition and, as we shall later discuss, that monopolistic approach to temperance was introduced and held sway from 1915 most conspicuously in Carlisle but also in Gretna and Cromarty in Scotland.

Balfour's Government in 1904 introduced major changes in licensing laws which in time had the effect of reducing the number of places where alcohol could be purchased and drunk, but the social welfare drive which gave us *The Goth* was for temperance. It preceded Balfour's reforms by well over half a century. It had been facilitated under the Industrial and Providential Societies Act of 1893 that allowed the proceeds of drink sold in co-operative public houses to be used to provide civic amenities. Put simply, the Gothenburg style pursuit of temperance was to be advanced by taking profiteering out of selling alcohol whilst at the same time promoting the sale of food. All forms of recreation were to be encouraged from the surpluses arising at the public house. To achieve this a different pattern of private ownership of public houses was believed to be required which, whilst seeking and being entitled to a reasonable return on the necessary capital investments made, would thereafter put all surplus profits back into the local community. These funds, managed by worthy trustees, were then to be used to engineer new opportunities for leisure for the working man and thereby divert his focus away from drinking alcohol as his major leisure pursuit.

2.1 Nelson and the Temperance Team that Built *The Goth* at Prestonpans

The East of Scotland Public House Trust was seemingly established by eight investors, subscribing immediately for 100 × £1 (= £20 000) shares each, after a meeting at 29 Rutland Square, Edinburgh, the offices of the Company's solicitors Young & Roxburgh and of the first Company Secretary, James Roxburgh. The funds were deposited with Clydesdale Bank in Edinburgh and the auditors appointed were J & W Pollard, C.A., of Edinburgh. They were an interesting grouping of a Member of Parliament, landowning Justices of the Peace who presumably regularly reviewed the results of alcohol excess, law officers, a doctor and a merchant. Why and how precisely they came together or who was the instigator is for us now lost in the mysteries of time but tangential literature suggests they would have known Earl Grey and those associated with him in broadscale British and Irish initiatives in 1901. The East of Scotland Trust is specifically mentioned in Rowntree and Sherwell's writings then – of which more later. One of their number, John Ross, with only a little artistic licence applied, could well have been the catalyst.

The initial eight investors were **R C Munroe Ferguson**, a landowner of Novar House, Rosshire who did not make the journey to Edinburgh so his signature was interestingly witnessed earlier at his home by his Chef de Cuisine, L Badelino. Nor was **George G Tod**, a Merchant of 19 Moray Place, Edinburgh able to be present and he asked E Denholm Young, WS, to act as his agent. The other six founding members of the Temperance Team were present on April 18th 1901 with Douglas Wilson as their common witness. They were **Will C Smith**, Advocate of 57 Northumberland Street, Edinburgh; **John Ross**, Solicitor of Dunfermline; **George Wilson**, Doctor of Medicine of Linden Lodge, Loanhead; **C H Scott Plummer**, landowner of Sunderland Hall, Selkirk; **Jas F Roxburgh**, Writer to the Signet already referred to above; and finally **Thomas A Nelson**, Publisher of St Leonard's, Edinburgh.

Thomas Nelson III

Thomas A Nelson III (Tommy) was one of the best known amongst them. He was to serve as a director until his death at the Battle of Arras in 1917 and was particularly significant in respect of *The Goth* in Prestonpans. He came from the quite exceptional family of Thomas Neilson who arrived in Edinburgh from Bannockburn in 1798 to open a second hand bookshop at the head of West Bow near St Giles' Cathedral, changing his name to Nelson in 1818. His name change was at a time when Lord Nelson was well remembered and he reputedly quipped: *"Like the naval hero of the same name, I have sacrificed an 'i' in a good cause"*.

He and then the next two generations of his family created one of Scotland's greatest book publishing enterprises, Thomas Nelson of Edinburgh, over the course of the next century and a half until it was sold out to Canadian media owner Lord Thomson and found an English base in London from 1968 most recently at Walton on Thames, Surrey. (Pleasingly Lord Thomson's family were of Scottish origin and he chose his baronial title as 'of Fleet, of Northbridge in the City of Edinburgh'.) The Nelsons' originating and sustaining motivation until well after the Great War was an evangelical zeal to spread the Word of God and secular publishing was the way to cross-subsidise that work. The focus until 1845 was on reprints of the classics, clearly seen to have an unsatisfied demand from their second hand book shop perspective. Selling spread to England with a branch at 35 Paternoster Row in London. In 1850 Thomas Nelson Yr. perfected a rotary press which was demonstrated at the Great Exhibition in Hyde Park in 1851 and was the parent of all newspaper presses until the later stages of the 20th Century. In 1854 a branch was opened at 42 Bleecker Street, New York and later still they extended to France and Germany. Their most famous American author was R M Ballantyne writing of his experiences with the Hudson's Bay Company in *Snow Flakes and Sunbeams, The Young Fur-Traders, Ungava, The Coral Island and Martin Rattler.* The family parted company with R M Ballantyne over the royalty/copyright assignment in his titles which worked most considerably to Nelson's advantage.

Later they had a longstanding editorial relationship with John Buchan who eventually became Governor General of Canada as Lord Tweedsmuir, an office also held earlier by the active temperance reformer Earl Grey (founder of the English Trust Houses Company in 1903 that acquired *The Goth* in 1919 after Thomas Nelson III's death). John Buchan's most famous book, *The Thirty Nine Steps* was published in 1915 whilst Thomas Nelson was at war and dedicated:

> *"To Thomas A Nelson, Lothian and Border Horse. My dear Tommy, you and I have long cherished an affection for that elementary type of tale which the Americans call the dime novel and which we know as 'the shocker' – the romance where the incidents defy the probabilities and march just inside the border of the possible. During an illness last winter I exhausted my store of these aids to cheerfulness, and was driven to write one myself. This little volume is the result, and I should like to put your name on it, in memory of our long friendship, in these days when the wildest fictions are so much less improbable than the facts".*

Tommy's death left the family publishing enterprise in the hands of his brother Ian who remained with it until his death in 1958. Ian lived in Aberdeen married to the daughter of an Australian. Tommy's wife Margaret had borne him two sons and two daughters after their marriage in 1903. After his premature death at 41 she was to later remarry to Paul Maze from Le Havre but that ended in divorce in 1949. She died in 1967.

C H Scott Plummer

C H Scott Plummer was 18 years Tommy's senior, but also served as a Major in the Great War in the Lothians & Border Horse. They surely knew one another well before that tragic episode. Scott Plummer survived the slaughtrous conflict later becoming Convenor of Selkirk County Council and H M Lieutenant from 1919 until his death in 1948 aged 89.

R C Munro-Ferguson, later Lord Novar

Perhaps the most internationally famous member of the founding Temperance Team was he who was unable to make the original subscribers' meeting and got his Chef de Cuisine to witness his signature at his home in Ross-shire, namely R C Munro-Ferguson of Raith & Novar. At the time he joined the subscribers he had already been a Member of Parliament since age 24 as his father and grandfather had been before him. But he did not follow them into an army career per se although he served in the Grenadier Guards and the Fifeshire Light Horse. He chose and shone in politics becoming Private Secretary to the Earl of Rosebery at 26 and a Junior Lord of the Treasury aged 34 when the Earl became Prime Minister. And his future life after 1901 held a very great deal more in store for him than the work of the East of Scotland Public House Trust. In 1910, he became a Privy Councillor. He necessarily resigned as an MP and was knighted in 1914 before departing to become Governor General and C-in-C of the Commonwealth of Australia where he served throughout the Great War. He returned after six years in Canberra to become the first and only Viscount Novar and within two years he held office from the House of Lords as Secretary of State for Scotland under both Bonar-Law and Baldwin between 1922 and 1924. His final honour was to be made a Knight of the Thistle in 1926. He had married Lady Helen, eldest daughter of the Marquess of Dufferin and Ava in 1889, but he died in 1934 aged 74, without an heir. Before he died he did however play a significant further role in the temperance movement of which more later.

John Ross, later Sir John

The notion that John Ross, the Solicitor from Dumfermline, was the vital catalyst stems from the Prospectus issued in 1901 which gives key details of the initiatives with which John Ross had already been engaged. There is also an extensive discussion of his previous work elsewhere by Rowntree and Sherwell.

His significant involvement in temperance activities arose from being solicitor to the Fife Coal Company whose Managing Director, Charles Carlow, had asked him in 1896 to assist in getting a Gothenburg going at the Hill of Beath, near Crossgates. He proved not only to have the legal skills, but also the determination and organising skills to help mean-gooders actually do some good. If he brought the necessary energy to the challenge, the other founding investors could bask in the goodwill they achieved by association. Certainly many distinguished figures in Scotland were signing up in Glasgow.

The Hill of Beath Tavern was originally funded in 1896 by the Fife Coal Company with a dividend cap of 4%, but was sold in 1900 for £1300 (£260 000) to a local Public House Society in which miners were amongst the shareholders. The Society significantly included a rule that no matter how many shares an individual might hold, each was only entitled to one vote, a notion that many social reformers at the time felt to be a wise way forward. There were no Trustees as such. The Society in general meeting was empowered to allocate the surpluses after a 5% dividend cap. It took a determined decision that recreation should *not* be provided at the public house but away from it completely. This led to quite separate provision of an Institute and Reading Room, a bowling green, singing classes, a football club and, top of the list, electric lighting of the village. All this had been achieved before 1901. John Ross was clearly an experienced temperance activist.

However, John Ross' reputation as a man who got results did not come without its critics. Rowntree and Sherwell were critical that village electricity should have been paid for out of the surplus proceeds from the public house. Since the coal mine owned the village they saw that as the mine's responsibility not the customers at the public house. Their criticism did not stop there however. They were doubtful about John Ross' second major initiative as solicitor to the Fife Coal Company, that at the Kelty Public House Society. This had arisen from an invited lecture he gave in Kelty on the Gothenburg system in 1899 and his subsequent Proposal (based entirely on the Hill of Beath Society but with 5/- [£50] rather than £1 [£200] shares) to go into action there by seeking an *additional* licence in the town. His Proposal found no Seconder at a public meeting whilst a Resolution against it was carried. However, after much further debate it was resolved to take a plebiscite on the question and a committee was formed to see it through. The Gothenburg promoters elected not to join the committee which issued 1200 Voting Cards. 381 (32%) voted For, 738 (68%) voted Against, a majority against of 357 (29%).

The question put in the plebiscite was: "Are you opposed to the granting of a licence to the Kelty Public-House Company?" It was a double headed question in truth because it begged both the need for an additional facility and whether it should be a Gothenburg or not. But most significantly, John Ross would not take no for an answer. The Society proceeded. It issued 3473 shares @ 5/- fully paid realising £868 (£175 000), took a loan of £2000 (£400 000) from the Fife Coal Company and a further loan of £240 (£56 000) from John Ross personally. By year end 1900 the Society had profits of £602 (£120 000) on sales in excess of £3000 (£600 000). The Society had already allocated its surplus to support the local library and made plans to lay a bowling green for £500 (£100 000). By any measure this was no mean achievement. Its promoter was ready now for greater things perhaps. In responding to Rowntree and Sherwell they quote him as characterising his Fife initiatives as "little more than experiments ... picking their way ... having been in existence for too short a time to show decisive results." Was the East of Scotland Public House Trust his brainchild, and the broadscale initiative that he must surely have dreamt of ?

2.2 The Administration of Surplus Profits and Paying the 5% Dividend

As will be more specifically discussed later, the Gothenburg principles implied a moderate rate of return to the capital invested, set by the Trust Company at 5% pa Cumulative, and the distribution of surplus profits arising thereafter to appropriate community causes. This latter task was initially to be undertaken for *The Goth* and all the other public houses owned by the East of Scotland Public House Trust by a truly most eminent independent Board of Trustees including three Baronets, two medical scholars and a Writer to the Signet viz. **Sir Ralph Anstruther** of Balcaskie, Pittenweem; **Sir T D Gibson Carmichael** of Castelcraig, Dolphinton; **Sir Michael Thomson** of 6 Charlotte Square, Edinburgh; a neighbour **Professor John Chiene** CB FRCSE of 26 Charlotte Square; **Dr T S Clouston** MD FRCP of Tipperlinn House, Morningside, Edinburgh; and **J P Wood** W S of 16 Buckingham Terrace, Edinburgh.

Records in *Burke's Landed Gentry: The Kingdom in Scotland* show Sir Ralph Anstruther serving as a JP and as H M Lieutenant of Fife after a Victorian military career in Egypt and Bechuanaland with the Black Watch. *Burke's* also shows Sir Thomas David Gibson Carmichael as Lord Lieutenant of Peebles; as Governor of Victoria, Australia from 1908–11; as Governor of Madras 1911–1912; of Bengal 1912–1917. He was knighted for his work in Australia and created 1st and only Baron Carmichael on his appointment in Madras. He had married Mary on July 1st 1896 but died in 1926 without a direct heir.

No specific records have so far come to light as to how long this initial Board of Trustees remained in office or what their particular allotments were or where they went. Certainly Sir Thomas's career overseas would have made his participation impractical by the time *The Goth* opened.

The best general indication we can derive from the accounts are that sums as high as £700 (£140 000) were available in 1910 to the Trustees for distribution across all the communities served by the Company. However that was the high point. Other good years showed £500 (£100 000) but the sums available collapsed from 1912 until 1916. By 1918 they had recovered handsomely so that £400 (£80 000) was available. By 1918 all the accumulated dividend arrears had been paid but of course there was no accumulation of any funds for distribution in the community. One cannot see John Ross as particularly pleased with such performance however. It should be borne in mind that these surplus allocations were across as many as 16 public houses and were scarcely better than what John Ross had achieved in Kelty from a single premises in 1900. In fact, he was no longer a director by 1910 and never acquired more than his initial 100 × £1 shares (£20 000), although he was alive and still holding them in 1919. His skill in the East of Scotland initiative had been in mobilising major funding from mean-gooders well beyond the single owner of a coal mine and its employees. But perhaps it was fools' gold. The absence of any deep sense of local connectivity might well have contributed to the undoing of the endeavour, making selling out to the English in 1919 a simple step.

As will be seen below, in 1918 the East of Scotland Public House Trust surplus was approximately equivalent to the 5% pa dividend being paid, indicating an overall notional rate of profit for distribution of 10% pa on the total capital employed after tax. That 5% was the measure of the philanthropic gesture made by the 79 investors who had subscribed for the shares at various times during the decade. The Trustees were at all times mandated to use it to provide funding for recreational activities which it was anticipated would divert the menfolk's attention away from alcohol. As Maggie Fewell has already recounted, free coffee and bread on the way home from the early morning shift was a permanent feature at *The Goth* right up until 1919 as were Scotch broth soup kitchens in times of Pit strikes and lock outs.

It is worth noting that the Trust Company never actually issued all its Authorised Capital of 50 000 × £1 (£200) shares at par (= £10m). Only £13 162 10/- (£2.6m) was realised from those 79 investors. Even the 13 160 shares issued were not all called up at once. By 1908 only 15/- (£150) had been called, but the final 5/- (£50) to make par value of £1 (£200) was called in 1910.

The dividend policy was set by the Memorandum and Articles of Association as 5% pa Cumulative. This was fully paid over the lifetime of the Trust Company although during The Great War its payment for years 1912/1917 was delayed. 1916 saw payment of the 1912 dividend arrears of £559 (£111 800) and the remaining accumulated arrears for 1913/ 1917 of £2467. 10/- (£493 400) were paid in 1918.

The 1908 Loan Note for £2 000 (£400 000) held by the Thomas Nelson Family Trust which funded the *The Goth* was also serviced at 5% pa until its repayment on June 30th 1915. It was secured against the lands and building erected in 1908 known significantly therein as The Trust Tavern, *not* The Gothenburg, and the owners were required to take out annual assurances of £2500 (£500 000). Other Debenture holders, notably C H Scott Plummer & Others from 1913 until August 3rd 1918, were similarly accorded no more than 5% pa. The repayment of the Nelson Loan that funded building *The Goth* had been the main reason for passing/ allowing the dividend to accumulate in 1913.

The land at High Street and Redburn Road on which *The Goth* was to be built was acquired early in 1907/1908 from the Executors of Margaret Stevenson and Trustees for the Bellfield Company for, respectively, £625 (£125 000) and a Ground Annual Rental of £12 (£2 400) and £12 payable every 19th year *in the name of grassum*. The Rev William Boag was persuaded at the same time to waive his claim over a parcel of the land in his Bond of Security for a loan to Bellfield and Company of £250 (£50 000). In 1909 the East of Scotland Public House Trust acquired a further piece of land for £115 (£23 000) from George Mackie, formerly of The Soap Works, in West End.

Whether or not 5% as a Cumulative Dividend on the shares or as interest on loans and debentures was satisfactory over any reasonable period of time depended on the beliefs and expectations of the investors. There was no opportunity under the Memorandum & Articles of Association for any capital gain on the shares issued. Certainly both the *Royal Commissions on Licensing in England & Wales* and in *Scotland* in 1931/ 1932 later found there was an inevitable limit on how many apparent philanthropes would step forward as the years went by particularly if the challenge of temperance was seemingly less great and even though the benchmark dividend had often increased after the Great War to 7.5% Cumulative per annum.

However, the macro perspective over the long term was not the concern of those at *The Goth* in Prestonpans. They had their excellent establishment with its fine lavatory equipment, and as it prospered we can estimate on a pro rata basis for the 16 licences it eventually held that sums might have been available in each of the communities served by the East of Scotland Trust of say £50 pa (£10 000). But as already reported there is thus far no precise evidence of how the Trustees determined their allocations across the communities or the potential beneficiaries.

2.3 Why Did They Sell Out to the English?

One of the most fascinating questions has to be: why did they sell out to the English in 1919? The accounts show that the Trust overall had a very good year in 1918. Net Profits from the Houses to year ending November 30th 1918 stood at £6 554 (£1.3m) before central overheads (including taxation of £607 (£121 400)) of £2 570 (£524 000) leaving a profit for the year to be taken to reserves of £4 074 (£814 800). Commission paid on Temperance Sales included in the central overheads was £56 (£11 200). £400 (£80 000) went to the Trustees. There were no loans outstanding at all.

1918 can be usefully compared with the pre-war year of 1911. The Houses were much more highly valued in the assets register then at £20 850 (£4.2m) after depreciation of £906 (£181 200), but assuming straight line depreciation was apparently being applied it was not surprising to find the book value of the Houses stood in 1918 at £12 681 (£2.5m) after depreciation that year of £839 (£167 800) which was probably a very substantial underestimate of realisable market value. 1911 Net Profit from Houses was £2 721 (£544 200) but central overheads and taxation – £100 (£20 000) – were much lower.

A higher level of some £83 (£16 600) on much lower sales was paid as Commission on Temperance Sales, an important aspect of The Gothenburg principles. Dividends at 5% on the Share Capital called up were paid at £522 (£104 400) and the Trustees received £500 (£100 000) for allocation. The loans outstanding were £5 000 (£1 000 000) but the interest paid thereon is seemingly taken into account elsewhere than in the final accounts presented since only £14 (£2 800) is shown therein which is less than the as yet not repaid £2 000 (£400 000) loan from Thomas Nelson would have required at 5% i.e. £100 (£20 000).

Trade creditors were well managed in both years standing at £1 884 (£376 000) in 1911 and at £1 417 (£283 400) in 1918, which latter figure is particularly satisfactory. Stock on hand was also satisfactory in both years once again but especially so in 1918. The comparative figures were 1911 £3 026 (£605 200) and 1918 £2 951 (£590 200).

By 1919 it was clear that the Trust had survived the Great War as a viable if not spectacular temperance entity. But it was also true that the shareholders were as much absentees from the public houses themselves as they had been at the Trust's foundation. None had ever lived in Prestonpans or indeed, apart from Edinburgh, in the other towns where the Trust's Gothenburg public houses were acquired or established. John Ross had been inactive for a decade. Maybe not surprisingly the four directors declared to the Registrar of Companies in Edinburgh on 26th June 1919, just four months before the sale to Trust Houses Limited at 227 Strand, London on October 21st, included just one of the original Temperance Team in the person of C H Scott Plummer, the landowner from Selkirk, who still owned 800 shares or 6%

The others were all new faces. Leslie Moubray from Aberdour owned 100 shares or under 1%; Charles Balfour from Kelso owned 350 or 2.6% and Charles Douglas from Lesmahagow who together with his wife Anne owned 2 500 shares or 19%.

The Executors of the late Thomas Nelson III, George Wilson and James Roxburgh held 2 000, 50 and 500 respectively (23.2%). George Tod, the Merchant at the time the Trust was established in 1901 and holder in 1908 of 4 000 shares or 30% had sold his stake completely which analysis shows Charles Douglas with his wife and a presumed relative Mrs Margaret Pantagalli of Villa del Gelsomino in Florence, Italy (who held 1 500) had between them acquired. Charles Douglas was a Member of Parliament incidentally when his name had appeared previously in temperance literature as a Trustee of the Glasgow Public House Trust established there one month ahead of the East of Scotland in March 1901.

Other Executors also held 805 shares or 6% for the estates of names from the first 10 subscribers in 1901. Maggie Fewell has been quoted earlier as saying that many of the founders had been lost in the Great War, and this must have implied more than just Thomas Nelson III at the Battle of Arras. So it was unavoidably the time to pass the baton to other hands and the hands it passed to clearly resolved, with the majority of shareholders, to sell to that enterprise in England that had greater critical mass and managerial leadership and which espoused similar temperance goals.

The shareholders did include senior figures who could have stepped forward. Sir William Haldane, who had married Thomas Nelson III's sister Margaret held a small stake. So did Sir Michael Nair and interestingly Sir Edward Tennant who was HM Lord Lieutenant for Peebles and had been Lord High Commissioner of the General Assembly of the Church of Scotland from 1911/1914 as well as MP for Salisbury from 1906–1910 during the Great Liberal Reform Government. Sir Edward was raised to the peerage as Baron Glenconner in 1911. His great nephew as Sir Anthony Tennant was later to become a director of Watney Mann & Truman then Chairman of Grand Metropolitan 1977–1987, and finally Chairman of Trust House Forte from 1989–1992, long after *The Goth* had been sold on by them to Bass.

It is not clear at what price the shareholders sold the Trust across to Trust Houses Limited in 1919, but since the true yield was nearer to 10% not 5%, unless Trust Houses agreed to sustain the allocation of surplus profits to local communities which clearly Maggie Fewell states that they did not in respect of *The Goth*, then a premium on the original par value should have been realised. The Memorandum of Association Clause F required that any surplus achieved above par value of £1 on the winding up of the Trust could not go to the shareholders if the cumulative dividend of 5% pa had been fully paid (and it had). Any surplus arising was quite specifically to go to the Trustees for the benefit of the local communities.

It seems more than likely that Maggie Fewell's conclusion was incorrect, even though the alienation of working for a London enterprise made it feel like the end of an era. Trust Houses Limited in England were an obvious and appropriate choice because of their common lack of particular local roots and they were far and away the largest and most successful practitioner of Trust House beliefs. They had also been spectacularly successful after the Great War in raising new capital, raising their cumulative dividend ceiling to 7.5%. Sums in the region of £1.5m (£250/300m) had reportedly been raised.

The exiting shareholders having received their dividend and par value were perhaps too careless of what happened to the local community benefits that could and should have arisen by the transfer of assets in such a way at below true market value. Perhaps they were very glad to be given consideration for their shares with a fixed ceiling of 5% pa when higher rates were available. In their defence, however, Trust Houses Limited in England was to stay loyally with the founding temperance goals right up until it was absorbed into Sir Charles (now Lord) Forte's Group in 1971 to become part of the Trust House Forte Group, although they had previously sold *The Goth* to Bass Ratcliff & Gretton in 1965 for £15 400 (£300 000) as a going concern. (For the record, it was still known in 1965 as The Trust Tavern but thereafter changed its name to The Forth Tavern under Bass ownership. It was only after a complete refurbishment in 1986 that *The Goth* was, finally, legally renamed The Gothenburg at its reopening under the Bass associate in Scotland, Tennent Caledonian.)

How the final shareholder value of Trust Houses Limited was allocated via Trustees when it merged with Forte in 1971 is less than apparent. That none of the benefit arising accrued to the community at large in Prestonpans at that time is crystal clear; and neither did any accrue to Prestonpans when the local *Goth* assets were sold by Trust Houses Limited to Bass in 1965. As such the protection deliberately written into Clause F was ignored. However, in the light of the ultimate financial collapse of *The Goth* in the 1990s the chances of success for any No Win No Cost legal action instituted to seek recovery seem remote in the extreme.

3. THE GOTHENBURG MOVEMENT IN BRITAIN AT LARGE

It was observed earlier, not unkindly, that the East of Scotland Public House Trust was a copycat initiative. And so it was although it preceded Earl Grey's London based Trust Houses Limited in the Home Counties by two years. The movement at the end of the 19th and start of the 20th Century is well described and analysed by Joseph Rowntree & Arthur Sherwell in *British 'Gothenburg' Experiments and Public House Trusts*. A choir of bishops, canons and lesser clergy, together with MPs gave support to the principles in an Appendix. Three especially famous figures of the times also gave support – Charles Booth who founded the Salvation Army, Sidney Webb and J Keir Hardie. Keir Hardie wrote:

"It is no figure of speech to say that this volume marks the beginning of a new epoch of the temperance movement. I cordially thank the authors for having brought temperance reform within the sphere of the practical."

That was truly its attraction at the turn of the Century – the chance to do something practical. The fact that the model could only act as an exemplar, and that it was unrealistic in the long run to expect a very extensive penetration of the market with this style of enterprise, was barely articulated. Maybe it was well thought upon by the likes of John Ross, but the literature was so alive with zeal there was little room for much downside discussion. It seems reminiscent of the dot.com zeal one hundred years later that we have so lately experienced.

3.1 The Principles and Conditions of Success

There were a series of well articulated principles that all Gothenburg style initiatives espoused which were seen as vital for 'success'. This was true whether they were philanthropic initiatives by sole individuals such as the Rev. Osbert Mordaunt who found himself trustee of the village pub the Boar's Head from 1877 as part of his living in Hampton Lucy, Warwick, or the institutional initiatives of Earl Grey in July 1901 before he left to take up office in Ottawa as Governor General of Canada that had by then already given rise to five 'non specific' Public House Trusts in Glasgow, Renfrewshire, Northumberland, Kent and Belfast as well as our own in East of Scotland. They also applied to a sister movement commenced in 1896 by the Bishop of Chester and Major Craufurd known as The People's Refreshment House Association. Major Craufurd had become involved because of his service with military canteens.

Success Meant ....
Success for the temperance movement meant: a substantial reduction in the normal expenditure upon drink. That was the beginning and the end of the matter. Some 6/- (£60) per week, one sixth of the average income of a working class family at the time, was estimated by social reformers as being expended on drink. It was too much. It was detrimental.

"It left no sufficient margin for the maintenance of that standard of physical and mental efficiency which is now seen to be of primary importance in the industrial competition of nations".

Means to Achieve Success ....
Wisely setting aside the prohibition of alcohol as unrealisable, the means available to achieve success were seen as follows:

- Pre-emption of new licences by Temperance Trust Houses
- Limitations of opening hours
- Elimination of credit
- Disinterested management of the sales of alcohol
- Bonuses for sale of non alcoholic drinks
- Sale of food in public houses
- Making the public house environment less conducive to heavy drinkers
- Publishing a Black List and banning badly behaved drinkers

- Encouraging alternative recreation activities

And if Trust Houses or Provident or Co-operative Societies could not achieve success for lack of sufficient access to capital or whysoever:

- Control by State or Municipal monopoly of retail ownership

Conditions for Success ....

Five Conditions were set forth for achieving success by Rowntree and Sherwell:

(i) *The elimination of private profit from the sale of alcoholic drink*

This principle was presented to ensure that those who owned or managed public houses would have no incentive to maximise alcohol sales. Indeed, by alternative bonus structures other sales, of less costly drink or beneficial food, could be made instead.

Shareholders such as are implicit in the model must be variously structured so as to be disinterested in alcohol sales.

(ii) *Public cupidity must not take the place of private cupidity*

This principle sought to avoid incentivisation to create surpluses for any public use other than diversionary recreation. In particular the diversion of surpluses to activities that should properly be undertaken by civic authorities should be abhorred. This latter feature was a great weakness in the Swedish/Norwegian structures of Municipal ownership, but was also occurring as with Fife Coal Company and John Ross' initiatives making Hill of Beath allocations to electric street lighting and giving Kelty sponsorship to a district nurse. How did this achieve a reduction of alcohol drinking? Did its undoubted usefulness as a source of funding not rather encourage it?

The People's Refreshment House Association reported similarly in 1900 and 1901 that much of its surplus was going into civic projects not recreation as follows:

Sparkford:	£15 (£3 000) to improved water supply and £14 (£2 800) to the local School
Hoar Cross:	£10 + £6 (£3 200) to the construction of a fountain
Tunstall:	£30 + £23 (£10 600) to the District Nurse Fund
Broad Clyst:	£15 (£2 000) each to the Nursing Fund, The Clothing Club and Village lamps on the green
Thorney:	£28 (£5 600) to the Mutual Improvement Society, £9 (£1 800) each to The Foal Show and the Horticultural Society, and £5 (£1 000) to Peterborough Infirmary.
Plymstock:	£11 (£2 200) to the Village Parish reading room
Flax Bourton:	£17 (£3 400) to the Voluntary School Fund.

Overall, Rowntree and Sherwell calculated that 65% was being allocated to civic activities across the British Isles with only 35% going to counter attractions to drinking alcohol.

(iii) *Trust Houses must have a Monopoly of retail on and off licences in any town where they were established*

In the absence of State or Municipal ownership structures this principle, whilst appreciated, is not likely to be realised except in small communities, such as mining towns and rural areas. The cost of acquiring all the houses in any large town would be prohibitive.

Its philosophical desirability was well illustrated in Kelty where John Ross had six others to compete with, and there was no evidence that temperance 'success' as defined above had been gained in 1901 according to its Chief of Police. What had been gained was an exemplar model of how to run a public house and the return of surplus profits to the local community.

(iv) *There must be full liberation of the progressive sentiment in the locality*

This principle required localities to have a large measure of self government in relation to traffic in alcohol so that they supported its activities. It will be recalled that John Ross was chastised for ignoring the plebiscite in Kelty and proceeding with those who were his supporters.

(v) *That the Companies concerned must have for their object a distinct temperance end to which commercial considerations must be strictly subordinated.*

This fifth principle, like the first which is partly duplicates, begs the question of where precisely the funding will come from apart from the State or Municipality. If the whole endeavour is to be careless of commercial considerations only the deeply conscientious or the ego-trippers will be willing to provide the necessary capital funding to make any major impact.

The People's Refreshment House Association interestingly side stepped this by not acquiring or building new premises but by renting them. If in-house purchases were high enough, and an annual surplus can be realised, then the working capital arising from a no credit policy and reasonable trade terms with suppliers can readily be seen to meet the needs of a going concern.

Perhaps not surprisingly, Rowntree and Sherwell conclude that their recommended way forward was to municipalise/ confer on a local monopoly company the power to organise and control the retail traffic in alcohol. It should be done within a framework of central State control which would receive all profits arising and allocate them to the provision and maintenance of counter attractions to the public house. The balance should accrue to the national exchequer. Each community would receive a grant from the State equal to its population not to the profits it generated. Finally each and every locality should have the right to prohibit the liquor traffic in part or altogether if it so chose.

These recommendations truly came of age in the British Isles in the State Management Scheme in Carlisle, introduced in 1915 and finally concluded in 1971 when the Member of Parliament for Penrith, William Whitelaw later Viscount Whitelaw, was Secretary of State for Home Affairs and held State responsibility for it. We shall return to that later.

3.2 Earl Grey's Central Association

Earl Grey's leadership and inspirational role in the Gothenburg movement was late arriving, but swiftly became clear. He wrote a definitive letter to the Licensing Magistrates in Northumberland, his home county on September 6th 1900 pointing out the commercial implications of a licence recently granted to him as chief landowner in the district of Broomhill. No sooner had he received it than it was pointed out to him that he had realised an asset that could be sold for £10 000 (£2m). He considered that such a monopoly being conferred by the State ought to belong not to any individual but to the community. Accordingly he made arrangements for surplus profits after a dividend cap of 10% (half for dividend and half for redemption of capital) to be expended by Trustees for the benefit of the community of Broomhill. He went further asking that in future the Licensing Magistrates should prefer those acting under Gothenburg principles in the grant of any new licences.

Writing subsequently to *The Times* on December 12th in the same year he announced that he was setting in hand the incorporation of several Public House Trust Companies for London and around the provinces. In due course Trust Houses Limited for the Home Counties was specifically established and went forward to become the major trust house actor across the nation over the next 70 years.

He wrote again to *The Times* on January 16th 1901 asserting that the establishment of the Central Public House Association and its campaign to develop a nationwide pattern of Companies and share the challenges together was not a threat to existing licensees. As he had originally postulated to the Licensing Magistrates in Northumberland, he wished to secure the new licences becoming available or to acquire for a fair price those who wished to sell or rent their premises.

4. 30 YEARS ON: THE ROYALCOMMISSIONS ON LICENSING

In the search for intelligence on how the Gothenburg Movement fared over the first three decades of the 20th Century there is no better source than the Minutes of Evidence provided to the Royal Commissions on Licensing established for England & Wales and for Scotland chaired by the Lords Amulree and Mackay respectively that reported in 1931. The major nationalisation initiative taken during the Great War to secure temperance in Carlisle, Gretna and Cromarty Firth was assessed, as were the activities of all the major activist groups still present at that time. Lord Novar gave evidence on his own Bill tabled in the Lords and on the conduct of affairs in the East of Scotland Public House Trust. The conclusions of Lord Southborough's Committee on Disinterested Management of Public Houses were debated. The outcomes of the several local option plebiscites authorised from 1920 under the Temperance (Scotland) Act of 1913 were evaluated.

4.1 State Management in Carlisle, Gretna and Cromarty from 1915/1916

The circumstances which gave rise to the nationalisation of the public houses and breweries first in Gretna and then in Carlisle and Cromarty were hardly those which Rowntree and Sherwell would have envisioned. The circumstances were wholly extraordinary, caused not by an omnipresent challenge of excessive drinking but a massive influx of some 15 000, mainly Irish, workers into munitions factories. The newly created factories were out of town but as with the coal mines of the late 19th century there were virtually no facilities on site for relaxation or merriment. Accordingly this army of munitioneers descended on Gretna and Carlisle of an evening turning the town and the City upside down. Convictions for drunkenness rose by more than 300% in 1916. At Cromarty Firth it was the massive expansion of the naval base that created the conditions for an equally disastrous outcome. The Ministry of Munitions and the Admiralty both asked the Control Board to seek a remedy. Rather than following the mining companies' earlier example and creating additional on site facilities with the cooperation of the breweries or on a Gothenburg model, the nationalisation option was swiftly adopted. That it was so swift was because it was wartime and the Central Control Board (Liquor Traffic) had sweeping powers under Defence of the Realm Regulations in 1915. Because there was such an apparent crisis it was conducted with little vocal opposition or complaint and those who were taken into State ownership were compensated at full market value.

Because of the previous twenty years of temperance debate the Control Board had a well thought through template to adopt. A State Management Scheme was introduced in Carlisle in July 1916 and was implemented by October. It was comprehensive, creating a local monopoly of retail trade. It took over 116 licences and all three local breweries, closing all but one. It did not seek to meet the excess demand for social activity and merriment by making greater provision, rather it swiftly closed 58 or 50% of the licences down. Off licences were also reduced by 87% from 100 to 13, and Grocers' licences eliminated altogether. Similar decisions were taken earlier for Gretna and Cromarty but they were on a much smaller scale and there were no local breweries. The smaller number of drinking premises available made the challenge of supervision and policing that much more tractable. In Gretna and Cromarty Firth taken together licenses fell to 30 with 4 off licences.

Simply withdrawing facilities alone was never likely to resolve the problem of course. It would simply have led to unsustainable overcrowding at those remaining. As rapidly as it could, the State Management Scheme introduced the principles of disinterested management in all its facilities; redesigned their interiors to discourage perpendicular drinking at bars by the provision of tables and chairs and removing snugs; banned treating others to drinks; introduced hot and cold meals at cheap prices; introduced games such as billiards and clock golf in association with and in the public houses; and removed all advertising to encourage drinking both inside and out.

When the war ended the exceptional cause of the crisis situation disappeared. But Carlisle, Gretna and Cromarty Firth had a fortunate legacy. Licences had been dramatically reduced by 50% and major improvements had been made to all the remaining facilities. In 1921 the patterns established by the Central Control Board under the wartime regulations were deliberately continued under Schedule III of the Licensing Act giving the Secretaries of State for Home Affairs and for Scotland power to continue the monopolies. It was opined by reformers that these areas were already exemplars of better temperance provision and that their continuance as experiments in peace time would provide comprehensive evidence of the superiority of such social

A few scenes in Carlisle after several months of state purchase and "disinterested management" under the Liquor Traffic Central Control Board

control processes over such provision as breweries and private landlords might make motivated, as they were characterised, solely by profit.

By the time of the Royal Commissions in 1930/1931 the temperance lobby that believed such monopoly social ownership was superior was called to the bar to provide the evidence. All three State Management districts were able to demonstrate that as even as disinterested monopolists they were effectively paying a dividend to central government of 10% on a mutually 'agreed' capital asset base, having already repaid the initial loan finance that was advanced by the Control Board from 1916 to compensate those who had lost their assets and to fund the programme of improvements. They had indeed followed their mandate well and not taken the opportunity inherent in a monopoly to exploit the situation. But there was no conclusive evidence that their activities as disinterested managers of the liquor traffic in the State Management Districts created greater sobriety than had been achieved elsewhere.

In Scotland Lord Mackay's Royal Commission recommended that the State Management Districts of Gretna and Cromarty Firth be returned to the control of the Licensing Boards and the State Management experiment discontinued. In England and Wales the recommendation was for the continuation of the Carlisle monopoly, indeed for its extension to cover small inconsistencies, under a Board of Management reporting to Parliament. Further for England and Wales, where appropriate to accelerate a restructuring of licences that local Licensing Authorities were unable or unwilling to achieve, the template was commended to the Home Secretary.

4.2 Trust Houses and People's Refreshment Rooms

Eric Spence was Chief Constable of Carlisle from 1913 till 1928. He had just retired when he gave evidence to Lord Amulree's Royal Commission and had of course continuous experience of the whole experiment there. Perhaps most significant was his expression of admiration for Trust Houses and People's Refreshment Rooms which he characterised as "not very much different from the Carlisle scheme. We know they were only able to get one house in any town or in two cases two houses, but they have improved their houses, and their great idea is the sale of food rather than the sale of drink." [Qn. 20692]

> "... I am a great believer in Trust Houses. I have been in practically every Trust House that the Company have [an almost unbelievable claim in fact], and I think their's is an ideal scheme. But of course they are limited by their capital...". [Qn. 20694]

Barry Holderness, General Manager of the People's Refreshment House Association also gave detailed evidence [Qns. 18067–18507]. He too had long experience having worked with the Association for 26 years but he seemingly disappointed the Commissioners by focusing almost exclusively on the problems posed by the emergence of Clubs as venues for alcohol. He said little of the successes achieved in the 180 Refreshment Houses created over the 30 years of the Association's existence.

Reginald Cripps, Secretary of the Central Public House Trust Association, also appeared [Qns. 17371–17793]. Arthur Sherwell, one of the Commissioners who had in fact written with Rowntree as described earlier on the Gothenburg Movement in 1906, led the questioning. After commencement in 1901 under Lord Grey's leadership before he went off to Canada as Governor General, the Central Association had 11 independent member Trusts in England, 4 in Scotland and one in Northern Ireland. By 1904 the Central association had, according to Cripps, practically completed its pioneering work and had 33 Members in England but still only 4 in Scotland and 1 in Ireland. Over the following years amalgamations took place and three major Trusts emerged – The People's Refreshment, Trust Houses Limited (which took over the East of Scotland Public House Trust its 16 licences in 1919 including *The Goth)* and the Western Counties Trust. Cripps reported that some £2.25 million (£340m) of capital excluding loans and mortgages was deployed nationwide by members of the Association and Trust Houses Limited – and Trust Houses Limited was the dominant participant with £1.5m (£250/ £300m) of share capital promising a 7% Cumulative dividend. They had some 181 public houses by 1930 out of the national Trust House total of 421. (421 was less than 0.5% of the total number of licences nationwide).

In cross examination Sherwell elicited from Cripps that no changes had occurred in the fundamental beliefs of the Trust House movement. But there was little zeal left for monopoly rights and quite specifically the Association asked for 'No Favours'. But there were unfair aspects to the licensing system including the increase of licence fees when improvements not connected with the licence were made to premises. And the matter of Clubs being able to compete unfairly was again raised. Furthermore the myth that Trust Houses were not tied was exploded. Certainly they were not tied to a brewery but each local manager had no discretion to choose which beers to carry. That was a given, and determined by central policies and deals.

William Madden was the main representative of management appearing before the Commission in England & Wales [Qns. 18508–18718]. He was Managing Director of 17 houses in the Surrey Public House Trust Company that had been founded in 1901. It had a ceiling on the shareholders dividend of 7% Cumulative and £100 000 (£15m) in 400 000 issued 5/- shares. He again showed no zeal after 25 years in the movement. His concerns were the pattern of opening hours at weekends and bank holidays and a desire for the reform of unlimited liability for safekeeping of cars (deemed in law to be a carriage) parked at premises that was a carry over from the Innkeepers' Liability Act of 1863 when the mode of conveyance was horse and carriage and they were housed in stables under careful supervision. He was also mesmerised by the challenge of necessarily serving food to anything up to 100 people emerging from a charabanc. Finally he was greatly concerned that Applications for Licences under The Licensing (Consolidation) Act 1910 must be attached to the door of the church or chapel in the area, which gave offence to abstainers in the churches and chapels concerned.

In Scotland, Lord Mackay's Commission heard evidence from three temperance advocates as well as from Lord Novar. Two were Justices of the Peace in addition to their temperance roles. *John Gordon* [Qns. 9174–9268] was Secretary of the Scottish Temperance Alliance and presented useful statistical analyses of licences across Scotland tabulated against population levels, death rates per 1000, infantile death rates per 1000 and the percentage of illegitimate births occurring. He then became hopelessly embroiled in cause and effect debate about alcohol, mortality and illegitimacy. He asserted licences must be reduced and that no compensation (as had satisfactorily occurred in the State Management Districts) should be paid to those who lost such licences.

Andrew Ballantyne appeared [Qns 8713–8959] on behalf of the Scottish Temperance Legislation Board and as General Manager the Public House Trust (Glasgow District). His Trust was formed in 1901 by Sir John Mann and by July 1930 had acquired ownership of eight hotels and two public houses, had licences for four additional hotels and three public houses, and a luncheon and tea room. His Trust paid a 5% Cumulative dividend with surplus profits going to Trustees.

Ballantyne urged the Commission to accept that the Temperance Act, 1913, had failed in Scotland and that a Liquor Control Board for Scotland should be appointed to replace Licensing Courts. The State Management Districts would be taken over by the new Control Board and a pattern of implementation of disinterested management would be installed for such other licences in areas wishing that outcome by local polls. Compensation was considered an appropriate approach. His Board believed they had failed to make major progress because Licensing Magistrates deliberately prevented it by granting competitive licences nearby but there had been noteworthy progress including a licence from Lord Glenconner at his works and at Harland & Wolff in Govan. In subsequent questioning he was proud to report that his Trust had provided *in cumulo* some £8 000 (£1.5m) for local community and recreational purposes. He cited a bowling green and a public park as major facilities, but went on to emphasise that three times as much as had gone to the Trustees had been spent on improving the properties to make them much more conducive to sobriety.

The third key Scottish witness was *William Reid,* [Qns. 8960–9033] on behalf of Disinterested Management Public House Societies from West Fife – the ancestral home of Scotland's Gothenburg Movement and of course where John Ross (now Sir John Ross) began at Hill o' Beath in 1899. William Reid had worked in those early days with John Ross. In comparison with the Trusts inspired by Lord Grey's Central Association, the far greater extent of benefits accruing to the local community by 1927 was immediately demonstrated. Every Society outperformed the Glasgow Trust by over 200% with far fewer houses and a quite different structure of its capital under Industrial and Provident Society Acts of 1893 & 1901:

Kelty Public House Society (3 houses)
Net Profits: £48 563 (£7.3m) *Interest Paid*: £12 236 (£1.8m) *Grants*: £13 924 (£2m)

Dunfermline Public House Society (5 houses)
Net Profits: £44 928 (£6.7m) *Interest Paid:* £8 879 (£1.3m) *Grants:* £16 884 (£2.5m)

Cowdenbeath Public House Society (3 houses)
Net Profits: £26 880 (£4m) *Interest Paid:* £3 935 (£600 000) *Grants:* £18 931 (£2.8m)

Reid argued that with such demonstrable benefits to the local communities, Licensing Magistrates should give preference in granting licences to Disinterested Management Gothenburg initiatives that limited themselves to a maximum 7.5% cumulative dividend or interest with the surplus devoted to the local community. This, it must be noted, was from a position of strength in the County of Fife where Gothenburgs held not 0.5% but just short of 10% of all licences (24/255). In Dunfermline they held just over 20% or 12/58.

At least one Commissioner was puzzled why, if so much benefit could be returned to the community, the Trust Houses would not seek to maximise alcohol sales so as to maximise grants available since the return on shares had a fixed ceiling. Reid affirmed that whilst that might seem to be a logical conclusion, the Trusts were committed to sobriety and to the sale of non-alcoholic merchandise to maximise grants.

4.3 Lord Novar's Contribution

It was one of the delights of historical research into *The Goth* to happen across the evidence given by Lord Novar [Qns. 2502–2632]. As we have seen earlier, he was one of the founding directors before departing to Australia in the Great War, returning to be Secretary of Sate for Scotland with Bonar Law and Baldwin. He appeared with Professor Bailey on behalf of the Scottish Public House Reform League, of which he was President and Professor Bailey was Vice Chairman, which had been founded in 1923. The League was neither for or against any given pattern of ownership; it sought sobriety through improvement of facilities everywhere.

Novar was uncompromising in the view that prohibition had failed in the USA and Canada, indeed had made matters worse. Public houses were part of the fabric of society and they had to change their nature, be reformed. He believed good progress had already been made over the last 30 years and that those who owned and managed the public houses must be encouraged in every possible way to continue. In particular perpendicular as opposed to sedentary drinking still persisted in many cities. To these ends, Novar had introduced his own Private Bill into the Lords in 1925, inter alia to encourage and facilitate disinterested management, but after successful 1st and 2nd Readings there it had been held over pending the Report of Lord Southborough on Disinterested Management that the Home Secretary had commissioned. That Report when it had appeared seriously questioned whether there was such a meaningful construct as dis-interestedness as opposed to interested-ness. No owner of a public house per se was seeking to encourage drunkenness and if it all too frequently occurred it endangered the licence held. They encouraged the creation of an appropriate surplus for their own declared ends.

However, Novar's Bill was perhaps most significant for its very shrewd intention to suspend the Triennial Plebiscites authorised throughout Scotland under the Temperance Act 1913 for a period of 11 years so that public house owners could bring their premises into appropriate good order. It was proposed that, with a prospective warning of this nature given, excellent and wholly congruent results could be anticipated. As a corollary to these proposals he paid especial attention to the compensation for licences lost in the best interests of the community with a general charge on those remaining as the basis for funding.

It was readily apparent from Novar's evidence, which Lord Mackay treated with more deference than had been shown to many other temperance witnesses, that he had not joined in the establishment of the East of Scotland Public House Trust in 1901 on a whim or for an ego trip. He described his career from his first involvement with public house licensing in 1881, but also acknowledged that his current mentor for his Bill was Lord Salvesen who was away in South Africa. He shared his experiences of temperance movements in Finland and visits to Gothenburg and Russia. Of especial interest he glowingly recalled and defended being "on the executive of (our) Scottish Public House Trust which held 16 licences, (which being) a larger trust system of handing over profits to another trust to be expended on counter-attractions in localities, with or without a licence, is superior to that under which the local committee of a migratory population supplies a village with benefits in proportion to the amount of liquor it consumes".

When invited to comment on Lord Southborough's conclusions in his Report on Disinterested Management he took the opportunity to observe that his experience with the East of Scotland Public House Trust had certainly seemed to him "fairly disinterested".

> *"That matter gave us a good deal of trouble and we had to look into how these public houses were conducted. A great deal depended on the managers we got. The managers had no bonus on the sales of alcoholic refreshments but they were paid a bonus on the non-alcoholic refreshments they sold. We thus stimulated the consumption of non-alcoholic refreshments. The money that was put into the trust yielded 5%. Everything else by way of profits was handed over to another body of trustees. One of them I know was the late convenor and present Lord Lieutenant of Fife, and they distributed the profits to counter-attractions.*
>
> *"They made dancehalls. In one village, in Glencraig, they danced in the public streets and in that case the trustees saw fit to erect a dance hall. Then there were bowling greens, and I think even the nurses got a grant from the trustees, but we had nothing to do with that. They divided our profits not only where the profits were made but in places without licences at all. I call that disinterested. "*

Novar was only too well aware of the difficulties of making the disinterested trust model work without a local monopoly and he was quick to point out, agreeing thereby with the Chief Constable of Carlisle, that the State Management Districts in Cromarty Firth and Gretna gave excellent examples of what could be achieved with a monopoly. But he felt his Bill in 1925 had offered a sensible approach to advancing the matter.

> *"I do not speak as a crank or fanatic; I speak as an administrator".*

4.4 Local Option Plebiscites

If the State Management Scheme in Carlisle was the high-water mark for nationalisation/ municipalisation in Britain then the Temperance (Scotland) Act of 1913 was the same for the prohibitionists. We have seen in discussion above that by 1930 commentators had written it off, but not because of its disastrous failure in the US. As enacted it was administratively impracticable as well as usurping the authority of Licensing Magistrates.

The 1913 Act authorised the holding of Triennial Plebiscites commencing June 1st 1920, i.e. eight years after the Bill's introduction, for each community to determine whether (i) to issue no licences for the sale of liquor except to those residing and/ or dining at inns, hotels and restaurants and even then no bar per se may be provided; (ii) to reduce the overall number of licences by 25%; or (iii) to make no change. Each elector had a single vote but if an insufficiency of votes occurred for (i) above, they were to be transferred to (ii). A sufficiency of votes meant 55% in favour being at least 35% of those entitled to vote. A valid Requisition to hold such a Plebiscite required not less than 10% of the locality's electors to sign it.

The moratorium on introducing the provisions was, as in Lord Novar's later unsuccessful Bill in 1925, intended to give local public house owners and breweries the opportunity to conduct their businesses in such manner as to make the local opt out unnecessary. But of course the Great War intervened and perhaps affected any major focus on achieving that. It was in many eyes, however, seen as ample justification for no offer of compensation when licences were discontinued.

The impracticality of the Act's provisions lay most especially in its triennial review. Licences lost either totally or by 25% limitation led to strenuous efforts for their reinstatement. There was no certainty that under a vote for limitation to 75% of the preceding levels that improvements would take place, indeed the imminent threat of withdrawal by plebiscite made them less likely since their investment payback was certainly well beyond three years. Prohibitionists who lost a first Plebiscite altogether continued to campaign for their cause thereby creating uncertainty. As Lord Novar argued, the Licensing Magistrates were better able than a popular vote to provide the necessary continuity for improved facilities to continue to emerge. But without coherent approaches to compensation there was little hope that Licensing Magistrates would take the decisive and at times draconian action necessary to eliminate large numbers of unnecessary licences.

As with prohibition in the US, the Temperance (Scotland) Act of 1913 was seen to exacerbate rather than ameliorate the problem.

4.5 The Temperance Verdict in 1931 as an Obituary

Temperance organisations singularly failed to gain any further institutionalisation of their goals in the laws of the land as a result of the two Royal Commissions. They had lost the zeal of their cause as the national provision by brewers and others emulated the very pattern of facility they had championed. The brewery trade had seen the writing on the wall of nationalisation and municipalisation and reformed itself. It will be recalled that James Fewell had moved in 1927 from *The Goth* to Catford, South East London, to work in a splendid facility there which provided all manner of recreation in a public house owned by Barclay Perkins.

The Royal Commissions accepted that Public House Trusts and People's Refreshment Rooms had demonstrated well a better way to design the public house as an important centre for a sober local social life, and that the State Management Districts in Scotland and Carlisle had honourably pursued disinterested management and improved facilities most specifically. But they saw no need or desirability to replace the emerging, reforming patterns of private provision along similar lines with a statutorily enforced provident/

fixed dividend/ disinterested preferred system of licences. They put their faith in Licensing Magistrates seeing the job through not the State or local Popular Opinion via triennial plebiscite. Only in 'exceptional circumstances' (such as had occasioned the Carlisle initiative in 1915) did Lord Amulree's Commission for England & Wales see any extension beyond Carlisle for State Management in any 'additional' areas. Indeed, Lord Mackay's Commissioners in Scotland recommended its total discontinuance in Cromarty Firth and Gretna forthwith. Carlisle, however was to be allowed to run on and so it did until 1970, when the only substantive element in the debate was the correct price at which to sell the whole State enterprise to a private brewer.

The Commissioners were also further convinced that it was inappropriate to confer a monopoly on disinterested management to overcome its obvious failure to raise sufficient 5% or 7.5% Cumulative funding, with no capital gains on realisation of equity stakes, to achieve its goals. It seemed far more likely then (in the depths of the 1930s Recession) just as it would in today's world of 21st Century perspectives on Public/Private Finance Initiatives (in the post-Socialist era of 1945/1979), that the private investor could be wisely led to achieve them. In particular they were unconvinced by what we today often hail as the greatest success of the Gothenburg Movement, the local provident society ploughing its surplus back into its own community's recreational infrastructure. Lord Novar robustly presented the view that that was less likely to bring about the macro societal changes required that would give us a more sober nation, north and south of the border.

Quite simply, Licensing Magistrates were called upon to ensure that their local communities sobered up by wielding the big stick of licence issue and withdrawal. And thus the temperance movement as a major national force was put to rest. What remained in play was not temperance campaigning but provident/ co-operative/ socialistic goals and objectives – and bravo for them. As we shall see when the future plans for *The Goth* are sketched that is what will be back in play on Redburn Road/ High Street Prestonpans. And of course, through it all, Alcoholics Anonymous still makes provisions for individuals in need.

5. THE GOTH AND DEAN TAVERN AT NEWTONGRANGE

The Verdict handed down in 1931 by the Royal Commissions meant that everything that has happened since that time has been down to the sheer native ability of disinterested parties to sustain the momentum or grow their portfolio. 'No Favours' were asked by Surrey Trust Houses and none were given to them or any others. Trust Houses Limited, which was eventually to merge with Forte in 1970 was the most spectacular residual beneficiary of the Verdict. It became the destination for Public House Trusts finding it all too difficult just as it had been a haven for the East of Scotland Public House Trust in 1919. And by coincidence it was that same year, 1970, that William Whitelaw, MP for Penrith later Viscount Whitelaw, and the Home Secretary in England and Wales, Reginald Maudling, determined the denationalisation of the Carlisle State Management Scheme.

Across this span of history it is an object lesson to see how *The Goth* and Dean Tavern at Newtongrange fared. Dean Tavern worked according to provident rules, *The Goth* under Lord Novar's "superior" approach.

The Goth's history has been educed here from legal records of property transfers/planning consents/listings and from several personal reminiscences captured for us by Julie Aitken. (We shall be looking for *more* to collate in the near future too.) Dean Tavern's history is readily available from the excellent book, derived from the Minute Books since 1899 plus extensive local research, *The Dean Tavern: A Gothenburg Experiment* penned by Alasdair Anderson in 1986. It has been supplemented by subsequent conversation with its long standing Trust Chairman, Jim Green, who has held that office since 1984.

5.1 The Goth at Prestonpans

The reminiscences collated by Julie Aitken were as follows:

Minnie Cowan was born in Prestonpans in 1912. She was a contemporary of Maggie Fewell, and Maggie's father James was Manager at *The Goth*. Her memories reinforce the description we have from Maggie Fewell in the twenties. It was a high class establishment determined to offer and maintain good social standards and offer good food. But by the late 1940s its profile had seemingly changed. Sobriety had lost its way under Trust Houses leadership from London.

> *"When I was at Prestonpans Public School [the "Grey School" – now demolished and the site of Grey School Corner amenity housing] the teachers used to go along to The Goth for their lunch – they did lovely meals. Some of the teachers from Preston Lodge used to go there too. It was considered a very high class establishment in those days.*
>
> *"I grew up in the Kittle (Cuthill) and the Gothenburg was a Kittle pub – the miners from the 'Grange socialised there and the ones that stayed home with their wives would send their bairns along to the jug bar for a pitcher of ale. I remember – I'd be about 10 or 11 years old [1922/1923]. Three auld*

Prestonpans – when trams ran and the pottery stood opposite and High Street had a bend

from Tulloch, Alister, "Prestonpans in Old Picture Postcards", *(European Library 1989) worthies from the Kittle were regulars at The Goth – Mathie Blair, auld Mrs Conner and Mrs Maguire. You would see them slip along the road to The Goth, a' happed up in their big shawls – sometimes with a bairn wrapped up inside. Guid-livin' folk used to turn their noses up at them for it was a disgrace, a married woman going into a man's pub. Folk would say: "There they go, runnin' the cutter.", and wee bairns used to run after them shouting "Runnin' the cutter, runnin' the cutter". I cannae remember now what it meant.*

"I was once invited to a wedding in the (Prestongrange) Miner's Institute. I only went along oot o' nosiness for folk were saying that they were having a five storey bride's cake – like Princess Elizabeth [in 1947] – and I wanted to see for myself. Right enough, the bride was lovely and there was a bride's cake wi' five storeys but when it came time tae cut it the happy couple were naewhere to be found. Somebody said they had nipped along to The Goth and we all trooped along to fetch them back. Just as we got there, the door to The Goth burst open and oot rolled the bride into the middle o' the road – she was fighting with some body or another – and the funny thing was – for all her braw white frock and her bride's cake like the royalty, she had on a pair o' navy blue gym knickers!"

Tammy Bogie was born in 1922, and he recalled memories as a young lad in the early thirties. He has no grand memories of sobriety at that date but what drunkenness there was stayed clearly under control.

"The Goth was the meeting place for the Grange miners, and on a Saturday night you couldnae move in the place, it was that busy. The Grinder – Auld Connachan – he would play the button box accordian for a sing song, and we laddies – I'd a been aboot eight or nine year old – would sit on the sea dyke tae watch for them coming oot at closing. The drink and discussions in the Goth would mean some tempers would be runnin' high and you would maybe get tae see a fight. It never got tae that though for Big Donald, the polis, he would wait at the door for them and as they cam oot he would point and say – right you, you're up that road – you, get along that road there – where are you gaun' you bide the other way, along at the Kittle. There was never any bother, Big Donald sorted them a' oot and made shair they a' got hame tae their ain hooses.

"The Grinder didnae just play the button box in the Goth. He was the trainer for the football team, and Sunday was the day the miner's played. Some o' the boys would have sair heids fi the Saturday night and they would kid on they were injured tae get off the pitch. They wud lie on the ground with their een shut, groanin' an' haudin' their leg or whatever, but you couldnae fool the Grinder. He would say, a' gentle like, "Are ye a'right laddie?" then chuck a basin o' cauld water oor them. The laddie wid jump up wi' the fright o' it and the Grinder would shout "Ye've made a miraculous recovery, ye're fine tae play on." We would a' stand on the side lines waitin' just for that – they [the players] never seemed tae get wise tae it!"

Fiona Hunter was born in 1972 so has much more recent memories of *The Goth*. She worked there after Trust Houses had sold to Bass/Tennant Caledonian. There is no mention from her of the finer points of a first class

A toast to the new Gothenburg tavern, formerly the Forth Tavern, in Prestonpans, reopened under the new name by Tennent Caledonian Breweries. Tennent's girl June Lake and Councillor Tom Wilson and guests raise their glasses to wish success to the new venture.

(Edinburgh Evening News *November 18th 1986*)

establishment that James Fewell managed. Quite the reverse it seems although entertainment was being provided.

> *"When I was 16/17 years old, I earned pocket money working as a waitress for John Blair's catering business. I remember working at a funeral tea in The Goth and behind the bar there were all these pottery bowls with names on them – I later found out they were water dishes for the regulars' dogs, and each one had its particular owner's name stamped on it. That was service for you!*
>
> *"A friend – who will remain nameless to save his embarrassment – was telling me recently that he and two friends were celebrating a forthcoming wedding through the back of The Goth. They were a bit drunk and started playing a drinking game which involved removing articles of clothing when you lost. An old wifie who was drinking through the front happened to come in on them on her way to the loo, and before the three young men knew what was happening, she had shouted to all her friends to "Come here, there's strippers on through the back". The three lads rose to the occasion and put on a show for the ladies, and later learned that the women had gone in the next day, thanked the barman for putting on such great entertainment and requested that strip shows become a regular thing in the Goth!*
>
> *"The Goth was a right "spit and sawdust" pub, a right working man's pub, but there's hardly a local that doesnae have some kind of memory of it".*

The Edwardian bar at The Goth

***The Goth's* Chronology** (See Appendix 7) captured from legal documents shows that Tennent Caledonian made a major refurbishment of *The Goth* in 1986, finally adopting *The Gothenburg* as the formal name. But by the mid 1990s, after being sold on with the benefit of brewery loans to three Landlords by Tennent Caledonian, it was in a state of total financial collapse in the hands of the third. The Banks, brewery and others were compelled to repossess and sell the property on to recover their own loans. By all accounts *The Goth* was no longer any credit to the town whatever, it was certainly not a pillar of temperance, and the lavatory equipment was not of the standards set in 1908. Mention was made of drugs and prostitution and wild parties; and the beer was reportedly uninspiring. It was into such a context that John & Scott Murray and family stepped in 1998. They closed the Public House and received Planning Consent to turn it into a private residence. They had plans to preserve the fine architectural heritage and the interiors re-opening in due course as a Bistro style facility. It was well past the appointed day for Lord Novar, George Tod, Thomas Nelson, Sir John Ross and the others to turn in their graves.

5.2 The Dean Tavern at Newtongrange

Good to tell for that township but sad to record for Prestonpans, Dean Tavern just a few miles away, without benefit of the "superior" system is alive and in good health. Over its 100 + years of uninterrupted trading at today's values it has contributed in excess of £1 million to the good of the local community. And from its Minutes Books we know where those surplus profits went. [Not for the first time Prestonpans has lost out to Newtongrange, which also took the Scottish Mining Museum from under our noses.]

The Dean's birth was nowhere as easy as it had been for *The Goth*. Sponsored by the Lothian Coal Company in 1897 their application for a licence on Gothenburg lines was rejected. In 1899 it was subsequently accepted by the Licensing Magistrates voting 19–10, with the support of the Marquis of Lothian whose ancestors had held the Barony of Prestoungrange at the start of the 16th Century and on whose lands it would be located. But that was not the end of the matter. The Licensing Board included three shareholders in the Lothian Coal Company and the losers being those with licences already in the area since 1897 cried foul. An action was raised in the Court of Session. In July Lord Darling reserved judgement and, the licence being still valid, Dean Tavern opened on October 29th 1899. However, Lord Darling ruled in December, after the case continued, that the licence was invalid and so the matter had to go to appeal, but an alternative device to resolve the issue was found before a determination of the appeal had been given. Dean Tavern, on behalf of the Lothian Mining Company, applied for a new licence and those with shares left the bench when the vote was to be taken and yet the application was still carried by 24–7. With this new evidence to hand, Lord Darling was content on May 29th 1900 that a valid licence existed.

The Dean Tavern never issued any share capital. It has been funded throughout by loans. From the Lothian Coal Company and bankers, and from its accumulated surplus. The Committee of Management was a self-perpetuating oligarchy, with members only replaced on their death and then by determination of those remaining, until 1971 when the present Trust was established. The original premises were three houses in a row rented from the Lothian Coal Company, but by 1910 it had accumulated sufficient funds to repay the 5% Start Up loan and to fund a wholly new building which is still in use today. A visit today shows an orderly premises with as much sobriety as might be desired, and good facilities for meetings. It is very much in need of modernised kitchens however. But its magnificent legacy from the past and its continuing pathway to the future arises from its support from its profits for local causes.

In typical Gothenburg tradition this began with a fine bowling green opened in 1902. After that the focus was on a new premises but the leadership was emboldened to mortgage future profits in 1911 by taking out a loan of some £3 000 (£600 000) from the Lothian Coal Company to build the Newbattle Institute. It provided 3 billiard tables, with settees all around and an alcove for other games; the reading room had eight long tables, newspaper racks and shelves for thousands of books; together with a temperance refreshment room. It had, they asserted, unsurpassed facilities and the membership fee was 1d (say 90 new pence) per fortnight. An extension to provide more scope for billiards, extra games rooms including noisy dominoes and a smoking room opened in March 1914, once again funded by a Lothian Coal Company loan of £2 500 (£500 000). But this was not the end of the provision made as the Great War dawned. In the week before Christmas 1914 the Newtongrange Picture Palace opened at a cost of £6 440 (£1.25m). A second Institute at Easthouses had also been planned but did not occur until 1925 at a cost of £4 000 (£600 000), and that was one of the last substantial buildings constructed by Dean Tavern. Thereafter the surplus funds were largely used to maintain and improve the building already in place.

It might be wondered who were the dynamic entrepreneurs behind this major programme of social improvement because by any comparison today it was most impressive. The answer is that James Hood, who became Managing

Director of Lothian Coal Company in 1902 in succession to his father Archibald as joint owner, and Mungo MacKay a brilliant engineer who came to Newtongrange at the turn of the century, were largely the driving force. They both served on the Management Committee and saw to it that what needed to be done was done, and that included housing as well as the social facilities created. Mungo MacKay served until his death in 1939 and through all that time dominated its decisions. He was there when the Local Option Plebiscite was taken in 1920 under the Temperance (Scotland) Act, 1913, seeing the Prohibitionists/ Limitation of Licences electors off by 863/ 217. Indeed it was that year and the next when the sales at the Dean Tavern reached their peak of £15 000 (more than £2m) but fell back by one third the following year. Profits averaged 10% of gross turnover each year. In 1923 this enabled the Dean tavern to fund the building of a new pavilion for Newtongrange Star FC. It was no mean facility and included a boxing ring, and rooms for the Pigeon, Quoiting and Miniature Rifle Clubs and yet another for the Radio Association just then founded with the launch of the BBC in 1922. A running track was also provided. The total cost was £5 000 (£750 000).

The Second World War brought a massive fall in profits with the worst results at £500 (£50 000) in 1943 since the Committee began. At that time the Institutes were sold to the Welfare Committee of the Coal Owners that was to be replaced after nationalisation by CISWO. But as soon as peace arrived profits soared to £4 800 (£480 000) in 1945/ 1946. But nationalisation loomed and in 1947 the Lothian Coal Company ceased to trade. The final audit of that Company's books showed every penny ever borrowed had been repaid. Murray's Brewery provided free beer to celebrate the Dean Tavern's 50th anniversary in 1949 and the Clerk to the Committee, John Gilmour, proudly announced he had been Clerk for every one of them.

However, new competitive forces were coming into their market, with their sibling bowling club gaining a licence and more besides. The Picture House closed in 1962. The result of these changes was that the Dean Tavern increasingly became a nostalgic spot in the community especially after the mine was eventually closed. Today it is clearly part of the social fabric of the town but not the sine qua non of social and recreational progress. It makes surpluses and distributes them broadly and wisely in the town. It has repaid the loans it received in the 1960s from the brewers Murrays to extend and modernise the premises. But it had no demonstrated plans to reinvent itself with the panache of a Hood or MacKay that will help it fly and show any and all competitors a clean pair of heels. Indeed the Committee since the formation of the Trust in 1970 is made up of institutionally nominated members. Its original driving purpose has long since gone and it is surely only a matter of time now until it too will fade away. The grants made annually are still, of course, appreciated but they are but a miniscule fraction of what they once were. An important restoration project was recently completed with a grant from CISWO not from internally generated reserves.

Anderson had concluded his book in 1986 with the observation that "The Dean is looking remarkably hale and hearty after its 86th birthday and has a long way to go yet" But he did not hint at where that might be … Certainly its next destination needs articulating sooner rather than later.

It is perhaps a long overdue moment for the baton that we so ignobly dropped at *The Goth* in Prestonpans as long ago as 1919 to be picked up again, to encourage a renascent momentum. Certainly there is a new vision of

Restoration Plans – North Elevation

Improvements and Restoration Plans – East Elevation

what might and we must certainly hope that we can muster just a fraction of the competence and skill Hood and MacKay brought to the Dean Tavern's affairs in the first quarter of the 20th Century making it such a fine exemplar of the Gothenburg System.

6. WHAT REALLY HAPPENED IN SWEDEN IN THE LATE 19TH CENTURY

The name of Sweden's second largest city has been bandied around in the British Isles for nearly 125 years as a pioneer in encouraging temperance by municipal socialism. Edwin Pratt wrote the definitive early 20th Century book on the subject, *Licensing and Temperance in Sweden, Norway and Denmark, 1906,* and the author here followed in his footsteps nearly a century later in August 2002. How much was myth and how much was fact?

6.1 The Establishment of the Vodka Bolag Monopoly in Gothenburg in 1865

Sweden had a problem of nationwide significance in the 19th Century. Almost all rural households distilled their own branwin or vodka from potatoes or corn with 40%/50% alcohol content. To help overcome the problem and at the same time to provide a major source of revenue for State and Municipal governments, such distilling was made illegal unless a fee was paid in 1855, and the counties and municipalities were given authority to govern the retail trade in vodka. It should be noted that the control related only to vodka. Gothenburg (Goteborg in Swedish) was the first City to come up with a scheme that captured the imagination.

After a Committee of Enquiry into Poverty and Drinking, in April 1865 the City's Licensing Magistrates agreed that all licences for the sale of vodka in the City would expire and only 40 of the previous 60 licences would be given instead to the newly established Vodka Bolag. In most instances the old licensees now traded under the authority of the new Bolag so their premises were not purchased. As can be imagined the uncompensated and dispossessed were un-amused. This new company, owned by local businessmen, agreed that after a Cumulative Dividend of 5% and appropriate provisions for Reserves, the balance of profits would be allocated 70% to the Municipality, 20% to the State Government in Stockholm, and 10% to local area Agricultural Associations. There was no requirement to allocate these surpluses to recreational activities by any party although good works were demonstrably accomplished. Neither was there any limitation on the prices at which shares in the Bolag could exchange hands as came to be the case in Scotland and England. However, the Bolag was very much

Swedish bar managed by the Gothenburg Bolag

Reading Room provided by the Bolag in Gothenburg

expected to spend its income and reserves on the improvement of facilities most particularly the provision of Reading Rooms.

In order to maximise the surplus funds available to government, the reduction of sales revenues was clearly not desirable, and as Pratt demonstrates although some success was achieved with food and non-alcoholic refreshments, the sale of alcohol in off-licences owned by the Bolag grew extensively. Kungsbacka, a market town of 1000 inhabitants but with heavy consumption on market days by incomers held some 30 km from Gothenburg, reputedly managed for many generations to levy no taxation at all on its citizens using its 70% of the surplus profits from its Bolag instead.

As an exercise in the encouragement of temperance, and it was emulated in Norway, it had far less to commend itself than the Danish approach that sought to make Public Houses and Refreshment Houses more open and to ensure that lower alcohol drinks were served. In this movement Carlsberg spotted the trend very early on and made great progress with its sales. It was not until 1917 that rationing was introduced in Gothenburg of 4 litres of vodka per month for men, with only maids permitted to make a similar purchase for ladies. It was a blessing to be old in those times, because the aged had a greater entitlement. A Sweden-wide Prohibition Plebiscite in 1922 was (fortunately for the Bolags and their beneficiaries) marginally defeated. The rationing continued until 1956.

6.2 Why Did Gothenburg So Influence Scotland

There is no formal documentary evidence explaining how precisely it was that Charles Carlow, as Managing Director of the Fife Coal Company, with John Ross as his solicitor, decided to adopt what they termed a Gothenburg approach. The most frequently proffered idea is that Scottish merchants had visited Gothenburg and seen what was happening. Swedish iron ore was being exported to Scotland from Gothenburg, and records at Morrison's Haven also showed strong trade links to there. Interestingly, founding director George Tod of the East of Scotland Public House Trust was described as a 'Merchant', and Lord Novar in 1930 had described him as a key activist, not mentioning Sir John Ross at all. But such a late 19th Century connectivity with Gothenburg is to greatly understate the real shared affinity with Scotland.

When modern Gothenburg was finally constructed as the third successor township on the estuary of the Gota Alv in 1640 by Dutch engineers, with the customary panoply of canals that still determine the City centre today, Scottish merchants were not far behind. If Scots could colonise as far afield as Nova Scotia and Darien in Panama they could certainly trade with Gothenburg straight across the North Sea. As Lord Mayor Jorgen Linder was able to inform the author in 2002, Scotland's early contribution was phenomenal. Chalmers University of Technology in the City was an original creation of David, a Scot of that name; Keiller helped to create the City's first great shipyard; Colin Campbell was the entrepreneur behind the 132 voyages to Canton and the Spice Islands by the Swedish East India Company between 1731 and 1819; Carnegie built the porter brewery and the recipe is still available today albeit as a Carlsberg brand; Scottish merchants including Dickson introduced cotton textile manufacture to the City and its workers staged the first recorded Swedish game of football there in 1892. During the Continental Blockade of mainland Europe by Napoleon from 1806–1815 designed to exclude English and Scottish goods, Gothenburg was the centre for almost all the illegal trade inwards via Denmark and Germany whilst the post-Nelson *Victory* and the fleet stood guard offshore. So great was the influence of the British at that time the City became known as Little England.

6.3 The Myth and Facts

It will be readily seen that the Gothenburg System was not much more than a nationwide authorisation of county and municipal monopolies for the traffic in vodka. It was a monopoly conducted by private companies funded by capitalist investors who could see their investment grow per se as well as receiving their guaranteed return of 5% Cumulative per annum. A nice proposition frankly. The Municipalities depended on the surplus profits arising as a major contribution to their revenues, even as all their revenues in Kungsbacka! It was a far cry from Scotland's proposition of no capital gains available, no monopoly, trading through Public House Trusts which frequently built or purchased their properties, and covering all alcoholic refreshment not only vodka.

The Gothenburg System was sold in Scotland and England as a philanthropic approach to the encouragement of temperance by disinterested management. And that is indeed what it came to mean in Britain at large for perhaps 50 years or more. Sweden was not doing the same thing at all. In truth in Sweden it was much better characterised as an excellent opportunity greatly to tax the poorer members of the community as they sought merriment and distraction in their vodka, with a subdued and tardy concern for sobriety.

7. *THE GOTH'S* SPECIAL ARCHITECTURAL AND/OR HISTORIC INTEREST

On January 4th 1985, in particular after the urgings of local Councillor (now Provost) Pat O'Brien who had himself had his wedding reception at *The Goth*, East Lothian District Council wrote to Bass, its owners at that time, giving Notice that The Forth Tavern (as it was then called) had been included in the consolidated list of buildings of special architectural or historic interest Category B ... compiled by the Secretary of State on 21st December 1984. "Such buildings contribute a great deal to the character of our towns and villages," the letter said, "... and one of the main purposes in preparing the list is to support ... the efforts already being made to repair and restore them ... and so they can receive the special consideration they merit."

The preceding pages have surely been well able to demonstrate the Historic Interest which *The Goth* has for our particular town. At the time of the Listing little of what has been written above was known to the current inhabitants of Prestonpans, however. The predominant belief was that it was like the Dean Tavern and had been started by a local group of enthusiasts, which has been shown as very far from the truth. It was in fact the product of Lord Novar's "superior" system for encouraging temperance and quite unlike the provident approach in Newtongrange or for that matter in Kelty which was given as a comparator. Neither were *The Goth* or the others cited in the Listing "essentially charitable companies".

As for Architectural Interest, the great happiness is that despite its several refurbishments over the past 90 years including the Murrays recent commencement of conversion to a private dwelling, almost all the original features are intact except for that famous lavatory equipment.

The Listing ascribes, possibly, Dunn & Findlay as the architects in 1908, and we certainly know it was a loan from the Thomas Nelson family Trusts that funded it. The Arts & Crafts style of the exterior is very widely to be seen south of the border, but in Prestonpans it is quite unique. The north facing façade is accordingly certainly remarkable if not especially imposing but all other elevations are less than distinguished. "The main elevations are in red sandstone ashlar with base course to the ground floor, upper floor brown harled with some sandstone dressings and some timber features".

The full details of the Listing are given in the exhibit included here, but of particular note for the exterior is what is termed "very varied fenestration". The windows are indeed a bizarre mixture, with those in the north elevation in particular giving minimal visibility in or out. Early pictures show that they have been changed somewhat over the years but it would still seem to be contradictory to the notions of openness for public houses espoused by temperance at the time it was built.

The interior of *The Goth's* bar is such that all who enter for the first time are impressed. It is certainly exceptional. The island bar and gantry has survived largely intact from 1908. The Jug Bar is also intact including its glazed doors. Throughout the bar area Art Nouveau decorative tiles are used above timber panelled dado. Several of the windows have decorative stained glass. The fireplace surrounds both in the bar and throughout the premises continue the Art Nouveau designs in carved wood and beaten copper. So too does the dumb waiter.

The other facilities mentioned in the original press report of the opening in

1908, the spacious refreshment rooms and the glorious views of the Firth of Forth are still intact and several of the doors of the original lavatories.

Altogether *The Goth* is a handsome architectural legacy and its Category B Listing means that the Secretary of State through Historic Scotland and the East Lothian Council are committed to ensuring it receives the "special consideration it merits ...when proposals for its development are contemplated."

8. A CONTINUING PURPOSE FOR THE GOTH AND SUSTAINABILITY

Any and all objective analysis of the fate of the Gothenburg System, however defined or manifest in Scotland, or England or in Gothenburg itself, makes clear that the challenge of drunkenness and abject poverty is not what it used to be. There are similar challenges at the top of our social agendas today, such as drugs, but it is not alcoholism and the focus is not the public house. Indeed, if Rowntree, Sherwell, Booth, Ross and the others were here today they would (i) be well pleased with the transformation that is still proceeding apace to bring food and families into public houses, and (ii) would probably put their reforming zeal into alleviating the challenge of drugs. They would see there the same issues precisely as they wrestled with a century ago – of public and private cupidity, of choosing between prohibition and limitation, of how profit drives the trade and the search for disinterested management.

They would probably smile at the realisation that the final nail in the coffin of alcoholic excess in public houses has been driven from outwith the trade altogether by the public approbation given to Don't Drink and Drive. It has been less the horrors of alcohol excesses as a cause of poverty that has brought about the change than an escalating public awareness of the mayhem caused on the roads by drivers with alcohol in their blood. They would not be surprised that Sweden had led the world in reducing alcohol blood level limits to zero tolerance. Their smile would broaden when further regaled with contemporary statistics about fitness and diet, and the way personal vanity not cupidity has transformed so many of our life styles. And finally they would break into a chuckle when told of the phenomenal growth of the sale of lagers, spritzers, non and low alcohol beers, sports drinks and colas, and the widescale development of coffee shops, pavement cafes, Sunday lunches and everyday bistros.

So it is wholly appropriate for Dean Tavern to let the temperance matter rest if it so chooses, not because Dean Tavern failed as we surely failed at *The Goth*, but because the strife is o'er, the battle won. But what to do with our legacy? Is it just for the history books like this one here or Anderson's 1986 classic *The Dean Tavern*? Is it just the subject for one more mural painted on the walls in Prestonpans?

The answer is, not necessarily. In the language of management experts today, how can Prestonpans 'leverage' the past? How can both the architectural legacy and the providential philosophy that Thomas Nelson's funds and Lord Novar, George Tod, Sir John Ross, and their managers at *The Goth* like James Fewell all espoused be given renascent meaning and leadership in the 21st Century?

8.1 A Continuing Purpose

It is one of the readily accepted truths in Prestonpans that when Johnny Moat keeled over in the Great Storm of December 1952 the unhappy predictions envisaged indeed came true. In the next decade the town's economy and its social life went from very good and very proud, to not so very good or proud after all. Now, there seems little likelihood that anything *The Goth* might come to achieve in the years ahead will be able to bring everything that needs to come better in Prestonpans into that blissful state. But oak trees from acorns grow, and if the Public House Trust Movement of 100 years ago has shown anything it has shown that you do not have to do it all yourself. Folk simply need to stand up and be counted. And that is what is now planned.

The East of Scotland Public House Company was re-incorporated on April 22nd 2002, exactly 101 years after its original incorporation. Its shareholders are raising the necessary capital faithfully to restore and extend *The Goth* for the 21st Century merriment and benefit of Prestonpans and all others who wish or can be persuaded to visit. The Memorandum & Articles of Association confirm that after a 5% return on the investment made, the surplus available will be given to Trustees for the benefit of the registered charitable activities of the Baron Courts of Prestoungrange & Dolphinstoun. The Charity is now based at *The Goth* and its major activities over the next decade are built around the Prestoungrange Arts Festival which seeks, via the Arts, to stimulate Tourism.

There is a global equivalent of the Gothenburg System underlying what is now being attempted. It is called the Global Association for Arts & Tourism and it was launched in the 1980s in British Columbia, Canada, at Chemainus – a small timber-mill township of 2000 inhabitants. Today that small town has 400 000 visitors each year, its own Dinner Theatre with 240 seats, a School of Theatre Studies and upwards of 50 associated townships around the world including Prestonpans that have adopted its principles. Its most obvious manifestation is the painting of murals telling the history of the town over the ages, and this is already in hand in Prestonpans. Karl Schutz, the inspiration of Chemainus has visited Prestonpans three times already to share his experiences and the challenges met and overcome.

The continuing purpose adopted therefore is to reinvest in Prestonpans the surpluses arising from trade at *The Goth,* not in recreational facilities and the encouragement of temperance thereby, but in Arts and Tourism initiatives. In doing so we confidently expect to deploy the Arts as a catalyst for the local economy, and to create additional and valued social facilities.

8.2 How Will The Goth Prosper Anew

The renovations and extensions at *The Goth* take place against a backdrop of abject failure there in the mid 1990s, both socially and commercially. So why will a renascent Gothenburg succeed? Nothing in life is certain, but some considerable care has gone into planning the next steps.

The first and most significant proposition is that, since it is Arts and Tourism that is the continuing purpose, *The Goth* must, and must be seen to, do justice to that purpose. The architectural interest inside and out must be something the town can once again take great pride in. *The Goth* must become a focus for the Arts and for Tourism, howsoever defined. Exhibitions will necessarily be a feature of this but the décor of the interior will also reflect the history of the town as captured in all the arts – pottery, poetry, painting, photography. In each of these areas and more besides, local societies and individuals will be encouraged to use the facilities available and they will be designed so that they serve their needs well.

Making this statement first is not for an instant meant to detract from the second proposition, that *The Goth* will once again join the local marketplace as a fine place to eat and to drink and to hold wedding feasts and personal anniversary celebrations. Then there are the community's own *Gala* celebrations which shall surely continue to include *St Jerome's Fair* each September 30th and *Goth Founders' Day* on April 22nd. The fascinating careers of the founders can be profiled. We can certainly honour the life and music of Davy Steele and anticipate interesting twinning with more than a few aspects of life in Goteborg. Can an annual pre-Christmas Domino's Competition lead to a *Fewell Challenge Trophy*?

Thirdly, *The Goth* plans to become home to its very own microbrewery producing some of the old Fowler's Ales. Fowler's Ales (Prestoungrange) Limited has also been incorporated and with the assistance of Fisherrow Breweries in Musselburgh will be launching the microbrewery and teaching all who truly care that much about their beer how to brew it well. But those who do not wish to go as far as trainee brewer status will have the opportunity to see the microbrewery at work through plate glass viewing areas.

The fourth and final proposition is Destination Tourism. The existing population of Prestonpans is, in all truth, scarcely large enough to sustain a viable renascent *Goth* solely from its own expenditures each week and month. It will contribute greatly and surely make regular visits to *The Goth* for a great series of special occasions, but incomers will be needed and must be welcomed too. The facilities will be of a standard that, as Hood and MacKay would have said at Dean Tavern 100 years ago, is "unsurpassed". *The Goth* will expect to become a destination in its own right as well as a meetings/ refreshment service facility for those who travel inwards for the Arts activities and those who simply find it a pre-eminently fine place to meet.

It is the combination of all four of these propositions that can make *The Goth* a sober and commercial success, giving the necessary return of 5% to the investors and a worthy surplus for the Charity's Trustees. Against this strategic framework, good management of *The Goth's* bar and catering operations is required and so is good marketing of the facilities to destination tourists and local users of meetings facilities alike.

8.3 Prestoungrange Online@www.prestoungrange.org

The greatest challenge of any activist group with zeal for its purpose is to inform and persuade much if not all the community at large in an acceptable proactive way, to invite their active participation and to sustain its own purposeful momentum. This is abundantly true of all the initiatives taken by the Baron Courts since 1998 which have been told out in the Baron Courts' Arts Festival *Brushstrokes* NewsSheet but also on the Internet – which has been used in a most imaginative way to inform and to archive a considerable part of the history of Prestonpans. This has been done where practicable in association with the Prestonpans Historical Society and of course the Industrial Heritage Museum.

In respect of *The Goth* in particular a similar facility has been created, but

The Gothenburg

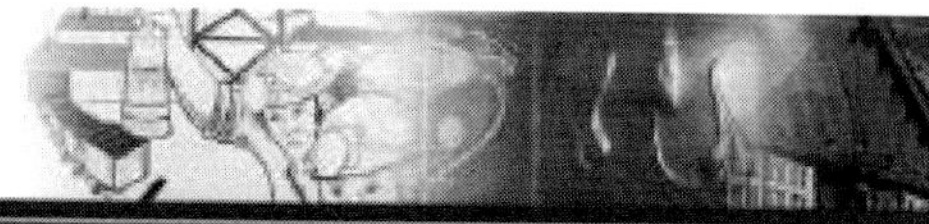

INDEX | GLOBAL MURALS | BARON COURTS | PRESTONPANS | ARTS FESTIVAL

- Home
- Chronology
- Pre-restoration
- Restoration
- Micro Brewery
- Belhaven Brewery
- The Future
- Goteborg, Sweden
- News & events

The Prestoungrange Gothenburg

The Prestoungrange Gothenburg was built in 1908 by the directors of the East of Scotland Public House Trust Company, a goal they had had since their establishment in 1901 in Edinburgh. It was to be a public house in the best traditions of the temperance movement, and was constructed on land acquired from Belfield, the potters, which had previously been within the Prestoungrange Baronial lands of the Grant Sutties. The founders were men of distinction including Thomas Nelson II and a future Governer General of Australia, Lord Novar.

The name Gothenburg was not formally adopted until the late 1980s having been originally named the Trust House and subsequently the Forth Tavern. But the name had strong roots from 19th Century Sweden where intemperance derived from had been a massive problem. Home manufacture was made illegal in Sweden and the cities were called upon to license public houses as well.

The City Fathers of Gothenburg resolved to address their duties by allowing only fixed interest rates on loan finance and diverting the profits to Public Sector Services. Public house managers were only bonus-ed for the sale of food and non alcoholic beverages.

By the start of the 20th Century more than a few public houses had been taken over by such Trusts and several built anew - in the manner of the Prestoungrange Trust House.

For nearly a century it served the mining community and its successors in Prestonpans, under a series of owners. It passed from the founding trustees to the London based Trust Houses in 1919 and then to Bass. Finally before John and Scott Murray acquired and closed it for conversion to a private home, two landlords conducted the business - James and Judith Bell and Malcolm McIlwraith .... By the late 90s trade had declined dramatically and there was no commitment to make it live again in the very different world Prestonpans had become.

Chronology of the Prestoungrange Gothenburg

The Baron Courts are determined to recreate the Gothenburg respectful of its traditions and mindful of contemporary needs and social behaviours. The Edwardian Bar area and the art deco design of the facilities will be restored and a microbrewery introduced alongside the meals/ bistro service. The upstairs Meeting Rooms will be restored to 21st Century standards for their traditional use for Weddings and Celebrations and for formal meetings and conferences. Access will also be given for local Clubs and Societies from Prestonpans.

Pre-restoration pictures of the Prestoungrange Gothenburg

The full history of the Gothenburg in Prestonpans is told in the historical Services Booklet published by Baron Courts:

The Prestoungrange Gothenburg: The first 50 years and the coming decade

Back to top

it can and shall have a more symbiotic relationship with each Panners' face to face experience of the renascent *Goth*. It is the deliberate intention to gather an email database of *Friends of The Goth* to whom all information on events and celebrations can be sent regularly, together with a metamorphosed *Brushstrokes* NewsSheet online and in the letterboxes of all.

9. FOUR YEARS ON: 2006

In 2006 The Prestoungrange Gothenburg was pronounced Scotland's Lothians, Edinburgh & Borders Pub of the Year by CAMRA. In 2005 it had been declared English Heritage/CAMRA UK's 'Pub Conservation' of the Year; and earlier in 2005, East Lothian's New Enterprise of the Year. As we pondered what it was that had so effectively captured the imagination of the judges for each of those wholly unexpected but truly worthy recognitions, it became crystal clear that the achievement was grounded in the vision set down in 8.2 above, and its four principles. The arts and crafts fabric of the original building had been scrupulously honoured in its renovation and redecorations, and extended in the new functions facilities where the foundation contribution by Thomas Nelson was honoured in the name given to them. Artists with the brush, in music, poetry and drama were making regular use and the Prestonpans real ales from the microbrewery were winning national acclaim. The James Park Bistro and the restaurant services have also been greatly appreciated. More than five hundred 'Friends' of The Goth have been enrolled, becoming members of the Arts Festival supporting charity.

The Chemainus model of Mural Arts & Cultural Tourism had been dramatically advanced across the town with some 22 murals completed and the Global Conference of some sixty + towns and cities across the world arriving in August. But as had been discerned all around the world, what begins with murals very speedily broadens its base. The fate of the town's 81 witches in the late 16th/ 17th centuries had also become an annual theatre focus at Hallowe'en, and a campaign for the 'better' interpretation of the Battle of Prestonpans 1745 was getting under way. In partnership with neighbouring Cockenzie and Port Seton a truly ambitious Three Harbours Festival had been staged with nearly 100 venues.

Much of this had been achieved, as all social entrepreneurs know, because of the omnipresence of naysayers and bureaucratic dilettantes, who have no faith in their own community's ability to regenerate its social and economic fabric; those who believe that regeneration is accomplished from above rather than from within. The frustrations they inescapably engender were fertile ground indeed for such a rebirth of community self-esteem, and so it transpired. Visitors from far and wide, both on the ground and virtually via the website, express appreciation and indeed surprise that such has been accomplished in Prestonpans. After all, Prestonpans was the former industrial hub of East Lothian with all the deprivation attendant on the restructuring of Scotland's industries in the later years of the 20th century.

Yet therein lay the second clue to the outstanding social success that has been achieved. The strength of community that is inherent in any industrial town cannot be snuffed out overnight. It was still there, in a state of aestivation, waiting to burst into flower. The reunions of Fowler's Ales old brewers and of local miners testifies to this as they resume their traditional places at The James Fewell Bar. Ancient they may be, but they and their descendants have taken the muralised history of the town, and the living personification of that history in The Gothenburg, very much to heart. They are well pleased. So are the countless couples who held their wedding reception long since upstairs in what is today known as The Lord Mayor's Bar in honour of the visit to The Gothenburg by that inspirational Swedish city's Lord Mayor Jorgen Linder on July 23rd 2003 as restoration proceeded.

9.1 Sustainable Renaissance Yet to be Proven

For the current configuration of services provided from The Prestoungrange Gothenburg to customers and the community at large to be sustainable under Gothenburg Principles in the medium term, sales of the order of £1 million each year are required by 2008/ 2009. By 2006 half that target had been reached. The shortfall after just 24 months trading is not cause for alarm but it remains a clarion call for unremitting commercial determination and leaves no room whatever for any complacency that might be engendered by national recognition in the media or awards rightfully received. To sustain its funding and its social purpose the requisite 5% return on capital employed must be reached then exceeded. Much still needs to be done.

Quite apart from the organic growth of sales at The Prestoungrange Gothenburg itself which can perhaps be realistically forecast at say 15% pa, plans are necessarily afoot to grow 'GothOutdoors'. This is being addressed through Arts and Music Festivals and Outdoor Catering services and the development of real ale sales across Scotland. Research and field studies are continuing to seek partners for the rebirth of salt making in Prestonpans, the industry that gave the town its name many centuries ago, to provide both an additional tourist attraction but also to recreate local employment.

Few who visit and appreciate The Prestoungrange Gothenburg care to comprehend these commercial realities that underlie its renaissance thus far, although they can hazard a guess at the investment that has necessarily been made. The commercial consensus, however, amongst those who are at the commercial coalface is that Gothenburg Principles can be reintroduced effectively but the scale of activity at present essayed is truly Herculean. The next 24 months will be just as challenging as the first and if targets cannot be met strategic adjustments and refocused ambition will necessarily be the consequence.

ACKNOWLEDGEMENTS, REFERENCES AND APPENDICES

This work was made possible by the help of a considerable number of proactive and reactive collaborators. Pre-eminently Jane Bonnar made an exhaustive search to find the details of the early commercial affairs of the East of Scotland Public House Trust at the Scottish Records Office, and she also located most of the Scottish photographs and press cuttings with the help of local library staffs in Haddington. Paul Zirkowski of the Planning Department of East Lothian Council assisted with leads to other Gothenburg houses in East Scotland and to microbrewers, as did Craig Ward.

Anne Taylor made all the arrangements for research in Carlisle and the Reference Library staffs there in the City Library led by Stephen White were magnificent in finding vital documents. Julie Aitken kindly conducted the contemporary interviews with Panners that are included in the text.

Sylvia Burgess took all the necessary steps with the British Lending Library and the Bodleian in Oxford to find details of the Royal Commissions' work in 1930/ 1931 and in particular the Minutes of Evidence that proved of inestimable value. She was also responsible for setting up the schedule in Goteborg in August 2002.

In Goteborg the staffs at the Regional and City Arkivet with Anna Connell taking responsibility for interpretation could not have been more helpful and they were able to provide CD copies of the key manuscripts and photographs in a matter of hours. Lord Mayor Jorgen Linder was most gracious and a fund of anecdotal information on Scottish merchants and linkages over the centuries. The City Museum, now located in its old Head Offices, provided invaluable information on Colin Campbell's role in the Swedish East India Company.

My thanks to everyone of you for enabling me to have such an exhilarating journey into an area of almost total ignorance on my part, and to learn so very much about The Gothenburg System as we lay our plans for the next decade.

The specific references consulted are listed below:

Adams, D.T., (1932) *The Carlisle Scheme,* The Temperance Legislation League, London

Amulree, Lord, Chairman, (1932) *Report of the Royal Commission on Licensing (England & Wales) 1929–1931,* HMSO Cmd 3988

Evidence to Lord Amulree's Commission for England & Wales:
- Cripps, R., Questions 17371–17793, April 1st 1930
- Holderness, B., Questions 18067–18507, April 10th 1930
- Madden, William T., Questions 18508–18718, April 10th 1930
- Spence, Eric H., Questions 20483–20743, May 8th 1930

Anderson, Alasdair, (1986) *The Dean Tavern: A Gothenburg Experiment,* Dean Tavern Trust, Newtongrange

Annual Accounts (1908–1918) *East of Scotland Public House Trust Company Limited*

Burke's Landed Gentry, 19th Edition, Volume 1. *The Kingdoms in Scotland* (2001), Stokesley

East Lothian Council, (1986) *Prestonpans Remembered,* Haddington, East Lothian Library Service

Goteborg Arkivet, (1865) *Minutes of the Licensing Magistrates; Minutes of the 1st Meeting of the Shareholders of Goteborg Bolag; Minutes of 1st Meeting of the Directors of Goteborg Bolag; Letter of Complaint from those Surrendering the Licences*

Goteborg Arkivet, (1905 est.) *Miscellaneous Photographs of interiors of Bolag Public Houses with Reading Rooms and Eating Tables*

Green, James, (2002) Chairman of Trustees at Dean Tavern, Newtongrange, *Conversations at the Dean Tavern (unpublished)*, May 2nd

Hansard, (20th April/ 27th May 1971) as reported in *Brewing Trade Review,* May 1971, Debates on the 2nd Reading and in Standing Committee D on Licensing (Abolition of State Management) Bill, pp. 432–493

Losman, Beata, (Ed.), (2001) *A Presentation for the EU Summit June 2001,* Regional, City & County Archives, Goteborg

Mackay, Lord, Chairman (1931) *Report of the Royal Commission on Licensing (Scotland),* HMSO Cmd 3894

Evidence to Lord Mackay's Commission for Scotland:

Ballantyne, A., Questions 8713– 8959, 1st July 1930

Gordon, John, Questions 9174–9268, 3rd November 1930

Novar, Lord, & Bailey, F.G., Questions 2502–2632, 18th February 1930

Patterson, J.G., Questions 3866–4537A, 27th March 1930

Reid, William, Questions 8960–9033, 1st July 1930

Sykes, Sir John C.G., Questions 3634–3865, 27th March 1930

Memorandum & Articles of Association, (2002) *East of Scotland Public House Company Limited*, Companies House

Memorandum & Articles of Association, (2002) *Baron Courts of Prestoungrange & Dolphinstoun Limited by Guarantee, a Charitable Company*, Companies House

Memorandum & Articles of Association, (2002) *Fowler's Ales (Prestoungrange) Limited,* Companies House

Forster, Jim, (Ed.) (2002) *Tales of the Pans,* reprinted, 2nd Impression, Baron Courts of Prestoungrange and Dolphinstoun

Hunt, J., (1971) *A City Under the Influence,* Lakescene Publications, Carlisle

Temperance (Scotland) Act, 1913, [3 & 4 GEO. 5 CH. 33], HMSO, Edinburgh

Pratt, Edwin A., (1907) *Licensing and Temperance in Sweden, Norway and Denmark,* John Murray, London

Prospectus & Memorandum & Articles of Association, (1901) *East of Scotland Public House Trust Company Limited*, Scottish Records Office

Punnett, R.M., State Management of the Liquor Trade, *Public Administration,* 44, pp. 193–211

Selley, E., (1927) *The English Public House as It Is,* Longmans, London

Stuart, Wilson, (1917) *The Carlisle & Annan Experiment,* Scottish Temperance League, Glasgow, 3rd Edition

Stuart, Wilson, (1927) *Drink Nationalisation in England & the Results,* James Clarke, London

APPENDICES

1. Temperance (Scotland) Act 1913 Poll Forms
2. Statutory Listing of *The Goth*
3. Troubled Times for Contemporary Gothenburg
4. Magistrates Protocol April 7th 1865 after consideration of report on the causes of poverty in the city of Gothenburg. Two Scottish families were instrumental in the report – the Dicksons and the Carnegies
5. City Council Protocol April 13th 1865 where by 29–12 it was resolved to establish the bolag's monopoly in Gothenburg
6. Letter of Complaint April 22nd 1865 from those who lost their rights to the new bolag
7. Chronology of The Gothenburg 1901–2002

APPENDIX 1

TEMPERANCE (SCOTLAND) ACT, 1913.

SCHEDULE I.

FORM OF REQUISITION FOR A POLL.

We, the subscribers hereto, being electors in [*here insert area for which the poll is demanded*] do hereby demand a poll under the terms of the Temperance (Scotland) Act, 1913.

Signature.	Name in full.	Address.	Number on register.

SCHEDULE II.

FORM OF BALLOT PAPER.

(Ballot Paper for [*here insert name of area*].)

Counterfoil No.

1	**No-Change Resolution** (Means that the powers and discretion of the licensing court shall remain unchanged).	
2	**Limiting Resolution** (Means that the number of certificates for the sale of exciseable liquors shall be reduced by one quarter *in accordance with the provisions of the Act*).	
3	**No-Licence Resolution** (Means that no certificate for the sale of exciseable liquors shall be granted except for inns and hotels or restaurants in special cases in accordance with the provisions of the Act).	

Indicate your vote by making a **X** in the right hand space opposite the resolution for which you vote. You have one vote, and may vote for one resolution only. If you vote for the no-licence resolution, and that resolution is not carried, your vote will then be counted as a vote in favour of the limiting resolution.

APPENDIX 2
STATUTORY LISTING OF THE GOTH

EAST LOTHIAN COUNCIL | PRESTONPANS BURGH

Information Supplementary to the Statutory List | STATUTORY LIST

ITEM NO 8

Group with Items: CAT: B

Map Ref: NT 382 742 Date of Listing: 21.12.84

227 HIGH STREET, THE GOTHENBURG (FORMERLY FORTH TAVERN)

Possibly Dunn & Findlay, 1908. Imposing public house in Arts and Crafts style with Art Nouveau interior. 2-storey, essentially 6-bay. Main elevations in red sandstone ashlar with base course to ground floor, upper floor brown harled with some sandstone dressings and timber features.

N (FRONT) ELEVATION: quasi-symmetrical, essentially 6-bay. 2 central bays slightly raised and projecting from upper floor: 2 tripartite windows to ground with stone mullions and transoms, separated by blank carved plaque; upper floor with Tudor style, mock-timbering, 2 canted timber oriel windows under jettied gablehead. Central bays flanked at ground to either side by tripartite windows and moulded round-arched doorways, that to the NE set in the corner angle. 1st floor with timber silhouette balustrade, projecting central bays flanked to each side by tripartite window and canted timber oriel windows clasping corner angles; angle of return with single window to W, with glazed door and single window to E.

S ELEVATION: irregular and undistinguished, including a variety of single, bipartite, tripartite and 1 large stair window. Flat-roofed extensions to rear.

E ELEVATION: projecting and piended ingleneuk with 3 small windows, flanked by single window to S (rear).

W ELEVATION: projecting and piended ingleneuk with 4 small windows, flanked by bipartite window to N and single window to S.

Fenestration very varied. To front elevation, ground floor has unusual diamond glazing pattern in timber below leaded upper lights; 1st floor windows in sections of 8 small panes, casement or top-opening. Other elevations have variety of sash and case, top-opening and fixed timber windows.

Roofs piended, with exception of front gablehead, in flat-profile red clay tiles, ridges in same material. Projecting chimney breasts on E and W elevations above ingleneuks, tall stacks harled with brick caps and plain cans. Similar projecting stack also to rear. Decorative rainwater hoppers to all elevations inscribed "1908".

INTERIOR: exceptional, surviving largely intact, with island bar, gantry and original fittings. Arcaded recesses and ingleneuk in bar, ingleneuk also in E room. Jug bar behind glazed panelled door to front. Glazed and decorative Art Nouveau tilework above timber-panelled dado. Some decorative stained glass.

REFERENCES: C McWilliam, Lothian, 1978, p 400.

EASTLOTH29.DOC 'PAGE NO' 11

APPENDIX 3

New probe into £600,000 grants for failed pub

Claims of cronyism as watchdog investigates council subsidies

JASON ALLARDYCE

SCOTLAND'S public spending watchdog is to launch an investigation into new claims of irregularities involving Fife councillors after the collapse of a pub which received £600,000 in public cash.

Audit Scotland, which is investigating links between the failed Third Age Charity and Fife Council, has been called in to examine the failure of the Number One Goth bar in the Fife mining town of Cardenden.

Scotland on Sunday has learned the bar is just one of a clutch of organisations that are funded by Fife Council and partly run by councillors.

'Young has sought a meeting with the council's head of legal services'

The revelations come just days after the council's own inquiry into the Officegate affair which toppled Henry McLeish identified a pattern of cronyism and patronage at the heart of the Labour run authority.

The Number One Goth, whose unsalaried director was Fife councillor Margot Doig, went into liquidation last year after failing to attract sufficient custom, despite a series of grants from the council and the European Union totalling £600,000.

The pub was made famous by the writer Ian Rankin, whose fictional character Detective Inspector Rebus bought his first round of drinks there.

Originally set up for local miners in 1904, it was based on the Swedish concept of Goth pubs, which began in the town of Gothenberg, where all profits were put back into the community.

Councillors invested £40,000 in the project in 1998 and handed over another £40,000 in 2000 in an effort to run the ground floor as a pub and the upper level as a training facility run by Fife College for local job-seekers.

But critics say the training arm of the operation never took off, that there was a high turnover of staff and that the grants awarded, despite council cash constraints, amounted to unfair subsidies not available to other local businesses.

Stuart Randall, the council's Conservative group leader whose complaint prompted the Audit Scotland inquiry, alleges that Doig chaired a key meeting on the group's future despite being its director – although there is no suggestion she broke any rules because she did not comment on the matter.

An Audit Scotland spokeswoman confirmed that the same team of external auditors examining the relationship between The Third Age and Fife Council will examine the council's links with Number One Goth.

However, the pub is not the only organisation that is raising concerns. It has also emerged that community transport companies co-run by Labour councillors are receiving thousands of pounds of council funding.

Councillor Robert Young is managing director of Gangforth Limited, which Fife Council admitted last week had received at least £27,000 in council grants since 1998.

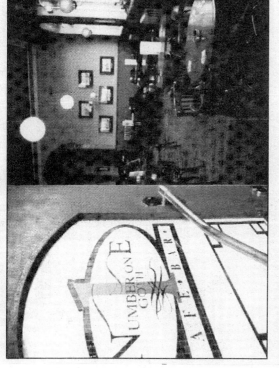

Closing time: the Number One Goth bar in Cardenden, made famous by Inspector Rebus, received £600,000 in grants but shut down after failing to attract enough custom. *Photograph: Dundee Press*

Returns to Companies House showed the charity has an annual turnover of around £300,000 and received local authority grants totalling £150,405 last year.

Young told Scotland on Sunday the charity has seven employees and is training 70 people, adding he did not believe there had been a conflict of interest between his role as managing director and a member of the council that helps to fund it.

'I have seen enough to have very grave concerns of cronyism and political bias'

Records also list Fife Labour councillor Michael Rumney as a former director of the project, which provides community transport for lunch clubs and other groups while training people to become drivers.

But he has sought a meeting with the council's chief executive and head of legal services this week to ask them to consider the matter. Company records also reveal that Young is one of four Labour councillors linked to Trans-Fife Community Transport, another local transport charity with a turnover of a quarter of a million pounds.

Young was a director of the transport charity until 1999 – as was Theresa Gunn, the Labour councillor.

Labour councillor William O'Sullivan was also a director until 1988 and the latest company returns continue to list Labour councillor Barbara Stocks as a director.

Since 1998, Trans-Fife has been awarded grants of at least £97,000 from the Fife Council.

Randall claims the disclosures reveal that Labour's links with The Third Age, criticised in last week's report by the council's chief executive, may be the tip of the iceberg.

He said there are too many "blurred distinctions" between councillors and organisations on which they serve.

He added: "I have seen enough of voluntary groups and companies limited by guarantee very closely connected to the council to have very grave concerns of cronyism and political bias in the selection of employees and the way that the public interest has been allowed to overlap substantially with Labour Party interests."

Following last week's damning council report, which highlighted Labour cronyism and patronage at the heart of the Officegate affair that brought down Henry McLeish, Fife Council will implement much tougher grant awarding procedures.

APPENDIX 4

1865. Göteborgs N:o 16.

Stadsfullmäktiges Handlingar.

Magistratens protokoll för den 7 April 1865, angående ansökan af ett tillernadt bolag, om öfvertagande af bränvinsutskänkningsrättigheter härstädes; jemte en skrift från nu varande innehafvare af dylika rättigheter.

Utdrag af Protokollet, hållet hos Magistraten i Göteborg, den 7 April 1865.

Till Magistraten hade i dag ingifvits en af handelsbolagen James Dickson & C:o, D. Carnegie & C:o, Ekman & C:o, Sv. Renström & C:o, C. F. Wærn & C:o, G. H. Hegardt & C:o, Aug. Abrahamson & C:o, H. J. Heyman & C:o, L. Levgren & Son och J. A. Kjellberg & Söner, grosshandlanderne Robert Dickson, J. W. Wilsson, Olof Wijk och B. E. Dahlgren, handlanderne Julius Lindström och G. Lundgren, boktryckaren S. A. Hedlund, medicine doktorn Elias Heyman, handelsfirman M. W. Rhedin och brukspatronen James Dickson undertecknad skrift, af denna lydelse:

"*Till Välloft. Magistraten i Göteborg.*

Sedlighet och välstånd bland arbetsklassen inom vårt samhälle hafva en svår fiende i bränvinet. Det är dock icke den berusande drycken allena och det omåttliga njutandet deraf, som alstra sedeförderfvet och fattigdomen, utan dertill bidraga i väsendtlig mån de oordningar, dåliga föredömen, tillfällen och lockelser till ondt af allahanda slag, som af kroglifvet i rikt mått uppstå. Lagstadganden, i förening med tillsyn af polismakten, förmå föga härvid uträtta, så länge utskänkningsrätten är öfverlåten åt enskilde personer, hvilkas fördel det är att uppmuntra supandet, utan afseende på stadgad ålder eller ungdom, fattigdom eller förmögenhet.

Undertecknade hafva derföre förenat sig om bildandet af ett bolag, under benämning: "Göteborgs Utskänknings-Aktie-Bolag", till öfvertagande, under en tid af tre år, af de utskänkningsrättigheter, 40 till antalet, hvilka vid den reglering af utskänkningen, som för hvarje utskänkningsår, räknadt från den 1 Oktober, enligt Bränvins-Förordningens 7 paragraf, före den 15 Maj bör företagas, kunna för öfverlåtande på annan man detta år blifva tillgängliga. De grunder och vilkor, på hvilka bolaget anhåller att få öfvertaga ifrågavarande rättigheter, äro:

att dessa rättigheter öfverlemnas åt bolaget mot de i Bränvinsförordningens 17 paragraf stadgade minimiafgifter; hvaremot bolaget förbinder sig att åt kommunen och länets Hushållningssällskap, efter afdrag af alla de utgifter, bolaget kan komma få vidkännas, öfverlemna nettobehållningen, intill ett belopp, motsvarande skillnaden emellan dessa minimiafgifter och den för dessa 40 rättigheter under innevarande försäljningsår utgående utskänkningsafgift, nemligen ⅓ af samma åt den förra och ⅓ åt den senare. Den denna summa möjligen öfverstigande vinst vill bolaget derjemte använda till något eller några för den arbetande klassen gagnande ändamål;

att åt bolaget förbehålles rättighet att bestämma utskänkningsställenas antal, inom detta 40-tal, samt placering.

Då af ofvanstående framgår, att bolaget med sitt förslag endast afser ett allmänt gagn, hvars betydelse icke af Välloft. Magistraten lärer undgå att behjertas, hysa vi den förhoppning, att Välloft. Magistraten skall, efter Herrar Stadsfullmäktiges hörande, gifva sitt bifall till vårt anbud.

Göteborg den 6 April 1865.

James Dickson & C:o, D. Carnegie & C:o, Ekman & C:o, Rob. Dickson, Julius Lindström, J. W. Wilson, Sv. Renström & C:o, C. Fr. Wærn & C:o, G. H. Hegardt & C:o, Olof Wijk, B. E. Dahlgren, Aug. Abrahamsson & C:o, H. J. Heyman, S. A. Hedlund, Elias Heyman, L. Levgren & Son, J. A. Kjellberg & Söner, G. Lundgren, M. W. Rhedin, James Dickson."

För ärendets utredning skulle här antecknas följande upplysningar:

Genom nådigt bref den 29 April 1851 har Kongl. Maj:t, till efterrättelse från och med 1852 och tills vidare, fastställt "stadga angående rättighet att i Göteborg distillera och i minut försälja bränvin och andra brända eller distillerade spirituösa drycker samt den afgift, som derföre bör till staden erläggas", innefattande: i *5:te §*, att de personer, som då stadgan först tillämpades, erhållit Magistratens tillstånd för idkande af traktörs- eller krogrörelse under löpande året, skulle än vidare dervid bibehållas, så framt de, år efter annat, fullgjorde hvad i sådant afseende föreskrifvits och framgent ställde sig de för yrkets utöfvande gällande föreskrifter till efterrättelse; och i *6:te §* att med beviljande af rättighet att idka traktörs- eller krognäring härstädes skulle så förhållas, att vid inträffande ledighet, näringsrättigheten utbjöds på auktion inför Magistraten till utöfvande under ett år, räknadt från och med den 1 påföljde Januari, och att för den, som sålunda vid yppad ledighet blifvit antagen till idkare af traktörs- eller krognäring, gällde, i afseende på näringens fortsatta utöfvande efter förloppet af första året, enahanda föreskrifter, som voro stadgade, beträffande de i 5 § omförmälde näringsidkare.

Efter kungörandet af Kongl. Förordningen den 18 Januari 1855, angående vilkoren för försäljning af bränvin och andra brända eller distillerade spirituösa drycker, genom hvilken nådiga förordning förut befintliga stadganden, rörande handel med bränvin och öfrige nyssnämnde drycker, blifvit upphäfne och nye föreskrifter i desse afseenden meddelade, hafva Magistraten och Borgerskapets äldste, vid öfverläggning den 13 April nyssnämnde år, funnit att, enär, enligt 60 § i högstberörda förordning, utskänkningsrätt, förlänad för tid, som före år 1855 icke tilländalöpte, fortfarande finge utöfvas i stad till den 1 Oktober 1855, mot de afgifter till stad eller kommunen, hvilka vid rättighetens förlänande åtagne blifvit, afgifterne till härvarande allmänna Fattigförsörjnings Inrättnings nybyggnadsfond, hvilka på grund af 1851 års Kongl. stadga utgjordes af de personer, som, enligt samma stadga, erhållit Magistratens tillstånd att här i staden utskänka bränvin, skulle för år 1855 påföras endast med tre fjerdedelar af de belopp, hvilka eljest bort till berörda fond för hela året utgöras; hvarjemte och i enlighet med Borgerskapets Äldstes tillstyrkande, Magistraten beslutat hos Konungens Befallningshafvande föreslå att, oberäknadt Restauratörerna å Börsen och Frimurarelogen, Traktören A. W. Jonsson och Traktörs-Enkan Sofia Jonsson, hvilka begge sistnämnde idkade sin rörelse med burskapsrätt, samt de Socker- och Schweitzer-Bagare, som erhållit eller undfingo rättighet att sälja likörer, försäljningsställenas antal för utskänkning af bränvin måtte för ett år från den 1 Oktober 1855 bestämmas å traktörsställen till tjugo och å krogar till trettio; med rättighet för sådana innehafvare af utskänkningsrätt, hvilka icke idkade annan handel, till hvars bedrifvande särskildt tillstånd erfordrades, att så vidt de för öfrigt pröfvades behöriga, ytterligare ett år, från berörde 1 Oktober räknadt, bibehållas vid rörelsen, under vilkor, som i 8 § bestämdes, hvaremot de utskänkningsrättigheter, som sålunda icke bibehöllos af dåvarande innehafvare, skulle, enligt 10 §, utbjudas på offentlig auktion för ett år och för hvarje rättighet särskildt; hvilket förslag Konungens Befallningshafvande den 22 Maj gillat, med undantag dock af utskänkningsställenas fördelning till bestämdt antal särskildt åt Traktörer och särskildt åt Krögare; Varande enahanda framställningar, som den nyssnämnda, hos Konungens Befallningshafvande årligen beslutade af Magistraten, efter det vederbörande hörde blifvit,

den 4 April 1856, och

den 24 April 1857, med anhållan tillika i senare tillfället, att Magistraten måtte för de 50 försäljningsställena få bestämma sådan fördelning af utskänkningen emellan traktörer och krögare, att de förre, i mån af afgång, minskades till 30, och krögarnes antal i förhållande derefter ökades till 20, samt

den 16 April 1858, likväl med den ytterligare förändring, att de utskänkningsrättigheter, som, efter det de för året antagne personer fortfarande blifvit bibehållne, såvidt de dertill pröfvades behöriga, då voro eller kunde blifva lediga, skulle, hvar för sig särskildt, utbjudas på offentlig auktion för tre år från den 1 påföljande Oktober, men vid de tre årens utgång för inroparne upphöra; hvilket allt Konungens Befallningshafvande bifallit, likasom dylika framställningar, som den sistnämnda, för åren från och med den 1 Oktober 1859 intill samma dag innevarande år 1865; Blifvande tillika antecknadt, att Borgaren och Traktören A. W. Jonsson år 1859 aflidit i enklingetillstånd, och att Gästgifvaren å Hotellet Göta Källare innehaft utskänkningsrätt sedan år 1860.

De 40 personer, hvilkas innehafvande utskänkningsrätt det bildade bolaget anmält sig önska öfvertaga, utgöras af följande, hvilka för innevarande försäljningsår erlägga afgift, efter nedan upptagne kannetalsberäkning, nemligen:

Traktörer.

1:o. Enkan Carolina Wennerlöf . . . . 4,000.
2:o. Enkan Eva Maria Pettersson . . . . 7,000.
3:o. Ogifta Carin Fryckstedt . . . . 3,500.
4:o. Enkan Ulrika L. Berggren . . . . 3,000.
5:o. Per Hallberg . . . . 1,200.
6:o. förre Tullvaktmästaren M. Schutz . . . . 3,000.
7:o. Enkan Anna C. Norgren . . . . 4,000.
8:o. f. Handlanden C. J. Majgrens hustru, Anna Sofia . . . 4,500.
9:o. Enkan Maria Gillström . . . . 4,500.
10:o. Petter Härström . . . . 3,500.
11:o. förre Bärareförmannen Sven Hellberg . . . . 7,000.
12:o. Enkan Carolina Thunholm . . . . 2,500.
13:o. förre Polisuppsyningsmannen C. J. Flygare . . . . . 5,000.
14:o. Enkan Anna C. Christensson . . . . 2,500.
15:o. Hustru Anna Catarina Lundahl . . . . 5,000.
16:o. Enkan Anna Charlotta Wenngren . . . . 3,500.
17:o. Enkan Johanna Edberg . . . . 4,500.
18:o. Enkan Maria Carolina Svensson . . . . 4,500.
19:o. Enkan Johanna Cecilia Ullgren, hvilken nyligen aflidit . . . 3,500.
20:o. Ulrika Andersson . . . . 4,000.
21:o. Inga Helena Zetterström . . . . 5,000.

Krögare.

22:o. Enkan Maria Catarina Westerberg . . . . 4,000.
23:o. Ogifta Gustafva Hasselqvist . . . . 4,000.
24:o. Ogifta Anna Maria Andersson, och . . . . 1,500.
25:o. Maria Christina Lindgren . . . . 5,000.
hvilka alla innehaft utskänkningsrätt förr än Kongl. Förordningen den 18 Januari 1855 utfärdades.

Traktörer.

26:o. förre Machinisten Carl J. Lundell, hvilken, såsom innehafvare af landeriet Lorensberg, fått, först år 1857 gemensamt med förre Handlanden C. B. Ekberg, och, sedan år 1859, ensam öfvertaga Musik-Direktören F. Cabrés före år 1855 derstädes bedrifna utskänkningsrörelse, på grund af upplåtelsevilkor, om skyldighet för landeriinnehafvaren att på stället tillhandahålla värdshusrum och betjena allmänheten med mat och lofliga förfriskningar . . . . 1,200.
27:o. Johan Christian Schlegel, som den 7 Augusti 1863 öfvertagit ut-

skänkningsrättigheten å Restaurationen Prins Carl, hvilken rättighet innehafts från och med 1851 af Traktören R. W. Ekström och från den 2 Januari 1863 af Emil Ekström och C. Svalander . 1,000.

28:o. förre Polisuppsyningsmannen B. Holmberg . . . . 4,000.

29:o. förre Snickaregesällen O. F. Landin . . . . 5,500.

30:o. Enkan Anna Cajsa Larsson 3,500,

hvilka tre sistnämnde innehafva sina rättigheter efter inrop å auktion för tid, från den 1 Oktober 1855.

Krögare.

31:o. förre Klamparen S. P. Andersson . . . . 3,000.

32:o. Enkan Maria Charlotta Rydström . . . . 2,400.

33:o. Hamninspektoren J. Wallgrens hustru Albertina . . . . 4,000.

34:o. förre Handelsbetjenten B. H. Möller . . . . 5,000.

35:o. J. A. Alldin . . . . 5,500.

36:o. förre Handelsbetjenten A. B. Larsson . . . . 7,000.

hvilka sex personer likaledes å auktion inropat utshänkningsrättigheterne, som innehafts af de begge förstnämnde från den 1 Oktober 1855, af Hustru Wallgren från samma dag 1856 och af de tre öfrige från den 1 Oktober 1857,

jemte fyra krögare, som å auktion år 1862 blifvit innehafvare af bränvinsutskänkningsrätt intill den 1 nästkommande Oktober, då denna deras rätt upphör . . . . 27,210.

tillhopa kannor 169,010.

I sammanhang härmed föredrogs en af hustru Lundahl den 24 nästlidne Mars till Magistraten ingifven skrift, innefattande anhållan om öfverlemnande till Stadsfullmäktige af en bifogad, utaf henne och 28 bland öfrige af de 36 här förut till namnen omförmälte traktörer och krögare, äfvensom af borgare-enkan Jonsson underteckuad skrift, uti hvilken de omförmäla sina bekymmer, i följd af uppstådd fråga om bränvinsutskänkningsrörelsens öfvertagande här i staden af ett bolag och åberopa sin rätt till bibehållande af denna rörelse.

Magistraten beslutade, enligt 10 § 2 mom. i Kongl. Förordningen den 18 December 1863, angående vilkoren för försäljning af bränvin, att utdrag af detta protokoll skulle tillställas Stadsfullmäktige härstädes, för yttrande, i anledning af utskänkningsbolagets framställning; och komme hustru Lundahls nyssnämnda skrift, med bilaga, att dervid till Stadsfullmäktige äfven öfverlemnas.

Ut supra

In fidem:

G. E. GIERS.

APPENDIX 5

1865 den 13 April

ledamöter, som i eftermiddag skulle utses, remittera handlingarna, för uppskattning af lägenhetens värde och afkastning, utredning af förhållandet mellan lägenhetsinnehafvaren och innehafvarne af de å lägenhetens område uthyrda tomtplatser, samt öfriga saken rörande omständigheter, och yttrande, angående lämpligheten af lägenhetens inlösen för stadens räkning.

§ 4.

Stadsfullmäktige företogo till fortsatt behandling det under § 4 i Protokollet för den 23dje sistlidna Mars antecknade ärende, angående yttrande, i fråga om bränvinsminuterings och utskänkningsrörelsen härstädes under nästa försäljningsår.

Uti detta ärende hade inkommit följande handlingar:

1) Utdrag af Magistratens Protokoll för den 27 sistlidna Januari, utvisande:

att Landshöfdinge Embetet i Länet, medelst Resolution den 14 Maj 1864, beträffande bränvinsförsäljningsrörelsen i minut och genom utskänkning under innevarande försäljningsår, bestämt:

a) att antalet af minuthandelsrättigheter skulle från sextio nedsättas till fyratio, på det sätt, att af de nio dylika å auktion inropade rättigheter, som den 1 Oktober 1864 upphörde, sex borde indragas och endast tre, medelst utrop hvar för sig, å offentlig auk-

1865. den 13. April.

tion för derpåföljande tre försäljningsår af
ytteras, och att af öfriga minuthandelsrättigh
ter, som antingen uppsades eller upphörde,
endast hvarannan bortauktionerades, intill
dess antalet minskats till fyratio;
b.) att de personer, som från 1855, hvarje
gång för ett år, berättigats till minuthande
med eller utskänkning af bränvin, vid så
dan rätt jemväl under innevarande förså
ningsår skulle bibehållas, derest de af Ma
gistratens fortfarande pröfvades dertill behör
ga och tjenliga;
c.) att, oberäknadt Borgareenkan Sofia
Jonsson, Socker- och Schweitzeribagaren T. W.
Paltzow, Konditorn J. Simen, Konditorsen
kan Celina Rubenson, Konditorn Josef
Frick, Konditorn C. M. Andersson, Restaura
törerna å Börsen och i Frimurarësamhället
hus samt Gästgifvaren å Gåla Källare, an
talet utskänkningsställen för innevarand
försäljningsår, under förbehåll, att rörel
icke finge idkas i den trakt af 12te roten,
som ligger utanför vägen till Underåsbro,
skulle förblifva femtio, med rätt för Ma
gistraten: dels att, i mån af afgång bland
traktörerna, minska deras antal till tjugo
och öka krögarnes antal till trettio; dels och
att, utöfver det sålunda bestämda antalet
utskänkningsrättigheter, ytterligare, derest
lämpliga sökander sig anmälde, för in
nevarande försäljningsår tillåta utskänk

1865. den 13 April.

ning, i förening med Konditors- eller restau-
rationsrörelse, mot afgift, beräknad efter det
kannetal, som af Bevillningstaxeringskom-
mittéen bestämdes; och

d) att utskänkningsrättigheter, som voro
eller kunde blifva lediga, skulle, i likhet
med sådana lediga minuthandelsrättigheter, hvilka icke borde indragas, å offentlig
auktion, medelst utrop hvar för sig, afyttras för lika lång tid som hittills, eller intill den 1 Oktober 1867;

att, under innevarande försäljningsår,
rättighet till minuthandel med bränvin
innehafts af:

trettiotre personer, som dervid årligen bibehållits från år 1855; och

tjugo personer, som å auktioner inropat
denna handelsrätt för tid af tre år, nämli-
gen femton intill den 1 Oktober 1865, två intill den 1 Oktober 1866, och öfriga tre intill
samma dag 1867; samt

Bränvinsutskänkningsrätt utöfvats af förr
bemälta enka Jonsson, Socker- och Schweitzeribagaren Paalzow, Konditorerna Frick, Simen
och Andersson samt Restauratörerna å Börsen och i Frimurarefamhällets hus, jemte
Gästgifvaren å Göta Källare, samt dessutom
icke allenast af Konditorn M. Rubenson, sedan hans moder, Enkan C. Rubenson, uppsagt sin innehafda, enahanda rättighet,
och af Konditorn Kristian Frick, som visat

1865 d. 13 April

sig hafva förhyrt Konditorilägenheten i Th
aterhuset; utan äfven af:
Tjugosex traktörer, och
tio krögare, hvilka, alla trettiosex, efter a
tagande årligen, fortfarit med utskänknin
rörelsen från år 1855; och
fjorton krögare, som å auktioner inro
pat denna rörelse, för tid af tre år, näm
ligen fyra intill den 1 nästkommande Okt
ber, sju intill samma dag år 1866, och tre i
till den 1 Oktober 1867; - samt
att en innehafvare af bränvinsminute
ringsrättighet, hvilken hans bolag inne
haft allt sedan 1855, uppsagt densamma f
re den 1 Juli 1864, och att denna rättighet,
i följd af beslutet om nedsättning i antalet
af dylika försäljningsställen, icke blifvit bor
auktionerad;
2) Förslag af Herrar Kommitterade för
undersökning af förhållandet med Pau
perismen m. m., om öfverlemnande af före
nämnda trettiosex Traktörs- och Krogrättighe
ter, som hitills årligen för innehafvarne
förnyats, äfvensom af de fyra utskänknings
rättigheter, hvilka blifvit å auktion försål
da för tiden intill den 1 nästa Oktober, åt
ett för öfvertagande af bränvinsutskänknings
rättigheter härstädes tillernadt bolag, på af
Kommitterade utsatta vilkor; varande försla
get, med dervid fogad reservation af Herr
Philipsson, under No 15 infördt bland ä

1865 d. 13 April

rets tryckta handlingar; samt
3.) och 4.) dels Utdrag af Magistratens Protokoll för den 7de dennes, innefattande ansökan af ett tillernadt bolag, om upplåtelse
till bolaget, på föreslagna vilkor och grunder, af ofvanomförmälda speralis brännvinsut-
skänkningsrättigheter under de tre nästkommande försäljningsåren, hvilken ansökan,
deri Sökanderna förklarat bolaget vilja använda den, efter afdrag af utfästa afgifter
återstående andel af nettobehållningen å rörelsen till något eller några för den arbetande
klassen gagnande ändamål, Magistraten,
med åtskilliga, för ärendets utredning nödi-
ga, upplysningar, remitterat till Stadsfullmäktige, för yttrande; dels ock en vid Protokollet fogad till Stadsfullmäktige ställd
skrift af 29 bland här ofvan omtalade traktörer och Krögare, äfvensom af borgareenkan
Jonsson; uti hvilken skrift de omförmäla
sina bekymmer i följd af frågan om ut-
skänkningsrörelsens öfvertagande af ett bolag,
och åberopa sin rätt till bibehållande af denna rörelse; Och finnas så väl Protokolls-
utdraget, som skrifvelsen införda under
No 16 bland årets tryckta handlingar.
Då föredragningen af ärendet skulle bör-
jas, begärde Herr Blomstrand, att hans under § 5 i Protokollet för den 23 sistlidna
Mars antecknade förslag, angående förbud
mot brännvinsutskänkning å sön- och helg-

1865 d. 13 April.

dagar, öfver hvilket förslag Kommitterade f
undersökning af förhållandet med pauperis
men, m. m, afgifvit ett, jemte dervid fogad
reservation af Herr Philipsson, under No 15
bland årets tryckta handlingar infördt be
tänkande, måtte afgöras, innan Stadsfull
mäktige fattade beslut om yttrande, rörande
de bränvinsminuterings- och utskänknings
reten; men denna begäran afslogs af Stad
fullmäktige, vid å densamma framställd
proposition; dock medgåfvo Stadsfullmäktig
att förslaget och betänkandet fingo anses s
som upplästa.

Beträffande minuthandel med bränvi
beslöto Stadsfullmäktige:
dels att tillstyrka att, i öfverensstämmelse m
det sistlidet år fattade beslut, antalet af
minuthandelsrättigheter från femtiotre ne
sättes till fyratio, på det sätt att af de fem
ton på auktion, för tiden till den 1 Okto
ber i år, inropade sådanarättigheter, sju
indragas, och endast atta, medelst utrop hva
för sig, å auktion afyttras för tre år, intill
den 1 Oktober 1868, då dessa rättigheter upp
höra; och att af öfriga minuthandelsrättighe
ter, som uppsägas eller af annan orsak upp
höra, blott hvarannan, bortauktioneras, in
tilldess antalet minskats till fyratio; samt
dels att till vederbörande myndigheters be
dömande öfverlemna frågan, huru med
de 33 minuthandelsrättigheter, hvilkas inne

1865 d. 13 April.

hafvare dervid årligen från 1855 bibehållits, skall
under nästa försäljningsår förfaras.

I fråga om ordnandet af utskänkningsrörelsen med brännvin, uppstod en längre di-
skussion, under hvilken yrkades: dels bifall
till det tillernade utskänkningsbolagets framställning, dels ock godkännande af Herr Phi-
lipsons förslag uti den af honom afgifna
reservation till Kommitterades hemställan
i ämnet, med det af Herr Philipson nu gjor-
da tillägg, att åt bolaget borde erbjudas öfver-
tagandet af icke allena de fem utskänkningsrättigheter, som, fyra i följd af utlupen försäljningstid och en genom dödsfall,
i år blifva lediga, utan äfven öfriga utskänkningsrättigheter, som af en eller annan orsak före den 1 nästa Oktober kunna komma att upphöra, och att, derest bolaget icke skulle vilja öfvertaga ifrågavarande åt
bolaget erbudna rättigheter, dessa genom
offentlig auktion hvar för sig, borde försäljas på ett års tid till den 1 Oktober 1866.

Derjemte upprepade Herr Blomstrand
sin begäran, att hans förslag om förbud
mot brännvinsutskänkning å sön- och helg-
dagar, måtte i främsta rummet afgöras;
hvilken begäran dock ånyo afslogs.

Efter slutad öfverläggning och sedan
Stadsfullmäktige förbehållit sig att, utan
hinder af blifvande beslut i hufvudsaken,
vidtaga sådan jemkning, som kunde för-

1865 d. 13 April.

anledas af den i Magistratens Protokoll för den 7de dennes meddelade upplysning, de om att förre Machinisten Carl J. Lundell hvars utskänkningsrättighet vore inbegripen ibland de fyratio rättigheter, bolaget begärt att få öfvertaga, utöfvade sin rörelse, såsom innehafvare af Landeriet Lorensberg, på grund af upplåtelsevilkor, om skyldighet för landeriinnehafvaren att på stället tillhandahålla värdshusrum och betjena allmänheten med mat och lofliga förfriskningar; - gjorde Ordföranden proposition på bifall till bolagets framställning.

Härvid begärdes votering, hvilken, sedan, Ordförandens, i anledning af yppade skiljaktiga åsigter, huruvida saken enskildt rörde de Stadsfullmäktige, som underskrifvit bolagets ansökan, framställda fråga, om Stadsfullmäktige ansågo ärendet vara af sådan beskaffenhet, blifvit med Nej besvarad, företogs, efter följande, justerade, Proposition:

"Den, som vill tillstyrka, att de trettiosex traktörs- och krogrättigheter, som hittills för innehafvarne årligen förnyats, jemte de fyra å auktion inropade krogrättigheter hvilka vid slutet af innevarande försäljningsår upphöra böra, i öfverensstämmelse med de uti senare momentet af § 10 i Kongl. Förordningen den 18 December 1863, angående vilkoren för

1865 d. 13 April.

bränvinsförsäljning, för dylikt fall meddelade föreskrifter, utan föregående auktion, öfverlemnas, på tre års tid, intill den 1 Oktober 1868, åt det bolag, som till dessa fyratio utskänkningsrättigheters öfvertagande sig anmält, röstar: ja.

Den, det icke vill, röstar Nej. Winner Nej, hafva Stadsfullmäktige beslutit tillstyrka, att nämnda bolag måtte få, för en tid af tre år intill den 1 Oktober 1868, öfvertaga: ej allena de fem utskänkningsrättigheter, hvilka, fyra i följd af utlupen försäljningstid och en genom dödsfall, i år blifva lediga; utan äfven de öfriga utskänkningsrättigheter, som af en eller annan orsak före den 1 nästa Oktober upphöra; och att, derest bolaget ej skulle vilja öfvertaga ifrågavarande, åt bolaget erbudna, rättigheter, dessa genom offentlig auktion, hvar för sig, försäljas på ett års tid till den 1 Oktober 1866; samt att de trettiofem innehafvare af de rättigheter, hvilka hittills år från år förnyats, ytterligare för nästa försäljningsår må tillgodonjuta enahanda förnyelseförmån; med uttryckligt tillkännagifvande likväl, att sådan förmån derefter ej är att påräkna, utan att rättigheterna vid den reglering, som 1866 förestår, ovilkorligen komma att till Kommunen återgå för den behandling, som i gällande författning är föreskrifven."

Wid upprop, röstade: Herrar J. J. Ekman,

1865 d. 13 April

Wijk, Kjellberg, Berger, Kobb, Frisell, Wickman, Jul. Lindström, Renström, Boman, Wedelin, Levgren, E. G. Lindström, Brusewitz, Hedlund, Levisson, Prytz, James Dickson, af Petersens, Ekström, O. Dickson, Lamberg, Willerding, Reuterskiöld, Francke, Boije, O. Ekman, Lundgren, och Ordföranden: Ja; men Herrar Billqvist, Magnus, Cavalli, Röhss, Philipsson, Jönsson, Blomstrand, Fleetwood, von Schoultz, Warburg, Lundström, och Greiffe Nej.

Med 29 röster mot 12, hade Stadsfullmäktige alltså bifallit Japropositionen.

Härefter gjorde Stadsfullmäktige den jemkning i beslutet, att, enär förre Machinisten Lundells rätt till utskänkningsrörelse vid Lorensberg grundades på vilkor vid upplåtelsen af nämnda landeri, och följaktligen Lundell borde vid ifrågavarande utskänkningsrätt å Lorensberg fortfarande bibehållas, antalet af de utskänkningsrättigheter, som, enligt hvad Stadsfullmäktige nu beslutit tillstyrka, finge af det tillernade bolaget vid slutet af innevarande försäljningsår öfvertagas, inskränktes till trettionio.

Widare beslöto Stadsfullmäktige tillstyrka:

att ifrågavarande trettionio rättigheter skulle till bolaget öfverlemnas, mot de i § 17 af Kongl. Förordningen den 18 December 1863,

1865 d. 13 April.

angående vilkoren för brännvinsförsäljning, stadgade minimiafgifter och förbindelse derjemte för bolaget att, intill en summa, motsvarande skillnaden mellan dessa minimiafgifter och de utskänkningsafgifter, som för rättigheterna under innevarande försäljningsår blifvit innehafvarne påförda, till staden erlägga nettobehållningen å utskänkningsrörelsen, för sådan fördelning, som för utskänkningsafgifter är eller kan varda bestämd;

att bolaget skulle förpligtas att till utskänkningsställen använda endast sunda, ljusa och rymliga lokaler, samt att så anordna rörelsen, att varm, lagad, mat vid vissa måltidstimmar dagligen komme att finnas tillgänglig;

att bolaget skulle tillförbindas att hålla tillsyn, deröfver att å utskänkningsställena snygghet, ordning och skick vidmakthållas, och spirituösa drycker icke på kredit utlemnades;

att bolaget skulle berättigas att bestämma sina utskänkningsställens antal; dock så att detsamma icke finge öfverstiga trettionio;

att bolaget likaledes skulle berättigas att bestämma utskänkningsställenas placering, utan hinder af nu gällande förbud mot brännvinsutskänkning i den trakt af tolfte roten, som ligger utanför vägen till Underåsbro; hvilket förbud i öfrigt borde fortfara äfven under nästa försäljningsår;

/

APPENDIX 6

Till Herrar Stadsfullmäktige i Göteborg.

Enligt hvad för oss blifvit kunnigt, hafva Herrar Stadsfullmäktige för afsigt att ordna utskänkningsrörelsen med spirituösa drycker på sådant sätt, att hela denna rörelse inom Göteborg och dess förstäder skulle öfvertagas af ett bolag, och således de förra innehafvarne af utskänkningsrättigheten derifrån skiljas.

Undertecknade, innehafvare af såbeskaffade rättigheter kunna på intet sätt underskatta värdet af de ansträngningar, som högt aktade ledamöter i samhället påtaga sig i riktning att mildra och om möjligt förekomma de sorger och olyckor fylleriet sprider omkring sig, till hvars afhjelpande

vi i vår ringa mån äfven vilja på att
sätt bidraga, men vi våga på samma gång
framhålla och göra gällande vår rätt, såsom
innehafvare af dessa rättigheter, hysande den
förhoppning att Herrar Stadsfullmäktige derå
fästa afseende.

Flertalet af oss och många andra innehafvare af utskänkningsrättigheter här i staden
hafva sedan många år idkat såbeskaffad
rörelse och på densammas bibehållande
byggt hela sin framtida utkomst.

Likaledes har mången af oss antingen
köpt eget hus, välbelägat för rörelsen och
derför dyrare än hvad de annars varit värdt,
eller ock för flera år hyrt dyra lokaler
samt till deras förbättring användt betydliga
kostnader, i de flesta fallen atth med uplånta
penningar, i den beräkning att rörelsen skulle
af dem under kommande tider få fortsättas
och ersättning så småningom erhållas.

Dessa och andra förhållanden, i hög grad
inverkande på vårt ekonomiska bestånd,
hafva framkallat beslutet hos oss att inför
Herrar Stadsfullmäktige uttala våra farhå-
gor för en behandling af den förevarande
angelägenheten, som kunde leda till vår
ruin.

Vi önska intet högre än att tillräckligt
verksamma åtgärder må vidtagas och un-
derkasta oss villigt alla erforderliga inskränk-
ningar, så att fylleriet kan minskas, eller än
hellre, alldeles utrotas, men vi anse att ord-
ningen å utskänkningsställena bör utan svårighet

kunna regleras på sådant sätt, att än-
målet vinnes och det utan att rättighete-
na behöfva fråntagas oss och dem som äro
lämpliga att utöfva dem, ty det är ostridigt
att en oberoende innehafvare af utskänkningsrörelse vårdar och handhafver den
med ojemförligt större intresse för sig
och det allmänna, än till exempel en
aflönad föreståndare; och då vi uttala
denna öfvertygelse måste vi på samma
gång förklara att ett hastigt afbrytande
af vår rörelse eller rättigheternas in-
dragning från oss är liktydigt med vår
ekonomiska undergång.

Vi tro oss kunna att afsigten är, att
i betydligare mån minska utskänkningsställenas antal, men vi kunna derom
ej tillbakahålla den anmärkning, att
de återstående, som då måste anläggas
i stor skala, blir förtäringen af starka
drycker öfver betydligen ökad, hvilket
synnerligen försvårar upprätthållande af
ordning å stället.

Hvad vi här i ödmjukhet vågat an-
draga, anhålla vi måtte komma i öf-
vervägande vid frågans behandling inför
Herrar Stadsfullmäktige.

Göteborg den 22 Mars 1865.

Sofia M. Svensson — P. H. Zetterström, Enka 67 år — A. M. Andersson, Jungfru 66 år [illegible]

C. [illegible] Fullmagt

Maria Carolina Svensson, 71 år gammal — Johanna Ekberg, Enka 83 år gammal — Eva Maria Pettersson, Tractörs Enka 77 år gammal [illegible]

Gustafva Hasselqvist — A. C. Larsson 65 år gammal, Traktörsrörelse [illegible]

Anna S. Mayggren Anna Catr Lundahl
Trackstörska

J. P. Hallberg B. Holmberg Ulrika Berggren
Traktör. 71 år gammal Traktör Traktörs Enka 63 år

J. P. Andersson, P. Hårström A. C. Christensson
m. j. c. p. Traktör Traktörs Enka

A. B. Larsson Mari C. Westerberg S. Hellberg

Carin Fryckstett Anna C. Norgren
72 år

Carolina Thunholm M. Schutz O. F. Lundin
65 år

Carolina Wennerlöf Ulrika Andersson
63 år m. j. c. p. 63 år

Maria Christina Gillström Marie C. Lindgren
Enka. 73 år 57 år
m. j. c. p.

Anna Charlotta Wengren B. K. Möller
Tracktörska
Enka c Sjuklig

APPENDIX 7
CHRONOLOGY OF THE PRESTOUNGRANGE GOTHENBURG 1901–2002

(Originally **The Trust Tavern** 1908–1965 and at onetime also **The Forth Tavern** 1965–1986)

(Document references are from Sasine where available and correlate to the Search for Incumbrances by Millar & Bryce 1908–1998 (GOTH 1908 NOV 12) All * information is derived from the Debenture Agreement concluded in 1908 with Thomas Nelson, Publisher for the Trustees of Nelson Halls (CH 214 190.195.) or Millar & Bryce above cited. CH=County of Haddington; EL/ELN=East Lothian; BP=Borough of Prestonpans; GOTH=Internal documents.)

1901 GOTH MEM & ART) East of Scotland Public House Trust Company Limited established in Edinburgh at 29 Rutland Square to acquire and build anew public houses that were owned and managed with temperance as their goal. The movement was inspired by developments in Sweden to combat widespread brandy drinking which the City of Gothenburg had pioneered. Publicans were incentivised to sell food and non alcoholic drinks not alcohol, and loan funds were restricted to modest rates of interest. It reached its high point with the nationalisation of Carlisle's Public Houses during World War I.

(GOTH 1901 MAY 20) The newly formed Company issued its Prospectus seeking 50 000 Shares of £1 each. Just over £13 000 was promised and gradually called up becoming fully paid by 1910.

1903* The East of Scotland Public House Trust makes its first two acquisitions:

- **White Hart Inn, Grassmarket, Edinburgh**
- **The Gothenburg, Glencraig, Ballingry, Fife**

1905* Further acquisitions are made of:

- **The Anchor Bar, Kincardine, Fife**
- **The Town Hall Bar, Dufftown, Banff**
- **Mansion House, Prestonpans**

1907* Acquisitions continue at:

- **The Red Lion Inn, Culross, Fife**
- **Land and subjects at Prestonpans** from Trustees of the late Margaret Stevenson, daughter of the late Adam Stevenson, Controller of Customs at Abroath, for the sum of £670 instantly paid on May 20th (GOTH 1907 100/206 Folios 42-47 May)

1908 (CH211 86.94) **Land purchased at Prestonpans from Belfield & Company by the East of Scotland Public House Trust to erect The Trust Tavern within 12 months** for a Ground Annual of £12 and £12 payable every 19th year in the name of grassum commencing 1927 on Whitsunday.

The sale was subject to any requirements arising from the Notarial Instrument in respect of George Syme (GOTH 1908 [1] and [2]) and with Rights retained by Belfield & Company to all coal, shale, limestone, ironstone, marl, peat, clay sand and all other minerals and metals but not by sinking a shaft or pit on the lands.

(CH 213 143.145) **Rev. William Boag waives his Claim over lands in his Bond of Security for a Loan to Belfield & Company of £250**

(CH 214 190.195) **Bond & Security over all The Trust Tavern and Lands to Thomas Nelson, Publisher and Trustees of Nelson Halls for a Loan of £2000 at 5% pa + Annual Insurances of Buildings for £2500** given by East of Scotland Public House Trust (November 4th)

1909 (CH 218 38.40) **East of Scotland Public House Trust acquires a small piece of land in West End, Prestonpans from Thomas and George Mackie, formerly of the Soap Works, for £115.**

1913 (CH 332 57) **Disposition to Debenture Holders Scott Plummer and Others as Trustees of all the assets of the East of Scotland Public House Trust** "for good and onerous causes and considerations".

1915 (CH 254 87.90) **£2000 Loan repaid to Trustees for the late Thomas Nelson** (June 30th)

1918 (CH 380 41.42) **Disposition from Debenture Holders by Scott Plummer and Others as Trustees of all the assets of the East of Scotland Public House Trust back to the Trust** (August 3rd)

1919 (CH 274 152.155) **The Trust Tavern acquired by Trust Houses Limited of 227 Strand, London** founded in 1903 under the leadership of the 4th Earl Grey, a leading temperance campaigner and grandson of the 2nd Earl Grey who as Prime Minister 1830– 1834 moved The Reform Act 1832 through the Parliament. The East of Scotland Public House Trust Company Limited having been placed in the hands of its Liquidator, James Black. The lands and buildings sold were those acquired from Margaret Stevenson (1907) and Bellfield & Company (1908) and the Mackies (1909) - (October 21st)

1921* **Disposition by Trust Houses Limited of The Trust Tavern in favour of Whitehall Trust Limited** (May 2nd)

1925* **Disposition by Whitehall Trust of The Trust Tavern in favour of Trust Houses Limited** (December 30th)

1930 (GOTH 1858 141.149 & GOTH 1930 JAN8) **Belfield & Company receives £12:10/- from Trust Houses Limited in respect of *any due or future casualties***

1950 (BP 5 EL 12-1 200.204) **Trust Houses Limited sells 66 sq yds of land on Redburn Road to Prestonpans Burgh Council for £15** to enable pavement widening (June 1st)

1965 (EL 65 574.168) **Bass Ratcliff & Gretton acquire The Trust Tavern from Trust Houses Limited for £15,400** (May 24th) who in the course of their ownership change its name to ***The Forth Tavern*** and indeed change their own name three times (GOTH 1888 + 1966 + 1969 + 1978) managing their activities in Scotland through Tennent Caledonian, the enterprise which in the sixties acquired and then closed Fowler's Brewery in Prestonpans.

1971* **Trust Houses Limited of London merge with Forte to become the largest British hotel and restaurant group, sacrificing its temperance goals as it had earlier when selling *The Trust Tavern* to Bass.**

1979 (GOTH 79 MAY28) **Bass pays £218.50 to East Lothian Council under Section 4 of The Land Tenure Reform (Scotland) Act 1974 in redemption of its Feu Duty and settled its final Annual Account of £11.50.**

1983 (EL 83 988.62) **Bass sells a garage area to David and Anne Brown of 2a Redburn Road.**

1984* **Bass receives two Improvement Grants for The Forth Tavern from East Lothian District Council of £2084.45 + £2291.23**

1985 (GOTH 85 JAN4) **The Forth Tavern designated a Building of Special Architectural or Historical Interest** (January 4th)

1986 **Planning Consent Given under the Town & Country Planning Acts for a new toilet** (GOTH 87 DEC14) **at The Forth Tavern (Gothenburg); Licensing Board Consent** (GOTH 86 JAN16) **for a new Lounge Bar to be formed from the existing Games Room; these Plans then receiving Approval from the Fire Brigade and a Building Warrant under the Buildings (Scotland) Acts** (GOTH 86/89 FEB13/SEP5)

1991 (EL 91 298.10) **Bass sells (*The Forth Tavern*) now *The Gothenburg* to James and Judith Bell for £109 250 including VAT (No. 227) and the attached Dwelling House (No. 229) for £10 000.** (August 29th)

(EL 91 298.14) **Bass (trading as Tennent Caledonian) grants a £100 000 Loan to James and Judith Bell secured against The Gothenburg** (August 29th)

1992 (EL 92 73.1) **James and Judith Bell sell *The Gothenburg* and the Dwelling House to Malcolm McIlwraith for £140 000** (March 14th)

(EL 92 111.48) **James and Judith Bell repaid their Loan to Bass** (March 31st)

(EL 92 268.49 & EL 92 73.4 & EL 92 283.4) **Malcolm McIlwraith receives Loans from Bass (£100 000) and the Bank of Scotland (£50 000)** secured against ***The Gothenburg*, with the loans ranked in the order shown** (November 5th)

1994 (EL 94 259.16) **Malcolm McIlwraith formally agrees with Bass and the Bank of Scotland in a Deed of Declaration that *The Gothenburg* and the Dwelling House are separate assets;** and Bass (EL 94 259.12) and the Bank of Scotland (EL 94 259.14) waive their Security Charge for their 1992 Loans over the Dwelling House at No. 229 (September 30th)

(EL 94 275.4) **Malcolm McIlwraith borrows £30 000 from the Woolwich Building Society secured against the Dwelling House, 229 High Street.** (October 14th)

1995 (EL 95 46.33) **Security Charge over *The Gothenburg* given to Heritage Management Company for a Loan of £50 000 ranking after Bass and the Bank of Scotland.** (January 16th)

(GOTH 95 MAR17) **Malcolm McIlwraith sells the land originally purchased in 1909 from the Mackies for £10 000 to Advanced Dimensions Stock Taking Limited** (March 17th)

(GOTH 95 APR5) ***Sequestration of the estate of Malcolm McIlwraith** (April 5th)

(GOTH 95 ELN 3870 APR7) **Demand issued to Malcolm McIlwraith from Bass for Principal and Interest of £6852.62 within 28 days or they will take possession of *The Gothenburg*.**(April 7th)

(GOTH 95 ELN 3870 SEP28) **Execution of Charge for Ejection from 229 High Street Dwelling House at request of Woolwich Building Society.** (September 25th)

1997 (GOTH 97 FEB18) **Coal Authority reports on The Gothenburg's proximity to two coal seams last worked in 1925 at 170m and 435m** (February 14th)

(ELN 98 26.24) **Bass and Woolwich Building Society advertise and then sell *The Gothenburg* and the Dwelling House for £75 000 to John and Scott Murray** (May 16th) **who gives Loan Security against the combined properties to the Royal Bank of Scotland** (EL 3870(1) 26.28) which Security is discharged November 6th 2001 (EL 3870(2)).

1998 (GOTH 99 MAR31) **John and Scott Murray cease trading as The Gothenburg and seek Planning Consent for Change of Use to 1 House and 1 Flat with Proposed Alterations** (May 20th), **with the Officer's Recommendation and rationale in support** (March 31st)

1999 (GOTH 99 FEB4 & GOTH 99 MAY4) **Planning Consent & Building Warrants issued with the Stipulation that if the Murrays or their Dependents cease to live there its Use shall revert to a Public House with 1st Floor Dwelling House.**

2001 (ELN 3870 (3)) **John and Scott Murray sell the 1 House and 1 Flat to the Baron & Lady of Prestoungrange for £160 000** (October

26th) and its Use automatically reverts to a Public House and Dwelling House.

2002 (GOTH et seq.) The Baron & Lady of Prestoungrange apply for Planning Consent to (i) restore the exterior and the Edwardian/ Art Deco Bar; (ii) to renovate the Dwelling House; and (iii) to extend the Workshops to accommodate Kitchens for a Bistro and a Microbrewery to brew old Fowler's Ales (March 5th) The whole to be accomplished so far as may be possible to meet the originating goals of the East of Scotland Public House Trust Company Limited in *The Trust Tavern* in 1908.

(GOTH 02 et seq) East of Scotland Public House Trust (2002) Limited and Fowler's Ales (Prestoungrange) Limited established by The Baron Courts of Prestoungrange and Dolphinstoun to facilitate the restoration and re-opening.

2003 GOTH 03 July 23rd) Lord Mayor of Goteborg, Sweden, Jorgen Linder, visits The Prestoungrange Gothenburg, to name The Lord Mayor's Bar and unveil The Goteborg/ John Muir Mural on the Foreshore.

2004 (GOTH 04 April 9th) The Baron & Lady of Prestoungrange sell the House and Flat, together with the car parking area known as 229A opposite, to Prestoungrange Gothenburg Inc. for £245,000 as it prepares to formally reopen as a public house.

(GOTH 04 June) [i] East of Scotland Public House Limited signs 10 year lease to run The Prestoungrange Gothenburg [using that name] under Gothenburg Principles; [ii] Fowler's Ales [Prestoungrange] Limited signs a 5 year lease to brew its ales at The Prestoungrange Gothenburg; [iii] Barons Courts of Prestoungrange & Dolphinstoun [1998], Charity, Prestonpans Salt Company Limited and Pandores Oysters Limited all sign management services agreement with East of Scotland Public House Limited.

(GOTH 04 July 1st) Lord Lieutenant of East Lothian, Garth Morrison, reopens The Prestoungrange Gothenburg; Thomas Nelson V names new functions facilities Thomas Nelson Suite; The Provost of East Lothian, Pat O'Brien, names the Bistro in honour of James Park; and June Lake who had attended the last reopening in 1986 as the then presiding Tennent's Lager Lady, attends again and renames the main bar in honour of its original Manager, James Fewell.

(GOTH 04 July 27th) Scotland's Final Sitting of a Baronial Court held at The Caput being The Prestoungrange Gothenburg, stocks used for the last time in Scotland on the baronial foreshore, and 81 Witches are Pardoned.

2005 The Prestoungrange Gothenburg receives the accolade from English Heritage and CAMRA as 'Best UK Pub Conservation of the Year'.

(GOTH 05 October) Prestoungrange Arts Festival [2006] Limited founded to lead arts activities forward and to launch The Three Harbours Festival June 2006.

(GOTH 05 October 31st) Memorial to 81 Witches dedicated in Gardens.

2006 The Prestoungrange Gothenburg receives the CAMRA accolade as Scotland's Lothians, Edinburgh and the Borders Pub of The Year.

(GOTH 06 May) Battle of Prestonpans [1745] Heritage Trust established to enhance the interpretation and remembrance of the Battle in the town.

(GOTH 06 August) Prestoungrange Totem Pole Raised and 6th Global Conference of The Global Association for Murals Arts and Cultural Tourism takes place at The Prestoungrange Gothenburg.

14
The Battle of Prestonpans

Reasons and its aftermath

Michael of Albany

INTRODUCTION

A battle, no matter how short a fight it might have been, can put a small town on the map forever. That, I think, was how everyone felt in September 1995, when we celebrated the 250th anniversary of the Battle of Prestonpans. It was a battle that had been a turning point in the Jacobite attempt to restore both the Stewarts[1] on the throne and the sovereignty of Scotland within Europe. Also, it was the first battle that the Jacobites had won since the demise of King James VII of the Scots[2] in 1688.

When I was asked by Prestoungrange to write this account of the battle, it very quickly became clear to me that, in view of the fact that the battle only lasted about seven minutes, this would be no easy task. I have therefore defined the structure of this analysis in order to examine *why* the Battle of Prestonpans took place at all. It is always difficult, even at the best of times, to get to the bottom of historical events that bring about the end of an era, so its seems appropriate to start from the beginning and explain why our ancestors came to fight upon the battlefield of Prestonpans in the first place.

1. BETRAYAL BY THE ANGLICAN CHURCH

We have to bear in mind that history, more often than not, is written by the conquerors, usually to keep those conquered firmly under their thumbs. In

Village of Prestonpans 21st September 1745 – battle field to the left of the picture immediately below the mill (Meadow Mill)

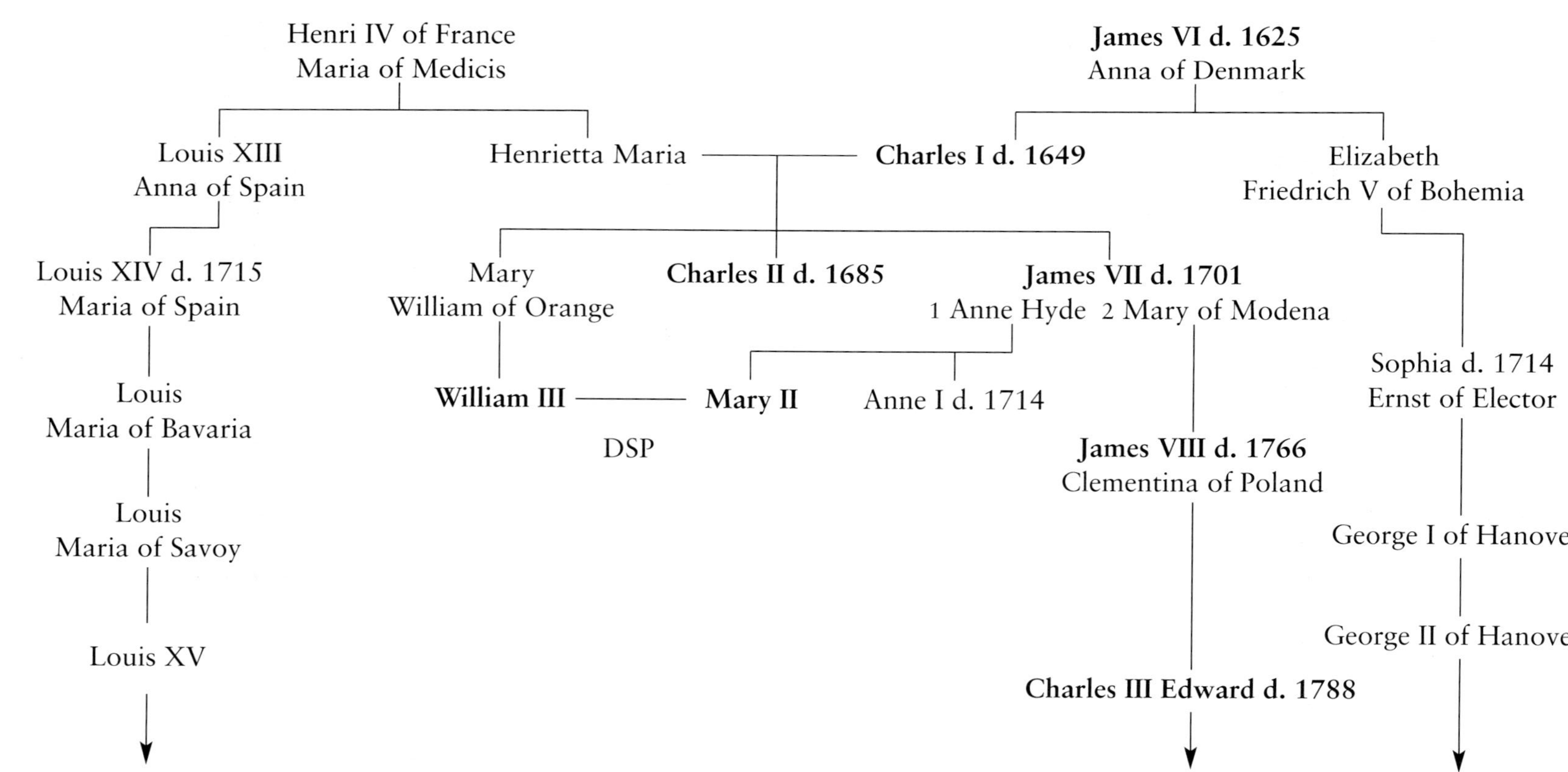
Henri IV of France
Maria of Medicis
James VI d. 1625
Anna of Denmark
Louis XIII
Anna of Spain
Henrietta Maria
Charles I d. 1649
Elizabeth
Friedrich V of Bohemia
Louis XIV d. 1715
Maria of Spain
Mary
William of Orange
Charles II d. 1685
James VII d. 1701
1 Anne Hyde 2 Mary of Modena
Sophia d. 1714
Ernst of Elector
Louis
Maria of Bavaria
William III
Mary II
Anne I d. 1714
DSP
James VIII d. 1766
Clementina of Poland
Louis
Maria of Savoy
George I of Hanover
Louis XV
George II of Hanover
Charles III Edward d. 1788

order to achieve this, an alternative course of history is then taught and, as the saying goes, 'tell them often enough and they will believe'. The same propagandist approach to history applies to the reasons why James VII of the Scots was betrayed by the Church of England, giving rise to Jacobitism. When James succeeded his brother Charles II in February 1685 the Church of England was in a quandary. Born an Anglican in St James' Palace on October 14th 1633, James converted to the Catholic Church in 1669 having reasoned that the Church of England had been created for the wrong reasons. His first wife, Anne, converted a year later. So, for some sixteen years before becoming king, James had worshipped in the old faith. But how could the Supreme Governor of the Church of England, the head spiritual of the church created by Queen Elizabeth I, be also a Roman Catholic?

Although the Anglican bishops saw James' declaration as a contradiction in terms, James conceived of no religious problems with his situation: as a private individual, he believed in Catholicism, as a king, he upheld the right of the Church of England as the State Church. However, James was unlike any other monarchs of his time. He had faced civil strife under Cromwell, had lived and worked abroad and had met enlightened individuals from many walks of life. They, and James, saw no sense in Protestant versus Catholic dogma and James worked with them all as equals, whether they were French Catholics, Huguenots or Dutch Protestants.

When he came to the throne and was anointed by the Archbishop of Canterbury, James received the Oath of Allegiance from all the bishops and peers, for himself and his heir. All of them felt quite safe with the fact that his heir at that time was his Anglican daughter Mary, wife of William of Orange. As long as James' second wife and queen, Mary Beatrix of Modena, produced no son, James' crown was secured. But it is, of course, the duty of kings to produce male heirs and in 1688 the happy event took place when the Duke of Rothesay, Prince James Francis Edward Stewart, Prince of Wales, was born in London. The Church of England's worst fear had come to pass. A Catholic succession was assured. Would England see itself reverting to the clutches of the Papacy and, if so, how would they fare under the yoke of Rome?

2. WILLIAM OF ORANGE AS THE ALTERNATIVE

There was, needless to say, another factor in play at the time. Church and politics usually went hand in hand and James' main problem was not so much his religious beliefs but rather the conflict between his cousin Louis XIV of France and his son-in-law, William in the Netherlands. It was all the more irritating in that all the parties concerned were closely related to one another as the small family tree opposite shows.

The 1680s had seen both Louis XIV and William of Orange at loggerheads over territorial rights and the supremacy of the sea. At that time Holland was supreme in all things naval. Britain had been at war with Holland for many years, since the Restoration of 1660, but the war was costly and in 1677 Britain decided to conclude a treaty with the Dutch. To seal the treaty, in the same year, James' eldest daughter Princess Mary was married to her cousin William of Orange. After succeeding as king, James also decided that Britain would remain neutral in the conflict between the French and the Dutch. While Louis was happy at this turn of events, William was furious: without British support the Netherlands would soon lose the war to the French foe and lose the trading supremacy it had held for so long. William needed British troops to fight for him against Louis XIV. From the day James succeeded to the throne of his ancestors, William was resolved to topple him from the royal steps and take the kingdom over himself. So William, a Dutch Protestant, turned to the one man who could turn the wheel of political fortune in his favour – Pope Innocent XI, head of the Roman Catholic Church.

This was not as surprising as it may seem. Holland was a member of the Holy Roman Empire and the spiritual head of that empire was, of course, the Pope. In order to topple a Roman Catholic king from his perch William needed two things from the head of the Roman Catholic Church: the first was his permission to do so and the second was the Pope's decree that Roman catholic mercenaries had the right to fight in the Dutch Protestant invading army. In the event, recent evidence[3] and press reports[4] suggest that Innocent XI did even better by giving William the money to be used for payment to the Catholic mercenaries who made up no less than two thirds of William's invading army in 1688. There were two reasons for Pope Innocent XI taking a stand against King James VII. Firstly, the French king Louis XIV was planning the creation of a Gallic Church of France, catholic in essence, but free and independent of Rome. Secondly, James VII was intent on giving British Jews, Quakers and Catholics the right to worship according to their conscience. While the Pope approved the removal of worshipping constraints on British Roman Catholics, he did not approve of Jews and Quakers enjoying the same rights. While it would have been difficult for the Papacy to remove the crown from the King of France, James of the Scots – particularly as King of England – was still in a precarious position and so the hammer blow fell on his head. By January 1689, having been deserted by most of his generals, James had to leave Britain. He landed in France where he was welcomed by King Louis XIV. The Palace of Saint Germain-en-Laye was made over to James and the British court in exile.

James VII had not, of course, abdicated and much of the English Parliament was anxious for his return, for they had not in fact offered the crown to William of Orange. A vote was taken and when the result was in favour of James, William became so incensed that he had the Houses of Parliament surrounded and word sent that he required a second vote to take place declaring that the 'vacant crown' of England was offered to him and his wife as joint rulers. It was made clear that the mercenary troops would be let loose on them if the vote did not favour William's wishes. Parliament did as William demanded. James, of course, rejected the notion of an elected monarch and stated the vote to be unconstitutional. He immediately set out to regain his inheritance through an Irish campaign with the financial backing of France.

3. BOYNE AND THE UNION

James VII fought and lost the Battle of the Boyne in 1690 and in 1701, just before James' death in Paris, the English Parliament passed the *Act of Succession* whereby 'no Catholic could succeed to the crown of St. Edward'. England and Scotland, however, had separate parliaments and thus the English Act could not be imposed upon the Scots. In fact, in 1703 the Scots Parliament passed the *Act of Security* keeping the succession in Scotland separate to that of England, though always within the royal line. The Scots Parliament ratified this Act every year until 1706 but, in 1707 Scotland saw herself stripped of her rightful sovereignty through the Treaty of Union. Her Parliament, the Three Estaites, was dissolved on May 1st 1707, at a cost of 12,000 English Pounds Sterling in gold – the money used to bribe the many Scottish Barons (which included Prestoungrange), Burgesses and Peers who voted in favour of the Union. In today's terms, this amounts to a paltry £750,000. The list of those who voted in favour of Union demonstrates that most of them were Presbyterians and, to quote Professor James Garden's speech in the new church of Aberdeen:

> "... they allowed and tamely permitted the nation basely and shamefully to be sold and enslaved contrary to the Express Remonstrances of most part of the Kingdom, under the specious name and pretence of an Union with England."[5]

He was right: the whole of Scotland was inflamed by the fact that a stroke of a pen had removed the nation's sovereignty. Riots flared everywhere and the Act of the Union, in leaflet form, was burned by the majority of the Scottish people.

With the Act of Union, Jacobitism was turned from Scots patriotism into Scots nationalism. Lockhart of Lee wrote to King James VIII that "as the aversion to the Union dayly encreases, that is the handle by which Scotsmen will be raised to make a general and zealous appearance ... as I am fully persuaded the better part of the English are far from thinking the Union beneficial to either Countrey. I cannot but see that it is expedient for the King to gratify his friends in Scotland".[6] James, in turn, replied that he would "... relieve our Subjects of Scotland from the hardships they groan under on account of the late unhappy Union and to restore the Kingdom to its ancient free and independent state ... We hope ... to see our just Rights, and those of the Church and People of Scotland, once more settled in a free and independent Scots Parliament on their Ancient Foundation".[7]

With Westminster then deciding to levy high malt tax and duty on the Scots, Jacobitism became ever more the political faction to follow since it advocated that it should only pay the hated tax and duty on the old Scots footing. The Union was seen by many as far too expensive to people north of the border – even the Cameronians were starting to think of catholic King James as a better bet both for themselves and the financial well-being of the people of Scotland.

4. 1708, 1715 AND 1718

In 1708, James VIII, Francis Edward, made his way to Scotland but was forced back to France by the English fleet before he could set foot on his ancestral kingdom. Following the succession of George I of Hanover, nicknamed 'The wee, wee German Lairdie' by the Scots, he came back in 1715 with the help of the Earl of Mar who unfurled the King's banner at Braemar, then a hotbed of pro-Stewart sympathisers. The Battle of Sherrifmuir, led by Mar, was one where both armed forces claimed victory. The Highlanders however, instead of staying put after the battle, made their way home with their booty and so the field was reclaimed by the Hanoverian forces soon afterwards. James was to be crowned at Scone but, before the ceremony could begin, the Duke of Argyll's pro-Hanoverian forces obliged him to make another escape back to France. A fourth attempt, this time with Spanish backing, took place in 1718 but failed due to adverse weather conditions which scattered the Spanish Armada at Cape Finisterre. The star of the Stewarts was at its lowest ebb and a restoration nowhere in sight.

With the birth of Prince Charles Edward in 1720, Scots aspirations were once more on the increase. Charles was brought up by mainly Scots and Irish people. His first tutor was chevalier Michael Andrew Ramsay, a man committed to the cause of Scottish freemasonry and an great enthusiast of all things Templar. As Charles' tutor he had a profound effect on Charles' way of thinking. Ramsay's intent was to create the first democratic king in the history of Europe. He resolved to restore Charles as king and set out to do this by making sure that Freemasonry would help achieve this. Ramsay created a secret service within Scottish and European Freemasonry that lasted well into the 19th century. In 1732 Charles Edward's training as a future 'crowned democrat' began when he joined the Jacobite study Lodge of Tobosco in Rome, which trained teenagers in the intricacies of Scottish Freemasonry. By 1743, the various members belonging to Charles' Lodge in Rome were travelling extensively, visiting Lodges all over Scotland. Murray, Charles' secretary, was high within the Scottish hierarchy and helped pave the way to Masonic support.

5. THE OPPORTUNITY PRESENTS ITSELF IN 1745

The summer of 1745 saw England at its lowest military ebb. The Hon. Henry Pelham, third Prime Minister of Great Britain, wrote to the Duke of Argyll that 'I never was in so much apprehension as I am a present ... the loss of all Flanders, and that of Ostend (which I am afraid must soon be expected), will, we apprehend, from the great superiority of the French in Flanders, be soon followed by some embarkation from Ostend, or Dunkirk, or both. And there is reason to believe that the French and Spanish ships which are now in the western ports of France, and in the Bay of Biscay, (amounting to between twenty and thirty, twenty of which are of the line), may be intended to support the embarkation either by coming up the Channel, where at present we have not a squadron sufficient to oppose them, or (as I find is apprehended by some), by coming up north, about Scotland to Ostend. Seven French men-o'-war sailed from Brest about five weeks ago. It is thought possible they may be somewhere lying to the westward to wait there till Ostend shall be in the hands of the French, and then proceed round Scotland thither. We are getting our ships ready, and I hope we shall soon have a tolerable squadron in the Channel. But if the French should come north about, they might surprise us. We are sending transports for 10,000 men to Campveer and Flushing, in order to bring part of our army from Flanders, if it should be necessary for the defence of this Kingdom'.[8]

In July 1745 Charles landed in Scotland. The Prince had come home to reclaim his grandfather's birthright. After his standard was unfolded in Glenfinnan on August 19th clan after clan joined him, carrying broadswords bearing the legend 'Prosperity to Scotland and no union'. They marched upon the capital city of Edinburgh, Athens of the North. Even then General Cope was trying to chase him away having travelled by ship to Dundee in an attempt to intercept the Prince's army before it became too big to deal with. Cope had not been keen to do this for it left Edinburgh undefended. Cope, of course, was right. To fight in a territory unknown to you is madness and the clans were excellent fighters in the manner we know today as 'guerilla warfare'. The

Prince Charles Edward (from a contemporary engraving)

hit and run tactic is one that no army can defeat, particularly when the geography of the land was so unlike that of the south of England. Moreover, they knew how to evade Cope's troops. The fact that Captain Switenham of Guise's regiment, together with his troops, had been taken prisoner by MacDonald of Keppoch's people five days before the raising of Charles Edward's standard did not help Cope either.

How had this twenty-five year old puppy, accompanied by only eight people (though history tends to mention only six), suddenly become so popular and so easily become a leader of the most disreputable men in Scotland? Courtesy and charisma were the keys by which Charles won their support. A contemporary report from one who was not a Jacobite sympathiser describes Charles Edward as being 'tall and handsome, with brown eyes and fair complexion, he wore a short tartan coat without a plaid, a blue bonnet and on his breast the star of the Order of St Andrew'.[9] Another stated Charles to be a 'goodlie person', 'physically fit and an excellent horseman', 'has the gift of projecting an aura of royalty and command', 'looked every inch a Prince with the manner of a very distinguished and well-bred person'.[10] That he should have appealed to so many thousands of people is not surprising, particularly if one adds the extra card of his willingness to tackle the Gaelic language.

There is another aspect of the '45 that is hardly ever dealt with: the fact that Charles' army was composed of even numbers of Catholics, Presbyterians and Episcopalians. Charles' emphasis during his opening speech at Glenfinnan was Scotland's god-given right to sovereignty, to freedom, civil rights and liberties. No Prince ever spoke like this before. The hated union with England was henceforth declared null and void. People were fighting for two things. First, for the restoration of Scotland's ancient rights and secondly for the restoration of the Stewarts, because the first could only happen if the second took place. One Covenanter Jacobite sympathiser, following the meeting at Edinburgh's Mercat Cross in 1707 whereby Queen Anne was deposed and her half brother, catholic James, proclaimed king, had declared 'No matter how much a Catholic tyrant he might grow to be, at least the ancient constitution and rights of our nation shall be preserved'.[11] The same thinking prevailed when Charles Edward set foot in Scotland some thirty-eight years later.

6. LORD LYON PROCLAIMS JAMES VIII KING OF THE SCOTS

Edinburgh was taken practically without the Jacobites firing a shot. The castle, then in Hanoverian hands, was not taken. This was a mistake. It had hardly any powder to fire its cannon, something Charles was unaware of, and the original plates once used to print our ancient Scottish notes were within the walls of Edinburgh's fortress. Moreover, the men manning the walls were elderly and few. With hindsight, Charles should have taken the castle and started to print cash, Scottish cash, straight away. The French would have recognised our ancient currency and this would have put both the Bank of England and the Hanoverian king in a quandary. One move which did terrify Prime Minister Henry Pelham was when the Lord Lyon, King of Arms, together with his Poursuivants at the Mercat Cross in the capital city of Edinburgh, proclaimed Charles' father 'King James VIII of the Scots' and Charles to be his rightful and lawful 'Regent' till the king could return home.

By this time, George II was having difficulties paying the troops who were fighting the French and was constantly requesting the British Parliament to pay the wages of his Hanoverian and Hessian soldiers. It was felt by many in London's political circles that the Hanoverian price was a hard one to pay. Britain, it was felt, was fast becoming Hanover's financial backer in a war that few perceived to be in England's interests. As for Scotland, few Scots were keen to enlist in the British Army. The idea of death on foreign soil was not a popular one. Moreover, Scots would have found themselves fighting one another on the battlefields of Europe. When James VII lost the Battle of the Boyne some 50,000 Irish and Scots followed him into exile in France. James quickly realised that unless these communities were transformed into something worth keeping by foreign rulers, they would be asked to leave. But they had vowed to go home only when their king was restored. James' answer to the Irish/Scots exodus was to create regiments that would fight on behalf of other rulers, sometimes even against England. They were to be paid, housed, watered and fed, not as mercenaries, but as hired military help. This was nothing new. The Duke of Hesse, for example, hired his soldiers to the first three Hanoverian Georges and their pay was settled by the British Parliament. James' concept, of course, gave a ready made army to many rulers in Europe, not least France, Spain and the few sovereign Dukes of Italy. With a Stewart restoration, it was understood that the map of Europe would change very quickly, due to the sudden lack of the Stewart warfare machine. Today, scarcely one aristocratic French and Spanish family is not diluted with the blood of those exiled Jacobite fighters, both Irish and Scots.

7. PREPARING FOR BATTLE WITH COPE

When Cope arrived with his troops in Stirling, most of his men were of foreign origin. They had fought battles in Europe and were therefore well hardened for a military campaign. Already, he had attempted to meet Charles' troops in battle, but two things had prevented this: firstly, General Lord George Murray knew the Highland area much better than Cope and secondly, most of the clans Cope thought he could count on simply turned their backs on him. In fact, once he had marched north of Perth, those Highlanders who had been forcibly enlisted simply went over to Charles' side. Fort Augustus proved the case against him, while Charles was marching happily onwards to Perth where he received a hero's welcome. Cope took ship for Dunbar where he arrived on September 15th, while the rest of his troops arrived two days later. On September 19th he left Dunbar for Edinburgh via Haddington. His problem was that the city of Edinburgh was already in Jacobite hands. However, he did not envisage that the Jacobite forces would be difficult to engage and destroy: his troops were rested and battle-ready. The Highlanders, the 'rabble of the north' as his officers referred to them, would be crushed and would probably run for their lives once they realised what they were up against.

On hearing that Cope had settled just a few miles from Edinburgh, Charles called his officers and advisers to attend a council of war. All were keen to meet Cope's army and send them packing over the border. George Murray, Charles' chief military officer, gave them his visualisation of how the clash would take place. Charles, of course, wanted to see the site beforehand and so they set off to scour the area and take a look at Cope's army. In the end, it was decided that the Jacobite army should pitch their tents slightly west of Tranent on the old post road. The army, then based at Duddington, marched by Musselburgh to the brow of Carberry Hill by Fa'side Castle through Tranent and lay all night on the high moorland to the east of the village. Cope had formed his army on the low ground between the sea and the high road, halfway between Prestonpans and Cockenzie, to the south of these villages. Charles retired for the night sleeping in the field, lying on the ground without any covering but his plaid. It was then that Robert Anderson of Whitburgh, a native of the area whose father had been active in Mar's army of 1715, decided to tell Hepburn of Keith that he had thought of a better way of fighting the Hanoverian forces. He and Hepburn decided to wake Lord George Murray to see if Anderson's plan could be put into action. Murray was so keen that he woke Charles in the middle of the night to tell him of this possible new plan of action.

Peter MacNeill, in his book, 'Prestonpans and Vicinity', has put it so well that I cannot but quote it:

> "Anderson being a native of the district knew every inch of the ground. His scheme was to go round the south side of Tranent eastwards, over Tranent Muir northwards, and down by Riggonhead to Seton; then coming in by Meadowmill westwards, to take the Royal forces unawares from behind. And on the Saturday morning, 21st, about three o'clock, the movement was begun."[12]

What began, of course, was the moving of some 2,400 Highlanders forming the Jacobite army. Macdonalds, Camerons, Stewarts of Appin, Drummonds, MacGregors, Athol men, Robertsons, MacLauchlans and many others including new recruits from Edinburgh, all came to teach the invaders a lesson. All this had to be done silently and without being seen by enemy. Anderson's involvement makes it clear that there were also Jacobite sympathisers in the area willing to help and fight.

It was just as well that Anderson came up with a new plan. Both Murray and Charles had felt that, although Cope had to be engaged, the Hanoverian general did have the better ground and the better chance of winning the battle. Cope was not a great general – far from it, but neither was he incompetent. Everything he did was by the book. Think of it: when he drew up his troops, he chose flat ground protected on three sides – by the sea, by park walls and by a few villages almost touching one another. Soft, boggy ground protected his south flank. At the time it was Cope who had the better deal, particularly for a combined action using his infantry and his cavalry, something that Charles' forces could not match. Jacobite reports of the site before the battle were of the opinion that it had been chosen with a great deal of skill. The more they examined it the more the Jacobites were convinced of the impossibility of attacking it. But in order to set the tone of this Jacobite enterprise this battle had to be won. Only then would the French send help, only if Prestonpans was favourable to Charles Edward would the other clans in the north rise to his call.

Nevertheless, the Jacobite troops were in high spirits, as conveyed in a popular ballad of the time by Adam Skirving, which was based on Charles' actual words to his troops:

> "Cope sent a letter frae Dunbar:
> Charlie meet me gin ye daur,
> An' I'll learn you the art o' war,
> If you'll meet wi' me in the morning
>
> When Charles look'd the letter upon,
> He drew his sword the scabbard from:
> Come, follow me, my merry men,
> And we'll meet Johnnie Cope i' the morning."

Cope's address to his men before the battle showed contempt for the Highlanders and offered the opportunity for plunder once the battle was won:

> "Gentlemen, you are about to fight with a parcel of rabble, a small number of Highlanders, a parcel of Brutes. You can expect no booty from such a poor, despicable pack. But I have authority to declare that you shall have eight full hours plunder and pillage of Edinburgh, Leith, and suburbs (the place which harboured and succoured them), at your discretion, with impunity."[13]

Charles' response was as follows:

> "On being told of Cope's words and of his reckoning that the day was his, Charles looked at his men and declaimed a prayer. No speech for Charlie, oh no, but a prayer that both defied Cope's barbarism and reminded everyone of the just cause they were fighting for. 'O Lord of Hosts who cans't see through the thickest vaill and disguise who vicisest the bottom of my heart and the deepest designs of my enemies who hast in thy hands as well as before thine eyes all the events which concern human life, if thou knowest that my victory will promote thy glory and the safty of thy people, if thou knowest that I have no other ambition in my soul but to advance the honour of thy holy name and the good of this state, favour O Great God the justice of my Arms and reduce all the Rebels to acknowledge him whom thy sacred decrees and the order of lawfull succession have made their soverigne. But if thy good Providence has ordered it otherwayes and thou seest that I should prove one of those Kings whom thou gavest in thine Anger, take from me O Mercifull God my life and my Crown, make me this day A Sacrifice to thy will. Let my death and the calamities of Brittain and let my blood be the last that is split in this quarrell."[14]

A major problem that Charles encountered in his preparations was one of tradition. Who should form the right wing? To the Highland mind this was important. Bruce had given that prerogative to the MacDonalds and so Clan Colla (or MacColl) under the Duke of Perth was awarded the place of honour. The centre, under the command of Captain James Drummond, would be held by the Duke of Perth's men and the MacGregors. The left wing, composed of the Camerons and Stewarts of Appin, was under the leadership of Lochiel and the command of Lord George Murray. Behind these stood Prince Charles and behind him a second line was formed with the Robertsons, McDonalds of Glencoe, MacLauchlans and the remainder of the Athol men, all under Lord Nairn.

8. LET BATTLE COMMENCE

On being told of the troops' movements Cope decided to change the position of his army. But it was to no avail. Even the weather was against him for there was a fog. Not a dense fog but that early, misty fog that tends to disguise the senses of both hearing and seeing. It was the kind of weather so beloved by the fighting highland forces, one that helps you slowly but surely move towards your foe without being seen or heard, particularly if you walk on all fours. By the time the Hanoverians realised what was happening and started to fire they knew they had already lost the day. When the various clans called

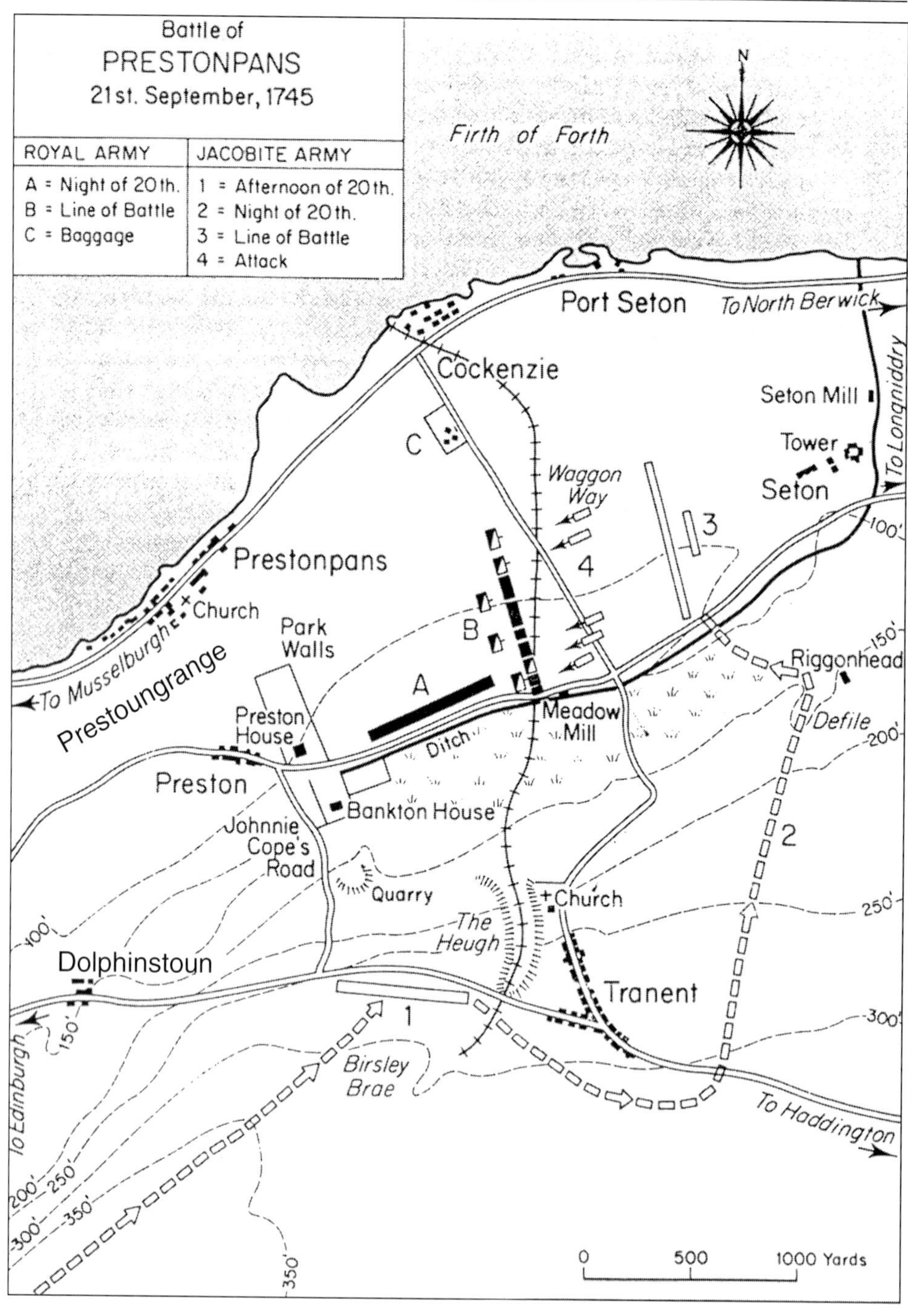

out their battle cries, the very blood of Cope's army was chilled. When Charles' troops attacked Cope's right wing, even his artillery shots were to no avail the Highlanders being too close and the cannon balls flying well over their heads. When they, the Jacobites, discharged their fire and threw their pistols down on the ground for hand to hand combat, the Hanoverian troops fled for their lives more so when they realised how the 'rabble of the north' fought.

'A Race from Preston Pans to Berwick': Sir John Cope brings the news of his own defeat (From a contemporary satirical print)

Having drawn their swords in their right hand and holding a spiky targe in their left hand, from which protruded the blade of their dirk, they then faced their opponents by bending their left knee in order to receive the thrust of the Hanoverian bayonet on the targe, killing the other soldier on their right with their sword while maiming the one on their left with either the spike of their targe or the blade of their dirk. Having fired once Hanoverians only had recourse to the bayonet of their musket, while the Highlanders had recourse to another two blades and the spike to inflict further damage. And then there were the dreaded scythes which could sever anything they touched. And they did swing and cut for heads, hands and legs were strewn everywhere on the battlefield. What terrified Cope's men was the fact that this was no rabble coming at them but rather a uniformed and orderly troop that was quick in movement. Cope faced a carnage he had never experienced before and fled the battle wearing a Jacobite white cockade so as not to be recognised.

Of Cope's fighting men, nine hundred were mortally wounded including Colonel Gardiner, and one thousand four hundred were taken prisoner. About two hundred, it is said, escaped. Of Charles' army, five officers died, thirty privates were killed and about eighty were wounded. The dead, as was the custom, are said to have been buried on the very field they died on. In fact, the same would later apply to the battlefield of Culloden. I was told by Jack Robertson that, should anyone dig a few inches below the ground where the Battle of Prestonpans took place, one would reach the remains of those fallen men, Jacobites and Hanoverians alike. In 1950, when a number of bones were found at the site of the battle, a religious service was held and the remains of a number of soldiers of both sides who died on the battlefield were re-interred,[15] close to the memorial cairn which was erected in 1932 by the Society for the Preservation of Rural Scotland and which stands on the B1377, just outside the town of Prestonpans at the turn off for Meadowmill Sports Centre.

REGISTERED.]

Numb. 380.

THE PENNY LONDON POST.

From Wednesday, October 2d, to Friday, October 4th, 1745.

BATTLE AT PRESTON PANS.

(NEAR EDINBURGH.)

LONDON.

From the LONDON GAZETTE,

Whitehall, Sep. 24.

BY an Express which arriv'd this morning, we are inform'd that Sir John Cope, and the Troops under his command, were attack'd by the Rebels, on the 21st instant, at day-break, at Preston, near Seaton, seven miles from Edinburgh; that the King's Troops were defeated, and Sir John Cope, with about 450 Dragoons, had retir'd to Lauder; Brigadier Fowkes and Colonel Lascelles had got to Dunbar; but as yet we have no account of the Particulars of this Action, nor of the Loss on either side. The Earls of Loudoun and Home, and some of the Gentlemen Voluntiers were at Lauder with Sir John Cope.

The following is the most exact List we have as yet receiv'd, of the Killed & Wounded at the Battle at Preston Pans, near Edinburgh:

Colonel Gardner's Dragoons.

SCOTLAND.

The following journal is taken from the *Caledonian Mercury*, that our Readers may see in what manner the Rebels have chosen to give an account of [illegible]ir atchievements.

EDINBURGH, Sep. 19. On Monday last, the Highland Army stood under Arms about Corstorphine, two miles west of this City, till about Four in the Afternoon; then their advanced Body march'd up to attack Hamilton's and Gardner's Dragoons, and the City Companies, who stood under Arms on this side the Colt Bridge, a mile west of this City; immediately after the Dragoons, &c. retired, rode off down the north side of this City towards Leith, then they filed away for Haddington, leaving their Baggage to the care of our Magistrates, who saw the same into the Castle. This Flight occasioned a general consternation here, so that the principal inhabitants, considering there was no expectation of General Cope's Army, and that the two Regiments of Dragoons had abandon'd them, address'd the Lord Provost, Magistrates and Council to capitulate, in regard the City was not tenable, lest, if the Highlanders took it by storm, the inhabitants might be pillag'd and destroy'd.—The Magistrates ordered the Fire-Bell immediately to be rung, to summon

JOURNAL OF THE PRETENDER'S ARMY.

AUG. 27. The Chevalier being inform'd that Lieut General Cope was to march that day over Corrieyerroig, order'd his whole Army to decamp, and at four in the morning march'd from Aberchalladree, in Glangary, over the hill of Corrieyerroig, with a resolution to fight Cope; every Man shewing by his behaviour the general inclination of the whole to attack him, and were determin'd all to a man to conquer or die on the spot; but to their great grief were disappointed, as Cope, the day before, having intelligence of our strength, was intimidated that he alter'd his Route from Corrieyerroig to Ruthvin in Badenoch, and made such dispatch to prevent our attacking his Rear, that in two days he perform'd four days' march. That night, after our arrival at Garvamore, the men were so vex'd at being disappoint'd of fighting that day, that 500 of them proposed to follow Cope, and march 24 miles under Cloud of Night, to intercept his march; but upon mature consideration, the proposal was not thought practicable. The 28th we march'd to Dalchrainy; the 29th to Dalnachairdach; and the 30th to Blair. From Blair the Army march'd, Sept. 2, from Dunkeld; and the 3d. to Perth, when they quarter'd 'till the 11th.

Major Bowles, wounded.
Cornet Nagh, killed.
Cornet Jacobs, killed.

Lascelle's Foot.

Captain Stuart, killed.
Captain Collier, killed.
Ensign Bell, much wounded.

Murray's.

Captain Blake, killed,
Captain Rud, killed.
Captain Leslie, slightly wounded.
Ensign Haldane, dangerously wounded.

Guise's.

Captain Pointz, dangerously wounded.
Captain Halwell, killed.
Captain Holmes, killed.

Leigh's.

Lieut. Colonel Hallet, prisoner, if not killed.
Captain Brewer, killed.
Captain Rogers, killed.
Lieut. Colonel Whileford, wounded.

Besides the above List, there are several Officers Prisoners, whose Names are not yet known.

Three Hundred Men Killed, and Five Hundred Prisoners.

Among the Rebels, the Duke of Perth and Fifty Private Men Killed.

EDINBURGH, Sep. 28. The Rebels are still here; but seem to be providing themselves with everything requisite for a long journey.

WHITEHALL, OCT. 1. By letters of the 28th of September from Berwick, we are inform'd that the main body of the Rebels had not been moved from Edinburgh, but that they had sent parties to Haddington and Dunbar.

as the Lord Justice, Clerk, Advocate, &c. had withdrawn from the City, and General Guest retir'd into the Castle, it was unanimously agreed, That a deputation should be appointed to go out of Town and treat with the young Chevalier's Army. These deputies accordingly went out to Gray's Mill and met with their Chiefs; but we don't hear that they came to any Agreement at all; However, the Citizens delivered up their Arms into the Arsenal, and all was very quiet till about Four this morning, when, as the gate of the Netherbow was opening, a few of the Highland Army enter'd thereat and were follow'd by about 1000 resolute and hardy Fellows, well arm'd, who took possession of the Gate, also the City Guard, making the Soldiers Prisoners of War, while the detachments march'd up to the Parliament Close and other Places; whereupon the Castle fired several Cannons as a Signal, and that the inhabitants should appear on the Castle Hill. The Pretender lay in his cloaths all that night at Slateford, two miles from hence, and set out yesterday for this City. The Highlanders behave civilly, and pay chearfully for what they get.

About noon the Pretender made his entry into the Abbey in a Highland dress, accompany'd by several persons of distinction, and alighting, took possession of the Royal Palace; all the rest of the Infantry (about 5000) remaining encamp'd in the King's Park. At one in the afternoon the Highland Party spread a carpet on the Cross; and, after cloathing the Heralds, Pursnivants, &c., carry'd them to the Cross; where with sound of Trumpet, they Proclaim'd the Declaration and Act of Regency, both dated at Rome, Dec. 23, 1744, and the Manifesto, in consequence of the said Act of Regency, dated at Paris, May 16, 1745.

This Evening the Highland Army march'd from St. Anne's Yards and encamp'd at Duddingston. They receiv'd a reinforcement of 1600 men yesterday from Athole and Perthshire.

... we durst attempt to cross the Fourth; but in Place of intercepting our Passage as soon as they heard of our crossing the River, they galloped away in great hurry and came that night to Falkirk; next day, the 14th, we march'd from Touch to Falkirk. The Town of Stirling, being left destitute of any Force, by Gardner's sudden flight, open'd the Gates to receive us.

That night we encamp'd at Falkirk, hearing of Gardner's being also within five miles of us encamp'd at Linlithgow, the Pretender order'd a Detachment of 500 men to attack him that night in his Camp; but Gardner, dreading the worst of it, in the greatest hurry, march'd off at seven o'clock in the Evening, and encamp'd at Kirkliston Water, the 15th. We encamp'd three miles to the East of Linlithgow, and the 16th march'd towards Corstorphine, where we heard Gardner had join'd Hamilton's Dragoons, and were ready to receive us: But their Piquet Guards seeing our number and the regularity of our march, took to their heels, and the whole Dragoons fled hastily that evening to Musleburgh. We encamp'd that night at Gray's Mill, where some of the Magistrates of Edinburgh waited on the Chevalier, to demand time to draw up a capitulation. His answer was, that he thought his Father's declaration, and his own manifesto, were sufficient terms of capitulation for all his subjects to accept of with joy, and that they had no other to expect. To consider of this he gave them four hours, and requir'd a positive answer by two a'clock in the morning but no such answers coming, and only a further delay asked, he refused to hearken to any thing further and order'd a Detachment of 900 men, under cloud of night to storm the Town, and accordingly early in the morning rushed in at the Nether-bow-Gate, and took possession of the Town. The Pretender march'd his army the 17th to Holyrood-House, and encamp'd in the King's Park, where he was met by a great Number of the citizens of Edinburgh.

"He came down to the Stirling plain in September, and at Prestonpans his terrible swordsmen scattered the only Government army in Scotland". Nineteenth-century Jacobitism here re-fights the battle. (North Britons, p. 299)

Cope had not coped at all. It was then the satirists and songwriters went into full flow. By the former he was called the 'pudding-headed general' and the latter let rip with comments on his troops' flight back over the border:

"But when he saw the Highland lads,
Wi' tartan trews and white cockades;
Wi' swords and guns, and rungs and gauds,
O, Johnnie he took wing in the morning" Robert Burns

and

"In faith," quo Johnnie, "I got sic flegs
Wi' their claymores and filabegs,
If I face them deil break my legs,
So I wish you a' good morning." Adam Skirving

From George II's point of view this was the worst news ever. What to do now? England had practically no troops to fight with if the Scots came south. All were busy fighting the French. Then, worse still, a Franco-Jacobite alliance was signed at Fontainebleau three weeks after the Battle of Prestonpans. The news of Charles' victory had been secretly sent to Paris and France, nay, Spain, France and all their allies were jubilant. The end of the usurpers, 'the idiot race, to honour lost, who know them best despise them most', to quote Burns, was nigh. Prestonpans had proved that Scotland, even though Charles was not fully in control of all of it, was still to be reckoned as a military power in her own right. The Auld Alliance was alive and well. With the restoration of the Stewarts, France's war against Britain and most particularly England, would come to an end, as would the wars of the Austrian succession, for lack of monetary backing. British interference in French interests in both India and Canada would abate. Moreover, the Union of 1707 had come to an end.

9. KING CHARLES III CROWNED AT HOLYROOD

The day after the Battle of Prestonpans, Charles Edward was privately crowned King Charles III by an Episcopalian minister at the Palace of Holyroodhouse. Great Britain was no more. Scotland had regained its sovereignty within Europe and the same thus applied to England and Ireland. The mood of the day was that a wrong had been righted.

Charles Edward's mind, however, was in a sober mood. He forbade any celebration of the Jacobite victory because so many of his father's subject had died that day. He asked that the ministers of the Presbyterian churches performed their Sunday worship as usual (some did, but most refused). Cope's wounded were treated as soon as the battle was over, water and doctors being provided to both armies and each of Cope's soldiers being asked never again to take arms against their rightful king. In fact, many of the survivors joined the Jacobite ranks. Among Cope's private baggage, the Highlanders found numerous boxes of chocolate, a luxury in those days, which Charles' highland men believed to be a healing salve. Colonel Gardiner's wounded body fell near a thorn tree and his man servant carried him to the Presbyterian manse at Tranent, where he died that evening in the arms of the minister's niece. Gardiner had fought valiantly and he would be recognised in 1853 by a monument funded by public subscription, which was erected facing Bankton House, once his property. The monument proclaims his valour as a man and a soldier and he certainly deserved it, unlike Cope, who deserted his post and fled over the border. Cope was tried for cowardice but was acquitted, which is surprising since he truly had deserted his troops and reached the safety of Berwick even before anyone had informed the authorities that the day had been lost.

For some six weeks Charles remained in Edinburgh, entertaining the city fathers and their families. Every morning he would have a levee of his officers and other sympathisers, then meet his councillors for several hours to listen to their very different opinions, and then would dine in public with his officers. Following dinner he would ride out with his guards, usually to Duddingston, where his army lay. In the evening, he would return to the Palace of Holyroodhouse and receive the ladies who came to his drawing room: he then supped in public. Generally there was music at supper and a ball afterwards. Most of the time, though, Charles was hard at work recruiting more men, sending for more troops from the Highlands, trying to persuade – in vain – MacLeod of MacLeod and Sir Alexander Macdonald, chief of the clan, to join him as soon as possible. This was counteracted by the arrival of the lords Kilmarnock, Balmerino and Pitsligo, Macpherson of Cluny and Gordon of Glenbucket with fresh Highland troops. Four French ships had also arrived with provisions, ammunition and money, but few men. Charles needed men if he was to overthrow the Hanoverians in England. It was the one thing which he and Lord George Murray agreed upon but even then the strain in their relationship was showing. Charles did not trust him – with good reason. Murray had been active in the Jacobite plots to restore the Stewarts in 1715 and 1718. He had been exiled by George I but had been pardoned in 1725 when he came back to Scotland. For twenty years he lived in Atholl, but was not particularly happy playing gentleman farmer. He was first and foremost a military man and loved both the power and glory of command. When Cope had reached Dalwhinnie in search of Charles Edward and his Highland army, Murray had offered his services, but Cope declined. Having been fobbed off Murray, out of spite, joined the Jacobite ranks. The Duke of Liria, Charles' cousin and rightful Duke of Berwick, describes Murray, whom he knew personally, as 'a man with plenty intelligence and bravery but … false to the last degree, and has a very good opinion of himself'. He did, however, bring Charles' army the much-needed military know-how and organisation. But Charles and Murray would soon be at loggerheads, particularly at Derby.

10. THE CAMPAIGN INTO ENGLAND

Charles' letters had the overall effect of giving him the army he needed to continue with the campaign. The Battle of Prestonpans had also provided

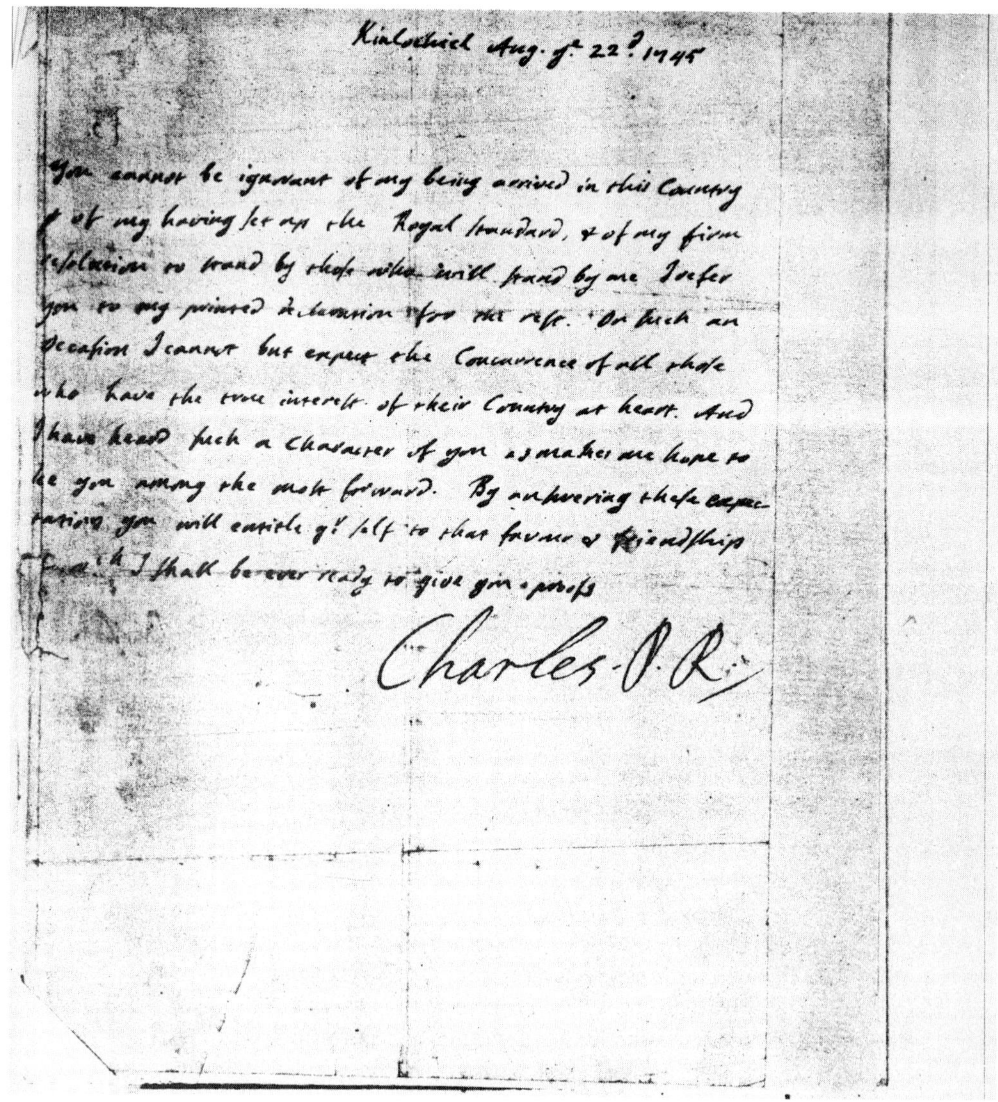

Kinlochiel Aug. ye 22d 1745

Sir

You cannot be ignorant of my being arrived in this Country & of my having set up the Royal Standard, & of my firm resolution to stand by those who will stand by me. I refer you to my printed declaration for the rest. On such an Occasion I cannot but expect the Concurrence of all those who have the true interest of their Country at heart. And I have heard such a Character of you as makes me hope to see you among the most forward. By answering these expectations you will entitle yr self to that favour & friendship which I shall be ever ready to give you proofs

Charles P.R.

Letter from Prince Charles Edward to Sir James Grant asking him to join him – 'You cannot be ignorant of my being arrived in this Country and of my having set up the Royal Standard, and of my firm resolution to stand by those who will stand by me'. Kinlochiel, 22 August 1745. Signed 'Charles P[rince] R[egent]'.

Charles' army with Cope's field pieces and several more Swedish guns were sent by the French. His army after Prestonpans was much more balanced and more like a modern fighting machine of the 18th century. Overall the Jacobite army totalled about 14,000 men (most of them kept in the Highlands) in all, but Charles planned to take only a little under six thousand men with him into England to eject George II from London and dispatch him back to his small electorate in Germany. It was thought that English Jacobites would swell the ranks of the Scottish troops, though Charles soon found that this would not be as easy as he thought.

He first marched to Carlisle and took it. Carlisle was quite a big city, bigger than Edinburgh and would be difficult to hold. Moreover, he could not afford to leave too many troops to hold it in his name and so he left less than three hundred men in charge of Carlisle Castle. They marched further south in two divisions, Murray commanding the first, while the second followed a day behind commanded by Charles himself. The route they took was that of Penrith, Shap, Kendal and Lancaster, and reaching Preston within a week. Calling a council Charles introduced a few English and Welsh Jacobite sympathisers, who confirmed there would be more though it would take time. Undeterred, Charles encouraged the chiefs, who were always reluctant to fight away from Scotland, to march on Manchester, where a small regiment was raised for Charles under the command of Francis Townley. By December 1st, the Jacobite army had reached Maccelesfield, two hundred miles from Scotland's capital city and one hundred and fifty miles from the English capital. It was, to say the least, a swift march through England and London was decidedly threatened. George II had to recall troops from Flanders, including the defeated troops under the command of his son, the Duke of Cumberland and required the Dutch government to give him six thousand men, as agreed in a treaty signed between George and Holland.

It is true that very few English people joined Charles' army, but it is equally true that Charles faced no resistance from anyone. When he appeared he was charming and his charisma attracted people. Nobody confronted him and town after town welcomed him as a deliverer. The truth was that, away from London, the Hanoverians were not particularly well-liked. They did not speak English, they did not like England, nor did they trust the English who had beheaded Charles I. None were born in Britain and they mostly lived in Germany. Moreover, they lacked Charles' personal magnetism and were expensive in their tastes. Charles, as far as the people were concerned, was the son of an Englishman and a prince of the true blood. Even better, there was nothing excessive in Charles' religious principles. He attended Episocpalian, Presbyterian, Anglican and Catholic ceremonies to make the point that, under the rule of his father, all would have equal rights. In other words, Charles appealed to the masses. He was every inch a Prince: courteous, approachable, an excellent horseman, and he listened to what the people had to say.

London too was starting to behave as though they were about to be delivered from unwanted Hanoverian rule. George had to witness hundreds of people wearing the while cockade, the Stewart symbol of restoration, and was so much in fear of his life that he had a barge standing ready on the Thames to take him aboard a ship that would take both him and the English crown jewels to Germany. A new hymn was written, *Onward Christian Soldiers*, that commemorated Charles Edward's march through England. The scene was set for a triumphant entry into London. If only he had known the mood of the city, if only he had marched on, the history of Europe might have been substantially different.

But Charles did not know. All he knew was that Hanoverian troops had been sent for from the continent. But these troops were slow moving, something that even Murray failed to capitalise on. Field Marshall Wade started his move in Newcastle but with few provisions and scant cash. By the time he arrived at Ripon, he was considered to be only a minor threat. Cumberland, in charge of Ligonier's forces, marched from Newcastle-Under-Lyme as far as Coventry and it was now that the Jacobites played a game of checkers with Cumberland. Murray and Charles decided to split their army in two, with Murray feigning a march to Congleton towards Wales. Turning east, Murray and his army crossed the Bow hills to Leek, where they rejoined Charles' troops and then advanced unchecked to Derby. Cumberland and his allies had been outmanoeuvred and found themselves facing a ghost army at Stone. Cumberland waited for the Jacobites in vain with his exhausted troops facing the chill of the wind and the coming winter without shelter while in Derby the Jacobites were sleeping in proper beds paid out of Charles' exchequer. And on Finchley Common, what little was left of the Hanoverian troops, quite untrained in the art of warfare, were gathering for what was probably to be their last confrontation with the Jacobite army.

11. THE FATAL DECISION TO WINTER IN SCOTLAND

But then the pendulum, as it always does, swung the other way. Murray and his chiefs informed Charles that they wanted to retreat to Scotland for the winter, in order to come back with more troops in the spring. Charles was appalled. Never had a winning army retreated before a deflated foe. The road to London, Charles Edward argued, was open to them. It was his gut feeling: he could not prove it to them. In fact, every intelligence gathering told Murray they would be facing a superior force. In this instance, Charles was right and Murray was wrong. The Hanoverian spies won the day. A few days later the Jacobite army left Derby to march back to Scotland. Welcomed as 'liberators' Charles' army had to face being called 'deserters' on their way back.

They were able to evade two English armies successfully and make their way back over the border. In Scotland, further successful fighting went on with Charles' army defeating General Hawley at Falkirk and Lord Loudon in Sutherland. Making his way back to Inverness Charles Edward, on the advice of O'Sullivan, decided to fight Cumberland on the ground of Drumossie Moor, the worst battlefield to choose: flat and boggy, with no opportunity for a Highland charge due to the lack of high ground. Culloden, as Drumossie Moor would be known, was the death knell of Scotland's ancient way of life. It lasted just twenty minutes and the butchery was, to say the least, atrocious. Unlike Charles Edward, who had issued a command that help should be given to Hanoverian survivors after a Jacobite victory, Cumberland issued the opposite order. No quarter was to be given. And none was given. Scotland, for the second time in its history (after Glencoe), faced an act of military genocide. Typically Cumberland, when back in London, entered the House of Lords and demanded that it pass a bill whereby all Highland women should be forcibly sterilised. To their credit, all the peers declined to back the bill and informed the press of Cumberland's demand, thus earning him the title 'Cumberland the Butcher'. Nor was the medal struck to commemorate his only victory ever claimed by any British regiment.

12. ABOLITION AND PROSCRIPTION

Until 1752, Scots Jacobites were forced by the thousands into slavery abroad or simply disappeared, never to be heard of again. From glen to glen, women, children, livestock and property were all ruthlessly assaulted by Cumberland's troops. Prohibitive laws were passed by Westminster forbidding the bearing of arms in Scotland, the wearing of tartan and playing of bagpipes. For forty-six years, anyone found disobeying these *Acts of Abolition and Proscription* was liable to imprisonment or transportation. Charles Edward, who had been forcibly removed from the battlefield when it became clear how badly things had gone, roamed the Highlands and islands evading the Hanoverian army and making his way back to France in September of that year. Even with a £30,000 reward for his capture no-one in Scotland betrayed him.

It is often stated by historians that Derby was the end of the Jacobite threat of a Stewart restoration but that is not true. Charles' army had successfully fought against several English generals winning battles in both England and Scotland and losing only one, at Culloden, the only battle Cumberland ever won in his military career. Even then Charles had made plans to gather his forces at Fort Augustus should the battle go against him. As far as he was concerned, losing a battle was hardly losing a war. But no-one had foreseen the degree of brutality that Cumberland would bring to the fight and its aftermath.

If Culloden was the end, Prestonpans was truly its beginning – the victory that gave the Jacobite army the impetus to march into England as far as Derby, only one hundred and thirty miles from London. Only one Scottish king had ever succeeded in marching unchecked into England before, when Alexander II of the Scots marched into England and met the Dauphin of France, then also on English soil, during the reign of King John, brother to King Richard the Lionheart. To believe that England has never been invaded is to believe an historical myth.

And Prestonpans, to quote AJ Youngson, was:

> "... a signal triumph of loyalty, courage and morale"[16]

Had it not been for the victory at Prestonpans there would have been no success in the attempt at a Stewart restoration in 1745. And the Stewarts were restored: James VIII had been proclaimed king in most of Scotland and his son had been symbolically crowned Charles III on Scottish soil. Nor was it an attempt by catholic Scotland to restore the Catholic religion in the most ancient kingdom in Europe. It truly was the last Scottish military attempt to restore the common laws and weals of our nation, that which our ancestors fought for so valiantly at the Battle of Bannockburn on St. John's Day 1314. Those fighting in 1745 on behalf of Charles Edward Stewart, Duke of Rothesay, fought for the restoration of Scotland's written constitution of 1320, the Declaration of Arbroath that confirmed all Scots were born equal under the law. Under the silent constitution of Britain, all Scots found themselves to be serfs rather than free men and women. British law cared little for the needs of 18th century Scottish people. Scotland's representation in both the Commons and the Lords was dismal, with forty-five seats being granted to the Scots in the former and sixteen peers being taken into the latter.

What should undoubtedly be understood is that the '45 (and thus Prestonpans) was, as FW Robertson puts it, the last great national move in Scotland:

> "... the real movement ... demanded a free Scotland ... We must not be deceived by the ridiculous trappings with which our enemies have covered the great tale of the '45. It is a living issue and not a mere dead end. The coming men will study it and its great men as the real Scotland."[17]

Prince Charles Edward wrote the following to King Louis XV after his defeat at Culloden:

> "The plight of Scotland as I left her calls for your Majesty's close attention. The Kingdom is about to be destroyed and the English government is resolved to treat alike those who supported it and those who took up arms for me."[18]

13. THE TOWN'S BATTLE HONOUR IN DANGER

At the outset of the analysis of the Battle of Prestonpans, its origins and its aftermath, I mentioned how a battle can put the smallest place on the map. It is clear that the local residents were aware of this. Only a short time after the battle took place the people of Prestonpans petitioned the *Scots Magazine*, on behalf of Prestonpans, Preston, Cockenzie, Seton and Tranent, that the battlefield should be referred to as Prestonpans and not as 'Gladsmuir', which is what most of the Highlanders called it during the 1745 campaign. If anything it appears that people were proud of the event that took place there on September 21st 1745 and were determined that future records should be historically accurate in identifying its location. The petition in part reads:

> "... whereas on 21st September last, there was a battle fought on a field which is in a manner surrounded by the petitioning towns and villages, from one or another of which the said battle ought undoubtedly to derive its title.
>
> Nevertheless the publishers of a certain newspaper, entitled the *Caledonian Mercury*, have most unjustly denominated the said battle from a moor on which it was not fought, nor near to it; in which they are followed by several people who, either through malice against your petitioners or through stupidity, have affected to call and still call it the 'Battle of Gladsmuir' by which practice your petitioners are, conjunctly and severally, deprived of that honour and fame which of right pertains to them, and which in all histories, future maps, and almanacs, ought to be transmitted as theirs, to latest posterity. [signed] Flying Shots."[19]

Whereupon, the editor tells his readers, 'to change or not, just as they have a mind.'

The Battle of Prestonpans was not the first and would not be the last military episode in the history of the area. In fact Prestonpans, a barony burgh since 1617 under a charter from King James VI, fell foul of Cromwell in 1650 when he burned the tower of Preston. Again, in 1797, the people of Prestonpans, in common with most of Scotland, refused to comply with the Militia Act which

Remains of those who fell in the Battle of Prestonpans being reburied – May 13th 1950 (The Scotsman) – at the site of the Memorial Cairn

required Scotland to provide six thousand men to fight in the British army. A document sent to the justices at Tranent stating the opposition among local people and their resolve not to comply with the Act reads:

> "... Although we may be overpowered in effecting the said resolution, and dragged from our parents, friends and employment, to be made soldiers of, you can infer from this what trust can be reposed in us if ever we are called upon to disperse our fellow-countrymen, or to oppose a foreign foe."[20]

Government reaction to this was swift. The following day, a demonstration turned into a riot whereby old and young, in and around Tranent, were massacred although the petitioners from Prestonpans escaped unharmed. The rebellious folk of Prestonpans also supported the Italian cause of General Garibaldi contributing £20 to the Garibaldian Patriotic Fund, and in 1868 Prestonpans was the scene of riotous opposition to the appointment of burgh commissioners. Some fifteen youths were arrested but all had their cases subsequently dismissed. This tradition of opposition, in the 20th century, translated into industrial action with the rise of trade unioinism and the miners of Prestonpans were closely involved with strike action and support for strikers elsewhere even after the closure of the collieries in the early 1960s.

The history of Prestonpans does not consist merely of one battle fought on September 21st 1745 and won by the Jacobite forces of Prince Charles Edward Stewart. Its history is the story of the independent spirit of a strong minded community believing in the causes of their fellow men and fellow Scots. Long may this continue.

NOTES

1 The English spelling 'Stewart' rather than the French 'Stuart' has been adopted throughout
2 Although James VI was the first James to become king of England, he was the sixth Scottish king of that name. Therefore, in this account, he and those who followed him are given their Scottish title and designated 'King of the Scots'
3 Monaldi & Sorti, *Imprimatur*, Mondadori, Italy 2002
4 J. Follian, *Sunday Times*, September 23 2001
5 Murray GH Pittock, *Myths of the Jacobite Clans*, p.100
6 ibid., p. 88
7 ibid., p. 96
8 Archives of the Ministry of Defence
9 V. Vitteleschi, *A Court in Exile*
10 Grant R. Francis, *Romance of the White Rose*
11 V. Vitteleschi, *A Court in Exile*
12 P. MacNeill, *Prestonpans and Vicinity: Historical, Ecclesiastical and Traditional, 1884*, p. 210
13 Jacobite website
14 Baron Porcelli, *The White Cockade*
15 *The Scotsman*, 13th May 1950
16 Murray GH Pittock, *Myths of the Jacobite Clans*
17 ibid., p. 88
18 ibid., p. 88
19 P. MacNeill, *Prestonpans and Vicinity: Historical, Ecclesiastical and Traditional*, 1884, pp. 217–18
20 ibid., p. 103

ANNEX 1
ADAM SKIRVING'S CELEBRATION SONG

This song, written about the Jacobite victory at Prestonpans, was composed by Adam Skirving (1719–1783), a farmer living near the battlefield, circa 1746

The Chevalier, being void of fear, did march up Birsle brae, man,
And through Tranent ere he did stent, as fast as he could gae, man;
While General Cope did taunt and mock, wi' mony a loud huzza, man,
But ere next morn proclaim'd the cock, we heard anither craw, man.

The brave Lochiel, as I heard tell, led Camerons on in clouds, man;
The morning fair, and clear the air, they loos'd with devilish thuds, man
Down guns they threw, and swords they drew, and soon did chase them aff, man
On Seaton crafts they buft their chafts, and gart them rin like daft, man.

The bluff dragoons swore, blood and oons, they'd make the rebels run, man:
And yet they flee when them they see, and winna fire a gun, man.
They turn'd their back, the foot they break, such terror seiz'd them a', man.
Some wet their cheeks, some fyl'd their breeks, and some for fear did fa', man.

The volunteers prick'd up their ears, and vow gin they were crouse, man!
But when the bairns saw't turn to earn'st, there werena worth a louse, man
Maist feck gade hame, O fie for shame, they'd better staid awa, man,
Than wi' cockade to make parade, and do nae gude at a', man.

Menteith the great, when hersel shit, un'wares did ding him owre, man,
Yet wadna stand to bear a hand, but aff fu fast did scour, man.
O'er Sourtra Hill, ere he stood still, before he tasted meat, man.
Troth, he may brag of his swift nag, that bore him aff sae fleet, man.

And Simpson, keen to clear the een of rebels far in wrang, man.
Did never strive wi' pistols five, but gallop'd wi' the thrang man.
He turn'd his back, and in a crack was cleanly out o' sight, man.
And thought it best: it was nae jest, wi' Highlanders to fight, man.

'Mangst a' the gang, nane bade the bang but twa, and ane was ta'en, man;
For Campbell rade, but Myrie staid, and sair he paid the kane, man.
Four skelpe he got, was waur than shot, frae the sharp-edg'd claymore, man;
Frae mony a spout came running out his recking het red gore, man.

But Gard'ner brave did still behave like to a hero bright, man;
His courage true, like him were few that still despised flight, man.
For king, and laws, and country's cause, in honour's bed he lay, man.
His life, but not his courage fled, while he had breath to draw, man.

And Major Bowle, that worthy soul, was brought down to the ground, man;
His horse being shot, it was his lot for to get mony a wound, man.
Lieutenant Smith of Irish birth, frae whom he call'd for aid, man.
But full of dread, lap o'er his head, and wadna be gainsaid, man.

He made sic haste, sae spurr'd his beast, 'twas little there he saw, man;
To Berwick rade, and falsely said rhe Scots were rebels a', man.
But let that end, for weel 'tis kend his use and wonts to lie, man.
The Teague is naught, he never fought when he had room to flee, man.

And Cadell, drest, amang the rest, with gun and gude claymore, man,
On gelding gray he rode that day, with pistols set before, man.
The cause was good, he'd spend his blood before that he would yield, man;
But the night before he left the core, and never fac'd the field, man.

But gallant Roger, like a soger, stood and bravely fought, man;
I'm wae to tell, at last he fell, and mae down wi' him brought, man
At point of death, wi' his last breath, some standing round in ring, man,
On's back lying flat, he wav'd his hat, and cried, 'God save the king!' man.

Some Highland rogues, like hungry dogs, neglecting to pursue, man
About they fac'd, and, in great haste, upon the booty flew, man
And they, as gain for all their pain, are deck's wi' spoils of war, man;
Fu'bauld can tell how her nain sel was ne're sae praw before, man.

At the thorn tree, which you may see, bewest the meadow mill, man,
There mony slain lay on the plain, the clans pursuing still, man.
Sic unco hacks, and deadly whacks, I never saw the like, man;
Lost hands and heads cost them their deads, that fell near Preston dyke, man.

That afternoon, what a' was done, I gade to see the fray, man;
But I had wist what after past, I'd better staid away, man:
On Seaton sands, wi' nimble hands, they pick'd my pockets bare, man;
But I wish ne'er to dree sic fear, For a' the sum and mair, man.

Michael Brander. *Scottish and Border Battles and Ballads.* (New York: Barnes & Noble, Inc., 1993), 273–276.

ANNEX 2
THE THORN TREE AT PRESTONPANS

The Thorn Tree, by Hugh Hannah, *East Lothian Antiquarian and Field Naturalist Society, Transactions Vol. 2, pp.154–7*

As the white hawthorn tree is dead, which for about a century and a half was a living landmark of the battle of Prestonpans (September 21st, 1745) and those who may remember it in its glory of white and fragrant "flourish", or scarlet haw, are few in number, the editors have pleasure in complying with a suggestion that there should be published in the *Transactions* one or two pictures of it. The tree was one of the famous historic trees of the county. Though never so wide spreading or imposing as the great yew tree at Whittingehame under which it is reputed the murder of Darnley was plotted in 1567, it was in its prime a handsome hawthorn.

The tree stood where the battle raged fiercest, and where the brave "Christian Hero", Colonel James Gardiner of Bankton, fell. It had originally three stems, standing out so markedly one from another that Peter McNeill in his *Tranent and its Surroundings* (2nd edition), 1884, speaks of the tree as a clump of three thorn trees; and J. Sands in his *Sketches of Tranent in the Olden Time*, 1881, writes that "strictly speaking there were three thorn trees". Like Bonnie Prince Charlie fighting to secure the crown of his ancestors the tree was young in years when the battle was fought. The hawthorn seldom lives to be two hundred years old, and the thorn tree was complete till 18th October 1899, though buttressed with iron rods and bands. On that date the largest stem was blown down as mentioned in a *Courier* of June 1990. In 1817 it was already regarded as venerable. In a letter written in that year it was so described by Andrew Bigelow of Medford, Massachusetts, and that letter is incorporated in his *Leaves from a Journal* or *Sketches of Rambles in North Britain and Ireland* published in 1824. Bigelow and a friend had walked over a part of the battlefield when a shower overtook them. They found shelter from the rain "under the lee side of a hawthorn row, about a stone's cast from the venerable thorn tree beside the meadow mill". Bigelow goes on to say "Our covert being on the declivity of a rising ground which commanded a view of the scene of combat we were enabled to calculate the relative advantages and disadvantages of the positions occupied by the two armies anterior to the engagement." Close to the tree in a field known as Thorntree Field many of the slain were buried. Both Jacobites and Royalists peacefully sleep their last sleep together under the ground that was stained with their life blood at the time of the battle with a deeper scarlet than that of the reddening haws on the thorn tree. Towards the close of the eighteenth century, as chronicled by Peter McNeill, "when this field was being drained

Thorn Tree – Original Tree

Reproduced from Chalk Drawing in flat water colour in possession of Mr James McNeill. Artist, Mr. F. W. Mason

the workmen came upon a number of bodies, the clothes covering the remains being so well preserved they could distinguish Royalist from rebel."

The Society has made two visits to the battlefields of Prestonpans (or Preston), and an account of both is given on pp. 207–212 of Volume I of the *Transactions*. On both occasions the thorn tree was visited. The first visit was made on 20th September 1924 under the leadership of the late W. B. Blaikie, LL.D., a well-known authority on the "Forty-five". The second took place five years afterwards (on 21st September 1929) and included a visit to Preston Tower and Cross, Hamilton House and Northfield House under the leadership of Mr James S. Richardson. The visit to the thorn tree was under the guidance of Mr Richardson and Mr Alexander Burnett. On the first visit it was noted that only one of the three limbs of the tree remained and it was dead; on the second Mr Burnett "gave a clear and concise account of how the dead and blackened stump which the members saw before them, had a special interest in connection with the history of the battle".

On the second visit a suggestion was considered that a Memorial be placed on the site of the thorn tree. The movement to erect a suitable Memorial Cairn gathered way. The tree was cut down by permission of the Earl of Wemyss as owner, the best portion of the trunk being presented to the Naval and Military Museum at Edinburgh Castle.

The thorn tree is mentioned in the verses on the "Battle of Prestonpans" by Adam Skirving, the East Lothian farmer who wrote the song "Hey, Johnnie Cope are ye waukin yet", which Sir Walter Scott in the *Tales of a Grandfather* says is "familiar in our mouths as household words over the whole length and breadth of Scotland". "'The Battle of Prestonpans' has preserved also" (Sir Walter says) "for its author, a memorial of his name outlasting the period of his own day and generation." The whole poem is given in Scott's *Tales of a*

Grandfather and is too long to be given (However, it appears as Annex 1 in this booklet pp. 32–34 above). The thorn tree stanza is:

At the thorn-tree, which you may see
　　Bewest the meadow mill, man,
There mony slain lay on the plain,
　　The Clans pursuing still, man;
Sic unco hacks and deadly whacks,
　　I never saw the like, man;
Lost hands and heads cost them their deads
　　That fell near Preston dyke, man.

Stemmed Tree
From photograph by Mr John R. Borrowman

Of the two illustrations of the tree, the first shows the tree as it originally stood with its three stems and represents the tree about 40 years ago laden with hawthorn blossom. It is from a chalk drawing, tinted in flat water colour, by Mr F. W. Mason which is in the possession of Mr James McNeill, Inveresk, youngest son of Mr Peter McNeill, the historian of Tranent and Prestonpans for whom the work was executed by Mr Mason. The editors tender their thanks to Mr James McNeill for his courtesy in allowing them to reproduce the drawing; and also to Mr John R. Borrowman for his courtesy in allowing them to reproduce the second illustration, which is from a fine photograph taken by him over 30 years ago after the tree had lost one of its main limbs. It should interest our members to know that in his garden at St. Michaels, Gilmerton, Mr Borrowman has a tall and sturdy thorn tree raised from a shoot of the battlefield thorn tree. Further illustrations of the thorn tree are to be found in the second edition of Mr Peter McNeill's book on Tranent published in 1884, and in his book on Prestonpans published in 1902. Both are from pencil drawings by James Veitch. The first shows the three stemmed tree, and the second two stems and a stump, but they are not so satisfactory as the illustrations presented here.

The erection in February 1932 of the Memorial Cairn to commemorate the battle is duly chronicled in the *Haddingtonshire Courier* of the 12th of that month. It was erected by the Society for the Preservation of Rural Scotland, and our Society gave a substantial contribution to the cost. The leader in the movement was Sir Iain Colquhoun, Bart, of Luss, and associated with him and others were our President, Major W. A. Baird of Lennox-love. And our member Mr G. A. Connor.

The cairn has not been erected on the actual site of the tree, which was near a colliery siding and could not readily be seen from the main road. It was ultimately decided to erect it in a more prominent position. The site chosen and granted by East Lothian County Council is a triangular piece of ground at a fork in the Edinburgh/North Berwick road at Meadowmill. It is within sight of the position occupied so long by the venerable hawthorn tree, and is close to the position occupied by the guns of Sir John Cope's ill-fated army.

The cairn which is about ten feet high and is hammer dressed is a stepped pyramidal structure "concave in plan above a square base with bevelled angles, with corner stones and coming into the square at the apex". It is finished off at the summit with a heavy top stone. On a panel on the main face is the arresting date "1745" carved in bold letters. A casket is built into the cairn containing a paper narrating the circumstances, and that the thorn tree was situated about 400 yards, 35 degrees west of north from where the cairn stands. The casket contains other documents relating to the thorn tree, along with photographs of it, a piece of the thorn tree itself and a set of new coins. The cairn was designed by Mr William Davidson, F.R.I.B.A. The builder was Mr John Henderson of Edinburgh.

While the cairn is not built on the actual spot where the thorn tree weathered the battle and two centuries, the actual site will, it is hoped, be preserved for generations yet to come through the transplanting from a private garden of an offshoot from it. A metal plate recording the circumstances should in due course be affixed.

Hugh Hannah

Postscript
In May 2006 The Battle of Prestonpans (1745) Heritage Trust was founded to seek to provide for 'the better continuous interpretation and presentation of the battle' for indwellers and visitors alike. The trustees intentions are ambitious and envisage creating a tourist destination for the town to continue its socio-economic regeneration.

15

Steamed Up at Prestongrange

Colin Boyd

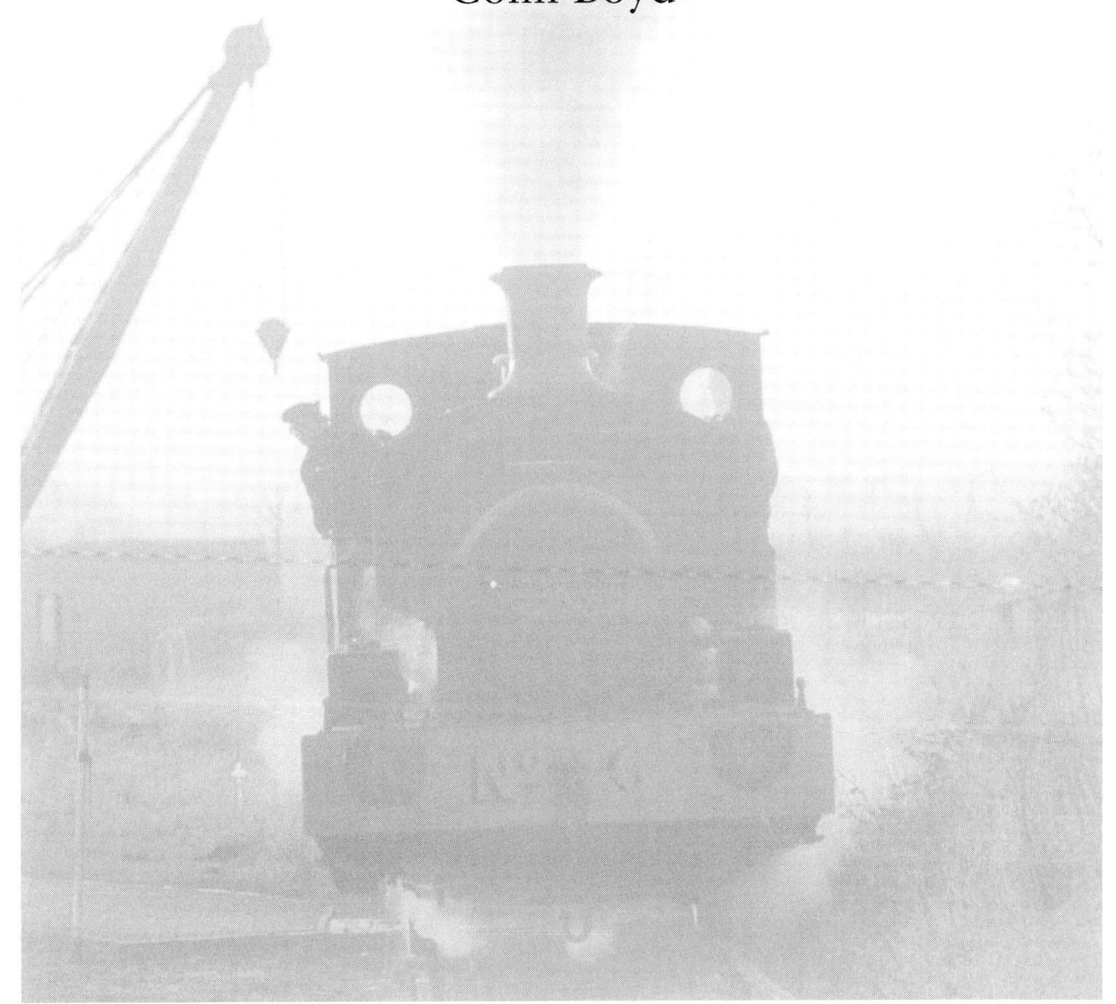

INTRODUCTION

The steam locomotive developed rapidly in the mining areas of the North of England and Cornwall. It was a necessary development of stationary steam power, and could quickly and cheaply move large tonnages of coal in preference to horse haulage or canal. The technology spread rapidly throughout the country as motive power for public railways and industrial premises alike. As coal mine complexes expanded some very large railway systems, known as "internal users", grew up while some lesser concerns made do with just a few sidings. Virtually every system was served by the company's own steam locomotives.

Rail transport would appear to have arrived at Prestongrange Colliery in the 1870s. It was served by a branch line diverging from the Edinburgh – Berwick main line, south of Prestonpans Station. It ran northwest over level ground above the Firth of Forth to a point atop an escarpment then turned east down a steep gradient to reach the sea level of the Colliery. It was approximately $^3/_4$ of a mile long.

Prestongrange Steam Engine No 7 entertains visitors to Prestongrange Industrial Heritage Museum

THE PRESTONGRANGE COAL AND FIRE-BRICK COMPANY (LIMITED),

PRESTONPANS, SCOTLAND.

Telegraphic Address: "Prestongrange, Prestonpans.

Priced Illustrated Catalogues on Application.

Telephone: No. 2201.

SHIPPING PORT,– MORRISONSHAVEN

Vessels can be loaded at Morrisonshaven up to about 14 feet draft, this Harbour having now been considerably deepened. We usually load Vessels of 100 to 300 tons capacity at Morrisonshaven. Ocean-going Steamers at Leith.

The Collieries and Brickworks are 100 yards from the Port of Morrisonshaven, being connected with it by Railways, the Property of the Company.

☞ Vessels loading Coals or Fire Clay Goods pay NO Harbour Dues.

p. pon. THE PRESTONGRANGE COAL AND FIRE BRICK CO., Ld.,

PRESTONPANS, 29th March 1889.

It was worked all its life by steam engines until closure in 1962. A total of nine locomotives have been recorded over this period. Of these only one survives – Andrew Barclay built No 2219 in 1946. The same builder's No 224, built in 1881, was still at work in 1962 and despite the efforts of an enthusiastic signalman at Morrisons' Haven Signal Box that locomotive, along with the rest of Prestongrange Colliery, was despatched for scrap. It would surely have been a fitting relic for Prestongrange.

In Scotland at large, steam lasted until 1981 working quietly away serving coal mining as it had done since the nineteenth century – 13 years after British Railways had itself dispensed with steam.

The mining complex lives on as The Prestongrange Industrial Heritage Museum, where railways and steam are an important aspect of its presentation. Steam re-appeared on rails in 1975 after a 13 year absence. This Historical Series booklet is proud to recount the tale of how and why the new railway was built.

FORMING AND STEAMING

For this author, at least, it began way back in 1963, through a series of coincidences, of which most people experience at least one in their lifetime. I have always been interested in railways, watching trains at pre-school age from my parents' bedroom window which overlooked the old station in Peebles. 1963 found me wandering cavernous Waverley Station in Edinburgh when I met Iain, now a lifelong friend. Iain was a railway signalman of the old school, shiny levers and continuous cups of tea, and his place of work was on the East Coast Mainline to London at Morrison's Haven, about 15 miles out from Edinburgh. Morrison's Haven was the now silted-up and filled-in harbour for Prestongrange Colliery and the signal box was named after it. Its purpose was to control the sidings for the wagons to-ing and fro-ing from Prestongrange Colliery. By the time I was paying my unofficial visits, the Colliery was closed but I enjoyed many sunny days, yes they appeared sunny then, observing railways.

Years passed. In 1969, exploring the Edinburgh outskirts in my faded blue aged Hillman Minx, re-designed at the back after the bus behind me one day did not stop, I discovered Lady Victoria Colliery at Newtongrange. I did not know the place existed but here were steam engines shunting this busy site, as they had done for over 60 years. I loved it!

More years passed. In 1976, I heard of a museum project being started at the site of Prestongrange Colliery and as it was close to home, decided this was the place to be. I investigated in my suave new White 1600E Cortina – no more beat-up Hillmans. What I found was the cleared site of the colliery, heaps of bricks and spoil and in the middle the embryo of what was to come. There, proud as punch in a gleaming coat of green paint, all on its own in a sea of dereliction, was the same locomotive I had watched in 1969. To the north, within shouting distance, Morrison's Haven harbour still lay waiting to be re-discovered and half a mile to the south, up the tree covered hill and across the North Berwick road was Morrison's Haven Signal Box, the site of my schoolday jaunts in 1963.

The locomotive was the first of many industrial-type railway artefacts to arrive at Prestongrange in 1975. It was being managed by three or four like-minded people and soon I was adorned in the traditional boiler suit and

No 6 in action with wagons. Beam Engine in the background, 26.12.93

getting happily filthy. The site at this time was basically managed by a retired Area Mining Manager whose influence gathered many of the items made available to Prestongrange, and thus the collection grew. Fortunately, so did the number of people willing to become involved, until at the peak, around 15 were actively involved. Fifteen doesn't sound much but it was adequate to manage the requirements and, after all, how many societies can claim 100% of active membership; 15 members; 15 active people!

The main group aim was to manage and operate items of equipment pertinent to the site, but principally the steam locomotive. All this was done on a somewhat ad-hoc basis, along the lines of – *Question: "Who will be here on Sunday?"; Answer forthcoming; "Oh good, then we can do this and/or that"*. This sporadic planning was fine up to a point but lack of continuity could hinder a planned project. One subject that was a total commitment was to steam the locomotive on the first Sunday of the month from April to September, and the Museum authorities expected this. Footplate "trips" were offered.

Thus in 1980, the members formally formed the Prestongrange Society. Along with the usual office bearers, it was recognised that groups managing certain disciplines were desirable and from this the Engineering, Permanent Way (P/way), and Operating Groups were formed, with a nominated "person in charge". Each member selected a group they would prefer to be associated with, usually determined by their skills. As in most groups, the membership's occupations ranged over a broad spectrum from engineers, farmers, lawyers, bankers, professional railwaymen, mothers, etc. However, those in charge were

Looking north over The Site. Pit Baths in background, 11.1.79

Lothians Southern Engine No 17 at work at Prestongrange

allowed to "poach" from other groups if manpower was required. One of the nice advantages in such a small working group is the ability for everyone to be involved in all tasks and the flexibility it produces. For example, during tracklaying, six people working in unison could manhandle a 30-foot length of rail with comparative ease.

Written rules was another item which had not been investigated before. Thus a Rules Committee was formed to produce formal rules for operations which would suit all the membership and embodying what was already being done in practice, and also to satisfy the Railway Inspectorate. This eliminated any discrepancy for people thinking they were doing the correct thing but misunderstood by someone else. "Did that strange hand signal mean stop?"

As expected with all groups, Annual General Meetings are held and minuted. At first, they were held "on site" at Prestongrange in the Beam Engine House. Unfortunately, this had its drawbacks. Chiefly, as the AGMs are usually held in December, the Engine House could be extremely draughty and cold – although this did make for very smart proceedings. However, the lady members declined the comforts and after one very cold meeting, it was decided to have the meetings at members' houses – why this was not done at first defies logic. The AGMs generated into social evenings going on until the small hours, with much food and drink being consumed. One lady member is renowned for her fresh raspberry and cream sponge and was dared to turn up at meetings without it! Latterly, these flourished into two or three gatherings a year with Belhaven beer being very popular.

For a number of years there was an outing, usually to another railway site, but as the membership had declined this has not happened for some time.

No 7 and Wagons. Colliery Power House Building in background, 5.10.81

Time has taken its toll on the size of the membership. Over the years people have moved, lost interest, had other commitments and unfortunately died. Despite efforts "lost" members have not been replaced and at this date the membership is down to eleven, not all of whom are as active as they were some 20 years ago.

The Society now owns one steam and two diesel engines. It is responsible for the maintenance and operation of the remaining steam and diesel locomotives and although not belonging to the Society the upkeep and expansion, where possible, of the track. All this is now enough to keep the level of membership fully employed and whereas it used to be involved with other museum artefacts, these responsibilities are no longer part of the Society's remit – hence the change of name in 1995 to "The Prestongrange Railway Society".

CALENDAR OF EVENTS

Initially, after Prestongrange Colliery closed in the early 1960s, the site was cleared leaving only the Beam Engine, the large building which was the colliery generating station, or Power House, and various sundry buildings. The brickworks were still in operation. Onto the virtual wasteland arrived locomotive No 7 in 1975. Acquired from Lady Victoria Colliery, Newtongrange, where it had recently ceased working commercially, this locomotive was built in 1914 by Grant Ritchie of Kilmarnock, a town which will appear again in the text. It was protected from curious youngsters, but

No 17 being offloaded at Prestongrange in snowstorm, 20.11.77

not the elements, by a vertical steel fenced compound. From this projected eastwards around 200 feet of track and on this short auspicious start the locomotive was steamed up and down, offering footplate rides.

Around this time a self propelled steam crane was acquired also from Lady Victoria Colliery. This vertical-boilered apparition is thought to date back to the 1860s. At the time of arrival, it was in working order. It proved useful for track laying, besides being of fun value.

The short section of track however, was not at all convenient for any steam engine to show a bit of pace, and to be honest, not very safe if anyone misjudged their stopping distance, so positive efforts were made to extend as far as possible to produce the "running line". As far as possible meant eastward for nearly a quarter of a mile to a point at the end of a small embankment in an area surrounded by trees, strangely dubbed by the membership as "the woods". To go any further would necessitate falling off the end of the embankment, 20 feet or so, and ending up in a local, long established scrap yard.

Up to around 1979, forays were made to various local coal mines that no longer used rail access to tranship coal, or had closed completely for business. Fortunately, one of the members is able to provide road transport, kindly supplied for the cost of his fuel. Lady Victoria Colliery at Newtongrange offered many yards and some pointwork. However, the drawback here was that much of it was in an area long disused beside the A7 road and was now so overgrown that we were working in a virtual forest, but it added to the interest of the job. If any reader cares to investigate the area today, I am sure some track will still be there that was not possible to extricate from around trees. Lady Victoria also donated some wooden wagons and weighing in at around 5½ tons were just within the capability of our member's transport.

No 7 at Prestongrange, 2.10.77

On the other side of the old railway to Carlisle from Lady Victoria was Butlerfield, a coal stocking site. Also derelict by now with no rail access, two of the shunting locomotives were marooned on a short section of track, one inside a corrugated iron shed. This locomotive interested the Society as, being a product of Andrew Barclay of Kilmarnock, it was supplied new to the Prestongrange Colliery in 1946. A homecoming was obvious, and the locomotive was eventually repatriated in a blizzard, to no-one's pleasure. As it was felt at this time that allowing passengers trips directly on the steam locomotive footplate was not acceptable, this new arrival was adapted to carry a few people and used as a "carriage".

1979 also saw the Society and the Museum gain the heights of TV stardom. Scottish Television were producing a series of programmes called "Treasures in Store" and wished to feature Prestongrange. Filming was done over a day of dismal, grey cold drizzle in January. The film crew reflected the weather, the director really was a "dearie" and everyone was glad to go home. However, the final showing on television looked very professional and a nice unexpected surprise was all the members who attended were paid as extras! I clearly remember getting for that day what I normally earned in a week!

Two of the members bought a very small diesel locomotive from a distillery in Tomatin. Described as virtually a lorry engine, a cab and flanged railway wheels, it existed in a previous life shunting loads of material during the construction of the Tay Road Bridge and is believed to have at one stage ended up in the water, rather similar to its more unfortunate bigger brother when the original rail bridge collapsed over a century ago. It arrived, once again, on our member's transport and as it was driven on to the trailer at Tomatin, it was literally driven off again on to the ground at Prestongrange, its diminutive nature allowing it not to sink up to its axles. Facing the wrong way, a couple

The steam crane being used for track laying 1.6.80

of ropes were attached to the front, some of the healthier members attached to the ropes and with some judicious grunting and tugging, the locomotive was driven and slewed simultaneously to line up with two old rails laid as a ramp. It was then driven up the ramp and with the whole exercise taking around half an hour, permanent track was found.

Using an old locomotive as a carriage for passengers had its drawbacks. The immediate one was capacity. As only three persons and a Society member acting as "guard" were allowed to travel at a time, the number of out and back journeys was considered excessive if the visitor numbers topped 300 in an afternoon. Something had to be better and the solution was found by a member who, at this time was a guard at the railway freight depot at Millerhill, near Edinburgh. He reported that an old van had recently been taken out of traffic as a departmental brake van, the type of vehicle that would accompany works trains. It was suitable as it was fitted with bench seating lengthwise along the sides, an open veranda, at one end with a powerful hand brake – admirable for a guard – and best of all, inside, right in the middle of the floor, central heating in the form of a cast iron stove, wood or coal, for the burning of. A deal was struck, low loader arranged, and disaster. At Millerhill the van was despatched to a remote area where it was convenient to winch up by our now well tried and trusted ramping, onto the low loader. The preceding evening, all was ready, material being deposited on the ground and on the trailer, bits of baulking, rail, etc. Next morning, SNOW and more SNOW hiding all the ground-loading material. However, after subduing initial panic, replacements were collected from Prestongrange and delivery eventually accomplished the next day – no snow of course! On site, the new arrival refused to run off the trailer by gravity so more brutal methods were adopted. A member – volunteering of course – manned the handbrake and with a bit of

Boiler of No 6 being re-assembled in frames, 20.5.89

persuasion by tractor and rope, the van was set in motion. And motion it was as it took off at about 15 mph and careered about 80 feet along our track, this vehicle weighing about 24 tons. However, it was home and dry.

Attention then turned to its décor. Like Henry Ford's Model T, it arrived in any colour as long as it was black – black outside, dark green inside. But metamorphosis took place over the winter and maroon exterior and maroon and cream interior hid the sombre black. Ready for the next season was a vehicle in which could be carried up to 16 souls. This greatly eased the queues at the little temporary platform that had been erected from redundant sleepers. The practice now was to propel the van in the direction of "the woods" and obviously pull it back. The van has two windows in the end next to the locomotive and this went down very well, especially with youngsters who could now observe the loco crew at close quarters. Was this appreciated by the loco crews now under minute scrutiny? – ask them!

A short "end to end" railway was now fully operational, with a nice wee green engine hauling a freshly painted maroon van, so thoughts now turned to "What can we do next?".

To date, everything was kept in the open, with the working steam loco, small diesel and the van secured in a high fenced compound when not in use. But at the north end of the site, behind the Visitor Centre, is the old colliery pit baths, once a scene of much scrubbing and activity as miners cleaned up at the end of their shift. Now derelict and home to the proverbial pigeon, one end had been converted by a haulage contractor to house lorries, necessitating a new concrete floor, but producing a long, wide empty gallery-like covered "shed". While not ideal – access was difficult, the roof leaked, it was not heated and headroom not much more than around 12 feet – at least it was indoors. What the Society did have in abundance was track, so the plan was

No 17 at Prestongrange. Heaps of discarded bricks from Brickworks in background, still to be removed, 11.1.79

hatched to build a sort of rough temporary railway to enable rail access to "the baths".

FORTUNE SMILES

Fortune smiled on the Society around this time. In 1980 another Andrew Barclay built locomotive was acquired. Last used at Cairnhill Colliery at the end of the 1970s, it was dumped at a withdrawn machinery store belonging to the NCB (National Coal Board) at Arniston, near Edinburgh. Incidentally, Cairnhill is in the middle of nowhere near Muirkirk, its solitude defies the fact that a colliery once operated here with steam engines and wagons crashing and clanking high up on the moors. This locomotive arrived by the easier method of low loader and crane; if only all our movements could have afforded the luxury of a crane. As this locomotive was not required to steam, and besides its condition was unknown, it was cosmetically restored (i.e. given a lick of paint) and put on display. A few years later, it was despatched to a new museum being established at Lady Victoria Colliery in fact a stone's throw from where the Society collected it from at Arniston a few years earlier.

Of even more consequence was the acquisition in 1982 of yet another Andrew Barclay steam locomotive. This loco was virtually the last steam loco to work commercially in Scotland, certainly for the NCB. It was taken out of service a bit worn but in working order at Bedlay Colliery near Glenboig, simply because the colliery had ceased production. Bearing in mind that the working locomotive at Prestongrange could not work for ever, this new

The railway developing No 7 with wagons, 5.10.81

manna from heaven was an opportunity not to be missed. It arrived unceremoniously on site in September but it took ten years to actually put it into service. Although basically sound as a locomotive, it was assessed by our boiler insurers that work was required and that would entail removal of the boiler from the rest of the loco and sending it to specialist repairers. This was fine, nothing unusual in this except the dreaded asbestos discovered lagging the boiler. And so our poor little engine was sent to Coventry in a distant corner of Prestongrange while the asbestos experts built what looked like not much more than a cub-scout make-and-mend venture hut of wood framing and polythene sheeting inside which the offending material was removed (apologies to the cub-scout movement).

A now scrubbed clean boiler was sent off, remedial work and painting being done in the interim, and by the time the boiler was returned the Society had claimed our stake under cover in the baths.

As previously mentioned, it was 1992 before this shiny black engine breathed steam for our delight.

While all this activity on the locomotive department was taking place, the stronger members calling themselves "The Permanent Way Group" had turned their fancies, as mentioned earlier, to linking the south end of the railway into the old pit baths. Included in the plan was the possibility of a platform on the large grassy area at the side of the visitors' centre. This would allow visitors to board the small train at the point of arrival at the site, and use it as a novelty trip to the beam engine and of course to return in the opposite direction. As things turned out, this option has never been realised, but the resultant track layout will still accommodate this when and if required. What did materialise is a railway of a very temporary nature which branches off near "the woods" runs around the north side of the pit baths, then doubles back on itself to enter the baths from the west. It serves only as an access track to the interior of the baths and is strictly a "non passenger" railway. All this effort was made over virgin territory. A shallow cutting on a gradient had to be formed behind the cottages at the east end of the site. This was dug out mostly by manual labour. Much of the ground is residue and in-fill from the years of industrial labour on the site and was full of broken earthenware pipes, drains and bricks. It was back-breaking work to remove due to the problem that no sooner was shovel thrust in than it came to an abrupt halt striking a jumble of broken rubbish. Perseverance paid off however, and the old road beside the cottages reached. Across the road our member with the mechanical shovel kindly dug and smoothed off the new track bed required to reach the east end of the pit baths. This was greatly appreciated, saving many months of pick and shovel. From this point a small embankment was required around the back of the baths. Much of the material for this came from the rubble dug from the cutting. The embankment took over two years to form, and was built largely by one member on his days off, utilising the Society's old tractor and trailer.

Embankments and cuttings alone are not enough, of course, and the next stage was laying the track. The only really difficult part was in the cutting which, also being on a slight curve, required a considerable amount of rail bending. Rail bending must be one of the most soul destroying railway activities known to mankind; it is slow, laborious, muscle-discovering work but all this activity was a means to an end and by 1992 the assault on the baths was accomplished. It had taken six years, all told! All that remained now was to move the locomotives down our new track to their new covered accommodation. This did not take place without mishap as at one particular temporary rail joint the six-wheeled locomotive decided to try and go round the easy way – on the ground. Derailments always seem to happen near the end of the day when everything else has gone to plan and going home for tea is becoming an attraction. Temporary hitches aside, within a month the baths were home to three steam locomotives, four diesels and three wagons.

By 1990 the ten year boiler certificate for the original steam locomotive being used had eventually run its course. This locomotive, with much cooperation from the boiler insurer, had served the Society well for fifteen years, and now in need of repair, was taken out of service and laid aside. As related earlier, the next locomotive was not put into service until 1992, so the passenger service was operated by the small diesel owned by some of the members. As this locomotive is about a third of the size of the van, aesthetically it was a very odd, unbalanced sight.

In 1991, word had spread that the then-named British Aluminium Company at Falkirk was disposing of a large four wheeled diesel shunter as their internal works transport system was being re-organised. Through the auspices of one of the members, the locomotive was offered to the Society, free of charge, on the condition that we, the Society collected it ourselves and that British Aluminium would receive some publicity from this gesture. With a free locomotive on offer, the conditions were quite acceptable, as all parties stood to benefit. The engineering group despatched themselves to Falkirk and reported favourably on the locomotive, it being assessed in need of a thorough

The English Electric Diesel off the rails at Alcan's Works, Falkirk, 20.1.91

service but no major disaster. British Aluminium had kindly pulled the locomotive out of its small shed for inspection. This transpired to be the gremlin in the works however, as the sleepers in the trackwork immediately outside the shed were so rotten they broke and de-railed the locomotive – sideways! – by about two feet. Undaunted, the next few weekends were spent jacking, packing, slewing, and repairing trackwork. The BA staff were friendly and helpful although on one of the Sundays torrential rain made them conspicuous by their absence. Thanks to everyone at BA, Falkirk, for their generosity. Eventually winched onto a low loader, the locomotive was sent on its way to Prestongrange.

At Prestongrange the Pit baths became the next obstacle, the locomotive being too high to fit in. Bearing in mind the building was not designed for railway locomotives, headroom to the concrete roof girders is fine for lorries but not our locomotives. Inside there is no congenital railway line built on sleepers, simply rails laid on edge directly onto the floor, so tight is the clearing. So out came the engineers with cutter and grinder and removed around six inches from the roof of the locomotive, transforming a beautiful elliptical cab roof into a flat slab, but needs must and a successful metamorphosis resulted in the locomotive being re-united with rails. Until this time it actually stood on its wheels directly onto the shed's concrete floor. The next task was a repaint. In service at the Falkirk foundry it was coloured "safety orange", a no-more better description of the colour would be appropriate. Whilst appreciating the reasoning behind this colour scheme, it was felt inappropriate for Prestongrange and something a bit kinder to the eyes and surroundings was deemed appropriate. At that time, British Aluminium's house colours were a pale blue and white and so the orange disappeared under lashings of undercoat and pleasant shades of blue. A little engraved plaque commemorating British Aluminium's generosity, mounted on the side of the cab, completed the picture.

While all this activity was going on, the re-assembly of our steam locomotive from Bedlay Colliery was progressing well. The boiler, returned from repair, was re-united with the chassis and without the water tank, was steam tested outside the baths to the satisfaction of our boiler inspector. Steam locomotives at this stage, partly dismantled, look somewhat alien and is something visitors do not normally get to see, but as this was done outside beside the main road along the coast, it certainly turned a few heads. With everything in place, the locomotive was ready to see service in 1992, although lining out and enhancing the black finish was still to be applied. The finished article now took first place in the queue of locomotives "on shed".

SETTLING DOWN

By the 1993 running season, the Society and its railway had settled down to a regular operation. Some initial problems with overheating axle-box bearings on our nice new engine were slowly overcome, the red lining was eventually applied and thus, once again, a passenger service was offered with steam. One of the main reasons the Society membership "does what it does" is to be involved with steam engines, and returning to steam brought a great deal of pleasure after ten years of slow, steady work. Not wishing to become complacent after this success, in the latter part of 1992, word had reached us that a diesel locomotive was available in Dumfries. We despatched our news-speaker member off to parts unknown and he reported favourably. In truth, the multi-national chemical company ICI was indeed disposing of a small diesel shunter, which was now inadequate to handle the ever-increasing rail-borne traffic on their site and was ours for the taking, the only conditions being that it was to be kept in its present livery, that being the manufacturer's original paintwork, that some form of ICI identification be displayed permanently on it, and of course, the beneficiary collects. Unlike Falkirk, however, this would be a straightforward operation. Once again, the locomotive was housed in a very impressive shed, accommodating two locomotives, at the back of the works complex. Access was easy and the area around wide open. Outside the shed, the ground was hard standing and the locomotive was definitely on the rails. Quite simply, it was in with our equipment, build the ramp up to low loader and the job was done, and so it was. Due to the nature of the goods being manufactured at Dumfries, security was tight. We were all, along with our vehicles, briefly searched, no cameras allowed, no naked lights and no smoking, except in designated areas, and signing in with name, address and ID, at the gatehouse. If this sounds daunting, it was not and was done in a very friendly way. Bear in mind a locomotive for the taking was just round the corner! At the loading site, we were given a brief lecture by the local Health & Safety Officer – brief because he noted that we were properly equipped with protective clothing, steel toe-capped boots, equipment in good

Danderhall. No 29 being lifted over the fence, 3.12.95

order and presumably presented a group who appeared professional enough to know what we were doing (of course we did!). One rather strange insistence, bearing in mind the "openness" of the site was the wearing of hard hats. To this day, I do not know what our heads were going to collide with. But rules are rules, and thanks to ICI, the Society were locomotive owners yet again, and without any hitches, and an overnight stay in the yard of the low loader contractor under lock and key, our new diesel was on the rails and running at Prestongrange within twenty four hours.

No 6 at Headshunt for Pit Baths, 8.3.92

Thus into the 1993 season, the Society was able to operate one steam and three diesel locomotives, any combination capable of running the brake van. This particular year saw the Society once again the subject of free gifts. GATX, an oil terminal in the Port of Leith, was dispensing with its rail-borne traffic and trackwork was available for the taking. Once again, "for the taking" was the effective expression, but this kind of thing could not be passed over, the distance this time from Leith to Prestongrange being just a hop, skip and jump away, and with the offer were some good quality sleepers, a commodity difficult to procure second hand. Our supply until now acquired from the closure of coal mine sites had virtually dried up, so the Permanent Way Group, temporarily dubbed the "track lifting gang" set about its business once again and thanks to GATX the trackwork was readily dismantled and transported via quite a number of trailer loads to Prestongrange.

Over the last few years, passengers boarded and exited the brake van via a temporary platform built up from redundant sleepers. While serving its purpose well, compared to boarding from ground level, it looked temporary, was slippery in the rain, and was inconvenient when a crowd gathered, being incapable of holding more than about six people. Platform, by the dictionary definition, it certainly was not. Therefore a decision was taken to construct a more substantial affair, complying with the latest minimum specifications. Along with this build, more substantial fencing of the track was desired. A start had been made on the latter in 1993, replacing an earlier wooden edifice which had suffered well the ravages of time, weather and to a lesser extent, vandalism. The new fencing is angle uprights supporting five strands of tensioned wire, all galvanised against the salty air. To accommodate the new platform, which would be straight, some track re-alignment was required at the west end of the layout, this being achieved quite quickly. By 1994, a start was made digging and laying foundations, slow and tedious work. By the next year, progress was enough to halt the train at the first 30 feet of the new improved platform.

On a sadder note, however, saw 1994 being the year the Ruston diesel was named "George Edwards". George Edwards was a stalwart member of the Society for a number of years, being a very practical person, who sadly died suddenly in 1991. It was felt that naming one of the locomotives after him would not be inappropriate and George's wife, Jean, accompanied by their daughter, Kathleen, performed a brief memorial unveiling of the nameplates, on a somewhat chilly day.

By now a pattern had set in, revolving around operating trains on Sundays during the summer months, and maintenance in between. Outwith that, nothing much was required, but as the Society was now fully committed to the railway, and very seldom had time or manpower to become involved with any other site activities, the title was changed to Prestongrange Railway Society in an effort to reflect where all loyalties lay. It was still recognised however, that the railway was still part of an overall theme, not just a railway on a site. As some members were shift workers, opportunities were now being taken to repaint some of the wagons on site, an occupation which could be done on a personal basis through the week without effort being required from the weekend squads. This resulted in a couple of wagons looking much the better.

In 1996 the Society was bequeathed yet another steam locomotive. This small tank locomotive was built by Barclays (why not?) of Kilmarnock in 1908, although how much of the 1908 construction is original is open to conjecture – many major parts are visually replacements. However, the essence of the locomotive is what now exists. This loco was still at work commercially for the National Coal Board until the 1970s at the Frances Colliery, Dysart near Kirkcaldy. When the usual "uneconomic to repair" symptom finally caught up with it, it was eventually despatched to the machinery store at Arniston. Someone took a liking to this wee loco however, and it found a new lease of life as a climb-on plaything in a public park in Danderhall near Edinburgh. Steam engines stripped of their more vulnerable fittings are very difficult to break, even by marauding children and teenagers and so it survived. Latterly however, some of the platework was rusting to the point that sections were becoming razor-edged. As a result of that, combined with a newer, politically correct attitude to people falling off steam engines in public parks, it was beginning to be felt by some locals that the locomotive had served its purpose. Thus it was offered to the Prestongrange Railway Society for – yes – we collect.

Now, de-railed diesels at Falkirk were one thing, but this locomotive was in a public park, at the bottom of a steep slope, with no road access into the park, and the nearest road about 100 feet away, over a fence, out of reach of a crane. The solution was to zig-zag it across and up the park, which was all grass, like tacking a sailing ship into the wind, and doing as little damage as possible to the local garden maintenance's pride into the bargain. Over a number of weekends, preceding the start of the move, a gang inspected and prepared the loco for movement, literally dowsing every moving part with old car engine oil, and transporting some track and sleepers to the site. With the

No 6 on the Road Crossing beside The Cottages, 5.9.92

help of one member's industrial Unimog tractor, fitted with a winch, and crowbars and pinches under the wheels, the plan was to move it along 30 feet of track at a time, relaying each 30 feet from behind to in front, somewhat like a cartoon film. But the plan worked, and over the weeks we became quite an organised team, moving rails, pinching, slewing, shouting orders ("stop" being the most common one used!) until slowly and surely 20+ tons of locomotive was inched up and across to a point near the road fence. It was then easy enough downhill, parallel to the fence, to the chosen spot nearest to the road.

All was secured for a few weeks until the crane and low loader were available. As the lift was still quite a reach and also over the fence, this was the largest crane yet that the Society has had to hire. A Sunday date was arranged, and as total occupation of the road was required, arrangements with the local police were made to have the road closed and signposted for the duration. On the day in question, however, the police never turned up and it was left to us to hastily erect some notices on large cards, which fortunately we had with us, and close the road ourselves. I've never closed a public road before or since – quite a feeling of power – but as Danderhall is quite small no-one complained and quite a few motorists stopped to watch the proceedings.

Between the inner edge of the pavement and the fence was soft ground and initially the crane was positioned in such a way that one of the spreader support legs was in this ground. As soon as the cable took the weight of the load, down went this leg into the ground and alarm bells went off in the crane cab. So, after some crane driver language, an hour later we had the crane repositioned and, in twenty minutes our locomotive was over the fence, swung round and down on to the low loader. By 3 o'clock in the afternoon it was on the rails at Prestongrange. Over the next few weekends it was inched down into the baths. The tank was removed, the cab already having been removed at Danderhall before the move, and over the winter the boiler was given an hydraulic pressure test which, after around 25 years of use, it performed very well, but to date no more work has been done.

Until a number of years ago, the demonstration line ran from the west end of the site, beside the beam engine, eastwards into the section described previously as "the woods". This wooded section is the only part of the railway that is actually built on original trackbed from the days of Prestongrange Colliery, the remainder being built on ground newly prepared by the Society. The point where it starts to curve away out of sight (the site of the Colliery Weighbridge from which large lumps of concrete had to be removed) to the bufferstop is formed on an embankment increasing in height as the land drops away. A visit from the railway Inspectorate one day incurred their displeasure insomuch as the rails themselves were too close to the edge of the embankment at the north side. Thus passenger trains would not be allowed to operate on this part until it was slewed over by about 2 feet. This virtually halved the operating distance but there was nothing else for it and the section was closed. Instead trains ran two short trips, back and forth – not a wholly satisfactory procedure. But "the woods" is a favourite part for the members as it can be quite pleasant and is out of sight from the start point, giving the impression of actually having been somewhere! It was a must to restore the track to operating condition. This was begun in 1997 when a vigorous effort was started to dismantle all the affected trackwork. Why does dismantling always seem easier and quicker than the re-build?

After stockpiling rails and sleepers at the side and removing to a safe haven anything that might appear useful to third parties, a new layout was surveyed and pegged out. Having thought that all our tracklaying days were over, once again it was back to the pick and shovel, levelling boards and hand operated rail saw and hole drill. When the section was originally built, much of it was done in winter and there were some days so freezing it was impossible to attack the ground with a pick, never mind a shovel. Now with milder winters and seemingly wetter summers, sometimes for the opposite reason, work had to stop as the ground simply slurried away. With membership declining somewhat, all this work took longer than originally planned and only by 2002 had the end been reached once again.

Much tidying up is still required, but once again a train can disappear among the trees, out of sight of the "starting point".

10 YEAR BOILER CERTIFICATES

1991 was now some time ago and the working steam locomotive was nearing the end of its ten year boiler certificate – 2001 obviously.

With no other steam locomotive available for service, the situation was beginning to appear unhealthy. As the locomotive was considered mechanically fit enough to perform its mundane duties at Prestongrange, it was decided that any expenditure would involve the boiler. Assuming that nothing drastic would be discovered by the boiler inspector, an estimate was produced to restore the boiler fit for another ten years use, and presented to the locomotive's owners. At first it seemed this would happen, but May 2001 came and went with no arrangements for restoration, and so it was withdrawn (fully operational) from service and joined the queue of locomotives in the baths. Services were run that year with one of the Society's diesels, but without the attraction of steam, and due to mechanical problems with the diesels, the service is now spasmodic. Interestingly, the steam locomotive reliability was probably better than the diesels, although the diesels have put in more days' work.

At the time of writing the Society has no working steam engines, there is no passenger service, the track is dangerously overgrown and the future is uncertain. But we've been there before.

REFLECTIONS

In its final layout the railway is easy to operate. The working steam locomotive is always second last into the baths and a diesel last. This had the obvious double advantage of the diesel being available to tow outside, for steam raising, the steam loco but also made the diesel available at any time without disturbing anything else. This has two advantages. As all the stock is kept in one long row, the steam loco can be "hauled" outside for steam raising purposes. The other advantage is that the diesel is readily available at any time without disturbing any other stock.

Passenger services began at 12 noon and ran until 4 pm. This required fire lighting around 9 am, but before the steam loco could be towed outside, oiling round and a thorough inspection is required, thus an early start of 7.30–8 am is necessary, although compared to most other steam railways in the country, 8 in the morning is a luxury. Oiling round, however, poses a problem. There is no pit so it necessitates crawling around under the locomotive, on the baths floor, and at one point limboing under some brake gear! Only three of our members are really slim enough to perform this task easily – please consult your colleagues when you book your holidays!

Once outside, the diesel will depart to collect the brake van, shunt it to the platform where the window shutters are removed. These are a great necessity as otherwise the brake van is not protected in any way. On a good day, the steam loco will be up by 11 am and some shunting will see it on the correct end of the van. It's now time for a short seat, and bacon cooked on the shovel for those who feel inclined. Most operating days are uneventful and come 4 pm it is starting to become a long day. The morning procedure is reversed and shunting is performed to release the steam loco. It will return to the baths first to have the fire dropped, while everyone else will remain to replace the shutters on the brake van, now an onerous task after a day's work. Having done it for so many years though, 5 pm can see everything away and shower and evening meal beckons.

Like everything else in life, things break, require maintenance, or simply wear out and need to be replaced. Without track, there is no railway. Initially, when much of the railway was being built, there was much help in the form of mechanical lifting gear and the steam crane – alas out of use for many years. This is now not readily available but as most of the track maintenance is now mainly replacing broken or worn-out sleepers, this can be done manually. The Society acquired an old tractor and trailer some years ago and it can be loaded with gear and penetrate far depths of the layout and is also useful for dragging lengths of rail. Alternatively, one of the diesels can be loaded up with tools and used instead; that's a bit more enjoyable anyway. Compared to any other railway system, the amount of running will certainly not affect wear and tear on the rails themselves, although there are plenty of spares. This does not mean that vigilance slackens and the track is inspected every 40 days and before any service day.

Locomotives however, like motor cars, rely on regular care. The biggest single item during winter is the preparation and passing of the annual boiler insurance. Basically, this requires dismantling the mud doors and washout plugs, wash out the boiler, and re-assemble, hydraulic test, hydraulic test in the presence of the inspector, steam test, steam test in the presence of the inspector. Depending on everyone's availability, this has known to take over three months! The washout is everybody's dread as Murphy's Law seems to apply. As this will take place, usually the beginning of January after the Santa Event, the chosen day more than likely will be cold and wet. Not enjoying the luxuries of hot running water, the washout is done with cold mains water. So there it is, outside in winter, on the banks of the River Forth estuary, the smallest members once again on their hands and knees underneath, and cold water going everywhere. It is not pleasant work, but the reward is a pass from the inspector and the satisfaction of operating steam during the summer months. Steam locomotives at Prestongrange are not hard worked and both locomotives that have been in service have been relatively maintenance-free – probably the single biggest recurring fault is overheating axle bearings. The Society does not have a workshop as such on site, but various members either work within the engineering industry and can get work done or have access to equipment. The disadvantage lies with the delay in taking a part off-site or waiting for tools to arrive. It is very much a spanner and hammer, block and tackle, lifting jack operation. Apart from boiler work, which is mostly specialist, many parts of a steam engine are basic engineering and to date have not proved unable to be remedied. Other preservation societies have also loaned parts and advice.

Diesels on the other hand are a bit like your car parked at the front door. They are fine when they work. Cold starting can be a real problem in the winter months. The baths are not heated and as the diesels, unlike most cars, are not run every day, sometimes weeks can go by, and therefore some mornings can be fractious. Usually, if it is known that a diesel will be required on a particular day, it is started up the week before. That has known to occupy a complete Sunday visit! The diesel problem is that spare parts are not readily available. They went out of production many years ago and quite often the best part on offer is the present day "nearest equivalent". Somewhere some modification will be required to make the part function, although recently in the case of the Ruston, one member has tracked down a gentleman who has a garage full of spares which has proved very useful.

The brake van however is probably the easiest. Mechanically, it asks for very little and only requires checking and oiling of the axle bearings and the brake gear. The wooden bodywork however, does suffer from being outside in the salty air, and has been patched up many times. There is no easy answer to this problem. It would be nice to have it under cover and have the time to strip the more vulnerable sections and replace them, but it is too tall to fit in the baths and no work could be left outside unfinished. Considering it has been on site since 1986, it has served its purpose well. In 1997 it was fitted with a new veranda floor, well overdue as the old one was partially rotten and, with uneven planking, was easy to trip over, especially older people coming and going. Two of the members made an exerted effort and emerged triumphant after a number of weeks, yacht varnish tin in hand. It received another coat in 2002.

The initiative to do something has led to some tentative work being started again on locomotive No 29 in October 2002. After jacking the boiler up a few inches to check clearances beside the axle spring hangers, it has been decided to remove the tubes then finish jacking with a view to a preliminary inspection from a Boiler Inspector. Perhaps this will be good news and will provide the necessary impetus to restore steam once again at Prestongrange.

Most recently news has arrived that funding will be available for reasonable work to be accomplished on No 7, the Prestongrange.

INVENTORY 2003

The following lists the locomotives on site at the Prestongrange Industrial Heritage Museum in 2003.

NCB – National Coal Board
ICI – Imperial Chemical Industries

NCB No 7	0-4-2 Saddle Tank. Built by Grant Ritchie of Kilmarnock, Scotland, in 1914. Works number 536 – The Prestongrange
NCB No 6	0-4-0 Saddle Tank. Built by Andrew Barclay of Kilmarnock, Scotland, in 1937. Works number 2043
NCB No 17	0-4-0 Saddle Tank. Built by Andrew Barclay of Kilmarnock, Scotland, in 1946. Works number 2219
NCB No 29	0-4-0 Saddle Tank. Built by Andrew Barclay of Kilmarnock, Scotland, in 1908. Works number 1142
NCB No 32	0-4-0 Diesel Mechanical. Built by Rustons of Lincoln, England, in 1962. Works number 458960
NCB No 33	0-4-0 Diesel Mechanical. Built by Rustons of Lincoln, England, in 1943. Works number 221647
	0-4-0 Diesel Mechanical. Built by Motor Rail (Simplex) of Bedford, England, in 1963. Works number 9925
ICI No 2	0-4-0 Diesel Mechanical. Built by Rustons of Lincoln, England, date unknown. Works number 398163
Alcan	0-4-0 Diesel Hydraulic. Built by English Electric of Newton-le-Willows, England, in 1964. Works number D908

16
The Glenkinchie Story since 1723

Craig Ward

INTRODUCTION

A little outside Pencaitland, in an idyllic dip among the gently rolling farmland of East Lothian, stands one of the two working distilleries in lowland Scotland, Glenkinchie. A wellpreserved example of red brick Victoriana, it supervises a pristine bowling green and pavilion, and two rows of terraced cottages. The hollow in which these lie is green and leafy, the Kinchie burn running through on its way to the Tyne. It is almost always still and peaceful, despite the presence of industry and the to and fro of curious visitors. That it should be here at all, when all but one of its various lowland competitors has fallen by the wayside (at one point there were one hundred and fifteen legally registered lowland distillers), is cause for curiosity. It has been a rough old ride for distilleries, this past couple of hundred years. Success stories are thin on the ground. But someone around here has been doing something right. Glenkinchie's is a story of adaptability, foresight and good fortune, from its stuttering beginnings through idealistic industrial progression to its solid and pragmatic present. It is a story of progress and compromise – one whose beginnings are cloudy but whose emergent threads speak of the economic patterns of past and present times and anticipate many contemporary questions and issues. We will look at the corporate, environmental, socio-economic and legal sides of the story, in the local, national and international contexts. Some periods are already reasonably well documented, others less so. The very early years of Glenkinchie certainly fall into the latter camp. What knowledge there is can be expressed as follows.

EARLY YEARS FROM 1723

In 1723, John Cockburn of Ormiston (known as the father of Scottish husbandry) founded the iconoclastic Society of Improvers of Knowledge of Agriculture, which would propel Scotland to the top of the European agricultural tradition.[1] The Society introduced the turnip and the potato, and imported agricultural experts from around Europe. It is largely thanks to their endeavours that East Lothian's crop farms would earn the area its reputation as "The Garden of Scotland". Indeed, prior to the society's introduction of barley to the area, East Lothian only produced coarser and less useful grain

crops. But by 1787 Burns would be calling East Lothian "*the most glorious corn country I have ever seen*", and, in 1832 the traveller William Cobbett would speak of "*Such corn fields as never were surely seen before in any country on earth*'.[2] The local barley was often grown on land fertilised by equally local seaweed. It would ripen earlier than those grown in other areas and was a considerably lighter grain.

The Milton Distillery (also known as Millton) was opened by farmer John Rate in 1825. He farmed the adjoining lands of Milton, Lempock Wells and Peaston Bank. Like most distilleries at the time it was very much a secondary concern of the farm – a way of supplementing income, rather than an example of autonomous enterprise. The precise location of the distillery is now unknown, although it was certainly in the proximity of the existing Glenkinchie distillery.[3] The business became a partnership consisting of John and his brother George who was also a farmer, and it remained in operation probably until 1834. At least, there are no records of any activity for a period lasting from 1834 to some time in 1837 (the year of Queen Victoria's coronation), when the Rate Brothers are recorded as licence holders (possibly in new premises) of the Glen Kinchie distillery (also known simply as Kinchie). The distillery took its name from the burn that ran through the dell and from which it took its water. (The name Kinchie was derived from de Quincey – the name of the family who had owned the land in the 14th century.) James Gray (of Leechman and Gray) took over the running of the distillery in 1840. This would be the beginning of a very long family association. However, in 1852 John Rate regained control in order to close down and sell the premises, which he did the following year, selling to Mr Christie, another farmer, who converted the building into a sawmill.

EXPANSION FROM 1880

It would remain such for almost thirty years, until, in the 1880s, it was reopened as a distillery by a consortium of wine merchants, brewers and blenders, which included R.H. Thomson, James Watt, J. Harrison and Mr Hannan of Alexander Melvin and Company, Boroughloch Brewery, Edinburgh.[4] The latter was the consortium leader. Much had changed in the period since 1853. A distilling concern was no longer a mere extra feature of a farm, but a fully-fledged, autonomous enterprise. This was as true then for Glenkinchie as for any other distillery, and was a reflection of the more general economic shift from agriculture to industry that characterised the Victorian era. Leith had also fully established itself as the centre of the blending industry – blending having only become popular in the early part of the 19th century – and, indeed, blends were becoming more and more popular all the time. And the bottling of Scotch was an industry changing innovation from 1860. The standard of distilling practise had also improved dramatically, mainly as a result of official intervention. Indeed, in 1880, a Spirits Act had

been passed, in which strict guidelines as to what constituted proper operation of the distilling process were laid out.

Some of the legislations of the 1880 Act were: the prohibition of operation of a still until at least two hours after the conclusion of a brewing period, thus ensuring the periods of brewing and distilling were 'alternate' and 'distinct'; the prohibition of wash and wort operations during the period of distilling; and the granting of a license to excise warehouses to add sweetening and colouring agents to whiskies at their own discretion.[5]

It was also around this time that the demand for whisky outside of Scotland began to take off. The major blenders (Dewars, Walkers, James Buchanan and Haigs) all opened offices in London in the 1880s. Tommy Dewar provided a pivotal moment at the Brewer's show at the Agricultural hall in London in 1885, when he famously responded to the popular use of musical boxes and barrel organs at a variety of stalls by playing the bagpipes at full tilt, thus drowning out all competition and greatly upsetting the chairman and committee members. He defied their pleas for him to stop and the ensuing press attention meant that all London knew him and his whisky.[6] Orders for bottled whisky soon escalated dramatically. And the increased demand for blends would at least keep the blender's demands for malts high, even if it did mean something of a marketplace marginalisation for the single malts themselves.

However, public knowledge of, and interest in, the variety of whiskies would soon be on the increase thanks to the efforts of one Alfred Barnard. In 1886 Glenkinchie's Mr Hannan would be guide to Barnard when he visited the distillery as part of the groundwork for his seminal publication, Whisky Distilleries of the United Kingdom. Barnard's account of his experience amounted to a glowing review. He provided a unique insight into the workings of the distillery at that time, and provided what could be considered a blueprint for the marketing of the whisky industry as a tourist attraction, something that would become very popular a century later:

> "...To the left of the entrance gate is one of the large Bonded Warehouses – of which there are two, the other being situated on the right of the gate – and at the back of this extending its entire length is the Barley Loft, immediately at the foot of the hill overhanging the Distillery, in which is stored the barley to be used in the manufacture of the whisky. On the top of this hill are placed two large Hoppers, into which the barley is emptied from the carts, and runs down shoots of about 100 feet in length to the Lofts, these are fitted with an overhead railway, fastened on beams, on which the carriers – large baskets suspended on wheels – run along and carry the barley to any place required. This railway is continued to the Steeps in the Malting House, a large two-storied building separated from the Barley Loft by a wide courtyard, across, on what may be termed, a suspension bridge, having on each side a reversed inclined plane. The carriers, filled with barley

> in the loft, are right across the courtyard to the Steeps, where they are emptied, and returned on the reverse plane to the Loft, to be again filled, and so on. The Malting Floors are also fitted with the same overhead railways, which convey the barley – changed to malt by germination, to a large Elevator, which lifts and deposits it in the centre of a large Kiln with a wire-cloth floor, where it is properly dried, and then it is shot direct into the Malt Deposits which lie alongside on a lower level. At the end of the deposits is the Grinding Room, on the same level, and into this the grist, as the malt is now technically termed, is easily conveyed when required for grinding, previous to the smashing process.
>
> "The Mash House is attached to the Grinding Room, and the ground malt is lifted to the Grist Hopper by elevators, worked by an engine placed in the Grinding Room, from which it falls into the large Mash Tun, just below it, where it is stirred by rakes driven by an engine specially used for this purpose. After standing the necessary time the infusion is drawn off and passed over a Refrigerator alongside, into the Underback from which it is lifted by a powerful steam-pump to the fermenting tuns in the Tun Room, where the process of fermentation goes on. When this is completed, the wash, as it is now called, is run into the Wash Charger, situated in the same room, and this supplies the Stills, of which there are two, of the kind known as Old Pot Stills, where by distillation, the wash is changed into whisky, and the process is completed; and at this point we saw what we had seen nowhere else – after the spirit is extracted from the wash, there is a very large residue known as *dreg,* which in towns is very largely used for cattle-feeding purposes but in remote districts is practically useless, and requires to be disposed of in some way; it cannot be emptied into the stream, for the riparian proprietors would object, so it is lifted by a steam-pump to a tank 500 yards from the distillery, and 70 feet above it, and used by the neighbouring farmer to irrigate his fields, and he is highly pleased with the result.[7]"

This practise is still evident today, albeit in a less strictly localised way – the wet draff (barley residue) is sold to farmers all around the Lothians for cattle feed, while pot ale is transferred to the local pig farmers. This is indicative of a desire to maintain a stable micro-economy, which has continued to be a prime concern ever since Barnard's time.

> "It will be seen from our description that each part fits into the other, and that the arrangements are such that manual labour is reduced to a minimum. Every facility was afforded us to examine everything, and in addition to the perfectness (sic) of the general plan, we were much struck with the absolute cleanliness which prevailed.[8]"

In the same year the Wine Trade Review published an article, which trumpeted, "The future of the wine trade is whisky". It is clear then, that the climate for the whisky industry was looking very favourable indeed (especially with the failure of the grape crop in France – which led to a cognac shortage and resulted in the need for a substitute after-dinner liquor). And the publication of Barnard's work, in 1887, would make sure whisky was securely situated on the economic map. Indeed, a four-page spread on the economic significance of the growth of the whisky trade in an 1890 edition of the Illustrated London News would confirm this.[9] As if in response to this increased consumer interest in Scotch, Glenkinchie would, at about this time, make moves forward in the way they operated. In a letter dated 28th March 1890, J. Harrison would sell his share of the company to Robert Harvey Thomson for the sum of £7600. The sale included all the equipment and dwelling houses 'with the exception, of course, of whisky, barley, malt and fuel and casks'. The deal included water rights, no (or negligible) feu duty, and the option to buy the remaining whisky, barley, casks etc at a price to be negotiated through William Sanderson (rectifier) of Leith.[10] Shortly afterwards (on 27th June that year), Glenkinchie would become a limited liability company. The company had eight members from four Leith-based firms. Three of these were wholesale wine and spirit merchants – Leechman and Company of 14 Quality Street would provide two members in John A. Leechman and Robert Gray; James Watt would be joined in the partnership by John Watt (their business operated from 7 Quality Street); and, similarly R.H. Thomson would bring in Alfred Thomson (of 130 Constitution Street both).[11] The other firm involved were spirit brokers, Robertson Sanderson and Company of 11 Quality Street, (blenders of the Celebrated Mountain Dew Scotch whisky) – Arthur and Fred Sanderson would be members of the board of The Glenkinchie Distillery Company Limited.[12] Gray, Watt and (R.H.) Thomson were the directors. The agreement between all parties was that the Sandersons would try to sell as much of the whisky as they could directly onto the market – whatever was left would be divided between the other three companies who would put it to use in their own businesses. The vast majority, therefore, ended up being used in blends. The total share capital of the company was £14,000, which consisted of 1400 shares, valued at £10 each.

The new company quickly set about restructuring the distillery, building an entirely new maltings and a worker's village in fashionable Victorian red brick, which, for the most part, still stands, well preserved, today. As well as the workers, the customs officers would live in the village. By law, all the working parts of the distillery needed to be locked and unlocked by the customs officer. For example, he would have to unlock the still for anyone to be able to put anything into it or to empty it. The officer would occupy one of the largest houses in the village.

The houses standing closest to the distillery today are the original Victorian constructions. Some of the buildings further up the hill towards Peaston Bank were built later (20th century). Glenkinchie and Peaston Bank were once quite separate villages but they look pretty much like the same place on a map nowadays. Glenkinchie still has a block that will, according to current manager, Charlie M. Smith, never be sold. The manager and two of the operators still live there, but do not own the premises they occupy. All the other remaining houses are privately owned – three of them by employees. A couple of retired employees also still live in the village. Another two houses used to stand in the space now occupied by the visitor's car park. The houses had all previously belonged to the distillery but began to be sold in the early part of the 1980s.

These were confident times (the Forth Bridge had opened in 1890 – towering over the Edinburgh scene as a symbol of progress and prosperity), and Glenkinchie, along with the whisky industry in general, moved as part of that confident surge. They were also idealistic times. The establishment of the worker's village in such idyllic surroundings displays a faith, in not only the product but in production itself, and a desire to create a satisfied and self-sufficient community. So much so that the owners followed the tradition started by the now long forgotten Yoker Distillery on the Clyde (founded 1770) by providing employees with a superb bowling green.

An article in the January 8th 1911 edition of the *Wine and Spirit Trade Record* entitled "A Famous Lowland Malt Distillery, Glen-Kinchie" makes mention of this and notes of Glenkinchie:

> "Not only are the natural surroundings everything that could be desired and calculated to bring out the best efforts of the workers, but the distillery buildings are perfect as they could well be from the sanitary and hygiene points of view, and the desire of the management to promote the health and comfort of the employees is further evidenced by the fact that they have provided them with a well laid-out bowling green".

Following the deaths of the Thomsons, the other members were worried that the Thomsons' share of the company might fall into the hands of someone not in any way connected with the company. To avert this possibility the registrar of the joint stock companies signed a special resolution on the 10th of March 1897, stating that the board may have first option on the shares of a member who dies or goes bankrupt.[13]

CONTRACTION DURING WORLD WAR I

This period of general expansion would continue until the years approaching the First World War. Only then did the economy enter a period of prolonged recession, and moves had to be made to consolidate the lowland whisky industry, pool resources, and tighten belts. The Glenkinchie directors began making preparations to sell shares in 1913. In a memorandum from that year the Sandersons and James Gray bind themselves to buying back first preference shares from new shareholders for the sum of £10 each, within five years of purchase, if given six months written notice – a condition which admits something of the potential unattractiveness of such shares as they were about to sell, given the general climate of recession.[14] The company was valued at £35,000 on 11th March 1913, and shares were put on the market the same day. By the 20th they had sold just 305 of the 3500 £10 shares, to a variety of speculators. Investors were clearly very cautious indeed.[15] Clearly, further action would have to be 8 taken, and, within months, discussions were taking place between Glenkinchie and four other lowland distillers towards the formation of Scottish Malt Distillers Ltd. (SMD). SMD would be born on 7th July 1914, 28 days before the outbreak of the First World War. The new company was comprised of Glenkinchie; the Clydesdale Distillery Company Ltd., of Wishaw; A. and J. Dawson Ltd. (ie: Saint Magdelene's Distillery), of Linlithgow (whose initial financial difficulties had been the original impetus for the merger); the Rosebank Distillery Ltd., of Falkirk; William Young and Company (ie: the Grange Distillery), of Burntisland; and Charles Ritchie, SSC, of Edinburgh.[16] The new company would bring on board James Risk as a consultant. His task was to advise on production methods, his reward, 20% of the net improvement. (He would be appointed general works manager in 1915, having made an average of £1390 per annum in commissions during his first two years consultancy).[17] The new company's total capital was £300,000.

The figure had been calculated thus – Clydesdale was valued at £65,950, Dawson at £54,380, Glenkinchie at £37,730, Rosebank at £60,000 and William Young at £81,940. The £300,000 consisted of £80,000 worth of ordinary shares and £220,000 worth of preference shares (5% cumulative). All shares were valued at £1. Glenkinchie's total shares would consist of 23,230 preference shares and 14,500 ordinary[18] (Glenkinchie wouldn't actually sell all of their available shares until October 1916. Between the 11th and the 30th of that month they sold 2530 ordinary shares (2030 of which were bought by an S.P. Sinclair, who was trustee to Leechman and Gray). This put them in a position to pay off their creditors in full).[19] The day after SMD was born, it was agreed that any assets and liabilities to be assumed by SMD would not include Glenkinchie's debtor and creditor balances (which, when the books had last been balanced on the 30th of September, 1913, had amounted to £17,419 5s 2d, and £29,327 12s 5d respectively).[20] This would make the ensuing liquidation a lengthy process. The company duly went into said voluntary liquidation on the 1st of August 1914. Gray would transfer his shares to the company in January 1915.[21]

During this period, much had been changing throughout the whisky industry, mainly due to a number of acts of legislation, some of which were designed to raise consistent standards throughout the industry as a whole, others to demonstrate a sensible response to war conditions. The Intoxicating Liquor Act of May 1914 proposed that the minimum spirits price, to the consumer, should be 8d per gill. The Edinburgh and Leith Wholesale Wine and Sprit Association (ELWWSA) would support this proposal wholeheartedly. The following year the Central Liquor Control Board (CLCB) was formed. They declared the minimum acceptable strength of whisky to be 32.7% alcohol. The Immature Spirits Act of that year would make it compulsory for the period of bonding to be at least two years, and the Scottish wholesale trade associations would agree a minimum price for whisky of 5s 6d per gallon under bond to the retailer, and 23s per gallon duty paid. Finally, in December 1915 a Finance Act would introduce an excess profits duty of 50%. The following year, the compulsory bonding period would be raised to three years. The CLCB would prohibit any distilling not licensed by the Ministry of Munitions. They also set a maximum limit for whisky strength of 42.9% alcohol. All grain distillers would also become obliged to cease making whisky, ordered, as they were, to make all of their spirit available for the manufacture of munitions. This ban though, did not yet extend to pot distilling, so Glenkinchie was among those who still continued to produce. The malt distillers were understandably apprehensive, however, and worried about the consistency of the many acts of legislation being passed. The CLCB were rumoured to be considering reducing the minimum strength limit to 30%, but fearing this would deal a serious blow to the trade in better class whiskies, the ELWWSA wrote them to formally protest against such a move.[22]

On 23rd May 1917 (only 6 weeks after the war had escalated to the extent that the United States had been forced to enter), the Whisky Association (which had been formed four years previously to represent the interests of the distilling industry) formed its own London section, thereby presenting a serious front against the real dangers presented to the industry by war and economic depression. But they were to have little serious clout for some time, as the following month a ban was placed on all pot distilling – barley being too important as a foodstuff to be squandered on such a luxury as whisky.[23] This ban would continue until March 1919. Ultimately, this break in production would allow Glenkinchie the breathing space to go about the business of closing the liquidation proceedings. On 6th October 1917 Lord Cullen was appointed to wind up said proceedings, only to be replaced in that position by Lord Ormidale, on the 14th of October the following year.[24]

1918 saw the introduction of a ban on all whisky exports, a fixing of the retail home trade price at 9s per bottle, a hike in income tax to 30%, and a whopping rise in duty from 14s 9d to 30s per gallon.[25] It also saw a bitter feud between the Clydesdale Bank and The Bank of Scotland over who was owed what by Glenkinchie. The Bank of Scotland hotly disputed a claim, which had been made the previous year by the Clydesdale Bank, for the sum of £6,589 4s 1d in unpaid bills. There is a more than tiny hint of bitterness in The Bank of Scotland's reaction to this situation. The final state of adjudications had been published on 17th April 1918 by the liquidator, William Cockburn (who had been given the job the previous May, one month after resigning from his position as manager of Glenkinchie). The total amount claimed from Glenkinchie, by various creditors, came to £33,916 4s 10d. The Clydesdale bank claim was among the £22,668 3s 4d worth of claims that were accepted by the liquidator. Among the £11,248 1s 6d worth of claims that were rejected, however, was a claim by the Bank of Scotland for £1690, which they had been pursuing since May 1916.[26] A letter from A.W. Robertson Durham dated 15th November 1916 puts forward the case for Glenkinchie's defence:

> In the early part of the century, Glenkinchie had been successful but short of capital – so the directors (who were the only major shareholders) allowed their dividends to remain with the company (as loans to the company). Later, in search of more capital, they requested a loan from the Bank of Scotland who, as security, requested the director's loan sums. This meant that if the company failed SMD would owe the Bank not only the money borrowed from the Bank but also the sum borrowed from the directors. The debt to the bank was later paid off – the bank thereby losing its right to any claim on the director's dividends – and the director's loans to the company were converted into shares. So Arthur Sanderson (for it was his particular loan to the company that was at the centre of all of this) received shares in lieu of his debt. The Bank of Scotland claimed that the terms of the loan included an absolute assignation of Sanderson's claim against the company (qualified, they claimed, by a back letter from Sanderson). As Sanderson's newly converted shares represented his claim against the company the Bank felt they were entitled to them. Glenkinchie responded that the assignation arrangement was based on the understanding that it existed for sole purpose of securing the debt, and with the debt having been paid off the Bank had forfeited any claim to the amount.[27]

Cockburn sided with his former employers,

> "...IV.169 *Second Preference Shares Of The Company In Liquidation.*
> The liquidator rejects this item (£1690) of the Claim. As these are shares of the company in liquidation, it is not proper subject matter by a Claim by a creditor... the company of Robertson Sanderson... (now in liquidation) is the registered holder of these shares and the liquidator of the company now claims... the right to them."[28]

This may have been the end of the Bank of Scotland's claim to Arthur Sanderson's shares but, preposterously, it was not the final end of squabbling over them. The business of where the dividends they had raised belonged was not settled until 1922. By this time, the amount (which was £146 5s 3d) had been made available to the five ordinary shareholders, but a Mr. Elgin, on behalf of James Gray's estate, demanded the sum in its entirety, as compensation for excessive income tax. Elgin would get his way.[29]

Most of the liquidation issues, however, had begun to settle in the summer of 1919 and, as reported in March that year, the amount of share capital to be made available, all debts having been settled, was £31,800 – not such a drastic slump from the £35,000 of 1913, considering all of this had happened through the recession which had preceded the First World War. (In 1916 a survey showed that 90.8% of all military age employees of Edinburgh and Leith's wholesale wine and spirit firms were serving in the forces.) On 27th June 1920, John Stuart Gowans published the final report on the liquidation. The share capital of the company, which had been stationary since the time of liquidation (some six years prior to the final settlement), was divided into 680 first preference shares, 500 second preference shares and 2000 ordinary shares. All shares were valued at £10 each.[30] The timing of the settlement couldn't have been better – the ban on pot distilling had been lifted in March 1919, which meant that the company were now able to put their attention again to the task of producing whisky. Unfortunately, economic and legislative constraints were making life difficult for the industry, and Glenkinchie would soon feel the pinch. Chamberlain increased duty from 30s to £2 10s, while increasing the retail price of a bottle by 3s to 12s, meaning the profit margin on a bottle for the producer would be notably reduced. Exports were permitted again, but at less than half the pre-war level, and, as if that wasn't difficult enough, the United States would introduce prohibition on 16th January 1920.[31] Unsurprisingly, SMD's profits had been on the slide for some time, as illustrated below:[32]

	1914–15	1915–16	1916–17	1917–18
DCL	£197,200	£277,500	£267,000	£264,200
SMD	£25,400	£22,000	£21,300	£14,900

Chances to get profits back on track were helped little by yet another huge increase in duty to £3 12s 6d per gallon. (Mercifully, though, this would be the last increase in duty until 1939). The accompanying rise in the price of a bottle was a mere 6d.[33] These were tough times for Glenkinchie and SMD, and it soon became apparent to the shareholders that they were going to have to make a few changes and become part of something bigger if they were to survive. SMD had already made a couple of significant moves to that end in 1919, buying the potentially profitable Edinburgh Distillery from Andrew Usher And Company then selling the struggling Clydesdale Distillery to DCL for £22,000, exclusive of plant.[34]

Many distilleries closed during this period, and the principal SMD distilleries were fortunate to have survived. In fact, their survival often depended on their practice of buying other lowland distilleries purely so they could close them. Glenkinchie, in particular, could be thankful for a number of important factors. For one thing, the quality of their produce was very good. Even at this stage, a consistency of standards throughout the industry had not emerged and much of the whisky on the market was really very poor. Location was also very important. The distillery's proximity to the administrative and business centre of Edinburgh, and to the hub of blending activity which was Leith, made Glenkinchie's an attractive and accessible supply. It was also great for export purposes. That there existed a railhead close to Glenkinchie (shut down by Dr. Beeching in the 1960s) also helped. Also, being run by a group of Edinburgh businessmen gave Glenkinchie a sense of business leadership and general savvy that other distilleries lacked.

GLENKINCHIE – 1923

BACK ROW: Sandy Boyd (Cooper), Archibald Wright (Greenkeeper), John Clark (Brewer), Andrew Purves (Maltman), John Sheils (Maltman), William Punton (Maltman), John Docherty Maltman), Peter Purves (Maltman), John Connell (Maltman), Tom Wilson (Effluent), John Scott (Electrician), Alex. Scott (Electrician).

MIDDLE ROW: John Renton (Cattleman), John Scott (Handyman), John Ferguson (Head Maltman), Edward Christie (Stillman), John Jackson (Excise), John Nicol (Manager), James Ellis (Assistant Brewer), James Halliday (Clerk), George Nicol (Blacksmith)(Engineer) Robert Harper (Kilnman).

FRONT ROW: Alex. Sheils (Maltman), Robert Nicol (Steam Engineer), John Keegan (Stillman), Dickie Wright (Boilerman), William Callander (Maltman), "BRUCE", Alexander Dewar (Horseman), William Hay (Maltman), John Christie (Horseman), David Beveridge (Tunroom-man).

FAR REAR: Robert Henderson (Driver), James Quinan (Driver)

TOWARDS RECOVERY FROM 1925

In 1925 the Distiller's Company Limited (DCL) bought SMD in its entirety. SMD had provided something of a model for DCL in their decision (in 1928) to form all their malt distilleries into a single group. The SMD amalgamation process had been overseen by W.H. Ross of DCL (who was repaying a debt to DCL by negotiating an amalgamation which was designed to help St. Magdalene distillery out of a tight financial spot). SMD were regarded as something of a runaway success, partly because they used identical pot distilling methods to DCL and had established a laboratory, staffed by a professional chemist, just as DCL had done previously, and partly because of James Risk's effective consultancy (Weir describes the lowland distilleries prior to the SMD merger as "backward"). The great amalgamation of the distilleries meant that the majority of SMD's produce was being bought by DCL, and it was this that led Risk to suggest, in 1925, that DCL should buy SMD. Weir quotes DCL as being "not particularly desirous of going in for any more amalgamations", but somehow Risk must have convinced them around their reservations, for amalgamate they did. DCL also acquired 33% of all shares in Risk's Clynelish distillery, thus making this distillery part of SMD. As a result of these arrangements it became possible, in agreement with the other malt distillers, to reduce industry production by 25%. In 1930, in the wake of the previous year's Wall Street Crash,

> "DCL placed all its malt distilleries under the control of its subsidiary SMD. The SMD board was reorganized: chairman, Thomas Herd, directors, Henry J. Ross, Alfred Horsfall, S.H. Hastie, OBE MC BSc FIC, J.B. Cumming, CA, David Black and T.C. Scott CA; secretary J.B. Wylie, CA. It was subsequently discovered that this arrangement deprived several DCL group companies of the right to call themselves 'Distillers'".

In agreement with customs and excise, some distilleries were formally leased to DCL-operating companies, in an attempt to fix this problem.[35]

As an indication of how bad things had become as a result of the extended depression, in 1931 Glasgow only had four whisky brokers, as compared to 25 in 1924. Indeed, the following year, DCL announced that they would be opening none of its distilleries in 1933, an example that was followed by everyone except Glenlivet and Glen Grant. This year of closure would, however, signal the lowest ebb of the industry at the end of a long recession. The recovery was just about to begin. Roosevelt brought prohibition to an end in 1933 and, in Great Britain the Chancellor's budget produced the first statutory description of Scotch whisky. A whisky could only claim the title if it "had been obtained by distillation in Scotland from a mash saccharified (sic) by the diastase of malt and had been matured in bond for a period of at least three years" (Finance Act, 1933).[36]

It is observed by one anonymous commentator of the time, however, that "Glenkinchie has at all times been a favourite Lowland malt of the largest firms in the trade, and this is testified (to) by the fact that it has worked almost continuously since its inception".[37] In anticipation of an approaching upward turn, DCL would move to more desirable premises in London, at 20/21 St. James Square in 1935.[38] The upward turn wouldn't last too long.

WORLD WAR II AND THEREAFTER

Needless to say, the outbreak of the Second World War on the 4th of September 1939 brought dire times for the whisky industry, but while other distilleries were forced to close during the Second World War (by October 1942 only 44 distilleries were still allowed to do any distilling – all others had been forced to stop in order to preserve barley as a foodstuff), Glenkinchie was allowed to continue distilling (albeit in a greatly reduced fashion – they were allowed to produce a small quantity during each year of the war). This privilege was almost certainly afforded the distillery by its proximity to Edinburgh and the clout of the Edinburgh business community.

A number of drastic measures were employed during this time:

- Duty on whisky was raised no less than four times during the war – from 72s 6d to 82s 6d per gallon in 1939 (the maximum retail price of a bottle rising to 14s 3d), then to 97s 6d per gallon the following year (maximum retail price per bottle: 16s), further to 137s 6d in 1942 (maximum retail price per bottle: 23s), and finally to 157s 6d in 1943 (maximum retail price per bottle: 25s 9d).
- Rationing of whisky was introduced in 1940.
- Grain distilling ceased entirely in 1941.
- A Finance Act of 1941 ordered that all excess profits be taxed at 100%.
- The Whisky Association had to be wound up and replaced by a new body, the Scotch Whisky Association (SWA). The reason for this was that the Whisky Association's constitution did not allow for a much needed amendment which would introduce a 'stop list' designed to cut off all supplies to retailers who flaunted the maximum retail price as set by the association.
- In August 1944 the government set a hard limit on distilling. 100,000 tons of barley would be allocated to the working distilleries and not a grain more.

These and other factors resulted in some equally drastic consequences:

- By March of 1940 pot-distilling output had dropped to about one third of the previous year's level.
- By 1941 home trade supplies had been cut to 50% of their pre-war level (although exports had increased).
- By the end of the war some 4.5 million gallons of whisky stock had been lost as a consequence of enemy action. Undoing this damage was of prime importance to Churchill. In April 1945 he would demand, "

  On no account reduce the barley for whisky. This takes years to mature and is an invaluable export and dollar producer. Having regard to all our other difficulties about export, it would be most improvident not to preserve this characteristic British element of ascendancy."

In order to undo some of the damage inflicted on the industry some regulations on the Manufacture Of Spirits (No.1588, 1945) were drawn up. The prohibition of Sunday working was lifted, as was the ban on concurrent brewing and distilling. When these measures came into effect, on New Year's Day 1946, distilling capacity was instantly doubled. Home trade supplies began rising rapidly again, but all these gains were suddenly halted when the cap on the amount of barley made available for distilling made itself felt again. Grain distilling would cease in May and malt distilling would follow suit in September. (Sufficient barley to resume distilling at pre-war levels wouldn't be released by the government until 1949, and with the capacity to produce suitably revived, sterling would be drastically devalued – from $4.02 to $2.80 – to encourage American buyers.) Another couple of hikes in duty would also make themselves felt – In 1947 the Chancellor of the Exchequer raised duty by 33s 4d to 190s 10d, and the following year Stafford Cripps would raise it a further 20s. At this point SWA would raise the maximum retail price of a bottle to 33s 4d. By 1957 it would be 37s 6d.

The ban on the importation of barley would finally be lifted in 1954, coinciding neatly with the end of rationing. In the SWA annual review of that year it was reported that whisky had come '*off quota* for the first time in fourteen years'.[39]

Throughout the 1940s and 50s Glenkinchie's distillery manager, W.J. McPherson, farmed the adjacent 85 acres. On this land he bred a prize-winning herd of Aberdeen Angus cattle (inspired, as he was, by the Smiths at Cragganmore, who had done the very same a few years previously). During the 1950s McPherson's cattle won the fatstock Supreme Championship for three successive years at Smithfield, Edinburgh and Birmingham. They did, in fact, win the Smithfield championship in 1949, 1952 and 1954.[40] These cattle were, of course, fed on the residual wet draff from the distillery. Clearly, this made a fine argument for using the leftovers of the malting and mashing processes to such ends. The farm grounds were also used as a holiday retreat for DCL's hard-working Clydesdale horses. These would pull dray-carts all around the country and, during the summer months, the Glasgow-based horses would be given a welcome break to amble around the Glenkinchie farm at their leisure, and duly recover from their toil.[41] In 1956 Glenkinchie decided to keep two of the horses. They would work for the distillery pulling carts loaded with coal and barley from nearby Saltoun station. This practice continued until the railway line closed in 1968.[42]

THE MUSEUM

It was the aforementioned James Risk who was primarily responsible for the scale model of a working distillery (one sixth actual size), which occupies pride of place in what is now the Museum of Malt Whisky Production (which itself occupies the area of the building where previously the maltings had been). The model is based on an amalgam of several lowland distilleries although the stills, specifically, are modelled on Glenkinchie's.

Risk employed the Northampton-based firm Bassett-Lowke to build the model (which he had designed along with George Cruikshank of the Linlithgow distillery), for the Scotch Whisky Exhibit in the Palace of Industry at the Empire Exhibition, Wembley, in 1924-25. When the Exhibition was over DCL lent the model (which is quite unique) to the Science Museum, London, where it was displayed continuously from 1926 to 1949.

In that year as a result of a drastic reorganisation of the Museum's collection, the model was dismantled and packed into 19 cases and put into store. It remained there until 1963 – undisturbed except for a twice yearly inspection by H M Customs & Excise to ensure the stills had not been

adapted for some more serious and practical purpose! It was returned to DCL that year and stored at Glenlossie Distillery near Elgin before being transferred to Mortlach Distillery about 1970. In 1974 Glenkinchie's Manager of the time, Alistair Munro, took it upon himself to rebuild the model from scratch.

As for the rest of the museum, it started life as a fine personal collection of tools and implements that had been used at various times throughout the distillery's history. There were the strange canvas boots that maltmen would wear while working in the maltings. These were designed to inflict minimum damage to the malt that lay on the floor. There were also pram-like barley-scoops and copper 'dogs'. The latter were extremely cunning devices used to smuggle illegal spirits out of distilleries – some in the form of thin tubes that could be hung inside a trouser leg, others in the form of a hot-waterbottle- cum-breastplate, which would be tied with a string around the torso, concealed beneath a shirt. All of this equipment had been discarded at Glenkinchie and had formed the nucleus of the museum until, with the support of SMD's directors other SMD distilleries were brought into the scope of the project. The museum was duly renovated and reopened as the Museum of Malt Whisky Production in 1995. The renovations included an extensive refurbishment of the model distillery.

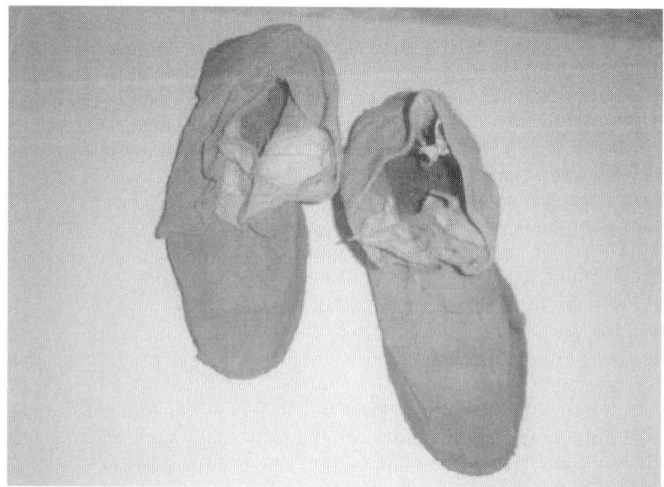

The museum was originally opened in 1969, following the closure of the maltings the previous year. (In 1968 SMD ceased floor malting at no less than 29 of its distilleries. It also temporarily closed the distilleries at Oban, Glenlochy and Glengarioch, but reopened Clynelish.[43]) These temporary closures were reversed in 1969 and Oban's fortunes, like Glenkinchie's, have flourished ever since that time. Alistair Munro, the manager at the time, would comment that this "brought home to me how much and how fast our industry was changing: and I felt that something of that disappearing past should be preserved and recorded for the future"[44] – hence the museum.

The closure had resulted in about half of the distillery's staff being made redundant. It was deemed sensible at that time to centralise the business of malting. (Glenkinchie would work with 25-ton batches of grain, compared to the modern-day typical batch size of about 300 tons.) DCL had opened a mechanical drum system malting plant at Burghead (at a cost of £1.25 million), which had achieved full-scale production by June of 1966 and was designed to produce 26,000 tons of malt per year.[45] All of this centralisation, and the use of larger quantities, led to a far more consistent standard. Since 1968 malting has been carried out at four different Diageo plc locations, two of which are in Speyside, one in Islay and one just north of Inverness, at Glen Ord. The Islay maltings services the Islay distilleries too, making it a very profitable enterprise for United Distillers. This does mean, however, that the Glenkinchie single malt is not made exclusively from East Lothian barley, as it was until 1968. The barley used now comes from various parts of Scotland.

MORE RECENT TIMES – FROM THE 1980s

The whisky industry went into a period of severe contraction in the 1980s. This was brought about by intensive over-production and over-stocking in the 1970s, when production was generally regarded, by government and industry, as king. The exponential sales forecasts of the 1970s didn't bear out in reality. Obviously, in distilling, companies produce well in advance of when the product will actually be sold. Forging ahead with production in expectation of 10–20% growth, when in reality it would turn out to be more like 3–5% growth, resulted in a huge surplus. Because of the surplus the demand for production fell and many distilleries started to take such measures as the 3-day week. Many ultimately closed down.

By 1981, SMD were operating a total of 45 malt whisky distilleries, associated maltings and bonded warehouses throughout Scotland, and still owned the 22 houses of Glenkinchie village.[46] Glenkinchie rebuilt its still house that year, converting the stills to the internal steam heating system.

In 1983, St. Magdalene would join the long list of those distilleries that didn't make it through this period of contraction to be followed by Bladnoch and Rosebank in 1993 thus leaving only Auchentoshan and Glenkinchie to represent the lowland distilling tradition. This state of affairs remains to the present, though there is a possibility that Bladnoch (in Wigtownshire) could reopen (see below). Since then, ownership of the SMD and DCL distilleries has changed considerably – the earliest hint of change came on 14th June 1985 when Guinness announced their intentions and their offer to buy Bells. The offer was flatly rejected by the managing director of the time, Raymond Miquel, but by mid- August, after an intense period of negotiation, a Guinness offer of £370 million had been accepted. Miquel would soon resign. Then, on 17th and 18th September, the DCL management committee met for what would be the last time for, in January 1986, Ernest Saunders of Guinness would begin a bidding war with the food group Argyll, for DCL. On 18th April their £2.5 billion offer was accepted and that particular war was over.[47]

Saunders won plaudits all around the business world, but was soon being quizzed by official inspectors from the Department of Trade and Industry. The arrest of American arbitrageur Ivan Boesky would be the beginning of Saunders' troubles. As part of a plea bargain Boesky had informed American authorities of a share dealing arrangement that had been designed to underpin Guinness' stock price while it was pursuing DCL. In December 1986 the DTI began their investigation into the takeover bid and, one month later, charged Saunders with a variety of financial offences. Saunders was ultimately convicted in 1990, along with businessman Gerald Ronson, trader Anthony

Parnes and consultant Jack Lyons. Saunders was sentenced to five years imprisonment, but later had his sentence halved on appeal.[48]

In 1987 DCL merged with Arthur Bell and Sons and all changed their name to United Distillers.[49] Only then did Glenkinchie begin the business of resurrecting its single malt from commercial oblivion. It hit the marketplace the following year. Some time after the formation of SMD Glenkinchie ceased selling bottled single malt, such was the whisky's success as a blender's favourite. It was only in the mid 1980s, when some of United Distillers marketing men in London dreamt up the Classic Malts package, that it would again see the light of day. The Classic Malts range capitalised on the emergent desire for knowledge of malt whisky, being a range of six malts each one representing a different region of Scotland (Cragganmore representing Speyside, Dalwhinnie representing the Central Highlands, Glenkinchie representing the Lowlands, Lagavulin representing Islay, Oban representing the Western Highlands and Talisker representing Skye). Many competitor companies followed suit with similar packages.

SMD finally ceased to exist as such in 1988 when United Distillers formed United Malt and Grain Distillers Limited (UMGD) to merge and take over SMD and the Scottish Grain Distillers (SGD).[50]

United Distillers had owned the aforementioned Bladnoch until the early 1990s, at which time it was sold to an Irish entrepreneur. He has often hinted at re-opening it but has yet to do so. It has been out of production since 1993. Glenkinchie's continued survival, however, seems fairly assured. Most blenders insist on having at least one lowland malt in their blends, to add mellowness to the flavour, and the blends in Glenkinchie's portfolio (Dimple, Bells, White Horse, Johnnie Walker) are no exception. Lowland whiskies tend to be softer, drier and milder than those from other areas of Scotland. Their flavour tends to be uncomplicatedly malty – there's no particularly strong presence of peatiness, smokiness, seaweed or brine. Limestone deposits in the local soil make the local water relatively hard by Scottish standards.

The lack of any serious competition surely secures Glenkinchie's usefulness. The museum also contributes greatly to Glenkinchie's continued prosperity. Finding out about Scotch whiskies didn't really become popular as a tourist activity until the 1980s. Glenkinchie is just one of the many distilleries who took to heart public requests for tours and information and opened museums and guided tours as a result. Again, proximity to the tourist magnet that is Edinburgh makes Glenkinchie an attractive package for visitors, who can make their visit part of a package that includes a stop at the Scotch Whisky Heritage Centre close to 23 Edinburgh Castle, which was opened by Magnus Magnusson in May 1988, again reflecting the new-found popularity of the industry as a tourist commodity.

In 1995 the mash house was rebuilt, although the existing wooden washbacks were retained.[51]

In December 1997 Guinness and GrandMet agreed to merge. A substantial part of this merger would be the coming together of the whisky and gin brands owned by Guinness' spirits division (ie. United Distillers) and the vodka and liqueurs owned by GrandMet's drinks business, International Distillers and Vintners (IDV) – which had been acquired by GrandMet in 1972. The new company was called Diageo plc with the new spirits arm called, perhaps not surprisingly, UDV. Today they own 27 malt and 2 grain distilleries with a 50% share of a third.[52]

Glenkinchie Staff – 2002

Back row L-R

***Sandy Rae** – started at Rosebank Distillery in April '91 and transferred to Glenkinchie in July '93 when Rosebank closed down – Process Operator*

***Adam Christie** – started in Jan '90 – latest in a long family tradition of Christies at Glenkinchie stretching back to 1800's – Process Operator*

***Colin Thomson** – started in March '91 – painter by trade who helps to keep the distillery up to scratch, was an active Territorial Army member until recently – Process operator*

***Hector MacDonald** – started in May '63 left for 9 months, came back in Jan '64 and been here ever since. Family has strong connections with Glenkinchie, father was horseman, brother was brewer, and sister-in-law was office cleaner. Hector is our local Mr. Fixit – Process Operator*

***Pud Gibson** – started with Bells at Dunfermline in Jan '84, moved to Aberfeldy in Sept. '94 then on to Glenkinchie in April '97. Has stayed in Rosyth all his working life and commutes approx. 80 miles round trip daily to get to work. – Process Operator*

***Bob White** – started in August '97, came from an engineering background and this experience is well used in keeping Glenkinchie together. When not busy doing that he looks after all the Warehousing operations.*

***Walter Barker** – started at Rosebank Distillery in June '90 and transferred to Glenkinchie in July '93 when Rosebank closed down – Process Operator*

***Ronnie Mcmurchie** – started in July '79. Was Bio Plant and warehouse operator until retiral in 2002.*

Front Row L-R

***Isobel Gardner** – started in March '91 as part time guide is now permanent staff as a Brand Home Lead guide*

***Mike Casey** – started in July '89 followed his dad into the distillery, brother also started at Glenkinchie and now works at Glen Ord – Process Operator*

***Duncan Tait** – started training at Aultmore in Dec '89, moved to Teaninnich, transferred to Elgin Group distilleries, trained as a Site Operations Manager (SOM), moved to Cardhu group before being appointed to Glenkinchie in June 2000 as SOM*

***Charlie Smith** – started with Bells in Jan '75 at Pittyvaich Dark Grains Plant, moved into distillery in Feb '78, transferred to Dufftown distillery in May '82, moved to Cardhu in June '93 and to Glenkinchie in Oct '98 – Distillery Manager*

***Mary Darling** – started April '86, as part time guide is now permanent staff as Brand Home Manager*

***Walter Cockburn** – started in March '77 and hasn't managed to get away ever since – Process Operator*

***Andrena Gray** – started in April '90 as part time guide is now permanent staff as a Brand Home Lead guide*

GLENKINCHIE TODAY

Glenkinchie still owns that 85 acres of the surrounding arable ground but doesn't use it. They currently rent it to a local farmer who, as chance would have it, used the ground for barley this year. The distillery still has an active relationship with the local farming community although not as direct as that described by Barnard back in 1887. Of the three waste products, only two are of any use to farmers. The wet draff, or barley residue, stays within the Lothian area where it is sold to farms as cattle feed. Pot ale is transferred to (very) local pig farms. Spent lees, on the other hand, don't constitute a viable foodstuff. They go through an effluent treatment system and are returned to the burn as clean water often of a higher standard than the burn water itself.

As well as that 85 acres of arable land, the distillery itself occupies an area of 17 acres. Its water supplies now come from a spring uniquely situated deep under the vast bulk of the warehouse and fed from the nearby Lammermuir Hills. The reservoir sits in the same catchment area that feeds the Kinchie Burn.

There are only nine full-time manual workers employed by the distillery now. (There are other distilleries which have as few as five). Glenkinchie had about 40 or 50 employees in the 1920s. The current manager, Charlie M. Smith, suggests there would have been about 20 staff at Glenkinchie when he joined the industry in 1975. Employees used to have to spread themselves around a variety of rooms to carry out a variety of tasks on a variety of pieces of equipment. The production process is now semi-automated and much more centralised than it was in the 1970s. (Some other distilleries have totally automated, but Glenkinchie has no plans to follow suit.) Only two operators are required to work at any one time.

Of course, Glenkinchie now employs a number of others on the tourism side. The Visitor Centre which incorporates the Museum, avoids the rigid timescales applied at some attractions because of its entirely rural setting and happily accepts the passing tourist on an 'as and when' basis. That way the tour and visit are as unhurried as the process itself and allow the traveller time to savour and reflect both on Glenkinchie – the malt and on Glenkinchie – the place where it is distilled.

Approximately 20 000 visitors make the journey each year to see this jewel of East Lothian. Large numbers are from the UK itself but the number and variety of overseas accents seems to increase every year. Many come almost as a pilgrimage; others because Glenkinchie is there. But it is sincerely believed all go away refreshed and enthused. To run this aspect of the operation successfully demands a manager and two other full time staff, augmented by six or seven part-timers in the summer.

Today duty on whisky is £20.56 per litre of alcohol.

Glenkinchie – The Classic Lowland Malt

Every race that can lay claim to producing a great drink has something that is so prized that it becomes the standard by which all others are judged.

For the Scots these are the single malts. Subtle variations in water, weather, peat and of course the distilling process itself, will lend to each single malt its singular characteristics. These variations are sometimes so local that within just a few miles of each other the fruits of neighbouring distilleries will display highly differing eccentricities.

Knowing that nothing can stimulate the palate or exhaust the vocabulary more than a journey by way of sips and sniff to each far flung distillery, the decision was taken in 1987 to launch a range of whiskies. Unique in their own right, each would convey to the eager consumer the deep, rich variety that is available in Scotch Malt whiskies. The range would divide Scotland into six regions and provide for the whisky traveller novice or expert, a journey of discovery as they travelled through the regional styles of six highly individual malts. They are quite simply Scotland's finest, the 'Classic Malts'.

It was no surprise that Glenkinchie, long admired and a favourite drink in the Edinburgh area, should be chosen to champion the Lowland style, with its pale golden colour, reminiscent of the local barleys, its sweet light grassy nose, its sweetly dry, warming taste, with its sudden intense spicy and for some a smokey finish.

Following consumer research and the knowledge that Classic Malt drinkers were keen to experiment with different versions of their favourite whiskies the Distillers' edition was introduced in 1998 to provide a range designed to complement the existing distillery character – so critical was this that considerable experimentation was required before the final selection was made. Ultimately Amontillado sherry cask wood was found to be the ideal partner for Glenkinchie.

This allows the sherry cask wood to stand alongside, rather than swamp, the malt giving the spirit a bright sunny gold colour, and imparting a delicate sweet fragrant nose. The taste is intense biscuity sweetness followed by sugar sweetness intertwined with an intense oaky dryness. Then follows an astonishingly long, dry, soothing finish, in total contrast to the short, spicy smokiness of Glenkinchie in its Classic Malt guise.

As well as a wonderful 'straight' dram this light lowland malt is excellent as both aperitif and digestif, but for those who might desire a longer drink, it also lends itself completely to the world of the cocktail. Sacrilege? Nonsense! Its distinguished history as a single malt has been achieved by being different and this is no less than would be expected of one of the few left to boast the Lowland style.

For those inclined to try, a simple recipe devised by Gary Regan, a noted creator of cocktails to celebrate the first 'Glenkinchie in the Gardens' concert is:

One shot (generous) of Glenkinchie
Splash of Cointreau or Triple Sec
Splash of Amaretto

Stir ingredients together and serve over ice. Alternatively, stir with ice and strain into a chilled martini glass. Garnish with maraschino cherry or slice of lemon.

Glenkinchie also works superbly well as a long summer drink, sometimes called a 'cooler' – try it in a long glass as an iced punch with ginger ale, lemons and mint or for the more formal version try soda water as a substitute for ginger ale.

But why stop here? To quote Rabbie Burns 'whisky and freedom gang th'gither' but what of whisky and food?

For a number of years now the concept of substituting grain for grape has gained favour and five course dinners exploring the idea of drinking malt whisky whilst eating have been tried and tested with fascinating results.

In the 1990s UDV took this on board and invited awardwinning writer and food consultant Richard Whittington, who is a specialist in this matter, to be responsible for the creation of Classic Malt whisky dinners. He notes that quite clearly there were some foods which by their preparation were never going to partner malt whisky, as the choice has to be based on good taste and balance of flavours on the palate.

A whisky dinner he concludes should encourage shared exploration, mutual discovery and vigorous debate. It should be lively but never raucous but above all be an event that provides education and pleasure.

One of the features of such events is the laying aside of any preconceptions as to how the whisky will be served. The standard 'pub' glass is nowhere to be seen. This is a dinner after all and the use of wine glasses gives an opportunity to play tunes with the presentation and the perception. Generally large wine glasses are better than small. They are aesthetically more appealing whilst giving every facility to nose and appreciate the strikingly individual bouquet of each malt.

Glasses where the whisky is to be drunk neat as with desserts and cheeses for example, may be dessert wine, port or brandy style. Champagne flutes can be used with startling effect with some of the lighter styles of malts.

Chilling whisky is normally not recommended but there are a few which are of a more floral and grassy aroma and these can be served from the freezer in a chilled glass. This suppresses the nose but still allows the flavour to come through particularly the thick texture of the Glenkinchie malt. As the whisky warms to room temperature it opens up revealing changing nuances of flavour with each sip.

Glenkinchie works very well when served in a champagne flute with poached salmon, potted shrimps, foie gras, smoked haddock and sweetcorn chowder such as the famous Cullen skink, prosciutto and black figs, deep fried oysters and mussels, sushi, scallops and when served in a red wine glass – wild mushroom risotto, or in a white wine glass – cock-a-leekie soup.

Glenkinchie – The Edinburgh Malt

Glenkinchie's beginnings as the Edinburgh Malt can reasonably be said to have been a result of the formation of the Glenkinchie Distillery Company in the 1870s.

When the re-opening of the distillery by the consortium of wine merchants, brewers and blenders took place in the early 1880s considerable quantities were readily available to an eager market and the light refreshing Glenkinchie was no doubt to be found in ample supply in the drawing rooms and studios of the time.

More recently, famed whisky writer – Edinburgh's own Charlie MacLean, wrote: 'Since the Scottish Assembly was established a few years ago, Edinburgh has enjoyed another renaissance and although it would be an over-statement to compare this with the golden age of enlightenment of the late 18th century, nevertheless the capital of Scotland is experiencing a boom today which once more gives it the atmosphere of a European capital. And once again Glenkinchie is finding its place as 'The Edinburgh Malt'. In the elegant drawing rooms of the classical 'New Town' you may well be offered Glenkinchie (with soda or water) as an aperitif, instead of gin and tonic. In pubs it is drunk as a chaser to a glass of Duechar's India Pale Ale. In stylish restaurants and cocktail bars it is becoming fashionable to drink it straight from the freezer in a Martini glass'.

The Lord Provost of Edinburgh, the Right Honourable Eric Milligan, (1995 – 2003) took Glenkinchie to heart as The Edinburgh Malt and took every opportunity to present it to visiting dignitaries, celebrities and politicians.

On his travels abroad to promote the interests of the City of Edinburgh he always carried Glenkinchie as a gift to those in the 'Airts and Pairts' he had travelled to impress.

One of the most famous recipients was Nelson Mandela, then President of South Africa, when given the Freedom of the City of Edinburgh by the Lord Provost whilst he attended the Commonwealth Heads of Government meeting in October 1997. More recently Nancy Sinatra was delighted to receive Glenkinchie as the result of a chance meeting/opportunity.

Glenkinchie – The Prestoungrange Malt

What is good for Edinburgh may not always be good for Prestonpans of course, but in choosing which whisky distillers to officially appoint for Prestoungrange there was never a moment's hesitation. It is served on all baronial occasions and takes especial pride of place at The Prestoungrange Gothenburg on the shores of the Firth of Forth established there in 1908 with commendable standards of sanitation and hygiene for its customers to equal those offered to the staff at Glenkinchie as reported in 1911

APPENDIX 1

THE WORKINGS OF THE DISTILLERY

Before 1968, when Glenkinchie still did its own malting on site, it employed coal during the drying process (and just a very little peat, compared to the western and highland distilleries – this contributes greatly to it's lighter flavour). These days malt is weighed into batches of about 9½ tons in the mill house. Ten batches are processed every week. The process is not continuous. A new batch is started only when the previous one has been completely processed. The entire process progresses as follows:

Malt is brought in from one of the four maltings and batched. It takes about two hours for one batch to pass over the rollers in the mill and become separated into grits between flour and husks, collectively known as grist. Although the grits fraction provides access to the starches essential in the production of scotch whisky, the husks provide important fibre to keep the mash "open" and allow for efficient drainage during the mashing process.

Milling is generally done at night because a) the process is too noisy and b) the fine dust produced during the milling (which can be hazardous in the wrong environment hence the No Flash Photography signs) does not easily accommodate distillery tours.

Two huge metal arms turn and mash the grist and water. The water enters the tun in three stages. The 1st quantity of water amounts to 28,000 litres. It is heated to 68° centigrade and meets the grist to mix at precisely 64° starting the conversion of starches to sugars. Over time the water becomes saturated with sugar and this is known as wort. As the wort is drained a further 12,000 litres of water are added to the mash at the higher temperature of 77° converting and dissolving any remaining sugars that still clings to the husks. The resulting wort is combined with the first worts to form a total quantity of 40,000 litres. This is passed through a cooling device on its way to the fermentation room – yeast would not survive such temperatures. Meanwhile back at the mashtun a third lot of water is added to the mash, this time at 83° and is only allowed a short residence time to draw out any remaining sugars This results in the water becoming slightly sugary but not adequately so to be considered wort. This is drained and returned to storage in a huge tank where it will become the first water of the next batch. No sugar is wasted. What is left in the mash tun is the sludgy, grainy mixture called wet draff, which is used as cattle feed. The fermentation room contains six wooden washbacks (four made from Canadian Larch, two from Oregon Pine) each large enough to hold 60,000 litres of wort. Yeast is added at this stage (the DCL company once had its own yeast factory in which they cultured their own yeast for distillery use but

the cultured yeast is now purchased externally) and the fermentation process begins. The wash for Glenkinchie Single malt has been fermented for a minimum of 60 hours – an unusually long time compared to some other distilleries – and ends up something like a flat beer of about 9½% alcohol. The wash then goes to the pot stills where it finally becomes the beginnings of what in the fullness of time will become whisky as we know it. Glenkinchie has two abnormally large pot stills (the largest of their kind in Scotland). Some other distilleries have up to 18 stills. The wash still has three sighting windows, which can be used to check what stage the boiling head has reached. In earlier days, a wooden ball would hang from the still on a string; when swung against the head of the still, the resulting note, sharp or dull, would indicate the level of the "boil" inside the head. It takes six hours for the first half of a washback to go through the first still – the wash still – and eight hours to go through the second – the low wines still. As the wash through in two halves, this means the total time taken to distil a single washback is approximately 20 hours The wash is gently heated in the wash still up to boiling point. The resulting vapours rise through the neck and out into an unusual twostory high, cast iron worm-tub condenser (an old fashioned type of condenser still preferred by Glenkinchie, as opposed to a more modern type – there is an argument that says the worm condenser adds more character and depth to the whisky). Herein, the vapours enter a coiled copper tube which runs around inside of a tub, which is in turn filled with cold water. The cold water causes the vapour to condense inside the tube. The resulting liquid is called low wines and is about 25% alcohol. This goes through the same process again in the low wines still, after which the first distillate to be received at the spirit safe is about 80% alcohol. (When the whole wash has passed through there is a huge residue left in the still. A mere 40% of the wash has turned to vapour. What is left is known as pot ale. It is used as pig feed and is less than 1% alcohol. The liquid residue from the second still has no feed value and is passed through an effluent plant before returning to the Kinchie Burn as clean water. The sludge produced in the effluent plant however does have a purpose and it is spread on the local fields as fertiliser.) This initial outpouring (the foreshots) is too strong to be of optimum worth and contains volatile flavour compounds not desired in the final spirit so is set aside and stored. Happily though, as the distillate comes through, its strength steadily weakens. 70% is considered the ideal strength (and anything between 75% and 65% is acceptable), and the next quantity of distillate comes through at that strength. This is known as the heart, and is passed directly on to the spirit receiver. When the distillate drops below 65% alcohol (known as tails or feints) it is too weak to be put into casks and is collected elsewhere. The feints and the foreshots will join the next quantity of low wines in the low wines still, to be distilled again. By this stage the initial 40,000 litres has been reduced to 5,500 litres of distillate at a strength of 70% alcohol, which is then reduced (by the simple addition of water), to 63.5% alcohol (considered the optimum strength at which to mature the whisky) before being put into oak casks, which have been imported from the United States, and which have previously have been used (only once) to hold bourbon. 1.8 million litres of alcohol are produced annually. The distillate has to stay in the cask for at least three years before it can be known, legally, as Scotch whisky.

East Lothian's relatively dry climate means Glenkinchie takes a relatively short time to mature – a mere 10 years. During those 10 years in the cask, the originally colourless liquid takes on a golden hue and gathers flavours by 'breathing' the surrounding air. 1½ to 2% of the liquid evaporates during the 10 years (equivalent to about 90,000 bottles per year). This is known as "The Angel's Share". When the maturation period is over, the whisky is watered down further to the familiar 43% alcohol, and bottled.

The special 'Distillers' Edition' is matured for a further period of time in an Amontillado sherry cask, which allows the fresh clean nutty sherry flavours to complement the light dry character of Glenkinchie.

APPENDIX 2

ENVIRONMENTAL ISSUES

Curiously, at the same time as Glenkinchie's late Victorian renaissance, an issue displaying great parallels with the modern industrial climate emerged. Amongst all the confident building and progress of that time was a voice of discontent and protest. On 21st March 1891, the distillery secretary received the first of many letters of complaint on behalf of the Fletcher family who were staying at nearby Saltoun Hall.[53]

Such letters would continue to arrive sporadically, often accompanied by threats of legal action, and concerned the foul state of the Kinchie Burn as a result of some of the distillery's practices. Another letter, dated 12th June 1895, from the Fletchers' solicitors, Strathern and Blair, to Glenkinchie's solicitors, Davidson and Syme, also complains about the shoddy condition of their mutual dyke.[54] Perhaps they were too distracted at that time by the death of one of their senior partners, Alfred Thomson (R.H. Thomson would also die in 1897), but clearly the Glenkinchie company were in no hurry to take action over their environmental laxity, as another two letters arrived three years later on 3rd and 6th June 1898,[55] this time complaining that the trout populations in the stretch of the Kinchie Burn between the distillery and the Tyne, and in the nearby Birns Water, had been decimated. These letters also deplored the distillery's use of the local haugh as a dump. Having still not taken any action three years later the distillery received a threat of litigation on 28th May 1901.[56] This threat came from Mr. G. Stevenson on behalf of the Fletchers, who now claimed that the contamination of the Kinchie Burn had also seeped into the Saltoun water which ran through their land. They reported dead fish floating in the stream. They also claimed that their cows refused to drink the water. How this long-running dispute was finally resolved is not well documented.

What is known though is that the Kinchie Burn finally ceased being used as the distillery's source of water in 1954. There was some concern that the quality of the water might have been adversely affected by the use of chemicals by farmers.[57] From this point on the distillery would use water from a spring deep below the warehouse which is fed through the limestone strata of the area all the way from the nearby Lammermuir Hills.

It is worth noting that Glenkinchie's present management have a very responsible and proactive attitude to protecting and enhancing the environment. In recent years in line with their 'green' credentials Glenkinchie as part of the 'Classic Malts' group are sponsors of the Wild Trout Trust – a body with strong environmental and conservation themes applied to freshwater fishing and river management. As manager Charlie Smith comments: "We rely on the quality of the natural products that make Glenkinchie the great whisky that it is, so it is incumbent on us to play our part in the environmental cycle to maintain and protect that situation for future generations".

BIBLIOGRAPHY

Primary Sources:

Copy Letter: J. Harrison to R.H. Thomson, 28th March 1890
Minute of The First Meeting of Directors, 30th June 1890
Letter to the secretary, on behalf of the residents of Saltoun Hall (signature indecipherable), 21st March 1891
Copy Letter: Messrs Strathern & Blair, W.S. to Messrs Davidson & Syme, W.S., 12th June 1895
Special Resolution of The Glenkinchie Distillery Company Limited, 10th March 1897
Memorial for Arthur Sanderson, Wine Merchant, Leith, for The Opinion of Counsel, 1897
Letter to William Cockburn Esquire, on behalf of the residents of Saltoun Hall (signature indecipherable), 3rd June 1898
Letter to William Cockburn Esquire, on behalf of the residents of Saltoun Hall (signature indecipherable), 6th June 1898
Stevenson, G.H., Letter to the secretary of the Glenkinchie Distillery Company Limited, 28th May 1901
Prospectus of the Glenkinchie Distillery Company Limited, 16th January 1913
Minute of Extraordinary General Meeting of Shareholders of The Glenkinchie Distillery Company Limited, 20th March 1913
Memorandum between Arthur Sanderson, Fredrick Reid Sanderson and James Gray, all Distillers, Leith, 1913
Agreement between and among The Clydesdale Distillery Company Limited and Others and Charles Ritchie on behalf of the Scottish Malt Distillers Limited, 7th July 1914
Memorandum and Undertaking by Glenkinchie Distillery Company Limited, 8th July 1914
Circular and Notice to Shareholders from William Cockburn, 9th July 1914
Minute of Extraordinary General Meeting of the Shareholders, 17th July 1914
Adopting Agreement between and among The Scottish Malt Distillers Limited Of the First Part; The Clydesdale Distillery Company Limited and Others of the Second Part; and Charles Ritchie of the Third Part 3rd October 1914
Letter from A.W. Robertson Durham, 15th November 1916
Minute of Meeting of The Shareholders of The Glenkinchie Distillery Company Limited (in Liquidation), 16th November 1916
Affidavit & Claim by The Clydesdale Bank Limited, 23rd July 1917
State of Adjudications prepared by The Liquidator, William Cockburn, on the claims lodged in the Liquidation, 17th April 1918
Copy Letter: Messrs Davidson & Syme, W.S. to Messrs Tods, Murray & Jamieson, W.S. and of their reply, 17th April 1918
Copy Letter: Messrs Ronald & Ritchie, W.S. to Messrs Davidson & Syme, W.S., 2nd July 1918
Note (no. 2) for William Cockburn, Liquidator of The Glenkinchie Distillery Company, Ltd. for Further Authority to Divide, &c., and close Liquidation, from David R. Scott on behalf of Lord Ormidale, 1st May 1919
Account of The Intromissions of William Cockburn, The Liquidator, from 1st August 1914 (date of the Liquidation) to 27th April 1920, 1920
Report by John Stuart Gowans, Chartered Accountant, Edinburgh, on The Accounts of Cockburn, Liquidator of The Glenkinchie Distillery Company, Ltd. from 1st August 1914 (date of the Liquidation) to 27th April 1920, 1920
Memorandum by The Glenkinchie Distillery Company Limited, 1922

Transcription of an interview with Charlie M. Smith, Manager of the Glenkinchie distillery, by the author, 18th September 2002

Secondary Sources:

Andrews, Allen – The Whisky Barons, Jupiter Books, London, 1977
Barnard, Alfred – The Whisky Distilleries of The United Kingdom, 1887
Craig, H. Charles – The Scotch Whisky Industry Record, Index Publishing Ltd., Dumbarton, 1994
Crammond, Dickens and Lerner – The Edinburgh Malt (Glenkinchie Heritage Leaflet), UDV, 1999
Hume, John R. and Moss, Michael – The Making of Scotch Whisky, Canongate, Edinburgh, 1981
Smith, Charlie – Discussions and editorial comments/ corrections at Glenkinchie, April/ June 2003
Spiller, Brian – Distillery Histories Series leaflet, 1981
Weir, Ronald – The History of The Distillers Company 1877- 1939, Clarendon Press, Oxford, 1995
The Wine and Spirit Trade Record, 1911

The Worldwide Web:

BBC News/BUSINESS/Guinness Four fail in fight for acquittal – http://news.bbc.co.uk/1/hi/business/1723136.stm
UISGE! Glenkinchie Distillery: All about it – http://www.uisge.dk/ ud/glenkinchie.html
Our history – http://www.udv.com/ad/company/our_history.html?15
The Six Classic Malts of Scotland from United Distillers review by AWA – http://www.awa.dk/whisky/clasmalt.htm
Images of Glenkinchie Distillery – http://www.activitypoint.co.uk/ en/e00/00583.htm

Notes

1 http://www.uisge.dk/ud/glenkinchie.html
2 Crammond, Dickens and Lerner
3 Spiller
4 Spiller
5 Craig
6 Andrews
7 Barnard
8 Ibid
9 Craig
10 Copy Letter: J. Harrison to R.H. Thomson, 28th March 1890
11 Minute Of The First Meeting of Directors, 30th June 1890
12 Spiller
13 Special Resolution of The Glenkinchie Distillery Company Limited, 10th March 1897
14 Memorandum between Arthur Sanderson, Frederick Reid Sanderson and James Gray, all Distillers, Leith, 1913
15 Minute of Extraordinary General Meeting of Shareholders of The Glenkinchie Distillery Company Limited, 20th March 1913
16 Minute of Extraordinary General Meeting of Shareholders, 17th July 1914
17 Weir
18 Adopting Agreement between and among The Scottish Malt Distillers Limited Of the First Part; The Clydesdale Distillery Company Limited and Others Of the Second Part; and Charles Ritchie Of the Third Part 3rd October 1914
19 Minute of Meeting of The Shareholders of the Glenkinchie Distillery Company Limited (in Liquidation), 16th November 1916
20 Memorandum and Undertaking by Glenkinchie Distillery Company Limited, 8th July 1914
21 Weir
22 Craig
23 Ibid

24 Report by John Stuart Gowans, Chartered Accountant, Edinburgh, on The Accounts of Cockburn, Liquidator of The Glenkinchie Distillery Company, Ltd, From 1st August 1914 (date of the Liquidation) to 27th April 1920, 1920
25 Craig
26 State of Adjudications prepared by the Liquidator, William Cockburn, on the claims lodged in the liquidation, 17th April 1918
27 Letter from A.W. Robertson Durham, 15th November 1916
28 State of Adjudications prepared by the Liquidator, William Cockburn, on the claims lodged in the liquidation, 17th April 1918
29 Memorandum by The Glenkinchie Distillery Company Limited, 1922
30 Report by John Stuart Gowans, Chartered Accountant, Edinburgh, on The Accounts of Cockburn, Liquidator of The Glenkinchie Distillery Company, Ltd, From 1st August 1914 (date of the Liquidation) to 27th April 1920
31 Craig
32 Weir
33 Craig
34 ibid.
35 Weir
36 Craig
37 Crammond, Dickens and Lerner
38 Craig
39 Craig
40 Spiller
41 http://www.uisge.dk/ud/glenkinchie.html
42 Spiller
43 Craig
44 quoted in Spiller
45 Craig
46 Spiller
47 Craig
48 http://news.bbc.co.uk/1/hi/business/1723136.stm
49 Craig
50 ibid.
51 Crammond, Dickens and Lerner
52 http://www.udv.com/ad/company/our_history.html?15
53 Letter to the secretary, on behalf of the residents of Saltoun Hall (signature indecipherable), 21st March 1891
54 Copy letter: Messrs Strathern & Blair, W.S. to Messrs Davidson & Syme, W.S., 12th June 1895
55 Letter to William Cockburn Esquire, on behalf of the residents of Saltoun Hall (signature indecipherable), 3rd June 1898 and Letter to William Cockburn Esquire, on behalf of the residents of Saltoun Hall (signature indecipherable), 6th June 1898
56 Stevenson, G.H., Letter to the secretary of the Glenkinchie Distillery Company Limited, 28th May 1901
57 Spiller

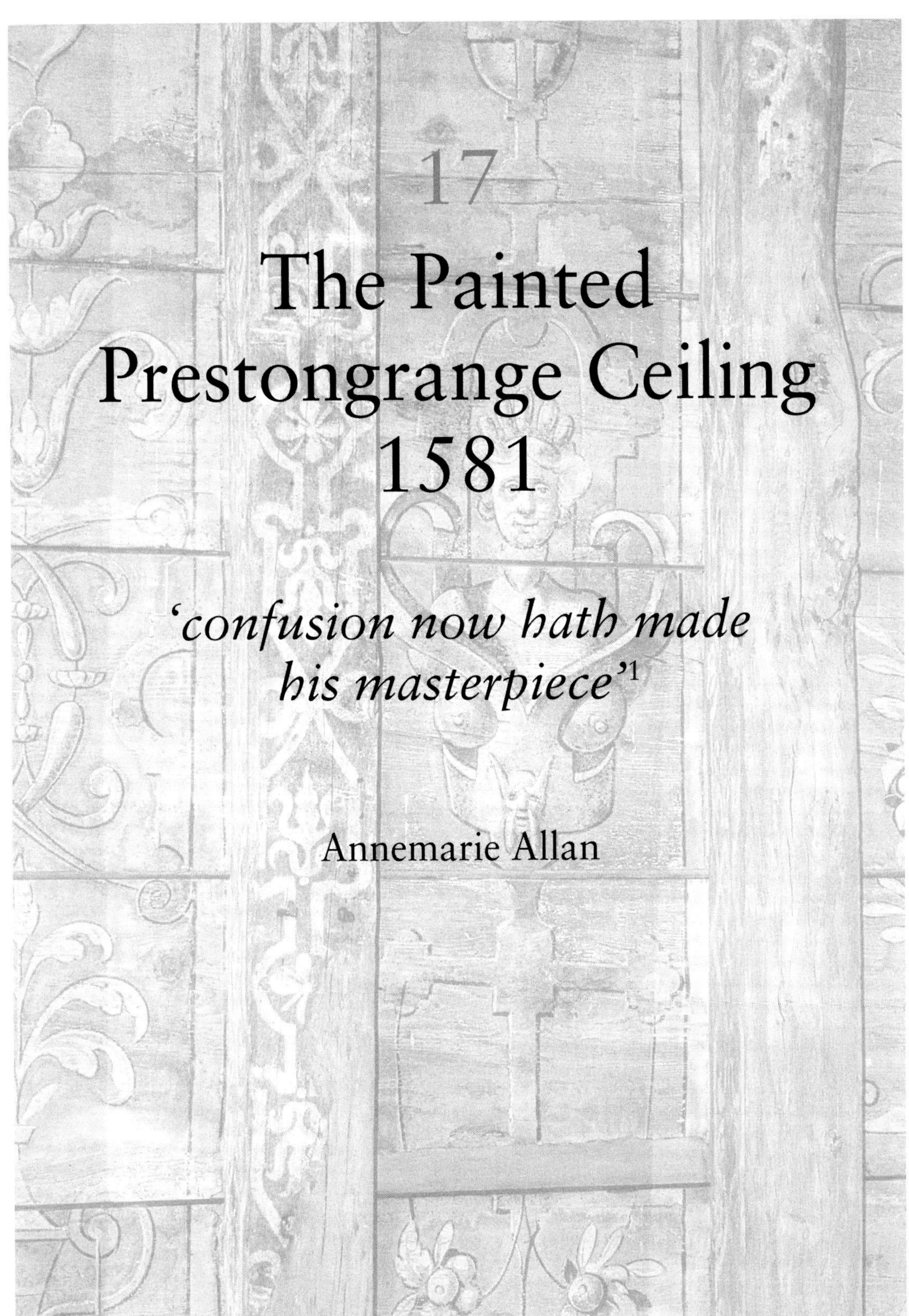

17

The Painted Prestongrange Ceiling 1581

'confusion now hath made his masterpiece'[1]

Annemarie Allan

… …/… … and, in 1962 transferred to Merchiston Tower in 1964 after cleaning and preservative treatment by staff of the National Trust and Ministry of Public Building and Works. The transfer was made by arrangement with the Coal Industry's Social Welfare Organisation and with the assistance of the Ministry. In order to fit its present site it has been reduced in size, the surplus pieces being preserved separately.

The paintings, on boards of Scots pine, bear the date 1581 on a scroll in the fourth bay of the ceiling from the east end. The motifs are painted in tempera (i.e. the pigments are applied with a size medium, not oil) in black, white, and grey; the background, which does not underlie the motifs but is painted round them, is of red lead. The motifs are arranged without reference to any particular theme; some of them occur on other painted ceilings of the period or in contemporary book illustrations. The ceiling as a whole is the best surviving example of what was known as Antique Work and is the earliest dated specimen in Scotland of painted Renaissance decoration.

Originally the oak beams were also painted, but most of the colour has been lost, partly as a result of the adzing of the undersides of the beams to provide a base for later plasterwork. The surviving decoration is not by the same hand as the paintings on the boards, & there are underlying traces of an earlier chevron pattern executed in pigments which match those on the boards.

Schemes of painted decoration such as this were comparatively common in Scotland towards the end of the sixteenth century & during the first half of the seventeenth century and are believed to be the work of local artist-craftsmen.

INTRODUCTION

In 1962, a unique piece of interior decoration was discovered during alterations at Prestongrange House by its current occupants The Royal Musselburgh Golf Club. Known now as The Prestongrange Ceiling it is the earliest dated example of a Renaissance painted ceiling in Scotland. It is one of the largest and best preserved examples of such work and is now admirably housed in the Council Chamber at the top of Napier University's Merchiston Tower in Edinburgh.

1 THE CEILING'S ARTISTIC BACKGROUND

In keeping with the rest of Catholic Europe interior painting in Scotland before the mid-sixteenth century was largely ecclesiastical. It is difficult to assess the true nature of early church interiors since little remains of the mediaeval structures where such painting might be found. However, the National Museums of Scotland and the National Gallery hold examples of painted church furnishings and these, together with surviving fragments such as those at Dryburgh Abbey and Glasgow Cathedral, as well as late 15th and 16th-century examples from Foulis Easter and Guthrie Castle, demonstrate its widespread presence in pre-Reformation Scotland.[2]

15th century Scotland was a nation turning its back on the vivid religious decorative traditions of the past in favour of a more austere style of worship. In terms of ecclesiastical art the most significant development was undoubtedly the reaction against the concept of idolatry. Reformers argued that places of worship furnished with statuary, relics and painted imagery turned the mind away from contemplation of the interior landscape of mind and soul, even to the extent of replacing the worship of God with worship of the object itself.

The social as well as theological impact of the Reformation was profound. Lands previously held by the great religious houses of Scotland were transferred into the ownership of individual families. Those whose influence rose with the acquisition of former church lands were keen to transfer the skills of journeymen painters into a wider secular environment. Prestongrange House, home of the Ker family, was one of the earliest of these conversions rebuilt between 1560 and 1581.[3] Alexander Seton's country house at Pinkie, enlarged in 1613, and Northfield House in Prestonpans, built in 1611, are also examples of East Lothian mansions built or extended around this time and all are liberally embellished with painted imagery on walls and ceilings:

> "*... almost without exception, at this period Scottish houses of any standing were extensively decorated with a gaiety, freedom and confidence which was the outward expression of a nation in the throes of intellectual expansion.*"[4]

The fashion for such domestic decoration was not limited to the nobility. It also extended to the dwellings of the growing merchant class. Merchiston Tower, home of the Napier family, burgesses and merchants of the city of Edinburgh is an excellent illustration of the rising status of these merchant classes.

These extensive building programmes were frequently financed by revenues from the estates which passed from the church to the crown and thereafter into the hands of the nobility and gentry. Before the 16th century the use of coal had been restricted to heating large dwelling places such as castles and great monastic houses and to industrial use, such as heating salt pans for the extraction of salt from sea water. However, land clearance in Scotland for agricultural and building purposes had been ongoing for generations and by the middle of the 16th century Lowland Scotland was almost bereft of trees. The need to find alternative fuels resulted in a significant increase in the value of coal despite the pollutants released when it was burnt.

Increased demand greatly added to the value of estates which contained coal deposits, such as those of Prestongrange and Culross in Fife. This increased the funds available for building which, in turn, increased pressure on dwindling supplies of timber. Building work was dependent on imports mainly from Scandinavia and the Baltic and much of the wood used for structural work lacked the aesthetic qualities of timber such as oak. There are twenty-four oak beams in the Prestongrange ceiling, for example, but the boards which they support (twenty-three in all) are pine.[5]

This combination of two different timbers is typical of such ceiling construction, a circumstance which provides at least a partial answer to the question of why such painted decoration was popular at this time. Paint represented a quick and effective means of disguising such inferior timber. It was:

> *"...the easiest and most cost-effective way to express exuberant display and to communicate the important symbols of the household."*[6]

The availability of journeyman painters previously employed on ecclesiastical decoration provided a source for the expertise required to carry out the work.

2 THE CEILING'S PAINTERS

It is possible that the skills required were imported along with the timber: limited documentary evidence exists of painters from Europe and England at work in Scotland at this time.[7] However, although the fashion for this style of interior decoration may have been imported, there is no evidence to suggest that the work was carried out by any painters other than local craftsmen, though little evidence remains of who these painter journeymen were. In Scotland the individuals who carried out such work were considered to be tradesmen, not artists, and painters were members of the same guild as wrights and masons. The only known example of decorative work signed by the artist during the period 1560 to 1660 is in the Montgomerie Aisle at Largs, inscribed *'J. Stalker fecit 1638'*.

Stalker is recorded as an apprentice in Edinburgh in 1632.[8] There is no record of a painter's identity on any other work except for the initials *'JM'* at

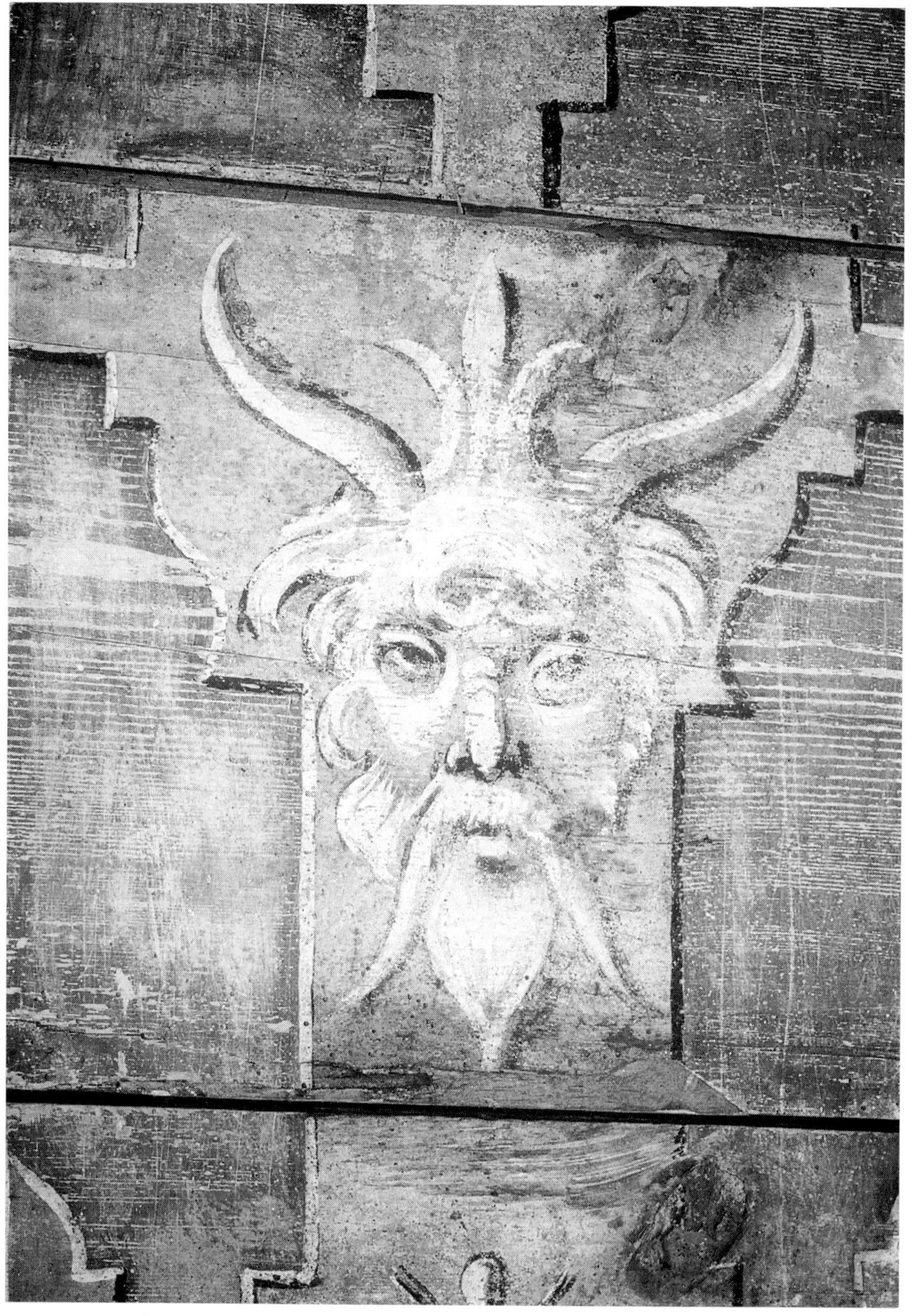

Delgaty Castle, thought to refer to a painter named John Melville or Mellin.[9] Stalker's work also offers interesting evidence that embroidery and painting not only used the same sources, but often relied on the same method, since some of the pattern is outlined in pounce work i.e. pricking out a pattern and using the holes to trace the outline of the finished work which is a technique more commonly associated with needlework.[10]

3 STRUCTURE AND TECHNIQUE

Where builders had to take account of the angles created by the roof above, ceilings were 'barrel vaulted' i.e. formed from wooden boards bent into a curved shape and nailed to the rafters thereby providing one large surface for decoration. This surface was generally divided into smaller areas for the artist to work within, as is the case with the Emblem Chamber at Culross Place, Fife, commissioned by Sir George Bruce, inventor and merchant.[11] More commonly the painting surface was formed from the underside of the floorboards of the room above as was the case at Prestongrange. These boards were supported by beams which remained visible from the room below, creating a long, narrow space interrupted by the beams running the length or breadth of the room:

> *"The painting was normally executed in situ with the artist working above his head. The surface was first prepared by laying on a white ground ... and the design was drawn onto this in a black outline which was then filled in with colour. The black outlining remains visible and should not be seen as the sign of crude or unskilful work."*[12]

Typically, such Scottish interior decoration of the period 1550 to 1650 was executed in glue-tempera:

> *"...a simple medium where dry pigments are mixed with glue or size generally made from the skins of such animals as the rabbit or the deer. The surface to be painted was usually first primed with several coats of size ... the final coat having some whiting or chalk added for the dual purpose of filling minor irregularities and giving a white ground on which to work the decoration."*[13]

The narrow surface available to work on was a major challenge to the painters' art. The subject matter of the paintings therefore relied heavily on images which lent themselves to such a surface. These images were rarely the invention of the journeymen painters who executed the work and, even where images are original, as is the case with much of the work executed for Sir George Bruce at Culross in the early 1600s, their conceptual origins derive from fairly specific sources.[14]

4 THE GROTESQUE ARTISTIC CONTEXT

It is important to bear in mind that, despite a rich variety of cultural traditions, the scholars of pre-Reformation Europe were unified by a shared language – Latin – and a shared body of concepts, both Christian and classical.

It was within this shared context that Scotland's journeymen artists created the vivid, richly decorated interiors demanded by their patrons. Decoration was not, of course, restricted to ceilings: walls and alcoves were also illustrated, with occasionally Christian but more frequently classical, scenes, as were ceramics, embroidered wall hangings, cushions and other soft furnishings.[15]

By the opening years of the 16th century refinements to printing techniques signalled a radical change in the nature of communication, when it became possible – and highly desirable – to obtain copies of books which were in simultaneous multiple circulation. Artists and writers embraced the opportunity to expand their audience while preserving the integrity of their ideas and images through the medium of the printed book. 'Pattern books' of engravings by artists mainly of French or Flemish background were in increasing circulation at this time.[16] These offered images in a style appropriate to the long narrow shape created by the ceiling beams and provided the source for much interior decoration.

Many of these pattern books are in the 'grotesque' style which in Britain is called 'antique work'. The Oxford Dictionary defines grotesque as, 'comically or repulsively distorted; monstrous, unnatural', but in its original form grotesque meant literally, 'in grotto style' and referred to the origins of such patterns in the painted walls of underground vaults or grottos of classical Rome. These antique *grotesqueries* were a strong contrast to the ordered formality more commonly associated with classical architecture and decoration. Painting or other ornamentation in the grotesque style comprises a bizarre disharmony of human, animal and plant forms combined in ways which contradict the laws of nature.

> *"Our contemporary artists decorate the walls with monstrous forms rather than reproducing clear images of the familiar world. Reeds are substituted for columns, fluted appendages with curly leaves and volutes [spiral scrolls] take the place of pediments."*[17]

This type of renaissance decoration is attributed originally to the painter Raphael, whose 16th century Vatican paintings are based partly on the images found in these grottos. Throughout the 16th century, the style became increasingly fashionable: between 1565 and 1571 Hans Vredeman de Vries of Antwerp published his *Grottesco: in diversche manieren*, a series of engravings which provided much of the imagery for ceiling decoration throughout Scotland, as did his *Caryatidum* published in 1565.[18]

In keeping with a more formal classical style, heraldic devices and emblem books also formed part of the source material for ceiling decoration. Heraldry, administered in Scotland by the Lord Lyon, King of Arms, records the genealogies, precedence and honours associated with noble families, and as such, offered a means of expressing a wide range of family attributes which was appropriate to the requirements of both painter and patron. Such heraldic devices frequently accompany images and text in emblematic style. The first emblem book in English was *A Choice of Emblemes* published in 1586 by Geffrey Whitney four years after the date inscribed on the Prestongrange ceiling.

Emblematic images combine a motto, usually in Latin, with a illustrative image derived from a range of sources – classical Greece and Rome, contemporary, biblical or mythological – allied with a short verse relating image to motto.[19] As demonstrated in the work commissioned by Sir George Bruce at Culross, the emblem format readily lent itself to modification to suit individual purposes.[20] The coherence and consistency of both emblematic and heraldic images, together with their clear intention of presenting a statement to the informed observer, is in strong contrast to the fantastical combining and recombining of an enormous variety of forms typical of the grotesque style.

Although it is difficult in many cases to identify reasons for the choice of images, it is nonetheless clear that such interior decoration was a highly individual statement of personal history, aspirations and beliefs by those who commissioned the work. Sir Alexander Seton, for example, when remodelling Pinkie House in 1613, used a number of sources to present an expression of his personal world view to the informed viewer:

> *"The houses Seton built or improve at Fyvie (Aberdeenshire) and at Pinkie (East Lothian) are notable for their use of an extended vocabulary of heraldic and emblematic devices which must be seen as making claims for his own and his family's role in bringing an implicitly neoclassical urbanitas and humanitas to Renaissance Scotland."*[21]

Indeed, uniquely among surviving examples, the source material at Pinkie has even been adapted to include a portrait of Seton himself.

5 THE BARONIAL HALL AT PRESTONGRANGE

Prestongrange House itself probably began life as an agricultural outpost for the Cistercian Abbey of Newbattle, the name Prestoungrange literally meaning priest's town farm. During the Reformation vast areas of land in Lowland Scotland including that of Prestongrange passed into the hands of Mark Ker. He was the former Commendator of Newbattle, a secular post concerned with Abbey lands and property. His family took over control of these Abbey lands initially as representatives of the Crown and subsequently as Barons of Prestongrange and Dolphinstoun and Earl and Marquis of Lothian. The house at this time underwent its first major conversion into the baronial hall of Prestoungrange or Prestongrange. By 1609, the house had passed from the Ker to the Morison family.[22] A plaster ceiling installed at some point in the early 1700s resulted in some damage to the painted decoration:

> *"Curvature caused by the weight of the ceiling made it impossible for eighteenth century reconstructors to affix their new plaster ceiling without first adzing the beams to a level."*[23]

The Morison family therefore were presumably familiar with the ceiling. Indeed, its presence may have been a factor in the dementia displayed by William Morison, described by Alexander 'Jupiter' Carlyle in his autobiography as a man widely believed to be a wizard. Morison inherited Prestongrange in 1684 and was:

> *"... so imaginary and credulous as to believe that close by his creek of Morison's Haven was the place where St. John wrote the Apocalypse."*[24]

The text of the Apocalypse is renowned for its visionary richness and variety not unlike the imagery on the Prestongrange ceiling.

By the 18th century, the house had passed into the hands of the Grant (later Grant-Suttie) family who occupied Prestongrange House almost continuously for more than two hundred years. During the 1830s Sir George Grant-Suttie commissioned William Playfair, one of the foremost Scottish architects of his day, to begin a radical programme of improvements. Playfair's modifications are to a large extent responsible for the survival of the ceiling since alterations to the existing house were minimal. Instead, the building was extended to create new external walls. Although the ceiling must have been visible in 1830 when the drawing room was panelled and plastered and again in 1837 when further work took place,[25] nowhere in the records of Playfair's work is there any mention of the existence of the ceiling.

The Grant-Suttie family were undoubtedly aware of the historical value of the ceiling. Sir George was a great-grandson of Lord Cullen of Monymusk House, a building which is notable for the preservation of the painted ceiling and walls of the Great Hall on the ground floor.[26] However, the Grant-Sutties were commissioning a building which would offer all the amenities of 19th century modernity. Furthermore, their Victorian sensibilities were no doubt offended by the coarse nature of some of the images. The family, models of respectability and Presbyterian rectitude, were unlikely to welcome such a riotous celebration of a world turned on its head on their new drawing room ceiling.

For the next 120 years the ceiling was once more consigned to obscurity behind a coating of plaster, until the purchase of the building and grounds by CISWO (Coal Industry & Social Welfare Organisation) in 1958 for the benefit of its current occupants the Royal Musselburgh Golf Club. The Club had already been tenants there for more than 30 years since the Grant-Sutties themselves finally moved away to Dunbar. CISWO initiated the first major repair and remodelling of the house undertaken since Playfair's work in the 19th century.[27]

6 THE CEILING UNCOVERED IN 1962

By the early 1900s there was a growing awareness of the value of Scotland's historic buildings, many of which had been reduced to partial remnants and many almost obliterated over time by war, reconstruction, neglect, environmental damage and in some cases misguided efforts at preservation. The need to create some means of preserving these buildings brought about the establishment of agencies responsible for their protection and restoration. The first recorded programme of conservation in the 1930s was commissioned by The National Trust for Scotland and undertaken by the Department's Office of Works, now known as the Conservation Centre at Stenhouse. Since that date the Conservation Centre has been involved in the provision of advice, specialist reports and practical conservation on behalf of the National Trust and others.

In 1962, when renovation work at Prestongrange was interrupted by the discovery of the painted figures on the boards and beams behind the old plaster ceiling, CISWO requested advice from the Historic Buildings and Monuments Department of the Scottish Office, which in 1991 became

Historic Scotland. It was this agency which provided specialists from Stenhouse Conservation Centre to free the ceiling from its plaster covering.

Its excellent state of preservation is rare in the context of such interior painting: apart from some damage to the beams and to some sections close to the fireplace, the Prestongrange ceiling, at 20′ by 40′ one of the largest in Scotland, emerged wonderfully intact from behind its layer of protective plasterwork. The technical report in 1963 to the National Trust for Scotland reveals the excitement generated by its discovery:

> *"The interest of the ceiling is manifold; the undoubted quality of design and draughtsmanship; the importance of content in relation to style and source development; and last but not least the original and untouched state in which the ceiling has survived ... its importance in the peculiar context of the development of Scottish Renaissance interior decoration is beyond doubt."*[28]

Although there is no clue either in contemporary documents or on the ceiling itself to the painter's identity Ian Hodkinson, a senior conservator with Historic Scotland, who was closely involved with the discovery and subsequent treatment of the Prestongrange ceiling, was confident that the painting on the ceiling boards was the work of a single master craftsman:

> *"The modelling is exceptionally well-rendered with a subtlety and sureness of touch ... intimate study of the brushwork and other stylistic and technical considerations obtained during restoration of the painting leaves me in no doubt that the entire ceiling was executed by one painter."*[29]

The painting which once existed on the oak beams has been almost completely obliterated and most of what remained appeared to be a later addition in a different hand. However,

> *"...there are underlying traces of an earlier chevron pattern executed in pigments which match those of the boards."*[30]

The colours used for interior decoration of this type were pigments derived from a range of natural sources. The addition of whiting or chalk to the glue tempera mix was an essential element in the preparatory work, creating a background with very specific properties:

> *"The ground ... reflects through subsequent layers of paint to give the work its characteristic sparkle."*[31]

Clearly the colour palette selected for use in individual cases was an essential element in determining the impact of the finished work. In the case of Prestongrange, the colours chosen were intended to achieve a striking effect.

> *"The entire surface of the beams and boards was primed with a middle tone of grey composed of whiting and carbon black. All the decoration was carried out in three simple pigments, black (carbon) and white (whiting) used for the grisaille of the motifs, and red oxide of lead for the background*

... *In its original state red lead, or minimum as it was called, is a brilliant orange and the decorative effect of the monochrome motifs against such a strong colour must have been quite extraordinary."*[32]

Fragments of other decorative work within the house show that at one time there was extensive painting throughout the building. These traces include the monogram of Mark Ker though it is not definite that this is the first Mark Ker since his son bore the same name. There is, however, no evidence of any wall painting in the room containing the ceiling and this, taken together with partial evidence of contemporary hooks and nails attached to the beams,33 suggests that the walls were originally hung with tapestry. The combination of the ceiling, together with wall hangings and presumably other fabrics within the room which echoed the painted surface in their colour and style, undoubtedly resulted in a striking piece of decoration; this must have been a showpiece room.

7 READING THE PAST

It has been mentioned earlier that such painted ceilings were often a means of expressing statements of individuality on the part of the patron who commissioned the work. The choice of sources and, most particularly, any variations from these sources is therefore closely bound up with the character of the patron. Although Whitney's *Choice of Emblemes* was not published until 1586, five years after the date when the Prestongrange ceiling was completed, this cannot necessarily be taken as confirmation that the Prestongrange ceiling lacks emblematic detail due to the unavailability of sources, since such books were extensively available on the continent from the mid-sixteenth century onwards.[34] The emphasis on grotesque imagery in the Prestongrange ceiling must therefore be interpreted as a conscious decision on the part of the patron who commissioned the work.

A feather-headed figure seated on a wheeled vehicle has been identified[35] as originating in an 1552 engraving by the Dutch designer, Cornelis Bos, whose work is typified by patterns incorporating dream-like, impossible figures and activities, but the major source for many of the ceiling images is the *Grottesco'* pattern book by Hans Vredeman de Vries. The images also include elements of his *Caryatidum* – pillars in the form of a human figure. These two pattern books were produced between 1565 and 1571. Therefore, in 1581, the date on the ceiling, they were of fairly recent publication. A further confirmation of the contemporary nature of the work is found in another source for the Prestongrange images, *Les songes drolatiques de Pantagruel.* This work, published in 1565 and probably illustrated by François Desprez was claimed by its printer Breton as a posthumous work by the great French humanist, Rabelais. This source, when taken together with the ceiling's significance as the most extensive example of 'antique' style, gives the work a unique flavour, since Rabelaisian imagery does not appear to have provided a source for other Scottish Renaissance decorative work of the period 1550 to 1650, when the fashion for such work was at its height.[36]

Today the term Rabelasian is synonymous with coarse humour but Rabelais himself was a subtle, complex individual. The humanist movement, of which he was an adherent, questioned the ethic of absolute obedience and subordination to higher authority, both secular and religious. An

accompanying interest in the values of individualism and intellectual freedom led to a reinterpretation of a world view previously based on the teachings of the Catholic church. This embraced the revisiting of classical traditions drawing on the civilisations of Greece and Rome, but Rabelais also drew on the oral traditions which had formed part of the community life of generations of peasantry. Such folktales bear little resemblance to sanitised modern versions of such stories now regarded as fit only for the nursery. Rabelais' tales comprise frequently ribald accounts of the adventures of Gargantua and Pantagruel, characters drawn from popular folklore and his own inventiveness. But their coarse and ribald nature does not indicate a lack of sophistication. On the contrary, these stories are subtle reinterpretations of the original tales offering a satirical commentary on contemporary life.

The Rabelasian images on the ceiling are not merely chosen for their general effect: those who commissioned such work were not seeking decoration 'bought by the yard': at Prestongrange this is evident from alterations made to the original, presumably intended to make some specific point which can now only be guessed at. One figure, for example, appears on the ceiling with a wooden leg, instead of the sound limb he enjoyed in the original engraving.

It is not unreasonable, given the unique nature of this particular choice, to assume that Mark Ker intended to establish an affinity between himself and Rabelais. Ker, like Rabelais, was both a man of the church and a man of the secular world. He, too, had a wife and children. As an educated man of his time the issues which occupied the Renaissance intellect were part of his mindset: faith in God balanced against the desire to question and discover, the reconciliation of established belief with newer, more independent thought and the life of the mind balanced against the earthy realities of everyday existence.

The sources for the images at Prestongrange are essentially the same as later ceilings such as those at Nunraw and Pinkie. However the structured, orderly mode of expression found most particularly at Pinkie is not that found on the Prestongrange ceiling. The disparate images, framed by ornate architectural fantasies, appear to have no discernible relationship other than that imposed by the patterns which surround them and the images themselves, many of them bizarre representations of human and semi-human figures – some displaying grossly exaggerated phallic attributes – appear, by and large, to have no specific individual meaning. The wealth of fruit and flowers surrounding the central images and the inclusion of several cereal crops in the images themselves are clearly copied from de Vries' *Grottesco* series. However, when this is taken in conjunction with the Rabelasian emphasis on the physical nature of existence, it would seem that the inference drawn when the ceiling was originally uncovered, ie that the work is intended to some degree as a celebration of fertility, of the natural cycles of birth, death and rebirth, may well be valid.[37]

It was partly due to this initial interpretation of its content that the discovery of the ceiling in the 1960s was taken as confirmation of occult practices and pagan beliefs associated with the Ker family. These rumours centred on the younger Mark Ker, 2nd Baron of Prestongrange. It was alleged that his wife, Margaret Maxwell, maintained an entourage of witches who harassed visitors to the house and that she brought about the death of her adulterous husband by the use of magic spells.[38]

It has subsequently become clear that the ceiling is not, in fact, based on

occult or pagan imagery but derives from sources which have no such association and that the work is, in fact, an innovative piece of contemporary decoration. However, this does not mean that witchcraft has no relevance to the history of the ceiling, most particularly when one considers that Prestongrange House is situated only a few hundred yards from the alleged site of events which triggered a period of witch mania unparalleled in the previous history of Scotland.

In 1591, John Cunningham, a Prestonpans schoolmaster, was executed for witchcraft. Cunningham, otherwise known as John Fian, together with Geilles Duncan of Tranent and Agnes Sampson of Humbie, confessed under torture to a catalogue of crimes involving the black arts, including a plot against the person of the king by raising a storm at sea in 1589, when King James I and IV was returning to Scotland with his bride. It was alleged that the witches assembled on the Prestonpans shore:

> *"...att the Newheavin callit Aitchesounes-heavin, betuix Musselburcht and Prestonpannis."*[39]

The sensationalist press of the day, in the form of a pamphlet, cheaply printed and widely distributed, were quick to take advantage of the public's thirst for detail. The earliest known tract on Scottish witchcraft, a pamphlet entitled *Newes from Scotland. Declaring the damnable Life of Doctor Fian a notable Sorcerer, who was burned at Edenbrough in Ianuarie last. 1591"*[40] enjoyed a wide distribution, largely thanks to its sensationalist account of sorcery maliciously directed at the highest in the land.

Witch trials had been on the increase throughout the second half of the 16th century, but it was the arrest and trial of Cunningham, Duncan and Sampson and the King's obsession with witchcraft which triggered a witch hunt lasting into the following century and beyond, until the last witch burning in Scotland in 1727.[41] Between 1580 and 1680, almost no-one in any community in Scotland was safe from the accusation of witchcraft. In Prestonpans alone, the year 1590 saw 39 persons out of a population of approximately 1,000 executed for witchcraft.[42]

Unlike many of the accused, the Ker family were favoured intimates of King James. But high position itself was not necessarily a guarantee of protection and rumour has a way of embellishing itself until the truth is wrapped in obscurity. A memoir from a recent publication illustrates this rather well:

> *'In the middle of Musselburgh there's a big house and it's supposed to be haunted by Lady Susan, but when they renovated it they took away a false ceiling and they found all these paintings of witches and warlocks up in the ceiling in the Royal Musselburgh. And it's that bad the men wouldn't take the ladies up to let them see them. It was really outrageous the things that was painted on the ceiling. So it must have been a witch's coven in the Royal Musselburgh years and years ago when it was Lady Susan's house. Now it's the Royal Musselburgh Golf Club.'*[43]

Betty Nisbet's words recorded not in the 17th century, but in the 1990s offer an insight into the social climate which existed in the years following the creation of the painted ceiling at Prestongrange and the possible reasons why

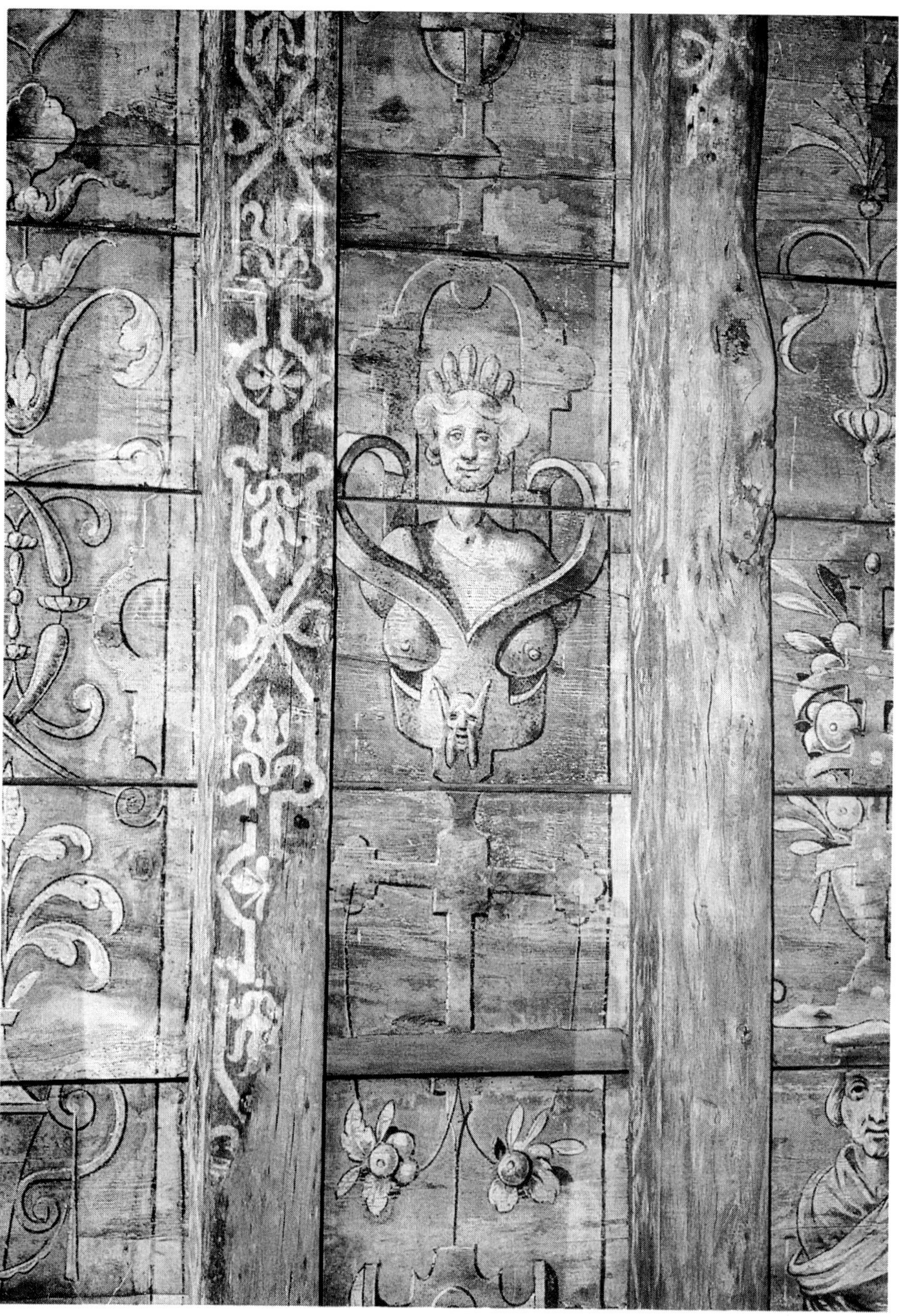

the ceiling, though no doubt admired, was never imitated. Its subject matter, though rooted in highly respected traditions of European art, may well have contributed to the rumours surrounding the Kers and if so, was clearly not worth the risk.

By the 1660s, the style of the ceiling was unlikely to be repeated for a somewhat more mundane reason. By this time, the fashion for 'antique work' had evolved far beyond its classical origins to the point where its exuberant imagery was considered fit only for the alehouse and the skill exhibited by the painter of the Prestongrange ceiling in terms of both brushwork and re-interpretation of de Vries' images had become merely:

> *"... a kind of unpolished painter's work."*[44]

The Prestongrange ceiling, as the earliest dated example of a Scottish Renaissance painted ceiling, was bound to be experimental, created before habits of style were fully formed. It offers an invaluable insight into the origins of the decorative style so typical of the 17th century Scottish interior. But its relevance goes beyond the artistic: it is a testimony to the spirit of the time, a means of reading the mood of a nation on the brink of a new era.

8 A NEW SCOTLAND

1581 as the inscribed date of the Prestongrange Ceiling's creation places it at the moment when the rigid structure of a Europe dominated by the medieval world view was being dismantled. According to Philip Thomson:

> *"It is no accident that the grotesque mode in art and literature tends to be prevalent in societies and eras marked by strife, radical change or disorientation."*[45]

Without rationality, endless possibilities beckon. The hidden ceiling from Prestongrange employs the art of the grotesque to open a window on a universe populated by the fantastic and the unreal. Imagination is unfettered by the constraints of any conventional reality. This freedom was an essential component in the development of the new world view. The period of the Enlightenment saw the birth of the application of scientific method to a rational universe where natural laws could be observed and quantified by means of deductive reasoning. However, such rationality also demanded the power to imagine what might be by observing what was. It was this reconciliation of the opposing elements of imagination and reason that encouraged the intellectual blossoming typified by men such as John Napier of Merchiston, who combined the ability to visualise new concepts with the rigorous mental discipline necessary for the development of valid mathematical rules.

Subsequent decoration placed far greater emphasis on symmetry and logic, where the grotesque exists as an element within a more orderly context. The decoration of Sir Alexander Seton's Pinkie House shows a formality of content, style and structure characterised by heraldic devices and emblematic imagery. These later ceilings emphasise restraint and dignity. Mark Ker's ceiling at Prestongrange was the antithesis of restraint employing the art of the grotesque as a celebration of the inventiveness of the human mind. It speaks

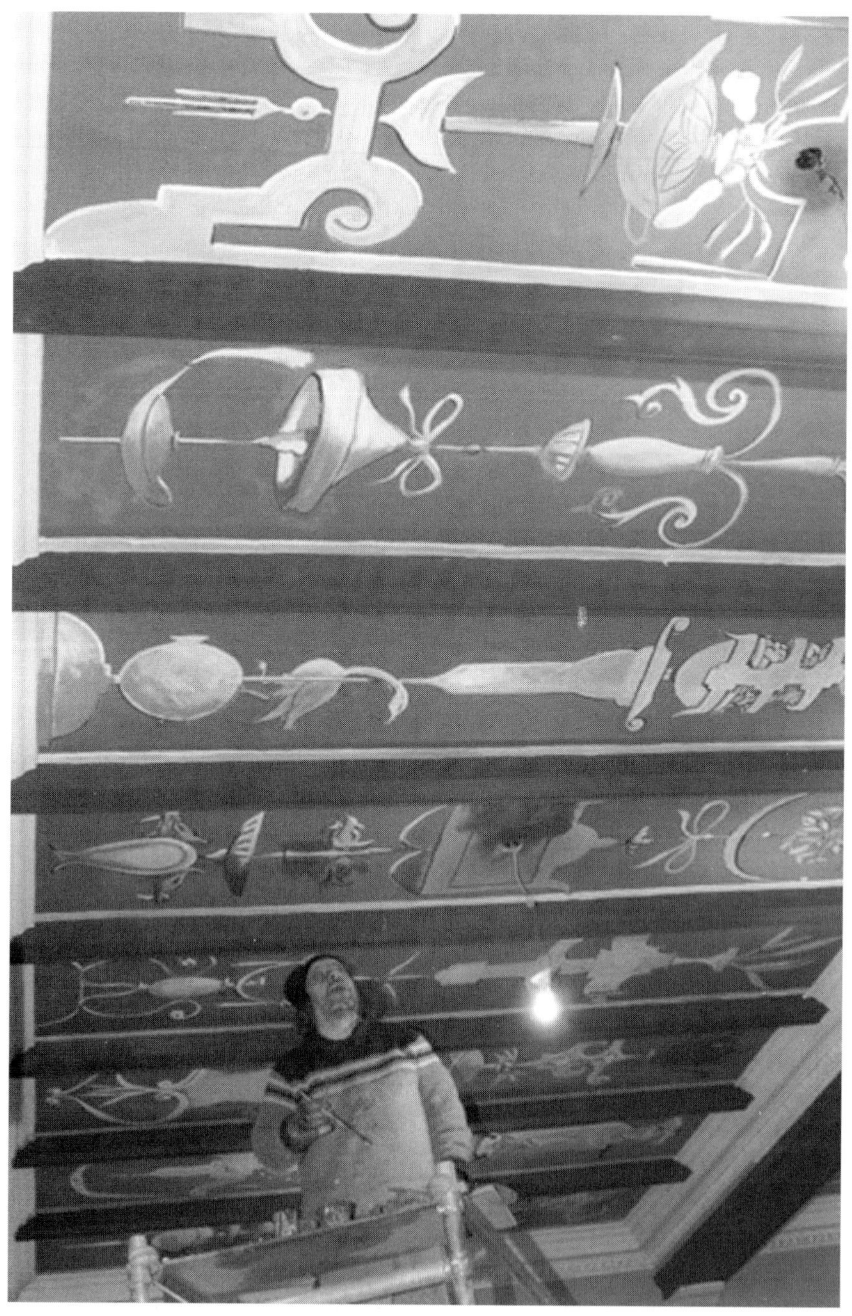

to us today across more than 400 years as a testament to the moment when the Scotland was poised on the brink of its philosophical and intellectual flowering which later became known as the Enlightenment.

9 THE CEILING'S PRESERVATION

The uncovering of the ceiling in 1962 was a moment of high excitement for the National Trust conservators who were called in to deal with its discovery. However, once the plaster was fully removed the conservators found themselves facing a number of preservation issues to do with the beams and boards, the paint layers, the ambient conditions and their likely effect on the uncovered painting.

The beams which supported the ceiling had suffered significant deterioration due to their age and the effect of building works since they were originally installed. Areas of the boards had been removed at some time in the past to allow the insertion of electric and plumbing pipes and to accommodate adjustments to the hearths in the room above.

> *"The beams are old, of inadequate dimensions to give support for such a span; in some places rotten at the ends, in some places weakened by subsequent cutting and in other places of frankly unsound construction."*[46]

The floor of the room above was found to be a later additional layer placed on top of the painted boards which had originally formed the floor of that room. Moreover the room above had been partitioned to create smaller rooms, a circumstance which had increased pressure on the beams which were supporting their weight. Together with deterioration due to the age of the ceiling these additions had caused the beams to bend under pressure.

> *"There is a notable sag in the floor above in some places as much as 3″ and considerable movement can be felt when walking."*[47]

Steel reinforcement of the beams was a possible solution but this would have prevented use of the rooms above since it would not prevent movement in the floor.

> *"The paint layers are not able to follow the movement of the boards and this together with the decomposition and loss of binding power of the glue medium by prolonged wetting or especially desiccation leads to flaking and powdering"*[48]

The only valid solution was the insertion of an additional floor in the room above suspended on steel beams. Next the nature of the paint layers also created issues in terms of protecting the boards from attack by wood boring beetles. Standard treatments were not an acceptable option since they were likely to have a damaging effect on the painted surface. Instead the use of methyl bromide gas would be necessary. The major preservation issue, however, was the nature of the painted surface. The vivid background shining through subsequent layers of colour so typical of such painting would not be possible without the glue-tempera mix. There is, however, no other method than the original to fix the paint to the surface while simultaneously retaining

the texture of the paint and providing protection.

> *"No binding medium has yet been discovered which completely fulfils the threefold function of re-fixing glue-tempera paint which has flaked or powdered off and retaining the important characteristic texture of the paint while at the same time providing a protective coating."*[49]

The purity of the glue, its chemical composition, the temperature of application, the skill required to fully impregnate the paint layers before the glue has set and the need to clean dirt, dust, cobwebs and other accretions from the surface were all vital components in the preservation of the ceiling, all taking place within the context of the conservators' determination to preserve the original work. The painting had never suffered from previous attempts to repaint or retouch the original and:

> *"... the necessity to preserve this integrity cannot be too strongly emphasised. All temptation to reconstruct or retouch areas of missing paint on original boards must be resisted...any kind of retouching on glue tempera results in the destruction of the original. Areas of new board should be tinted to match adjacent background colours and the missing areas on beams should be treated likewise ... all that should be necessary to achieve visual harmony while retaining antiquarian integrity is smoothing off and painting to match the original background colour of the beams."*[50]

However, perhaps the most significant issue of all faced by the conservators was that of its *future* preservation. The room in which the ceiling was found had been designated by CISWO for future use as a bar. Ambient air pollution was not a significant issue, but:

> *"...a much more serious menace arises from the decision to use the room in which the painted ceiling is situated as a bar thereby creating serious potential sources of pollution, firstly from the tendency for the spread of mould growths associated with fumes arising from the storage of liquor and more important from the contamination of the atmosphere and consequent deposit of nicotine from the intensive smoking which will take place when the bar is in use."*[51]

Ideally the requirements of preservation would be best served by re-designating the room for alternative use. Failing this it would be necessary to cover the ceiling once again, this time behind a modern ceiling, and to install an independently suspended floor in the rooms above to prevent further damage from vibration, using the space between the original and new floors to house preservation equipment such as an insulation quilt to equalise temperature and humidity on both sides of the boards and to allow fumigation for protection from insect damage.

Given the cost and complexity of these works, the possibility was raised that the interests of preservation might be best served by removing the ceiling from its original location either for storage or re-installation elsewhere. At the time this was considered by the conservators to be the most viable option.

> *"It could be argued that it is unethical to remove a work of this kind from its original context and to some extent it undoubtedly is. However it is*

equally true to say that the style and content of the work is valid in the context of the age in which it was painted as much as in the particular context of its relevance to Prestongrange House."[52]

There is some value to the argument that the impact of Prestongrange ceiling as a work of national importance would not be significantly diminished by its removal. However, the historic and artistic significance of any such work is heavily reliant on its preservation within its original context and the above discussion has exemplified this beyond any reasonable doubt.

In the case of Prestongrange the quality and extent of the work, the date of its creation and the nature and impact of its imagery at both a local and national level all contribute to a very considerably enhanced understanding of the social climate of the time and the thinking of the Baron at the time. For these reasons its removal has been subject to a considerable degree of criticism.

"The Prestongrange ceiling, removed for safe-keeping to Merchiston Castle in recent times, has lost its power of association with place forever."[53]

However in terms of its preservation for the future it was judged at the time to be the only valid solution bearing in mind the usage that CISWO and the Royal Musselburgh Golf Club had in mind for the room.

"We are all aware of the inevitable loss of significance when a work of art of this type is removed from its original context and this must be particularly true in the case of the Prestongrange ceiling in view of the special association which the painting had with the inhabitants of the house. It must be said that at the time of restoration this association was not fully appreciated but even then every attempt was made to bring about restoration of the ceiling leaving it in situ and in circumstances which would ensure its preservation for posterity."[54]

10 THE MERCHISTON TOWER

When the Prestongrange Ceiling was uncovered in the early 1960s a unique and ambitious project was already underway at Merchiston Tower in the City of Edinburgh. Although there are no records of the Tower's origins its history is inextricably linked with the family who occupied it almost continuously for a period of five centuries – the Napiers of Merchiston.[55]

The Napiers were merchant burgesses of the City of Edinburgh and close associates of the Royal family throughout the 15th century. But it is through John Napier, 8th Laird of Merchiston who was born in Merchiston Tower in 1550, that the family achieved international renown. John Napier is best known for his work on logarithms, an essential tool for subsequent mathematical advances. He also:

"published a treatise on ... multiplication ... which became known as Napier's 'Rods' or 'Bones'... In an appendix he explained ... a mechanical means of calculation ... which makes him the grandfather of our modern day calculator."[56]

In keeping with many other Renaissance thinkers, Napier did not confine himself to mathematics alone.

> *"Amongst his other 'Secret Inventions' ... is ... a precursor of the tank; a ship which could travel under water; a burning mirror which would consume enemy ships ... and an artillery piece ... His ingenuity extended also to farming ... using salt as a fertiliser [and] other novel ideas for tilling the soil"*[57]

By the time the Tower came into the hands of Edinburgh Corporation in 1935 it had been the subject of much alteration in the course of its history. Over the 30 years up to the mid 1950s, various additions were demolished and emergency repairs carried out, particularly with regard to strengthening the roof and replacing missing slates. Throughout this time the building remained unoccupied except for temporary use by the National Fire Service during the Second World War until, in 1956, it was proposed that the Tower should be restored as far as possible to its 15th century condition and should form the centrepiece of a new technical college planned by the City to be named after John Napier. This college was the precursor to the present Napier University.

The Historic Buildings Council for Scotland was involved from the earliest stages and it was on their recommendation that approval was given for a grant towards its restoration by the Ministry of Works. In 1958, as part of a shared initiative by the City Architect's Department, the Ministry of Works and the Royal Commission on Ancient Monuments, work was begun on integrating the Tower into a series of new buildings intended to house the college.[58]

Initial work on the Tower was largely concerned with making sure that weak or dangerous sections resulting from careless alterations and poor workmanship were rendered safe. However, the major task was the detective work required in differentiating original or early building from a host of later additions, both architecturally and structurally inferior. This was a complex process since the Tower had been the subject of many changes in its three centuries of history. These additions had almost obliterated the original building and the proposal to restore the Tower as an integral part of the new college buildings, while simultaneously establishing its separate identity, presented a significant challenge to architects and restorers.

> *"The alterations carried out after 1800, being for the most part incidental to the attachment of other buildings, naturally did nothing to enhance the appearance of the tower as a free-standing building, and indeed did much to mar it. In these circumstances a purely conservative preservation has not been feasible, and a bold policy of reconstruction has been adopted. The junction with the new College has been calculated to make the tower truly the heart of the College without compromising its essential free-standing character ...The resulting amalgam of fifteenth and seventeenth century features will in fact be of a kind which never existed at any one time in the history of the tower, but which will nevertheless be a fair reflection of its past, and – it is hoped – a seemly piece of architecture."*[59]

Decisions regarding external work were the first priority, the interior being left until further detective work on establishing as far as possible the nature of the original had taken place. However, once building work was underway external work was accompanied by a radical renewal and remodelling of the interior with conservators striving to identify as much of the original structure as possible. Merchiston Tower today is very much the centrepiece of the college buildings and is in no way diminished in impact by the 1960s architecture which surrounds it.

11 REMOVAL AND INSTALLATION AT MERCHISTON TOWER

The ongoing project at Merchiston Tower suggested the fortuitous possibility of a home for the ceiling which would allow conservators to maintain it within a context largely contemporary with the date of its creation. Indeed it is highly likely that the owners of Prestongrange were known to the Napiers, most particularly the Morisons, since John Morison, who bought Prestongrange in 1609, was treasurer of the City of Edinburgh in 1588 four years before Sir Archibald Napier received additional land from the Town Council in recognition of his contribution to the defence of the City.[60]

By May 1964 the decision had been taken by the National Trust and the Ministry of Public Building and Works to remove the ceiling from Prestongrange and transfer it to workshops provided by Edinburgh Corporation at Links Place in Leith, where preservation work would be carried out.

The painted surface was protected by covering with tissue and the location of each piece marked. The additional flooring in the room above was removed, followed by the boards themselves, and the beams were then lowered from the ceiling by use of block and tackle.[61]

The boards had suffered extensive damage on the back from woodworm infestation, which probably occurred when they came into contact with 19th century timber during Playfair's alterations and the laying of the additional floor in the room above.[62] Removal of the ceiling from its original location made the work of treating woodworm infestation easier, since the boards were fumigated in a special chamber. Extensive repair and strengthening work was carried out by the addition of timber supports to the back of the boards.

The painted surface itself required extensive work due to the flaking and powdering of the paint layers. This required the impregnation of the surface with a fungicide in a gelatin medium. However, emphasis was on preservation of the original with minimum restoration:.

> *"No repainting, design reconstruction or retouching of the paintings will take place. The integrity of the original work will be maintained throughout. Missing areas will be repaired and tinted in neutral tones to 'lose' them against the decoration of the ceiling."*[63]

This hands off approach offers an interesting contrast with the 'bold reconstruction' undertaken at Merchiston Tower by the same body of conservators, illustrating how each individual conservation and restoration project must be approached with an awareness of the unique nature of each project. While the painstaking process of repairing damage and protecting the ceiling from further deterioration was ongoing, work continued on the restoration and reconstruction of the interior of Merchiston Tower.

The eventual transfer of the ceiling to the Tower was not an easy task. Firstly, the ceiling in its present form was too large for its new home. Before installation it was necessary to record the original layout of the ceiling, remove sections for which space was not available and rearrange the boards. This offered the advantage of allowing for the removal of sections which had suffered damage when fireplaces were inserted in the room above. However, the paintings on these boards, now stored in an attic space above the ceiling include images from de Vries' 1565 *Caryatidum.*

> *"Movement of parts was kept to a minimum as far as the different room shape would allow...It was felt that altering the relationship of component parts was justified on this account and in view of the fact that the juxtaposition of motifs appear to be quite arbitrary and in no way following a continuous narrative."*[64]

Given the nature of the Tower with its fortress-like walls, limited doorways and narrow windows, the actual process of introducing the ceiling into the third floor board room presented a significant challenge. Beams and boards were delivered to the site by lorry, where they were lifted by block and tackle to the roof of an adjoining building then passed, beam by beam, through a narrow window on the upper floor measuring approximately 3′ square.[65] The component parts were then assembled to form the Council Chamber's ceiling.

Since its installation at Merchiston in 1964 responsibility for maintenance of the condition of the ceiling has been shared between Napier University and Historic Scotland. Equipment was installed to measure humidity to ensure that the environment provided is appropriate to its preservation and various maintenance tasks have been undertaken including the removal of dust layers[66] and further treatment against beetle infestation with a product selected to avoid undue staining of the painted surface.[67]

12 EPILOGUE FROM PRESTOUNGRANGE 2004

In 2001 the present and 14th Baron of Prestoungrange purchased the Prestoungrange Gothenburg Tavern in Prestonpans with the intention of restoring both its delightful arts and crafts interior and simultaneously returning the public house to the Gothenburg principles on which it had been founded in 1908. The Gothenburg movement of the late 19th and early 20th centuries was based on principles first enunciated by the City Fathers of Goteborg in Sweden i.e. to encourage the working population to avoid alcoholic excess. When The Gothenburg opened its doors in Prestonpans in 1908 it accordingly offered bonuses to its managers solely for the sale of food and non-alcoholic refreshment. After 5% return on capital invested had gone to the original investors the remainder of the profit was directed towards enhancing the recreational life of the local community. These principles have been re-established for The Prestoungrange Gothenburg as it opens its doors in 2004.[68]

Restoration has been a major project of great significance for the community. The opportunity has been taken inter alia to restore an element of local saliency to the 'lost' Prestongrange Ceiling. The main bar area named after the founding manager from 1908–1927, James Fewell, now provides a home for a piece of new Prestoungrange ceiling art consciously executed in the style that Mark Ker used some 423 years earlier at the baronial hall. Andrew Crummy, an internationally recognised painter and mural artist from East Lothian, received the commission. He had already made a significant contribution to the Prestoungrange Murals Trail which has unfolded across the town of Prestonpans since 2000.

Andrew Crummy researched and prepared the details now included on the 'new' Prestoungrange Gothenburg ceiling. As well as key elements from the original ceiling, in the best ancient traditions of the grotto the new ceiling contains images of people and places associated with the town's history. Amongst them are the 1st and 14th Barons of Prestoungrange, David Spence whose inspiration led to the foundation of the Prestongrange Industrial Heritage Museum, and East Lothian Provost Pat O'Brien who assisted the preservation of The Gothenburg in the 1980s. Not least are portraits of a local craftsmen who worked on the Prestoungrange Gothenburg restoration in 2003–2004 together with a human skull from the 1745 Battle of Prestonpans which he found as a lad, and of Jim Forster, President of the Historical Society.

As with the original Prestongrange ceiling the background colour is the very attractive red oxide with an intensity that would have been present in 1581. The colours used are red oxide, white, mid grey and black outline again as in 1581. The paints employed was a quality flat oil which gives no reflection and artist's oils. Such a use of oils is similar to English Renaissance painting of the period where oil was often substituted for size as a binding medium. It is intended to avoid the problems of deterioration that Hodkinson's Report to the National Trust Tempera Paintings Committee outlined and which are associated with tempera painting in an environment which also houses a bar and a micro-brewery. Additionally it allowed a varnish to be added to further protect the painted surface.

The 'new' Prestoungrange ceiling at The Prestoungrange Gothenburg is a most substantial work of art in its own right. But it is very much to be hoped and expected that it will act as a fillip for visits by arrangement to Merchiston Tower at Napier University to view the original in all its glory.

NOTES

1 This sub-title is taken from Shakespeare's *Macbeth* written less than 20 years after the completion of the Prestongrange Ceiling. The play echoes much of the thematic content of the Ceiling

2 Apted, M.R., *The Painted Ceilings of Scotland 1550–1650*, 1966, pp. 2–3

3 Baker, S., *Prestongrange House*, Prestoungrange History Series No. 1, 2000, p. 11

4 Murray, G., Apted, M.R., and Hodkinson, I., 'Prestongrange and its Painted Ceiling', in *Transactions of the East Lothian Antiquarian and Field Naturalist's Society*, Vol X, 1966, p. 112

5 Hodkinson, I.S. and Adams, W.R., *The 16th Century Painted Ceiling at Prestongrange House*, National Trust for Scotland – Scottish Tempera Paintings Committee, Technical Report 1963

6 Mackay, S., *Behind the Facade: Four Centuries of Scottish Interiors*, Royal Commission on Ancient and Historic Monuments of Scotland, 1995, p. 24

7 Op cit., Murray, G., Apted, M.R., and Hodkinson, I., p. 123

8 Op cit., Apted, M.R., p. 89

9 Bath, M., *Renaissance Decorative Painting in Scotland*, 2003, p. 10

10 Ibid, p. 131

11 Ibid, p. 57

12 Op cit, Bath, M., p. 8

13 Op cit., Murray, G., Apted, M.R., and Hodkinson, I., p. 126

14 Op cit, Bath, M.., p. 59
15 Op cit, Mackay, S., p. 25
16 Op cit, Bath, M., p. 107
17 Vitruvius, *Treatise On Architecture*, Book VII, circa 15BC
18 Op cit, Bath, M., chapter 5
19 Ibid, p. 30
20 Ibid, chapter 3
21 Ibid, pp. 79–80
22 Op cit, Baker, S.
23 Op cit, Murray, G., Apted, M.R., and Hodkinson, I., p. 125
24 Ibid p. 99
25 Ibid pp. 102, 104
26 Op cit, Bath, M., p. 223
27 Op cit, Baker, S., pp. 43–47
28 Op cit, Hodkinson, I.S. and Adams, W.R.
29 Op cit, Murray, G., Apted, M.R. and Hodkinson, I., p. 114
30 *Tower of Merchiston: brief notes on its history and restoration*, undated document, Napier University Library
31 Op cit, Hodkinson, I.S..and Adams, W.R.
32 Op cit, Murray, G., Apted, M.R., and Hodkinson, I., p. 126
33 Ibid, p. 127
34 Op cit, Bath, M., p. 57
35 Op cit, Bath, M., pp. 116–118
36 For a detailed survey of the sources for images which appear on the Prestongrange Ceiling, see *op cit*, Bath, M., chapter 5. I am greatly indebted to Dr. Bath for his exhaustive examination of these sources.
37 Snowden, R., personal communication
38 Scotstarvet, *The Staggering State of Scottish Statesmen 1550–1650*, as quoted in *Transactions of the East Lothian Antiquarian and Field Naturalist's Society*, Vol. X, 1966, p. 121
39 Murray, M., *The Witch Cult in Western Europe: a Study in Anthropology*, 1921, p. 28
40 Wright, W. (Publisher), *Newes from Scotland. Declaring the damnable Life of Doctor Fian*, 1592
41 Pugh, R.J.M., *The Deil's Ain*, 2001, p. xii
42 Ibid, Appendix 5
43 *Tell Us a Story: Memories of East Lothian*, East Lothian Library Services and School of Scottish Studies, 2002, p.137
44 Florio, J., '*A World of Words*', as quoted in *Transactions of the East Lothian Antiquarian and Field Naturalist's Society*, Vol. X, 1966, p. 113
45 Thomson, P., *The Term and Concept 'Grotesque': A Historical Summary*, Methuen Critical Idiom Series, 1972
46 Op cit, Hodkinson, I.S. and Adams, W.R.
47 Ibid
48 Ibid
49 Ibid
50 Ibid
51 Ibid
52 Ibid
53 Op cit, Mackay, S., p. 25
54 Op cit, Murray, G., Apted, M.R., and Hodkinson, I., p. 124
55 Smith, C.J., *Historic South Edinburgh*, Vol. 1, 1978, p. 87
56 Napier University, *Merchiston Tower Edinburgh*, undated
57 Ibid
58 Arnet, H. and Harris, S., 'The Tower of Merchiston', in *The Book of the Old Edinburgh Club*, Vol 31, 1962, pp. 13–14
59 Ibid, p. 29
60 Ibid, p. 6
61 Snowden, R., personal communication
62 Hodkinson, I., *The 16th Century Painted Ceiling from Prestongrange House*, National Trust for Scotland – Scottish Tempera Paintings Committee, Technical Notes, 1964
63 Ibid
64 Op cit, Murray, G., Apted, M.R., and Hodkinson, I., p. 124
65 Snowden, R., personal communication
66 Currie, J.W., *Merchiston Tower Painted Ceiling Report*, Historic Scotland Conservation Centre, 1988
67 Hemmett, R.F., *Merchiston Castle – Napier University: Prestongrange House – Painted Ceiling report*, Historic Scotland Conservation Centre, 1999

68 Prestoungrange, G., *The Prestoungrange Gothenburg: the Goth's first 90 years and the coming decade*, Prestoungrange History Series No. 13, 2002

BIBLIOGRAPHY

Baker, S., *Prestongrange House*, 2000, Prestoungrange History Series No.1, Prestoungrange University Press, 2000

Bath, M., *Renaissance Decorative Painting in Scotland*, NMS Publishing, 2003

Currie, J.W., *Merchiston Tower Painted Ceiling Report*, Historic Scotland Conservation Centre, 1988

Apted, M.R., *The Painted Ceilings of Scotland 1550–1650*, HMSO, 1966

Arnet, H. and Harris, S., 'The Tower of Merchiston', in *The Book of the Old Edinburgh Club*, Vol. 31, 1962, pp. 13–14

Hemmett, R.F., *Merchiston Castle – Napier University: Prestongrange House – Painted Ceiling Report*, Historic Scotland Conservation Centre, 1999

Hodkinson, I.S., *The 16th Century Painted Ceiling from Prestongrange House*, National Trust for Scotland – Scottish Tempera Paintings Committee, Technical Notes, 1964

Hodkinson, I.S. and Adams, W.R., *The 16th Century Painted Ceiling at Prestongrange House*, National Trust for Scotland – Scottish Tempera Paintings Committee, Technical Report 1963

Mackay, S., *Behind the Facade: Four Centuries of Scottish Interiors*, Royal Commission on Ancient and Historic Monuments of Scotland, 1995

Murray, M., *The Witch Cult in Western Europe: a Study in Anthropology*, 1921

Murray, G., Apted, M.R. and Hodkinson, I.S., 'Prestongrange and its Painted Ceiling', in *Transactions of the East Lothian Antiquarian and Field Naturalist's Society*, Vol. X, 1966

Napier University, *Merchiston Tower Edinburgh*, undated

Prestoungrange, G., *The Prestoungrange Gothenburg: the Goth's first 90 years and the coming decade*, Prestoungrange History Series No. 13, Prestoungrange University Press, 2002

Pugh, R.J.M., *The Deil's Ain*, Harlaw Heritage, 2001

Smith, C.J., *Historic South Edinburgh*, Vol. 1, 2nd Ed. Birlinn, 2000

Tell Us a Story: Memories of East Lothian, East Lothian Library Services and School of Scottish Studies, 2002

Thomson, P., *The Term and Concept 'Grotesque': A Historical Summary*, Methuen Critical Idiom Series, 1972

Tower of Merchiston: brief notes on its history and restoration, Napier University Library, undated

Vitruvius, *Treatise On Architecture*, Book VII, circa 15 B.C.

Wright, W., (Publisher), *Newes from Scotland: Declaring the damnable Life of Doctor Fian*, 1592

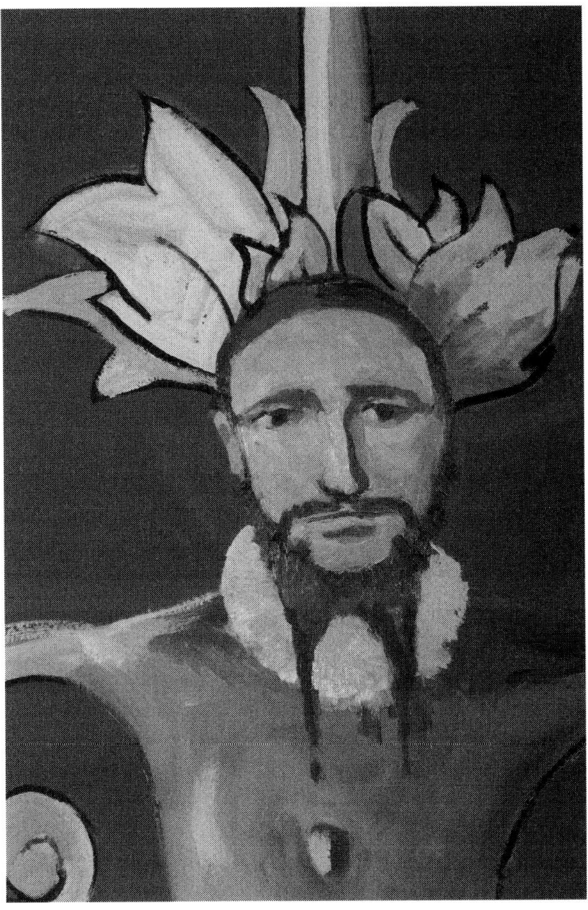

ACKNOWLEDGEMENTS

I am greatly indebted to Dr Michael Bath for his expertise and advice. Grateful thanks also to Mr. Rab Snowden, Senior Conservator (retired), Historic Scotland Conservation Centre, Sheila Barcroft of Napier University Library and Liz Wood of Historic Scotland. The majority of the images used in this booklet were created by Michael Tracey, a photographer with strong local connections, who was present when the ceiling was first uncovered in the 1960s. Finally my personal appreciation of Andrew Crummy as he brought back to Prestoungrange his bold and salient reminder of the baronial heritage, an appreciation shared by all his colleagues in the Baron Courts' Arts Festival team.

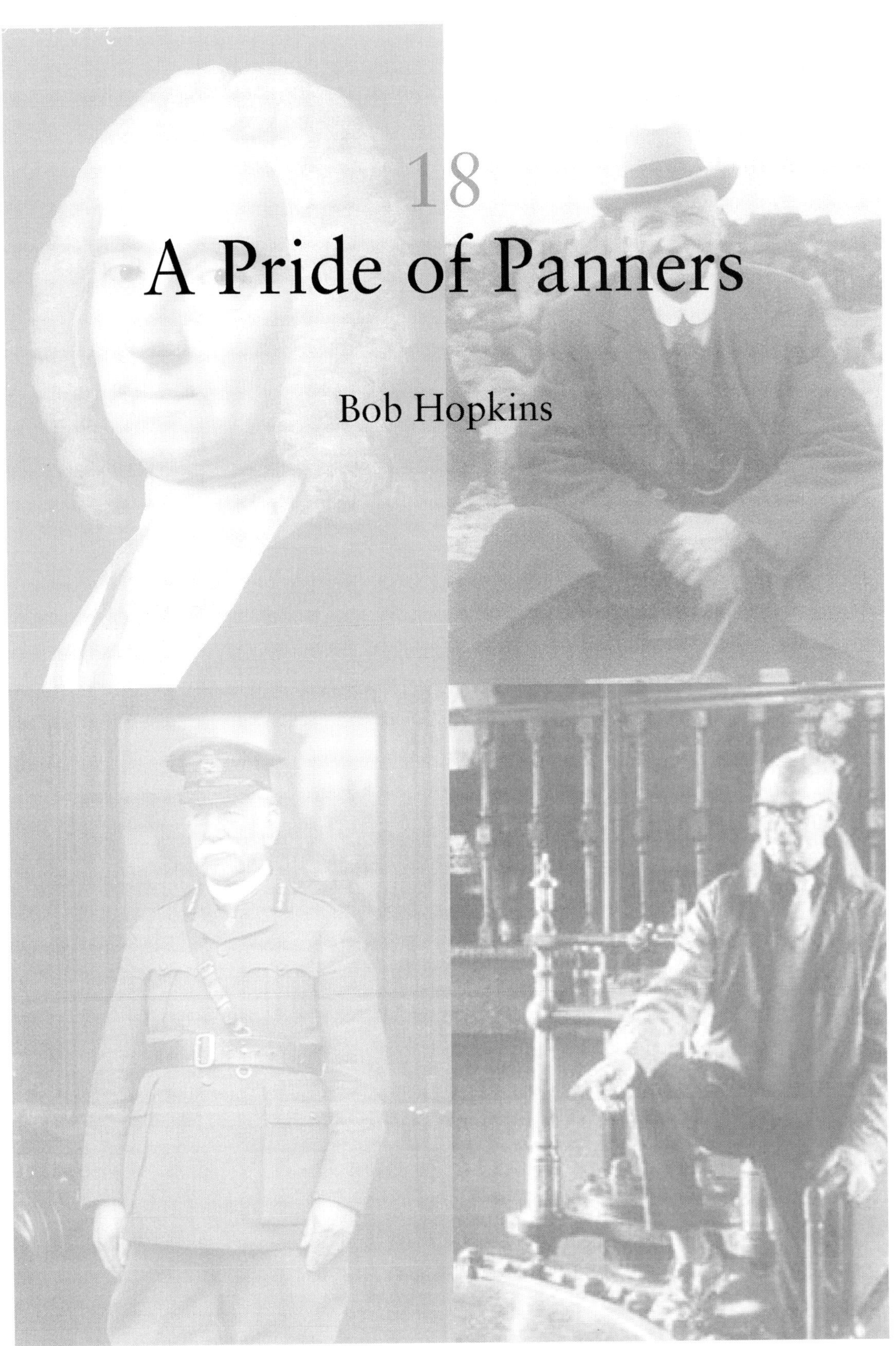

18
A Pride of Panners

Bob Hopkins

INTRODUCTION

It is a responsible pleasure to offer these thirteen short biographies of some of the most conspicuously successful people whose lives were associated with Prestonpans. What each one of them achieved in their quite disparate vocations re-lives again here as a beacon to us all of what could be done in their *can-do* worlds. They are indeed A Pride of Panners.

These pages share tales of the battlefield medicine of **Alexander Thomas** at work with Florence Nightingale in the Crimea and the inspiration during **Sir Walter Scott's** youthful convalescence for *Waverley's* recounting of the Battle of Prestonpans. The John Muir Way which passess along the shores of Prestonpans links us with the legendary **John Muir**, the inspirer of America's and later the world's National Parks Movement. They tell of the civic medicine of **William McEwan** aided by his two sons in Prestonpans across 40 years, his role as Provost in ensuring somewhat cleaner air, better education services and the town's new Library. They tell of **Alexander Hume**'s pioneering Latin grammar and the extraordinary benefactions of **James Schaw** and **Mary Murray** providing the burgh with an excellent 18th Century School for Boys and an equally admirable Victorian Girls' School for Domestic Servants.

They tell of Prestonpans' association with two Lords Advocate of Scotland and Lords of Sessions and of the outstanding lifetime contribution of **Lady Susan Grant-Suttie**. These larger than life aristocratic personalities presided as **Lord Prestoungrange** over the post 1745 attainders, served at Westminster in the Union Parliaments and on the Parish Council, ensured the establishment of a Coffee House in the town, the construction of the Town Hall after years of wrangling and the kidnapping of his own wife by **Lord Grange**.

Amidst such tales Church Ministers are not to be outdone. They are represented by **John Davidson** the founding Minister at Prestongrange Church, exiled to the burgh for his opposition to King James VI, and **Patrick Mackay**. Mackay was the second Free Church Minister who was a missionary across the Colonial world whilst conducting his ministry in Prestonpans where he successfully mediated in the Miners' Strike at Prestongrange of 1893.

And they tell most recently of the heroic role that **David Spence** played at Prestongrange in initially establishing the Scottish Mining Museum there, preserving key features including the pit's steam engines, beam engine, brickworks and shaping the Museum's parklands.

Inevitably there is a host of biographies that could, indeed *should*, have been included here of which we are unaware – some nationally famed some heroes of our local community. There are also many more of which we are only too well aware but they have already been honoured in this series Volumes 1–17 – such as our brewers, our potters and the distinguished founders of our Gothenburg.

For each and every one of these may we hope to understand the meaning of their lives and let us take pride in what they achieved in and for our burgh.

Stained glass at Grange Church to commemorate the life of Dr Patrick Mackay

1 THOMAS ALEXANDER

Adequate medical care for military personnel in the field regardless of nation is something which is now both expected and taken for granted. Any serviceman or woman, who naturally becomes ill or are injured in the course of their various duties will today receive a high standard of medical or surgical attention. It was not, of course, always thus. The lifetime of Thomas Alexander saw the comprehensive transformation of attitude and actuality.

Dr. Thomas Alexander, C.B., F.R.C.S. (Edinburgh), was born in Prestonpans, East Lothian on 6 May 1812 and spent his entire working life endeavouring to improve the medical and hygiene conditions experienced by service personnel on active service. He was the first child and the only son of William Alexander and his wife Helen Kemp. They had been married at Athelstaneford in East Lothian on 18 December 1809 but lived in Prestonpans where William worked as a flesher; and they remained in the Pans until both died in 1865. They also begat four sisters to Thomas – Isabella, Helen, Jane and Margaret.

Peter McNeill writing in *Prestonpans and Vicinity* asserts that during his early years in the town young Thomas Alexander always intended to become a doctor of medicine. He eventually followed that vocation at both the Universities of Paris and Edinburgh – funded by his father William who was by then a prominent and wealthy salt manufacturer in Prestonpans.

At Edinburgh, his primary tutor was the internationally acclaimed anatomist Robert Knox, who had himself previously served as an army surgeon at Waterloo. Knox had gone on record as being greatly disturbed by the truly basic amenities that were available to deal with the wounded among Wellington's troops in Belgium. It may well have been the influence of Knox, allied to the fact that Edinburgh University boasted a Regius Professorship of Military Surgery from as early as 1806, that persuaded Alexander to make his own medical career in the military. He qualified as a surgeon on 9 June 1831 – at what would seem the extraordinarily youthful age of 19 – and on 10 October 1834 accepted the position of Assistant Surgeon, Second Class, in the British Army. (There was no automatic commissioned rank accorded to army doctors at the time.)

Even on his first posting to the West Indies, where he spent the first five and a half years of his military service, he was appalled by the lack of hygiene and general deficiency of medical provision available to army personnel. From that moment on he made it his primary objective to ameliorate that situation – frequently to his own personal detriment. On numerous occasions during the early and middle parts of his service, Dr. Alexander was threatened by his commanding officers with the possibility that he might lose his post because of the unconventional methods he adopted to aid his patients. But he was seemingly never intimidated and continued to insist on proper sanitary checks and conditions throughout his service. Yet that insistence alone often failed to combat the prevalent disease and fevers which raged in the theatres of war where he served.

He returned to Britain for only a few months after his tour of duty in the West Indies and then spent time in Quebec. He had a serious difference of opinion there with his senior officer concerning the supply of wine to sick troops. Dr Alexander also served in the so called 'Kaffir Wars' in Africa from 1851 to 1853 where he was again dismayed with all the servicemen's living conditions – but particularly those who became sick – and was able to obtain reluctant permission for proper huts and the provision of gardens in which the soldiers could spend time while convalescing.

Over the years, everywhere he went Dr Alexander maintained his high standards relating to the health care of his men. In Bulgaria, for example, when pestilence appeared in his Division and men were sinking fast with little medicine or proper food available, as superintending surgeon, Alexander called the regimental officers to a meeting and said:

> *"Gentlemen, you are to purchase on my authority, at any cost, everything necessary for your sick that you can lay your hands on. You are to pour gold down their throats if it will save their lives; and if the country will not allow the charge, I will pay for it myself."*

Despite his undisputed surgical ability it took him twenty years to attain the rank of First Class Surgeon. There can be little doubt that this was due to his constant conflict with authority.

At Work in the Crimea

The true watershed so far as Alexander's ambitions were concerned, coincided with the "Eastern Expedition" – or Crimean War. The Doctor travelled with the Expeditionary Force to Gallipoli and Scutari in Turkey in 1854 where he was attached to the Light Division. In medical terms things were extremely bad at these initial staging posts. Typhus and cholera were rife and many soldiers died. At Gallipoli Dr. Alexander again incurred the wrath of commanders by impounding all the available blankets for his sick patients.

During the Crimean conflict, Alexander's efforts were greatly aided by *The London Times* correspondent, Dr. W. H. Russell, who had also traveled to Turkey with the Expeditionary Force and began to file alarming reports of deficiencies in overall organisation, administration and lack of proper medical facilities. In his later reports Russell often spoke favourably of Dr. Alexander's achievements in the field. The correspondent described the surgeon as *"a gentle giant of a Scotchman sitting on a beach with a man's leg on his lap while pouring out the vials of wrath on Sir John Hall (Senior Deputy Medical Inspector General) for landing an army without medical supplies"*. In another report Russell described how *"Dr. Alexander, at Inkermann, for hour after hour, day after day, toiled through scenes which those who have not witnessed a battlefield, and the terrors of a hospital tent, can neither imagine nor conceive, and upheld the noblest sense of duty"*.

At the end of August 1854 the allied armies transferred specifically to the Crimea peninsular where the British contingent was located at Varma although the main hospital complex remained behind at Scutari. Dr. Alexander went with the army to Varma and was shortly afterwards appointed Senior Medical Officer in the field. He remained always at the front line and served with distinction at the subsequent battles of Alma, Balaklava and the infamous carnage of Sebastapol – where the French lost no less than six thousand and the British three thousand men. Following the storming of Sebastapol during September 1855 Russell reported: *"it is most creditable to the medical officers in charge – Dr. Alexander and his surgeons – that all these men were in their bed, had their wounds dressed and their wants attended to, by eight o'clock that same evening"*.

The Doctor was now consistently being 'Mentioned-in-Despatches'. He ministered to those cavalry personnel that survived – following the ill considered, ill fated 'Charge of the Light Brigade' – 247 of the 'Gallant Six Hundred' died.

One of Thomas Alexander's greatest conflicts with authority arose during the Crimean campaign when he insisted on the use of the new anaesthetic, chloroform, which was still at that time considered unproven. (Dr. Alexander was an Edinburgh University contemporary of its developer, James Young Simpson, and to reinforce his argument for using the new anaesthetic he was able to point out the product's favourable effect on Queen Victoria during the birth of Prince Leopold!)

Dr. Alexander was now recognised as extremely efficient and very often – as with the use of chloroform – a pioneer in new medical and surgical techniques. An excerpt from the 1906 book, *From Midshipman to Field Marshall* by Field Marshall Sir Evelyn Wood, F.M. V.C. shows how the approach of Dr. Alexander was often at great odds with convention.

During the Crimean War, Sir Evelyn suffered severe damage to his right arm while on a gun emplacement. In his own account he states: "*I was taken to a doctor – an Irishman – whom I had known for some time, and was greeted warmly with the exclamation 'sit down, my dear boy', and 'I'll have your arm off before you know where you are'. I steadily, but with some difficulty, evaded his kind attention and was put into a stretcher and carried to camp by four Bluejackets.*"

Sir Evelyn waited in the operating tent for his turn to be seen. He continues: "*When my turn came, I had a heated argument with the surgeons who wished to amputate my arm above the elbow ... All but the Senior Doctor wished to take off my arm. ... The eight who were for removing the limb declared that it was impossible that any use could be obtained from the arm the elbow joint of which had been shattered. To prove that it was not I, doubling my fist, raised the arm as high as I could until the case shot met the fore and upper arm, on which the Senior Medical Officer decided he would at all events try to save the limb*". Dr. Alexander was the Senior Medical Officer.

In addition to battle injuries the entire Crimean project was continually blighted by diseases including cholera, typhus, scurvy and rheumatism. Loss of manpower was great. Those who became very ill, or so severely wounded that they would never likely fight again, were carried on stretchers to the dock and from there repatriated by ship to the Scutari hospital complex. At least in the early days, that was too often a pointless exercise as the soldiers' constitutions were too weakened to combat the prevailing bad conditions.

Late in 1854 however, Scutari was the locus of an event which proved to be of profound assistance to the endeavours of Dr. Alexander. Florence Nightingale, 'The Lady of the Lamp', arrived there from Britain and brought with her a group of experienced nurses. *The London Times* reports filed by Russell – and letters home from serving soldiers – are often credited with having given Nightingale the key motivation to make that journey.

Initially her presence, although unsought, was tolerated by most of the army authorities. But she was never accepted, indeed her actions were invariably condemned, by the Deputy Medical Director General Sir John Hall. There arose a strong mutual dislike of each other which was to last a lifetime – and from which Sir John Hall was to be an ultimate loser.

Working with Florence Nightingale

The overall tolerance evinced by the military authorities however, soon turned to annoyance. Unlike Dr. Alexander she was in no manner constrained by military rules and regulations, and she took no cognisance of what were considered "normal channels." Florence Nightingale was calm, determined and, despite opposition, usually succeeded in what she set out to achieve. She was also a consummate politician who had a long association with Sidney Herbert, and through him a direct line to Government. Her other long time friend and supporter, Lord Palmerston, became Prime Minister in January 1855 and appointed yet another personal friend Lord Panmure, as his Secretary for War.

On arrival at Scutari, Nightingale had observed that hospital mattresses were infected and unhygienic so she burned them and had them replaced with proper beds – regardless of cost. She also procured new dressings and blankets. Her overall success in improving general conditions can be measured by the mortality rate at Scutari Hospital – it fell from 42% to 4%. She was revered by her patients and not surprisingly became a good friend – and later mentor – of Dr. Alexander.

An enduring relationship of mutual benefit and respect developed between Florence Nightingale and Thomas Alexander. On returning home from the Crimea he was mentioned in a House of Commons address and recommended by the then Director General of the Army Medical Services – Dr. Sir Andrew Smith – for promotion to Local Inspector General for services during the Russian War. He had not however endeared himself to everyone in military authority – particularly Sir John Hall – and two months after his return to Britain, Dr. Alexander was posted to Canada as Principal Medical Officer, which some thought to be exile and a second class appointment.

But his tour in Canada was very brief. Developments and improvements in military medicine emanating from the Crimea, many of which were directly due to him and had been greatly enhanced by the efforts of Sidney Herbert and Florence Nightingale, had greatly improved his esteem in England. A Royal Commission was established, chaired by Lord Panmure, to examine the standards of hygiene and overall sanitary conditions which should in future be expected throughout the British Army. Florence Nightingale was asked to suggest members for that body of enquiry and her consultations included her personal doctor, John Sutherland. Dr. Sutherland advised Nightingale: "*Get Alexander. Nobody else if you cannot. He is our man.*"

So Thomas Alexander was recalled from what would be his last overseas posting to serve on Lord Panmure's Royal Commission. He was especially nominated to formulate the new rules for the hygienic administration of army barracks and hospitals. These proposals and changes, together with their implementation, would occupy him for the remainder of his life.

Director General in 1858

Early in 1858 the Director General of Army Medical Services, Dr. Sir Andrew Smith, indicated his intention to retire. Miss Nightingale, in keeping with her intense dislike which originated in the Crimea, denied Sir John Hall the promotion which he undoubtedly would have expected. Dr. Alexander had the honour to replace Sir Andrew Smith as Director General and was officially Gazetted on June 11 1858. He was also appointed as an Honorary Surgeon to

Queen Victoria and created Companion of the Order of the Bath. Of note however, it was a Companion not a Knight that he became – unlike his predecessor. In that same year he was also appointed Fellow of the Royal College of Surgeons in Edinburgh.

During the final two years of his life he was London based and worked from his study in Norfolk Square. His contact with Florence Nightingale continued and he met at her home on a daily basis with Sidney (later Lord) Herbert as together they explored new regulations and created reports to allow their implementation. Sidney Herbert considered Dr Alexander *"unquestionably the ablest man in the British Medical Service."*

The pressure of work was great and Dr. Alexander was continuously warned of related risks to his own health. On 1st February 1860, at the relatively young age of 47, he died while working at his desk. The cause of death is sometimes recorded as 'gout and inflammation of the nervous system.' The biographer Cecil Woodham Smith however in *Florence Nightingale,* claims that Dr Alexander died suddenly from a brain haemorrhage and goes on to suggest: *"behind his death lay a history of obstruction and petty intrigue. The departmental machine had been strong enough to break him. Men he had trusted, who had been placed in their positions through his recommendation, had betrayed him."*

Although he had effectively left Prestonpans on becoming an army surgeon, Dr. Alexander frequently returned to visit his parents, siblings and many friends in the town. The Census Return of 1851 shows him spending his leave at home with his family in Prestonpans. He therefore remained well known and appropriately his body was brought to Prestonpans and interred in the small family plot which is located just north of the parish church.

The Doctor was survived by his wife Mary Alice but there is little record of her – or of where they had married and they apparently had no children. The Doctor's father, William, dealt with all the funeral arrangements and issued personal hand written invitations to attend the event. On the day itself local shops and businesses closed as a mark of deep respect and our fishermen did not go to sea. The funeral procession is said to have "stretched the full length of the village".

Memorial in Prestonpans

Shortly after the burial, a memorial was commissioned by the townspeople from a public subscription that reached a total of two hundred pounds. And The Thomas Alexander Trust Fund was established for a triennial essay competition on matters relating to military medicine – the Prize being a gold medal and fifty pounds.

The Prestonpans statue was created by the well known artist William Brodie, R.S.A. It was one of Brodie's first works when he had then just completed his training in Rome. The sculpture stands some eight feet high, and shows the Doctor wearing full dress uniform of Director-General of the Army Medical Services including all his military decorations and especially the Cross of the Legion of Honour conferred by the French for Crimean Service. His figure has his left hand on his sword hilt and right hooked into the belt and proudly stands on an ornate plinth looking out across the sea. The plinth was also created by Brodie and on each side bears the condensed history of Alexander's service. The memorial is located in well tended gardens adjacent

Prestonpans setting of the Alexander statue

to Prestonpans High Street on ground gifted by his father just to the north of the Doctor's grave.

The memorial statue was the first ever to be erected in Prestonpans. The dedication ceremony on 9th September 1862 was attended by many people from throughout East Lothian and elsewhere. Lord Elcho, a long serving 19th Century Member of Parliament for the County, delivered a speech of dedication. Local politicians were also invited to attend. William Alexander was heard to comment more than once on how much the finished statue captured the image of his late son. Florence Nightingale was also invited but was prevented by illness from doing so. She did however write a letter read by Lord Elcho prior to dedication of the statue, most of which is recorded in the *Medical News* of 4 October 1862.

Miss Nightingale wrote as below and hearing the contents of her letter formed the culmination of Lord Elcho's speech as the statue was uncovered:

> *"I must be ill indeed, not to say my word for Doctor Alexander ... I can truly say I have never seen his like for directness of purpose, unflinching moral courage and honesty ... ... Everywhere – at Gallipoli, where he seized the blankets for his sick – in Bulgaria where he fought such a fight for his men in the opening prologue to the Crimean tragedy itself he showed the same fearless devotion, incurring thereby a serious personal responsibility, in*

order that his men might not perish. ... ... When the "Royal Commission on the Sanitary State of the Army" was issued, Dr. Alexander's service on it was considered so necessary that he was sent for from Canada. He afterwards served on a no less important, though less well known commission ... as was predicted more than once to him, he fell at his post as true a sacrifice to duty as if he had fallen in the field ... ..."

Bibliography

The British Expedition to the Crimea by W. H. Russell, LL.D., Routledge, 1858
From Midshipman to Field Marshall, Sir Evelyn Wood, Methuen & Co., 1906
Letters from the Crimea, Captain Robert Portal, 1900
The Light Cavalry Brigade in the Crimea (extracts from the letters and journal of the late General Lord Paget, 1881)
Medical & Surgical History of the British Army in the years 1854, 1855, 1856. 2434, Vol.2
Florence Nightingale, Cecil Woodham Smith, Constable, 1949
Prestonpans and Vicinity, Peter McNeill
Florence Nightingale and The Crimea, H.M. Stationery Office, 2000
The Haddingtonshire Courier (reports)
Medical News and Gazette (reports)
Caledonian Mercury (Sept 12 1862)
Weekly Scotsman (Sept 13 1862)
United Service Gazette (1860)
News of the World – Portrait Gallery of Eminent Personages (Oct 4 1862)

The author of the following poem, 'C.D.E. Prestonpans, 6 February 1860' is unknown. It was written on the day of Dr Alexander's funeral and subsequently published in the *Haddingtonshire Courier.*

THOMAS ALEXANDER

Lay down now his noble head,
Sorrowing ye who loved him best,
He has fought a gallant fight,
Let him take his quiet rest.

Not mid crowded piles of dead,
'Midst a city's strife and roar,
In an acre of the Lord,
Sloping to a rockbound shore.

Fitting 'tis that he should lie,
In the ancient sea washed town,
Where 'midst needy ones his hand,
Often shed rich bounties down.

Let no show of funeral pomp
Seek to blazon forth his fame;
For the greatness of his worth
Clasps in deathless arms his fame.

Let a grateful country tell,
How he toiled by night and day;
'Mid the dying and the dead
Casting thought of self away.

Let us thank the God who gave
Grace to be and strength to do,
Made him generous, gentle, kind,
Truly brave and bravely true.

2 JOHN DAVIDSON

Among what written history of Prestonpans endures the lasting contribution of the Rev. John Davidson is constantly mentioned. The church of Preston, together with many others in East Lothian, was summarily destroyed in 1544 by a vengeful invading English army commanded by the Earl of Hertford. In his book *Prestonpans and Vicinity* the 19th Century Tranent historian Peter McNeill states: "*There was still no church or chapel, priest or minister, in Preston or Prestonpans district and this state of affairs continued from the destruction of the church in 1544 till the appointment of Maister John Davidson in 1595.*"

Sketchy 16th century records suggest that Davidson was born circa 1549 in Dunfermline. He died in Prestonpans during September 1604. The contention, that Davidson was a 'Roman Catholic priest before adopting the new teachings of the Reformation' is very unlikely. In 1560, when the Reformation began to take effect, he would have been only 11 years of age. However, an extract from McCrie, John Knox's biographer, if taken at face value, appears to cast doubt on Davidson's correct birthday. McCrie states: "John Davidson, who was Melville's predecessor at Glasgow, was a clergyman before the Reformation, and had studied at Paris along with Quintin Kennedy, Abbot of Crossraguel who died in 1564. Having returned to Scotland, Davidson was placed in 1557 at the head of the college in Glasgow." Andrew Melville was certainly Principal of Glasgow University from 1574 so if McCrie is accurate Davidson must have been born earlier than 1549.

It is thought much more likely that he entered St. Leonard's College at St. Andrews in 1567 where he gained his Bachelor in 1569 and Masters in 1570 (which are shown in the records of St Leonard's College). He may well have continued his studies in Paris before returning to Scotland and Davidson was indeed raised initially as a Roman Catholic in Dunfermline. However, prior to leaving that town for St Andrews he became something of a protégé to an early Reforming minister named Ferguson and it was probably at St Andrews that he first met John Knox since he preached there regularly.

At odds with Regent Mortimer and James VI

Apart from debate regarding his birth date there is a consistency about

Davidson's lifetime work, achievements and tribulations. Like other prominent Reformers such as Knox and Melville he was constantly at odds with the monarchy and its thoughts concerning church administration. Despite the infant King James VI being educated in a manner intended to encourage his wholehearted adoption of the new religion, attempts were often made by the King, his Regents and advisors to reintroduce an episcopacy to an unwilling people.

Davidson was a prolific, if not greatly accomplished, author of both prose and poetry. Throughout his career, he constantly confronted the monarchy. One of his first poems entitled *Ane Dialog, or Mutual Talking betuix a Clerk and ane Courteour* was responsible for the first recorded serious repercussion of this confrontation.

The Regent Morton had decided to amalgamate several parishes under the control of one Minister contrary to the wishes of the General Assembly. Davidson considered, in all probability correctly, that the real reason for that amalgamation was to provide Morton personally with funds from the church. This motivated Davidson to write his poem which was printed by Robert Leprevick without authority in St Andrews during 1573.

On reading the publication the Earl of Morton was furious. The printer Leprevick was subsequently held captive for a time in Edinburgh Castle. Davidson was called to account in Haddington where he was held captive but for only a day. Davidson admitted authorship of the offending poem but was released in the hope that he would retract his allegations and be censured by either or both the University of St. Andrews or the General Assembly. No such censure occured nor did Davidson ever retract his allegations. He did, however, voluntarily exile himself from Scotland for the next three years to avoid the wrath of Regent Morton.

The Kirk made strong representation to Regent Morton concerning the exiled Davidson and the Regent permitted his return to Edinburgh in 1577. Two years later in 1579 Davidson was appointed to his first church at Liberton, Edinburgh.

Morton fell from Royal favour and while awaiting execution in June 1581 for alleged involvement in the murder of Lord Darnley, he made his peace with Davidson. The disgraced Earl allegedly embraced Davidson and said: "Yee wrote a little book indeed; but trulie I meant never evill towards you in my pairt: forgive yee me, and I forgive you". That pre-execution statement of forgiveness is said to have reduced Davidson to tears.

Davidson still courted controversy. By his constant condemnation of King James and his court, together with an outspoken opposition to all religion other than the reformed Kirk, he consistently fell foul of the Duke of Lennox, close friend of the King, and the 'Iron Chancellor' James Stewart, Earl of Arran. It soon became necessary for Davidson to abandon his Liberton post and flee first to England, then briefly to the Continent. He returned to Scotland in November 1585 when James Stewart was stripped of the Arran title and post of chancellor. Lennox had also fallen into temporary disfavour with the King

Davidson declined returning to Liberton Kirk. Instead he preached for some years in various city churches then, latterly, at the second charge of Holyrood. During this time, he continued to preach against the King and nobility so that his presence in Edinburgh again became uncomfortable and he was advised by the General Assembly to 'seek a rural charge'.

Arrival in Prestonpans

On November 5th, 1595 the Presbytery of Haddington initiated procedures for Davidson's introduction to the ministry "at South Preston and ye Panns east and west, and ye haill bounds yairabout belonging as well to my Lord of Newbattle as to ye Laird of Preston". (South Preston is now known locally as the Upper Pans and Panns East and West or Salt Preston as the Lower Pans.)

Davidson agreed to accept this rural charge if the people of Preston found him suitable. As a result of sermons delivered to his potential parishioners he was invited to become their minister – the first since the Reformation. Lord Newbattle of Prestongrange provided his necessary agreement and the induction proceeded on 5 January 1596 when Davidson made a lengthy speech to his new congregation, emphasising the importance of prayer within the household. Prayers and graces prepared by Davidson for this purpose can still be found in old manuscripts including *A Memoir* – published in 1876 by Dr. Charles Rodgers.

The Rev. Davidson was installed but was still without a church in which to preach. He applied first to Mark Ker, Baron of Prestoungrange and Lord Newbattle but Newbattle would not agree to provide any assistance unless the proposed church was built on his lands of Prestoungrange. Indications are that Davidson and Mark Ker were never friendly. The fact that Ker's father made a convenient and swift post Reformation conversion from Abbot of Newbattle Abbey to Lord Newbattle in order to retain Abbey holdings at Prestoungrange would scarcely have helped their relationship. There was also a later incident of Newbattle not allowing Davidson to bury one of his congregation in the West Graveyard with Davidson predicting bad times for his lordship.

On being refused building land by Lord Newbattle Davidson approached George Hamilton of Preston. Hamilton also wanted the proposed church in a preferred location but soon relented and provided, free of cost, land on which to build a church, a manse, and school. The land adjoined 'Pinkerton's Garden' which was soon afterwards adopted as the new graveyard. Davidson met the greatest cost of building the new church and manse by using personal funds which also provided for the new school.

Davidson's health began to deteriorate from 1598 and as a result he was unable to be as actively involved as before in church politics. He continued however to criticise policies advanced by King James through writing to the General Assembly. Davidson's last great confrontation came when the King insisted that church ministers should sit in parliament. On that occasion the Reverend Davidson wrote to the General Assembly which sat in Burntisland during May 1601 renewing his protest against ministers sitting in parliament.

Davidson declined to withdraw his opposition and on 26th May 1601 was sentenced to detention in Edinburgh Castle. He was detained there for his second one day spell in prison but then released on condition that he would never again be allowed to travel outwith his own parish. This restraint applied for the remainder of Davidson's life despite constant entreaties for revocation from both the Haddington Presbytery and by Davidson himself.

When the now bankrupt King James was traveling south in 1603 to assume the now united English and Scottish thrones in London he passed through Prestonpans. The Edinburgh Presbytery suggested to Davidson that he should take the opportunity of meeting the King in Prestonpans to congratulate him on the English accession and to seek personal clemency.

Davidson agreed, even first seeking permission to kiss the King's hand. But King James would not relent and still maintained an intense dislike of this parish Minister. A final attempt to obtain clemency was made by the Provincial Synod but that also failed.

So the Rev. John Davidson now sick and infirm remained confined within the bounds of his rural charge until he died during the autumn of 1604 "being not older than 56 years." Of those 56 years he had spent only eight in Prestonpans perhaps surprisingly given his legendary status in the town. His contribution was undoubtedly substantial not only in building the parish church where none had existed since 1544 but also in creating a school. Throughout his entire turbulent adult life John Davidson was immersed in politics. Overall he lived the life typical of many reforming Ministers in whose minds the power of the church must be absolute and certainly not challenged by monarchs. Many of his copious writings all on a theological theme have been well preserved and are still often items of significant clerical reference.

Bibliography

Prestonpans and Vicinity, Peter McNeill
Life of John Davidson of Prestonpans, R. Moffat Gillon
Three Scottish Reformers, Charles Rogers
Scotland, A Story of a Nation, Magnus Magnusson
Presbytery of Haddington, Synod of Lothian and Tweedale, W. Bruce Cunningham

3 JAMES ERSKINE – LORD GRANGE

James Erskine, later Lord Grange, was born the second son of Charles, 10th Earl of Mar in 1679. Though not born in Prestonpans he was to have a long association with the town. Here as elsewhere he lived an enigmatic existence which would undoubtedly, without his saving family connections, have seen him executed or at best committed to a long spell of custody.

He studied law but according to Alexander (Jupiter) Carlyle he had "neither talents nor learning nor ability." That assessment may have been harsh for Carlyle was renowned for his unfavourable considerations of everyone but himself, but Erskine's rapid advancement within the legal hierarchy was without doubt due to the influence of his brother and his own position in society not to any demonstrated talent. He became a member of the Faculty of Advocates on 26 July 1705 when still only twenty six years old and thereafter advanced with abnormal rapidity. He was appointed to the Bench in March of 1707 and that same year became a full Lord of Justiciary as Lord Grange.

Such an appointment while still only twenty eight years old was astonishing but his career was to become even more astonishing when on 27 July 1710 at the age of thirty one he replaced Lord Ormiston as Lord Justice Clerk. Even at a time when patronage was an accepted fact of life Lord Grange's rapid progression through the ranks of Scottish Justiciary caused much controversy and created many enemies.

He habitually swore allegiance to the Hanoverian monarchy unlike his brother the 11th Earl of Mar who was quite open in his support of the exiled Stuarts. Lord Grange consistently presented a facade of piety, and facade it must have been when considering his overall way of life. He was held in high esteem by the strict presbyterians and was always involved in the workings of the General Assembly. Despite his own benefits from patronage he presented a staunch assertion that church Ministers should not be constrained by either government or lay patrons. Yet despite this presbyterian involvement enemies often accused him of being both a closet Jacobite and Jesuit.

Meteoric Career Questioned

His association with Prestonpans coincided with his appointment as a Judge. Early in the 18th century he acquired the old Preston House on what is now Preston Road just east of the Mercat Cross from the heirs of the previous owner, Dr. Oswald. This was to be his country residence as he had a town house in Edinburgh. He developed the four acres of garden surrounding Preston House creating a complex maze which took a full two hours to navigate successfully which became an early visitor attraction in Prestonpans. Despite his assertions concerning the appointment of church ministers he was primarily responsible, in 1724 for the appointment of the Rev. William Carlyle, Jupiter's father, to Prestonpans Parish Church. Lord Grange and William Carlyle, with their respective children, were close friends but that friendship waned when Carlyle began to openly disapprove of his mentor's general bad habits and debauchery.

Just before his elevation to Lord Justice Clerk Lord Grange married Rachel Chiesly, described by 'Jupiter' Carlyle who knew her well as "very beautiful but of violent temper." She was also the daughter of a murderer, her father Chiesly of Dalry having earlier murdered Court of Session Lord President Lockhart in Edinburgh's Lawnmarket after that judge had ruled against him in court.

The marriage was not entirely voluntary. The lady had become pregnant by his lordship and in keeping with contemporary requirements, particularly within the clerical circles to which he professed allegiance, a marriage took place. Their eldest son Charles was born soon afterwards on 27 August 1709. The marriage began as a marriage of necessity but despite later turbulence it begat four sons and four daughters by 1720.

Lord and Lady Grange alternated between their town and country residences. Lord Grange himself was also often absent in London or elsewhere on legal business and perhaps covert Jacobite missions. By 1730 Lady Grange with ample cause suspected her husband of infidelity and even employed the equivalent of private detectives to shadow his movements. There were instances of bad behaviour by both partners but that of Rachel was said to have caused her husband a great deal of embarrassment as she drank to excess even in public, and was not above openly accompanying the occasional male friend in the absence of her husband.

Separation was perhaps inevitable and that she achieved together with enforced payment of legal maintenance. Lord Grange paid perhaps because she threatened to report her husband for his treasonable association with the Jacobites. Rachel was also said to be insane, but that was a term then often confused with unconventionality.

Kidnapping his Wife

In 1732 Lord Grange formally announced the sudden death of his wife and arranged an elaborate funeral which was attended by many. There was undoubtedly a burial – but what or whom did the coffin contain? It was certainly not Rachel who was still alive and well in Edinburgh. But the arrangements for the funeral and third party involvement in this tragic farce demonstrate the extent of the influence Lord Grange exercised at that time

Being dead Lady Grange could scarcely be allowed to reside in Edinburgh any longer where she had lodged with a Mrs MacLean. On the night of 22 January 1732 as Rachel was about to leave for London intending to expose her husband as a Jacobite, Mrs MacLean allowed four highlanders in Lovat tartan to enter the lodging place. These men overpowered Lady Grange and tied her securely before taking her to the Linlithgow home of Advocate Murdo McLeod.

That initial brief stopover with McLeod was but the start of a tortuous journey. The unfortunate Rachel, still captive, went next to Falkirk, then to Pomeise, where she is said to have been 'concealed in a closet' for 13 weeks before travelling at night via Stirling through the Highlands, then eventually by boat to the island of Hesker. The entire operation was managed by Alexander Foster of Carsbonny in association with Lord Grange's page, Peter Fraser. In addition, several Highland Chieftains were involved including Sir Alexander Macdonald, MacLeod of Muiravondall and Lord Lovat – Jacobites to a man. According to Carlyle, Lady Grange later claimed that Lord Lovat stole her from her Edinburgh lodgings. While Lord Grange would later try to justify his wife's abduction and detention because of her supposed insanity it was almost certainly Rachel's threat to expose Jacobite intrigues that caused her incarceration. The Clan Chiefs would almost certainly not have been interested in solving a simple domestic problem.

Lady Grange was held prisoner on Hesker for ten months in deplorable conditions before being moved far off shore to St. Kilda where she remained captive for a further seven years. She was of course no longer locked up there and allowed to move around the island because without assistance escape was impossible. She even had a single male servant who alas spoke little English. Nobody was prepared to help her return to the mainland.

A church minister who arrived at St Kilda during January 1741 and learned of Lady Grange's predicament refused to assist her return to the mainland but shortly afterwards a servant girl did pass details of her predicament to friends in Scotland. By the time a rescue vessel was sent to St Kilda, Rachel's captors had removed her first to Sutherland, then later to Dunvegan on the Isle of Skye, where she died and was buried in May of 1745. The entire abduction story later became common knowledge. Lord Grange provided an explanation of both abduction and false funeral which was apparently fully accepted affording yet further evidence of his position and influence.

Off to Westminster

Following the 1732 abduction of his wife Lord Grange remained at Prestonpans, but now with political ambitions. He fervently opposed the policies of Whig Prime Minister, Sir Robert Walpole, and in 1734 he unwisely resigned his judicial post in protest against a new Act precluding any member of the Scottish Bench from concurrently becoming a Member of Parliament. As James Erskine that same year he was elected Member of Parliament for Stirlingshire. At Westminster on the opposition benches he joined forces with fellow Scottish Bar Member, Dundas of Arniston, in opposition to the policies of Walpole.

Overall his parliamentary sojourn was not a success. For a short time he was Secretary to the Prince of Wales but never achieved his declared ambition of becoming Scottish Secretary. He did not make his Maiden Speech until early 1736, and chose the occasion to produce a pedantic monologue opposing the Witches Bill, a subject on which he considered himself an expert. His library allegedly contained many books on the subject. The speech made him the object of much derision and effectively curtailed any prospect of a real parliamentary career. It is undoubtedly strange that a former senior member of the Scottish Justiciary even in the early 18th century should retain a belief in witches.

With the failure of his parliamentary venture James Erskine returned to the Scottish Bar. However his enemies were still many and work scarce. His brother, 11th Earl of Mar, had also fallen from grace so was no longer able to help the failed Member for Stirlingshire.

James Erskine had by this time formed an enduring liaison with Fanny Lindsay, an expatriate Scotswoman who owned a coffee house in London's Haymarket. He spent the remaining years of his life in London and Fanny became his second wife. Her business seems to have been his only means of financial support. There is no record of when he left Prestonpans but Preston House and the Edinburgh town house had both been sold. What could have been a distinguished legal career with a prominent position in Edinburgh society was lost through ill conceived ventures and political ambition. He died in London on 20 January 1754.

Bibliography

Tales of a Grandfather, Sir Walter Scott
Prestonpans and Vicinity, Peter MacNeill
Dictionary of National Biography Anecdotes & Characters of The Times, Alexander Carlyle
Lord Advocates of Scotland Omonds
Dictionary of National Biography Encyclopaedia of Scotland Collins
Registers of Scotland Old Parish Records

4 WILLIAM GRANT – LORD PRESTOUNGRANGE

The Grant dynasty including the Grant-Sutties owned and occupied Prestongrange House for some two centuries, regular occupation only ending with the death of Lady Susan in 1909. The founding member was William Grant who acquired the Barony of Prestongrange and Dolphinstoun in 1746 for £160 000 Scottish from the bankrupt Morrison family.

William Grant was the second son of Sir Francis Grant, Lord Cullen. According to the *Dictionary of National Biography* he was probably born in 1701 and his mother is wrongly recorded as Sarah Fordyce the second wife of Lord Cullen. Parish Records for Edinburgh confirm absolutely that Grant was born in the City on 4 May 1701 and that his parents were undoubtedly Sir Francis Grant and Jean Meldrum.

William Grant read law at Edinburgh and was called to the Bar on 24 February 1722. As was then common in legal circles he was involved with the

Church of Scotland and, on 13 May 1731, was appointed Procurator and Principal Clerk by the General Assembly. Like many of his contemporaries he claimed to despise patronage. In 1736 he wrote a paper on the subject: *Remarks on the State of the Church of Scotland with Respect to Patronages*. But there is evidence that both he his family arranged that chosen Ministers were granted the living at Prestonpans.

His progression through the legal ranks can be described as steady rather than meteoric. It was not until 20 June 1737 – some 15 years after becoming an advocate – that he was appointed Solicitor General when Charles Erskine moved up to become Lord Advocate. Grant sought, and was granted permission, by the Church of Scotland to appoint a deputy for his clerical commitments should they conflict with his new obligations as Solicitor General.

When Charles Erskine resigned as Lord Advocate in 1742 Grant did expect to take his place but Robert Craigie was appointed new Lord Advocate. It is perhaps a measure of the man that Grant wrote Craigie a letter of congratulations on his appointment.

William Grant – Lord Prestoungrange
Courtesy of The Scottish National Portrait Gallery and the National Gallery of Scotland

Lord Advocate 1746

William Grant eventually became Lord Advocate on 26 February 1746, receiving something of a poisoned chalice. He had already been elected Member of Parliament for Elgin and now had to balance his Scottish legal responsibilities with those of a parliamentarian. He found favour at Westminster with Prime Minister Walpole in his efforts to achieve justice and, where appropriate, compensation following the ill fated Jacobite rebellion in 1745. The new Lord Advocate resisted the absolute Crown annexation of *all* Highland estates and resolved to contain such impounding to those estates of perceived Highland rebels. He introduced the Bill at Westminster on 24 February 1752 annexing the forfeited estates to the Crown for all time.

Grant was fortunate in not personally having to prosecute many of the rebels who were taken south to Penrith, York or London where they were tried and perhaps inevitably executed. He probably had some undeclared sympathy with the rebels. When the impeachment of the old Jacobite Lord Lovat was considered he wrote to advise London "*there is too much ground to doubt whether a Bill of Indictment would be found against Lord Lovat by a grand jury to be summoned in the County of Inverness.*" That protectionist measure if indeed that is what it was failed. Lord Lovat who had never actually borne arms for the Prince was instead taken to London and suffered the obligatory show trial prior to his execution.

The Church of Scotland would no longer allow Grant to continue as Procurator and Clerk following his appointment as Lord Advocate, but it is likely he would have had to relinquish those posts anyway because of other commitments. A position on the Bench became available in 1748 but he was passed over and continued as Lord Advocate.

The Appin Murder Trial

What may be seen as a considerable blemish on his career as Lord Advocate was the charade which became known as the Appin Murder Trial. Many Highland estates became Crown property after 1745 with administrators appointed with their duties including rent collection. While under control of the deposed Highland Chiefs such cottage rents were often ignored as the Chiefs saw tenants primarily as sources of power. But the rents for small cottages were now to be vigorously collected for the Crown and failure to pay resulted in eviction.

Colin Campbell of Glenure managed the forfeited estates of Lochiel and Ardshiel and intended to evict a number of tenants on 15 May 1752. But on 14 May Campbell was shot dead while riding at the entrance to Glencoe in the company of an Edinburgh lawyer, a Sheriff Officer and servant. Allan Breck Stewart of Ardshiel, later to figure in Robert Louis Stevenson's *Kidnapped,* and his kinsman James Stewart were soon suspected of the crime, Allan Stewart as the murderer and James as an accessory.

Allan Stewart escaped to France and only James could be arrested. His trial was a farce and by becoming involved where he could have delegated the prosecution to a depute, William Grant did himself no credit. The Circuit High Court of Justiciary was constituted in Inverary, home of the Campbells. Archibald Campbell, 3rd Duke of Argyll and Lord Justice General, assumed personal charge of the trial. In keeping with the procedure at the time Argyll personally selected the Jury. Not surprisingly eleven of the fifteen chosen members were Campbells like himself. Never before had a Lord Advocate gone on Circuit and there is no known reason why William Grant personally conducted the prosecution of James Stewart, unless he felt some moral obligation because the presiding Judge's father had earlier aided his own career.

Such records as remain leave little doubt that the proceedings were biased, contrived from the start, with no fair hearing accorded to the defence. James Stewart was inevitably found guilty and hanged. *Collins Encyclopaedia of Scotland* states "James Stewart was Ardshiel's half brother and there is little doubt of his being guilty as charged." A sweeping assumption based on an undoubted travesty of justice. Why else were all trial records ordered to be destroyed though one copy of Precognitions has survived to be seen today in the National Library of Scotland. From what evidence is available there it is extremely unlikely James Stewart would have been convicted today.

Lord Prestoungrange in 1754

Apart from that Inverary debacle as Lord Advocate Grant was consistently moderate and usually fair in his Scottish prosecutions. That attribute was later recognised in his appointment to the Bench as a Lord of Session on 14 November 1754 and taking the name Lord Prestoungrange. Earlier that year he had also been returned for the third time as Member of Parliament for Elgin but had to resign that Commons seat on becoming a Lord of Session. As Lord Prestoungrange he remained on the bench until his death in Somerset a decade later on 23 May 1764. He was subsequently buried under the aisle of Prestonpans church and a monument was erected in his memory on the church walls constituting perhaps Prestonpans first mural. The inscription is still to be read inside the organ loft although the that outside is now illegible.

Lord Prestoungrange enjoyed a good domestic life. He married Grizel Millar, daughter of a Renfrewshire Minister, in 1729 and they had four daughters. The eldest, Janet, was heir to the baronial lands of Prestoungrange and Dolphinstoun and married John Carmichaell, 4th Earl of Hyndford, in Edinburgh on 8 January 1749. In her turn Janet mapped and managed those estates with skill and in 1787 when nearby Wintoun Estates were broken up added the Tranent farms of Myles and Birslie and Fallside to Prestoungrange. As Countess of Hyndford she remained at Prestoungrange until her death in 1818. She survived her husband by many years and became a great favourite and benefactor in the locality. On her death the baronial lands passed to her nephew Sir James Suttie Bart., and the family henceforth adopted the name Grant-Suttie.

Grizel Millar, wife of William Grant – Lord Prestoungrange, died in 1792 and so survived her husband by 28 years, but there is no record to show whether she spent her latter years with her daughter Janet at Prestoungrange House.

Bibliography

Lord Advocates of Scotland, Omonds
Dictionary of National Biography Encyclopaedia of Scotland, Collins
Registers of Scotland Old Parish Records

5 LADY SUSAN GRANT-SUTTIE

There is no comprehensive biographical record of Lady Susan who during the latter part of the 19th and into the 20th centuries was an integral part of Prestonpans life. The local historian Peter McNeill only briefly and favourably mentions her in *Prestonpans and Vicinity* but he was unique in that respect. In the absence of any formal record her many good deeds simply became the subject of legend and with the passage of time those legends have begun to diminish.

Born on 13 November 1837 at the Roxburghe ancestral home of Floors Castle, Kelso and christened Lady Susan Harriet Innes Ker, she was a daughter of Sir James, 6th Duke of Roxburghe, 1st Earl Innes and Viscount Broxmouth. His wife was Susanna Stephaina Dalbiac, daughter of Lt. General Sir Charles Dalbiac. As Duchess of Roxburghe, Susanna was Lady of the Bedchamber to H.M. Queen Victoria.

As the daughter of a Duke she was known as Lady Susan from birth. She inherited her mother's striking beauty and from an early age is said to have displayed a high degree of intelligence and a great interest in politics both local and national. An old report in the *Haddington Press* describes her as "like her mother, of great beauty, slim, lithe of figure, with an elegant carriage and healthy complexion." That same report suggests she retained all of these attributes throughout life.

Unfortunately no late portrait photographs of Lady Susan have been found but in the Billiard Room at Floors Castle there is a full length portrait of Duchess Susanna and on another wall, a picture of Lady Susan with her sister Lady Charlotte in a garden setting. The portrait of their mother is thought to be by McKenzie of Graves but the 19th century artist Henry Wyndham Phillips certainly painted Lady Susan and her sister. The pictures display a remarkable likeness between mother and daughters.

Lady Susan (left) with her sister, Lady Charlotte
From the painting by Henry Wyndham Phillips
By kind permission of Roxburghe Estates

At Kelso Church, on 6 August 1857, when she was still only nineteen, Lady Susan married James Grant-Suttie, who was seven years her senior, the son and heir of the extensive estates of Sir George Grant Suttie, 5th Baronet of Balgone and Prestongrange. Lady Susan's husband who would later, but for only a short time, succeed his father as 6th Baronet, was a serving soldier at the time of their marriage. By 1878, he was Colonel Commanding the Haddington, Berwick, Linlithgow and Peebles Militia.

James and Lady Susan set up home within the Mansion House of Maines in Chirnside, Berwickshire. Three daughters were followed by a son on November 2, 1870, George Grant-Suttie who was destined eventually to become 7th Baronet. Another second son James who was born prematurely on 13 September 1874 survived only two days.

Sir James' Inheritance

Apart from the sad loss of young James no record exists of serious problems affecting Lady Susan or the family until 1878. But in June Lady Susan's father in law Sir George died while on holiday at Grantham House, Putney Heath in Surrey. Her husband Sir James succeeded his father as 6th Baronet but did not immediately or automatically inherit his father's moveable estate of £46,609/11/8d., or all the heritable Prestongrange property. Sir George, as legal records in the National Archives of Scotland confirm, had always been extremely litigious and new Wills, with inevitable codicils thereto, were an almost annual event. He had been a widower for some twenty years at the time of his death and had heavily entailed Prestongrange. He had consistently sought to ensure that all his surviving children, and not just his immediate heir, were made financially secure from the Prestongrange estate.

Resolution of Sir George's Estate was in its early stages when his immediate heir, Lady Susan's husband Sir James, died of typhus on 30 October 1878 at their Chirnside home. He left a Will written on 10 September 1878 and personal Estate of £15,059/15/2d. That testament also nominated and appointed Lady Susan to be his sole Executrix and Memorialist. He further named his brother in law James, soon to be the 7th Duke of Roxburghe, and a friend Major John Dawson as additional Memorialists, Tutors and Curators to his children.

Although only eight years old, his son Sir George became 7th Baronet – with *prima facie* rights to Prestongrange Estates. The premature death of his father however, when the estate of his grandfather had yet to be fully resolved, was to create many problems before young Sir George could be seen as Laird of Prestongrange.

The then prevailing Law of Scottish Succession was more primitive than that of the current Succession (Scotland) Act 1964. Sir James' brother and two sisters, aided by their father's trustees including the formidable legal mind of Robert Dundas of Arniston, actively pursued their prescribed legacies. Fundamentally for cash flow reasons these bequests could not be met and much controversy inevitably arose between the trustees and Lady Susan acting as her husband's Executrix and in the interests of her son Sir George.

It has been suggested that the controversy led to a position where Prestongrange was run by "a large group of lawyers" to the exclusion of Lady Susan and her son. That is not strictly true. Legal opinion was obviously necessary to resolve the numerous problems but Lady Susan was not the type of person to be excluded from negotiations. She was after all a Roxburghe and had direct links to Queen Victoria.

Frequent legal meetings were invariably attended by Lady Susan, her brother James and Major Dawson. Chaired by Lady Susan's kinsman Mr J Innes they dealt with all administrative matters concerning Prestongrange including such renting land and houses, the state of local industry in which there was an interest, local fishermen complaining about ship captains disturbing the oyster beds, even the relatively small matter of agreeing not to collect rent from the local bowling club. In addition these meetings attempted to reach an amicable resolution with the legal representatives of her husband's siblings.

Lady Susan played a key role and her strong signature *Susan H. Grant Suttie* is always first on related Minutes and other legal documents dealing with her son and his inheritance. On the odd occasion when she could not attend a meeting the Minutes were sent to her first for approval and signature.

By early 1879 Innes with the approval of Lady Susan had taken advice from the Accountant of Court who as an interim measure proposed: *"that there should be paid to Lady Susan Grant Suttie an annual allowance (from Prestongrange Estate) of £400 for the maintenance of the Heir, this allowance to begin from 30 October 1878, and that there should be a further allowance to Lady Susan of £140 per annum to cover the salary of Mr Adamson who had been engaged by Lady Susan as Tutor to the Heir"*. Innes also advised the meeting that: *"in addition to the aforesaid allowances, it has been arranged that Lady Susan shall occupy Prestongrange House rent free in view that the Heir is to reside with her. That the garden and grounds shall be upheld at the expense of the Heir and that Lady Susan shall pay, at market rates, for all produce taken."*

That interim measure was agreed by all involved and by mid 1879 all bills and invoices relating to Prestongrange Estate were being dealt with by the Tutors and Curators of the Heir. Any lawyers involved in such actions were therefore acting on the instructions of Lady Susan, her brother and Major Dawson. An ante nuptial agreement drawn up by the elder Sir George in 1857 at the time of his son's marriage to Lady Susan, granted her an annual income of £2000 per annum from Prestongrange Estate. That payment apparently continued throughout the years of protracted negotiations. Apart from legal negotiations, 1879 was a year of mixed emotions for Lady Susan. Her father died on 23rd April and her first grandchild, John James Dalrymple a future Earl of Stair, was born on 1st February

Not surprisingly with such diverse interests no amicable agreement could be reached concerning settlement of the Prestongrange inheritances so the entire matter was referred for resolution to the Court of Session from which a Judgment was delivered on 12 May 1881. That Judgment, even though it resulted in lesser amounts being settled on the siblings of Sir James, was accepted by all participants and moves were initiated to at last establish young Sir George as 7th Baronet at Prestongrange.

Residence at Prestongrange House

No actual date can be determined to show when Lady Susan and her family took up formal residence at Prestongrange. During his later years her father in law Sir George had badly neglected the big house and much work was required to render it fully habitable. The Census of 1881 shows only six servants in residence, probably in some maintenance capacity, but she was certainly recognised as the Lady of the Manor by 5 September of that year when she formally opened the new Prestonpans Public School. The 1891 Census records Lady Susan in residence at Prestongrange with youngest daughter Victoria Alberta, her son Sir George and eighteen live-in servants. In 1886 daughter Harriet had married Sir Daniel Cooper, 2nd Baronet of Woolahara and taken up residence at Warren House, Newmarket, Suffolk where her husband had sporting interests.

So by 1891 Lady Susan was undoubtedly established with her son at Prestongrange. He was 21 that year and really no longer required any kind of guardianship. But his absences were frequent and Lady Susan was recognised locally as head of the Prestongrange household with effective control of administration.

Lady Susan became a member of Prestonpans Parish Church soon after her move to the town from Chirnside. Such folklore and legend that remains suggests that from an early stage she became actively and physically involved with church work. In 19th century Prestonpans there was very little help available to sick or unemployed workers and their families. On learning of such cases Lady Susan begun an enduring habit of home visits to offer assistance. When income to purchase food and medicine was practically non existent such visits must indeed have been welcome. At the time houses in miners rows at Cuthill had an average of six residents living in what were very cramped conditions.

Those visits were not without personal health risk to Lady Susan. Town Council records consistently showed a sustained presence of many infectious diseases such as scarlet fever, smallpox, typhoid fever and cholera which were often treated at home with attendant chances of further infection. There was also ongoing concern about obtaining a clean water supply in Prestonpans. The lack of good clean water served to perpetuate typhoid and cholera.

Those same Town Council records dealing with infectious diseases highlight another of Lady Susan's commendable activities. In association with Mrs. Stirling Boyd of Edinburgh she dealt with the Fortnight Holiday Children. Again there is a dearth of historical record detailing that activity but fundamentally it concerned children of Edinburgh and Leith who lived in deprived conditions. Under a scheme organised by Lady Susan and her friends the children were given a free holiday for two weeks beside the sea in Prestonpans. They did not holiday in 1894 however. A medical report to Prestonpans Town Council concerning an exceptionally high incidence of smallpox in Edinburgh caused the Council to ask Lady Susan that she should ensure The Fortnight Holiday Children stayed at home that year.

Prestonpans Town Hall

From the time of her arrival at Prestongrange she became a familiar figure walking around The Pans talking with people and showing a genuine interest in their lives. An old *Haddington Advertiser* report speaks of her "happily walking around the town in short skirts (doubtless relative to what was then the norm) and habitually using third instead of first class rail travel so she could meet people."

She became actively involved in the protracted construction of Prestonpans Town Hall. The need for one had first been identified in 1874, long before she came to Prestongrange. A committee was formed back then to explore the situation, find a suitable site, and raise funds. Some £400 was soon raised but no construction took place. It was ten years later in 1884 before a suitable site was identified opposite old Aldhammer House. A benefactor with a Prestonpans connection offered to bear the entire cost of design and construction. There was, however, continued political argument which resulted in the offer being withdrawn.

However, a core of residents was determined that construction of a Hall should proceed so pressure was maintained on the Town Council. Much later on 4 June 1895 a Poll of Householders in Prestonpans resulted in 50 votes for and 38 against such a new Hall from the electorate of 384.

Plans for construction of the Hall were well advanced when Lady Susan became involved. She suggested an extensive Fair within Prestongrange grounds to raise the building funds and that offer was readily accepted and proved to be a great success. After purchase of the chosen site £1000 still remained available towards building costs. There was still some political argument but eventually the Town's Hall, designed by Peter Whitecross, was opened by R. B. Haldane, Member of Parliament for the County.

Lady Parish Councillor

Lady Susan had been resident in Prestongrange for a relatively short time but her active involvement in the Town Hall project and ready friendship with the people probably led to what was in 1895 arguably her greatest achievement. In the elections held that April she was elected as a Parish Councillor for Prestonpans' Landward Area. This political success was of only parochial effect yet of national significance though no newspaper reported it as such. It was achieved at a time when women had no vote so by implication all of her electors were men. This success was achieved 24 years before the high profile election of Lady Nancy Astor at Plymouth in 1919 as the first ever female Member of Parliament. Although Lady Susan's success may have been tempered somewhat initially by the death of her mother The Dowager Duchess Susanna on 6th May 1895, she stayed as a Parish Councillor for the remainder of her life. That same year her eldest daughter Susan was divorced from the Earl of Stair soon afterwards marrying Sir Neil Menzies.

Some twelve months after her election success Lady Susan's youngest daughter Victoria Alberta married Prestonpans' Church of Scotland Minister the Rev. George Stuart Smith at Prestonpans Church. The lifelong family association with Dunbar was continued with the Dunbar Minister William Borland conducting the ceremony. Sadly Victoria Alberta died prematurely on 5 January 1900 of a fever soon after the birth of her second daughter. She is buried just within the gate of Prestonpans Churchyard. In his book Peter McNeill refers to that sad event and emphasises the subsequent greater involvement of Lady Susan in raising her two granddaughters.

Despite such examples of adversity Lady Susan sustained active community work. She initiated and was first chair of Prestonpans Women's Guild. She was also executively involved with and one time president of the local YWCA. That organisation had evolved from classes held during the mid 19th century by the Misses Alexander of Aldhammer House, sisters of Thomas, Director General of Army Medical Services. She was also a member of the School Board as indeed was her son in law the Rev. George Smith.

Coffee Shop and Recreation Centre

A new Coffee House and Recreational Centre was opened in the town on 28 July 1887. That new establishment, in addition to providing refreshments, contained a series of games such as draughts, bagatelle and billiards. Lady Susan was the motivating force behind the project which issued share capital of £300 being 1200 × 5/- shares and she was its major shareholder. The prospectus for that company states: *"It is felt that a great need exists in Prestonpans of a place of resort for the inhabitants, where they can meet together for social intercourse and recreation without the necessity of partaking of intoxicating liquors."* Unfortunately, due to illness, Lady Susan was unable to attend the formal opening but local businessman James Mellis deputised and opened the project in her name.

Closure at Prestongrange

Lady Susan died at Prestongrange on the morning of Saturday 16 October 1909 after a short illness just one month before her 72nd birthday. Next day the Prestonpans morning church service was curtailed as a mark of respect and the evening service was cancelled. During Sunday afternoon between two and three o'clock the church bell tolled in her memory.

On Thursday 21 October a funeral service took place within Prestonpans Parish Church conducted by the Rev. Smart of Chirnside, preserving the association of Lady Susan and her family with that village. The burial took place later in the day at Dunbar.

After the Prestonpans service her oak coffin was carried in relays from Prestongrange House to the local railway station. Estate workers carried it first to the south gate from where it was borne by members of the Kirk Session before her fellow Parish Council members carried her on the last leg of the journey.

All Prestonpans shops and businesses were closed from mid day as a mark of respect. School children many of whom had been personally known to Lady Susan lined the route followed by her cortege. A special train carried the coffin plus a large number of friends and relatives from Prestonpans to Dunbar railway station.

On arrival at Dunbar the coffin was carried shoulder high from station to churchyard. Pall bearers were her sons in law Sir Neil Menzies and the Rev. George Smith, her grandson Viscount Dalrymple, her nephew the Duke of Roxburghe together with Lord Charles Innes Ker, Robert Grant Suttie, Lord Montgomerie and John Russell.

The pre-burial service at Dunbar was attended by many hundreds of people including a large representation of the people of Prestonpans along with many members of the aristocracy. An unusual feature was the considerable female presence at a time when women did not normally attend burials. The service was jointly conducted by the Rev. Donald MacLeod of St Columba's London and the Rev. William Borland of Dunbar. The grave was surrounded with ivy and chrysanthemums.

It may seem strange that Lady Susan and her family are buried at Dunbar rather than within the family vault at Prestonpans. Perhaps it was simply due to the long family association with Broxmouth – which was particularly strong at the time of her husband's death. However, when Prestonpans Parish Church was reopened on 10 September 1911 after extensive renovations the internal changes included a plaque in memory of Lady Susan. In addition to that church memorial the only other obvious indication of her name within Prestonpans is at *The Lady Susan* inn which is situated on what was once part of the Barony of Prestoungrange.

Lady Susan left personal estate of £10,267/3/3d. Her daughters Dame Susan Menzies and Lady Harriet Cooper were appointed and confirmed at

Haddington on 17 January 1910 as Joint Executrices.

Unlike his sisters, Lady Susan's son Sir George never married. Therefore there was no direct line of descent bearing the Grant Suttie name. Sir George was never a regular occupant of Prestongrange House after the death of his mother and the house was for a long time unoccupied before passing to the Royal Musselburgh Golf Club as their clubhouse which use it still has some 80 years later. Lady Susan, from the Roxburghe family, was ironically the last private resident there just as Mark Ker of the same Roxburghe family had been its first post-Reformation owner.

Acknowledgements

Information contained in this record derives mainly from the Prestongrange legal records, Minutes of Prestonpans Town Council and other biographical documentation held within the General Archives of Scotland together with *Haddington Press* articles accessed within the History Department of Haddington Library. The research assistance provided by staff at both venues is most gratefully acknowledged. Information contained in Peter McNeill's ubiquitous reference work *Prestonpans and Vicinity* also provided considerable basis.

6 ALEXANDER HUME

The education of its young has always been a major preoccupation for the Scottish nation. Indeed, the first attempt in Europe to prescribe a system of compulsory education was the 'First Book of Discipline' in 1560, which proposed a national plan for schools at all levels, from elementary to university, to be set up throughout Scotland.

During the period immediately following the Reformation, the newly-established parishes and their ministers were concerned with the issue of educational provision for their congregations. The first post-reformation minister of Prestonpans, the Reverend John Davidson, shared this preoccupation and, although he did not live to see it open, one of his major contributions to the parish was the founding and financing of a school for the education of the sons of gentlemen in 'Latin, Greek and Hebrew Toungis'.

Thanks to Davidson's generous endowment, the school attracted staff of high quality and its first master was the highly respected figure of Alexander Hume, known as 'The Grammarian'. By the time Hume arrived in Prestonpans in 1606, he had already established a considerable reputation as an educator of the young. He came to his post after a period as master at the Edinburgh High School. Previous to this, Hume spent many years teaching in England, including two years as a private tutor at Oxford.

Although Davidson's intended curriculum included three languages, by far the most important of these was Latin. Fluency in Latin was an essential element in the education of the young at this time. Lectures at university were customarily delivered in Latin, while many of the essential texts were written in this tongue. Latin was the language of government and the law, and provided an international means of communication amongst scholars. Anyone who lacked fluency in both spoken and written Latin would have found it impossible to participate in the intellectual and political society of the day.

It was during his ten-year period as a teacher at Davidson's school in

Prestonpans that Hume completed the work which established his reputation as one of the foremost educators of the day. His 'Grammatica nova in usum juventutis Scoticae ad methodum revocata', was a Latin grammar intended to provide a sound basis in the language for young students between the ages of ten and fourteen. This grammar was a response to the concern at this time that a lack of uniformity in the teaching of Latin in Scottish schools meant that some pupils were not developing the level of skill required for their later studies.

In 1612, in response to the need for a consistent approach to the teaching of Latin, Hume's work was adopted as the standard text in all Scottish schools. Interestingly, although the grammar created a standardisation in terms of Latin, a number of peculiarly Scottish words provided in some of the book's translations demonstrate that standardisation of the English tongue in an educational context was far from complete at this time.

Although Davidson had originally emphasised a combined curriculum of Latin, Greek and Hebrew, these latter languages were taught to provide basic understanding. The majority of the curriculum was devoted almost entirely to developing fluency in Latin, even to the extent of requiring pupils to use Latin when talking not only to their teachers, but among themselves, so long as they remained on the school premises.

Hume maintained his responsibilities at Prestonpans for a period of ten years, until 1626, when he left to become master of the grammar school at Dunbar. It is a testimony to the considerable respect he enjoyed in the parish that the inheritor of Davidson's personal papers, John Johnstone, subsequently left these papers jointly to Alexander Hume and Robert Wallace.

The school at Prestonpans flourished for over a hundred years and continued to maintain its reputation. However, as the value of the original endowment shrank, the school gradually declined until, by the date of The First Statistical Account of Scotland in the 1790s, Davidson's school was no longer in existence.

Bibliography

Arbuckle, W, 'School Exercises of the 17th Century from Prestonpans', in *Transactions of the East Lothian Antiquarian and Field Naturalists' Society*, Vol X, 1966

Keay, J&J, *Collins Encyclopaedia of Scotland*, 1994

MacNeil, P, *Prestonpans and Vicinity*, 1902

Tales of the Pans, Prestonpans Local History Society, 2000

7 PATRICK MACKAY

Dr Patrick Mackay, C.B.E., was born at Latheron, Lybster, Caithness on the 6th July 1854. Patrick's father, Free Church Minister the Rev. John Mackay, was greatly interested in education and four of his sons gained their doctorates – two in medicine, one in law and Patrick as doctor of divinity.

On entering St Andrew's University at the age of fourteen, Patrick Mackay's initial studies included literary subjects and philosophy and he obtained honours in both. He was awarded the Gray Prize in his year for the best essay on Metaphysics. On graduation Mackay enrolled in the University of Edinburgh with the intention of following his father into the Free Church. In 1878 he

Patrick Robson Mackay, CBE, Doctor of Divinity
Photo, Courtesy Executors of the late Mrs Jean Mackay

became a licensed preacher then spent nine months gaining experience as Assistant at North Leith Free Church.

In February 1879 he was ordained as only the second Free Church Minister of Prestonpans in succession to the Rev. Bruce Cunningham. He was to remain incumbent there for almost twenty years.

Prestonpans School Board

His ministry differed in several ways to that of Davidson in Prestonpans almost two centuries earlier. He took a hands on approach to religion and was very interested in the social well being of his congregation. Over the years due entirely to his influence that congregation doubled in number and his work became recognised and acknowledged throughout the county. Mackay like his father had a strong belief that education should be available to all children and was soon elected chairman of the Prestonpans School Board. Although funds from old educational trusts existed including those from James Schaw and Mary Murray they were not always administered to best advantage. As chairman he was able to direct those funds more beneficially to provide a greater standard of general education for children of the town.

Patrick Mackay's interests during his Prestonpans ministry were not entirely parochial. In 1882 he was asked by the Colonial Committee of the Free Church to consider an expedition to Luxor in Egypt to determine whether that place was a suitable venue for an expansion of the Free Church.

Colonial Missions to Luxor Gibraltar and India

Permission of his congregation for such a venture was obtained with some degree of reluctance. Mackay arrived in Egypt soon after the battle of Tel-el-Kebir and in addition to the primary reason for his visit he volunteered his services as Temporary Chaplain to the Highland Brigade and remained with that Regiment until he returned to his Prestonpans post late in 1883.

In April 1884 not long after his return to the town the Colonial Committee made a further request for Patrick Mackay to travel on their behalf to Gibraltar but his congregation did not welcome that new proposal. All 243 members of the congregation wrote their Minister a note stating "*We the undersigned, members and adherents of your congregation ... ... take the liberty of asking you to consider the matter well before coming to a decision. ... ... We earnestly hope you will consider the great work which is yet to be done, in this place and neighbourhood and the risk which all congregations must necessarily run where a change such as this takes place.*" That plea dated Prestonpans 28 April 1884 was presented to the Minister in scroll form.

The plea was successful. Mr Mackay subsequently declined the offer of a Gibraltar expedition on behalf of the Colonial Committee and continued with his normal ministerial duties until 1887 when, with the reluctant permission of his congregation, Patrick Mackay went overseas once more, this time to India. On this occasion he spent a year on behalf of the Anglo-Indian Evangelical Society acting as Minister of the Union Church at Mussoorie while also working in a military sanatorium and directly with the British troops stationed in the Province. The Rev. Mackay also began to write long articles containing details of India, his work and travels which were sent home to Scottish newspapers.

It was during that trip to India that he met Harriet Sprot whom he later married at her family home in Edinburgh on 11 June 1890. Patrick Mackay was then almost thirty six years old and Harriet eight years younger. Her father had emigrated to New Zealand to farm sheep and Harriet was born at Diamond Bay near Christchurch on the South Island. When she met Patrick Harriet was working in India as a children's governess.

On resumption of his Prestonpans duties Harriet proved to be of great assistance to The Rev. Mackay and involved herself wholeheartedly in caring for the working people of the town. After Harriet's father died in New Zealand her mother had returned to Scotland and settled in Edinburgh. After Harriet's marriage her mother with her still unmarried sisters and an aunt moved to Prestonpans where they rented accommodation at Northfield.

Mediation in 1893 Miners' Strike

Patrick Mackay's involvement in community matters was often greater than would be expected of the town Minister. In 1893 there was a strike at Prestongrange Colliery which threatened to be disastrous, in a financial sense, for the miners and indirectly for the economy of Prestonpans. The mine workers were becoming organised and most were Federation members but no proper union or political representation existed locally. During May 1893 the colliery was in liquidation and the liquidators had attempted to impose a ten per cent wage reduction on the workforce to allow the mine to operate until a new owner was found.

Not surprisingly the miners would not accept that reduction of income and from the second week of May 1893 staged a protest strike. The Mid and East Lothian Miners' Federation had a working fund of £1600 from which each striking miner was paid eight shillings per week, a sum increased by one shilling for each child of their families. Even for the time that was barely a subsistence income.

After three weeks, recognising the impasse between miners and the liquidators, Patrick Mackay voluntarily assumed the role of mediator. He successfully achieved a solution acceptable to both parties and the miners returned to work on the same wages as before the strike. To achieve the settlement the Rev. Mackay personally volunteered responsibility for six per cent of the miners' wages until a new colliery owner was found. There were 250 miners involved so that six per cent represented a formidable commitment by the Minister and also suggests a personal wealth not entirely dependent on his ministerial stipend. Another indication of some personal wealth was displayed when he became a shareholder and director of the Prestonpans Coffee House Company Limited with Lady Susan Grant-Suttie.

At the Miners' Federation of Mid and East Lothian Annual General Meeting during August 1893 it was formally agreed to recognise the assistance provided by Patrick Mackay. He was subsequently presented with a silver watch which the miners paid for personally by subscription.

Back to India Alone with a Dream

After the first Indian mission which among other benefits had resulted in his marriage to Harriet the Reverend Mackay remained in Prestonpans Free Church Manse with his wife, his children and two domestic servants until his tenure in Prestonpans came to a formal end late in 1898.

It was at that time that the Rev. Mackay is reported to have "received a Call which a servant of Christ may not without dishonour decline." However Harriet gives a different version in her short autobiography. She suggests that in 1898 the Anglo-Indian Society required a deputy to undertake an expedition to India where the appointed person would conduct evangelical work, carry out surveys to determine the areas occupied by Europeans and their numbers, and assess the religious requirements of each sector.

Patrick Mackay was never in fact 'called' but rather volunteered to undertake the Indian expedition. His offer was initially declined by the Anglo-Indian Society because he was a married man with three young children. So the minister gave the Society two months to identify a suitable replacement, and if they failed to do so he would again offer to go.

Mrs Mackay's autobiographical account continues: "*You* may be sure I was not willing to let him go, indeed I was most unwilling, especially as another baby was coming. I was constantly haunted with the thought." However, before the aforementioned two months deadline expired Mrs Mackay had a dream in which she says: "the Saviour appeared and spoke to me." As a direct result of that divine intervention she withdrew her objection to her husband going to India and in fact instead insisted that he *must* go.

So Patrick Mackay with some familial reluctance and at some personal expense, which would somewhat be defrayed by his resumed activities as newspaper correspondent, resigned as Minister of Prestonpans Free Church. The family had to find suitable alternative accommodation prior to the Patrick's departure. And because of her condition Mrs Mackay insisted that any new accommodation should still be within reach of her doctor, William McEwan. Since Mrs Mackay's mother had moved from Prestonpans to Stair Park in nearby Tranent she too moved out of Prestonpans and set up home with her children there in Hopetoun Cottage.

Mackay sailed to India leaving his wife at home pregnant with daughter Harriet. He travelled extensively preaching as he went. During those travels he assimilated the required information and met with people of all faiths and levels of society. Such was his success that he was able to arrange joint Anglican, Presbyterian, Hindu and Muslim meetings where the different religions were amicably discussed which could not even have been contemplated in immediately post-Reformation times.

At Darjeeling, following an earthquake, which became known as the Darjeeling Disaster, Mackay became physically involved in the rescue of an entire family from beneath a collapsed house. For that successful involvement, he and others were presented with a specially struck gold star medallion and a silk bound record of the presentation proceedings.

Shortly after he became ill and was ordered home but he recovered during the voyage and after a short spell with the family in Tranent, including his first sight of daughter Harriet, he therefore returned to complete his Indian mission. When his youngest son Patrick Hugh Robson Mackay was born on 23 January 1901 Patrick Mackay Senior was still apparently absent and in addition to being present at the delivery the child's birth was registered by eminent Prestonpans doctor and Town Provost William McEwan.

Although the Census of April 1901 shows the infant Patrick still living in Tranent there is no record anywhere in Scotland of his mother or father in the Census. But later in 1901 the Rev. Mackay was most certainly back in Scotland because for his achievements both at home and abroad he was granted the degree of Doctor of Divinity by St Andrews University.

Military Ministry and the Great War

Following his return from India Dr Mackay served as a locum in Perth and subsequently at Bonar Bridge near Inverness. From there he traveled fairly extensively throughout Scotland on behalf of the Anglo-Indian Society until he was invited to become Minister of the Free Church congregation in Wick. An entry in *The Fasti of the United Free Church of Scotland 1900 – 1929* records him being translated from Prestonpans to Wick in 1902.

While at Wick Dr Mackay undertook much deputation work visiting places where "the feeling was difficult about the union" of the Free Church. He also edited a monthly magazine *The Highland Witness* and never lost his interest

Patrick Robson Mackay, CBE, Army Chaplain

Photo, Courtesy Executors of the late Mrs Jean Mackay

Mrs Harriet Mackay

Photo, Courtesy Executors of the late Mrs Jean Mackay

in military matters. That military interest was recognised in 1908 when he was offered a post at Army headquarters in Edinburgh.

Dr. Mackay resigned his Wick ministry and with his family returned to live at Chalmers Street in Edinburgh. He remained associated with the military for the remainder of his life and never returned to parish ministry.

Whitefoord House became the first of three residences for destitute veteran soldiers in Edinburgh and there is an engraved stonework dedication to Dr Mackay outside the hospital wing of these premises. The doctor was also founder and chairman of the Naval and Military Institute in Edinburgh.

During the 1914–1918 Great War he served as an Army Chaplain and was created Commander of the Order of the British Empire (Military Division) at Buckingham Palace on June 3rd 1919 "in recognition of valuable services rendered in connection with the war."

Patrick Mackay died at 11 Cumin Place, Edinburgh two years later on 17 June 1921 at the age of sixty six. He was apparently still employed in an ecclesiastical capacity for in addition to being described as a Minister of the United Free Church he was also shown as Chaplain of the Scottish Commons. He was buried in Prestonans cemetery in what would later become the family grave. Later two stained glass windows *The Good Samaritan* and *The Children* were placed in Grange Church, the former Free Church of Prestonpans, in his memory.

Patrick Mackay was survived by Harriet for over twenty nine years. After the death of her husband she returned to East Lothian and lived with her daughters Sabina and Peg at Ivy Lodge, Levenhall where she died on 5 December 1950 and was buried beside her husband at Prestonpans. Their youngest son Patrick Hugh Mackay was the only one of their children to marry. With his wife Jean, Patrick Hugh also returned to East Lothian in retirement and both died at North Berwick during 1994 and 2003 respectively to be buried in the family burial ground within Prestonpans cemetery.

Bibliography

Prestonpans and Vicinity, Peter McNeill
Fasti of the United Free Church
Haddingtonshire Courier
The Scotsman
Records of the Central Chancery, St James's Palace.
Papers on the Sprot and Mackay families 1707 – 1984, Rev. Patrick Hugh Robson Mackay, General Archives of Scotland, GD 483
Autobiography of Harriet Mackay, General Archives of Scotland GD483/30

Thanks also for the assistance provided by Mrs Elizabeth Dewar, Executor of the Estate of Mrs Jean Mackay.

8 WILLIAM MCEWAN

Dr William Crawford McEwan was born on 2 October 1859 in the Scottish Border village of Ancrum in Roxburghshire, eldest son of John Knox Free Church Minister the Rev. John McEwan and his wife Mary Crawford. After spending some years in the Borders where he attended primary school, William's father moved to a new charge in Edinburgh and the family took up residence at 36 Lauder Road on the south side of the city. They remained there until William attended Edinburgh University as a student of medicine and surgery.

Following graduation and the obligatory period gaining experience the new Dr. McEwan moved to Prestonpans where he became an integral part of village life for over four decades. He was already established at Prestonpans when he travelled to Paisley to marry Agnes Clazy. Dr. McEwan and his new wife were 'a son and daughter of the manse' and their wedding service was jointly conducted by their fathers.

William McEwan set up his surgery and living quarters in Walford House at the end of what is now Ormiston Place then known as Doctor's Wynd. That surgery bore little resemblance to its modern equivalent. Patients simply presented themselves at the published surgery times, rang the big brass door bell at Walford House and were admitted by his Highland born housekeeper Jane Stewart to the waiting room. From there they were eventually summoned by the doctor simply calling "Next." Allegedly there was never any problem in deciding who that was.

William McEwan came to Prestonpans when there was a great deal of deprivation in the town and from the outset he became involved in alleviating that situation, often at great financial cost to himself.

Cleaner Air for Prestonpans and Regatta Patron

Dr William C. McEwan

Photo – courtesy of Mrs Priscilla Miles

By 1893 McEwan had been elected to the Town Council and two years later in 1895 was elevated to the position of Town Provost which office he retained for nearly a decade until 1904. A long while before impure industrial emissions were considered a legal nuisance, as Town Provost he was instrumental in achieving a better standard of air quality within the town.

Parish Minister the Rev. George Stuart Smith wrote to the Town Council expressing concern on behalf of his parishioners regarding excessive smoke and other pollutant emissions from the various industries operating throughout Prestonpans. There was then absolutely no statutory control over what today would certainly be considered illegal production methods leading to air pollution. Provost McEwan would certainly have been well aware of the medical conditions likely to be made worse through breathing such unclean air. Accordingly he constituted two Council committees each of which were detailed to visit all the production units throughout Prestonpans in order that the overall situation should be investigated. Ultimately, where fault was found the industrial owners were asked to implement improvement measures. Although pollution was not at the time a criminal offence thanks to Dr McEwan there was a discernable improvement in air quality. In many cases it was not at all difficult. Some industrial owners already possessed air filter equipment but simply had never used it prior to the Town Council's initiative.

His election as a councillor also coincided with the ongoing controversy regarding the need for a Town Hall in Prestonpans. Dr. McEwan perceived a real need for such a centre and, in his new position as a councillor, ably assisted by others such as Lady Susan Grant-Suttie, he was able to overturn the negative decision of 1892. Prestonpans Town Hall was formally opened some years later in 1899 by Lord Haldane, the sitting Member of Parliament for East Lothian.

William McEwan made extensive use of the Town Hall as a venue for his many welfare projects, which usually contained some religious element. It seems he and his wife never did abandon the religious input of their formative years. He was also joint patron of the annual Prestonpans Regatta.

Prestonpans Library Opened

Another early and important project initiated by Dr. McEwan was the provision of a public library for the burgh. Libraries today are taken for granted but during the early 20th century were scarce outwith major conurbations. The Provost was already an active member of the School Board and considered a library to be an integral part of all educational processes. It was opened in 1904 whereupon he was appointed as its first Chairman.

During 1910, the doctor was also instrumental in forming the Men's Club which regularly met in the Town Hall during the winter months. Its members in addition to the almost mandatory religious instruction were encouraged to engage in debates covering diverse subjects as yet another extension of Dr. McEwan's interest in education. Most of the men were miners and were also instructed in the general principles of First Aid which as a doctor he considered an absolute necessity given the unsafe conditions associated then with working underground.

The Men's Club only lasted until 1914 when at the outbreak of the Great War most of its members enlisted in the armed forces. However, ably assisted by the local newsagent Dr. McEwan replaced the now defunct club with a similar gathering for boys of the burgh which became known as The Lad's Club. In addition to being something of a winter months' Bible Class and general social gathering, the club arranged an annual outing for the boys to some location outside the town such as North Berwick. Similar classes for Girls were also offered during the summer months. And somehow, at the weekends, he still found time to attend women's meetings at the old Cuthill Mission Hall.

His work over the years as a general medical practitioner gave rise to many stories concerning the individual experiences of residents of old Prestonpans. One who knew him well and worked beside him in public service said: "He was sympathetic with real illness but had little toleration for those who made much of their maladies." However he gained the overall respect of his patients, though not always prompt payment for his services. Many were too poor to pay, but that never detracted from the doctor's willingness to help. Initially in his horse drawn carriage and later in one of the first motor cars seen in the town, he was regularly seen on his rounds visiting those too infirm to attend his Walford House surgery.

For over forty years, the doctor was an Elder of Grange Church and a good friend of its late 19th Century Minister Patrick Mackay. When the latter was serving abroad in India during 1901 Dr. McEwan travelled to Tranent to deliver Mrs. Mackay's baby and, in the absence of its father, also registered the birth.

Dr William McEwan and Sons

Mrs. Agnes McEwan died on 26 June 1925 at the age of 65 but William McEwan worked on for quite a few more years before he formally retired from practice in 1934 at 75. For some time he had been assisted in the practice by his two sons Doctor Willie and Doctor George, both of whom would continue as general practitioners in the village through the advent of the National Health Service and beyond. Dr. George McEwan emigrated to Kenya in the fifties and unfortunately died there soon afterwards, but his brother remained in practice at Prestonpans until retiring to Longniddry. From the time his sons were co opted as assistants Dr. McEwan became affectionately known as Old Doctor McEwan.

In 1934 the Doctor returned to live in Edinburgh though he did not completely sever his links with Prestonpans. In Edinburgh he energetically pursued involvement with various Christian bodies including the Scottish Evangelistic Council, the Y.M.C.A. Fellowship and especially the Religious Tract Society of Scotland, of which he had been Chairman of the Board of Directors since 1933. He lived in formal retirement for some ten years until 9th July 1943 when he died suddenly at his Edinburgh home aged eighty five.

Dr William McEwan did indeed become a legend in his lifetime. In a mini-biography published in the September 1943 issue of *Monthly Visitor* a contemporary Andrew Stewart described his late friend as 'a man of great force of character, sterling honesty, fearless courage and a born leader who, for over half a century was probably the most influential figure in Prestonpans.'

Bibliography

The Haddingtonshire Courier
The Monthly Visitor
Minutes of Prestonpans Town Council 1893 – 1904

And grateful thanks for the assistance provided by Priscilla Miles, granddaughter of Dr. McEwan, and members of the Prestonpans Local History Society, especially Annette Gilroy.

9 JOHN MUIR

John Muir was born on 21 April 1838 in the town of Dunbar on the east coast of Scotland. His native country is naturally deeply proud to be associated with his name but it was his adopted homeland of the United States of America which has made John Muir an international hero and honoured in Scotland.

At the age of eleven John Muir's formal childhood schooling ended when he travelled with his family to farm at Fountain Lake, Wisconsin. Muir worked there on the family farm until the age of 21 when he left to pursue further studies and subsequently travel across the USA and Canada.

He arrived in California on 28 March 1868 aged 30. And it was there that he found his life's work. Extensive travelling had revealed to him the grandeur and wonder of the natural landscape, a grandeur he communicated brilliantly to others through his writings during this time. By 1876 Muir was actively involved in the fight to conserve the beauty of the wilderness country, not only in California but throughout the American west. It was largely through John Muir's efforts that Yosemite was established as a National Park in 1890. He continued to campaign successfully for the preservation of many other areas of outstanding natural beauty both as an individual, as a writer and as President of the Sierra Club which he co-founded in 1892 until his death from pneumonia on Christmas Eve 1914.

On his visit to Europe in 1893, Muir spent much of his time visiting his childhood haunts as well as undertaking expeditions further afield to the Scottish Highlands. He also found time to visit with a family friend who had moved to Prestonpans though he does not record his impressions of the locality which, at that time, was heavily polluted with industrial waste and emissions notwithstanding the best efforts of Dr William McEwan as Town Provost.

John Muir

In 1976 the John Muir Country Park on the East Lothian coast was opened near Dunbar, and in 1981 the former home of the Muir family was opened as a museum. 1983 saw the establishment of the John Muir Trust in Scotland which, for thirty years, has worked successfully to preserve large areas of wild land in Scotland. And since the establishment of the John Muir Award in 1997 it has also encouraged many hundreds of young people to become involved in conserving their environment.

An East Lothian study on coastal access for leisure purposes resulted in the establishment of the John Muir Way, which weaves its way mainly along the coast from Musselburgh just outside Edinburgh to John Muir's birthplace in Dunbar. And that Way includes the shores of Prestonpans on the Forth and the baronial foreshore opposite the Prestoungrange Gothenburg.

Those who walk the John Muir Way through Prestonpans are bound to ask themselves what this inspiring individual who gloried in untouched beauty in his adopted homeland but also in Scotland made of the ancient industrial landscape used and often abused by its residents over one thousand of years or more. Human presence was everywhere: in the coal bings which now he would be delighted to see form grassy slopes close to the sea; at the old infilled harbour of Morison's Haven; and in the jumbled collection of buildings which hug the shore, their varied architecture a testament to generations who lived and worked on the land and sea and yes even below that sea itself.

John Muir Way's myriad walkers who pause at the mural opposite the Prestoungrange Gothenburg at the junction of Redburn Road and High Street will see John Muir himself seated there, in the landscape of his much loved Yosemite, overlooking the shoreline of the country which gave him birth, as painted by Kate Hunter in memory of such a great man.

10 JAMES SCHAW AND MARY MURRAY

Although their involvement with Prestonpans began one hundred years apart these two extraordinary benefactors shared remarkable similarities as providers of residential education in Prestonpans, a town with which neither had any recorded previous connection.

In 1780 most of the old Preston Estate including Preston House, which had been in Lord Grange's ownership in the first half of the century, was purchased by Dr. James Schaw. He has no personal recorded history prior to that acquisition nor does he appear in any formal Scottish biographical records other than in abbreviated form relating to his endowment of the Prestonpans School. A family named Schaw living at Saltoun, East Lothian may have been related but there is no other possible East Lothian connection prior to his appearance at Prestonpans that year. And relatively soon afterwards in 1784 Dr. James Schaw died at Preston House bequeathing a legacy which provided handsomely for some of the young males of Prestonpans and the surrounding area.

Dr. Schaw bequeathed the majority of the Barony and Lands of Preston, together with the proceeds thereof, to create a trust for old Preston House "to be fitted up for the maintenance and education of boys of poor but respectable parents." He also left a small legacy to his daughter, Mrs. Sawyer, with the proviso that should she die without issue her inheritance would also revert to his Prestonpans Trust which it duly did.

Schaw's Hospital for Boys

There had always been a school of sorts in Prestonpans ever since the high profile establishment set up by John Davidson during the 17th century where Alexander Hume 'The Grammarian' taught Greek, Hebrew and Latin. In contrast Schaw's Hospital as it was to become known had a more fundamental educational purpose.

Not unexpectedly Dr Schaw attached many conditions to his legacy. Boys could only be admitted to the school between the ages of four and seven and remain there until they attained the age of fourteen. They were on admission to be absolutely free from the King's evil and from all contagious distempers. Preference was to be accorded to those with the surnames Schaw, MacNeill, Cunningham and Stewart. There was never any reason given for the preferential treatment accorded to the latter three surnames.

Schaw's Hospital opened as a school in Preston House during February 1789 initially run by a master, a housekeeper and two maid servants. There is no known reason for the five year delay in opening the establishment but initially and for many subsequent years there were only fifteen students enrolled at the school. The students were taught English, writing and arithmetic and also received some instruction in how to knit stockings and mend their clothes and shoes.

No fewer than 19 Trustees were appointed to supervise and administer these 15 boys and in keeping with the practice of the time they included the Parish Ministers of both Prestonpans and Tranent. On completion of their education those Trustees were empowered to "bind the boys as apprentices or otherwise let them out to businesses as they judge best." A Matron was later appointed with responsibility for the fundamental schoolhouse administration.

Preston House was eventually extended and adapted to successfully accommodate twenty four pupils. The Trustees, through prudent investments, had greatly enhanced the original bequest and decided to use the funds to create larger accommodation so more pupils could benefit. A new site was chosen just to the north of Preston House and in 1832 a new building designed in the old English Jacobean style by William Burn was completed at a cost of £3 000. The students together with their headmaster Mr. McBride moved to their new home and Preston House was abandoned.

Old Registers held within the Scottish Archives in Edinburgh do list names of many pupils who benefited from a Schaw education but those lists are thought to be incomplete. It cannot therefore be absolutely certain how many boys passed through the school. Some boys are known to have benefited greatly from their early education and many emigrated to America and elsewhere. William Jelly became a distinguished doctor of medicine in San Francisco and George Goldie a gymnastics instructor at Princeton University in the USA whilst John Chisholm became an eminent dental surgeon in

Edinburgh. The first pupil with the surname Shaw – without the 'c' – was not admitted to the school until 1804 and he later became Chief Accountant of the old Eastern Bank.

The school was brought to an end by the Endowed Hospitals Act of 1881. Schaw's funds were appropriated and the establishment ceased to operate coincidentally in the same year as the high profile opening of Prestonpans Public School by Lady Susan Grant-Suttie. Despite the closure of Schaw's school a financial legacy remained which provided an annual award well into the 20th century for the best pupil attending secondary school in Prestonpans.

****

Mary Murray died at the age of 86 at her High Street home in Dysart, Fife on 26 November 1861. She was born in Edinburgh the daughter of wine merchant William Murray and his wife Margaret. Neither Mary or her parents have any traceable connection with Prestonpans. Her exact place of birth and parentage are unclear but her Will made provision for girls that was strikingly similar to that made by James Schaw a century earlier in respect of boys. Her bequest was to found "an hospital for the training of female children of poor but respectable parents as domestic servants".

On her death, the Estate was worth some £20 000 but she, perhaps unusually, expressed a primary condition that the sum should be allowed to accumulate for a period of twenty one years under the care of named Trustees – John Dundas, William Wilson, Samuel Davidson and Alexander Montgomery Bell. By 1882, Mary Murray's legacy had increased to £36 000. By then unfortunately the original trustees had passed away but alternative trustees – the Keeper of the Signet and his Deputy together with their Commissioners – had assumed administration of the Mary Murray Trust.

In 1882 those new trustees proceeded to take a twenty five years lease of the old and empty Schaw's Hospital building to implement the directions of Miss Murray in setting up her proposed school for girls. Like Schaw a century previously Miss Murray's Will contained copious conditions, provisos and strict rules to be absolutely observed by her trustees.

The Murray Institute for Girls

Children with the surname Murray, if their claims in all other respects appeared to her trustees to be equal, were to be given preference of admission to the school. Children were to be accepted between the ages of six and eight and remain there until age fourteen, at which time they were to be found a place in domestic service. Whereas Schaw's directions had allowed some discretion regarding employment subsequent to the boys' formal education all pupils of the Mary Murray Institute were invariably to be placed in domestic service.

To equip them for such employment the girls were to be instructed in reading, writing, arithmetic, sewing, spinning, knitting 'and such other plain, useful acquirements as my said Trustees shall think best calculated for them'. However, the most important requirement was that all the pupils were to be taught the principles of religion, honesty and truth. Reading of the Scriptures together with prayers were to be a morning and evening necessity.

No male teacher or chaplain was ever to be admitted or employed in the school, the whole establishment to be controlled by a 'proper mistress' or matron appointed at the discretion of the trustees. Miss Isabella Meikle, previously of Donaldson's School in Edinburgh, was appointed Matron and apparently remained in that position throughout her working life as indeed did many of the later teachers.

Miss Murray empowered the trustees to determine rules for actual management and general administration of the school. It was decided that the establishment would be run by eight directors all of whom were appointed from the Office of the Signet. They were the Keeper of the Signet, his Deputy and six of his Commissioners. These men formulated specific rules which effectively guaranteed the smooth running of the school.

Unlike the delay in setting up Schaw's school the Mary Murray Institute opened in 1882 with an initial intake of twenty six students including two from Dysart in Fife, where the Magistrates and Town Council had been invited annually to nominate two girls for admission to the institution. This was not a prescribed requirement of the Will so the Dysart invitation must supposedly have been a gesture of good will by the administrators.

There was never any breath of scandal associated with the Murray Institute and a report dated 1901 revealed that by that year many girls had completed their education and been placed successfully in domestic service. During 1901 the yearly roll of students had increased to sixty eight and Miss Meikle was confirmed as still in charge. Another teacher, Miss Thomson, had already recorded sixteen years service giving an indication of stability within the teaching and administrative staff.

Miss Murray's concern for the pupils obviously extended beyond the years of their formal education. If a student had remained with her first employer until the age of twenty then "provided she had at all times conducted herself with decorum (she) would receive a present not exceeding £10 from Miss Murray's Trust either on the occasion of her marriage or attaining the age of forty". In practice because of the excellent management of funds by the Trustees every girl who successfully concluded her formal education was given a present of £10 on leaving the Institute. It was further provided that any former pupil attaining the age of sixty, and having no home of her own, could return to live in the Institute where she would be given work in accordance with her age and strength, subject to the woman having throughout her life, conducted herself with "proper propriety".

Extensive changes in the provision of formal education during the first half of the 20th century saw the gradual demise of the Murray Institute. The old Schaw School building survived for many years as a venue for other purposes.

Bibliography

Prestonpans and Vicinity, Peter MacNeill
Old Scottish Statistical Account, Vol. 17.

11 SIR WALTER SCOTT

Sir Walter Scott has achieved world-wide renown for his poetry and his historical novels. He was born on 15th August 1771 and is primarily associated with the Border country where his estate at Abbotsford has become a place of pilgrimage for his many devotees. But Walter Scott also had very strong associations with the East of Scotland including our small coastal village of Prestonpans.

After an attack of polio left the young Walter with a damaged leg his parents sent him away from the unhealthy atmosphere of Edinburgh to his grandfather's Sandyknowe Farm at Smailholm in Roxburghshire. And it was at Sandyknowe that he first developed his lifelong enthusiasm for the old tales and ballads of his native Scotland.

Sir Walter Scott

By the age of eight he had returned to Edinburgh but efforts to restore mobility to his damaged leg continued and he was sent to Prestonpans just 10 miles from Edinburgh where it was hoped that the sea water would assist his lameness. His visit is commemorated by a plaque in the High Street at the location where Scott resided and in Walter Scott Pend which would have been the route taken by him for sea bathing.

At Prestonpans he continued to seek out local tales and legends and made the acquaintance of two men who were to have a significant influence on his later writings. They were family friends George Constable and Captain Dalgety, a retired soldier who continued to take a great interest in military campaigns. George Constable had a fund of interesting tales from many sources particularly including memories of the Jacobite rebellion in 1745. Young Walter also spent many hours debating the progress of British military campaigns with Captain Dalgety.

Prestonpans had of course been the site some 34 years earlier of the battle at which the Young Pretender Charles Edward Stuart had routed the Hanoverian forces led by Sir John Cope and opened the way for a victorious advance towards the City of London. To the young boy this must have given the area strong romantic associations. It provided the source for one of the most dramatic episodes in *Waverley*, his first novel published in 1814. That his early visits to Prestonpans influenced his description of the Battle of Prestonpans is clear from the wealth of local detail he includes in his description of the battle. This includes his precise account of the death of Colonel James Gardiner, a local landowner who fought courageously for the Hanoverian cause that day.

Other memories of his days at Prestonpans appear in Sir Walter Scott's writings such as *The Antiquary*, where the title character is based on George Constable who spent a great deal of time with the young Walter and his aunt during their time at Prestonpans. Sir Walter Scott died in 1832.

Bibliography

Wilson, E. (2000), 'Sir Walter Scott's Memories of Prestonpans', in *Tales of the Pans*, Prestonpans Local History Society, 2000, pp 72–73.

12 DAVID SPENCE

David Spence, M.B.E., is famed not only in Prestongrange and East Lothian but throughout the Scottish mining history. His long association with mining in The Lothians and Fife for most of the 20th century, together with his enduring passion to ensure the creation of Prestongrange Heritage Mining Museum, is comprehensively recorded elsewhere. The major source is the David Spence Archive within East Lothian Library headquarters at Haddington.

'Davie' Spence was not a native of Prestonpans. His association began as a local employee who eventually went on to have a lasting influence on the area. He was born at 10 Arniston Place, Bonnyrigg, Midlothian on 2 October 1900 to David Spence and his wife Margaret Gordon. His father was a miner as indeed were the majority of workers of the time in that area and it was certainly by choice that Davie Spence followed in his father's footsteps.

The young David showed early signs of academic ability which could, had he been so inclined, have removed him from involvement with mines and mining industry. The family moved to Tranent where David attended primary school. Some of his class mates were Bertie Wood, Archie Buchanan, William Sheddan, Adam Shields, James Yorston, Alex Tennant and Thomas Watson. At the age of 13, David obtained a bursary to cover three years study at Broughton High School in Edinburgh. Among his papers Davie Spence kept newspaper cuttings regarding that Traill Bursary which was open to all children attending schools in East Lothian during the early part of the century.

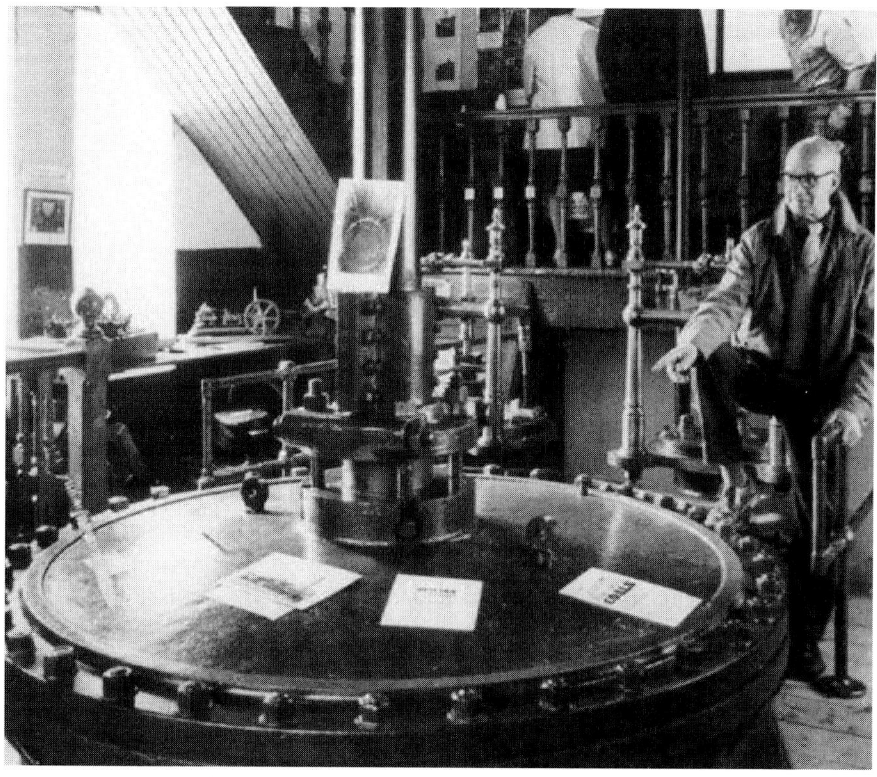

David Spence in the Beam Engine Room at Prestongrange Colliery
Courtesy East Lothian Museum Service

Determined to be a Miner

Broughton School did not retain Davie Spence long as a pupil. After a relatively short experience of Edinburgh education he returned one evening to Tranent to advise his parents that he had "left school and was going to the pits." The motivation for what some might see as a foolish decision is unrecorded. Young Davie was told by the Broughton headmaster: "Spence, you will regret this day for the rest of your life." Happily, although his decision to abandon education was also a big disappointment to his mother, there is no evidence that Davie ever did regret his chosen way of life. However, the unused part of his bursary was necessarily refunded and the used portion repaid which would have been difficult for a mining family.

On the Monday following his momentous and life changing decision, Davie Spence joined his father working underground in nearby St. Germains Colliery then owned by the Ugston Coal Company. His father stripped the coal which Davie loaded on to hutches before manhandling those conveyances out to a main underground despatch point. He remained at St. Germians until becoming unemployed, without warning or notice, when the mine ceased production and shut down in 1922. The closure certainly cannot have been for lack of coal reserves. Coal was still being produced from open cast operations in the adjacent area of Blindwells some sixty years later. Indeed when David Spence was given a conducted tour of the East Lothian Open Cast Mine project at that location during the early nineteen eighties he was able to identify the same seams of coal which he had worked from underground at St Germains.

There were however many coal mines in the East and Mid Lothian area which could provide alternative employment. Davie soon found a new job at Oxenfoord Colliery near Pathhead, Midlothian. That pit was between five and six miles from Tranent and the travelling was scarcely convenient and after only a year at Oxenfoord Davie moved again. This time he went to the old Fleets Colliery owned by the Edinburgh Coal Company located between Tranent and Ormiston. He was still in that employment during 1927 when the Fleets mine was temporarily flooded. Underground water in that pit, as with most of those in East Lothian, was a continual hazard. Davie was not himself underground when the flooding occurred and fortunately all those who were reached the surface safely. The colliery was however out of action for some days until all the floodwater had been pumped out.

Many sporting and social activities were available to young men during the early 20th century. Local track and field Games were regularly held in Tranent and surrounding villages and every village had its own football team, often affiliated to the Scottish Junior League. Davie Spence excelled as a wing half with nearby Macmerry St. Clair apparently attracting the attention of senior clubs which, had he chosen, could have provided another exit from a miner's life. He was also a dancer of considerable ability and won numerous medals in local competitions.

Despite the privations created by the Miners' Strikes of 1921 and 1926 David Spence continued in his chosen occupation. On 2 January 1931 when he married Violet Hastie Beale in Edinburgh he was a colliery oversman living at 34 Lammermoor Terrace, Tranent. Perhaps his new marital responsibilities brought the realisation that he should not have been so impulsive in abandoning Broughton High School. That same year he enrolled for a course of study

which, due to the necessities of shift working, meant Saturday evening was the only time he could regularly attend classes. The qualifications he obtained after six years' study he could probably have obtained in three years at Broughton High School.

Into Management and Nationalisation

In 1937 he was appointed Under Manager at Michael Colliery in Fife, his first taste of managerial experience. Coal mines were of course then still privately owned and it was possible in a managerial capacity to negotiate personal terms with the mine owners. Through that system Davie returned relatively soon to the Fleets Colliery now as Deputy Manager.

He remained at 'The Fleets' for only a short time. Just prior to World War II Davie moved to the Klondyke pit at Newcraighall to fill the post of Manager. During the first week of February 1941 he received a letter from an old school mate, Thomas Watson, who was employed by the Binley Colliery near Coventry containing a job offer in the post of Colliery Under Manager with a weekly wage of £8/10/- plus 17/- per week 'war bonus' together with a house, free coals and 'other perquisites'. But Davie chose not to accept the offer. No reason can be determined for his decision – perhaps he was still considering it a few months later when Coventry was blitzed by the German Luftwaffe or perhaps he simply preferred to remain in Scotland. He spent the war years as Manager of Newcraighall.

David Spence was still at Newcraighall and a well known local colliery

Manager when on 1st January 1947 the newly created National Coal Board assumed responsibility for all British mining. Many of the old mine owners in addition to being financially well compensated for the loss of their pits were also co-opted as Coal Board administrators and board members. That co-option would have undoubtedly been partly responsible for recognition of ability which resulted in David Spence's appointment as Group Manager of the Wallyford Group of collieries, which then included the mines at Carberry, Prestonlinks and Prestongrange. Promotion was rapid and after a relatively short interval he was moved again this time to oversee the much larger Newbattle Group.

As Newbattle Group Manager David Spence oversaw the gradual run down of pick and shovel coal production and the introduction of massive coal cutting machines. In his time old wooden pit props were also gradually replaced with steel thereby enhancing the safety of workers. Miners' welfare also assumed greater importance with the appearance of pit head baths and canteens where hot food was available if required. First Aid Centres, usually permanently staffed with a nurse, also appeared on pitheads.

Progress in mining was a double edged sword. During the later years of Davie Spence's administration the smaller Lothian pits such as Carberry, Newcraighall, Fleets, Easthouses, Lingerwood, Lady Victoria (which would later also house the Scottish Mining Museum) Rosewell and Burghleigh all closed in favour of larger mines. Monktonhall colliery was opened on the border of East Lothian and Bilston Glen colliery at Loanhead in Midlothian.

In December 1962 almost coincidental with the opening of Monktonhall Colliery coal production ceased at Prestongrange mine. That pit which in 1947, when the National Coal Board assumed ownership, employed 500 producing 144,000 tons a year, was not considered economically suitable for improvement largely due to the high incidence of underground water. Demand for coal was already beginning to decline and Prestongrange was considered expendable.

Almost inevitably following closure neglect of the site led to it becoming overgrown together with a progressive degree of vandalism. The presence of underground water which had been considered a prime factor leading to the mine's closure had, until 1954, been controlled with pumps operated by the Cornish Beam Engine on the pithead. This engine, installed in 1874 and the only surviving one of its type in Scotland, became so badly vandalised that in 1968 the National Coal Board decided it should be demolished in the interest of safety.

Creating Prestongrange Museum

By this time in his sixty-eighth year Davie Spence, though long retired, was an acknowledged mining historian still much in demand as a speaker and columnist. Indeed he often claimed to have retired early so he could write about mining history. He had observed with growing dismay and indignation the steady degeneration of his former Prestongrange workplace and was appalled at the proposition to destroy the beam engine. He initiated urgent action primarily to save the engine, but along with it he carried the entire site to create a Scottish mining museum.

Details of his actions in that respect are much too extensive to record here but after enlisting the invaluable assistance of Frank Tindall, East Lothian's legendary County Planning Officer, agreement was reached with the National Coal Board that East Lothian Council would acquire the old Prestongrange colliery site.

On 16th July 1968 a committee with representatives of the National Coal Board, National Union of Mineworkers, East Lothian Antiquarian and Field Naturalists Society, Institute of Mechanical Engineers, The Royal Scottish Museum and the Council together with David Spence was constituted. Its mission was: "*To explore the possibility of establishing a historical site for the East Lothian Mining Industry at Prestongrange and report back to the Planning Committee*".

As the explorations began a team of some twenty volunteers was recruited to repair and restore the Cornish Beam Engine. That team worked under the direction of Davie Spence, James Blaik – a retired colliery electrician – and William Scott. There was also input from Moray House College of Education in Edinburgh. The initial restoration was successful and over the ensuing years the mining museum steadily took shape. A group of secondary schoolboys from Portobello began to provide help twice weekly at the embryo museum. Their technical teacher at Portobello, Colin Oswald, claimed the restoration work made the boys keener on an engineering career.

With the assistance of the National Coal Board and many other bodies there was a progressive expansion. The Council also later acquired the old Morison's Haven site together with the Prestongrange Brick and Fireclay Pipe Works and the pithead baths. Some other enthusiastic volunteers formed *The Prestongrange Society* which became engaged in the ongoing refurbishment and restoration of the site.

From its inception, David Spence was acknowledged as the Museum's prime administrator and procurer of services. He was responsible for obtaining many fine exhibits of colliery equipment and associated items of interest including working examples of 'pugs' or colliery locomotives, cranes and winding gear. Later in life he also donated all his many personal mining artefacts. Although initial progress was relatively slow by 1980 the growth of the museum had made it necessary to employ a full time caretaker. Also in that year, a Management Committee and Working Party were formed with Davie involved in both at nearly eighty years of age. He was appointed lifetime Honorary Curator of the Museum and all his efforts resulted in the award of his M.B.E.

During 1981/1982 the Scottish Development Agency carried out final re-grading and landscaping at the museum including better road access, foot paths and car parks.

The official opening of the Mining Museum took place at Prestongrange on 28th September 1984. Development expenditure on the project up to that time was given as £1m. The inauguration took place at a time of some turbulence within the mining industry which was in the throes of a protracted national strike. National Union of Mineworkers officials decided at the last moment not to attend the opening, probably due to the attendance of Members of Parliament and ranking National Coal Board officials – which was a most unfortunate political distraction for such proceedings. And the other absentee alas was David Spence himself who had been hurt in a fall the previous evening and was in hospital.

It can be unequivocally observed that without the Herculean leadership of David Spence there would be no mining museum at Prestongrange. And to honour his memory today's stewards face the challenge of making it live again.

He died the following year on 28th December at Longmore Hospital Edinburgh. *The East Lothian Courier* Obituary published on 10 January 1986 provides a condensed and factual biographical account of his life and achievements which justifiably describes David Spence as 'Founder of the Scottish Mining Museum at Prestongrange', a view echoed by East Lothian Local Councillor Tom Wilson in the September 1986 issue of *Coalface*. Tom Wilson wrote: "The Scottish Mining Museum remains indebted to him for it was his drive and enthusiasm which laid the foundations on which the Scottish Mining Museum Trust continues to build."

Acknowledgements

Coalface Magazine
Edinburgh Evening News
The Scotsman
East Lothian Courier
David Spence Archive, East Lothian Library H.Q.
Registers for Scotland
John Muir Papers, Holt Atherton Special Collections, University of the Pacific Library

19

The Roads that led by Prestoungrange

a journey through the landscape

Andrew Ralton

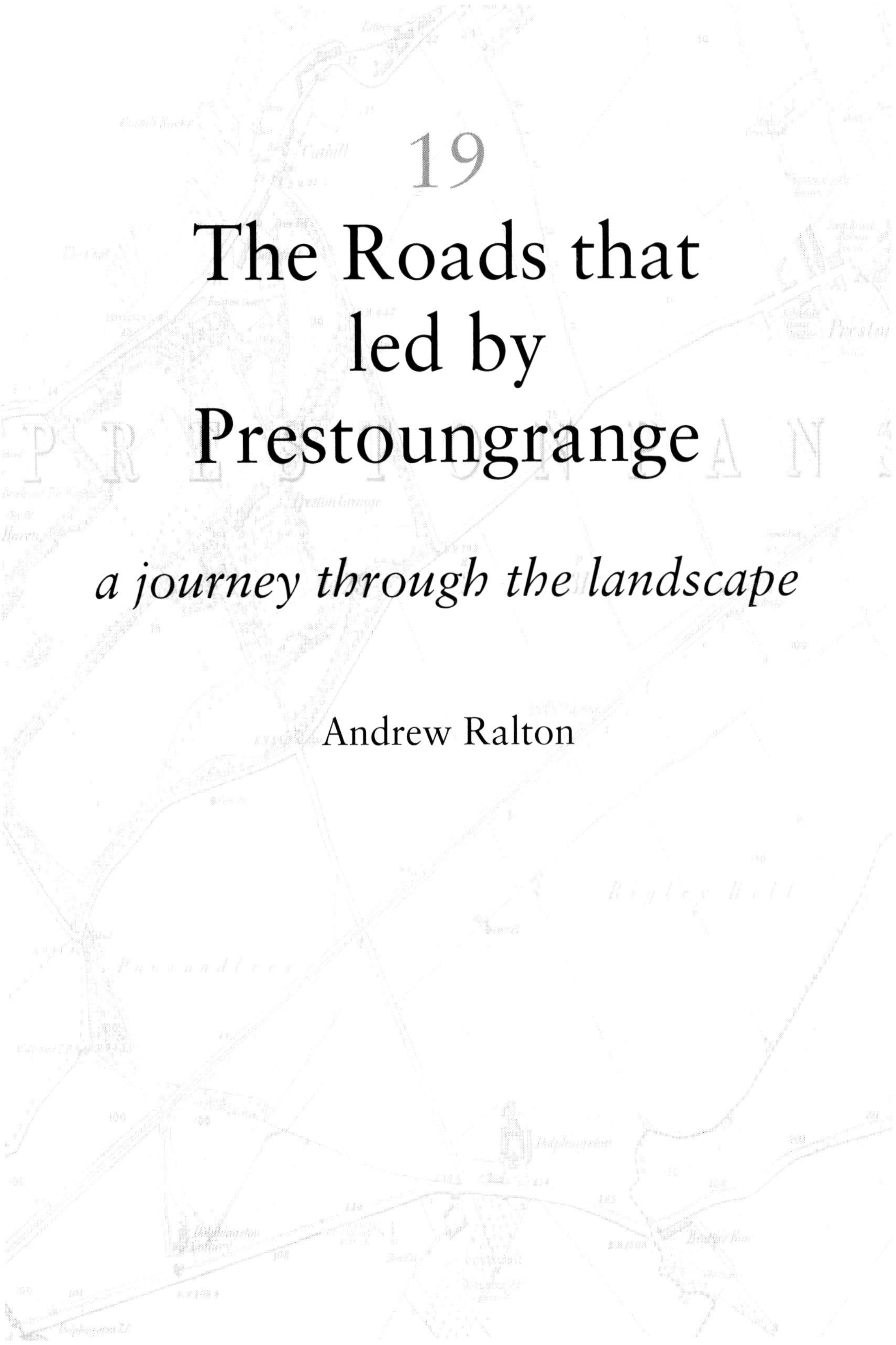

INTRODUCTION

This book is about roads and the how, why and where of their occurrence in the Prestonpans area through the ages. It has also been necessary to venture beyond the bounds of Prestonpans to show the reader where these roads led to and from, and where archaeological evidence has been found. In any study of roads the landscape must feature prominently if one is to show the natural obstacles man has had to overcome, or indeed the 'natural highways' that the landscape has provided. This landscape has been much modified by man, including development of roads and ways, and many prominent, and not so prominent, features in the landscape of Prestonpans will also be pointed out. The title of this book indicates that while it is possible to trail and explore the town of Prestonpans and vicinity in a single day it is however much better to explore 'The Pans' over a much longer period.

It is also important to note that although many of the routes described in this book are public roads, or perhaps even public rights of way, not every route will be so and it is not intended that the reader should assume that they may access every route freely without consideration for the rights of the proprietors to manage their land safely and efficiently.

Finally, the scope of this work, covering a huge period of time has inevitably meant that I have only scratched the surface; and with this in mind I have included an extensive bibliography for future researchers to explore should this publication spark a greater interest in any of the themes or time-periods mentioned.

THE LANDSCAPE OF PRESTONPANS AND VICINITY

The original settlement of what is now known as Prestonpans was called Aldhammer. It was as the land passed in ownership to the Cistercian order of monks of Newbattle (originally Neubotle)[1] that the town came to be known as the 'Priests toun,' although there are indications that other priestly establishments were linked with the town before this, or near to this time.

However, some time before 1189 Robert De Quinci granted the monks of Newbattle a portion of the land in his possession, De Quinci owning the lands of Traffernent (Tranent).[2] A translation[3] of the Charter states the boundaries thus:

> *As the burn of Whytrig falls into the sea, on the east, to the Marches of the Abbot of Dunfermling's lands of Inveresch and Pontekyn* [Pinkie], *namely as the rivulet runs from Fauside to the sea, and that I, in presence of good men, perambulated the march between my own mains and Meduflat, and cast ditches for a memorial.*

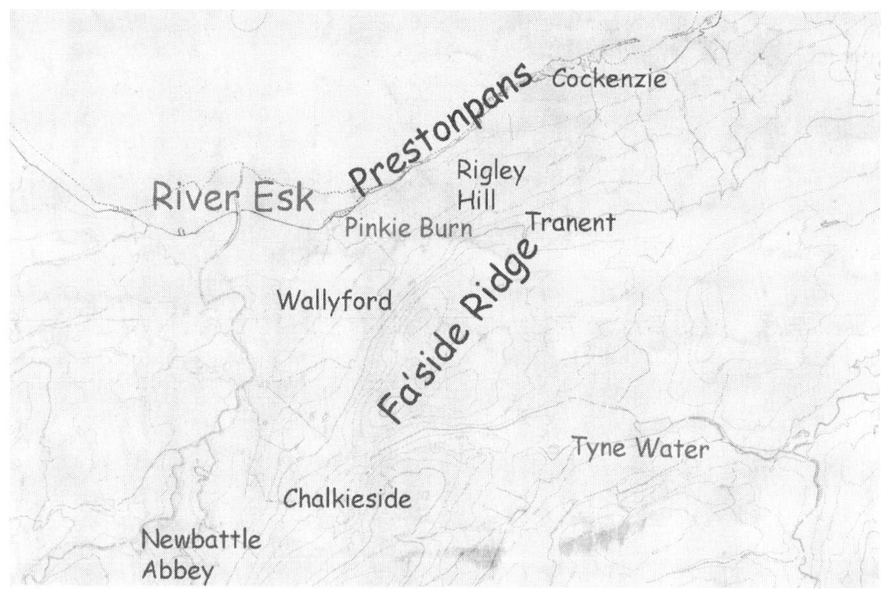

Prestonpans in its surrounding Landscape

Titles superimposed on Sheet 74 of the Ordnance Survey, 1930, OS One Inch Popular Edition [Water-Contour-pull map] © National Library of Scotland

This grant of land was extended by Robert's heir Seyer De Quinci, Earl of Winchester, in successive charters from 1200– 1210 and was thus extended to include half of the marsh nearest the De Quinci properties, as well as the right to work and quarry coal (*carbonarium*) and the rights to the foreshore between aforementioned boundaries.[4] The Charter of 1209 is the earliest known granting of rights to mine coal in Great Britain.

The Charter refers to the natural landscape and environment of the area, and I will attempt to describe that landscape and how it formed a natural compartment for man through the ages, and how this landscape has governed man's activities including travel.

Fauside (Falside) is part of the Tranent/Falside ridge looking over the western bay of the Firth of Forth at East Lothian. It is part of the D'Arcy / Crossgatehall geological fold,[5] which is part of the range of higher land created through tectonic movements from the Southern Uplands geological fault line forcing the Midland Valley of Scotland against the Highland boundary fault line. The burn of Whytrig refers to a stream, now not obvious on the ground but possibly the same as the "dribbling burnie" described by McNeill and others.[6] This ran from the prominence of Whytrig Hill, (Rigley Hill) approximately 200 feet above sea level, currently sandwiched between the new A1 and the main Edinburgh to London railway line, and down on the approximate line of what was to become known as West Loan.

The Ice Age also significantly shaped this part of lowland Scotland, leaving its mark in the form of 'raised beaches.' This is where the land, after having been compressed for thousands of years by an enormous weight of ice, covering both land and sea, springs back again over a period of thousands of years so that land on the edge of the sea rises up. In the Prestonpans / Musselburgh area evidence for this can be seen where the raised beach comes 25 to 75 feet above present day sea level. Such land is well drained and made an excellent location for settlement, agriculture, and of course transport.[7]

Ice age glaciers, which affected the Forth Valley during the Loch Lomond Readvance about 11,000 years ago,[8] left evidence of their activity as they carried rock debris for miles and deposited as they receded. These 'glacial erratics'[9] are generally rounded boulders smoothed by the scouring action of the ice. (Johnny Moat, named after a former excise man,[10] is one such rock on the Prestonpans shoreline.)

MAN IN THE PREHISTORIC ENVIRONMENT

Early man's arrival in the landscape of this part of Scotland around about 7,000 B.C.[11] was probably by sea, and he is likely to have been met by the view of the dominant Tranent ridge, which at that time was likely to have been covered in oak and hazel woods.[12] Much of the lower lying land would have been swamp and marsh and probably very dangerous to cross.

Prehistoric man's need for food, clothing and shelter meant he had to hunt and gather for life's essentials. Ridgeways, such as the Tranent ridge, afforded dry, safe routes where the wider countryside could be seen, and were free of places where enemies might hide. Such prehistoric ridgeway routes as the Icknield Way in South East Anglia were 'made and maintained' by usage – perhaps following existing animal tracks.[13] These routes were not fixed carriageways. Instead "the traveller would pick, within the whole width of the ridge, the best, firmest, hardest and driest way."[14]

Alternatively, man's ingenuity was utilised to the full in making tracks and routeways across the swamps and moors, such as 'The Sweet Track' in the Somerset Levels.[15] The Sweet Track was a remarkable piece of engineering and planning in which wood, especially managed and harvested for this purpose, was split and laid to form a platform with supporting posts, and this afforded a safe passage across hazardous swamps.

The evidence for such structures and routes in Scotland, let alone our part of East Lothian, is sparse it has to be said. However, it seems likely that there would have been many routes from prehistoric times, particularly over high and naturally well drained land, such as at Tranent ridge. Evidence of prehistoric trade and communication can be seen in the archaeological finds, particularly where petrological evidence is found i.e. the study of where a particular kind of stone that is known to outcrop in only a few places in Great Britain is found out of its natural area. An example of this is the stone axe found in Tranent dating from the Neolithic age and thought to have originated in the prehistoric 'stone-axe factory' at Langdale Pikes in Cumbria.[16] Conversely, deposits of shells and other coastal artefacts inland from Prestonpans may well indicate that these relics have been brought as a special commodity. It is most likely, however, that sea and water routes were the most important means of travelling long distances in prehistoric times rather than land routes.[17]

Early man's way of life changed as his knowledge and mastery of the environment grew. From the hunter and the gatherer nomadic life, he developed over time a system of agriculture and learned to grow food on the land. The earliest known record of the people of this region names them the *Votadini,* ascribed to them by the Greek geographer Ptolemy.[18] These people spoke a language akin to modern day Welsh. The territory of the Votadini

(Guotodin in Welsh[19]) spanned from Clackmannan at the head of the Forth to the river Weir or Tyne in England,[20] and included Traprain Law where extensive settlement remains have been excavated.

THE LEGACY OF THE ROMANS

No history of roads should fail to mention the Roman period of occupation in North Britain. We must take a jump through time to the years 78–82 AD when the Romans brought new skill and experience to road construction in Britain. Each road that the Romans built was precisely planned and took the most direct route to its destination; not always straight and sometimes following the natural highways of some of the prehistoric and later routes. The main purpose of the Roman road building in Scotland was to facilitate their military campaign to extend the bounds of the Roman Empire. This was pursued by General Julius Agricola through the building of military roads such as Dere Street (built circa 80 AD), which ran from Corbridge, across the line of what was to become Hadrian's Wall (built 120 AD), to Rochester, to Newstead (Trimontium), and beyond to Lauder, Pathhead, Ford, to Dalkeith and the Elginhaugh Fort, and, it is believed, continued to Cramond (later to be part of a chain of forts across the isthmus that separates the Firths of Clyde and Forth, known as the Antonine Wall, circa 143 AD).[21]

The connection with our part of East Lothian becomes stronger when the Roman Fort is examined at Inveresk, where St Michael's church was later to be built. This Fort belongs to the later Antonine period (142–163 AD) of the Roman occupation.[22] A road link is suggested leading from Dere Street to Inveresk by the account of the 'Expedecion of His Grace of Somerset) by his Chronicler Patten[23] in the lead up to the Battle of Pinkie (10 September 1547):

> *Fro this hil of Fanxside Bray descended my Lorde's grace, my Lorde Lieutenant and another along before their cape (Camp) within less than two flights shottes, into a lane or street of a thirty feet brode, the fenced on either side with a wall of turf, an elle of height; which way did lead straight northwards, and nie to a church called St. Mighaels, of Undreske.*

That the road 'did lead straight northwards' towards St Michael's church is highly suggestive that this was indeed a Roman road and approaching from Falside suggests a line similar to that taken by the current road leading past Carberry to Pathhead and joining the known alignment of Dere Street. 'Strete' is the forerunner of our word 'street' and its original meaning referred to a paved road the type of which was constructed by the Romans.

It has also been put forward that the Fort of Inveresk was linked to the other Roman roads coming from the west via Biggar and the Pentland Hills. One may speculate as to what line this connecting road may have taken. If we are to look at the Ordnance Survey Dalkeith map of 1853 one can make out a straight line leading along existing tracks or field boundaries and from the Old Cow Bridge over the South Esk at Dalkeith through the policies of Dalkeith Palace, towards Smeaton Dairy where there appears to be a rectangular land formation suggestive of a fort. This is also shown on Roy's map of 1755, and rather gives the impression that this straight line from the medieveal bridge pre-dates the surrounding fields. The fact that in the vicinity there is a farm called Castlesteads, and that there has been an archaeological dig uncovering *paved areas*, is very suggestive that there may well be remains of Roman road-building activity. This is at the moment without further supporting evidence, and is surely worthy of further investigation.

The Roman road continued from the Fort at Inveresk beyond to the Roman Harbour at Fisherrow and along the coast, on Fishwives Causeway[24] behind what is now Portobello, to what was to become the Edinburgh village of Restalrig. As Anderson[25] has stated, there is no direct evidence of Roman presence at Prestonpans; although, recent finds of chards from a Roman amphora (a jug-like storage vessel) at Prestonpans again raises this idea as a possibility.[26]

SALT: A VITAL TRADING COMMODITY

There is a strong link between the Romans and salt making of course. The Romans had their *Via Salaria* as we have our *Salters Road* (leading from Prestonpans to Dalkeith, of which more later). The importance of salt to the well being of all living things cannot be underestimated.[27] As well as providing essential minerals to the body, salt was also used to preserve food. The Romans, as an advanced and refined society, knew this well and they had even coined several words in this respect. The word 'soldier' comes to us from 'Saldare'[28] meaning to give salt; and 'salary' has its meaning from the same origin, as the Roman soldiers were paid in salt.

The Celtic word for salt was *Halen*,[29] and evidence of the use of this word in lowland Scotland may possibly be seen in the settlement of Halltree, (also known as Kirkcoltoun when it was the property of the Monks of Newbattle[30]), to the east of Heriot and near to the current line of the A7. This meaning, if correct, would suggest that this was a *Salt Settlement* and may have been an important centre of salt trading, during the resurgence of the Celtic peoples after the decline of the Roman Empire. That there must have been a localised centre for trade would seem highly probable as the position of the settlement is at the crux of three main valleys (Wedale of the Gala Water, the valley of the Armet Water, and the Heriot Water valley); and these valleys today form main lines of communication into the Borders. This point of time in the history of Scotland is known as the Dark Ages.

The presence of the Votadini acted as a 'buffer' between the two Roman walls and kept marauding Picts at bay. When the power of the Roman Empire began to wane in the fifth century the territory of the Votadini became more susceptible to incursions from beyond the walls.

Not long after this time the Firth of Forth would have been frequented by people from Continental Europe. The 12th century account of the sixth century St Kentigern by Jocelyn the Monk of Furness[31] states that when Theneu, Kentigern's mother, was cast out into the Firth of Forth as a punishment by Loth, her father, for being pregant against his wishes, her simple boat drifted by the Isle of May where the people of Belgae and Gallia (the people of the Low Countries and France) fished.

The Firth of Forth was at this time a highway to the North Sea. It is possible that the incursion of the Anglic peoples from Friesia[32] (part of the Low Countries to the north of Germany), who themselves had mastered the technology of salt production,[33] coincided with the establishment of the settlement of Aldhammer (Old Village) in the mid seventh century at what was to become Prestonpans. Although not much is known about land routes in Scotland at this time we can infer that any organised transport networks over land may have been similar in method to those that were developing in parallel in Ireland at this time for which there is some evidence.[34]

SALINA DE PRESTUN

Little is known about the life of Aldhammer, as Prestonpans was known during these Dark Ages. We can however generalize from what was going on elsewhere in Scotland at that time, as Christianity first took hold over the land with the preachings of holy men and women like St Columba and St Monenna. The latter saint founding five churches in Scotland at the beginning of the sixth century, one of which was on 'Dunpeledur Law' (Traprain Law today), at which it is supposed that Theneu served. However, we must return to where we started this book, the the Middle Ages and the industry of the Newbattle Monks. To this period we look to King David I and his religious reforms that founded several monasteries in Scotland at this time and introduced continental monastic orders such as the Augustinians of Holyrood, and the Cistercians of Melrose and Newbattle, all of which are linked to Presonpans.[35]

According to Lord Wemyss when writing his appendix to the First Statistical Account of Prestonpans, evidence of the Newbattle Monks with Prestonpans can be seen in the name Olivestob: meaning Holy Stop, or the place where the *Host* stopped,[36] and this place was meant to mark a stop on the procession of the Newbattle Monks from Preston.

McNeill has speculated that the old Church of Preston was in this vicinity, and that the walls enclosing Northfield House, and perhaps also its ancient Doocot, may in fact contain stone from an ancient Church, the stone reused in McNeill's time in *Katie Herrin's Close*.[37] The Church, as well as the Tower of Preston, was subsequently destroyed by the Earl of Hertford, prior to the Battle of Pinkie. However, it is quite likely that there was more than one church in the district of Prestonpans at this time, as the Canons of Holyrood also had lands in Preston.

Furthermore, the presence of the west Churchyard lying off Prestonpans High Street, where there are some very ancient tombstones, also suggests that there may have been a church connected to this, and it would seem quite probable that a church, if it existed there, could well have been the property of the Monks of Newbattle; with the Canons holding a church at Preston.[38]

Elsewhere, a strange engraved stone is alluded to by McNeill as possibly belonging to the original Church of Preston and being built into a field wall on Wygtrig Hill (Rigley Hill). McNeill[39] describes it thus:

> *Facing Bankhead House, on the south, right over Wygtrig Hill, runs an old stone dyke, and in this dyke, a little distance down, may be found the very curious memorial stone shown elsewhere. What may be termed its base or foundation stone, almost on a level with the soil, is rounded at the corners, and has the appearance of a heavy doorstep. Directly above the foundation lies another stone, a little over four feet in length, and about eight inches thick, reminding us of a sculptured window lintel, but lying in a reversed position; it is of light sandstone. Directly over this again, and in the centre of it, stands a piece of yellowish sandstone in pyramidal form; this is about eighteen inches broad at the base and about eighteen inches in height, running to a narrow point at top. There seems to have been a deal of labour*

spent on this, which may be termed the chief stone, the chiseling evidently having been attended to with great care. In the first place, it has been "cut out" all round about an inch in depth, leaving a border about an inch in breadth, the central part being cut out several inches deeper. Crowning all, and directly on the point of the pyramid, is a crescent, its horns pointing skywards. There is other sculptured work in the dyke, but no more of the same yellowish sandstone; while the foundation stones of the dyke at this point are large hewn blocks, which had evidently been used previously for a very different purpose.

The memorial slabs have an aged appearance compared with their surroundings, and this has called attention to them previously. The late Dr Struthers, half a century ago, examined the stones. He expressed no opinion as to them being there; but the inscription we give elsewhere is said to have been copied by him. Part of the original inscription may still be found there, but it will be found difficult to decipher. The late Mr J F Hislop, another antiquarian of standing in the district, tried also to unravel the mystery, but without success. It seems to us that this dyke, which is a mutual wall between the Northfield and Castlepark lands, must have been built by old Laird Fowler, laird of Wygtrig, and the proprietor of Northfield at that period, with stones taken from Katie Herrin's close, for there may be found blocks of the very same sort, the whole of which, including the memorial stone, may have belonged to the original church of Preston.

On further investigation this stone was located in a field to the north of the A1 by Prestonpans. The stone does indeed bear marks of having been extensively worked. It does however also carry what strongly resembles the Seton Family Heraldic Crest of the half crescent (signifying the Earl of Winton's time spent on the Crusades perhaps). The stone is undoubtedly of great antiquity, but it seems more likely to have come from Olivestob House or perhaps Seton Palace when it was beaten down, or maybe even Winton House (also owned by the Setons).[40]

THE TRAVELS AND INDUSTRY OF THE NEWBATTLE MONKS

Newbattle Abbey plays a pivotal role in the history of Prestonpans and particularly in our study of roads. Looking at the charter evidence of the Newbattle Abbey in the Bannatyne Club's "Registrum S. Marie de Neubotle"[41] one can find numerous references to their lands, travels and industry. The Newbattle Monks' properties and lands were extensive. They owned most of the Moorfoot Hills, parts of Leith, Haddingtonshire, Peeblesshire and Clydesdale.[42] In this latter area their property became known as the *Monklands* and this was also an important centre of coal mining in Scotland. The Monks of Newbattle constructed a road to the Monklands, and this was to become the main line of communication between Edinburgh and Clydesdale, taking the line of road through the Melville lands of *Retrevyn* (from the Gaelic or Welsh *rath*,[43] and possibly relating to the ancient fort or settlement by Mavisbank on the River North Esk by Lasswade), by *Strabroc* (Broxburn), and *Bathcat* (Bathgate).[44] The Monks were also engaged in lead mining in the Leadhills of Lanarkshire, perhaps used for making salt pans. Both of these enterprises required serious road building at which the monks were adept.

There would indeed be a strong need to retain open communication between all these properties. In 1189 Alexander II granted travellers the right to cross over land with cattle and to pasture them on common land 'saving corn and meadow'.[45] The Monks, in order to stay on good terms with landowners, often paid landowners on a yearly basis with a gift of a Newbattle Cart filled with timber or building materials.[46]

The industry of the Newbattle Monks was recognised by James V who granted the Monks permission to build a harbour at the site known as Gilbertis-draucht.[47] James V's subsequent Acts of Parliament of 1555 commanding all highways, especially those from burghs to sea ports, to be kept open[48] would no doubt have helped give fresh impetus to the Monks to keep the Salters Road maintained to Newbattle. As well as salt the Monks' coal workings at Newbattle would have been carted to their seaport for export, and rather than return empty, the famous 'Newbattle Cart'[49] would return with salt, shellfish and other imports from the Continent.[50]

The extent of the Newbattle monks' landholdings in southeast Scotland can be seen in the charters passed in favour of Mark Kerr, Commendator of Newbattle Abbey, by the Old Scottish Parliament on 28th July 1587. The lands encompassed: 'Prestoungrange and Sowter Cloute, in Haddington; *Eisthouse* [Easthouses] and *Westhouse* [now lost but then south of Mayfield], Morphat-toun [Moorfoot, where the Monks had a Grange], *Huntlawcoit* [Huntly Cot], *Toksyde Hill* [Toxside Hill], *Coitlaw* [unknown] and *Gledhouse* [Gladhouse], in Edinburgh; *Lethinghoipis*, [Leithen Hopes], in *Peblis* [Peebles] were all united into the Barony of Prestoungrange.'[51]

SALTERS ROAD ON THE ORDNANCE SURVEY MAPS

Looking at a modern day Ordnance Survey Map of East Lothian one would see several other references to 'Salters Road.' When the OS Surveyor was gathering information on the county to enable him to include place names on the first edition map of 1849, he would have talked to local landowners and proprietors and recorded this information in his Object Name Books. Some of this evidence has to be treated with a degree of caution, and perhaps some entries are based on local folklore. However, much of this pertaining to our subject can be backed up by reference to other material such as old charters.

The reference to *Salters Road* is made for the name given to the road running between Prestonpans and Newbattle Abbey. In addition, there is also Salters Road north of the village of Fala Dam in Midlothian, which crosses *Salters Burn* over the *Salters Ford* or the *Salters Bridge*; and also *Salter Sykes* outside Penicuik. There is also the *Salters Ford* which crosses the Loch Burn by Toxside, Midlothian; as well as the *Salters Ford* at Darnick by Melrose.

Of our first reference to Salters Road, the OS Surveyor tells us that this was:

> *A small piece of bye road frequented by smugglers conveying salt from Preston Salt Pans. It leads off the line of road from Dalkeith to Lauder near Newmills Toll Bar joining the public road from Dalkeith to Cousland.*[52]

The earliest map showing fragments of the Salters Road is the first edition Ordnance Survey map of Dalkeith in 1853, and it runs along the line of road, as described, heading for Newbattle, (which is still called Salters Road today in the community of Woodburn) shown at OS map reference NT 337 670, and then heads for the 15th century 'Maiden Bridge.' Salter's Road is then shown running south eastwards to the north of *Queen Margaret's Burn* and then to the north of Easthouses at NT 344 660; it then is shown as heading east at the field edge at approximately NT 363 660 to the south of 'Fuffet Wood'.

The name *Salters Road* is not given to the road through Wallyford (later to become the A6094) on this map until the second edition in 1893. The most direct line from Dalkeith to Prestonpans would have followed this general line of a route through, or near Inveresk where the Abbots' dwellings were, and on to Wallyford.

It is also possible that the route from Prestonpans to Newbattle would have gone via Cousland gaining access to the Fa'side ridge and down the coast to Prestonpans. In support of this, there have been aerial photos taken which do indeed suggest a line of ancient routeway between two woods on either side of it at nearby Chalkieside.[53] This would indeed line up with Newbattle Abbey if one was to follow the 'lay of the land' and the occurrences of the Monks' properties – Whitehill and Cowden.

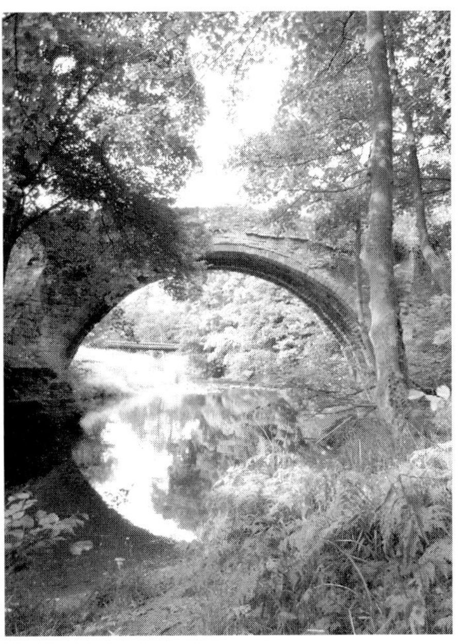

Maiden Bridge, in the grounds of Newbattle Abbey, dating from the late 15th century © A Ralton, 2004

Woodlands near Chalkieside demarcate the possible line of Salter's Road © A Ralton, 2004

Northfield Doocot © A Ralton, 2004

The curious stone described by McNeill. The crescent was part of the armorial badge of the Setons.
© A Ralton, 2004

THE ROUTE OF SALTERS ROAD SOUTH

As well as the East-West Salter's Road there was also a North-South route. The OS Surveyor attributed the name 'Salters Road' to the straight stretch of road just north of the village of Fala Dam, and immediately bordering Whitburgh House on the west. He then shows it skirting to the east of the ancient Fort of Dodridge Law and heading north on a line for 'The Murrays' and Peaston. The OS Surveyor makes the following entry in the Object Name Book:[54]

> *Salters Road:*
> *A portion of a road which passes through Whitburgh Estate to Prestonpans. Its name is derived from being a thoroughfare of those employed in Salt trade with Prestonpans.*

The occurrence here of the Salters Road is strongly indicative of this part of the route linking to the road over Soutra – the old Roman road of Dere Street and also the later medieval Via Regia (The Royal Road)[55] – as this route was one of the main routes into Scotland (as it still is, now known as the A68). The route of Salters Road just north of Fala Dam is straight running along a NNW – SSE line. The straightness of this road might deceive us into thinking that it had been left to us by the Romans; rather, this road was straightened through the agricultural improvements in the mid eighteenth century. This process was widespread throughout the country as fields were enlarged and enclosed and roads were made to take sharp turns around the boundaries of walled estates. This can be clearly seen in this case as Salters Road here makes a sharp turn to the west beyond Whitburgh House, and likewise at its southern end at the Fala Dam burn, the road turns sharply to the east – the

Salter's Road north of Fala Dam, overlooking Salter's Bridge
© A Ralton, 2004

natural obstacles in the landscape of Dodridge Law and Fala Dam burn obviously curtailing further 'improvement'. We know this road was improved circa 1755 when the Midlothian Turnpike Trustees deemed that it should receive improvement and the Minutes of the Trustees record the building of a 'new road called Salters Road' near Fala;[56] this was an improvement of the older Salters Gait (the old Scots word for road).

The investigations into the medieval hospital Soutra have put forward the case that the line that Salters Road would have taken between Prestonpans and Soutra was as follows[57] via Dodridge, The Murrays, House-o'-Muir, Ormiston, Clutes (now known as North Elphinstone Farm), Corse House just north of Elphinstone, Tranent and Bankton House (formerly Olivestob).

As aforementioned, Olivestob is reputedly the 'Holy' stop of the Monks of Newbattle. Corse-house was the house at the Crossroads, as Corse was often used in Scots language to signify a crossing. Corse House no longer exists as a building, yet the place where it used to be is still a crossroads of the Elphinstone – Tranent public road (B6414), the road eastwards past North Elphinstone; and also the two routes that are still public rights of way today, passing to the north at Myles Farm and onwards to Birsley, and continuing on westwards towards Fa'side Castle. From this crossroads the route past Clutes is interesting in that the name of this place gives a clue to a possible former Prestoungrange property. It is possible that the name Clutes may be contracted from *Sowtercloute*, which was confirmed in a charter as part of the Prestoungrange estate as inherited by Mark Kerr in 1584,[58] and subsequently by Robert Kerr in 1620.[59]

Following the road south via Ormiston from Prestonpans is also very logical as this line makes for the higher ground between the Tyne water and its tributaries – the two strands of the Keith and Humbie waters – and the route would also cross the Tyne where it is relatively shallow and weak. This would possibly follow the same general line of the path called 'The Howden' (probably meaning a narrow valley) crossing the Bellyford (possibly indicative

Roy's map of 1755 (Sheet 8/5a) showing Prestonpans and vicinity, including Ouylystob.
© British Library; By permission of the British Library

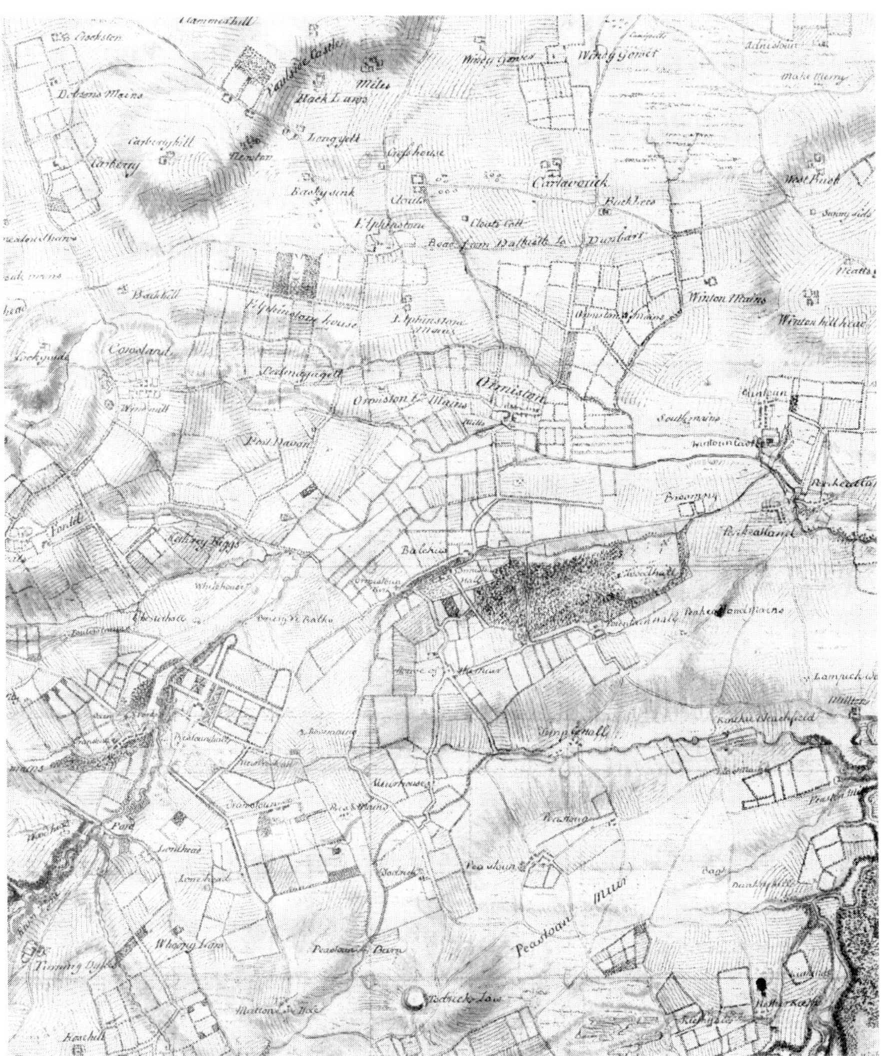

Roy's map of 1755 (Sheet 8/5d) showing Corse House, Clouts, etc.
© British Library; By permission of the British Library

of pack-horse traffic: 'bag' or 'belly', which could refer to characteristic use by pack animals, and ford – water crossing[60]). The route may well have continued to the north of Ormiston passing the ancient Cross of Ormiston, where no doubt much bartering was entered into. From Ormiston the River Tyne was crossed and the road past House o' Muir would possibly have been taken, and then The Murrays (the name being corrupted from 'The Muirhouse'), and heading for the high ground of Dodridge Law and Salters Road as marked on the First Edition Ordnance Survey Map.

That there were many tracks over this part of the moor is evident today with the village now known as Pathhead (formerly Peth-heid)

The medieval hospital of Soutra would likely have been a key stopping off point, and no doubt the hospital would have used vast quantities of salt in their day-to-day work and life. However, besides Soutra there are clear documented links between Prestonpans, or Salt Preston as it was known, and Melrose Abbey, which was the Mother house of Newbattle.

In the Bannatyne Club's *Liber Sancte Marie de Melros* there is an early charter which grants the Melrose monks one Saltwork at Preston, and the right to cut wood from the wood at Preston to fire the salt pans at *Salina de Prestun*.[61]

The connection between Salt Preston and Melrose may be seen in the place name of the First Edition Ordnance Survey Map of Roxburgh: 'Salter Ford.' This was the ford crossing the Tweed above the rivulet of Darnick. This ran "to the East of the Pavilion Cottage then by Gattonside Bank, Easterhouses Byres through Mosshouses then Bluecairn and Blainslie."[62]

The OS Surveyor says of this as follows:

> *Salters Ford*
> *This was a ford across the Tweed between Melrose beside Melrose Bridge when the Salt Cadgers, were in the habit of crossing, with their salt on pack horses. It is not now used as a ford. This ford is ridden every second year by a gentlemen living near Melrose so as to keep a right of use for the public.*[63]

This route described is in fact using parts of an ancient track from Darnick and linking in to the Roman Dere Street. The references to cadgers, as with the other Salters Road's reference to smugglers, may well have some truth, and is supported by Whatley's assertion of smuggling being rife in the two preceding centuries before this entry.[64] However, it seems more than likely that this route pre-dates this to the time of the Monks of Melrose. The whole of this route from Darnick to Blainslie is now part of the long distance walking trail – the 'Southern Upland Way.'

Further evidence linking Prestonpans to this part of the Borders is found in the charter granting in Feu farm to William Hall the lands of Nether Blainslie, and Overtown of Blainslie, to which fish or salt was to be brought from North Berwick or *Salt Preston*, or neighbourhood 'for the sustenation of the Convent and household in the summer'[65] by John Thornton, "Prothonotory Apostolic Precentor of Moray" and also by Steven Culross, Treasurer of Orkney confirming a Charter (dated at Melrose 8th March 1546–7). We also have the charters of Sir Robert Hamilton of Fingalton (who lived in Preston Tower) in the year 1460 giving over the rock-cut Salt Pans and a farm to the Monks of Melrose.[66]

As mentioned above, there was a Salters Ford at Toxside crossing the Loch Burn,[67] which was also owned by the Newbattle Monks. Furthermore, an ancient droveway has recently been uncovered here.[68] It is quite possible that this route was on the line of the way the Monks would have taken to their Grange at Rommanoch in Peeblesshire; now the settlement of Romannobridge – from the Gaelic Rothmaneie meaning 'Monk's Dwelling.'[69] This is also intriguing in that the Gaelic language would pre-date the time of the Monks of Newbattle and may give us clues to an early route between the ancient monastery of Iona on the west coast of Scotland, who may be the monks referred to. The first abbey founded at Melrose between 635 AD and 651 was by St Aidan, Columba's disciple.[70]

THE KIRK ROAD

The difficulties that the Church was facing at this time of religious Reformation in the 16th Century were considerable. As mentioned above, the original Church of Preston was destroyed by Lord Hertford in the 'rough

The line of road formerly known as the Kirk Road, and the Brickworks Road, leading from Johnnie Cope's Road.
© A Ralton, 2004.

wooing' of 1544. However, it may well have been that the religious powers of the day knew that times were changing and the Churches were never rebuilt here in Preston or Prestonpans. Prestonpans was to be without a Church for over fifty years until Mr. John Davidson was appointed Minister of "*South Preston, including Ye Pannis East and West.*"[71]

During the intervening period, the people of Prestonpans attended the Old Kirk at Tranent. There is a road shown on John Adair's map linking the Tranent Church with the village of Preston, and this follows roughly the line of Johnnie Cope's Road but takes a more direct route diagonally to the south east across to the Church. Indeed, the direct line of the route was probably diverted onto the line of the route running today from the 'Roupin Steps' heading east to the Church. This track has been known as the 'Brickworks Road', owing to the presence of a brickworks along its length at one time, but before this it was known as 'The Kirk Road' and on the 1829 "Plan of the improvement made on the Turnpike Road at Tranent" by William Kempt[72] it was shown as such. This route is still in existence today, following a public right of way.

THIEVES WHILLIWHAES AND UNSEEN DANGERS

To travel on the roads in these times was not a pleasant, or altogether safe, experience. The following extract from Mr James Melville's diary in 1572 gives us a graphic description of what the roads were like then:

> *For, first ryding from Hadington to Smeton, reposing on our gyde, we want fordward, who be it under night, far, lot when we war in graittest danger of*

> *collpittes and sinks, the darknes was sa grait, that our gyde knew nocht whar he was, nor whom to gyde, sa that iff God haid nocht gydet us, we haid bein lyk Thales wha compased the erthe, and dyed in a draw-well at his awin dur! When we haid spent a guid part of the night, at last ane of our hors rashed on his nes* [nose] *upon a gevill of a hous, lot whether at was hous or stak or henche, we knew not, nether saw hors or man na nocht our awin finger-end til light and doon grapes, ellanges and find a dur, and chapping, we gat some folks that tauld us we war in Tranent, fra the quhilk conducing a gyde, with a lantern knit to his hors teall to schwa us the way with grait fas cherie throw the coll hors gett, we cam to Smeton.*[73]

Smeton was of course Smeaton and the 'Coll-hors-gett' could well have been any of the roads used for transporting coal, perhaps even leading to Acheson's Haven on the coast at Prestonpans.

Apart from the poor condition of the roads, the traveller had to be wary of those that lay in wait to rob, steal and murder. Writing in 1615, Calderwood calls these people 'The Whilliwhaes.'

> *About this tyme, certaine bair and idle gentlemen lay in wait upon passengers, by the ways about Edinburgh and in other parts of Eist Lothian, en route wold needs have money from them. The commone people call them Whilliwhaes.*[74]

There are many 'Thieves Roads' indicated on OS maps of Scotland, particularly in the Scottish Borders, where cattle reiving was rife. In Lothian, part of the ancient route of the Great North Road route to England is called the 'Thieve's Dykes' just outside Haddington in the Garleton Hills. However this is probably not because of cattle reiving, but because of it being frequented by these robbers or 'Whilliwhaes'. This part of this ancient route is now ploughed over but it used to be the place called 'Yellowcraigs' in the Garleton Hills near to the ancient Barnes Castle. 'Holloways' – the sunken tracks made by the pressure of many passes by wheel, hoof and foot can still be seen here. This part of the road is also known as 'Cope's Road' as this was the road that General Cope took from landing at Dunbar to proceed to Prestonpans and his inglorious defeat in 1745 at the hand of Bonnie Prince Charlie and his Jacobite rebels at Prestonpans.[75]

THE GREAT NORTH ROAD AND ITS ROYAL CONNECTIONS

The coastal route was used by Edward I in 1296 on his return from his mission to quell the rebellious Scots in the Wars of Independence.[76] From Edinburgh, the road would have led to Musselburgh over the Figgate Whins, possibly following the line of an ancient Roman road later to be known as the Fishwives Causeway, crossing over the Roman Bridge (actually built 1529–1530 at the behest of Lady Seton, but quite possibly on the site of a far more ancient crossing of the Esk), then to Preston, Seton, Cantyhall, Seton Hill, Cottyburn, Coates, Gatefoot, Pencraig, Upper Hailes and Linton.[77]

A common element in the eastern part of the road from Preston was the way it joined up with property of the Seton family, also known as the Earls of Wintoun. Not only did they own Seton Castle, but they also had properties in the Garleton Hills in the early seventeenth century (Garmylton-Noble or Garleton-East and Barnes Castle were owned by the Setons). The Setons may even have owned substantial parts of Preston village at that time[78] as well as owning Pinkie House in Musselburgh. The establishment of the roads between major landowner properties no doubt helped to keep them in at least serviceable condition.

McNeill states that between Holyrood House and Seton Palace

> *there were [...] continual royal processions along this way, and that these were often more the scene of merriment than discretion.*

Therefore, not always were the processions as solemn as those on the Holy stop (Olivestob).[79]

The information carried north by Sir Robert Carey in 1603, when he rode from London to Edinburgh along this way, a journey of almost four hundred miles in sixty hours – a considerable achievement – was of a more sombre nature, confirming the death of Queen Elizabeth of England.[80]

At this time James, the son of Mary Queen of Scots, was to ascend to the throne of the Kingdom of Great Britain and become James I of England, Ireland and Wales as well as VI of Scotland.

England had by this time made some progress in establishing a network of postal routes for conveying the King's despatches, and various staging posts were set up throughout the country.[81]

On his journey south to his coronation on 5th April 1603 James no doubt became well aware of the condition of the roads in Scotland in comparison with those south of the border, although English roads were not without their own difficulties. With his retinue of five hundred noblemen he would stop at the south west corner of the orchard of Seton Castle as Robert, the seventh Lord Seton, was buried,[82] since the Setons were a most influential and powerful family, particularly in the reign of the Stewart monarchs.

The importance of good communications between England and Scotland in order for James to keep up to date with the Scottish Parliament in Edinburgh became of great significance. The condition of cross-border routes at this time was generally extremely hazardous. Prior to the Union of the Crowns, the continual warring between England and Scotland meant there was very little incentive to improve these routes. The steep ravines of 'Ye Peaths'[83] at Pease bay in Berwickshire were a significant obstacle to overcome.[84]

In 1617, on his first trip north after his Coronation, James I and VI made a request for a total of three hundred and thirty six horses over fifteen stages in Berwickshire alone.[85] In anticipation of this journey Sir John Hamilton of Preston petitioned the Scottish Lords of Council to improve the road through Preston.

McNeill comments on Hamilton's shrewdness in convincing the Lords to sanction the mending of the roadway through Preston 'Lest strangers with His Majesty should observe its poverty strickenness'[86] and he pleaded for the authority to levy a toll to remedy the poor state of the road as follows:

> *That altho the Lords have taken great course for enlarging and mending all highways and passages throu which his Majesty will pass on his approaching visit to Scotland, there is a very eminent and open place oversine, to wit, the high gait throu the town of Preston which is so broken after a small rayne and*

weit as hardlie is passible.

Now it is quite a schame that the common streit of a throu fairing toune so neir to the burgh of Edinburgh sail not be mendit; and unless it is mendit in tyme, and a good calsay made throu the same, it will be a grit discredit quhan that the strangers that accompanie his Majesty sail sie the same.

The time limit was for three years and to this effect, "that he should levy a duty of 2d. on any 'horse-load' of whatever goods should pass through the village, 4d. on every 'cart-load', 2d. on every 'ox or cow', and 4d. on every 'ten sheep' that should pass that way." But an exception was made on all green wood that was conveyed through the town, on horse or cart, for use at Salt Preston.[87]

On James I and VI's return journey south on 1st July 1617, there were great demands made on the Parishioners of the land through which he was to travel to supply horses and carts to carry His Majesty, his Retinue and Chattels onwards to Dunbar. Those assisting with this move were to meet at:

Haliruid Hos about tua of the cloke in the moirning' and that the Parrochynneris were to supply a number of carts including from Tranent 'fourty cairtis with a three horss in everi cairt, and the Parrochynnaris of Prestoun, tuentie cairtis with twa horss in everye cairt, – and thair to lift His Majesteis cariadge and to carye the same thairfra to Dunbar, under the pane of £20 for everye horsse that salbe absent.[88]

THE BURGH OF BARONY AND THE MERCAT CROSS

1617 the village of Preston and Prestonpans became a joint Burgh of Barony, after much influence from Sir John Hamilton.[89] This gave the people of Preston the right to free port and anchorage, and the right to hold a fair in honour of St. Jerome on the 1st, 2nd and 3rd of October every year.[90]

With the fair came the building of Preston Cross, one of the finest examples of its kind in Scotland. It was reputed to have been built by William Wallace, the King's Master Mason who was also the builder of Wintoun House in Pencaitland and Heriot's School in Edinburgh.[91]

The Chapmen of Lothian subsequently acquired a right to the cross in 1636.[92] They would no doubt agree prices of goods for the coming season and they acted in effect as a form of traders' guild. This set them apart from other *packmen*. Without some form of friendly society, life would have indeed been hard. Freemen and artisans of the burgh had a right to trade at the burgh market, but those who did not have such a privilege, such as the itinerant packmen, were taxed heavily for enjoying the benefits of attending markets. The Chapman (the word perhaps derived from the old English Ceapman: 'ceap' meaning barter or dealing, thus a man who barters or deals)[93] was often victimised, and the regular occurrence of the 'Packman's grave' particularly noticeable on the OS Maps of the Lammermuirs, betrays the hard and dangerous life they led. Packmen were a frequent sight around farms of East Lothian even until early in the twentieth century.[94]

Preston Cross is divided into eight compartments, two of which are doorways and six which form alcoves with semi-circular mouldings at the top in the form of scallop shells. The scallop shell was the badge of the pilgrim,

Preston Cross with an ancient pillar in the foreground; and also a contemporary drawing of the curious stone
From the 1st Edition of Peter McNeill's book of Prestonpans and Vicinity; 1884.

and it was frequently worn by those travelling on known pilgrim routes such as the way to Santiago de Compostella in northern Spain or, closer to home, the Pilgrims travelling over the Forth from North Berwick to St. Andrews (where the bones of St. Andrew are reputed to be buried).

STATUTE LABOUR ROADS I

James' experience of the relatively poor state of roads in Scotland compared to England prompted him in 1610 to direct his Privy Council to take corrective action.

The Justices of the Peace of the County of East Lothian or Haddingtonshire were made responsible for mending and repairing the highways, which had been the case in England since 1555, following James' direction.[95]

This means that the Justices of each County relied mainly on voluntary labour for four days per year for: *'upholding and repairing of the briggis that ar not utterlie ruined'* and also to *'provyde for helping of the Kingis Heicheways alswell for the benefite of careagis as ease of passingeris'*.[96]

This proved to be a most unreliable means of organising and going about the repair of roads as it seems that very seldom was anything substantive achieved and many roads were in very poor condition, even for foot and horse traffic.

When Charles I succeeded to the throne the Privy Council was instructed in March 1627 that *'hiewayes be made faire and passable for coaches and utherwayes,'*[97] in anticipation of his journey north for Coronation in Scotland. Nothing appears to have been done in this respect as the orders were repeated in 1628 and 1629.

EDGEBUCKLING BRAE

The highway between *Edgebuckling Brae* and the water of Almond was singled out in particular for the Sheriff of Edinburgh to repair by the Privy Council.[98]

Edgebuckling Brae was where Somerset's troops camped prior to the Battle of Pinkie in 1544 after ransacking Prestonpans. Blaeu, in his notes to his Atlas of 1654 calls this brae 'Bush Hill' separating the Shires of Edinburgh and Haddington.[99] On the other side of this hill is nearby Ravenshaugh Road and also nearby is a house named Beggars Bush, as well as Drummore House, meaning 'The Great Ridge' in Gaelic. Edgebuckling Brae is thought to be on the line of the road off the A199 just outside Wallyford and bordering Drummore Estate. Part of the road at one time crossed the grounds of Drummore Estate as it descended to Ravenshaugh Bridge.[100]

Ravenshaugh Bridge is now long gone, with the Pinkie Burn being channelled into a conduit under the former line of the B1348 road, which has been superseded by a road nearer the coastline but still can be walked along today.

In 1633 Charles I did finally venture north into Scotland for his Coronation; and the two months prior to his visit the prominent landowners of the day in Lothian were nominated by the Lords of Secreit Counsell for:

> *surveying and ryding the hiewayes betuix Seatoun and Edinburgh and fra Seatoun to Dalkeith and frome that to Edinburgh, and to have considderit what parts of the said hiewayes needed to be enlarged or repaired.*[101]

The said nominated landowners were William, Erle of Lothiane, William, Lord Ramsay, Sir John Hamiltoun of Prestoun, David Crichtoun of Lugtoun and Mr. James Raith of Edmistoun (formerly the hamlet lying near Brunstane now on the A199 – Milton Road). They found that there were indeed defects in the highway at the back of Prestoungrange and Edgebucklin Brae and they reported this accordingly. They were however rebuked by the Privy Council for failing to order how and by whom these defects were to be corrected.[102]

For Charles's journey from Dunglass to Seatoun the Lords of Privy Council directed the Constables of each of the Parishes in East Lothian should supply a total of five hundred and ninety one carts and one hundred and forty six horses and be waiting at a given point to deliver these to the King's Master of the Carriage. In particular thirty carts were to come from the Parish of Prestoun and forty carts from the Parish of Tranent. Failure to provide the required horses and carts at said time meant a fine or a poinding of goods to the value of £6.[103]

STATUTE LABOUR ROADS II

Reliance on the voluntary principle was persisted with, and the 1669 Act for repairing highways and bridges, gave the Justices of the Peace powers to order all Parishioners to undertake six days work each year at any time most convenient except seed time or harvest.[104] Those who lived a considerable distance away could opt out by paying 6/– per annum instead and this money was to be used to hire suitable labour.

The Act was to all intents and purposes largely ignored, resulting in the Privy Council fining the County's Justices of the Peace. It was slightly strengthened in a further Act of 1686[105] by the joining to the Justices of the Peace those landowners appointed to collect tax on behalf of the King, ie the Commissioners of Supply.

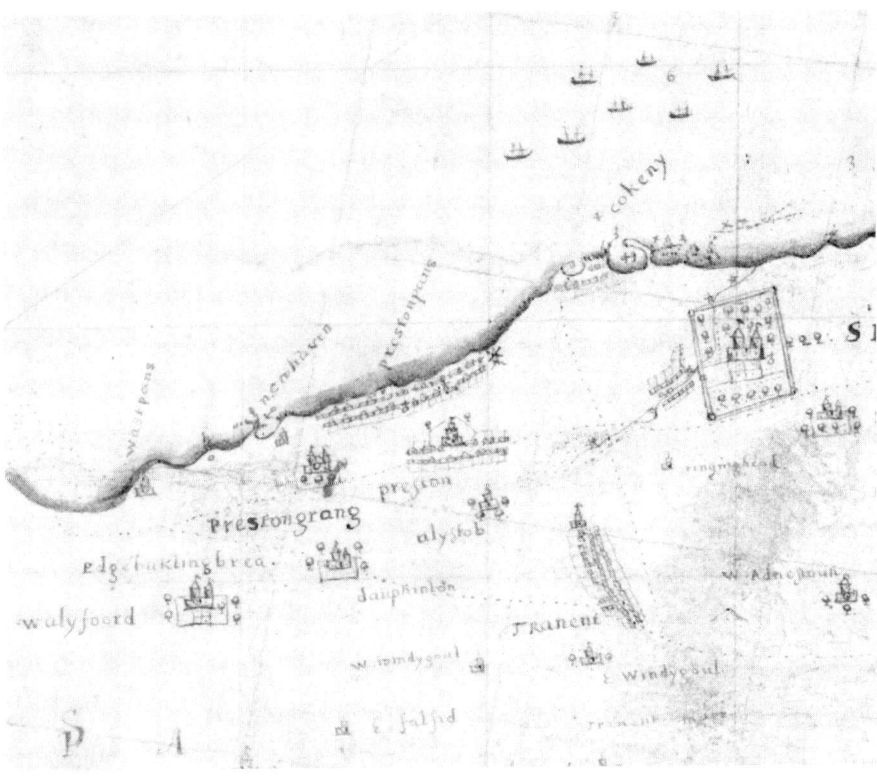

The Adair map of 1682 showing Edgebuckling Brae, and the line of the Great Post Road; Adair, J; 1682; East Lothian; Shelf Mark: Adv.MS.70.2.11 (Adair 10) *© National Library of Scotland.*

ENCLOSURE AND AGRICULTURAL IMPROVEMENT

An Act of the Scottish Parliament of 1661 gave protection to landowners' enclosures and allowed them to 'cast about highways to their conveniency, providing they do not remove them above 200 ells upon their whole ground.'[106] This had the effect of creating sharp right-angled bends as estates built walls around their land, which roads were diverted around. In some cases this made transport difficult – especially for carriages – and concentrated traffic in a single channel where before the line of the road varied across quite a wide area of land, taking the most convenient and driest line.

Examples of enclosure can be seen in the great walls surrounding the Prestoungrange and Drummore Estates, as well as at Whitburgh Estate where the Salters Road was subsequently straightened. Looking at the 'Plan of the Battle of Preston 21st September 1745' (anon) one can also see where the extensive gardens of Preston House have encroached directly over the roads, forcing them to go around the walls, McNeill corroborates this when he mentions that the building of Preston House blocked off the old highway through the village.[107] On the Battle map the Great North Road is named as a '*defile leading to the village of Preston*' another defile being the road now known as East Loan.

THE BATTLE OF PRESTONPANS

It is worth at this point to mention the Battle of Prestonpans, as contemporary descriptions give some indication as to the landscape of the time. Cadell[108] details that the roads beyond Haddington took two different ways, which gave General Cope a choice of route from landing at Dunbar. The route by Haddington, Gladsmuir, and Tranent, was not suitable for Cope's troops, being broken up by hollow roads, coal pits and walls. The northern road went over the Garleton Hills past former residencies of the Setons. Cope took the latter route and eventually encamped in the vicinity of Seton West Mains to the east of Prestonpans. The rebel forces of Prince Charlie took the high ground from Musselburgh, encamping at Tranent, where he had three options for crossing the great morass and bog that intervened between Tranent and Seton: a footpath passing near the farm of Riggonhead; the cart way between Cockenzie and Tranent; and the waggonway for taking coal from Tranent coal pits down "The Heugh" to Cockenzie Harbour (the first railway in Scotland dating from 1722,[109] part of which is still in use as a walkway today).

Cadell notes how Cope ordered the walls surrounding Lord Grange's Preston House to be knocked down in case these were to be used as cover for rebel troops. Although occupying only four or five acres, it is said that because of the many walkways, it would have taken someone at least two hours to walk round the whole estate grounds. The outcome of the Battle of Prestonpans is well known, as is the final outcome of the Rebellion and the defeat of the Jacobites. Johnny Cope's Road is the road that General Cope took when fleeing the scene of the battle and the carnage inflicted on his own troops – he continued on to Soutra and the road south.

After the Rebellion, there was a sense that more information was needed about the geography of the country as this knowledge was especially critical for the Hanoverian control of Scotland. General William Roy was thus commissioned to carry out a survey of Scotland and these, at a scale of 2 inches to the mile,[110] were the first detailed maps of the countryside.

TURNPIKES AND TOLLS

The condition of the roads was obviously noted at this time also. The Great Post Road was one of the first turnpike roads in Scotland. The name *turnpike* was given to describe the horizontal bar that spanned the road and could be swung aside to allow toll payers through.

In 1750 the Great Post Road Bill was published, entitled 'An Act for repairing the roads leading from Dunglass Bridge to the town of Haddington; and from thence to Ravenshaugh Burn in the County of Haddingtoun.'[111]

Its opening preamble sets out the reasons for its enactment:

> *Whereas the high roads leading from Dunglass Bridge to the town of Haddingtoun, and from thence to Ravenshaugh Burn, all in the County of Haddingtoun (being the Great Post Road from Edinburgh to London), are, by reason of the deepness of the soil, and many heavy carriages passing along the same, in many parts ruinous, and so much out of repair, that travellers cannot pass thereon without great danger:*
>
> *And whereas the said road cannot by the ordinary course provided by the laws for repairing the highways of this Kingdom, be effectually amended, and kept in good repair, unless some provision be made for raising money, be applied for that purpose.*

The Route of the Great Post Road from the Garleton Hills to Musselburgh; from Blaeu, C; and Blaeu, J; 1654; Lothian and Linlitquo; Shelf Mark: WD3B/8

The Act was not universally welcomed in East Lothian. The Justices of the Peace of the County of Haddington in the Minutes to their quarter session meeting of 4th May 1751 express strong opposition to it, even so far as to lobby the East Lothian MP Sir Hugh Dalrymple and also to lobby the Lord Advocate in order to persuade them to strongly oppose the Bill in Parliament.[112]

The Commissioners of Supply of East Lothian also felt that such an Act would be injurious to their affairs. Sir John Hope of Dunglass indeed offered to repair the roads around his property himself; and it was generally thought that the Post Road was in sufficiently good condition not to need the measures of the aforesaid Bill.[113]

Sir Hugh Dalrymple and Sir Andrew Fletcher, both Senators of the College of Justice and Justices of the Peace for East Lothian proposed that the Trustees of the turnpike road should have powers to erect the toll bar within the lands of the County of Edinburgh by up to 120 yards.[114]

This no doubt would allow those going about their business in East Lothian District, and in particular Prestoungrange, enough latitude to be able to avoid the toll and not to be unduly penalised. Further reasons against the turnpike of the Great Post Road were given in the 'Memorandum for the Gentlemen of East Lothian' namely, there was already a tollgate at Jock's Lodge which raised sufficient funds for the repair of the Great Post Road throughout East Lothian; that there were already tolls levied on loaded horses and carriages at *Canty* (near Longniddry) and at the *Watergate (Haddington)*, and it would be unjust to increase this; the toll prices proposed were at best not any less, and in some cases higher than those already existing. Supporters of the Bill also thought that because the East Lothian part of the Great Post Road

Prospectus Oræ maritimæ LOTHIANÆ a Prædio de Stony hill. The Coast of LOTHIAN from Stony hill.

Ships sailing into Morrison's Haven and Prestonpans can just be seen in the distance in this image from Slezer's 1693 Theatrum Scotiae. The beginnings of early field enclosures are also evident.
Plate 22; Shelf Mark: EMS.b.5.1; © National Library of Scotland.

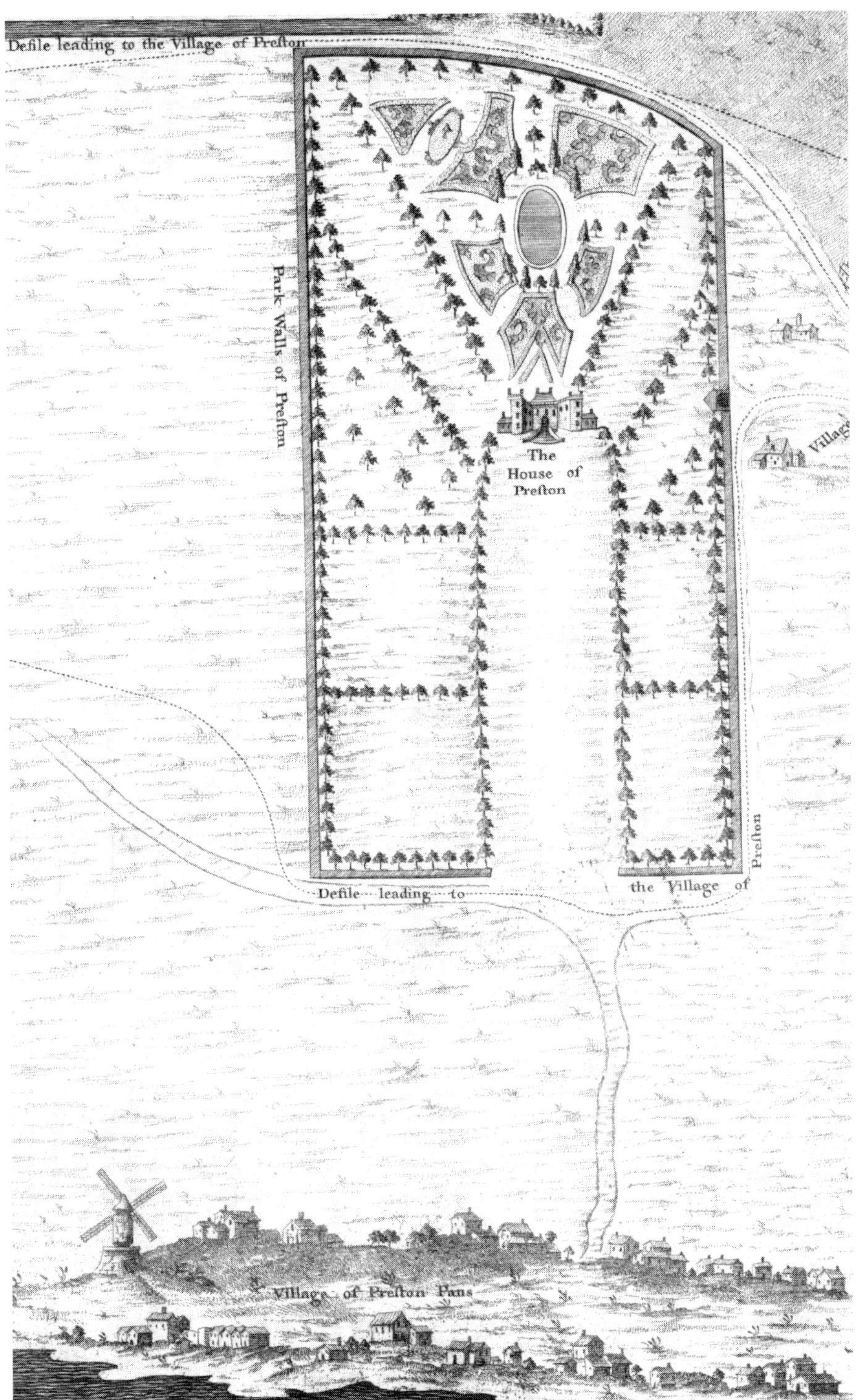

The Battle of Preston Map by Christopher Seton shows the Great Post Road, and also East Loan as 'defiles'. Note the windmill in the foreground, presumably next to Nethershot House and also the Church.
Christopher Seton; 1745; Plan of the battle at Preston, 21st Septemr. 1745. By an officer of the Army who was present; Shelf Mark: EMS.s.90 Case.6.4; © National Library of Scotland.

was currently not turnpiked then that would allow coal merchants, in particular the Laird of Woolmet, to exploit this road to avoid other turnpike roads, but this was stated as being unlikely.[115]

The Bill, however, was successfully enacted despite the protests of the East Lothian Justices of the Peace and Commissioners of Supply.

In addition to the turnpike legislation, the statute labour roads continued, especially on the lesser roads but also in relation to the Great Post Road. A Committee of the Turnpike Trustees Meeting on 7th August 1750 proposed that:

> *All Heretors, Tenants and others, liable to send out wains and carts to the highways, shall be allowed to compound for three of the six days for which they are liable, at the rates following, viz. For every labouring horse above three years old, kept by such person, at the rate of 10d per annum, and for every labouring ox, at 5d per annum.*
>
> *That all householders, cottagers and labourers shall be allowed to compound for the whole six days for which they are liable, at the rate of 1/8d per annum.*[116]

This would also apply to the Great Post Road with regard to all persons living within the space of two computed miles from the Post Road.[117] The original road would appear to have stuck to the line aforementioned going by Riggonhead to the north of Tranent and over the Garleton Hills and bypassing Haddington. In Roy's map of 1755 the road over the Garelton hills carries the legend '*the short road from Edinburgh to Dunbar;*' which implies that the alternative road through Haddington was the main route of the Great Post Road. It is shown as such on Taylor & Skinner's map of 1776.

The Great Post Road led to Edinburgh via Prestoungrange, which indicates the importance of the colliery and Haven in supplying coals, salt and other goods, which would have been in high demand for the grand houses of the New Town of Edinburgh.

The Taylor and Skinner Map of 1776 shows the tolls on the Great Post Road at Ravenshaugh near West Pans; and also at the Wallyford By-bar on the Prestonpans to Wallyford road. The Ravenshaugh Toll was one of the five tolls established on the Great Post Road in Haddingtonshire. The Trustees directed that walls should be built to stop people evading tolls, and this cut off the route across Drummore Estate, which was probably the earliest line of the road.[118]

THE NETHERSHOT ROAD DISPUTE

There is a line of road shown on the Roy map running behind the main street of Prestonpans along the back of the houses. Looking at a modern town map of Prestonpans we would recognise this road as Nethershot Road.

The land at Nethershot was part of the land owned by the Laird of Preston House, Lord Grange, who subsequently disposed of it to Mr William Ramsay, his factor some time after the 1745 rebellion (another part of Lord Grange's estate was sold to Watson's Hospital). It was not long before Ramsay settled on improving the land at Nethershot, and part of those plans involved stopping up the back lane to the public, and this he duly did by building walls and ditches across the road and turning people away from using it.[119]

The public used this road due to the High Street of Prestonpans at that time being in a very ruinous state, with the sea also encroaching on to this road making it doubly hazardous. William Ramsay, alongside David Dalrymple and James Erskine, advocates, tried to put a stop to this use by claiming that there never was a public right to use the road, that Lord Grange had only allowed the public to use it at his discretion as an indulgence to his feuars – who used the road as a servitude access to their properties – that no one had complained when he had stopped up the road to the east of Nethershot commonly called the Links Park Road. (This road is open today as a right of way leading to Cockenzie.)

A lengthy legal battle then ensued between the Justices of the Peace of East Lothian and Ramsay, Erskine and Dalrymple and others over the road called Preston Loan.

The Justices' response was to get a '*proof*' from seven witnesses to attest that they had used the road since time immemorial and this proof was served on William Ramsay in 1752. The Justices claimed that the branch of the road which led to the west from the '*windmiln*' was a kirk road, and led to a seaport and that the road to the south led to a school and to a market town; and the encroachment of this was contrary to the Act of 1661 they also claimed that Lord Grange never attempted to block this route as he had accepted it as public. Both sides employed legally trained advocates and the issue still appeared to be bubbling to the surface in 1762 (10 years later), despite the Justices' belief that they had previously done enough to secure access on the road.

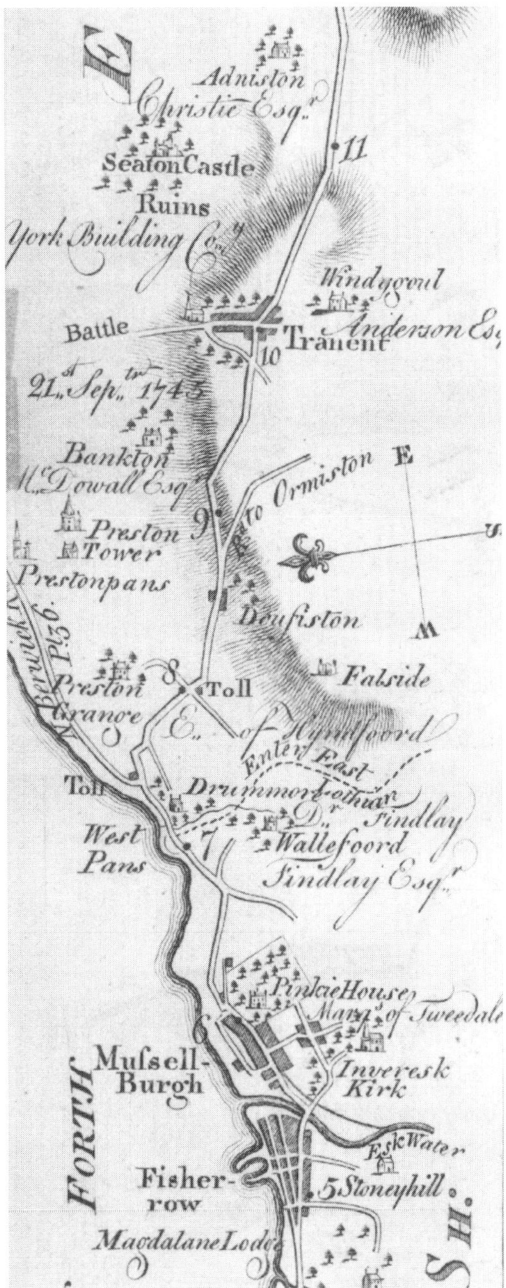

Taylor & Skinner's Road maps were published in 1776 in strips showing the main roads of the day. This extract is from Plate 1 of their "Survey and maps of the roads of North Britain or Scotland"; and shows part of the road from Edinburgh to Berwick upon Tweed; Shelf Mark: EMS.b.3.48;
© National Library of Scotland.

Ramsay would have preferred the public to use the High Street at this time and he did in fact plea to the Justices to improve this road along the coast. The Justices stuck to their guns and one presumes that they made the Preston Loan into a proper turnpike. The advocate for the Justices considered that the High Street was not sufficient for the public to use, it being less than ten feet wide between the walls on the one side and the sea on the other 'so that many times when the sea overflows it cannot be passed with safety.'[120] The road that William Ramsay tried to stop up is shown on his 1767; *Plan of the Lands of Preston,*[121] which implies he had accepted this by then and which continues to be part of the road system in Prestonpans to this very day.

TO TOLL OR NOT TO TOLL? OR HOW TO AVOID PAYING

A relic of the turnpike era can still be seen on the outskirts of Prestongrange near the the southwest corner of the Estate. There is a very finely built tunnel running under the old road (which is now fenced off to vehicular traffic). The tunnel is 133′ long, 13′6″ wide and 13′6″ high. It is believed that this was built by Sir William Grant in order for coals to be transported between his colliery and Dolphingston to Morrison's Haven, and also for salt from Prestonpans to be taken back on the return journey. Using the tunnel avoided the Wallyford By-bar and Ravenshaugh Tolls. Sir William was known to have pressed for concessions for coal and salt works he owned when the Great Post Road Bill was being debated. Research by Graham[122] has revealed what was agreed at a meeting of the Trustees in August 1750:

> *At a meeting of the Trustees on 7th August 1750 at Haddington House a petition from the Rt. Hon. William Grant of Prestoungrange, Advocate showing that, in July 1745, Petitioner purchased Barony of Prestoungrange and Dolphingston with Coals and Saltworks lying in the Parish of Prestonpans at a judicial roup and sale before the Court of Session. That these Coal and Saltworks were estimated in that sale by taking a medium of the free produce for 12 years preceding same and providing £200 per annum and price set upon them by the Lords was 5 years purchase of this supposed medium of the casual rent or £1,000.*
>
> *The Petition goes on to make a case for relief of toll duty as most of the trade was westward to Edinburgh and was being subject to tolls at Ravenshaugh and also in Midlothian.*
>
> *In the first instance the Trustees excused tolls for one year for carts carrying coal or salt westwards on production of a certificate from the "Coall or Saltwork Grieves" and refunded tolls collected from empty vehicles from the*

The tunnel built by Laird Prestoungrange to avoid tolls on his coal wagons. © A Ralton, 2004.

west on the return loaded journey. Vehicles proceeding to and from the east had to pay tolls. Subsequently after further discussion it was agreed that all tolls would be excused on production of receipts and that refunds of tolls collected from empty vehicles from east and west would be made on the loaded return journey.

Another view of the tunnel, and in particular the fine masonry work.
© A Ralton, 2004.

Tolls were payable regardless of the distance travelled to cross them, and Sir William would obviously have been liable for them as much as anyone else. It must have made good economic sense to go to the expense of building a tunnel so that tolls could be avoided, which implies that there was considerable traffic making this journey. A roadway is clearly seen shown on the Roy Map leading to Dolphingston and after a one field length it splits into two branches with the eastern branch heading to Dolphingston Colliery and the western branch heading to Prestoungrange North Lodge.

Transport of coal was clearly a very large part of the traffic from Prestongrange. There was also a road named the "Coal gate loan" running southwards from Bankfoot and following a line close by the east garden wall of Prestoungrange House to reach the '*Middle Road*' as noted in Robert Fowler Hislop's unpublished memoirs.[123] This may be the same road as the '*Clinking Gate*' as shown on

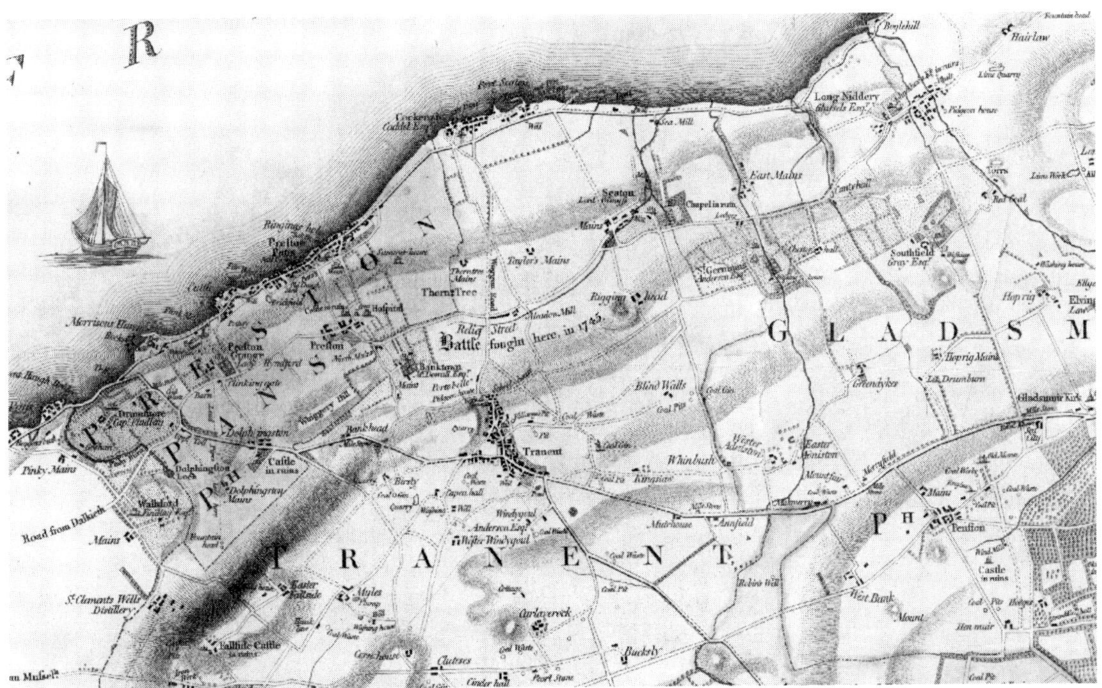

Forrest's map of 1799, showing the "Clinking Gate," Beggars Bush (in the far left hand corner), and the "Wagon Road" to Tranent, etc: "Map of Haddingtonshire," NW; Shelf Mark: EMS.s.637; © National Library of Scotland.

William Forrest's Map of 1799. This was shifted to the east at some point in its history (60 years before Robert Hislop wrote his undated reminiscences, therefore probably around the early 1800's).[124]

Some people went to extreme lengths to avoid paying tolls. The tollkeeper at Ravenshaugh had the misfortune to experience the heavy-handed brutality of the occupying British Army on 5 October 1760 when he requested payment for allowing a troop of light dragoons through. For his troubles he received a severe beating, as did a few women who happened to be there with him at the time.[125] A satirical pamphlet of the time portrays the soldiers as bold defenders against French impostors disguised as tollkeepers, in fact these were innocent tollkeepers subject to a violent attack. The incident reveals the brutality of certain officers of the army at this time which came to a head with the Tranent Militia Riots and massacre of innocent people in 1797. The pamphlet says:

> *A report still prevails, that those Frenchmen in Petticoats were really Women, and that the one disguised in the Toll-keeper's Garb was in fact the tollgatherer appointed by the Trustees for Turnpike Roads. The Improbability, nay the utter Impossibility of this Account, will appear from the following reasons: First, It is agreed, that none but Cowards, Dastards and Poltroons Would beat women*

The Dragoons were to receive some form of punishment at least, paying £200 damages on top of a £5 fine for each officer.[126]

A more unusual means of avoiding tolls is light-heartedly recounted by McNeill. The first passage concerns the tollkeeper at Ravenshaugh in the early 1800's and the second a group of youths who wished to avoid paying tolls for their pony. McNeill captures the stories as follows:[127]

> *RAVENSHEUCH HOUSE.*
> *This ever-clean and tidy-looking building is better known to many as "Ravensheuch" or "Raven's Hauch Toll," and it was indeed a "toll-house." It was built a little previous to the year 1800 by Peter Kerr, a sterling old highlander, and somewhat of a character in his day. He was great-grandfather, by the mother's side, of a well-known and worthy character of the present day, Mr Charles Forman, salt manufacturer in Cockenzie. Mr Peter Kerr became contractor for and looked after a great many tolls in East Lothian, and held them for quite a series of years; but after building Ravensheuch House he kept the toll there also, and, while keeping a strict lookout after the others, made it his headquarters. One of his chief peculiarities was his constant refusal to charge toll for blackfaced sheep. Sheep were always charged at so much per score. When counting the flock, he was always observed to miss the black ones; but any time he was reminded of the evident mistake, "Na, na," was his invariable reply, "it's nae mistake o' Peter's, but ta Tevel never peys toll."*

> *THE PONY WHICH DID NOT PAY TOLL AT RAVENSHEUCH.*
> *Some five-and-fifty years ago, half-a-dozen youths, ranging from twelve to sixteen years, left Seton West Mains one morning to spend a holiday in Musselburgh. They took a pony with them to get rides time about by the way. They paid toll both at Ravensheuch and West Pans when going, but forgot they had to pay toll again when returning, and spent all their coppers*

in the sweetie and bun shops at Musselburgh. On coming back to West Pans Toll on their way home, they just remembered they had to pay again, and had nothing wherewith to pay. They made a dash to get through behind a machine, but were caught. "Not so fast, my lads!" said the keeper, "not so fast!" "We dinna pay double toll on a wee beast like that?" queried the leader of the party. "Oh yes," was the reply. They all set to rifling their pockets, and one did find as much as pay the fee. On getting to Ravensheuch they made a dash again, but it was of no avail. Again every pocket was turned inside out, but there were no coppers forthcoming, and the keeper threatened to stable the pony. They knew enough, however, to defy him to lay hands on it.

The half-dozen retired for a brief consultation, and a hearty laugh was the outcome. They again approached the keeper, with, "I say maister, if the pony doesna gang through the toll you dinna charge onything?" "Oh no," was the reply; "if the gate doesna open, no pay." "A' richt," quoth the leader, "come on boys," when four of them laying hold of a leg a piece, one the head, and another the tail, they carried him amid great laughter right through on the footpath. The toll-keeper became so hilarious over the device that he laughed too, then ran and helped them.

THE NEED FOR ROAD IMPROVEMENTS

The difficulties experienced on the roads of this time can be seen to some extent to be as a consequence of the agricultural improvement and enclosure of fields, cutting off former routes that took a more convenient line. The growth of agriculture however was also one of the main drives for road improvement, given the necessity for transporting lime and manure for fertilising the fields.

An anonymous writer, under the pseudonym of 'An East Lothian man' writing in the *Farmer's Magazine* of 1805 is critical of the lack of scientific principles in maintaining the Great Post Road in East Lothian.[128] He proposed a completely new line of the route on account of the steepness of the road travelling westwards after Linton Bridge, after which the road levelled, and then also after Tranent, as the road is noted as descending steeply to the banks of the Forth. Travelling eastwards from Prestongrange this called for a very severe pull up to the high ground. The road is shown as descending from the Tranent road to the west side of Dolphingston Farm, which eventually would be crossed by the main Edinburgh to London railway.

This road may still be traced, but it has in fact been stopped up due to the dangers of crossing a railway line. It then ran along the south of Prestoungrange and around to the west, crossing the aforementioned tunnel and turning north between the enclosure walls of Drummore and Prestongrange estate.

An old milestone of the old road can be seen at the East Lodge Gatehouse of Drummore Estate. Martine[129] suggests that the lettering on the milestone, now barely legible, said at one time: '*Edinburgh 7' on one face and on another face 'Haddington 8*', although in fact the actual distances are 8 and 9 miles respectively. Martine also mentions that the road was indeed '*A very severe and steep one to travel.*'[130] This latter section of road was superceded by the section of road from Levenhall to Dolphingston via Edgebuckling Brae in 1816.

The road to Dolphinston from Levenhall, Edgebuckling Brae, has been known by the name of Bluchers Brae and it is curious to note that there is still

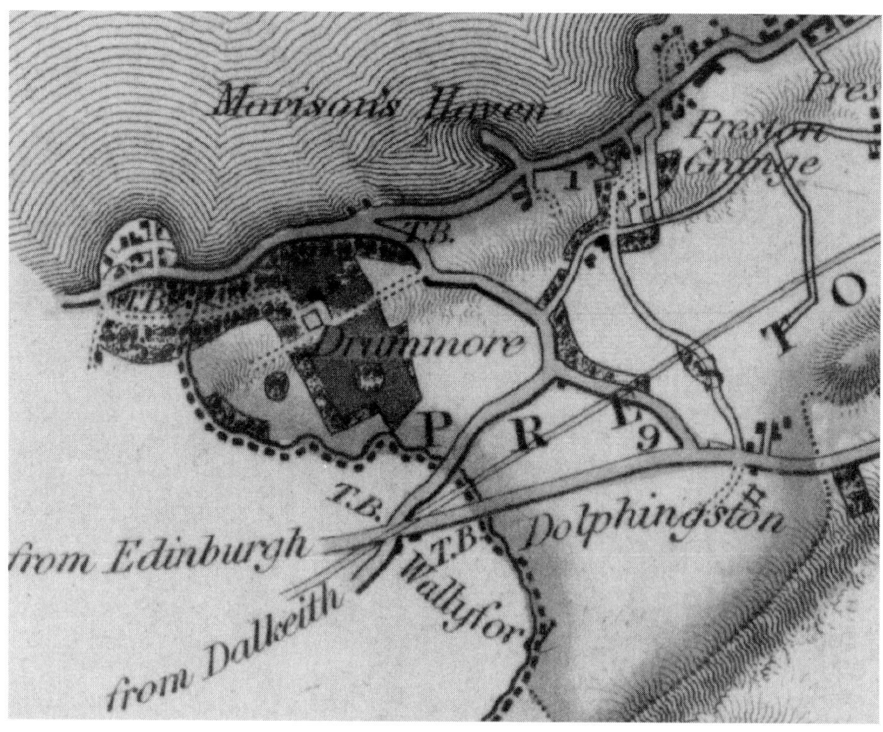

The "Map of the County of Haddington;" by Greenwood, Fowler, Sharp and Dower (1844), shows the first part of the Edinburgh to London railway line. Shelf Mark: EMS.s.532; © National Library of Scotland.

The old milestone on the Great Post Road, as described by Martine, just outside the East Lodge of Drummore Estate.
© A Ralton, 2004.

An old milestone on Edgebuckling Brae;
© A Ralton, 2004.

a house called Bluchers Hall near Mrs Forman's Pub at Levenhall. Blucher was the famous Field Marshal of Prussia in the Napoleonic Wars of the early 19th century. He was known for his courage and forcefulness.

Blucher was also the name of a type of four-horse coach,[131] named in honour or even perhaps as a way of marketing certain qualities of the vehicle after the great General's part in the Battle of Waterloo and the name of this house gives an indication that there was probably some kind of change stop here at this time; indeed nearby '*Mrs Forman's*' was originally a coaching house.

The road was subject to various improvements over the years and some of the old sections of road can still be used today by non-motorised transport. Examples are at Tranent[132] and at Prestoungrange.[133]

The Milestone built into the Fowler's Court development on the High Street; © A Ralton, 2004.

THE AGE OF RAIL

The coming of the railways and the opening of the Edinburgh to London line in 1846 also had an acute effect on how people used the roads. This doubtless curtailed the use of the tunnel and the road to Dolphingston from Prestoungrange. However, on the first edition OS Map there is still a clear line of the route shown from the tunnel to the West Lodge on the Wallyford road which neatly avoids the toll bars. It is interesting to note that in the great industrial age of canal and railways a canal was also proposed that would follow roughly the same line as the current A1; however this did not go ahead.[134]

The wider effect of railways amongst the travelling public was to increase the arbitrary nature of whether the public used tolls or not, and of course if they could avoid them they would. It was possible now that farmers could get their produce to Edinburgh by taking a road that led to the station either avoiding all tolls, or at least tolls that would have been paid prior to the railway. The effect of the railways was to encourage shorter travel distances and a denser network of routes.[135]

It did however mean that those whose journeys did not involve the railway, or whose location meant that they could not avoid tolls, still continued to pay, and one can understand the sense of injustice that some no doubt felt as they saw other parts of East Lothian managing to escape toll-free. This was possibly compounded by the fact that an Act of 1844 rendered all former statute labour roads in the County of Haddington into turnpike roads.[136]

Robert Hislop, brewer and owner of Fowler's Brewery in Prestonpans, speaking at the Government Enquiry into public roads in April 1860 stated:

I have long been established in my present business at Prestonpans. I employ in my business five non-agricultural horses; these are employed chiefly in carrying goods to the railway station, and also to Edinburgh, Haddington and the other towns around. We send almost all our goods to Edinburgh by our own carts; but what goes through Edinburgh, we send by railway. Our Brewery is 9 miles from Edinburgh. The annual amount paid in tolls for these horses is estimated at £20 per annum. We pay two tolls to Edinburgh, three to Leith (9 miles distant), two to Musselburgh (3 miles distant); and these last are paid for travelling over little more than two miles up road. The people of Prestonpans consider the tolls to which they are subjected as very oppressive, and I concur in that opinion. It was at one time proposed to put on certain new tolls between Prestonpans and the railway, but this was successfully resisted. If those tolls had been put on, the parties paying them would on an average not to have used more than about a mile of the road before passing through them. It would have been quite impossible to have gone out of Prestonpans in any direction without paying tolls. The present rate in our Parish for statute labour is 37/6d per plough gate. For our Brewery horses we pay annually £3. Nothing is paid for my dwelling house.[137]

ROAD REFORM

The Haddington Courier of 25th February 1870 records numerous lengthy debates on how the roads and their administration could be improved. There also seems to have been some rivalry between the east and the west parts of the county and questions were asked as to why the west appeared to get a greater amount of money spent on their roads. Sir George Grant–Suttie of Prestoungrange was to reply to this by arguing that the whole of the County was to benefit from good roads at the west on account of the need for coals throughout the county originating from Prestoungrange.[138]

Part of the former Great Post Road, now a right of way for non-vehicular access, at the west end of Tranent near Birsley Brae. © A Ralton, 2004

The end was in sight for the toll system of raising funds for road improvements.

The Editorial of the *Haddingtonshire Courier* of 20th June 1862 states:

It is now generally admitted that the tollage system, as it at present exists, is quite inadequate to maintain roads in the condition befitting a County like East Lothian, and a remedy has become imperatively necessary.

Not all the people of East Lothian were enthusiastic about the abolition of tolls, however. The Heritors and Tenants of the Parish of Humbie in their meeting of 5th October 1857 unanimously resolved to oppose the scrapping of tolls. Situated at the south end of East Lothian there seemed to be a general fear amongst the Humbie Parishioners that as their nearest market town was Dalkeith and their nearest railway station Tynehead, both in Midlothian, they could be in the undesirable position of having to pay rates for road improvements based on an assessment of the annual value of land and heritages (as was proposed for East Lothian) and also having to pay tolls which would continue in Midlothian.[139]

The County Road Act of East Lothian was passed in 1864, but to most people's disappointment tolls were not in fact repealed and the worst fears of the Humbie Parishioners were realised i.e. tolls remained and rates were also extracted for the upkeep of roads. A continuation of tolls no doubt had something to do with the outstanding debts remaining for road works.

An account in the *Haddingtonshire Courier* of 30th March 1860 of the Government Enquiry into the public roads in Haddingtonshire, gives us a detailed note of revenue and debts outstanding as follows:

Detailed Note of Revenue

	1844–45			*1845–46*		
Great Post Road	£4,484	12	0	£4,565	18	0
North District Road	1,353	0	0	1,479	0	0
South District Road	628	5	6	630	2	3
Killpallet District Road	330	0	0	357	0	0
Ormiston District Road	348	0	0	223	0	0
	£7,143	17	6	£7,264	0	3

	Bonded and Floating Debt 1844 – 45			*Postponed Debt 1845–46*		
Great Post Road	£4,800	0	0	£2,500	0	0
North Road	578	10	8	0	0	0
South Road	1,800	0	0	707	7	2
Killpallet Road	2,300	0	0	870	12	3
Ormiston Road	425	2	10	184	17	8
	£9,403	18	6	£4,263	7	1

It was not until 1878 and the Roads and Bridges Act that tolls were finally abolished. This Act vested the management and maintenance of highways and bridges in the Burgh Local Authority.[140] The Police Burgh of Prestonpans had been set under the 1850 'Act to make more effectual provision regulating the police of towns and populous places in Scotland, and for paving, draining,

This extract from the OS 1'st Ed of Haddingtonshire (1854) map shows the recognisable pattern of main roads in Prestonpans and vicinity today, as well as the viaduct over the tunnel with a clear track marked to West Lodge; and also a routeway to Dolphinston Colliery. © National Library of Scotland.

cleansing, lighting and improving the same (15th July 1850).' This was not implemented until 1868 and such was the strength of feeling regarding tolls and taxes, its introduction caused great concerns and even riots[141] much akin to the Poll Tax protests in the late 1980s.

AN EARLY RIGHT OF WAY DISPUTE

The rights of access to Preston Cross came under dispute when, in 1889, the Cross was enclosed by a high wall and a gate which was padlocked by Wright, the market gardener. This created something of a 'stushie' at the time. with a Dr. William Ireland of Preston Lodge writing in the *Evening Dispatch* of August 31st 1889 of his long use of the route past the Cross as a public right of way.[142]

The scene today is of course much different, with open access to the Cross at all times. Then, however, the market garden had ploughed right up to the base of the Cross and a high wall enclosed the whole garden. The enclosure of the Cross may in fact have helped to preserve it although the old village surrounding it had long since gone by this time.

Two other agencies were also involved in this episode not least the Trustees of Schaw's bequest, named after Dr James Schaw who bequeathed his property of Preston House in 1784 to be made available for the "maintenance and education of boys".[143] Part of the lands owned by the Trust was tenanted to the Wrights. Secondly, the Scottish Rights of Way and Recreation Society was concerned. The papers in the National Archives of Scotland detail the correspondence between Dr Ireland and the Society. Although they do not give information as to how this dispute was resolved (probably without going to Court), the end result is that today all can access the Cross.

SOME LOCAL ROADS AND STREETS OF NOTE IN PRESTONPANS

There are two *Loans* in Prestonpans: East and West. Why there should be two roads running in the same line of direction very close to each other is on the face of it puzzling. However, both roads could be part of an early form of one-way system: a Loan was generally a grassy track for animals to be driven between a township and common grazing,[144] and it might well be awkward for two herds of cattle to pass each other from opposite directions. An alternative reason for the establishment of the two roads so close together was perhaps the use of one route being diverted or stopped up at one time; from the Plan of the Battle of Preston, East Loan can be seen to have been moved. Alternatively, given that a line east of West Loan marks the boundary between the former burghs of Preston and Prestoungrange – owned by the Canons of Holyrood and the Monks of Newbattle respectively – perhaps the existence of two roads results from various land disputes between those two parties.

What is certainly known is that, as late as the 20th century, animals were still driven on to the 'killing houses' located where the War Memorial is now and at the Co-operative store house at the bottom of Redburn Road.[145]

The *Double-Dykes* road was a path not more than about a yard wide where the Co-op workers walked the bullocks to the Redburn Road Killing House. Jimmy Burns recounts that if you happened to be travelling through

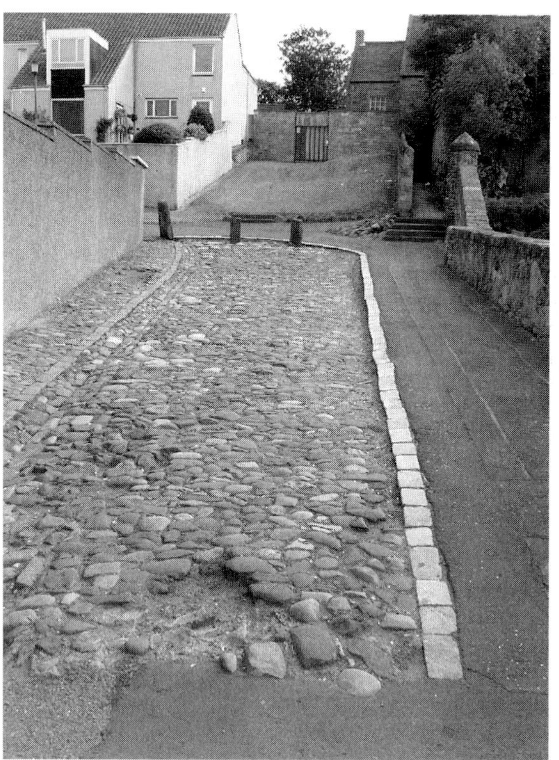
Mill Wynd and its causey stanes;
© A Ralton, 2004

the path at the same time as the bullocks they always won![146]

Local folklore tells us that *Redburn* Road is supposed to have been named as such because of it running red with the blood of the massacred Hanoverian troops at the Battle of Prestonpans. It may also have been blood from the nearby Killing House; or even water that had been contaminated by runoff from all the coal mines nearby which turns water a rusty red colour.

Low's Wynd is no longer in existence. It used to be where the Kinetic Sculpture and the monument to Robert Burns are located. On the south side of the High Street by the Church gardens, the lane is called *Mill Wynd*, and it preserves the characteristic causewayed paving typical of the time. There is a fine picture of this road in Alistair Tulloch's book[147] "Prestonpans in Old Picture Postcards." This shows the lane paved with *causey stanes*. The name for a causeway is thought to have been derived from *calsay* meaning a hard paved road.

Housing estate streets have been built rapidly in the last century and their names reflect either local councillors and great people or events associated with Prestonpans.[148] The Battle of 1745 is an obvious theme: *Gardiner's Road*, or *Johnnie Cope's Road*, for example, and *Thorntree Crescent* and *Hawthorn Road* from the tree where Colonel Gardiner was wounded; *Bankton Terrace* reflecting Bankton House, formerly the property of Lord Bankton after Colonel Gardiner lived there. Lately there is even a *Jacobite Way*.

Other local worthies and former councillors commemorated are: Mackie, McLeod, Nimmo; Ormiston, Robertson, and Wilson; and *Ayres Wynd* after a favourite walk of the Reverend Logan Ayre (although this street name exists today the original layout has been changed); *Alexander Drive* after the famous surgeon who worked alongside Florence Nightingale in the Crimean War, and whose statue occupies a prominent place in the town; *Sir Walter Scott Pend*; *Schaw Road* after Dr James Schaw the philanthropic owner of Preston House; *Oswald Terrace* after Dr William Oswald, heir to the Hamilton properties in Prestonpans; and also lately a *Robert De Quinci Place*. *Polwarth Terrace*, etc is thought to be named after Lord Polwarth, a local County Councillor representing Humbie who was instrumental in getting a direct water supply to Prestonpans from reservoirs in the Lammermuirs in the early 1920's.[149] *Pyper's* and *Cookies Wynd* also echo other local characters.[150]

Names from the industrial age are *Summerlee Street*, after the company that owned Prestongrange Colliery in the late 19th Century; *Fowler's Court*, situated in the former Brewery buildings; and *Rope Walk*, named for the rope manufactory behind the west end of the High Street; *Bellfield Square* after the owner of one of the many potteries which flourished in Prestonpans and not forgetting *Acheson Drive*, named after the 16th century entrepreneur Alexander Atkinson (Acheson).[151]

Other geographical or agriculturally derived names are: *Rigley Terrace*, after Rigley Hill; *Inchview*, looking over the Firth of Forth to the islands named from the Gaelic – *Inchcolm* and *Inchkeith*; and *Nethershot*, *Middleshot* and *Longdykes*, after field names. A '*shott*'[152] was a measurement of land used in pre-improvement agriculture to indicate a block of arable land divided into strips or *selions*.[153]

Fowler's Court, with milestone built into wall;
© A Ralton, 2004.

The name of the hamlet of Cuthill has claim to being perhaps one of the oldest surviving settlement names in Prestonpans, as it possibly derives from the Gaelic *Comhdhail*, meaning: assembly; conference; or tryst; not necessarily indicating a court of law.[154]

Harlaw Hill is also of some interest, possibly of ancient heritage from the old English *here hlaw* meaning army hill, although a degree of caution is necessary, as the name may also have been transferred from another place when a landowner established a house there.

There are others, and probably those elder residents of Prestonpans whose knowledge will doubtless be superior to mine could add and expand on this list.

THE MODERN ERA

The proliferation of coach travel meant that streets had to be widened to accommodate these vehicles in Prestonpans and elsewhere. In July 1899 the Western District Committee of the County Council formed a sub-committee to consider how to widen West Loan, which had been narrowed as a result of a field being enclosed. The report states:

> *The sub-committee inspected the road at Prestonpans West Loan, and have to report that the road is narrow throughout its entire length. The road opposite the Glebe, including the footpath, is 20 feet wide at the widest part. The hedge, or wire fence appears to encroach a little on the road, while the portion of the road opposite the north end, where a wall has been erected to fence the field from the road, is a little narrower (17 feet).*[155]

This situation was resolved by the Council feuing a strip of land 130 yards long and moving the wall three feet for the landowner.

Road surfaces were also considerably improved by the laying of tarmac (named after John Louden MacAdam, one of the great Scottish road engineers of the 19th Century who made great improvements in road surfacing) and this was used widely on roads from 1910 onwards.[156]

The beginning of the 20th Century also saw the development of tramway systems in East Lothian. The line from Edinburgh extended to Musselburgh in

The line of the former coastal road, now superseded by a new road on reclaimed land from the sea; Jim Corsiter's excellent mural of the Cornish Beam Engine and James Watt [from the Prestoungrange Arts Festival's collection] is seen on the wall.
© A Ralton, 2004.

1904, and then on to Port Seton in 1909.[157] An original stretch of that tram rail line can still be seen just outside to the east of the Prestongrange Industrial Heritage Museum at Morrison's Haven. The development of tramways meant that some streets had to be widened and consequently some fine old buildings in Prestonpans High Street were demolished or altered with parts shaved off to accommodate the wider road.

The trams were replaced by buses from 1928; and in 1935 the first stretch of dual carriageway in Scotland was laid down between Seton and Cantyhall north of the railway, supplanting the original Great Post Road which lay to the south of the railway line and which had necessitated several level crossings of the line. The development of the internal combustion engine and the emergence of the motorcar, which was to see a further revolution in transport and the roads on which they travelled. This was especially the case after the Second World War, when the stability of peacetime and the growing economy meant that motorcars were being acquired as consumable products by many more households.

The Great Post Road became known as the A1 as a result of the establishment of the Ministry of Transport in 1919. The Road Act passed in 1920 standardised the system for road classification and numbering. Class 1 roads were to be denoted by the prefix 'A'; Class 2 roads were to be denoted by the prefix 'B'; class 3 roads were to be denoted by the prefix 'C'.

Thus in Prestonpans the Mid Road, part of which was formerly the Great Post Road, became known as the A198; Prestonpans High Street became the B1348; West Loan became the B1349 and East Loan was categorised as a class 3 road.

The B1348 to the north of Drummore, using part of the old road past Ravenshaugh and West Pans, had several difficulties with landslides which necessitated the building of a retaining wall for the Drummore Estate until a new line of road was created out of the sea by the laying of waste ash from Cockenzie Power Station and the reclaiming of land. The new line of road was opened along the coast in 1975.[158]

The A1 travelled through Tranent and Musselburgh into Edinburgh. However the increasing use of the car meant that the new phenomenon of 'gridlock' became a serious issue for travellers. Calls were made for a Tranent By-pass and also a Musselburgh By-pass and on 27th March 1986 the latter was opened by Sir Malcolm Rifkind after works costing £9M.[159] The dual carriageway was then extended eastwards to Haddington in 1996 at a further cost of £26M.[160] By this time, there were strong calls made for the further improvement of the A1 eastwards to Dunbar and this too was accomplished in early 2004. Inevitably all such changes and development raised wider issues concerning loss of countryside, and the wider environmental impact on the landscape.[161]

Tolls have not completely disappeared, and whenever they recur in the media it is almost guaranteed to cause heated debate; the continuation of tolls on the Forth Road Bridge and the proposal of the City of Edinburgh Council to charge tolls electronically on vehicles entering the city being just two recent examples.

In this respect there have also been initiatives for greater non-motorised transport, as Government has recognised the need for people to become more active and thereby healthier. Laws have been changed to seek to facilitate greater access to the countryside. The legacy of coal mining in Prestonpans has left several former mineral railways leading to the former collieries of Preston Links, Northfield (Penny Pit) and Bankton (where the path to the 'Blue Knowe' was a former coal miner's path[162]) used by local walkers. The coastal trail along the Firth of Forth now called the John Muir Way, after the famous conservationist, is also part of the North Sea Trail.

Thanks to this developing awareness of the need to promote ways of achieving a healthier population, these old roads are no longer simply of historic interest. Instead, they offer a valuable resource which is likely to be increasingly used in the future.

NOTES

1 Nicolaisen, W F H; 2001; *Scottish Place Names, their study and significance (Second Edition)*; John Donald Publishers; Edinburgh
Baker, S; 2000; *Prestongrange House*; Prestoungrange University Press; Milton Malsor

2 Barrow, G; 1951; "A Twelfth Century Newbattle Document" in *Scottish Historical Review, Volume XXX*

3 Innes, C; 1849; *Registrum S. Marie de Neubotle. Abbacie Cisterciensis Beate Virginis de Neubotle chartarium vetus. Accedit appendix cartarum originalium. 1140–1528;* The Bannatyne Club; Edinburgh

4 Ibid

5 Cameron, I B and Stephenson, D; 1985; *The Midland Valley of Scotland* (Third Edition); Her Majesty's Stationery Office; London

6 McNeill, P; *Prestonpans;* op. cit
Ireland, W; 1898; "Notes on the Scottish De Quency's of Fawside and Leuchars" pp275–94 in *Proceedings of the Society of Antiquaries of Scotland*; The Society of Antiquaries of Scotland; Edinburgh.
McKenzie, J; 1987; "Prestonpans water, Past, Present and Future" pp 49–65 in of the *Transactions of the East Lothian Antiquarian and Field Naturalist Society Volume 19*; East Lothian Antiquarian and Field Naturalists Society; Haddington
7 Meiklejohn, G; 1927; *The Settlements and Roads of Scotland, a study in human geography*; Oliver and Boyd; Edinburgh
Dennison, E P and Russel Coleman; 1996; *Historic Musselburgh*; Historic Scotland in association with Scottish Cultural Press; Edinburgh
McNeill, P and Hector L MacQueen (Editors); 1996; *Atlas of Scottish History to 1707*; The Scottish Medievalists and Department of Geography; Edinburgh
8 Cameron and Stephenson; op. cit.: pp 134–5
9 Gregory, J W; 1926; *Geology*; J M Dent & Sons Ltd; London
10 Macaulay, J; 1981; *A Short History of Prestonpans*; Janet D Macaulay; Prestonpans
11 Dennison, & Coleman; op. cit.
12 Rackham, O; 1995; *The History of the British Countryside*; Weidenfeld and Nicolson; London
13 Coles, J M; 1984; "Prehistoric Roads and Trackways in Britain: Problems and Possibilities" pp 1–21 in Fenton and Stell; 1984
14 Ibid. p 10
15 Ibid
16 Royal Commission Ancient and Historical Monuments of Scotland; 1996; NT47SW 9; [Find of a polished stone axe at Wilson Walk, Tranent]
17 Coles, op. cit.
18 Rivet, A L F and Colin Smith; 1979; *The place-names of Roman Britain*; Batsford; London
19 Watson, W J; 1926; *History of the Celtic Placenames of Scotland*, (reprinted 1993 by Birlinn, Edinburgh)
20 Ibid
21 Macdonald, J; 1893; "Notes on the 'Roman Roads' of the One Inch Ordnance Survey Map of Scotland" in *Proceedings of the Society of Antiquaries of Scotland*; The Society of Antiquaries of Scotland; Edinburgh.
22 Ibid
23 Stirling, R M; 1894; *Inveresk Parish Lore from Pagan Times, pp 46–7*; T C Blair; Musselburgh
24 Russell, J; 1922; *The Story of Leith*; Thomas Nelson and Sons Ltd; Edinburgh
25 Anderson, D; 2000; *Sourcing brickmaking, salting and chemicals at Prestongrange*; Prestoungrange University Press; Cockenzie
26 Royal Commission Ancient and Historical Monuments of Scotland; 2001; *NT 37 SE [CANMORE entry for find of Roman amphora at Edinburgh Road, Prestonpans]*
27 Johnman, W A P; 1899; *"Saut Ha'" and its tragedy: with an excursus on the ancient salt industry*; W Morrison and Company Ltd; Hawick
28 Twigg, G D; 2002; *Salt History–salt in Roman times [Online]*; http://www.saltinfo.com/salt%20history2.htm
29 Johnman; op. cit: p 4
30 Anderson, J; 1899; *Calendar of the Laing Charters* AD *834–1837*; James Thin; Edinburgh
31 Jocelyn, a monk of Furness; Twelfth Century; *"The Life of Kentigern" (Transcribed by Cynthia Whiddon Green, 1998) [Online]*; http://www. gypsyfire.com/Translation.htm
32 Stirling; op. cit.
33 Anderson, *Sourcing Brickmaking* ... op. cit.
34 Graham, A; 1951; "Gleanings from the Dark Age Records" pp 64–91 in *Proceedings of the Society of Antiquaries of Scotland*; The Society of Antiquaries of Scotland; Edinburgh.
35 Cowan, I B, and David E Easson; 1976; *Medieval Religious Houses in Scotland (Second Edition)*; Longman; London
36 Wemyss, W; 1799; "Parish of Prestonpans Appendix to the Statistical Account of Prestonpans" in *The Statistical Account of Scotland 1791–1799 (Edited by Sir John Sinclair)* [East Lothian District Library 1995 Reprint]; East Lothian District Library; Haddington
37 McNeill; *Prestonpans*: pp 174 & 229

38 Reid, A; 1907; "The Churchyards of Prestonpans" pp 18–39 in *Proceedings of the Society of Antiquaries of Scotland*; The Society of Antiquaries of Scotland; Edinburgh
39 McNeill; Prestonpans; op. cit: pp 177–8
40 Personal communication with Ian Fraser of RCAHMS; 2004
41 Innes; op. cit.
42 Innes; op. cit.
43 Nicolaisen; op. cit. p 217
44 Innes; p xxxvii
45 Innes; op. cit.
46 Ibid
47 Aitken, J; 2000; *Acheson / Morrison's Haven*; Prestoungrange University Press; Cockenzie.
48 Anon.; General *Index to the Acts of the Parliament of Scotland Vol XII – General Index*; p 642; H M General Register Office; Edinburgh
Graham, A; 1962a; "Archaeology on a great post road" pp 317–47 Reprinted from the *Proceedings of the Society of Antiquaries of Scotland*; The Society of Antiquaries of Scotland; Edinburgh
49 Carrick, J C; 1908; *The Abbey of S. Mary, Newbattle. A memorial of the royal visit, 1907*; George Lewis & Co; Selkirk
50 Aitken, J; op. cit.
51 Thomson, J M; 1892; *The Register of the Great Seal of Scotland* AD *1609–1620:* pp 770–2 ; HM General Register House; Edinburgh
52 Royal Commission Ancient and Historical Monuments of Scotland; No Date; *Ordnance Survey Object Name Books [on Microfilm]; Midlothian (Edinburghshire), 1853 "Parish of Newbattle": Reel 119, Book 20, Page 60.*
53 Royal Commission Ancient and Historical Monuments of Scotland; 1996; NT 36 NE; [Aerial Photographs and sketch map of Salter's Road – possible]
54 Royal Commission Ancient and Historical Monuments of Scotland; No Date; Ordnance *Survey Object Name Books [on Microfilm]; East Lothian (Haddingtonshire), 1853 "Parish of Humbie": Reel 78, Book 7*; Royal Commission Ancient and Historical Monuments of Scotland; Edinburgh.
55 Hardy, R; 1942; *The Roads of Medieval Lauderdale*; Oliver and Boyd; London
56 Williamson, M G; 1996; *The Origin of Street Names in Dalkeith*; Midlothian Council Library Services; Dalkeith
57 Moffat, B; 1995; *The Fifth Report on Researches into the Medieval Hospital at Soutra, Lothian / Borders Region Scotland*; SHARP; Fala
58 Innes; page xxviii & xxix
59 Thomson, J M; 1892; *The Register of the Great Seal of Scotland* AD *1609–1620:* pp 770–2 ; HM General Register House; Edinburgh
60 Personal communication with Mr Bill Paterson of the Scottish Place Name Society
61 Primus, T; 1837; *Liber Sancte Marie de Melros. Munimenta vetustiora Monasterii Cisterciensis de Melros*; The Bannatyne Club; Edinburgh
I am grateful to Mr Bill Paterson of the Scottish Place Name Society for helping with the Latin translation of this text
62 Jeffrey 1826 cited in Mackay, J J; 1999; *Border Highways*; John James Mackay; Kelso
63 Royal Commission Ancient and Historical Monuments of Scotland; No Date; *Ordnance Survey Object Name Books* [on Microfilm]; Roxburghshire, 1860: Reel 182, Book 28, Page 135
64 Whatley, C A; 1987; *The Scottish Salt Industry, an economic and social history*; Aberdeen University Press; Aberdeen
65 Anderson, J; 1899; *Calendar of the Laing Charters* AD *834–1837:* pp 148–9.; James Thin; Edinburgh
66 Oram, R and Richard Fawcett; 2004; *Melrose Abbey*; Tempus Publishing; Stroud
67 Royal Commission Ancient and Historical Monuments of Scotland; No Date; *Ordnance Survey Object Name Books* [on Microfilm]; *Midlothian (Edinburghshire), 1853 "Parish of Temple"*
68 O'Sullivan, J and A Smith; 1994; *Forestry Survey: Toxside, Roseberry Estate*; AOC; Edinburgh
69 Carrick; op. cit: p. 76
70 Cowan and Easson; op. cit: p. 51
71 Reid, A; op. cit: p. 18
72 NAS; RHP21113

73 The Haddingtonshire Courier; 1922; "East Lothian Roads 350 Years Ago"
74 Dickinson, W C; 1961; *A Source Book of Scottish History, Vol 3 1567–1707*: p. 353; Thomas Nelson and Sons Ltd; Edinburgh
75 The Haddingtonshire Courier; 20 May 1938; "East Lothian Antiquarian and Field Naturalists Society, Annual Meeting in Haddington, Excursion to the Garleton Hills" Haddingtonshire Courier
76 McNeill, P G B & Hector MacQueen; op. cit: p. 87
77 Inglis, H R G; 1915; "The Roads that Led to Edinburgh" pp 18–49 in the *Proceedings of the Society of Antiquaries of Scotland*; The Society of Antiquaries of Scotland; Edinburgh.
78 McNeill; Prestonpans and Vicinity; op. cit.
79 McNeill; *Prestonpans*; pp 174–5.
80 Haldane, A R B; 1971; *Three Centuries of Scottish Posts:* p. 52; University Press; Edinburgh
81 Ibid
82 McNeill, P; 1883; *Tranent and its Surroundings* (1984 Reprint): p. 188; Remploy; Leicester
83 Graham, A; 1962a; op. cit.
84 Ibid: p. 325
85 Mackay; op. cit.
86 McNeill, P; *Prestonpans;* op. cit.
87 Ibid: p. 176
88 Masson, D; 1891; *The Register of the Privy Council of Scotland Vol V* AD *1613–1616:* pp. 162 & 646; H M General Register House; Edinburgh
89 McNeill; Prestonpans; op. cit.
90 Thomson, J M; 1892; *The Register of the Great Seal of Scotland* AD *1609–1620:* pp. 610–11; HM General Register House; Edinburgh
91 National Archives of Scotland (NAS); *Preston Cross Rights of Way papers*; Scottish Rights of Way and Recreation Society; GD335/8/9
92 McNeill; Prestonpans and vicinity: p. 200
93 Leitch, R; 1990; "'Here chapmen billies tak their stand': A pilot study of Scottish chapmen, packmen, and pedlars" in *Proceedings of the Society of Antiquaries of Scotland*, Volume 120; Society of Antiquaries of Scotland; Edinburgh
94 As described by Sarah Robertson: pp 45–53 in East Lothian Council Library Service; No Date; *Thank You For Listening, Memories from Prestonpans*; East Lothian Library Service; Haddington
95 Moir, D; "The Roads of Scotland II: Statute Labour Roads: The First Phase pp 101–10 in the *Scottish Geographical Magazine*; The Royal Scottish Geographical Society; Edinburgh.
96 Ibid: p. 102
97 Ibid: p. 104
98 Ibid: p. 105
99 National Library of Scotland; 2004; *Blaeu Atlas of Scotland, 1654 [Online]*; http://www.nls.uk/digitallibrary/map/early/blaeu/index.html
100 Graham, A; 1962a; op. cit.
101 Hume- Brown, P; 1904*; The Register of the Privy Council of Scotland Vol V* AD *1633–1635:* p. 77; H M General Register House; Edinburgh
102 Ibid
103 Ibid
104 Moir, D; "The Roads of Scotland II: Statute Labour Roads: The Second Phase pp 167–75 in the *Scottish Geographical Magazine*; The Royal Scottish Geographical Society; Edinburgh.
105 Ibid
106 Pagan, W; 1845; *Road reform: a plan for abolishing turnpike tolls and statute labour assessments, etc:* p. 297; Blackwood and Sons; Edinburgh
107 McNeil; op. cit: p. 223
108 Cadell, R; 1898; *Sir John Cope and the Rebellion of 1745*; William Blackwood and Sons; Edinburgh
109 Worling, M J; 1991; *Early Railways of the Lothians*; Midlothian District Libraries; Dalkeith
110 Roy, W; 1755
111 George I
112 NAS; 1750; *Copy Minute, Heretors of Haddington*; GD110/630

113 Ibid
114 NAS; 1751; *Turnpike Certificate of Measure*; GD110/630
115 NAS; 1751; *Minutes of the Justices of Peace for East Lothian anent Turnpikes*; GD110/630
116 NAS; 7 August 1750; *Act of the Trustees anent the Turnpike Roads in East Lothian*; GD110/630
117 Ibid
118 Graham, A; 1962b; Unpublished manuscript appendix to "Archaeology on a great post road" from the *Proceedings of the Society of Antiquaries of Scotland*
119 NAS; 1752; *Extracts – Acts of the Quarter Sessions of the County of Haddington relative to the road on the south side of Prestonpans*; CS27143296
120 NAS; 1762; *Answers for the Justices of the Peace for the County of East Lothian to the Bill of Suspension offered for Mr James Erskine and Mr David Dalrymple advocates; Mr William Ramsay of Preston and others*; CS271/43296
121 NAS; 1767; *Plan of the Lands of Preston, The property of William Ramsay Esq. Surveyed and drawn up David Mather*; RHP23475
653122 Extract from General Road Trustees Sederunt Book, Vol. 1 – Ref 2/1/1/ *in* Graham, A; 1962b; Unpublished manuscript appendix to "Archaeology on a great post road" from the *Proceedings of the Society of Antiquaries of Scotland*
123 Hislop, R F; No Date; *Prestonpans: Reminiscences by Old Inhabitants relative to the Locality* [Unpublished work]
124 Ibid
125 Anon.; 1760; *The Surprising and Heroic Atchievment at Ravenshaugh Toll* {Satirical Pamphlet]
126 National Register of Archives (NRA); 31 June 1761; *The Surprising and Heroic Atchievment at Ravenshaugh Toll [Unknown Newspaper Report]*
127 McNeill; op. cit: pp 254–5
128 An East Lothian Man; 1805; "On the Management of Roads in East Lothian" pp 349–52 in *The Farmers Magazine*
129 Martine, J; 1894; *Reminiscences of Ten Parishes of the County of Haddington*; William Sinclair; Haddington
130 Ibid: p. 157
131 Mackay; op. cit: pp 181–2
132 NAS; 2 March 1829; *Plan of the Improvement made on the Turnpike Road at Tranent, 1829 – William Kempt (Surveyor)*; RHP21113
133 NAS; 17 May 1844; *Plan of a Proposed Improvement on the line of Road south of Prestongrange, County of East Lothian – James Hay (Surveyor)*; RHP41331
134 NAS; 1817; *A Map of the Environs of Edinburgh marked to show the Proposed Canal from Edinburgh and Haddington*; RHP9647
135 Morris, A S; 1980; "The Nineteenth Century Scottish Carrier Trade: Patterns of Decline" pp 74–82 in the *Scottish Geographical Magazine*; The Royal Scottish Geographical Society; Edinburgh.
136 Pagan; ibid
137 The Haddingtonshire Courier; 13 April 1860
138 The Haddingtonshire Courier; 25 February 1870
139 Anon.; 1857; Excerpt from minute of a meeting of the heritors and tenants of the parish of Humbie: held in the school-house, Upper Keith, on Monday the 5th October 1857
140 Hunter, W A; 1882; *Handbook of the Roads and Bridges (Scot.) Act 1878 containing a dictionary index and a chronological view of procedure for bringing the act into operation*; Edinburgh
141 Anon.; 4 May 1868; [*Poster giving notice of meeting of occupiers of premises in Prestonpans to elect Police Commissioners, 4 May 1868*]
142 NAS; GD335/8/9
143 McNeill; ibid: p. 223
144 Adams, ibid: p. 119
145 Burns, J; No Date; "Prestonpans as I Remember it" pp. 1–4 in Prestonpans Local History Society; 2000; *Tales of the Pans: a collection of memories from Panners about Prestonpans*; Prestonpans Local History Society; Prestonpans
146 Ibid
147 Tulloch, A P; 1989; *Prestonpans in Old Picture Postcards*; European Library; Zaltbommel

148 East Lothian County Council; 1953; *Burgh of Prestonpans in County Surveyors Report 1953*; East Lothian county Council; Haddington
149 Barbour, G F; 1947; *Lord Polwarth, 1864–1944; Oliver and Boyd; Edinburgh*
150 McNeill; Prestonpans: pp 189–90
Burns, op. cit: p. 1–4
151 Aitken, J; 2000; *Acheson/Morrison's Haven*; Prestoungrange University Press; Cockenzie
152 Adams, I H; 1970; *Provisional Glossary of the Agrarian landscape*; University of Edinburgh; Edinburgh
153 Ibid
154 Barrow, G W S; 1981; "Popular Courts in Early medieval Scotland: Some Suggested Place-Name Evidence" pp 1–24 in *Scottish Studies* Vol 25; School of Scottish Studies; Edinburgh
155 *Haddingtonshire Courier*; 7 July 1899; "A Prestonpans Road Question"
156 Hindle, P; 2001; *Roads and Tracks for Historians*; Phillimore and Co Ltd; Chichester
157 Tulloch, A P; 1989; *Prestonpans in Old Picture Postcards*; European Library; Zaltbommel
158 The Edinburgh Evening News; 19 July 1974; "Coasting Along ..." *Edinburgh Evening News*; Edinburgh
159 Baker, S; 2003; "The Story of the A1 in the County" pp 128–31 in Baker, S; 2003; *East Lothian 1945–2000, Fourth Statistical Account, Volume One: The County*; East Lothian Council Library Service for the East Lothian Fourth Statistical Account Society; Haddington
160 Ibid
161 Hoyle, D, Nigel Doar and Peter Smith; 1996; *Head On Collision Scotland*; Scottish Wildlife Trust; Edinburgh
162 McKenzie; ibid

BIBLIOGRAPHY

A Traveller; 1814; "On the Roads of East Lothian" pp 223–32 in *The Farmers Magazine*

Adams, I H; 1965; "The Salt Industry of the Forth Basin" pp 153–62 in *Scottish Geographical Magazine* Volume 81; The Royal Scottish Geographical Society; Edinburgh

Adams, I H; 1970; *Provisional Glossary of the Agrarian landscape*; University of Edinburgh; Edinburgh

Aitken, J; 2000; *Acheson/Morrison's Haven*; Prestoungrange University Press; Cockenzie

Aitken, J; No Date; *Tynewater, People and Places, Fala, Soutra, Pathhead, Ford, Edgehead and District* [Edited by Jean Blades and Alan Reid; Fala and District Historical Society]

Allan, A; 2000; *Horses, steam and electric engines at Prestongrange*; Prestoungrange University Press; Cockenzie

Allan, C; 2001; *Agricultural Improvement at Dolphinstoun*; Prestoungrange University Press; Cockenzie

An East Lothian Man; 1805; "On the Management of Roads in East Lothian" pp 349–52 in *The Farmers Magazine*

An East Lothian Man; 1806; "On the Management of Roads in East Lothian" pp 63–8 in *The Farmers Magazine*

An Old Roadmaker; 1806; "On the Forming and Repairing of Roads" pp 467–71 in *The Farmers Magazine*

Anderson, D; 2000; *Sourcing brickmaking, salting and chemicals at Prestongrange*; Prestoungrange University Press; Cockenzie

Anderson, J; 1899; *Calendar of the Laing Charters* AD *834–1837*; James Thin; Edinburgh

Anon.; General *Index to the Acts of the Parliament of Scotland Vol XII – General Index*; p 642; H M General Register Office; Edinburgh

Anon.; 1760; *The Surprising and Heroic Atchievment at Ravenshaugh Toll* [Satirical Pamphlet]

Anon.; 1787; "Observations on the Manufacture of Salt in Scotland in 1787" pp 760–5 and 817–22 in the *Scots Magazine*; Edinburgh

Anon.; 1814; "On Roads" p 205 in *The Farmers Magazine*

Anon.; 1857; Excerpt from minute of a meeting of the heritors and tenants of the parish of Humbie: held in the school-house, Upper Keith, on Monday the 5th October 1857

Anon.; 4 May 1868; [*Poster giving notice of meeting of occupiers of premises in Prestonpans to elect Police Commissioners, 4 May 1868*]

Armstrong, M J; 1776; An *Actual Survey of the Great Post Roads Between London and Edinburgh*; London

Arnold, J; 1979; *All Drawn by Horses*; David and Charles; Newton Abbot

Baker, S; 2003; *East Lothian 1945–2000, Fourth Statistical Account, Volume One: The County*; East Lothian Council Library Service for the East Lothian Fourth Statistical Account Society; Haddington

Baker, S; 2000; *Prestongrange House*; Prestoungrange University Press; Milton Malsor

Barbour, G F; 1947; *Lord Polwarth, 1864-1944;* Oliver and Boyd; Edinburgh

Barrow, G; 1951; "A Twelfth Century Newbattle Document" in *Scottish Historical Review, Volume XXX*

Barrow, G; 1983; "Midlothian or the Shire of Edinburgh" pp 141–8 in the *Book of the Old Edinburgh Club; Old Edinburgh Club*; Edinburgh

Barrow, G W S; 1981; "Popular Courts in Early medieval Scotland: Some Suggested Place-Name Evidence" pp 1–24 in Scottish Studies Vol 25; *School of Scottish Studies*; Edinburgh

Barrow, G W S; 1992; "Land Routes" pp 201–16 in *Scotland and its Neighbours in the Middle Ages*; The Hambledon Press; London

Batey, C and Muriel King; 1994; *Discovery and Excavation*; Council for Scottish Archaeology; Edinburgh

Batey, C and Muriel King; 1995; *Discovery and Excavation*; Council for Scottish Archaeology; Edinburgh

Bishop, M C (Editor); 2002; *Roman Inveresk*; The Armatura Press; Duns

Bourhill, J; No date; *The History of Wallyford*; East Lothian Council Library Service; Haddington

Cadell, R; 1898; *Sir John Cope and the Rebellion of 1745*; William Blackwood and Sons; Edinburgh

Caird, J B; 1964; "The Making of the Scottish Rural Landscape" pp 72–80 in the *Scottish Geographical Magazine Volume 80*; The Royal Scottish Geographical Society; Edinburgh

Cameron, I B and Stephenson, D; 1985; *The Midland Valley of Scotland* (Third Edition); Her Majesty's Stationery Office; London

Campbell, R H; 1971; *Scotland Since 1707: The Rise of an Industrial Society*; Basil Blackwell; Oxford

Carrick, J C; 1904; *Around Dalkeith*; Carrick, J C; Dalkeith

Carrick, J C; 1908; *The Abbey of S. Mary, Newbottle. A memorial of the royal visit, 1907*; George Lewis & Co; Selkirk

Carter, M and Julian Wills; 2002; *Geology and the Environment at Prestoungrange*; Prestoungrange University Press; Cockenzie

Corporation of the City of Glasgow; 1988; *Horse Drawn Carriages a Descriptive Guide*; The Glasgow Museums and Art Galleries Department, Art Gallery and Museum; Glasgow

Cunningham, I; 2001; *The Nation Survey'd, Timothy Pont's Maps of Scotland*; Tuckwell Press in association with the National Library of Scotland; East Linton

Cunningham, W B; 1839; "Parish of Prestonpans Presbytery of Haddington Synod of Lothian and Tweeddale" in *New Statistical Account 1839* [East Lothian District Library 1995 Reprint]; East Lothian District Library; Haddington

Davidson, J L; 1986; "The collection of antiquarian information for the early Ordnance Survey maps of Scotland" pp 11–16 in *Proceedings of the Society of Antiquaries of Scotland*; The Society of Antiquaries of Scotland; Edinburgh

De Brisay, K W and K Evans; 1974; *Salt the study of an ancient industry : report on the Salt Weekend held at the University of Essex, 20, 21, 22 September 1974*; Colchester Archaeological Group.; Colchester

Dennison, E P and Russel Coleman; 1996; *Historic Musselburgh*; Historic Scotland in association with Scottish Cultural Press; Edinburgh

Dennison, E P and Russel Coleman; 1998; *Historic Melrose*; Historic Scotland in association with Scottish Cultural Press; Edinburgh

Dickinson, W C; 1961; A Source Book of Scottish History, Vol 3 1567–1707; Thomas Nelson and Sons Ltd; Edinburgh
Dixon, P; 2002; *Puir Labourers and Busy Husbandmen*; Birlinn with Historic Scotland
Duckham, B F; 1967; *The Transport Revolution, 1750–1830*; The Historical Association; London
East Lothian Council Library Service; No Date; *Thank You For Listening, Memories from Prestonpans*; East Lothian Library Service; Haddington
East Lothian County Council; 1953; *Burgh of Prestonpans in County Surveyors Report 1953*; East Lothian county Council; Haddington
East Lothian District Council Library and various contributors; 1986; *The Pans Remembered*; East Lothian District Council Library; Haddington
Edina; 2004; *Statistical Accounts of Scotland [Online]*; http:// edina.ac.uk/statacc/
Edinburgh Evening Dispatch; 31 August 1889; "Prestonpans Cross and Right of Way" *Edinburgh Evening Dispatch*; Edinburgh
Edinburgh Evening News; 1954; "The Changing Face of Levenhall" *Edinburgh Evening News*; Edinburgh
Edinburgh Evening News; 19 July 1974; "Coasting Along ..." *Edinburgh Evening News*; Edinburgh
Fenton, A and Geoffrey Stell; 1984; *Loads and Roads in Scotland, Road Transport over 600 years*; John Donald Publishers; Edinburgh
Field, J; 1990; *Place Names of Britain and Ireland*; David and Charles; Newton Abbot
Forbes Gray, W and James H Jamieson; 1941; "East Lothian Biographies" *Transactions of the East Lothian Antiquarian and Field Naturalists Society* Fourth Volume; East Lothian Antiquarian and Field Naturalists Society; Haddington
Forbes Gray, W and James H Jamieson; 1941; "East Lothian Biographies" from *Transactions of the East Lothian Antiquarian and Field Naturalists Society Fourth Volume*; East Lothian Antiquarian and Field Naturalists Society; Haddington
Geddes, A; 1938; "The Changing Landscape of the Lothians, 1600–1800 as revealed by old estate plans" pp 130–40 in the *Scottish Geographical Magazine Vol 54*; The Royal Scottish Geographical Society; Edinburgh
George I; 1749; *An Act for repairing the roads leading from Dunglas Bridge to the town of Haddingtoun; and from thence to Ravenshaughburn in the county of Haddingtoun*
Gilchrist, I, J Wood and L Baxter (Editors); 1983; *Neubottil Newbattle*; Newbattle Schools Council; Newbattle
Gordon, A; 1988; *To Move with the Times*; Aberdeen University Press; Aberdeen
Graham, A; 1951; "Gleanings from the Dark Age Records" pp 64–91 in *Proceedings of the Society of Antiquaries of Scotland*; The Society of Antiquaries of Scotland; Edinburgh
Graham, A; 1960; "An Old Road in the Lammermuirs" pp 198–206 in the *Proceedings of the Society of Antiquaries of Scotland*; The Society of Antiquaries of Scotland; Edinburgh
Graham, A; 1960; "More Old Roads in the Lammermuirs" pp 217–35 in the *Proceedings of the Society of Antiquaries of Scotland*; The Society of Antiquaries of Scotland; Edinburgh
Graham, A; 1961; "Notes on Seven Lammermuir Roads" in Berwickshire Naturalist Club Volume 35; *Berwickshire Naturalist Club*
Graham, A; 1962a; "Archaeology on a great post road" pp 317–47 Reprinted from the *Proceedings of the Society of Antiquaries of Scotland*; The Society of Antiquaries of Scotland; Edinburgh
Graham, A; 1962b; Unpublished manuscript appendix to *"Archaeology on a great post road"* from the *Proceedings of the Society of Antiquaries of Scotland*
Green, C E; 1907; *East Lothian*; W A Green; Edinburgh
Gregory, J W; 1926; *Geology*; J M Dent & Sons Ltd; London
Gregory, J W; 1938; *The Story of the Road* [second edition, revised and enlarged by C J Gregory]; Adam and Charles Black; London
Haddingtonshire Courier; 2 December 1859
Haddingtonshire Courier; 30 March 1860
Haddingtonshire Courier; 6 April 1860

Haddingtonshire Courier; 13 April 1860
Haddingtonshire Courier; 2 November 1860
Haddingtonshire Courier; 22 March 1861
Haddingtonshire Courier; 1 May 1861
Haddingtonshire Courier; 20 June 1862; "The Roads Question."
Haddingtonshire Courier; 24 February 1865
Haddingtonshire Courier; 4 August 1865
Haddingtonshire Courier; 16 March 1866
Haddingtonshire Courier; 1 March 1867
Haddingtonshire Courier; 23 August 1867
Haddingtonshire Courier; 11 October 1867
Haddingtonshire Courier; 25 June 1869
Haddingtonshire Courier; 25 February 1870
Haddingtonshire Courier; 11 August 1876
Haddingtonshire Courier; 27 February 1889
Haddingtonshire Courier; 30 August 1889
Haddingtonshire Courier; 29 August 1890
Haddingtonshire Courier; 6 April 1894
Haddingtonshire Courier; 7 July 1899; "A Prestonpans Road Question."
Haddingtonshire Courier; 1922; "East Lothian Roads 350 Years Ago."
Haddingtonshire Courier; 16 May 1930; "East Lothian Antiquarian and Field Naturalists Society, Annual General Meeting, Visit to the Garleton Hills."
Haddingtonshire Courier; 20 May 1938; "East Lothian Antiquarian and Field Naturalists Society, Annual Meeting in Haddington, Excursion to the Garleton Hills."
Haldane, A R B; 1962 [1995 Reprint]; *New Ways Through the Glens*; House of Lochar; Isle of Colonsay
Haldane, A R B; 1971; *Three Centuries of Scottish Posts*; University Press; Edinburgh
Haldane, A R B; 1997; *The Drove Roads of Scotland*; Birlinn; Isle of Colonsay
Hamilton, A; 1976; *Prestonpans: Scotland's last Saltworks*; Outlet Design Service; Edinburgh
Hands, S; 2002; *Road Signs*; Shire Publications; Princes Risborough
Hardy, R; 1942; *The Roads of Medieval Lauderdale*; Oliver and Boyd; London
Harper, C G; 1901; *The Great North Road: the old mail road to Scotland*; London
Haverfield, F; 1899; "Note on the Antiquity of the Wheel Causeway" pp 129–30 in the *Proceedings of the Society of Antiquaries of Scotland*; The Society of Antiquaries of Scotland; Edinburgh
Heddle, R G; 1981; "Road Administration in Midlothian in the Early Eighteenth Century" pp 105–18 in the *Book of The Old Edinburgh Club*; Old Edinburgh Club; Edinburgh
Hindle, P; 1998 [2002 Reprint]; *Medieval Roads and Tracks*; Shire Publications; Princes Risborough
Hindle, P; 2001; *Roads and Tracks for Historians*; Phillimore and Co Ltd; Chichester
Hislop, R F; No Date; *Prestonpans: Reminiscences by Old Inhabitants relative to the Locality* [Unpublished work]
Hoyle, D, Nigel Doar and Peter Smith; 1996; *Head On Collision Scotland*; Scottish Wildlife Trust; Edinburgh
Hume Brown, P; 1891 [Facsimile Edition, 1973]; *Early Travellers in Scotland*; James Thin; Edinburgh
Hume-Brown, P; 1904; *The Register of the Privy Council of Scotland Vol V* AD *1633–1635*; H M General Register House; Edinburgh
Hunter, M; 1974; *The Lothian Run*; Puffin Books; Middlesex
Hunter, W A; 1882; *Handbook of the Roads and Bridges (Scot.) Act 1878 containing a dictionary index and a chronological view of procedure for bringing the act into operation*; Edinburgh
Inglis, H R G; 1912; "The Ancient Bridges in Scotland" pp 151–77 in *Proceedings of the Society of Antiquaries of Scotland*; The Society of Antiquaries of Scotland; Edinburgh

Inglis, H R G; 1913; "The Roads and Bridges in the Early History of Scotland" pp 303–33 in the *Proceedings of the Society of Antiquaries of Scotland*; The Society of Antiquaries of Scotland; Edinburgh

Inglis, H R G; 1915; "The Most Ancient Bridges in Britain" pp 256–74 in the *Proceedings of the Society of Antiquaries of Scotland*; The Society of Antiquaries of Scotland; Edinburgh

Inglis, H R G; 1915; "The Roads that Led to Edinburgh" pp 18–49 in the *Proceedings of the Society of Antiquaries of Scotland*; The Society of Antiquaries of Scotland; Edinburgh

Innes, C; 1849; *Registrum S. Marie de Neubotle. Abbacie Cisterciensis Beate Virginis de Neubotle chartarium vetus. Accedit appendix cartarum originalium. 1140-1528;* The Bannatyne Club; Edinburgh

Ireland, W; 1898; "Notes on the Scottish De Quency's of Fawside and Leuchars" pp 275–94 in *Proceedings of the Society of Antiquaries of Scotland*; The Society of Antiquaries of Scotland; Edinburgh

Jamieson, J, Eleanor Hawkins and W Forbes Gray; 1936; *Bibliography of East Lothian*; East Lothian Antiquarian and Field Naturalists Society; Edinburgh

Jocelyn, a monk of Furness; Twelfth Century; *"The Life of Kentigern" (Transcribed by Cynthia Whiddon Green, 1998) [Online]*; http://www.fordham.edu/halsall/basis/Jocelyn-LifeofKentigern. html

Johnman, W A P; 1899; *"Saut Ha'" and its tragedy: with an excursus on the ancient salt industry*; W Morrison and Company Ltd; Hawick

Jusserand, J J; 1891; *English Wayfaring Life in the Middle ages (XIVth Century)*; T Fisher Unwin; London

Kelly, K; 11 May 1934; *"From Prestonpans to Port Seton" [Unknown Newspaper article]*

Keppie, L; 1998; *Scotland's Roman Remains*; John Donald Publishers; Edinburgh

Laing, J M; "Packmen's Graves" p. 89 in *Scottish Notes and Queries Vol XI*

Leighton, A C; 1972; *Transport and Communication in Early Medieval Europe* AD *500–1100*; David and Charles; Newton Abbot

Leitch, R; 1990; "'Here chapmen billies tak their stand': A pilot study of Scottish chapmen, packmen, and pedlars" in *Proceedings of the Society of Antiquaries of Scotland*, Volume 120; Society of Antiquaries of Scotland; Edinburgh

Macaulay, J; 1981; *A Short History of Prestonpans*; Janet D Macaulay; Prestonpans

Macdonald, J; 1893; "Notes on the 'Roman Roads' of the One Inch Ordnance Survey Map of Scotland" in *Proceedings of the Society of Antiquaries of Scotland*; The Society of Antiquaries of Scotland; Edinburgh

Mackay, J J; 1999; *Border Highways*; John James Mackay; Kelso

Mair, C; 1988; *Mercat Cross and Tolbooth*; John Donald Publishers Ltd; Edinburgh

Margary, I D.; 1973; *Roman roads in Britain (Third Edition)*; J Baker; London

Martine, J; 1894; *Reminiscences of Ten Parishes of the County of Haddington*; William Sinclair; Haddington

Masson, D; 1891; *The Register of the Privy Council of Scotland Vol V* AD *1613–1616*; H M General Register House; Edinburgh

McKenzie, J; 1987; "Prestonpans water, Past, Present and Future" pp. 49–65 in the *Transactions of the East Lothian Antiquarian and Field Naturalist Society Volume 19*; East Lothian Antiquarian and Field Naturalists Society; Haddington

McNeill, P; 1883; *Tranent and its Surroundings* (1984 Reprint); Remploy; Leicester

McNeill, P; 1883; *Prestonpans and vicinity: historical, ecclesiastical and traditional (1984 Remploy Reprint);* Remploy; Leicester

McNeill, P and Hector L MacQueen (Editors); 1996; *Atlas of Scottish History to 1707*; The Scottish Medievalists and Department of Geography; Edinburgh

Meiklejohn, G; 1927; *The Settlements and Roads of Scotland, a study in human geography*; Oliver and Boyd; Edinburgh

Miller, T R; 1958; *The Monkland Tradition*; Thomas Nelson and Sons Ltd; Edinburgh

Mitchell, I R; 2001; *Walking Through Scotland's History*; NMS Publishing Ltd.; Edinburgh

Moffat, B; 1995; *The Fifth Report on Researches into the Medieval Hospital at Soutra, Lothian / Borders Region Scotland*; SHARP; Fala

Moir, D; "The Roads of Scotland II: Statute Labour Roads: The First Phase" pp 101–10 in the *Scottish Geographical Magazine*; The Royal Scottish Geographical Society; Edinburgh

Moir, D; "The Roads of Scotland II: Statute Labour Roads: The Second Phase" pp 167–75 in the *Scottish Geographical Magazine*; The Royal Scottish Geographical Society; Edinburgh

Moody, D; 1986; *Scottish Local History, an introductory guide*; B T Batsford Ltd; London

Moore, J; 1984; "The Early Printed Maps of East Lothian" pp 23–42 in *Transactions of the East Lothian Antiquarian and Field Naturalist Society*; East Lothian Antiquarian and Field Naturalists Society; Haddington

Morris, A S; 1980; "The Nineteenth Century Scottish Carrier Trade: Patterns of Decline" pp 74–82 in the *Scottish Geographical Magazine*; The Royal Scottish Geographical Society; Edinburgh

National Archives of Scotland

NAS; 1750; *Copy Minute, Heretors of Haddington*; GD110/630

NAS; 7 August 1750; *Act of the Trustees anent the Turnpike Roads in East Lothian*; GD110/630

NAS; *Memorial for the Gentlemen of East Lothian anent the Turnpike Road*; GD110/630

NAS; 1751; *Minutes of the Justices of Peace for East Lothian anent Turnpikes*; GD110/630

NAS; 1751; *Turnpike Certificate of Measure*; GD110/630

NAS; 1752; *Extracts – Acts of the Quarter Sessions of the County of Haddington relative to the road on the south side of Prestonpans*; CS27143296

NAS; 1752; *Replies Anent Preston Road*; CS271/43296

NAS; 1757; *Plan of Tranent Muir done to a scale of 100 feet in an inch from a survey taken Aug 1757 by David Mather*; RHP29/3

NAS; 1760; Replies for Mr James Erskine and Mr David Dalrymple advocates and suspenders to the Answers offered for the Justices of Peace for the County of East Lothian; CS271/43296

NAS; 1762; Extracts Acts of the Quarter Session of the County of Haddington relative to the road on the south side of Prestonpans; CS271/43296

NAS; 1762; Answers for the Justices of the Peace for the County of East Lothian to the Bill of Suspension offered for Mr James Erskine and Mr David Dalrymple advocates; Mr William Ramsay of Preston and others; CS271/43296

NAS; 1762; *Statement of Alexander Gray, Notary Public in support of Mr James Erskine, Mr David Dalrymple, Mr William Ramsay, of Preston, Archibald Forrest, Thomas Warrock, and James Dow feuars in Prestonpans*; CS271/43296

NAS; 1767; *Plan of the Lands of Preston, The property of William Ramsay Esq. Surveyed and drawn up David Mather*; RHP23475

NAS; 1775; *Plan of the runrig lands of Tranent*; RHP29/6

NAS; 1790; *Sketch of the Road in Dispute near Preston House*; RHP758

NAS; 1817; *A Map of the Environs of Edinburgh marked to show the Proposed Canal from Edinburgh and Haddington*; RHP9647

NAS; 1825; *Prestongrange Estate upon a reduced scale from the plan or survey J Ainslie, 1796 and W Forrest 1812, 1825; Shewing the cropping in 1877 and 1878*; RHP41333

NAS; 2 March 1829; *Plan of the Improvement made on the Turnpike Road at Tranent, 1829 – William Kempt (Surveyor)*; RHP21113

NAS; 1832; *Plan of the Lands of Riggonhead belonging to James William Hunter Esq. of Thurston*; RHP13612/1

NAS; 1838; *Plan of the Lands of Birsley, Myles and Easter Falside*; RHP41330

NAS; 1840; *A Plan of the Water Courses Ravenshaugh and Pinkie Burn and their localities at the boundary of the counties of Edinburgh and Haddington by John Mason, surveyor*; RHP5972

NAS; 17 May 1844; *Plan of a Proposed Improvement on the line of Road south of Prestongrange, County of East Lothian – James Hay (Surveyor)*; RHP41331

NAS; No Date *[Mid 19th Century; Plan of part of street leading through Prestonpans]*; RHP21115

NAS; 1856; *Plan of the Lands of Preston*; RHP20591
NAS; 1898; *Preston Cross Rights of Way papers*; Scottish Rights of Way and Recreation Society; GD335/8/9
NAS; RHP626
NAS; No Date [late 19th Century]; *Plan of the damaged ground to be occupied by Summerlee and Mossend Iron company*; RHP49302
NAS; 1909; *Roads used by inhabitants of Cockenzie*; RHP24025
NAS; 1921; *Plan of the proposed Road Diversion at Meadowmill*; RHP36861
NAS; 1925; *Plan of Road at Meadowmill*; RHP13865
National Library of Scotland; 2004; *Blaeu Atlas of Scotland, 1654 [Online]*; http://www.nls.uk/digitallibrary/map/early/blaeu/ index.html
National Library of Scotland; 2004; *Maps Collections [Online]*; http://www.nls.uk/collections/maps/index.html
National Register of Archives (NRA); 31 June 1761; *The Surprising and Heroic Atchievment at Ravenshaugh Toll [Unknown Newspaper Report]*
Nicholson, J; 2000; *A1, portrait of a road*; Harper Collins Illustrated; London
Nicolaisen, W F H; 2001; *Scottish Place Names, their study and significance (Second Edition)*; John Donald Publishers; Edinburgh
O'Sullivan, J and A Smith; 1994; *Forestry Survey: Toxside, Roseberry Estate*; AOC; Edinburgh
Oram, R and Richard Fawcett; 2004; *Melrose Abbey*; Tempus Publishing; Stroud
Ordnance Survey; 1966; *Map of Britain in the Dark Ages*; Ordnance Survey; Southampton
Pagan, W; 1845; *Road reform: a plan for abolishing turnpike tolls and statute labour assessments, etc.*; Blackwood and Sons; Edinburgh
Parry, M L and T R Slater; 1980; *The Making of the Scottish Countryside*; McGill University Press; Montreal
Postan, M; 1952; "The Trade of Medieval Europe: the North" in *The Cambridge economic history of Europe, trade and industry in the Middle Ages;* Cambridge University Press; Cambridge
Pratt Insh, G; 1932; *The Study of Local History and Other Essays*; The Educational Institute of Scotland; Edinburgh
Prestonpans Local History Society; 2000; *Tales of the Pans: a collection of memories from Panners about Prestonpans*; Prestonpans Local History Society; Prestonpans
Primus, T; 1837; *Liber Sancte Marie de Melros. Munimenta vetustiora Monasterii Cisterciensis de Melros*; The Bannatyne Club; Edinburgh
Rackham, O; 1990; *Trees and Woodland in the British Landscape* (1996 paperback edition); Phoenix; London
Rackham, O; 1995; *The History of the British Countryside*; Weidenfeld and Nicolson; London
Reid, A; 1907; "The Churchyards of Prestonpans" pp 18–39 in *Proceedings of the Society of Antiquaries of Scotland*; The Society of Antiquaries of Scotland; Edinburgh
Rennie, S (Editor); 2004; *The Dictionary of the Scots Language [Online]*; http://www.dsl.ac.uk/dsl/
Renville, A; 1990; *Historical Landscapes of East Lothian: A study of settlements, roads, and woodlands between 1590–1854 A. D. Maps drawn to a common scale; based on old historical surveys*. [Unpublished work]
Rivet, A L F and Colin Smith; 1979; *The place-names of Roman Britain*; Batsford; London
Robertson, D M; 1993; *Longniddry*; East Lothian District Library; Haddington
Royal Commission Ancient and Historical Monuments and Constructions of Scotland; 1924; *Eighth Report with Inventory of Monuments and Constructions in the County of East Lothian*; Royal Commission Ancient and Historical Monuments of Scotland; Edinburgh
Royal Commission Ancient and Historical Monuments of Scotland; 1996; NT 36 NE; [Aerial Photographs and sketch map of Salter's Road – possible]; Royal Commission Ancient and Historical Monuments of Scotland; Edinburgh
Royal Commission Ancient and Historical Monuments of Scotland; 2001; *NT 37 SE*

[CANMORE entry for find of Roman amphora at Edinburgh Road, Prestonpans]; Royal Commission Ancient and Historical Monuments of Scotland; Edinburgh

Royal Commission Ancient and Historical Monuments of Scotland; 2001; *NT46 NW [CANMORE entry for excavation of ancient roadway at Templehall*; Royal Commission Ancient and Historical Monuments of Scotland; Edinburgh

Royal Commission Ancient and Historical Monuments of Scotland; No Date; *Ordnance Survey Object Name Books [on Microfilm]; East Lothian (Haddingtonshire), 1853 "Parish of Prestonpans": Reel 81, Book 37*; Royal Commission Ancient and Historical Monuments of Scotland; Edinburgh

Royal Commission Ancient and Historical Monuments of Scotland; No Date; *Ordnance Survey Object Name Books [on Microfilm]; East Lothian (Haddingtonshire), 1853 "Parish of Tranent": Reel 81, Book 38*; Royal Commission Ancient and Historical Monuments of Scotland; Edinburgh

Royal Commission Ancient and Historical Monuments of Scotland; No Date; Ordnance *Survey Object Name Books [on Microfilm]; East Lothian (Haddingtonshire), 1853 "Parish of Humbie": Reel 78, Book 7*; Royal Commission Ancient and Historical Monuments of Scotland; Edinburgh

Royal Commission Ancient and Historical Monuments of Scotland; No Date; *Ordnance Survey Object Name Books [on Microfilm]; Midlothian (Edinburghshire), 1853 "Parish of Newbattle": Reel 119, Book 20, Page 60*; Royal Commission Ancient and Historical Monuments of Scotland; Edinburgh

Royal Commission Ancient and Historical Monuments of Scotland; No Date; *Ordnance Survey Object Name Books [on Microfilm]; Midlothian (Edinburghshire), 1853 "Parish of Penicuik": Reel 120, Book 33*; Royal Commission Ancient and Historical Monuments of Scotland; Edinburgh

Royal Commission Ancient and Historical Monuments of Scotland; No Date; *Ordnance Survey Object Name Books [on Microfilm]; Midlothian (Edinburghshire), 1853 "Parish of Temple";* Royal Commission Ancient and Historical Monuments of Scotland; Edinburgh

Royal Commission Ancient and Historical Monuments of Scotland; No Date; *Ordnance Survey Object Name Books [on Microfilm]; Midlothian (Edinburghshire), 1853 "Parish of Inveresk": Reel 118, Book 8*; Royal Commission Ancient and Historical Monuments of Scotland; Edinburgh

Royal Commission Ancient and Historical Monuments of Scotland; No Date; *Ordnance Survey Object Name Books [on Microfilm]; Roxburghshire, 1860: Reel 182, Book 28, Page 135*; Royal Commission Ancient and Historical Monuments of Scotland; Edinburgh

Royal Scottish Geographical Society; 1973; *The Early Maps of Scotland to 1850 Volume 1*; Royal Scottish Geographical Society; Edinburgh

Royal Scottish Geographical Society; 1983; *The Early Maps of Scotland to 1850 Volume 2* (Third Edition, edited by D G Moir); Royal Scottish Geographical Society; Edinburgh

Russell, J; 1922; *The Story of Leith*; Thomas Nelson and Sons Ltd; Edinburgh

Scottish National Dictionary Association; 1985; *Concise Scots Dictionary*; Polygon at Edinburgh; Edinburgh

Scottish Place Name Society; 2004; *Welcome to the Scottish Place Name Society [Online]*; http://www.st-andrews.ac.uk/institutes/ sassi/spns/

SCRAN; 2004; *SCRAN Online [Online]*; http://www.scran.ac.uk

Seton, G; 1896; *A History of the Family of Seton*; Edinburgh

Silver, O; 1987; *The Roads of Fife*; John Donald Publishers; Edinburgh

Silver, O; 1987; "The Roads of Scotland: from Statute Labour to Tolls – the first phase, 1700 to 1775" pp 141–9 in *Scottish Geographical Magazine Vol. 103, No 3.*; The Royal Scottish Geographical Society; Edinburgh

Sinclair, C; 1994 1996 Reprint; *Tracing Scottish Local History, A Guide to Scottish Local History Research in the Scottish Record Office*; Scottish Record Office; Edinburgh

Smith, R F & Rev. Norman Johnston; 1949; "Quarry to Abbey: an ancient Fife Route" pp 162–7 in the *Proceedings of the Society of Antiquaries of Scotland*; The Society of Antiquaries of Scotland; Edinburgh

Smout, T C; 1998; *A History of the Scottish People, 1560–1830* (Second Edition); Fontana Press; London

Snodgrass, C P; 1953; "The Parish of Prestonpans" in *The Third Statistical Account of Scotland 1953* [East Lothian District Library 1995 Reprint]; East Lothian District Library; Haddington

Stirling, R M; 1894; *Inveresk Parish Lore from Pagan Times*; T C Blair; Musselburgh

Thomson, J M; 1883; *The Register of the Great Seal of Scotland* AD *1513–1546*; HM General Register House; Edinburgh

Thomson, J M; 1892; *The Register of the Great Seal of Scotland* AD *1609–1620*; HM General Register House; Edinburgh

Torrance, D R; 1991; *Scottish Trades and Professions, A Selected Bibliography*; The Scottish Association of Family History Societies

Touche, J E D; 1970; *Tollbars in South East Scotland [unpublished]*; John E D Touche; Edinburgh

Trotter, J; 1799; "Parish of Preston-pans" in *The Statistical Account of Scotland 1791–1799* (Edited by Sir John Sinclair) [East Lothian District Library 1995 Reprint]; East Lothian District Library; Haddington

Tulloch, A P; 1989; *Prestonpans in Old Picture Postcards*; European Library; Zaltbommel

Turner, R; 2002; *Discovery and Excavation*; Council for Scottish Archaeology; Edinburgh

Twigg, G D; 2002; *Salt History – salt in Roman times [Online]*; http://www.saltinfo.com/salt%20history2.htm

Urquhart, R M; 1989; *The Burghs of Scotland and the Police of Towns (Scotland) Act 1850*; Scottish Library Association; Motherwell

Vernon, B; 2003; A1-*The Great North Road [Online]*; http://www.biffvernon.freeserve.co.uk/contents.htm

Waterston, R; 1958; "Timothy Pont Map of the Tyne Valley" pp 44–6 in *Transactions of the East Lothian Antiquarian and Field Naturalist Society Volume 7*; East Lothian Antiquarian and Field Naturalists Society; Haddington

Watson, W J; 1926; *History of the Celtic Placenames of Scotland*, (reprinted 1993 by BIRLINN, Edinburgh) [Online]; Scottish Place Name Society; http://www.st-andrews.ac.uk/institutes/ sassi/spns/

Webster, N; 1974; *The Great North Road*; Adams and Dart; Bath

Wemyss, W; 1799; "Parish of Prestonpans Appendix to the Statistical Account of Prestonpans" in *The Statistical Account of Scotland 1791–1799 (Edited by Sir John Sinclair)* [East Lothian District Library 1995 Reprint]; East Lothian District Library; Haddington

Whatley, C A; 1987; *The Scottish Salt Industry, an economic and social history*; Aberdeen University Press; Aberdeen

Wilkes, M; 1991; *The Scot and His Maps*; The Scottish Library Association; Motherwell

Wilkie, J; 1919; *Historic Musselburgh*; William Blackwood and sons; London

Williamson, M G; 1996; *The Origin of Street Names in Dalkeith*; Midlothian Council Library Services; Dalkeith

Worling, M J; 1991; *Early Railways of the Lothians*; Midlothian District Libraries; Dalkeith

Wright, G; 1997; *Turnpike Roads*; Shire Publications; Princes Risborough

Yeoman, P; 1999; *Pilgrimage in Medieval Scotland*; BT Batsford Ltd/Historic Scotland; Edinburgh

ACKNOWLEDGEMENTS

The following people and organisations have made the writing and researching of this book possible:

Annemarie Allan; Frances Baird for typing services; East Lothian Local History Centre, Haddington; George Edmond; Jim Forster of Prestonpans Local History Society; Midlothian Local Studies, Loanhead; National Archives of Scotland, Edinburgh; National Library of Scotland, including the Map Library, Edinburgh; National Monument Record Library, Edinburgh; Bill Paterson of the Scottish Place Name Society. However, any errors of fact or interpretation are mine alone.

Finally above all, thanks are due to Kate for her support and forbearance whilst I was writing and researching this work.

APPENDIX

Byrlaws Governing Passage Across the Baronial Foreshore at Prestonpans by the Publick

Unto All Whom it May Concern
Be Aware These ByrLaws are:
"maid and determined be Consent of Neichtbors, elected and Chosen be Common consent, in our ByrLaws courts. The quhilk me so Chosen as judges and arbitratars to the effect foresaid are called ByrLawmen [Skene 1597]."

Preamble: It is the earnest wish of The Much Honoured Barons of Prestoungrange and of Dolphinstoun that all members of the public shall be able to make passage between sunrise and sunset at all times tides and weather permitting across the Baronial foreshore which lies within their Crown Baronies on the Firth of Forth between Prestongrange Road and Redburn Road at Prestonpans, precise maps of which are available for inspection at the Caput of the Baronies at all reasonable times.

In order to give proper effect to their wishes through ByrLaws in this respect the Barons together have taken advice of those in Scotland most particularly well informed upon the implications of granting such permission for passage by the public being *Scotways* – The Scottish Rights of Way Society which advice was readily given in good faith but wholly without recourse.

1. **Proper Notice of Permission for Daylight Passage Shall Be Prominently Displayed** at both ends of the Baronial foreshore at all times and the Baron Sergeand being the ByrLawman in this

respect shall ensure that this is accomplished and that it be kept in good repair.

2. **These ByrLaws Shall be Displayed at All Times at the Caput of the Crown Baronies being The Prestoungrange Gothenburg** – this to be ensured by the ByrLawman.

3. **The Publick Makes Passage at its Own Risk** since it is proclaimed hereby that any dangers arising when making such passage across the tidal foreshore which is extensively covered at high tide by the sea itself which can make the ground underfoot slippery and difficult to traverse, and which on occasions is affected by stormy weather- these are the *'obvious dangers' [after Lord Shaw in Glasgow Corporation v Taylor (1922) I AC 44 @ p.60]* which the public must always assess and accept when electing to make their passage and parents or guardians the same in respect of their children or wards.

4. **The Barons Courts Shall Ensure All Dangers That Are *Not* Obvious are Brought to the Publick's Attention** – by the posting of Notices from time to time as may be required and *in extremis* by closing the Baronial foreshore to the public altogether with such formal Notices properly placed both at each end of the foreshore and at the Caput of these Baronies by the ByrLawman.

5. **Access is Granted for Passage Not for Assembly.** These ByrLaws expressly forbid members of the public to loiter or pause during their passage along the Baronial foreshore [except for a reasonable time to ensure and enhance their enjoyment including the launching and recovery of their own navigable craft or viewing and studying the Barons Courts murals art] and under no circumstances are members of the public permitted to hold an assembly thereon or to fish other than by gathering shell fish therefrom *[after Lord Moncrieff at 131 in Marquis of Bute v McKirdy and McMillan 1937 SC 93]*. Any wishing to spend periods of time or to hold assemblies or conduct other activities upon the Baronial foreshore shall make proper application to the ByrLawman the reasonable approval or rejection of which shall necessarily be given in writing.

6. **No Despoliation of or Scavenging on the Foreshore.** These ByrLaws expressly forbid the despoliation of the Baronial foreshore by the publick in any manner whatever nor may any member remove from the foreshore any materials whatever or any trove there discovered. The discovery of any trove should be notified to the ByrLawman who in the event that considerable value is found to attach thereto will pay a commission of 25 per centum to the finder and the balance to the Scottish Charity which

is established to further the work of the Barons Courts across the ancient Lands and Crown Baronies.

7. **No Right of Passage At Night.** The permissions accorded under these ByrLaws apply only during the hours between sunrise and sunset and at all other times the public shall not have any right of passage across the Baronial foreshore the justification for this restriction being that during such hours the *'obvious dangers'* associated with a tidal Baronial foreshore are invisible and not wisely to be entertained. The Notice granting Daylight Access displayed under 1. above shall also include detail of this restriction.

8. **Scottish Power's Responsibility for Keeping its Pipeline in a Reasonable and Safe State of Repair.** Under Deed of Servitude GRS East Lothian 6 October 1983 the Baron of Prestoungrange granted SSEB [now Scottish Power] the right to construct a pipeline 'as operational equipment' along the entire length of the Baronial foreshore to carry Ash away from Cockenzie Power Station and that pipeline is now covered with concrete. Whilst such concrete may seem to members of the public to afford a convenient foot route along the foreshore it is *not* a walkway and Scottish Power has no responsibility nor do the Barons Courts for maintaining it as such. Its condition at anytime provided it is kept in a 'reasonable and safe state of repair' is to be assessed by members of the public making their passage and to be regarded at all times as an *'obvious danger'* if slippery howsoever.

9. **Bringing Animals and Vehicles onto the Foreshore.** The permissions hereby granted to the public are intended for passage by members of the public and although there is no objection to the simultaneous passage of appropriate animals and vehicles under the care of a member of the public such animals and vehicles must always be controlled in a manner that occasions no inconvenience or damage including any excessive noise and never left unattended on the foreshore nor must any despoliation occur.

10. **Penalties for Breaches of These ByrLaws.** The ByrLawman is authorised hereby to levy penalties for breaches of these ByrLaws up to the sum of ten shillings or one daylight hour in the stocks. Determinations of the ByrLawman shall at all times be executed as given and when given but any and all who feel that their determinations were not fair or proper are at liberty to Appeal to the Barons Courts of Prestoungrange & Dolphinstoun for a binding judgement in the matter such Appeal to be submitted in writing to the Clerk to the Courts at the Caput of these Our Baronies within one week of the determination, and

the Appeal shall be heard within not more than one further week by the Barons or their Bailie.

11. **Conformance with Any and All Other Laws Extant in Scotland –** The ByrLawman shall act not only in respect of these ByrLaws but also seek as best he may to ensure conformance at all times with such the other laws and regulations governing the Baronial foreshore not least in respect of applicable health, hygiene and safety requirements and the caring provision of service for those with disabilities howsoever all arising from proper risk assessments thereof.

By Order of These Our Barons Courts

Trinity Session [Elizabeth II. 53. 2004 P&D 08/02]
July 27th

Dolphinstoun Bailie Prestoungrange

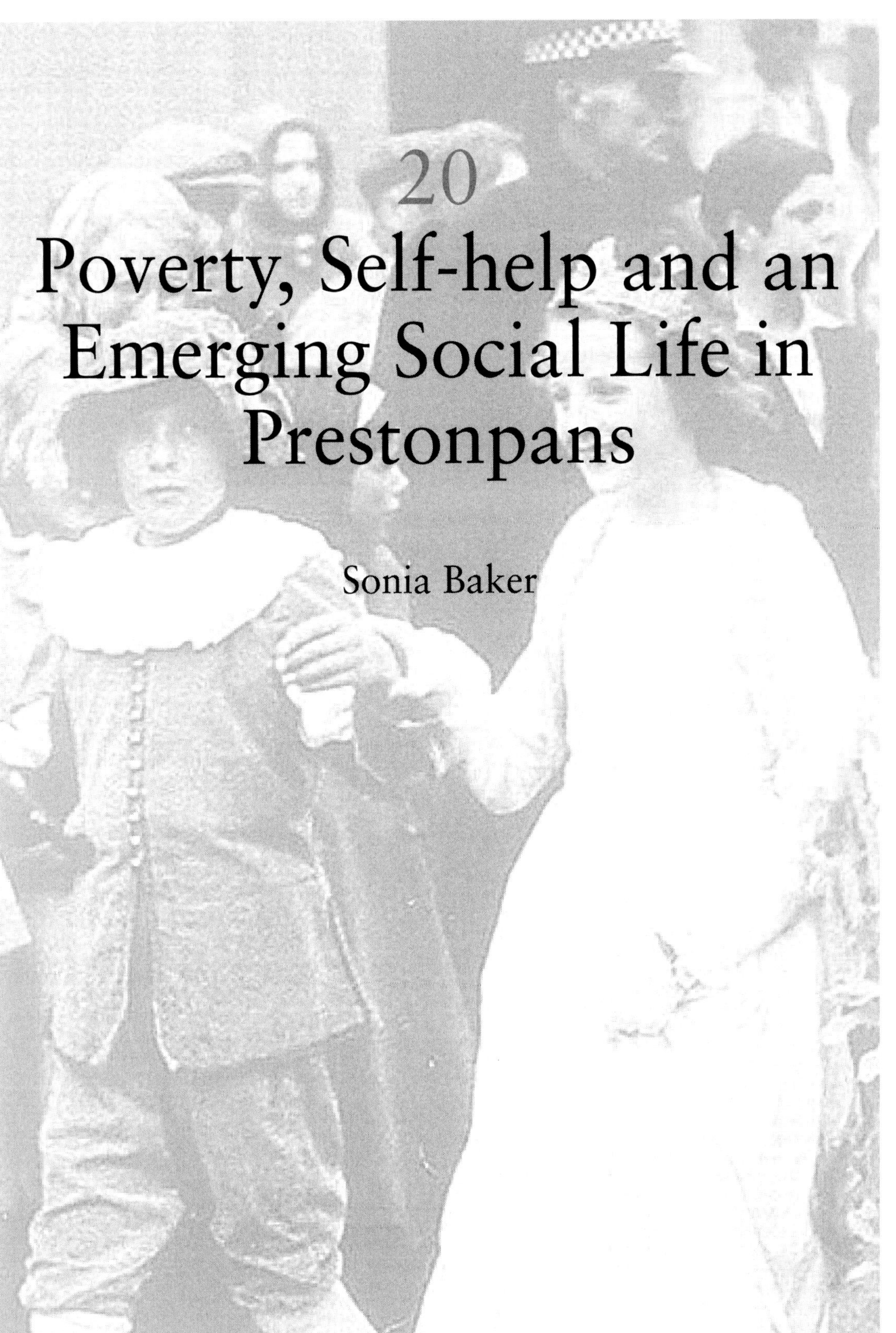

20
Poverty, Self-help and an Emerging Social Life in Prestonpans

Sonia Baker

The photographs throughout this chapter are from the collection of Mr. Bert Renton – to whom we are most grateful.

1 INTRODUCTION

It is difficult today, when longer lives and general good health are the norm, to understand how hard life was for the majority of people in the past. The state did not make any provision for welfare until the middle of the 20th century. Until then, the emphasis was on 'care' within the parish community, which was often care of the most minimal kind, particularly for those who lived on the margins of society. The experiences of these less fortunate people are difficult to unravel, especially those relating to the earlier periods of history, and broad assumptions often have to be made. Research carried out on other communities (such as Dingwall's work on late 17th century Edinburgh[1]) is a useful aid to explain what was probably happening in Prestonpans, where the wide range of industries attracted workers in. This 'fluid' workforce tended to dip in and out of destitution, never earning enough and, without a permanent income, never moving far from poverty. Together with the old and the young, the sick and disabled, these 'able-bodied' poor – often termed the idle or 'sturdy beggars'[2] – comprised a sizeable part of Prestonpans' population. Some of the destitute children were taken in by the several endowed 'hospitals' or schools in the parish and given the chance to improve their lot with education.

The slightly more fortunate people, who were employed in the many industries of the parish, drew on the support networks of their own people, namely the many and varied friendly societies. These were essentially self-help societies where, for a regular weekly payment, the sick, the widowed and the orphaned were provided for. Prestonpans had many such societies – for the potters, the sailors, the carters – many of which list members from other trades and occupations. By the end of the 19th century, societies were emerging that served other groups too; for example the Rechabites' Friendly Society catered for those 'of a temperate mind' from 1893. The Co-operative Wholesale Society (Co-op) provided a more general service, not being affiliated to any particular group. Gradually, too, over time, came more and more state intervention; legislation eased the lot of many, although the view of social welfare that pervades today has its root in the 19th century.

From the self-help groups emerged a whole gamut of leisure activities, firstly with the various society walks, when the society 'box' was paraded through the town, accompanied along the way by music and with a dance at the end of the day, and later with the miners' gala days and work-related sports clubs. Other social events were church-led, initially by the established Church of Scotland and, from the 19th century onwards, by the increasing number of other churches within the community. By the time the police burgh was created in 1862,[3] Prestonpans was home to a broad social mix of people, many of whom participated in the various social activities the town had to offer. Women had always played an important role in the informal social networks of home and community, and as the 20th century progressed, they

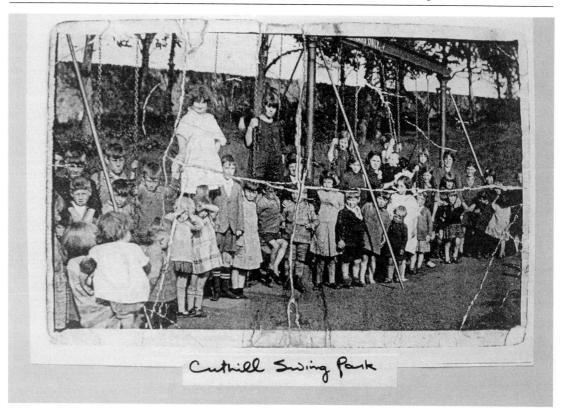

Cuthill Swing Park

A Bit of Time to Play

The Band Tradition Lives On

came to take a more prominent public role in the burgh, with their own branches of political support groups, and more electoral rights. For many years, the working communities tended to keep apart from each other; similarly so the Catholics and Protestants.

2 PRESTONPANS IN THE 18TH AND 19TH CENTURIES

2.1 The settlement

While Prestonpans did not achieve burgh[4] status until the latter part of the 19th century it had long been a busy industrial centre, with the important port of Acheson's Haven nearby. This port dated back to the 17th century, when its exports were chiefly of coal and salt (to Germany and the Baltic) and also hides, corn, eggs and stockings.[5] Imports included pitch, lead and iron plate.[6] After his purchase of the barony of Prestoungrange in 1617, Alexander Morrison renamed it Morrison's Haven. A thriving harbour, together with the range of industries based at Prestonpans, meant that there was generally work available for temporary day-labourers as well as for those employed in the more permanent workforce. In 1793, the population of the parish was 1092 women and 936 men – 2028 in total. Of these, 769 were born outwith the parish. There were 19 day-labourers, and 614 people and their families were employed in the various industries in the town.[7]

Over time, the economic makeup of the parish changed, as different industries – including oyster fishing, coal, salt, glass, brownware, stoneware (beginning c1750), chemicals (in 1784 the Prestonpans Vitriol Company was apparently the largest acid works in Britain[8]), soap and brick/tile production[9] – all thrived and declined (and in the case of coal revived and finally declined again); their workforces similarly ebbed and flowed. Morrison's Haven harbour also experienced fluctuating fortunes.

During the first 50 years of the 19th century, Prestonpans had become increasingly urbanised; it had progressed from a collection of different groups of industries to a busy centre that provided small town life to its many communities. Its elevation to a police burgh in 1862 signified that it was a settlement of some importance, and thereafter came under the aegis of its burgh council.

2.2 Control of the people – heritors and the kirk session

From the earliest times, parish life was structured – whether that structure was applied to work, to leisure or to faith – and it went hand in hand with social control. Control was implemented through the kirk session, which worked with the heritors – the landowners – of the parish, who had responsibility for both assessing the funds required to meet the session's obligations, and for providing that money. In 1751–2, the Court of Session decided that the heritors should take over complete control of the funds for the poor, a move initiated by the many landowners who were Episcopalian absentee landlords.[10] However, as the owner of Prestoungrange from 1745–64 was William Grant, a staunch supporter of the established church,[11] Prestonpans is unlikely to have experienced such problems. Understandably, the dual role made the heritors very cautious and, as the wealthiest people in the parish, their opinions coloured the kirk session's decisions. This often left the poor and destitute in an even more desperate situation.

In rural Scotland, the Crown exerted control in each locality by gifting lands to the nobility – heritable jurisdictions – known as baronies. The baron or laird had a franchise from the Crown to administer justice, in the baron court. Prestonpans parish was administered by two such baronies.

> The barony of Prestoungrange was granted to Mark Ker under the Great Seal of Scotland in 1587, ratified 1591. By 1622, it had passed to John Morrison, and was referred to as the west barony of the parish. By 1684, Prestoungrange barony had come into common ownership with that of Dolphinstoun.
>
> The east barony was established c1617 when it was granted to Sir John Hamilton; it encompassed the old villages of Preston and Prestonpans.

So the two holders of the baronies in the parish were the most influential of the heritors, and each had the right to hold a court. Many misdemeanours were dealt with at kirk session level, but more serious cases were referred to the baron court.[12] In the *Statistical Account*[13] (1790s) there were as many as 20 heritors referred to with the following listed: the Countess of Hyndford – Prestoungrange and Dolphinstoun; Mr Finlay of Drummore; Mr Syme of Northfield; Mrs Ramsay of Burnrigg; the trustees of Schaw's Hospital (owners of Preston House and parts of Preston estate); and the trustees of George Watson's Hospital (a charitable hospital for the less advantaged founded in 1741 by an Edinburgh merchant, the trust fund owned parts of Preston estate).

After 1845, social control continued, often in the hands of the same individuals as before, but through the new parochial boards that took over responsibility for the poor. The *New Statistical Account*,[14] published in 1845, listed the chief proprietors as: Sir George Grant-Suttie, Bart, Balgone and Prestoungrange; William Atchison, Drummore; George Sime, Northfield; John Fowler, Hallidoun and Burnrigg; the trustees of Schaw's Hospital; the trustees of George Watson's Hospital; Colonel Macdowell, Logan; Mrs Gowans; Sir William Hamilton, Bart, Preston and Fingalton; the heirs of the late Mrs Clapperton; and William Cockburn, Preston Cottage. The heritors' responsibility for the church, manse and school continued until 1925,[15] effectively maintaining their influence on parish life, and of course many of them remained active on the parish boards. So the running of the parish was the responsibility of the same group of people (with generational changes) until gradual alteration came with the formation of the burgh in 1862 and the social changes of the period.

This need to control was the manifestation of the concern of parts of the community (mainly the upper and middling classes) to control the lives of the rest of the community (the working classes). Everyone was keen to control the lives of the destitute, as they placed demands and expense on the community as a whole, but on occasion, members of the 'better' classes had to be brought under control as well. Any activity that was perceived as a threat – rowdy and unseemly behaviour in particular – was deemed necessary to be controlled; the Kirk Session Minutes[16] throughout the 18th and 19th centuries are full of censure for antenuptial fornication – for which punishment took the form of three weeks of public penance in the kirk for the poor, while the wealthy were fined. For example, on 15 December 1717,[17] John Grahame, salt officer, was to be fined two guineas or 40 shillings sterling (he negotiated a reduction) for his 'irregular marriage'. Irregular marriages were carried out away from the parish, and so the church lost money (which was used for the poor). Many accused of antenuptial fornication claimed they were married elsewhere. Other 18th century sins (all committed on the Sabbath) included being drunk, carrying water, dancing before the sacrament, the taking of ale, and putting fire to the malt kilns. Two boys, John Fin and George Amos, were reprimanded for 'being on the streets during the time of divine service throwing stones at dogs'. Stealing apples, wife-beating and fighting (between women and men) were also censured. On 17 April 1717,[18] one couple were having an 'alliance' when neighbour Christian Spence suggested that Helen Reid should stop seeing William Crooks. Her response – 'Go to hell you and all them together; God's plague come on you Presbyterian devils' – came to the kirk session's notice, which demanded that she should be 'publickly' rebuked before the congregation. She was threatened with certification if she continued with such 'scandalous' behaviour; Crooks' transgressions were not seen as being so shocking.

Bad behaviour could affect whether a pension was granted or not; in June 1717, 'a poor woman' Jean Cane begged at the church door, but did not attend, and she had no certificate of good behaviour from her last parish of residence. Her application for a pension was only considered after she agreed to behave in a more Christian manner; she was awarded 2d a week (in November the same year £2 Scots was given to a church officer for a pair of shoes). Similarly, in March 1718, Christine Preston's pension was stopped and she was called before the kirk session when found cursing and swearing; her pension was reinstated when she apologised. Elders who recorded those who 'abused the Lord's day by idling it away in the fields or by walking or otherwise' monitored behaviour on the Sabbath; such behaviour was reported back to the kirk session.

3 THE POOR, THE SICK AND THE IDLE

3.1 Managing the needs of the less fortunate – early poor relief until 1845

For the aged, the sick, the poor, the widowed and the orphaned, the difference between life and death was often on the say-so of one's 'betters' who sat in judgement on one's behaviour. The kirk session would pay small pensions, and provide clothes for the orphaned and other poor children. The years from the end of the 16th to the middle of the 17th centuries were a period when even the workers lived in poverty.[19] Those of 1782–83 were ones of scarcity and the number of poor increased, as did the amount of money required to maintain them, and this continued for a number of years afterwards. By the 19th century the process of industrialisation and urbanisation impacted on parishes on an unprecedented scale, and the problems worsened in the post-Napoleonic war period, 1815–22, when the country was beset by an economic depression. Work was hard to find, even in the lowlands. As the unemployed were classed as able-bodied poor, and were regarded as the lowest of the low, they were excluded from any form of relief; this was reinforced by legislation of 1819. In practice, during the 17th century there were exceptions to this, as in 1663 when manufacturers were permitted to 'press able-bodied vagrants into service',[20] and most kirk sessions would not see the children of an able-bodied pauper starve.

A letter written in 1829 (for quite another purpose) reveals much about the obstacles that the destitute had to overcome before getting any aid – *'the degradation of living on public and extorted charity, and ... the inquisitorial examinations, and even cruel insults, to which applications, though for the smallest of pittance, frequently ...give rise'*.[21]

The parish itself, through the heritors and the kirk session, had, since the Poor Law Act of 1575, a responsibility for the *deserving poor* born within its boundaries, or those who had lived there for five years; conversely it had no responsibility for those born elsewhere, although help was given on occasion, and the debt reclaimed from the claimant's home parish. Paltry pensions[22] were paid weekly to those in regular need (the aged, the infirm, the widows and the children; the needy were predominately female) and occasional funds were released to keep the temporarily inconvenienced from destitution. The funds for the poor were collected in a number of ways: by fundraising (including the fines imposed on better-off parish residents for 'wrong-doing', and the fees imposed for the declaration of banns of marriage); by voluntary collections at the church door; by mortcloth dues (payments for the hire of a coffin cover[23]); by donations (made into an open ladle so that the donor's generosity or otherwise could not be hidden), mortifications and legacies; and by taxation, or assessment of the heritors – which of course was to be avoided if at all possible. Records from 1623 indicate that, at a time when two successive harvest failures brought famine to many, the county of East Lothian refused James VI's call for money to sustain the needs of the poor.[24] Dingwall comments that, in the Edinburgh parishes c1700, the *'kirk session had the expense of dealing with those who died on the street or with the corpses of exposed children'*.[25]

In 1740, the following blunt information was given relating to claimants of poor relief in Prestonpans:[26]

John Petegroes wife is dead got two pence weekly
Robert Flinn criple
Janet Choicely
Helen White
Jean Flight
Jean Banks for her children
Stopped George Fforsyth pension was 6 pence weekly in room of his wife deceast
James Bickerhorn
John Charles wife and married daughter
Margaret Ross
John Cannie
Patrick Horseburgh
6 pence added to Isabell Grant weekly pension because she is in great distress and most have come to serve her
John Charrel
Janet and Rachel Wood

Marie Barnard
John Thomson
Kathrine Mark for her children
Isabell Spears and daughter
Margaret Hepburn
Margaret Beaton
Margaret Mathieson
Rebecka Christie
Rachel Robertson and lame daughter
Widow Reid in Preston for her son
Janet Smart for her child
Elizabeth Reburn
Jean Clark
George Forsyth
Margaret Hooker and Elizabeth White
Elizabeth Henderson for her child
Margaret Reid
Janet Haley and Margaret Davidson

The kirk session records of 1745 state that the parish supported 46 poor; of whom three were bedridden, one was blind, 11 were children aged about 10, and eight more who were able to work. The rest were generally old and infirm. The comment is made that '*but most of them are capable of doing something*'; payment is also noted for '*the big bell rung at funerals*'.[27]

In 1753, Prestonpans' heritors had provided accommodation for the poor, raising the funds to pay for the purchase of a house by making an impost (2d Scots) on each pint of Scotch ale brewed. It soon became evident that the plan was not successful: the house was rented out, with the income going into the poor funds. The reason given for the abandonment was '*besides the utter aversion which many in actual want had against entering into the house the expenses was found to be greater than when the pensioners had a stated allowance given to them and permitted to spend it after their own way.*'[28] [This impost was re-introduced by the Barons Courts on July 27th 2004 to be payable by Fowler's Ales (Prestoungrange) Limited to the Arts Festival Charity – EII. 53. P&D 2004.05.]

In 1793, some £30 was required to pay the 42 regular pensioners; the amount received could be increased or decreased as the recipient's circumstances changed. A pensioner with a family received 2/– weekly at most, and an individual 1/4d.[29]

As well as the sources of income listed above, Prestonpans' kirk session had an income from the interest accrued on £250 sterling of 'sunk' money that had been left by various people specifically to be used in support of the poor. £100 of this money was a bequest by '*Andrew MacDowal of Bankton one of the senators of the College of Justice who bequeathed a like sum to the poor of every parish in which he had property*'.[30] There was also an income from the rental of a house in Preston (see 1753 above). Some of the funds were '*distributed by the kirk session to those suddenly reduced to want by misfortune or disease*' and used for '*wages for the education ... poor scholars ... for clothes for the poor; and funeral expenses of the pensioned poor*'.[31] Money was used from the same fund to pay the wages of church staff and the schoolmaster.

Examples of the process in practice can be seen from kirk session records; applications for parochial aid were considered at a meeting of the heritors and the kirk session on 12 February 1845.[32] At the meeting were the great and the good of the parish, namely George Syme, Rev Mr Struthers, Robert Hislop, Mr Turnbull, Mr Stevenson, Mr Spence, Sir G Grant-Suttie Bt., and Mr Knox. Applications had been received for consideration of allowances from the following since the last kirk session meeting:

Margaret Richardson	*1/6*
Marrion Baxter	*1/–*
James Bell	*1/6*
Thomas Dobson & wife	*1/6*

These seem to be ongoing claimants, because the next group are given as new applicants:

Widow Stewart	*6d*
James Renton	*2/1*
John Howden & wife	*6d*
Elizabeth Simpson	*1/–*
Walter Nicol	*1/6*

The other matters for consideration were the cases of two men whose illegitimate children had received some support from the session, and the session were seeking repayment through petitions to the sheriff. The men concerned were James Marr junior (fisherman) *'father of Elizabeth Simpson's child'* and James Burns (labourer) *'father of Mary Crombie's illegitimate child'*.

SCHAW'S HOSPITAL 1789–1881[33]

This school for boys *'whose parents are in poor circumstances'* opened in Preston House in 1789; it was funded by the considerable income from a trust fund set up by Doctor James Schaw, owner of most of the old Preston estate from 1780 until his death four years later. Boys aged between four and seven could be admitted, educated until aged 14; those with the names of Schaw, MacNeill, Cunningham and Stewart, were preferred. For many years the 19 trustees outnumbered the students (15). The trustees were to 'bind the boys as apprentices, or otherwise let them out to businesses as they shall judge best'. The number of students later increased to 24.

In 1832 the school left Preston House, moving to a new building nearby, designed by William Burn. The school closed in 1881, a few years after the 1872 Education Act made parish schools a legal necessity.

Schaw's funds (£100 pa in 1883[34]) continued to aid poor parish families in the form of bursaries for a number of years, and this and Stiell's fund meant that children were taught Latin and French[35] in order that they might be eligible for the bursaries on offer. From an account of the bequest in the *Haddingtonshire Courier* 14 January 1898, it is clear that the provision of funds to pay for higher education was not without strings, as a special report was to be provided on *'conduct ... attendance and progress'*. In 1916, Schaw's Bequest gave out 275 grants, 115 of which were for evening continuation classes. In 1921 £12–12s was granted to the County Education Authority for the purchase of lantern slides for the public school. In 1925 the trustees granted £90 towards a playing field for Preston Lodge School, and £40 for the same purpose at Prestonpans Public School. It seems that the funds were incorporated into the county's education fund sometime during the 1930s.

3.2 Increasing concern about the conditions of the poor

By the middle of the 19th century, the scale of the problem of the poor – able bodied included – generated a need to find alternative solutions, not primarily through concern for the poor themselves, but more due to concern over social order. In 1840, Dr William Pulteney Alison produced a report condemning the way the Scottish poor law was working in the urban areas, highlighting the health problems posed by urban living, claiming that poor health was the result of low wages, and that low incomes and periods of unemployment created a poverty trap. He argued his case in 1840/41 against the ideas of William Chalmers, who had long held that there was no need for poor relief from the authorities and that family, community or philanthropy could provide the needs of the poor.[36]

In 1842, the Chadwick Report on the condition of the labouring poor of Great Britain focused on the poverty and squalor in which they lived – and pointed out that it was largely unseen/ignored by the middle and upper classes. It was this concern that led to the emergence of the ragged schools of the 1840s; Edinburgh's Thomas Guthrie was an important figure in this, and support was forthcoming from Charles Dickens and Lord Shaftsbury. Gradually the social issues of health, housing, education and the needs of the poor rose up the middle class agenda:[37] it was increasingly seen that poverty and immorality were not necessarily one and the same, and that the poor needed more help to escape their fate.

From the 1730s onwards, when dissenting voices began to be heard, the established church no longer had control over the whole population; this had implications for the administration of poor relief. The truly destitute could also seek help from local charitable foundations, although it was usually only orphans who could claim. So ineffective was the old Scottish poor law once the pace of urbanisation increased, that the whole system was revised in 1845; the new poor law lasted until the introduction of the National Health Service in 1948.

For the able-bodied poor, judgement was most censorious; it was only when periods of economic depression threw increasing numbers of unemployed people onto the streets that it was acknowledged that some action had to be taken. By the early 20th century, the state had begun to intervene with legislation.

The situation was not helped when the body that managed the funds for the care of the needy and destitute – the kirk session of the established church – was beset by problems of its own. The Disruption of 1843, when breakaway members of the Church of Scotland formed the Free Church of Scotland, coincided by chance with the culmination of some 20+ years of argument over the rights and wrongs of the Scottish poor law. The recession of the 1840s decided the matter once and for all; there was no way that the old system could cope, and the report and evidence gathered by the Royal Commission on the Scottish Poor Law 1844 proved the point further. The result was the

Poor Law (Scotland) Act 1845, and responsibility for the poor became a matter for the state not the church.

3.3 Poor relief 1845–94: the Board of Supervision

Under the new laws, membership of the parochial boards was based on a property qualification; in towns this generally meant a change in personnel, but in places such as Prestonpans membership of the kirk session and the board were virtually the same. Minimum standards were drawn up (and they were *very* minimal) and claimants subjected to testing; parochial inspectors were appointed – in 1887, the Inspector of the Poor was Mr G Hunter. As a result there was a rise in the number of eligible poor, which was matched by an increase in expenditure on poor relief. It became necessary for each parish to raise money to support the poor and, although widely variable across the country, by 1894, 95% of parishes had decided to levy compulsory rates in the form of a tax; control of the finances remained within the locality. The able-bodied poor were still left out of the equation, but parishes made their own decisions on these 'occasional poor'. Many wandered the roads, seeking work where they could, as they had in previous years.

Problems arose in many parishes, especially those under pressure from the rapid urbanisation that marks this period; demand often exceeded the supply of funds. The fostering of urban children to rural families was one solution, and this provided the foster family with a welcome source of income, as well as removing children from the influence of their 'unfit' parents.

In Scotland, 'outdoor relief' was generally preferred to the more expensive option of the provision of accommodation in a poorhouse (a very different solution to that adopted in England). The limited poorhouse provision was seen as an effective deterrent to abuse of the system, while providing a catch-all option for the very poor. The Scottish view of poor relief was moralistic; it was a necessity to counter the destitution that was a result of improvidence and fecklessness. What's more, *'social inequality was seen as divinely programmed'*.[38]

Nonetheless, the system provoked comment from all levels: in cold weather *'the paupers grumble at their allowance and think it too little, while the ratepayers grumble at the rate of assessment and think it too great. But surely the latter ought to pocket their grievance with the best grace they can, when they allow a man who is earning above 20 shillings weekly to receive every Monday morning 5/– from the Parochial Board'*.[39] In 1868, almost one person in every 10 was in receipt of relief in Prestonpans parish,[40] and in an East Lothian context, Prestonpans had fewer poor people to maintain than the rural parishes.

While the local papers,[41] said that those 'below the grade of the working class' being in a state of *'such a mass of vice, ignorance and poverty'* they also commented that it was *' ... better that we should know it than remain unaquainted with its existence...'*. Within the locality there was an understanding that poorer people benefited from help from other sources. In 1900 collections were made to raise funds for 'the poors' coal' and the coal companies 'promised liberal terms'. At a more basic level during the 1920s, potted hough would be made and left on the outside windowsill, and collected by the needy; after the next payday, a penny would be left to pay the debt.[42]

The Inveresk Combination Poorhouse – 1861–1995

Proposed in October 1853, by 1861 Wedderburn House was built to the south of Inveresk (then in the county of Midlothian), near Musselburgh. Designed by Peddie & Kinnear,[43] it sports crow-stepped gables, skewputts and finials. The term 'combination' refers to the combination of parishes that shared the cost of the poorhouse and which had a right to send residents there. These parishes were Duddingston (in Edinburgh), Inveresk (Midlothian) and the western parishes of East Lothian: Gladsmuir, Haddington, Humbie, Ormiston, Pencaitland, Saltoun, Tranent and Prestonpans. It was never a workhouse, which was a term more used in England than in Scotland, but its residents were reluctant nonetheless. They slept in separate male/female dormitories, and there was no provision to accommodate couples. Prestonpans' share was eight places. The original 1853 Peddie & Kinnear drawings declared Wedderburn to be 'the building for the idiots',[44] leaving us in no doubt how the residents were regarded at that time. In 1863 there were three Prestonpans paupers – John McLeod, D Brown and Ann Lauder – who refused the offer of the comforts of the poorhouse; Ann Lauder had previously been there for 12 weeks and refused to return.[45] At least one *Courier* correspondent understood their desire to remain in their own homes, poor though they were (in the lengthy correspondence over the issue). In 1881, the staff comprised a governor, his wife (the matron), a children's nurse, three servants and a cook.

In 1883, a printed letter from the Board of Supervision[46] to the Inspectors of the Poor – commonly referred to as the poorhouse test – encouraged the withdrawal of outdoor relief from some paupers, which was to be substituted with relief in the poorhouse; the accompanying appendix gives no East Lothian examples of any resultant reduction in pauperism (perhaps implying that the county already had a tight rein on its poor, or that the county's residents already did as much as possible to avoid incarceration). The letter indicates that the poor sought maintenance from *'relatives legally or morally liable for their support'* before they applied to the parish. Further it indicates that the poorhouse was to be used for two particular classes of the poor; those who could not care for themselves (both mentally and physically), and *'all persons of idle, immoral or disported habits... who would squander their allowances in drunkenness and debauchery or otherwise misapply them'*.

The letter continues

'The experience of the administrators of the Poor Law since 1850 is that it is hurtful in practice to grant relief otherwise than in the poorhouse to:

> *mothers with illegitimate children and widows with legitimate families who may fall into immoral habits*
> *deserted wives*
> *persons having grown up families either settled in this country or abroad*
> *persons having collateral relations in comfortable circumstances*
> *wives of persons sentenced to terms of imprisonment or penal servitude*
> *generally all persons of idle, immoral or dissipated habits'*

It concludes that:

> *'Judicious but firm and vigilant use of the poorhouse test has had:*
>
> > *A marked effect on diminishing pauperism.*
> > *That it is not attended with any evil consequences such as the increase of crime or vagrancy*
> > *That the great majority of paupers by whom an offer of the poorhouse has been refused have become self-supporting or are supported by their relatives'*

The letter comments that it was regrettable that some parochial boards had again offered outdoor relief after poorhouse relief had been refused. The accommodation at Inveresk was extended in 1897.

Janet Naysmith's recollection serves as a reminder that attitudes during the early 20th century were very different from those of today:

> *'During the [first world] war, many a girl was put to shame for being too trusting and a few were put into mental care. The registrar took care of administrative costs, still most of these young healthy women had to work hard for their keep. One, whom I knew very well, escaped from such an institution in Haddington and managed to keep her movements secret for six months. As she had been able to maintain herself for that time she was set free from the institution and later married, she was one of the lucky ones'.*[47]

Minute books of the poorhouse board are mostly concerned with the day to day running of Wedderburn. They do, however, reveal a few other items of interest, in particular referring to the treatment of children. In July 1922,[48] there is reference to a child from Prestonpans *'that had been the cause of much trouble'*. While the preference was for the home parish to board out children, this child was to be returned to Wedderburn as he *'was of unsatisfactory habits'*. The board decided that this child was to be sent to an institution (other than Wedderburn) as the poorhouse was not appropriate, and no permanent carer could be found in Prestonpans. Where they intended to send this child is not given, and the health board too had no idea what could be done. By April 1923, the child was still at Wedderburn and so were a number of other children (many from Inveresk parish), a situation that the board felt was untenable, as there were no facilities for children. This was then a change of approach as initially it was seen appropriate that mothers and children would be accommodated in the poorhouse – generally these were unmarried mothers. An entry on 25 October 1923 indicates that efforts were again made to board out the Prestonpans child in the parish; he is not mentioned again. One child from Inveresk had, by 31 October 1929, spent some two years at Wedderburn. From 12 June 1930,[49] the home was under the management of the East Lothian County Council Midlothian County Council and the City of Edinburgh Council. The general policy was of no children, but they continued to be accommodated, with 12 resident there in October 1932.

Wedderburn became a home for the aged and infirm, providing both residential care downstairs for the local authority (Midlothian County Council) and nursing care upstairs for the National Health Service from 1948 until it closed in 1976. There is one reference[50] to it being where 'people without resources' could be sent by the Local Government Office. Oral evidence points to the fear in which a stay at Wedderburn was regarded: seemingly, the general view was that if you were put in the lift and taken upstairs, then the next stop was the mortuary.[51]

Affleck[52] has commented on the role of the Inspectors of the Poor:

'In 1945, the front-line welfare service was provided by local government officers acting as Inspectors of the Poor... Some were still in post in 1970 such as Mr Lowe in his ground floor office in an adapted council house in Prestonpans ...They also operated as registrars, managed the local county council office and dealt with welfare assistance, including issues of school attendance and the need for care in the two poor law institutions run by the county councils for Midlothian [Wedderburn] and East Lothian [Prestonkirk]. They had a wealth of local knowledge but by 1948, their duties had started to decline, with central government dealing with the need for National Assistance from 1948.'

After 1976, Lothian Regional Council used Wedderburn as a day centre for adults with a learning disability, and the social work service used it as a 16-bed hostel. From 1990 onwards it was managed by ELCAP,[53] but by 1995 institutional care had finally ended, and all residents had been rehoused in the community. The Church of Scotland used Wedderburn until it finally closed in 1998. In 2001 it was sold for housing development. Thus ended over a century of 'care' for the old, the sick and the needy at Wedderburn.

Janet Naysmith commented:

'I was delighted when the town had its first lady Provost, a Mrs Mary Polick. I remember one meeting of the Woman's Guild when Mrs Polick was the speaker and I asked her what had happened to old folks' pension rises and to mentally retarded people who were in homes such as Wedderburn ... As she was on the health committee, she ... went out to visit these places for themselves. She was furious at the nutrition supplied to the patients and fought the health board to ensure that they were given a cooked meal every day. Later she invited me along to observe how the patients' disposition had improved. I very much appreciated this and found that they were very well cared for apart from the incontinent patients, of course hygiene has greatly advanced since those days'.

3.4 Hospitals and other funds

Mary Murray Trust & Institute 1883–1930s[54]

Mary Murray left a bequest to found *'an hospital for the training of female children of poor but respectable parents as domestic servants'*. As a result, her trustees leased the (new) Schaw's Hospital building, and brought her rather particular requirements into play, opening on 2 February 1883. These included a preference for girls with the surname Murray; acceptance of entrants aged six to eight, who remained at the institute until aged 14, when they would then be placed in domestic service. They were trained accordingly, and religion featured prominently in their education. Initially 26 students were enrolled, increasing later to 68.

Ex-pupils met up at annual reunions, and they were eligible for other payments (on achieving a certain age, or on marriage); they could even return to live at the institute after they were 60 (under a range of provisos). The role of the institute declined during the 20th century, and by 1939 the building was being used as a community centre. It became a day nursery during the war, reverting to community use afterwards. In the 1950s, demand for school accommodation from Preston School returned part of the building back to education.

During the early 1970s, the site was earmarked for development of a new day centre, but this did not proceed past the feasibility study phase as much of the site was deemed unstable. The building was finally demolished in 1979; the new community centre on the site was completed in 1984.[55]

George Stiell's Hospital Trust 1821–84[56]

Prestonpans fell under the aegis of the George Stiell's Hospital Trust (Scheme No 12), which also covered Tranent, Gladsmuir and Pencaitland. This was an educational endowment scheme that was set up on the death of Tranent native George Stiell, builder and smith. Stiell left property earning £900 pa for the education of a few boys and girls as inmates and also a free day school, which was run in a rather austere looking building at Meadowmill, designed by William Burn in 1821. The school provided 140 children with an education, and lunchtime bread and milk. Change came with the Endowed Institutions (Scotland) Act 1878, and in 1883 it was proposed that the school should close;[57] funds (£20pa) were to be administered by Tranent parish. Supported by Free Church minister Mackay, his fellow Prestonpans representative on the Stiell's Hospital board, John Fowler Hislop was in there fighting for his Prestonpans community to retain its claim on Stiell's funds: *'The parish is small and its inhabitants belong chiefly to the mining and fishing classes whose occupations are hazardous and emoluments precarious'*.[58] The parochial school board used their share of the Stiell money to pay the fees of 68 children in standards V and VI upwards (ie beyond the age at which schooling was compulsory). The board also assisted 71 children by paying 2d a week of their 5d a week school fees, and paid the fees of 32 children *'whose cases are most necessitous'*. Nearly £10 was used for books *'the price of these being a serious obstacle to many'*. If Prestonpans lost this funding the impact on the children of the parish would be considerable; the public school had 490 children on the roll, and an average attendance of 360, so nearly 50% of these were in receipt of some sort of support from the funds.

The problem seemed to lie with the role of Tranent minister Dr Caesar; he even lacked support amongst his own Tranent school board. Dr Caesar was accused of being in an *'iniquitous position'* with the Earl of Wemyss and Fred Pitman WS, both of whom were members of the Stiell board, but not resident within any of the four parishes. All three were opposed to the *'disembursement of free school fees by school boards'*. By October 1883, the Prestonpans school board had written to the Education Endowment Commission regarding the *'large sums of money squandered'* and were pleading for the parish to receive a greater share of the funds because of the greater increase of population compared to that in the other three parishes. When it was proposed that selection for funding was to be by competitive examination, the response from Prestonpans was typical. The school board considered that *'a child's poverty is its greatest claim to free elementary education under this trust deed'*. Competitive examination was acceptable for pupils of the sixth grade upwards, and the sum provided for evening classes should be increased. The building was sold and the funds put to use as two-year bursaries for children going into higher education from state aided schools in the four parishes. Evening class funding was also increased. In 1890, Thomas Tulloch was awarded a bursary of £60 over three years and Joseph Hunter £40 over two. From 1892, secondary education also became free.

The building became St Joseph's Industrial School in 1888, a Roman Catholic school for young offenders under the East Lothian Educational Endowment Trust; it was run from 1914 by the de la Salle Brothers, with the Passionists of Drummohr (see 6.2.3. below) looking after the boys' spiritual welfare. St Joseph's closed in 1998.

Prestonpans Rev. John Davidson's Mortification (Scheme No 307) 1882–89[59]

This was an educational trust scheme funded by an endowment left by John Davidson (c1549–1604) minister of Prestonpans, who organised the building of (and who provided much of the money for) the present church in 1596. This flamboyant character left funds to provide for the teaching of Latin, Hebrew and Greek. Under the Education Endowments (Scotland) Act 1882 these funds were to be transferred to the School Board of the parish. By 1889, the funds had still not been transferred.

The Infant School Fund dispute[60]

The records provide evidence of the power struggle that continued between adherents of the different churches. In his role as chairman of Prestonpans School Board in 1884 Free Church member John Fowler Hislop of Castle Park, wrote to the Education Endowment Commission regarding the sum of £80, which had been collected c1845 towards the erection of an infant school in the burgh. Originally it was lodged with the Established Church minister Struthers, and after the 1872 education changes, Hislop wanted to know where that money was. Struthers *'dissents from the present application'* – ie would not respond; just before his death later that year, he had suggested that the money should be used to erect a hall near the established church. Hislop pursued the matter with the kirk session, suggesting that the fund should be relinquished to the school board.

The kirk session took the view that, now that education was provided free, the funds could not be re-allocated to be used to assist the children of the poorest families. However they released some funds to pay for clothes and books for these same children.

3.5 After 1894

In 1894, the Local Government (Scotland) Act set up the Local Government Board, which took over responsibility for the operation of the Poor Law. Although legislation was gradually introduced during the early 1900s, aimed at improving provision for the poor and destitute, many of the poorest in society remained so. Only gradually did their rights improve, and many continued to resist claiming the benefits to which they were entitled. The degradation associated with 'going into the poorhouse'[61] lingered on into the 20th century.

3.6 Children

Wherever possible children – whether orphans or from families unable to cope – were boarded out. This was cheaper than placing them in Wedderburn House (see 3.2.2. above) and the like. Nonetheless, there were instances where some children did end up at Wedderburn, probably either because they were difficult to place in the community, or because they were too young to be separated from their mothers who were also there, or because the family's stay at Wedderburn was to be for a short while only.

The people who accommodated boarded-out children were paid a welcome pension to cover their costs. One orphaned pair of sisters (their mother had died in the 'flu epidemic of 1919) was given a home in Morrison's Haven by their paternal aunt, who already had 12 children of her own. During the General Strike of 1926, the family's sole income was the children's money from the welfare agencies.[62]

Wartime saw the emergence of various charitable societies. A shilling fund was begun in 1899 for the widows and orphans of soldiers who died in the Boer war (Charles Belfield was the treasurer). In 1900 a collection for the War Relief Fund raised £24/14s.

By 1901 a general UK-wide concern[63] was being expressed in the newspapers that children were working before and after school, and that in agricultural districts their school holidays were taken during the peak times in agriculture. Prestonpans was not specifically mentioned, but as a prime market gardening area, it seems likely that children were expected to work.

4 SELF-HELP

Self-help was something of a tradition in East Lothian. Haddington man Samuel Smiles had published the widely acknowledged *Self-Help* in 1859 and *Thrift* in 1875, and the Co-op movement had self-reliance as a core quality.

4.1 Mutual and friendly societies

In the burghs, the mediaeval guilds looked after their own and vigorously excluded non-members, operating a closed shop. In a small industrial settlement like Prestonpans – which was a burgh of barony for three centuries – groups of workers operated friendly societies that provided a safety net of financial support for the sick and for the families of the dead. Like modern insurance policies, money was paid into the fund by members when they were healthy and able, and paid out when they were sick. A death fund ensured that the family was able to at least pay for the funeral. Acknowledged problems of these societies included fraudulent claims and membership of more than one society; rules were put in place to try to prevent this.

The requirements of the craft organisations also stated rules on apprenticeships – many lasted seven years. In burghs like Edinburgh, it was necessary to be a freeman of the city and to pay a burgess fee before being permitted to employ anyone.[64] In burghs of barony like Prestonpans, it was unlikely that such rules were enforced; indeed one of Edinburgh's problems was the amount of competition that came from settlements outwith the city.

Most friendly societies used rather arcane language – of lodges, tents, brother, warden, master etc – and followed particular rituals; some were trade incorporations, and involved members of higher social groups, while others were solidly based in working communities. These last groups of workers also came together for social events, when banners and parades brought a little relief to their lives; they often lived in close proximity to each other and formed tight-knit communities of their own, relying on the informal bonds of family and work for support.

Some of the ministers of the established churches felt great concern about the situation that was developing in the increasingly urban parishes. In 1827 the Rev Adam Thomson[65] delivered an address proposing the formation of 'The Coldstream Congregational Friendly Society', being open to all members of the congregation – male and female, young and old (but only if they joined during the first year, thereafter those over 40 were excluded) – and that it would mean a payment of 1d a week out of an income of 8d a day from a bondager, for five shillings a week in case of inability to work. There would be a delay of five years before the fund would become effective. There was a proviso that payment of five shillings a week was payable 'provided the funds allow it'. Without further research it is unclear whether the venture succeeded, and whether Thomson's true aim was to save the heritors money. The destitute would of course still be excluded.

Prestonpans' friendly societies

The numbers of societies changed over time, with some closing down and re-opening later. Many processed through the town on the traditional fair day of the first Wednesday in June. In 1835 one author[66] stated:

> *'At one period, this parish had more than enough of such institutions. The only survivors now are the Carters', Gardeners', several yearly societies, and the Sailors' Incorporation.'*

He considered that only the latter and the yearly societies managed their funds well enough to ensure their survival.

The oldest recorded of these societies in Prestonpans is the *Masonic Lodge of Aitchison's Haven*, with unique extant records from January 1598 to 1764.[67] The signatories were George Aitoun, John Fender (warden of the lodge) and Thomas Petticruiff. The lodge membership was evidently drawn from a large area – with meetings held as far away as Dalkeith and Musselburgh. The lodge ceased in 1862.

In 1886,[68] there is mention of the self-help lodge of *Good Templars* – the Guiding Star Lodge No 312, Cuthill – which met at the Mission Hall, Cuthill. There was also a juvenile lodge. The following year, reference is made to the lodge's 17th anniversary, indicating it was formed in 1870. It is also noted that the Temperance Society and the Good Templars fought against the common foe – strong drink – and not against each other.

The *Thorntree Masonic Lodge* No 1038 was formed on 2 February 1908; by 1946 the lodge was meeting twice monthly in the Church of Scotland hall. In May 1909, the Free Church kirk session recorded that a request was made by the freemasons for permission to hold special service in the church in connection with their lodge; permission was given – but that the lodge was to get a United Free church minister to hold service. Lodge tenets remain brotherly love, relief and trust.

Some Prestonpans residents maintained membership in other lodges. On 12

August 1898 the *Haddingtonshire Courier* reported the death of a Prestonpans butcher who was a member of the Dunbar Castle Lodge of Freemasons.

Extant records of the *Prestonpans Incorporation of Seamen* run from 1668–1747, and then from 1798–1801, being still extant in 1824.[69] It seems to decline thereafter, but the group evidently revived as it was running in 1835 (see above). By 1898, the *Sailors' Walk* (held on a Friday in September) was an event of some note in the parish; the walk progressed through 'the village' and on to Prestongrange, calling also on Cockenzie, raising £4 and 8 shillings for Edinburgh Royal Infirmary. The procession was headed by Newtongrange Band, and model ships were held high. 'As the day advanced they were joined by a large number of girls and young women'; street dancing followed later. In 1902, the walk was led by the Gilmerton Band.

The potters' society was erected on 26 March 1766[70] – as the *Society of the Potters' Box Meeting*. No members over 30 years old were admitted, or anyone who was involved in any other business; no benefits were paid until three years of membership. Initial joining fees were 5/–. Meeting day was early June (2 June in 1775). It seems that members attended meetings wearing white aprons; they were fined for non-attendance at meetings, and for uttering oaths during meetings. A potter's mortcloth was available. By 1775, it was clear that membership came from outwith practising potters, with members listed as a labourer, a spirit dealer, a pilot, a thatcher, and a watchmaker. It seems that the potters' society ceased sometime in the first decade of the 19th century.

The Statistical Account of 1793 provides information about the *travelling chapmen*, who were 'itinerant sellers of wares'; this was a wealthy group which paid money to needy members, or to members' families. One source suggests the meetings at Prestonpans began in 1530.[71] They met annually at Preston Cross (from 1636) and from 1732–52 at Prestonpans on the second Thursday of July, drawing their membership from across the Lothians. By 1793, it was estimated that there were fewer than six chapmen in the county, and only 24 in all; the declining numbers was attributed to the increase in town-based shopping. Martine (1890) deemed the group extinct, commenting that 'many years ago' the cross was 'rescued' by the Bannatyne Club (1817–67), which revived the guild and 'made gentlemen chapmen – including Sir Walter Scott ... after the manner of antiquarian good fellows'.[72]

On 29 May 1829, the *Prestonpans United Society of Carters*[73] was instituted. From 22 December 1876 the society's registered office was at Cuthill, moving later to Moat House, and from 17 June 1905 to 16 Kirk Street, where George Thomson lived. Members included potters, labourers and gardeners. In 1844, procession day was the third Wednesday in June, from 9am; there were to be no drunks, and the horses to be run were workhorses. The Riding of the Marches would take place, and the cost to members (for music) would be 6d each. In 1893, they gathered at the Black Bull, and the boxmaster, the holder of the Farrier's Cap, and the standard bearer led a small procession. In 1897 'my lord' William Fraser was mounted on a 'gaily caparisoned horse'. In 1900, the procession was preceded by 'my lord' Peter Dudgeon, and an equerry on horseback. Penston Band marched in support, and the event ended with a dance. The popularity of this society waned with declining numbers between 1889 and 1901; in 1901 'for the first time in half a century' their procession did not take place. Until the society applied for dissolution on 21 February 1912 (awarded on 28 March 1912) it had a good record for paying out as necessary on sickness and death.

On the same Wednesday in both 1897 (74 members) and 1900, the *Cuthill Benevolent Friendly Society* also had its annual procession; in 1900, 40 marchers, wearing silk tartan sashes, and with banners and flags were preceded by two officers with drawn swords, and Gilmerton Brass Band. They visited Provost McEwan's home, then went on to Cockenzie. The day ended with a dance.[74] The group was still meeting in 1901, but further references have not been located.

Records[75] are extant for the *Prestonpans Caledonian Lodge of Free Gardeners* from c1820; in 1872 and 1873, they marched on the same day as the carters. Support evidently waxed and waned over the years, and the society actually closed in 1884 as funds ran out.[76] It evidently drifted on as there are references to there being no procession in the 1890s. The naming of Alexander Gradison as the secretary in 1897 indicates the society remained active. In 1925, it was suggested that there were 80 members. In July 1925, the annual walk took place. Members (and many from other lodges) met at the town hall and, preceded by the Newhaven Silver Band, marched to Cockenzie; there they visited their property at Gardener's Close. Returning to Prestonpans, there was dancing in the town hall.

A few references[77] are found to the *Hammermen of Prestonpans* with a fair day in June. It seems that they were active before the 19th century and are listed in the 1821 East Lothian Register. It may be that they were an adjunct to the hammermen of either Haddington or Musselburgh. Hammermen incorporated the craft groups of blacksmiths, pewterers, locksmiths, saddlers and armourers.

Similarly a single reference in 1897 hints at the existence of a *Mechanics' Friendly Society* in Prestonpans.

Other groups, too, emerged in Prestonpans, among them those societies keen to promote temperance. The *Rechabite Friendly Society* was founded in 1835 in Salford, by a group of teetotallers for people of like mind to provide for them in time of sickness or to cover funeral arrangements. The name of the order was taken from Jeremiah 35. There were two tents in Prestonpans (district 35) – Preston Tower and John Davidson, which began in 1893 with a membership of 10; it held its annual social gathering of the 75 members in March 1901 in the United Free Church hall, where Provost McEwan presided over the songs and recitations provided by the ladies. The groups had both senior and junior lodges; it was open to men and women, and peaked in the 1930s and 1940s, by which time they were using the Church of Scotland hall for meetings. Local meetings were still held at least to c1950. In the 1970s there was a change of social habits and the Rechabites faced a decline in membership as the original membership died off; new teetotallers were few and far between. Tents merged, and groups were consolidated into districts and then into regions; by 2000 the society had centralised at Salford. In 1995 the board decided a change of approach was essential and so the society modernised its slant, being now for those with a healthy lifestyle, and was renamed Healthy Investment – a non-profit making mutual friendly society.[78]

In 1887 a Prestonpans branch of the *Scottish Legal Life Assurance Society* (Haddington district) appears.

Registered under the Friendly Society Acts 1896 and 1908 on 4 April 1911, the *St Andrew's Catholic Total Abstinence and Benefit Society, Branch 'Father John Hughes' Branch No 36, Prestonpans*[79] held its meetings in Cuthill Hall on alternate Sundays at 5pm. Members within three miles were fined for non-attendance, 'courtesy and respect' being desired virtues. Both sexes were eligible, as long as they were abstainers from 'intoxicating liquors' as well as 'practical Catholics'. Junior members were covered for funeral benefit. The registered office was at Easter Road, Broxburn. Trustees of the branch were all miners: John McKenna, 36 Middle Street; Cornelius Lafferty, 83 Back Street; and Thomas Banks, 26 Summerlee Street, all Cuthill, Prestonpans. The 'Father John Hughes' branch ceased to exist when all members 'withdrew from the membership' by 30 April 1912; it briefly revived in April 1914, and finally closed by June 1914.

The other 'big' temperance presence in Prestonpans was of course the *Gothenburg*; between its building in 1908 and its decline in the 1960s it provided a gathering and eating place for ordinary people, and their families, of Prestonpans. Following the lead of the Industrial and Providential Societies Act 1893, any profits above 5% return on capital were recycled into the local community 'to provide civic amenity'. The aim was to provide alternative leisure activities to drunkenness,[80] credit was prohibited, as were gambling games. [It re-opened in 2004 once again true to its original principles, spurred on by a visit from Jorgen Linder, Lord Mayor of Gothenburg in Sweden, in July 2003.]

4.2 The Co-operative Wholesale Society[81]

Concern about the poverty of the 1830s stimulated the rise of the co-operative movement in England. The ideas of Robert Owen (later of New Lanark) were a driving force behind the development of the co-operative self-help ethos. The modern co-operative movement began with a model developed by the Rochdale pioneers in 1844. The Co-op sought to 'bring the producer and the consumer into more immediate contact, and thus enhance the profits of co-operation, by diminishing the costs of distribution'.

In 1863 the North of England Co-operative Wholesale Society was founded, being renamed the Co-operative Wholesale Society in 1872. The Scottish Wholesale Co-operative Society was founded in 1868, and worked with the CWS from 1876, for example on activities such as organising butter supplies from Cork. The SWCS merged with the CWS in 1973.

The Co-op provided a source of reasonably priced (bulk buying helped, as did the wholesale practice of paying in cash), quality goods; in a world where short weights and adulterated food (such as powdered glass in sugar, white lead in flour, red lead in cheese, and mahogany shavings in tea) was common, the Co-op's guarantees were welcomed. In mining and manufacturing communities it offered an alternative to the exploitative shops operated by the employers where goods were provided 'on tick', and the costs deducted from the wages before the workers got them (although legislation against these truck shops had helped to reduce this exploitation).

The nearby Tranent society[82] opened in 1862; members joined by purchasing shares of £1 in total, and there seemed to be no limit on the number of shares they could have. Interest was paid on the investment. Poorer members were able to pay for their shares at 6d a week (so took 40 weeks to pay), but they could not benefit from the quarterly dividend until they had paid the complete £1.

When the Tranent society decided that they needed to buy a shop, they did not want to take on a loan, and so the cost of the shares was increased to £2, the same arrangement as before being employed by the poorer members. At the time a miner's average wage was 2/6 a week, so it would take eight weeks for the miner to earn £2. For funding the second shop, the share price was increased to £5.

The credit available to each member depended on the value of the shares held, with the credit offered matching their investment, so it was offset against a member's own money, and cleared once the 'divi' paid out. Each member's book was coded so that the shopkeepers knew how much credit they could be offered. In Tranent, this was the means by which ordinary people managed to save for events such as weddings and the buying of extras at Christmas; it also enabled them to afford death insurance. The fear of penury that followed a death in the family was a very real one.

Most co-ops observed how nearby co-ops worked and adopted the best practices from them in their own shops. The Tranent Co-op seems unusual in several ways; most co-ops stuck with the £1 shares, and most offered no credit. Modern co-ops still have the £1 share today, and individuals can invest up to £20,000; while it was acceptable to have more that a single share, there was only one vote per person. In general it was possible to pay for your share by instalments; however at the end of the quarter (or half-year) the store took what would have been paid in the dividend or 'divi', and that went towards the share cost. The 'divi' could be taken as cash or added to one's share capital. Often the 'divi' payouts coincided with a time of year when the need was greatest – when winter clothing was required or for school uniforms.

The original Rochdale principles were very anti-credit; trading was always in cash, and so people were encouraged away from the previous truck-shop practice of always being one week in arrears.

As time went on, the Co-ops expanded into many other areas of life, and often employed their own members. The Scottish society had a factory at Shieldhall, Glasgow, that produced foods (like semolina and custard), metalware and furniture.

Different co-ops adopted friendly society-type benefits at different times. The CWS introduced a 'sick and burial club', which ran from 1887–1908, thereafter 2d was collected each week from employees. In 1920, the Musselburgh and Fisherrow Co-operative Society agreed to enter the Collective Life Assurance Scheme, whereby a small percentage of the cost of any purchases was collected, and entitled their next of kin to claim death benefit.[83]

By the late 1920s, most co-ops were under compulsory union membership, which ensured that every member had sickness, death and unemployment benefit. Most co-ops gave credit to miners and their families during the 1926 general strike. Prestonpans adopted collective life assurance in 1923.

Like many of the larger employers in the area, the Co-op supported a range of social and leisure activities for its workers and their families. The Scottish Co-operative Woman's Guild was formed in 1892, and was linked to the Scottish Labour Party until the first world war. There were 12,000 members of the guild by 1913;[84] it was effective in promoting the role of women, and also provided education for them. The Co-op guild supported the temperance societies, including the Band of Hope.

Prestonpans Co-op[85]

One significant addition to the town was the Prestonpans Co-operative Society,[86] which was registered in 1869 (it became part of Scottish Midland Co-operative Society in 1994). Its workforce was considerable and its very ethos supported workers and customers.

The Co-operative Society in Prestonpans moved into new premises at Beach House (purchased for £1150 in February 1898) in August 1899; celebrations began with the 100th psalm 'accompanied by Messrs Miller & Richard's brass band'. Chairman Joseph White gave a brief history[87] – with the store beginning in what was later a plumber's, moving into the old Parochial Grammar School and erecting the bakery there, and then purchasing and converting Beach House. The society's motto was 'the greatest good for the greatest number'. At this time the 'shops are arranged with grocery and drapery departments under one roof, the bakery adjoining the grocery and communicating therewith. The fleshing department has a separate entrance ... also stabling for four horses, with hay and straw lofts'. The band played on as tea was served to members, while delegates, management and committee retreated to the hall for dinner. One visiting store representative, Mr Taylor of St Cuthbert's store, commented that 'Edinburgh had pauperised itself by accepting Mr Carnegie's gift and that, great as the gifts of Mr McEwan and Mr Usher to the city were, they were nothing in comparison to what co-operation was doing for the people. During the last two years, St Cuthbert's had returned to its members upwards of a quarter of a million of money and not a word said about it'.

Prestonpans Co-op's half-yearly general meetings were held in the Free Church hall, an indication of where the society's loyalties lay at the time. The Golden Jubilee celebrations were reported at length in *The Scottish Co-operator* of 4 July 1919. This account revealed that the early days of the society were beset by internal squabbles and the inevitable instability that followed. This only ceased with the appointment of David McCairn as secretary (1869–1915), David Fraser as treasurer (1869–1911) and Peter Robertson as manager (1873–1903). From 1871 there was a healthy social aspect to the society, with the annual 'do' an event of note right until the beginning of the war in 1914. In 1912 a dairy was opened, and later a piggery. Redundant earlier premises were recycled into housing, and in 1918, the society purchased Castle Park estate, with the intent of converting the house into workmen's houses and to build more on the grounds, as well as a bowling green for members and the public. By 1925 it was estimated that the society served some 1060 members; from at least 1918 there was an annual picnic organised for the employees. They went to Gifford that year and on a motor tour of southern Scotland in 1920.

The Golden Jubilee was marked by a Band Competition on 7 June, followed by a Gala Day a couple of weeks later, complete with skipping competition and football match; the adults' celebrations were to be marked with a social event in the autumn. The society's Diamond Jubilee was held in January 1929, and Belfield's pottery produced a commemorative teapot, perhaps the memento valued at 10/– mentioned in the account? The aim was that 'no one connected with the society will be forgotten'. A social and dance were held in the Town Hall in January. One recollection of the time was that the bank had stopped the society's credit, which was only reinstated because of the esteem in which treasurer William Fraser was held.

Gala Day Memories (from the collection of Mr Bert Renton)

Gala Day Memories (from the collection of Mr Bert Renton)

As the population grew, so did the society; the new Cuthill store opened in 1925,[88] with music from the Prestongrange silver band and tea afterwards in the parish church hall. The Preston branch opened in 1926, followed by drapery at Cuthill in 1927, and hairdressing and confectionary in the High Street in 1926.

> *'As the Co-operative grew it began to take over other premises such as Cooper's joinery in Kirk Street and the Borland drapery and house. Front Street [was] where Mrs Gray had a sub-post office and Mrs Nisbet sold groceries and cheques [sic] from the co-operative to poor families, collecting the money on pay day. For taking this risk Mrs Nisbet received a dividend from the Co-op. Another option for the less-well-off was to contribute to the Co-op savings scheme which allowed them to buy goods on credit that could be paid off weekly using a 'store book'.*[89]

In 1948[90] the Prestonpans Co-operative Society employed over 100 people. These were distributed amongst its various outlets thus: four grocery shops (34 employees); two butchers' shops (11); one confectionary and fruit shop (two); a gents' hairdressing saloon (two); a modern bakery (12); a boot and a boot repairing shop (four); a drapery (four); a hardware shop; a painting department (nine); a joinery & undertaking department (two); a smithy (two). There were also eight transport workers, three packers, two cleaners, and 14 clerks, as well as seven motor and three horse-drawn vans.

In Prestonpans, there was still a Co-op youth club active in the 1950s; the society had also constructed a bowling green, and rented it to the Castle Park bowling club. Most of the members were also members of the Co-op society.

4.3 THE MINEWORKERS' STORY

Prestonpans' long history of mining began in the 12th century and lasted until the 1960s. The twin industries of coal mining and salt panning ran side-by-side; following legislation of 1606, both sets of workers (and their families) were tied by a type of serfdom to their place of work. If they ran away they were pursued and punished, although the 18th century kirk session records recount the tale of one miner from another parish whose behaviour was so awful that 'his' parish (and his owner) did not want him back. At the same time the miners were a workforce of noted belligerence, with no compunction about striking, knowing that their owners had no alternative workforce on which to draw. Whatley comments that 'miners, nominally serfs, had an effective trade union system which enabled them to resist pressure by the mine owners to increase output'.[91]

The desperate need for more workers forced through the Emancipation Act of 1774, and this meant that new workers from 1 July 1775 were not held under serfdom; the ruling was extended to existing serfs when serfdom was abolished entirely in 1799.[92]

Women were banned from underground working in 1842; the resultant lower incomes for families meant that miners became more vulnerable to threats of dismissal from the mine owners. Nevertheless, the miners found ways of presenting a united front to mine owners, forming 'combinations' or unions (long deemed illegal by owners). Coal mining moved into the industrial age from c 1818; by 1837 it seems that all Lothian's colliers were members of the Dalkeith Union.[93] One of the key roles of the combinations was to collect contributions from the workers (1/6 a week in 1837), which were then used to fund sickness benefits. The Scottish Federation did not introduce funeral benefit until 1895. No provision was made for periods of unemployment although later, limited funds were drawn on to sustain members during strikes. The Insurance Act 1911 provided free medical care for employees; miners, but not their families, were included. By 1925 there were reports of the annual general meetings of the Prestonpans branch of the Scottish Miners' Friendly Society; David Allan was the secretary, and Robert Stein the sick visitor. Prestonlinks Colliery had an employees' Sick & Accident Fund certainly between 1920–24, if not longer.

Various groups[94] were formed then closed, attracting members during good times, and losing them through bad. These included the Coal & Iron Miners' Association (1855–63); the anti-Catholic and anti-Irish Free Miners' Society (1860s)–70; the Mid and East Lothian Association and the Mid and East Lothian Miners' Association (M&ELMA) finally settled as the latter in 1889 (with one branch at Prestongrange).

The 1890s saw the mining industry in the eastern coalfields at its most intensive, and most mines had an average of over 400 workers. In 1899 M&ELMA joined a Scottish Federation, itself becoming the Coal Conciliation Board for Scotland. In 1914 M&ELMA became part of the National Union of Scottish Mineworkers (NUSM) and members were able to participate in the range of friendly society schemes offered by the NUSM. Previously the association had supported its own funeral benefit scheme. Branch delegates of M&ELMA in 1918 were Alex Murray (Prestongrange) and Joe Colquhoun (Prestonlinks). The association lasted until 1944/5 when it was succeeded by the National Union of Mineworkers (Scottish area).

The mining community was well known for its strong ties of comradeship and community. This was particularly evident during the number of strikes that occurred[95] (including 1894, 1912, 1921, 1926, 1984/5), when mining communities shared their limited resources; in 1926 a soup kitchen was run from Cuthill school,[96] itself only opened in 1901. Janet Naysmith recalled:

> *'My husband, father and two brothers were on strike again for seven months in 1926... soup kitchens were situated in the basement of Bank House and various events were organised to aid mining families such as night-time concerts which could last till midnight. Being young we did not fully realise the hardships our parents were subjected to. Yet again the miners returned to work worse off'.*[97]

More happily, the community ethos was also manifest in the building of miners' welfare institutes, in social clubs and groups, and in galas that often continue today under the auspices of the local communities. In 1922 the Prestongrange gala day saw 1200 children being entertained at Bankfoot with processions, bands and sports. Outings, too, were a regular social event; in 1925 700 went to Dunfermline, taking the silver and pipe bands with them. On weekday evenings, chara-banc trips to the Borders, Dumfries and Lanark were common. In 1952 the Coal Industry Social & Welfare Organisation (CISWO) took on the caring role within mining communities.

The social responsibilities, and the responses, of the local landowners were varied: c1908 'Lady Susan Grant-Suttie would visit the church families. If at times things were hard for the miners' families, we children would be sent to the kitchen door of Prestoungrange House for a pitcher of roast dripping'.[98] Other support came from the wider community; for example Dr McEwan Senior was running first aid classes for miners from c1910, and in 1916, a plot of wasteland near the links colliery was being used for gardens for mine employees.

Welfare Institutes

The creation of these was included in the Mining Industries Act 1920; a penny was raised for every ton of coal produced, and the monies were used to pay for welfare institutes. The funds were extended by a further levy in 1926, which was to be used to fund the building of pit-head baths. Both institutes in Prestonpans opened in 1925.

Prestonlinks Institute was known as the East Institute; it was situated at the eastern end of Prestonpans next to the football ground. It had a large billiard room, a games hall, a ladies' room and a committee room,[99] together with offices and a caretaker's house. It was proposed that baths could be added later. In 1917, this busy pit had 1100 employees. Prestonlinks closed in February 1964 and the institute sometime after.

The brick and roughcast Prestongrange Welfare Institute – the West Institute – was located at Bankfoot, Cuthill, on the road that ran north from the East Lodge of Prestongrange House. The provision of education was a key aim and the institute had a reading and recreation room, as well as a billiard room with two tables, and a large hall that could accommodate 400. Nearby was a house for the caretaker.

At the opening it was commented that it was to be hoped that the gambling spirit would not be part of the games played at the institute.[100]

One of the earliest uses for the institutes was as soup kitchens during the strike; miners' wives could use the kitchen facilities (their own were often minimal), and for perhaps the first time there was suitable accommodation for dances, weddings and other functions. In the 1930s concerts were held there. In spite of the earlier intentions, it was not until September 1952 that pit-head baths opened at Prestongrange. Those at the Links seem to have opened

Miners' Welfare Institute, East Prestonpans (from the collection of Mr Bert Renton)

earlier. The end came when the mining industry finished in the 1960s; Prestongrange pit closed in December 1962. Quite what happened to the institute is unclear; from 1978–83, the Salvation Army used it for their meetings, and by 1984, it had become derelict. Sometime after that it was demolished.

Bands and sports groups

In 1887, Prestongrange fielded a *cricket team* against Strathear. Team members were P Whitecross, J Govan, P Thomson, G Thallon, A Tait, W Sheppard, J Wood, J Rennie, R Frazer, E Johnstone and A Mitchell. In 1888 the team played against Cliftonville and later against Musselburgh, and in 1900 against Newbattle.

In 1918 *Prestonlinks Colliery Band* was founded; once the Links Pit closed in 1962 the band continued under a number of different names, merging with the Dalkeith burgh band as the Dalkeith & Monktonhall Colliery Band in 1987. It continues to entertain today, recently celebrating 80 years of music-making.[101]

Prestonlinks Pipe Band was formed in 1922; it continues today as the Royal British Legion Pipe Band, after the last Lothian link with coal mining disappeared in 1999 with the closure of Monktonhall.[102]

Prestongrange Colliery Band, conducted by Mr R Malcolm, was fifth in a contest for the championships of Scotland in 1925.

The *Star of the East Flute Band* was formed in May 1925.[103]

Galas

Both pits held galas, and these were the highlight of the summer for local children: Janet Naysmith again, c1914

> *'I will not forget our first Grange miners' gala held there [Prestongrange] when we were given tea and a bag of sticky buns. Prize races were organised at the event ... The miners at Prestonlinks had a gala day of their own which allowed me to have another shot at winning a prize'*

The Grange gala was held at Cuthill Park. The two mining community galas were combined for the first time on 24 June 1946, as a gala for the district, held in the field of Prestonpans public school.

4.4 Fishermen

As well as the sailors' friendly society, the fishermen were unionised. From 5 May 1899 the group was to be known as the East & West of Scotland Fishermen's Association. They met at the Free Church hall.

5 IMPROVEMENT THROUGH LEGISLATION

From the middle of the 19th century, central government was increasingly willing to take on a role in the social and economic matters throughout Britain. *Some* examples of the legislation enacted relating to the poor, the sick and the needy, as well as the able-bodied poor, are given below.

The Poor

1844	Poor Law Amendment (Scotland) Act – introduced Boards of Supervision
1885	Part of the Medical Relief Grant for Scotland could be used to encourage the employment of trained nurses in the parish poor-houses; this was the start of nursing as an accepted profession
1894	The Local Government (Scotland) Act set up the Local Government Board, which took over responsibility for the operation of the Poor Law from the Board of Supervision.
1906–14	The Liberal Government introduced a raft of legislation, all of which was targeted at improving the lot of the poor and destitute; however, they kept the poor law legislation in place to ensure that those who still did not benefit from the new legislation were provided for including:
1908	Old Age Pensions Act; limited pensions were introduced; these were fairly restrictive, providing a maximum of 5/– a week for the 'poor but deserving' aged 70+. They were also non-contributory and means tested. More pension legislation followed in 1919
1925	Widows', Orphaned and Old Age Contributory Pensions Act; the latter were paid from age 65, and widow's benefits were introduced.
1937	The Children & Young People's (Scotland) Act 1937; this was the first legislation that recognised the need for children to be in the care of a fit person, as well as the need for delinquency to be addressed. It was the forerunner of the Kilbrandon Report 1964 which looked at 'those juveniles alleged to have committed crimes or offences, children in need of care and protection, children who are refractory or beyond parental control and who are persistent truants.'[104]
1945	The Family Allowance Act provided funds to help families.
1980	State Retirement Pension to increase in line with prices, not earnings

The Mentally Ill

1855	Royal Commission on Lunacy was set up, and the first mental health legislation enacted. The General Board of Commissioners in Lunacy for Scotland followed.
1857	The Lunacy (Scotland) Act; this was followed with amendments in 1862 and 1866. This legislation lasted until 1913. It made it possible for patients to be admitted into asylums as 'voluntary boarders' and was designed to promote more positive and enlightened attitudes towards the humane care and welfare of the mentally ill.
1885	Beginning of use of trained nurses in asylums
1907	Introduction of three-year training programme for nurses.
1913	The Mental Deficiency and Lunacy Act
1913–60	The General Board of Control (Lunacy)
1960–date	The Mental Welfare Commission. Under this was enacted the Mental Health (Scotland) Act 1984, and the Adults with Incapacity (Scotland) Act 2000.

The Sick

1867	Public Health (Scotland) Act.
1875	Public Health Act enabled local authorities to set up hospitals out of the rates.
1911	Insurance Act – free medical service for all employees.
1919	Registration of Nurses Act; England and Scotland set up separate General Nursing Councils.
1925	State Registration for Nurses began.
1948	National Health Service. Since when the NHS has provided for the sick, including taking over from the Queen's Nursing Association, a national organisation that had been operating in Prestonpans since 1899.

The Unemployed

1905	The Unemployed Workmen's Act gave local authorities powers to establish labour exchanges and to create work for the unemployed at the ratepayers' expense.
1906	The Workmen's Compensation Act made provision for disablement or death due to certain industrial diseases.
1909	The Labour Exchange Act created a national network of offices through which the unemployed could seek work.
1911	The Unemployed and National Insurance Act brought in a contributory national insurance scheme. This had limited coverage; the death of an employee was not covered. A short-term loss of earnings was covered.
1946	The National Insurance Act.

Education

1872	Education (Scotland) Act. In 1906/07 legislation was introduced to provide free school meals; a school medical service was begun after the Education (Scotland) Act of 1908 was introduced.
1918	Education (Scotland) Act.

6 KIRK

6.1 Competing for souls

From c1730, other Scottish Presbyterian churches began to compete with the established Church of Scotland. In many instances, the trigger for discontent in the parish was the issue of patronage; the established church was in thrall to the landowners (and thus the Crown and state) and they decided who was appointed as minister (lay patronage was abolished first in 1649, again in 1690, reinstated under the Patronage Act of 1712 and repealed in 1874).[105] By and large the breakaway groups, though each was very different, sought ministerial appointments through congregational elections, and appealed mostly to the working class.

Scottish Presbyterian church history is complex and confusing, with these many 18th century splits and re-unions. These included, for example, 1733 the Seceeders (that in 1747 split into Burghers and Anti-burghers); 1761 the

Relief Church; 1799 old light and new light (a split of the Seceeders); 1820 the United Secession Church brought some of the Burghers and Anti-burghers back together.

In Prestonpans, the influence (or otherwise) of the established church in this period can be assessed from information given in the *Statistical Account* of 1793:

> *'The great body of the people adhere to the established church. About a twentieth part of the whole number are Seceeders, of whom nearly two thirds are of the Burgher persuasion. There are 10 or 12 Episcopalians.'*[106]

As the total population for the parish was just over 2000 in 1793, about 100 people were seceeders. The Burghers probably went to Tranent to worship as there was an active group there from c1740.

By the 1830s it was considered that *'Dissenters of all denominations and ages amount to 100 individuals'*.[107]

The Free Church of Scotland emerged after the Disruption of 1843; it was largely led by the middling classes, and was more egalitarian than the established church, but even it had its problems. Many of the dissenting groups were driven by an evangelistic agenda, and found support in the burgeoning urban and industrialised areas. It became increasingly difficult for the established church to maintain its role as arbiter of society and fundraiser in chief. The middle classes – the shopkeepers and professionals – were increasingly drawn to the Free Church and other congregations, taking their funds with them. Claimants of poor relief had to apply to the established church kirk session, even if they did not worship there. John Fowler Hislop, a key member of the Prestonpans community, was a Free Church member; his name arises in many of the records of the period – the session minutes, school board records and so on.

Post-1843, splits and unions continued: in 1847 the United Secession and the Relief Church joined forces as the United Presbyterian Church. In 1898 the Free Church and the United Presbyterian Church proposed and supported union becoming the United Free Church of Scotland in October 1900. Eventually, the United Free Church of Scotland and the Church of Scotland re-united as the Church of Scotland in 1929. In Prestonpans both Preston and Grange churches continued to serve their separate congregations until 1981 when they united as Prestongrange church.

While the established church and its scions were dealing with fractiousness and discontent, other churches were making headway amongst communities. The migrant workforces of the west of Scotland brought their religions with them, and Prestonpans saw an increase in the numbers of Roman Catholics and members of the Orange Order too (see 7 below). Within East Lothian, Methodism was popular, and Episcopalians also maintained a foothold. All these groups were active in their community, holding social meetings and supporting associated groups for both adults and children; each had their own agenda as they impacted on the town's social life.

6.2 Kirk-related leisure

It is difficult to disentangle the social groups of the two main Prestonpans Presbyterian churches – Preston and Grange – especially during the 19th century, as at times each had a group of the same name active at the same

Preston Kirk Award Winning Drama Group (from the collection of Mr Bert Renton)

time. Where the references come from the kirk session minutes, then it is possible to attribute a group to one or the other church. The information gleaned from newspapers is less clear.

The established Church of Scotland – Preston Church 1595–1981 (see also 2.2 and 3.1 above)

In 1902, church halls were built in Preston and at Cuthill; these provided venues for fundraisers such as jumble sales.

The *Young Men's Christian Association* (YMCA) was founded across Scotland in 1841; in Prestonpans it existed from c1890 (although possibly not continuously thereafter).

The *Boy's Brigade* was revived in 1899, and it reappeared in the 1930s, when John Buchanan was the first captain, and activities included drills, marching and even boxing one night a week.[108] Their camps included one stay under canvas at Belhaven.

The *Woman's Guild (*formed 1909 see 7.1 below) and Praise Committees co-ordinated congregational social events from at least the 1940s. During the war they formed the Troops' War Comfort Fund (a joint effort between Preston and Grange churches); this ended in September 1945. The guild members also organised choirs and fetes, and the Sunday school picnics, when children went to Prestongrange House in the early days, and later to Roslin and Craigmillar. By the 1920s favourite locations were Eskside and Gullane and, by the 1950s, they ventured to places like Peebles, North Berwick and Burntisland. In more modern times the church supported a broad range of groups for all ages, including the bible class, girl guides, drama group and so on.

The *Boys' or Lads' Club* was started by Dr McEwan and Mr HT Laidlaw in May 1914 with 20 boys aged 10+, who met in the Town Hall. Outings

Scouts: a Long Tradition (from the collection of Mr Bert Renton)

were part of the attraction, a favourite being to Longniddry by bus via Macmerry and Tranent. By 1924, the club was very popular with 200+ members, 80 of whom were in training to be Scouts. In 1947 the club was raised to status of a YMCA.

The *Preston Church Drama Club* grew out of the church *Literary & Debating Society* which itself ended in 1949. The drama club was founded in 1939 and thrived until the end of the 1970s.

The Free Kirk – Grange Church 1843–1929; Church of Scotland 1929–81

In the age of social philanthropy, the evangelising character of the free kirk pervaded all corners of parish life, as the kirk concerned itself with all and sundry. It was very popular in Prestonpans: in its first months there were 162 names on the communal roll, and by 1899 the Free Church hall had been extended to provide additional accommodation. Some 300 children of the congregation went for tea and cake to the Manse, and by 1905 the roll had 344 names. Like the established church, the free kirk was obsessed with antenuptial fornication, recording the misdeeds of labourer David Shaw (1864), John Richie and his wife (1867), and Archibald Buchanan, fisherman (1871). The obsession continued into the new century.

In January 1884, the free kirk presbytery was calling for assistance in carrying on mission work amongst the miners in the neighbourhood; Grange church had already begun a Sabbath school at Cuthill[109] – where 120 children were on the roll (ten years later the roll was 156), and were cared for by 13 teachers. By 1907, the need for a 'proper hall' was seen as hindering mission work at Cuthill, although the suggestion that the Cuthill school could used for Sabbath meetings was rejected (21 January 1908). In February 1910, the Summerlee Iron Company Ltd granted permission for a new mission hall to be built at the east end of the space between the back of Cuthill and Summerlee Street, at a rental of one shilling a year. (The mission hall was taken over by the military in 1942, and was condemned in 1945).

Groups abounded, and in the late 1880s–90s, the magic lantern show operated by Mr Belfield was a popular entertainment, and was shown to the Bible Club, the Band of Hope and to the *Young Ladies Christian Association* in the Free Church hall. By 1888 this had become the Young Women's

Christian Association, and was another of John Fowler Hislop's projects. He chaired the group, with Lady Susan Grant Suttie as president. The YWCA lasted at least until the end of the second world war.

Miss Lilias Taylor of Bankton was an active church member, and her work with the *Women's Foreign Mission Association* is of note.[110]

The Free Church hall was a popular venue for many meetings, including a Limelight Lecture, by Miss Brown of London, on 'Slum life in London'[111] (reported in the *Haddingtonshire Courier* 25 February 1898), and a series of lectures including, perhaps a little surprisingly, one on Witchcraft in 1886.

'Good works' societies emerged in the 1860s, including the temperance movement. Supporters included James Belfield and John Fowler Hislop.[112]

In 1875 the Edinburgh Band of Hope was formed with the aim of attaching a band to 'every congregation, mission hall, Sabbath school and temperance society.' The *Band of Hope in Prestonpans* had both junior and senior bands, and in 1884 held a concert in the Free Church hall. The *Prestonpans British Women's Temperance Association* was established c1876, and had their weekly meetings in the Cuthill Mission hall; by 1925 the group was meeting in the parish church hall.

Grange kirk session proposed and began a *Boys' Brigade* (29 October 1888); it had evidently ceased at some time, as in 1908, the kirk session approval was given to Mr Edmonston for the organisation of a boys' brigade, probably based at Cuthill.

In the first decade of the new century, the Free Church doubled its efforts to encourage the non church-going people of *Cuthill*[113] into the kirk. More time was to be devoted to visiting the sick, the idea being that if one could get into the home, there was more chance of success. Sabbath school, bible classes, a children's service, a Cuthill Boy's Brigade, and a faith mission were set in train. An early success seems to have been the Cuthill mission church choir that was trained by Mr Grimwood.

By the 1930s, the mission hall was '... used at times for the *Sisterhood, Home League, Boys' Brigade or rehearsal for the Christmas Kinderspiel.*'[114]

Other churches

Roman Catholic – Parish of St Gabriel's 1932–date[115]

From small beginnings, Catholicism grew in Prestonpans after the influx of miners from the west of Scotland, who moved from one Summerlee pit to another at Prestongrange. More came to the parish during the 1950s in search of work. From c1845, Prestonpans was a Mission Station of St John's in Portobello; in 1907, mass was celebrated in Prestonpans – the first for three centuries. The Passionist Retreat of St Mary's at Drummohr opened in March 1932 (and closed c1980), and the parish of St Gabriel's was established at the same time. While Mass was also celebrated at a number of venues within Prestonpans (including at St Gabriel's Chapel Hall built in 1934), the monastery served as the parish church until 1966, when the new St Gabriel's Church on West Loan was opened. There were close links between the Passionists and the de la Salle Brothers at St Joseph's School at Meadowmill (see 3.4. above).

Social activities organised through the church have included Sunday school; men's and women's guilds – the latter of which evolved out of the Union of Catholic Mothers and St Anne's Guild; football and badminton teams; boxing and golf clubs; prayer groups; St Vincent de Paul Society (from 1983–date); various youth groups, and the Operetta Group

St Andrew's Episcopalian Church 1911–date[116]
From 1911–1939, St Andrew's was variously run as a mission from other churches in the area. It was then associated with St Peter's, Musselburgh, and remains thus linked to date, having had a period of independence 1959–76. Worship eventually settled at a wooden (later clad in stone) church on the High Street; this was demolished in 1993, the congregation having moved to the former Grange Church in 1992. Today a creche is provided during services, and the church runs a Sunday school, and weekday prayer meetings.

The Salvation Army 1919–date[117]
Established within the parish in 1919, until 1978 the Salvation Army was based on the High Street; from 1978–82, it used the redundant Prestongrange Miners' Institute (now demolished), and from 1983 on, the former Grange church hall. The army leisure groups have varied but have included the Songster Brigade, Women's Home League, Young People's Corps, the Legion (boys' group), Sunbeams (for girls), Sunday school, prayer meetings, brownies, bible study, parents & toddlers, and the junior youth club.

7 THE EMERGENCE OF A SOCIAL LIFE IN THE BURGH

From the latter part of the 19th century onwards, social groups of all sorts emerged in Prestonpans as they did in communities across Scotland. While impossible to cover all of these, a flavour is summarised here; tracking the fate of some has proved impossible, but an up-to-date summary of clubs and societies in the parish today can be found in the *East Lothian Fourth Statistical Account: 1945–2000.*

Holidays gradually became more abundant; in 1864, it seems that the traditional Hansel Monday in the last week of January was still kept in Prestonpans, when the labouring classes and the fisherfolk went shooting on the sands, before attending a ball.[118] In 1865, there was a move towards an early closing – earlier, that is, than 7pm. In 1885 it was noted that New Year's Day was increasingly seen as a holiday; in 1899 there was a merchants' holiday and by August 1902 this was taken on the same day that the annual regatta was held. In June 1900, when the carters and the Cuthill benevolent society had their processions, many merchants and public workers had a holiday too. They were entertained by the 'usual gathering of hobby horses, merry-go-rounds, high flyers shows and Aunt Sallys which were well patronised.'[119] In 1901, 600 people went on an excursion to Aberdeen provided by the Summerlee & Mossend Coal Company, and the following year 700 went by train to Stirling. This latter trip catered also for brickworks employees. In 1902, the annual outing for Co-op employees ventured to Hopetoun.

In the 1920s, fishing families often took a month away in the school holidays to favourite places like the Isle of Man and Whitby.[120]

Later still, the Queen's Arms was owned by the two Miss Grants and managed by Mr Pow who also groomed and hired out horses with brakes (buggies). This was very popular with families going on day trips to Gullane and North Berwick.

Nevertheless, life continued to be a struggle for many; in January 1894, the parochial board instructed that a soup kitchen be set up. Sea coal, thrown up on the beaches after a storm, was generally collected for free. In September 1894, two little girls from Cuthill were charged with stealing coal from a wagon, and their parents fined 3/6d or four days' in prison. Others were found guilty of theft for gleaning potato leavings. In 1921, prosecutions were made for the theft of coal and wood from a cart as the effects of the strike took hold.

7.1 The changing role of women

Lady Susan Grant-Suttie began the *Prestonpans Woman's Guild* (an off-shoot of the Church of Scotland), and was its first chairwoman; she died later the same year – 1909.

The *Prestonpans & Cockenzie District Nursing Association* was formed in November 1899 when members of the public were asked to fund a nurse for the district. Reports of the meeting reveal that the guest at the meeting, Miss Guthrie Wright, was 'not allowed to address public meetings at any length' so her speech was read for her by the Rev Mr Iverach. Her comments included that 'by employing a Queen's nurse there was to be no pauperising of the people. It preserved their feeling of independence to employ her and added to their comfort'.[121]

Affiliation to the *Queen Victoria's Jubilee Institute for Nurses* and to the Scottish branch of the Queen's Institute of District Nursing followed soon after. From 1901, miners at Prestongrange had subscribed 1d a month to support the nurse. The same year, the nurse had visited 170 patients with 2933 visits. Things had evidently moved on from Miss Wright's visit of 1899; by 1901, all the office bearers were female, except for the two reverends, Smith and Iverach. The nurses' group was still in being from 1916–28;[122] Miss Wilson was appointed district nurse in 1916 (out of 20 applicants). The East Lothian Nursing Federation was constituted in 1932, and the NHS absorbed the association's role in 1948.

From 1921–26, the ladies of Prestonpans had supported the *League of Pity,* which was concerned about the welfare of children, and organised fund-raising.

The *Prestonpans Red Cross Society* was evidently in place by 1916, as the group endowed a bed in Rouen Hospital by raising £50 pa. In 1925,[123] there was a *Red Cross Society* meeting that considered the forming of a Voluntary Aid Detachment in the burgh. Dr McEwan was in the chair, and Major General Hunter Blair, of Inglisfield, explained the scheme to the meeting; Mrs G Bertram Sheilds, of Dolphistoun, was appointed commander, Mrs Geo. McEwan was elected assistant commander and Mrs Logan Ayre quartermaster. Dr McEwan was lecturer.

In the 1920s women began to play an increasing role in the political life of the burgh. With the new groups of the *Women's Labour Guild, the Woman's Co-op Guild* and the *Eastern Star Order*. It appeared that *'the formation of these latter organisations seemed to make women more independent.'* Janet Naysmith[124]

Guides: a Long Tradition (from the collection of Mr Bert Renton)

Some of these had annual meetings and outings – for example in 1925 the Co-op Woman's Guild went on a chara-banc trip to Lochgilphead.

Other groups included guides, brownies, which perhaps grew out of earlier church groups. There was no Scottish Women's Rural Institute in the parish.

7.2 For the people, by the people

Only over the later years of the 20th century did the social life of the parish gradually move out of the aegis of the churches, and was increasingly run by interested members themselves. People also sought entertainment further afield, and when the trams came to Prestonpans in 1909, they were well used.

In 1901, Andrew Carnegie[125] gifted £1000 (later increased to £1500) towards the cost of building a *free library* in Prestonpans. The architect was Mr Allison. The library on Station Road was opened by Dr Hew Morrison in December 1905. There was a reading room, which could accommodate 100 readers, complete with reference section, and lending library of some 3000+ books – for which separate funds were raised; a recreation room and a separate house for the librarian.

Earlier efforts to improve the literary facilities in Prestonpans had begun in the early 1820s, when there was a subscription library. In 1858 a circulating library was started; in 1875 a literary institute was mooted, and in money raised towards this. However, by 1887, the literary group was reduced to just five members. The project eventually manifested itself in the building of the new town hall.

The new *Town Hall* opened in 1897; designed by Peter Whitecross, a Prestonpans architect, it could seat 450. As the records relate, protests from the established church about concerts held in the town hall in March 1844, there was evidently an earlier hall.[126]

Events held included in 1899 a concert with Mr Glass and his 'ventriloquial séance' singing and step dancing; and in the same year a lecture on the Transvaal by the Presbyterian minister of Johannesburg. On a Wednesday in February 1902 the merchant's ball saw 50 couples dancing to music by Mr Aithies' string band from Tranent. In the 1930s, concert party groups were popular, and the dances soon revived after the war years.

> *'The dances, or assemblies as they were also known, generally started at 10pm on Friday nights and could go on until 5.30am. Thus we had just enough time to get home, changed and have something to eat. Most of us had to be at work for 6.30am on the Saturday, which was a half day, thus we could afford to miss out on our beauty sleep. On other weekdays the dances would stop much earlier. At 16 or 17 years old you didn't seem to get exhausted and could always manage to keep going, one night it would be the drill hall and next the town hall. The entry fee for the dances was threepence for ladies and sixpence for gents.'*[127]

The *Gladsmuir Jacobite Club*[128] was formed in 1899 in Prestonpans and district. Its purpose was to stimulate interest in all things associated with the events of 1745, 'song, story, history and romance', and for 'suitably observing' the anniversary of the battle of Prestonpans. The 155th anniversary was celebrated with a gathering of the members of the club at the old thorn tree; it was noted that the tree was a little past its best, and it was proposed that a memorial be erected.

Other early clubs included the *Prestonpans & Musselburgh Colportage Society* (late 1890s), which met under the eye of Colonel Cadell in the Free Church hall.

The *Mutual Improvement Association (MIA) Conversazione*, for both men and women, was certainly extant in 1886. Readings were given and elocution improved, followed by singing and tea. There was a monthly magazine, and poetry readings.

Discussion topics ranged far and wide: in 1887 the topic was 'Ought the suffrage to be extended to women' with J. Belfield opposing and Adam Tait supporting. The latter won, but interestingly the ladies present refused to vote. In 1898, the Reform Bill, women's suffrage, Ruskin, whether schoolchildren get their books free, should ladies cycle, should cyclists be taxed, should Prestonpans have free recreation rooms and grounds were all up for discussion. In 1899, the topic of the South African war was discussed. The MIA continued at least until 1902, perhaps longer.

The Comrades of the Great War Club Ltd.[129] was registered at 46 High Street, Prestonpans, on 30 September 1920, and was affiliated to the United Services Fund Club. The comrades' club registration was cancelled on 1 September 1924 when all the club members resigned. It followed the rules set out in the 'Model rules for ex-servicemen's clubs and institutes in Scotland', and was effectively a social club, open from 4–9.30 pm. on weekdays. There were 152 members.

The democratic and non-sectarian *British Legion*[130] was set up after the 1914–18 war to care for ex-servicemen, many of whom faced starvation and ruin; the Scotland wing was established in 1921 and the Prestonpans branch was formed in 1936, with a ladies' section by the 1950s.[131] Care extended to the children of members, who could go on the annual legion bus trip.

In 1925 there was a *Prestonpans Burns Club*; members attended the annual conference in Edinburgh. There were annual Burns competitions for schoolchildren, for singing and recitation.

There was a branch of the *Territorial Army* (TA) in Prestonpans.[132] The TA began in Britain in 1920; in Prestonpans the 51st Lowland Heavy Regiment emerged in 1939 and used the drill hall until the middle of the 1960s (the building is now used by the Prestonpans Labour Club).

In 1899, the weekly meeting of the local group of *The Christian Endeavour Society* was recorded – 'tea and sacred solos'.

Politically aligned societies included:

The *National Liberal Association* – in 1886 this was chaired by Dr Ireland and the group met at the Queen's Arms Hotel.

The Order of the Loyal Orange Lodge

A chance find of a newspaper cutting revealed that on 21 September 1907, the first Orange Lodge of the area – the Inniskilling Purple Guards L.O.L. No 184 – was inaugurated at Prestonpans (although the ceremony took place at the Free Church hall in Cockenzie). It was one of a number of lodges run under the umbrella of the No. 5 John Knox District, Edinburgh, and took members from Prestonpans, Tranent and Cockenzie. The speech given by Alexander Prophet Profit included the advice that members should be 'very careful who they admitted... for they would find people who said they were Protestant but who all the same were worse than many Roman Catholics [hear, hear] while many others joined the order to see what they could get out of it'.[133]

However, the official Orange Lodge website suggests that the Order of Orange Lodge was established within the parish c1911. A female lodge – Lily of the East – was formed in Prestonpans in 1922; there were 200 members in the 1960s. Prestonpans District Lodge (44) was part of the new County Grand Lodge of Lanarkshire, the Lothians, Stirlingshire & Fife when it was created in November 1967. Late in 1968, five districts, including Prestonpans, formed the County Grand Lodge of the East. The lodge bought Castle Park House, using it as a Social Club until 1996. In its time, the lodge supported youth meetings and had a flute band. The building was demolished, and in 2000 the site lay vacant.

The kirk session minutes of 13 February 1945 provide a small insight: the Orange Lodge was told off by the session as it was running dances on Saturday nights after the business meetings had ended.[134] Two years later, the lodge had asked that it might use the church hall every first Saturday of the month for the formation of a new chapter.[135]

The Prestonpans Labour Club began c1967.

The *Unionist Association* was recorded having whist drives and dances in 1925.
In 1925, the *League of Private Enterprise* met in the town hall and discussed the 'red menace'; 250 attended, and the speakers criticised socialism.

The Pictures
The cinema played a key role in Prestonpans' social life. In 1899 Scott's Cinematograph visited the town, showing, in the town hall, a film about the life of Christ. Later the 'Scratcher' run by the Codona family attracted full houses,. In 1916 it was said to be 'well lighted and sanitary' with seats at 4d, 5d, and 7d. Star turns, vocals and dancing completed the entertainment on offer. It closed in 1960.

Sport
Football had long been popular, with informal games in the streets; on 11 March 1898 the *Haddingtonshire Courier* reported that eight young men and lads had been charged with playing football in the burgh at the brewery; 'carriages could not get past and it was undoubtedly a bad habit and should be put down'. Despite the lads' claim that the game had been played there for the past 10 to 11 years, they were fined 2/–.

The Scottish Football Association was founded in 1873. While the history of the local football teams is still to be written, a few indicators of the importance of this game to the community have been located. In 1916 a football benefit match was played between Prestonpans & Musselburgh Select and the East of Scotland team, on behalf of the widow and family of Thomas Killen, a well-known Musselburgh Athletic player who was killed at the Front.

The two main teams in the town were Prestongrange Athletic and Prestonpans Thistle, and it seems then that the teams emerged out of the sports tradition of the two collieries. Odd though it might seem today, a smoking concert was held by Prestongrange Athletic in 1918.

By the 1930s, Summerlee Thistle, Thorntree United, Wemyss Athletic and the Bing Boys appear to have been the league teams for boys; support was forthcoming from Prestonpans for the Tranent Juniors.

The mining community continued its involvement with football into the 1940s with the formation of Preston Athletic, who took over the pitch vacated by Prestongrange Rovers, close to Prestongrange Colliery. By the 1950s, Preston Athletic were attracting large crowds of supporters. In 1995, Preston Athletic became a member of the Scottish Football Association. Although support for local teams waned after the 1960s, the team is still well supported in the local community and is sponsored, among others, by the Prestoungrange Gothenburg under the traditional Gothenburg Principles.

Rugby is well represented in the area; founded in 1929/30 with Dr Boyle as its first president, Preston Lodge Former Pupils Rugby Football Club continues to enjoy significant success up to the present day, with a number of players having caps for their country. The club encourages the participation of young people (including girls) by running a variety of teams for different age groups.

Golf has long been of importance in the parish, with the Thorntree golfers' ball recorded in the late 1890s – 65 couples dancing to Mr Archibold's Quadrille Band. Thorntree Ladies' Club was extant in 1899. The relationship between the Royal Musselburgh Golf Club, Prestoungrange House and the Coal Industry Social Welfare Organisation (CISWO) is more fully explored elsewhere,[136] but golf and the mining community are closely linked in Prestonpans.

There was a *Prestonpans Swimming Club*, and swimming was taught in the sea during the inter-war years. In 1932, the Port Seton Swimming Pond opened and the club decamped to there.

Morrison's Haven Quoiting Club appears between 1888 and 1925.

There was for a number of years an *annual regatta*; it appears to have existed between 1897 and the 1920s.

The Pennypit sports facility opened in 1970 on the site that was once Northfield colliery, then a sports field.

Other interests were also catered for in the past: sources mention *whippet racing* at Tranent and *homing pigeons*; the *Draughts Association* – an attempt to revive this was made in 1925; *billiards*; and the *badminton* club (1942).

8 CONCLUSION

The experiences of this small, busy, industrial settlement are probably typical of similar parishes across Scotland. People were drawn to Prestonpans by the promise of work, and the population expanded quickly; the social networks already in place probably struggled to cope with the rising demands, and this is reflected in the records that have been consulted. It is clear that the importance of the friendly societies and the Co-op to the community cannot be over-stated. With no state-funded support, there was often very little standing between poverty and outright destitution. Yet alongside this daily struggle emerged a small town community, with its interests evidently reaching beyond the parochial. The Free Church worked at encouraging people to become educated, and many of the key players of the period played a major role in the development of the community. It is clear that, by the beginning of the 20th century, ordinary people were far more aware of the wider world than perhaps was previously thought.

NOTES

1 Dingwall, Helen (1994) *Seventeenth century Edinburgh: a demographic study* Scolar Press
2 Ibid p. 248
3 Urquhart, RM (1991) *The Burghs of Scotland; The General Police & Improvement (Scotland) Act 1862* ('The Lindsay Act') Motherwell Scottish Libraries Association p. 6
4 Prestonpans was never a mediaeval burgh; it split from Tranent in 1606 to become a parish in its own right.
5 Smout, T C 'The trade of East Lothian at the end of the 17th century' *in East Lothian Antiquarian & Field Naturalists' Society Transactions Vol IX* pp. 67–78
6 Aitken, J (2000) *Acheson/Morrison's Haven: what came and went and how?* (Booklet 2) Prestoungrange University Press pp. 39, 40
7 Sinclair, John (ed) (this edition Withrington, D & Grant IR 1975) *The Statistical Account of Scotland 1791–1799 Volume II: The Lothians* (EP Publishing Ltd) p. 586–589
8 Anderson, D (2000) *Sourcing Brickmaking, Salting & Chemicals at Prestongrange* (Booklet 3) Prestoungrange University Press p. 17
9 The range of industries is covered in detail in other booklets in this series, particularly booklets 2, 3, 4, 6, 9, 12
10 Lenmen, Bruce (1997 reprint) *Integration & Enlightenment: Scotland 1746–1832* Edinburgh University Press pp. 19, 20
11 Baker, Sonia (2000) *Prestongrange House* (Booklet 1) Prestoungrange University Presss pp. 26, 27
12 NAS CH2/307/1 p. 174 1719 is an example
13 op cit Sinclair, John (ed) pp. 578
14 Cunningham, WB (1845) 'Parish of Prestonpans' in *New Statistical Account of Scotland: Haddingtonshire* 3 Vols, Edinburgh Blackwood p. 311
15 Sinclair, Cecil (first ed 1990) *Tracing Your Scottish Ancestors* The Stationary Office, Edinburgh p. 64
16 National Archives of Scotland, CH2 collections
17 NAS CH2/307 1716–27
18 NAS CH2/307 p. 28
19 op cit Dingwall, p. 248
20 Houston, R. A. & Knox, W. W. J. Eds (2002) *The New Penguin History of Scotland: from the earliest times to the present day* p. 220 Penguin op cit Mitchison, R (1974) pp. 67, 68
21 Thomson, Adam (1829) *A Cure for Pauperism proposed in a letter to The Rev Thomas Chalmers* document held by the new College Library, University of Edinburgh pp. 16, 17
22 op cit, Dingwall, p255 states an average of 8 shillings a week for individuals in 1683
23 As many of the friendly societies had their own mortcloths, this cost was largely borne by the poorer in society
24 Mitchison, R (1974) 'The Making of the Old Scottish Poor Law' in *Past & Present* 1974 pp. 66, 67
25 op cit Dingwall, p. 257
26 NAS CH2/307/14 Prestonpans Kirk Session Poor Accounts 1732–1741 p. 39
27 NAS CH2/307/25 p. 56
28 op cit Sinclair John p. 580
29 ibid p. 579
30 op cit Sinclair, John (ed) pp. 579, 580
31 ibid
32 NAS CH2/307/20 Prestonpans Kirk Session Poor Accounts 1835–1858 p. 110
33 Hopkins, Bob (2004) *A Pride of Panners* (Booklet 18) Prestoungrange University Press pp 54–58; Martine, John (1890, this ed 1999) *Reminiscences & Notices of the Parishes of the County of Haddington* East Lothian Council Library Service p 183; McNeill, P (1902) *Prestonpans and Vicinity; historical, ecclesiastical and traditional,* Remploy, Leicester pp. 222–225; op cit Sinclair John p 582 from which the first two quotes are taken
34 NAS ED13/16
35 *Haddingtonshire Courier* 27.3.1885
36 op cit Houston & Knox p382 ; Checkland, Olive & Sydney (1989 2nd ed) *Industry &*

Ethos: Scotland 1832–1914 Edinburgh University Press pp. 99–103
37 ibid p. 99
38 Mitchison, R (2000) *The Old Poor Law in Scotland: the experience of poverty, 1574–1845* Edinburgh University Press p. 230
39 *Haddingtonshire Courier* 4.11.1859
40 *Haddingtonshre Courier* 1.1.1868
41 *Haddingtonshire Courier* 18.12.1863
42 Oral recollection via A. Allan
43 The designs are held by the Royal Commission on the Ancient & Historical Monuments in Scotland (RCAHMS), Sir John Sinclair House, 16 Bernard Terrace, Edinburgh
44 RCAHMS DPM/1850/3/1/1–10; NO 6 – ground plan (Dick Peddie & McKay collection)
45 *Haddingtonshire Courier* 30.1.1863
46 NAS GD176/1959 letter of 1883 from Board of Supervision to the inspectors of the poor
47 Naysmith (nee Cunningham), Janet 'As I Remember' in Prestonpans Local History Society 2001 *Tales of the Pans: a collection of memories from Panners* p. 33
48 NAS CO2/97/1 Inveresk Combination Poorhouse Minute Book of the Board 1913–29
49 NAS CO2/97/2 Inveresk Combination Poorhouse Minute Book of the Board 1930–44
50 Stiven, David 'Inveresk' in (1985) *The Third Statistical Account of Midlothian* pp130, 131
51 Affleck, David – comment made to him during the period c1970–76
52 Affleck, David K 'Social Welfare: the Promotion of Social Welfare in Communities' in Baker, S. (2003) *East Lothian Fourth Statistical Account: 1945–2000 Volume One: the County* pp. 104–110
53 East Lothian Care and Accommodation Project
54 op cit Hopkins pp. 56–58; *Haddingtonshire Courier* 2.6.16
55 additional information from Allan, Annemarie 'Prestonpans' in Baker, Sonia (ed) yet to be published *East Lothian Fourth Statistical Account 1945–2000: Volume Five* East Lothian Council Library Service
56 NAS ED13/573 1889–1890; NAS ED13/16 1882–6; McWilliam, C (1978) *Lothians excluding Edinburgh* p452 suggests it was taken over by the Catholic church in 1884, but the Scottish Catholic Archive, 16 Drummond Place, Edinburgh is unable to confirm this; Henderson, J (1845) 'Parish of Tranent' in *New Statistical Account of Scotland: Haddingtonshire* 3 Vols, Edinburgh Blackwood p. 302
57 *Edinburgh Gazette* 7.8.1883 quoted in NAS ED13/16
58 NAS ED13/298 letter (January 1888) to the Educational Endowments (Scotland) Commission
59 NAS ED13/298; NAS ED13/761; *Haddingtonshire Courier* 10.12. 1886
60 NAS ED13/298 and NAS CH2/307/25 25.6.1889–5.2.1894
61 as was pointed out in the Rev Adam Thomson's letter to The Rev Thomas Chalmers in 1829 p. 3, available from the New College Library, Edinburgh University
62 Information provided by Annemarie Allan
63 *Haddingtonshire Courier* editorial 16.8.1901
64 Information from The Peoples' Story Museum, Edinburgh
65 Thomson, Adam (1829) *A Cure for Pauperism proposed in a letter to The Rev Thomas Chalmers* document held by the new College Library, University of Edinburgh
66 Cunningham, WB (1845) 'Parish of Prestonpans' in *New Statistical Account of Scotland: Haddingtonshire* 3 Vols, Edinburgh Blackwood p. 314
67 Wallace-James, RE *The Book of the Lodge of Aitchison's Haven, 1598–1764*. The Minute Book of Aitchison's Haven Lodge is in the possession of the Grand Lodge of Scotland, 96 George Street Edinburgh.
68 *Haddingtonshire Courier* 19.11.86
69 National Library of Scotland MSS 1993–4 Accounts of the Prestonpans Incorporation of Seamen 1668–1747; NAS CH2/307/28 excerpts from minutes of Prestonpans Sailors' Incorporation 1743–6; list of members of Incorporation of Sailors of Prestonpans 1711–41; and Edinburgh University Library – Report on the Affairs of the Incorporation of Sailors of Prestonpans as of December 1824 by James Cleghorn
70 NAS CS96/299 Articles for the Potters Box. The last entry in the first section is 14 June 1802; see also Bonnar, Jane (2000) *Decorative Pottery at Prestongrange* (Booklet 9) Prestoungrange University Press pp. 25–27
71 *Haddingtonshire Courier* 17.7.1863
72 Martine, John *Reminiscences & Notices of the Parishes of the County of Haddington*

(1890, this ed 1999) East Lothian Council Library Service p. 180
The Bannantyne Club was founded for the 'printing & publication of works illustrative of the history, literature and antiquities of Scotland'

73 NAS FS4/868 Prestonpans United Society of Carters; NAS FS1/9/8 also; *Haddingtonshire Courier* 12 March 1912; however *Haddingtonshire Courier* 23.6.1893 holds that there was an earlier Carter's Society

74 *Haddingtonshire Courier* 22.6.1900

75 NAS FS 1/9/7 Prestonpans Caledonian Lodge of Free Gardeners

76 *Haddingtonshire Courier* 20.6.1884

77 *Haddingtonshire Courier* 23.6.1893

78 See www.healthyinvestment.co.uk I am grateful to William Turnbull, chief executive for his assistance. It has not been possible to pinpoint when meetings ceased in Prestonpans.

79 NAS FS4/565

80 Prestoungrange, Gordon (2002) *The Prestoungrange Gothenburg: the Goth's first 90 years and the coming decade* (Booklet 13) Prestoungrange University Press.

81 Unfortunately the records of the Prestonpans Co-op were destroyed in a flood during the 1990s examples of Co-op practices have been drawn from records of nearby Co-ops. Each Co-op operated independently, each with its own rules and regulations.
Redfern, P (1913) *The Story of the C. W. S.: the jubilee history of the Co-operative Wholesale Society Ltd. 1863–1913* The Co-operative Wholesale Society, Manchester

82 Thanks are due to Margaret Ward for her assistance with information about Tranent Co-op

83 Musselburgh & Fisherrow Co-operative Society (1962) *One Hundred Years of Progress: the history of your society* M&FCS p. 9

84 Checkland, Olive & Sydney (1989 2nd ed) *Industry & Ethos: Scotland 1832–1914* Edinburgh University Press pp. 207–208

85 see also Fraser, Henry 'Prestonpans Co-operative' in Prestonpans Local History Society (2001) *Tales of the Pans: a collection of memories from Panners* pp. 41,42

86 *The Scottish Co-operator* (1919, 1929); thanks to Gillian Lonergan, Archivist at the Co-operative College, Manchester for providing extracts

87 *Haddingtonshire Courier* 25 August 1899

88 *Haddingtonshire Courier* 20.11.25

89 op cit Naysmith (nee Cunningham), Janet 'As I Remember' in Prestonpans Local History Society 2001 *Tales of the Pans: a collection of memories from Panners* p. 34

90 Snodgrass, C (1953) *The Third Statistical Account of Scotland: the County of East Lothian* Oliver & Boyd pp. 214, 215

91 Whatley, CA 'The Fettering Bonds of Brotherhood: Combination and Labour Relations in the Scottish Coal Mining Industry, 1690–1775' in *Social History XII* (1987) pp 139–54 quoted in Mitchison, R & Leneman, L (1998) *Girls in Trouble – sexuality & social control in rural Scotland 1660–1780* Scottish Cultural Press p. 13

92 op cit Houston & Knox p300 Burnett, Allan (2000) *Industrial Ownership & Relations at Prestongrange* (Booklet 4) Prestoungrange University Press pp. 8 – 13

93 Scottish History Society (2003) *Mid & East Lothian Miners' Association minutes, 1894–1918* Scottish History Society; 5th series; 12 p. 424

94 ibid all 7 pages of article

95 op cit Burnett, pp. 29–32

96 Robert Donaldson 'From 6–12' in East Lothian District Council (1986) *The Pans Remembered* ELDC p. 7

97 op cit Naysmith (nee Cunningham), Janet 'As I Remember' in Prestonpans Local History Society 2001 *Tales of the Pans: a collection of memories from Panners* p. 35

98 op cit Naysmith (nee Cunningham), Janet 'As I Remember' in Prestonpans Local History Society 2001 *Tales of the Pans: a collection of memories from Panners* p. 31

99 *Haddingtonshire Courier* 18.4.24

100 *Haddingtonshire Courier* 25.12.25

101 see also Baillie, Margaret 'Dalkeith & Monktonhall Colliery Band: 1920–2000' in Prestonpans Local History Society (2001) *Tales of the Pans: a collection of memories from Panners* pp. 91, 92

102 see also Muir, Andrew 'Prestonlinks Pipe Band' in Prestonpans Local History Society (2001) *Tales of the Pans: a collection of memories from Panners* pp. 70, 71

103 see also Gibbons, Linda 'Star of the East Flute Band' in Prestonpans Local History Society (2001) *Tales of the Pans: a collection of memories from Panners* p. 90

104 HMSO, 1964 p. 9; I am grateful to David Affleck for drawing my attention to this report

105 Lynch, M (1991) *Scotland: a new history* Pimlico pp. 278, 399; Daiches, D ed. (1993) *The New Companion to Scottish Culture* Polygon p. 77
106 op cit Sinclair, John p. 579
107 op cit Cunningham p. 314
108 op cit Donaldson, R 'From 6–12' pp. 8, 9
109 NAS CH3/267/1 28 January 1884
110 CH3/ 267/ 1 her death on 21 February 1911 was reported at length
111 *Haddingtonshire Courier* 25 February 1898
112 John Fowler Hislop was a key member of the Prestonpans community; his work is acknowledged in the free church session minutes CH3/ 267/ 1 after his death in September 1894
113 *Haddingtonshire Courier* 18 July 1905
114 Davie, Bing 'Schooldays' in Prestonpans Local History Society (2001) *Tales of the Pans: a collection of memories from Panners* p. 40
115 Information from St Gabriel's Parish Directory. Also Allan, Annemarie 'Prestonpans' in Baker, S (not yet published) East Lothian Fourth Statistical Account: 1945–2000 Volume Five – the parishes of Cockenzie & Port Seton, Inveresk, Prestonpans and Tranent, East Lothian Council Library Service
116 Tulloch, Harriet 'St Andrew's Church' in Tales of the pans op cit p. 50
117 see also McLeod, Agnes & John 'The Salvation Army' in tales of the pans pp. 57, 58
118 *Haddingtonshire Courier* 22.1.1864
119 *Haddingtonshire Courier* 22.6.1900
120 Interview by Annemarie Allan with Bob Brown, Fisherrow, Musselburgh 2001
121 *Haddingtonshire Courier* 3.11.99
122 NAS IRS21/1062
123 *Haddingtonshire Courier* 20.11.25
124 op cit Naysmith, J p. 34
125 *Haddingtonshire Courier* 19.12.1905; NAS GD281/3/258
126 CH2/307/26
127 Naysmith p. 33
128 *Haddingtonshire Courier* 29.9.1899
129 NAS FS12/300 Although NAS has this listed under Friendly Societies it seems unlikely that this ever fulfilled such a role. It was more of a social club
130 Malcolm, George (1959) *We Will Remember – the historical record of the British Legion* British Legion, Edinburgh
131 see also Keenan, Isa 'British Legion (Ladies Section)' in Prestonpans Local History Society (2001) *Tales of the Pans: a collection of memories from Panners* p. 69
132 Bunyan, Stephen in Baker, S (2003) *East Lothian Fourth Statistical Account 1945–2000: Volume*
One the County East Lothian Council Library Service pp 239–243; Davie, Bing 'Prestonpans Territorials' in *Tales of the Pans* op cit pp. 47, 48
133 *Belfast Weekly News* 26 September 1907
134 CH2/307/26
135 CH2/307/26
136 Baker, Sonia (2000) *Prestongrange House* (Booklet 1) Prestoungrange University Press pp. 42–47; Ironside, R & Douglas, H (1999) *Royal Musselburgh Golf Club 1774–1999* Royal Musselburgh Golf Club

REFERENCES

Primary sources as given in footnotes: NAS – National Archives of Scotland

Thomson, Rev Adam (1829) *A cure for pauperism* Letter to Chalmers available from Special Collections, New College Library, Edinburgh University (refs: A.c.8.10/6 and S.c.38/2)

The Scottish Co-operator (1919, 1929) provided by Gillian Lonergan Archivist, The Co-operative College, Manchester

Baker, Sonia (2000) *Prestongrange House* (Booklet 1) Prestoungrange University Press

Bonnar, Jane (2000) *Decorative Pottery at Prestongrange* (Booklet 9) Prestoungrange University Press

Checkland, Olive & Sydney (1989 2nd ed) *Industry & Ethos: Scotland 1832–1914* Edinburgh University Press

Cunningham, WB (1845) 'Parish of Prestonpans' in *New Statistical Account of Scotland: Haddingtonshire* 3 Vols, Edinburgh Blackwood

Davie, Bing 'Schooldays' in Prestonpans Local History Society (2001) *Tales of the Pans: a collection of memories from Panners*

East Lothian District Library (1986) *The Pans Remembered* East Lothian District Library

Fraser, Henry 'Prestonpans Co-operative' in Prestonpans Local History Society (2001) *Tales of the Pans: a collection of memories from Panners* pp. 41, 42

Henderson, J (1845) 'Parish of Tranent' in *New Statistical Account of Scotland: Haddingtonshire* 3 Vols, Edinburgh Blackwood

Hopkins, Bob (2004) *A Pride of Panners* (Booklet 18) Prestoungrange University Press

Houston, RA & Knox, WW eds (2002) *The New Penguin History of Scotland from the earliest times to the present day,* Penguin

Lenmen, Bruce (1997 reprint) *Integration & Enlightenment: Scotland 1746–1832* Edinburgh University Press

Lynch, M (1995 reprint) *Scotland: a New History* Pimlico

Malcolm, George (1959) *We Will Remember – the historical record of the British Legion* British Legion, Edinburgh

McNeill, P (1902) *Prestonpans and Vicinity; historical, ecclesiastical and traditional* Remploy, Leicester

Mitchison, R (2000) *The Old Poor Law in Scotland: the experience of poverty, 1574–1845* Edinburgh University Press

Mitchison, R & Leneman, L (1998) *Girls in Trouble: sexuality & social control in rural Scotland 1660–1780* Scottish Cultural Press

Mitchison, R 'North & South: the development of the gulf in poor law practice' in Houston, RA & Whyte (eds) (1989) *Scottish Society 1500–1800*

Musselburgh & Fisherrow Co-operative Society (1962) *One Hundred Years of Progress: the history of your society* M&FCS

Naysmith (nee Cunningham), Janet 'As I Remember' in Prestonpans Local History Society (2001) *Tales of the Pans: a collection of memories from Panners* pp. 31–37

Prestoungrange, Gordon (2002) *The Prestoungrange Gothenburg: the Goth's first 90 years and the coming decade* (Booklet 13) Prestoungrange University Press

Redfern, P (1913) *The Story of the C. W. S.: the jubilee history of the Co-operative Wholesale Society Ltd. 1863–1913* The Co-operative Wholesale Society, Manchester

Ironside, R & Douglas, H (1999) *Royal Musselburgh Golf Club 1774–1999* Royal Musselburgh Golf Club

Royle, E (reprint 1993) *Modern Britain: a social history 1750– 1985*, Arnold

Scottish History Society (2003) *Mid & East Lothian Miners' Association minutes, 1894–1918* Scottish History Society; 5th series

Sinclair, Cecil (first ed 1990 revised ed 1997) *Tracing Your Scottish Ancestors* The Stationary Office, Edinburgh

Sinclair, Cecil (1994) *Tracing Scottish local history* Edinburgh HMSO

Smout, T C 'The trade of East Lothian at the end of the 17th century' in *East Lothian Antiquarian & Field Naturalists' Society Transactions Vol IX* pp. 67–78

Snodgrass, C (1953) *The Third Statistical Account of Scotland: the County of East Lothian* Oliver & Boyd

Whatley, Christopher A. (1987) 'The Fettering Bonds of Brotherhood: Combination and Labour Relations in the Scottish Coal Mining Industry, 1690–1775' in *Social History XII* (1987) pp. 139–54

Withrington, D & Grant, I eds (1975 ed, 1790s) *The Statistical Account of Scotland: Volume II the Lothians* EP Publishing Ltd.

Wormald, Jenny (reprint 1997) *Court, Kirk & Community: Scotland 1470–1625* Edinburgh University Press

21
81 Witches of Prestonpans

– pardoned they are

Annemarie Allan

PROLOGUE – PRESTONPANS 1590

It is late autumn and the people of Saltpans, later to become Prestonpans, go about their business, unaware of the doom that will shortly engulf them.

From the harbour at Acheson's Haven, fishing boats head out over the water, threading their way between the seagoing trading ships which come laden with timber, iron and luxuries for the Lords of Prestoungrange, Preston and Seton. They will leave soon, anxious to avoid the winter storms, their holds filled with the coal and salt they will carry to their home ports across the North Sea – including Gothenburg in Sweden.

At the salt pans that give the town its name, workers are red-faced from the heat, sweating with the effort of piling coal beneath the huge pans where the salt is boiled out of the sea water. There are others outside, shivering with cold, passing bucket after bucket of water back to the shore. Colliers labour beneath the ground: men hacking out the coal, women and children loading the wicker baskets on their backs to lug the coal up endless stairs to the surface. The Lords of Preston and Prestoungrange are affluent men: salt is almost as valuable as gold in 16th century Scotland, and the town of Saltpans has the biggest concentration of industrial workers in the whole of Haddingtonshire.

Rumours are flying: it is said that David Seton, Bailie of Tranent, has instituted an accusation of witchcraft against his servant, Gelie Duncan. Whispers suggest that he has his eye on the estates of his kinswoman, the heiress Euphemia MacAlzean of Edinburgh, and Gelie has named her for a witch. This is exciting news. Though many witches have been arrested and executed elsewhere in Scotland, there has been no hint of witchcraft in Haddingtonshire since Jonet Fultoun fled the town of Saltpans in a great hurry over ten years ago. People still talk of her, and of her burning as a witch at Edinburgh.

Soon, the news spreads that Gelie Duncan has named two others: Agnes Sampson, the wise woman who cured Robert Bailey's lad of a sickness is one of them. It seems she got her healing powers not from God, but from the Devil. There is one other – and here the voices dip even lower in outraged glee – John Cunningham, respected local schoolmaster has been up to much mischief in and around the town, chasing one woman after another, working enchantments where his charm was not enough – even flying through the air at night when his neighbours thought him fast asleep in bed. There have been dark doings in the Kirk at North Berwick – people shiver as they repeat stories of corpses raided for bones to make corpse powder, of dancing and lewdness in the presence of the Devil himself. There is a delicious shivering dread in repeating the accusations – there is nothing to fear. North Berwick is a goodly distance from Saltpans.

The excitement reaches a new pitch of intensity with the news that King James himself has taken an interest in the three witches – it seems that the plot unearthed by David Seton was worse than anyone had suspected: it was

King James I & VI. Reprinted by kind permission of Glasgow University, Department of Special Collections

treason, directed against the reigning monarch and instigated by that devil in the form of a man, Francis Stewart, Earl Bothwell. There are those who scorn such rumours, pointing out that this is no magic conspiracy, merely an attempt by David Seton to feather his own nest at the expense of another – as everyone knew at the outset. The voices of reason are ignored.

Jonet Straton has been named by Agnes Samson and taken for a witch – she has reported another more serious witch convention and this one not at North Berwick, but at Acheson's Haven. Though the boats ply their trade in daylight, at night it seems the harbour at Saltpans has been a meeting ground for many witches – as many as a hundred have gathered there to practice their evil art. Some say this is not surprising. My Lord Prestoungrange, Mark Ker, has long been known for his association with the arcane – those who serve in his great house tell of a whole room given over to a celebration of sorcery, richly panelled and painted in red, and the ceiling covered in figures of lewd demons and serpents. And all agree that Acheson's Haven itself has a strange reputation for mystical doings. But these things are only whispered of, not spoken aloud. Lord Prestoungrange is a close friend of the King.

Rumour slows as the witch hunt moves closer to home but then comes further news. John Cunningham – renamed Fian by the Devil, his master – had escaped! No-one saw him return to Saltpans, nor his recapture. But this is not surprising for one who can call on the supernatural power of hell itself to come to his aid. There are those who breathe easier when further news comes that Fian has retracted his confession, denying his pact with the Devil. But the die is cast. The King has his eye on the people of Saltpans.

Agnes Sampson is persuaded by torture to name many others. There is no more salacious gossip, no laughter at the antics of the witches, no excited rumour-mongering concerning the doings of Earl Bothwell. People eye each other uneasily, wondering who it was that took part in the spellmaking at the Fiery Hills of Acheson's Haven, casting a cat into the waters to create violent storms at sea, crossing the water in leaky vessels to sink the ships that pass up and down the busy waterway of the Firth of Forth, passing an image of the King from hand to hand to create an evil enchantment and bespelling poison from a toad, one drop of which will see an end to His Majesty's life.

Others, less credulous, nonetheless still fear their neighbours, knowing that

Newes from Scotland.
Declaring the damnable life of Doctor Fian a notable Sorcerer, who was burned
at Edenbrough in Ianuarie laſt.
1591.

Which Doctor was regiſter to the deuill,
that ſundrie times preached at North Baricke
Kirke, to a number of notorious
Witches.

With the true examinations of the ſaid Doctor and
witches, as they vttered them in the preſence
of the Scottiſh king.

Diſcouering how they pretended to bewitch and
drowne his Maieſtie in the ſea comming from Den-
marke, with ſuch other wonderfull matters
as the like hath not bin heard
at anie time.

Publiſhed according to the Scottiſh copie.

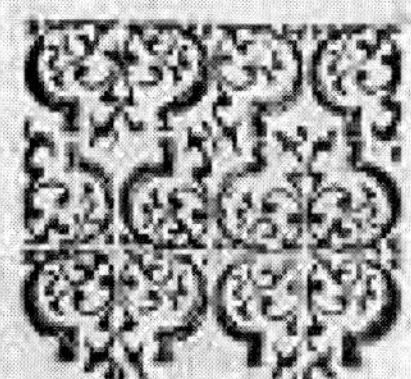

Printed for William Wright.

Front cover, Newes from Scotland. *Reprinted by kind permission of Glasgow University, Department of Special Collections*

accusation alone is enough to condemn them. George Mott's wife, a pillar of the community, has been arrested as an associate of the Devil. She has plotted treason with other witches at her home, as has Rob Grierson a skipper out of the Haven. They are both part of a conspiracy stretching all along the coastline. Women tremble at the news of their daughter's, their sister's, their mother's arrest. They know that the prickers who drive their sharp spikes into soft flesh in search of the witch's mark can bend even the most determined to their will. And if that does not suffice, then a few days or weeks – or even months – with little food and no sleep in the chill stone prison of the tolbooth will do the job.

It is not acceptable to hide from the enactment of punishment. Strangulation and burning are public spectacles. No-one wishes to draw attention to themselves by refusing to attend. While children watch their mothers burn, the smell of roasting meat fills the air, bringing a shameful response in those who see meat on their table not more than once or twice a year. This is the Devil's work, they tell themselves as they turn away. Not hunger, but the Devil's work.

Those who have lost family, friends, tenants and workers to the witch hunters are well aware that it is dangerous to draw attention to themselves. Instead they turn to God. But how can the people beg God for release? There has been no church for more than fifty years, not since it was burnt by the Earl of Hertford in reprisal for the Queen Regent's refusal to honour a marriage contract between her daughter and the son of the English King.

The people pray earnestly and desperately for a minister and at last their prayers are answered. The man is John Davidson and he is known to all for his fearless confrontation of the King in the pursuit of God's law. With Davidson's help, the people of Saltpans establish their church, bury their dead and look to the future.

The eye of the witch hunter turns elsewhere and the shattered community begins the painful process of rebuilding. But the eye will turn back. Saltpans has been marked. And for a further one hundred years, it is God and not the King who will root out those who have accepted the Devil's mark and made their pact with Satan.

The pricker

INTRODUCTON

The Scottish witch hunts of the 16th and 17th centuries formed part of a witchcraft panic which engulfed Europe from the early 1500s onwards. In Scotland, the witch fever took on a national dimension in 1590, when the entire nation, monarchy, nobility, church and people, were persuaded that witches sought to undermine the fabric of legitimate government in Scotland by focussing their malice on the person of King James VI, later King James I of England. These allegations were to have a profound effect on the residents of the small community of Prestonpans.

1. CONTEXT

From the 11th century onwards, Christianity in Western Europe had undergone a process of consolidation until, by the end of the 15th century, the authority wielded by the Roman Catholic church was immense. All religious and philosophical debate took place within this vast sprawling religious empire and huge areas of land throughout Europe were administered by the great monastic houses. Archbishops and cardinals were a significant political and religious presence in every country, with ultimate power vested in the hands of the Pope and his cardinals in Rome.

The relationship between European nobility and the clergy was close: higher clerics were members of the noble families and European monarchies often benefited from the affluence of the great monastic houses:

> "James V, for example, in 1532...had wrung permission from the Pope to appoint three baby sons, all illegitimate, to be titular abbots...The King thus got his bastards beautifully provided with an income at the churches' expense, but the monasteries were lumbered with the farce of a baby master."[1]

From its earliest days, the Christian church in Europe had faced divergence in religious belief: in Scotland, for example, the emergence of Roman Christianity included the absorption of a more localised Celtic form of Christian worship.[2]

However, by the late 15th century, the questioning and reinterpretation of established belief was moving gradually towards the establishment of alternative systems of worship. This splintering of Christianity was triggered by changes in the social framework: feudal society, with all its members integrated into an hierarchical structure reaching from peasant to monarch and its spiritual life guided by the Pope in Rome, could not accommodate the growing numbers of urban middle class who sought greater economic, social and political autonomy. In addition, many noble families such as the English Tudors resented the affluence of the church and its power to interfere in national politics.

Although often driven by secular issues, religious debate was nonetheless a genuine, deeply felt response to moral and philosophical issues. The rise of the Protestant faith was marked by an increased emphasis on personal responsibility: instead of worship mediated by the priest through the mass, scripture was seen as the source of religious truth and authority. And in the emergent technology of the printing press, dissenters found a powerful weapon for the spread of new ideas. Critics of the established church, such as Martin Luther, were able to disseminate their ideas swiftly and permanently: once printed, pamphlets could not be easily recalled and destroyed. This was, of course, a two-edged sword: John Davidson, for example, appointed first Reformation minister of Prestonpans in 1595 was, as a young man, obliged to flee the country when his criticisms of the Earl of Morton appeared in print without his consent.[3]

These religious changes were part of a wider philosophical revolution taking place at this time. A growing interest in the pre-Christian civilisations of Greece and Rome and in the native pre-Christian traditions of Europe produced a new breed of philosophers such as Desiderius Erasmus and, later, Francis Bacon, who challenged the absolute nature of the medieval world view. These Renaissance humanists sowed the seeds of individualism and the application of deductive reasoning typified by Scottish mathematician John Napier, who evolved his sophisticated system of mathematical calculation, known as 'Napier's Bones', during the late 16th century.[4]

To the modern mind, the growth of rationalism and deductive reasoning seems in conflict with a developing obsession with witchcraft. However, these efforts to create a rational structure for the universe were conducted within the context of deeply held religious belief, and the existence of God was proof that supernatural power did exist. There was no absolute means of determining whether the reality of magic and witchcraft was fact or fantasy since belief was based on a particular interpretation of observed events. There was nothing contradictory, for example, in the publication in 1685 of 'Satan's Invisible World Discovered', by George Sinclair, Professor of Natural Philosophy at Glasgow University and inventor of an early 'diving bell'.[5] Sinclair had already proved a man could breathe underwater and saw no reason to reject the notion that people might fly through the air as witches did. His publication of a collection of material on witches and fairies is anomalous only from a 21st century point of view.

Moreover, the presence of unseen influences was evident everywhere in everyday life. This was a period when epidemic diseases killed large numbers in town and country and these diseases clearly moved by some invisible means from one person to another.[6] In 1584, for example, when plague broke out in Perth, King James took immediate action:

> "...his majesty departed the same night...leaving his whole household servants enclosed in the place of Ruthven, with express command to them not to follow, nor remove forth from the same, until they saw what became of them upon the suspicion."[7]

The birth of rationalism, therefore, with its emphasis on deductive reasoning, in many cases actively contributed to the belief that witchcraft was a real and often malevolent force in society. It was in fact the attempt to provide a logical explanation for supernatural phenomena within a Christian context which encouraged the belief that witchcraft and magic were part of the arsenal of weapons wielded by Satan in his struggle against God.

2. THE DEMONIC PACT

In the pre-Reformation medieval period, charms, prayers and practical remedies used by healers, particularly among the poor, were an accepted fact of everyday life. Many pre-Christian beliefs were woven into the fabric of daily life and the practise of magic was not necessarily regarded as proof of demonic involvement. In Scotland, as in the rest of Europe, many customs and beliefs from pre-Christian religion were common and some, such as Halloween, survive even today.[8] In other cases, many of those who claimed supernatural powers were considered simply misguided, or insane.[9]

However, this relatively relaxed attitude to magic began to change as the supremacy of the Catholic Church was challenged:

> "Previously, the church had accepted and incorporated a great deal of popular folk belief; now it was consistently hostile to popular 'superstition', including both surviving Catholic practices...and rituals involving such things as fairies."[10]

For practitioners of both the old and the new religions, it was necessary to demonstrate adherence to a specific set of beliefs – there was no room on either side for alternatives. Those who rejected the dominant faith, whether by practising alternative forms of Christian worship or by employing magic, were acting on behalf of Satan, who sought the overthrow of God's kingdom on earth. Across Europe, Catholics and Protestants alike pursued a policy of apprehending and punishing the heretic. In Scotland, when the Catholic religion was in the ascendant, there were:

> "168 accused of heresy or otherwise identified by contemporaries as Protestant sympathisers in the period up to 1546"[11]

Any group bent on establishing conformity will seek a means to consolidate its sense of self by identifying 'outsiders', and the concept of heresy was applied to all alternative belief systems. Since the use of charms and spells did not conform to accepted practice, their use came to be viewed as a deliberate rejection of the true faith. Furthermore, in Protestant societies, the growth of the concept of personal responsibility facilitated the notion that those who indulged in heretical practices did so not through lack of understanding but through personal choice.

The '*Malleus Maleficarum*' or '*Hammer of Witches*', compiled in Germany in 1486 by two Dominican friars, demonstrates the growing belief that witchcraft was heretical and therefore merited severe punishment. Indeed, this document argues that not only those who practised witchcraft were guilty of heresy, but also those who refused to acknowledge its reality.[12] The conflict over belief systems was seen as the earthly representation of the battle between God and Satan. Witches could therefore only receive their powers by entering into a pact with Satan, whereby they renounced their baptism and undertook to be his servants:

> "the devil asks whether she will abjure the Faith, and forsake the holy Christian religion...then the devil stretches out his hand and so does the novice, and she swears with upraised hand to keep that covenant"[13]

Whether or not they used their power for good or for acts of 'malefice', ie to do harm, was irrelevant. Such power was a denial of true religion. Any evidence of magical practices was considered an indication that such a pact had been entered into. As to the question of why women were more frequently found guilty of the practise of witchcraft, the *Malleus Maleficarum* is quite clear:

> "...since they are feebler both in mind and body, it is not surprising that they should come more under the spell of witchcraft."[14]

This belief in the Demonic Pact was prevalent in both Catholic and Protestant cultures and the suggestion that someone had entered into such a pact was enough to secure a conviction in many subsequent trials:

> "The Pact was not universal in European countries which prosecuted witches. It featured relatively insignificantly, for example, in England...but [elsewhere] it became more important than accusations of malefice or sorcery in securing a conviction in a court of law."[15]

3. SCOTLAND IN TURMOIL

In common with the rest of Europe, Scotland in the 16th century was a nation in upheaval. New concepts of social order, new approaches to human understanding of the natural world and new systems of religious observance were to bring about radical social change, including the emergence of a religion ratified by the state but, unlike England, largely independent of its control.

The opening years of the 16th century saw Scotland poised between alliance with two others: France, a Catholic country, and England, which had rejected the authority of Rome. In 1503, the royal families of Scotland and England were united through the marriage between James IV and Margaret, eldest daughter of Henry VIII. By 1513, however, the Scots were invading Northumberland in support of France, a campaign which culminated in the disastrous battle of Flodden in which 8,000 Scots were killed, including the King.

The uneasy relationship between these three nations was acted out against the tide of religious change sweeping across Europe. There can be no argument that the most profound event in terms of the Scottish nation during the 16th century was the gradual establishment of the Presbyterian Church of Scotland. However, it is important to bear in mind that this was not simply a struggle between two forms of faith. What began as a debate conducted by disaffected catholic clerics on the flaws within the existing church became a separatist movement only in response to their frustration at the pace of change from within. In these early years, Presbyterianism was only one of a range of options. Moreover, this impetus for change was driven not only by religious considerations, but also by the nobility's eagerness to benefit from the affluence of the great monastic houses. From the twelfth to the sixteenth centuries, Prestonpans, for example, was part of the lands of Newbattle Abbey.[16] By 1549, Mark Ker, first Lord of Prestoungrange, was the abbey Commendator, responsible for the management of abbey lands and in charge of the income derived from these lands. In the years which followed, the Ker family gradually took over ownership of most of the land and property previously governed by the monks of Newbattle.[17] The progress of the Reformation movement towards establishment as the official church in Scotland was therefore inextricably linked with social and political issues, including not only the struggle for power between French and English sympathisers within Scotland but also those determined to retain Scotland's independent sovereignty.[18]

In 1527, the first designated martyr to the Protestant faith in Scotland was created when Patrick Hamilton's outspoken criticism of the Catholic church attracted the attention of David Beaton, Archbishop of St. Andrews. He was found guilty of heresy and burned in 1527.[19] Hamilton was a Catholic cleric who had been exposed to new ideas while studying abroad. The accusation of heresy, initially employed against clerics such as Hamilton, was later used to justify the arrest, examination and punishment of witches. Archbishop (later Cardinal) Beaton conducted a campaign of some force against the growing Protestant population and was responsible for the death of George Wishart, who arrived in East Lothian in 1546, when John Knox, Scotland's greatest religious reformer, was a resident at the house of Hugh Douglas in Longniddry:

> "Wishart was...conducted to the mansion of Longniddry. There he had an opportunity of communing with Knox, who, deeply interested in his missionary labours, became his companion from place to place, armed with a two-handed sword."[20]

After Wishart's arrest and imprisonment at Elphinstone Tower, home of the Johnstone family, Sir David Hamilton of Preston became involved in efforts to save his life. A daughter of this family later married John Ker, stepson of John Knox and the second post-Reformation minister of Prestonpans.[21] Knox's widow lived for a number of years with her son in Prestonpans[22] and his grandson, Samuel Pont, was baptised in the parish in 1609.[23] Wishart was executed in 1546: Cardinal Beaton was assassinated by several Protestant sympathisers later that same year.

4. THE GODLY STATE

It was against this background of religious dissent that the Scottish monarchy moved closer to France in 1538 with the marriage of James V to Marie de Guise. The year 1542 saw both the birth of their daughter, Mary and the death of King James V. An attempt to enforce a marriage proposal between the English and Scottish crowns triggered an English invasion which came to be known as the 'Rough Wooing', a period of considerable turbulence for East Lothian. However, by 1548, the infant queen was resident at the French court, with the government of Scotland in the hands of a succession of regents.

In 1557, the rise of Scottish Presbyterianism was confirmed when Protestant nobles signed a bond rejecting among other things, the 'Congregation of Satan', ie the Catholic church.[24] In the two years which followed, many others across all ranks of society added their names to this bond. During this period John Knox continued to express his discontent with the governance of his country, despite his enforced residence in England and Europe. In his pamphlet of 1558, 'The First Blast of the Trumpet against the Monstrous Regiment of Women', famous for its title if not for its content, he argues that any woman who exercises temporal or spiritual power over men is an instrument of the devil:

> "...it is a thing repugnant to the order of nature that any woman be exalted to rule over men. For God has denied unto her the office of a head...the nobility both of England and Scotland...[are] not only subjects to women, but slaves of Satan and servants of iniquity."[25]

This deep suspicion of women in positions of authority undoubtedly contributed to the much greater likelihood of a woman being accused of witchcraft than a man. In Scotland, 85% of accused witches were female.[26]

Within days of his return from exile in 1559, a sermon preached by Knox in Perth triggered a riot which resulted in the burning of two monastic houses.[27] The reformers subsequently expanded their influence across Scotland, allying themselves with England through the Treaty of Berwick. In spite of vacillation on the part of many of its supporters, in 1560 the Scottish Parliament declared the abolition of the mass, rejection of papal authority and the adoption of the Protestant faith. The 'First Book of Discipline', presented to Parliament in 1561, though not ratified by the monarch, Mary Queen of Scots, is nonetheless an important document, outlining a system of social control which was later successfully put in place and which had significant implications for the witchcraft outbreaks of the 17th century. The Protestant ministry was to be organised into superintendents, ministers, elders and deacons, a combination of ordained ministry and local laymen. Superintendents were considered to have the following responsibilities:

> "...to erect kirks, appoint pastors...examine the life, diligence and behaviour of the ministers...and the manners of the people: they must see how the youth were instructed and the poor provided for; and finally take cognisance of any crimes which called for the correction of the Kirk."[28]

In 1561, Mary returned to Scotland, the Catholic Queen of a country divided by religion and still enduring an uneasy relationship between France, England and its own sense of national identity. The conflict between Mary Queen of Scots, and John Knox, Scotland's greatest religious reformer, was a significant element in the turbulent years following her return.

Mary declined to ratify the edicts of the 'Reformation Parliament'. There seems, however, to have been perfect agreement between the various factions over one particular piece of legislation. In 1563, two years after her return to Scotland, Catholic and Protestant alike were united in the passing of the Scottish Witchcraft Act, part of a series of Acts aimed at criminalising unsocial behaviour. This Act, among the most draconian of such legislation in Europe and without expressing any definite belief in what it terms 'vain superstition', forbade, on pain of death, any use of magic. In addition, anyone who consulted a magic user was subject to the same penalty.

> "...na maner of persoun nor persounis of quhatsumver estate, degre, or conditioun they be...to use ony maner of Witchcraftis Sorsarie or Necromanccie nor gif thame selfis furth to have ony sic craft or knawlege thairof... Nor that na person seik ony help response or consultatioun..... the pane of deid, alsweill to be execute aganis the user abusar as the seikar of the response or consultatioun."[29]

The Scottish Act took:

> "The most extreme position with regard to the conflation of black and white magic...consulters of witches were said to be worthy of death in the same manner as practitioners...England continued to tolerate cunning men and women (who were quite distinct from black witches)...Major witch hunts in Scotland and on the continent on the other hand tended to engulf the healer along with the cursed."[30]

5. KING JAMES VI

In 1567, Mary Queen of Scots abdicated in favour of her infant son, King James VI, (later James I of England) handing him over to the care of Protestant nobles. In securing the person of the King, these nobles also secured the opportunity to educate him in the Protestant faith. As a child, James was little more than a game piece in the power play between various court factions. Once he reached adulthood and began his personal reign at the age of 21, suspicion and mistrust were ineradicable aspects of his personality, a fact which was to have significant implications in the context of the witch hunts which gripped the country throughout his reign and beyond.

Although the Earl of Morton eventually established himself as Regent for a considerable number of years, as a child James was constantly at risk from the political manoeuvring of various factions. Much of his childhood was spent at Stirling Castle under the guidance of his tutor, George Buchanan, a man of significant intellectual achievement and a fervent Calvinist.[31] Buchanan endowed James with a fondness for learning and a considerable facility in Latin. This intellectual precocity was allied to a strong sense of self-preservation and James learned very early to manoeuvre his way through the various court factions by avoiding confrontation wherever possible. Physically weak, it was his mental agility which allowed him to survive the often violent world of 16th century court politics. A contemporary description of the King as a young adult highlights the conflicts in his character, including his awareness that he lacked the physical presence necessary to gain the respect of his court. He was:

> "...wonderfully clever...full of honourable ambition and has an excellent opinion of himself...he is timid with great lords and seldom ventures to contradict them, yet his especial anxiety is to be thought hardy and a man of courage...his gait is sprawling and awkward; his voice is loud and his words sententious...His body is feeble...he is an old young man...he is prodigiously conceited."[32]

6. DEMONS AND DIVINE RIGHT

Nonetheless, as an adult, James successfully presided over a nation riven by different factions. The rising middle class saw the Protestant church as both a spiritual entity and a route to power, not merely independent of the state, but with significant control over the government of the country. At the same time the nobility – at war with itself in its quest for power – saw control of the person of the King as a route to supremacy. Lacking physical presence and with neither the willingness or the competence for confrontation, the King was nonetheless determined to establish his right to rule, basing his mandate for kingship on the authority of a higher power, ie as God's representative on earth.

The concept of 'divine right' was more usually associated with Catholic monarchs and it brought him into conflict with his Protestant subjects. George Buchanan, his childhood tutor, refused to acknowledge the concept of divinely appointed kingship, arguing that no monarch could act without the mandate of the people.[33] James, however, saw a true monarch as one:

> "...ordained for his people, having received from God a burthen of gouernement whereof he must be countable."[34]

According to James, a true King is created by God, and the power vested in him is of divine origin and therefore absolute:

> "...love that God, whom ye have a double obligation; first, for that he made you a man; and next, for that he made you a little God to sit on his throne and rule over other men."[35]

The concept of divine right has a direct bearing on the witch hunts which took place in Scotland: any supernatural act directed against the King or the godly society was seen as part of Satan's efforts to destroy God's kingdom on earth and was therefore undoubtedly demonic in origin. The King's interest in witchcraft was intense. His 'Demonologie', published in 1597, specifies both the dangers of witchcraft and the methods of dealing with it which were enforced during his reign, first as King of Scotland and subsequently of Britain.[36]

The Demonologie, though published in 1597, was probably written at some time in the course of the witch hunt of 1590–91.[37] As the wording of the 1563 Act implies, belief in witchcraft at this time was by no means universal and in part, the Demonologie is an attempt to refute the arguments of those who refused to acknowledge its reality. Reginald Scot, for example, writing in 1584, ridiculed the credulity of those who entertained such beliefs:

> "I for my part have read a number of their conjurations, but never could see anie divels of theirs, except it were in a plaie."[38]

Not only did King James strongly object to such disbelief:

> "...such assaults of Satan are most certainly practised, and that the instruments thereof merit most severely to be punished."[39]

but he also maintained the validity of torture as a means of extracting a confession, the reality of the Demonic Pact and its associated 'witch's mark' – the spot on the body marked by Satan and subsequently insensitive to pain:

> "...experience daily proves how loath they are to confess without torture, which witnesseth their guiltiness."...he [Satan] makes them to renounce their God and baptism directly, and gives them his mark upon some secret place of their body. Which remains ...thereafter ever insensible, howsoever it be nipped or pricked by any (as is daily proved)."[40]

Amongst a range of acceptable proofs for the practice of witchcraft he includes accusations by neighbours, a sorcerous reputation and the naming of another individual by a witch under interrogation. All these, he argues, are valid, since no innocent person can be falsely identified by servants of the devil. Once guilt is established, the penalty should be death with no exemption for sex, age or rank, including children.[41]

7. WITCHES AND THE NEW RELIGION

The new Protestant Church of Scotland strongly supported the King's desire to eradicate the perceived threat of witchcraft. In the 17th century in particular, witch hunts were frequently driven by local ministers, but even as early as the 1570s, John Knox is recorded as having harangued a woman accused of witchcraft from the pulpit at St. Andrews, afterwards watching her being burned to death.[42]

The process by which an individual came under suspicion of witchcraft often began with an accusation either by another witch under examination, by the local minister, or the local laird and, very commonly, accusations from neighbours. In the latter case, the issue of 'habit and repute' was crucial to any defence.[43] Unlike modern legal practice, a person's reputation was considered a valid element in the assessment of evidence. Some accusations were dropped early thanks to proof of respectability, but clearly, such an accusation would have an impact on the individual's reputation, who, once accused, would be more likely to come under suspicion in the future.

Evidence was collected from neighbours while the witch underwent local imprisonment and interrogation by the accuser and often by local church elders. Torture was, technically, not permitted without the issue of a legal commission. However, such legal considerations were often ignored in the witch hunts of the 15th and early 16th centuries. Suspect witches were 'walked', ie prevented from sleeping, for days and even weeks at a time. Often, clothing was removed, food was withheld and imprisonment was made as uncomfortable as possible – all of this before being convicted of any definite crime. During Cromwell's interregnum in the 1650s his commissioners reported a:

> "...woman that was suspected...to be a witch, was twenty-eight days and nights with bread and water, being stript stark naked, and laid upon a cold stone, with only a hair cloth over her. Others had hair shirts dipp'd in vinegar put on them to fetch off the skin."[44]

'Witch prickers' such as John Kincaid of Tranent, toured the country, inserting needles into the bodies of the accused in search of the 'witches mark'. Kincaid's:

> "method of testing witches was to stick a brad-awl, or a pin three inches long, into various parts of their bodies...Probably his awl...could be retracted into the hilt when the operator pleased, so as to deceive the eye of spectators."[45]

These practices – and further tortures if the crime was tried at a higher court – were all considered acceptable in compelling a witch to confess. If found guilty, sentence of execution, usually by strangling and burning, was often carried out locally. The final indignity was that, once convicted,

> "prisoners had to reimburse the courts for the costs of their torture, trial and execution."[46]

It is perhaps for this reason that the cost of execution for John Fian of Saltpans, the most famous of Scotland's alleged witches, is carefully itemised in the records:

> **"Cost of Execution of John Fian or Cuninghame :**
>
> Item, to the wricht for setting the stoupe 10s
> Item, for ten laid of coillis at vs viij the laid 64s 4d
> Item, for twa turs of hedder 9s
> Item, ane turs of brome 3s 6d
> Item, vj tar barrellis and for careing of thame to the hill 20s
> Item, 2 dry barrellis 5s
> Item, for towis 3s
> Item, for waiting upon the fyre 2s
> Item, for carying the stoupe to the hill 8d
> Item, to the lokman and his man 6s 8d
> Total £5 18s 2d"[47]

8. A FRAGMENTED HISTORY

Although the witch hunts clearly had a profound impact on society in Scotland during this time, a study of the impact of these events is subject to certain limitations:

> "...the total number of executions, let alone the number of prosecutions, for witchcraft, can never be known...far too many records have been lost or destroyed...the surviving records demonstrate the indifference to formal and regular detail of a pre-bureaucratic age. Names are not always given. There are frequent references to 'many witches'. Verdicts are omitted."[48]

In addition, these records often ignore additional deaths among those who were suspected but did not suffer the full process of the law:

> "... those who had committed suicide while in prison...those who died from torture, ill-treatment or neglect in prison...those who had committed suicide or fled before their arrest, those who had been acquitted...given minor punishments, banishment or merely admonished..."[49]

In the case of Prestonpans, the ministers of the 16th century parish are recorded as having participated in a number of witchcraft trials. However, direct access to the parish minutes is not possible: The original records have disappeared and material held in Scotland's National Archives comprises a heavily edited version produced in the 18th century which makes no reference to witchcraft.[50]

Difficulties in terms of such fragmentary documentation – much of it lost, destroyed, held in undocumented private collections or in many cases never recorded at all – is compounded by the complex and varied legal processes from accusation to trial and verdict. Scottish law was administered by a range of courts: baronial courts trying local offences; Regality Courts exercising central authority on a devolved basis which functioned in tandem with Sheriff Courts; the central criminal court or Court of Justiciary, which tried cases either centrally or through travelling courts, the 'Justice Ayres' and the Privy Council, which operated at the highest level, but could intervene in the legal process at any point.[51]

Furthermore, the laws governing witchcraft were not static. Before 1563 the church dealt with witchcraft, but punishment was enacted by secular powers. In 1563, the Witchcraft Act criminalised witchcraft and in October 1591 the privy council established six commissioners to enquire into witchcraft cases. This commission, empowered to send suspects for trial and authorise the use of torture, encouraged a proliferation of prosecutions of the early 1590s.[52] Between 1592 and 1597, commissioners from the Kirk and Privy Council were permitted to distribute standing commissions for the prosecution of witches at local level, after which this power was withdrawn and the privy council thereafter considered each individual request for a commission to hold a witchcraft trial.[53]

The 17th century saw further changes to the law. In contrast to the state-driven witch panic of 1590–91, much of the subsequent business of identifying, imprisoning and interrogating witch suspects was, as mentioned above, the preserve of the Kirk Session.[54] The Kirk, however, was not significantly involved in Prestonpans in 1590. At this time the town had no minister and indeed, no church, the original having been destroyed by the Earl of Hertford during the 'Rough Wooing' of 1544.[55]

It is also difficult to determine why witchcraft persecution should occur in one place and not another. The Highlands of Scotland, for example, appear to have experienced relatively little in the way of 'witch panics' compared to Fife and the Lothians.[56] In the case of East Lothian, or Haddingtonshire as it was formerly known, of all the cases recorded prior to the late 1580s, only one refers to a case in East Lothian. Witchcraft trials did occur during this period: the University of Edinburgh database, the 'Survey of Scottish Witchcraft lists 112 witchcraft cases between 1550 and 1588.[57]

However, in the case of Haddingtonshire, the trigger seems to have been the national panic of 1590–91. Between the years 1590 and 1690 Haddingtonshire recorded a total of 542 cases, the highest of any county in Scotland, despite the fact that relative to other lowland counties of Scotland, its population was fairly small.[58] Although there is no valid means of determining why Haddingtonshire did not pursue witches with any great vigour before the 1590s, the trigger for its subsequent witchcraft obsession is, by contrast, relatively easy to pinpoint: the marriage of the King, by proxy, to Anne of Denmark at Copenhagen on 20 August 1589.

9. THE WITCH PANIC OF 1590–91

It was intended that the King's bride would travel to Scotland in autumn, 1589. However, the Queen's fleet was hindered by both bad weather and a leaky vessel. On several occasions the ships were forced back and, after a final effort in November 1589, the Queen settled in Oslo to wait for better weather. The storms which plagued the fleet also resulted in the sinking of the ferry between Burntisland in Fife and Leith, just outside Edinburgh, with the death of most of the passengers and crew, including Lady Mary Melville of Garvock, on her way to welcome the queen.

> "...Sche being willing to mak deligence, wald not stay for the storm to saill the ferry; wher the vehement storm drave a schip forceably upon the said boit, and drownit the gentilwoman, and all the personnes except twa."[59]

King James, waiting anxiously for news of the fleet, spent his time close to Edinburgh, including a stay near Prestonpans, at the home of Robert, 6th Lord Seton. From Seton House he no doubt had a clear view of the stormy waters which separated him from his bride. By the end of summer, he had waited long enough and undertook the journey to Norway to meet his bride – an uncharacteristically decisive choice which placed him in some degree of personal danger. James sailed in October 1589 and despite contrary winds, arrived safely in Oslo six days later. He and his bride spent the winter in Denmark and by May 1590 they were in Scotland.[60] These three events: the sinking of the ferry, the delayed arrival of the Queen and the contrary winds affecting the King's voyage were the core of truth at the centre of the various 'dittays' or indictments in the witchcraft trials which followed.

In the summer of 1590, two women were burnt at Kronborg in Denmark, having been found guilty of using witchcraft to raise storms to impede the Queen's voyage.[61] By July, news of this witch hunt had followed the royal couple to Scotland. Physically weak and fearful of personal injury, it is probable that James welcomed this news: it confirmed that his fear was not for personal reasons, but for the future of a state without its divinely appointed King.

According to Walter Scott:

> "James was self-gratified by the unusual spirit which he had displayed on his voyage in quest of his bride and well disposed to fancy that he had performed it in positive opposition ...to the malevolent purpose of Hell itself."[62]

Clearly, the King's determination to fetch his bride in the face of opposition from Satan himself gave him, in his own mind at least, the heroic stature which he craved.

10. CONSPIRACY

The accusation of treason through witchcraft was not new to Scotland. In 1479:

> "The Earl of Mar, brother of James III...fell under the King's suspicion for consulting with witches and sorcerers...the unhappy Mar was bled to death in his own lodgings without either trial or conviction."[63]

In 1577, a little over ten years before the arrests of 1590, Violet Mar of Perth had been tried and executed for treason by attempting to kill Regent Morton through witchcraft. These two examples clarify the social changes Scotland had undergone between the late 15th and late 16th centuries: the King's brother was executed without trial – Violet Mar, thanks to the Witchcraft Act of 1563, was tried and executed by established legal process.

It is clear that that East Lothian's involvement in the events which followed the King's return was to some extent the result of geographical factors: any supernatural plot against the well-being of the King and his family would require the conspirators to be placed at various locations along the coastline of the Firth of Forth,[64] and in November 1590, when David Seton, bailie of Tranent, instigated the examination of his servant, Gelie Duncan, on charges of witchcraft, the King took an immediate interest in the case.[65]

It seems likely that Gelie Duncan's arrest was motivated by personal gain supposedly to assist David Seton in acquiring the estate of his relative, Euphemia MacCalzean.[66] No doubt Seton was encouraged by the family feud centred on Lady Foulis of Rosshire, which smouldered on in a series of accusations and counter-accusations of witchcraft from 1576 up to the end of the 16th century,[67] reaching one well-reported climax in the summer of 1590.[68] Among those named by Gelie Duncan in early depositions were John Fian, a schoolmaster from Saltpans and Agnes Sampson, a healer, of Nether Keith, near Humbie. This discovery of witchcraft in Tranent, close to the coast, was enough to persuade the King that this might provide the answer to the question of who was responsible for the dangers that had plagued him and his household.

The case of Gelie Duncan would have been known to King James through his association with James Carmichael, a Haddington minister who may well have participated in an earlier interrogation of Agnes Sampson at Haddington in May 1590. Carmichael is widely believed to have been the author of 'Newes from Scotland' a sensationalist pamphlet published in 1591, describing the arrest, torture and confession of John Fian and others.[69] This pamphlet attempts to take events to a new level of conspiracy, describing a plot by the devil to destroy his greatest enemy on earth, Scotland's divinely appointed King.

By December 1590, when the first of those accused of treasonably plotting the death of the King and members of his court were interrogated in Edinburgh, a link between Denmark and Scotland had been established:

> "...in the midst of the firth they met with the [witch] of Coppenhown [Copenhagen], where they commoned together."[70]

The names of those implicated by the North Berwick witches extended beyond the affluent middle class into the nobility, including the English ambassador, Robert Bowes who, though briefly mentioned, was never seriously considered a likely suspect.[71] But the most famous of the alleged conspirators was undoubtedly Frances Hepburn, fifth Earl of Bothwell and the King's cousin.

The King's relationship with his cousin was an uneasy one. Unlike James, Bothwell was a dynamic individual of a type becoming anachronistic in a society which placed increasing emphasis on social order and control. James was:

> "...bookish and machiavellian, Bothwell was intelligent and with an aristocratic pride comparable to James's sense of royal privilege."[72]

Bothwell was also aggressive. In 1584 he participated in an attack on members of the Hume family and:

> "killed all three, but hewed Davy Hume...all to pieces."[73]

Bothwell frequently disrupted the King's life, often arousing fear and consternation by forcing his way into the King's presence supported by men and weaponry. James, typically, attempted to appease this alarming figure: when James set off to fetch his bride, Bothwell was not only, as lord high admiral in charge of the fleet which brought the royal couple home, but was also named second in command of the government during the King's absence.[74]

James appears to have used a typically double-sided approach in his efforts to control his unruly cousin, part conciliatory, part accusatory. By 1593, James took advantage of the various accusations against his cousin when Bothwell was tried for employing witches in various attempts on the life and well-being of the King. Bothwell defended himself vigorously, but ultimately unsuccessfully, and left Scotland. He died in exile in Naples in 1612.[75]

Of the high ranking individuals named as conspirators, only one, Euphemia MacCalzean, was executed. In June of 1591, she was found guilty of various acts of both witchcraft and treason. Her death was horrific. She was not so much burned as baked alive:

> "...taken to the castle hill of Edinburgh and there bound to a stake and burned in ashes, quick [alive] to the death and all and sundry her lands, heritages...and gear to be forfeited and escheat to our sovereign lord's use."[76]

Almost immediately after her death, officially notarised documents were signed by those who had testified against her, proclaiming her innocence[77] and most of Euphemia MacCalzean's forfeited estates were returned to the family – presumably including David Seton – in June 1592.[78]

11. THE RANK AND FILE

Although high ranking individuals such as the Earl of Bothwell and Euphemia MacCalzean were an essential component in the existence of a conspiracy aimed at the highest in the land, the validity of such a conspiracy is also dependent on large numbers of supporters. In the case of the Earl of Mar in 1479:

> "...twelve women of obscure rank and three or four wizards, or warlocks, as they were termed, were burnt at Edinburgh, to give a colour to the Earl's guilt."[79]

In terms of those who were identified as conspirators at local level, the earliest surviving records of the events of 1590–91 are the interrogations of Gelie Duncan and Agnes Sampson in Edinburgh in December 1590. The only official record relating to John Fian is the 'dittay' from his trial that same December. However, Fian's fame was assured by the notorious 'Newes from Scotland':

> "declaring the damnable life and death of Doctor Fian, a notable sorcerer, who was burned at Edinburgh in January last, 1591."[80]

'Newes' is typical of the type of prurient, sensation-mongering journalism which remains with us to the present day. It includes elements which, even without the account of witchcraft and sorcery, make it clear that its publisher was not excessively concerned with the truth. It describes how Fian accidentally charmed a cow which followed him:

> "forth of the church and to what place soever he went, to the great admiration of all the townsmen of Saltpans"[81]

This is clearly a fabrication, not simply because of the magic but, in purely practical terms, because Saltpans at this time had no church.

It is therefore difficult to judge the truth of the pamphlet's descriptions of torture inflicted on the accused. However, if these are valid, then the accused were subjected to extreme pain. In the case of Fian, torture instruments included the 'bootes' (an iron frame which used wooden wedges to crush the legs and bones) and the 'turkas' used to tear out fingernails. Gelie Duncan was subjected to the 'pilliwinkes' or thumbscrews and 'thrawing', ie securing her head with ropes and jerking it from side to side.[82]

Both the official records and 'Newes from Scotland' agree that it was through the King's own interrogation that Agnes Sampson confessed her treasonable actions,[83] although 'Newes' declares torture was used to encourage her. The King participated in a number of interrogations and followed the trials with interest, even to the extent of questioning the verdict of the assize in the case of one of the accused, Barbara Napier.[84]

This case of Barbara Napier, where the King made clear his resentment of the court's failure to enact the sentence of execution, also offers an insight into the attitude of the kirk to witch persecution and highlights the continuing struggle between church and state even in the pursuit of a common goal:

> "Mr Johne Davidsone said likewise, in the morning doctrine, that it appeared by the evill successe he [James] had in executioun of justice, so farre, that he had not power over a carline witche, naming Barbara Naper; that he and his counsell were not assisted by God, and that, because he had not repented sufficiently for his former sinnes."[85]

The statement that the King was not supported in his actions by God was not likely to be well received by a monarch who claimed his Kingship was divinely appointed. Two days later:

> "...Davidson was brought before the court with other members of his Presbytery when the King demanded that they should desist from using such public censures... discussion turned upon that ever-recurring question – the power of the King and the jurisdiction of the Kirk."[86]

It is clear that the Kirk, at least, did not see James as having higher authority than their ministers:

> "Mr Johne Davidson went doun to the Palace, to speeke with the King...He admonished him of neglect of justice, carelesse appointing of the ministers of justice, placing unfit men in offices, granting remissiouns."[87]

The most famous event described in the various documents associated with the witch persecutions of 1590–91 is undoubtedly the alleged convention at North Berwick Kirk, the place chosen by the witches to meet with the devil to celebrate their successes and make future plans. The earliest map of the area of sufficient detail, by John Adair in 1736, offers a possible reason for this: North Berwick, located at the point where the river meets the sea, was the only settlement with a church overlooking the coast.[88]

However it was not the citizens of North Berwick who became the focus for this witch hunt, but the residents of Tranent and Prestonpans.

12. A COMMUNITY UNDER SUSPICION

Prestonpans was the closest coastal settlement to Tranent, source of the original accusation by David Seton. It provided an appropriate mid point for a conspiracy stretching from Leith to North Berwick and boasted a well established harbour. Moreover, by 1590, the town already appears to have had some degree of sensitivity towards the issue of witchcraft: Jonet Fulton of Leith, who was strangled and burned in 1579, was obliged to move from Prestonpans some time before this due to a reputation for witchcraft.

Apart from its geographical suitability and close proximity to Tranent, there are a number of other possible reasons why the town was likely to attract suspicion. The area around the harbour at Acheson's (Later Morison's) Haven, formerly Prestongrange Colliery and now the site of the Prestongrange Industrial Heritage Museum, has been mined for coal for many hundreds of years. Local tradition reports that coal deposits did catch fire at various times[89] and Janet Stratton's description of the area around Morison's Haven as the 'Fiery Hills'[90] suggests that the coal workings there may have been on fire at some time. This would give the landscape a somewhat fearful appearance, as such fires continued to smoulder on, often underground, for many years.

Acheson's, or Morison's Haven itself also has another claim to fame, as the location of the earliest records of any Masonic Lodge in the world, dating from 1599.[91] Masonic guilds had a reputation for interest in arcane matters such as geometry and alchemy which came to be associated in the popular mind with the use of magic. Although there is no record of the date when this lodge was established, the mason's guild had an official presence in Scotland from 1475[92] and it is therefore a reasonable assumption that the lodge at Acheson's Haven existed for some time before 1599. Though there is no evidence of significant involvement in the witch hunts on the part of the Masonic community, the King's master of works, William Schaw, undoubtedly knew the members of the lodge of Acheson's Haven and is recorded as participating in the interrogation of Agnes Sampson.[93]

Documents relating to the confessions and trials of the alleged conspirators establish Prestonpans as a significant locus for the conspiracy against the King, with the activities of witches in Edinburgh, Leith and elsewhere orchestrated by John Fian in Prestonpans. According to the various depositions, dittays and 'Newes from Scotland', a number of events allegedly took place in the area both prior to and following the infamous witch convention at North Berwick. These included meetings at various locations, including a number of houses in and around Prestonpans, such as Robert Grierson's house, from which the witches progressed to a Halloween meeting with a ship at sea, causing the ship to sink[94] and 'George Mot's backhouse' where they baptised a cat and tied bones from a corpse to its feet, then cast it into the water at Prestonpans in order to raise the storms which sank the Burntisland ferry and caused difficulties for the King's ship on its way to fetch his bride during September and October 1589.[95] Most damaging of all, however, were the activities alleged to have taken place during a witch's convention at the 'Fiery Hills' beside Aitcheson's Haven, the port of Prestonpans, on Lammas Eve (31 July) 1590, when:

> "Agnes Sampson, Barbara Napier and Euphame MacCalzean being at the Fiery Hills, Agnes Sampson raised the devil."[96]

This meeting was of primary importance in establishing guilt, for it was here that the witches took forward their treasonable plans for the death of the King by means of an enchanted picture and the use of poison extracted from the body of a toad. It was also the occasion for a number of damaging statements concerning the role of Francis, Lord Bothwell. Documents refer to up to eighty persons present at this meeting.[97] and Agnes Sampson in particular identified many individuals by name in the course of her enforced:

> "retelling of a story of witchcraft until that story becomes convincing as a narrative of treason."[98]

It is probable that Tranent, located on the lands of the Seton family, suffered equally with Prestonpans, which was under the control of the Kers of Prestongrange and the Hamiltons of Preston. However, it was Prestonpans, as the largest settlement in the area, which provided a ready supply of victims. The Adair map shows the town was not a great deal smaller than Haddington. It was surrounded by land farmed on the 'runrig' system mainly by residents of tiny 'farmtouns' – the First Statistical Account of Scotland, as late as the 1790s, lists a total of 60 resident in 13 houses at Dolphinston and Dolphinston Mains combined.[99] Tranent, situated slightly inland, and the coastal fishing hamlets also appear on the Adair map as much smaller settlements than Prestonpans, which was at this time already engaged in a range of rural and industrial activities including coal mining, saltmaking, fishing, farmwork and market gardening.

Furthermore, the population of Prestonpans, its salters and colliers, were considered to be among the lowliest of classes. Although their vital function in terms of the Scottish economy was recognised in various late 16th century statutes which brought them under the special protection of the crown, a further act of 1606 aimed at preventing people from escaping this difficult and extremely dangerous work declared these two types of worker tied to the land in perpetuity: they were, in effect, slaves to the landowner.[100]

It is also important to bear in mind when considering the impact of the witch hunts on a specific community that local settlements were closely linked through family ties. Beigs Wallace, of Preston in the parish of Prestonpans, who was burned in 1629, named her daughter, Jean Craig of Tranent as a witch. Twenty years later in 1649, her daughter was tried, found guilty and strangled and burned at Tranent.

13. THE LOCAL LORDS

Although the Kirk Session, with its rigid system of social order later became the major source of witchcraft accusations:

> "The Kirk Session, which identified so many witches, was a fully inquisitorial body. There was no jury, and the minister and elders combined the roles of prosecutor and judge...their primary role was coercive, stamping out ungodliness wherever it could be found."[101]

this was not yet fully the case in the 1590s, when the system of parish kirks was still in the process of establishing itself. Prestonpans, without a church or minister, had no local system of authority which might have mediated between its residents and the attentions of the nobility. This may in part explain why the first witch hunt, a relatively local affair, was colonised by the crown for its own purposes:

> "...the lord could, if he chose, dominate it [the town] completely."[102]

There is no record that the three major land-owning families in the area, the Setons, the Hamiltons and the Kers, took any steps to prevent the witch hunting on their lands. Indeed, the Seton family, in the person of David Seton, had already established their agenda in the witchcraft trials. In terms of the Setons, an important element in the progress of these accusations would undoubtedly have been the fact that the Setons were a Catholic family. A significant number of executions of 'catholic heretics' took place in Scotland throughout the early Reformation period[103] and the family must have been well aware that their religious affiliation put them at particular risk of the charge of heresy. Despite their interest in the outcome of the trials, they would undoubtedly have attempted to ensure that Seton lands did not figure too largely as named focus points for witchcraft activity.

It has been mentioned above that the Hamiltons of Preston were fervent supporters of the Protestant cause. Given their significant presence as commissioners and investigators of cases of witchcraft in the area during the course of the 17th century it would seem that some of the family at least were also committed to the hunting of local witches. Robert Hamilton, Bailie of Preston, was a commissioner in the cases against Margaret Mathesoun of Prestonpans and Beigs Wallace of Preston, both of whom were burnt locally in 1629. John Hamilton, bailie of Prestonpans was involved in the cases against 7 women in 1661 and, between 1628 and 1630, Patrick Hamilton of Preston was commissioner in a total of 24 accusations of witchcraft.

The remaining family, the Kers, are probably the most important in terms of the first witchcraft outbreak of 1590– 1591, since it was on the Prestongrange land owned by the Kers that much of the alleged activity took place. If the Setons were representative of the old Catholic nobility and the Hamiltons of the new Protestant hierarchy, then the Kers may be said to typify another group, the Renaissance humanists, who sought greater intellectual freedom than that allowed by adherence to the authority of the established church. Scotland's largest and best preserved example of renaissance ceiling decoration, the Prestongrange Ceiling, was commissioned by the first Mark Ker and completed in 1581. The wealth of images on this ceiling are a homage to the humanists of 16th century Europe, including the great French humanist Rabelais. It is an unequivocal statement that the Ker family considered themselves part of this cultured society.[104]

The family's religious affiliations are uncertain. Though not a catholic family like the Setons, there is some evidence that the first Mark Ker was not as confirmed a Protestant as his de-secularisation of the abbey lands of Newbattle might suggest: in 1560, during the early Parliamentary declarations of Protestant independence, John Knox commented:

> "...the chief pillaris of the Papisticall Kirk gave their presence, sick as the abbotis of Lendorse...Newbottill... and dyverse otheris..."[105]

Moreover his brother George was implicated in the treasonable affair of the 'Spanish Blanks' in 1592, when an alleged attempt at a Catholic conspiracy ended with George Ker's capture off the island of Cumbrae.[106]

There is also evidence of Mark Ker's attitudes to those who subsisted on land through his favour: in 1563 he was summoned before the Privy Council for evicting four of his tenants and ordered to pay a sum for their living expenses.[107] Although there is no record of the Ker family directly involving themselves in the witch hunt, this, together with the general attitude to salters and colliers mentioned above, suggests that the people who lived and worked on the lands of Prestongrange were not particularly valued by their lord.

The Prestongrange Ceiling, uncovered in the early 1960s, was originally thought to be evidence of satanic involvement on the part of the Ker family. Although this was not, in fact, the case[108] it seems likely that its existence may have contributed to a contemporary belief that the lands of Prestongrange were associated with satanic ritual. The death of Mark Ker the younger in 1609 was reputedly brought about by witchcraft[109] and sorcery was also blamed for the death of his son, the 2nd Earl of Lothian, when the Ker family's ownership of the lands of Prestongrange ended with the suicide of the debt-ridden Earl.[110]

14. WHO WERE THE ACCUSED?

It is difficult to arrive at precise figures for how many of those accused in the witch hunt were residents of Prestonpans. Many women, as was customary at this time, are listed in the records under their original, not married name. The 'wife of George Mot', for example, may therefore appear elsewhere under another surname.

Christina Larner lists 51 for Prestonpans/Preston during 1590–1591.[111] However, the Survey of Scottish Witchcraft lists only five. This second, much smaller, total is due to a number of people in the Survey who are listed under the presbytery of Haddington instead of their place of residence. The actual number for this particular outbreak of persecution is no doubt somewhere between these two extremes.

Local records can also help in identifying residents of Prestonpans. However, there are no church records for 1590–91, before the parish was established. Furthermore, as mentioned earlier, the Minutes of Prestonpans Kirk session for the 17th century are no longer available and the existing record contains no information about the years of witchcraft persecution in Prestonpans, despite the fact that two ministers of the parish are recorded as participating in trials. The only surviving record in what remains of the parish minutes of an individual who may be one of the accused is the marriage of Issobel Griersoun to William Nicholson in 1598.[112] A woman of the same name was the first recorded witchcraft suspect in Prestonpans during the 17th century. Records of wills can also be useful in determining whether at least the family names of witchcraft suspects were resident in Prestonpans during the 16th and 17th centuries. These wills were made by rich and poor alike, since the poorer classes used a will as a means of claiming goods, even of minimal value, or outstanding wages.[113] These wills confirm that a number of families, such as Grierson, Chouslie, Mott and Acheson, were residents of Prestonpans during this time. However, certain names, such as Acheson, were common all along the East Lothian coastline. Other names, such as Richesone or Carington can be traced through records of births, marriages and deaths[114] but, although these local records confirm residence, this does not necessarily confirm a family relationship.

The total numbers of accused collated from various sources for the 17th century correlate much more closely, comprising a figure between 38 and 41. Together with the figures from the 16th century, this indicates a minimum of 43 and a maximum – allowing for duplicates in Larner, who identified the number of trials rather than the number of individuals – of 81. These figures exclude those whose trial record is no longer available and those who died, fled or suffered in other ways.

In terms of establishing motive for the targeting of specific individuals, there is little evidence remaining. However, the saltpans were an enormously valuable resource and, given that David Seton appears to have a clear financial motive for instigating the original accusation against Gelie Duncan, it is possible that others, too, saw the witch hunt as an opportunity. There were a number of individual salt pan owners in Prestonpans in the 16th century, including George Mott, in whose home an alleged witches' meeting took place, Mott had a charter for a saltpan from Mark Ker in 1559 as did the Achesons, two of whom appear in the lists of accused.[115] Robert Griersonn may be the same Robert Griergsoun, skipper in Prestonpans, for whom a will is recorded in 1593.[116] However, as has been stated above, such relationships can only be speculative.

Despite these difficulties, it is clear that Prestonpans was a focus for the persecution of witches. Those who were imprisoned, tortured by the witch prickers and deprived of sleep until they were incapable of distinguishing fantasy from reality were likely to confirm and elaborate anything their examiners chose to introduce into their interrogations and, even from this distance in time, it is not difficult to imagine the ravaged community, where every mother, daughter or sister was only a whisper away from torture and execution. The damage that could be done to a single family is evident in the case of Margaret Hall of Prestonpans, who was investigated for witchcraft in 1661. Both her daughter and her mother were also accused of witchcraft. And not only women, it seems, were at risk: some cases also record the denunciation of husbands and fathers.

15. THE KIRK ESTABLISHED

The establishment of the parish of Prestonpans in 1595 is possibly one indication of how the community responded to their dire circumstances. In

1595, the Presbytery of Haddington proposed the appointment of a minister for:

> "South Preston and ye Panns, east and west and ye haill bounds yairabout, belonging, alsweill to my Lord Newbottle, as to ye laird of Prestoun."[117]

These were the lands belonging to the Kers, the Barons of Prestoungrange, and the Hamiltons. The Presbytery's choice for this ministry was none other than that perennial thorn in the King's side, the Reverend John Davidson.

Davidson was a man with a fervent belief in God and a clear understanding of the implications of individual responsibility. He gave part of his own personal fortune to the establishment of a church and school in Prestonpans. This was a new breed of Scottish Protestant; not a disenchanted cleric, but one whose whole upbringing was steeped in the Protestant faith. He was still a child when the Reformation Parliament of 1560 made its attempt to establish the Protestant faith as Scotland's official religion. Davidson was firmly against royal intervention in the affairs of the Kirk. While the crown was engaged in efforts to establish bishops within the church, Davidson was determined to reject any interference with the 'liberties of Presbyterianism'.[118]

No doubt this appointment contained elements of political expediency. Davidson was outspoken in his condemnation of anything he considered detrimental to the church and he may well have been something of an embarrassment to his more conciliatory colleagues:

> "...preaching against the King, denouncing the nobles as oppressors of their tenantry and condemning the Commons for imitating their vices."[119]

However, it seems that Davidson was not merely sequestered to a country parish to keep him out of trouble. This appointment was something the people welcomed. After Davidson's first sermon in Prestonpans, taking, perhaps significantly, for his text 'the people which sat in darkness saw great light', a 'great multitude' expressed their eagerness for his ministry and in 1596, Davidson became first minister for the newly established parish in Prestonpans.[120]

After some difficulty with Mark Ker, Lord Newbattle, Davidson gained permission to build a church and manse on lands belonging to the Hamilton family. It is doubtful if Ker had any fondness for John Davidson, who was probably the author of a tract giving an account of the Spanish Blanks episode involving George Ker.[121]

The people had their wish and a godly community was born, under the leadership of a man who was fearless in confronting the King and with a reputation for defending the people against the power of the nobility. With such a recent example of what befell those who were judged to have denied God, it is not surprising that Davidson's parishioners strove to lead a blameless life. Among those listed as participating in the first baptism following Davidson's appointment are the families of Acheson and Wallace.[122] Both of these names appear in the list of prosecuted witches in 1590–91.

In spite of Davidson's apparent enthusiasm for the pursuit of witches during his time at St. Giles, it does appear that his parishioners enjoyed a degree of relief from witchcraft prosecution once their minister was appointed: the 'North Berwick' case continued to rumble on but, as the witch panic gathered momentum elsewhere, by and large the remainder of the 16th century passed peacefully for the people of Prestonpans. Between 1592 and 1600, there were 146 recorded witchcraft cases in Scotland, only two of which were in East Lothian, despite a national panic in 1597 during which an estimated total of 400 cases occurred. It was:

> "another North Berwick – a major panic over treasonable witchcraft that was thought to be directed against the King personally."[123]

Despite his removal from Edinburgh, Davidson continued to irritate the King: in 1601 he was imprisoned in Edinburgh Castle for a day and subsequently confined to the bounds of his parish.[124] In 1603, when the King passed through the parish of Prestonpans on his way to set up permanent court in England, Davidson experienced at first hand the King's ability to bear a grudge. The King was leaving Scotland and John Davidson, now old and frail, would no longer be a source of irritation. The Presbytery entreated the King to allow Davidson the freedom to leave the parish bounds, to which the King replied, "he may lie and rot there".[125] Davidson died later that same year.

16. THE WITCH HUNT CONTINUES

By the time of the appointment of John Ker, stepson of John Knox, as minister to replace Davidson,[126] it would seem that the power of the church was affirmed in Prestonpans. But unfortunately for the town, it was the church and not the departed King which ensured the continuation of witchcraft persecution into the 17th century. By the 1640s, the Protestant witch hunt was in full force in Prestonpans. In many cases, the imprisonment and examination of suspects took place in Prestonpans itself and the enactment of sentence too, was frequently local.

By this time, much of the local policing of antisocial behaviour had been taken over by the Kirk session and this brief included crimes of witchcraft. John Oswald, minister of Prestonpans between 1646 and 1653, was an investigator in the 1649 case of Jeane Craig, the daughter of Beigs Wallace. Patrick Cook, his successor, is recorded as investigator in the trials of Helen Gibesone in 1661 and Christian Blaikie in 1662. There is no record of the Ker family participating in the witchcraft trials: however, this changed when ownership of Prestoungrange passed into the hands of the Morison family in the first decade of the 17th century.[127] Alexander Morison, later Lord of Sessions, was one of the commissioners in the case against Agnes Kelly in 1678.

Unlike the previous century, the pattern of witch hunting in Prestonpans was by this time a reflection of national patterns. But once a neighbourhood was established as a locus, it was permanently identified as a potential place of witchcraft activity and Prestonpans, together with Tranent, was firmly established in the national consciousness as a place where witches congregated:

> "Within these general areas there were certain small towns and villages which appear again and again. Tranent and Prestonpans were places which featured both in the first witch-hunt and in all the major hunts...Where there were local memories of actual burnings it was relatively easy to stimulate them again."[128]

Between 31 and 39 persons from the parish of Prestonpans were recorded as being involved in witch trials between 1600 and 1679, the date of the last recorded accusation of witchcraft in the town. Compared with the totals from the 1591 witchcraft trials, this may seem a relatively small number over a period of almost eighty years. However, these figures reflect specific periods of intense witch hunting activity. During the period 1628–29, seventeen people from Prestonpans were tried on charges of witchcraft, almost 50% of the total for the period, twelve in the years 1659–62, a major period of witch hunting across Scotland, then a further four in 1678–79.

The earliest recorded witchcraft trial in Prestonpans in the 17th century was the case of Issobel Griersoune in 1607. Although it is certain that the Grierson family were long established residents of Prestonpans[129] there is no record of whether she was related to the Robert Griersonn who was at the centre of many of the allegations in 1590–91. Issobel was not particularly well off. Her husband is recorded as a working man. She appears to have been a woman of intemperate habits, a dangerous thing at the time, given to colourful cursing and involved in various disputes with her neighbours. She was strangled and burnt on Castle Hill in Edinburgh. David Seton's involvement in the trials of Beigis Tod, first implicated in 1591, but tried and executed in 1608 and Isobell Griersoune in 1607 is the final record of his activities as a hunter of witches. His existence, however, is still recorded in the town of Tranent:

> "To the north of the churchyard of Tranent...stands an old dove-cot...Above the now doorless doorway of the dovecote a tablet of sandstone is still to be seen...now all but effaced by time and the weather, and still bears the name of David Seton, and the date, 1587...On reading the inscription, one remembers with a shudder that this was the name of the deputy bailiff in Tranent...who, in the year 1591, was the prime mover in the crusade against witchcraft."[130]

This inscription is still faintly visible today.

The witchcraft trials of 1628–29 are not recorded in any great detail. However, as well as the Hamilton family, the Johnstones of Elphinstone are also recorded as participating in many of these trials. This family have already been mentioned as close associates of John Knox: a member of this family was the wife of John Ker, stepson of Knox and minister of Prestonpans parish from 1605 to 1644.[131]

During the period 1658–1662, a number of individuals in Prestonpans were denounced, some of whom appear to have come under suspicion because of James Welsh, a young beggar boy who offered a rich resource for witchcraft investigators with his descriptions of witches, fairies and various magical events and whose childish imaginings foreshadow the future pattern of many witchcraft accusations, including those at Salem in Massachussets in 1692 and the case of Christian Shaw in Paisley in 1697. These young people became involved in witchcraft accusations from a variety of motives: in the case of James Welsh, presumably he was fed and sheltered while his evidence was taken. Christian Shaw may have been ill. The Salem outbreak was, perhaps the most tragic since it appears likely that the trigger for this savage witch hunt was simple boredom:

> "These Salem Village children had little to occupy their time but the drudgery of routine indoor tasks and the strict demands of their Calvinist

parents. Activities which stimulated mental or physical excitement were considered sinful by their elders."[132]

The last major local outbreak of witch hunting, in 1678, seems to suggest that the witch frenzy might be abating, since on this occasion it was the accusers, not the accused, who received censure from the law. Church and state seem to be concerned to distance themselves from the violence associated with witch hunting. Catherine Liddel:

"...exhibited a complaint against Rutherford, baron bailie to Morrison of Prestongrange, and against David Cowan in Tranent, bearing that they had seized upon her, an innocent woman, and had defamed her as a witch, and detained her under restraint as a prisoner; and that the said Cowan had pricked her with his pins in sundry parts of her body, and bled and tortured her most cruelly."[133]

Cowan, it appears, had learned his trade from John Kincaid the witch pricker from Tranent. Rutherford was discharged by the Privy Council with a reproof. David Cowan was sent to prison. The remainder of those involved in this case were an assortment of salters, mariners and others who do not appear to have any official standing, except perhaps William Atcheson, an officer. The minister of the parish of Prestonpans, James (or possibly John) Buchan, does not appear to have had any involvement with these events, which suggests that the malefactors were acting without community approval as well as legal authority.

Rutherford and Cowan did not limit their attentions to Catherine Liddel. In 1677 and again in 1678, in company with a different band of men, they had forced their way into the home of Elspeth Chousley and subjected her to the same ordeal as Catherine Liddel. On this occasion, local residents came to her aid, which suggests that by this time, or at least in this case, they had no fear of guilt by association. The malefactors also targeted Agnes Kelly and her servant Marjorie Anderson in an attempt to persuade them to incriminate Elspeth Chousley: this situation appears to have been a little more serious than Catherine Liddel's, since they were faced with a commission including Patrick Brown of Coulston, who was involved as commissioner in a large number of trials, and Alexander Morrison, baron of Prestongrange, whose bailie, Rutherford, was closely involved with the actions against Elspeth Chousley. Catherine Liddel, Elspeth Chousley and Agnes Kelly appear to have been relatively well-to-do: two at least were widows whose estates were their own. Perhaps these episodes were more to do with robbery than with fear of demonic activities.

17. SCOTLAND'S WITCH PANIC ABATES

Up until 1662, large-scale witch panics were the norm, with government commissions for trials being granted with minimal reference to individual circumstances. However, from 1662 onwards, there was a gradual decline in the pursuit of witches. To a large extent, this was the result of a wider process of centralisation of authority. Before this date,

"in more than 90% of all the trials conducted by local commissioners, the accused were convicted and executed."[134]

However, the national hysteria of 1661–1662, when 664 named witches in four counties were subjected to unauthorised arrests, torture and in many cases execution, (including 'several persons' recorded as burnt at Saltpreston in 1661) seems to have triggered a determination on the part of central government to prevent such illegal activities in the future.

From April 1662 onwards, the conduct of witchcraft trials was passed into the hands of professional legal representation and judgement.[135] The Privy Council expressed disapproval of the fact that:

> "many persons had been seized and tortured as witches, by persons having no warrant for doing so, and who only acted out of envy or covetousness. All such unauthorised proceedings were now forbidden."[136]

The proclamation issued by the Privy Council at this date did not immediately effect a reduction in the numbers of those arrested and tortured on suspicion of witchcraft. However, it did establish the illegality of many of these proceedings.

> "...a caution was given that there must be no torture for the purpose of extorting confession. The judges must act only upon voluntary confessions; and even where these were given, they must see that the accused appeared fully in their right mind."[137]

The system of circuit courts, initially enforced under the rule of Cromwell was continued after the crowning of Charles II in 1660. Commissions required the presence of a justice-depute from Edinburgh, ensuring that their verdicts were subject to central scrutiny.[138] Under this system, the practice of arrest and interrogation based on local 'habit and repute' was clearly no longer a validation for the arrest and torture of witchcraft suspects.

In 1689, the 'Claim of Right' by which Scotland accepted the rule of William of Orange increased the individual's legal protection from torture. Whereas before this, torture was considered a valid means of gaining evidence and extracting a confession, the Claim of Right specified that use of torture without evidence of crime was contrary to the law:

> "The Declaration of the Estates containing the celebrated Claim of Right (April 1689) asserted that 'the imprisoning of persons, without expressing the reasons thereof, and delaying to put them to trial, is contrary to law.' It also pronounced as equally illegal 'the using of torture without evidence in ordinary crimes.'[139]

This would not, however, have made any significant difference to the fate of the original victims of 1591, since their crime was not merely witchcraft, but treason, and torture was still considered acceptable in such cases. Nor does this increasing centralisation of authority mean that unauthorised witch hunting no longer took place, as can be seen from the 1678 cases in Prestonpans and elsewhere. In 1705, Janet Cornfoot from Pittenweem was tortured, stoned and eventually crushed to death, all without legal authorisation and the last recorded case of execution for witchcraft in Scotland, in Dornoch in 1727, was also carried out without reference to any valid judicial framework.[140]

18. THOU SHALT NOT SUFFER A WITCH TO LIVE

However, these changes in the law and society were still many years distant when James VI inherited the throne of England and was crowned in 1603 as James I of England. James brought with him the attitudes and beliefs formed as a child and developed during his years as Scotland's monarch. His 'Trew Law of Free Monarchies' published in 1603 reiterates the idea of sovereignty divinely granted, the belief which permitted him to interpret any act against that sovereignty as an act of the devil. One of his first acts as King of England was to strengthen the law against witchcraft in his new kingdom. The English Witchcraft Act passed, like the Scottish Act, in 1563, had limited the use of the death penalty to those found guilty of causing death by witchcraft. The Witchcraft Act of 1604 extended the English Act to include death by hanging for anyone attempting to bring about harm to another person through magic. This Act brought a significant increase in executions for witchcraft in England, most particularly during the 1640s.[141]

The King's attitude to witchcraft was clearly expressed not only in his Demonologie, but in the bible which bears his name, the King James version, published in 1611. Although a work of undoubted scholarship and vivid language, it is famous not only for its widespread popularity, but also for its famous – and probably deliberate – mistranslation of the phrase 'thou shalt not suffer a poisoner to live' as, 'thou shalt not suffer a witch to live'.[142]

However, it was not only the publications of the King and the church which fixed the concept of the malevolent witch in popular imagination. The exact publication date of Shakespeare's Macbeth is not known, but it was certainly at some point close to the early days of King James' arrival in England.

The tale of a kingdom torn apart by the murder of its lawful King, of the unnatural signs and portents which accompany the murder of Duncan, God's ordained monarch and the treasonable sorcery on the part of the witches incorporates all the major themes of the witch panics of the 1590s. References to the ancestry of King James in the character of Banquo make it clear that Shakespeare was linking his work of fiction to the person of the King and the details included within the play clearly reveal the author's familiarity with the description of events contained within 'Newes from Scotland'.[143]

The pursuit of witches did not, however, limit itself to England. By the time James succeeded to the throne of England, colonisation of the eastern seaboard of the American continent had already begun and the witchcraft act of 1604 has been identified as a primary cause of the most famous episode of witch persecution in America, the Salem witch trials of 1692.[144] Although the Protestants of England did not have the rigid social control which allowed witches to be pursued on the scale they were in Scotland, this did not mean they were not aware of the dangers of demonic power and willing to take steps to deal with it: Matthew Hopkins, the most notorious of English witch hunters, was the son of a Puritan clergyman. There were close links between the various Protestant communities in England and Scotland. John Davidson, for example, while exiled from Scotland due to his outspoken criticisms of the government, spent some time with the leaders of the English Puritan communities.[145] The Puritan settlements of New England and Massachusetts incorporated the attitudes and beliefs they had developed in England.

Large scale Protestant immigration to America began in 1620 and the colony at Salem was established only a few years later, in approximately 1626. As in Britain, the crime of witchcraft was punishable by death and from 1650 onwards, a number of cases were recorded in New England, often involving the accusations of children. Cotton Mather, a church minister and son of the colonial ambassador to England, Increase Mather, was closely involved in one case of 1688, publishing a detailed account of the sorcerous practices conducted in particular by one woman, Mary Glover.[146] To some extent, Salem Village represented a meeting of cultures between the European belief in witchcraft and the 'voodoo' magic known to servants in the village. As with the arrests and trials associated in Scotland with James Welsh, it was young people who were the driving force behind the witch panic, which culminated in 1692 with the arrest of 200 people, and the execution of 24. Although the total number of those executed for witchcraft in America compared to Scotland and England is, relatively speaking, very small, it nonetheless stands as a major example of the savage potential of witch panic: in a single year, 20 people were executed in the tiny community of Salem.[147] It is ironic to consider that the attitudes which drove the witch panics of Scotland and arrived in England with the coronation of King James VI, then travelled thousands of miles to impact upon the communities of those who had left Britain in protest against persecution for their beliefs.

It is interesting to note that once again, a major contributor to our appreciation of the significance of witchcraft persecution is a work of fiction: 'The Crucible' by Arthur Miller. Though written more than 250 years after the events at Salem the play clarifies the reasons why these events should not be forgotten. Its purpose is not so much to tell a story of 17th century America, but to use those events as a warning against contemporary persecution at a time when the 'House Committee on UnAmerican Activities', driven by a panic-fuelled fear of Communism during the 1950s interpreted the refusal of witnesses to speak or to incriminate others as proof of guilt.[148] 'The Crucible' is a warning against complacency, a reminder that what has happened in the past can, in another form, impinge upon the present.

It is no accident that the Columbus Centre for the study of the dynamics of persecution and extermination took as its two major area of study both the program of Jewish extermination in Nazi Germany and the European witchcraft persecution of the 16th and 17th centuries.[149]

19. AFTERMATH

In 1736, amendments to the Witchcraft Act reduced penalties to imprisonment or a fine. This Act took the stance that witchcraft was non-existent and its implementation was reserved for those who sought to profit from faking such abilities. This does not mean to say, however, that belief in witchcraft could be eradicated by statute:

> "People growing up in Caithness and Sutherland in the 1870s 'all believed in the reality of witchcraft' because they all personally knew witches."[150]

Belief in witchcraft has persisted throughout the years since the witch panics of the 16th and 17th centuries and indeed in recent years, has gained ground, as is evident from the numerous 'wiccan' sites accessible through the

Helen Duncan of Callander. The last person convicted under the Witchcraft Act

internet. In Acheson's Haven itself, as late as the 1920s, a woman who could cure warts was considered to be a witch of the healing variety.[151]

A comparison between various areas of Scotland reveals that East Lothian, and Prestonpans in particular, suffered more from witchcraft persecution than any other location in Scotland, with the largest recorded number of accusations for any town, even much larger settlements such as Aberdeen.[152] It is clear that, acknowledged or not, these events are deeply embedded in the national consciousness. A junior school history of Scotland, published in 1854, gives the following account:

> "...it was alleged that, in conjunction with certain witches, he [Bothwell] had modelled a waxen image of the King, which was afterwards held before a slow fire with the intent that, as it melted away, James should grow sick and die. He was further accused of preparing a very potent poison from the skins of adders and toads, with an essence extracted from the head of a young foal, and which was to be so placed that it might fall on the King's head, a single drop being sufficient to destroy life."[153]

Despite changes in the law, the spectre of witchcraft continued to haunt British society: In 1944, Helen Duncan from Callander was convicted under the

Witchcraft Act of 1736, a trial which generated interest throughout the United Kingdom, including the involvement of the Prime Minister, Winston Churchill. Although this act specified witchcraft as a practice of charlatans, it was used in this case because the authorities feared her clairvoyant powers enabled her to predict details of wartime movement of shipping. She spent nine months in prison. Not until 1951 was the Witchcraft Act finally repealed when Sir Winston Churchill was once again in office at 10 Downing Street.

20. AT LAST A PARDON WAS GRANTED

In July 2004 the Barons Courts of Prestoungrange and Dolphinstoun issued their Pardon, four months before their right to exercise such an option was removed from Scotland's remaining Barons Courts by Act of Parliament. This Pardon was similar in intent to the General Court Resolve issued at Salem, Massachusetts in August 1957, absolving those accused of witchcraft of any guilt.[154] Since many of those tried and executed in Prestonpans were also found guilty of treason, a crime which can only be tried by Higher Courts, the Barons Courts also petitioned the Crown personally for a review of these cases in the hope of a further Pardon from Her Majesty. It was alas referred to Her Ministers who indicated only the most extraordinary quantum of research could enable the matter to be considered and that even then there was no precedent for successful outcome.

The Pardon for witchcraft issued by the Barons Courts of Prestoungrange and Dolphinston in 2004 lists eighty-one names.[155] It could be argued that the Pardon is a case of 'too little, too late': these events are over four hundred years distant in time and little, if any interest remained in the fate of these people. However, this was not the case. The event at the Prestoungrange Gothenburg on October 31st 2004, when Roy Pugh, author of 'The Deil's Ain', delivered copies of the Pardon to local named descendant families, made it very clear indeed that residents of Prestonpans still wished to honour the memory of those who suffered. The local Pardon ceremony attracted press and tv interest around the world: particularly in America, Australia and New Zealand, where many Scottish emigrants have made their homes. Links for the future have been forged with Salem in Massachusetts USA. The history of working people is rarely recorded and the modern-day residents of Prestonpans clearly welcomed a rare opportunity for recognition of themselves and their ancestors. The name descendants were content in the context of such global awareness to agree that no further steps should be taken by the Barons Courts to secure the long overdue Pardon for Treason.

The Barons Courts not only resolved to Grant their Pardon however. They specifically required that each succeeding October 31st, Hallowe'en, should be a Remembrance Day in Prestonpans for the 81 Witches. Murals have since been painted and dramatic re-enactments of the period have been created. And this historical study was commissioned by Prestoungrange University Press quite specifically so that visitors to Prestonpans [who are being specifically encouraged to come] can take away a comprehensive and respectful version of these tragic times.

***

It is very easy for all of us to acknowledge and rail against the crimes that others perpetrate against humanity, but it is an altogether different thing to

Pardon ceremony

acknowledge that such inhumanity can occur within one's own community. The Pardon granted already stands as a distinctive memorial to those who lost their lives. But it must surely act forever as a warning that no-one amongst us can confidently state that they would never participate in such a process of persecution. The Kirk was right: there were indeed demons loose in their Godly state. Sadly, these demons were not supernatural – they were man-made, and still dwell amongst us.

NOTES

1 A History of the Scottish People 1560–1880, Smout, TC, Fontana Press, 1998 pp. 50
2 The New Penguin History of Scotland from the Earliest Times to the Present Day, Houston & Knox eds, Penguin, 2002, pp. xxxviii
3 John Davidson of Prestonpans: Reformer, Preacher and Poet in the Generation after Knox, Moffat Gillon, R, Clarke & Co., London 1936 pp. 41–43
4 A History of the Scottish People 1560–1880, Smout, TC, Fontana Press, 1998 pp. 172–173
5 Enemies of God: the Witch Hunt in Scotland, Larner, C, Chatto & Windus, London 1981, p. 32
6 A History of the Scottish People 1560–1880, Smout, TC, Fontana Press, 1998 pp. 151–152
7 Domestic Annals of Scotland from the Reformation to the Revolution, Chambers, R, Edinburgh, 1874, Vol 1, ch. 7
8 For a detailed study of Scottish folklore, see 'Scottish Folklore and Belief', Vol 1, 'The Silver Bough', F. Marian MacNeil, Canongate, 1989
9 The Scottish Witch Hunt in Context, Goodacre, J, ed, Manchester University Press, Manchester, 2002, p. 3
10 Ibid, p. 4
11 Scotland: A New History, Lynch, M, Pimlico, London 1992, pp. 188
12 The Deil's Ain, Pugh, R, Harlaw Heritage, Balerno, 2001, p. XV
13 Malleus Maleficarum, Part II, Q 1, Chap II, transcribed by Lovelace, W & Rice, C, http://www.malleusmaleficarum.org/mmtoc.html, accessed Feb 2005
14 Ibid
15 Enemies of God: the Witch Hunt in Scotland, Larner, C, Chatto & Windus, London 1981, p. 11

Absolu

FINDINGS OF THE BARONS COURTS

On 27th July 2004 in the Trinity Session of our Baron Courts of Prestoungrange and Dolphinstoun we *pronounce* the following interlocutor [EII. 53. 2004 P&D. 02]:

Finds in Fact:

1) That it appears that a gross miscarriage of justice was inflicted upon many persons convicted of 'conjuration or sorcery' within the jurisdiction of the Baron Courts of Prestoungrange and Dolphinstoun and executed for the same before the enactment of *The Witchcraft Act 1735.*

2) THAT before the enactment of *The Witchcraft Act, 1735*, thousands of people through out Scotland and their cats, were executed for 'conjuration or sorcery' under the Statute 1603, 1 Jac. I, c. 12, upon legally insufficient 'spectral evidence' under Scots Law: That is to say, the 'voices' or actions of 'spirits' given as 'evidence' of the 'guilt' of the accused.

3) THAT those persons condemned for witchcraft within the jurisdiction of the Baron Courts of Prestoungrange and Dolphinstoun were convicted on the basis of 'spectral evidence', that is to say, the 'voices' or actions of 'spirits' given as 'evidence' of the 'guilt' of the accused.

4) THAT this gave rise to a situation of waging private vendettas by accusing one's enemies of witchcraft.

5) THAT all those persons and their cats were convicted of 'conjuration or sorcery' within the jurisdiction of the Baron Courts of Prestoungrange and Dolphinstoun and executed for the same were convicted on the basis of legally insufficient "spectral evidence" and were probably the victims of personal vendettas by personal enemies who alleged the commission of 'Witchcraft' solely as a means to getting rid of the accused.

Finds in Law:

1) THAT 'spectral evidence', consisting of the 'voices' or 'actions' of evil spirits, is impossible to prove or to disprove in a court of law; nor is it possible for the accused to cross-examine the 'spirit' concerned: One is convicted upon the

In Re

Margaret Aitchesoun
Masie Aitchesoun
Agnes Aird
Marjorie Andersone
Margaret Auchinmoutie
Marioun Bailzie (Baillie)
Christian Blaikie
Meg Bogtoun
Janet Boyd
Bessie Broune (Brown)
Thomas Brounhill (Brownhill)
Wife of the above
Duncan Buchquhannan
Margaret Butter
Martha Butter
Jonett Campbell
Elspeth Cheuslie
Thomas Cockburn
Marioun Congilton
Bessie Cowane
Beatrix Cuthbertson
Janet Darlig
Agnes Dempstar
Gelie Duncan
Catherine Duncane
Thomas Fean
John Fian or Fiene
Jonett Gall
Malie Geddie
Helen Gibesone (Gibson)
Johnne Gordon
Catherene Gray
Jonnett Gray
Robert Griersoune
Issobell Griersoune
Issobell Gylloun
Margaret Hall
Agnes Kelly
Cristian Kerington
Helene Lauder
Issobell Lauder
Agnes Liddell
Katherine Liddell
(Acquitted on ca
Jonett Logan

Pardon

brance

McCalzean	1590T
emia McLean)	
e McGill	1590T
AcGill	1590T
AcGill	1590T
Mathie	1628B
George Moitis	1590T
Nichol Murray	1590T
n	1591T
icolsoun	1590T
Nicolsoun1590T	
Oliver	1628B
tersoune	1590T
Seton, wife	1590T
uhyte (White)	1590T
er Quhytelaw (Whitelaw)	1590T
ohn Ramsay	1590T
Ranking	1590T
id	1628B
iddell	1628B
t Ridpeth	1628B
Robinson	1590T
cheson	1590T
ers of Agnes Sampsoun	1590T
ampsoun	1590T
ne Schaw	1590T
ison	1591T
Smythe	1590T
n Steven	1629
traitton	1590T
rauchane (Strachan)	1628B
tt Thomson	1590T
homsoune	1590T
ne Wallace	1590T
Wat	1591T
Wrycht (Wright)	1590T
et Young	1628B

ried by local commission ordered
y the Privy Council or the
Committee of Estates acting for
arliament
reason and witchcraft

very making of such charges without any possibility of offering a defence against such 'spectral evidence'.

2) That, at the least, the verdict of "Not Proven" should have been rendered in all cases and situation where those accused of witchcraft were convicted on the basis of legally insufficient 'spectral evidence'.

3) That all those persons and their cats convicted of 'conjuration or sorcery' within the jurisdiction of the Baron Courts of Prestoungrange and Dolphinstoun and executed for the same were wrongly convicted upon the basis of "spectral evidence" legally insufficient under Scots law to sustain a conviction.

HELD:

1) The Baron Courts of Prestoungrange and Dolphinstoun rule that weightily and sufficient grounds of both fact and law exist for vacating the conviction of all those persons and their cats who were convicted of 'conjuration or sorcery' within the jurisdiction of the Baron Courts of Prestoungrange and Dolphinstoun and executed for the same before the enactment of *The Witchcraft Act 1735*: In all cases such convictions were based upon 'spectral evidence' legally insufficient under Scots law to sustain a conviction. In all such cases the verdict of "Not Proven" ought to have been rendered by the Baron Courts of the day.

2) Accordingly, the Baron Courts of Prestoungrange and Dolphinstoun grant an Absolute Pardon to those persons convicted of 'conjuration or sorcery' within their jurisdiction before the enactment of *The Witchcraft Act 1735* as well as to the cats concerned.

3) Furthermore, the Baron Courts order that this most unfortunate carriage of justice inflicted upon such persons and their cats be remembered: (i) in murals to be painted in the baronies depicting their plight; (ii) by an historical record being published that both recounts their alleged crimes and punishments and records such Absolute Pardon; and that (iii) the tragic events involved be re-enacted each year on Hallowe'en and from time to time as a living reminder of this earlier process of justice in Scotland.

16 Industrial Ownership and Relations at Prestongrange, Burnett, A, Prestoungrange History Series no. 4, Prestoungrange University Press, Northamptonshire, 2000, p. 3
17 Prestongrange House, Baker, S, Prestoungrange History Series no. 1, Prestoungrange University Press, Northamptonshire, 2000, p. 10
18 For a more detailed examination of the rise of the Protestant faith in Scotland, see Scotland: A New History, Lynch, M, Pimlico, London 1992, pp. 186–202
19 Biographia Scoticana, Howie, J, Nelson, 1812
20 Life of George Wishart the Scottish Martyr, Rogers, C, Grampian Club, Edinburgh, 1876, p. 16
21 Ibid, p. 19
22 Prestonpans & Vicinity, McNeil, P, Menzies & Co., Edinburgh 1902, p. 54
23 NAS GB234/CH2/307/28
24 Collins Encyclopaedia of Scotland, Keay, J & Keay, J, eds, HarperCollins, London 1994, p. 185
25 The First Blast of the Trumpet against the Monstrous Regiment of Women, Knox, J, Geneva, 1558
26 The Scottish Witch Hunt in Context, Goodacre, J, ed, Manchester University Press, Manchester, 2002, p. 7
27 A History of the Scottish People 1560–1880, Smout, TC, Fontana Press, 1998 p. 55
28 John Davidson of Prestonpans: Reformer, Preacher and Poet in the Generation after Knox, Clarke & Co., London 1936 pp. 15–16
29 from Acta Parliamentorum Mariae, Acts of the Parliament of Scotland, Vol II, p. 539
30 Enemies of God: the Witch Hunt in Scotland, Larner, C, Chatto & Windus, London 1981, p. 9
31 Scotland: A New History, Lynch, M, Pimlico, London 1992, pp. 200
32 Dictionary of National Biography, Lee, S, ed, London, Smith, Elder & CO, 1892, Vol XXIX, p. 163
33 De Jure Regni Apud Scotos, Buchanan, G, 1579, transl. MacNeill, D, http://www.kuyper.org/main/publish/books_essays/article_16.shtml, accessed Jan 2005
34 Basilicon Doron, James I, 1599, Scolar Press, England 1969, p. 28
35 Ibid, p. 4
36 Witchcraft in Early Modern Scotland: James VI's Demonology and the North Berwick Witches, Normand, L & Roberts, G, eds, University of Exeter press, 2000, pp. 353–425
37 Ibid, p. 328
38 Discoverie of Witchcraft, Reginald Scot, Booke XV, Chapter XXVI, London 1584, e-text http://www.horrormasters.com/Texta0506.pdf, accessed February 2005
39 Witchcraft in Early Modern Scotland: James VI's Demonology and the North Berwick Witches, Normand, L & Roberts, G, eds, University of Exeter press, 2000, p. 353
40 Ibid, pp. 381–383
41 Ibid, pp. 421–424
42 Perspectives in Scottish Social History: Essays in Honour of Rosalind Mitchison, Leneman, L, ed, Aberdeen University press, 1988, p. 8
43 Enemies of God: the Witch Hunt in Scotland, Larner, C, Chatto & Windus, London 1981, p. 103
44 Ibid, p. 75
45 Sketches of Tranent in the Olden time, Sands, J, 1881, chap 3
46 Cassell Dictionary of Witchcraft, Pickering, D, Brockhampton Press, 1996, p. 244
47 Bothwell and the North Berwick Witches: A Chronology, Edward H. Thompson http://homepages.tesco.net/~eandcthomp/Chronology1.htm, accessed Nov 2004
48 Enemies of God: the Witch Hunt in Scotland, Larner, C, Chatto & Windus, London 1981, pp. 15–16
49 Ibid, p. 62
50 NAS GB234/CH2/307/28
51 Witchcraft in Early Modern Scotland: James VI's Demonology and the North Berwick Witches, Normand, L & Roberts, G, eds, University of Exeter press, 2000, chap 5
52 Enemies of God: the Witch Hunt in Scotland, Larner, C, Chatto & Windus, London 1981, p.70
53 Witchcraft in Early Modern Scotland: James VI's Demonology and the North Berwick Witches, Normand, L & Roberts, G, eds, University of Exeter press, 2000, p. 88
54 Enemies of God: the Witch Hunt in Scotland, Larner, C, Chatto & Windus, London 1981, pp. 104–107

55 John Davidson of Prestonpans: Reformer, Preacher and Poet in the Generation after Knox, Moffat Gillon, R, Clarke & Co., London 1936 p. 132
56 Enemies of God: the Witch Hunt in Scotland, Larner, C, Chatto & Windus, London 1981, p. 82
57 'The Survey of Scottish Witchcraft', Goodacre, J, Martin, L, Miller, J, Yeoman, L, http://www.arts.ed.ac.uk/witches/, archived January 2003, accessed December 2004
58 Statistical Account of Scotland 1791–1799, Sinclair, J, Edinburgh, 1799, Vol 21 p 472, table of rents by county
59 Memoirs of his Own Life from the Original Manuscript, Sir James Melville of Halhill, Bannatyne Club, Edinburgh 1827, pp. 369–370
60 Witchcraft in Early Modern Scotland: James VI's Demonology and the North Berwick Witches, Normand, L & Roberts, G, eds, University of Exeter press, 2000, pp. 31–34
61 Bothwell and the North Berwick Witches: A Chronology, Thompson, E, http://homepages.tesco.net/~eandcthomp/Chronology1.htm, accessed Sep 2004
62 Letters on Demonology and Witchcraft, Sir Walter Scott, London, Routledge & Sons, 1884, Letter IX, p . 249
63 Letters on Demonology and Witchcraft, Sir Walter Scott, Routledge & Sons, London 1884, letter IX
64 Witchcraft in Early Modern Scotland: James VI's Demonology and the North Berwick Witches, Normand, L & Roberts, G, eds, University of Exeter press, 2000, p. 38
65 Ibid, p. 22
66 The Scottish Witch Hunt in Context, Goodacre, J, ed, Manchester University Press, Manchester, 2002, pp. 107–108
67 The Deil's Ain, Pugh, R, Harlaw Heritage, Balerno, 2001, p. 12
68 Witchcraft in Early Modern Scotland: James VI's Demonology and the North Berwick Witches, Normand, L & Roberts, G, eds, University of Exeter press, 2000, p. 21
69 Ibid, pp. 292–293
70 Ibid, doc 1, p. 137
71 Ibid, p. 163
72 Ibid, p. 39
73 Ibid, p. 39
74 Ibid, pp. 35, 39
75 Bothwell and the North Berwick Witches: A Chronology, Thompson, E, http://homepages.tesco.net/~eandcthomp/Chronology1.htm, accessed Sep 2004
76 Witchcraft in Early Modern Scotland: James VI's Demonology and the North Berwick Witches, Normand, L & Roberts, G, eds, University of Exeter press, 2000, pp. 273–274
77 Ibid, docs 16–18, pp. 191–199
78 Ibid, docs 16–18, p. 220
79 Letters on Demonology and Witchcraft, Sir Walter Scott, Routledge & Sons, London 1884, letter IX
80 Witchcraft in Early Modern Scotland: James VI's Demonology and the North Berwick Witches, Normand, L & Roberts, G, eds, University of Exeter press, 2000, doc 27, p. 309
81 Ibid, doc 27, p. 320
82 Ibid, doc 27, pp. 309–326
83 Ibid, doc 2, p. 146
84 Ibid, pp. 212–214
85 The History of the Kirk in Scotland, Calderwood, D, Thomson, T ed, Wodrow Society, Edinburgh, 1844, Vol V, pp. 130
86 John Davidson of Prestonpans: Reformer, Preacher and Poet in the Generation after Knox, Moffat Gillon, R, Clarke & Co., London 1936 pp. 107–108
87 The History of the Kirk in Scotland, Calderwood, D, Thomson, T ed, Wodrow Society, Edinburgh, 1844, Vol V, p. 140
88 A Map of East Lothian/surveyed by Adair, J, ca 1736, National Library of Scotland, EMS.s.737 (15)
89 Prestonpans & Vicinity, McNeil, P, Menzies & Co., Edinburgh 1902, p. 9
90 Witchcraft in Early Modern Scotland: James VI's Demonology and the North Berwick Witches, Normand, L & Roberts, G, eds, University of Exeter press, 2000, doc 7, p. 168
91 http://www.grandlodgescotland.com/glos/Literature/Articles/400html accessed Jan 2005
92 http://www.kena.org/hirams/phl-de99.htm accessed Jan 2005
93 Witchcraft in Early Modern Scotland: James VI's Demonology and the North Berwick Witches, Normand, L & Roberts, G, eds, University of Exeter press, 2000, p. 154

94 Ibid, doc 19, p. 229
95 Ibid, doc 20, pp. 239–240
96 Ibid, doc 7, p. 168
97 Ibid, doc 8, pp. 170–173
98 Ibid, doc 8, p. 220
99 Statistical Account of Scotland 1791–1799, Sinclair, J, Edinburgh, 1799, Vol 17, p. 83
100 Industrial Ownership and Relations at Prestongrange, Burnett, A, Prestoungrange History Series no. 4, Prestoungrange University Press, Northamptonshire, 2000, pp. 7–8
101 The Scottish Witch Hunt in Context, Goodacre, J, ed, Manchester University Press, Manchester, 2002, p. 140
102 A History of the Scottish People 1560–1880, Smout, TC, Fontana Press, 1998 p. 166
103 The Deil's Ain, Pugh, R, Harlaw Heritage, Balerno, 2001, p. 200
104 The Painted Prestongrange Ceiling 1581, Allan, A, Prestoungrange History Series no. 17, Prestoungrange University Press, 2004, p. 17
105 Prestongrange and its Painted Ceiling, Transactions of the East Lothian Antiquarian and Field Naturalists Society, Vol X, p. 95
106 John Davidson of Prestonpans: Reformer, Preacher and Poet in the Generation after Knox, Moffat Gillon, R, Clarke & Co., London 1936 pp. 114–115
107 Prestongrange and its Painted Ceiling, Transactions of the East Lothian Antiquarian and Field Naturalists Society, Vol X, p. 95
108 The Painted Prestongrange Ceiling 1581, Allan, A, Prestoungrange History Series no. 17, Prestoungrange University Press, 2004 p. 18
109 Prestongrange and its Painted Ceiling, Transactions of the East Lothian Antiquarian and Field Naturalists Society, Vol X, p. 121
110 A History of the Scottish People 1560–1880, Smout, TC, Fontana Press, 1998 p. 189
111 A Sourcebook of Scottish Witchcraft, Larner, C, Glasgow: SSRC Project on Accusations and Prosecutions for Witchcraft in Scotland, 1977
112 NAS GB234/CH2/307/28, p. 102
113 Threads of the Past, Baker, S, Prestoungrange History Series no. 23, in preparation
114 Mormon Index to Old Parish Registers, LHC Haddington
115 Sourcing brickmaking salting and chemicals at Prestongrange, Anderson, D, Prestoungrange History Series no. 1, Prestoungrange University Press, 2004 pp. 7–8
116 http://www.scottishdocuments.com, accessed 21/02/05
117 John Davidson of Prestonpans: Reformer, Preacher and Poet in the Generation after Knox, Moffat Gillon, R, Clarke & Co., London 1936 p. 133
118 Ibid, p. 29
119 Prestonpans & Vicinity, McNeil, P, Menzies & Co., Edinburgh 1902, p. 40
120 John Davidson of Prestonpans: Reformer, Preacher and Poet in the Generation after Knox, Moffat Gillon, R, Clarke & Co., London 1936 p. 134
121 Ibid, p. 116
122 Prestonpans & Vicinity, McNeil, P, Menzies & Co., Edinburgh 1902, p. 45
123 The Scottish Witch Hunt in Context, Goodacre, J, ed, Manchester University Press, Manchester, 2002, p. 62
124 Prestonpans & Vicinity, McNeil, P, Menzies & Co., Edinburgh 1902, p. 44
125 Ibid, p. 51
126 Ibid, p. 54
127 Prestongrange House, Baker, S, Prestoungrange History Series no. 1, Prestoungrange University Press, 2000, p. 18
128 Enemies of God: the Witch Hunt in Scotland, Larner, C, Chatto & Windus, London 1981, pp. 81–82
129 http://www.scottishdocuments.com, accessed 21/02/05
130 Sketches of Tranent in the Olden time, Sands, J, 1881, chap 3
131 Prestonpans & Vicinity, McNeil, P, Menzies & Co., Edinburgh 1902, p. 32
132 Salem Witchcraft Trials, Katherine W Richardson, Peabody Essex Museum, Salem 1994 p. 6
133 Prestonpans & Vicinity, McNeil, P, Menzies & Co., Edinburgh 1902, p. 101
134 The Scottish Witch Hunt in Context, Goodacre, J, ed, Manchester University Press, Manchester, 2002, p. 171
135 Ibid, p. 169
136 Domestic Annals of Scotland from the Reformation to the Revolution, Chambers, R, Edinburgh, 1874, Vol II: Reign of Charles II.: 1660 – 1673 Part B

137 Ibid, Vol II: Reign of Charles II.: 1660 – 1673 Part B
138 The Scottish Witch Hunt in Context, Goodacre, J, ed, Manchester University Press, Manchester, 2002, p. 173
139 Domestic Annals of Scotland from the Reformation to the Revolution, Chambers, R, Edinburgh, 1874, Vol III, Reign of William and Mary: 1689–1694 Part A
140 The Scottish Witch Hunt in Context, Goodacre, J, ed, Manchester University Press, Manchester, 2002, pp. 180–181
141 Cassell Dictionary of Witchcraft, Pickering, D, Brockhampton Press, 1996, p. 83
142 Ibid, p. 20
143 Thompson, pp. Macbeth, King James and the Witches, http://homepages.tesco.net/~eandcthomp/macbeth.htm, accessed November 2004
144 Cassell Dictionary of Witchcraft, Pickering, D, Brockhampton Press, 1996, p. 83
145 John Davidson of Prestonpans: Reformer, Preacher and Poet in the Generation after Knox, Moffat Gillon, R, Clarke & Co., London 1936 p. 83
146 Salem Witchcraft Trials, Katherine W Richardson, Peabody Essex Museum, Salem 1994 p. 5
147 Ibid, p. 5
148 The Oxford Companion to English Literature, M Drabble ed, 5th ed, 1985, p. 650
149 Enemies of God: the Witch Hunt in Scotland, Larner, C, Chatto & Windus, London 1981, p. ix
150 The Scottish Witch Hunt in Context, Goodacre, J, ed, Manchester University Press, Manchester, 2002, p. 216
151 Maria Grayson, personal communication
152 Enemies of God: the Witch Hunt in Scotland, Larner, C, Chatto & Windus, London 1981, p. 81
153 A History of Scotland for Junior Classes, Henry White, ed., Edinburgh 1854 p. 72
154 Salem Witchcraft Trials, Katherine W Richardson, Peabody Essex Museum, Salem 1994 p. 24
155 The Deil's Ain, Pugh, R, Harlaw Heritage, Balerno, 2001, Appendix 5, p. 211

ACKNOWLEDGEMENTS

I am deeply indebted to the 'The Survey of Scottish Witchcraft', Goodacre, J, Martin, L, Miller, J, Yeoman, L, http://www.arts.ed.ac.uk/witches/, accessed September 2004– February 2005 for statistical material and most particularly for information on the commissioners and investigators involved in trials associated with the people of Prestonpans. Unless stated otherwise, the names of individuals and statistical information have been taken from this survey.

I am also grateful for the invaluable survey of historical context and contemporary documents published by Normand and Roberts in 'Witchcraft in Early Modern Scotland: James VI's Demonology and the North Berwick Witches'.

BIBLIOGRAPHY

Acta Parliamentorum Mariae, Acts of the Parliament of Scotland, Vol II Dictionary of National Biography, Lee, S, ed, London, Smith, Elder & Co, 1892

Basilicon Doron, James I, 1599, Scolar Press, England 1969

Biographia Scoticana, Howie, J, Nelson, 1812

Cassell Dictionary of Witchcraft, Pickering, D, Brockhampton Press, 1996

Collins Encyclopaedia of Scotland, Keay, J & Keay, J, eds, HarperCollins, London 1994

The Deil's Ain, Pugh, R, Harlaw Heritage, Balerno, 2001

Domestic Annals of Scotland from the Reformation to the Revolution, Chambers, R, Edinburgh, 1874

Enemies of God: the Witch Hunt in Scotland, Larner, C, Chatto & Windus, London 1981
The First Blast of the Trumpet against the Monstrous Regiment of Women, Knox, J, Geneva, 1558
A History of the Scottish People 1560–1880, Smout, TC, Fontana Press, 1998
John Davidson of Prestonpans: Reformer, Preacher and Poet in the Generation after Knox, Moffat Gillon, R, Clarke & Co., London 1936
The History of the Kirk in Scotland, Calderwood, D, Thomson, T ed, Wodrow Society, Edinburgh, 1844, Vol V
A History of Scotland for Junior Classes, Henry White, ed., Edinburgh 1854
Industrial Ownership and Relations at Prestongrange, Burnett, A, Prestoungrange History Series no. 4, Prestoungrange University Press, Northamptonshire, 2000
Letters on Demonology and Witchcraft, Sir Walter Scott, London, Routledge & Sons, 1884
Life of George Wishart the Scottish Martyr, Rogers, C, Grampian Club, Edinburgh, 1876
Memoirs of his Own Life from the Original Manuscript, Sir James Melville of Halhill, Bannatyne Club, Edinburgh 1827
The New Penguin History of Scotland from the Earliest Times to the Present Day, Houston & Knox eds, Penguin, 2002
The Oxford Companion to English Literature, Drabble, M ed, 5th ed, 1985
The Painted Prestongrange Ceiling 1581, Allan, A, Prestoungrange History Series no 17, Prestoungrange University Press, 2004
Perspectives in Scottish Social History: Essays in Honour of Rosalind Mitchison, Leneman, L, ed, Aberdeen University press, 1988
Prestongrange and its Painted Ceiling, Transactions of the East Lothian Antiquarian and Field Naturalists Society, Vol X
Prestongrange House, Baker, S, Prestoungrange History Series no. 1, Prestoungrange University Press, Northamptonshire, 2000
Prestonpans & Vicinity, McNeil, P, Menzies & Co., Edinburgh 1902
Salem Witchcraft Trials, Katherine W Richardson, Peabody Essex Museum, Salem 1994
Scotland: A New History, Lynch, M, Pimlico, London 1992
'Scottish Folklore and Belief', Vol 1, 'The Silver Bough', F. Marian MacNeil, Canongate, 1989
The Scottish Witch Hunt in Context, Goodacre, J, ed, Manchester University Press, Manchester, 2002
Sketches of Tranent in the Olden time, Sands, J, 1881
A Sourcebook of Scottish Witchcraft, Larner, C, Glasgow : SSRC Project on Accusations and Prosecutions for Witchcraft in Scotland, 1977
Sourcing brickmaking salting and chemicals at Prestongrange, Anderson, D, Prestoungrange History Series no. 1, Prestoungrange University Press, 2004 pp. 7–8
Statistical Account of Scotland 1791–1799, Sinclair, J, Edinburgh, 1799
Witchcraft in Early Modern Scotland: James VI's Demonology and the North Berwick Witches, Normand, L & Roberts, G, eds, University of Exeter press, 2000

National Archives of Scotland:

Prestonpans Kirk Session Records: NAS GB234/CH2/307/28

National Library of Scotland:

A Map of East Lothian/surveyed by Adair, J, ca 1736, National Library of Scotland, EMS.s.737 (15)

Local History Centre, Haddington:

Mormon Index to Old Parish Registers

Web based sources:

Bothwell and the North Berwick Witches: A Chronology, Edward H. Thompson http://homepages.tesco.net/~eandcthomp/ Chronology1. htm, accessed Nov 2004

De Jure Regni Apud Scotos, Buchanan, G, 1579, transl. MacNeill, D, http://www.kuyper.org/main/publish/books_essays/ article_16. shtml, accessed Jan 2005

Discoverie of Witchcraft, Reginald Scot, Booke XV, Chapter XXVI, London 1584, e-text http://www.horrormasters.com/ Texta 0506. pdf, accessed February 2005

Malleus Maleficarum, Part II, Q 1, Chap II, transcribed by Lovelace, W & Rice, C, http://www.malleusmaleficarum.org/ mmtoc.html, accessed Feb 2005

The Survey of Scottish Witchcraft, Goodacre, J, Martin, L, Miller, J, Yeoman, L, http://www.arts.ed.ac.uk/witches/, archived January 2003, accessed December 2004

http://www.grandlodgescotland.com/glos/Literature/Articles/ 400html accessed Jan 2005

http://www.kena.org/hirams/phl-de99.htm accessed Jan 2005

http://www.scottishdocuments.com, accessed 21/02/05

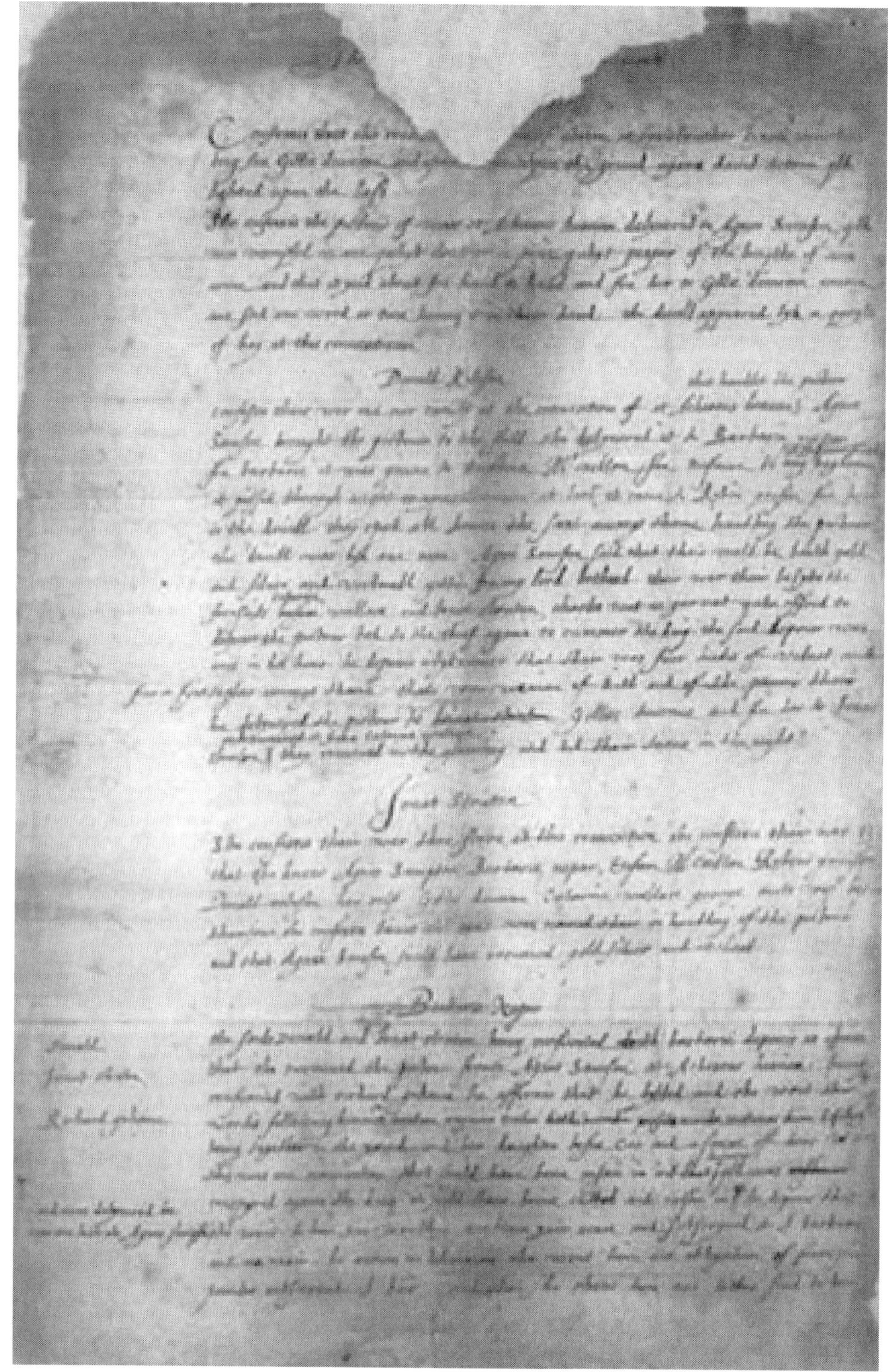

From High Court records 1581/82 [sic] – 1591/92?

From High Court records [Scotland]

Confesses that she rec[?eived pie]ces of glass at Foulstruther beside Ormiston Bridge fra Gillie Duncan and spread [?the]m upon the ground against David Seton, which lighted upon the lass.
She confesses the picture of wax at Acheson's Haven delivered to Agnes Sampson, which was wambled [rolled] in a white clout or a piece white paper of the length of an arm, and that it gaid about fra hand to hand and fra her to Gillie Duncan. Every one said a word or two, having it in their hand. The devil appeared like a quoyle [bundle] of hay at this convention.

Donald Robson
Confesses there were more nor twenty at the convention at Acheson's Haven that handled the picture. Agnes Sampson brought the picture to the field; she delivered it to Barbara Napier. Fra Barbara it was given to Euphame MacCalzean; fra Euphamie to Meg Begtoun of Spilmersford. It passed through eight or nine women. At last it came to Robin Grierson; fra him to the devil. They spake all 'James the Sixth' amongst them handling the picture. The devil was like a man. Agnes Sampson said that there would be both gold and silver and victual gotten fra my Lord Bothwell. There were there besides the forsaid, Catherine Wallace and Janet Stratton, Charles Wat in Garvet, who offered to deliver the picture back to the thief again to cummer [trouble] the king. The said deponer [deponent, Robson] was once in his house. He depones in like manner that there was four hoods of velvet and four or five taftas [taffeta gowns] amongst them [meaning that there were four rich women there]. There were women of Leith and of 'Pans there. He delivered the picture to Geillis Duncan and fra her to Janet Stratton and received it from Catherine Wallace. They convened in the gloaming [evening twilight] and did their turn in the night.

Janet Stratton
She confesses there were three score at this convention.
She confesses there were thirteen that she knew: Agnes Sampson, Barbara Napier, Euphame MacCalzean, Robert Grierson, Donald Robson, herself, Geillis Duncan, Catherine Wallace, George Mott's wife, Bessie Thomson. She confesses 'James the Sixth' was named there in handling of the picture and that Agnes Sampson should have received gold, silver and wheat.

Barbara Napier
The said Donald and Janet Stratton being confroned with Barbara, depones as above that she received the picture from Agnes Sampson at Acheson's Haven.
Being confronted with Richard Graham he affirms that he dited [dictated] and she wrote these words following: 'Hominum aratum regnum valui kethi imundum prosita munda metanas dium sipilus' being together in the yard, and her daughter Bessie Car and a son of hers with her. This was a conjuration that should have been cast into that liquor which was conspired against the king. It should have been cutted and cast in and was delivered by Marion Loch to Agnes Sampson. He depones that she wrote to him a writing eighteen year since and subscrived it 'I Barbarie' and no more. He avows in like manner she wrote him an obligation of four score pounds subscrived 'I Bar'. And that she showed him a letter sent to her...

22

Threads of the Past

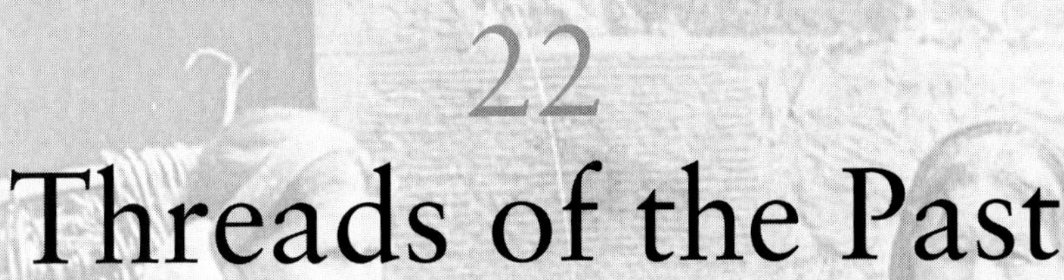

Prestonpans' Parish, Burgh, Community & People, 17th–19th Centuries

Sonia Baker

INTRODUCTION

If you would understand anything, observe its beginning and its development

Aristotle

Over the years, communities evolve, adapt and change. The communities of Prestonpans burgh and parish have coped with perhaps more changes than many over the past 300 years and more. Drawing on material produced at the time, this essay looks back at the Prestonpans' community – its history and its development – from about the 17th to the 19th century. The area's early industries (for example chemicals, salt, pottery, coal) have been covered in detail elsewhere in this series of booklets. Using the surviving information on wills and testaments, of maps made at the time, and a diverse range of other records, it is possible to add a human dimension to this picture. While the story is far from comprehensive – early material is often elusive and fragmentary – the picture that emerges provides enlightenment on the nature of the Prestonpans communities from the end of the 16th century until about 1900. It is the people who worked in the industries, as well as the toilers of the soil, the market gardeners, those who worked in the locality at the port, on the boats and the fisherfolk, the merchants and the townspeople, whose lives are reviewed. Their communities, both rural and industrial, evolved over a period of intense economic and social change.[1]

This booklet is divided into two: those readers familiar with historical documents may choose to skip the first part where the sources of the information used – the *records* – are discussed, and move onto the second part. The records rarely fall neatly into time–slots, and some overlap; others have simply not survived. Those for the earlier times are elusive. The later 19th century 'official' records that relate to the parish and (from 1893) the burgh of Prestonpans complement the information gleaned from the early records. The Victorians' obsession with statistics and analysis has left valuable information in a number of forms, including the census returns, and reports from various Parliamentary Commissions on living and working conditions.

From this apparently disparate array of sources, sense can be made. It is this that is presented in the first section *Threads of the past*: here the story of Prestonpans is summarised and described through the centuries until the turn of the 20th century. It addresses in turn the themes of *landscape* and *life & death*, and ends with *people*.

1 TC Smout *A History of the Scottish People 1560–1830* (1985) and *A Century of the Scottish People 1830–1950* (1986) remain the best economic and social history summaries, especially for the background of the period

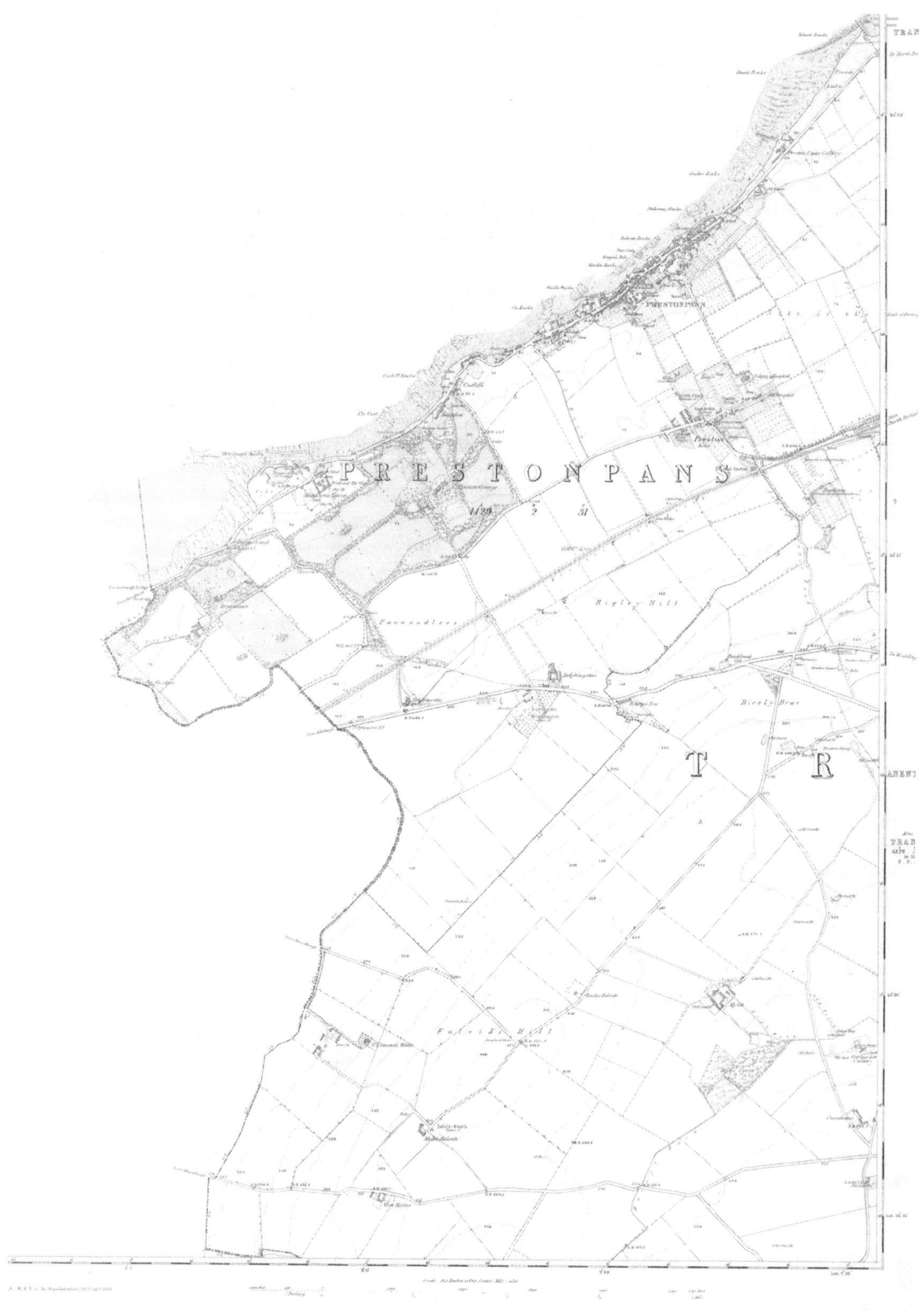

6 inch OS Map of Prestonpans Parish 1854
Reproduced by permission of the Trustees of the National Library of Scotland, ref: 2920/05

SECTION ONE: THE RECORDS

This section provides the background to the records, when they were created and (perhaps) why, and whether there is any inherent bias therein.

1 Parish records – hatches, matches and despatches to 1855

Genealogists and family history researchers use many of these records to locate specific family members; they start with the modern-day family and work back in time. For general information it is possible to interpret the information more broadly[2]. Until the middle of the 18th century, these records were written in Latin or Scots, and later in English. Time has faded ink, damaged paper, and for many parishes only a fraction of the records remain.

The various religious institutions were the main record keepers in this period. As the established church, the Church of Scotland recorded the majority of baptisms/births, the reading of the banns/marriages, and burials/deaths. The quality of these records varies considerably, but nevertheless can provide valuable information on the parish community. Record-keeping was generally the task of the session clerk, and many were in post for years, as their handwriting bears witness.

A 14th century directive required the clergy to record parish deaths. Records of baptisms and the reading of banns were similarly required by 1552. Registration of all three was not introduced until 1616, and even then there was no guarantee that they would be religiously maintained.

Between 1783 and 1794, registration itself was taxed. This was a big disincentive to accurate and up-to-date record keeping, and many parishes foundered in their task during this period. The established church itself – already under attack by the dissenters – did not benefit from its new role as tax collector of the state. It is hard to say whether the Prestonpans records were well maintained or not between 1783 and 1794; some remain extant, but may or may not be complete.

For Prestonpans, the earliest of these records[3] that survive are: birth 1596–1854 (none 1681–86); marriages 1687–1854 (none 1717–1787); deaths 1799–1854. The quality of these records is variable and some are simply illegible.

2 Taxation on householders in the 1690s

Seventeenth century listings of taxable people were made for much the same reasons that modern records are kept – in order to target specific individuals to enable the raising of revenue for the government. It seems that historical tax-gathering was as fraught as it is today, with a variable degree of success; under-recording was a particular problem, as was accuracy. As well as the hearth tax of 1691 (see below), a poll tax was charged on anyone over 16 in 1693, 1695 and 1698. The only poll tax records for East Lothian (or Haddingtonshire) that remain are for the parish of Dirleton[4]. It is unfortunate

2 Flinn, M (ed) *Scottish Population History* (1977) Cambridge University Press remains the best summary of population trends and guide to interpreting the records Sinclair, Cecil *Tracing Your Scottish Ancestors* (revised edition 1997) Scottish Record Office

3 Microfilm copies of NAS OPR718/vols 1–10 are held at the Local History Centre, Haddington Library

4 NAS E70/3/1 Poll tax returns for East Lothian 1698 – Dirleton

that there are no extant returns for Prestonpans, as they are a useful check for accuracy against the hearth tax returns. The tranche of taxes of the 1690s was particularly untimely as this was a period marked by crop failure and subsequent famine.

2.1 The hearth tax

In 1691 a tax was charged on every hearth in Scotland, and only those living off the parish were exempted. Forges, locksmiths and bakers' ovens were included. Generally some houses listed had more hearths than others – the minister's manse would often have four to six – and mansion houses considerably more. According to poll tax data from elsewhere in Scotland, rich Scottish households perhaps comprised 7–10+ individuals in the rural areas and 5–7 in towns.[5] Hearth tax lists cannot provide population numbers, but do provide valuable information on the likely size and composition of settlements at the end of the 17th century.

3 Where there's a will: something to leave – 1514 and beyond[6]

Although it would initially seem that a lot of people left wills, the records or testaments might be a little misleading. If there was no will, even poorer people could appear on the testament registers. If the term *testament dative* appears on the record, it might indicate that the deceased's relatives were seeking monies owed (like outstanding wages), or that those owed money by the deceased were trying to get recompense via the court. A detailed examination of the wills would clarify this, although this is outwith the scope of the present work.

People can appear several times; if there is an *eik* (a supplement to a testament), then this is listed separately, as are any later amendments or additions. Women can appear several times – especially if they have remarried; they are generally listed under their maiden name, and any husband's name as well.

Even the lists alone are enlightening; they provide an overview of the types of work being carried out by some of the people in Prestonpans in the 17th, 18th and 19th centuries. Of the women listed, none seems to have an occupation. They are included as spouses, and widows or relicts of their husbands.

3.1 Heritable property – land and buildings[7]

In the past, land and property ownership was the province of the few. The complexities of the topic preclude detailed investigation for this paper.

3.2 Moveable property – money, furniture etc

The Commissary Court dealt with this until the 1820s. For Prestonpans' matters this was Edinburgh Commissary Court – 1514–1829, and thereafter the Sheriff Court – Haddington 1830–1901. There was a degree of overlap with this, but fortunately recent computerisation of these records makes

5 Flinn, *Scottish Population History* p 196

6 Sinclair, C (1997 revised ed) *Tracing Your Scottish Ancestors* National Archives of Scotland pp 32–45

7 Sinclair, *Tracing* pp 46–53

locating the records much easier.[8] Records are also available from Edinburgh Sheriff Court as wills (1844–1901) and as inventories (1808–1901), and from Haddington Sheriff Court as wills (1898–1901).

4 Maps[9]

These provide wonderful visual impressions of a landscape at a given time. Maps may be of particular locations, or with digitisation, it is possible to home in to the detail on county maps too. There are other maps available than are detailed here.

4.1 John Adair (c1650–1722)

Adair was commissioned by the Scottish Privy Council to survey and map Scotland. His survey was completed in 1682, but the maps were not published until 1736. They show fermtouns, and settlements. His manuscript version was later engraved; the engraved version tidies up some of his text, for example the harbour is 'Morrison's or New Haven'. Adair's original merely states 'New Haven'. This fits in with the remodelling of the harbour by William Morison c1700 and its consequent renaming.

4.2 Roy's Military Survey of Scotland 1747–55[10]

Roy produced a series of splendid maps of Scotland. They were part of the response of the British government to the upheaval of Culloden, when it was seen as necessary to impose rule on the unruly. Essentially the survey provided a means of informing the government forces on how to get around Scotland; the highlands were surveyed first and the lowlands later. The survey concentrated on the access routes through the countryside, depicted roads and bridges and the location of the scattered fermtouns. Recent digitisation enables the landscape to be closely examined.

4.3 William Forrest

He surveyed the area in 1799, and his Map of Haddingtonshire was produced in 1802. By this stage early industry is a key feature.

4.4 The Ordnance Survey (OS)

The first ordnance survey maps date from the 1850s, and were thereafter updated. Together these make it possible to track the physical development of the landscape over time, right up to the present day.

5 The Statistical Accounts[11]

The statistical accounts are parish-by-parish summaries of the economic and social history (and more) of Scotland. The title is misleading as they provide some of the best information on the social life of the period, and there are few actual statistics given The early two are known respectively as the OSA and the NSA – the old (or first) and new (or second) statistical accounts. More

8 Search until 1901 on www.scottishdocuments.com; the advanced search can be made by location

9 See www.nls.uk/digitallibrary/map for the National Library of Scotland's online collection

10 Viewable on www.scran.ac.uk roy map 08/5a SCRAN 000-000-190-753-C *The British Library*

11 The OSA and the NSA are available on-line at www.edina.ac.uk

correctly they are *The Statistical Account of Scotland* by Sir John Sinclair of Ulbster (1790s), and *The New Statistical Account of Scotland* (1835). The OSA was largely written by parish ministers who responded to Sinclair's lengthy questionnaire. Many entries were strongly biased towards matters of concern to the church, for example on the poor, and on the drinking habits of the working population. Nevertheless, the accounts also provide some of the most vivid descriptions there are of the day-to-day lives of ordinary people of the time; the OSA is a valuable source of information relating to the size of the population at the time (although there was a degree of guesswork with some data) and to the new industries that were located in each settlement. The contributor of the Prestonpans material, minister John Trotter, provided an extensive and comprehensive summary of the parish. A broader range of contributors produced material for the NSA, and here too the industrial development described is of particular interest; minister Bruce Cunningham wrote at length about Prestonpans. For both accounts the amount of editing by the editors was minimal, probably due to the mammoth scale of each project.

A third account by county was produced variously between the 1950s–90s, compiled from material produced by a range of people. Dr Catherine Snodgrass edited *The County of East Lothian*; published in 1954, it was one of the earliest of the third series.

East Lothian is the only county to have brought the accounts up to date with *East Lothian 1945–2000: the Fourth Statistical Account*, Sonia Baker (ed) East Lothian Council. Of the seven volumes, the first was published in 2003, the second in 2004; and the balance to 2007. Contributions were gathered from 300+ individuals, and each parish was overseen, and often written, by a parish representative. Some worked with, and on behalf of, local history groups, others alone.[12]

6 Censuses

6.1 Webster's census

The first population count that is regarded as even remotely reliable is Webster's *Account of the number of people in Scotland, 1755*: this is a private census collected by minister Alexander Webster. It is thought that his data was later utilised by Sir John Sinclair of Ulbster for the *Statistical Account of Scotland* (see below) of the 1790s. Webster produced 3 schemes, which variously include parish size, patrons, stipends, and population, number of papists and number of fighting men aged 18–56.[13] The accuracy of Webster's figures is debateable; fortunately Sinclair's *Account* followed within about 40 years and the information given therein enables any widely erroneous figures from Webster to be identified and queried.

6.2 19th century government censuses[14]

For England and Wales the censuses began in 1801, with the count taken by the overseers of the poor in each parish. In Scotland, enumerators were often the local schoolmasters. Ambitiously it was intended that estimates were to be made on previous populations using the parish records to provide decennial

12 See also www.el4,org.uk

13 Flinn *Scottish Population History* pp 58–61

14 This information is summarised from Flinn *Scottish Population History* pp 80–83

estimates back to 1700. This proved patchy in England and Wales, and a non-starter in Scotland. The count was taken in March/April, when most people were at their home base; with so many people moving around the country at harvest time, this period was best avoided.

The 1801 information was produced in a single volume, and asked only the most basic of information – the number of people, occupation of the household head and the number of houses. From 1841, Scottish returns were published separately, and from 1851, the information gathered was more extensive; more was asked about name, birthplace, marital status, and even those on ships in harbour were included. Occupation was broken down into trade and employment, or 'of independent means'; the 'occupations etc of wives living with their husbands, or of sons or daughters living with their parents, and assisting them but not apprenticed or receiving wages, need not be set down'. A series of abbreviations was suggested – including Ag. Lab. for agricultural labourer – 'whether in the fields, or as shepherd, ploughman, carter, waggoner or farm servant generally'. H.L.W. for hand loom weavers. M.S. to be used to denote male servant – to include 'all bailiffs, game-keepers and domestic servants, butlers, coachmen footmen grooms, helpers, boys etc'. Female servants – F.S. to 'include all females employed in houses'.

The introduction of civil registration in 1855 meant that the census returns were augmented by the births, deaths and marriages data. From 1861 the Scots conducted their own census from Edinburgh. The 1861 census asked name, sex, age, birthplace, address and census place, rank/profession/occupation, relationship to head if household, marital status, blind, deaf or dumb, number of children attending school, number of rooms with one or more windows, and 'imbeciles, idiots or lunatics'. By 1881, householders were asked about Scots Gaelic speakers.

For most parishes in Scotland the 1841 returns are the earliest for which the enumerator records are extant. In East Lothian, original parish returns (1801, 1811, 1821 and 1831) only survive for the parish of Ormiston. Many of *New Statistical Account* (1835) entries provide the early census figures by parish – see 5 above.

For practical use, the Prestonpans census of 1861 is one of the first to be useable, being mostly legible. Faded ink makes that of 1851 indecipherable. In the 1861 census, the parish was divided into six enumeration divisions. The urban core was divided first into north and south by the north turnpike road – now Prestonpans main street – and then into the east and west sections by the Market Strand. This is indiscernible today but was possibly West Loan.

Division One extended from the **north side** of the turnpike road from the **east boundary** to the Market Strand separating the baronies of Preston and Prestongrange.

Division Two extended from the **north side** of the turnpike road from the Market Strand separating the baronies of Preston and Prestongrange **westward** to the Red Burn.

Division Three covered the area on the **south** of the turnpike road, as far south as to include the Manse and from the **east boundary** to the Market Strand separating the baronies of Preston and Prestongrange. This included all to the east of John Davieson Street and all the old potting buildings and to the east of the Custom House.

Division Four covered the area on the **south** of the turnpike road and including all north of Preston from the Market Strand separating the baronies of Preston and Prestongrange **westward** to the Red Burn.

Division Five covered the **western edge of the village** to the parish boundary with Inveresk, and included Cuthill, Bankfoot, Morrison's Haven and Ravensheugh.

Division Six covered the parish from the eastern boundary and encompassed most of the rural hinterland. **Preston, Prestongrange, Dolphinston, Drummore** and 'various isolated dwellings in the neighbourhood' were included. Similar Divisions applied in 1891. These two census returns are used for the discussion in Section Two 3.3.

Until 1901 when the boundaries were revised, the earlier registration districts coincided with the ecclesiastical parishes, but these often bore no relationship with county boundaries. This creates problems when trying to relate information over time; boundary changes play havoc with comparisons of population figures.

7 Civil registers from 1855

Registration of births, marriages and deaths was made compulsory from 1 January 1855. Again, overly ambitious intent had to be reined in. We are left with what is fairly accurate data collected and processed within an impressive timescale. Each parish had its own registrar; some were based at the main village or town, which often meant that people had to travel a long way to register.

With the changes to Scotland's religious make-up following the 1843 Disruption, the introduction of civil registration removed the problems that were arising when some of the 'new' churches proved reluctant to register marriages. The United Presbyterian Church was both opposed to registering marriages and to the new civil registration.

8 Valuation rolls from 1855

These record each household, the address – though house numbers are not always included – the use made of the premises, the names of the owner and the tenant and the value of the property. Used alongside the civil registers and the census, the valuation rolls provide a valuable checking mechanism. They also provide a means of checking when a property changed hands. The Prestonpans valuation rolls for 1893/4 were used for the discussion on people in the 19th century in Section Two, 3.3 below.

9 Parliamentary papers (PP) & reports

The 19th century saw an explosion of official reports on the state of the nation. From the numbers of poor in a parish to working conditions in factories, the Victorian ethos of civic pride motivated concern about all facets of society. The parliamentary reports that resulted provide an enormous amount of information about 19th century working people and their lives.

Examples include:

Children's Employment (Mines) Commission, ***PP 1842*** *Vols XVI–XVII*

The Poor Law Inquiry (Scotland), ***PP 1844***, *Vols XX–V*

Fourth Report of the Royal Commission on the Employment of Women and Children in Agriculture ***PP 1870*** *Vol XIII & Appendix II*

10 Gazetteers or geographical dictionaries

A number of gazetteers were produced during the 19th and early 20th centuries, all of which described the small settlements and burghs of Scotland. They ceased when change progressed at too fast a pace for the publishers to keep up to date. Colin Hinson has transcribed the 1868 Gazetteer on-line[15], and Groome's has been added to and brought up to date by editors Dr D Munro and BM Gittings.[16]

In **1832**, Robert Chambers' *Gazetteer of Scotland* offered 3/4 page on Prestonpans.

The *National Gazetteer of Great Britain and Ireland* appeared in **1868**, as did John M Wilson's *Imperial Gazetteer of Scotland.*

Francis H. Groome's *Ordnance Gazetteer of Scotland* was first published in 6 volumes between **1882 and 1885**.[17]

SECTION ONE: THREADS

1 17th century & earlier – a struggle to survive[18]

For many years, Prestonpans' success was due to its role as a small port on the firth of Forth. The inhabitants exploited the area's natural resources to develop a number of industries, the earliest of which were the interrelated industries of coal and salt. A brownware works began in the parish c1693, and William Morison established a glass works in 1697 – making luxury items[19] like mirrors, spectacles and window glasses – which survived until c1720. For many years the royal burghs held a monopoly on foreign trade, but, by the middle of the 17th century, settlements around the firth of Forth – including Prestonpans – gradually increased their trading position to Leith's (and therefore Edinburgh's) cost. The goods produced were exported from the harbour at Acheson's/ Morrison's Haven that lay between Cuthill and West Pans. Trade through Morrison's Haven exceeded those from the Dunbar ports further south, and exports[20] included coal (1540s–1660s, 1684–90s), salt (1540s–1690s, with the market changing after the civil war – before to Holland and England, after it Germany and the Baltic); hides (1540s–1600s); others recorded were eggs, stockings, cloth, kelp, tallow, skins, malt, tobacco and French & Dutch goods.

Local trade along the coast was also of importance, including coal to feed Edinburgh's domestic fires, and imports too (like English wool, Swedish iron plate, and pitch and lead from the Netherlands) contributed to the local economy.

Prestonpans survived during the 17th century because the town was economically diverse, and did not rely on a single industry, although salt remained the most important. Whilst trade was plied along the eastern

15 See www.genuki.bpears.org.uk for Colin Hinson's 2003 transcript

16 www.geo.ed.ac.uk/scotgaz/

17 www.clerkington.plus.com/GENUKI/ELN/Prestonpans/prestonpans.html provides a 1903 edition

18 Flinn, *Scottish Population History* pp 168–9

19 Anderson, David (2000) *Sourcing Brickmaking, Salting & Chemicals at Prestongrange* Booklet 3 Prestoungrange University Press pp 21–23

20 Aitken, Julie (2000) *Acheson/Morrison's Haven: what came and went and how?* Booklet 2 Prestoungrange University Press pp 6–27, 39, 40

seaboard, to the Baltic, Scandinavia and to the Netherlands, the Forth ports thrived. After the 1670s, when Scotland's trade shifted away from Europe and towards the Americas and the West Indies, Glasgow became the pre-eminent port. Thereafter local trade became of greater importance, and Prestonpans 'fed' off Edinburgh's prosperity.

1.1 Landscape

At this point, the settlement was still referred to as Saltpreston. Early settlements – often denoted by the suffix 'ton' or toun, as in Dauphinston and nearby Seaton – comprised a cluster of small buildings, some homes, some barns – set alongside the toun's land. Each tenant and their family had a share of the better land, which was cultivated in strips – hence the stripy appearance of Roy's map – and each tenant or sub tenant also had a right to graze stock on the poorer land. Communal working was essential for the well being of all.

Adair's 1682 survey reveals settlements at Preston, Prestonpans, West Pans, Prestongrang (sic) and Dauphinton (sic), as well as the more obscure Alystob (tidied by the later engraver, c1730s, to Olivestob, the land on which Bankton House was later built). Ringinghed lies to the east and, at the western edge of the parish is Edgebucklingbrae (which by the time of the 1894 OS map is shown as the name of the road that leads down the hill into Musselburgh now the road to the east of Pinkie Braes[21]).

In 1682, Prestonpans itself is shown as a single meandering run of houses following the coast for much the same distance as it does today. No tracks appear to link the Pans with any other part of the parish. There is one through Preston that leads to Prestongrange, and a track from nearby Tranent leads to Musselburgh via Dolphinton; another heads from Tranent north to Cokeny (sic).

1.2 Life & death

Earlier times were a struggle. The 17th century was a particularly grim time, marked by civil war, famine, epidemics (including plague) and religious upheaval, although it is noted that in the 1640s Prestonpans had few deaths from plague when the disease was rife elsewhere, including nearby Edinburgh and Leith, which were devastated.[22]

Day to day survival was dependent on successful harvests; in a good year, grain was exported from Morrison's Haven – as in 1679 and 1685. However, the century ended with a decade of hunger across the country and beyond. Harvests were bad in 1695, 1696 and 1698; the stress placed on populations was often manifested in a fall in the birth rate nine months to a year afterwards following an increase in the death rate amongst child-bearing aged parents. For Prestonpans the birth figures are inconclusive – but perhaps are an indicator that the urban population's survival was due to the proximity of a rich and productive agricultural hinterland.

Snow fell in nearby Tyninghame on 3 May 1698, and the remainder of the year was marked by endless wind and rain. Harvest was late or non-existent, and as this was experienced all over northern Europe, it was difficult to import food from elsewhere to counter the shortfall in Scotland. In this pre-

21 Martine, John (1999 orig published 1890) *Reminiscences and Notices of the Parishes of the County of Haddington* p 177 states this 'new road from Levenhall ... was made about 1816')

22 Flinn, *Scottish Population History* p 140

turnip and potato society, most surplus animals were killed in the autumn, and families struggled to keep their breeding stock going through until spring. When the harvest failed, the breeding stock too had to be killed and eaten. What followed was a period of hunger and, in the towns, destitution and increased vagrancy followed, and the death rate was heightened further by outbreaks of disease.

1.2.1 Urban Prestonpans

The settlements of Musselburgh, Tranent and Prestonpans are all recorded as having over 500 hearths, making them sizeable settlements, their populations reliant mainly on industry, not farming. For comparison, Tranent lists 1142 hearths, Haddington 1496. The Prestonpans hearth tax of 1691 has survived[23]; the detail is not easy to decipher, but the number of hearths totals 830. The information is given in six sublists, but there is no geographical distinction apparent – so it is not possible to allocate one list to, say, Preston and another to Prestonpans. The lists show many householders as having 4 or more hearths; this is unusual.

Flinn's table[24] relating to the occupational groups in Perth in 1694 suggests the professions as averaging 3.9 hearths, and merchants 3. He also points to the whole county of West Lothian having only 17 houses with 10 or more hearths.[25]

Eight householders are listed as having hearths in double figures and, while all properties are not identifiable, some are.

'Lady Preston has 20'; Prestongrange, 15 hearths; another had 14; Dolphinston and another property 'in Preston' had 12; 'Mistress Lothian in Preston' and James Oswald of Singleton both had 11, and Bailzie Charteris 10.[26] Still more properties had between 5 and 9 hearths: 28 in total,[27] although at least two of which were salt pans – one of 7 hearths 'belonging to the laird of Goshen' and 6 hearths for John Sanderson 'for the Earl of Winton's salt pans'. A further 21 had 4 hearths.[28]

So 62 householders/tenants were listed as having 4+ hearths. The remaining taxed households had 1–3 hearths.

With almost half of the hearths[29] listed for Prestonpans parish apparently accounted for by larger properties, this then is an indication that in 1691 the town supported a sizeable wealthy population, many of which were the merchant class, which Flinn[30] stated included 'professionals, maltmen, dyers, as well those described as merchants'.

This picture concurs with Smout's findings;[31] based on the salt trade, Morrison's Haven was a prosperous port even by 1650, and there is evidence that Prestonpans was importing luxury goods. In February 1693/4,[32] one

23 National Archives of Scotland (NAS) E69/9/2 13 March 1691; microfilm copy held at Local History Centre, Haddington
24 Flinn *Scottish Population History* p 194 Table 3.8.4
25 Flinn, *Scottish Population History* p 195
26 These 8 account for 105 hearths
27 These average 7 hearths each, total 196
28 21 with 4 hearths, total 84
29 385 in number – 46% of 830
30 Flinn *Scottish Population History* p 187
31 Smout, TC 'Trade of East Lothian at the end of the 17th century' IN *East Lothian Antiquarian & Field Naturalists' Society Transactions Vol IX* pp 67–78
32 NAS GD406/1/3874 correspondence of the Dukes of Hamilton

Daniel Hamilton, Edinburgh, reported to the Earl of Arran that his garden seed and 12 peach trees had arrived at Prestonpans from Holland. Untaxed goods were smuggled both ways.

1.3 People

The Prestonpans baptismal registers of 1698 provide an indication of the occupations of the children's fathers. While statistically not valid, this listing does provide an idea of the sorts of people – of all classes – the residents were. The following male occupations are given:

baxter – baker
carpenter
coal hewer to the laird of Preston Grange
cordwainer – shoemaker
fisher
gardener to laird of Singleton
maltman – processes barley into malt
mariner
mason
mealmaker
oversman to the laird of Preston Grange
portioner
sailor
salter
skipper
taylor
weaver
workman to the earl of Wintoun

From the wills (see Section One, 3 above) the following can be added to the listing. The date given is the year the document was lodged with the court. Most of those listed are male. There is one female given as 'resident', another as 'indweller'.

When the wife (spouse) had died, the occupation of her husband was given; occasionally it was the widow (the relict) who had died and the occupation of her late husband was given. There is one example of a daughter having died, and her father's occupation was given. The names of those that were possibly related are in bold type. *Umquile* means deceased.

16th century
Cordiner – shoemaker: James Lowis 1588
Mariner: Alestare Mansoun 1571

17th century
Baillie – 4 town magistrate: spouse of John Thomeson 1632; Alexander Hendersone 1671; William Scott 1675; Niniane Henderson 1682
Baxter – baker: James Allane 1667;
Chirurgeon – carries out medical operations and makes own drugs: spouse of Mark Hamiltoun 1668 who had been a burgess of Edinburgh
Coalhewar (sic): Adame Mathisone 1622;
Cooper – 2: spouse of Alexander Bailzie 1657; relict of Mark Lockhart 1690

Cordiner: James Clerk 1677 *at the Cutle*
Indweller – inhabitant – 6: spouse of James Cuthbertsoun 1633; Alexander Hendersoun 1640; William Wood 1643; Patrick Thomas 1653; Marion Baillie 1657; Hendry Vauss 1696
Mariner – 9: relict of Alexander Hammyltoune 1607; Walter Lyndsay 1611; Robert Hamiltoun 1618; Alexander Bisset 1630; spouse of George Pincartoun 1637; John Cubie 1648; Robert Humble 1651; John Thomsone 1662; George Forrest 1697
Mason – 3: Thomas Petticruis 1608; Hew Cunynghame 1635; John Pittincruiff 1662
Merchant – 6: James Hammiltoun 1622; Nicoll Meassone 1681; William Birnabie 1684; George Spence 1692; Robert Fairlie 1694; John Tait 1695
Minister – 3: John Oswald 1654; Patrick Cooke 1673; George Monipennie 1678
Portioner – not quite an occupation, but an owner of perhaps a very small plot of land – 5: relict of George Smailholm 1637; Mark Achesoun 1634; Alexander Auchinleck 1665; James Browne 1666; George Deanes 1699
Resident – NB different to indweller: Aliesone Wilkie 1646
Sailor – 13: **spouse of David Thomeson 1632**: spouse of Robert Broun 1633; **David Thomsoune 1635**; William Hendersone 1637; James Huntar 1646; **spouse of James Robertsoun 1648; daughter of unquile James Robertsone 1648**; James Robeson & his spouse 1648; Robert Cra[w]ford 1658; Thomas Graye 1658; John Hamiltone 1658; James Johnstoune 1658; Patrick Melvin 1658; Thomas Avaes 1672; Robert Lockhart 1676;
Seaman – 3: James Donaldsone 1673; Adam Mitchell 1690; John Conbie 1692
Servitor – servant: David Foster 1642
servitrix – servant, female – 2: Jonnet Dudgeone 1667; Helen Heriot 1687
Skipper – 14: James Broun 1624; Johne Wilsone 1625; **Robert Thomesone 1633; Williame Thomesone 1635**; Robert Crawford 1638; John Wood 1649; Robert Griersone 1650; George Pinkertoune 1650; John Ker & his spouse 1656; Robert Crauford 1663; George Nicolsone 1666; Johne Wilsone 1670; Walter Bezet & spouse 1699; Robert Padden 1699
Smith – 3: Williame Nicolsoune 1632; Alexander Griersone 1634; James Deanes 1699
Tailor – George Riddell 1691
Traveller – 2 (sells to customers in their own house): **Johnne Broun 1603**; Robert Browne 1637; **relict of John Broun 1637**
Wobster (sic) (weaver): Johnne Cuming 1603
Weaver: George Thomson 1666

Although any full analysis from this information is impossible, the large numbers of skippers (14), mariners (9), seaman (3) and sailors (13) supports the notion that Prestonpans in the 17th century was, above all else, a port, and earned its wealth from trade at sea. The Thomesone (1633, 1635) and the Crawford (1638, 1658, 1663) families were seemingly long-time sea-based families.

Interestingly, no jobs associated with salt (or its taxation) are included in the wills (although 'salter' is amongst the occupations in the birth register) at a time when salt was being produced (albeit by smaller producers). As salt production remained important, it is notable that no occupations related to salt appear on the wills. This may be coincidental but it also ties in with Anderson's[33] suggestion that the smaller pans were absorbed by larger-scale owners and landed interests during this period, and these individuals do not appear as 'salter' etc. A further point is that the salt pans might have been opportunistically acquired by others during the witch hunts of the early 17th century.[34] There is little direct evidence for this, but it is known that female members of the Mott and Achesone families (both salt pan owners in the 16th century) were targeted and persecuted; perhaps this was how the persecutors benefited economically.

2 18th century – a time of improvement & technology[35]

During the early 18th century, Morrison's Haven[36] was busier than ever, dealing with ships from Europe, Scandinavia and even North America; however, by 1743, trade through here had ceased altogether. This was probably due to the new duties imposed post-Union. Things did not improve when coal extraction at Prestongrange declined from c1740s and ceased altogether in the parish between 1765 and 1830. It was deemed that coal could be produced more cheaply elsewhere – possibly from around Tranent and from the Prestonlinks pit, to the east near Cockenzie. However, many new industries took off in the Prestonpans area during the second half of the century. Salt production continued throughout, and was joined by the brewing business (1720s) and the manufacture of chemicals, soap, and pottery, all began about the same time in the 1750s. The impact of the manufacturing development of the town was probably mainly environmental.[37] Between 1749 and the end of the century, the Vitriol Works would have belched out toxic gases, and the sulphur-based fumes were noted to have turned brass green. The smell was 'suffocating'. Add this to the smells associated with the salt works, where part of the extraction process involved the addition of buckets of animal blood to the boiling brine to remove impurities, and the poor quality coal that gave off sulphur smells (like bad eggs) and Prestonpans must have been a very unpleasant place to live.

By the 1790s, trade through Morrison's Haven had begun again. Imports were increasingly important, especially of luxury goods – much in demand by the newly wealthy. Silk, leather, spirits, copper and brass goods, dried fruits and wine came into Morrison's Haven beside less glamorous goods like timber (for pit props), bar-iron and barrels for the Dunbar fish trade. Exports of

33 Anderson, David (2000) *Sourcing Brickmaking, Salting and Chemicals at Prestongrange* pp 8,9 Booklet 3 Prestoungrange University Press

34 Allan, Annemarie (forthcoming 2005) *The Witches of Prestonpans* Prestoungrange University Press

35 It seems likely that merchants and industrialists who cut their teeth on the east coast had interests on the west also. Further research is needed to clarify how extensive the relationship was, but certainly Garbett and Roebuck, who with William Cadell from Cockenzie had started up the production of sulphuric acid (oil of vitriol) at Prestonpans in 1749, moved on to open the Carron Iron Works together in 1759. The Glassford (see Smout, TC (1985) *A History of the Scottish People 1560–1830* Fontana p 359, p 362) family invested in the vitriol works at Prestonpans in 1774; later they were Glasgow-based tobacco barons with interests in Virginia and elsewhere.

36 Aitken, Julie (2000) *Acheson/Morrison's Haven: what came and went and how?* Booklet 2 Prestoungrange University Press pp 15–23

37 Anderson, David (2000) *Sourcing Brickmaking, Salting & Chemicals at Prestongrange* Booklet 3 Prestoungrange University Press and pp 15, 16 for environmental information

glass, pottery, vitriol and its associated products were matched by imports of the raw materials needed for their production.

The Statistical Account provides a picture of the parish's manufacturies (sic) c1793: the comparison with Forrest's survey of 1799 indicates that the health of the economy had declined in those six years – perhaps a sign that the Darien disaster (see 2.3.1 below) had begun to impact on the local economy? In 1793, only six of the ten salt pans were being worked. By 1799, the 6 had declined to just two. Cadell's stoneware in the town continued to thrive until the end of the period, as did one of the two brownware works at the Cuttle. Brownware was exported to Europe, the Americas and the West Indies.

Of the two tileworks (one producing bricks as well) of 1793, only one brickwork was recorded in 1799. The Vitriol Works had also gone by 1799 – overtaken by new technology.

2.1 Landscape

Early 18th century agricultural improvements made land use more efficient and profitable. Longer tenancies of 19 years encouraged tenant farmers to manage the land better, and across the Lothians farmers keenly adopted the new ideas. By mid century, the trend towards enclosure was well under way. Drainage tiles – local demand for these possibly led to the opening of the brick and tile works in Prestonpans in the 1790s – enabled more ground to be cultivated, and improved crops and crop rotations increased productivity. New inventions saved time and labour, and many were developed in the Lothians. James Small, of Dalkeith, designed a new plough in 1763, which reduced the number of horse or oxen required; Andrew Meikle, of East Linton, invented the (water) power-driven threshing machine in 1786. Tenant farms, rented from landowners, replaced the scattered ferm touns, and the surplus displaced population migrated towards the towns in search of work and accommodation.[38]

The best picture of the parish later in the century comes from local minister John Trotter writing the Prestonpans' contribution to Sinclair's Statistical Account in 1793, when the population had risen to just over 2000. While his record implies that rural Prestonpans was an important agricultural area, and 'modern' methods were practised, he also stated that 'though nine tenths of the land is rented there is not one family in the parish who depends for their livelihood solely on farming'. Oddly though, he later listed the professions – stating that there were 18 gardeners and 29 farmers! He went on to, perhaps, hint at the main use of the land: 'the principal market for garden productions is Edinburgh', and at least one baillie was listed in the wills as being also a farmer. Later still Trotter stated that 'land is parcelled into lots of a few acres amongst different tenants who labour it themselves' which seems concomitant with small-scale market garden enterprises.

The ground was well-manured – with either street- or stable-dung – and ploughed several times with Small's plough, using horse power. It was then harrowed to give crops the best chance of success, and peas and beans were sown in drills – making weed control easier. Other crops grown included wheat, Scotch barley, oats – although bird damage was such that this was of less importance than other grain crops – and potatoes and turnips, as well as

38 see also Allan, Chris (2001) *Agricultural Improvement at Dolphinstoun* Booklet 9 Prestoungrange University Press

hay. Cabbage plants were raised in the parish and sold locally and to Glasgow (supposedly 150,000 plants a year) and 70,000 to Falkirk and Carron. Roy's 1755 map[39] shows how much of the parish had been enclosed, and how much remained under the older agricultural system of runrig. The land around Preston House, Drummore and Preston Grange was enclosed by 1755; the fact that the park land of Preston House was enclosed by stone walls is made clear in Groome's description[40] of the 1745 battle site of Prestonpans. It was portrayed as a 'boggy morass, criss-crossed with water-filled ditches; along the margins were fields enclosed by low walls or hedges and scattered with willow trees'.

At this point, Prestonpans remained essentially a single street, with characteristic burgage plots stretching away at right angles to the street frontage. Here the residents would perhaps keep livestock, a pig or chickens, or develop the backlands for small-scale workshops. Adair's Alystob has become Ouyly Stobb; to the east is Triggin Hede – modern day Riggonhead – which was in 1745 a farm. Near Seaton there is a lake, perhaps a precursor of the waterlogged land that presented the 20th century A1 road builders and the opencast mine workings at Blindwells with major problems.

Again, 'roads' are difficult to differentiate from field boundaries; the track from Tranent to Musselburgh remains, and there are 'two roads' described in the Groome account. One passed by Colonel Gardiner's house (ie Olivestob/Bankton) and another to the west of Preston House. It seems likely that the residents of the coastal strip relied more on boats than carts. Certainly there was a lot of traffic across the firth of Forth, between the small settlements. This is borne out to a certain extent by the diary[41] that relates how some Fife folk crossed from Pittenweem to Prestonpans in a small boat to view at close hand what became later known as the Battle of Prestonpans – 21st September 1745. The tourists, Sanders Donaldson, the 'gudeman' Martin and Colin Fowler found their efforts were repaid by a very short – some say 15 minutes – rout of the highlanders, which they viewed from the top of Preston Tower. As strangers and 'Whigs', they were threatened by the Preston natives and fled back to their boat and scurried off home, taking one of the fleeing English soldiers and his son along with them.

2.2 Life & death

In spite of the town's prosperity, and its proximity to the productive acres of the Lothians, the people were still vulnerable to the vagaries of the climate. Harvests remained variable; in 1716, crops in the Lothians were poor after a period of drought, and food riots occurred in Prestonpans in October 1740 after harvest failure. The introduction of the new crops of the turnip, first sown in 1734 by Lee of Skateraw near Dunbar, and the potato, which was grown as a field crop in the Lothians from c1760s on, meant that for the first time, farmers could feed both stock and people through the winter. These tougher crops were better suited to poor weather conditions.

However, nothing was guaranteed: further crop failure followed in 1782,

39 reproduced in Ralton, Andrew (2005) *The Roads that led by Prestoungrange: a journey through the landscape* Booklet 19 Prestoungrange University Press pp 18, 19

40 Quotes from Groome, F ed (this version 1903) *Ordnance Gazetteer of Scotland* on www.clerkington.plus.com/GENUKI/ELN/Prestonpans/prestonpans.html

41 Annemarie Allan was made aware of the existence of this document after a chance meeting with Morag Hood who preserved this memoir of the Horsbrugh family

with famine the following year. Extra supplies were imported from England, Europe and the Baltic countries,[42] and distribution was easier as transport links had improved. Nonetheless, lean years returned in 1799 and 1800. Industrial towns like Prestonpans kept their populations, as earnings in the non-agricultural sectors were paid in cash and were much higher. But if food was unavailable, then no amount of money would overcome the problem.

Disease continued to take its toll and any disease spread quickly though the towns.[43] Hungry people were weak people and so more prone to infection. Poor food contributed to their problems, and failed to meet the dietary needs of those whose work was hard and physical. Because few washed, dysentery and the louse-borne typhus had a free rein. Death was so common it is thought likely that attitudes to the value of life were affected. If a child died, then it was common to re-use the name for another child; and most working families had lots of children, on *average* about 6, of whom only 3 would live into their 30s. Physical work wore people out very quickly and it was important in a society where poverty was rife, that children were able to earn a living and support their parents. The orphaned often lived with aunts and uncles. About 35% of all deaths were of children under 5 years old. There was a measles epidemic in 1735 and, in the 1750s, eastern Scotland suffered a rise in infectious diseases. Whooping cough came in 1755, 1767 and 1776. Smallpox was the greatest threat and many Prestonpans children died of smallpox during the epidemics in 1766 and 1768;[44] Mitchison suggests that 15% of all deaths in Tranent can be attributed to smallpox. Infant diarrhoea – known as bowel hives at the time – was a regular killer, especially when babies were weaned.

2.3 People

During the 18th century, less than half of the population was aged under 25, and few lasted into old age. Single people were either apprentices or farm servants, and marriage only occurred once one could afford to support a family – the average age being the mid 20s – and two parents were essential to the successful raising of a family. If death intervened through childbirth for example, then remarriage was common, and followed the death of a partner fairly quickly. As some 20% of marriages involved at least one bereaved person, many children experienced living with step-parents with all that that entailed.[45]

By the end of the 18th century, the population was increasingly mobile, and society seemed to be less concerned about 'poor people's bed habits'.[46] The age at which marriages occurred fell to 22.6 years, and a greater number of women were pregnant at marriage. These changes in behaviour were probably largely due to the improving economic situation, which enabled couples to set up their own households earlier. Few households comprised several generations together.

42 Flinn, *Scottish Population History* pp 218, 233, 234

43 Mitchison, Rosalind 'Death in Tranent: 1754–81' IN *East Lothian Antiquarians & Field Naturalists' Society Transactions Vol 16* 1979 pp 37–44 Burial registers for nearby Tranent 1754–81 are unusually complete, and some generalisations can be drawn from Rosalind Mitchison's work on these.

44 Flinn, *Scottish Population History* p 226

45 Information from notes provided by Professor Mike Anderson, Edinburgh University 1995/96

46 M Anderson

Prestonpans Fishwives: Mrs Marshall and friend
Photograph Bert Renton

This was a youthful society, and one where many were looking for employment, and each settlement supported an enormous diversity of occupations.

In the marriage registers for Prestonpans 1739, the following occupations of males are given:

barber and pirry wig maker [periwig]
baxter – baker
brewer
candlemaker
carrier
coal hewer
coallier (sic)
dyer – dyes cloth and produces dyes
fisher
gardiner
maltman
maltster – processor of barley into malt
mason
mealmaker
merchant
officer of excise
plowman
portioner – holder of a small feu/proprietor or joint proprietor of land
sailor
salt master
salt officer
sievewright
shoemaker
soldier
tobacconist
tylemaker
weaver
workman
wright

and from the wills (see also Section One, 3) the following occupations are mentioned:

baillie – 2: Richard Sherriff 1706; John Lewars (also tenant farmer) 1746
Baker: Thomas Bower 1710
brewer – 4: Richard Sherriff (also merchant) 1739; John Couper 1755; **James Whitson 1757; James Whitson 1771**
captain – 2: Robert Pinkertoun 1709*
clerk of the custom house – 2: James Smith (resident in Cockeny) 1709; George Skinner (also merchant in Edinburgh) 1713
Collector of the customs – 3: James Baillie 1709; relict of John Haldane 1739; John Ross 1794
Comptroller in the Custom House – 2: William Lem 1759; James Reid 1790
Dyer/dyster/litster – 2: John Liddel 1727; Luke Vallange 1770
Gardener: William Grieve & his widow 1759

Grocer: Archibald Cockburn 1791
Indweller – 2: Walter Martine 1721; William Henderson 1743
Land-waiter – 2 (watcher of the landing of goods): Joseph Wake 1739; Archibald Forrest 1789
major of Strathnaver's regiment: William Reid 1721
Maltman: James Jollie 1704
Mariner – 2: relict of Thomas Hempsteid 1704; widow of [?] Simpson 1766
Merchant – 11: Alexander Deans 1710; Charles Smith 1714; Alexander Dunbar 1724; Archibald Hamilton 1725; William Mathie 1726; John Bartleman 1728; William Melvill jnr (also shipmaster) 1728; **Patrick Sheriff 1729; Charles Sherriff 1740; John Hogg 1750; John Hogg 1756**
Messenger: Robert Spence 1750
Minister: Mathew Reid 1772
Officer of the salt duties: Robert Ferguson 1749
Officer of the customs: Charles Ogilvy 1714 (was Provost of Montrose)
Officer of the excise: Christopher Rapier 1791
Portioner – 3: relict of [?] Henderson 1741; George Vint 1752; Mary Robertson 1762
Sailor – 6: William Cubie 1704; George Grant 1707*; James Pedden 1707*; John Spence 1707*; Thomas Waddell 1707*; relict of Andrew Ormistoun
Salter: daughter of David Thomson 1791
Saltmaster: John Grieg 1759
Salt officer: relict of Hugh Hay 1753
Seaman – 2: William Bartleman 1702; James Gibson 1717
Shipmaster – 8: William Forrest 1720; George Jollie 1725; Stephen Jolly 1730; William Melvill 1733; David Reid 1733; **John Hogg 1736**; James Sherriff 1739; **Robert Hogg 1769**
Shoemaker: son of John Cumming 1731
Skipper – 4: William Cuthbertsone 1702; **Thomas Mathie 1706; John Mathie 1733**; Stephen Tough 1710
Supervisor of the salt duties – 2: John Heriot 1744; Archibald Campbell 1765
Surveyor of His Majesty's Customs – 3: George Lochhart 1707; William Cochran 1724; Robert Halyburton 1777
Tailor: Thomas Brown 1728
Tidewaiter – watcher of the tide for customs: relict of Thomas Campbell 1756
Tobacconist: John Banks 1738
Waiter – watcher: Luke Potts 1712
Weaver: spouse to John Doughtie 1745
Writer – lawyer or notary: Andrew Darling 1735

The link remained between each of the seafaring groups, with the notable exception of fishermen, although the term 'skipper' possibly referred to fishing boat owners; otherwise, sailors, mariners, skippers and shipmasters all feature. The Mathie, Hogg and Sherriff families appear to link both shipmasters and merchants, and merchants and skippers.

In 1793, John Trotter summarised the Prestonpans' workforce: 12 men worked the salt pans; Cadell's pottery employed 40 men and 30+ boys; the brownware pottery at Morrison's haven employed about 20 men and 15 boys. Six men worked at the brick and tile works; and 3 at the seaside works. Fifty men used to work at the Vitriol Works. Trotter stated that there was no butcher in the parish – hence the twice-weekly meat market. Evidently there were a lot of people employed on a very casual basis around the parish, and this probably included most of the women and children, who were expected to help with whatever work the family was involved with. Many women worked as domestic servants. What is notable is that some occupations mentioned in the wills do not appear in Trotter's lists: there are no mariners, merchants or shipmasters.

Business at the port had evidently perked up since the Union in 1707 – or at least the business of taxation, with a comptroller, clerk, collector and officer of the customs all occupied at the Customs House. Trotter stated that a Customs House was extant in 1793, with a wide jurisdiction, and that there were 19 officers of the customs. In case anyone considered smuggling goods in, they were under observation by land- and tide-waiters as well as general waiters or watchers. Monitors of the salt trade had also appeared – with an officer of the salt duties and a salt officer listed – to ensure taxes and dues were paid; salt producers remained elusive.

2.3.1 Impact of Darien

After Union in 1707, there was a flurry of requests made to the compensation fund to claim monies by relatives of those lost* on the ill-starred Company of Scotland trip to Darien, on what later became known as Panama. The Company was set up in 1693, with backing from many of Scotland's wealth-holding sector as well as numerous ordinary folk. The withdrawal of support from English backers did not have an immediate impact on the venture that set off from Leith in 1698. Arguably the destination was poorly chosen – infested with mosquitoes, disease and already under Spanish rule – and by the time the next two groups of settlers had arrived at Darien, it was increasingly clear that there was no other choice but to go home. Only one of the original 16 ships got back to Scotland. The refusal of the Crown under William & Mary to aid the Scots against the Spaniards when the settlers got into trouble at Darien has since been seen as an early step towards ensuring that Scotland chose Union as the way forward, as the country was tipped into near bankruptcy as a result of the failure.

Compensation was agreed as part of the Union settlement. The five testament datives lodged from Prestonpans' folk in 1707 are probably part of the claims, and provide a slightly surprising insight on Prestonpans in the early 18th century, bringing national events into a local context.

'George Grant, sailor on the Unicorn'
'James Pedden, sailor aboard the Rising Sun'
'Robert Pinkertoun captain, sometime commander of the Unicorn'
'John Spence younger, sailor aboard the Rising Sun ... son to umquhile James Spence, boatswain on ... said ship, nephew to Gavin Spence seaman in Prestonpans...'
'Thomas Waddell, sailor aboard the Rising Sun... son to unquhile William Waddell, mariner in Prestonpans.'

2.3.2 Fishing

In his contribution to the *Statistical Account* of 1793, Trotter wrote at length about the fishing industry. It seems that fishing was indeed a part of Prestonpans' life, despite the lack of people listed in the various other sources as 'fishermen'. It was evidently a job that was irregular, low earning, and not a job where wages would accrue over time – and as no monies tended to be outstanding, there was no call for testament datives (see Section One, 3). Fish were caught in season, and were sold locally.

Between c1770–86, the Prestonpans' oyster crop was an important, although seasonal, (January – May) part of the fishing industry. Sixteen boats regularly worked the beds, and a Leith merchant exported the oysters to London where they were relocated on the Thames and the Medway and left to fatten until autumn. Over-fishing led to the trade's decline, and the London oyster market went elsewhere. By 1793, there was a regular workforce of 23 fishermen working 10 boats, plus a further 27 casual workers, harvesting the crop from September – April; the oysters were exported to Newcastle, and also sent overland to Glasgow. The shells were ground for agricultural use as lime.

3 19th century – boomtime

During the 19th century, changing technology carried on apace, and innovation continued to drive the Lothians' prosperity in both industry and agriculture. From c1810 onwards, steam engines fuelled by coal gradually superseded water-power and, although the location of industry was no longer limited to riversides, water remained an essential requirement in the steam age. In the Lothians the early 19th century was a period of agricultural prosperity, accompanied by a phase of house and steading rebuilding – for example at Dolphinston farm, Prestonpans.

As with urban settlements all over Scotland, the crowding of people into poor quality accommodation led to increasing problems with disease. Ultimately it was concern over public health and the associated need to improve water supplies and sewage processing that led to the creation of police burghs with all the authority they needed to implement reforms. In Prestonpans' case the police burgh was created in 1862. By 1892 it had acquired a provost, two bailies and six commissioners.

This is the best-documented period and records abound; the census returns are particularly informative, and for the first time permit the separate parts of the parish to be reviewed.

3.1 Landscape

In 1832 Chambers sang the praises of the good quality agricultural land of the parish, which continued to be enclosed and improved. In 1844, the parish extended to 800–900 acres, with the farms 30–40 acres in size. The whole parish was described as 'arable'. However, Cunninghame wrote in the 1839 *Statistical Account* that 'the arable lands in the parish are very limited in their extent'. Perhaps his admission of the limitations of his agricultural knowledge that followed coloured his view? Certainly the picture of land use that emerges from the 1861 census is rather different – see 3.3.2 below.

Prestonpans town was described thus in the 19th century:

> 'though improved in modern times it is still a straggling dingy town, chiefly consisting of a single street parallel with the Firth, and studded here and there with salt or other manufactories, which keep the place almost continually enveloped in smoke'[47]

47 Chambers 1832 p 876

and Groome (writing in 1903) stated that the manufacture of 'fine earthenware and soap ... a brewery the produce of which is much celebrated and a large distillery' took place, with 'brown earthenware' manufactured at Morrison's Haven. He also related that the salt works – long the backbone of Prestonpans' economic health – had declined during the years following the new salt duty legislation of 1825, leaving the buildings long associated with the industry to decay – though they were still in evidence early in the 20th century.

By the middle of the 19th century, when the Ordnance Survey (OS) produced the first of its maps, the various villages along the northern coastal strip were still separate entities. At Morrison's Haven, there were two clay pits, a school, a brick and tile works, three kilns and a saw mill beside the jetty. At Cuthill, four buildings were labelled as ruins; there was a colliery near to Dolphinston. Wilson's *Gazetteer* of 1868 termed both Preston and Dolphinston as 'villages', and Prestonpans as a 'post-town'. *The National Gazetteer* of the same year called it a 'market town', and added the Cuttle and Preston Grange to the tally of villages.

According to the OS map of 1854, orchards still separated Prestonpans from Preston, but the Free Church manse had been built on West Loan – well away from both the Free Church and Preston itself. Preston was still compact and named places included the remains of Preston Castle, Preston Cottage, the North British Railway Tavern, Preston Cross, a bowling green, the old hospital and Schaw's Hospital. The railway passed to the south, calling at Tranent Station: by 1894, it had become Prestonpans Station.

Mid century, the built-up area of Prestonpans still hugged the coastal strip, but extended to the road immediately south of the established church. The town was beginning to creep south along West Loan, ending at the Free Church (built 1878). The town boasted two potteries, a salt works, a soap manufacturer, brewery – called by one source as a 'good ale brewery', post office, Preston Links Colliery and an Established Church and school. A Custom-house and a 'works for the manufacturer of oil of vitriol' associated with the manufacture of spirits of salt and Glauber salts and soap was noted.[48] Brick and tile manufacturing continued, and the oyster trade kept residents busy. Others were 'engaged in the coasting trade'. Martine, writing in 1890, commented that there were a 'number of substantial well-built houses on each side of the streets and lanes', with 'new tenements as recent additions'.

3.2 Life & death

Disease continued to devastate the population, with each of the 19th century killers affecting a different sector of the community.

The following all appear as cause of death in Prestonpans' burial registers of 1835:

apoplexy
bowel hives (infant diarrhoea)
cancers
consumption – TB
decline

48 The earlier chemical works of the Prestonpans Vitriol Company had disappeared by 1800

dropsy
drownded
fever
hooping cough (sic)
inflamation
measles
mortification
old age – aged 57!
palsy
rheumie
scarlet fever
teething
typhus
water on chest
weakness

Many of these are mere descriptions – an understanding of disease was one of the great breakthroughs of the period.

Deaths continued to be high amongst children; at times the burial registers give separate listings of children's deaths – including cause of death and the location of the burial. Measles, scarlet fever, dysentery, diarrhoea and whooping cough were devastating illnesses; unfortunately it took a number of years before the various links were made, and understood, with living conditions – poor sanitation, overcrowding and contaminated water supplies being the main culprits. The Old Parish Register for Prestonpans, 1833[49] makes for sad reading.

The typhus outbreak of 1818–19 was accompanied by measles and whooping cough,[50] which affected mostly children. In Prestonpans, measles killed at least 15 children in November 1839. Supported by the Church of Scotland, smallpox vaccinations had begun in Musselburgh in 1801, so it should have been the non-vaccinated infants that died from the disease in Prestonpans between April and November 1840: Mary Thomson, 4 months; Margaret Little's child, 5 months; Isobel Whitson, 3 months all followed Margaret Mackay, aged 22, Peter Ritchie, 1 year and Ann Stonehouse, 2 1/2 years, to their graves. Three children died in June 1844 from whooping cough.

Typhus struck again in 1847 and 1849, again accompanied by measles, and scarlet fever and smallpox. TB was bad during the 1840s.

Older adults suffered most from the cholera epidemic of 1831/1832.[51] Water-borne, the disease moved into Haddington on 17th December 1831, and reached Tranent in January 1832, taking about 6 weeks to pass through each town:

> 'The disease cholera morbus, which has made such ravages in all parts of the world, visited the Cuthill, Prestonpans upon the 22nd January 1832'.

By mid March, 29 people had died, and one more died in April.

By the time of the Poor Law Inquiry of 1844, people of the town were 'not

49 NAS OPR 718/9 1833 – copy in Local History Centre, Haddington
50 Flinn *Scottish Population History* p 369
51 Flinn *Scottish Population History* pp 370, 371, 380, 381

allowed to accumulate dung hills at their door' and it was noted that the streets were cleaned daily 'by the person to whom the dung is let'. Some effort was evidently being made to reduce the squalor, even though many homes remained without effective sanitation.

Between November 1848 and January 1849, a second wave of cholera killed off 26 people in Prestonpans, as it again spread across the Scottish lowlands. Spasmodic outbreaks occurred, including the death from cholera, in September, of 'a stranger man said to be 42 years old' followed by 2 more in October. The disease reappeared in October 1854.

East Lothian's death rate was at its highest between 1871–1875, but the population levels were maintained as workers came into Scottish towns from the highlands and from Ireland, as they had on a seasonal basis for years. The 19th century immigrants sought to escape the Irish famine and many settled in Scotland, especially on the west coast. Later, these migrants moved again, this time to the east coast where they sought to use their industrial skills in the mines.

3.3 People

This period provides an abundance of information on local people, though most is available for the post 1850 period.

Male occupations in 1833[52] included:

baker
blacksmith
carter
enginman (sic)
excise officer
fisherman
flesher
gardener
labourer
mason

An idea of the types of employment in the parish can be gleaned throughout the wills of the 19th century (again those individuals possibly linked by family are in bold):

Baker – 5: John Aitchieson 1806; Matthew Smith 1848; Andrew Cathic 1852; Charles Smith 1868; **John Rennie 1884; James Rennie 1897**
Banker: Richard Clark Belfield 1899
Baron baillie: James Watt 1827; James Watt 1846
Blacksmith – 3: William Hay 1890; Thomas Merrylees 1898; Richard Fortune 1899 (Preston Links)
Brewer – 2: John Fowler 1841
Builder: Alexander Knox (also grocer) 1862
Butcher – 2: Robert Ketchen 1881; Alexander Instant 1899
Brickwork manager:
William Dun 1899 (Cuthill)

52 NAS OPR 718/9 gives some occupations

Carrier – 3: **Peter Whitecross 1858; Charles Whitecross** (and farmer) **1868**; Thomas Johnston 1892

Chelsea Pensioner: Malcolm McNaughton 1807

Cloth merchant: Robert Turnbull 1867

Collector of the customs – 3: Francis Buchan Sydeserf 1822; Andrew Watson 1826

Colliery agent: George Alexander Proctor 1893 (Rosemount)

Colliery manager: George Goodwin 1897 (Ravensheugh)

Commander, Royal Navy: George Syme of Northfield House 1886

Controller of customs: Adam Stevenson 1857

Farmer –2: relict of Adam Robertson, Prestonpans 1821; John Taylor, Prestonpans 1822

Farmer & gardener – 2: **William Wright, Preston 1862; George Wright, Preston 1867**

Fisherman: Archibald Buchanan 1885

Flesher: George Hume 1879

Gardener – 6: John Goodsir Preston Grange 1829; wife of John Taylor 1831; John Ferguson 1864; William Wright 1869; Alexander Inglis 1880; Robert Allison 1885 (Castle Gardens, Preston); widow of Thomas Aitken 1899; John Henderson 1899 (Castle Garden, Preston)

Gas manager: John Mann 1889

Grocer – 4: John Heriot 1838; James Walker 1864; John Porter 1883; John Davie 1884 (High Street); Elizabeth Stewart or White 1887 (High Street)

Joiner: Samuel Rogerson 1873

Market gardener – 2: Thomas Sibbald 1876; George Halliday 1892

Mason: relict of John Howieson 1808; son of John Howison 1813 (tenant of the lands of Preston); **James Pettgrew 1859; James Petticrew (and merchant) 1876**

Matron Schaw's Hospital: Elisa Ann Webb 1884

Merchant – 8: **Alexander Nimmo 1813; Andrew Nimmo junior 1824; George Nimmo 1825**; David Pearson 1837; Andrew Alexander 1843; William Baird 1844; Robert Hunter 1847; David Walker 1859; relict of Charles Aitken 1872; Joseph Drysdale 1875; widow of James Brown 1892

Mine overseer, Prestonlinks: John McCairn 1875

Minister –3: Peter Primrose 1833; William Bruce Cunningham 1878; John Struthers 1888

Potter – 7: spouse of Robert Gordon, Bankfoot 1832; Thomas Brown 1854; sister of Duncan Thomson 1858; Andrew Mitchell, Cuthill 1862; James Allan 1865; **James Belfield 1878; Charles Belfield senior 1890; Francis Sinclair Belfield 1892**; James Fraser 1897 (Whitefield Place)

Residenter: Margaret Dick 1801; Jean Murray 1824; Peter Dougall 1846

Salt manufacturer – 3: **Andrew Alexander 1840; William Alexander 1865**; wife of John Maxwell Sharpe 1877

Soap boiler: John Dickson 1887

Soap maker – 2: Thomas Paterson 1848; Richard Johnston 1874

Soap manufacturer: James Mellis 1899

Surgeon – 3: James Williamson 1834; Robert Ritchie 1860; James Lumsden King 1874

Tailor & clothier: John Borland 1886

Teacher – 4: *female*: Isabella Trotter 1847; Janet Harper 1853; *2 male*: Alexander Hane Cowan at the Grammar School 1856; George Inglis Bird

1869
Watchmaker: Andrew Smith 1857
Wright: George Clark 1829; daughter of Thomas Cowan 1869
Writer to the Signet: daughter of Thomas Cowan WS in Prestonpans 1869

More unusual members of the community also appeared in the wills, and included the following:

A Prestonpans resident, **Andrew Graham** (1816) was 'formerly Governor of the British Settlements of the Hudson's Bay Company'; **Alexander Bisset** (1864) another Prestonpans resident was the 'Minister of the English Presbyterian Church Amsterdam'; **William Aitken Carmichael Shand** (1871) 'Professor of English literature in St. Petersburg, thereafter residing in Edinburgh latterly at Prestonpans'; and **George Alexander** (1872) 'merchant in Prestonpans thereafter in Halifax Nova Scotia'.

Jane Boyd (1879) was the daughter of Adam Stevenson, Controller of Customs at Prestonpans as well as being the widow of John Boyd master mariner, Arbroath.

William MacKinlay (1889) 'sometime residing in South Leith Manse, Leith thereafter Keeper, Wallace Monument, Abbey Craig, Stirling, latterly residing at Broomhill House, Prestonpans.'

David Stevenson (1899) 'sometime officer of H.M. Customs, Grangemouth, residing at West End, Prestonpans.'

These people are an indication of Prestonpans' role in the wider world. Today it has become an ex-coal town and commuter settlement; in the past it had greater standing.

In 1844,[53] it was said that the population comprised 'agricultural and other labourers, colliers and fishermen, but chiefly fishermen. None of these classes are provident in their habits'. However as the Poor Law Inquiry went on to say that there were friendly societies in existence – the gardeners with 160 members and 'artists and sailors also', surely an indication that some residents were provident enough to try to provide for their future?[54]

As will be seen below, a range of jobs was available in the parish during the 19th century, and there are indications too that the parish proved attractive to workers from elsewhere. Unfortunately there was not always enough work for them all. At the end of the 1891 census return for Enumeration Area 5, there is a list of 10 men and 2 women, classified as 'Migratory Poor etc found in a brick kiln at Morrison's Haven'. All are noted as 'unemployed', with occupations thus: coal miner 2; general labourer 3; harness maker; butcher; farm servant 2 male, 1 female; bootmaker; and jute factory worker (female). Their ages varied from 64 to 35, their places of birth included Ireland 3; Leith; Auchterarder; Renfrew; Dumbartonshire 2; Dundee (but not the jute worker); Neilston; Portobello and Queensferry. If life was hard for those in work, things could always get worse for the unemployed.

3.3.1 *Fishing*

In 1839 the continuing importance of the oyster fishing was noted. By 1861, there were about 90 ordinary fishermen, aged between 13 and 70, listed in the

53 Parliamentary Paper various volumes (including 22, 25) 1844.
54 See Baker, S (2005) *Poverty, Self-help and an Emerging Social Life in Prestonpans* Prestoungrange University Press pp 21–26

census. Members of the Ritchie, Thomson and Baleny/Ballenie families abounded. Some 50 fishermen lived in the burgh north of the turnpike road; other surnames included Edmund, Cunningham and Fraser. Harrie Thomson and the husband of Georgina Fraser were 'away at the whaling'. A further 33 lived south of the turnpike road; John and Ellen Cunningham and their family appear typical. He and his 3 eldest sons – James 21, Adam 19, and John 15 were all fishermen; his remaining 4 sons were not old enough to work. Just 5 fishermen lived in the Cuthill and Morrison's Haven part of the parish.

The three named female fish dealers – Euphemia Thomson aged 54, Janet Ritchie aged 60 and Susan McLeod aged 35 – lived in the town. Margaret Baillie was listed as a herring net worker.

At the time of the 1891 census, fishing continued to be important to the burgh. The same names appear as before – Ritchie, Cunningham, Baillie, McLeod, Thomson – although the number of branches of each family had greatly multiplied. A Peter Thomson from Cuthill and a William Thomson of Morrison's Haven were both recorded as 'sea pilot', perhaps developing further the Thomson family link with the sea; a later Thomson was the last sea pilot recorded.

3.3.2 Prestonpans' agriculture – landowners, tenants etc.

By combining information from the census, the voting lists and the valuation rolls it is possible to unravel the intricacies of the agricultural sector in Prestonpans parish. In 1861, most of the gardeners lived between Preston village and Prestonpans, or in the rural parts of the parish. Many were listed as both farmers and gardeners, and indeed many worked large acreages of land.

The only farm as such in the parish was **Dolphinston**, owned by the Grant-

Plough horses at Dolphinston Farm
Photograph © copyright East Lothian Museums Service

Sutties of Prestongrange, where 10 households were listed. No farmer was given, just 2 stewards – John White, farm steward and James Fysh, land steward. James Gray and his nephew William Gray were both given as gardeners there, though neither held land of their own. By 1893/4, Dolphinston was being farmed by James Shields, and William Gray, gardener, was working the market garden there. In the 1891 census William Gray (aged 54) is listed as a market gardener and employer. Other land at Dolphinston was tenanted by James Morrison, and by John Gilles, gardener from West Pans.

In 1861, the occupation of Robert Binnie, Seton Mains was given as Agent & Farmer, but as no acreage was listed his role perhaps was as a manager; he does not appear in the voters roll of 1855. The entry for Robert Hislop (aged 30 in 1861 and son of brewer Robert Hislop (71)) states he farmed 200 acres, but no more information is given.

Continuing the earlier trend for Prestonpans folk being involved in a range of activities, in 1861, salt manufacturer William Alexander (72), was also a farmer of 42 acres, employing 2 agricultural labourers.

Market gardens

The amount of land worked by the most influential gardeners is given in the 1861 census. There were 6 key individuals; Mark Aitken, Alexander Inglis, Alexander Lauder, Thomas Sibbald, and two men who in all likelihood had family links – William Wright and William Wright (Preston). The 1855 Voters' Roll lists William Wright senior, Prestonpans and William Wright junior, Preston, and both are designated as gardeners. By comparing these names with the will lists above and the voters' lists (Appendix Five), it is clear that the designation of gardener, farmer, market gardener and so on was a fairly random process. Mark Aitken is on the 1855 Voters' Roll as a gardener, and on the census as a farmer.

These 6 individuals – all variously designated as 'farmer & gardener' – are discussed below in order of the amount of land held according to the 1861 census, which perhaps reflects their importance in the market garden sector in the parish. The information from the 1893/4 Valuation Roll is also given: much of this last seems to indicate that gardening was a skill passed down through the generations. However it should be noted that the writer has assumed family relationships where there may be none. More work would be needed to confirm these relationships.

In 1861, the unmarried Tranent-born Alexander Lauder, aged 60, lived in the Drummore area; he held 152 acres and employed 9 men, 1 boy and 10 women. He lived with his 30-year old niece Isabella Lauder who was his housekeeper, his nephew Alexander Radelin (?) (23), farm foreman and Jane Kemp (20) who was a domestic servant.

By 1891, 90-year old farmer and employer Alexander Lauder was living at Goshen House, and late in the day had married. He lived there with his wife Elizabeth (65), and unmarried son Alexander (23). The 1893/4 valuation roll states that Drummore farm, owned by Colonel William Aitchison, was tenanted by Alexander Lauder junior.

William Wright was a widower aged 87 in 1861, living in the south-eastern part Prestonpans town. He held 5 acres of garden and 120 acres of farmland, and employed 4 men and 1 boy. His unmarried grandson Archibald Greenfield, 23, was also a gardener. William's 22 year-old grand-daughter

Margaret was the household's housekeeper. His great grand-daughter Jane Clerk, 5, was a scholar. William was on the Voters' Roll of 1855, and may have died in December 1869.

In 1891, gardener and employer Archibald Greenfield was living at Prestonlinks with his wife Mary, daughter Alice (11) and 13-year old son, George.

In 1893/4, Archibald was a tenant of the Shaw Bequest, renting 9 houses (he had 7 subtenants) and land. He also rented market garden land at Prestonpans from James Scrymgeour, gardener, Tranent. George Greenfield is on the 1904 Voters' Roll.

In 1861, Mark Aitken (39) was probably based at Preston. He farmed 80½ acres, and employed 4 men, 3 boys and 4 women. He and his wife Helen (45) had 6 children, one of whom was James born in 1851, and employed a domestic servant Ann Mathieson (19).

In 1891, James Aitken was listed as the farmer's son at Northfield, though Mark cannot be located on the census. James lived at Northfield with his wife Isabella, 3 daughters and 2 sons (Mark and Andrew). The census entry suggests that he was no longer an employer. The 1893/4 Valuation Roll entry makes it clear that James Hunter Aitken, rented Northfield Farm and offices from James McNeil of Northfield, and land from John F Hislop in Preston.

Also of Preston, gardener William Wright (65) worked 60 acres in 1861; he employed 5 men and 2 boys. He lived with his wife Margaret (57), daughter Mary (24), son clerk Archibald (17) and son George (23) who was also a gardener. His other sons John (14) and Thomas (12) were scholars. A William Wright died in October 1862. In 1891, John Wright, market gardener and employer, was living at Preston Cottage with his wife, Catherine, and their 3 sons (the eldest being William, who was born in 1876) and 4 daughters. John also appears in the 1893/4 valuation roll: he rented houses, gardens and buildings from the Schaw Bequest, and land from John F Hislop at Preston.

From the south-eastern part of town, Alexander Inglis (62) worked 12 acres and employed 4 men in 1861. His unmarried sons Alexander (30) and William (22) also worked as gardeners and lived at home with their parents and wife Margaret's (54) mother Catherine Smith (75). An Alexander Inglis died in July 1880. In 1891, Alexander Inglis (22), gardener and employer, lived with his mother Agnes and his 4 brothers and sister on the High Street. In 1893/4 he rented land at Harlawhill from John F Hislop, and appears on the Voters' Rolls of 1904.

Also a resident of the south-eastern part of Prestonpans, gardener Thomas Sibbald (51) employed 2 men to work his 11 acres. His son William (22) was also a gardener and his daughter Catherine (16) a milliner; both lived with Thomas and his wife Ann (48). The wills list refers to Thomas as market gardener, and it seems likely that retired gardener Robert Sibbald (76) was his father. A Thomas Sibbald died in March 1876.

In 1891, market gardener and employer William Sibbald was living at Rose Lane Cottage, Preston with his unmarried sisters Catherine (aged 46) and Margaret (39), and brother Thomas (39). In 1893/4, William Sibbald was renting 2 houses and land from the Schaw Bequest, and the glebe land from the minister. By 1904 he was on the Voters' Roll.

Others who were evidently more than just labouring gardeners also appear in the records; fortunes evidently rose and fell over time.

In 1861, George Halliday (28) was referred to as a garden master; in 1891

Workers at Fowlers Brewery circa 1915
Photograph Bert Renton

he was living in Kirk Street with his son, David (also a gardener, 26) and daughter Marina, and called gardener and employer. On his death in 1892 he was referred to as a market gardener. In 1891, gardener John Halliday (29) was living elsewhere on Kirk Street with his wife and children, Catherine (5) and George (4). Referred to as a market gardener, he rented land at West Loan from John F Hislop in 1893/4: it is likely he was another of George's sons.

In 1891, market gardener and employer Robert Allison was living at Tower Cottage, Preston with his wife, Margaret and 3 daughters and 2 sons. He rented land at Dunbar Butts from John F Hislop, part of the glebe from the church, and land from Sir William Hamilton of Preston.

In 1891, head gardener and employer John Henderson lived in the burgh at Rose Cottage. By 1893/4 he was also a tenant of John Fowler & Company, renting land at Burnrig. The Rodger family also appear regularly in the records: in 1891, William Rodger (gardener and employer aged 67) was living on the High Street with his wife, son and 3 daughters.

Others named as gardeners included James Sanderson, William Robertson and John Ferguson.

The Taylors of Seton Mains appear on the Voters' Roll of 1855 – indicating that they owned land within Prestonpans. By 1893/4, they were renting out their own land in the parish – for example a market garden was rented to

William Robertson, and they also rented additional lands in Prestonpans from land owners like the Schaw Bequest and George Watson's College (at Upper and Middle Shotts). One James Duncan Taylor, farmer, rented part of Bankton farm from owner James McDonall of Stranraer.

3.3.3 Agriculture – general workers

The agricultural depression that affected arable farmers all over the country impacted the Lothians between 1870–90; the wheat growers were the worst hit. Prestonpans' mixed farms and market gardens perhaps fared better. Here, the land was divided into smaller acreages than elsewhere in the Lothians. It is likely that the women field workers adopted the same distinctive headgear as the other female agricultural labourers of the area – the bonnets of the bondagers.[55]

Most workers in Prestonpans were employed as fishermen or field workers, and the census of 1861 has many workers listed as agricultural labourers, farm servants, gardeners, out workers etc. Those who laboured in the fields earned lower wages than those in manufacturing or industry. In 1844, the average wage of an able-bodied agricultural labourer in the parish was 1/6 day; women and children who laboured in the fields got 8d a day.[56] Cottagers paid 30 shillings to £2 per year for a cottage (with no garden), and meal was 16 shillings a boll.[57] Potatoes were 10/– a boll.

The female labour force was essential to the success of both market garden crops – cabbages, leeks and so on – and arable farm crops – turnips and potatoes – all of which required a large amount of care in the pre-mechanised era. More hands were required at harvest time and again women provided the labour. With at least three market gardens within the Preston area alone, demand for workers was high. Female highland migrant workers were still coming south on a regular basis to work on the land although, over the course of the 19th century, male workers from Ireland increasingly replaced them.

The proximity of Edinburgh provided demand for local products and the local women took their goods – kail, salt and fish – into the town to sell. It seems likely that other local produce – vegetables and fruit – was also touted round the town.

3.3.4 Industry

In 1839, Bruce Cunningham's account noted that the two brownware potteries and the tile manufacturie (sic) at Preston Grange colliery remained in business. Paterson's soap works was described as thriving. The salt works of William Alexander and Fowler's Brewery 'under Mr Hislop's care' continued to do well. By 1890, Morrison's Haven was trading well in coal and drain pipes. Mr Meek traded salt, and James Mellis had taken over the soap works from the Patersons sometime during the 1860s.

Coal mining

Mining in Prestonpans was very much an on and off industry during the 19th

55 The labour of the ploughman's bondager paid for the rent of his cottage. Sometimes she was his wife, or daughter, or an unrelated single female. She was paid by the ploughman and lived in his cottage. Her hooped bonnet protected against sun and wind.

56 There were 12 pennies in a shilling, and 20 shillings in a £1; the women and children got 8 pennies, less than half the rate of the male workers who got 1 shilling and 6 pennies a day

57 Boll – in Scotland equal to 6 imperial bushels or a weight of 140lb of such as flour

Prestonlinks Colliery
Photograph Bert Renton

century.[58] The *Report on Children Employed in Mines*[59] stated that work at Prestongrange was 'suspended from overflowing occasioned by cutting through a dyke', or flooding. It is unclear where the erstwhile miners were in 1861 – there are few empty houses noted, so possibly they decamped to nearby Tranent or Inveresk. By 1848, the mine was again operational.

The occupier of Preston Links, John Grieve, gave evidence. In 1842 there were 31 adult males employed there, 12 males under 18 years old, and 9 boys under 13. In addition there were 5 adult females, 9 females under 18 and 5 girls under 13. Children began work in the mines aged between 7 and 8.

Concern was expressed that although the school was located close to the mining community, and it was free, few collier children attended. Teacher Thomas Furzie commented that the 'avarice' of the parents led them to get the children to work as soon as possible, often aged less than 8. 'I have known children of 5 left at home in charge of still younger members of the family as their mothers are employed in the pits'.

John Grieve commented 'it is my opinion that it would be advantageous to exclude children under 10 years of age and their mothers, so that the children might be educated and looked after'. Children were used as 'pumpers'

58 see also Burnett, Allan (2000) *Industrial Ownership and Relations at Prestongrange* Prestoungrange University Press Booklet 4; Allan, Annemarie (2000) *Horses, Steam & Electric Engines at Prestongrange* Prestoungrange University Press Booklet 5

59 1842 Parliamentary Paper Vol XVI

working in the deepest part of the mines; standing up to their waists in water they worked 6-hour shifts, followed by 12 hours of rest.

The following children were named as working[60] at Preston Links in 1842. None could write, those who could read, read badly:

Jane Cumming, aged 14 – working in the mine for 8 years
Isabel Cumming, 10 – working in the mine for 3 years
Janet Gibb, 8 – working in the mine for 7 months
John Gibb, 10 – working in the mine for nearly 3 years
Mary Hood, 10 – working in the mine for 1 year
Nicoll Hood, 12 – working in the mine for below 5 years
Marrion Lamb, 11 – working in the mine for 1 year
Jane Peacock, 10 – working in the mine for nearly 5 years

In 1851, coal miner **Nicoll Hood**s (aged 22, born Dalkeith) married Angelina aged 19 in Prestonpans; they resided at Prestonlnks. Of the remaining children interviewed for the Inquiry, only **Mary Hood**, born 1832 at Cowpits, Inveresk appears in the 1851 census. None appear in the 1881 census, which is searchable electronically. One wonders if they survived long beyond childhood.

The 1842 Report summarised that the 'whole district of Preston Links and the Pans though containing 2 large potteries, a distillery and breweries, well attended parochial and infant schools, appeared to contain a very ignorant and destitute population.'

By the time of the 1861 census, there were just half a dozen men in the area near Preston Links whose occupations were given as 'coal miner'. At Bankfoot there were 6, and at Cuthill there were about 20. It was not unusual for men of entire families to work in the mines, such as Robert Naysmith and his 3 sons, James McKinley and his 2 boys, and John Davidson, his son former coal miner John (at 21 already an invalid), and another coal mining son (19).

There were two cases where the miners and their families had come from Ireland and settled in Prestonpans. These examples indicate that the families would do anything to earn a few pennies. Miner Felix Mowbray (47) was born in Ireland, as was his wife Catherine and son Thomas (18), also a coal miner; his daughter Jane (14) worked as a farm labourer, and there were 2 more small children.

Thomas Heart (48) came from Sligo; his wife Mary was an agricultural labourer and their 12-year old son William worked as a labourer in a pottery. They had a daughter Maria (9) and a boarder Thomas Airley (24) also from Ireland.

In 1874, there were 182 men employed in coal mining in the parish: 47 at Preston Links and 135 at Prestongrange.[61] By the time of the census in 1891, there were 134 miners living in the west of the parish; 90 in Middle Street and 33 in Front Street, Cuthill and 7 at Bankfoot and 4 at Morrison's Haven. There were 28 empty houses in Middle Street.[62] Most were born in the Lothians, other came from Fife; just a few originated from Ireland.

60 Unfortunately their own comments on their work and lives have been lost

61 Archibald, G 'Overview of Mining' IN Baker, S (unpublished) *CD-ROM: East Lothian Fourth Statistical Account 1945–2000 Appendix 3*

62 Lyall, Annie (2000) *Model Housing for Prestongrange Miners* Prestoungrange University Press Booklet 7, pp 9–11

3.3.5 The burgh

In 1844, there were 4 resident heritors and 6 absentee heritors - the landowners – who worked with the kirk session and who had responsibility for both assessing the funds required to meet the session's obligations, and for providing that money. By 1861, demand for servants was high within the burgh itself, and many women were working as domestic servants. It seems that young girls were content to work in the fields for a few years, but later moved towards domestic service

The lack of a savings bank in the town was noted, as was the fact that a 'pawn broker recently came to Prestonpans'. There were also '19 public houses or licensed for sale of spirits' and 'shops – not public houses that sell spirits – 11'. In 1839, Cunningham declared that by stopping the sale of spirits on a Sunday, drunken behaviour and 'brutal merriment' had been reduced.

According to the 1844 Poor Law Inquiry, the parish supported the education of 14 pauper children and a total of 30 pauper children aged 12–14 attended the 3 schools. A number of vagrant beggars from Tranent were in evidence.

The poor were made up of '113 retired paupers' and a 'great number of widows with small children' – perhaps inevitable in a mainly fishing town. The total number of paupers was 144, and 22 were wholly disabled from work, 44 partially disabled and 5 were insane. By 1861, there were 25 male paupers with no stated occupation; 10 male and 22 female lunatics; and one male and two female vagrants. In 1861 the Inspector of the Poor was David McQueen who lived at Cuthill.

Prestonpans became a Police Burgh in 1862,[63] as did nearby Tranent and North Berwick. At the time it was known as a seaside resort and the townsfolk were 'conscious of a special responsibility to the many visitors that came to the town'. A range of laws was adopted in quick succession including one against 'obstructions and nuisances in the streets', others on 'cleansing', 'lodging houses', 'slaughterhouses', 'improving streets' and 'public bathing'.

It was considered unnecessary to adopt water and drainage laws until it was realised that Prestonpans had no claim for water from the entailed estate from which it was drawn. Wells sufficed until 1900, when a water trust was formed.

Conclusions

By the turn of the century, the town extended about 3/4 mile along the coast, occupying about the same area as it did a century before, so this seems to be a tale of use and re-use of the same land over time. However, the impact of the decline of the salt industry had left redundant buildings standing 'ruinous and forlorn' giving the town a 'decayed appearance'. The big chemical works too were long gone.

> 'The houses have a blackened, time worn appearance, scarcely two of them stand in a line ... the town was zigzag ant both ends and crooked in the middle'[64]

63 Urquhart, R.M. (1989) *The burghs of Scotland and the Police of Towns Act 1850* The Scottish Library Association

64 Quotes from Groome, F ed (this version 1903) *Ordnance Gazetteer of Scotland* on www.clerkington.plus.com/GENUKI/ELN/Prestonpans/prestonpans.html

The two key industries by this time were the soapworks and the brewery; at Morrison's Haven there was a small pottery turning out brown and white ware. Oysters were still harvested but it seems likely that the beds offshore were beginning to suffer from pollution. The same thing happened at Musselburgh. This is unsurprising considering the amount of effluent being discharged by the various industries along the river Esk. Prestonpans own industrial heritage too contributed to the damage along the coast.

The town boasted 'a post office (with telegraph), a branch of the Royal Bank, two hotels, a gas company and waterworks'.

Inevitably more research could be carried out on the wills themselves, which in turn would provide more detail about trade and family connections but unfortunately time constraints preclude this.

It is apparent that Prestonpans parish and burgh went through a number of identities over the years. This was evidently a fairly wealthy community in the 16th and 17th centuries, with merchants, a busy port and a high standard of living for many of its residents. The industries provided opportunities for a range of both skilled and unskilled work, and generally as one declined in importance another rose to take its place. The rich soils of the parish produced an ample harvest that was sold to nearby burgeoning Edinburgh, and provided work for the younger and unmarried women of the parish in the process. Edinburgh continued to draw in slightly older single women to work as household servants, who found this work more attractive than fieldwork.

APPENDIX ONE
CHRONOLOGY OF PRESTONPANS' INDUSTRIES[65]

22 Apr 1526	permission to build harbour granted by Royal Charter
1700	harbour remodelled by William Morison
1712–59	decline
(1711–41	*records extant of the Members of Incorporation of Sailors of Prestonpans)*
1753	harbour repaired
1875–7	harbour improved
1957	harbour filled in

Coal – exported 16th century, late 17th, late 18th –1930s.
Produced at least from 12th century. Coal was needed to heat the seawater to extract the salt; small scale until new technology enabled deep workings

1680s	half of all boats trading from the Prestonpans' harbours (ie all from Fisherrow to Aberlady) were colliers; some went overseas, rest to Edinburgh or other Forth ports
c1765–1830	coal mining ceased at Prestongrange (supplies brought from other parishes)
1797	Tranent militia riot – Prestonpans colliers involved
1799	Serfdom banned
1830	No 1 shaft sunk

65 All of these have been covered in detail in other booklets in this series

1843	Women banned from underground working
c1919	End of peak phase of industry
1962	Prestongrange pit closed
1964	Prestonlinks pit closed

Salt – 1543–1800s, salt exported
Produced at least from 12th century, peaking in the 16th and 17th centuries; big business in the 26th century with 38 pans. Salt was essential in an age when meat and fish preservation was the only way to feed the people over the winter. It was also used in agriculture, leather making, to glaze pottery, in soap and cloth making and metallurgy.

Pre 1640s	salt exported to Holland and England from Morrison's Haven
Post 1640s	salt exported to Germany & Baltic; English cod fishing boats collected salt en route to Iceland
1685	An 'infinite innumerable number of salt works'[66]
1707	Union beginning to impact on salt sales; decline evident by 1727 (Morrison had 11 pans, of which 8 in ruin)
1740s–50s	salt industry boom again. Demand high for salt in nearby Edinburgh
1780s	Prestonpans had 10 salt pans; salt sold in Edinburgh & other towns by salt wives
1825	repeal of salt duties marks beginning of the end for Scottish salt
1903	one surviving salt works, working 2 pans
1959	end of salt works in Prestonpans

Glass – exported from 1698

c1610–27	produced by Sir George Hay; some production continued until 1646
c1698–c1720s	one of William Morison's enterprises – bottle making – goods exported

Pottery[67] – exported late 1690s on

1690s	brownware manufactured in Prestonpans (OSA footnote p 571)
1750–1838	the works begun by William Cadell & Co (Kirk Street and Bankfoot) continued under various owners and managers including Gordon, Thomson and Watson
1772	record[68] of flowerpots from Cadell's being sold to the Duke of Buccleuch
1764–1817	Littler's, West Pans (1764–77)was later owned by Bangle (1784–92). Others took it on from 1792–1817
1772–1841	Gordon's
1835–1935	Belfield & Co

66 Smout, TC 'Trade of East Lothian at the end of the 17th century' IN *East Lothian Antiquarian & Field Naturalists' Society Transactions Vol IX* p 67

67 Information from Bonnar, Jane (2000) *Decorative Pottery at Prestongrange* Booklet 9 Prestoungrange University Press

68 NAS GD224/209/13

Bricks, tiles etc

c1790s–1975s	Owners changed many times, and companies came and went, including the Prestongrange Coal & Firebrick Company (1882–93)

Brewing

1720s onwards	several different breweries
1745–1969	Fowler's Brewery

Chemicals

1749–1799	Roebuck & Garbuck set up a sulphuric acid manufactury. Continued under Glassford from 1774, and later as the Prestonpans Vitriol Company. By 1784 this was the largest acid works in Britain. Export trade was important. Decline came once chloride of lime became preferred bleach after it was patented in 1799

Soap

Mid 18th century–1950s, under first Patterson, then Mellis (1860s on).

APPENDIX TWO
POPULATION SUMMARY – PARISH & BURGH

NB These figures are variable depending on source
The estimated population in Prestonpans parish in 1755 was 1596.

Civil parish including the burgh,[69] and Cuthill, Preston and Morrisons's Haven

1801	1964
1811	1995
1821	2055
1831	2322
1841	2234
1851	2123
1861	2080
1871	2069
1881	2573
1891	2659
1901	3382
1911	4722
1921	5154
1931	5986
No data was collected during the war period	
1951	7593
1961	8339
1971	8561

69 From listing held at Local History Centre, Haddington Ref A21.3

The Police Burgh of Prestonpans – created a police burgh in 1862[70]

1871	1597		
1881	1610	843 male	767 female
1891	1606		
1901	1721		
1911	1923		
1921	2021	1043 male	978 female

The burgh was extended in 1923

Population from the General Registrar's office[71]

By parish			By burgh		
1931	5986	3150M 2836F	1931	2426	1273M 1153F
1951	7593	3799M 3794F	1951	2907	1433M 1474F
1961	8339	4151M 5188F	1961	3105	1525M 1580F
1971	8561	4252M 4309F	1971	3132	1531M 1601F
1981	7726	3822M 3904F	1981	7609	— —
1991	7152	3439M 3713F	2001	7341	3541M 3800F

APPENDIX THREE
DISEASES

Lung disease – a disease of urban living

Bronchitus – inflammation of the bronchial membranes in the bronchial tubes. Made worse by environmental pollution (including smogs)

Pneumonia – bacterial inflammation of the lung(s)

Tuberculosis/TB – also known as psthisis- bacterium spread by coughs & sneezes (and spitting), discovered 1882. Nutritionally dependent – socially deprived are vulnerable – and overcrowding makes problem worse – open windows

Gut diseases – improved hygiene & sanitation essential

Diarrhoea – bowel infection caused by infected meat, milk, water, and dirty environment and flies

Dysentery – inflammation of the intestine; spread reduced by hygiene

Typhoid/enteric fever – Salmonella typhosa. Enters body through contaminated food or water; into bloodstream and then blood poisoning. After 7 days – spots, then after 10–14 days, particular fever diarrhoea/constipation. Can cause heart failure. Cause discovered 1880–1884

Typhus – cause discovered 1916 – spread via lice – and victim scratches bite and rubs lice faeces into wounds – control by washing self and clothes weekly.

Childhood infectious diseases

Diphtheria/croup – infectious bacterial disease of the throat

Measles – viral disease – nutritionally dependent – socially deprived are vulnerable

70 From summary of data held 1931 census Volume One part 16 – East Lothian p 614

71 From listing in Baker, S (2003) *East Lothian 1945–2000; Volume One the County*, pp 265, 266 East Lothian Council Library Service

Scarlet fever/Scarlatina – infectious bacterial fever
Smallpox – spread person to person, airborne and by contact with pustules cause discovered 1886–92. From c1801, inoculation with same virus; vaccination with cowpox gives temporary protection.
Whooping cough – infectious bacterial disease
Cholera was not endemic but an occasional visitor

APPENDIX FOUR
OCCUPATIONS LISTED IN THE STATISTICAL ACCOUNT 1793

Professions	
Barbers	2
Brewers	5
Clergyman	1
Employed at a distillery in a neighbouring parish	9
Licensed to sell spirits & ales	32
Farmers	29
Gardeners	18
Officer of the customs	19
Officer of the excise	2
Teachers – private	3
Salters & salt agents	14
Schoolmaster	1
Shopkeepers	23
Surgeon	1

Masters, journeymen & apprentices	
Bakers	10
Candlemaker	1
Carpenters	22
Carriers	4
Coopers	2
Masons	16
Ropemakers	4
Shoemakers	19
Slaters	3
Smiths	11
Taylors	13
Watchmakers	3
Weavers	13
Midwives	2
Washerwomen	8

Other	**male**	**female**	**total**
Domestic servants	9	73	82
Farm servants	24	5	29
Day-labourers			19
Coal drivers			3

Mothers meeting at Castlepark
Photograph © copyright Local History Centre, Haddington

Seamen	20	
Regular fishermen	23	

Persons employed in manufactories (and their families)

Potteries	252	
Vitriol works	188	
Regular fishery	94	
Salt pans	47	
Brick & tile works	33	
Persons serving in the navy – last & former wars	28	
Persons serving in the army – last & former wars	20	(7 Chelsea pensioners)

APPENDIX FIVE

Haddingtonshire Annual Register of Voters 1855[72]

County Electors
(d) deceased; others twice enrolled

Prestonpans Parish 50 in number (Haddington 44, North Berwick 13, Tranent 111, Dunbar 36) *NB 48 listed and only one 'twice enrolled'*

David Aitchison, Episcopal clergyman
Francis Aitchison, late of Borlands
John Aitchison, London
Robert Aitchison, Southampton (d)

72 Voting rights depended on property ownership. Women were not entitled to vote.

William Aitchison, of Drummore (twice enrolled)
M. Aitken, gardener, Preston
Thomas Alexander, staff-surgeon, St John's, New Brunswick
William Alexander, salt manufacturer, Prestonpans
Charles Bellfield, potter, Cuthill (d)
James Bellfield, potter, Cuthill
James Brown, baker, Prestonpans
Dr William Brown, Duddingston
Charles Clark, baker, London
Alexander Cumming, joiner, Preston
Alexander Home Cowan, schoolmaster, Prestonpans (d)
Joseph Drysdale, merchant, Prestonpans
John Ferguson, gardener, Prestonpans
Richard Forbes, maltster, Prestonpans
James Grant, innkeeper, Prestonpans
John Grieve, Preston Colliery
Sir William Hamilton, Bart. Edinburgh
R. Hislop, brewer, Prestonpans
John Howison, draughtsman, Edinburgh
George Inglis, fisherman, Prestonpans (d)
James Kemp, wine merchant, Musselburgh
A. Knox, builder, Prestonpans
J. Mitchell, feuar, Prestonpans
James Mellis, soapmaker, Prestonpans
Andrew Mitchell residing Cuthill
Alexander Nimmo, innkeeper, Tranent*
James Pettecrew, building mason, Prestonpans
Thomas Pow, flesher, Prestonpans
John Pursell, ironmonger, Dalkeith
James A. Robertson, solicitor, Edinburgh
James Sanderson, gardener, Prestonpans
Adam Stevenson, proprietor, Prestonpans
John Stewart, Prestonpans
Rev. John Struthers, minister of Prestonpans
George Syme of Northfield
Alexander Taylor, farmer, Seton Mains
John Taylor, farmer, Seton West Mains
Robert Turnbull, cloth merchant, Prestonpans
William Wallace, merchant, Edinburgh
Peter Whitecross, carrier, Prestonpans
William Wright senior, gardener, Prestonpans
William Wright junior, gardener, Preston
J. Walker, grocer, Prestonpans
Thomas Yule, baker, Hadddington (d) **

* not listed on Tranent list
** not listed on Haddington list

APPENDIX SIX
HADDINGTONSHIRE ANNUAL REGISTER OF VOTERS 1904

Number of voters in Prestonpans parish 552 (North Berwick 136)

William Aitchison, Colonel, Drummore
R. Allison, gardener
John Anderson, contractor
Daniel Arbuckle, colliery manager
Charles Barett, customs officer
John Bellfield, potter, Cuthill
Alexander Black, ironmonger
John Bower, brewer
Alexander Brownlee, smith
James Bryce, shoemaker
Robert Buchanan, dairyman
Robert Buchanan, grocer
R. Clark, ropemaker
George Clark, cashier, Bankfoot
James Cowper, joiner
S.Y. Crichton, farmer, Dove Cote
James Dickson, mason, Dolphinston
Charles Farrow, grocer
Henry Fraser, potter
James Fraser, commercial traveller
John Gilles, farmer, Preston
George Greenfield, gardener, Preston
James Grosset, spirit merchant
Sir William S. Hamilton, Bart.
James Hamilton, clerk, Preston
Walter Henry, drill instructor, Preston
Thomas Hume, grocer
James Hunt, insurance agent
George Hunter, teacher
George Hunter, joiner
Alexander Inglis, gardener
Rev Donald Iverach, clergyman
Alexander Lauder, farmer Drummore
James Mackie, fisherman
George Mackie, soap maker
David T. Marr, baker
William A. Meek, salt manufacturer
George G. Moncur, hothouse builder, Preston
David McCairn, superintendent of soapworks
William C. McEwan, medical practitioner
James McNeil of Northfield
Rev James McPhail, clergyman
John Neilson, brickwork manager
James R. Pow, flesher
Adam Prentice, teacher

Andrew J. R. Purves, clerk, Preston
Thomas Rennie, baker
William Rennie, baker
John Richardson, tailor & clothier
P. W. Robertson, store manager
G. Rodger, soapmaker
William Rodger, carter
James Scott, retired grocer
James Shields, farmer, Dolphingston
W. Sibbald, gardener, Preston
Rev. G. S. Smith, clergyman
Sir George Grant Suttie, Bart.
Rev W. B. Turnbull, clergyman
James Wallace, teacher
James Watt, smith
R. Weatherhead, joiner
David White, shoemaker
Peter Whitecross, architect
Robert H. White, brewer
John Wright, farmer, Preston

APPENDIX SEVEN
NAMES ON THE WAR MEMORIAL REPORTED IN *HADDINGTONSHIRE COURIER* 5 MAY 1922

1914–18 – 143 fell

John Aitken
Thomas Aitken
McKenzie Allan
Garret Allison
Robert Amos
David Anderson
George Anderson
George Anderson
Robert Anderson
James Arnott
William Arnott
William Baillie
Peter Baird
James Banks
John Barr
Arthur Baxter
Thomas Bell
Walter Bell
William Blackley
Archibald Blyth
George Bowes
Peter Brackenridge
Andrew Brown
John Brown
Andrew Buchanan
James Burns
James Burns
William HP Calder
William Clark
James Clelland
Alexander Cochrane
Martin Condron
Owen R Cullen
George R Cunningham
James Cunningham
Robert D Cunningham
James Darroch
David Darling
Robert Darling
William Darling
James Davie
Joseph Donachue
Patrick Douglas
Alexander Edgar
James Edmond
John Edmond

Thomas Edmond
William Edmond
George Fairlie
George Findlay
John Findlay
George Flockhart
Thomas Forbes
Andrew Fraser
Andrew Fraser
Andrew Fraser
Robert R Fraser
Robert Fraser
Walter Gilroy
James Gordon
Peter Gunn
John Hamilton
James Hawthorn
Thomas K Henderson
Archibald Herriot
Joseph Hewitt
Charles Horne
Richard Hulbert
Charles Hunter
Charles Inglis
John Inglis
George Jenkins
Robert Jenkins
Andrew Johnston
Benjamin Johnston
Martin Keenan
Robert Kelly
Alexander Kennedy
Peter Lourie
Alexander Lumsden
James Lumsden
Andrew McFarlane
William McKie
Thomas Main
Alexander B Melrose
George Melrose
Andrew M Millar
John Moodie
John McAuley
James McFarlane
Dennis McGroarty
Alfred McKenzie
W A S McKerrell
Peter H McKinlay
James J McLagan
Robert D McLean
John McLeod
Robert McLeod
David McMurdie
Charles Neilson
James Nisbet
Robert H Nisbet
Samuel Nisbet
David Peden
John Porter
Robert AL Purves
Patrick Rafferty
Thomas Rafferty
James Reid
A W Renwick
David Ritchie
George Ritchie
Charles Robertson
John Russell
George Samuel
Walter Samuel
Alexander Scott
Alexander Smith
Charles A Smith
George R Smith
John M Smith
William I Smith
Thomas Spiers
Thomas Stevenson
John Stewart
David Stirrat
John Tennant
John Thomson
Charles Tonner
John C Vanbeck
Thomas Vevers
Alexander Waddell
Andrew Wallace
Harold S Wallace
W Ernest Wallace
James Waters
John S Weir
David Williams
Henry Cross Wilson
William Wood
William Yorkston
Thomas Yorkston

BIBLIOGRAPHY

Flinn, M (ed) (1977) *Scottish Population History* Cambridge University Press

Sinclair, C (1997 revised ed) *Tracing Your Scottish Ancestors* National Archives of Scotland

Smout, TC (1985) *A History of the Scottish People 1560–1830* Fontana

Whittington, G & Gibson, AJS (nd) *The Military Survey of Scotland 1747–55: a Critique* Historical Research Series ISBN 1870074 009

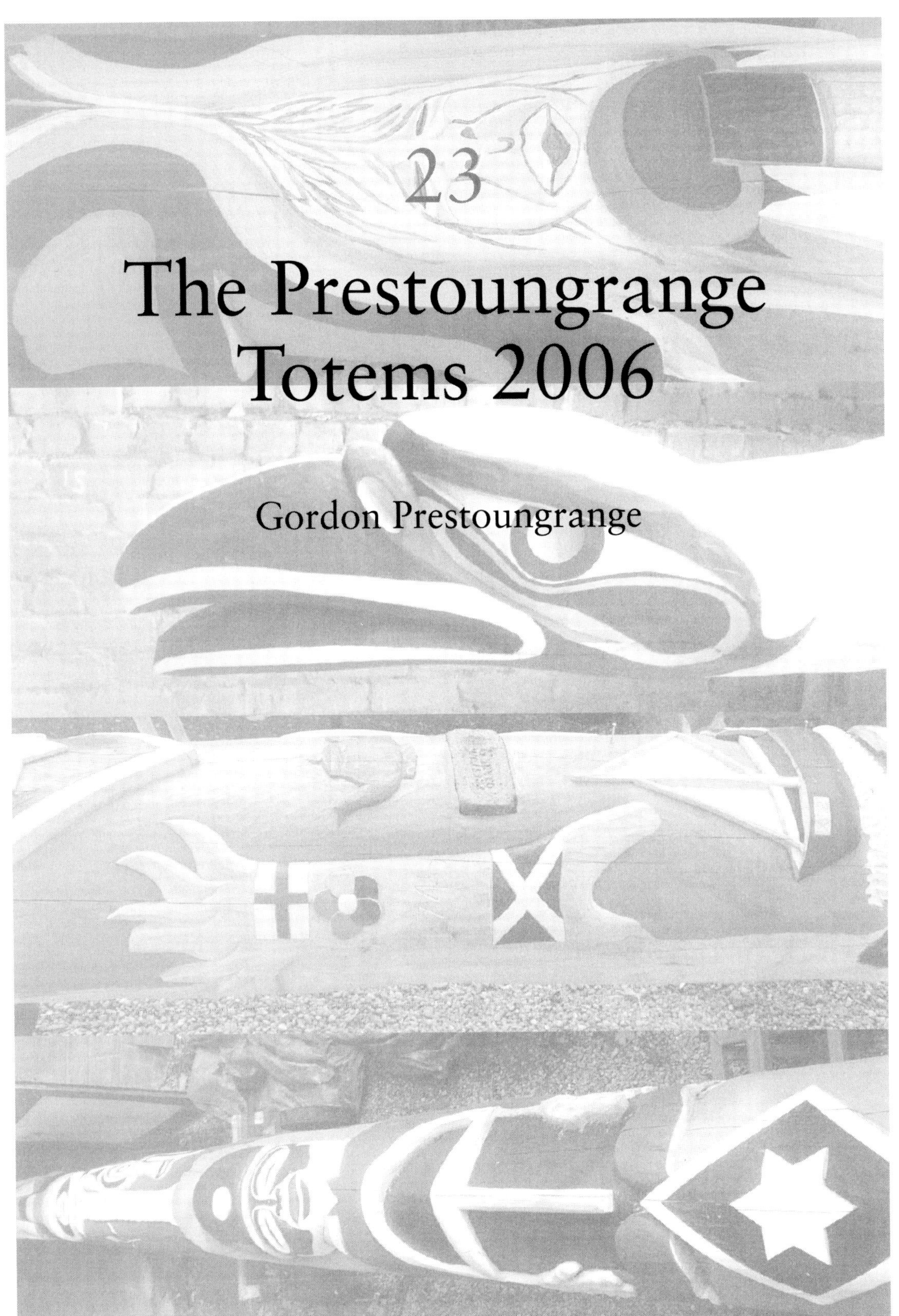

23

The Prestoungrange Totems 2006

Gordon Prestoungrange

1. ORIGINS AND NATURE OF TOTEMS

Free standing totem poles, house posts and talking sticks are present throughout the NW Pacific Coast of Canada and the USA. The unique artistic symbolism used is common to all tribes there and is thought to have emanated before Contact with Western civilizations from the Nass River region [Barbeau,1932]. Chemainus, the inspiration for the Prestoungrange Arts Festival Murals Programme, lies in this region on the ancient lands of the Cowichan tribe of the Coast Salish people, which today is known as the east coast of Vancouver Island, British Columbia. The Coast Salish people are relatively recent adherents to free standing totem pole carving having traditionally preferred house posts and external longhouse wall painting. Their art was more minimalist than their northern neighbours, and designs to infill were simple and geometric. They also had very strong artistic traditions using the same designs in basketry, rugs and blanket making. Most recently they have created Cowichan sweaters and hats that are world famous and examples of this were specially created and brought to the Potlatch held in Prestonpans on August 18th 2006.

In common with all other tribes their totems, whether free standing poles or posts or talking sticks, were the first 'public' art form in the area that sought to tell out local tribal and family history. Contrary to popular belief it seems clear that the greatest flowering of free standing totem pole carving came after Contact, as far better tools for carving became available and demand from anthropologists and souvenir hunters reached fever pitch at the end of the 19th century more than a century before Chemainus launched the world movement for historical mural painting. Yet by the mid 20th century there was a very real danger the traditions and skills would be lost and those totems which remained would end up in museums. However, a small group of family descendants of Charley James including Ellen Neel and her step-uncle Mungo Martin, with the encouragement of the University of British Columbia, ensured that a renaissance in carving took place with revenues eventually enhanced by increasing flows of tourism and the emerging policies and funding by governments intended to foster greater respect for and preservation of local cultures. The Northwest School of Native Art was established near Hazelton in 1969. Duncan just to the south of Chemainus became *The City of Totems* with a carving shed and Native Heritage Centre. Victoria, the capital of British Columbia saw a BigHouse dedicated to Mungo Martin at a potlatch and totems raised in its Beacon Hill Park in 1956 standing at 127' 7" – at that time the tallest totem pole in the world.

Poles tell of rights and origins

Early missionaries had misunderstood the purposes of totems, which were certainly not raised to heathen Gods nor were they worshipped. Neither was the great tribal gathering known as the potlatch, which was outlawed from 1884 until 1951, a heathen festival. It was a grand opportunity for chiefs of tribes to demonstrate their wealth by lavish entertaining and gift giving ... and the opportunity for the rights and stories recorded on the totems to be spoken aloud and re-enacted since there was no written language beyond the artistic symbols. The same occurred at the less lavish winter dance celebration the tribes arranged at the conclusion of their nomadic lifestyle in the summer months of the year. This tribal requirement to winter together but to roam in the other months seeking food and surpluses for barter trade meant that many of the small villages they built with their accompanying totems were short lived. Not only did the red cedar tree which they always used have a life of no more than 50 years as a totem, but the tribe would probably have migrated earlier [Harold, 1996]. But the winter months, snowed in as they normally were, did provide ample time for the carvers and basket makers and blanket weavers to accomplish their work.

The history captured in the totemic art was most frequently mythological, and associated with the animals and birds that were such a significant part of their lives. The stylized images of the animals and birds carved on the totem not only reminded the tribe's story tellers and dancers of their tribal ancestry but also, by their presence on the totem, conferred the very 'right' to tell the story and dance the dance at all. Those looking for an analogous symbolism in Western civilization compare the totem figures with uniquely held heraldic family coats or arms, badges and crests.

Raven's Role

Within the tribe are clans and each clan or phratry is frequently based on common matriarchal descent, depicted with its own particular animal or bird on its totems. Each animal or bird had a wide range of tales to tell and many tell of times before the world was as it is now, of a time when animals and birds could be transformed into humans and back again. This can be well illustrated by the stories from throughout the region associated with the Raven, which is the symbolic bird included on the Prestoungrange Totems because of its existing place in the heraldic arms of the Barons of Prestoungrange and of Dolphinstoun. It can be represented with beak and wings either down or up.

The Raven is one of the most significant birds in Pacific NW Coast totemic art, and the quintessential *organizer* or transformer. He is also characterised as a *trickster, a relentless schemer, a practical joker without remorse, a catalyst, lustful, a teacher, impulsive, shameless and cunning*. Quite a portfolio and sufficient to embellish and accommodate almost any Clan tale. The Raven is accordingly a figure to be both honoured and derided. He is both inventive, intelligent and innovative yet also greedy and selfish and especially mischievous.

In order to accomplish one of his greatest feats, freeing the Sun Moon and Stars for us all, he needed all his adjectival talents [Stewart, 1993]. ***'Raven was going along'*** ...long ago and heard of a greedy chief who kept the world in darkness by holding the sun, the moon and the stars in three wooden boxes in his house. He would occasionally raise the lids and let light spill out for a short time but always closed them back again quickly. Hearing of these boxes Raven though it would be a grand idea to bring light to the world but since he could not gain access himself to the boxes knew he would need a most cunning plan. Fortunately there was a pretty daughter to the chief who went to collect water every day from a stream and he resolve to seduce her by transforming himself into a hemlock needle [or was it a speck of dust] that floated into the water pitcher and thence into her drinking supply. Having swallowed the hemlock needle Raven ensured that she became pregnant and gave birth to a dark, beady eyed boy who grew at an astonishing rate. He was forever tearful and cried most especially for the box with the shiny ball inside. But the greedy chief refused to allow him to play with it until one day, exasperated with the crying he succumbed to his grandson's wishes and opened the boxes. Raven immediately transformed himself into bird form, released the moon and the stars and, grasping the sun ball in his beak flew up and out of the smoke hole in the tepee. Higher and higher he flew and farther and farther, spreading light all across the world for us all to enjoy. And having done that he threw the sun ball high into the sky where as one can see it still remains to this day. As if such an accomplishment was not sufficient, other Clans will tell how ***'Raven was going along'*** and gave the world fire, gave it humans and created the salmon.

Similarly compelling myths about vital aspects of daily life are shared by Clans that have been granted their retelling rights at potlatch, who claim their descent from Bear or Bear's Mother, from Beaver; from the mythical beings Thunderbird, Kolus, Hoh-Hok, Sisiutl, Dzoonkwa or the Watchman; from Eagle, Hawk, Shark, Frog, Wolf or Whale. Just as Raven has its common symbolic representation in all totems so do each of these beings have their own.

Preserving Authenticity for Totemic Art

The art form of red cedar tree carving and painting, and the meaningful symbols that have evolved and are used in association with it are, as already noted unique and comprehensively stylized in presentation. They tell not another person or another tribe's stories but their own. There can be no rationale for imitation elsewhere in the world when the authentic work is capable of creation through its traditional owners' leadership and craftsmanship.

As such the First Nations of the NW Pacific Coast of Canada and the USA have developed patterns of partnership around the globe as well as continuing their work on the home soil. Most significantly they are prepared to travel worldwide demonstrating and employing their skills at carving and finishing totems that celebrate their culture and heritage whether the totem is to remain in a natural wood, be feathered, grain blasted or painted. They will share in carving work with local craftsmen as their apprentices and educate those who are involved in their own stories underlying the symbolic representations, helping new tribes and families to select and represent their own stories and rights. They will share the meaning and substance of the ceremonies associated throughout including the final raising ceremony and potlatch after which the art and the stories contained therein 'become public'. They seek to ensure that the new stories of such totems at large, and of the particular totems now created, are told and retold, in print, on film and at potlatches for the future, just as they are now and in the past in their own homelands.

In this way their culture and their wholly unique art form in carved red cedar is preserved and maintains its proper authenticity.

The Copper and The Hat

Two final items also widely represented must be mentioned. Firstly, the Copper, created from the metal after which it is named, was created after Contact with Western civilization gave access to such material. Its ownership became a symbol of wealth and normally chiefship. On its unique shape are depicted the requisite symbols of rights. It became an ostentatious act of extravagance to break a piece off the Copper and give it to another and a demonstration of 'extreme wealth' to throw the whole Copper into the sea. The Copper increasingly took its place as an additional symbol of authority on totems equaling the symbolism accorded by the Hat and the cylindrical accumulation atop it of further Hats in a tower. Each segment of such a cylinder reflects an act of especial recognition of the individual whose Hat it is often recording an additional potlatch held.

2. WHY THE PRESTOUNGRANGE ARTS FESTIVAL RAISED THE PRESTOUNGRANGE TOTEMS IN 2006

The Prestoungrange Arts Festival's own first Contact with Chemainus, British Columbia arose from a chance visit by the author and Lady Prestoungrange to that town to see Shakespeare's *Midsummer Night's Dream* in 1999 on mid-summer's eve. It had long been an aspiration that never seemed to get met until a family vacation with the author's sister living in Victoria BC afforded the opportunity. The venue was the Chemainus Dinner Theatre, a truly significant outgrowth of the town's original and highly successful programme of historical mural painting. The impact of the murals was so obvious that it was inevitable that the question was asked: who was the visionary and driving force behind the original and ever evolving notion of using the arts to stimulate an otherwise declining/ threatened community? The local store keeper selling the 3rd Edition of the Chemainus Murals' Souvenir Book was able at once to direct us to Karl Schutz. He lived just out of town off the main highway but had been a worker at the local sawmill, the sole significant employer, that had closed down leaving almost the whole community without work. Karl Schutz was always willing to discuss what his small town had accomplished – he had indeed developed a break even consultancy service to advise others who might wish to follow a similar path.

The Chemainus Story

The Chemainus story has been told and retold across four continents. But it merits repeating and repeating because it has all the elegance of simplicity and the most extraordinary powers of socio-economic achievement. Some sixty small towns and cities have deployed the approach and many now belong to the Global Association for Murals Art & Cultural Tourism that was founded in 1998. Perhaps the most authoritative account appeared in the *Smithsonian Magazine*, entitled '*The Little Town That Did*'. It recounts how, when faced with the most dire of all consequences for the township, Karl Schutz suggested an approach that he had observed in Rumanian monasteries on a recent holiday there. The medieval church had told the story of Christianity and of its many Saints in paintings on their walls so that pilgrims and regular visitors could see for themselves what they could not comprehend in Latin or might never have the opportunity to hear as the Word. Karl Schutz proposal was that, taking advantage of a history of the area already available, mural painting should be used to attract tourists to the town. There were two major objections from those who Schutz calls the nay-sayers: firstly it would not work; and secondly if it did it would transform the town into a tourist mecca. Reluctant approval was eventually won for the first work of art on the understanding that if it was unacceptable it could always be painted out. It worked. It is indeed a tourist mecca but local people took great pride in it and the town's economic future became assured –even more so when the saw mill reopened. The rest is history. Today Chemainus attracts of the order of 400,000 tourists each year, enjoying the public art, purchasing souvenirs and murals books and taking food and refreshments. And the Dinner Theatre, with its own student population, affords countless opportunities for return visits by those who have already seen and enjoyed the murals. A Suites Motel has just been completed.

Seeing and hearing this amazing story occurred at an opportune moment for the Prestoungrange Arts Festival. During its first two years under Jane Bonnar's leadership it had sought to work with Education Officer Annette MacTavish at the Prestongrange Heritage Museum. A series of Historical Research Studies had been conceived for use with schools and Teachers' Guides had been developed. But abrupt personnel changes meant that such a goal was increasingly unlikely to be achieved. However, if the example of Chemainus was followed, the history already researched, analysed and elegantly published could act as formal briefings for mural artists and for all who wanted to understand the stories told in murals in much greater depth. And so it transpired. Not only were the initial ten studies thus used but research and publication has continued apace and the murals programme continually draws upon it. The studies both inspire the artists and those who gaze upon the murals seeking a more comprehensive understanding of the issues and the personalities addressed.

Global Lessons to be Learnt

At a direct level, the Prestoungrange Arts Festival simply intended to run with the murals idea. It obviously worked. But there was clearly a great deal more to the Chemainus success story, and the successes gained elsewhere around the globe, that should appropriately be understood to gain maximum advantage. And fortunately in 1998 Karl Schutz had, along with another dozen Charter Members, established a 'Global Association for Murals Art and Cultural Tourism'. Accordingly the first deliberate learning step was taken when Karl Schutz, working with Doris Bucklin from 29 Palms California, was invited to Prestoungrange to give a two day Public Workshop. He was listened to most carefully. Designs for the first two murals were soon thereafter commissioned and tabled with the local Council for their approval, but nay-saying was encountered. Unperturbed, the murals were painted on the baronial sea walls looking across the Firth of Forth accessible along the foreshore; and 'virtually' displayed on land where they would have been if the nay-sayers had not prevented it.

The second learning steps involved a programme of visits to as many of the other murals towns around the globe as possible over a period of four years. It entailed traveling across the globe to Foxton and Kati Kati in New Zealand, to Sheffield Tasmania, to Mendooran, Kurri Kurri and Kyogle in New South Wales, to Bowen in Queensland, to Exeter, Lompoc and Tulare in California, to Vale Oregon, to Philadelphia with more than 3000+ murals, to Scarborough Ontario, to Legal, Grand Prairie and Stony Plains in Alberta, to Vernon and Saanich British Columbia and then as far north at Whitehorse in the Yukon. And in tandem with such field visits, where friendships were built with many members of the local murals societies and splendid press coverage achieved for the benefit of their local initiatives, the team made a particular point of attending and contributing at two biennial Global Association Conferences [Moosejaw Saskatchewan 2002 then Ely Nevada 2004], at two Californian Regional Seminars [Lindsay 2003 and Bishop 2005], and at the Pacific Mural Gathering [Bowen 2005].

Invitation to Convene the Global Conference in Prestonpans

Such willingness to work hard at understanding the global achievements of so many towns and cities [now in excess of twenty have been visited], and the fact that Prestoungrange was the first European member of the Association, sufficiently endeared us to the Association's Board in Moosejaw in 2002 when it was resolved that the 2006 Biennial Global Conference should be convened in Prestonpans by the Prestoungrange Arts Festival. That was a signal honour because there were then and there remain many towns and cities with surely more to share than we can aspire to after just eight years. But in accepting the honour bestowed on us by the Association we resolved to make sure its members who attended received something special. We further resolved to make 2006 a target date for the achievement of a wide range of goals that we had already set for ourselves. And finally we agreed to develop the Global Association's own website @ www.globalartsandtouurism.net to ensure better communications one with another between each Conference. But the 'something special' for 2006 was resolved to be the Prestoungrange Totems. They afforded, we felt, a magnificent opportunity to say thank you:

Firstly, by using the most ancient art form known to the Cowichan Valley where Chemainus stands, a fitting tribute could be given.

Secondly, by representing the Global Association's Gala Dinner as both a Civic Reception and a Potlatch a proper and fitting tribute could be paid to all those in the global murals community who had welcomed us so warmly and shared all their experiences with us whilst at the same time reminding them of how much they owed to Chemainus.

The 2006 Prestoungrange Potlatch and the Raising of the Totems thereat was not however the first occasion on which the Arts Festival had had the opportunity to say thank you to the inspiration of Chemainus. At a Civic Reception at the Arts Theatre in Chemainus for the author and Lady Prestoungrange in 2002 the Prestoungrange Arts Festival was granted the Freedom of Chemainus and given the Key to the Town. In return, we promised to organize a celebratory 2003 Burns' Supper at the Chemainus Arts Theatre in partnership with local Scottish cultural societies of which there are many – British Columbia was extensively settled by Scots in the late 19th century. It was at that outstandingly successful Supper that Jon Lefebure, the Mayor of North Cowichan [which includes Chemainus], agreed that if the Prestoungrange Totems were to be carved they must be carved from red cedars and that his Council would be honoured to donate such trees for the purpose. All that the Prestoungrange Arts Festival had to do was to ship the trees to Scotland - in which task they fortunately had on the ground assistance from the author's sister and Dr Karl Schutz himself.

Scotland's Earlier Experience of Totems

One of the most intriguing aspects of the decision to carve the Prestoungrange Totems for 2006 was the *subsequent* discovery that there was already a totem heritage at the National Museums of Scotland from an exhibition many decades ago. Furthermore a contemporary Scottish wood carver, Kenny Grieve of Brotus Rural Crafts, had since *Treefest* 2002, [The Year of The Tree], been vigorously pursuing a truly flourishing programme of totem pole carving in partnership with NW Pacific Coast First Nations carvers who had been making regular visits to Scotland supported amongst others by the Scottish Arts Council. He was embarked on a programme to raise at least thirteen totem poles right around the nation. Accordingly, notwithstanding the wholly discrete rationale for our own particular excursion into totemic art, it was clearly appropriate to work together with this much broader scale initiative, and a joint working group was formed with Kenny Grieve and the National Museums of Scotland. Kristine Cunningham from the Prestoungrange Arts Festival was appointed overall Team Leader. The access which Kenny Grieve had to the most distinguished First Nations carvers in the American NW Pacific was to prove invaluable.

The poles carved under the leadership of Kenny Grieve at Brotus Rural Crafts had involved thousands of school children across the country. Prince Charles had donated a 130' Douglas Fir log from the Queen's Balmoral Estate and the National Trust for Scotland a similar Fir standing at 170' from The Hermitage, to create poles for Dunkeld and Dundee; poles had also been carved at Bennachie, at Strathdon, at Dalbeattie, at Kelty, at Stranraer, at Port Patrick, at Vane Farm near Kinross, at Dunblane, and at Peterhead. In all instances the local history and folklore of the town was represented and each and every community was actively involved in the carving. In Bennachie this included a man's betrayal by his sweetheart and a key to the big cave there. Kenny Grieve had lately offered an Exhibition at The Scottish Parliament in March 2005.

As more and more communities in Scotland have come to realize what a powerful moment the carving and raising of a totem pole can be, more and more townships are seeking to follow suit.

3. SYMBOLS TO BE CARVED FOR PRESTONPANS

'*Raven was going along and ...*' decided that the symbols to be carved on the Prestoungrange Totems should also be debated and discussed throughout the community and especially in the schools in the town of Prestonpans and right across the former baronial lands. And they should deliberately reflect the history of the town and in some proper manner the sharing of cultures with Chemainus. A competition was run at The Prestoungrange Gothenburg by the National Museums of Scotland to select symbols designed by youngsters in three historical areas – coal mining, Morrison's Haven and the Battle of Prestonpans 1745. Contributions from others community groups were captured. Additional inspiration came from the 1995 Commemorative Banner created for the 250th Anniversary of the Battle of Prestonpans which is on display at the Industrial Hertitage Museum in the town.

After six months **'Raven was going along and...'** resolved:

At the top of the pole **Raven wished his own image to appear**, wings folded with a Pacific North West Coast Indian Face in his care.

Directly beneath himself Raven wished to see the **Face of Barony** in Prestoungrange and Dolphinstoun which had led the town's industrial and agricultural pursuits for five centuries, and inaugurated the Arts Festival five years ago, the Face of Barony to be wearing five hats to celebrate the many potlatches known as Chapmen's Fairs held on St Jerome's Day in the town for so many years. Two of the hats were to be baronial chapeaux and the other three Indian First Nations. The Face of Barony was to be robed proper in scarlet to the left with a record of the 81 witches pardonned in 2004 together with five brass buttons being Pound coins and to the right in an Indian blanket with Wolf Eye design and below Xwa Lack Tun's own signature. The robe and blanket were to be held together by five silver buttons being Canadian Quarters.

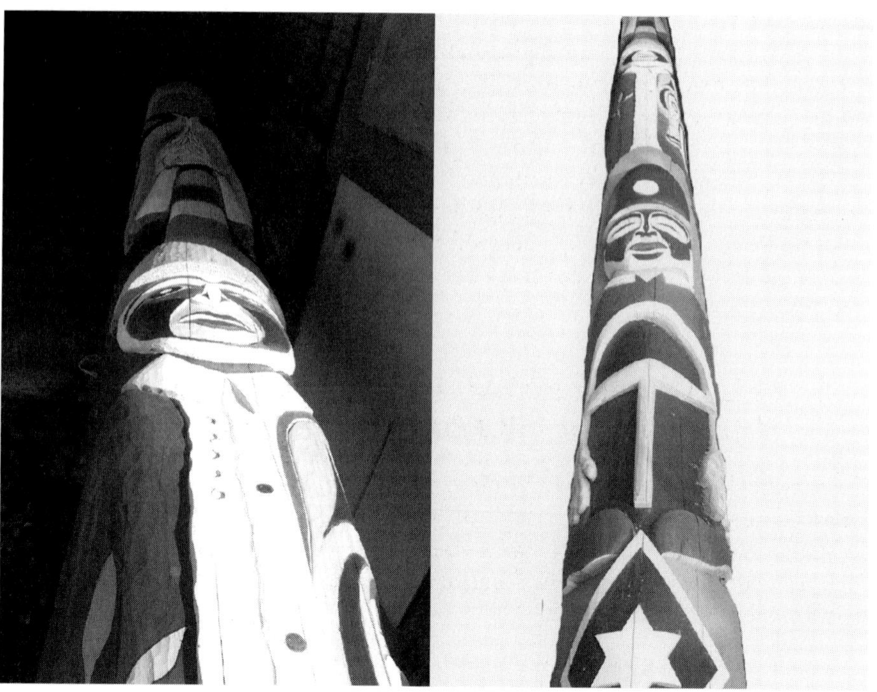

Beneath the Face and the Robe of Barony was to come the **Face of The Prestonpans Miner** with lamp aglow [created at St Gabriel's Primary School by Declan]. Coal was the energy source in Prestonpans which fuelled the Industrial Revolution in Scotland and for some four centuries coal mining provided much of the town's employment. When all the pits closed in the 1960s the town fell wounded. Further mining symbolism created by Erin [also from St Gabriel's] was to show the Miner's hands and a **Pick in a Tunnel,** and beneath it the **Heraldic Symbols of Coal and Salt** – the black diamond and the six pointed white star – as granted in the Prestoungrange Coat of Arms.

Beneath those symbols Raven determined that the derived industries of Prestonpans should be shown the first being **Pottery** represented by a Bellfield 'broon coo' teapot which had originally been made in the 1920/ 30s on the site of the Prestoungrange car park where carving of the pole was eventually to take place. Beneath the teapot there should be a **Prestongrange Brick,** being one of those made in the town's own brickworks and used when The Prestoungrange Gothenburg was originally built in 1908. Behind it should be a representation of the charitable goals of that public house in the form of a Scottish five Pound note and a Canadian five Dollar bill.

To the left of the Brick should be carved the **Thorn Tree** made famous at the Battle of Prestonpans in 1745 where Colonel Gardiner was mortally wounded together with the date 1745 and the Scottish Saltire and the Cross of England's St George. [This symbol was contributed by Melissa of Prestonpans Primary School.] And to the right of the Brick should stand a **Garb of Corn** from the Barony of Dolphinstoun as depicted in its Grant of Arms.

The final grouping of symbols should represent **Morrison's Haven,** with a **Ship Afloat** on the Firth of Forth, a wavy sea, filled with **Fish** [images created by Jamie and Jack from Prestonpans Infant School]. And last, beneath those waters, **Salt and the Coal** once again depicted heraldically.

'Thus Raven, going along, decreed that it should be .....'. Yet before any carving could begin red cedar trees must be felled and the logs transported to Scotland.

4. FELLING CHEMAINUS RED CEDARS AND THEIR TRANSPORTATION TO SCOTLAND

The logistical tale began early in November 2004 when the two magnificent, donated, red cedars were felled in the forests of Chemainus in North Cowichan by Tim McTiffon under the direction of Forester Darrell Frank. They also attended to their limbing and peeling [which meant they gave up their branches and their bark].

Step 2 was to get the trees from their home forest to a carefully chosen 'timber yard' with access for a spacious container, and this was accomplished by one Scotty Thomson, needless to say born in Scotland with an accent to prove it. [*'No problem. Just let me know where and when you want them.'*]

Step 3 involved securing a 40' container. Tim Strang of Hill's Native Art in Vancouver who ships finished totems across the world was able to introduce Karl Schutz to Anjali Sadarangani of Wilson Freight. [*'No problem shipping 40' trees to Scotland. Just give me the dates and we look after the rest.*] They scheduled November 29th for collection but did have a wee problem and the container arrived a day late. So loading was eventually accomplished, most auspiciously, on St Andrew's Day.

Step 4 saw the loading of the trees at the 'chosen timber yard', and where better than the world-famous Chemainus 'sawmill' that closed in the early 1980s thus creating the challenge that Karl Schutz and others met with their murals programme. Nowadays reopened for business and owned by Weyerhaeuser, it is managed by Jason Kearns, a former neighbour of Karl Schutz who until recently led Chemainus based Planks Window Factory which was purchased by Weyerhaeuser. Jason Kearns and his colleague David Turnbull from South Island Reman Division quickly agreed that: *'Weyerhaeuser would love to handle the loading and if Scotty brought the logs they'd do the forklift truck work, push them in, fasten them down. Nothing to it!'* In fact one log was a tad too long but a saw helped it fit the box. Daniel Derby directed three forklifters as the logs were transferred from Scotty Thomson's trailer to the container in record time. The *Ladysmith-Chemainus Chronicle* told the story on December 7th .

Step 5 was the journey to Vancouver and Montreal. For this the container took the night ferry across from Vancouver Island to the mainland where fumigation of the logs was undertaken under Anjali Sadarangani's direction. Routing by sea in the Pacific then through the Panama Canal had been considered but the more direct route across Canada was eventually selected. So the logs boarded a freight train for Montreal, Quebec, and from there made their passage along the St Lawrence Seaway on the opposite Atlantic coast.

Step 6 was the journey across the Atlantic Ocean from Montreal to Edinburgh. The vessel selected by Anjali Sadarangani of Wilson Freight Canada was *Canmar Pride*, Voyage 216E, Reference # 15732130, departed December 9th which then arrived in Europe in time for transfer to a feeder line for the final sea journey to Scotland to be on dockside by December 24th, Christmas Eve. Another auspicious date.

Step 7 took place in the docks in Edinburgh where the trees required Forestry Commission authorization before they could be moved along to Prestonpans. Here Sylvia Burgess, the Baron Sergeand at the Prestoungrange Arts Festival, and Kristine Cunningham took over co-ordination from Karl Schutz and

Anne Wills. And once the MasterBill of Lading was to hand Paul Armstrong of Wilson Freight UK began arranging inspection times for Tom Francis of the UK Forestry Commission shortly after Christmas. [Because the trees had been limbed and peeled in the forest, and fumigated in Vancouver, no formal Import Licence was necessary from the Department of Trade and it was anticipated that Forestry Commission protocols had been met.] The relevant Plant Health Order read:

'*Wood of Thuja L., including that which has not kept its round surface, originating in Canada. Without prejudice to Article 3(1) Part A of Schedule 2 and Schedule 3, the wood shall be stripped of its bark and shall be free from grub holes which are larger than 3mm across. Phytosanitary Certificate or Industrial Certificate required to accompany the trees.*'

Notwithstanding such seeming comprehension of the necessary issues, however, the Forestry Commission quarantined the logs on arrival since there was no Phytosanitary Certificate, only an industrial notice of fumigation which alone would not suffice. [The *Ladysmith-Chemainus Chronicle* picked up on that story January 18th 2005 when Prestoungrange met with the shipping team in Chemainus to make 'thank you' presentations of Glenkinchie Single Malt.] However, before too much demurrage expense was incurred the Forestry Commission released the logs to proceed by road accompanied by an Order on the Baron Sergeand that the final remains of bark must be peeled and burnt. [Since we had no professional competence in this respect the Officer concerned was gracious enough to undertake this final task for us pro bono.]

Step 8 followed the logs release under Order from the docks. It involved moving the cedars by road to a temporary resting place in the neighbourhood of Prestonpans as all the other arrangements for their carving came gradually together over the following three months. It needed to be able to receive the large container in the first instance, have room for its unloading and indoor cover for the logs protection. Sir Francis Ogilvy at Winton House was able to offer the use of the main barn behind Winton Hill Farm, and by January 5th 2005 the trees had completed that stage of their journey.

Step 9 took place at 07.30 am on Monday April 11th 2005 when under the Baron Sergeand's command, A.G. Thomson's *Bonnie Scotland* low loader and JCB arrived to load the logs with great skill and finesse and take them to The Prestoungrange Gothenburg's seashore on the Firth of Forth in Prestonpans for their first Scottish photocall; and most importantly their blessing by First Nations carvers. [These carvers were led by Xwa Lack Tun of the Squamish Nation in Canada's Pacific NW and were already in Scotland working with Kenny Grieve of Brotus Rural Crafts in association with the National Museums of Scotland, which has had five years of Scottish Arts Council support for a series of millennium totems around Scotland carved from Scottish logs.]

The logs, already well accustomed to media attention in British Columbia, lay proudly side by side in the East Lothian sunshine at Prestonpans as photographers from the *Glasgow Herald, East Lothian Courier, Edinburgh Evening News and East Lothian News* chose their preferred angles – and cast of characters. *Reporting Scotland,* the BBC TV News programme each evening for the whole nation, also attended and recorded interviews with Xwa Lack Tun, Kenny Grieve and the Baron of Prestoungrange.

The BBC camera crew indeed followed the logs on A.G. Thomson's low loader to St Joseph's at the back of the Pans to see them safely lodged in their carving shed, where carving was eventually to begin in August 2005 – with many a community group and school visit sharing in the excitement and learning a great deal as they talked and watched and 'helped' a little.

Step 10 followed a summertime residence for the logs with St Joseph's and saw the carving there in August 2005 of a 6' high totem taken from one end of the second log. Xwa Lack Tun and colleagues met with members of the Prestoungrange Arts Festival and school groups to share their culture and music and to explain the nature and purpose of totemic art forms.

The 6' totem depicts the Raven with the heraldic crosslet held in its beak and for the winter months it stood attracting a great deal of attention in the James Park Bistro at the Prestoungrange Gothenburg, prior to painting in March 2006 under the supervision of Xwa Lack Tun. This 6' totem also served as a model for the youngsters who were to create designs prior to the carving of the main pole.

5. CARVING AND PAINTING THE POLE

'Raven was going along and carved the main totem pole'

The original intention was that the main pole [it will be recalled that there are two logs] should be carved at St Joseph's but it was soon accepted that there was inadequate room for the visitors expected as work progressed. So the potential venue was moved to the Prestongrange Heritage Museum but even that was frustrated by local Council health and safety regulations on chain saw use on the site. So finally the car park at The Prestoungrange Gothenburg, where BBC TV had first shown the logs, was selected. Yet these little local difficulties were dwarfed by the events at Glasgow Airport when Xwa Lack Tun and Tawx'sin Yexwullo [*alias Splash*], the invited carvers, were denied permission to enter Scotland since they had no work permit. Immigration officials were adamant and it took a final appeal by Viscount John Thurso MP to the UK Minister for Immigration at Westminster, Tony McNulty, before common sense prevailed.

Kenny Grieve provided a small marquee to cover the carving which certainly kept the rain away although the NE winds at times got the better of it. More than 400 visitors came from far and wide to observe, discuss and in many instances participate in the carving. They included Englishman Paul Colbert who created the Baronial Ellwand in 1998, who had been entrusted on this occasion with carving Talking Sticks for each Baron.

The depictions of Prestonpans industrial history created by youngsters were faithfully incorporated in the overall design.

The press came to visit and wrote as glowingly as the visitors from far and wide, including John Muir Walkers and those from earlier Scottish totem pole towns. A selection of comments from the book provided tells it all:

> *'Brilliant idea; fantastic work'. 'Very good to see other countries' culture and skills'.*
>
> *'Absolutely stunning'. 'This is a very interesting project and totally different from anything ever done in this town before'.*
>
> *'Truly represents Prestonpans town'. 'Wonderful to see craftsmen so at ease with their tools and materials'. 'So impressive what can be achieved in well less than 2 weeks.'*
>
> *'Amazing, its such a beautiful gift. Great project for the community'. 'Absolutely amazing wood and people. The meeting of cultures is something to celebrate'.*
>
> *'Just great to watch it take shape from a tree!'. 'Like being back in Canada ... great memories'.*
>
> *'Brilliant; Great idea; Awesome; Fabulous; Amazing - culture in the Pans!!'*
>
> *'At once creative and traditional. This tree stood for 75 years in Canada, it knows what it is doing'.*

The pole, still weighing well over a ton and as carved 32' 8" long, was carried aloft to the grounds of Prestoungrange House in Prestonpans by Preston Athletic Youth Football XI fresh from their victory in the East Lothian Cup Final. And week commencing May 17th painting began. Tom Ewing and Adele Robertson, under the leadership of Andrew Crummy, took responsibility. They collaborated with Kenny Grieve and Peter Hill so that the steel spine could be applied for the pole's raising on August 18th and Quantity Surveyor Gordon Eadie made the calculations for the concrete base and plinth on which it now stands. [This pattern of raising was deliberately used so that the pole could be moved around to different locations to tell the story of Prestonpans.]

6. TALKING STICKS AND COWICHAN KNITTING

In addition to the totem pole itself, two other First Nations artifacts were created for the potlatch to be held on August 18th and Hudson Bay Company blankets [used as currency in earlier days] and reproduced as souvenirs by the Hudson Bay Company to this day were brought to Scotland.

The most significant artifacts were the two Talking Sticks crafted by Paul Colbert, who had earlier created the Baronial Ellwand. One each was carved for the Barons of Prestoungrange and of Dolphinstoun.

"***Raven was walking along ...***" and firstly invited Paul Colbert, Walking Stick Maker from Kempston Bedford but a regular at all Scottish Game Fairs,

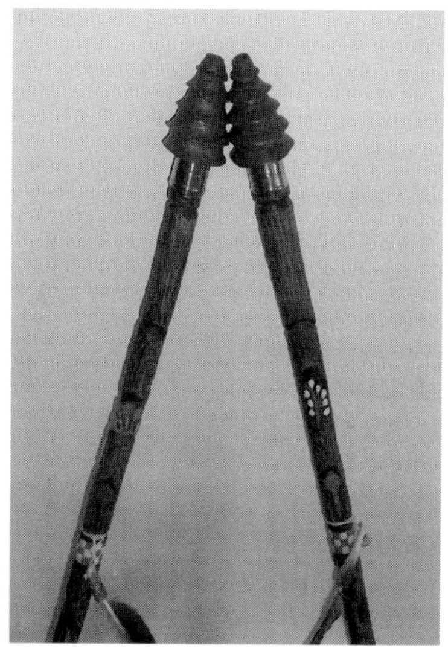

to carve two Pacific West Coast style Talking Sticks one for each Baron. It was he who had created the widely admired Prestoungrange Baronial Ellwand with Hamilton & Inches in the last century. The Talking Sticks are ceremonial mini-totem poles and are carried to all significant meetings and potlatches by their proud owners.

Both Dolphinstoun and Prestoungrange, said Raven, shall receive a Talking Stick carved in hazel which shall have been dremelled to remove its bark with a round headed router. It shall be treated overall with rosewood stain and have chevrons interspersed throughout. It shall be finished with coats of Danish oil derived from natural tung vegetable oil.

Both shall have five hats atop the hazel carved in mahogany with gold balls proper to their rank. The hazel shall have red and white chequers at intervals which are common to both shields on their Arms. Finally, both shall have a band of copper at their top, a red deer horn holding one of Raven's own feathers, and a copper ferrule at their base.

In all other respects they shall differ. Dolphinstoun shall have the garb of corn and green crosslet from his Arms and the Man in The Moon and poppies from his espoused Compartment. His name D O L P H I N S T O U N shall be carved around the stick with green lettering and the H and O set amongst the chequers.

Prestoungrange's differencing shall include the coal black diamond and six pointed white star for salt from his Arms and his red crosslet. The Sun and the Thorntree shall be derived from his espoused Compartment and the name P R E S T O U N G R A N G E shall be carved around the stick with black lettering, the O and G set amongst the chequering.

"***Raven was going along …***" and secondly asked Emily living in Duncan, City of Totems on Cowichan lands, to knit four sweaters for the male members of the family of Prestoungrange. And Emily so knitted them to the traditional Cowichan patterns and travelled to the Potlatch in Prestonpans in August 2006 to give them as Raven had wished to Duncan, to Mathew Yr of Prestoungrange, to Julian of Dolphinstoun and to Gordon of Prestoungrange [The full story of Cowichan knitting is recorded by Meikle (1987)]

REFERENCES

Barbeau, M., [1932,1984], '*Art of the Totem*', Hancock House, Surrey, BC

Grieve,K., [2002] Scottish Totem Poles Project reported @: http://www.brotus.co.uk/Brotusfiles/poles/polenews02.html

Harold, H., [1996], '*Totem Poles and Tea*', Heritage House, Surrey, BC

Jensen, V., [1992], '*Where the People Gather: Carving a Totem Pole*', Douglas & MacIntyre, Vancouver BC

Jensen, V., [2004], '*Totem Poles of Stanley Park*', Subway Books, Vancouver, BC

Joniatis, A., [ed] [1991], '*Chiefly Feasts: The Enduring Kwakiutl Potlach*', Douglas & MacIntyre, Vancouver, BC

Kramer, P., [1998, 2004], '*Totem Poles*', 2nd Edition, Altitude Publishing, Canmore, Alberta

McGrail, S., [2005], '*Stories in Wood*', The Scots Magazine, November, pp 496-499.

Meikle, M., [1987], '*Cowichan Indian Knitting*', UBC Museum of Anthropology, Vancouver, BC

Meisler, S., [1994], 'Take a Look at the Little Town That Refused to Die', *The Smithsonian Magazine*, May.

Meyer, G., [1992], '*American Folk Art Canes*', Sandringham Press & University of Washington Press

Muckle, R., [1998, 2003], '*The First Nations of British Columbia*', UBC Press, Vancouver, BC

Reid, B. and Bringhurst, R., [1996], '*The Raven Steals The Light*', University of Washington Press

Stewart, H., [1979], '*Looking at Indian Art of the NorthWest Coast*', Douglas & MacIntyre with University of Washington Press

Stewart, S., [1993], '*Looking at Totem Poles*', Douglas & McIntyre, Vancouver, BC

Shearer,C., [2000], '*Understanding Northwest Coast Art*', Douglas & McIntyre, Vancouver, BC.

Wyatt, G., [1999], '*Mythic Beginnings: Spirit Art of the NorthWest Coast*', Douglas & MacIntyre with University of Washington Press